CONSTANTINE PORPHYROGENITUS AND HIS WORLD

CHRIST CROWNING CONSTANTINE PORPHYROGENITUS
(Ivory relief *c.* 944. Museum of Fine Art, Moscow)

Constantine Porphyrogenitus

AND HIS WORLD

ARNOLD TOYNBEE

LONDON
OXFORD UNIVERSITY PRESS
NEW YORK   TORONTO
1973

Oxford University Press, Ely House, London W. 1

GLASGOW   NEW YORK   TORONTO   MELBOURNE   WELLINGTON
CAPE TOWN   IBADAN   NAIROBI   DAR ES SALAAM   LUSAKA   ADDIS ABABA
DELHI   BOMBAY   CALCUTTA   MADRAS   KARACHI   LAHORE   DACCA
KUALA LUMPUR   SINGAPORE   HONG KONG   TOKYO

ISBN 0 19 215253 X

© *Oxford University Press 1973*

*Printed in Great Britain
at the University Press, Oxford
by Vivian Ridler
Printer to the University*

PREFACE

LIKE Constantine Porphyrogenitus, I was educated on the study of Greek texts. 'Ancient' Greek and Latin literature was still the staple of higher education in the humanities in Britain in my generation. Long before my education was over, I had come to feel that my vocation lay somewhere in the field of the humanities, and I thought of this field, first of all, in terms of the work of scholars to whom I had been indebted. These were the devoted modern Western editors of the works of Greek and Latin authors. I was aware, from experience, of the value of a skilled editor's work.

By that time there were already first-rate editions of most of the extant works written in Greek and Latin down to the beginning of the seventh century of the Christian Era, but the extant works in Greek of a later date than that were, by comparison, still inadequately edited for the most part. In the first decade of the present century, C. de Boor's fine editions of the Patriarch Nicephorus's chronicle and Theophanes's *Chronographia* and Georgius Monachus's chronicle, which had been published by Teubner in 1880, 1883–5, and 1904 respectively, and A. Reifferscheid's edition of Anna Comnena's *Alexias*, published by Teubner in 1884, stood out as exceptions to the general rule. Most Greek works written in and after the seventh century were accessible only in antiquated editions: the seventeenth-century French corpus and the early-nineteenth-century Bonn corpus. Here, then, there was editorial work still to be done. I was assuming, at this stage, that my own work would be editorial; and, by the time I had arrived at my last year as an undergraduate at Oxford—this was the university year 1910–11—I had put one particular piece of editorial work on my agenda. I had cast myself for the task of editing one group of the works of the East Roman Emperor Constantine VII Porphyrogenitus.

I was not so much interested in the extant collection of excerpts, made under his direction, from the works of Greek authors dating from before the débâcle of the Roman Empire and the Graeco-Roman civilization in the seventh century. These examples had already been edited by the scholars who had reassembled the surviving fragments of the books from which Constantine's excerpts had been culled. My ambition was to edit Constantine's works dealing with East Roman affairs that were of later date than the seventh-century break in the continuity of civilization in the Levant. I put this ambition of mine on record in some Greek verses that I wrote towards the end of the year 1910.

Χαῖρέ μοι ὦ μεγάλου μεγάλη πόλι Κωνσταντίνου,
τοὺς Κωνσταντίνου χαῖρ' ἐφέποντι λόγους,
οὐ κτίστου γ', ἑτέρου δέ, σοφὸς σοφοῦ ὅς ῥα Λέοντος
υἱὸς ἐγεννήθη πορφυρέῳ 'ν θαλάμῳ.
καὶ Δάναπριν Περάτης τε καὶ 'Ηοῦς ἱστορεῖ ἔθνη
ἐσθλά τε 'Ρωμαίων ἐξέτασεν θέματα.
νῦν δ' ἐγὼ ἐκ γῆς ὀψὲ Βαράγγων ἐξανέτειλα
τερπνὰ διορθώσων τοῖο γέροντος ἔπη.

What had led me to set my heart on editing Constantine Porphyrogenitus's works, and this group of them in particular? My mother had
been giving me the volumes of Bury's edition of Gibbon in instalments,
and it was Bury's appendix to volume vi, published in 1902, that had set
me off. Bury's summary here, on pp. 536–7, of the contents of Constantine's *De Administrando Imperio* had opened up for me a panorama of the
tenth-century world as viewed from Constantinople. For me, this had all
been new and exciting. It had made me realize that Gibbon's slighting
account of Constantine Porphyrogenitus in the forty-seventh chapter of
the *Decline and Fall*, which I had previously read in volume v of Bury's
edition, was not the last word about Constantine—that it was, in fact,
misleading. Bury's revision of Gibbon's jaundiced view had caught my
imagination and had whetted my appetite. (This is only one item in my
immense debt to Bury—a debt that has increased with every additional
year of my working life.) My resolve to become Constantine Porphyrogenitus's modern editor had thus been implanted in me directly by
Bury and indirectly by my mother.

In 1910, Constantine Porphyrogenitus's works on East Roman affairs
certainly did require re-editing. The latest edition was Bekker's in the
Bonn series (three volumes, published in 1829, 1830, and 1840). The first
two volumes were simply a reprint of Reiske's edition of the *De Caerimoniis*
and his commentary on this work of Constantine's; and Reiske's text and
commentary had been published in 1751–4, and were already nearly a
quarter of a century old by the time when Gibbon cited them. Reiske's
commentary was a magnificent feat of scholarship for its age, but it had
fallen out of date in the course of the century and a half that had gone by
between Reiske's generation and Bury's. Bekker's third volume contained
the texts of the *De Thematibus* and the *De Administrando Imperio*, with
Banduri's commentary on these two works.[1]

In 1972 the Bonn edition is still the only one that we have for the
De Caerimoniis, Book I, chapters 84–97; for all except chapters 52–3
of Book II; and for the memoranda on campaigning. The rest of

---

[1] Bekker's editorial work in this volume was perfunctory (see J. B. Bury, 'The treatise *De
Administrando Imperio*', in *Die byzantinische Zeitschrift*, 15. Band, 3 and 4 (1906), pp. 517–77, on
p. 518, n. 3).

Constantine's works on East Roman affairs have now been re-edited. Chapters 52–3 of Book II of the *De Caerimoniis* (Philótheos's *klêtorolóyion*), were republished in 1911, by Bury himself, in a revised text, based on a first-hand study of the Leipzig and Jerusalem manuscripts, and accompanied by a monograph of his own on *The Imperial Administrative System in the Ninth Century*.[1] I have a copy of this that was sent to me, at the time, for review. Most of Book I of the *De Caerimoniis* was re-edited in 1935–40 by A. Vogt[2] in the Collection byzantine de l'Association G. Budé. The *De Administrando Imperio* was re-edited in 1949–62, with an English translation and a commentary, by Gy. Moravcsik and R. J. H. Jenkins.[3] The *De Thematibus* was re-edited in 1952, with an introduction and a commentary, by A. Pertusi.[4]

How is it that I have not had a hand in this work, in spite of my early ambitions? One answer is that, less than four years after I had declared these aspirations in the Greek verses already quoted, the First World War turned my activities into other channels. After that, I might have started on the task of re-editing Constantine's works on East Roman affairs in the years 1919–24, when I was the first holder of the Koraes Chair of Byzantine and Modern Greek Studies in the University of London. By that time, however, I had realized that my *métier* was to use texts, properly edited by textual scholars, as materials for historical study,[5] but not to be a textual scholar myself. Anyway, my tenure of the Koraes Chair ended abruptly in 1924, and for the next forty-two years I was engaged on intellectual enterprises in which East Roman affairs played a relatively small part.

However, this field of study never receded from its original place— a high place—in my historical interests. A set of Bekker's edition of

---

[1] J. B. Bury, *The Imperial Administrative System in the Ninth Century*, with a revised text of the *Klêtorologion of Philótheos*, The British Academy, Supplemental Papers, I (London, 1911, Oxford University Press); reprinted in 1958 by Burt Franklin.

[2] Vol. i contains Book I, chaps 1–46 (37), Part I (text), Part II (commentary), both published in 1935; vol. ii contains Book I, chaps. 47 (38)–92 (83), Part I (text), 1939, Part II (commentary), 1940.

[3] The text, edited by Moravcsik, and the English translation, made by Jenkins, were published in one volume (Budapest, 1949, University Institute of Greek Philology); the commentary was published separately (London, 1962, Athlone Press). The commentary was produced by Moravcsik and Jenkins in co-operation with Dvornik, Lewis, Obolensky, and Runciman. It was edited by Jenkins. A slightly revised second edition of Moravcsik and Jenkins's text and translation (but not the commentary) was published in 1967 by the Dumbarton Oaks Center for Byzantine Studies at Washington, D.C.

[4] Città del Vaticano, 1952, Biblioteca Apostolica Vaticana: Studi e Testi, 160.

[5] 'It is now generally recognized as a fundamental principle in historical work that philological criticism (literary and *quellenkritisch*) is the necessary preparation for a satisfactory use of authorities. Documents are not ready for the constructive operations of the historian till they have been submitted to the analytical operations of the philologist' (J. B. Bury, 'The treatise *De Administrando Imperio*', in *Die byzantinische Zeitschrift*, 15. Band, 3 and 4 (1906), pp. 517–77, on p. 517).

Constantine's works on East Roman affairs, which I had acquired in 1923, was sitting on my shelves to remind me of my early ambition. When these three volumes were joined successively by Vogt's and by Moravcsik's and Jenkins's,[1] I was delighted that these skilful contemporary hands had done a large part of the job that I had left undone and that I should certainly not have been so competent to do as these fine scholars of my own generation have proved themselves to be. Yet, though my aspiration to be Constantine's latest editor had evaporated, my concern with Constantine had remained alive. When, in the spring of 1966, I found that I had finished all the pieces of historical writing that had come on to my agenda since 1913, I started, at last, to read Constantine's works on East Roman affairs systematically. The result is not a new edition—not even of the residue that has not yet been re-edited by other hands; the outcome is only the present historical essay. I publish this as a small tribute to Bury, who, besides being a very great historian, was also a masterly editor of Greek texts.

My essay's field is indicated in its title *Constantine Porphyrogenitus and His World*, and I have covered even this limited field only partially. I have concentrated on aspects of Constantine's world in which Constantine himself evidently took a special interest, and here I have gone the most into detail in discussing interests of Constantine's that happen also to be mine: for instance, the East Roman army-corps districts ($\theta \acute{\epsilon} \mu a \tau a$); the Slav settlements to the south of the Danube and the eventual conversion of the southernmost of the settlers into Greek-speaking Eastern Orthodox Christians; and the Empire's foreign relations, particularly those with Bulgaria, the Eastern Muslims, the Armenian and Caucasian principalities, and the peoples to the North. But I have not written a separate chapter on the Eastern Orthodox Church (though there are few chapters into which the Church does not enter); nor, within the province of ecclesiastical affairs, have I given special attention to Byzantine monasticism, except in so far as the richer of the monasteries in the Empire's territory were large-scale landowners. This feature of tenth-century Byzantine monasticism was important fiscally, economically, and socially. The year 961, which is the date of the foundation of the Great Lávra on Mount Athos, is a landmark in the history of Byzantine monasticism. But monasticism was a more active force in Byzantine Greek religious life in other periods: for instance, during the transition from the Hellenic to the Byzantine Age of Greek history, during the conflict over eikóns (726–843), and during the fourteenth-century controversy over Hesychasm.

I have left out these historically important episodes in the history of Byzantine monasticism because I have limited my field chronologically.

---

[1] Pertusi's edition of the *De Thematibus* was already out of print by the time when I was seeking for a copy of it. I have read, and taken my notes from, the copy in the British Museum.

I have tried to confine it within the smallest chronological compass that would suffice for making Constantine's world intelligible. I have not carried my narrative any farther forward beyond the year 959, in which Constantine Porphyrogenitus died, than the earliest subsequent date at which I could wind it up without breaking off in the middle of the story. I have followed the Emperors' agrarian legislation as far as Basil II's Novel No. 29 of 1003–4, the Empire's relations with the Eastern Muslims as far as the reconquests of Crete, the Eastern Cilicia, and Cyprus in 960–5, its relations with Armenia as far as the annexation of Taron in 968, and its relations with the North as far as the conversion of Vladímir in 989. But, in tracing the history of the Paulicians and the Bogomils, I have been led on into the thirteenth century, and even into the nineteenth. I have also been led back into the seventh century in tracing the origin of the army-corps districts, and into the sixth century in trying to ascertain the date of the beginning of the Slav *Völkerwanderung*.

Thus this essay is not an attempt at a comprehensive history of the Byzantine Greek civilization. This has been provided recently in the two parts of the second edition of volume iv of *The Cambridge Medieval History*, edited by Professor Joan Hussey and published in 1966–7, and, still more recently, in the second revised edition, translated into English by Professor Hussey and published by Thames and Hudson in 1971, of H. W. Haussig's *A History of Byzantine Civilization (Kulturgeschichte von Byzanz)*. The first of these two works appeared in time for me to make full use of it in my own present work, but the script of this was already in the hands of the Oxford University Press before I received an advance copy of Professor Haussig's work through the kindness of Mr. Thomas Neurath of Thames and Hudson. I have therefore only been able to take account of Professor Haussig's brilliant book at the last moment, here and there.

Professor Dmitri Obolensky's *The Byzantine Commonwealth: Eastern Europe 500–1453*, published in the autumn of 1971, is noted in my Bibliography, but unfortunately I had not been able to read it in time to take any account of it in the text.

ACKNOWLEDGEMENTS

I am deeply grateful to Sir John Wolfenden, the Director of the British Museum, for his most considerate hospitality. Before I had finished the work in the British Museum Library that I needed to do in order to write the present book, I was overtaken by illness, and, after convalescence, I might not have been physically capable of working in the British Museum again if this stint of work had not been eased for me by Sir John Wolfenden's kindness.

Professor Paul Lemerle of the Collège de France has read, in typescript, Annex III of this book, and Professor Robert Browning has read the whole typescript. Both these learnèd scholars have given me very valuable information and advice. I am most grateful for the time and trouble that they have spent on doing this. Their help has made it possible for me to improve the book, but of course they themselves are not implicated in the result.

I am also grateful to colleagues who have coped with my manuscript. There are many footnotes and many quotations in Greek, and there have also been numerous corrections and additions. The chapters that I wrote first were typed by Mrs. H. L. Rocke. In an emergency, part way through, Miss Carola Piggott and Mrs. F. Ilic came to my rescue. Miss Louise Orr has not only completed the typing of the manuscript; she has also put the whole of the printer's copy into presentable shape—a most exacting task, which included writing a number of Greek passages by hand. Without this kind aid, the book could not have been set up in print.

The index has been made by Mrs. Sally Bicknell. This analysis, in detail, of the contents of the book will, I believe, be as greatly appreciated by the reader as it is by the author. Thanks to Mrs. Bicknell's care, I have been able to correct a number of inconsistencies and slips before the book finally passed out of my hands.

ARNOLD TOYNBEE

July 1972

CONTENTS

PART V

CONSTANTINE PORPHYROGENITUS'S WORKS

MAPS[1]

at end of book

[1] Map 1 has been based on a map in *The Annual of the British School at Athens*, No. 65, (1970), p. 38. Maps 2, 3, 4, 5 have been based on maps in the author's earlier book *A Study of History*, vol. xi: *Historical Atlas and Gazetteer* (London and New York, 1959, Oxford University Press), maps 38, 42, 39, 40 respectively.

NOTE ON THE TRANSLITERATION OF RHOMAIC GREEK WORDS

When the Romans transliterated Greek words, they did not reproduce them in the Latin alphabet letter for letter; they re-cast the words themselves into Latin forms. This Roman practice has been followed by the Romans' Western successors, and by now it has become so well established that it would be pedantic to depart from it in transliterating the Greek of the Hellenic Age into any of our modern Western vernaculars. In Latinizing this Hellenic Greek, we are following a bad Roman example; we are taking an impertinent liberty with a finer language than Latin; yet here, all the same, it seems better to conform to custom, since custom has made the Latinized forms of Hellenic Greek words so familiar to Western eyes that the original Greek forms actually look uncouth.

This consideration, however, does not apply to Rhomaic Greek. In the long history of the Greek language, the transition from the language's Hellenic phase to its Rhomaic phase was, no doubt, gradual; but the change must have gone with a run in the anarchic seventh century of the Christian Era, and we have evidence that, at least by the tenth century, Greek was already being pronounced as it is today. This is attested by the spelling of 'fossil' Latin words in the Greek alphabet in Constantine Porphyrogenitus's works, and by the spelling of Greek words in the Latin alphabet in the works of Constantine Porphyrogenitus's contemporary, Bishop Liutprand of Cremona. In transliterating Rhomaic Greek words into the Latin alphabet—i.e. into the phonetic values given to the Latin letters in one or other of the present-day Western vernaculars—there is no reason why we should denature these Greek words by Latinizing their form. East Roman proper names—e.g. the personal name Várdhas Phokás and the geographical name Laghouvardhía—are not household words in the West, as many Hellenic proper names are, so it would be gratuitous for twentieth-century students of East Roman history to Latinize these Rhomaic Greek names into 'Bardas Phocas' and 'Langobardia', the forms in which they would have been travestied by Cicero or by Virgil. In contrast to the Hellenic World, the Byzantine World is relatively unfamiliar to present-day Westerners; Byzantine Greek names will look exotic to them, in whatever form they are transliterated; so we might just as well transliterate them accurately. 'Lekapênós' does not look more uncouth to us than its Latinized equivalent 'Lecapenus', nor 'kameláfkion' than 'camelaucium'.

Moreover, we should be putting the history of the Byzantine World into a false perspective if we were to 'process' Byzantine Greek words as we 'process' Hellenic Greek words. In Latinizing Byzantine Greek words too, we should be suggesting that Byzantine history is a prolongation of Hellenic history, and that, at Constantinople, Hellenic history did not come to an end till A.D. 1453. We should be obscuring the historical truth; and this truth is that the Byzantine Christian civilization which arose in the Levant after the great break there in the seventh century was just as new and as original a growth as the Western Christian civilization which arose, contemporaneously, side by side with the Byzantine.

For these reasons, I have, in this book, transliterated Byzantine Greek proper names and other Byzantine Greek words according to the system set out below. The only names that I have Latinized are those of writers. I have made this exception for convenience of reference, since these names have been cited in Latinized forms ever since their bearers' works were first edited and printed in the West—i.e. ever since the fifteenth and sixteenth centuries. I have therefore resigned myself to writing 'Leo Grammaticus' instead of 'Léon Ghrammatikós', but I have not been able to bring myself to write 'Cedrenus' instead of 'Kedhrênós'.

TRANSLITERATION

The Greek Alphabet	*The Latin Alphabet*	*Approximate Pronunciation*[1] (In the illustrative words the letters that represent the Rhomaic pronunciation of the transliteration are printed in italics)
α	a	b*u*tt
αι	ai	b*e*t
αυ (except before voiced sounds)	af	cu*ff*
αυ (before voiced sounds)	av	lo*v*e
β	v	o*v*er
γ (except before 'soft' vowels and 'soft' diphthongs, namely αι, ε, ει, ευ, η, ηυ, ι, οι, υ, υι)	gh	(Spanish) fue*g*o (the sound of the Arabic letter ghayn)
γ (before 'soft' vowels and 'soft' diphthongs)	y	*y*ield
γγ	ng	fi*n*ger
γκ (initial)	g	*g*et
γκ (medial)	ng, ngk	fi*n*ger, i*nk*
γξ	nx	sphi*nx*
γχ	nkh	an*x*ious
δ	dh	fa*th*er

---

[1] Following closely J. T. Pring, *The Oxford Dictionary of Modern Greek* (*Greek–English*) (Oxford, 1965, Clarendon Press), pp. xii–xiv.

The Greek Alphabet	*The Latin Alphabet*	*Approximate Pronunciation*
ε	e	b*e*t
ει	ei	b*ea*t
ευ (except before voiced sounds)	ef	ch*ef*
ευ (before voiced sounds)	ev	*ev*er
ζ	z	la*z*y
η	ê	b*ea*t
ηυ (except before voiced sounds)	êf	*lea*f
ηυ (before voiced sounds)	êv	*leave*
θ	th	au*th*or
ι	i	b*ea*t
κ	k	s*k*in
λ	l	*l*eave
μ	m	*m*ay
μπ (initial)	b	*b*et
μπ (medial)	mb	hu*mb*le
ν	n	*n*ot
ντ (initial and final)	d	*d*o
ντ (medial)	nd	a*nd*
ξ	x	bo*x*
ο	o	b*ou*ght
οι	oi	b*ea*t
ου	ou	b*oo*t
π	p	s*p*in
ρ (initial)	rh	th*r*ee
ρ (medial, between two vowels)	rrh	th*r*ee
ρ (medial, not between two vowels)	r	th*r*ee
σ (not before voiced consonants)	s	*s*ee
σ (before voiced consonants)	z	la*z*y
τ	t	s*t*ick
τζ	dz	a*dz*e
υ	y	b*ea*t
υι	ui	b*ea*t
φ	ph	*ph*ysic, *f*at
χ (except before 'soft' vowels and 'soft' diphthongs)	kh	lo*ch*
χ (before 'soft' vowels and 'soft' diphthongs)	h	*h*ew
ψ	ps	ta*ps*
ω	o	b*ou*ght

The Rhomaic Greek stress-accent has been represented uniformly by an acute accent, and no accent has been placed on the transliterations of monosyllabic Greek words, since, in a monosyllable, a stress-accent is superfluous. That is a justifiable simplification of the present-day Greek system of accentuation, since this is a legacy from a stage in the evolution of the Greek language in which the accent was still a pitch-accent and had not yet turned into a stress-accent. The Greek system still preserves two out of the three different symbols—the grave, the acute, and the circumflex accent—that originally distinguished different tones, though these differences have not survived the change in the Greek accent's character. For instance, the accent on Σχολῶν is still represented by a circumflex, though there is now no difference in the quality of the accent between Σχολῶν and Σχολή. Accordingly, Σχολῶν, Χερσῶν, etc., have been transliterated as Skholón, Khersón. In Hellenic Greek, the acute accent on the last syllable of a word, or on a monosyllabic word, was turned into a grave accent except at the end of a sentence or a clause. In present-day Rhomaic Greek, the grave accent has been eliminated, and this practice has been followed in the transliteration of Rhomaic Greek words into the Latin alphabet in the present book. On the other hand, the Hellenic system of accentuation has been followed in passages of works, written in the Attic *koiné* by Byzantine Greek authors, that have been quoted here.

NOTE ON SYSTEMS OF CHRONOLOGY

THE East Romans had a double system of recording dates: by fiscal years ('indictions', meaning literally 'assessments') and by years of the (supposed) age of the Universe. Both the Indiction Year and the 'Year of the World' ran from 1 September to 31 August. Thus every indiction coincided exactly with some Year of the World, and vice versa. The Years of the World ran in a single continuous series; the indictions ran in cycles of recurrent runs of fifteen years in each round. The Muslims reckoned by a continuous series of years starting from the Prophet Muhammad's withdrawal (*hijrah*) from Mecca to Medina in A.D. 622. The East Roman years in both series were Julian solar years. The Muslim years of the Era of the *Hijrah* were, and are, lunar years, none of which can ever coincide exactly with any solar year, whether Julian or Gregorian.

The numbers attached to years in the present work are those of years of the Christian Era. When a pair of consecutive year-numbers is written thus—913/14—the stroke means that this is a single year (either a single East Roman solar year or a single Muslim lunar year) that straddles parts of two consecutive years of the Christian Era. When a pair of consecutive year-numbers is written thus—913–14—the hyphen means that these are two separate solar years of the Christian Era. The formula 913–59 means that these are forty-seven separate solar years of the Christian Era.

The East Roman system of double dating—by indictions linked with Years of the World—ought to have made for accuracy. It does provide a test; for if an indiction and a Year of the World that are cited by an East Roman annalist or historian as being identical turn out not to correspond with each other in fact, it is evident that at least one of the two figures must be wrong, and the whole of this particular dating then becomes suspect. In the datings given by East Roman writers the ratio of proven inaccuracies is high. Datings given by Muslim writers sometimes supply the trustworthy chronological information that East Roman writers have failed to provide. Yet there are a number of important events in East Roman history that cannot be dated with certainty, even with the aid of our Arabic sources.

PART I

CONSTANTINE PORPHYROGENITUS HIMSELF

1. *Constantine Porphyrogenitus's Life*

It is a misfortune to be born into a position in society from which there is no possibility of escape, however uncongenial this inescapable position may be to the victim's temperament, gifts, and consequent inclinations. This misfortune is a rare one. There are few stations in life that have held everyone that has been born into them as their life-long prisoner. One prisoner in a thousand, or one in a million at least, has succeeded in breaking his way out of even the most cramping and most crushing original confinement. At least one person, out of the many born into this position, will have found his position uncongenial enough, and will have had importunate enough incompatible ambitions, to have nerved him to make the necessary effort of will for breaking out, hard and painful though the act of self-liberation may have been.

Perhaps the only social position from which escape is impossible for those born into it is royalty; for this continues to haunt its victim psychologically even if he has managed to extricate himself from it officially. A royal personage who, so long as he has remained officially royal, has been longing to enjoy the satisfactions and amenities of private life, is apt to find, if and when he has had his way, that he now misses the servitude that was so irksome to him so long as he was officially subject to it. He now discovers, too late, that, unconsciously, he had been wishing to have the best of both worlds; and he has actually got the worst of both as an ironical result of his apparently successful fight to win his freedom. Moreover, the royal personage who is free to divest himself of his royalty officially is relatively fortunate. Even this limited degree of self-liberation can be attained by a royal personage only in a society that has become so orderly, or that has reduced royalty to so insignificant a social role, that, in this society, it has ceased to be dangerous either to wear a crown or to doff one. In most societies, at most times and places, the wearer of a crown has been holding a wolf by the ears.

In the present-day Western World, to be royal has ceased to be dangerous, yet royalty continues to be awkward for inheritors of it who are irked by it. *A fortiori*, in the East Roman Empire in the tenth century of the Christian Era, the Imperial crown was a heavy incubus for a wearer on whose head it had proved to be a misfit. Whether the sovereignty associated with a crown is still effective or has become little more than nominal, the crown attracts to itself a constantly growing burden of obligatory ceremonial. This is burdensome enough in the surviving constitutional monarchies of the present-day Western World, but their load of ceremony is light by comparison with the load imposed on an Egyptian Pharaoh or a Chinese Son of Heaven or an East Roman Vasiléfs. Try with yourself, as I have tried with myself, the experiment of reading Constantine Porphyrogenitus's massive work on the ceremonies of the East Roman Court, without giving in to the temptation to skip. The book is big because the set formulae, prescribing what each actor in the ritual drama is to do, to wear, and to say are repeated so remorselessly that the reiteration produces a hypnotic effect on the reader. How much more potent must have been the effect on the actors, and, above all, on the protagonist, namely the Emperor himself. Unless this nonsense happened to be congenial to an Emperor's temperament, he was bound to be irked by it, and, if he had any incompatible positive personal bent, he was bound to repine and—in an extreme case of uncongeniality—bound to revolt.

However, in the East Roman Imperial Palace, an Emperor revolted at his peril. A conforming Emperor lived dangerously; a recalcitrant Emperor, in ceasing to obey convention, was courting death. Michael III achieved a *tour de force* in managing to reign unconventionally for nearly twenty-six years before meeting his inevitable death by assassination. Constantine VII Porphyrogenitus reigned for perhaps almost twice as long. He was crowned, while his father Leo VI was still alive, on a Whit Sunday which may have been that of 908,[1] and he died in office on

---

[1] Reasons for thinking that 908 was the year are given by Ph. Grierson and R. J. H. Jenkins, 'The Date of Constantine VII's Coronation', in *Byzantion*, vol. xxxii (1962), pp. 133–8. If this dating is right, Constantine was Emperor for more than 51 years. Pseudo-Symeon's date for Constantine's coronation is Whit Sunday 911 (pp. 711–12). *Georgius Monachus Continuatus*, p. 874, *Leo Grammaticus*, p. 288, and pseudo-Symeon, p. 718, all reckon Constantine VII's reign as beginning at the death of his uncle the Emperor Alexander on 6 June 913, and they all give identical numbers of years for each of the three sections of Constantine VII's reign. These figures add up to 48 years, but only pseudo-Symeon gives the total correctly. The other three chroniclers make it come to 55 years, i.e. to longer than Constantine VII's whole life-time. The figure 48 itself is nearly two years too high (the year in which Constantine fell under Rhomanós I's tutelage and the year in which he escaped from it have each been counted twice). Constantine reigned, not for 48 years, but for 46 years and six months, if he is reckoned to have come to the throne at the date of his uncle's death, and not at the earlier date, whatever that may have been, at which Constantine was crowned.

15 November, A.D. 959, in the fifty-fifth year of his life.[1] If Constantine Porphyrogenitus's death was a natural one, he could have summed up his career in the Abbé Sieyès's words 'J'ai vécu'. His survival would have been a greater achievement than his scholarship had been.

Constantine did survive on the Imperial throne for perhaps fifty-one years in spite of his having allowed himself to follow his private interests to some extent; but, then, Constantine's private interests did not fly in the face of Byzantine convention, as Michael's did. Michael's private interests were mainly in low life; Constantine's were in scholarship—a field in which an Emperor could follow a private pursuit without provoking scandal. Even so, it is not certain that Constantine did die a natural death. It is recorded as an established fact that an unsuccessful attempt to poison him was made by his son and colleague Rhomanós II and by his daughter-in-law, Rhomanós's second wife, Theophanó.[2] It is also recorded—though this only as an unverified report—that his subsequent death, at an age sixteen years short of threescore and ten, was due to a second dose of poison, administered by Rhomanós and Theophanó, which, this time, was successful.[3]

Some of those private pursuits of Michael III's that shocked East Roman public opinion would have shocked any public at any time and place. Michael was a drunkard; he surrounded himself with a band of disreputable boon companions whose pastime was to burlesque, for the Emperor's amusement, the liturgy of the Church;[4] and Michael's own principal personal passion was for charioteering in the races in the

---

[1] Constantine VII Porphyrogenitus died in November 959. The month is recorded in *Theophanes Continuatus*, pp. 468–9; pseudo-Symeon, p. 756; Leo Diaconus, p. 5. *Theoph. Cont.* and pseudo-Symeon both make the date 15 November. The November of 959 fell in the third indiction, i.e. the third year in the current round of the fifteen-year cycle of East Roman fiscal years running from 1 September to 31 August. The number of the indiction is given correctly in *Theoph. Cont.* and by Leo Diaconus and by Kedhrênós, and Kedhrênós also gives correctly the corresponding Year of the World, namely A.M. 6468 (see C. B. Hase's note on p. 6 of his edition (Bonn, 1828, Weber) of Leo Diaconus's *Historiae*). On the other hand, *Theoph. Cont.*, pseudo-Symeon, and Leo Diaconus all give wrong Years of the World (A.M. 6469, 6456, and 6467 respectively); and both *Theoph. Cont.* and pseudo-Symeon make Constantine live a year longer than he did live. Pseudo-Symeon makes him over 55 at the date of his death; *Theoph. Cont.* makes him exactly fifty-five years five months and two days old. A comet is said to have appeared at the time of both his birth and his death (*Theoph. Cont.*, p. 370; pseudo-Symeon, p. 756; Leo Diaconus, p. 5). Whatever may have been the precise date of Constantine's birth in 905 (see p. 8, n. 1), he died in the fifty-fifth, not in the fifty-sixth, year of his life.

[2] Yeóryios Kedhrênós = Georgius Cedrenus Joannis Scylitsae Ope ab I. Bekkero suppletus et emendatus, tomus alter (Bonn, 1839, Weber), pp. 336–7; Johannes Zonarás, *Epitomae Historiarum*, vol. iii, Books XIII–XVIII, ed. T. Büttner-Wobst (Bonn, 1897, Weber), p. 488; Michael Glykas, *Vívlos Khronikḗ*, ed. I. Bekker (Bonn, 1836, Weber), pp. 563–4.

[3] Kedhrênós, op. cit., ed. cit., vol. cit., p. 337; Zonarás, op. cit., ed. cit., p. 489.

[4] *Theophanes Continuatus*, Book IV, Reign of Michael III, chaps. 38–9, pp. 200–2; pseudo-Symeon Magister, Reign of Michael III, chap. 18, pp. 661–2; Kedhrênós, vol. ii, pp. 176–8; Genesius, *Basileiai* (Bonn, 1834, Weber), Book IV, pp. 102–3.

Hippodrome. His gross neglect of his professional duties in order to engage in frivolity and vice would have been as reprehensible in a private profession as it was in the Imperial office. However, the Byzantine historians' condemnation of Michael III ought not to be swallowed whole without reservations. Even his drunkenness had some excuse; the boringness of the East Roman official protocol was enough to make a puritan take to drink. As for the burlesquing of the liturgy, this was aggravated by the vulgarity of the performance; yet, here again, we can diagnose a natural human reaction to the irksomeness of having to be in attendance, *ex officio*, at genuine ecclesiastical rites that sometimes lasted for hours, and even days, on end.[1]

Moreover, Michael was blamed, with equal severity, for activities which, to our minds, were harmless and indeed were meritorious. He was criticized, for instance, for roaming the streets of Constantinople without an escort.[2] The gravamen of this charge was that he did this 'needlessly'.[2] A present-day critic would concede that Michael had a genuine psychological need to take occasional breaths of fresh air after being half-asphyxiated by the stifling atmosphere of the East Roman Court. One incident, recorded to discredit him, will win a modern reader's sympathy.

His passion for charioteering was positively pathological, and it is not as if this was the worst of his offences against decency. He went beyond bounds in trying to keep within bounds [that would have been suitable for someone in a private station]. This led him into the worst of his offences against decency and of his breaches of Imperial decorum.

Once, in the street, he ran into a woman to whose son he had stood god-father. She was on her way home from the public baths, and she had a pail in her hand. Michael jumped off his horse, dismissed his senatorial attendants to the palace in the neighbourhood, picked up a party of disreputable vicious creatures, and went off with the woman. Taking her pail from her, he said to her: 'It is all right, lady. I want you to entertain me in your home. I am dying for some branny bread and for some fresh-made cheese.' (Please excuse the vulgar language; it is Michael's own, verbatim.) The strangeness of the performance struck the woman dumb. She did not know what to do. She had no table and no table-linen. But, as quick as a thought, Michael turned; seized the towel, still soaking wet, that the woman was carrying home from the baths; spread it in lieu of proper table-linen; snatched the woman's key from her hand; and filled every role simultaneously. He was Emperor, waiter, cook, and guest. He emptied out the pauper woman's larder and dined with her festively—telling her that he was following the example of Christ Our

---

[1] This irked Phótios too, when he was Ecumenical Patriarch, if there is any truth in the story that, during the liturgy, he used to whisper snatches of Hellenic poetry in lieu of the breviary (pseudo-Symeon, Reign of Michael III, chap. 33, p. 672). See further p. 609, with n. 7.

[2] Glykás, op. cit., p. 541.

Lord. After that, he went back to the Palace on foot, abusing his predecessors on the Imperial throne for their stupidity and hocus-pocus and pomposity.[1]

In reading the account of the reign of Michael III in Genesius and in *Theophanes Continuatus*, and the description of Michael given by Constantine Porphyrogenitus in his biography, in the same series, of Michael's beneficiary, colleague, murderer, and successor, Constantine's grandfather Basil (Βασίλειος) I, we have to keep constantly in mind the pertinent fact that Constantine and his anonymous employee the writer of Book IV of *Theophanes Continuatus*, as well as his other employee Genesius, had a motive for denigrating Michael. This was an indirect way of carrying out the difficult enterprise of whitewashing Basil. The less excusable that Michael was made out to be, the more excusable could Basil be made to appear. However, Michael is condemned no less vehemently by later chroniclers—Kedhrênós, Zonarás, Glykás—who were under no pressure to appease the now defunct Basilian dynasty and who did, in fact, use their liberty to give frank accounts of the crimes by which Basil I made his way to the Imperial throne. This concordant testimony suggests that those of Michael's acts that were faults in Byzantine eyes—including those that are not faults in our eyes—are authentic.

Constantine Porphyrogenitus's indulgence in the pleasures of private life took less provocative forms. He did not neglect his official duties. So far from that, he took a positive intellectual interest in the Imperial protocol that Michael had found exasperating. Constantine was a natural-born scholar and a competent self-taught painter,[2] and he had enough practical knowledge of sculpture, architecture, goldsmiths' and silversmiths' and blacksmiths' work, shipbuilding, and music, to be an effective critic, as well as an active patron, in all these fields.[3] These private

[1] *Theoph. Cont.*, ed. by I. Bekker (Bonn, 1838, Weber), Book IV, Reign of Michael III, chap. 37, pp. 199–200. The story is repeated, almost verbatim, by Kedhrênós, ed. cit., vol. ii, pp. 175–6. The story is also told by pseudo-Symeon Magister, with two variations. He omits Michael's alleged comparison of his own conduct with Christ's, and he adds, after reporting Michael's request for bread and cheese, that Michael imagined that the woman would have had something in hand out of the fifty gold pieces that he had given to her husband when he had stood godfather to their son (pseudo-Symeon, Reign of Michael III, chap. 17, pp. 660–1).

[2] *Theoph. Cont.*, Book VI, second bout of Constantine VII's sole reign, chap. 22, p. 450. *Theoph. Cont.* is the composite work of four different hands, three of them anonymous, while the fourth is Constantine VII Porphyrogenitus. Books I–IV are by the first anonymous author, who was Constantine's employee. Book V, the biography of Basil I, is by Constantine himself. Book VI, pp. 353–441 in the Bonn edition, was written by the second anonymous author in the reign of Nikêphóros II Phokás (*imperabat* A.D. 963–9), and drew on the genuine Symeon, the magister and logothete (reproduced by Leo Grammaticus and in *Georgius Monachus Interpolatus* (A.D. 813–42) and *Continuatus* (A.D. 843–948). From p. 441 onwards (i.e. from after the notice of Rhomanós Lekapênós's death), *Theoph. Cont.*, Book VI, is the work of a third anonymous author. This is an original work. K. Krumbacher dates it *circa* A.D. 961–3 (*Geschichte der byzantinischen Literatur*, 2nd ed. (Munich, 1897, Beck), pp. 348–9).

[3] *Theoph. Cont.*, Book VI, second bout of Constantine VII's sole reign, chap. 25, p. 451; chap. 36, p. 457.

pursuits of Constantine's gave him some of the psychological relief that he too needed, without their being invidious, as Michael III's private pursuits were.

In the opening chapter of his biography of his grandfather the Emperor Basil I, Constantine Porphyrogenitus avows that his inescapable official position has been a serious hindrance to the fulfilment of his ambitions as a scholar and historian.

> For a long time past, I have had an eager longing to convey to serious minds, through the mouth of the memorable and immortal [muse of] history, a knowledge, based on experience, of public affairs. My ambition, supposing that I could achieve this, was to write the story of the outstanding events of the whole Byzantine period of Roman history, including the acts of the Emperors and their civil and military subordinates, as well as other significant affairs. However, this enterprise would have required much time and continuous labour and a first-rate library and leisure from public duties; and none of these facilities were at my disposal. So, as a *pis aller*, I have had to content myself with writing the life of a single Emperor . . . If I were now to be granted a further instalment of life, and could have even a short respite from ill health, and if no public business were to get in my way, perhaps I might manage to continue my narrative farther. I should like to cover the whole story of Basil's house down to my own generation.[1]

This last-mentioned project of Constantine's, like his earlier more ambitious one, remained unfulfilled. He is wistful about the impediments to the work which was his true vocation. Undoubtedly he would have produced more than he actually did produce if he had been born in a private station and if he had lived to the age that was the normal expectation of life in his society. On the other hand, much of the scholarly work that he did do could not have been done by anyone who had not a right to explore the Imperial archives and to receive oral reports from officials returning from missions abroad. Moreover, though Constantine was conscious that the Imperial Crown was, on balance, a handicap to him as a scholar, and that the duties that the Crown carried with it were uncongenial to him, he was nevertheless determined, not only to retain the Crown, but to reign in reality and not just in name, though he was aware that the exercise of real power was bound to increase his burdens and his anxieties. If he had been sole Emperor throughout his reign, he might have imagined that he would have been happier in a private station; but he could not cherish this illusion after having had the experience of being eclipsed politically for nearly twenty-six years, from his fourteenth to his thirty-ninth year,[2] and possibly also being pro-

---

[1] *Theoph. Cont.*, (Bonn, 1838, Weber), Book V, Reign of Basil I, chap. 1, pp. 211–12.

[2] i.e. from 25 March 919, the date on which Rhomanós Lekapênós occupied the Palace at Constantinople, to 27 January 945, the date on which Constantine Porphyrogenitus

gressively degraded, in the course of this long eclipse, from the first to the fifth place in the Imperial consortium which the intruder Rhomanós Lekapênós had created for his own purposes.[1] When Constantine did at last recover his original position, thanks to a division in the Lekapenid house which led to its fall, he did not succeed in becoming a fully effective ruler up to the standards set by Rhomanós Lekapênós and by Constantine's own grandfather Basil I. Yet, in the light of his humiliating previous experience, Constantine preferred to be a semi-effective Emperor rather than to remain a shadow Emperor or to become a commoner—which he could hardly have achieved except at the price of being tonsured or castrated or blinded.

Throughout his reign, Constantine Porphyrogenitus always found himself on a bed of thorns. His life was a series of tribulations. These assailed him one after another. Even after the fall of the Lekapênoí, he had few spells of peace and quiet.

Constantine's earliest trouble was bequeathed to him by his father the Emperor Leo VI, who was acclaimed as 'the Wise' but who deserved the title as little as Solomon did. Leo's lack of wisdom revealed itself, like Solomon's, in his marital escapades. When Leo had married his fourth wife, he had split the Eastern Orthodox Church, and the whole of Byzantine society with it, into a condoning and a condemning faction. This split in A.D. 906 was a tragedy, coming, as it did, only sixty-three years after the final settlement, in A.D. 843, of the conflict between iconoclasts and iconodules. That previous split, grievous though its effects had been, had at least been concerned with an important question of religious principle. The split precipitated by Leo VI was more wanton than the one produced by Leo III. The whole of Byzantine society suffered from this second split too, but the chief individual victim was Leo's infant son Constantine; for Leo's controversial fourth wife, Zoe Karvounopsína (Coal-eyes),[2] was Constantine's mother. She had borne

---

arrested, deposed, and exiled his two surviving co-Emperors, Rhomanós I's sons Stephen and Constantine, who had already deposed and exiled their father Rhomanós on 16 December 944.

[1] See Kedhrênós, vol. ii, p. 321. On the other hand, *Theoph. Cont.*, p. 435, says that Rhomanós Lekapênós made a will giving precedence to the Porphyrogenitus, and Kedhrênós's statement is challenged by H. Grégoire in *C. Med. H.*, vol. iv, 2nd ed., Part I, p. 143. Grégoire holds that Rhomanós had always given Constantine Porphyrogenitus precedence over his own sons Stephen and Constantine; that he confirmed this in November or December 944; and that this was why his sons deposed him. If Kedhrênós in loc. cit. is mistaken, his mistake may have arisen from there being two co-emperors named Constantine. Since Constantine Porphyrogenitus is named before Christopher in Novel No. 2, he may also be the first of the two Constantines named in No. 5. This is, indeed, probable, since Constantine Lekapênós is not likely to have been named before his elder brother Stephen.

[2] For the spelling of the name, see pseudo-Symeon, Reign of Leo VI, chap. 12, p. 705 in the Bonn edition.

Constantine to Leo out of wedlock in 905,[1] before Leo had married her[2] as his fourth wife.

When, in A.D. 912, Leo died and Leo's brother Alexander succeeded him, with Leo's son, the child Constantine, as his nominal co-Emperor, Alexander deposed Efthýmios, the Patriarch who had condoned Leo's fourth marriage, and reinstated Nikólaos, the Patriarch who had been deposed by Leo for condemning the marriage. The implication of this act was that the marriage was illegal and that Constantine was therefore illegitimate. According to the anonymous author of the first part of Book VI of *Theophanes Continuatus*,[3] Alexander was with difficulty dissuaded from having Constantine castrated—a mutilation that would automatically have voided his title to the Imperial Crown.[4] Fortunately for Constantine, his uncle Alexander died on 6 June 913 after having been on the throne for only thirteen months; but the chairman of the council of regency which now took control was the Patriarch Nikólaos, who had no reason for loving Zoe and her child. One of the blandishments by which the Patriarch cajoled Khan Symeon of Bulgaria into withdrawing from his investment of Constantinople in 913 may have been a promise that the Patriarch's Imperial ward would marry one of the Khan's daughters;[5] and though, in A.D. 914, Zoe emerged from retirement and managed to gain control of the government, her own and Constantine's position remained precarious so long as the conflict between Nikolaites and Efthymians persisted.

[1] On 18 May 905, according to Grierson and Jenkins, 'The Date of Constantine VII's Coronation', p. 135, n. 2. However, Jenkins dates Constantine's birth in September, not in May, 905, in a later paper ('The Chronological Accuracy of the "Logothete" for the years 867–912', in *Dumbarton Oaks Papers*, Number Nineteen (1965), pp. 91–112, on p. 108).

[2] Symeon Magister in *Georgius Monachus Continuatus*, Reign of Leo VI, chaps. 32 and 34, p. 865, and Leo Grammaticus, p. 279; pseudo-Symeon, Reign of Leo VI, chaps. 17–18, pp. 708–9.

[3] Reign of Alexander, chap. 3, p. 379. Cf. *Georg. Mon. Cont.*, Reign of Alexander, chap. 2, p. 872; Leo Grammaticus, Reign of Alexander, p. 286; pseudo-Symeon, Reign of Alexander, chap. 1, p. 716; Kedhrênós, vol. ii, p. 276.

[4] In the second of three poems on the death of Leo VI, written, in the main scribe's hand, in the margin of folio 116ʳ of the Madrid manuscript of Scylitzes's chronicle, the poet makes Leo commend his son Constantine to Leo's brother and Constantine's uncle and co-successor Alexander (lines 1–2). The poet also (lines 32–3) makes Leo assure Constantine that Uncle Alexander is going to be benevolent towards him. What are these lines intended to convey? Confidence or anxiety? They are printed on pp. 196 and 197 of I. Ševčenko's paper: 'Poems on the Deaths of Leo VI and Constantine VII in the Madrid Manuscript of Scylitzes', in *Dumbarton Oaks Papers*, Numbers Twenty-three and Twenty-four (1969–70), pp. 185–228. Ševčenko holds (ibid., p. 225) that, like the poem on the death of Constantine Porphyrogenitus, these three poems on the death of Leo were composed as obituary notices, immediately after the Emperor's death, i.e., in the case of the poems on Leo, 'shortly before 913'. If so, the lines cited here from the second of the three poems on Leo VI express a view of Alexander's attitude and intentions towards Constantine which is contemporary, whether the sense in which we interpret these lines is creditable to Alexander or is discreditable to him.

[5] See S. Runciman, *A History of the First Bulgarian Empire* (London, 1930, Bell), pp. 156–8, with Appendix IX on pp. 299–301. See also the present work, p. 366 n. 2.

This conflict was ended by agreement in June 920;[1] but this hardly improved Zoe's and Constantine's position canonically, while politically their position was now undermined. The formula of reconciliation did not explicitly condemn Leo VI's fourth marriage, but it banned fourth marriages for the future. The imputation on Constantine's legitimacy was manifest though indirect; and it was a humiliation for him to have to take part in the annual celebration of the reconciling compromise.[2] Moreover, the reconciliation between the two factions in the Church had been negotiated by a man who was elbowing his way on to the Imperial throne, pushing the youthful incumbent Constantine to the wall.

The intruder, Rhomanós Lekapênós, had been Admiral of the Imperial Fleet, and, with his ships' crews overawing Constantinople at close quarters, Rhomanós had had himself made máyistros and méghas etaireiárkhês; had then had his daughter Elénê married to Constantine by the Patriarch Nikólaos,[3] and had had himself elevated to the rank of vasileopátor (honorary father of the Emperor),[4] passing on the etaireiarkhate to his son Christopher. After crushing an armed rebellion by Leo Phokás (a member of a distinguished and powerful military family) and quashing a second hostile conspiracy, Rhomanós had relegated Zoe to a convent, had exiled Constantine's tutor Theodore and his brother, and had had himself created first Caesar and then Emperor on 17 December 920. The Patriarch Nikólaos had done the crowning, but Constantine had to take part in this and all the subsequent coronations of members of Rhomanós's family. Rhomanós proceeded to make his wife Theodora avghoústa and his son Christopher co-Emperor. (When Theodora died, as she did soon after, Rhomanós made Christopher's wife avghoústa in Theodora's place.)

As a precedent for his high-handed seizure of the Imperial crown, Rhomanós could have cited the career of Constantine's grandfather Basil I. He could have gone on to point out that Basil had made his way to the throne by murdering first the Caesar Várdhas and then the Emperor Michael III, whereas he, Rhomanós, had reached the same goal without shedding blood. (Leo Phokás, after his defeat and capture, had merely been blinded, and this without orders from Rhomanós, so

---

[1] *Georg. Mon. Cont.*, Reign of Rhomanós I, chap. 2, p. 890; Leo Grammaticus, p. 304; *Theoph. Cont.*, Book VI, Reign of Rhomanós I, chap. 1, p. 398; pseudo-Symeon, Reign of Constantine VII, chap. 18, p. 731.

[2] For the protocol, see *De Caer.*, Book I, chap. 36, pp. 186–7.

[3] On 4 May 919 (Jenkins, 'The Chronological Accuracy of the "Logothete" for the years 867–912', p. 108).

[4] The creation of this office—honorary in itself, but a well-placed stepping-stone for mounting the Imperial throne—had been one of the numerous inept acts of Constantine Porphyrogenitus's father Leo VI. Leo had invented the title for his minister Zaoúdzas (Ζαούτζας), with whose daughter he had fallen in love. See *Georg. Mon. Cont.*, p. 852; Leo Grammaticus, p. 266; *Theoph. Cont.*, p. 357; pseudo-Symeon, p. 701.

it was said.)[1] Rhomanós might have told Constantine that, considering how Constantine's grandfather had disposed of an Emperor who had been standing in his way, Constantine himself was lucky to have escaped without having been blinded or castrated or tonsured. This parallel, had Rhomanós drawn it, would have been specious, but it would have been fallacious. When once Basil I had been made co-Emperor by the disreputable Michael III, the only practical alternative, for Basil, to liquidating Michael would have been to allow himself to be implicated in Michael's discredit, which by then was approaching the point of political bankruptcy. Indeed, Michael might have murdered Basil before coming to grief himself if Basil had not struck first. Constantine VII never presented any comparable problem to Rhomanós I. On 25 March 919, when Rhomanós occupied the Palace, Constantine was only thirteen. On 16 December 920, when Rhomanós assumed the Imperial crown, Constantine was still only fifteen, and by temperament he was no fighter. For the next twenty-four years, Constantine put up with being subordinate to Rhomanós, without giving Rhomanós any trouble. When Rhomanós was overthrown in A.D. 944, the deed was done by two of his own sons whom he had associated with himself as co-Emperors. It is true that all accounts agree that the other co-Emperors—i.e. Christopher Lekapênós's son Michael and Constantine Porphyrogenitus himself—were privy to Stéphanos and Constantine Lekapênoí's plot to depose Rhomanós Lekapênós; but only Kedhrênós's and Zonarás's common source[2] says that it was the Porphyrogenitus who put the idea into Stéphanos's head.

Rhomanós Lekapênós did all that he could to ensure that his family should remain on the Imperial throne. He made his second and third sons, Stéphanos and Constantine, and his eldest son Christopher's son Michael too, co-Emperors. However, in crowning his sons, Rhomanós proved merely to have been laying up trouble for himself. Christopher's father-in-law, the máyistros Nikĕtas, was tonsured before Christopher's death, on the charge of having incited Christopher to overthrow Rhomanós. Stéphanos and Constantine Lekapênoí lived to succeed in overthrowing Rhomanós and tonsuring him, only to be overthrown within forty-two days,[3] and to be tonsured in their turn, by Constantine

---

[1] *Georg. Mon. Cont.*, p. 889; Leo Grammaticus, p. 303; *Theoph. Cont.*, first bout of Constantine VII's sole reign, chap. 13, pp. 395–7; pseudo-Symeon, joint reign of Constantine VII and Rhomanós I, chap. 15, p. 730. These authorities all say that Rhomanós I was vexed at this, but Kedhrênós, vol. ii, p. 295, says that, according to some accounts, Leo Phokás was blinded on secret orders from Rhomanós.

[2] Kedhrênós, vol. ii, pp. 321–4; Zonarás, vol. iii, p. 480. They drew upon this original common source via Skylídzês (Scylitzes).

[3] Forty-one days according to the Egyptian Eastern Orthodox Christian physician and historian Yahyā b. Saʿīd; but he dates the deposition of Rhomanós 16 December 944, and the deposition of Stéphanos and Constantine Lekapênoí 27 January 945 (see the passage

Porphyrogenitus—or, it might be more accurate to say, by their sister Elénê, Constantine Porphyrogenitus's wife, who had inherited her father's intelligence[1] and initiative. It was through marrying his daughter to the Porphyrogenitus, not through making three of his sons and one of his grandsons co-Emperors, that Rhomanós I did succeed in keeping descendants of his on the Imperial throne so long as the Basilian dynasty lasted.

Thus Constantine Porphyrogenitus had recovered his previous position of being sole Emperor, after having been under eclipse for nearly twenty-six years. This had been his reward for having taken the one decisive political action that he is known, for certain, to have taken[2] during his forty-six and a half or fifty-one years on the throne. Stéphanos and Constantine Lekapênoí had been paid out for overthrowing their father by being overthrown in their turn; but, in getting rid of all his former Lekapenid co-Emperors, Constantine Porphyrogenitus had not got rid of the Lekapênoí. His wife Elénê Lekapênê survived him[3]—luckily for him, for, now that he was effectively on the throne, he could not have 'got by' without drawing on her capacity for taking action. As has been noted already, Elénê is credited with having spurred her husband into deposing her brothers before they deposed him.[4] Rhomanós, Stéphanos, and Constantine Lekapênoí were now all monks interned in monasteries; but, though this was enough to disqualify them technically from being reinstated on the throne, Constantine Porphyrogenitus had to pay for his clemency in not taking more drastic action against them. They were an anxiety to him as long as they lived. Rhomanós Lekapênós lived till 948; Constantine Lekapênós got himself killed in trying to break out of his internment by force of arms. Constantine Porphyrogenitus had to cope with one plot to restore Rhomanós and with another to restore Stéphanos.[5] The first of these two plots had been hatched by Constantine Porphyrogenitus's brother-in-law Theophýlaktos, who had been installed in the Patriarchate by his father Rhomanós. Fortunately for Constantine Porphyrogenitus, Theophýlaktos was a light-weight. He had a passion for horses, and he thought of little besides that.

Theophýlaktos and Elénê were not the only Lekapênoí who were still at large. There was the youthful co-Emperor Michael, Christopher's son.

translated in Vasiliev, *Byzance et les Arabes*, ii, II, pp. 93–4; see also Mas'ūdī, translated ibid., pp. 397–8).

[1] ᾗ, πρὸς κάλλος σωματικόν, προσήκμασεν καὶ σύνεσις (*Theoph. Cont.*, first bout of Constantine VII's sole reign, chap. 13, p. 394).

[2] The story that Constantine Porphyrogenitus was the instigator of Stéphanos Lekapênós's plot against Rhomanós Lekapênós is told only by Kedhrênós's and Zonarás's source.

[3] *Theoph. Cont.*, Book VI, Reign of Rhomanós II, chap. 6, p. 473.

[4] Kedhrênós, vol. ii, p. 324; Zonarás, vol. iii, p. 481.

[5] *Theoph. Cont.*, Book VI, second bout of Constantine VII's sole reign, chap. 5, pp. 440–1, and chap. 6, p. 441, and the authorities cited on p. 23, n. 1.

Constantine Porphyrogenitus disqualified him for continuing to wear the crown by making him take orders, but he subsequently appointed him to the posts of máyistros and rhaíktor.[1] He castrated Stéphanos's son Rhomanós, but afterwards made him sevastophóros. He also castrated the ex-Emperor Rhomanós I's bastard son Basil.[2] In castrating Basil, Constantine Porphyrogenitus made his victim's political fortune. He now appointed Basil to be his parakoimómenos; and Basil and his half-sister Elénê, between them, managed the Imperial Government on Constantine's behalf. By the time Constantine had associated his half-Lekapenid son Rhomanós II with himself as co-Emperor, he had surrounded himself with Lekapênoí once more.

Constantine VII was not a porphyrogenitus[3] for nothing. His birth in the purple chamber of the Imperial Palace, when his father was on the Imperial throne, was his title to legitimacy; and this title evidently counted for much with the Imperial Court and with the Constantinopolitan public—especially at the crucial moment when Stéphanos and Constantine Lekapênoí discredited their family by deposing their father, and so gave their brother-in-law his opportunity for recovering his long-lost rightful status.

Legitimacy in virtue of the physical place of one's birth is an unfamiliar concept to Westerners. Like the 'Osmanlis who eventually became the 'Caesars of Rome' in virtue of their having conquered the former dominions of the East Roman Empire, Westerners are familiar with the concept of legitimacy deriving from physical descent.[4] The Ottoman dynasty actually gave its name to the empire which it built up and to the Muslim Turkish people who were this empire's ruling element. It was not till the Ottoman Empire had broken up and till the house of 'Osman had been deposed that the 'Osmanlis began to take pride in calling themselves by their national name 'Turks'. By contrast, in the Roman Empire, as in the Egyptian and Chinese empires, no dynasty ever succeeded in making its claim to legitimacy good.

Many other Roman Emperors, before and after Basil I and Rhomanós I and Constantine VII, sought to ensure the transmission of the Imperial crown to their descendants by associating one or more of these with them during their own lifetime, but none of these would-be legitimate dynasties managed to hold the Imperial throne for long. Each in turn was ousted, sooner or later, by some able outsider, and these successive intruders

---

[1] *Theoph. Cont.*, Book VI, chap. 3, p. 438; Leo Grammaticus, p. 330; *Georg. Mon. Cont.*, p. 923; pseudo-Symeon, p. 754.

[2] Kedhrênós, vol. ii, p. 327; Zonarás, vol. iii, Books XIII–XVIII, p. 482.

[3] In Greek, porphyroyénnêtos, i.e. born in the purple (chamber of the Palace).

[4] This point is made by A. Rambaud, *L'Empire grec au dixième siècle: Constantin Porphyrogénète* (Paris, 1870, Franck), p. 24. See the whole of chapter IV, 'Progrès des idées de légitimité', ibid., pp. 23–38.

could not fairly be called usurpers; for they were following in the footsteps of the original founders of the Roman Empire more closely than
those Emperors who came to the throne on the strength of being their
fathers' sons. Monarchical power in the Roman state had been seized,
first by Julius Caesar and then by Augustus, in a struggle for existence
between rival competitors in which the ablest won the prize. This prize
was an unconstitutional one; so it is no paradox to say that the Roman
Empire had no constitution or, alternatively, to say that its constitution
rested on unconstitutional foundations. At any time during the fifteen
centuries covered by the long series of Roman Emperors, the Imperial
Crown could be seized legitimately by any aspirant who had the ambition
to seize it and who also had the ability to translate his ambition into
accomplished fact. Originally the competition was limited to members
of the Roman nobility. Julius was not only a noble; he was a patrician.
But his adopted son Octavianus Augustus was a plebeian by birth, and
after the enactment, in A.D. 212, of the Constitutio Antoniniana, the
great majority of the subjects of the Empire became eligible for contending
for the prize. The winning of it by an able man of humble origin who,
like Basil I and Rhomanós I, had risen in the world, was not only
a frequent occurrence; it was a fulfilment, not a breach, of the Imperial
tradition.

This revolutionary tradition, which was inherent in the institution,
was beneficial to the Roman Empire in as much as it made it certain
that ability should come into power from time to time. On the other
hand, this tradition was detrimental in as much as the price of it was
periodical civil war and chronic intrigue, assassination, and consequent
political instability. The device of conferring legitimacy by virtue of
birth in the purple chamber of the Imperial Palace was an attempt
to obtain the political stability which Imperial descent failed to
provide.

The Palace was the physical embodiment of the Court, and the Court,
which had originated in Caesar's private household, was a much more
solid and permanent element in the Imperial system than the Emperor,
or Emperors, of the day, whom the Court served with such a show of
loyalty and veneration. Actually the Emperors were the Court's creatures. Emperors might and did come and go; able adventurers might
and did oust an ephemeral dynasty; but the Court lived on; and the
ablest upstart Emperor had to come to terms with it—which, from the
time of Diocletian onwards, meant submitting to becoming the prisoner
of the Court's oppressive annual round of ceremonies. Birth in the purple
chamber of the Palace was tantamount to legitimization by the Court;
and since, in the Roman Imperial system, the Court, not the reigning
Emperor, had the last word, to be a porphyrogenitus, as Constantine VII

was, came the nearest to being politically legitimate that it was possible to come under the Roman Imperial dispensation. Perfect legitimacy had been lost for ever in the Roman state when the republican constitution had been undermined and eventually overthrown, as it had been during the century of revolution that had ended in 31 B.C.

2. Constantine Porphyrogenitus's Character

LIGHT is thrown on Constantine's character by his own writings, as well as by what has been written about him by other people. Among these views of Constantine seen from outside, we shall be suspicious of contemporary accounts by writers who were Constantine's subjects, and who therefore could not offend him with impunity. We shall give more weight to independent first-hand contemporary evidence than to posthumous accounts—though these must have been derived ultimately, at least in part, from candid contemporary impressions that must have been committed to writing secretly at the time or have been handed down orally. Among the posthumous accounts, again, we shall give more weight to those which were written when Constantine's descendants were no longer on the throne than to accounts written after Constantine's death but while the Basilian dynasty was still reigning. The East Roman subjects who wrote these earlier posthumous accounts could not afford to publish anything that was seriously critical of a reigning Emperor's ancestor.

If we accept these criteria for assessing the value of the sources other than Constantine's own works, we shall pay the most attention to the evidence of Liutprand, Bishop of Cremona. Though Liutprand's acquaintance with Constantine was slight, it was contemporary and first-hand, and Liutprand was free to write what he chose, since he was not under the East Roman Government's thumb. On his two visits to Constantinople, Liutprand was a foreign ambassador, and, as such, was sacrosanct, while at home, in Lombardy, he was beyond the reach of the East Roman Government's arm. Next to Liutprand, we shall pay attention to the East Roman chroniclers—Kedhrênós, Zonarás, Glykás—who were writing after the Basilian dynasty had expired. On the other hand, we shall take with a grain of salt the more flattering account of Constantine by the anonymous author of the second part of *Theophanes Continuatus*, Book VI,[1] who was probably writing while Constantine's son Rhomanós II was on the throne. The first part of Book VI was probably written while the young Emperors Basil II and Constantine VIII were being overshadowed by the intruder Nikêphóros II Phokás, as their grandfather Constantine VII had been overshadowed by their great-grandfather Rhomanós I Lekapênós. The writer of this part has followed his source the logothete Symeon in treating Rhomanós I more handsomely than was feasible for anyone who was writing during Constantine VII's or even Rhomanós II's lifetimes.

[1] i.e. the part that begins immediately after the notice of Rhomanós Lekapênós's death (pp. 441–81 in the Bonn edition).

In Constantine's own writings, we can find one good touchstone of Constantine's character in those references to Rhomanós I that date from after Rhomanós's fall, when Constantine was no longer inhibited from writing about Rhomanós freely. In the *De Administrando Imperio*, which appears to have been written between A.D. 948 and perhaps 952, Constantine does give vent to his resentment against Rhomanós when he is castigating him for the bad precedent that he had set in giving his granddaughter in marriage to Tsar Peter of Bulgaria. The context is a passage[1] in which Constantine is instructing his son Rhomanós II (Rhomanós I's grandson) how to parry requests from northern barbarians for marriage-alliances with the Imperial family of the day. The barbarians are to be told that it had been laid down by Constantine the Great that the Imperial family must not intermarry with any foreign nation except the Franks.

If they [the barbarian suitors] retort that the Lord Emperor Rhomanós did make a marriage alliance with the Bulgars when he gave his own grand-daughter to the Lord Peter the Bulgarian, you must parry by pointing out that the Lord Emperor Rhomanós was an uneducated commoner. He had not enjoyed the advantage of having been brought up, from infancy, in the Palace or of having been initiated into Roman traditions from the start. His family was not Imperial or even noble, and accordingly he was apt to be head-strong and arbitrary in his conduct of affairs. In the case in point, he did not attend to the Church's veto and did not obey Constantine the Great's explicit injunction. He went his own headstrong and self-willed and vulgar way, without regard for what was right and proper or for his duty to conform to ancestral rules. This accounts for his having presumed to do what he did.[2]

These strictures are caustic, and Constantine gives the impression of being pleased that his argument has given him an opportunity for censuring Rhomanós incidentally. However, for a scholar, this censure is fairly mild. Many scholars have written more tartly about colleagues who have offended against them much less grievously than Rhomanós had offended against Constantine.

Moreover, Constantine is fair-minded enough to add that 'Rhomanós has one plausible line of defence. This action of his led to the redemption of a large number of Christian prisoners. Also, the Bulgars are Christians of the same persuasion as ourselves.'

Constantine would have done better for his own reputation if he had ended here; but he could not resist going on to make the point that María Lekapêně's marriage to Tsar Peter was not really a breach of Constantine the Great's alleged injunction, because María was not an

---

[1] *De Administrando Imperio*, chap. 13, pp. 85–9 in the Bonn edition.
[2] *De Adm. Imp.*, chap. 13, p. 88.

authentic Imperial princess, since her father Christopher was not a legitimate emperor but was a mere subordinate without effective power.[1] (Constantine must have been forgetting, when he wrote this, that his own wife Eléné was María's aunt.) This is all very human, and it is not very reprehensible.

Constantine criticizes Rhomanós I again, in the *De Caerimoniis*,[2] for not having respected a traditional rite.

The celebration of the Vroumália according to the procedure just described was denatured, to the point of being virtually annulled, in the reign of the Lord Rhomanós. He suppressed the Vroumália in the name of [Christian] piety. He did not think it right for the Romans [i.e. the contemporary Greeks] to keep up the ancient [pagan] customs of the Ausones [the ancient Romans].

Rhomanós had not paused to reflect that the celebration of the Vroumália had been countenanced by all the famous Christian Emperors who had been his predecessors. 'In Rhomanós's eyes what seemed good to him was tantamount to civil law, common law, rectitude, and piety.'[2]

Rhomanós's vandalism had offended Constantine's antiquarianism, and Constantine prided himself on having rehabilitated an antique festival that Rhomanós had sought to abolish. Once again, he castigates Rhomanós for his wilfulness; yet, once again too, he has the honesty to mention that Rhomanós did at least have a respectable motive for his wrong-headed action.

Few scholars, I believe, would have let Rhomanós off so lightly if they had suffered all that Constantine had suffered at his hands and if they had had the opportunity of taking a literary revenge on Rhomanós that Constantine did have after Rhomanós's fall in 944.

If Constantine's own works cast little discredit on his character, Bishop Liutprand's testimony shows it in a positively favourable light. Liutprand was not an easy person to deal with. He was flamboyant, vain, and touchy; and, since he was inordinately proud of his own prowess in the Latin culture, he is likely to have been particularly sensitive when he was on Byzantine ground, where he found himself in the presence of a culture which he must have recognized as being superior to his own. On the second of his two diplomatic missions to Constantinople, which was in 968–9 and thus fell within the reign of Nikêphóros II Phokás, Liutprand quarrelled with everyone, from the reigning senior Emperor downwards, with whom he had to do business, and he came away cursing Byzantium and all its works. Constantine Porphyrogenitus, on the other hand, got on well with Liutprand when Liutprand paid his first visit to Constantinople in 949.

---

[1] *De Adm. Imp.*, chap. 13, p. 88.   [2] Book II, chap. 18, p. 606.

After the ultra-formal preliminary Imperial audience, in which it was taboo for the Emperor to have any direct communication with his visitors, Constantine invited Liutprand to dine with him *proprio mecum ore locutus*, and he 'tipped' (*munere donavit*) the ambassador and his suite after dinner.[1] Noting, during dinner, that Liutprand was entranced by the skill of the acrobats who were entertaining the company, the Emperor asked him which of their turns seemed to him the most marvellous; and, when Liutprand declared that he did not know, Constantine laughed and said that he did not know either.[2] Having thus shown himself human to Liutprand when he was entertaining him, the Emperor invited Liutprand to be present when he was on duty. After watching Constantine handing out tips, in the form of coin and robes, to the dignitaries of the Imperial Court on three consecutive days in Holy Week, Liutprand concluded that the Emperor's performance was as remarkable as the acrobatic display had been.[3] At the close, the Emperor asked Liutprand whether he had enjoyed the spectacle, and Liutprand answered that he might have enjoyed it if he had been a beneficiary. Odysseus himself could not have been more adroit in conveying a hint. According to Liutprand, the Emperor smiled, showed signs of embarrassment, nodded to him to signify that he was to come forward, and presented him with a big robe and a pound of coin. 'He gave this gift with alacrity, and I received it with greater alacrity still.'[3] On this occasion, Liutprand left Constantinople well content, and the credit for this result is manifestly due to Constantine.

Constantine got on well with other Franks besides the difficult Liutprand, and the secret of his success with them evidently was that he liked and esteemed them.[4] He might have been prejudiced against the Franks by Rhomanós I's act—a truly high-handed one—of imposing a Frankish daughter-in-law on him. Bertha's father, Hugh of Provence,

---

[1] Liutprand, *Antapodosis*, Book VI, chap. 7.

[2] Ibid., chap. 9.   [3] Ibid., chap. 10.

[4] Constantine Porphyrogenitus justifies Imperial marriage alliances with Franks on the two grounds that Constantine the Great had made an exception in the Franks' favour 'because his own family had originated in those parts' and 'because of the age-old illustriousness and nobility of those parts and those peoples' (*De Adm. Imp.*, chap. 13, p. 86). In the catalogue of formulae for addressing foreign rulers that was in force in Constantine VII's and Rhomanós II's joint reign (*De Caer.*, Book II, chap. 48), the formula for Frankish rulers is 'our (dear and) well-beloved spiritual brother the (noble and) illustrious Rhêx' (pp. 689 and 691).

This Francophilism of Constantine Porphyrogenitus's was remembered by his second successor, Nikêphóros II Phokás, as a bad mark in Constantine's record. Liutprand, on his second mission to Constantinople in 968–9, bought five purple robes of state to take home with him. Before he left, the Imperial authorities re-purchased them from him compulsorily on the ground that they were in a category scheduled as 'too good for export' (κωλυόμενα). When Liutprand cited, as a precedent, the licence that he had been given to export robes of this kind when he had come on his previous mission, Nikêphóros's officials reminded him that this had been under Constantine Porphyrogenitus's regime, and that Nikêphóros was an Emperor of a different kidney (*Legatio*, chaps. 53–5, quoted in II, 1 (ii), on pp. 65–7).

was only a minor Frankish prince; he was not a successful one; and Bertha was not even Hugh's legitimate daughter.[1] Yet Constantine valued his Frankish daughter-in-law, prized the connection with Hugh, and devoted a whole chapter of the *De Administrando Imperio*[2] to 'The Genealogy of the Illustrious King Ougon'. Bertha's escort, Siegfried, Bishop of Parma, happened to be in Constantinople when Stéphanos and Constantine Lekapênoí deposed their father Rhomanós. The news of this *coup d'état* caused an uproar in the City, and there were popular demonstrations in favour of Constantine Porphyrogenitus. There were fears that, having got rid of their father, the conspirators might take still more drastic steps against their brother-in-law. At this critical moment in Constantine Porphyrogenitus's career, Bishop Siegfried came to his rescue at the head of the Latin residents in Constantinople:[3] Amalfitans, Romans,[4] Gaetans. No doubt this incident had left grateful memories in Constantine's mind.

When we come to Constantine's own countrymen's accounts of him, we find them agreeing on two points. His critics agree that he was an eminent scholar, and that, in this field, he had done outstandingly good service.[5] His supporters agree that he was too fond of food and drink.[6] Constantine can hardly have drunk greatly to excess; if he had been another Michael III, he could not also have been the industrious intellectual worker that his literary output proves him to have been. It is also significant that he is not criticized on this score by Liutprand, who did dine with him and who had a malicious love of scandal. On the other hand, the impression of good nature, which Liutprand's account of Constantine gives, is confirmed explicitly by the anonymous author of the second part of *Theophanes Continuatus*, Book VI. This writer declares that Constantine was 'affable to everybody',[7] and that 'he never lost his temper with anybody—aristocrat, bourgeois, or proletarian—though he came up against serious misdemeanours committed by numerous offenders against the public interest as well as against the Emperor personally.'[8] The same writer also lays stress on Constantine's humaneness as this was manifested in his public acts. For instance, he sent John Kourkoúas to carry out an exchange of prisoners at the frontier between

---

[1] Liutprand, *Antapodosis*, Book V, chap. 20.   [2] Chap. 26, pp. 114–18.

[3] Liutprand. *Antapodosis*, Book V, chap. 21.

[4] i.e. Romans in the Western sense of inhabitants of the City of Rome, not in the Eastern sense of subjects of the East Roman Empire.

[5] See Zonarás, vol. iii, Books XIII–XVIII, pp. 482–3 (Bonn edition); Kedhrênós, vol. ii, p. 326 (Bonn edition); Glykás, p. 561 (Bonn edition).

[6] *Theoph. Cont.*, Book VI, second bout of Constantine VII's sole reign, chap. 54, p. 468, confirmed by pseudo-Symeon Magister, p. 756, Kedhrênós, vol. ii, p. 325, Zonarás vol. iii, p. 483.

[7] Προσηνὴς τοῖς πᾶσι (*Theoph. Cont.*, p. 468).

[8] *Theoph. Cont.*, Book VI, second bout of Constantine VII's sole reign, chap. 10, p. 444.

the East Roman Empire and the Caliphate in Cilicia.[1] When he received reports of social injustices in the provinces, he sent out commissioners to see that justice should be done to the poor against their rich oppressors, and he followed up this investigation with legislation.[2] He reviewed the cases of persons serving sentences in prison in the provinces as well as in the capital, and released a number of them.[3] He enlarged the public hospital in Constantinople,[4] and he turned his brother-in-law the late Patriarch Theophýlaktos's palatial stables into a home for old people.[5]

This writer also gives Constantine good marks as an administrator. He worked hard at his desk on reading dispatches and drafting instructions.[6] He also made good appointments to posts of every kind—civil, naval, military, academic. Constantine's revival of higher education paid dividends to the state by improving the quality of the field from which Constantine selected his judges, civil servants, and senior prelates.[7] In the administration of justice Constantine took a hand in person.[8]

This portrayal of Constantine as being an effective ruler as well as a distinguished scholar seems, at first hand, to be contradicted flatly by the common source of Kedhrênós's and Zonarás's portraits of him.

According to Kedhrênós,

> It looked as if a fine Emperor had [now] turned up—one who would make it his business to take care of the Empire's interests if he became sole ruler. [This expectation was disappointed.] Constantine proved to be weaker than he had been taken to be (μαλθακώτερος ὤφθη τῆς ὑπολήψεως). His performance quite belied what had been expected of him. He drank. He shirked laborious tasks and preferred to take the easiest line. He was implacable in dealing with offences and was hard-hearted in meting out punishments. He was no good at making appointments. He did not choose to follow the policy of selecting by merit, as is incumbent on a ruler invested with majestic authority. Constantine entrusted the first comer with the responsibilities of office—a provincial governorship (στρατηγίαν), say, or a civil post (πολιταρχίαν). He made no inquiries, with the result that quite vulgar and discredited people were appointed to the most important civil offices. His wife Eléné and the parakoimómenos Basil played a big part in this. They did not shrink from putting offices up for sale.[9]

According to Zonarás,

> As a public administrator he [Constantine] was decidedly weak (διέκειτο μαλθακώτερον). At the same time, he was vindictive towards offenders and was implacable in meting out punishments. He drank to excess. In making appointments, he did not put the provincial governorships and the posts in

---

[1] *Theoph. Cont.*, Book VI, second bout of Constantine VII's sole reign, chap. 9, p. 443.
[2] Ibid., chap. 10, pp. 443–4; chap. 15, pp. 447–8.
[3] Ibid., chap. 15, p. 447.   [4] Ibid., chap. 18, p. 449.   [5] Ibid., chap. 19, p. 449.
[6] Ibid., chap. 17, pp. 448–9.   [7] Ibid., chap. 14, pp. 445–6.
[8] Ibid., chap. 16, p. 448.   [9] Kedhrênós vol. ii. pp. 325–6.

the central government into worthy hands. He appointed unsatisfactory and disreputable candidates—in fact, whatever candidates the Empress and the parakoimómenos presented to him—and these two put up the public offices for sale.[1]

These two critical retrospective verdicts on Constantine Porphyrogenitus are manifestly derived, via Skylídzês (Scylitzes) from a single original source, which was presumably contemporary with Constantine, though it could not be given publicity so long as descendants of his were on the throne.

It is credible that Constantine may have shrunk from the ordeal of wrestling with forceful personalities and may therefore have been too ready to delegate this essential part of an administrator's duty to his wife and brother-in-law. If this is the truth, the source will have been justified in accusing him of being 'weak'. Even the anonymous author of the second part of *Theophanes Continuatus*, Book VI, admits that Constantine was generally timid.[2] These indications make it credible that Constantine did owe it to his wife Elénê Lekapênê's prompting that, for once in his life, he struck first, when, in his confrontation with his brothers-in-law Stéphanos and Constantine after the deposition of his father-in-law, he was faced with an inescapable choice between either smiting or being smitten—the choice that Constantine's grandfather Basil I had faced, and had decided for himself without a woman's help, when he had struck down first the Caesar Várdhas and then the Emperor Michael III. At the same time, it is also credible—though Kedhrênós's and Zonarás's common source[3] is our sole evidence for this story—that Constantine, on his own initiative, put the idea of deposing Rhomanós Lekapênós into Stéphanos Lekapênós's head. The story, as told by Kedhrênós, is circumstantial. According to Kedhrênós, Constantine did not approach Stéphanos direct, but employed, as a go-between, Basil Peteïnós, a soldier in the guards' regiment called the Etaireía who had been a personal friend of the Porphyrogenitus's since childhood. Peteïnós succeeded in persuading Stéphanos to embark on the enterprise; Stéphanos tried to enlist his brother, Constantine; but Constantine Lekapênós was reluctant, and, in the end, it was Stéphanos who carried out the coup, with his brother Constantine's half-hearted assent. If this is the true story of the overthrow of Rhomanós Lekapênós, it throws

---

[1] Zonarás, vol. iii, Books XIII–XVIII, p. 483.

[2] ὡς τὰ πολλὰ δειλός (*Theoph. Cont.*, second bout of Constantine VII's sole reign, chap. 54, p. 468). Constantine had shown his timidity when, on the eve of Rhomanós Lekapênós's usurpation, he had given orders for ousting his mother and had then countermanded these orders when his mother wept (*Theoph. Cont.*, p. 392; *Georg. Mon. Cont.*, pp. 884–5; Leo Grammaticus, p. 298; Kedhrênós, vol. ii, p. 291). This was weak, but it was good-natured too.

[3] Kedhrênós, vol. ii, pp. 321–4; Zonarás, vol. iii, Books XIII–XVIII, p. 480.

light on Constantine Porphyrogenitus's character. It does not show him to have been any bolder or more resolute than the rest of the evidence about him indicates that he was; for, according to this story, he had been careful to cover his tracks in the event of the plot that he had initiated miscarrying. What the story, if true, reveals is that Constantine Porphyrogenitus was more sly and less amiably incompetent than he would otherwise appear to have been. However, this story, though not incredible, seems unlikely to be true if Stéphanos's grievance against his father was that Rhomanós had confirmed Constantine Porphyrogenitus's precedence over the Lekapenids. In these circumstances, to have engineered the overthrow of Rhomanós would have been an insensate rejoinder, on the Porphyrogenitus's part, to Rhomanós's recognition of his rights.

The charge that Elénê and Basil were financially corrupt is not substantiated; and, as far as Basil is concerned, it is flatly contradicted by pseudo-Symeon Magister, who says that Basil was 'judicious and intelligent and gave the Emperor good and true service in all affairs of state.'[1] The contradiction between the anonymous writer's praise of Constantine's appointments and Kedhrênós's and Zonarás's source's condemnation of them is resolved when we find that, as is not surprising, some of these appointments were bad, while others were good. Constantine appointed an incompetent officer to the command of the expeditionary force sent against Candia in A.D. 949,[2] and this unfortunate choice was largely responsible for the expedition's failure. Even the well-disposed anonymous writer testifies to the knavery of Constantine's éparkhos Theóphilos,[3] and Constantine did not mend matters by transferring Theóphilos from the eparkhate to the kuaistorship[4]—a post which offered almost equally lavish opportunities for misconduct. On the other hand, Basil appears to have been a capable and worthy incumbent of the parakoimomenate; and Constantine certainly did well in rehabilitating John Kourkoúas[5] and the house of Phokás,[6] whom Rhomanós Lekapênós had disgraced,[7] and in strengthening Várdhas Phokás's hands by appointing good officers to serve under him.[8] Whether Constantine reversed these un-public-spirited acts of Rhomanós's on his own initiative or at Basil's and Elénê's instance, this move was undoubtedly in the public interest. It brought back into the East Roman

---

[1] Pseudo-Symeon Magister, Reign of Constantine VII, chap. 4, on pp. 754–5 of the Bonn edition of *Theoph. Cont.*   [2] Kedhrênós, vol. ii, p. 336.

[3] *Theoph. Cont.*, Book VI, second bout of Constantine VII's sole reign, chap. 8, pp. 441–2.

[4] *Theoph. Cont.*, ibid., chap. 10, p. 444.   [5] Ibid., chap. 9, p. 443.

[6] Ibid., chap. 1, p. 436: chap. 41, p. 459; chap. 45, p. 462.

[7] *Theoph. Cont.*, Book VI, first bout of Constantine VII's sole reign, chaps. 13–15, pp. 395–7; Reign of Rhomanós I, chaps. 40–2, pp. 426–9; Kedhrênós, vol. ii, pp. 317–18. Rhomanós had disgraced John Kourkoúas reluctantly (see p. 381).

[8] *Theoph. Cont.*, Book VI, second bout of Constantine VII's sole reign, chap. 14, p. 445.

Empire's service a fund of military ability of which Rhomanós had deprived the Empire.

Constantine's prowess at his desk-work, which the anonymous writer praises and which Kedhrênós's and Zonarás's source does not deny, is something that we should expect in a man who was an administrator perforce while he was temperamentally a scholar. As for the contradiction between the amiability with which Constantine is credited by the anonymous writer and the vindictiveness of which he is accused by Kedhrênós's and Zonarás's source, we may perhaps conjecture that Constantine was amiable by nature, but that he was capable of plotting cunningly if his resentment was aroused, as it was by Rhomanós Lekapênós's shabby treatment of him, and that he was also capable of reacting savagely if and when he was distracted from his beloved scholarly occupations by some political crisis that was too serious for him to ignore. He will have resented being forced into playing the hateful power-game even more than he will have resented the danger to his crown and life that he was being compelled reluctantly to parry. It is not surprising if, in these circumstances, Constantine did sometimes hit back more violently than would have come naturally to a born man of action who enjoyed living dangerously. Several accounts[1] confirm the anonymous writer's statement[2] that Constantine detected and suppressed two pro-Lekapênoí conspiracies. The first of these aimed at reinstating Rhomanós I, the second at reinstating Stéphanos. The anonymous writer himself records that some of the participants in the second conspiracy had their ears and noses cut off, and that others were flogged beyond endurance.[3]

Atrocities are culpable, even when committed under provocation. There is not, however, any evidence that Constantine committed them habitually. For the most part, his subjects will have had little cause to be afraid of him unless they went out of their way to exasperate him by threatening his security and—still worse—disturbing the peace and quiet without which he could not pursue his scholarly activities.

There is, however, a story, told by Kedhrênós alone,[4] which does give some colour to the charge that Constantine was vindictive and implacable, and this in a case in which he had not the excuse that his victim had sinned against him by bringing his crown or his life into jeopardy. After the death of his disreputable brother-in-law, the Ecumenical

---

[1] e.g. *Georg. Mon. Cont.*, p. 923; Leo Grammaticus, p. 330; *Theoph. Cont.*, pp. 440–1; pseudo-Symeon Magister, pp. 753–4; Kedhrênós, vol. ii, pp. 327–8; Zonarás, vol. iii, Books XIII–XVIII, pp. 483–4; Yahyā b. Saʿīd, loc. cit. on p. 10, n. 3.

[2] *Theoph. Cont.*, Book VI, second bout of Constantine VII's sole reign, chaps. 5–6, pp. 440–1.

[3] *Georg. Mon. Cont.* and Leo Grammaticus and pseudo-Symeon say that Constantine meted out severe punishments on the first occasion too.

[4] Kedhrênós, vol. ii, pp. 334 and 337–8.

Patriarch Theophýlaktos, Constantine replaced him by a worthy successor, the monk Polýefktos, whose character was irreproachable.[1] This appointment belies the charge that Constantine's appointees were invariably worthless, but it confirms the charge that there was a decidedly unamiable vein in Constantine's character. According to the story, Polýefktos, after his appointment, was insistent in urging Constantine to correct injustices that had been caused by the greed of Rhomanós Lekapénós's kinsmen. At the worst, Polýefktos was being importunate in a good cause; but it was a cause that was naturally displeasing to Constantine's Lekapenid wife and Lekapenid brother-in-law the parakoimómenos. They set Constantine against Polýefktos, and for the rest of his life Constantine carried on a vendetta against the excellent patriarch whom he himself had appointed to his own credit. According to Kedhrênós's story, Constantine's pilgrimage to the hermitages on the Mysian Olympus—the expedition on which he died—was cover for a meeting with the bishop of Kýzikos to discuss ways and means of getting Polýefktos deposed. If this story is true, it shows Constantine in an extremely unpleasant light.

All the same, I lose my heart to the Porphyrogenitus, as his contemporary my fellow-Frank Liutprand lost his, when I picture Constantine as he is portrayed by the second of the two anonymous authors of *Theophanes Continuatus*, Book VI[2] and, in almost identical words, by pseudo-Symeon.[3]

In his personal appearance the Emperor Constantine Porphyrogenitus was tall in stature. His complexion was milk-white. He had fine eyes; their expression was genial.[4] He was beaky-nosed (hook-nosed). He had a long face, ruddy cheeks, and a long neck. He held himself as erect as a cypress tree. He was broad-shouldered. He was amiable: affable to everybody and generally timid. He was fond of food and drink. His talk was full of charm. His scale of presents and rewards was generous.[5]

The earliest and most authoritative description, after Liutprand's, of the impression made by Constantine's countenance may be

ἥμερος ὄψις, εὔλαλα χείλη, χάρις ὀμμάτων.

---

[1] τὸν εἰλικρινῆ αὐτοῦ βίον (the first of the two anonymous authors of *Theoph. Cont.*, Book VI, p. 434); μοναχὸς ἀσκητικὸν βίον διαλάμπων καὶ μονάσας ἐξ ἁπαλῶν ὀνύχων καὶ διαπρέψας ἐν πάσῃ ἀρετῇ καὶ ὀρθῷ δόγματι· καὶ ὡς ἄλλος Ἰωάννης Χρυσόστομος παρὰ πολλῶν ἐγνωρίζετο καὶ ἐλέγετο, καὶ οὐκ ἐλέγετο μόνον, ἀλλὰ καὶ ἐφαίνετο (the second of the two anonymous authors of *Theoph. Cont.*, Book VI, pp. 444–5); τίμιος ἀνὴρ καὶ ἁγιώτατος (pseudo-Symeon, p. 755); chosen by Constantine διὰ τὸ τοῦ ἔθους σεμνὸν καὶ τὸ τῆς σοφίας ὑπερβάλλον καὶ τὴν ἀκτημοσύνην (Kedhrênós, vol. ii, p. 334). Polýefktos took a strong line not only with the timid Constantine but with Constantine's formidable successors Nikêphóros II Phokás and John Dzimiskês.

[2] On p. 468.

[3] Second bout of Constantine VII's sole reign, chap. 5, p. 756.

[4] χαροποίους (*Theoph. Cont.*) χαροπούς (pseudo-Symeon) ἔχων [τοὺς ps.-S.] ὀφθαλμούς.

[5] *Theoph. Cont.*, Book VI, p. 468.

This is line 20 of a poem on Constantine's death which is written, in the main scribe's hand, on the margin of folio 116ʳ of the Madrid manuscript of the chronicle of Scylitzes. This manuscript was written in the second half or third quarter of the thirteenth century—at latest *circa* 1300; but the editor of the poem[1]—which is headed Συμεὼν πατρίκιος καὶ ἀσηκρῆτις, τοῦ νυνὶ μαγίστρου καὶ στρατιωτικοῦ, εἰς Κωνσταντῖνον τὸν πορφυρογέννητον βασιλέα—holds that the poet is the celebrated Symeon Metaphrastes,[2] and that the poem was composed, as an obituary notice, immediately after Constantine's death in 959.

The traits noted in this line of verse are reported at first hand by Bishop Liutprand and described in the passage, just quoted, from *Theophanes Continuatus*. The beauty of Constantine's eyes, which is remarked in both these descriptions, indicates that both are authentic.

An imaginary picture of Constantine Porphyrogenitus on his deathbed, in the Madrid MS. of Scylitzes, folio 138ʳ, is reproduced by Ševčenko.[3]

---

[1] I. Ševčenko, 'Poems on the Deaths of Leo VI and Constantine VII in the Madrid Manuscript of Scylitzes', in *Dumbarton Oaks Papers*, Numbers Twenty-three and Twenty-four (1969–70), pp. 185–228. The text of this poem is printed ibid., pp. 210–12.

[2] See ibid., pp. 216–19 and 222–3.

[3] In his Plate 7, in loc. cit.

PART II

THE EAST ROMAN EMPIRE

1. *The Economy since the Seventh Century*

(i) *General Considerations*

THE Emperor Constantine Porphyrogenitus lived and reigned towards the close of a quarter of a millennium during which the East Roman Empire was prosperous. This prosperity was only relative. Throughout this period too the Emperors and their subjects underwent many severe trials. They were, nevertheless, relatively well-off by comparison both with their predecessors in the seventh century and with their successors from the latter part of the eleventh century onwards until the East Roman Empire's eventual extinction at the end of a long-drawn-out death-agony. The East Roman Empire's seventh-century crisis had been as desperate as the fifth-century crisis in the Roman Empire's western provinces and as the third-century crisis in the Empire as a whole. But, like the Empire in the third century, and unlike its western provinces in the fifth century, the Empire's eastern remnant had emerged, in the seventh century, out of a sea of troubles that, for a number of decades on end, had seemed bound to overwhelm it. On the other hand, its decline and collapse in the eleventh century was never retrieved, though, even after this, it struggled hard and long to survive, in contrast to the feeble collapse of the fifth-century Imperial Government in the West.

The seventh-century blizzard had raged, with hardly a lull, from the overthrow and murder of the Emperor Maurice in 602 till the raising of the first siege of Constantinople by the Arabs in 678. This first of the two Arab sieges of the East Roman Empire's capital city had been the more formidable ordeal of the two. At that date the *élan* of the Muslim Arab world-conquerors had not yet been spent. By 717–18, which was the date of the second siege, the Umayyad dynasty of Caliphs had been verging towards its fall and the Arabs' original ardour and self-confidence had begun to abate. After their second failure to capture Constantinople, they tacitly renounced their ambition to conquer the whole of the East Roman Empire, as they had conquered the whole of the Empire's peer and rival, the Empire of Iran. Thus the year 718, if not the year 678, may be taken as the initial date of the East Roman Empire's *floruit*. Its terminal date was 963, the year in which Constantine Porphyrogenitus's son Rhomanós II died, and in which his two grandsons were treated by his brilliant general Nikêphóros Phokás as Constantine himself had been treated in 920 by Rhomanós Lekapênós, the admiral of the Central Government's fleet.

At first thoughts it may seem surprising to find the terminal date of the East Roman Empire's quarter of a millennium of relative prosperity in the accession-year of an Emperor who, after his accession as well as before it, achieved a rapid series of dazzling military successes. Within less than a decade, Nikêphóros II Phokás reconquered for the East Roman Empire more territory than had been recovered for it by the cumulative efforts of his predecessors during the preceding three centuries and a half. But Nikêphóros II's military triumphs were purchased at a fatally high social cost.

In his single-minded pursuit of military efficiency, Nikêphóros keyed up the demand on those members of the rural population who were under obligation either to serve personally in one of the thematic army-corps or alternatively to provide the equipment, or a quota of it, for a serving soldier. Nikêphóros found money more welcome than only semi-professional men; for, with monetary commutations of service, he could employ fully professional soldiers in place of the semi-professional levies of the army-corps districts. These onerous and, on a long view, unpropitious, military innovations of Nikêphóros's are discussed in the chapter on the East Roman Army.[1] In the present context, we may note the effect of his ambitious wars of conquest on the East Roman Empire's domestic food-supply. It has been pointed out[2] that the beginning of the period of chronic food-shortage and high prices at Constantinople coincides in date with the beginning of the East Roman Government's large-scale offensive military operations. The famine at Constantinople in 960 can be accounted for by the demands for the supply of Nikêphóros's expeditionary force in Crete in the winter of 960–1. The famine of 968 can be accounted for similarly by the demands of Nikêphóros's campaign in that year in Osrhoênê and Syria. This is attested by Otto II's ambassador, Bishop Liutprand of Cremona, who was in Constantinople in 968.[3]

Famine at home was, indeed, the inevitable price of the new style of East Roman warfare that had now replaced the guerrilla tactics and

---

[1] See Part II, chap. 6, pp. 311–14 and 320–1.
[2] By J. L. Teall, 'The Grain Supply of the Byzantine Empire, 330–1024', in *Dumbarton Oaks Papers*, Number Thirteen (1959), pp. 87–139, on pp. 114, 116, 117.
[3] Liutprand, *Legatio*, chaps. 34 and 44.

diversionary raids with which the East Romans had countered the Saracens' incursions in the border warfare along a frontier that, for more than two centuries, had remained static. The East Roman Army was now making distant and protracted expeditions in force into Muslim territory. Its strategy was to break the enemy's spirit and to drive the rural population to take shelter within the walls of the cities by systematically devastating the countryside, and then to take the cities themselves, not by storm, but by starving them into surrender. This strategy required a constant flow of food supplies from East Roman territory to feed the East Roman armies operating far afield.[1] Famine at home was a high price to pay for victories that brought in returns solely to the 'Establishment'.

It is no wonder that Nikêphóros became unpopular and that his comrade-in-arms, John Dzimiskês (*Τζιμισκῆς*), was able, with impunity, to murder him and to step into his shoes.[2] The murderer was himself a militarist of his victim's school, but, unlike Nikêphóros, John had not quarrelled with the Church, as Nikêphóros had done for a legitimate reason and with a reputable motive. Nikêphóros had an unfortunate personality. His austerity could compel respect and his professional ability could win admiration, but his rigidity and his harshness could arouse the violent antipathy that envenoms Liutprand's report of his encounter with him. Nikêphóros is a tragic figure. In devoting himself whole-heartedly to the aggrandizement of the East Roman Empire, he confirmed its already impending doom.

To outward appearance the East Roman Empire stood at its apogee in the century 963–1071, not in the preceding quarter of a millennium 718–963. This outward appearance was not deceptive in the fields of literature and visual art; but in the economic and social fields, and consequently in the political and military fields as well, the Empire's imposing appearance was illusory.[3] Ominous signs of the times had become apparent already to predecessors of Nikêphóros II, for instance to Constantine Porphyrogenitus's unwelcome senior colleague Rhomanós I and to Constantine himself. A series of Emperors, ending with Con-

---

[1] See Anonymus Vári, *Liber de Re Militari*, chap. 21.

[2] Leo Diaconus, Book IV, chapter 6, mentions four causes of Nikêphóros II's unpopularity. The immediate particular cause was the loss of life in a panic among the audience in the Hippodrome at Constantinople over a military tournament that Nikêphóros had staged. The three chronic causes were the sharp increase of taxation to meet the demands of Nikêphóros's swollen military budget; the famine; and the alleged exploitation of the famine by Nikêphóros's brother, Leo the Kouropalátês. Leo Kouropalátês was believed to have made profits by manipulating the grain-market. Leo Diaconus records this damaging allegation against Leo Kouropalátês without going bail for it. But it is significant that he has not ignored it, considering that he himself was not a partisan of Nikêphóros's murderers. Leo Diaconus gives a gruesome account of the murder, and his condemnation of John Dzimiskês for his perpetration of this crime is forthright (see Book V, chaps. 7–9).

[3] See the Appendix to chap. 1, section (i), on pages 36–8.

stantine's grandson Basil II, tried to restore the Empire's social health by legislation and were foiled. In the light of their failure, they would probably have been surprised, not that the Empire was eventually overtaken by disaster, but that the disaster did not come sooner than it did.

The dynasty that had been founded in 867 by Constantine's grandfather Basil I 'could build upon firm foundations in agriculture and commerce laid by their predecessors'.[1] 'Many characteristics of the flourishing society' over which this dynasty ruled 'can be traced into the earlier years of the ninth century and even further back.'[1] Commercial vitality and urban growth had become apparent in the reigns of Nikêphóros I (802–11) and Theóphilos (829–42).[1] The reign of Basil I's predecessor, colleague, and victim, Michael III (842–67), had been particularly fruitful. In the stubborn military confrontation between the East Roman Empire and the Arab Caliphate, the tide had turned decisively in the Empire's favour in 863, when Michael's uncle Petronás had annihilated a Muslim expeditionary force led by the Amīr of Malatīyah. Next year, in 864, the Khan of Bulgaria, a state that had intruded itself into the Empire's former domain in the heart of the Balkan Peninsula, had yielded to an East Roman show of military force and had submitted to be converted to Christianity. In 860 Constantinople —bravely succoured by the Emperor Michael in his swift return from an eastern campaign—had repulsed a surprise attack by water, through the Bosphorus, from the Rhos, a barbarian power that, till then, had been hardly within the East Romans' ken. Within seven years of that terrifying experience, the Ecumenical Patriarch, Phótios, had retorted to the military offensive of the Rhos's Scandinavian war-lords by launching a counter-offensive on the religious plane. He had lodged a Christian mission in Kiev,[2] the Rhos's distant capital; and, though most of the seeds scattered at this first sowing were trampled away before they could germinate, the progressive conversion and progressive expansion of Russia eventually extended the bounds of Eastern Orthodox Christendom northward and eastward to the Arctic and Pacific Oceans.

Eastern Orthodox Christianity took root in Russia because, within those same seven years, two Thessalonian Greek missionaries, the brothers Constantine-Cyril and Methódhios, had invented an alphabet for conveying the language of the Slav settlers in Thessaloníkê's

---

[1] J. L. Teall in loc. cit., p. 90.

[2] Phótios's letter of 867, announcing this, is printed in Migne, *Patrologia Graeca* (hereinafter Migne, *P.G.*), vol. cii, cols. 736–7. See also Obolensky in *C. Med. H.*, vol. iv, 2nd ed., Part I (1966), p. 496. Constantine Porphyrogenitus, in *Theoph. Cont.*, Book V, pp. 342–3, gives the credit to Basil I and to his Patriarch Ighnátios. Professor Dmitri Obolensky, in *The Byzantine Commonwealth: Eastern Europe 500–1453* (London, 1971, Weidenfeld & Nicolson), p. 184, suggests that, after Phótios had sent a bishop to the Rhos at some date before 867, Ighnátios sent an archbishop to them, perhaps *circa* 874. In 946 there were βαπτισμένοι 'Ρῶς soldiers at Constantinople in the Imperial Government's service (*De Caer.*, Book II, chap. 15, p. 579).

hinterland, and had made a start in the translation of Greek literature, secular as well as religious.[1] At about the same time there had been a renaissance at Constantinople of the study of Hellenic Greek literature. In this intellectual enterprise too, Phótios—a morally ambivalent personality but a pre-eminent intellect—had been the moving spirit, while the Emperor Michael's uncle Várdhas, a brother of Petronás, had used his power as Caesar to give the Photian renaissance practical effect before he was assassinated by Constantine Porphyrogenitus's grandfather Basil with the acquiescence of Basil's next victim, Várdhas's nephew the Emperor Michael.

Michael's accession-year 842 was near the mid-point of the East Roman Empire's spell of relative prosperity, and the achievements that distinguished the quarter of a century during which Michael was on the throne are evidence of the vitality of the East Roman state and of the Byzantine civilization. The evidence is so conspicuous that it has been proof against Constantine Porphyrogenitus's assiduous efforts to expunge it.[2]

If a foreigner who had some cognizance of the East Roman Empire at its zenith had been asked to declare what struck him as being its most prominent and characteristic feature, he would probably have said 'solvency'. If the same question had been put to one of the Empire's contemporary subjects, his reply would probably have been 'taxation'.

Ever since the Empire's astonishing recovery from its third-century collapse, its Government had been determined not to fall again into the financial chaos that had been perhaps the most painful feature of the third-century crisis—more painful, even, than civil war and barbarian invasion. For a time the Graeco-Roman World had actually relapsed into a barter-economy from the monetary economy that had been its practice since the seventh century B.C. From the reign of Diocletian until the reign of Aléxios I, the Roman Government never went bankrupt and never suspended payments.[3] In 618 the Emperor Heraclius had found himself compelled to issue a silver currency that had been debased to the extent of 50 per cent,[4] but this seventh-century lapse had been retrieved, and the gold solidus (nómisma) had not depreciated in the long time of troubles that had followed the death, in 565, of the Emperor Justinian I.[5] An alleged depreciation of the currency in the reign of

[1] See D. Obolensky in *C. Med. H.*, vol. iv, 2nd ed., Part I (1966), p. 500; F. Dvornik: *The Slavs: Their Early History and Civilization* (Boston, 1956, The American Academy of Arts and Sciences), pp. 80–115.

[2] For these efforts of Constantine's, see Part V, chap. 2.

[3] J. B. Bury: *A History of the Eastern Roman Empire from the Fall of Irene to the Accession of Basil I (802–867)* (London, 1912, Macmillan), p. 221.

[4] A. N. Stratós: *Byzantium in the Seventh Century* (Amsterdam, 1968, Hackert), p. 100.

[5] Stratós, op. cit., pp. 6–7.

Constantine Porphyrogenitus's second successor Nikêphóros II Phokás, is, though probable, non-proven.[1]

In Ostrogorsky's opinion the East Roman Empire was the only effective state, in the modern sense of the term, in the medieval Christian oikoumenê. It was this in virtue of a number of its features: for instance, the close-knit centralization of its administration, staffed by an educated bureaucracy; the regularity of the collection of its tax-revenue, which gave it a budget that, at its apogee, balanced at a figure equivalent to nearly 100 million gold marks.[2] Bury has estimated[3] that in the ninth century the East Roman Empire's revenue was half as large again as that of the contemporary 'Abbasid Caliphate—an empire that dwarfed the East Roman Empire in the size of both its territory and its population. Ostrogorsky draws attention to the East Roman Empire's money economy and to its role in international trade.[4]

Ostrogorsky also points out[5] that the taxation-system was the governing factor in the life of the East Roman Empire and of its subjects. It played this role because the Imperial Government's solvency was a *tour de force*. In the age in which the Roman Empire had embraced the whole perimeter of the Mediterranean Sea, its three principal industrial and commercial power-houses had been Egypt, Syria, and western Asia Minor. All three had been retained by the Constantinopolitan Roman Empire when the economically backward western provinces had dropped off; but, in the seventh century, the first two had been lost, first temporarily to the Persians and then permanently to the Arabs, while the coasts and off-shore islands of western Asia Minor had been cruelly ravaged in the course of the Arab naval offensive that had been launched in 649 and had culminated in the assault on Constantinople in 674–8.

[1] See Kedhrênós–Scylitzes, vol. ii, p. 369 (Bonn), cited by E. Bach: 'Les Lois agraires byzantines du Xe siècle' in *Classica et Mediaevalia* V (1942), pp. 70–91, on p. 100, and G. Schlumberger: *Nicéphore Phocas*, 2nd ed. (Paris, 1923, Fontemoing), p. 443. According to Kedhrênós–Scylitzes in loc. cit. (cf. Zonarás, vol. iii, Books XIII–XVIII, p. 507), Nikêphóros II issued a new gold nómisma, the so-called tetartêrón, which was below the standard weight, and then made his payments in tetartêrá, while still exacting the Imperial Government's dues in standard nomísmata. According to Bach, loc. cit., Scylitzes's allegation is supported by numismatic evidence. However, according to F. Dworschak, in *Numismatische Zeitschrift*, Neue Folge, no. 29 (1936), pp. 79 seqq., cited by G. Ostrogorsky, *Geschichte des byzantinischen Staates* (Munich, 1940, Beck), p. 247, n. 1, the tetartêrón was only slightly lighter than the standard nómisma. The standard coin continued to circulate as an international currency, and, no doubt, also continued to be issued, side by side with the tetartêrón, by the East Roman mint. The standard nómisma was not debased till the reign of Constantine IX (1042–55), and it did not collapse until after the disastrous year 1071. See J. M. Hussey: *The Byzantine World* (London, 1957, Hutchinson), p. 51.

[2] G. Ostrogorsky, 'Die wirtschaftlichen und sozialen Entwicklungsgrundlagen des byzantinischen Reiches', in *Vierteljahrschrift für Sozial- und Wirtschaftsgeschichte*, 22. Band (Stuttgart, 1929, Kohlhammer), pp. 129–43, on p. 129.

[3] Bury, op. cit., p. 220.　　　　　　　　　　　　　　[4] Ostrogorsky, loc. cit.

[5] G. Ostrogorsky, 'Agrarian Conditions in the Byzantine Empire in the Middle Ages', in *The Cambridge Economic History*, vol. i, 2nd ed. (1966), pp. 205–34, on p. 205.

In the subsequent age of the East Roman Empire's *floruit*, the Imperial stud-farms, managed by the loghothétês ton ayelón, were located in what had once been the Roman provinces of Asia and Phrygia.[1] Of these, Phrygia, except for its fertile south-western corner in the Maeander valley, had always been a pastoral country, but Asia, between the west coast of Asia Minor and the western edge of its central plateau, had been one of the most intensely cultivated and densely urbanized regions of the Mediterranean World. The seventh-century Arab naval offensive seems to have ruined the former province of Asia permanently.[2] Most of the interior of Asia Minor to the north-west of the Távros Range is arid. The fertile soil of théma Armeniakoí (the former kingdom of Pontic Cappadocia) is exceptional here. Yet Asia Minor was the region from which the East Roman taxation-officers wrung the major part of the East Roman Empire's ample tax-revenue. This *tour de force* goes far towards accounting for both the recovery of the East Roman Empire after the seventh century and its downfall in the eleventh century.

During the intervening period the mainstay of the Imperial revenue was the taxation of the communities of peasant freeholders[3] in the Empire's Asiatic territories. These peasant communities seem not to have possessed any formal institutions of local self-government,[4] but they were responsible collectively for the payment of the taxes due from each of their members, and this formidable collective liability created a social bond, since every member's interests suffered if any single member defaulted or decamped. Consequently the villagers became accustomed to taking collective action, and, in some circumstances, they were entitled *de jure* to take it. The survival of the small freeholds was of vital importance for both the fiscal and the military strength of the Empire.[5] It is surely untrue that the progressive transfer of the ownership of land from small holders to big landowners did not diminish the amount of the tax-revenue that the land was made to yield.[6] Legally, of course, the land was

[1] See A. Vogt, *Basile Ier* (Paris, 1908, Picard), p. 358.

[2] H. Ahrweiler, 'L'Asie Mineure et les invasions arabes', in *Revue historique*, 86e année, tome ccxxvii (1962), pp. 1–32, on p. 14.

[3] P. Lemerle, 'Esquisse pour une histoire agraire de Byzance' in *Revue historique*, vols. ccxix, pp. 32–74 and 254–84, and ccxx, pp. 43–94 (1958), in vol. ccxix, on pp. 279–80. Cf. R. J. H. Jenkins: 'Social Life in the Byzantine Empire', in *C. Med. H.*, vol. iv, 2nd ed., Part II, pp. 79–103, on p. 93.

[4] See G. Rouillard, *La Vie rurale dans l'Empire byzantin* (Paris, 1953, Maisonneuve), p. 99. 'Die byzantinische Gemeinde ist also eine finanzielle und administrative Einheit, aber auch *nur* das.'—Ostrogorsky, 'Die ländliche Steuergemeinde des byzantinischen Reiches im x. Jahrhundert', in *Vierteljahrschrift für Sozial- und Wirtschaftsgeschichte*, 20. Band (1928), pp. 1–108, on p. 45. Cf. eundem, 'Agrarian Conditions', pp. 212 and 213; Haussig, *A History of Byzantine Civilization*, p. 274.

[5] Ostrogorsky, 'Agrarian Conditions', p. 216.

[6] This is E. Bach's thesis in 'Les Lois agraires byzantines du Xe siècle', in *Classica et Mediaevalia*, v (1942), pp. 70–91, on p. 75.

taxable at the same rate, whoever the owner of it might be. In practice, the fiscal merit of the collectively assessed and taxed communities of free peasants was that the full amount of the tax demanded (and perhaps more) could be extracted from them, whereas the big landowners were able to get off with paying less than their due. Like the senior taxation-officers themselves, the big landowners were members of the 'Establishment'. They had friends at Court and in the metropolitan central bureaux of the civil service. All members of the 'Establishment' were tacitly in league with each other to promote their respective private interests,[1] and, when the 'Establishment' conspired against the Crown, the 'Establishment' could count on being the winner, though officially the Emperor was an autocrat.

The free peasantry was as important for the Army as it was for the Treasury; for the peasantry furnished the great majority of the Empire's troops. The Emperor Leo VI declares, in one of the rare passages in his *Taktiká* that he has not copied out of someone else's book, that 'two occupations' ($\epsilon\pi\iota\tau\eta\delta\epsilon\acute{u}\mu\alpha\tau\alpha$) are 'absolutely essential' ($\lambda\acute{\iota}\alpha\nu$ $\dot{\alpha}\nu\alpha\gamma\kappa\alpha\hat{\iota}\alpha$), namely agriculture ($\gamma\epsilon\omega\rho\gamma\iota\kappa\acute{\eta}$) and military service ($\sigma\tau\rho\alpha\tau\iota\omega\tau\iota\kappa\acute{\eta}$). 'These occupations take precedence over all others.'[2] This declaration is repeated in the agrarian law promulgated in 934 in the names of the Emperors Rhomanós Lekapênós, Leo VI's son Constantine, and Rhomanós's sons Stephen and Constantine. 'The presence of a numerous population brings with it a number of practical benefits: the co-operative payment of taxes and the co-operative discharge of military obligations. If the population gives out, there will be a complete breakdown of these services.'[3]

By the year 934 the free peasantry of the East Roman Empire was manifestly in danger of being reduced to vanishing point by the expansion, at its expense, of the properties of the big landowners. It is amazing that the free peasants should have survived for so long as they did, considering that successive Emperors proved powerless to save them, and that the peasants had to withstand the assaults of three enemies: the Imperial Government's own taxation-officers and enemy raiders from beyond the Empire's frontiers,[4] as well as the peasants' big-landowner neighbours. Of these three assailants, the tax-officers were perennial, the foreign raiders seasonal, and the native big landowners permanent, when once they had begun to add field to field. The date at which the

---

[1] Ostrogorsky, 'Die wirtschaftlichen und sozialen Entwicklungsgrundlagen', p. 136.

[2] Leo VI: *Taktiká*, Dhiátaxis 11, § 11, in Migne, *P.G.*, vol. cvii, cols. 793–6.

[3] ἡ γὰρ τῶν πολλῶν κατοίκησις πολλὴν δείκνυσι τῆς χρείας τὴν ὠφέλειαν, τὴν τῶν δημοσίων συνεισφοράν, τὴν τῶν στρατιωτικῶν συντέλειαν, ἃ πάντως ἀπολείψει τοῦ πλήθους ἐκλελοιπότος.— *Jus Graeco-Romanum*, ed. by C. E. Zachariä von Lingenthal, Part III (Leipzig, 1857, Weigel), p. 247.

[4] See II, 1 (iii), (b).

free peasants make their first appearance in numerical strength is significant. This date is towards the close of the seventh century, the probable date of the Farmers' Law (*Νόμος Γεωργικός*).[1] This was soon after the end of a virtual interregnum, three-quarters of a century long, during which the Central Government's writ had almost ceased to run in the provinces, while its taxation-officers had had to run the gauntlet of foreign invaders.

It may sound paradoxical, yet it is the truth, that the East Roman peasants had a good turn done to them by the seasonal Saracen raiders who burnt their crops, cut down their fruit-trees, looted their cottages, and carried off the peasants themselves and their livestock if they could catch them. The raiders were a pest, but they kept two greater pests in check. They made the Imperial taxation-officers' work difficult and risky, and they made investment in rural land unattractive for the minority of the Imperial Government's subjects who had funds to invest and who were looking for larger and more lucrative openings than those that were offered by industry and trade—a field in which private economic enterprise was more effectively hampered by governmental controls and restrictions.[2]

Dates are significant in this connection too. It has been mentioned already that, in the border warfare between the East Roman Empire and the Arab Caliphate, the tide had turned decisively in the Empire's favour in 863. In 926 the East Roman Army took the offensive, and, though there were fluctuations in the fortunes of war, this offensive was maintained, and the eastern frontiers of the Empire were carried farther and farther eastwards, in the course of the next hundred years. It is no mere coincidence that the same century witnessed first the successive attempts, by legislation, to save the free peasants from the expansion of the big estates, and then the big landowners' victory over the Crown and its peasant protégés.[3] The earliest of the tenth-century agrarian laws, the law allegedly promulgated in 922, may be spurious, or, if genuine, it may be misdated, but the law of 934 is undisputedly genuine, and it was promulgated in the year in which Malaṭīyah was finally captured and annexed. Malaṭīyah and Tarsós were the two principal bases of operations for the Muslims' seasonal raids into East Roman territory, and these raids will not have ceased entirely before 965, the year in which Tarsós fell. Long before that date, however, both the range and the scale of the raids must have diminished to a point at which they had ceased to be anything more serious than an occasional local nuisance.

[1] Text edited and interpreted by W. Ashburner, in *J.H.S.*, vol. xxx (1910), pp. 85–108, and vol. xxxii (1912), pp. 68–95. Ostrogorsky, 'Agrarian Conditions', p. 209, attributes this law to the Emperor Justinian II.

[2] See A. R. Lewis, *Naval Power and Trade in the Mediterranean, A.D. 500–1100* (Princeton, 1951, University Press), p. 176.

[3] See Ostrogorsky, 'Die wirtschaftlichen und sozialen Entwicklungsgrundlagen', p. 133.

The victorious East Roman armies whose advance had thus reduced to vanishing point the long-sustained Saracen incursions into East Roman territory were mainly composed of peasant soldiers, and it is ironical that the peasants themselves should have cleared away the barrier to their eviction by the big landowners. From start to finish there were at all times some large-scale rural estates in the Roman Empire and in its East Roman avatar. There are no extant statistics of the ratio between big properties and small holdings for any period in this span of fifteen centuries; but we may guess that the aggregate extent of the big properties varied inversely with the degree of security. Big estates, containing luxurious country houses flanked by elaborate farm-buildings, will have been the first objectives of raiders in search of easily won loot; and, when once a country house had been gutted, its farm buildings wrecked, its herds of livestock lifted, and its host of labourers and administrators, slave and free, dispersed, it would not have been worth while to incur the expense of putting the sabotaged estate into working order again so long as there was any danger that the catastrophe might recur. The big estates must have suffered relatively more severely than the peasant holdings during the invasions in the seventh century and after.[1] A peasant could take refuge temporarily in the mountains with his family and his scanty stock; and if, after the raiders' departure, he and his neighbours found that their village had been burnt down, they could quickly rebuild their huts with their own hands by a united effort.[2]

Though, in the seventh century, the big properties in Asia Minor are likely to have been greatly reduced in number, we have no evidence that they were extinguished.[3] We cannot infer this from the fact that they receive little notice in either the seventh-century Farmers' Law[4] or in the handbook for the use of taxation-officers which appears to have been produced at some date between 912 and 1139,[5] perhaps in the second quarter of the tenth century.[6] Taxation-officers, lawyers, and civil

---

[1] 'The seventh century saw the liquidation of the old aristocracy and the breakdown of large estates in most of the provinces.'—A. S. Lopez, 'The Role of Trade in the Economic Readjustment of Byzantium in the Seventh Century', in *Dumbarton Oaks Papers*, Number Thirteen (1959), pp. 69–85, on p. 84.

[2] I myself, during and after the Graeco-Turkish war of 1919–22 in Asia Minor, saw a particular Turkish village intact in one year and restored, as a going concern, in the next but one, after it had been rased to the ground in the year in between. Villages in Asia Minor in the heyday of the East Roman Empire were probably as easily reparable as they were in the 1920s.

[3] See P. Charanis, 'On the Social Structure of the Later Roman Empire', in *Byzantion*, vol. xvii (1944–5), pp. 38–57, on p. 43; Rouillard, op. cit., p. 85; Lemerle, 'Esquisse', *Revue Historique*, vol. ccxix (1958), pp. 65 and 67–9.   [4] See p. 34.

[5] See F. Dölger, 'Beiträge zur Geschichte des byzantinischen Finanzverwaltung, besonders des 10. und 11. Jahrhunderts', in *Byzantinisches Archiv*, Heft 9 (1927). The text, which has been preserved in Codex Marcianus gr. 173, has been edited by W. Ashburner, in *J.H.S.*, vol. xxxv (1915), pp. 76–82, and again by Dölger in loc. cit.

[6] Lemerle, 'Esquisse', *Revue Historique*, vol. ccxix (1958), pp. 258–9.

servants were interested in the communities of free peasants because they had these at their mercy. On the other hand, treatises on the legal rights and obligations of big landowners, or notes on how to extract the full amount of the tax due from them, would have been both ineffective and indiscreet. This point is illustrated by the ineffectiveness of the tenth-century Imperial agrarian legislation, including the ferocious laws promulgated by the grim Emperor Basil II.

As soon as the East Roman peasant-soldiers began to bar out from Asia Minor the seasonal Saracen raiders, all branches of the East Roman 'Establishment' began to move in with an eye to getting hold of the peasants' land. By 967, if this is the date of Nikêphóros II Phokás's Novel No. 22,[1] some of these investments had been profitable enough to pay for the building of large and expensive country-houses on land bought from the purchasers' fellow members of a taxation-unit in villages (χωρία) or in outlying hamlets attached to villages (ἀγρίδια) in which the purchasers already had ancestral holdings of real property. By the time in the tenth century when these luxurious mansions were erected, security in Asia Minor must have been, once again, almost as good as it had been there in the first two centuries of the Christian Era. For members of the 'Establishment', this spelt lucrative investments in rural property. Consequently, for the free peasants, it spelt the alienation of their freeholds, by means that might be fair theoretically but were, in reality, foul.

Appendix

RECENTLY, at any rate, the prevalent view among students of East Roman history has been that, in the century 963–1071, the East Roman Empire was economically and socially sick; that the debasement of the coinage in the course of this century was a symptom of this sickness; that a disease which had long been sapping the Empire's strength without being recognized and acknowledged was made flagrantly apparent by the double military disaster in 1071; and that, although, after that, the Empire twice rallied—first in the reign of Aléxios I Komnênós and for a second time in the thirteenth century, at Níkaia—it was fighting a losing battle. The fall of Constantinople in 1204 was a more devastating disaster than the fall of Bari and than the débâcle at Melazkerd in 1071; the second fall of Constantinople in 1453 was never even partially retrieved; it was the end of the East Roman Empire's history.

This is the view taken in the present book. It is presented brilliantly by Haussig in the most recent version of his authoritative work.[2] It has,

---

[1] Text in Zachariä, op. cit., vol. cit., p. 299.

[2] See Haussig, *A History of Byzantine Civilization*, pp. 301–50, Part Four: 'Byzantine Civilization in Decline', especially the introductory piece, 'Political decay and cultural flowering', on pp. 301–2. The four chapters in this Part of Haussig's book are 'Byzantine culture in

however, now been challenged by M. F. Hendy. He considers that the East Roman Empire was not, in truth, 'culturally brilliant but economically decadent' in the period 1081–1204,[1] and, if he is right apropos of these later years, presumably his thesis also holds good for the years 963–1081.

Hendy points out[2] that the interior of Asia Minor, which was occupied by the Saljūqs permanently after 1071, was economically the least valuable part of the peninsula. We may add that, for the Imperial Government, the loss of the rebellious magnates and the alienated peasantry of the forfeited region may have been a good riddance. Coins and archaeological excavations provide indices of economic life which show that 'it is the eleventh and twelfth centuries . . . that represent the apogee of Byzantine mercantile development'.[3] 'The debasement of the gold coinage, which normally assumes such importance in accounts of the Byzantine coinage during the eleventh century, was in fact a temporary phenomenon.'[4]

Hendy praises Aléxios I's currency reform *circa* 1092,[5] but he does not say that Aléxios restored the nómisma's pristine gold-content and weight. He mentions[6] that, from the twelfth century, the increase in the volume of coin-finds is 'quite overwhelming' in the Empire's European territories, which, since 1018, included the whole of the interior of the Balkan Peninsula up to the south bank of the lower Danube. However, he does not mention the economic misery of the Bulgarian peasantry that favoured the spread of Bogomilism on the testimony of Cosmas the Priest;[7] nor does he mention the hardly less acute misery of the East Roman peasantry that is attested by the tenth-century East Roman agrarian legislation. Agriculture and animal husbandry were always the mainstay of the East Roman Empire's economy. If Hendy is right in holding[8] that 1081–1204 was a period of expansion in urban population, industry, and trade—particularly in the Empire's European territories— the expansion in these sectors must surely have been unaccompanied by a proportionate expansion of the rural economy, and this would explain why the twelfth-century urban boom was ephemeral. Hendy suggests[9] that the progressive consolidation of the holdings of rural property into

---

bondage to feudalism and the new economic forces', 'The end of the supremacy of monastic culture and the beginning of the Byzantine enlightenment', 'The rise of secular Byzantine literature', 'Enlightenment and humanism in representational art'. In this set of chapters Haussig makes a strong case for his thesis.

[1] M. F. Hendy 'Byzantium, 1081–1204: An Economic Reappraisal', in *Transactions of the Royal Historical Society*, Fifth series, vol. 20 (1970), on pp. 31–52.

[2] In loc. cit., on pp. 32–4 and 36.   [3] Ibid., p. 50.

[4] p. 45, n. 3.   [5] pp. 42–3.

[6] On p. 46.   [7] See the present work, pp. 684–8.

[8] p. 48.   [9] On pp. 38–9.

large estates may have resulted in an increase in economic efficiency. But we know from Nikêphóros II's agrarian legislation[1] that the management of estates acquired by monasteries and bishoprics was inefficient. By comparison, large landowners who were laymen made better use of the land in Nikêphóros's judgement; but surely nothing could compensate for the ruin of the peasantry—and the plight of the East Roman peasants went from bad to worse, whether they remained nominally independent economically or whether they sank to the status of serving as πάροικοι on large landowners' estates.

Perhaps Hendy takes up these questions in his book *Coinage and Money in the Byzantine Empire, 1081–1261* (*Dumbarton Oaks Studies*, xii), which was in the press when he published the article discussed in the present Appendix.

(ii) *Trade and Industry*

The size of the tax-revenue of the East Roman Empire in its heyday is the more remarkable considering that it was mainly raised from the produce of the land. The Empire's other sources of revenue, namely its trade and industry, were ebullient by comparison with those of pre-eleventh-century Western Christendom, though they were stagnant by comparison with those of the contemporary Islamic World or with those of the Greek World itself in earlier and later chapters of its history.

At the present day, Greek shipping is plying on every sea-route, and Greek traders are to be found doing business in most parts of the World. This modern Greek commercial activity has been expanding ever since the East Roman Empire was supplanted by its Ottoman successor. For the four centuries before that event, the Italians had been capturing from the Greeks even the trade in the Greeks' own home waters and lands. Under the Ottoman regime, and under the subsequent regime of re-established Greek independence, the Greeks have not only recaptured the economic mastery of their own house; they have carried their commercial activities far beyond those limits. They have held their own in the Levant against the competition of the Syrians, the Lebanese, and the Sephardic Jewish refugees from Spain and Portugal whom the 'Osmanlis deliberately planted in Istanbul, Thessaloníkê, and Smyrna to serve as a counterpoise to the Greeks' commercial prowess. The Greeks have also held their own in the World at large against the economic prowess of the modern Westerners.

This is not the first time that the Greeks have come to the fore in trade and industry. In the Roman Empire before its first breakdown in the third century, Alexandria was the workshop of the Graeco-Roman

---

[1] See p. 165–6.

World, and Alexandrian traders were doing business as far north-westward as Britain and as far eastward as Gandhara and the east coast of India. In the last millennium B.C. the Greeks got the better of their Phoenician and Etruscan competitors in the race for the exploitation of the western basin of the Mediterranean. In the Mycenaean Age they were as versatile as the Rhos were in the Byzantine Age in practising either commerce or piracy, whichever of these two alternative activities offered them the greater opportunity at the moment for making profits. The Byzantine Age was an exceptional interlude in the Greeks' economic history. In this age, their commercial and industrial performance was relatively sluggish.

The cause of this sluggishness is manifest. In the Byzantine Age the East Roman 'Establishment' was uneconomic-minded, or was even positively averse from manufacturing and trading with a view to making profits. It may seem paradoxical that a people with an aptitude for business, and with a tradition of exercising this aptitude with success, should produce, and should maintain in power, a native 'Establishment' that looked down upon manufactures and commerce with disdain. Yet the East Roman 'Establishment' is not the only one in the course of Greek history that has adopted this attitude. In the Hellenic Age the aristocrats of the city-state of Thebes despised, and penalized politically, their fellow citizens who were artisans and traders; and the 'peers' who came to dominate the Spartan city-state recoiled from the industrial and commercial activities in which pre-'Lycurgan' Sparta had made a promising start. However, the closest counterpart to the situation in the Greek World in the Byzantine Age is to be found in China in her Imperial Age—an epoch of Chinese history that lasted for more than twenty-one centuries, as against the eight centuries of the Roman Empire's East Roman avatar. In the Chinese World, as in the Greek World, the people's genius for industry and commerce could be discouraged by an unsympathetic 'Establishment', but it could not be eradicated. In the Chinese World too, this genius has asserted itself beyond the damping Empire's frontiers and since its demise.

There is a story[1] that the Emperor Theóphilos (829–42), watching a particularly fine merchant-ship coming into port in the Golden Horn, inquired who the owner was and was horrified to learn that the ship and its cargo belonged to his wife. By going into the shipping business the Empress Theodora had compromised the dignity of the Imperial office. 'God', Theophilos is reported to have exclaimed, 'has made me an Emperor, and my consort the Avghoústa has turned me into a shipowner (ναύκληρον). Who has ever seen an Emperor of the Romans and his wife

---

[1] See *Theoph. Cont.*, pp. 88–9 (Bonn); Genesius, Book III, pp. 75–6 (Bonn); Zonarás, vol. iii, pp. 357–8 (Bonn); Kedhrênós, p. 980 (Bonn).

engaging in trade?'¹ The outraged Emperor gave orders that the ship and its cargo were to be burned. This story is at any rate *ben trovato*. It expresses correctly the East Roman 'Establishment's' attitude of mind. 'Economic profit', the Emperor Leo VI writes, 'is not Our Majesty's objective in seeking to subjugate Our opponents.'²

East Roman Emperors had to assume airs of pomp and state when once they had climbed on to the Imperial throne, because so many of them were adventurers of obscure origin. The fictitious genealogies that Basil I and his like procured for themselves after reaching the summit did not carry conviction. By contrast, the contemporary Caliphs of the Islamic Empire—both the Umayyads and their 'Abbasid kinsmen and sup-planters—were hereditary rulers whose authentic lineage was as re-spectable as the Medicis'. The Caliphs' Meccan ancestors had been 'a nation of shopkeepers'. The Prophet Muhammad himself had been in business before he received his call. Indeed, no Meccan could have afforded not to be in business, for Mecca's only assets were a spring, a shrine, and the people's commercial ability. Meccans had either to trade or to starve. Consequently the rulers of the Muslim World regarded traders with respect so long as the Caliphate remained in the hands of the Quraysh—the Meccan clan to which Muhammad and the Umayyads and the 'Abbasids all belonged—and this ancestral commercial-mindedness of the Islamic Empire's Qurayshite 'Establishment' proved to be stimulating for the Caliphs' subjects. In the age in which the East Roman 'Establishment' was damping down Greek commerce and industry, the Caliphs' subjects of all religions were the leading traders and industrialists in the Oikoumenê.

The East Roman 'Establishment's' anti-commercial-mindedness re-vealed itself in a number of ways. The volume of private business, so far from being encouraged to expand, was deliberately restricted. Business-men were hindered from travelling even within the Empire's frontiers and, *a fortiori*, from going abroad. It was assumed that foreigners and provincials would find it worth their while to come to Constantinople, and that the members of the business community in 'the City' could therefore count on being able to do their business with outsiders within the walls, where they, as well as the outsiders, would be conveniently under the Imperial Government's eye. At the same time, things were not made easy for foreigners who did come to Constantinople to do business there. Trade between the Empire and the rest of the World was chan-nelled through a small number of points on the frontier; and, when the foreign traders arrived at Constantinople with their merchandise, their

---

¹ *Theoph. Cont.*, loc. cit.

² Οὐ γὰρ κέρδους ἕνεκεν τὴν ὑποταγὴν τῶν ἀντικαθισταμένων ἐπιζητεῖ (Leo VI, *Taktiká*, Dhiátaxis 15, § 39, cols. 896–7).

activities were jealously supervised and restricted. The products of the Imperial Government's own factories were reserved exclusively for governmental use. They were not for sale either to natives or to foreigners. Even some of the products of private East Roman industry were placed on an index of commodities that were withheld from export (κωλυόμενα or κεκωλυμένα were the technical terms for these articles that were subject to a permanent embargo).

However, before we review these various evidences of the East Roman Government's anti-economic-mindedness, we shall do well to remind ourselves that our principal source of information about the East Roman Empire's trade and industry is a document that does not give, and was not designed to give, a comprehensive and well-balanced account, and that the evidence provided by this document must therefore be discounted and corrected. This master document is the Ἐπαρχικὸν Βιβλίον, the manual of the Prefect of the City of Constantinople, which appears to have been compiled during the reign of Leo VI (886–912).[1] This work takes cognizance of a number of the guilds in the capital city, but this number does not include some of the most important of these associations.[2] The book does not cover the corresponding guilds in other cities;[3] and Constantinople, like all capital cities, was not a fair sample of the life of the country beyond the capital's bounds. All capital cities resemble each other more closely than any of them resemble their respective countries. All alike are parasitic. Moreover, the Book of the Prefect is not concerned with the probably unrepresentative Constantinopolitan guilds' business activities except in so far as these were regulated and controlled by the Prefect and his staff.[4] We should be better informed about East Roman industry and commerce in general if we had the minute-books of one of the local guilds at Thessaloníkê or at Trebizond, or if we had the ledgers of some individual member of one of these non-metropolitan business associations. With these reservations in mind we may sift the evidence provided by the Book of the Prefect, taking it *cum grano salis* and supplementing and correcting it from other sources, in so far as these are forthcoming.

---

[1] J. Nicole, who discovered and edited the unique manuscript of this book, argues, convincingly, that it was compiled in Leo VI's reign, though, in his opinion, parts of it are older (*Le Livre du Préfet*, ed. by J. Nicole, (Geneva, 1893, Georg), pp. 4–8). G. Zoras comes to the same conclusion (*Le corporazioni bizantine* (Rome, 1931, Editrice Studium), pp. 30–40). A. Stöckle dates the compilation in the reign of Nikêphóros II (*Spätrömische und byzantinische Zünfte* = *Klio*, Neunter Beiheft (Leipzig, 1911, Dieterich), pp. 142–8). This dating of Stöckle's is unconvincing, but his analysis of the contents of the book is acute and exhaustive.

[2] e.g. the smiths, wool-weavers, and linen-weavers (G. Mickwitz: *Die Kartell Funktionen der Zünfte* (Helsingfors, 1936, Societas Scientiarum Fennica), p. 226. Cf. Stöckle, op. cit., pp. 6–7, and Nicole, op. cit., p. 11. One profession that is conspicuously left unmentioned is the shipowners (ναύκληροι).

[3] Stöckle, op. cit., p. 3.   [4] Ibid., pp. 3–4 and 55.

At Constantinople there was a considerable 'restraint of trade'—as it would be called in the parlance of the modern World, in which governments are eager to expand trade to a maximum, and this whether they leave trade in private hands or take it into their own hands.

For instance, jewellers (arghyráprátai, khrysokhóoi) were allowed to deal only in gold, silver, pearls, and precious stones.[1] The Vestioprátai (dealers in silk clothing) might buy silk garments only, but no other merchandise except for their own use.[2] There was a veto on doing business as a dealer in silk clothing and as a manufacturer of silk clothing (sêrikoprátês, sêrikários) simultaneously. Membership in either of these guilds disqualified a candidate for membership in the other.[3] The prandioprátai (dealers in 'wrappings') must not poach on the vestioprátai's preserve. The prandioprátai must confine their purchases to clothes (of all kinds) exported from Syria, and χαρέρια (silks, the Arabic word harīr) from Seléfkeia and from elsewhere.[4] Dealers in raw silk (metaxoprátai) were debarred from exercising any trade other than their own.[5] So were the candle-manufacturers,[6] the bakers,[7] the dealers in unguents (myrepsoí),[8] the grocers (saldhamárioi)[9]—this last-mentioned pair of trades might not be combined—, and the inspectors and valuers (vóthroi) of livestock brought to market at Constantinople.[10] If a non-slave processer of raw silk (katartários) wanted to become a dealer in raw silk (metaxoprátês), he had to produce witnesses to testify that he was giving up his original trade.[11]

There were also limitations on the quantity of raw material that a manufacturer might have in hand. A goldsmith, for instance, might not buy more than one pound at a time of silver, either wrought or bullion. If he exceeded this limit without immediately notifying the president of his guild, he rendered himself liable to severe penalties.[12] Processers of silk (katartárioi) might deal only in the quantity of imported raw silk that they could work up.[13] The cutters of leather piece-goods (lorotómoi) were forbidden to deal in more hides than they required as material for their products.[14] Bakers might not buy more than one gold piece's (nómisma's) worth at a time of grain (síton).[15]

Thus, at the turn of the ninth and tenth centuries, the state was still laying a heavy hand on the Constantinopolitan guilds.[16] Yet the Book of the Prefect shows that, even at Constantinople, the guilds had now succeeded in raising themselves above their depressed condition in the

---

[1] *Livre du Préfet*, chap. 2, § 1, p. 22 of Nicole's edition.

[2] Op. cit., 4, 1, pp. 26–7.   [3] 4, 7, p. 28, and 8, 6, p. 37.   [4] 5, 1, p. 29.

[5] 6, 1, p. 31.   [6] 11, 2, p. 44.   [7] 18, 5, pp. 54–5.

[8] 10, 6, p. 43.   [9] 13, 1, p. 47.   [10] 21, 7, p. 59.

[11] 7, 3, p. 34.   [12] 2, 8 and 9, p. 24.   [13] 7, 1, p. 34.

[14] 14, 1, p. 49.   [15] 18, 1, pp. 53–4.   [16] Stöckle, op. cit., pp. 138–9.

age that had been inaugurated by Diocletian and Constantine I and that had been brought to an end by the cataclysm in the seventh century.[1]

In the Book of the Prefect there is only a single provision for the commandeering of private artisans' labour for the public service. The leather-cutters alone were at the state's disposal. When they were working for the Government they were under the Prefect's command, though this without being annexed to his staff; when they were working for the Emperor himself, they took their orders from the Master of the Emperor's Stables (protostrátor), by agreement with the Prefect. They were paid for this governmental work, though the rate of pay was at the Emperor's discretion.[2] Neither the leather-cutters nor the members of any other of the Constantinopolitan guilds that are mentioned in the manual were under the hereditary servitudes which had been such an onerous feature of the Roman Empire's economic regime between the third century and the seventh.[3]

So far from that, the members of the guilds were now recruited by voluntary enlistment.[4] Candidates' professional, financial, and moral qualifications were scrutinized; for some guilds the candidates had to give written assurances and to produce testimonials and guarantors, and, if admitted, they had to pay an entrance fee. Conversely, expulsion from the guild was now one of the penalties for misconduct.[5] Under the Diocletianic regime, release from a guildsman's burdensome obligations would have been, not a punishment, but a boon, supposing that it had ever been attainable. 'The individual's personal freedom is now much greater.'[6] It may be added that his prospects were also much brighter if he chose to use his freedom by engaging in industry or trade. For membership in a guild was now evidently desirable, and its attractiveness implies that it was likely to be lucrative.[7] Though the quantity of silver that a silversmith might buy was limited to one pound at a time, the silversmiths were able to lend the Prefect gold and enamel and chased silver work, as well as hangings, to decorate the City, and the Palace too, on state occasions.[8] Nor did the Government merely borrow from

---

[1] See Mickwitz, op. cit., p. 231.

[2] *Livre du Préfet*, 14, 1, p. 49.

[3] C. M. Macri: *L'Organisation de l'économie urbaine dans Byzance sous la dynastie de Macédoine (867–1057)* (Paris, 1925, Guillon), pp. 8–9.

[4] Stöckle, op. cit., p. 140.

[5] Ibid. Fees and guarantees figure prominently in the procedure for the election of members of the guild of notaries (*Livre du Préfet*, 1, pp. 13–22); of bankers and money-changers (trapezítai) (ibid., 3, 1, p. 20); of dealers in silk clothing (vestioprátai) (ibid., 4, 5, pp. 27–8); of dealers in raw silk (metaxoprátai) (ibid., 6, 6, p. 32); of soap manufacturers (ibid., 12, 2, pp. 45–6). No less than 27 instances in which expulsion from the guild, either alone or in combination with other penalties, is ordained in the Book of the Prefect are noted by Stöckle in op. cit., pp. 128–9 and 130.

[6] Stöckle, op. cit., p. 140.   [7] Mickwitz, op. cit., pp. 210–11.

[8] Constantine Porphyrogenitus, *De Caer.*, Book II, p. 572. See the present work, Part III, chap. 7, p. 500.

the stocks of private dealers; it made purchases from private sources—for instance, when it was acquiring stores and equipment for the expedition of 949 against the Cretan Muslims.[1]

Moreover, though a Constantinopolitan manufacturer or dealer was debarred from engaging in more than a single trade at a time, he was free to choose the guild in which he would seek admission to membership, and in one case, so long as he was not a slave, he was also free, as has been noted, to transfer from an inferior trade to a superior one, on condition that he did not stay in business in the inferior trade as well.

Personal freedom in the pursuit of gainful occupations was not limited to guildsmen and other traders on a large scale. The sheep merchants (provatémboroi) were forbidden to hinder the peasants from coming, as the sheep merchants themselves came, to the capital and doing their own petty business there, side by side with the big men and on the same terms and conditions.[2]

Employees, too, were free, as well as their employers. An employee might not be hired for more than thirty days at a time, and his wages had to be paid to him in advance.[3] The employee must complete the work for which he had contracted, but, if the carrying out of the work by the employee was delayed owing to remissness on the employer's part, then the employee, after giving notice to the employer, lodging a complaint with the Prefect, and obtaining the Prefect's approval, was free to undertake other work.[4]

The shipowners were perhaps the greatest beneficiaries from the relaxation of the Imperial Government's grip on private business enterprise. They had been among the worst sufferers from this during the Empire's Diocletianic Age, when the Government's policy had been to re-establish and maintain the pre-third-century dispensation at all costs. One feature of the Empire's *ancien régime* that had then been maintained was the provision of free food for the metropolitan urban proletariat, and this burden had been doubled by the duplication of the capital through the creation, at Constantinople, of a New Rome endowed with the same parasitic privileges as the Old Rome. The population of the Old Rome had been liquidated during Justinian's reconquest of Italy from the Ostrogoths (537–53); the provisioning of Constantinople from Egypt had been interrupted by the Persian occupation of Egypt from 616 to 628/9 and had been ended once for all by the Arab conquest of Egypt in 642. After that, the corn exported from Egypt, now reduced in volume, had been diverted permanently from Constantinople to Medina

---

[1] Constantine Porphyrogenitus, *De Caer.*, Book II, pp. 673–6.
[2] *Livre du Préfet*, 15, 4, pp. 50–1, read together with 15, 1, p. 50.
[3] Ibid., 6, 2, p. 31; 8, 12, p. 38.
[4] Ibid., 21, 1, pp. 60–1.

and Mecca.[1] Meanwhile, the Emperor Heraclius had stopped the corn dole at Constantinople,[2] and this stoppage of the dole under *force majeure* had the effect of liberating the East Roman shipowners.[3]

The earliest evidence for this is in the provisions of the Maritime Law, which, like the Farmers' Law, is thought to have been published in its present form towards the close of the seventh century. Its title 'the Rhodian Law' suggests that, like some other East Roman official or semi-official documents, it may have included material that was ancient and out of date. It therefore has to be used with caution as evidence for late-seventh-century practice, but, in so far as we can rely on it, it does suggest that, by that date, the East Roman merchants who dealt in maritime trade owned their own ships and were free to use them for their own private purposes.[4] While the Slav and Nomad invasions of the Balkan Peninsula seem to have disrupted overland traffic there, the Arab naval offensive of 649–78 does not seem to have paralysed maritime trade. The East Roman mercantile marine seems to have responded to the challenge of Arab naval power at this stage by technical improvements which made the ships lighter and swifter.[5] The biography of Saint Antony Dekapolítês indicates that, about the year 820, East Roman sea-traffic was lively, notwithstanding the activities of Arab corsairs—in contrast to the state of the overland routes, which were dangerous and were in some cases closed.[6] The persistence of the East Roman merchant marine's activity in the Tyrrhene, Ionian, and Aegean Seas right on into the later decades of the ninth century is attested by the biographies of St. Elías of Enna and of St. Vlásios.[7] The prosperity of East Roman shipowners (ναύκληροι) in the reign of the Emperor Nikêphóros I (802–11) is revealed in the ninth of the ten ingenious acts of oppression (κάκωσιν, κακόνοιαν) that are debited to Nikêphóros's account by Theophanes.[8]

Ninth: he compelled the shipowners (ναυκλήρους) whose homes were on the seaboard, especially in Asia Minor, to buy, at his own valuation, some of the properties that he had confiscated—and this though they had never been agriculturists and made these purchases only under coercion.[9]

---

[1] Teall in loc. cit., p. 97; Lewis, op. cit., p. 82. 'Amr, the conqueror of Egypt, had re-opened the canal from the Nile Delta to Suez (Lewis, ibid.).

[2] In 618 and finally in 626, according to Teall in loc. cit., p. 89; in 618 according to Stöckle, op. cit., pp. 50 and 140–1, following *Chronicon Paschale*, p. 711. See also Nicephorus Patriarcha, Ἱστορία Σύντομος, p. 12. Cf. Stratós, op. cit., pp. 100–1.

[3] Lewis, op. cit., p. 83.   [4] Teall in loc. cit., p. 104.   [5] Lopez in loc. cit., pp. 70–72.

[6] G. Ostrogorsky, 'The Byzantine Empire in the World of the Seventh Century', in *Dumbarton Oaks Papers*, Number Thirteen (1959), pp. 1–21, on pp. 11–12.

[7] E. Eickhoff, *Seekrieg und Seepolitik zwischen Islam und Abendland: Das Mittelmeer unter byzantinischer und arabischer Hegemonie (650–1040)* (Berlin, 1966, de Gruyter), pp. 112–13. Cf. pp. 48–9 and 210.   [8] p. 487. Cf. Kedhrênós, vol. ii, p. 38.

[9] The purpose of this 'ninth oppressive act' of Nikêphóros's was presumably to convert into liquid assets, on terms favourable to the Treasury, some of the real estate that he had

Tenth: he assembled the leading Constantinopolitan shipowners and forced them to accept loans from him of twelve pounds gold per head at the rate of 16⅔ per cent interest, without letting them off from paying the regular dues as well.

These two measures of Nikêphóros's show that he believed that, at the date at which he introduced them, shipowners were an affluent class, and, since the Emperor was an ex-treasury official, he is likely to have been well informed.

In the Aegean and in the seas to the west of the Straits of Ótranto, East Roman maritime trade fell into adversity after the year 827 or 828,[1] when the Spanish Muslim refugees at Alexandria conquered Crete, and after the beginning, in 827, of the progressive Arab conquest of Sicily that was virtually completed in 902. Even then, however, the East Roman navy and merchant marine retained their command of the Black Sea, in spite of the occasional naval raids of the Rhos, which may have begun half a century before the Rhos assault on Constantinople in 860.

The continuing importance of Greek maritime trade in the Black Sea is attested by a provision in the Romano-Russian treaty of 912, which reappears, in shorter form, in the treaty of 945.[2] The Rhos undertake to come to the help of any Greek ship that they find in distress and to repatriate the ship, with its cargo and its crew. If the cargo cannot be repatriated, the Rhos will sell it on the owners' account and will pay over the proceeds on their next visit to the East Roman Empire. In the treaty of 945, the Rhos also undertake not to molest Khersonite fishermen if they meet them at the mouth of the Dniepr. In this latter treaty the Rhos also renounce the right to spend the winter at the mouth of the Dniepr, either at Belobereg or at St. Eleíthérios. When autumn comes, they will return home. We may guess that the Rhos would not have

acquired by the first of the 'oppressive acts' on Theophanes's list. Nikêphóros had sold up the real estate of the deportees from all the thémata whom he had transplanted to the Sklavinías in 809 (see II, 1 (iii) (a), p. 94). The compulsory purchase of real estate by shipowners resident along the seaboard of Asia Minor had nothing to do with the endowment of the seamen of the Asiatic naval thémata with στρατιωτικὰ κτήματα. The unwilling purchasers were owners of merchant-ships (ναύκληροι), not captains of warships (πρωτοκάραβοι). The captains could not have accumulated the capital for buying real estate out of the pay that they received at irregular intervals. Nor was it only the captains that were endowed with στρατιωτικὰ κτήματα. Every seaman in a naval théma had to have a strateía of the same minimum value—four pounds gold—as a trooper in a cavalry théma (Constantine VII Porphyrogenitus's Novel No. 7, cited in II, 1 (iii) (d), p. 134).

[1] See A. A. Vasiliev, *Byzance et les Arabes*, vol. i (Brussels, 1935, Institut de Philologie et d'Histoire Orientales), p. 55.
[2] See *The Russian Primary Chronicle*, Laurentian text, translated and edited by S. H. Cross and O. P. Sherbowitz-Wetzor (Cambridge, Mass., 1953, The Mediaeval Academy of America), pp. 67 and 76.

accepted this last stipulation if, at the time, East Roman naval power in the Black Sea had not been strong enough to enforce observance.

The materials imported by the Constantinopolitan dealers in linen from Póndos and Kerasoús[1] and by the dealers in unguents (myrepsoí) from théma Khaldhía and Trapezoús (Trebizond)[2] were presumably conveyed to Constantinople by coastwise shipping;[3] Khersón imported its grain from Asia Minor;[4] and there is evidence for sea-borne trade between Bulgaria and Constantinople via the ports of Mesêmvría and Ankhíalos.[5] The Book of the Prefect does not inform us whether this was the route by which the Bulgars and other barbarian peoples (éthnê) dispatched their exports to Constantinople for barter on a scale that required co-operation between the Constantinopolitan dealers in linen (othonioprátai) and grocers (saldhamárioi) and other trades for assembling the goods of the requisite kind, quality, and value for negotiating the exchange.[6]

After the East Roman Empire's reconquest of Crete in 961 and of Cyprus in 965 the Empire's merchant marine revived.[7] The East Romans did not begin to lose their sea-borne trade till the last quarter of the eleventh century.[8] They lost it to the Italians. It is significant that this happened at the time when the East Roman gold piece (nómisma) was at last being disastrously depreciated.

The activities of the East Roman merchant marine are a reminder that the Empire's trade and industry was not monopolized by the city of Constantinople. Trebizond and Attáleia (Antalya) and Thessaloníkê were important focuses of international trade. The Pelopónnêsos rapidly became an important industrial region, for the first time in its history since the fourth century B.C., when, towards and after the turn of the eighth and ninth centuries, the Imperial Government re-established its authority over all but two of those Peloponnesian districts that had been overrun by the Slavs. Greece became an important seat of silk production,[9] and Thebes, in théma Ellás, became one of the seats of the silk-manufacturing industry.

---

[1] *Livre du Préfet*, 9, 1, p. 39.

[2] The Χαλδαῖοι of the *Livre du Préfet*, 10, 2, p. 42, were the inhabitants of the East Roman théma Khaldhía, of which Trebizond was the capital (see Stöckle, op. cit., pp. 36–7).

[3] G. Le Strange, *The Lands of the Eastern Caliphate* (Cambridge, 1905, University Press), p. 136.

[4] Constantine Porphyrogenitus, *De Adm. Imp.*, chapter 53.

[5] Teall in loc. cit., pp. 117–18.   [6] *Livre du Préfet*, 9, 6, p. 40.

[7] H. Ahrweiler, *Byzance et la mer* (Paris, 1966, Presses Universitaires de France), pp. 77, 144, and 164–5.

[8] H. Antoniadis-Bibicou, *Études d'histoire maritime de Byzance à propos du 'Thème des Caravisiens'* (Paris, 1966, S.E. and P.E.N.), p. 14.

[9] Silk-worms had been imported from China into the East Roman Empire in the reign of Justinian I (527–65). We have no information about the date at which silk cultivation and the silk industry were introduced into Greece in particular.

The channelling of international trade through a few points on the Empire's frontiers evidently produced large local customs receipts. In Leo VI's reign (886–912) the military governor (stratêghós) of the army-corps district (théma) of Khaldhía had his comparatively low salary of ten pounds gold supplemented by an additional ten drawn on the customs dues collected along the sector of the Empire's frontier that was the outer border of his district,[1] and the military governor of théma Mesopotamía, a rugged and unproductive frontier district in the angle between the two arms of the upper Euphrates, received all the customs dues collected in his district for himself, in lieu of a salary,[2] though, as governor of a district of the 'Eastern' class, he ought to have received a salary from the Central Government. Naturally the governor of Khaldhía instructed the local customs-officers to be strict, and Saint George, the bishop of Amastrís, interceded at this governor's court of justice at Trebizond on behalf of some merchants whom the customs-officers had falsely accused of fraud.[3]

The Byzantine writers' Arab contemporaries give economic and statistical information about the East Roman Empire that is not to be found in the Byzantine sources. Ibn Hawkal, who died at some date in the last quarter of the tenth century, records that he has obtained his information about the Empire from escaped or ransomed Muslim prisoners of war.[4] He cites, as two of the most important sources of the Empire's public revenue, the customs dues collected at Trebizond and the tax on prize of war collected at Attáleia, which was the headquarters of the naval théma of the Kivyrrhaiótai.[5] He notes that the trade between Trebizond and the 'Abbasid Caliphate was in Armenian hands, but that in Trebizond there were also many resident Muslim merchants.[6] This piece of information is significant. It bears out Lewis's contention[7] that the East Roman Government's policy of channelling international trade through a small number of points played into the hands of foreign traders. The prize brought in to Attáleia did put money into Greek pockets. This prize consisted of loot seized in raids (by privateers?) on Syrian ports, prize captured by East Roman warships, and the proceeds of the sale of Muslim prisoners of war, their ships, and their cargoes.[8]

Antālīyah [Attáleia] is both a strong fortress and [the capital of] an extensive district attached to the fortress. Neither the household tax [kapnikón, i.e. hearth-tax] nor any other tax, great or small, is levied there. No one

---

[1] *De Caer.*, Book II, pp. 696–7.   [2] Ibid.
[3] L. Bréhier, 'Les Populations rurales au ixme siècle d'après l'hagiographie byzantine', in *Byzantion*, i (1924), pp. 177–90, on p. 187.
[4] See the passage translated in Vasiliev, *Byzance et les Arabes*, vol. ii, Part II, pp. 413–14.
[5] Vasiliev, op. cit., ii, II, p. 414.   [6] Le Strange, op. cit., p. 136.
[7] In op. cit., pp. 120–1.   [8] Vasiliev, op. cit., ii, II, p. 414.

exercises authority there except the Emperor himself. There is only a post-master.[1]

Greek sources of information indicate that Ibn Hawkal has exaggerated the degree of Attáleia's immunity from taxation and administration, yet his account suggests that at any rate the East Roman Government's hand lay more lightly on the activities of the Empire's subjects at Attáleia than at Constantinople.[2]

As for Thessaloníkê, its revival was assured as soon as the dust raised by the Slav *Völkerwanderung* had begun to settle. Thessaloníkê shares with Marseilles the topographical advantage of being sited near the mouth of a river whose valley provides a natural highway from the seaboard of the Mediterranean into the interior of continental Europe. By the year 904, in which Thessaloníkê was sacked by a Syrian corsair squadron, the city's population had expanded to a size at which it needed organized imports of food, as we know from the narrative of one of the victims of the catastrophe, John Kameniátês.[3]

Nor was trade monopolized by the major cities. At Éphesos, which had declined lamentably from its pre-seventh-century industrial and commercial pre-eminence, there was still a periodical fair; and this was made tax-free by Constantine VI (780–97),[4] perhaps in an attempt to arrest Éphesos's decay. The profits from the ownership of rural fairs were substantial enough to move an owner to resist the transfer of his fair to another location in which the dues would no longer fall into his pocket. By the year 996 the control of fairs had come to be so lucrative that it was now worth while for the 'influential' (οἱ δυνατοί) to wrest this asset out of their 'uninfluential' fellow citizens' hands. This piece of hotly contested ground in the contemporary class-war had come to the attention of Basil II and had caused him to legislate on the subject in section 7 of his Novel No. 29. The importance of the part played by fairs in the economic life of the East Roman Empire has been noted by Jenkins.[5]

The importation of silk-worms into the East Roman Empire in the reign of Justinian I had endowed the Empire with a new and valuable economic asset, and this had survived the seventh-century débâcle. It has been mentioned that one region in which the production of silk was acclimatized was central Greece, round the city of Thebes. This region

---

[1] Ibid., p. 419.

[2] For instance, Constantine Porphyrogenitus notes, in *De Thematibus*, pp. 228–9, that Stavrákios, whom Leo VI had appointed to the post of katepáno of the Mardaïte community at Attáleia, 'stayed in office for a considerable number of years, although his handling of the taxes was unsatisfactory'.

[3] Ch. 6 *ad. fin.*, on p. 496 of *Theoph. Cont.* (Bonn). See Teall in loc. cit., p. 122.

[4] See H. Ahrweiler, 'L'Asie Mineure et les invasions arabes', in *Revue Historique*, 86ᵉ année, tome cxxvii (1962), pp. 1–32, on p. 25.

[5] R. J. H. Jenkins in *C. Med. H.*, vol. iv, 2nd ed., Part II, p. 96.

had had the good fortune not to lie on the main track of the Slav *Völker-wanderung*, and it produced silk for spinning and weaving and dyeing and converting into garments. We may guess that Greece supplied most of the raw silk for the silk industry at Constantinople as well as at Thebes; and, now that silk was being produced for the East Romans at home instead of having all to be imported, either raw or in the form of piece-goods, from the opposite end of the Old World, the Imperial Government no longer needed a monopoly in order to meet its own requirements for supplying the Imperial factories that produced the Government's silk robes of state. Purple dye continued to be an Imperial monopoly[1]—for political rather than for economic reasons, since there were purple fisheries in East Roman territorial waters—but silk, and the products made from it, no longer needed to be kept in the Government's hands exclusively.[2]

The post-seventh-century East Roman Empire was not the sole pro-ducer of silk and of silk products at the western end of the Old World. When silk production had been acclimatized in the Empire in the sixth century, Syria had lain within its frontiers, and silk production had established itself there. Since then, Syria had been conquered from the Empire by the Arabs, and the Syrian silk industry had acquired the vast market of the Caliphate. However, Syria under Arab rule still had a surplus of silk piece-goods for export, and the East Roman Empire had a demand for silk beyond its own domestic production[3]—a demand that Syria could and did meet. At Constantinople there was a guild, the prandioprátai, that did no other business except the trade in Syrian piece-goods made of silk or other materials.[4]

Of course, silk clothing was a luxury, not one of the necessities of life, as linen or woollen garments were. But it was a luxury that, in this age, had enormous social and political prestige, and the market, though inevitably confined to a rich and powerful minority, was valuable be-cause it was world-wide and because a handsome profit could be earned even on a limited volume of sales. We do not know whether Syrian silk goods competed with East Roman silk goods in Western Christendom, or whether the East Roman prandioprátai succeeded in interposing them-selves as middlemen between Syria and the Christian West. In any case, East Roman silk had a market in the Christian West till the year 1147, when, two centuries and a half after the Empire had lost all but one last foothold in Sicily, the Norman king of Sicily, Roger II, deported some East Roman adepts in the silk industry from Corinth and Thebes to

---

[1] Vasiliká, xix, 1, 80 = *Cod. Just.*, IV, 40, 1, cited by Stöckle, op. cit., p. 30.
[2] Lopez in loc. cit., pp. 76–7 and 78.
[3] Stöckle, op. cit., p. 24.
[4] *Livre du Préfet*, 5, pp. 29–31.

Palermo. We may guess that, throughout, the East Roman prandio-prátai and vestioprátai (dealers in silk clothing of better quality than the wares to which the prandioprátai's dealings were confined) suffered less from Syrian commercial competition than from their own Government's anti-commercial-mindedness.

A present-day government that had such heavy calls upon its financial resources as the East Roman Government had would have seen in its country's silk production a prime economic asset which must be exploited to the full for the two purposes of raising revenue and achieving a favourable balance of trade with the rest of the World. For the East Roman Government, silk was primarily a political asset. Silk production was a means for enabling the East Roman Court to make a display of pomp and state with which foreign courts would not be able to vie, with the one exception of the 'Abbasid court (the Chinese court was too remote to be a competitor in this game of prestige at the western end of the Continent). In the East Roman Government's eyes, silk was not an economic commodity; it was a sacrosanct treasure. Its value lay not in the price that it might fetch but in the prestige that it might confer. Therefore silk must be safeguarded against falling into unworthy hands. Constantinopolitan dealers in raw silk (metaxoprátai) were forbidden to sell to Jews, and to non-Jewish merchants too, who designed to re-sell the silk outside Constantinople.[1] Constantinopolitan processers of silk (katartárioi) might not sell their products without first registering with the Prefect, in order that the Prefect might satisfy himself that they were not slaves and were not paupers or bad characters, but were respectable people who would see to it that their silk was not put to unworthy uses.[2] Silk was, indeed, the most conspicuous, though by no means the only, product of the East Roman Empire that was subject to the haughtily unbusinesslike institution of the embargo on the export of products of East Roman industry and art that were too good to be degraded by being delivered to barbarians.

While the central Greek section of théma Ellás became the focus of East Roman silk production and processing, théma Pelopónnêsos appears, as has been noted, to have developed a remarkable industrial activity after the re-establishment of the Imperial Government's authority there. We have a glimpse of ninth-century Peloponnesian industry in Constantine Porphyrogenitus's account of a visit—via the overland route from Pátras to Constantinople—that was paid to Constantine's grandfather, Basil I, by Basil's benefactress the Patran millionairess, the widow Dhanêlís, after Basil had eliminated his Imperial benefactor and colleague Michael III in 867.

---

[1] *Livre du Préfet*, 6, 16, p. 33.
[2] Ibid., 7, 5, p. 35.

There was a state reception for her in the Maghnávra, of the kind that Roman Emperors customarily give when they are going to entertain some famous and important head of a foreign state. Dhanélís was introduced to the Emperor as ceremoniously and as magnificently as that; and, for her part, she brought the Emperor costly gifts such as hardly any foreign ruler had ever brought so far.

There were five hundred slaves, one hundred of whom were handsome eunuchs. This plutocratic old lady seems to have been aware that, in palaces, there is always room for more of these creatures.[1] In palaces they are to be found in greater swarms than flies in a sheep-fold in springtime. Accordingly, Dhanélís had provided herself with these eunuchs in advance—reckoning, perhaps, that their customary service would make them an ideal guard of honour for her when she entered the Palace. There were also one hundred women whose complexions had been preserved in the shade (σκιατρίαι); one hundred Sidonian piece-goods of many colours (nowadays called *sendaí*; the general state of ignorance has led to this corruption of the correct name); two hundred napless linen *amalia*; and another hundred that were finer spun than spiders' webs—so fine that Dhanélís had been able to have each of them stowed in a section of a hollow reed. There were also quantities of costly gold and silver vessels of many varieties.'[2]

During her stay in Constantinople, Dhanélís took the measurements of the floor of the 'New Church' that Basil I was building at the time;[3] and, after returning to Pátras, she had huge deep-pile carpets (νακοτάπητας) made and dispatched to Constantinople to protect the mosaics with which the floor of this church was covered.[4]

In this age the Peloponnesians—Greeks and Graecized Slavs alike—were unmilitary-minded, except for two recalcitrant Slav tribes, the Ezerítai and the Mêlingoí, in southern Laconia. Twice in Leo VI's reign and once in Rhomanós I's, the Pelopónnêsos, and also the Empire's other western thémata in Europe except for the warlike Mardaïte communities that had been planted there, opted for making payments in money, or in both money and kind, in lieu of supplying the contingents of troops that were due from them. On the last of these three occasions the Pelopónnêsos commuted its military service for 1,000 horses and 100 pounds gold in specie.[5] Evidently here the local temper was very different from what it was in théma Kivyrrhaiótai as described by Ibn

---

[1] Liutprand was as well informed on this important point as Dhanélís had been. The *pièces de résistance* among the presents that he brought for Constantine Porphyrogenitus, when he came to Constantinople in 949 on a mission from Berengar of Ivrea, were four eunuchs that he had bought from dealers in Verdun. He records, in *Antapodosis*, Book IV, chap. 6, that these dealers made large profits by selling Kwarizmian eunuch boys in Spain.—A. J. T.

[2] Constantine Porphyrogenitus, Biography of Basil I, in *Theoph. Cont.*, Book V, chap. 74, pp. 317–18.

[3] See II, 2, p. 187.   [4] Constantine, op. cit., chap. 76, p. 319.

[5] Constantine Porphyrogenitus, *De Adm. Imp.*, chaps. 51–2, pp. 242–4.

Hawkal[1]—and this Muslim observer was recording his co-religionists' dire experience.

The East Roman Empire's economy was, in fact, not so static as it might appear to be at first sight.[2] It may be guessed—though no statistics have survived—that, by the date of the composition of the Book of the Prefect at about the turn of the ninth and tenth centuries, the public sector of East Roman industry and trade had been surpassed by the private sector, and this in both volume and value.[3] The introduction of silk-production and silk-processing at home may have been the turning-point. The principal surviving state monopolies were gold-mining,[4] the use of purple dye,[5] the manufacture of robes of state and other consumer-goods for official use at Court,[6] and, since 539, the manufacture of military equipment[7]—the most important and most legitimate monopoly of all. The private sector was still controlled by the state meticulously, at least at Constantinople, though not so oppressively as it had been under the Diocletianic dispensation; but this state control was not to the manufacturers' and merchants' disadvantage on all points. For instance, the state's insistence, at Constantinople, on collective buying, within the city limits, from provincial or foreign dealers probably enabled the Constantinopolitan guildsmen to make larger profits than they would have made if they had competed with each other, even though, in impos-ing this rule, the state was concerned primarily, not with putting money into the guildsmen's pockets, but with keeping prices low for the metro-politan consumer. Collective buying on the consumer's home ground at places and on terms dictated by the state probably kept the importers' prices down to a low enough level to give the guildsmen as well as the consumers an advantage at the suppliers' expense.

Again, though the state monopolized the business of buying any silk that still had to be bought from abroad,[8] it handed over any surplus, beyond its own requirements, to the private sector, and this at cost price, though not tax-free.[9] Moreover, this is the only tax levied by the East Roman Government on trade and industry of which we have a record.[10] This is surprising, considering the Government's ever-pressing need for revenue and also considering the mercilessness with which it taxed the produce of the land. The explanation may perhaps be found in the pre-ceding chapter of the Empire's history. Under the Diocletianic dispensa-tion the Government's first concern with industrial and commercial

---

[1] See pp. 48–9.   [2] Lopez, op. cit., p. 69.
[3] Cf. Macri, op. cit., p. 11.   [4] Macri, op. cit., p. 16.
[5] Stöckle, op. cit., p. 111.   [6] Macri, op. cit., pp. 17–18.
[7] Macri, ibid.; Stöckle, op. cit., p. 111, citing Justinian I, Novel No. 85, §§ 1 and 4, and *Vasiliká*, lvii, 9.
[8] Stöckle, op. cit., p. 25; Macri, op. cit., pp. 20 and 88–9.   [9] Macri, op. cit., p. 29.
[10] Dölger, 'Beiträge zur Geschichte der byzantinischen Finanzverwaltung', p. 62.

businessmen had been to conscript their services for meeting the state's needs, and these compulsory services had been so onerous that the public authorities may have feared that the victims would collapse under the load if they were to be saddled with taxes as well. Now that the private sector had become more prosperous, it may have been profiting from one of the consequences of its previous adversity.

Though the private sector of industry and trade had expanded in volume and had also, apparently, remained tax-free, it was still unable to absorb all the private capital that was seeking investment.[1] This is indicated by the vigour of the influential minority's drive to acquire rural land[2] as soon as this had been made an attractive investment by the deliverance of the Empire's Asian dominions from the scourge of Saracen raiders. Why did the magnates invest in heavily-taxed land rather than in tax-free industrial and commercial enterprises? Three reasons for this can be discerned. Overt engagement in 'business' would have been as much beneath a grandee's dignity as it was beneath the Emperor's. *Sub rosâ*, business deals with guildsmen, and a proportionate participation in the guildsmen's untaxed profits, would have been acceptable to metropolitan grandees if the Prefect had not prohibited such practices and had not also been able to make his vetoes effective.[3] Investment in heavily-taxed rural property was attractive, after the cessation of Saracen raids, because the prospective 'influential' investor could reckon confidently that, unlike a free peasant, he would be able to fob off the taxation-officers with less than their due, regardless of the demands for more than their due that they were sure to make.

For a metropolitan magnate the Prefect was a formidable official, however much influence the magnate might have. The Prefect outmanœuvred the magnate by making the guildsman who was caught transacting illicit business with the magnate pay penalties that the guildsman would hesitate to risk incurring. Expulsion from his guild was the penalty for a Constantinopolitan dealer in raw silk (metaxoprátês) who made purchases under his own name, at a profit, on behalf of some influential person or plutocrat or silk-weaver (sêrikários, sêrikoprátes).[4]

---

[1] There is no evidence for the existence, in the East Roman Empire, of an appreciable number of great bankers or merchants, 'and in view of the continual governmental restrictions placed upon private economy this is hardly surprising' (Hendy in *Transactions of the Royal Historical Society*, Fifth Series, vol. 20 (1970), p. 42, n. 1).

[2] For this, see F. Dölger, 'Beiträge zur Geschichte der byzantinischen Finanzverwaltung', pp. 64–5.

[3] Ostrogorsky, 'Die wirtschaftlichen und sozialen Grundlagen des byzantinischen Reiches', p. 134, suggests that the reason for the land-hunger of the δυνατοί, after rural land had become a safe investment, is to be found 'above all in the fact that, in the Byzantine city, the δυνατοί were unable to make their weight felt either politically or economically. The centralizing autocratic Byzantine régime gave the δυνατοί no scope in that field.'

[4] *Livre du Préfet*, 6, 10, pp. 32–3.

A Constantinopolitan dealer in pigs would be flogged and cropped if he were caught hiding his pigs in a magnate's mansion and selling them secretly,[1] after the presidents of the guild had notified the Prefect of the arrival of a herd from the countryside and had given him an assurance that their guildsmen would not sell to middlemen but would do the selling all together in the Távros Market.[2] Árkhondes and others might buy direct the imports from Syria, but only as much as would suffice to supply their own needs.[3] On the other hand the taxation-officer who would be an adept in wringing tax, and surtax too, including 'gratuities', out of the peasants, might be defeated by the task of taxing a large estate in Asia Minor, at a long distance from Constantinople, if the owner were a metropolitan absentee landlord with friends at Court.

One of the most cramping and frustrating of the restraints on the business activities of the members of some of the Constantinopolitan guilds was the veto on their travelling.[4] For a dealer in raw silk (metaxoprátês) who was convicted of having travelled abroad to buy silk, the penalty was expulsion from his guild.[5] The Constantinopolitan butchers might not go out to meet the dealers in livestock (provatárioi) who had brought their droves as far as Nikomědheia, for fear that butchers and dealers might do profitable business there at the Constantinopolitan consumer's expense.[6] The livestock dealers must come all the way into the City to sell to the butchers in the Stratěghion Market there with the Prefect's cognizance and at prices fixed by him.[7] If the pork-butchers

---

[1] Εἰς οἶκον ἀρχοντικὸν ἐναποκρύπτων τοὺς χοίρους καὶ λάθρα πιπράσκων (ibid., 16, 4, p. 52).

[2] Ibid., 16, 3, p. 52.

[3] Ibid., 5, 4, p. 30.

[4] According to Hendy, in loc. cit., p. 40, this embargo was no longer in force in the twelfth century. 'Despite the assumption that the Byzantine merchant class was in decline, twelfth-century documentary evidence indicates the presence of its members at both ends of the Mediterranean: Alexandria, Barcelona, and Beziers.'

[5] *Livre du Préfet*, 6, 12, p. 32.

[6] Ibid., 15, 3, p. 50. The text of the (sole) manuscript of the book runs, in this passage, as follows: οἱ μακελάριοι μὴ συναντάτωσαν τοῖς ἀπὸ τῶν ἔξωθεν προβαταρίοις, τοῖς τὰς ἀγέλας ἐμπορευομένοις καὶ εἰσάγουσιν ἢ ἐν Νικομηδείᾳ ἢ ἐν πόλεσιν, ἀλλ' ἐν τῷ πέρα τοῦ Σαγγαρίου, ὡς ἂν εὐωνοτέρα ἡ πρᾶσις τοῦ κρέατος ᾖ, δηλονότι τοῦ ὀφειλομένου κέρδους τοῖς σφάττουσιν ἐγγινομένου, ἀλλὰ μὴ τοῖς ἐμπόροις. The words ἐν πόλεσιν can hardly be correct as they stand. Nicole, the editor of the document, has inserted ἄλλαις between ἐν and πόλεσιν, but this insertion has the effect of making the edict debar the Constantinopolitan butchers from doing business with the dealers in the environs of the City, while permitting them to do it farther afield. This seems illogical. Nicole's insertion has been defended by Mickwitz in op. cit., p. 114, on the strength of an analogous provision in the statutes of medieval Pisa. Beyond the Sangários, Mickwitz points out, the dealers might have had other markets besides Constantinople. This, however, would have made the dealers' bargaining-position stronger, not weaker. An alternative to inserting the word ἄλλαις before πόλεσιν would be to change the immediately following word ἀλλ' to ἄλλαις. This would have the effect of making some cities on the far side of the River Sangários forbidden ground for the Constantinopolitan butchers, as well as Nikomědheia on the near side. Stöckle, in op. cit., p. 42, assumes that this is the meaning of the text.

[7] *Livre du Préfet*, 15, 1, p. 50.

were caught meeting the pig-merchants somewhere outside Constantinople or clandestinely inside the City, with the object of raising prices, the penalty was expulsion from their guild after a preliminary flogging and cropping.[1] Like the butchers and the pork-butchers, the inspectors and valuers of livestock (vóthroi) were forbidden to go out to meet the stock and to make purchases.[2] They must not do any business anywhere except in the Amestrianoú Forum at Constantinople.[3]

While Constantinopolitan guildsmen were thus being hobbled and tethered, their contemporaries who were the Caliphs' subjects were travelling to the ends of the Earth. In the ninth century in the ports of southern and south-eastern China there were colonies of Arab and Persian businessmen, from Siráf and other ports on the Persian Gulf, who did business there until they were constrained to withdraw by the T'ang dynasty's inability to continue to maintain law and order. Other Arab mariners were feeling their way southward along the east coast of Africa. Arab camel caravans were reconnoitring the Sahara and were on the eve of reaching the Senegal and the Western Sudan. Northwards, the Muslims were reaching out at least as far as the Bulgaria at the confluence of the Volga and the Kama—some of them travelling by water from the south-west corner of the Caspian Sea, while others trekked overland across the steppes from the 'Abbasids' dominions in Transoxania. In this direction the Eastern Muslims had encircled the East Romans. The oldest East Roman coins that have been found at Kiev are said all to be dated later than 867,[4] and no East Roman coins of older date have been found in Scandinavia, whereas there is numismatic and other archaeological evidence for extensive commercial contacts between Northern Russia and the south coast of the Caspian from the seventh century onwards.[5]

These far-reaching travels bore fruit in the literal sense. The East Romans' feat of introducing silk-production into the Mediterranean basin in the sixth century was surpassed by the Muslims' feat of introducing there in the tenth century citrus-fruit, saffron, rice, cotton, and paper.[6] At the turn of the ninth and tenth centuries the East Roman Empire was emulated, and Northern Italy was anticipated, in 'Iraq, Iran, and the Indian Ocean by the transition from silver to gold as the medium of exchange, and the 'Iraqis and Iranians became the World's bankers.[7]

These Muslims travelled not only on business but also out of curiosity, like the fabulous Sinbad the Sailor, doing business in order to pay their way. The great corpus of the works, in Arabic and Persian, of the Muslim

---

[1] *Livre du Préfet*, 16, 2, pp. 51–2. [2] Ibid., 21, 9, pp. 59–60.
[3] Ibid., 21, 3, p. 58.
[4] I. Boba, *Nomads, Northmen, and Slavs* (The Hague, 1967, Mouton), p. 35, n. 56.
[5] S. H. Cross and O. P. Sherbowitz-Wetzor, *The Russian Primary Chronicle*, English translation of the Laurentian text, Introduction, p. 44.
[6] Lewis, op. cit., p. 172. [7] Ibid., pp. 170–2.

travellers and geographers had no counterpart in medieval Greek except Constantine Porphyrogenitus's *De Administrando Imperio*, and Constantine got his information at second hand. So far as we know, he himself never travelled farther than the Mysian Olympus[1]—hardly farther, that is to say, than the limits of the range that his Prefect allowed to the Constantinopolitan butchers.

Ibn Hawkal reports more extensive travels of East Roman businessmen than any that are recorded or sanctioned in contemporary Byzantine official or unofficial documents. The East Roman public authorities at Attáleia, Ibn Hawkal tells us, sent ships with commercial cargoes to ports in Dār-al-Islām, and the crews then travelled far and wide in the interior with the goodwill of the Muslim masters of the country, who hoped that these East Roman visitors were going to bring their Muslim hosts some profitable business. However, the visitors' own purpose, according to Ibn Hawkal or his source, was, not to make commercial profits, but to obtain military intelligence.[2] Whether or not there is any truth in this tale, it makes the valid point that the medieval Greeks, too, did travel, but did so mainly for other than commercial purposes, even when they were posing as traders to gain an entrée.

Medieval Greeks travelled widely for political purposes, not only for obtaining intelligence but for conducting diplomatic negotiations. There were frequent East Roman embassies to the Court of the ʿAbbasid Caliphs[3] and to the courts of the Carolingians and their successors in Western Christendom. There were also occasional embassies to the Muslim rulers of North-West Africa and of Spain. No less than four East Roman embassies are said to have been sent to China between 643 and 719.[4] According to a letter from the Ikhshid to Rhomanós I,[5] this East Roman Emperor, at any rate, was not too proud to send trade-goods with an embassy. (Rhomanós I was of humble origin, and he has been castigated by his unwilling colleague and son-in-law, Constantine Porphyrogenitus, as an incorrigible vulgarian.)[6] The Ikhshid plumed himself on his *bonhomie* in having allowed Rhomanós's ambassadors to buy and sell to their hearts' content. Some East Roman diplomatic missions were less profitable and more hazardous than this one. The annual mission to the Pechenegs in Constantine Porphyrogenitus's time is a case in point.[7]

---

[1] See I, 2, p. 24.

[2] The passage is translated in Vasiliev, *Byzance et les Arabes*, ii, II, p. 416.

[3] An East Roman embassy that came to Baghdad in 917 to negotiate an exchange of prisoners was given a reception that was designed to impress on the ambassadors the ʿAbbasid Caliphate's wealth and power. The proceedings evidently did impress contemporary Eastern Muslim observers. Five accounts, by Arab historians, will be found in Vasiliev, *Byzance et les Arabes*, ii, II, on pp. 60–1 (ʿArīb), 66–9 (Miskawaih), 73–9 (Hatīb), 146–7 (Ibn al-Athīr), 169–71 (Sibt b. al-Jawzī).

[4] Lopez in loc. cit., p. 75.

[5] See Vasiliev, *Byzance et les Arabes*, ii, II, p. 213.

[6] See I, 2, pp. 16–17.

[7] See III, 5 (iii), pp. 458–60.

However, the East Roman Empire's secular missions were surpassed by its ecclesiastical missions. These were more intrepid, more enterprising, and more imaginative.

The pioneer East Roman missionary, Theodore of Tarsós,[1] did not change the course of history on so grand a scale as this was changed by his successors Constantine-Cyril and Methódhios two centuries later. Theodore gave a new turn to the history of one Western country only; the two Thessalonian brothers gave a new turn to the history of the whole of Eastern Orthodox Christendom.[2] But in courage, statesmanship, energy, and sheer physical vitality, Theodore set standards that were never surpassed. Theodore received his call when he was already sixty-six years old, and he died in harness at the age of eighty-nine, after twenty-one years' service (669–90) in the mission-field that had been entrusted to him. He had been born in the year before the catastrophe that the East Roman Empire had brought upon itself in 602. In the year of Theodore's birth, Egypt, Palestine, Syria, half of Mesopotamia, and two-thirds of Armenia still lay within the East Roman Empire's frontiers. In 672/3, within three years of Theodore's arrival at Canterbury, his native city—which had also been St. Paul's—was taken by the Arabs, and it subsequently became the principal base of operations for the almost ceaseless Muslim raids into the remnant of the East Roman Empire's Asiatic dominions.[3] By the year 668, in which the Pope consecrated Theodore Archbishop of Canterbury, Theodore was already established in Rome,[4] some 1,150 miles, as the plane flies, away from his birthplace. We may guess that both Theodore and his North-West African companion Hadrian had been moved to migrate from their respective homelands to Italy by the irresistible advance, on all fronts, of the East Roman Empire's Arab invaders.

In 668 the sixty-six-year-old refugee started to travel onward again another 750 miles, as the plane flies, farther from Tarsós. The journey from Rome to Canterbury took Theodore and Hadrian a whole year, but Theodore did not rest. He proceeded to travel intensively over his English archdiocese, he reorganized its ecclesiastical administration, and he cleansed the Church in England of some of the flagrant abuses into which it had fallen while it had been left in the hands of a recently converted barbarian people. The Greek prelate Theodore of Tarsós was the unifier of England. During his episcopate, the

---

[1] See F. M. Stenton, *Anglo-Saxon England* (Oxford, 1947, Clarendon Press), pp. 131–40.
[2] See IV, 1, pp. 515–18.   [3] See II, 1 (iii) (b), pp. 107–22.
[4] In migrating as far afield as Rome, Theodore was not singular. Out of the thirteen popes who held office between 678 and 752, eleven came from Greek-speaking regions (P. Charanis, 'Ethnic Changes in the Byzantine Empire in the Seventh Century', in *Dumbarton Oaks Papers*, Number Thirteen (1959), pp. 25–44, on p. 42).

country's unity was consolidated on the ecclesiastical plane, and, but for this, the subsequent political unification of the Roman Empire's petty English successor-states on that island might never have been achieved. England was unified ecclesiastically by Theodore as a province of the Patriarchate of Rome, within whose domain Britain lay, and one of the most admirable features of Theodore's career was his loyalty to the Roman See and to the Roman rite, though he had been an Eastern Orthodox Basilian monk. A comparable loyalty to the Roman See was shown by Constantine-Cyril and Methódhios when they, in their turn, evangelized another part of the Roman Patriarchate's domain.

Though Theodore of Tarsós was a Greek and a subject of the East Roman Empire, the initiative in sending him on his mission did not come from either the Government or the Patriarchate at Constantinople. On the other hand, the Greek bishop who had been installed in Kiev between 860 and 867 had been sent there by the Patriarch Phótios and the subsequent archbishop by the Patriarch Ighnátios.[1] The representative of the Constantinopolitan Church must have been courageous and persuasive. He had made his way to Kiev, the Rhos lion's den, across steppes that were haunted, at that date, by the ferocious Magyars, and, having reached his goal, he had contrived that his presence there should be tolerated. Meanwhile, between 860 and 863, the Thessalonian linguist, Constantine-Cyril, had gone first on a mission to Khazaria and then, with his brother Methódhios, on a mission to Moravia[2]—two journeys that were as arduous and as perilous as the journey to Kiev.

For economic purposes, however, the East Romans preferred to stay at home[3] and to leave it to the foreigners who wanted to do business with them to take the trouble to do the travelling that one or other party had to do if they were to meet. This policy, which was deliberate, was also short-sighted. It suited the Byzantine Greeks' un-Greek commercial sluggishness, it flattered their pride, and, on short term, it gave them the advantage in making their bargains. Its nemesis was that eventually it enabled one set of commercially enterprising foreigners, the North Italians, to capture from the Greeks the domestic as well as the foreign trade of the East Roman Empire.[4]

The foreigners who did come to do business at Constantinople were hampered there by vexatious regulations. We do not know whether the

---

[1] See II, 1 (i), p. 29, with n. 2.

[2] See Obolensky in *C. Med. H.*, vol. iv, 2nd. ed., Part I, p. 500; F. Dvornik: *The Slavs, their Early History and Civilization*, pp. 80–115; and the present work, II, 1 (i), pp. 29–30.

[3] East Roman commercial travellers beyond the Empire's frontiers were mostly East Roman Jews (see Haussig, *A History of Byzantine Civilization*, pp. 171–3).

[4] This point is made by Lewis in op. cit., p. 121, p. 122, n. 107, and pp. 176 and 215, and by Macri in op. cit., pp. 46–7.

citizens of the autonomous city-states that recognized the East Roman Government's suzerainty[1] counted as foreigners for this purpose. Officially the citizens of Khersón, Venice, Amalfi, Naples, and Gaeta were the Empire's subjects. Were the Amalfitans and Gaetans who rallied to Constantine Porphyrogenitus's support at the crisis of his career in 944[2] permanent residents in Constantinople, or were they temporary visitors like Hugh of Provence's envoy Bishop Siegfried, who mobilized his fellow-Latins in the interest of his Latin sovereign's Byzantine father-in-law? Whatever the status of these five peoples may have been, all visitors who were unquestionably foreigners were subject, at Constantinople, to governmental supervision and restrictions.

The Prefect had a subordinate, his lêghatários[3] (i.e. deputy, probably a synonym for the sýmbonos (aide) attributed to the Prefect in Philó-theos's klêtorolóyion).[4] This lêghatários was an important official, for his appointment by the Prefect had to be ratified by the Emperor. It was the Prefect's lêghatários's duty to report to the Prefect the arrival of all persons entering Constantinople 'from outside' (i.e. from the provinces as well as from abroad) who brought with them any kind of merchandise. He was to name the place [within the Empire] or the [foreign] country from which they came. He was to keep an eye on their wares and to lay down the conditions and the time-limit for the sale of these. He was then to present these foreigners or provincials to the Prefect with a list of their purchases, to make sure that nothing that was under embargo ($\mu\eta\delta\grave{\epsilon}\nu$ $\kappa\omega\lambda\upsilon\acute{o}\mu\epsilon\nu\upsilon\nu$) should leave the precincts of the capital.[5] The Prefect was not authorized to permit the visitors to stay in Constantinople for longer than three months.[6] The penalty for a foreigner who over-stayed this term was expulsion, after his goods had been confiscated and he himself had been shaved and cropped.[7] The three months' time-limit was laid down specifically for Syrians[8] and for merchants, native as well as foreign, who imported into Constantinople the materials for the dealers in unguents.[9]

Certain categories of foreigners paying temporary visits to Constantinople on business were granted some alleviations. For instance, foreign silk-importers were exempted from all exactions except for the cost of their board and lodging during their stay.[10] Syrian visitors who had

---

[1] See Part II, chap. 5.　　　　　　　[2] See Liutprand, *Antapodosis*, Book V, chap. 21.

[3] *Livre du Préfet*, 20, 1, p. 56.

[4] *De Caer.*, Book II, p. 717, where he is mentioned first in the list of the sixteen members of the Prefect's staff. He also appears in the Prefect's company in *De Caer.*, Book I, p. 13. See also Nicole, *Le Livre du Préfet*, p. 89; Stöckle, op. cit., pp. 90–2.

[5] *Livre du Préfet*, 20, 1, p. 56.　　　　　[6] Op. cit., 20, 2, p. 57.　　　　　[7] Ibid.

[8] 5, 5, pp. 30–1.　　　　　　　　　　　　　　　　　　　　　　　[9] 10, 2, p. 42.

[10] Mὴ διδότωσαν πρατίκια, εἰ μὴ τὰ ἐνοίκια καὶ μονήν (6, 5, p. 32). τὰ ἐνοίκια presumably includes board as well as lodging. If μονήν is not a synonym for ἐνοίκια, it might mean a visitor's tax for the duration of the visitor's stay, and this would be a πρατίκιον from which the visitor was not exempt.

imported garments for selling to the Constantinopolitan prandioprátai or unguents for selling to the myrepsoí were to declare to the Prefect the still-unsold merchandise that they had on their hands when their three months' term had run out, in order that this surplus 'should be suitably disposed of'.[1] Presumably this means that the surplus was to be taken off the departing Syrians' hands at a valuation that was acceptable to both parties. Moreover, notwithstanding the explicit limitation of the Syrian silk-importers' stay to a term of not more than three months, there were Syrians in Constantinople who had been in residence there for ten years, and these were given the privilege of sharing with the guild of the prandioprátai the profits of the trade in Syrian wares at Constantinople.[2]

Special pains were to be taken to give satisfaction to the Bulgar merchants who came to Constantinople to barter Bulgarian linen and food-stuffs, especially honey, in exchange for East Roman goods.[3] The Constantinopolitan grocers and dealers in linen were to have the co-operation of all the other guilds for offering to the Bulgars goods of the kinds, and in the quantities, that they and the Bulgars agreed to be equivalent in value to what the Bulgars had brought, and that also met the Bulgars' various needs. The other guilds were required to accept from the Bulgars only as much as they required for their own needs, and presumably they were not under an obligation to give the Bulgars more of their own wares than the amount that was considered to be equivalent in value to what they accepted. The dealers in linen and the grocers were required to take over from the Bulgars any surplus of the Bulgars' wares that still remained, and for this they were to receive a commission of one kerátion per nómisma (i.e. one twenty-fourth) of the estimated value of the surplus, to compensate them for their trouble and for their possible financial loss on this transaction.[4] Evidently the East Roman Government was concerned to make sure that the Bulgar merchants should return home feeling that they had been given a fair deal.

This suggests that the Book of the Prefect was compiled after the peace-settlement at the end of the Romano–Bulgarian War of 894–6; for the cause of this war—a war that turned out badly for both belligerents— had been a well-justified Bulgarian grievance over the East Roman Government's handling of the conduct of the trade between the two countries. The Emperor Leo VI had been cajoled by his minister Zaoúdzas into giving a monopoly of the Romano–Bulgarian barter trade to two businessmen from théma Ellás who were Zaoúdzas's protégés and allowing them to transfer the emporium from Constantinople to

---

[1] τοῦ οἰκονομεῖσθαι ταύτην κατὰ τὸ ἁρμόζον (5, 5, pp. 30–1).
[2] 5, 3, pp. 29–30.
[3] See p. 47, with n. 6.
[4] *Livre du Préfet*, 9, 6, p. 40. For a commentary, see Stöckle, op. cit., pp. 65–6.

Thessaloníkê.[1] Thessaloníkê's access to the interior of the Balkan Peninsula is better than Constantinople's; but the motive for the transfer was not to re-channel the trade through this better route but to move the emporium away from Constantinople, where business had to be conducted under the Prefect's eye, in order to make it possible for the pair of monopolists to impose unfair terms on the Bulgarian traders without risk of being called to order by their own Government. They had succeeded so well in this that they had provoked Khan Symeon into going to war; and, after Leo had experienced this extremely disagreeable consequence of his own irresponsible behaviour, he must have been anxious to take precautions against the possibility of another outbreak of war between the East Roman Empire and Bulgaria from the same cause.

Among the foreign visitors to Constantinople there was a third nationality, the Rhos, besides the Bulgars and the Syrians, to whom special consideration was shown. This is apparent from the texts (probably translated from Greek originals) of the Romano–Russian commercial treaties that are cited in the Russian Primary Chronicle. In the treaty of 907[2] it is said to have been agreed that Rhos visitors, if they came with merchandise, should receive as much grain as they required; six months' supplies of provisions, in monthly deliveries, including bread, wine, meat, fish, and fruit; baths *ad libitum*; and rations and ship's tackle for their journey home. They were also allowed to do business tax-free. They were to lodge in the St. Mámas quarter (on the south-west shore of the Golden Horn, just outside the northern corner of the city walls). They were to enter the city by one gate only, not more than fifty of them at a time, and escorted by an East Roman official.[3] These provisions, together with those of the treaty of 912, were reproduced in the treaty of 945.[4] But in this treaty two restrictions on the Rhos visitors' activities were introduced which diminished their previous privileges, though they still enjoyed better terms than visitors of other nationalities. The treaty of 945 stipulated that, 'when the Rhos enter the City, they shall not have the right to buy silk above the value of fifty nomísmata. Whoever purchases such silks shall show them to the Imperial official, who shall mark them with his seal and return them'. In the second place, the Rhos, though still not limited to a three months' stay, were now prohibited from staying on in the St. Mámas quarter over the winter.

During their stay in Constantinople, foreign and provincial traders were kept under police control exercised partly by the public authorities directly

---

[1] *Theoph. Cont.*, Book VI, p. 357 (Bonn); *Georg. Mon. Cont.*, p. 853; Leo Gramm., pp. 266–7. See also the present work, pp. 519–21.

[2] Cross and Sherbowitz-Wetzor hold that this treaty is authentic (*Russian Primary Chronicle*, p. 236, n. 33).

[3] Op. cit., pp. 64–5. The text of the supplementary treaty of 2 September 912 is on pp. 65–8.   [4] Text in op. cit., pp. 73–7.

and partly through the compulsory agency of the guilds. If a jeweller is offered gold or silver ware or pearls or precious stones, he must inform the Prefect.[1] If he is offered gold or silver, wrought or unwrought, by anyone from outside the precincts of Constantinople, he is to discover from the would-be seller where he has obtained the goods, and he is to pass on this information to the president of the jewellers' guild.[2] The money-changers must notify the Prefect if they see the sakkoulárioi (? black-market money-changers) standing about in the piazze (πλατεῖαι) and in the streets, to prevent them from carrying out any illicit transactions. Penalty for non-observance, the cutting-off of one hand. The money-changers must not charge a premium on good coins, and must accept bad coins at a valuation. Penalty for non-observance, flogging and cropping and confiscation of property. A money-changer who has received a piece of bad money must notify the Prefect, not only of the counterfeit coin, but of the person by whom it has been tendered.[3] Penalty as for the last-mentioned offence. A dealer in silk garments (vestioprátês) is forbidden to sell to outsiders any articles that are on the embargo list (τῶν κεκωλυμένων), in order to make sure that these articles, which are scheduled in technical language, shall not be transmitted to barbarian peoples.[4] If a vestioprátês (dealer in silk garments) buys from anyone, either a magnate (ἀρχοντικός) or a silk-weaver (sêrikoprátês, sêrikários), goods valued at more than ten nomísmata, he must inform the Prefect.[5] If he sells merchandise for export, he must show it to the Prefect for marking with the Prefect's seal.[6] A seller of raw silk must do the business in the Forum only, not at home.[7] He must not sell either to Jews or to non-Jewish merchants for retailing outside the City's precincts.[8] The stuffs that the silk-weavers and purple-dyers may and may not manufacture are scheduled in technical language, and those that they may manufacture must be declared, when made, to the Prefect—as well as any garments whatsoever that are valued at more than ten nomísmata, even if they are motley (πολύχροα).[9] A sêrikários who sells to non-Constantinopolitans (τοῖς ἐξωτερικοῖς) a garment valued at more than ten nomísmata is to be flogged and cropped.[10] A sêrikários who sells goods to foreigners without the Prefect's knowledge is to have these goods confiscated.[11] A candle-manufacturer who does not denounce to the Prefect persons who are deliberately manufacturing candles out of forbidden materials is to be subject to the same penalties as the offender himself. He is to be flogged and to be put out of business.[12]

---

[1] *Livre du Préfet*, 2, 4, p. 23. [2] 2, 6, p. 23. [3] 3, 2 and 3 and 5, pp. 25–6.
[4] 4, 1, pp. 26–7. [5] 4, 2, p. 27. [6] 4, 4, p. 27.
[7] 6, 13, p. 33. [8] 6, 16, p. 33 (see p. 51).
[9] 8, 1, pp. 35–6. [10] 8, 3, p. 27.
[11] 8, 5, p. 37. [12] 11, 6, pp. 44–5.

The regulation about outsiders offering gold or silver for sale appears to have been imposed primarily with a view to detecting thefts, and the regulation against selling raw silk to Jews appears to have been motivated by the public authorities' general policy of eliminating middlemen. All the rest of the regulations that are listed above are designed expressly to make sure that articles on the embargo list (τὰ κωλυόμενα, τὰ κεκωλυμένα) shall not find their way from Constantinople to foreign countries, and in some cases shall not even find their way into East Roman territory outside the capital's precincts. A fuller list of these contraband goods than can be gleaned from the Book of the Prefect is given in the *Vasiliká*.[1]

There seem to have been several degrees of embargo.[2] The strictest embargo of all was the one that was imposed on goods that were reserved for being manufactured exclusively in the factories that were owned and operated by the state. Weapons came within this category,[3] and the stuffs that private silk-weavers and purple-dyers were forbidden to manufacture must have come within it too. But there was at least one other commodity—the Gallic kind of soap—which was manufactured by the soap-makers and soap-merchants (saponoprátai) but which they were forbidden to offer for sale[4]—presumably because it was reserved for exclusive use by the Court, or even, within the Court, by the Imperial household.

There were other commodities that fell within the private, not the public, sector but that might not be exported. A case in point is non-military iron tools and iron in general. These might be manufactured, wrought, mined, and sold within the Empire, but only within its frontiers, by private entrepreneurs.[5] At least one commodity might be held by private persons domiciled permanently or even temporarily in Constantinople, but might not be exported beyond the capital's precincts. A silk-weaver (sêrikários, sêrikoprátes) might own a slave or hire an employee or engage a foreman (ἐκλέκτης),[6] but, if the sêrikários sold one of these human commodities to provincials or to foreigners, he was to have one hand cut off.[7]

Out of the eighty-eight cases in which the Book of the Prefect imposes punishments for breaches of its regulations, this savage punishment is imposed in only seven cases. It is the most severe of all the various punishments and combinations of punishments that are prescribed, except for a single case of the imposition of the death-penalty. This was incurred

---

[1] *Vasiliká*, xix, 1, 81–4, cited by Stöckle, op. cit., p. 120, n. 2. See also Macri, op. cit., pp. 25 and 55.

[2] Stöckle, op. cit., p. 111.

[3] *Vasiliká*, loc. cit.　　　　　　　　　　　　　　[4] *Livre du Préfet*, 12, 4, p. 46.

[5] *Vasiliká*, loc. cit.

[6] For the meaning of this term, see Stöckle, op. cit., p. 70.

[7] *Livre du Préfet*, 8, 7, p. 37.

by a saponoprátês who gave or sold soap-suds to anyone for causing injury (by poisoning?) to a third party.[1]

What was the motive for the severity of the sanction against the export of live contraband goods? Was it humanitarianism? Or was it a fear that this live contraband might carry with it the knowledge and practice of industrial secrets? A soap-manufacturer was fined for teaching his art to someone who was not a member of his guild without the cognizance of the Prefect and of the guild-president of the day.[2] Silk was a more important commodity than soap, and eventually, about two and a half centuries after the date at which the Book of the Prefect had been compiled, some silk-workers who had been exported—not by sale but by capture—from Greece to Sicily did break the East Roman Empire's monopoly of the silk industry by introducing this industry into the Empire's Norman successor-state in Sicily.[3]

The regulations governing the embargo on the export of privately manufactured silk garments (the products of the state factories were, of course, not in question) were particularly strict. Foreign visitors and lodgers (τοὺς συνδημίτας καὶ μιτατευομένους) in Constantinople were strictly forbidden to buy either articles on the embargo list (κεκωλυμένα) or any 'unstitched' garments,[4] except for their own wear, and this only within the confines of the capital. On leaving Constantinople they must declare all such articles to the Prefect. The penalty for being caught in the act of trying to smuggle out such articles was castigation and confiscation.[5] Bishop Liutprand came up against this regulation in 968 on the second of his two ambassadorial visits to Constantinople, when he was getting his clearance for his departure. His account of his experiences under this ordeal[6] tallies exactly with the prescriptions of the Book of the Prefect.

'We believe', said the East Roman officials, 'that you have bought some robes for your personal adornment. Kindly produce these for us. Those that are not too good for you will be marked with a lead seal, and these you may keep. But those that are κωλυόμενα, i.e. on the embargo list for all nations except us Romans, will be taken from you. The purchase price will be returned to you.' They then proceeded to deprive me of five particularly choice purple robes, because they consider that your majesties [Otto I and Otto II] and all Italians, Saxons, Franks, Bavarians, and Swabians—in fact, all foreign peoples—are not fit to go adorned with garments of this kind. How insulting and humiliating! To think that effeminate milk-sops, dressed up in long-sleeves and female tiaras and mantles—liars, eunuchs, idlers—should go clad

---

[1] 12, 7, p. 46.   [2] 12, 1, p. 45.   [3] See pp. 50–1.

[4] Ἄρραφα ἱμάτια (4, 8, p. 28). Does this mean garments made of a single piece of stuff, in contrast to those made of several diversely coloured pieces sewn together? Motley garments seem to have been less sacrosanct (see 8, 1, pp. 35–6).

[5] 4, 8, p. 28.   [6] *Legatio*, chaps. 53–5.

in purple, while this is denied to heroes, I mean mighty men of valour, good soldiers, honourable, amiable, God-fearing, virtuous characters. What can one call this except 'humiliating'?

'Well', I said, 'but what about the Emperor's word? What about his promise? When I said goodbye to him, I asked him to allow me, for the honour of the Church, to buy robes without any limit on the price. His answer was: *By all means: of whatever kind and in any number that you wish.* He spoke simply in terms of ποιότητα καὶ ποσότητα, i.e. quality and quantity. It is obvious that he drew no distinctions. He did not say *except for this and that.* The Emperor's own brother, Leo the curopalates, can bear out what I say. So can the interpreters Euodisius, John, Romanus. Indeed, I can be my own witness. I understood what the Emperor said. I should have understood it even if no interpreter had been present.'

'But these articles are κωλυόμενα', i.e. under embargo, was their reply. 'And, when the Emperor said what you assert that he said, he could not imagine that you were even dreaming of articles of this quality. We are the superiors of other nations in wealth and wisdom, so we ought to be their superiors in dress too. We are graced with unique virtues. It is only fitting that we should wear uniquely beautiful clothes.' 'Not unique at all', I retorted. 'You cannot make out that this kind of garment is unique when in our country it is worn by two-penny whores and by stage impostors.'[1] 'From where have you got them?' they ask. 'From Venetian and Amalfitan dealers', I tell them. 'Their food-supply depends on their conveying these things to us. We give them our food-stuffs in exchange.' 'They won't have any more opportunities', my Greek interlocutors say. 'From now on, they will be searched, we may tell you, and, if anything of this kind is found in their baggage, they will be punished. They will be flogged and cropped.'

'In the reign of the late lamented Emperor Constantine', say I, 'I came here once before. I wasn't a bishop then; I was only a deacon; I wasn't representing an emperor or a king, but only a marquess: Berengar. Yet, on that visit, I bought a larger number of robes of greater value, and they were not examined or even seen by any of you Greeks, and there was no marking of them with lead seals. Now I am, by God's indulgence, a bishop, and I am the ambassador of their highnesses the Emperors Otto and Otto, father and son, and in this capacity I am being subjected to this gross indignity. My robes are to be marked as if I were a Venetian dealer. Those that are deemed by you to be of any value at all are to be taken from me, when they are being exported for the use of the church of which I have the honour to be in charge. Are you not yet tired of humiliating me—no, not just me, but my Imperial masters, for whom, in my person, you are showing contempt? I have been held in custody; I have been tortured by hunger and thirst; I have been detained all this time from returning to my principals. Wasn't this enough for you? Must you put the last touch on your insulting treatment of my Emperors by robbing me of my own property? Take from me, if you insist,

---

[1] Here Liutprand is showing off his knowledge of the classical Latin playwrights' works. Some of his Western readers would catch the allusions, but his Greek interlocutors would not, for they knew no Latin, either classical or vernacular. See IV, 2 (vii).—A. J. T.

my purchases, but at least let pass the articles that are gifts to me from friends.'

'The Emperor Constantine', they answered, 'was an easy-going man. He never left his Palace, so he appeased foreign nations with things like these. Nicephorus is a man of a very different stamp. He is a proper basileus; he is a man of action—ταχύχειρ, quick on the draw, in other words a dedicated soldier. He hates the Palace like the plague. He has a reputation here for spoiling for a fight and liking nothing so much as an altercation. Our Nicephorus does not buy the friendship of foreign nations; he subdues them—yes, by the sword, if they have not been terrified into submission. So now we are going to show you just how little regard we have for those kinglets who are your masters. None of your talk of distinguishing between purchases and gifts! Whatever is of this colour is going to come back into our hands—yes, all of it, all alike!'

The most significant single point in this illuminating ambassadorial report is that the East Roman Government in the year 968 chose to retain articles that were on the embargo list in preference to earning foreign exchange by parting with them. They confiscated Liutprand's purple robes and refunded his money. (If they had not refunded it, as they had said that they were going to, Liutprand would certainly have told us.) In East Roman eyes, τὰ κωλυόμενα were not merchandise for sale; they were decorations to be awarded; and the value of decorations lies in the rarity of awards, whereas the value of merchandise is measured by the volume of sales. The East Roman Government's embargo on the export of decorations was not businesslike in economic terms, but this is beside the point, for governments do not transact economic business only. They have diplomatic and military business to transact as well, and for diplomatic purposes the East Roman Government's embargo on the export of decorations was as businesslike as, for economic purposes, its nursing of its famous gold coin, the nómisma, was. In both cases, the East Roman Government was seeing to it that an important asset should be insured against the risk of depreciation.

The diplomatic value of the embargo is illustrated by Constantine Porphyrogenitus's lists[1] of two sets of articles that, in the year 935, were placed in the hands of an East Roman diplomatist, Epiphánios, by the Emperor Rhomanós I, when he was sending Epiphánios on a diplomatic mission to Hugh of Provence, who was at that date king of Frankish Italy. One set was not for sale, and would not have been purchasable from any source by King Hugh or by his Venetian or Amalfitan agents. This set was offered to Hugh as a gift, but not gratis. The offer was conditional upon Hugh's performing certain military services for Rhomanós. The other set of articles consisted of garments that were not

---

[1] In *De Caer.*, Book II, chap. 44, pp. 661–2.

on the embargo list and that Epiphánios was therefore at liberty to cash, like travellers' cheques, to the extent required for covering his expenses.

The conditional gifts were one kentênárion of spice, ten under-garments, one onyx cup, seventeen Heliopolitan (?) glasses, thirty bags of incense, and 500 aleiptá for Hugh himself; six citron-coloured skaramángia for six of his bishops; five skaramángia (one each of four different colours) for the king's count and marquess in charge of the march adjoining Laghouvardhía, making nine skaramángia in all. (There is a discrepancy in these figures.) Item, four more under-garments and three fine-spun ones, making seven in all, and three pieces of gilded silver-work.

The diplomat Epiphánios was also given, to cover the expenses of his mission, six skaramángia of different colours and makes, thirty 'eight-size' under-garments, twenty lorotá, and twenty purple robes. Of these, Epiphánios spent two skaramángia, seventeen 'eight-piece' under-garments, twelve lorotá, fourteen purple robes. He refunded the balance after returning to Constantinople.

The evidence surveyed in this chapter suggests some tentative general conclusions. The first of these is that, during the time-span of slightly less than five centuries between the political and military collapse of the East Roman Empire in 602 and the First Western Christian Crusade, the volume and value of maritime trade in the Mediterranean were perhaps considerably smaller, on the average, than they had been in the time of Justinian I and than they came to be, again, in the later Middle Ages, when the commercial hegemony in the Mediterranean basin had passed into the hands of the northern Italian city-states. Within this period of relative commercial depression there were fluctuations in the Mediterranean peoples' commercial fortunes; but the second conclusion that suggests itself is that there was no sudden sharp breach of economic continuity either in the seventh century—a century which did bring with it a sudden sharp political and cultural break—or in the ninth century. Henri Pirenne's thesis that there was a breach of economic continuity in the seventh century evoked a prolonged and detailed discussion of the evidence,[1] and the prevailing opinion seems now to be that this thesis is non-proven. It is also non-proven that economic continuity was broken by the Muslim conquest of Crete in 827 or 828 and by the beginning of the Muslim conquest of Sicily in 827. The Book of the Prefect informs us that, at the turn of the ninth and tenth centuries, there was still an active trade between Constantinople and Syria.[2]

A third conclusion suggested by the evidence is that, in so far as there was a diminution of Mediterranean maritime trade between the opening

---

[1] See the bibliography in Eickhoff, op. cit., p. 266, n. 34, and p. 268, n. 39.
[2] See the present chapter, pp. 50 and 60–1.

of the seventh century and the close of the eleventh century, this was due, not to Arab conquests and piracy, but to restrictions imposed on the business activities of East Roman traders by their own government. The East Roman Imperial Government was uneconomic-minded by comparison with the governments and peoples of the Empire's city-state satellites, with the Arabs and their subjects, and with the Lombard northern Italian city-states that eventually competed with Venice for the economic heritage of both the East Romans and the Eastern and Western Muslims.

The East Roman Government's primary concern with manufactures and with trade was, not to promote them, but to control them, and it did control them at the cost of restricting them. Its purpose in controlling its subjects' economic activities was to use the Empire's economy as a weapon in the service of its foreign policy. The Arabs' conquest of Syria and Egypt and their bid for the naval command of the Mediterranean had not cut off the trade between what was left of the East Roman Empire and its former dominions that were now under Arab rule. The Empire had continued to buy from its lost dominion, Egypt, the papyrus, that it had not ceased to need, with the Imperial gold coin that the Caliphate needed for use in business transactions in its ex-Roman provinces. A provocative change, made by the Caliph 'Abd-al-Malik, in the watermark on Egyptian papyrus processed in Egypt for export to the Empire had been countered by an East Roman threat to make a provocative change in the superscription on East Roman gold pieces. This, in turn, had provoked 'Abd-al-Malik into minting a gold coinage of his own. This had led the Emperor Justinian II to go to war with him; and, when the military operations had turned out badly for the Empire, the Imperial Government seems to have resorted to a commercial boycott as a more promising weapon for imposing its will on a militarily stronger opponent.[1] 'It was not the Arabs, but Byzantium who destroyed the ancient unity of the Mediterranean.'[2] Trade was cut off, not by the Empire's Arab assailants, but by the Imperial Government itself.

A fourth conclusion that emerges is that the East Roman Imperial Government's policy of using trade-control as a political weapon proved, in the end, to be disastrous for the Empire's trade and consequently also for its political power. The Government's control of its subjects' foreign trade, and, above all, its channelling of this trade through a limited number of points on the frontiers in order to facilitate the control of it, resulted in the capture of the trade by alien hands. It was captured

---

[1] See Theophanes, p. 365, sub A.M. 6183; Al-Balādhurī: *Kitāb Futūh al-Buldān*, English translation by P. K. Hitti and F. C. Murgotten (New York: Columbia University Press), vol. i (1916), pp. 383–4, and part ii (1924), pp. 263–6; A. R. Lewis, *Naval Power and Trade in the Mediterranean, A.D. 500–1100*, pp. 87–97; Eickhoff, op. cit., pp. 31 and 266–8.

[2] Lewis, op. cit., p. 97.

first by the Empire's city-state satellites[1]—nominal subjects who enjoyed the advantages of East Roman citizenship without being handicapped by the disabilities imposed on their fellow subjects whose subjection was effective. These satellites had no sooner won the Empire's trade from the non-autonomous majority of the East Roman Empire's population than their lucrative business in the Empire was challenged by the rising city-states in the Lombard part of northern Italy, and only Venice and Ragusa succeeded in holding their own against this Lombard competition. Amalfi, Gaeta, Naples, and all the Dalmatian city-states except Ragusa succumbed.

The economic conquest of the Empire by the northern Italian city-states was accelerated by the strain that was imposed on the Empire's economy by the Empire's military conquests during the reigns of three warlike Emperors, Nikêphóros II Phokás, John Dzimiskĕs, and Basil II. These reigns extended over the years 963–1025. The military emperors' civilian successors maintained their policy of territorial expansion by the expensive expedient of employing native professional and foreign mercenary troops. Both variants of the expansionist policy played into the hands of the northern Italian city-states from 963 till 1071—the year in which the Saljūq warlord Alp Arslan defeated and captured the Emperor Rhomanós IV Dhioyénês and in which, at the opposite extremity of the over-extended Empire, the Normans took Bari, the capital of théma Laghouvardhía.

(iii) *The Utilization and Ownership of the Land*

(a) *Depopulation and Resettlement*

Depopulation and resettlement were not unprecedented social phenomena in those portions of the East Roman Empire over which the Imperial Government succeeded in retaining or re-establishing its rule after having survived the seventh-century cataclysm.

The Roman Empire as a whole had been suffering from depopulation since the third century, and, in the Balkan Peninsula, the malady had set in much earlier. Macedonia, for instance, had never recovered from the draining away of its man-power by Alexander the Great in his *tour de force* of conquering and garrisoning the vast dominions of the First Persian Empire. The population explosion that had enabled the Greeks to colonize first the coasts of the western basin of the Mediterranean and the Black Sea and then the new world in the east that Alexander had opened up for Greek enterprise had subsided in the second century B.C. Polybius has described this demographic revolution in second-century-B.C. Boeotia.[2] In the second century of the Christian Era—a century in

---

[1] See Part II, chap. 5.　　　　[2] See Polybius, Book XX, chap. 6.

which, to outward appearance, the Graeco-Roman World stood at the peak of its prosperity—the malady had gone to further lengths in European Greece, which had once been the Graeco-Roman World's cultural nerve-centre. A second-century-A.D. Greek man of letters, Dio Chrysostom of Prusa in north-western Asia Minor, has described how, on the European Greek island Euboea (Εὔβοια), he was guided by local country-folk to the site of a decaying city, whose public monuments were fighting a losing battle against the resurgence of a bucolic pre-urban way of life.[1] After that, for about three and a half centuries beginning with the temporary débâcle of the Roman Empire in A.D. 235, the Illyrian provinces and Thrace were drained of their man-power, as their neighbour Macedonia had been drained during the two centuries ending in 168 B.C., by military demands that were likewise both heavy and unceasing.

In and after the seventh century, the resettlement, by which the depopulation of the remnant of the East Roman Empire was counteracted, took several different forms. There were settlements of intruding barbarians who established themselves by force without asking the Imperial Government's leave. There were other settlements of barbarians that were carried out by the East Roman Government itself. There were also settlements of civilians who had fled or had been evacuated, and of troops that had been expelled or been withdrawn, from the ex-Imperial territories that the Empire had failed to hold.

There were precedents for all these various forms of resettlement. Both the Balkan Peninsula and Asia Minor had received uninvited increments of population from the seventh-century-B.C. Eurasian Nomad *Völkerwanderung*, the third-century-B.C. Celtic *Völkerwanderung*, and the fourth-century-A.D. Gothic *Völkerwanderung*. After the Romans had conquered Macedonia in 168 B.C., they had found that the Macedonian Government had planted extensive settlements of Illyrians and Celts on depopulated Macedonian territory.[2] From the second century of the Christian Era onwards, this local Macedonian precedent had been followed in many regions of the Roman Empire. Civilian refugees had been evacuated in the third century of the Christian Era from Dacia to new homes south of the River Danube, and in the fifth century from Raetia and Noricum to new homes in peninsular Italy.[3] In the third century, Roman troops had been withdrawn not only from Dacia but from the *limes* that had bridged the gap between the 'natural frontiers'

---

[1] See Dio, Oratio VII, Εὐβοϊκὸς ἢ Κυνηγός. Though Dio professes to be recounting a personal experience, this essay is, no doubt, a *jeu d'esprit*. All the same, it is also probably true to life. Dio refers to the depopulation of Thessaly and Macedonia in Oratio XXXIII (*Tarsica Prior*), §§ 25 and 26.

[2] See Livy, Book XLV, chap. 3.

[3] See Eugippius, *Vita Sancti Severini*, ed. Sauppe (Berlin, 1877, Weidmann).

provided by the River Danube and the River Rhine, and in the fifth century the Roman troops from Britain had been withdrawn before the whole of the Roman military establishment in the Empire's western provinces had melted away.

The distinctive feature of the corresponding phenonema in the seventh century was a difference from these precedents that was one, not of kind, but of degree. In the Balkan Peninsula the Slav *Völkerwanderung* which began in 581/2[1] was more massive[2] than any that this region had experienced since the twelfth century B.C., when there had been a migration, comparable in magnitude, of Greeks speaking the North-West-Greek dialect, with Illyrians and Thracians following at their heels. Moreover, in the Balkan Peninsula in the Christian Era, there was a two-way movement. Besides the influx of barbarian settlers from the north side of the River Danube, there was a counter-movement of renegades and deportees across the Danube from Roman territory into country that either had never been under Roman rule or that was now not under it any longer.

For instance, we have a report by the East Roman ambassador Priscus, who visited Attila's camp on the Hungarian Alföld in A.D. 448, of a conversation which he had had there with an ex-Roman prisoner of war who had thrown in his lot with captors who had been willing to accept him as a comrade.[3] The author of a treatise, compiled at about the turn of the sixth and seventh centuries, on the contemporary East Roman art of war,[4] mentions the presence, in Slav territory in what is now Wallachia, of ex-Roman 'refugees' or 'deserters' who had become pro-Slav, and he warns the commanders of Roman expeditionary forces operating there to be on their guard against offers of military intelligence from these gentry.[5]

'Mavríkios'[6] advises a Roman commander on campaign against the Slavs in Wallachia to linger there long enough to give Roman prisoners of war a chance to escape, which they could do safely so long as the woods were in leaf. On the other hand, the Emperor Maurice is said to have

---

[1] John of Ephesus, *Historia Ecclesiastica*, Book VI, chap. 25. The Slav settlements in the Balkan Peninsula are discussed in greater detail in Annex III.

[2] The Slav tribes were πολυανδρότατα ('Mavríkios', *Ars Militaris (Stratêghikón)*, ed. by J. Scheffer (Uppsala, 1664, Curio), Part II, chap. 5, p. 272; πολύανδρα (*Mauricii Strategicon*, edited by H. Mihăescu (Bucarest, 1970, Academy of the Socialist Republic of Rumania), Part II, chap. 4, p. 276). For the text of 'Mavríkios's' *Stratêghikón*, see further Annex II.

[3] See Priscus, fragm. 8, in *Historici Graeci Minores*, ed. Dindorf, vol. i (Leipzig, 1870, Teubner), pp. 305–9.

[4] 'Mavríkios', cited in n. 2 above.

[5] τοὺς δὲ λεγομένους ῥεφούγους ἤτοι προσφούγους ἐπαγγελομένους . . . κᾂν γὰρ 'Ρωμαῖοί εἰσι, τῷ χρόνῳ ποιωθέντες [? ἀλλοιωθέντες] καὶ τῶν ἰδίων ἐπιλαθόμενοι, τὴν περὶ τοὺς ἐχθροὺς εὔνοιαν ἐν προτιμήσει ποιοῦνται (op. cit., p. 282 Scheffer, following N, P; τοὺς δὲ λεγομένους ῥεφούγους ἐπιστελλομένους, p. 284 Mihăescu, following M).

[6] p. 282 Scheffer, p. 286 Mihăescu.

refused to ransom prisoners of war[1] who had not proved their good faith by escaping, and it has been suggested[2] that this was because some of the *soi-disant* prisoners were really deserters. The Khaqan of the Avars is said to have been instigated by spokesmen (ἀποκρισιαρίους) of the deserters to undertake the third of the three Avar sieges of Thessaloníkê.[3] The deserters are said to have offered to serve as a 'fifth column'.[4] By this time, Thessaloníkê was (so the deserters' spokesmen are said to have reminded the Khaqan) the only still unconquered city in the whole of Illyricum. All the cities and provinces of this region had been depopulated by the Avars already, and Thessaloníkê had given shelter to all the refugees who had escaped from the Danubian regions: i.e. Pannonia, Dacia, Dardania, and the other provinces and cities.[5] The Avars, together with their Slav subjects, had, in fact, devastated almost the whole of Illyricum, i.e. the provinces of the two Pannonias, the two Dacias, the Dardanias, Moesias, Praevalis,[6] Rhodhópê, and Thrace as well, right up to the Anastasian Long Wall, and they had carried off the whole population to the Avars' own territory in the portion of Pannonia adjoining the River Danube,[7] the province whose capital was formerly the city of Sirmium.[8] The date of this great deportation may have been 582/3.[9] A possible alternative date is the fifth year of Maurice's reign, 586/7. This is Theophanes's date for the second Avar invasion of the Empire,[10] and in 586/7 the Avars and their Slav subjects still held the Roman dominions in the Balkan Peninsula at their mercy, since the East Roman Government was then still at war with the Persian Empire and had no troops to spare from the front in Asia. The process of depopulation did not cease. During the third siege of Thessaloníkê, the inhabitants' morale was threatened by the defeatism of refugees from Naïssus and Sardica.[11] There was a second deportation, on a smaller scale, 231 years later than 582. In 813 the Bulgar Khan Krum took Adrianople and carried off from there twelve thousand males, with their families, to his dominions on the north side of the Danube, in what is now Wallachia.

---

[1] Zonarás, vol. iii, p. 297.   [2] By Stratós in op. cit., p. 43.

[3] *Sancti Demetrii Miracula* in Migne, *P.G.*, vol. cxvi (1891), cols. 1203–1398: Book II, chap. 2 (cols. 1336–7). This siege was laid when John was archbishop of Thessaloníkê (col. 1337). This John was in office from 610 to 649 (H. Grégoire, 'L'Origine et le nom des Croates et des Serbes', in *Byzantion*, vol. xvii (1944–5), pp. 88–118, on p. 105). The date of the third siege is discussed in Annex III, on p. 640.   [4] *S. D. Miracula*, ibid.

[5] Ibid.   [6] The Τριβάλεως of the MSS. should be emended to Πρεβάλεως.

[7] i.e. Pannonia Secunda.   [8] *S. D. Miracula*, Book II, chap. 5, col. 1361.

[9] P. Lemerle, 'La Composition et la chronologie des deux premiers livres des Miracula S. Demetrii', in *Byzantinische Zeitschrift*, 46. Band (1953), pp. 349–61, on p. 360. Cf. eundem, 'Invasions', p. 273, n. 2. See also the present work, Annex III, pp. 634–5. Bulgar raiders are said to have deported 100,000 people as early as 558 ('Invasions', p. 285).

[10] Theophanes, p. 257, sub A.M. 6079.

[11] *S. D. Miracula*, Book II, chap. 3, col. 1337.

Both these sets of East Roman deportees maintained their social and cultural identity in exile, and at least a portion of them, or of their descendants, managed to make their way back home eventually. After possibly as long as a quarter of a century in exile, the Adrianopolitan deportees fought their way to an East Roman naval squadron which had been sent to repatriate them.[1] The East Romans who had been deported by the Avars remained in exile for more than sixty years, so it is said,[2] preserving their Roman tradition and their Christian religion and always longing to escape, though they inter-married with Avars, Bulgars, and other aliens (ἐθνικοί) and thus increased their numbers.[3] When the new generation of the exiles grew up, most of them were made freemen, like the ex-prisoner of war whom Priscus had met in Attila's camp, and the Avar Khaqan then gave them a governor of their own, a Bulgar named Koúver.[4] Under Koúver's leadership, this community of half-caste East Roman exiles fought their way home into East Roman territory across the Danube and asked the Imperial Government to receive them back into the cities, including Thessaloníkê.[5]

According to the story, these repatriated exiles then split into two factions. One faction wished, bona fide, to settle down again at home as loyal citizens of the Empire. The other faction wanted to set up a state of its own on East Roman territory, with Koúver as Khaqan and with Thessaloníkê as his capital, if they could get possession of the city. Some of the repatriated exiles then asked permission from the Praetorian Prefect of Eastern Illyricum,[6] whose seat had been removed to Thessaloníkê, and the Prefect parried their request by sending them to Constantinople by sea.[7] Koúver then schemed with one of his counsellors who spoke Greek, Latin,[8] Slavonic, and Bulgar to feign allegiance to the Emperor, infiltrate their partisans into Thessaloníkê, seize the city, and install Koúver there. An adherent of this faction named Mávros, who did enter Thessaloníkê as a refugee,[9] won the confidence of the local authorities, was decorated by the Emperor with the consular insignia, and was given

---

[1] *Georg. Mon. Interpolatus*, pp. 817–19; Leo Grammaticus, pp. 231–3; *Theoph. Cont.*, pp. 216–17. See further J. B. Bury, *A History of the Eastern Roman Empire, A.D. 802–67* (London, 1912, Macmillan), pp. 370–1; S. Runciman, *A History of the First Bulgarian Empire* (London, 1930, Bell), pp. 85–6; and the present work, III, 5 (i), p. 424. The Adrianopolitan exiles were repatriated in the reign of Theóphilos (829–42).

[2] *S. D. Miracula*, Book II, chap. 5, col. 1364. But see the present work, Part III, chap. 5, Appendix I.

[3] *S. D. Miracula*, ibid.

[4] Ibid. The question whether this Bulgar Κοῦβερ is or is not identical with the Bulgar Koúvrat, the leader of the Onoghoúndouroi (Onogurs) who likewise seceded successfully from the Avars, is discussed in III, 5, Appendix I, pp. 461–4.

[5] *S. D. Miracula*, ibid.

[6] οἱ τὴν ὕπαρχον ἔχοντες φροντίδα.   [7] *S. D. Miracula*, cols. 1365–8.

[8] τὴν Ῥωμαίων γλῶσσαν (op. cit., col. 1368).

[9] πρόσφυξ.

command of the whole body of Koúver's escapees,[1] whom Koúver had stationed provisionally on the Keramêsian Plain.[2]

Mávros had planned to seize Thessaloníkê on Easter Saturday, but the Emperor had ordered the Admiral of the Imperial Fleet,[3] Sisínnios, to make for Thessaloníkê. The Admiral, who was conscious of the urgency of his mission and was aided by a timely change of wind, left Ellás on Palm Sunday and arrived at Thessaloníkê, via Skíathos, on the Wednesday before Easter at the hour of seven.[4] The Admiral made Mávros's people camp outside Thessaloníkê side by side with a landing party of his own, pending the arrival of the loyal faction of the escapees stationed on the Keramêsian Plain.[5] Mávros's own son finally denounced him, and the Emperor deprived Mávros of his command and interned him on a rural estate (προαστεῖον).[6]

This story should, no doubt, be treated with considerable reserve. It has been written, not to inform historians, but to glorify a saint. Still, it is evidence that in the 630s or 640s, as, in the 830s, a body of deportees did return to East Roman territory. According to the *Chronicle of Monemvasía*,[7] those portions of the Greek population of the Pelopónnêsos that were dislodged by the Avar [*sic*: actually Slav] *Völkerwanderung* escaped extermination or deportation partly by retreating to the east coast and partly by taking refuge in East Roman territory overseas, and these refugees' descendants eventually returned home, when, after the turn of the eighth and ninth centuries, the East Roman Government succeeded in re-establishing its rule over the independent Slav settlers in the Pelopónnêsos, except for the Mêlingoí and Ezerítai in southern Laconia. The author of the *Chronicle* states[8] that the people of Pátras found asylum at Rhíyion (Reggio di Calabria) in the 'toe' of Italy; the Argives on Oróvê ('Ορόβη) Island,[9] the Corinthians on

---

[1] ἀποφύγους.

[2] τὸν Κεραμήσιον κάμπον (ibid., col. 1365; cf. col. 1368: τοὺς Κερμησιάνους ἀποφύγους). This plain was near Thessaloníkê. Perhaps it was the plain on either side of the lowest reach of the River Vardar (Axios). The route up the Morava and then down the Vardar would have been the easiest avenue for escapees from Sirmia. The Dhragouvítai Slav tribe who were ordered to supply the refugees with rations were located near Vérrhoia (M. Vasmer, *Die Slaven in Griechenland* (Berlin, 1941, De Gruyter), p. 177).

[3] στρατηγὸς τῶν καράβων.

[4] Op. cit., cols. 1369 and 1373. According to the story, Sisínnios hurried because, at Skíathos, he had been warned by St. Demetrius in a dream to lose no time (col. 1372). It is also implied in the story that the timely change of wind was St. Demetrius's doing (col. 1373).

[5] Op. cit., col. 1373.   [6] Col. 1376.

[7] The MS. in the library of the Ivĕron Monastery on Mount Athos (Athous 4449; Ivĕron 329), lines 38–50 and 61–9.

[8] Ivĕron MS., lines 39–44.

[9] The place-name on the map of Hellenic-Age Greece that most closely resembles this name 'Ορόβη is 'Οροβίαι (the present-day 'Ροβιές) towards the northern end of the coast of the island of Évvoia that faces the mainland. An asylum on Évvoia would not be nearly

Aíyina,[1] the Laconians in Sicily, where they are still to be found at Dheménna.[2] If these statements are authentic history, the eventual return of these refugee communities brought another reinforcement to the pre-*Völkerwanderung* population of the East Roman Empire's former domain in the Balkan Peninsula. However, such partial restorations of the demographic *status quo ante* in the Balkan Peninsula cannot have reversed, in any substantial measure, the revolutionary effects of the exoduses and the *Völkerwanderung*, taken together.

In Asia Minor, in contrast to what had happened in the Balkan Peninsula, the demographic effects of the seventh-century cataclysm were not so great. In the *Völkerwanderung* in the twelfth century B.C. the Thraco–Phrygian wing of the migrants had surged across the Straits from Europe into the interior of Asia Minor, while the west coast of Asia Minor had been occupied by the advance-guard of the North-West-Greek-speaking Greeks and by fugitive survivors of the older strata of Greek-speakers in European Greece who had also made their way across the Aegean. In the seventh century of the Christian Era, fortress Constantinople, together with the East Roman Imperial Navy, prevented the Slav migrants into the Balkan Peninsula from invading Asia Minor as well. Meanwhile Asia Minor was being depopulated nevertheless, for it was a war zone almost continuously from the year 609 till the East Romans recaptured Malaṭīyah in 934 and Tarsós in 965. A Persian expeditionary force reached Chalcedon, the Asiatic suburb of Constantinople, in 609,[3] perhaps also in 616,[4] and again in 626. The Arabs besieged Constantinople

so distant from Argos as Reggio is from Pátras and as the north-east corner of Sicily is from Sparta. However, Évvoia has already been mentioned in the Ivĕron MS. of the Chronicle as being one of the parts of Greece that were attacked by the barbarian invaders, so a place on the coast of Évvoia facing the mainland would not have been a promising asylum from these selfsame invaders. Moreover, 'Oróvê' is called an island, not a town on an island. Lemerle, in 'La Chronique improprement dite de Monemvasie' (*Revue des Études Byzantines*, vol. xxi (1963), pp. 5–49, on p. 14), points out that the island Lévinthos in the Sporádhes, to the east of Amorghós, was also called Orovís. (He cites C. Müller, *Geographi Graeci Minores*, vol. i, p. 498, with n. on p. 499.) This identification of the Chronicle's 'Oróvê Island' is convincing. Lévinthos was a safe asylum till Mu'āwīyah launched his fleet in 649. It is a tiny island, but the number of refugees from Argholís may have been small if it is true that in the eastern part of the Peloppónnēsos the Greek population held its own against the barbarian invaders. The refugees on Péra Island in Peráni Bay, on the south coast of Salamis, whose presence there at about the turn of the sixth and seventh centuries is attested by archaeological evidence, may have been another party of Argive refugees (see Sinclair Hood in *The Annual of the British School at Athens*, No. 65 (1970), p. 43).

[1] This statement is corroborated by the fact that, on Aíyina, there are no Slavonic place-names (see Annex III, p. 630).

[2] The date of the earliest mention of this name that has been found by Amari is 902, the date of the latest is 1223 (Lemerle in loc. cit., p. 14). After the Norman conquest of Sicily, the north-east corner of the island was called in Latin Vallis Demeniae and later, in Italian, Val di Demone. Δεμέννα looks like a colloquial alternative of the Greek perfect participle passive, nominative neuter plural, δεδεμένα. The *Etymologicum Magnum* says that Δεμέννα was so called ὅτι ἐν αὐτῇ δέδεται ὁ Τύφων (Lemerle in loc. cit., p. 14, n. 16).

[3] Stratós, op. cit., p. 65.   [4] Op. cit., p. 115.

in 674–8 and again in 717–18, and these were not the only two occasions on which the Arabs reached the Straits.[1] However, neither the Persians nor, after them, the Arabs were able to occupy Asia Minor, even temporarily,[2] as the Persians did occupy Mesopotamia, Syria, and Palestine temporarily[3] and then the Arabs permanently. Consequently, in Asia Minor, the problem of resettling a depopulated East Roman territory was not solved by the East Roman Empire's invaders taking the country for themselves, as the Slavs took the interior of the Balkan Peninsula right down to the western side of the Pelopónnêsos and to Laconia save for the Tainaron Peninsula (the Máni).[4]

The East Roman Empire retained possession of Asia Minor to the north-west of the Távros and Andítavros ranges, from the Mediterranean coast, west of Tarsós, to the Black Sea coast at the Black Sea's south-eastern corner. The Empire also retained possession, in the Balkan Peninsula, not only of Constantinople but also of Constantinople's hinterland as far westward as the east bank of the lower Hebrus (Maríca) River, including the city of Adrianople—the Empire's European bastion, which was never taken by the Avars and was never held permanently by the Bulgars, though these did take Adrianople three times—for the first time in 813 and then again in 914 and in 923. In Europe on the far side of Adrianople, the Empire succeeded in retaining or recovering only isolated enclaves of its former territory, and the communications of these enclaves with each other and with Constantinople remained in some degree precarious till 1018, when the subjugation and annexation of West Bulgaria was completed by the Emperor Basil II.

Thus, for the East Roman Empire, the problems of resettlement were different to the east of Adrianople and to the west of it. To the east of this barrier-fortress, the Empire had on its hands the task of re-peopling a depopulated territory that remained in its possession. To the west of Adrianople, the Empire's scope for carrying out its demographic policy was narrower. The greater part of the Balkan Peninsula had been re-peopled by Slav invaders after these, under Avar command, had drastically reduced the numbers of the previous Latin-speaking and Greek-speaking population of this region. Here the most that the East Roman Government could achieve was to subjugate the southernmost of the intrusive 'Sklavinías' and then re-Graecize the reconquered territory, partly by Graecizing the subjugated Slavs[5] and partly by repatriating Greek

---

[1] In Arab parlance, the Khalij (Channel). See further II, 1 (iii) (b), p. 112.

[2] Stratós, op. cit., p. 117, 258, 274, 360–1, apropos of the Persians.

[3] Mesopotamia from 606–10 to 629, Syria and Palestine from 613–14 to 629; Egypt from the end of 616 to 629 (Stratós, op. cit., pp. 62–3, 107–9, 113–14, 232–58, 283).

[4] See further Annex III, pp. 641–51.

[5] Vasmer, op. cit., p. 325, points out that this Graecization of the immigrant Slavs must have started early, since some Slavonic place-names have been Graecized in an archaic form.

refugees and by introducing Greek-speaking settlers from other parts of the Empire. This was a minor concern for the Imperial Government by comparison with the problem of solving the demographic crisis[1] in its territories to the east of Adrianople.

The problem here was how to replenish, by resettlement, the Empire's depleted supply of taxpayers and soldiers. If the Imperial Government had not accomplished this, the Empire could not have survived.[2] The crisis was severe; for enemy action in the forms of the massacre and deportation of the population and the devastation of the countryside was aggravated by three successive outbreaks of plague: in 541–4, in 619, and in 746–7.[3] Throughout the fourth, fifth, and sixth centuries, the ratio of population to land was low.[4] After the plague of 541–4, in the reigns of Tiberius II and Maurice (578–602), man-power had a greater value than territory for the East Roman Government, and recruiting and supplying were more important considerations than tax-yield. In 580 Tiberius II was willing to evacuate Persarmenia, but he wanted to keep the refugees who had migrated from there to East Roman territory.[5] From the end of Justinian I's reign in 565 onwards, the East Roman Imperial Government was combating the depopulation caused by successive plagues and by persistent enemy action. For this purpose it was planting new settlers in the devastated and depopulated countryside, and it was encouraging the growth of communities of free peasants, which were likely to yield more tax-money for the Treasury and more recruits for the Army than could be extracted from big rural estates.

The Imperial Government won this long and arduous demographic and economic battle. As a result of its policies, the Empire's labour force increased till eventually the total acreage of potential arable and pastureland in Asia Minor came once again to be fully utilized and exploited[6]—fully, that is to say, up to the capacity of the rather backward and stagnant East Roman techniques of agricultural and pastoral husbandry.[7] By the turn of the ninth and tenth centuries the Emperor Leo VI was able to maintain[8] that the Romans were so many times more

---

[1] See Lopez in loc. cit., pp. 70–1.

[2] 'Il n'est pas douteux qu'aux viie–ixe siècles le peuplement des provinces restées byzantines a subi de profondes modifications. C'est peut-être la principale explication de la vigueur que montra alors l'Empire' (Lemerle, 'Esquisse', vol. ccxix, p. 64, n. 6).

[3] Teall in loc. cit., pp. 100–1.

[4] Ibid., p. 96.

[5] Ibid., p. 96, with n. 26. Cf. Lemerle, 'Esquisse', vol. ccxix, p. 37.

[6] Teall, ibid., pp. 131, 132, 133–4. However, according to Ostrogorsky, 'Agrarian Conditions', p. 231, 'Byzantium never lacked idle land'.

[7] See Teall, ibid., pp. 128–9, and Ostrogorsky, 'Agrarian Conditions', p. 231. By the tenth century the barbarians of Western Christendom were forging ahead of the East Romans. For instance, they were adopting a method of harnessing draught-animals that made it possible for these to exert their muscle-power to the full.

[8] In his *Taktiká*, Dhiátaxis 18, §§ 129–30 (Migne, *P.G.*, vol. cvii, col. 977).

numerous than the Arabs that the Romans could be sure of being the victors if only they would supply their troops with equipment of the Arabs' standard.

This slow but sure restoration of the East Roman Empire's man-power was a magnificent achievement. It was a tragedy for the Empire that it had no sooner won this social and economic victory than its Government became engaged in a losing battle with an influential minority (the δυνατοί), which now proceeded, in the teeth of successive acts of agrarian legislation, to add field to field at the expense of the peasant freeholders who were the source of the Empire's strength—as the Emperors, and no doubt also their powerful antagonists in their own household, were well aware.

The East Roman Government's main sources of reinforcements of man-power for settlement on the land in Asia Minor were soldiers ex-pelled or transferred from elsewhere, prisoners of war, and refugees. The refugees might be either the dissident alien subjects of a foreign power or deserters from a foreign power's own ruling 'establishment'. The earliest of these reinforcements of the population of Asia Minor, after this had been reduced during the Romano–Persian War of 604–28, were the troops of the army-corps of the magistri militum per Orientem and per Armeniam, who were driven into Asia Minor by the Arabs' onslaught, and the troops of the magister militum per Thraciam, who were transferred to Asia Minor to support their hard-pressed comrades from the Empire's lost dominions farther to the east. These military settlements are dealt with at later points in this book.[1]

The future Emperor Maurice is said to have augmented the Empire's military forces notably in 577 by settling Armenian deportees from Arzanênê in large numbers on depopulated lands.[2] Enlisting prisoners of war was evidently a hazardous experiment. The Emperor Leo VI is said by the Muslim chronicler Tabari[3] to have played this game successfully in A.D. 896–7, when 'the Slavs' (i.e. the Bulgars, led by Khan Symeon) were under the walls of Constantinople. In this emergency, Leo, accord-ing to Tabari, mobilized the Muslim prisoners in Constantinople, put arms into their hands, and asked them for their help against the enemy at his gates. The Muslims agreed and repulsed the 'Slavs', whereupon Leo took alarm, disarmed his Muslim saviours, and dispersed them among different parts of his dominions. Justinian II had tried the same experi-ment with Slav prisoners of war, and had fared less well. In 692, 20,000 out of 30,000 Slav troops, recruited from the Slavs whom Justinian had

---

[1] See II, 1 (iii) (d) and 4.

[2] Evagrius, *Historia Ecclesiastica*, Book V, chap. 19, p. 215; John of Ephesus, *Ecclesiastical History*, Book VI, chap. 15.

[3] In a passage translated in Vasiliev, *Byzance et les Arabes*, ii, II, pp. 11–12. See also the present work, III, 3, p. 385.

deported from Europe to théma Opsíkion in 688/9,[1] deserted to the Arabs.[2] Justinian had been warned; for 5,000 Slavs had deserted to the Arabs already in 664/5.[3] All the same, Justinian exterminated the families of his Slav deserters.[4]

The East Roman Government could not count on the loyalty even of refugees and deserters, and *a fortiori* not of prisoners of war, unless they had become converts—and genuine converts—to Eastern Orthodox Christianity. Charanis observes[5] that, in the East Roman Empire, the two unifying forces were the Greek language and Orthodox Christianity, and it may be added that, of the two, Orthodox Christianity was the more important, but that only recruits who were still pagans could be converted easily.

Of all the Christian immigrants, compulsory or voluntary, the Armenians were among the readiest to adopt Orthodoxy.[6] The Armenian national variety of Monophysite (alias pre-Chalcedonian) Christianity was slightly closer to Orthodoxy than the Syrian and Egyptian form. Nevertheless the Armenians, on their home ground, resisted repeated attempts, by blandishments or by coercion, to bring them over into the Orthodox fold. The Armenian national church was obdurate, and in this it had the nation's support; for in Armenia—incorrigibly disunited as the country was, politically—the Armenian version of pre-Chalcedonian Christianity was the distinguishing mark of Armenian nationality and was the bond of national unity.[7] On the other hand, for Armenian émigrés in the East Roman Empire, the acceptance of Orthodoxy was virtually obligatory,[8] and, when once they had made this ecclesiastical break with their Armenian national past, they, or at least their descendants, could, and did, rise to the highest positions in the Empire.[9] Fourteen East Roman Emperors (among them, Heraclius and Basil I) are reckoned to have been of Armenian origin, but, of these, all but one came from families that had long since become naturalized, and the single exception proves this rule. This exception is Mjej Gnouni (*Graecè* Mizizios), an Armenian immigrant of the first generation. Mjej succeeded in 668 in assassinating his master Constans II, but he did not achieve his objective of reigning in his victim's stead.

[1] Theophanes, p. 364, sub A.M. 6180.   [2] Theophanes, p. 366, sub A.M. 6184.
[3] Theophanes, p. 348, sub A.M. 6156.   [4] Theophanes, p. 366, sub A.M. 6184.
[5] P. Charanis, 'Ethnic Changes in the Byzantine Empire in the Seventh Century', in *Dumbarton Oaks Papers*, Number Thirteen (1959), pp. 25–44, on p. 44.
[6] Ibid., p. 36.
[7] See J. Laurent, *L'Arménie entre Byzance et l'Islam* (Paris, 1919, Fontemoing), pp. 129–37.
[8] Op. cit., p. 195.
[9] See the lists in P. Charanis, *The Armenians in the Byzantine Empire* (Lisbon, 1963, Bertrand), pp. 18–28; in eodem, 'Ethnic Changes in the Byzantine Empire in the Seventh Century', in *Dumbarton Oaks Papers*, Number Thirteen (1959), pp. 25–44, on pp. 32–6; and in A. Rambaud, *L'Empire grec au dixième siècle* (Paris, 1970, Franck), pp. 535–8.

Moreover, even the apparently assimilated Armenian citizens of the East Roman Empire continued to feel a certain ethnic solidarity with each other—especially, perhaps, those who had risen in the world; for these were aware that their eminence was enviable and therefore vulnerable. Basil I came from an obscure Adrianopolitan family of Armenian origin,[1] and his feat of wading out of obscurity through slaughter to a throne was facilitated in its earlier stages by Armenian patrons,[2] and in its culminating stage by Armenian accomplices,[3] who were attracted to Basil by the identity of their and Basil's ethnic origin. Basil's principal victims, the Caesar Várdhas and Várdhas's nephew the Emperor Michael III, also had Armenian blood in their veins.[4]

The Syrian refugees in the East Roman Empire may have been as readily assimilable as the Armenians—indeed, even more readily, since the Syrians had been exposed to the influence of the Greek language and culture at close quarters ever since the overthrow of the First Persian Empire by Alexander the Great; and the cultural, as well as the commercial, links between Syria and the East Roman Empire survived the Empire's loss of Syria to the Arabs. The leading polemical theologian in the anti-iconoclast camp was St. John of Damascus, a Syrian Orthodox Christian whose family had supplied senior civil servants to the Umayyad Caliphs. St. John was able to play his role—an effective role because he wrote in Greek—just because he was a subject of the Caliphate and was consequently beyond the reach of the East Roman Government's arm. The Emperor Leo III (717-41) was a Syrian whose family were refugees of recent date from Yermaníkeia (Mar'ash), in Commagene, to Thrace; and Leo III may fairly be judged to have been the greatest of all Emperors after Heraclius who ever attained the East Roman Imperial throne, while the second greatest may be judged to have been Leo III's son, Constantine V (741-75), a ruler who was a worthy successor to his father.

Since Yermaníkeia lay on the border between the pre-Chalcedonian and the Chalcedonian fraction of the Christian World, we cannot be sure which sect was the original religion of Leo III's family. Some of the refugees from this borderland are recorded to have been Monophysites,

---

[1] For Basil's I's origin, and his grandson Constantine Porphyrogenitus's attempt to ennoble Basil's lineage, see Laurent, op. cit., p. 263, n. 1; N. Adontz, 'L'Âge et l'origine de l'empereur Basile I', in *Byzantion*, viii (1933), pp. 475–500, and ix (1934), pp. 223–64; and the present work V, 2, pp. 587–8.

[2] e.g. the dhroungários Constantine. Charanis conjectures, in op. cit., pp. 25–6, that Basil I's first employer at Constantinople, Theophilídzês, too, was an Armenian. He was a kinsman of the Empress Theodora and the Caesar Várdhas, who had an Armenian uncle (see n. 4, below).

[3] An instructive list of these is given by Laurent in op. cit., p. 263, n. 2.

[4] Várdhas's uncle and Michael's great-uncle, Manuel, was an Armenian (*Theoph. Cont.*, p. 148, cited by Bury, *Eastern Roman Empire*, p. 81, n. 1).

but, whether Leo's family were Monophysites or not, their place of origin makes it certain that they were Syrians. The civil war of 742–3 between Constantine V and his brother-in-law Artávasdhos, ex-stratêghós of théma Armeniakoí, was ostensibly a contest between an iconoclast and an iconodule but was in truth one between a Syrian-descended and an Armenian-descended aspirant to the East Roman Imperial throne. It was no accident that, before the Arab conquests had shorn away Syria and the Roman portion of Armenia from the East Roman Empire, the Anatolic army-corps, which was Leo III's and Constantine V's mainstay, had been stationed in Syria, while the Armeniac army-corps, which was Artávasdhos's mainstay, had been stationed in Roman Armenia. The Syrian-descended Leo III and the Armenian-descended Basil I were more successful than any East Roman Emperors of native stock in founding dynasties—a practice that went against the grain of the Roman Imperial tradition.

As for the Paulician refugees and deportees who were planted in Thrace, we may guess that their compulsory conversion to Orthodoxy—in so far as they submitted to conversion—was insincere. On the other hand, the religious tenets of the Mardaïtes are not known to have given the East Roman Government any anxiety. The Mardaïtes were anti-Muslim freedom-fighters first and foremost, and, whether or not these northern Syrians were Jacobites (i.e. Syrian pre-Chalcedonians) in origin, Orthodoxy, in virtue of its being anti-Muslim, was acceptable to them.

The rarest converts among all the foreigners who came into East Roman hands as prisoners of war or as deserters were the Eastern Muslims (οἱ Σαρακηνοί), and these were also the most highly prized and the most handsomely treated. They were recognized by the East Romans as being civilized men,[1] and those of them who were willing to change their religion were offered particularly advantageous terms of settlement in the East Roman Empire. The legendary hero of the Byzantine Greek epic, 'Vasíleios the Mestizo Borderer' (Βασίλειος Διγενὴς Ἀκρίτας) is presented as being the son of an Arab amīr who, for love of an East Roman girl whom he has taken captive on a raid, becomes a convert to Christianity, migrates with his bride to Rhomanía, and is welcomed by the bride's family. This piece of poetic fiction is a faithful reflection of historical fact. The official instructions[2] for the treatment of Muslims who have accepted baptism in an army-corps district are remarkable.

For information: Each one of them is entitled to receive three nomísmata per man from the protonotários of the district, and six nomísmata for their

---

[1] 'Byzance accordait aux Arabes une sorte de prééminence sur ses voisins occidentaux' (Vasiliev, *Byzance et les Arabes*, vol. i, p. 12).

[2] In *De Caer.* Book II, chap. 49, pp. 694–5.

ploughing-oxen, together with fifty-four módhioi of corn each for seed-corn and rations. Note concerning prisoners who are adopted into land-owning families (οἴκους) as sons-in-law. A family that has adopted an [ex-]Muslim son-in-law is entitled to a three-years' immunity from the produce-tax (συνονήν) and the hearth-tax (καπνικόν), whether this family is a military (στρατιωτικός) or is a civilian (πολιτικός) one. (After the expiry of the three years, the said family is once again under an obligation to pay the two taxes aforementioned.) Note: prisoners of war or other persons who have been given land for settlement (εἰς κατασκήνωσιν) are, for three years, to remain unmolested by demands for the performance of any kind of public service, and they are not to pay either produce-tax or hearth-tax. (They have to pay both after the three years have run out.)

We have a record of two bodies of Muslim deserters from the dominions of the 'Abbasid Caliphate and its successor states who took refuge in the East Roman Empire and did accept conversion to Eastern Orthodox Christianity.

In 834 a body of Khurramīyah—an unorthodox Iranian Muslim sect that had rebelled against the Caliph Mu'tasim under the leadership of Bābek—escaped into East Roman territory after Bābek had suffered a serious defeat. The captain of these Khurramite Persian refugees, Nasr, was christened under the name Theóphovos,[1] and the Emperor Theóphilos took him and his men into his service, settled them at Sinópê and Amastrís, put them on his military pay-roll, and gave them East Roman wives.[2] Their number, said to have been originally 14,000,[3] rose,

[1] For the identity of Theóphovos with the refugee Khurramite Nasr, see Vasiliev, *Byzance et les Arabes*, i, p. 124, with footnote 3, and the additional note by H. Grégoire on pp. 413–17. According to Grégoire, there has been some confusion, partly deliberate, between the legends of Theóphovos-Nasr, the refugee and renegade Muslim, and of Manuel, the refugee and renegade East Roman. For instance, though Theóphovos-Nasr is duly credited with having saved Theóphilos's life on campaign (see p. 84, n. 3), the Greek authorities who record this have entered it under a wrong date, because the authentic incident, which occurred in 838, has been attributed, under that date, to Manuel. The securely dated events in Theóphovos-Nasr's career are his participation in the campaigns of 837 and 838. The accounts of his lineage and early life in Genesius and *Theoph. Cont.*, of which Bury was already suspicious (*The Eastern Roman Empire*, p. 252, n. 3), have been rejected definitely, as being apocryphal, by the editors of Vasiliev, *Byzance et les Arabes*, i, in loc. cit. The Greek sources are *Georg. Mon. Interpolatus*, pp. 793, 803, 810; Leo Grammaticus, p. 215; *Theoph. Cont.*, pp. 110–14, 124–5, 135–6; Genesius, pp. 52–61. The Syrian source is Michael Syrus, ed. and tr. by J. B. Chabot (1905–6), vol. iii, pp. 50 and 73. The Arabic source is Tabari.

[2] Tabari, sub A.D. [837/8], translated in Vasiliev, op. cit., vol. i, p. 294. The East Roman Imperial Government attached to itself not only settlers from abroad but also foreign potentates by supplying them with Greek wives. The Emperor Basil II, for instance, purchased the aid of Prince Vladímir of Kiev by giving him his sister Anna for a bride. Theóphovos-Nasr was given either Theóphilos's own sister (*Theoph. Cont.*, p. 112; Genesius, p. 55) or Theóphilos's wife the Empress Theodora's sister (*Georg. Mon. Interpolatus*, p. 793; Leo Grammaticus, p. 215). St. Athanasía of Aíyina, a widow who wished to become a nun, was compelled, by an Imperial edict applicable to all unmarried women and widows, to marry a barbarian settler (see L. Bréhier, 'Les Populations rurales au ixᵉ siècle d'après l'hagiographie byzantine', in *Byzantion*, i (1924), pp. 170–90, on p. 186).

[3] *Georg. Mon. Interpolatus*, p. 793; Leo Grammaticus, p. 215.

through subsequent accessions,[1] to 30,000.[2] In 837 Theóphilos responded to an appeal from Bābek, who was now being pressed harder than ever by the 'Abbasid forces, to make a diversion in Bābek's favour. Theóphilos attacked and captured the 'Abbasid frontier fortress Sozópetra (Zápetra, Zibatrah) and treated the garrison and population cruelly. The Caliph Mu'tasim retorted in 838 by invading the East Roman Empire and capturing and rasing Amórion, Theóphilos's family's home town and the principal fortress on the road from the Cilician Gates to the Bosphorus. Theóphovos-Nasr took an active part in both these campaigns, and is said to have saved Theóphilos's life.[3] According to Grégoire,[4] it was after the campaign of 838 that Theóphilos became distrustful of Theóphovos-Nasr's troops and took action which led these to mutiny and to proclaim Theóphovos-Nasr emperor,[5] but Theóphovos managed both to pacify the mutineers and to make his peace with the Emperor Theóphilos, who amnestied the mutineers but now distributed their *tághma* among a number of *thémata* in *toúrmai* of not more than 2,000 men each.[6] Perhaps this was the proposed precautionary measure which had caused the mutiny. According to the Arabic sources,[7] Theóphovos-Nasr was killed in action against the 'Abbasid forces *circa* 840. According to the Greek sources,[8] Theóphilos had Theóphovos-Nasr arrested and put to death.

The second of the two recorded large-scale secessions of Eastern Muslims to the East Roman Empire has been described by Ibn Hawkal of Nisībīn.[9] Ibn Hawkal's native city and its territory had been acquired by the Hamdanids in 941/2, and, according to Ibn Hawkal, they taxed the population so extortionately that their kinsmen, the Banu Habīb, migrated with their families, slaves, partisans, cattle, and movable property to East Roman territory. According to Ibn Hawkal, the Banu Habīb's combatant strength was 10,000 horsemen, magnificently equipped. They became Christians, and the East Roman Government gave them a choice of good land and furnished them with livestock. After this, the Banu Habīb raided Muslim territory as energetically as

---

[1] Tabari (sub anno A.D. 833). [2] *Theoph. Cont.*, p. 125.

[3] See *Theoph. Cont.*, pp. 113–14; Vasiliev, op. cit., i, p. 124, n. 3.

[4] In loc. cit.

[5] *Theoph. Cont.*, p. 124–5, dates this between the end of the Sozópetra campaign and the beginning of the Amórion campaign. This is a most improbable dating. However, on pp. 135–6, *Theoph. Cont.* recounts, in a different form and with a different ending, what seems to be the same incident. This second version of *Theoph. Cont.*'s agrees with *Georg. Mon. Interpolatus*, pp. 803 and 810, and Leo Grammaticus, p. 228.

[6] *Georg. Mon. Interpolatus*, p. 793; Leo Grammaticus, p. 215; *Theoph. Cont.*, p. 125; Genesius, p. 61. [7] See Grégoire, ibid., on p. 416.

[8] *Georg. Mon. Interpolatus*, pp. 803 and 810; Leo Grammaticus, p. 228; pseudo-Symeon, p. 646; Genesius, pp. 60 and 61. This account of Theóphovos's end is rejected in Vasiliev, op. cit., i, p. 124, n. 3, *ad fin.*

[9] This passage is translated in Vasiliev, *Byzance et les Arabes*, ii, II, pp. 419–21.

they had raided East Roman territory previously, and many of their fellow-countrymen followed their example in changing sides. In contrast to the story of Theóphovos-Nasr and his men, this story of the Banu Habīb can be accepted without reserve, since the events occurred in the narrator, Ibn Hawkal's, home country, and within his own lifetime.

The major sources of man-power for re-peopling Asia Minor were, however, not these occasional secessions of Eastern Muslims but influxes from Armenia and the Sklavinías, two regions, adjoining Asia Minor, that were populous.

After the year 653, in which the Armenians had come to terms with the Arabs on the understanding that they were to enjoy religious toleration,[1] there was nevertheless a flow of migration from Armenia to the East Roman Empire,[2] since the Arab–Armenian compact of 653 was not observed faithfully by either of the parties to it.[3] There were waves of migration after the temporary reconquest of Armenia by the East Romans in 683–93, after the unsuccessful Armenian revolt against the Arabs in 749–50, when the Arabs were paralysed momentarily by the civil war between the Umayyads and the 'Abbasids, and after the crushing of Armenia by the 'Abbasids in 772 and in 852–5.[4] The flow of Armenians, Paulicians,[5] and Syrians seems to have been directed mainly to Western Asia Minor and Thrace by the East Roman Government.

Already, in 571, refugees from Persarmenia, including the Katholikós, had been settled at Pergamon.[6] This settlement subsequently produced the Emperor Philippikós Vardhânês (711–13). By the year 911 there were Armenian settlements at Platánion, in théma Anatolikoí, and at Prínê, in théma Thrakěsioi, which were populous enough to be able to provide 500 soldiers each for the expeditionary force that Leo VI sent to Crete in that year.[7] Leo VI himself planted Armenians in the region to the east of Kaisáreia,[8] which suffered from incessant Muslim raids.

---

[1] Laurent, op. cit., p. 139. (See also the present work, pp. 108, 395, 398, 678.)

[2] Op. cit., pp. 4–5, 184, n. 4, 190–8. According to Laurent, p. 193, n. 8, there was no mass migration from Armenia into the East Roman Empire before the tenth century. However, the previous flow was copious enough to produce important demographic results.

[3] Laurent, ibid., p. 154.

[4] Ibid., pp. 190–2. 12,000 Armenians, together with their women, children, retainers, and horses, entered East Roman territory *circa* 790 (Charanis, *The Armenians in the Byzantine Empire*, p. 14; see also Charanis, 'Ethnic Changes in the Byzantine Empire in the Seventh Century', in *Dumbarton Oaks Papers*, Number Thirteen (1959), pp. 25–44, on pp. 29–31.

[5] According to N. G. Garsoian, *The Paulician Heresy* (Paris, 1967, Mouton), the original Paulicians were Armenians, but a branch of the sect was established in East Roman territory in 654 (pp. 90, 117, n. 13, 124, n. 34, 132).

[6] Charanis, *The Armenians in the Byzantine Empire*, p. 13; 'Ethnic Changes', p. 29.

[7] See *De Caer.*, Book II, chap. 44, p. 652 and pp. 655–6, for these two communities of Armenian settlers. Platánion lay in théma Anatolikoí (chap. 44, pp. 675–8). The Armenian settlers in théma Thrakěsioi, who served in the expeditionary force sent to Crete in 949 (chap. 44, p. 663; chap. 45, p. 667), were presumably those at Prínê.

[8] M. Canard, in *C. Med. H.*, vol. iv, 2nd ed., Part I (1966), p. 717.

There were other Armenian settlements on the Asiatic side of the straits.[1] Some of the Armenians deported in 577 from Arzanênê had been settled in Cyprus,[2] and Nikêphóros I (802–11) planted some Armenians as far afield as Sparta[3] when he was assembling colonists for reconstituting Sparta as one of his measures for 'de-Slavizing' the Pelopónnêsos.[4] Leo VI's general Nikêphóros Phokás planted Armenians still farther afield, in Calabria, after his campaign in South-Eastern Italy in 885,[5] and his grandson and namesake, the Emperor Nikêphóros II (963–9), planted Armenians in Crete after his conquest of the island in 961, in the reign of Rhomanós II.[6]

However, the majority of the non-Muslim refugees and evacuees from territories on the Caliphate's side of the East Roman Empire's retreating eastern frontier appear to have been directed to Thrace. Already a small settlement of Armenians had been planted there by Justinian I (527–65).[7] This settlement was reinforced on a larger scale by Tiberius II and Maurice (578–602).[8] In 745 or 746 Constantine V occupied Yermaníkeia and Dholikhê, and in 751/2 he rased Malatīyah and Qālīqalā (Theodosiópolis). These East Roman territorial gains were ephemeral,[9] but they produced a yield of evacuees. Constantine V settled in Thrace Monophysites from Yermaníkeia in 745 or 746,[10] and Paulicians from Theodosiópolis and Malatīyah in 755 or 756 or 757.[11] Leo IV (775–80) settled in Thrace Monophysite evacuees from Yermaníkeia in 778.[12] After the East Roman annexation of Eastern Bulgaria in 972, John Dzimiskês (969–76) settled 2,500 Paulicians round Philippópolis.[13]

The Mardaïtes,[14] alias Jarājimah,[15] were Syrian Christian freedom-

---

[1] The Armenian settlers in this region were assimilated and were loyal to the Empire. Many stratêghoí of théma Opsíkion were of Armenian origin. (H. Ahrweiler, 'L'Asie Mineure et les invasions arabes', pp. 18–19).   [2] See p. 79, with n. 2.

[3] Charanis, *The Armenians*, p. 16; idem, 'Ethnic Changes', p. 31.

[4] See the present chapter, pp. 95–6.   [5] Charanis, *The Armenians*, p. 16.

[6] Leo Diaconus, Book II, chap. 8, p. 28 (Bonn).

[7] Procopius, Book III, chap. 37, § 7.

[8] Charanis, *The Armenians*, pp. 14–15; idem, 'Ethnic Changes', pp. 29–30.

[9] V. M. Anastos, 'Iconoclasm and Imperial Rule, 717–842', in *C. Med. H.*, vol. iv, 2nd ed., Part I (1966), pp. 61–104, on pp. 73–4 (following Theophanes, p. 427, sub A.M. 6243).

[10] Theophanes, p. 422, sub A.M. 6237; Nic. Patr., p. 65.

[11] Theophanes, p. 429, sub A.M. 6247; Nic. Patr., p. 66. For Constantine V's settlements in Thrace, see also Michael Syrus (ed. Chabot), vol. ii, pp. 518, 521, 523. The year 757 is D. Obolensky's dating (see his *The Bogomils* (Cambridge, 1948, University Press), p. 60, n. 5).   [12] Theophanes, pp. 451–2, sub A.M. 6270; Michael Syrus, iii, p. 2.

[13] Anna Comnena, *Alexias*, Book XIV, chap. 8.

[14] This name is derived from a Semitic root meaning 'rebel'. See H. Antoniadis-Bibicou, op. cit., p. 30, n. 3, citing R. Dozy, *Supplément aux dictionnaires arabes*, tome ii (Leiden and Paris, 1927), p. 550ᵃ: 'mardd' means 'rebellion'; 'maradat Lubnan' means 'Lebanese rebels'.

[15] This name is derived from the name of a town in the Amanos Range called Jurjūma (Antoniadis-Bibicou, op. cit., p. 30, following Balādhurī, *Kitāb Futūḥ al-Buldān*, P. K. Hitti's translation, vol. i (New York, 1916, Columbia University Press), p. 247).

fighters against the Arab conquerors. The Arabs' military forte lay in swift and sweeping cavalry operations in open country. The Mardaïtes baffled these hitherto invincible horsemen by engaging in guerrilla operations against them in mountainous forested country. Starting in their native Amanos Range, they gained a foothold in the Lebanon, within close range of the Umayyad Caliphs' capital Damascus, in 677,[1] and here their numbers were swollen by large numbers of slaves, (Roman) prisoners of war, and (Christian) natives, who joined them. This was a telling East Roman riposte to the Arabs' disastrously unsuccessful siege of Constantinople in 674–8. The Caliph Muʿāwiyah was reduced to suing for peace, and obtained an annual truce on condition of paying tribute to the East Roman Imperial Government. This peace was renewed, on the Caliph ʿAbd-al-Malik's initiative, in 685.[2] However, the East Roman Emperor Justinian II decided to sell a military advantage that he presumably considered to be a wasting asset, and to extract, in exchange, additional favourable terms from the Umayyad Government while the Mardaïtes were still creating alarm and embarrassment at Damascus. In 688/9 or 689/90 Justinian II made a treaty with the Umayyad Government in which, in consideration of their paying him a greatly increased tribute and also dividing equally the revenues of Cyprus, Armenia, and Iberia, the Emperor agreed, for his part, to withdraw the Mardaïtes to the East Roman side of the border and to put a stop to their incursions for the future.[3]

In execution of this Romano–Arab treaty, Justinian II withdrew 12,000 Mardaïtes from Umayyad territory.[4] He received his Mardaïte evacuees in Armenia[5] and settled them at Attáleia (Antalya). By the dates of the East Roman expeditions against Crete in 911 and 949, there were also Mardaïte settlements in some of the thémata to the west of Adrianople: in Pelopónnêsos, Kephalênía, and Nikópolis;[6] in Kórphous (Kérkyra);[7] and perhaps in Dhyrrhákhion too; for, though there is no record of a Mardaïte settlement there, the present-day Albanian tribe called Mirdita, in Northern Albania, is of Mardaïte origin, to judge by its name.

[1] Theophanes, p. 355, sub A.M. 6169.

[2] Theophanes, p. 361, sub A.M. 6176. Cf. Balādhurī, Hitti's translation, vol. i, pp. 247–8.

[3] Tabari, sub A.D. 689/90 (cited by E. W. Brooks in 'The Arabs in Asia Minor (641–750) from Arabic Sources', in *J.H.S*, vol. xviii (1898), p. 189); Theophanes, p. 363, sub A.M. 6178.

[4] Theophanes, p. 363, sub A.M. 6178.   [5] Theophanes, p. 364, sub A.M. 6179.

[6] *De Caer.*, Book II, chap. 44, pp. 654, 655, 656, 657, 660; chap. 45, p. 665. For the Mardaïtes in the Pelopónnêsos, see also *Theoph. Cont.*, Book V, chap. 70, p. 311. See also Rambaud, *L'Empire grec au dixième siècle*, p. 214; Antoniadis-Bibicou, op. cit., p. 31; H. Glykatzi-Ahrweiler, 'Recherches sur l'administration de l'Empire byzantin aux ixe–xie siècles', in *Bulletin de Correspondance Hellénique*, lxxxiv (1960), pp. 1–111, on p. 32. In loc. cit. G.-A. locates the Peloponnesian Mardaïtes in the Máni (Tainaron).

[7] See Antoniadis-Bibicou, loc. cit.

Justinian II has been severely blamed by Theophanes[1] for his having agreed to withdraw the Mardaïtes; and the high price, in terms of money, that the Arabs paid for this, taken together with the military sequel, shows that the Arabs thought that they were getting the best of the bargain and that they proved to have been correct in their calculation. The withdrawal cost the East Roman Empire the possession of eastern Cilicia. In 702/3[2] or 703/4[3] the Arabs fortified and garrisoned Mopsouestia (Massīsah). By 705/6 or 706/7 the Mardaïtes were fighting a battle with the Arabs at Tyana, on the north-west side of the 'Cilician Gates' pass through the Távros Range—a battle that ended in the Mardaïtes being defeated and Tyana, together with four other fortified places, falling temporarily into the Arabs' hands.[4] Those of the Mardaïtes who remained on the Arab side of the frontier came to terms with the Caliph Walīd, on favourable conditions, in 708.[5]

The settlement of Slavs in Asia Minor was more convenient for the East Roman Imperial Government in several ways than the settlement there of Armenians and Syrians. In the first place, the transportation of Slavs to Asia Minor from the Balkan Peninsula served two purposes at once. While increasing the number of the Empire's taxable and conscriptable Asiatic subjects, it simultaneously diminished the number of the barbarian trespassers on the Empire's former territories in the Balkan Peninsula. Transfers of Slav population could be carried out on a large scale, since the Sklavinías were populous.[6] Moreover, the Slavs were comparatively amenable. The Syrians and Armenians, who were on a par with the East Romans in point of civilization, were unaccommodating. The Slavs, though they were barbarians, were mild and even amiable. They were kind to prisoners of war,[7] and hospitable to travellers.[8] In

---

[1] On pp. 363, 364, 365.

[2] Ya'qūbī and Theophanes, p. 372, sub A.M. 6193 (two of the sources cited by E. W. Brooks, ibid., p. 191).

[3] Tabari, following Wākidī (cited by Brooks, ibid.).

[4] Tabari, (following Wākidī sub A.D. 705/6 and again sub A.D. 706/7 (cited by Brooks, loc. cit., on pp. 191 and 192); Theophanes, pp. 376–7, sub A.M. 6201; Nic. Patr., pp. 43–4. According to Theophanes in loc. cit. and to Balādhurī (*Kitāb Futūh al-Buldān*, English translation by P. K. Hitti, vol. i (New York, 1916, Columbia University Press), pp. 248–9, the Arab assault on Tyana was in revenge for the previous annihilation by the East Romans of a force led by Maïoumá (in Arabic, Maymūn). According to this account, Maymūn was a partisan of the Arabs. Tabari, however, represents him as being a partisan of the East Romans (Brooks in loc. cit., p. 203). Perhaps he was a Mardaïte captain who changed sides (see Balādhurī, loc. cit.).

[5] Balādhurī in Hitti's translation, vol. i, p. 249.

[6] πολυανδρότατα: 'Mavríkios', *Stratēghikón* Part 11, chap. 5, p. 272 Scheffer; πολύανδρα, Part 11, chap. 4, p. 276 Mihăescu (cited already on p. 72, n. 2; reproduced in Leo VI, *Taktiká*, Dhiat. 18, § 100 (Migne, col. 969).

[7] 'Mavríkios', *Stratēghikón*, Part 11, chap. 5, p. 273 Scheffer, p. 278 Mihăescu, reproduced in Leo VI, *Taktiká*, Dhiat. 18, §§ 102–3 (Migne, col. 969).

[8] Ibid., pp. 272–3 Scheffer, p. 278 Mihăescu, reproduced in Leo VI, *Taktiká*, Dhiat. 18, §§ 102–3, col. 969.

the third place the Slavs were liberty-loving, factious, and insubordinate.[1] They split into a large number of small communities (in Greek, 'Sklavi-níai'), under chiefs who were quarrelsome and who could therefore be played off against each other.[2] Besides being ill organized, the Slavs were ill armed,[3] and therefore they were an easy prey.

The first bout of the Slav *Völkerwanderung* into East Roman territory— the invasions in the years 581/2–586/7—occurred at a time when the East Romans were preoccupied by the Romano–Persian War of 572–91. The second bout occurred after the Empire's temporary lapse into anarchy in the sequel to the overthrow and murder of the Emperor Maurice in 602. On both occasions, the Slav invaders were directed by the highly organized Eurasian Nomad Avars.[4] When the Avars lost control over the Balkan Peninsula as a result of their failure to take Constantinople in 626, the Slavs were at the East Romans' mercy whenever the Persians and their heirs the Arabs gave the Empire a breathing-space. The Sklaviníai were not under East Roman control, but they were not organized states;[5] and, if the Eurasian Nomad Bulgars had not won a foothold on the south bank of the lower Danube in 680, it seems probable that, before the close of the seventh century, all the Sklaviníai that had been established beyond that bank of the river would have been subjugated by the East Roman Government—though they might not all have been assimilated ethnically by the remnants of the local Latin-speaking and Greek-speaking population and the meagre reinforcements of Greek-speakers that the Imperial Government could scrape together.

After crossing the Danube and consequently, as Leo VI puts it,[6] 'being forced, more or less, to submit to servitude, [the Slavs] preferred to suffer detriment from rulers of their own race to submitting with a good grace to the Roman rule of law'. Leo VI adds that, down to his own day, even the converted Slavs still clung to their ancient tradition of liberty in so far as they were free agents. He does not, however, also add that the salient feature of Roman law for the East Roman Empire's subjects was its taxation-legislation, and that, in this department, the rules were

---

[1] 'Mavríkios', p. 272 Scheffer, p. 276 Mihǎescu, ἐλεύθερα, μηδαμῶς δουλοῦσθαι ἢ ἄρχεσθαι πειθόμενα; p. 275 Scheffer, p. 280 Mihǎescu, ἄναρχα καὶ μισάλληλα, reproduced in Leo VI, Dhiat. 18, § 99, cols. 968–9.

[2] 'Mavríkios', p. 281 Scheffer, p. 284 Mihǎescu.

[3] 'Mavríkios', p. 275 Scheffer, p. 280 Mihǎescu, reproduced in Leo VI, Dhiat. 18, §§ 106–7, cols. 969–72.

[4] The Avars had organization, the Slavs had numbers (P. Lemerle, 'Invasions et migrations dans les Balkans depuis la fin de l'époque romaine jusqu'au viiie siècle', in *Revue Historique*, vol. 211 (1954), pp. 265–308, on p. 293).

[5] See G. Ostrogorsky, 'The Byzantine Empire in the World of the Seventh Century', in *Dumbarton Oaks Papers*, Number Thirteen (1959), pp. 1–21, on pp. 4 and 6.

[6] In Dhiat. 18, § 99, cols. 968–9. Cf. § 79, cols. 964–5. Cf. also 'Mavríkios', Part 11, chap. 5, p. 272 Scheffer, p. 276 Mihǎescu.

traditionally transgressed by the taxation-officers for the benefit of the Treasury and of the officers' own private pockets.

The earliest piece of evidence for a deportation of Slavs from the Balkan Peninsula to Asia Minor may be a seal inscribed τῶν ἄνδρας δόντων [i.e. τῶν ἀνδραπόδων] τῶν Σκλαβόων τῆς Βιθύνων ἐπαρχίας. This seal is dated 'the eighth indiction', and this might be either the year 649/50 or the year 694/5. Since it is on record that 5,000 Slavs deserted from the East Romans to the Arabs as early as 664/5,[1] Charanis dates the seal 650, and this dates the first deportation of Slavs from the Balkan Peninsula to Asia Minor in the reign of Constans II (641–68).[2] It is, in fact, recorded that, in 657/8, Constans II subdued (ὑπέταξεν) the Sklavinías and took many prisoners.[3] The victorious expedition against the Strymonian Slavs by an unnamed Emperor may have been made in 679, in which case the Emperor will have been Constantine IV.[4] In 688/9, Justinian II marched through the Sklavinías as far westward as Thessaloníkê, took prisoners in his turn, and settled these in Bithynia.[5] A further settlement of 208,000 Slavs was planted in Bithynia (part, by then, of théma Opsíkion), on the River Artánas,[6] in 762, in the course of Constantine V's twenty years' war (755–75) with Bulgaria.[7] The Slav settlers in this batch were not prisoners of war from Sklavinías that had been subjugated, permanently or temporarily, by the East Romans. They were refugees from Sklavinías that had been subjugated by the Bulgars, and they had taken refuge in the East Roman Empire in order (we may guess) to escape being conscripted for military service in the Bulgarian army.

Our surviving record of Slav settlements in Asia Minor may not be complete, but we may assume that the Sthlavêsianoí (Σθαβησιανοί) in théma Opsíkion were descendants of these settlers, however many batches of them there may have been. We may also guess that the 3,000 slaves of the widow Dhanêlís whom the Emperor Leo VI liberated and settled in théma Laghouvardhía[8] were Peloponnesian Slavs, and that, in thus

---

[1] See p. 80.

[2] P. Charanis, 'The Slavic Element in Byzantine Asia Minor' in *Byzantion*, xviii (1948), pp. 69–83, on p. 70. The date 694/5 is preferred by H. Grégoire, 'Un Édit de l'empereur Justinien II daté de septembre 688', in *Byzantion*, xvii (1944–5), pp. 119–24a, on p. 123. The year 694/5 is also preferred by Lemerle, 'Invasions', p. 307.

[3] Theophanes, p. 347, sub A.M. 6149. Lemerle notes in loc. cit., p. 300, that this is the first occasion on which Theophanes uses the word 'Sklaviníai'.

[4] For the date of this expedition, which is reported in *S. D. Miracula*, Book II, chap. 4, see Lemerle, 'La Composition et la chronologie', p. 359.

[5] Theophanes, p. 364, sub A.M. 6180, and pp. 365–6, sub A.M. 6184; Nic. Patr., pp. 36–7; see also Rambaud, op. cit., pp. 218 and 249–50.

[6] The River Artánas flows into the Black Sea between the River Sangários and the Bosphorus.

[7] Theophanes, p. 432, sub A.M. 6254; Nic. Patr., pp. 68–9.

[8] Constantine Porphyrogenitus, Biography of Basil I, in *Theoph. Cont.*, Book V, chap. 77, p. 321.

disposing of this part of the widow's bequest to him, Leo was concerned, not only to strengthen the Empire's hold on a recently re-acquired piece of territory, but also to reduce, by 3,000, the Slav element in the population of the Pelopónnêsos.

Some, at least, of the communities of settlers in Asia Minor were autonomous in the sense that their captains were under the direct authority of the Emperor, and were not subordinate to the provincial, or to the subsequent thematic, authorities. The administrative conflicts that could arise from this arrangement are illustrated by the story[1] of a clash between the captain of the Mardaïtes of Attáleia and a deputy governor of théma Kivyrrhaiótai. The direct responsibility of the captain of the Mardaïtes to the Emperor was upheld. The Sthlavêsianoí in théma Opsíkion were autonomous likewise.[2] Even prisoners of war who were enrolled in the East Roman armed forces served under officers of their own.[3] This local autonomy did not, of course, carry with it any exemption from the ubiquitous activities of the Imperial taxation-officers. Tax was assessed and levied on all land that was utilized.

The East Roman Imperial Government had to limit its ambitions to more modest objectives in the European territories to the west of Adrianople that had once been, or that still remained, under East Roman rule. 'Asia Minor was the basis and foundation of medieval Byzantium.'[4] Possessions west of Adrianople were not indispensable for the Empire's survival. The Imperial Government's first objective here was to link up, by a continuous belt of territory under its own control, the isolated enclaves that it still held in the Balkan Peninsula on the far side of Adrianople. The Government's second objective was to re-Graecize as much as it could of this belt of territory when it had been consolidated.[5] The first of these objectives was the less difficult of the two to attain.

Constans II had attacked the Sklavinías,[6] and, during the Pervoúnd affair, an unnamed Emperor had sent a successful punitive expedition against the Strymonian Slavs.[7] On Justinian II's return march from Thessaloníkê to Constantinople in 688/9, however, his army, which had won easy victories over the local Slavs, was attacked, and was severely handled, by the Bulgars in a pass.[8] Considering that it was only nine years since the Bulgars had made their permanent lodgement to the south of the Danube, this feat of theirs was ominous for the East Roman Empire.

[1] In *De Adm. Imp.*, chap. 50, pp. 228–31.
[2] *De Caer.*, Book II, chap. 44, pp. 662, 666, 669. For this Sklavisía, see also *Theoph. Cont.*, p. 379.
[3] *De Caer.*, Book II, chap. 45, p. 667.
[4] Ostrogorsky in *Dumbarton Oaks Papers*, Number Thirteen, p. 1. Cf. p. 20.
[5] See Haussig, *A History of Byzantine Civilization*, p. 209.
[6] Theophanes, p. 347, sub A.M. 6149, cited already on p. 90, n. 3.
[7] *S. D. Miracula*, Book II, chap. 4, col. 1357. See p. 90, with n. 4.
[8] Theophanes, p. 364, sub A.M. 6180.

The first East Roman army since the Empire's temporary collapse in 602 that succeeded in marching right through from Constantinople to the Pelopónnêsos was probably the Patrician Stavrákios's in 783,[1] and, from that time on, this route was usually under the East Roman Government's command more or less, except at some moments during the Romano–Bulgarian wars of 807–13, 894–6, 913–27, and 976–1018. Stavrákios entered the Pelopónnêsos and took prisoners and loot in the Sklavinías there, but he is not recorded to have subjugated these Sklavinías permanently. He did, however, annex to the Empire all the Sklavinías as far to the south-west as théma Ellás. From 783 onwards the Empire held a continuous belt of territory along the north and west coasts of the Aegean; and this belt was eventually prolonged, along the north shore of the Corinthian Gulf and the east shore of the Ionian Sea and the Adriatic, to about as far north as the Adriatic end of the present Albanian–Jugoslav frontier, in order to reopen a through-route to Nikópolis and Dhyrrákion;[2] but the belt was narrow along the greater part of its length, and, at one point in the immediate hinterland of Thessaloníkê, which was the most vulnerable sector of all, the belt was only 21 kilometres wide after the year 904.[3] Nevertheless, the overland route seems normally to have been open after 904 as well as before that date.

It has been mentioned already[4] that, after Basil I had made himself sole Emperor in 867, the widow Dhanêlís travelled overland from Pátras to Constantinople and back.

She came up to the capital with a big escort (δορυφορίας) and a host of attendants (ὑπηρεσίας). She was [physically] incapable of doing the journey by carriage or on horseback, and perhaps she had also been spoilt by her boundless wealth; so she sat herself in a chair, and had herself carried to Constantinople by three hundred of her slaves whom she had picked out for their youth and their physical strength. The litter was borne by teams of ten at a time, who relieved each other in shifts and so brought Dhanêlís all the way from the Pelopónnêsos to the capital.[5]

On her outward journey, Dhanêlís was carrying with her gifts of great value for the Emperor. On her return to Pátras, she dispatched a consignment of valuable carpets to Constantinople for Basil I's 'New Church' in the grounds of the Imperial Palace. After Basil's death and Leo VI's accession in 886, Dhanêlís travelled once again from Pátras to Constantinople and back in the same style as in 867.

---

[1] Theophanes, pp. 456–7, sub A.M. 6275.
[2] See D. M. Metcalf: 'The New Bronze Coinage of Theophilus and the Growth of the Balkan Themes', in *American Numismatic Society Museum Notes* x (1961), p. 95.
[3] See p. 106. [4] In II, 1 (ii), pp. 51–2.
[5] Constantine Porphyrogenitus's biography of Basil I in *Theoph. Cont.*, Book V, p. 317.

There is no record of any attempt having been made to plunder any of these three valuable caravans en route. We must conclude either that the total military forces of the six thémata through which Dhanêlís's three successive convoys passed were mobilized, on each occasion, to guard the Imperial highway, or else that the Slavs were less enterprising than their predecessors the Thracians had been. In 188 B.C., when the Roman robber proconsul Vulso was bringing his army back by this route to Italy, laden with Asiatic loot, the Thracians had swooped down on the road like kites and had relieved Vulso and his men of a substantial part of their ill-gotten gains. If those dare-devil Thracian brigands, who had not been in awe of Roman arms, had been still extant in Dhanêlís's day, they would have made short work of the old lady and her valuable freight.

Perhaps Dhanêlís was lucky in her dates. Both her journeys, as well as her consignment of carpets after her first journey, were made after the final pacification of the Pelopónnêsos *circa* A.D. 842 and before the outbreak, in A.D. 894, of the first of the wars between the East Roman Empire and Khan Symeon of Bulgaria. The Romano–Bulgarian wars of A.D. 894–6 and A.D. 913–27 may well have shaken the East Roman Government's hold over the Slav tribes under East Roman sovereignty that bestrode parts of the overland route between Pátras and Constantinople. A Palestinian prisoner of war, Hārūn b. Yahyā, who was conveyed from Attáleia to Constantinople and who managed eventually to travel on to Rome via Thessaloníkê at about the turn of the ninth and tenth centuries[1]—that is to say, probably during the interval between these two wars—has recorded[2] that the journey to Thessaloníkê from Constantinople took him twelve days, and that his route lay through a continuous plain, on which there was cultivated land, with villages. However, when, in A.D. 927, Liutprand's father was travelling along this route in the opposite direction on a mission from Hugh of Provence to Rhomanós Lekapênós, his party had to beat off an attack by dissident Slavs on the outskirts of Thessaloníkê. They captured two of their Slav assailants, brought them along with them, and handed them over to Rhomanós at Constantinople. According to Liutprand, Rhomanós professed gratitude;[3] but he cannot really have been pleased at being presented with this material evidence of his government's inability to police the most important of all the roads in his European dominions. As for the branch of this road that led, not to Pátras in théma Pelopónnêsos, but to Náfpaktos in théma Nikópolis, Liutprand, on his way home from his

---

[1] For the date, see Vasiliev, *Byzance et les Arabes*, ii, II, pp. 380–2.
[2] Ibid., p. 394. Hārūn's account of the East Roman Empire has been transmitted by Ibn Rustah.
[3] *Antapodosis*, Book III, chap. 24.

second mission to Constantinople, travelled over this section safely between 2 October and 20 November 968.[1]

There were three enclaves of territory along the north and west shores of the Aegean on which the East Roman Empire had never lost its hold. The nearest to the main body of the Empire was the city of Thessaloníkê, which was never captured by the Slavs or the Avars or the Bulgars and never by any other enemy until 904, when it fell to a fleet of Saracen corsairs and was held by these captors for a few days. The second enclave was Ellás, i.e. east central Greece, the districts formerly known as eastern Thessaly, Boeotia, and Attica,[2] together with the Island of Évvoia (Euboea). The third was the eastern side of the Pelopónnêsos, except for a part of southern Laconia in which two Slav tribes, the Mêlingoí and the Ezerítai, had established themselves. The East Roman Government's second objective, after regaining its hold on a continuous belt of territory from the west bank of the River Maríca to the Pelopónnêsos, was to close the gaps between these three enclaves by recolonizing them, as far as possible, with East Roman settlers or, as a second best alternative, by Graecizing the subjugated Slav population.

In pursuing this objective, the Empire was confronted with the limitations of its reservoir of man-power. In the execution of its policy of re-peopling its dominions, its first priority was Asia Minor and Thrace. Its second priority was Constantinople. After the depopulation of the capital by the plague of 746–7, Constantine V re-peopled it by bringing whole families (συμφαμίλους) from the Islands and Ellás and 'the lower regions' (τῶν κατωτικῶν μερῶν),[3] which might mean the territory still held by the Empire in the Pelopónnêsos.[4] The colonization of the gaps to the west and south-west of Adrianople was the lowest priority; but Nikêphóros I (802–11) made a determined effort to provide for this too. Between September 809 and Easter 810, 'he conscripted Christian colonists from all the thémata for the Sklavinías, and he imposed forced sales of the conscript-colonists' real estate'.[5] This measure was arbitrary and harsh;

---

[1] *Legatio*, chap. 57.

[2] In the *Völkerwanderung* of the twelfth century B.C., Attica had staved off the invaders but Boeotia had been overrun by them.

[3] Theophanes, p. 429, sub A.M. 6247. It is surprising that Constantine V should have drawn on these parts of the Empire for re-peopling Constantinople; for on pp. 422–3, sub A.M. 6238, Theophanes records that the plague had spread to Constantinople from Sicily and Calabria via 'Monemvasía and Ellás and the adjacent islands'.

[4] See P. Charanis, 'Hellas in the Greek Sources of the Sixth, Seventh, and Eighth Centuries', in *Late Classical and Mediaeval Studies in Honor of Albert Mathias Friend, Jr.* (Princeton, 1955, University Press), pp. 161–76, on p. 172. Cf. Bury, *A History of the Later Roman Empire from Arcadius to Irene (395 A.D.–800 A.D.)* (London, 1889, Macmillan, 2 vols.) vol. ii, p. 350, n. 8. Theophanes's 'the lower regions' on his p. 429 would then correspond to his 'Monemvasía' on his p. 422.

[5] Theophanes, p. 486, sub A.M. 6302 (cf. Kedhrênós, vol. ii, p. 37). In this passage, Theophanes alleges that Nikêphóros's purpose was 'to humiliate the troops in every way' (τὰ

and, though Theophanes's record of it is an item in a vehement indictment of Nikêphóros, it is credible that this Emperor's forcible transfer of population did cause great hardship and did arouse proportionately strong resentment. In the panic that followed Nikêphóros's disastrous defeat and death at the hands of the Bulgars in 811, 'Ankhíalos, Vérrhoia, Níkaia, Provátou Kástron, and other fortresses, as well as Philippoúpolis and Phílippoi, were abandoned by their Christian inhabitants. These did not wait to be evicted. The settlers in the Strymón district, too, seized the excuse for decamping and returning to their original homes'.[1]

The *Chronicle of Monemvasía*[2] gives details of Nikêphóros I's reinforcement of the non-Slav element in the population of the Pelo-pónnêsos. According to the Chronicle, the Avars (*sic*) had held all of the Peloponnêsos except its eastern side, from Corinth to Cape Maléa inclusive, without being subject to the East Roman Emperor or to anyone else, till A.M. 6313 (A.D. 804/5) or till the fourth year of Nikêphóros I's reign (A.D. 805/6).[3] The Imperial governor of the eastern Peloponnêsos then made war on the Slav (*sic*) nation (τῷ Σθλαβινῷ ἔθνει) [in the Peloponnêsos], conquered it and completely annihilated it (ἠφάνησε εἰς τέλος),[4] and thus opened the way for the repatriation of the original inhabitants.[5] When the

στρατεύματα πάντῃ ταπεινῶσαι σκεψάμενος). This allegation tells us that the compulsory colonists were thematic soldiers (see Lemerle in loc. cit., p. 29, n. 40), but we need not believe the allegation itself. It seems more likely that Nikêphóros's motive was to reinforce the western army-corps. The districts in which these corps were domiciled had just become exposed to a threat of invasion and conquest by the Bulgars, because Khan Krum had gained possession of the barrier-fortress Sardica and had rased its fortifications, and, though Nikêphóros had re-occupied the city, his troops had refused to rebuild the city-walls. A reinforcement of the western army-corps was therefore now the only alternative means of safeguarding the Empire's possessions in the Balkan Peninsula; and to provide for this is more likely to have been the Emperor's motive than mere spite. The troops' insubordination at Sardica had left the Empire's hinterland, to the west of Rhodhópê, exposed. The probable motive for the compulsory colonization was a concern for military security. Theophanes has his knife into Nikêphóros, and he puts the worst possible construction on all his acts. It is also probable that Theophanes does not tell us the whole truth. He makes much of the forced sales of the colonists' real estate in the Asiatic thémata, but Lemerle guesses convincingly, in loc. cit., p. 29, n. 40, that Nikêphóros compensated the colonists by endowing them with estates in their new domiciles in Europe.

[1] Theophanes, p. 496, sub A.M. 6304.
[2] The text cited in this work is that of the MS. in the Ivêron Monastery on Mount Athos (Athous 4449; Ivêron 329), as printed by P. Lemerle in 'La Chronique improprement dite de Monemvasie: le contexte historique et légendaire', in *Revue des Études Byzantines*, vol. xxi (1963), pp. 5–49, on pp. 8–11. This is the best MS. in Lemerle's judgement (ibid., p. 8).
[3] The Chronicle erroneously equates A.M. 6313 with Nikêphóros I's fourth year. We do not know whether the author was reckoning by years of the World or by the regnal years of Emperors, so we cannot tell whether the year that he intended to designate as the terminal year of the Peloponnesian Sklavinías' independence was 804/5 or 805/6.
[4] The sequel shows that this is untrue.
[5] According to the Chronicle (Ivêron MS., lines 39–44), at the time when the barbarian invaders of the Peloptónnesos had evicted and replaced the original inhabitants everywhere except along the east coast, the population of Pátras had emigrated (*en masse*, apparently) to Reggio di Calabria. The Lákones had taken refuge, some at Monemvasía on the east coast of

aforementioned Emperor Nikêphóros heard this news, he was delighted, and he made plans for rehabilitating the Peloponnesian cities, for rebuilding the churches, and for converting the barbarians themselves to Christianity.[1] So, when he had ascertained where the people of Pátras were living in exile, he gave orders for them to be repatriated, on the original site of their city, with their bishop (the name of the bishop then in office was Athanásios). At the same time he gave the see of Pátras metropolitan status (formerly it had been only an archbishopric). He also rebuilt the city of Pátras from the foundations, and its churches. This was during the patriarchate of Tarásios, now deceased.[2] Nikêphóros also re-created the city of Lakedhaímon from the foundations and settled in it a mixed population—Káfêroi[3] and Thrakêsioi[4] and Arménioi[5] and others who had been collected from different places and cities.[6] The Emperor decreed that [the episcopal see of] Lakedhaímon should be subject to the metropolitan see of Pátras, and he also consecrated to Pátras two other sees as well, namely those of Methónê and Korónê. So, by God's help and grace, the barbarians were instructed and baptized and converted to Christianity.[7]

The Chronicle can be believed[8] when it states that some of the Peloponnesian Greeks had fled overseas to parts of the East Roman Empire that were still relatively secure, and that others had ensconced themselves, in the Pelopónnêsos itself, in the natural fastness provided for them by Kynouría. We can also believe that the descendants of the Peloponnesian refugees overseas did return when, in the sequel to Stavrákios's military expedition in 783, the East Roman Government's authority in the Pelopónnêsos was re-established effectively in the reign of Nikêphóros I (802–11)—in either 804/5 or 805/6. There have been other instances in which the descendants of exiles have returned to their ancestral homes as soon as an opportunity has presented itself. The Adrianopolitans who were deported beyond the lower Danube in 813 returned after having been in exile for possibly as long as quarter of a century; the half-caste descendants of the East Romans who were deported to Sirmia—probably in the ninth decade of the sixth century—

the Pelopónnêsos and some overseas at Dheménna in north-eastern Sicily. The Argives had found asylum on Oróvê (? Levinthos) Island and the Corinthians on Aíyina. See the present chapter, p. 75, with n. 9.

[1] This is convincing, since it is in line with the subsequent policy of Basil I as described by Leo VI (see p. 98).

[2] Tarásios died in 806.

[3] Καφήρους looks like a transliteration of the Arabic word 'kāfir', which means 'non-Muslim'. Possibly these Κάφηροι may have been Syrian Christian ex-subjects of the Caliphate who had become refugees or evacuees.   [4] i.e. inhabitants of théma Thrakêsioi.

[5] Either inhabitants of théma Armeniakoí or actual Armenians.

[6] E. P. Kyriakídhês, Οἱ Σλάβοι ἐν Πελοποννήσῳ (Thessaloníkê 1947, No. VI in the Βυζαντιναί Μελέται series), points out, on p. 49, that this notice of the rebuilding and re-peopling of Lakedhaímon is found in the Ivêron MS. only. However, this is no reason for doubting its accuracy.

[7] Ivêron MS., lines 60–75.   [8] See Lemerle in loc. cit., pp. 33 and 37–8.

are said to have returned after more than sixty years. The successive batches of Messenian refugees from Spartan oppression waited still longer for the liberation of their country that followed the Spartan disaster at Leuktra in 371 B.C. Some of the descendants of the Jews who were evicted from Palestine by the Romans in A.D. 135 have been returning to Palestine in our own day.

We do not know what other regions, besides the Strymón district and Laconia, Nikêphóros I attempted to colonize, nor how many of his reluctant colonists settled down permanently in the European districts in which he had planted them; but we may guess that colonization played a lesser role than assimilation in the re-Graecizing of the Pelopónnêsos and other, more northerly, parts of Greece in which the former Greek population had been supplanted by Slav intruders.

Greek culture, in all its successive metamorphoses, has proved attractive, and it soon began to attract the Slavs who had settled in those parts of the Balkan Peninsula in which their predecessors had been Greeks and in which some enclaves of Greek population had survived the Slav *Völkerwanderung*. For instance, by the eighth decade of the seventh century at the latest,[1] Pervoúnd (*Περβοῦνδος*), the kinglet of a Slav tribe called the Rhýnkhinoi (*Ρυγχίνων*),[2] was living in Thessaloníkê, wearing Greek dress and speaking Greek.[3] No doubt his tribesmen, out in the countryside,

---

[1] The dating depends on whether the 25 July of the fifth indiction, in which Thessaloníkê was assaulted by some of the neighbouring Slav peoples (*S. D. Miracula*, Book II, chap. 4), was that day of this month in 662 or in 677. (See Lemerle, 'Composition et chronologie', pp. 357 and 358–9; eundem, 'Invasions et migrations', p. 302; cf. H. Grégoire, 'L'Origine et le nom des Croates et des Serbes', in *Byzantion*, xvii (1944–5), pp. 88–118, on p. 107, n. 19). If 25 July 677 is the true date of the first day of the Slavs' three days' assault on Thessaloníkê, the arrest, deportation, and eventual execution of Pervoúnd may have been prompted by a suspicion that Pervoúnd might be secretly collaborating with the Arabs who were besieging Constantinople from 674 to 678. The length of the Slavs' siege of Thessaloníkê on this occasion, and the wide range of their maritime raids (they penetrated the Propontis, apparently with impunity), would be explained by the Imperial Government's preoccupation with the Arabs' siege of Constantinople. The dispatch of an Imperial expeditionary force from Constantinople overland to the Strymón district, the defeat of the Strymonian Slavs, and the dispatch of ample food-supplies to Thessaloníkê from Constantinople by sea would have followed immediately upon the conclusion, in 678, of peace between the Empire and the Caliphate. See Lemerle's convincing reconstruction of the chronology in 'Composition et chronologie', p. 359.

[2] Their habitat, Rhýnkinos (*Ρυγχίνου*), perhaps lay somewhere to the west of the lower course of the River Strymón (Struma, alias *Ρήχιος*). See Vasmer, op. cit., p. 177.

[3] The seventh-century-A.D. Slav kinglet Pervoúnd had a fifth-century-B.C. predecessor in Skylês, king of the Skythians along the north shore of the Black Sea. Skylês had a Greek mother from the Greek colonial city-state Istros, and, with his kingdom, he inherited a colonial Greek wife who was his father's widow (his father had married more Greek wives than one). Skylês could not bear the Skythian way of life, so, when his own people's annual trek on the steppe brought them to the gates of the Greek colonial city Borysthenes (alias Olbia), at the mouth of the (southern) River Bug, Skylês used to leave his tribesmen outside the gates, enter the city himself, change into Greek dress, and pass the time of day there in the agora, staying in Olbia for a month or more in the year. Skylês did this annually, and he built a

were still speaking Slavonic and were also still leading their barbarian way of life. Yet there was already a pacific *modus vivendi* between the Thessalonians and their Slav neighbours. When the unfortunate Pervoúnd was accused by the Praetorian Prefect of Eastern Illyricum of plotting treason, and when, in consequence, this kinglet was arrested in Thessaloníkê and was sent in chains to Constantinople on written instructions from the Emperor, the local Slav tribes sent envoys to the Emperor in agreement with the Thessalonians,[1] before taking up arms against the Imperial Government and eventually assaulting the city of Thessaloníkê itself. Even after the local Slavs had engaged in hostilities against the East Roman Government and had made their unsuccessful assault on Thessaloníkê, they revealed their abiding friendliness towards the Thessalonians. They sent them a secret message that it would now be safe for them to venture out into the countryside and to gather in their harvest, because they (the Slavs) were evacuating the Thessalonian territory that they had overrun.[2]

Some two centuries after Pervoúnd's generation, the spontaneous self-Graecization of some, at least, of the descendants of the Slav settlers in the Balkan Peninsula was followed up by the Emperor Basil I (867–86). Basil I's son and successor Leo VI records, in one of the rare original passages in his *Taktiká*,[3] that his father

persuaded the Slav tribes to give up their traditional manners and customs. He 'Graecized' them ($\gamma\rho\alpha\iota\kappa\omega\sigma\alpha\varsigma$), put them under rulers in the (East) Roman style, and did them the honour of having them baptized. Thus he liberated them from their servitude to their own rulers and trained them to perform military service against the (East) Romans' enemies. Basil took great pains over the implementation of this policy, and its success relieved the (East) Romans of the anxiety that they had suffered previously from the Slavs' constant insubordination ($\dot\alpha\nu\tau\alpha\rho\sigma\iota\alpha\varsigma$). In the past, the Romans had had to endure frequent disturbances and hostilities at the Slavs' hands.

No doubt we do not have a complete record of the Slav revolts against East Roman rule after Stavrákios's expedition in 783,[4] but we do have a notice of a coup that was attempted in 799 by the chieftain of a Sklavinía

house for himself in Olbia and married a local Greek wife. He took strict precautions to prevent his tribesmen from discovering his goings-on in Olbia, but he was betrayed thoughtlessly by one of his adopted fellow-citizens, and his tribesmen deposed him, hounded him down, and put him to death (Herodotus, Book IV, chaps. 78–80). We do not know what the Emperor Constantine IV did to Pervoúnd.

[1] *S. D. Miracula*, Book II, chap. 4, col. 1351 (Latin summary); Lemerle, 'Composition', p. 357; 'Invasions', pp. 301–2.

[2] *S. D. Miracula*, Book II, chap. 4, col. 1357.

[3] Dhiat. 18, § 101, col. 969.

[4] See p. 92.

named Velzêtía (Βελζητία).¹ We also have from Constantine Porphyrogenitus² an account of a general revolt of the Peloponnesian Slavs in the reign of Nikêphóros I (802–11). This revolt—which must have been made between either 804/5 or 805/6 and 811—culminated in an unsuccessful siege of Pátras; and Constantine Porphyrogenitus mentions that the Slav insurgents had the help of African Muslims in this. A Muslim fleet is known, from independent evidence, to have been cruising in East Roman waters in the year 807,³ and this date for the revolt and the siege would fit in with the date—804/5 or 805/6—which is given in the *Chronicle of Monemvasía* for the re-establishment of the East Roman Government's effective authority over the Pelopónnêsos and for the consequent return of the descendants of the Greek refugees from the Pelopónnêsos—the people of Pátras among them—to their ancestral homes.⁴ Indeed, the reassertion of the East Roman Government's authority, followed by the repatriation of the refugee Peloponnesian Greek communities, might have been the events that provoked the Peloponnesian Slavs' insurrection. However, Constantine gives his readers no inkling that the city of Pátras had been refounded, perhaps less than two years before the date of the siege, to receive the repatriated descendants of its original Greek inhabitants, and we should not have guessed this if Constantine's narrative had not been supplemented, on this point, by the *Chronicle of Monemvasía*.⁵

¹ Theophanes, pp. 473–4, sub A.M. 6291. Theophanes's notice implies that Velzêtía was in touch with théma Ellás. The Elladhikoí had prompted the chieftain of Velzêtía to try to liberate the sons of Constantine V, and these had been interned at Athens (Zonarás, vol. iii, p. 300 Bonn). If this Velzêtía is identical with Veleyezêtía (Βελεγεζητία) (see Vasmer, op. cit., pp. 85–6), it must have lain somewhere near the north-eastern end of théma Ellás, i.e. somewhere in Eastern Thessaly, since the Veleyezêtai are one of the five Slav peoples mentioned by name in *Sancti Demetrii Miracula*, Book II, chap. 1, col. 1325, as having taken part, with others, in the second of the sieges of Thessaloníkê (the first of those in the time of Archbishop John) that the authors of the book describe. Another of the five tribes named in this context, the Dhraghouvítai (Δραγουβῖται), are known to have settled in the neighbourhood of Vérrhoia in Southern Macedonia (Vasmer, op. cit., p. 177). During the siege of Thessaloníkê by the local Slavs that followed the arrest and deportation of Pervoúnd, the Thessalonians sent ships to (Phthiotic) Thebes and Dhêmêtriás to obtain food-supplies from the Veleyezêtai (*S. D. Miracula*, II, 4, col. 1351 (Latin summary)). If Velzêtía was within striking distance of Athens, and if the Veleyezêtai lived in the hinterland of the Gulf of Vólos, this Slav people's name may survive in the name of the modern town Velestíno (Βελεστῖνο), on the site of the Hellenic city Pherai.

² *De Adm. Imp.*, chap. 49, pp. 217–20 (Bonn).

³ R. J. H. Jenkins in his and Gy. Moravcsik's edition of *De Adm. Imp.*, vol. ii (*Commentary*), p. 183.

⁴ See pp. 75–6 and 95–6.

⁵ Though the statements made by Constantine Porphyrogenitus and by the author of the *Chronicle of Monemvasía* do not merely harmonize with each other but positively support each other, Jenkins is well advised in counselling us, in loc. cit., to treat both these authorities with some reserve. Constantine derived his information from a source which, like *Sancti Demetrii Miracula*, was concerned primarily, not to inform would-be historians, but to glorify a saint. The patron saint of Pátras was the Apostle St. Andrew, and, in glorifying him, the

Constantine records a second general revolt of the Peloponnesian Slavs 'in the days of the Emperor Theóphilos and his son Michael [III]', i.e. within the two years—841–2—of their joint reign.[1] The Slav insurgents succeeded, for the moment, in shaking off East Roman rule, and a strong expeditionary force had to be sent against them.[2] Contingents were provided not only by thémata Thrákê and Makedhonía but by all the rest of the Western[3] thémata, and the command of this force was given to a protospathários, Theóktistos Vryénnios.[4] On this occasion, all the Peloponnesian Slavs except the Mêlingoí and the Ezerítai appear to have been reduced, once again, to the status of ordinary taxpaying subjects of the Empire that had been imposed on them originally perhaps in 804/5 or 805/6 or perhaps in 807 after the suppression of their revolt,[5] and the Mêlingoí and Ezerítai too were now compelled, for the first time, to recognize the East Roman Government's suzerainty by paying tribute. Theóktistos settled with these two tribes for annual payments at moderate rates—60 nomísmata for the Mêlingoí and 300 for the Ezerítai. In view of the natural strength of the fastnesses in which they had established themselves, he prudently refrained from attempting to subdue them, too, by force.[6]

The Emperor Leo VI issued a siyíllion (khrysóvoullon) defining in detail the obligations of the Peloponnesian Slavs who had been under servitudes to the see of Pátras since 807, and forbidding the bishop of Pátras to subject them to any arbitrary additional afflictions or exactions.[7]

episcopal see of Pátras was vindicating the Emperor Nikêphóros I's alleged elevation of the see of Pátras to metropolitan status at the expense of the see of Corinth. On the other hand, Kyriakídhês's extreme scepticism about the veracity of the *Chronicle of Monemvasía* is partly inspired by a motive that is not disinterested. Kyriakídhês's non-historical motive is not ecclesiastical ambition; it is Greek nationalism.

[1] For this convincing interpretation of Constantine's words, see Jenkins in loc. cit., p. 185.
[2] Probably in 842, immediately after Theóphilos's death (Jenkins, ibid.).
[3] *Sic*, though thémata Thrákê and Makedhonía ranked, not as 'Western', but as 'Eastern'.
[4] *De Adm. Imp.*, chap. 50, pp. 220–1.
[5] See Jenkins, ibid., following A. Zakynthinós, *Οἱ Σλάβοι ἐν Ἑλλάδι* (Athens, 1945), p. 49, with nn. 2 and 3. *De Adm. Imp.*, chap. 49, p. 219, reads as if the taxes imposed, perhaps in 807, on the Peloponnesian Slavs (except for the Mêlingoí and Ezerítai) were made payable, not to the civil government of théma Pelopónnêsos, but to the see of Pátras. These Slavs were also subjected to the additional servitude of providing free board and lodging for all official travellers, both East Roman and foreign, who passed through Pátras (*De Adm. Imp.*, chap. 49, p. 220).   [6] *De Adm. Imp.*, chap. 50, p. 221.
[7] *De Adm. Imp.*, chap. 49, p. 220. Kyriakídhês in op. cit., Epiphýlaxis III, *Συνοδικὸν Γράμμα τοῦ Πατριάρχου Νικολάου πρὸς τόν Ἀλέξιον τόν Α'*, pp. 22–32, on pp. 24–9, considers that Leo VI issued two separate khrysóvoulla, one (mentioned by Constantine Porphyrogenitus in loc. cit.) safeguarding the rights and interests of those Peloponnesian Slavs who were under servitudes to the see of Pátras, and a second endorsing the see of Pátras's claim that it had been given metropolitan status. According to Kyriakídhês, the two khrysóvoulla issued by Leo VI were re-enactments of the provisions of corresponding khrysóvoulla that were alleged to have been issued by Nikêphóros I, but texts of these alleged original documents were not forthcoming, and Leo VI's reconstructions of these were based on oral

Presumably this was one of the measures taken by Leo VI for reconciling his European Slav subjects to the East Roman regime as a first step toward Graecizing them. However, the Mêlingoí and Ezerítai, at any rate, continued to be recalcitrant,[1] and in Rhomanós I Lekapênós's reign, probably in the year 921,[2] a newly appointed stratêghós of théma Pelopónnêsos, Krinítês Arotrás, subdued the Mêlingoí and Ezerítai by military force and increased the amount of the tribute payable by each of the two tribes. But this successful punitive action was almost immediately followed by internal dissensions among the officials of théma Pelopónnêsos after a new stratêghós had taken office; the Pelopónnêsos was then invaded by the Bulgars;[3] and the Emperor Rhomanós, fearing that the Mêlingoí and Ezerítai might join forces with the invaders, granted a petition to him from the two tribes that their tribute should be reduced again to the amounts originally imposed by Theóktistos Vryénnios.[4] When the Franks occupied the Pelopónnêsos after sacking Constantinople in 1204, they found the Mêlingoí and Ezerítai still autonomous. In 1412–15 the Greek traveller Láskaris Kananós found the Zyghiótai (i.e. the inhabitants of Mount Taÿgetos) still speaking Slavonic, and he recognized the affinity of their language with that of the Sthlavounía round Lübeck.[5]

These two tribes, who had penetrated the farthest south of all in the sixth-century and seventh-century Slav *Völkerwanderung*, were assimilated eventually. When I myself was walking about in southern Laconia in 1912, there were still Slavonic place-names there, but the Slavonic language had long since become extinct there. The Peloponnesian Slavs, however, were a small advance-guard that had been insulated politically

tradition (i.e. on assertions made by the representatives of the see of Pátras who were in office at the date when Leo VI took action). Kyriakídhês points out that the subjugated barbarian settlers in the Pelopónnêsos are called Σκλαβηνοί in his Document I, but he holds that they were called Avars in his hypothetical Document No. II; he infers that at least one of the two documents must have been a forgery, and maintains that the document which names the Avars cannot have been genuine. This argument is fine-drawn; it is rejected by Lemerle (in loc. cit., p. 46, n. 71); and Kyriakídhês's Greek nationalist motive makes it suspect. Kyriakídhês asserts that there was no independent record of the date at which the see of Pátras was raised to metropolitan status. Charanis, 'On the Question of the Slavonic Settlements in Greece', p. 256, points out that, actually, Nikêphóros I's khrysóvoullon is mentioned not only by Constantine Porphyrogenitus, *De Adm. Imp.*, chap. 49, p. 220, but also by the *Chronicle of Monemvasía* and the scholion of Aréthas.

[1] *De Adm. Imp.*, chap. 50, pp. 221–2.

[2] For the date, see Jenkins in loc. cit., p. 186; eundem in *Late Classical and Mediaeval Studies in Honor of A. M. Friend Jr.* (Princeton, 1955, University Press), pp. 204–11.

[3] In *De Adm. Imp.*, chap. 50, p. 223, the invaders are called Σκλαβησιανοί. Jenkins points out (*Commentary*, pp. 186–7) that these Sklavêsianoí are the Danubian Bulgars, who by this date had been Slavized. They are not the Sthlasvesianoí, mentioned in *De Caer.*, Book II, chap. 44, pp. 662, 666, 669, and in *Theoph. Cont.*, p. 369, who were East Roman subjects domiciled in théma Opsíkion (see p. 91).

[4] *De Adm. Imp.*, chap. 50, pp. 221–4.   [5] Vasmer, op. cit., p. 18.

since 805 from the main body of their kinsmen in the northern hinterland of Greece. How far northward into the interior of the Balkan Peninsula did Graecization, spontaneous or induced, extend? It is significant that, at some date earlier than the tenth century, detachments of Mardaïtes had been settled in théma Nikópolis, and perhaps in théma Dhyrrhákion too.[1] Moreover, at a date that is not on record,[2] Turkish-speaking converts to Eastern Orthodox Christianity had been settled in the valley of the River Vardar (Axios)[3] and another batch

---

[1] See p. 87.

[2] Rambaud in op. cit., p. 214, and F. C. H. L. Pouqueville, *Voyage en Grèce* (Paris, 1820–1, Didot, 5 vols.), in vol. ii, p. 416, n. 1 (on pp. 416–18) state that these settlements of Turks were planted by the Emperor Theóphilos (829–42). They identify the Vardariot Turks with Theóphovos-Nasr's Babekite Persian refugee followers (see the present chapter, pp. 83–4), whom the Emperor Theóphilos did take into his service and eventually distributed among a number of thémata. This identification had been made already in a note by J. Gretser and P. J. Goar on Codinus, *De Officiis*, which will be found on p. 267 of Bekker's edition (Bonn, 1839, Weber), but there is no warrant for it. The thémata among which Theóphovos-Nasr's followers were distributed are not specified in our sources, and the Vardariots were not Persian-speaking; they were Turkish-speaking, as Pouqueville found by first-hand acquaintance with their descendants. 'Ces . . . Guèbres, qui avaient pour évêque le prélat de Poliana (aujourd'hui Cogliana, ville ruinée voisine de Cara-Verria), suffragant de Thessalonique (*Oriens Christianus*), parlaient le turc tartare, puisque j'ai vu des fragments des évangiles traduits dans cette langue pour leur usage lorsqu'ils étaient Chrétiens?' (Pouqueville, vol. ii, n. 1 from p. 416, on p. 418). The modern scholars have been misled by Codinus's statements that the Vardariots wear a Persian headdress called ἀγγουρωτόν (Bonn edition of *De Officiis*, p. 38); that τούτους πάλαι Πέρσας κατὰ γένος ὄντας ὁ βασιλεὺς μετοικίσας ἐκεῖθεν εἰς τὸν Βαρδάριον ἐκάθισε ποταμόν (ibid.); and that the Vardariot contingent of guardsmen at the East Roman Court wish the Emperor 'many years' (πολυχρονίζουσιν) κατὰ τὴν πάλαι πάτριον . . . φωνήν, ἤτοι Περσιστί. By 'Persian', Codinus means 'Turkish'. This misapplication of the word 'Persian' is frequent in pedantic Byzantine Greek literary works. This is because the word 'Persian' occurs in Classical Hellenic Greek literature, whereas the word 'Turk' does not.

It seems probable that the Turks were planted in the Vardar valley and in the Okhrida region by the Emperor Nikêphóros I when, between the years 809 and 811, he was competing with Khan Krum of Bulgaria for the acquisition of the Sklavinías in the hitherto independent no man's land to the south-west of the East Roman Empire's former barrier-fortresses Philippópolis and Sárdica (see the present chapter, pp. 94–5 and 105–6). The objective will have been to hold, for the Empire, the line of the former Via Egnatia, in the section of it that linked Thessaloníkê with Dhyrrhákhion. After Nikêphóros's defeat and death in 811, the East Roman Government would hardly have had the power to plant settlers so far to the north and to the west as this.

[3] Pouqueville found descendants of the Vardariot Turks living, not in the Vardar valley, but in the upper basin of the Vistríca (Aliákmon). At Lepchista (Lapšista), which is 19 miles to the SSE. of Kastoriá, he found a community of Vardariot converts to Islam who told him that they had established themselves there in the fourteenth century (Pouqueville, op. cit., vol. ii, p. 337). We may guess that they had been converted and been transplanted from the Vardar valley in or soon after 1371–2, the date of the Ottoman Turkish occupation of Macedonia (i.e. of the former Hellenic Kingdom and subsequent Roman province; the East Roman théma mis-called 'Makedhonía' had been occupied by the 'Osmanlis in 1366). The 'Osmanlis colonized, in force, the plain to the west of the lower Vardar, and, to make room there for themselves, they may have displaced the previous Vardariot Turkish inhabitants. On the road from Lapšista to Kastoriá, at the approaches to Kastoriá, Pouqueville found two villages, Toûri and Coustourachi, whose population was a mixed one of Christians and Vardariot converts to Islam (vol. ii, p. 344). At Bogatzico, which is 11½ miles SSE. of Kastoriá and 7½ miles NNW. of Lapšista, Pouqueville, *en route* from Kastoriá to Šatista,

of them in the neighbourhood of Lake Okhrida,[1] and the Christian Scriptures were translated into Turkish for their benefit.[2] This suggests that Nikêphóros I had not found Greek-speaking colonists—or, at least, not many permanent colonists—for the more northerly Sklavinías,[3] and indeed the pre-1922 ethnic map of the Balkan Peninsula more or less faithfully revealed the northern geographical limits of the effectiveness of Basil I's policy of Graecization. The exodus of the Greek diaspora from Asia Minor and Thrace in 1922, which was confirmed and completed by the subsequent Graeco–Turkish, Graeco–Bulgarian, and Bulgaro–Turkish treaties for the exchange of populations, achieved, at long last, most of the colonizing work that Nikêphóros I had attempted to carry out. Today the whole of northern Greece, right up to Greece's present northern and eastern frontiers, is inhabited by Greeks, with the exception of Western Thrace, where the Graeco–Turkish Convention of 30 January 1923 provided that the existing Turkish population should be left undisturbed.[4] However, until 1922, Thessaloníkê, together with the Chalcidic Peninsula, was still, as in King Pervoúnd's day, an isolated enclave of non-Slav territory[5] surrounded by a Slavonic-speaking population on all sides, and the boundary between the areas in which the local population was predominantly Greek-speaking and in which it was predominantly Slavonic-speaking coincided approximately still in 1922 with the watershed

found a community of Vardariots who were still Christians (vol. ii, pp. 417–18). The distances and locations given in this footnote are taken from *A Handbook of Macedonia and Surrounding Territories*, compiled [during the First World War] by the Geographical Section of the Naval Intelligence Division, Naval Staff, Admiralty (London, no date, H.M. Stationery Office), pp. 206–7.

For the Vardariot Turks, see also G. Finlay, *A History of Greece, B.C. 146 to A.D. 1864*, edited by H. F. Tozer (Oxford, 1877, Clarendon Press), vol. iii, p. 77, addition by Tozer to n. 2; vol. iv, p. 27; K. Dieterich: *Byzantinische Quellen zu Länder- und Völkerkunde (5.–15. Jhd.)* (Leipzig, 1912, Wigand), Zweiter Teil, note on pp. 144–5.

[1] A contingent τῶν περὶ τὴν Ἀχριδὼ οἰκούντων Τούρκων served in the Emperor Aléxios I's army in 1081 (Anna Comnena, *Alexias*, IV, 4 (Reifferscheid's ed., vol. i, p. 138)).

[2] See Pouqueville, op. cit., p. 418, cited already on p. 102, n. 2. Rambaud, op. cit., p. 215, n. 1, cites, from the Emperor Leo VI's *Ýpotýposis*, the title of a bishop ὁ Βαρδαριωτῶν ἤτοι Τούρκων. Presumably this is the episcopal see mentioned by Pouqueville in loc. cit. The Vardariot Turks were placed under the ecclesiastical jurisdiction of the Archbishop of Okhrida by the Emperor Basil II in a siyíllion promulgated at some date later than May 1020 (Dölger, *Regesten*, I. Teil, p. 104).

[3] The evidence of Slavonic place-names shows that, in Épeiros, Slavonic continued to be spoken long enough for the language to undergo changes (Vasmer, op. cit., pp. 318–19).

[4] See V. M. Boulter in *Survey of International Affairs, 1925*, vol. ii (London, 1928, Oxford University Press), p. 257.

[5] The Chalcidic Peninsula, except for its easternmost prong, which culminates in Mount Athos and was μιξοβάρβαρος in Thucydides' day, has been Greek-speaking continuously, ever since its colonization by southern Greeks in and after the seventh century B.C. Thessaloníkê, too, is a Greek-speaking city again today; but in 1912, when I paid my first visit to it, the predominant language in the city was Castilian, and the majority of the population was Jewish. These Castilian-speaking Jews were descendants of Jews who had been expelled from Spain and had been given asylum in the Ottoman Empire.

between the upper part of the basin of the River Vistríca (Aliákmon) and the basin of the Črna tributary of the River Vardar.

It is instructive to read our notices of the plantations of Turks in Macedonia, and Leo VI's account of Basil I's policy of Graecization, in the context of our information about Khan Borís of Bulgaria's ecclesiastical and cultural activities in the Okhrida region (its Slavonic name was Kutmitčevica), in which the East Roman Emperor Nikêphóros I, or one of his successors, had planted a settlement of Turks. Kutmitčevica was on or near the south-western frontier of Bulgaria in Khan Borís's reign (852–89). It was also the south-westernmost region in which the Slavonic language was then still holding its own (and it still holds it there today) against the resurgence, to the south and to the west of it, of the Greek and Albanian languages, whose bounds had been pushed back temporarily by the Slav *Völkerwanderung*.

When, after St. Methódhios's death in 885, the Slavophone missionary church that he and his brother Constantine-Cyril had founded in Moravia[1] had been destroyed and this church's clergy had been persecuted, Borís welcomed those of them who had managed to escape into Bulgaria, and, with their aid, he made the Eastern Orthodox Church in Bulgaria Slavophone and equipped it with a Slavonic version of the Eastern Orthodox liturgy, and also with Slavonic translations of works of Greek literature, not only ecclesiastical but secular.[2]

Borís installed his refugee Slavophone clergy at two points. One of these was naturally in the north-eastern corner of Danubian Bulgaria, in the region in which the Turkish-speaking Bulgar founders of the state had gained their first foothold to the south of the river, and in which the first capital, Aboba-Pliska, and the second capital, Preslav,[3] lay. At the monastery of Titča,[4] near Preslav, the refugee St. Naum founded a school of Slavonic translators and copyists. The second point, however, on which Borís concentrated his efforts was Kutmitčevica, in the extreme opposite quarter of his dominions. Here Borís posted the refugee St. Clement; and, when, in 893, Khan Symeon (893–927) made Clement bishop of Velika (?)[5], near Okhrida, Naum was sent to reinforce Clement in Kut-

---

[1] See iv, 1, pp. 515–18.

[2] See F. Dvornik; *Les Slaves, Byzance, et Rome au ixe siècle* (Paris, 1926, Champion), pp. 298–9 and 311–312; eundem, *The Slavs: Their Early History and Civilization* (Boston, 1956, American Academy of Arts and Sciences), pp. 121 and 177–83; G. Sergheraert (C. Gérard), *Syméon le Grand* (Paris, 1968, Maisonneuve), pp. 53 and 99–111; S. Runciman, *A History of the First Bulgarian Empire* (London, 1930, Bell), pp. 124–6 and 135–41; D. Obolensky in *C. Med. H.*, vol. iv, 2nd ed., Part I, pp. 501–2; G. C. Soulis, 'The Legacy of Cyril and Methodius to the Southern Slavs', in *Dumbarton Oaks Papers*, Number Nineteen, pp. 19–43; Vlasto, A. P., *The Entry of the Slavs into Christendom* (Cambridge, 1970, University Press), pp. 164–6.

[3] The capital was moved to Preslav by Khan Symeon (Runciman, op. cit., p. 136, n. 4).

[4] See G. Sergheraert, op. cit., p. 53; Vlasto, op. cit., p. 166.   [5] Vlasto, p. 169.

mitčevica, where he was made bishop of Devol.[1] Clement is said to have educated 3,500 pupils in the course of the seven years 888 to 893.[2] He is also said to have worked for the economic development of Kutmitčevica —for instance, by importing fruit-trees from Constantinople.[3] In Kutmitčevica the Slavophone church clung to the Glagolitic alphabet, which was the original one that had been invented by Constantine-Cyril for conveying the Macedonian Slavonic dialect. The Glagolitic alphabet departed farther from the Greek alphabet[4] than the so-called Cyrillic, which was invented, perhaps in 892, and in any case after Constantine-Cyril's death, in the Preslav school.[5]

These facts, taken together, suggest that Khan Borís and his second son and second successor Khan Symeon were consciously competing with their East Roman contemporaries for the linguistic and cultural and ecclesiastical, as well as political, allegiance of the Sklavinías in the interior of the Balkan Peninsula. We may guess that the competition had been initiated on the Bulgarian side, and that it had started in Khan Krum's and the Emperor Nikêphóros I's reigns. The final partition, in 805, of the Avars' domain between Charlemagne's empire and Bulgaria had brought to Bulgaria large territorial gains to the north of the Danube, and the consequent increase in Bulgaria's strength may have been the consideration that moved Khan Krum to take the offensive, two years later, in the opposite quarter, against the East Roman Empire. Nikêphóros's defeat and death in 811 in the Romano–Bulgarian war of 807–13 had two consequences which, between them, inclined the scales in Bulgaria's favour. In the first place, Nikêphóros's disaster brought with it, as has been noted already,[6] a grave set-back for his colonization scheme in Europe. In the second place, this scheme itself seems to have been prompted, at least in part, by a previous loss in the war of 807–13.

Until 809 the East Roman Empire had succeeded in holding the fortress of Sardica (the present-day Sofia), the half-way house on the old Roman road running north-westward from Constantinople to Sirmium. So long as Sardica remained in East Roman hands, the Bulgars were debarred from expanding beyond their foothold, south of the lower Danube, from which Constantine V had failed to dislodge them. In 809[7] Khan Krum captured Sardica; Nikêphóros quickly retook it, but he was

---

[1] See F. Dvornik, *Les Slaves, Byzance, et Rome*, pp. 313–15; eundem, *The Slavs*, p. 177; Sergheraert, op. cit., pp. 59–60; Runciman, op. cit., pp. 127–8; D. Obolensky in *C. Med. H.*, vol. iv, 2nd ed., Part I, p. 502; Soulis in loc. cit., pp. 23–4 and 27–8; Vlasto, op. cit., pp. 166 and 168–9.

[2] Sergheraert, op. cit., p. 53; Vlasto, op. cit., p. 168.   [3] Sergheraert, ibid.

[4] See Dvornik, *Les Slaves, Byzance, et Rome*, pp. 162–4.

[5] See Soulis in loc. cit., pp. 27 and 29–31; Vlasto, op. cit., pp. 38–44 and 174–5.

[6] See p. 95.

[7] For this date, see Obolensky, op. cit., p. 490. The fall of Sardica is recorded by Theophanes on p. 485, sub A.M. 6301.

prevented from reconditioning it by a mutiny in his army;[1] so, though the town had been regained for the moment, the fortress had been lost permanently, and thus the barrier to Bulgaria's expansion had been removed. The peace treaty of 817[2] re-established the territorial *status quo ante bellum*,[3] but since Adrianople (weakened by Krum's deportation) was now, in reality, the farthest outpost of the East Roman Empire towards the north-west,[4] Bulgaria could, and did, turn the Empire's flank during the ensuing period of peace. Bulgaria now expanded, in competition with the Empire, into those of the Sklavinías that neither of the two rival powers had previously succeeded in appropriating.[5] At some date between 864, the year in which Bulgaria was converted to Christianity, and 889, the year in which Khan Borís abdicated, one, at least, of Nikêphóros I's surviving colonies—New Tiverioúpolis (near Strumica), which had been peopled with citizens of Tiverioúpolis in Bithynia—came to be on the Bulgarian side of the frontier.[6]

When Thessaloníkê lay at Bulgaria's mercy after the city had been taken and sacked by a squadron of Saracen corsairs in 904, the Emperor Leo VI had to ransom Thessaloníkê by making cessions of territory all along the line. Two of the boundary stones, dated A.M. 6412 (A.D. 903/4) and bearing a Greek inscription on which Symeon is named,[7] have been found at the village of Naranch or Naresh, on the River Ghallikó, only twenty-two kilometres inland to the north-north-west of Thessaloníkê itself.[8] The territory ceded on this occasion appears to have included Kastoriá, in the upper basin of the River Vistríca (Aliákmon), and a

[1] Theophanes's account of this affair does not explain the reasons for the East Roman army's refusal to do the work of refortifying Sardica. All that is clear is that Theophanes, or his source, was bitterly hostile to Nikêphóros I.

[2] *Theoph. Cont.*, p. 31; Genesius, p. 41. A fragment of the Bulgarian copy of the Greek text of the treaty of 817 has been preserved (see V. Beševliev: *Die protobulgarischen Inschriften* (Berlin, 1963, Akademie-Verlag), No. 41, on pp. 190–206 of the text). For the date, see Beševliev, pp. 204–6.

[3] As had been proposed by Khan Krum in 812 (Theophanes, p. 497, sub A.M. 6305 (812)). The *status quo ante* had been established in the peace treaty of 717.

[4] In the panic after Nikêphóros I's disaster in 811, Ankhíalos, Vérrhoia (i.e. Stara Zagora), Níkaia, Provátou Kástron, Philippoúpolis, Phílippoi, and théma Strymón, had been abandoned by their inhabitants (Theophanes, p. 496, sub A.M. 6304, cited on p. 95).

[5] This expansion of Bulgaria south-westwards is dated between 831 and 842 by Obolensky in *C. Med. H.*, vol. iv, 2nd ed., Part I, p. 498, with n. 1. Ostrogorsky, however, holds that it was gradual ('The Byzantine Background of the Moravian Mission', in *Dumbarton Oaks Papers*, Number Nineteen (1965), pp. 1–18, on pp. 8–11).

[6] See Runciman, op. cit., pp. 128–9.

[7] Ὅρος Ῥωμαίων καὶ Βουλγάρων ἐπὶ Συμεὼν ἐκ Θεοῦ ἄρχοντος Βουλγάρων, ἐπὶ Θεοδώρου ολγου τρακανου, ἐπὶ Δριστρου κομίτου.

[8] See Sergheraert, op. cit., pp. 87–8; Runciman, op. cit., p. 152, n. 3; Vlasto, op. cit., p. 172; Beševliev, *Die protobulgarischen Inschriften*, pp. 215–19. One of these two stones, on which the inscription was almost effaced, has been lost. Symeon was prompt in staking out his territorial claims. A.M. 6412, the year in which the legible inscription at Naranch is dated, ended on 31 August 904. The Muslims' three-days' siege of Thessaloníkê had started on 29 July 904 (John Kameniátês, on p. 519 of the Bonn edition of *Theo h. Cont.*).

corridor to a port on the Adriatic which cut théma Dyrrhákhion's overland line of communcations with théma Nikópolis and the rest of the
Empire's European dominions.[1] In most of the ceded territory, the population was probably still Slavonic-speaking, but in the Kastoriá district it
may have already been re-Graecized, since it was Greek-speaking in
1922, as it continues to be today. At the western end of Bulgaria's newly
acquired corridor to the Adriatic, the population must have been
Albanian-speaking.

(b) *The Effect of Muslim Raids on Rural Life in East Roman Asia Minor*

The resettlement and the economic redevelopment of East Roman Asia
Minor were achieved in spite of incessant Muslim raids, not only overland but also by sea round the peninsula's southern and western coasts.
The first Muslim raid into the Romans' country is dated 640/1 by Ibn
al-Athīr.[2] Presumably Ibn al-Athīr means by 'the Romans' country' that
part of the former dominions of the East Roman Empire in which the
majority of the local population were Chalcedonian Christians (in their
own parlance 'Orthodox', but, in their pre-Chalcedonian Christian
subjects' parlance, 'Melchites', i.e. 'Imperialists'), as distinguished from
Syria, Egypt, Mesopotamia, Roman Armenia, and the Roman slice of
Persarmenia, whose peoples were predominantly pre-Chalcedonian
('Monophysite') Christians.

The Arabs' conquest of the non-Orthodox territories of the East Roman
Empire had been as amazingly swift as their contemporary conquest of
the Persian Empire had been. Within the decade 634–44, spanned by the
brief reigns[3] of the second and third Caliphs, 'Umar and 'Uthmān, the

---

[1] Sergheraert, ibid., says that the ceded port was Khimárra. This seems improbable,
considering that Khimárra is cut off from its hinterland by the Acroceraunian Range.
Kánina, on the east shore of the Gulf of Avlóna, is the port shown as being Bulgarian in
Spruner–Menke: *Hand-Atlas für die Geschichte des Mittelalters und der neueren Zeit*, 3rd ed.
(Gotha, 1880, Perthes), Maps 79, 80, 84. Kánina is on the list of places assigned to the
Archdiocese of Okhrida (Ákhridha) in Basil II's siyíllion (promulgated at some date earlier
than May 1020) that sets out the original extent of this archbishopric's domain (Dölger,
Regesten, I. Teil, pp. 103–4). Khimárra was one of the additions granted to the Okhrida
Archdiocese in Basil II's siyíllion of May 1020 (ibid., p. 104). However, in this siyíllion of
20 May 1020, Basil II states that the additions, granted in this instrument, have been made
in response to a request from the Archdiocese of Okhrida that its ecclesiastical domain,
hitherto coextensive with the former political domain of Tsar Samuel, should be enlarged
to include the rest of the territory that was once politically subject to Tsar Peter (927–69).
This implies that Khimárra, as well as Kánina, had been included in Tsar Peter's dominions
and therefore probably already in Khan Symeon's. See G. Schlumberger: *L'Épopée byzantine
à la fin du dixième siècle*, seconde partie (Paris, 1900, Hachette), pp. 124–7.

[2] E. W. Brooks, 'The Arabs in Asia Minor (641–750) from Arabic Sources', in *J.H.S.*,
vol. xviii (1898), pp. 182–208, on p. 183.

[3] 'Chairmanships' (in the sense in which the title was being given in 1972 to 'Chairman
Mao') would be a more apt word than 'reigns' for describing the early Caliphs' regime.
Theophanes's Greek word for 'Caliph' is πρωτοσύμβουλος, which means 'President of the
Council'.

East Roman Empire's frontier had been cut back as far north-westward as the Amanos Range; the Arabs now held both Antioch and Alexandretta.[1] Moreover, the frontier did not come to rest finally at this line. The Armenians, ex-Roman and ex-Persian subjects collectively, came to terms with the Arab viceroy of Syria, Muʿāwīyah, in 653.[2] On the south-western sector of the front, the East Roman Empire's frontier was cut back still farther, from the line of the Amanos to the line of the Távros Range, after the Mardaïtes' successful counter-offensive against the Arabs had been called off by the Emperor Justinian in 689/90.[3] As early as 672/3, the Arabs had already taken Tarsós, which occupied a strategic position at the west end of the plain of eastern Cilicia and at the southern approaches to the 'Cilician Gates', the principal pass through the Távros Range.[4] By 705/6 or 706/7, the Arabs were through the Cilician Gates at Tyana.[5]

After this, the frontier between the East Roman Empire and the Caliphate remained stationary for more than two centuries. It was not till 926 that this frontier became unstable again, and from that date onwards, for the next 120 years, it moved back eastwards in the East Roman Empire's favour. The stable frontier of the eighth and ninth centuries and the first quarter of the tenth century was a 'natural' one, provided by the Távros and Andítavros Ranges, by the right (west) bank of the more northerly of the two headwaters of the River Euphrates, from just above their confluence to Kamakha, and from there by the serried ranges of mountains, running approximately parallel to the south-east shore of the Black Sea, that bound the Euphrates basin on this side. During those two centuries and a quarter, some of the key forts and fortresses along the frontier—for instance Kamakha,[6] Adhatá (Hadath), Loúlon (Lu'lu'a), Tyana—repeatedly changed hands, but the consequent variations in the *tracé* of the frontier were very slight.

Along this natural rampart there were no more than three principal passes giving access to East Roman Asia Minor from the regions over which the Arab Caliphate had now expanded. The first was the Cilician Gates, from whose north-western exit at Lu'lu'a a main road 431 miles long, according to Ibn Khurdādbih,[7] led to the Asiatic suburbs of

---

[1] Balādhurī, *Kitāb Futūh al-Buldān* (P. K. Hitti's translation, vol. i (New York, 1916, Columbia University Press), p. 253, cited by Brooks, loc. cit., pp. 203–4.

[2] Laurent, op. cit., p. 33. See also the present work pp. 85, 395, 398, 678.   [3] See pp. 87–8.

[4] See p. 58 of the present work. The date is given by Yaʿqūbī, cited by Brooks in loc. cit., p. 187. Presumably Tarsós was captured by naval operations, since the Cilician plain to the east of Tarsós was not occupied by the Arabs till 703/4.   [5] See the present work, p. 88.

[6] For the vicissitudes in the history of Kamakha during this period, see Vasiliev, *Byzance et les Arabes*, vol. iii, *Die Ostgrenze des byzantinischen Reiches von 363 bis 1070*, by E. Honigmann (Brussels, 1935, Institut de Philologie et d'Histoire Orientales), pp. 56–7.

[7] For the details of Ibn Khurdādbih's itinerary, see Le Strange, op. cit., pp. 134–5. Ibn Khurdādbih reckons the distance to Lu'lu'a from Tarsós to be 32 miles.

Constantinople. The second led from Adhatá (Hadath)—a fort lying to the east-north-east of Yermaníkeia (Mar'ash)—through the Andítavros to the Cappadocian Kaisáreia. The third led fromMelitênê (Malatīyah), near the right bank of the united Euphrates, not far below the confluence of its two headwaters, across the Andítavros to Kaisáreia and to Sevásteia (Sivas) in the upper valley of the Qyzyl Irmāq.[1]

Considering the strength and the almost unbroken continuity of this natural rampart of East Roman Asia Minor, it might have been expected that the East Roman Army, which had now been concentrated in Asia Minor, would have sought to plug the three gaps (all of which were 'strait and narrow'), and so to keep Asia Minor immune from Arab raids. Actually, this strategy is discountenanced in the three surviving East Roman manuals of instructions[2] for the conduct of war during the period when the frontier was stationary. Possibly the East Roman military authorities had taken to heart the Mardaïtes' disastrous experience in 705/6 or 706/7, when they had tried and failed to plug the Cilician Gates. For whatever reason, the standing instructions were to avoid pitched battles with an invading enemy force if this force was numerically equal or superior to the East Roman defending force.[3] The East Roman commander was warned, further, that it was dangerous to engage an enemy invader who had penetrated far into the interior of the Empire, since, if the enemy was cornered in this situation, he was likely to fight with the courage of desperation (εἰς ἀπόνοιαν τρέπεται).[4] An

---

[1] A fuller list of possible alternative exits from East Roman territory for enemy invaders is given in Περὶ Παραδρομῆς Πολέμου, chap. 23, p. 250: (i) The Kleisoúrai in théma Seléfkeia, i.e. the Kalykadnós valley route; (ii) those of théma Anatolikoí, where the Távros Range forms the dividing line between Cilicia and [thémata] Kappadhokía and Lykandós (the principal pass on this section of the frontier was the Cilician Gates); (iii) the Kleisoúrai adjoining Yermaníkeia and Adhatá; (iv) Kaêsoún (between Yermaníkeia and Samósata); (v) Dhaouthá (south of Malatīyah); (vi) Malatīyah (Melitênê) and ta Kaloúdhia (Klavdhiás), both on the Tokhma Su, ta Kaloúdhia being downstream from Malatīyah; (vii) to the east of the Euphrates, the Kleisoúra at Rhomanópolis, a short way below the headwaters of the Tigris, on the frontier between the Armenian district of Khanzit, which had been annexed to the East Roman Empire, and the adjoining territory to the south-east that was still in Muslim hands.

[2] The Emperor Leo VI's *Taktiká*; Περὶ Παραδρομῆς Πολέμου (written *circa* 976 by an officer of the late Emperor Nikêphóros II Phokás's who had served his apprenticeship under Nikêphóros's father Várdhas Phokás); the 'Anonymus Vári' (of about the same date as the *Π. Π. Π.*).

[3] Leo VI, *Taktiká*, Dhiátaxis 17, Περὶ Ἐφόδων Ἀδοκήτων, § 76, col. 932 (Migne). Leo's precept is endorsed by Nikêphóros II Phokás in his Στρατηγικὴ Ἔκθεσις καὶ Σύνταξις, ed. by J. Kulakovskij in *Mémoires de l'Académie Impériale des Sciences de St.-Pétersbourg*, viiie série, Classe Historico-Philologique, vol. viii, no. 9 (1908), pp. 17–18. The experienced and warlike Nikêphóros II, like the academic and unsoldierly Leo VI, has taken over this precept from 'Mavríkios's' *Stratêghikón*, Part 7, chap. 4, p. 139 Scheffer, p. 168 Mihăescu; Part 8, chap. 2, pp. 183, 186, and 197 Scheffer, pp. 204, 208, 218 Mihăescu; and Part 10, chap. 2, p. 241 Scheffer, p. 252 Mihăescu.

[4] Leo VI, *Taktiká*, Dhiat. 17, § 78, col. 933. In 863 a major battle, deep in the interior, had been fought by Petronás with brilliant results. The Amîr of Malatīyah's invading force

invasion should be countered, not by fighting pitched battles, but by laying ambushes (ἐγκρύμματα), by practising tricks (ἐπιτηδεύσεις), and by the procedure that is called nowadays 'scorched earth'.[1] 'If you feel that you must engage the enemy, wait to do it till he is on his way back from his looting, or till he is actually making his exit. At that stage he is distracted by his concern for salvaging his loot, and he is tired—especially by the time when he is approaching his own country.'[2]

The author of Περὶ Παραδρομῆς Πολέμου gives the same advice as the Emperor Leo VI, with the proviso[3] that, at the time of writing (which seems likely to have been after the death of the Emperor John Dzimiskĕs), the traditional tactics are no longer applicable on the Empire's eastern front, since the Muslims' power has now been weakened and their offensives have been repulsed. Nevertheless, he too still advises that it pays better not to go out to meet (προσυπαντᾶν) the enemy when they are preparing to make a raid into Rhomanía. Wait to pounce on them till they are returning from our country to theirs. By that stage they will be tired; they will be encumbered with loot, prisoners, and cattle; and they will be eager to get home. If we drag out the operations, this gives time for the (East) Roman forces—not just those near the kleisoúrai, but the more distant forces as well—to concentrate.[4] If you attack at this stage, you can count in advance on being victorious.[5] Till this auspicious moment arrives, the author advises the (East) Roman commander to confine his operations to 'dogging' or 'shadowing' (παραδραμεῖν) the enemy invader, and especially never to lose touch with him when he is on his retreat.[6] The title of this manual—Περὶ Παραδρομῆς Πολέμου—can be translated 'How to Make War by Dogging-Tactics'. The whole treatise is an expansion of Leo VI's instructions to lay ambushes and to practise tricks.

From the professional military point of view, this policy of refraining from fighting pitched battles except when the enemy was on his way home through the passes,[7] jaded and encumbered, seems to have been justified by its general success—though Petronás's bold and masterly

had been wiped out, and the Amīr himself had lost his life. But the cornered enemy force had, it is true, put up a desperate resistance.

[1] Leo VI, *Taktiká*, Dhiat. 17, § 76, col. 932. Cf. Dhiat. 18, § 40, col. 956. See also Dhiat. 12, §§ 130–3, col. 841.

[2] Op. cit., Dhiat. 17, § 77, cols. 932–3. Cf. Dhiat. 18, § 134, col. 977. In these passages, Leo VI is copying 'Mavríkios', Part 10, chap. 2, p. 241 Scheffer, p. 252 Mihăescu.

[3] In his preface, on p. 183 of the Bonn edition of Leo Diaconus.

[4] Ἐπισωρεύονται, which means, literally, 'accumulate'.

[5] Π.Π.Π., chap. 4: περὶ τοῦ ποιῆσαι λάθρα τὰς κατὰ τῶν ἐχθρῶν ἐπιθέσεις, καὶ περὶ τοῦ προσυπαντᾶν τοῖς πολεμίοις πρὸς τὴν ἰδίαν ὑποστρέφοντας, pp. 192–3.

[6] Ibid., p. 193.

[7]
> ῥύμαι γὰρ καὶ στενώματα ἀποκτείνουν ἀνδρείους·
> εἰς δὲ τοὺς κάμπους ἄνανδροι τολμητροὶ ἐκποιοῦνται.
> *Dhiyenĕs Akrítas*, lines 1552–3
> as numbered in Mavrogordato's edition.

breach of the rule in 863, when he engaged the rash Amīr of Malatīyah in the interior of Asia Minor, resulted in an East Roman victory[1] that proved to be the turning-point in the long-drawn-out series of Romano–Arab hostilities. However, the prescribed strategy of avoidance, dogging, and then pouncing at the last moment probably had a larger number of successes to its credit. The following three instances illustrate this strategy's efficacy.

In 778, when an invading Muslim army penetrated as far as Dhory-láïon,

the Emperor [Leo IV] ordered the commanders of the army-corps districts (τοῖς στρατηγοῖς) not to oppose the invaders by fighting pitched battles (δημόσιον πόλεμον), but to secure and garrison the forts (the Emperor posted a senior officer in every fort). The corps-commanders themselves were ordered to mobilize picked troops, three thousand strong per corps, to dog (παρ-ακολουθεῖν) the enemy in order to prevent him from dispersing his strength on forays, and to forestall the enemy's arrival by burning the pasture for his animals and any other provisions. After the enemy had been in occupation of Dhorylaïon for fifteen days, he ran short of supplies and his animals starved; the rate of mortality among these was high. The enemy turned back, invested Amórion on his way for one day, found that the place was strongly fortified and amply munitioned, and accordingly returned home without having achieved any results.[2]

Successful pounces were made on a Muslim force, on the last stage of its way home through the passes, in 878[3] at Podhandós (Bozanti),[4] at the north-western approaches to the Cilician Gates,[5] and in 950 at two successive passes on the route running southwards from Aravissós (Yarpūz) and Lykandós (Albistan) to Yermaníkeia, on the Muslim side of the frontier, at the northern end of the Great Rift Valley. In 878 the retreating enemy force was almost wiped out, and its commander was taken prisoner. In 950 the victim of the standard East Roman strategy was the redoubtable Hamdanid Amīr of Aleppo, Sayf-ad-Dawlah, the adventurous leader, during the years 936–58, of the last series of Muslim raids into East Roman territory.[6]

---

[1] See II, 6, 300.   [2] Theophanes, p. 452, sub A.M. 6271.

[3] This appears to be the correct date. See M. Canard in Vasiliev, *Byzance et les Arabes*, ii, I, pp. 82–4. The Greek authorities' date is 883. The Arabic authorities' date is 877/8.

[4] When I was travelling through the Cilician Gates by road on 11 November 1948, the patch of relatively open ground round Bozanti was covered by the encampments of Yuruk nomads, who were breaking here their annual trek from their summer pastures on the Anatolian plateau to their winter pastures on the East Cilician plain.

[5] Genesius, Book IV, pp. 114–15; Constantine Porphyrogenitus's biography of Basil I, in *Theoph. Cont.*, Book V, chap. 50, pp. 284–5. See also Vasiliev, *Byzance et les Arabes*, ii, I, pp. 82–4, and ii, II, p. 166, citing Sibt b. al-Jawzī.

[6] In the final engagement in the second of the two passes, Sayf-ad-Dawlah lost 5,000 men killed and 3,000 taken prisoner. He had to jettison all his loot, and he himself only just

Evidently the East Roman strategy of dogging and pouncing was militarily correct, but it was not a strategy of defence—not even of 'defence in depth'. It left at the invaders' mercy all civilians who did not live within the shelter of town walls,[1] and the unprotected civilians included the whole of the rural population that made the land productive by carrying on agriculture and animal husbandry.

It is true that, even by sea, and *a fortiori* overland, the Muslim raiders seldom reached the west coast of Asia Minor or the Asiatic shores of the narrow seas (Dardanelles, Sea of Marmara, and Bosphorus, known collectively in Arabic as the Khalīj, meaning 'the Channel').[2] The East Roman Navy kept its command of these waters until the conquest of Crete by Spanish Muslims in 826 or 827. Moreover, when the invaders did get as far as the west coast of Asia Minor, their expeditions ended disastrously more often than not. Though the central plateau of Asia Minor is rolling country, with only a few outcrops of mountains here and there, it was not yet so thoroughly deforested as it is today. For instance, Ibn Khurdādbih, in his description, written in 864, of the main road from the Cilician Gates to the Asiatic suburbs of Constantinople, notes the beginning of one forest twenty-three miles to the west of Êrákleia (Eregli) and another between Amórion and Dhoryláïon.[3] In these forests, as well as in the perilous defiles of the Távros and the Andítavros through which the Muslim invaders had to pass at both the beginning and the end of an expedition, Nature favoured the East Roman military authorities' strategy of 'dogging and pouncing', and this combination of impediments made long-distance expeditions hazardous.

Mu'āwīyah reached the Bosphorus as early as 652/3.[4] The Arabs besieged Constantinople by sea and land in 674–8 and again in 717–18. Hārūn-ar-Rashīd reached its Asiatic suburbs in 780/1 (Ya'qūbi) or 781/2 (Tabari).[5] In 798/9, Arab raiders reached Éphesos.[6] *Circa* 869–70 Khrysókheir, the leader of the Paulicians—a sect that had been driven into the Amīr of Malatīyah's arms by the East Roman Government's

---

managed to escape to Aleppo. See Vasiliev, ii, I, pp. 344–5, and, for details, citing the Arabic authorities, op. cit., vol. cit., Part II, pp. 95–6, 126–7, 181, and 242. The author of Περὶ Παραδρομῆς Πολέμου claims that three reverses were inflicted on Sayf-ad-Dawlah by these tactics, two of them in Constantine Porphyrogenitus's reign and one in Rhomanós II's reign, and that the same tactics had been used with the same success against the Tarsans (*Π.Π.Π.*, p. 191).

[1] The Arabs seldom captured East Roman towns (Ahrweiler, 'L'Asie Mineure et les invasions arabes', p. 10).

[2] Ahrweiler, ibid.

[3] Le Strange, op. cit., pp. 134–5.

[4] Brooks in *J.H.S.*, xviii (1898), pp. 182–208, on p. 184, citing Ibn al-Athīr and the Armenian historian Sebeos.

[5] Brooks in *The English Historical Review*, vol. xv (Oct. 1900), pp. 728–47, on pp. 737–8.

[6] Brooks, ibid., p. 740, citing Tabari.

persecution of them since 843—reached Níkaia and Nikomědeia and sacked Éphesos.[1] On this occasion, Khrysókheir came and went unscathed, as Mu'āwīyah, characteristically, had succeeded in doing in 652/3. But both the Arab sieges of Constantinople ended disastrously for the invaders. The island of Rhodes, which had been occupied by the Arab Navy as a half-way base of operations during the overture to the first Arab siege of Constantinople, was evacuated after this siege had failed.[2] Hārūn's arrival on the Asiatic shore of the Bosphorus forced the Empress Eirĕnê to agree to pay a heavy annual tribute for a three-years' truce, but Hārūn was not negotiating altogether from a position of strength. According to Tabari, he 'stipulated for guides and markets on his way [home], and that because he had come by a road that was difficult and dangerous for the Muslims'. According to the Monophysite (pre-Chalcedonian) Christian historian Michael Syrus, Hārūn found that he had caught himself in a trap, and asked for peace.[3]

It is significant that Hārūn subsequently concentrated on strengthening the Arab Empire's own defences.[4] On his return from the Bosphorus, he rebuilt Massīsah and the fort guarding the bridge at Adhanah. When he succeeded to the Caliphate (*fungebatur* 786–809), he organized a forward zone of defences, the Thughūr, and a rearward zone, the 'Awāsim, and built, or rebuilt, there a number of major fortresses and minor forts.[5] It is also significant that in 838, when, in reprisal for the Emperor Theóphilos's cruel treatment of Sozopetra (Zápetra, Zibatrah) in 837, the Caliph Mu'tasim had mounted his great expedition against Amórion, the principal East Roman fortress on the road from the Cilician Gates to the Bosphorus, and when he had duly succeeded in taking Amórion, he then advanced only one day's march beyond Amórion before withdrawing, and gave orders not only to rebuild Sozopetra but also to build four new forts in the neighbourhood.[6] Mu'tasim in 838 resisted the temptation to which in 863 the Amīr of Malatīyah succumbed with fatal consequences for his army and himself. The Amīr, intoxicated by a success of almost the magnitude of Mu'tasim's, insisted on advancing still farther, against the advice of his council of war, and so gave time for the East Roman forces to concentrate and converge upon him.

The East Roman Empire suffered more constant damage, which was cumulatively more serious, from seasonal short-range raids launched

---

[1] Vasiliev, ii, I, pp. 27–8; N. G. Garsoian, *The Paulician Heresy* (Paris, 1967, Mouton), p. 128.

[2] Brooks in *J.H.S.*, xviii, pp. 187 and 189. Tabari records the taking and garrisoning of Rhodes in both 672/3 (the year in which Ya'qūbī dates the taking of Tarsós) and in 673/4. Wākidī records it in 679/80 (probably the date of the evacuation, not of the occupation, of Rhodes according to Brooks, ibid., p. 189).

[3] Brooks in loc. cit., pp. 737–8, with p. 738, n. 85.

[4] M. Canard in *C. Med. H.*, vol. iv, 2nd ed., Part I, p. 708.

[5] Canard, ibid., pp. 706–7; Le Strange, op. cit., pp. 120–4 and 128–33; Honigmann in Vasiliev, op. cit., vol. iii, p. 42.   [6] Vasiliev, vol. i, pp. 170 and 173.

from permanent bases at Tarsós and at Malatīyah. This seasonal raiding was not brought to an end by the decline of the 'Abbasid Caliphate's power. This decline became manifest after the assassination of the Caliph Mutawakkil in 861; but the raiding was still kept going by the ability of the Caliph's local representatives or successors,[1] by the zeal and energy of the Tarsan and Melitenian Muslims themselves,[2] and by the continuing influx of temporary or permanent volunteers[3] from all parts of the Caliphate's disintegrating dominions. The rural population of the eastern half of East Roman Asia Minor was not finally or completely relieved of this perpetual scourge till the East Romans conquered and annexed Malatīyah in 934 and Tarsós in 965, and, in between these two red-letter dates in East Roman military history, the eastern thémata underwent a final bout of tribulations at the hands of Sayf-ad-Dawlah of Aleppo.

Considering that, from 649 to 678, and again from 826 or 827 to 961, the southern and western coasts of Asia Minor were continually being raided from the sea, and this right through the Dardanelles and into the Sea of Marmara, it will be seen that, even if we discount the damage done by the Arabs' occasional long-distance overland expeditions, few parts of Asia Minor except the north-west corner were immune from devastating enemy action.[4] An Arab fleet never made its way through the Bosphorus into the Black Sea,[5] but in 860 a Rhos fleet did make its way from the Black Sea through the Bosphorus, and only just failed to capture Constantinople in a surprise attack; and, for half a century before that, the zone in northern Asia Minor that was beyond the Arab overland-raiders' range may have been raided occasionally by Rhos pirates.

Ibn Hawkal claims to have seen Tarsós still serving as a base for seasonal raids into East Roman Asia Minor in 978. His description—which, in its vivid detail, bears the stamp of authenticity—must have been derived either from the oral evidence of surviving Muslim inhabitants or from some written source dating from before 965; for Tarsós had been taken in 965 by Nikêphóros II Phokás. According to Ibn Hawkal,

from all the great towns within the borders of Persia and Mesopotamia, and Arabia, Syria, Egypt, and Morocco, there is no city but has in Tarsós a hostelry (dār) for its townsmen, where the warriors for the Faith (ghāzī) from

---

[1] See Canard in *C. Med. H.*, vol. iv, 2nd ed., Part I, p. 712.

[2] In 877, a new governor, sent to Tarsós by the Caliph Mu'tamid, failed to pay and provision the Slav garrison of Lu'lu'a; the Tarsans raised a private subscription for the garrison; the governor embezzled the money; the garrison delivered the fortress to the East Romans; at Tarsós there were riots (Ibn Sa'īd (died in 1274 or 1286) in Vasiliev, vol. ii, Part II, pp. 200–1).

[3] These volunteers were equipped, not by their respective governments, but by their kinsfolk, especially by the women (Leo VI, *Taktiká*, Dhiat. 18, col. 976).

[4] Ahrweiler, 'L'Asie Mineure et les invasions arabes', p. 8.   [5] Ahrweiler, ibid.

each particular country live. And, when they have once reached Tarsós, they settle there and remain to serve in the garrison; among them prayer and worship are most diligently performed; from all hands, funds are sent to them, and they receive alms rich and plentiful; also there is hardly a sultan who does not send hither some auxiliary troops.[1]

In 756–9, Malaṭīyah had been rebuilt by the governor of Mesopotamia (al-Jazīrah) and had been equipped with large barracks for ghāzīs[2] of the kind seen at Tarsós by the eyewitness who was Ibn Hawkal's source of information.

Kudāmah, writing *circa* 932, but probably reproducing al-Garmī, who was taken prisoner by the East Romans in 845,[3] gives the calendar of the raiding seasons.[4] The winter-raid season ran from the end of February to the beginning of March, the spring-raid season from 10 May to 10 June; the summer-raid season from 10 July to 8 September. Of these three seasonal raids, the summer-season raid was the principal one according to the author of the Greek treatise on how to make war by dogging-tactics. He notes that big enemy forces used to build up in August; 'for, at that season, large masses used to assemble in Cilicia and in the regions of Antioch and Aleppo. They came from Egypt, Palestine, Phoenicia, and Coele Syria; they were joined by Arabs; and they made their sortie against the (East) Romans in September.'[5]

'There was a raid of some kind nearly every year.'[6] The frequency of these raids is brought out in Brooks's careful chronicle of them, as recorded by Arabic and Syriac writers, whose notices Brooks collates with the corresponding notices in Greek texts.[7] In the translations of excerpts from Arabic writers in the first volume[8] and in the second part of the second volume[9] of Vasiliev's *Byzance et les Arabes*, Brooks's record for the years A.D. 640/1–807/8 is carried down to 959, the year in which Constantine Porphyrogenitus died. The victims of the Muslim raids and of the East Roman Army's strategy for dealing with these were the country people in the East Roman war zone.

As soon as intelligence has been received that the raiders are on the move, the village communities (τῶν χωρίων), together with all their

---

[1] Ibn Hawkal, translated by Le Strange in op. cit., p. 132.
[2] Canard in *C. Med. H.*, vol. iv, 2nd ed., p. 704.   [3] Mas‘ūdi, *Tanbīh*, p. 190.
[4] Kudāmah, ed. De Goeje, p. 259, cited by Brooks, 'Byzantines and Arabs in the Time of the Early ‘Abbasids, I', in *The English Historical Review*, vol. xv (October, 1900), pp. 728–47, on p. 730.
[5] *Π.Π.Π.*, p. 196. The two other seasonal raids were carried out by the Cilician Muslims alone. The winter-raid was the most favourable occasion for attacking the raiders. There was a greater chance of being able to destroy them then than when they assembled in full force in large numbers (Leo VI, *Taktiká*, Dhiat. 18, § 126, col. 976).
[6] Brooks, ibid., p. 731.
[7] Brooks in *J.H.S.*, vol. xviii (1898), pp. 182–208, and in *The English Historical Review*, vol. xv (October, 1900), pp. 728–47, and vol. xvi (January, 1901), pp. 84–92.
[8] pp. 267–394.   [9] The whole of this part.

livestock, are to be chevied (φυγαδευομένων) by the eksplorátores into the forts (τοῖς κάστροις), or, where there are no forts, into mountains high enough to serve as natural fastnesses where the refugees cannot be got at.[1] Sometimes the enemy's sortie will be so sudden and so vigorous that the local corps-commander will not have had time to mobilize even his own corps; there will have been no possibility of any general concentration of the Imperial forces; and the local corps-commander will have only a handful of troops in hand. If he is informed that the population of the district for which the enemy is heading has not yet been evicted (ἐκσπη-λευθεῖσαν)—i.e. by the commander's own military police—and has not yet been chevied into the forts and the natural strongholds, the commander's local subordinates are to evict and chevy the inhabitants and their live-stock, as far as possible, before the enemy arrives.[2]

However, it may not be expedient that quite all the peasants should be salvaged; for, if the enemy captures some of them before he starts making forays (πρὸ τοῦ ἐξελάσαι), and if he learns from these prisoners that the (East Roman) corps-commander is in the neighbourhood, the enemy may not venture out and may make haste to get home without having gained anything by his exertions.[3] The enemy's cavalry will go ahead of his infantry because they will be keen to surprise and capture any villagers who have stayed at home.[4] The East Roman commander is to set a decoy consisting of 100 picked troops who are to keep an eye on villages in the vicinity of the enemy's route. When the enemy cavalry who have been detailed for foraging in the adjacent villages dismount and begin to ransack the peasants' houses, this is the ideal moment for the 100 picked troops to fall upon the enemy, kill or capture as many of them as they can, and then make a feigned flight, so as to lure the enemy along the road between two ambush-parties (ἐγκρύμματα) who will be lying in wait for the enemy on either flank.[5] Another effective way of using the 100 decoy-troops is to make them wait to attack the enemy cavalry till these have dismounted in order to round up the horses belonging to the villages[6] (so not all the peasants' livestock will have been evacuated).

For the combatants on both sides, raiding and dogging was an exciting game of hide-and-seek which gave play for the intellectual gifts of skill, cunning, resourcefulness, and judgement in arriving, in each situation, at the right compromise between caution and daring. For the East Roman peasantry, whose homeland was the war zone, this war game spelled misery. However, one of the objectives of the dogging-tactics was to save the peasants from being victimized by the enemy, in so far as this could be done without exposing the East Roman dogging force to unacceptable

---

[1] *Π.Π.Π.*, chap. 8, p. 197; chap. 22, p. 248; *Τὰ Βασιλικὰ Ταξείδια*, p. 447.
[2] *Π.Π.Π.*, chap. 12, p. 215.   [3] Chap. 6, p. 195.   [4] Chap. 10, p. 205.
[5] Chap. 10, pp. 206–7.   [6] Chap. 11, p. 214.

risks. The enemy can be deterred from making forays on the villages;[1] the villagers can be given time to take refuge in the natural fastnesses and in the forts;[2] captured peasants and their looted property can be retrieved.[3] More active steps have to be taken if, after the rural civilian population has been evacuated, the enemy insists on pursuing them into the fastnesses in which they have taken refuge. If the enemy sends infantry to comb these fastnesses, the East Roman commander must conduct the refugees to still more remote and still less accessible hiding-places, and in this extremity he must commit the whole of his own force to occupying and holding the tracks leading to the civilians' last refuge.[4]

However, the luckless East Roman civilians must sometimes have prayed to be saved from their military friends. In the Emperor Leo VI's *Taktiká*, there are some revealing passages on this subject. When on the march in East Roman territory, the commander is to order the troops to spare the country, and not to plunder it or devastate it.[5] Do not linger on home ground when once you have decided to invade enemy territory.[6] If possible, traverse uncultivated lands, even if this involves you in making a detour.[7] The commander must intervene personally to prevent his troops from damaging cultivated lands.[8] But *quis custodiet ipsos custodes?* Officers had been known to exact money from the villages. If they were convicted, the penalty was a fine of double the amount that they had exacted.[9] In East Roman territory, arrange for the troops to be able to purchase what they need by providing markets and traders.[10] Look after these traders. Do not let the troops ill-treat them. If the traders are aggrieved, they will stop bringing supplies of provisions.[11] Evidently the troops had the money to pay for what they needed—they must not commandeer; they must be able to buy[12]—but they preferred, unless restrained, to save their own pockets by living off the country on their own side of the frontier as well as in enemy territory. This is a bad mark against them, for, in local campaigns, the troops were thematic troops, that is to say only semi-professionals whose homes were in the villages and who lived the same life as their non-military peasant neighbours. They might have been expected to show greater sympathy and consideration for their own kind. On the other hand, when the crews of warships

---

[1] Chap. 12, p. 216.   [2] Chap. 12, p. 217.
[3] Chap. 14, p. 223.   [4] Chap. 20, pp. 244–5.
[5] Leo VI, *Taktiká*, Dhiat. 9, § 1, col. 768; cf. Dhiat. 11, § 7, col. 793.
[6] Dhiat. 9, § 2, col. 768.
[7] Dhiat. 9, § 17, col. 772, paraphrasing 'Mavríkios', *Stratêghikón*, Part 1, chap. 9, p. 42 Scheffer, pp. 68 and 70 Mihăescu.
[8] Ibid., paraphrasing 'Mavríkios', ibid.
[9] Περὶ Στρατιωτικῶν Ἐπιτιμίων, text and commentary by W. Ashburner in *J.H.S.* xlvi, Part I (1926), pp. 81–109, on p. 102.
[10] Leo VI, *Taktiká*, Dhiat. 9, § 26, col. 773.
[11] Dhiat. 11, § 7, col. 793.   [12] Dhiat. 6, § 23, col. 728.

plundered their fellow citizens, apparently they were not so blameworthy. Seamen were supposed to be supplied with rations, and they resorted to robbery when their rations were not forthcoming.[1]

Inevitably, this degree of insecurity was reflected in a decrease in the productivity of agriculture and animal husbandry,[2] and the Government's efforts to re-people the country were partly frustrated by the country people being taken prisoner[3] and being carried away captive, or by their decamping in order to escape this fate. Amnía in théma Paphlaghonía, the home of the eighth-century saint Philáretos, lay in the relatively immune zone of northern Asia Minor, yet this saint's grandson Nikĕtas, in his biography of his grandfather, attributes Philáretos's impoverishment to the depredations of Muslim raiders[4] as well as to the saint's own generosity. Nikĕtas's testimony must be treated with some reserve, since he has cast his biography of his grandfather in the form of a folk-tale. However, the evidence of the tenth-century handbook for taxation-officers, preserved in *Codex Marcianus Graecus 173*,[5] is cogent. Here it is noted[6] that an inspector of taxes remits, for a term of thirty years, the tax on land that has been ruined (ἐξαλιφείσης, 'wiped out') by, say, an incursion of barbarians or by some other act of God.

There is also credible evidence of decampments to escape the clutches of invaders in the lives of ninth-century East Roman Saints. St. Theodora and her husband fled to Thessaloníkê from Aíyina to escape from Muslim raiders.[7] At the close of the ninth century the parents of St. Luke the Greek fled from Aíyina, first to Phokís, then to Kastoriá.[8] St. Joseph the hymnographer and his parents fled from Sicily to the Pelopónnêsos *circa* 820.[9] The parents of St. Athanásios, bishop of Methónê, fled to Pátras after the fall of Katánê in 828.[10] There was not, however, any general emigration from the war zone in eastern Asia Minor.[11] The rural population held its ground, in spite of the tribulations that it suffered at the hands both of its official defenders and of its overt enemies.

This long-suffering East Roman peasantry had a more effective ally in General Winter than in the commanders of the East Roman army-corps districts and their predatory troops. The Arab invaders' sufferings from

[1] Dhiat. 19, § 17, col. 996, and § 28, col. 1000.
[2] Ahrweiler, 'L'Asie Mineure et les invasions arabes', p. 13.
[3] Ibid., pp. 13–14.
[4] Nikĕtas of Amnía = *Life of Saint Philáretos*, ed. by M.-H. Fourmy and M. Leroy in *Byzantion*, vol. ix (1934), pp. 85–170, on p. 115. Philáretos died on 1 December 792, at the age of ninety.
[5] Text first published by W. Ashburner in *J.H.S.*, vol. xxxv (1915), pp. 76–84; revised text edited by F. Dölger, in *Byzantinisches Archiv*, Heft 9 (1927), pp. 113–23, with a commentary on pp. 123–56. Dölger's work has been reprinted, with corrections and additions (Hildesheim, 1960).
[6] Dölger's text, p. 116; commentary, p. 152.
[7] Bréhier, 'Les Populations rurales', p. 186.   [8] Ibid.
[9] Ibid.   [10] Ibid.   [11] Ahrweiler in loc. cit., p. 16.

the severity of the winter climate in the interior of Asia Minor and along the central plateau's mountain rim come to light both in Leo VI's *Taktiká*[1] and in the notices of the Arabic annalists. The occasions on which an invading Arab army went into winter quarters in East Roman territory were rare enough to be thought worth recording.[2] In both the Arab sieges of Constantinople, General Winter was one of the besiegers' most formidable adversaries. Taranta (Derende), far up the basin of the Tokhma Su tributary of the Euphrates, was conquered by the Arabs in 702/3. At first it was garrisoned seasonally by troops from the Jazīrah, but these children of a warmer region used to evacuate Taranta every year when the snow fell. The Caliph 'Umar II (717–20) abandoned Taranta altogether in 718/19 and moved its inhabitants to Malatīyah, farther down the valley.[3] When the Caliph Mansūr (754–75) garrisoned Malatīyah with 4,000 troops from the Jazīrah, he gave them additional annual pay of 10 dinars each, together with a bounty of 100 dinars each.[4] In a summer raid on Ikritiyah (the Akrítai's country?) in 791/2 the raiders 'met with such cold that their hands and feet dropped off'.[5] In 802/3, Hārūn invaded Asia Minor for the second time that year, in spite of the cold.[6] The Caliph Mahdi (775–85) fortified Adhatá and garrisoned it with 4,000 men, but the newly-built fortress, which had been completed at the moment of Mahdi's death, was wrecked by winter snow and rain, and the East Romans seized the opportunity to occupy it and to drive out the Muslim garrison.[7] In 845/6, snow and ice inflicted a disaster on an Arab raiding-force.[8] In 914/15 the Tarsans suffered from cold and snow in a winter raid.[9] In 939/40 Sayf-ad-Dawlah prudently waited for the snow to melt before invading Armenia.[10] In 931/2 the Tarsans, in a spring raid, had to wade through snow up to the poitrails of their horses.[11] In spite of the snow this raid was successful.[12]

The winter climate was certainly rigorous in Asia Minor by comparison with Arabia and Egypt and 'Iraq and the Jazīrah. Does this climatic

---

[1] The Arabs cannot stand cold, winter weather, or rain; so engage them when the weather is bad. In their raids in bad weather they have often been caught and destroyed by the Romans (Leo VI, *Taktiká*, Dhiat. 18, § 124, col. 976).

[2] e.g. sub annis 666/7, 667/8, 669/70, 672, 674/5, 676/7, 678/9 (Brooks in *J.H.S.*, vol. xviii (1898), pp. 185, 185–6, 186–7, 188, 189).

[3] Brooks in loc. cit., pp. 197 and 206.

[4] Balādhurī, *Kitāb Futūh-al-Buldān*, English translation by P. K. Hitti, vol. i (New York, 1916, Columbia University Press), p. 293.

[5] Tabari, cited by Brooks in *The English Historical Review*, vol. xv (October, 1900), p. 740.

[6] Tabari, cited by Brooks in loc. cit., pp. 743–4.

[7] Balādhurī, pp. 296–7, in vol. i of Hitti's translation, following Wākidī and other authorities.

[8] Vasiliev, *Byzance et les Arabes*, vol. i, p. 204, citing Tabari (text of Tabari, ibid., p. 315).

[9] Tabari, in Vasiliev, *Byzance et les Arabes*, ii, II, p. 23.

[10] Ibn Zāfir, ibid., pp. 122–3.

[11] Ibn al-Athīr, ibid., p. 152. [12] Dhababī, ibid., p. 238.

factor account for the Arabs' failure to gain any permanent foothold in Asia Minor? This question is answered in the negative by the Arabs' success in conquering and holding Armenia and Iran and Transoxania. In Armenia the altitudes are higher than in Asia Minor, and consequently the winter climate is still more severe. Yet the Arabs compelled the Armenians to submit to their suzerainty, and they planted colonies in the heart of Armenia, to the north of Lake Van, at Akhlat, Arjish, Perkri, and Melazgerd. As for Iran, the Arabs conquered it, held and colonized it,[1] and converted it to Islam with ease, though the Iranian plateau has as severe a winter climate as the plateau of Asia Minor and is many times larger. The Arabs did not find it so easy to conquer Transoxania, but they did conquer it in the end, though latitude does the work of altitude in making the winter climate of Transoxania inclement.

A convincing explanation of the Arabs' failure to conquer and hold Asia Minor is to be found, not in physical, but in ecclesiastical, geography. The regions in the Levant that the Arabs did conquer with ease were those whose inhabitants were Zoroastrians and pre-Chalcedonian Monophysite and Nestorian Christians. The region that the Arabs failed to conquer was one whose inhabitants were Chalcedonian Christians who called themselves 'Orthodox' and were called 'Melchites' ('Imperialists') by their Monophysite Christian former subjects. No doubt, the winter snow and the perennial mountain rampart of Asia Minor helped the East Romans to hold their own here; but the examples of Armenia and Iran suggest that Asia Minor would have succumbed to the Arabs, as these other regions did, if the local population had not reacted more valiantly to the common ordeal.[2] It also looks as if this valour was inspired by the Imperial religion. At any rate, the line along which the frontier between the East Roman Empire and the Caliphate came to rest during the two centuries and a quarter beginning *circa* 700 coincided with the line of

---

[1] Under the Umayyad regime, Iran was held by the Arab cantonments (junds) at Basrah and Kūfah, on the Arabian bank of the lower Euphrates. The north-east frontier province, Khurāsān, was colonized, particularly intensively, with drafts of Basran and Kufan Arab families (see J. Wellhausen, *Das arabische Reich und sein Sturz* (Berlin, 1902, Reimer) pp. 79 and 266). The revenues of the cities and districts of Dīnavar and Nihāvand, both on the great north-east road, were payable to the Arab junds at Kūfah and at Basrah respectively (Le Strange, op. cit., pp. 189 and 197).

[2] Perhaps the reason why the Eastern Orthodox Christian Greek-speaking population of Asia Minor reacted valiantly against the Arabs in the seventh, eighth, ninth, and tenth centuries was that—unlike the seventh-century Monophysites and Zoroastrians—they were not yet alienated from their own government. The peasantry in Asia Minor did become alienated, in their turn, in the tenth century, and in the eleventh and twelfth centuries they failed to resist the Saljūq Turks as they had previously resisted the Arabs. Indeed, they acquiesced in the Turkish conquest as readily as the peoples to the south-east of the Távros and the Andítavros had acquiesced in the Arab conquest in the seventh century. By the eleventh century, Turkish Muslim rule had come to seem, in the eyes of the peasantry of Asia Minor, to be preferable to the exactions of East Roman taxation-officers and to the encroachments of East Roman magnates, lay and ecclesiastical.

demarcation between Chalcedonian Christians to the west and pre-Chalcedonian Christians (Monophysites and Nestorians) to the east and the south.

The endurance displayed by the Orthodox Christian population of Asia Minor during those two centuries and a quarter was not emulated by their Muslim antagonists when, in and after 926, the tide turned and the war zone shifted eastwards out of Rhomanía into Dār-al-Islām. By that time the Muslims had come to take it for granted that it was their role to be the invaders and that it was the East Romans' role to be their victims; and, when the Muslims suffered, in their turn, the tribulations that they had formerly inflicted, they lost their tempers and their nerve.

In 926/7, Malatīyah was taken, sacked, and occupied for thirteen days by the East Romans. A deputation from the people of Malatīyah then came to Baghdad to demand military aid.[1] In 928/9 the East Romans forced the Muslim enclaves at Akhlat and Bitlis to capitulate, and the inhabitants of Arzan, to the south-west of Bitlis, fled. The victims appealed to the Caliph for help, but without success.[2] Another East Roman raid on the territory of Malatīyah in 929/30 led the people of Āmida, Mayyā-fāriqīn, and the whole of Diyār Bakr to send a deputation to Baghdad to protest against the Caliph's failure to give them effective protection.[3] By this date the population of the north-western marches was so thoroughly terrified that it played with the idea of offering to pay tribute to the East Romans and of surrendering to them Samosata and other cities.[4]

In the spring of 932, representatives of the population of the north-western marches and of Jibāl made a demonstration in front of the Caliph's palace in Baghdad and stirred up the inhabitants of the capital. They described their sufferings at the hands of the East Romans and the Daylamis, and declared that the first charge on the land-tax that was levied from them and from their fellow subjects ought to be for the provision of protection for the whole population and for the repulse of the enemy to beyond striking distance. This demonstration provoked a riot, and many lives were lost before peace was restored.[5]

Mayyāfāriqīn was now in the front line on the Muslim side—the ordeal that the cities along the road from the Cilician Gates to Constantinople had endured for two centuries and a quarter. A tenth-century preacher whose home was Mayyāfāriqīn, Ibn Nubātah, sought to re-animate the Jihād, but his exhortations fell flat.[6] Ibn Nubātah's contemporary and neighbour, Ibn Hawkal of Nisībīn, observed sadly that the East Roman

---

[1] Miskawaih, translated in Vasiliev, ii, II, p. 69.
[2] Ibn al-Athīr, translated in Vasiliev, ii II, p. 151.
[3] Ibn al-Azraq al-Fāriqī, translated in Vasiliev, ii, II, pp. 113–14.
[4] Dhahabī, translated in Vasiliev, ii, II, p. 238.
[5] 'Arīb, translated in Vasiliev, ii, II, pp. 62–3.
[6] One of Ibn Nubātah's sermons is translated in Vasiliev, ii, II, pp. 292–4.

Empire was a minor power by comparison with Muslim North-West Africa, but that the disintegration and demoralization of the Islamic World had given the East Romans a free hand.[1]

(c) *The Peasant Freeholders, circa 700–925*

In the Diocletianic Age (284–602) of the Roman Empire's history, peasant freeholders had not ceased to exist. Conversely, some large-scale landowners survived the Diocletianic Empire's seventh-century collapse[2] and continued to exist, side by side with the peasant freeholders, till the way was opened for these large-scale landowners once again to add field to field at the peasants' expense, thanks to the opening of the East Roman Army's counter-offensive against the Eastern Muslims in 926 and thanks also to the great famine that afflicted the East Roman Empire itself during the terrible winter of 927/8.[3] During the preceding two centuries and a quarter, big estates seem to have been the exception[4] and small holdings the rule; yet the two scales of ownership, perhaps with different ways of utilizing the land,[5] seem always to have co-existed.[6] Whatever may have been their respective ratios of the total amount of land that was being utilized in the period 700–925, the East Roman rural economy was in a relatively flourishing condition in the reign of Constantine V (741–75).[7]

---

[1] Ibn Hawkal, translated in Vasiliev, ii, II, pp. 418–19.   [2] See p. 35.

[3] The date is 927/8, not 928/9, according to Lemerle, 'Esquisse', vol. ccxix, p. 271, n. 1, and Ostrogorsky, 'Agrarian Conditions', p. 216.

[4] G. Ostrogorsky, 'La Commune rurale byzantine', in *Byzantion*, vol. xxxii (1962), pp. 138–66, on pp. 141–2; idem in *The Cambridge Economic History*, vol. i, 2nd ed. (1966), p. 208. However, Theophanes, sub A.M. 6302, does mention πάροικοι (i.e. the labour-force on large-scale estates) and κτήματα (the large-scale estates themselves) as having existed in the reign of Nikêphóros I (802–11).

[5] The large-scale estates might be made up of topographically scattered parcels of land (Lemerle, 'Esquisse', vol. ccxix, p. 44, n. 1, and p. 48. G. Ostrogorsky, 'Die ländliche Steuergemeinde des byzantinischen Reiches im X. Jahrhundert', in *Vierteljahrschrift für Sozial- und Wirtschaftsgeschichte*, 20. Band (1928), pp. 1–108, on pp. 36–7. The properties of the more affluent of the peasants are known to have been scattered (ibid., pp. 35–7; idem, 'Agrarian Conditions', p. 210).

[6] There are no surviving direct descriptions of rural economic and social conditions in the East Roman Empire during the years 700–925. It is perhaps improbable that any works of this kind were ever written. Our information is derived from the texts of laws and of a handbook for taxation-officers (*Codex Marcianus Graecus 173*). The relevant laws are the Nómos Yeoryikós, which was probably promulgated towards the close of the seventh century (Lemerle, 'Esquisse', vol. ccxix, p. 54), and the novels, promulgated by Emperors during the last three-quarters of the tenth century, with the object of protecting the small freeholds from being swallowed up by the big estates. Of these three sources of information, the first two deal with the small freeholds only. The Nómos Yeoryikós 'is not a complete agricultural code. . . . It is concerned exclusively with a village community, composed of farmers who cultivate their own land.' There is 'no ground for maintaining that the other classes of the agricultural population . . . have in the meantime ceased to exist' (Ashburner in *J.H.S.*, vol. xxxii (1912), p. 77).

[7] Nic. Patr., p. 76.

Meanwhile, it was the peasant freeholders who were adding field to field. Apparently they were expanding their holdings, not at the expense of their neighbours, but by bringing into utilization unutilized land[1] that had either never been utilized before or had been left derelict when its former owners had been harried beyond endurance by Roman taxation-officers or by barbarian raiders or by both these scourges. However, the effect of expansion was to create, or at any rate to increase, inequalities of wealth within the peasant class.[2] The more enterprising peasants, if their ventures were rewarded by economic success, acquired property on a scale that raised them to the level of a middle class, intermediate between their fellow peasants, owning holdings of average size, and the large-scale landowners.[3] In rare cases,[4] a peasant raised himself to equality with the large-scale landowners in the extent of his property.

The Emperor Basil II records, in his Novel No. 29 of 1 January 996[5]— a law that was the last but one in the series of abortive attempts to save the small landowners by legislation—how, in a village through which the Emperor had happened to pass on one of his journeys, he had received, and taken cognizance of, the complaints of the poorer inhabitants against a fellow villager of theirs, Philokálês, who had started as just an ordinary peasant in a small way but had contrived to obtain some official rank and had then gained possession of the whole village and had turned it into a large-scale estate (προάστιον) of his own. It is significant that his obtaining official rank was the achievement that had made his fortune. In itself, this was not an economic achievement, but, by giving him the entrée into the coterie of the δυνατοί—'the people with influence'—his ennoblement had enabled Philokálês to build up an estate on the scale of those possessed by men of influence who were investing their money now in rural land. Basil II reveals, with undisguised self-satisfaction, the vindictiveness of his redress of a social injustice in this case.

I rased to the ground Philokálês's edifices, which were sumptuous; I restored to the indigent inhabitants [of the χωρίον] the property that was rightfully theirs; and I left in Philokálês's possession only his original property. In fact, I reduced him to being once again just one of the local peasants.

The thunderbolted tenth-century *kulak* Philokálês had an eighth-century counterpart in St. Philáretos of Amnía (702–92), if the saint's grandson Nikétas's biography of his grandfather is to be taken *au pied de la lettre*. According to Nikétas, his grandfather had inherited property that put him in the category of the large-scale landowners. He was very

[1] Rouillard, op. cit., pp. 90–1; Ostrogorsky, 'Agrarian Conditions', p. 210.
[2] Ostrogorsky, 'La Commune rurale', pp. 148–9; idem, 'Agrarian Conditions', p. 211.
[3] Bréhier in loc. cit., p. 190; Rouillard, op. cit., p. 96.
[4] Their rarity is emphasized by Charanis, 'On the Social Structure of the Later Roman Empire', p. 44, with n. 22.
[5] C. E. Zachariä von Lingenthal, *Jus Graeco-Romanum*, Part III, pp. 306–18, on p. 310.

rich. He possessed enormous numbers of livestock: 600 cattle, 100 yokes of oxen; 800 horses out at grass; 80 saddle-horses and sumpter-mules; 12,000 sheep; and no less than 48 extensive estates (προάστια), all delimited (μονώτατα).[1] These estates were splendid, and their value was immense. Every one of them had a spring supplying more than enough water to irrigate the land. Philáretos possessed numerous slaves and, in fact, a huge amount of property.[2] Even after he had been ruined—or had ruined himself—Philáretos kept his fine house—the finest in Amnía—and, though he no longer had food for entertaining distinguished guests, he still had his ivory dining-table.[3] Philáretos ranked as a local aristocrat,[4] and inevitably he married a wife of his own social standing.[5] Nikḗtas represents his grandfather as having started life as a super-*kulak*, and his statistics lend his story an air of authenticity. These figures may be delusive, for Nikḗtas has given his work the form of a folk-tale, as has been noted already. In any case, neither Philáretos's nor Philokálês's fortune was typical of even the most successful representatives of the peasantry in the peasantry's halcyon days. In this age some peasants evidently did succeed in improving their economic position, but few improved it so far as to become members of the class of large-scale landowners—a class which, anyway, was apparently more or less in abeyance in this age.[6]

Nevertheless, as has already been noted, the inequalities among the peasants who had not risen into the large-scale landowner class were already considerable by the time when the Nómos Yeoryikós was promulgated,[7] and these inequalities were also evidently increasing.[8] This was, as has also been noted, a consequence of the expansion of the area of rural economic activity.

The normal village (χωρίον) had evidently, to begin with, been a compact built-up settlement. The technical name for this built-up nucleus seems to have been καθέδρα.[9] It had a boundary (περιορισμός),[10] and the term ἐνθύρια may mean 'walled villages' (which was its meaning in the fiscal terminology of Egypt under the late Roman regime).[11] Compact

---

[1] The extent of a peasant freeholder's holding in his village community was proportionate to his tax-quota. Normally he had no boundary-marks, not to speak of title-deeds (Dölger, *Beiträge zur Geschichte der byzantinischen Finanzverwaltung, besonders des 10. und 11. Jahrhunderts* (*Byzantinisches Archiv*, Heft 9 (Berlin and Leipzig, 1927, Teubner), p. 123).

[2] Text and translation of Nikḗtas's biography in Fourmy and Leroy, loc. cit., on pp. 113–15.

[3] Ibid., pp. 135–7.   [4] Ibid., p. 113.

[5] Ibid., p. 115.   [6] Bréhier, 'Les Populations rurales', p. 190.

[7] Ostrogorsky, 'Agrarian Conditions', p. 211.

[8] Ostrogorsky, 'La Commune rurale', pp. 148–9.

[9] The Handbook for taxation-officers, §§ 2 and 4 (see G. Ostrogorsky, 'Die ländliche Steuergemeinde des byzantinischen Reiches im X. Jahrhundert', in *Vierteljahrschrift für Sozial- und Wirtschaftsgeschichte*, 20. Band (1928), pp. 1–108, on p. 105; cf. Lemerle, 'Esquisse', vol. ccxix, p. 260).   [10] Lemerle, ibid.

[11] Rouillard, op. cit., p. 87. Ostrogorsky, however, in 'Die ländliche Steuergemeinde', p. 105, translates ἐνθύρια 'Landsteile, Parzellen'.

walled villages would be the form of settlement that we should expect in a country in which insecurity was as extreme as it was in the East Roman Empire from 602 to 925. However, before the close of the seventh century, if that is the date of promulgation of the Nómos Yeoryikós, the nuclei of the East Roman villages had begun to ramify into outlying homesteads (ἀγρίδια).[1] There were even some rural communities (ὁμάδες, alias μετουσίαι, alias ἀνακοινώσεις, alias κοινότητες) without any village centre. These were called κτήσεις,[2] and they consisted entirely of separate 'properties' (κτησίδια). There was no difference between χωρία and κτησίδια in fiscal status,[3] and therefore none in administrative status either. The difference was solely in their topographical layout. The communities, which were primarily fiscal units, also contained properties (προάστεια, literally 'suburbs') that were large enough to need the labour of slaves and hired hands.[4] The owners of proásteia were in some cases absentee landlords. They might be either peasants who had made their fortunes or members of the 'Establishment' (δυνατοί). These proásteia seem to have been included for fiscal purposes in the community within whose area they lay.[5]

The sprouting of ἀγρίδια and κτησίδια and προάστεια was the consequence of an increase in population that resulted in the utilization of a larger area of land. At the date of promulgation of the Nómos Yeoryikós, rural communities still had unutilized lands,[6] and, from time to time, portions of these were divided up among the members of the community for individual ownership[7] and development.[8]

---

[1] Ostrogorsky, 'Die ländliche Steuergemeinde', p. 19, with n. 2, and p. 103; idem, 'Agrarian Conditions', p. 212; Rouillard, op. cit., p. 88.

[2] Ostrogorsky, 'Die ländliche Steuergemeinde', pp. 16 and 106.

[3] Dölger, *Beiträge*, p. 115.

[4] Ostrogorsky, 'La Commune rurale', p. 149; idem, 'Die ländliche Steuergemeinde', p. 20; idem, 'Agrarian Conditions', p. 212; Dölger, *Beiträge*, p. 115.

[5] Ostrogorsky, 'Die ländliche Steuergemeinde', p. 21.   [6] Ibid., p. 23.

[7] Ostrogorsky, 'Agrarian Conditions', p. 210.

[8] If a distribution of hitherto unutilized and undistributed common land proved to have been unfair, it had to be revised (Nóm. Yeory., Art. 8). Lemerle holds ('Esquisse', vol. ccxix, pp. 60–1) that there were periodical redistributions of land belonging to a community. This is his interpretation of N.Y., Arts. 8, 32, 82. Ostrogorsky, 'La Commune rurale', p. 144, n. 2, holds (surely correctly) that there is no evidence for there having been any redistributions, and Lemerle himself holds that there were only redistributions of land that was taxed because it was potentially productive though it was being left unutilized. He holds that the tax was redistributed and that, in consequence of this, the land was redistributed in the same ratio. The N.Y. used to be interpreted as indicating that the whole of a community's land was redistributed periodically, and this practice was attributed to the influence of Slav customary law. There is no evidence for this conjecture, and the theory is, indeed, anachronistic. This Slav theory was still upheld by E. E. Lipšic, *Byzance und die Slaven* (Weimar, 1951, Böhlaus), but it has been rejected by other recent students of the subject, e.g. by Ostrogorsky, 'Die ländliche Steuergemeinde', pp. 12, 40, 43–4; eodem, 'La Commune rurale', pp. 146–7; Lemerle, 'Esquisse', vol. ccxix, p. 59, with n. 2, and p. 64. Lemerle, loc. cit., pp. 69 and 74, holds that the seventh-century cataclysm produced changes, not in the

Here was the opportunity for an able and enterprising peasant to better himself, so long as there was still undistributed land belonging to his community, and so long as the people with influence (οἱ δυνατοί) had not yet found it worth their while to compete with the peasant freeholder for the acquisition of rural land. A peasant who had acquired one or more ἀγρίδια could bequeath these 'outside' (ἐξώθυρα) properties to some of his sons and his 'inside' (ἐσώθυρα) property to other sons.[1] East Roman rural society, as revealed in the Nómos Yeoryikós, consists of 'paysans apparemment libres de leur personne, de leurs mouvements, et de leurs biens'.[2] The ownership of land,[3] livestock, and movable property was individual, not collective.[4] The peasant could change his domicile, and, though recorded instances of this are rare, there is no evidence that migration (as distinct from flight to escape fiscal or military obligations) was illegal.[5] As for a free peasant's property, it was his permanent possession; there is no question of there having been periodical redistribution of property within a peasant community;[6] and the property-owner could bequeath what he possessed,[7] and, during his own lifetime, he could lease it, sell it, exchange it for other property,[8] or give it away.[9]

The peasant freeholder's freedom to dispose of his property was, however, limited by the fact that his community was a fiscal unity in the sense that all members of it were responsible collectively for the payment of the total amount of the tax assessed on the community as a whole. For this reason, the peasant's συγχωρῖται—his fellow members of his ὁμάs— had the right of first refusal (προτίμησις) of any offer made by any one of them to sell any of his land.[10] The Emperor Basil II, in his Novel No. 29 of

institutions, but in the facts, of rural life. Ostrogorsky, 'La Commune rurale', p. 147, holds that there were no new institutions but that there was new vitality. Ashburner, in *J.H.S.*, vol. xxx (1910), p. 85, holds that the Nómos Yeoryikós was largely a compilation of existing customs. It did not make a break with Roman tradition (Ostrogorsky, 'Die ländliche Steuergemeinde', pp. 12–13).

[1] Handbook for taxation-officers, Dölger's text, p. 115. Cf. Ostrogorsky, 'Die ländliche Steuergemeinde', p. 19.   [2] Lemerle, 'Esquisse', vol. ccxix, p. 63.

[3] Ostrogorsky, 'La Commune rurale', p. 144.

[4] Ostrogorsky, 'Agrarian Conditions', p. 210.

[5] Ostrogorsky, 'La Commune rurale', p. 144; Ashburner in *J.H.S.*, vol. xxxii (1912), p. 78; Charanis, 'On the Social Structure of the Later Roman Empire', p. 46; John the Psychaïte's father moved from théma Voukellárioi to a village near Nikomēdeia (Bréhier, 'Les Populations rurales', p. 184). Charanis, loc. cit., p. 45, guesses that the laws restricting migration and change of occupation had never been repealed, but had become dead letters.

[6] Ostrogorsky, 'Die ländliche Steuergemeinde', pp. 43–4.

[7] Ostrogorsky, 'Agrarian Conditions', p. 210; idem, 'Die ländliche Steuergemeinde', p. 37. A property was booked and re-booked by the taxation-officers in the names of successive inheritors (ibid., p. 40, citing the Handbook, § 20).

[8] Ostrogorsky, 'Die ländliche Steuergemeinde', p. 44.

[9] Ostrogorsky, 'Agrarian Conditions', p. 210.

[10] Ostrogorsky, 'The Peasant's Pre-emption Right', in *J.R.S.*, vol. xxxvii (1947) pp. 117–26; idem, 'Die ländliche Steuergemeinde', p. 32. The community's right of προτίμησις is dealt with further in Part II, chap. 1 (iii) (e).

996 (section 3), was concerned to vindicate a community's rights when one of its members had built a church on his own piece of land and had dedicated this land to this church's upkeep. This gave the ecclesiastical authorities an opening for trying to have the dedicated property scheduled as a monastery,[1] with a monastery's fiscal privileges,[2] and the effect would be to increase the community's fiscal burden, since the community would now have to pay the same aggregate amount of tax on a reduced area of tax-paying productive land. Basil II sought to redress this hardship by ruling that the dedicated property should revert to the community. This was a case in which the individual peasant's freedom to dispose of his property was overruled by an act of Imperial legislation in order to safeguard the legitimate rights of the community to which the individual belonged.

Private property-rights were thus, in fact, restricted by fiscal considerations. Yet, considering the extent to which taxation governed rural life, it is remarkable that private property-rights should, nevertheless, have had as much free play as they prove to have had on the evidence of the Nómos Yeoryikós. The whole of this late-seventh-century collection of laws is concerned with private property in various forms: the land itself, the produce of the land, the equipment for utilizing the land, and livestock. The population of a rural community was not homogeneous in status. Among the freeholders who were responsible collectively for paying the tax assessed on the community as a whole, there were evidently different degrees of relative affluence and indigence. There were other inhabitants who were freemen but who possessed no land, or at any rate possessed so little land that they had to earn their living mainly by hiring their labour either to individual affluent freeholders or to the community. Examples of wage-earning freemen are the (communal?) herdsman (ἀγελάριος βοῶν) (Art. 25), the crop-watchman (ὀπωροφύλαξ) (Art. 33), and the hired shepherd (Art. 34). There were also slaves who were the affluent freeholders' property.

The Nómos Yeoryikós is a miscellany. Its contents are not even as orderly as Ashburner makes them out to be. Ashburner analyses the collection into three successive parts: Articles 1–22 dealing with the cultivation of the land and with the peasants' relations with each other; Articles 23–55 dealing with livestock, large and small, and with sheepdogs; and Articles 56–66 dealing with the produce of the land, with agricultural implements, and with farm buildings.[3] But the arrangement

---

[1] By the tenth century the monasteries, like the lay big landowners, were seizing opportunities for enlarging their estates at the expense of the freeholding peasantry (see D. Savramis, *Zur Soziologie des byzantinischen Mönchtums* (Leiden/Köln, 1962, Brill), pp. 45–52.

[2] Monastic land was not exempt from taxation in principle, but in practice it enjoyed great alleviations of tax (op. cit., p. 47).

[3] Ashburner in *J.H.S.*, vol. xxxii (1912), p. 69.

of the articles is not really so systematic as this, and Ashburner himself
concedes that Articles 67–85 are addenda that have not been distributed
under Ashburner's three hypothetical headings. However, it is possible to
discern a certain number of fundamental principles that are applied
consistently throughout the collection. First and foremost, a party to an
agreement must abide by his undertakings unless the other party fails to
abide by his. In the second place, private persons must not take the law
into their own hands. In the third place, unintentional damage to another
person's property must be made good, except in certain special circumstances. In the fourth place, stealing and fraud must be punished severely.
In the fifth place, vindictive or sheerly malicious damage to property
must be punished ferociously. Finally—and this is the most significant
principle of all—anyone who has been enterprising enough to extend the
area of land-utilization or to increase the land's productivity must be
assured of reaping a fair reward for his initiative.

An agreement, made in the presence of witnesses, for a permanent
exchange of parcels of land was binding (Art. 3). If an agreement has
been made for a temporary exchange during the sowing season, and if one
of the parties then revoked, this revocation was invalid if the seed had
been sown already, but was valid if the seed had not yet been sown.
However, in that case the party that had revoked must still do the
ploughing if the other party had already ploughed the land temporarily
taken over by him (Art. 4). If the parcels of land that had been exchanged,
temporarily or permanently, proved to have been unequal, the inequality
must be rectified unless it had been provided for specifically in the agreement (Art. 5). If someone took over some land from an indigent peasant
(γεωργοῦ) and undertook only to plough and then to divide the produce,
the agreement was to stand; but, if it had been agreed that the contractor
should sow as well as plough, the agreement was to stand in this case too
(Art. 11). If someone took over half a vineyard from an indigent peasant
and did not do the work on it properly, the contractor was to have no
share in the produce (Art. 12). The same rule applied to arable land
(Art. 13). If the indigent peasant had gone away (ἀποδημήσαντος, a
neutral word that would cover both illegal and legal change of domicile),
and if the other peasant who had taken over half the indigent peasant's
land then failed to cultivate it, the contractor was to pay double the
value of the lost harvest (Art. 14). If, however, the contractor reported his
inability to cultivate before the beginning of the working season, and if
the owner of the land ignored this notification, the contractor (ἡμιαστής,
meaning 'halver') was to be quit of his obligation (Art. 15).

If a peasant undertook to cultivate a vineyard or a farmstead (χώρα),
if he then took delivery of part-payment in advance, and, if he started
work and then gave up, he was to pay the proper price for (the use of ?)

the land, and the owner of the land was to have the land (Art. 16). If a lender accepted from a borrower, in lieu of interest, the temporary possession of the borrower's land and the right to take this land's produce, there was to be an adjustment of accounts in the borrower's favour if the lender had kept the land, and had taken its produce, for more than seven years (Art. 67). In this case, the agreement was governed by customary law, and so it was also in a crop-sharing agreement between a landlord (χωροδεσπότου) and a tenant (μορτίτου). The tenant's share was nine sheaves out of ten; the landlord's was one sheaf. Any landlord who contracted for a larger share was accursed (θεοκατάρατος) (Art. 10). Conversely, any tenant who reaped without the landlord's permission and harvested his (the landlord's ?) share was to be treated as a thief (Art. 9).

Taking the law into one's own hands, and, *a fortiori*, behaving high-handedly without provocation or excuse, was frowned upon and, in most cases, was punishable. In ploughing, a peasant must not encroach on his neighbour's furrows (Art. 1), and anyone who ploughed or sowed someone else's land without the owner's knowledge was to forfeit the fruits of his labours (Art. 2). A plaintiff who, while a suit was still pending, reaped the defendant's harvest against the defendant's will was not to retain any of the harvest even if the suit went in his favour, and he was to pay double the value of the harvest if the suit went against him (Art. 6). If, again while a suit was still pending, the plaintiff lawlessly (ἀνάρχως) cut down the defendant's vines or any other tree, the offender was to have one hand cut off (Art. 80). If a peasant cleared and cultivated another's woodland without the owner's knowledge, he was not to get any of the produce (Art. 20). It was not permissible to prune a tree, belonging to someone else, even if it overhung one's own ground, but there was one exception to this rule. If the land that the tree overhung was garden-land, the owner of the garden might prune the tree (Art. 31).

Anyone who caught someone else's animal making depredations (πραῖδαν ποιοῦντα) on his land should return the animal to its owner and should then put in a claim on the owner for damages. If the aggrieved party killed or damaged the marauding animal, he must give the animal's owner another animal in compensation (Arts. 38 and 85). If he mutilated a marauding animal, he must replace it with an intact one (Art. 48). If anyone killed a marauding animal, after the first or the second offence he must pay the owner the animal's value (Art. 54), but a third offence entitled the aggrieved party to do anything that he chose to the marauding animal (Art. 49). No compensation was payable for an animal that had got itself killed, while trying to maraud, by falling into a ditch surrounding a vineyard or a garden (Art. 50) or by impaling itself on the stakes of a fence (Art. 51). No compensation was payable, either, if someone set a trap at harvest-time and a dog or a pig was killed by it (Art. 52). Nor was an ayelários punishable if he killed, injured, or blinded with a stone; but he was punishable if he did the deed with a stick (Art. 29).

Sheep-dogs, being particularly valuable, were more fully protected by the law. If two dogs were fighting, and if the owner of one dog blinded, killed, or injured the other man's dog even with a stone, and, *a fortiori*, with a stick or with a sword, the offender must pay compensation and receive a beating (twelve strokes) as well (Art. 76).[1] The same combination of penalties was prescribed for the owner of a champion dog (κύνα δυναστήν) who set his champion on weaker dogs, with the result that one of these was injured or killed (Art. 77).

Unintentional damage created rather more difficult legal problems. If an ox that had been committed to the ayelários's keeping was killed by a wolf, the owner had no claim against the ayelários, if the ayelários reported the loss (Art. 23); but, if the ayelários lost an ox, the owner did have a claim against him if he failed to report the loss on the same day (Art. 24). If someone reported an injury to an animal, and if he was suspected by the owner of having done the injury himself, he could clear himself by protesting his innocence on oath (Art. 73). If an ox in the ayelários's keeping strayed and made depredations on fields or vineyards, the ayelários was not to have his wages docked, but he was to pay compensation for the damage done (Art. 25). If an ox in the ayelários's keeping disappeared (Art. 26), or if an ox in his keeping was injured or blinded (Art. 27), the ayelários was cleared if he testified, on oath, that he had not been an accessory. If, however, he subsequently proved to have perjured himself, he was not only to compensate the ox's owner but was to have his own tongue cut out (Art. 28).

If someone carelessly killed an animal, belonging to someone else, while felling timber in an oak-wood (Art. 39) or by letting an axe drop (Art. 40), he had to provide another animal in compensation. If an animal belonging to someone else was rounded up among a peasant's own animals, and if this animal was then lost or was caught by a wolf (λυκωθῇ), the unintentional recipient of the animal must replace it unless he had reported the occurrence to the animal's owner, had shown him the place where the mishap occurred, and had demonstrated that he had been unable to control the animal (Art. 43).

---

[1] When I was walking about in Greece in the years 1911–12, the customary rule, at that date, was that, if I was attacked by a sheep-dog and if I injured or killed it with a stone, the shepherd was not entitled to take any reprisals against me. If, however, I knifed or shot the dog, the shepherd was entitled to knife or shoot me. In the course of twelve centuries, the dog's rights had been diminished, and the dog's victim's rights had been increased, by a stone's-throw. By 1911–12, making the motion of picking up a stone was usually enough to make the dog retreat hastily till he was out of range.

If someone started a fire in woodland or other land of his own, and if the fire then spread and destroyed other people's houses and crops, the man who started the fire was not guilty if he had done this when there was not a high wind blowing (Art. 56). On the other hand, restitution was due from anyone who, with however good an excuse (ἐξ οἱασδήποτε προφάσεως), destroyed an animal belonging to someone else (Art. 74). If someone had harvested the crop on his own land before his neighbours had harvested the crops on theirs, and if he then brought in his own cattle on to his own land and his cattle injured his neighbours' crops, he was to pay damages and to be given thirty strokes (Art. 78). The penalty was to be the same if the damage was done, not to arable land, but to vineyards (Art. 79). A miller, too, had to pay damages if his mill-race devastated other people's fields and vineyards. If he refused to pay, his mill was to be put out of action (Art. 83). The owners of land were entitled to veto the passage, through their land, of the miller's water (Art. 84).

Stealing and fraud seem to have been rife. There were fines in cash and kind for stealing agricultural implements (Art. 22), and for stealing a cow-bell or a sheep-bell (Art. 30). The fine for stealing implements was 12 phólleis *per diem* for the period during which the thief had had the implements in his possession (Art. 62). A crop-watcher who purloined the crop that he had been hired to guard was not only to forfeit his pay; he was also to be given a very severe flogging (Art. 33). The same combination of penalties awaited the hired shepherd who milked or sold his master's animals on the sly (Art. 34). A straw-thief was to be fined double the value of the straw that he had stolen (Art. 35). An employee who took an animal belonging to his master and hired it out for his own profit was to be fined double the amount of the hire money, and, if the animal died on the road, he was—if he had the wherewithal—to give his master two animals in compensation (Art. 36). If an ox died doing work that it had been hired to do, there was no penalty, but, if it died doing other work, the full value of the ox was payable in compensation (Art. 37).

The penalty for proven theft of an animal was a fine of double the value of the animal itself and of its work, together with a flogging (Art. 41). If a herd was devoured by wild beasts in consequence of an animal's having been stolen out of the herd, the thief was to have his eyes put out (Art. 42). If someone found an ox straying in a wood, killed it, and took the meat, he was to have one hand cut off (Art. 44). If a slave committed this offence, the ox was to be replaced by the slave's master (Art. 45). If a slave drove cattle out of their pen at night to steal them, and if they were lost or were devoured by wild beasts, the slave was to be given a murderer's death by hanging (Art. 46). If the slave committed this crime repeatedly, the slave was to be hanged and his master was also to pay compensation (Art. 47).

The fine for impounding and killing someone else's pig or dog was double the value of the animal (Art. 54). There was the same fine for burning (the timber on) someone else's mountain or cutting down his trees (Art. 57).

The penalty for stealing corn-crops or pulse (δέματα ἢ σταχύας ἢ ὄσπρια) was for the thief to lose his shirt and to be given a whipping (Art. 60), and there was the same penalty for entering a vineyard or a fig-orchard in order to steal (for profit), though there was no penalty for doing the same in order to satisfy one's hunger (Art. 61). For burning or stealing a waggon the fine was double the value of the waggon (Art. 63). The penalty for burning down houses or demolishing fences lawlessly (ἀνάρχως), as if these had been houses built, or fences erected, on land that was one's own, was to have one hand cut off (Art. 66). For stealing grain from a barn, the penalty for a first offence was restitution plus one hundred strokes; for a second offence it was a fine of double the value; for a third offence the thief was to have his eyes put out (Art. 68). There was the same gradation of penalties for stealing wine at night (Art. 69).

People who used false measures were to be beaten—the punishment for impiety (Art. 70). If someone entrusted cattle, for putting out to pasture, to someone else's slave without informing the slave's master (and without paying the master for the service), and if the slave then sold these cattle or deprived their owner of them in some other way, the owner had no claim against either the slave or the slave's master (Art. 71). On the other hand, a slave's master had to make restitution if, with his cognizance, his slave stole someone else's animals and ate them or destroyed them in some other way (Art. 72).

Deliberate damage, prompted by vindictiveness or by sheer malice, seems to have been a disagreeably frequent form of crime. For instance, someone might kill someone else's sheep-dog and might not confess, and the sheep-fold might be attacked by wild beasts. If the offender was subsequently identified, he had to pay (the price of) the entire flock, as well as the price of the dog (Art. 55). If the offender had poisoned the sheep-dog, he was to receive one hundred strokes, besides paying the value of the dog. If the flock was then lost, the killer was to pay for the whole of it. The severity of the penalty was to be decided by the dog's character. If the dog was capable of fighting wild beasts (εἰ θηριομάχος ἦν), the penalty was to be as stated above, but, if the dog was just an ordinary dog (εἰ δὲ ἁπλῶς καὶ ὡς ἔτυχε), the offender was to get off with just a beating and the payment of the price of the dog (Art. 75). The penalty for burning down the fence enclosing a vineyard was flogging and branding on the hand, besides paying double the cost of the damage (Art. 58). The penalty for cutting down or uprooting someone else's vines when they were bearing fruit was to have one hand cut off, besides being fined (Art. 59). For vindictive arson, in which corn on a threshing-floor or in stacks had been set on fire, the penalty for the criminal was to be burnt alive (Art. 64). For arson in which a barn full of hay or chaff had been set on fire, the penalty was to have one hand cut off (Art. 65).

Enterprise that increased production was encouraged. If a peasant penetrated woodland belonging to another peasant and brought it under cultivation (with the owner's consent),[1] the peasant who had opened this woodland up was to have the produce of it for three years, after which he was to return the land to its owner (Art. 17). If a peasant built a house and planted a vineyard on an absentee family's land, and if the absentees then returned after a lapse of time, they did not have the right to pull down the house or to uproot the vines, but they did have a right to be compensated by being given an equivalent piece of land (ἀντιτοπίαν), and, if the occupier refused to provide this, then, and then only, the owners had a right to evict him (Art. 21). If someone had nursed a tree on the community's common land, and if the common was then divided up into private allotments and if the allotment containing the tree fell to someone else, the tree was still the property of the peasant who had nursed it. If the man who had acquired the allotment was dissatisfied, he might have the tree if he would give another tree in exchange (Art. 32).

If one of the inhabitants of a village perceived a place, in the community's common land, that was a good location for a (water) mill, and if he took possession of this place while it was still common land, and if, after he had completed the installation of his mill, the community (ἡ τοῦ χωρίου κοινότης) denounced the mill-owner for having occupied common land as if it had been his private property, it was open to the community to pay down the whole sum due to the mill-owner for the work that he had done in advance, and, on these terms, they could become his partners (Art. 81). If, however, the community's common land had already been divided up, and someone then found on his own allotment a good location for a mill and developed this asset, in this case the recipients of the other allotments had no claim (Art. 82).

It will be seen that the picture of rural life which is given in the Nómos Yeoryikós is not only vivid but is also enlightening. It shows that the rural population was increasing; that it was taking advantage of its augmented man-power by bringing previously unutilized land into utilization; and that it was expanding the utilized area because land-utilization was now profitable. We can infer that, at the date at which the Nómos Yeoryikós was compiled, taxation, however heavy it may have been, was not so

---

[1] 'With the owner's leave' is implied, though this proviso is not explicitly stated; for a peasant who did the very same thing without the owner's cognizance was to get none of the produce (Art. 20, cited above on p. 129).

heavy as to make the ownership and utilization of taxable land a liability and not an asset.[1]

(d) *The Στρατιωτικὰ Κτήματα*[2]

The earliest certain surviving occurrence of the term στρατιωτικὰ κτήματα[3] is in section 1 of Constantine Porphyrogenitus's Novel No. 7. This novel bears no date, but, since it was promulgated in Constantine's name only, its date must have been between 945, when Constantine had become sole Emperor once again, and 959, which was the year in which he died, and presumably it is later than March 947, which is the date of Constantine's Novel No. 6. In this section, Constantine enacts, as law, a rule which, so he here declares, had previously been sanctioned only by unwritten custom (ὅπερ ἡ συνήθεια ἀγράφως πρῴην ἐκύρωσε).[4] This rule was that persons who were under the obligation to provide a serving soldier (for one of the thematic army-corps) were not at liberty to sell the real estate from which a soldier's service was financed (μὴ ἐξεῖναι τοῖς στρατιώταις[5] τὰ ἐξ ὧν αἱ στρατεῖαι ὑπηρετοῦνται κτήματα διαπωλεῖν). In this novel, Constantine prescribes the minimum amounts of the property that was to be inalienable. For a cavalryman and for a seaman in any of the three naval thémata Aiyaíon Pélaghos, Sámos, and Kivyrrhaiótai, the minimum capital value of the soldier's or seaman's inalienable real estate was to be four pounds gold; for a seaman in the Imperial Fleet it was to be two pounds gold. (The seamen in the Imperial Fleet received pay in cash, besides the income from property in the form of real estate.)[6]

It is possible that the term στρατιωτικὰ κτήματα may have been coined for the first time when a customary rule was thus converted into formal

[1] Rouillard, op. cit., p. 91.

[2] See the bibliography in H. Antoniadis-Bibicou, *Études d'histoire maritime de Byzance, à propos du 'Thème des Caravisiens'* (Paris, 1966, S.E. and P.E.N.), p. 97, n. 2.

[3] The term occurs also in Novel No. 2 of the Emperors Rhomanós I, Constantine, and Christopher, which bears the date April 922, but the authenticity of this dating is suspect (see II, 1 (iii) (e), pp. 148–9). However, the novel itself is probably authentic, and its true date is probably 929. The text is printed in C. E. Zachariä von Lingenthal, *Jus Graeco-Romanum*, Part III, *Novellae, Constitutiones* (Leipzig, 1857, Weigel), pp. 234–41. The term στρατιωτικὰ κτήματα will be found on pp. 237 and 241.

[4] The statement that the rule had hitherto been only customary is made five times over in this novel (Lemerle, 'Esquisse', vol. ccxix, p. 266; vol. ccxx, p. 47, n. 2).

[5] A στρατιώτης was the owner of a piece of real estate that carried with it, as a legal servitude, the obligation to provide a soldier (a στρατευόμενος). The στρατιώτης might serve in person; alternatively, he might finance the equipment of a substitute (H. Glykatzi-Ahrweiler, 'Recherches sur l'administration de l'Empire byzantin aux ixᵉ–xiᵉ siècles', in *Bulletin de Correspondance Hellénique*, vol. lxxxiv (1960), pp. 1–111, on p. 13; Antoniadis-Bibicou, op. cit., p. 101).

[6] Constantine Porphyrogenitus, Novel No. 7, section 1 (*J.G.-R.*, Part III, p. 262). Constantine raises the figures for the desirable minima in *De Caer.*, Book II, chap. 49, p. 695: 'A cavalry soldier ought to possess real property (περιουσίαν ἀκίνητον), i.e. land (τοπία), of the value of five pounds (gold), or anyway not less than four pounds. For a seaman in the Imperial Fleet, the figure should be three pounds.'

and obligatory law. On the other hand, properties burdened with this military servitude, and kept intact, by custom, to the extent required for meeting the obligation, must have been in existence in East Roman Asia Minor ever since the date at which the Anatolic army-corps from Syria, the Armeniac army-corps from the Roman portion of Armenia, the Thracensian army-corps from the dioecesis of Thrace, and the Obsequium (Opsíkion), which had been the mobile force attached to the Emperor, had been cantoned in Asia Minor to hold this peninsula at the cost of leaving the outlying parts of the Empire undefended.

These four corps must have been concentrated in Asia Minor before the year 641, which was the date of Heraclius's death; for Heraclius had had the misfortune to live to see the whole of Syria, including the city of Antioch itself, wrested from the East Roman Empire by the Arabs after it had been recovered for the Empire from the Persians by Heraclius's own heroic counter-offensive. The innovation introduced by Constantine Porphyrogenitus's Novel No. 7 was that any land that had been registered in the military ledgers (ἐν τοῖς στρατιωτικοῖς κώδιξιν) was henceforth under an embargo. Henceforth it was not merely contrary to custom, but was positively illegal, for any registered land to be sold, even if the value of the amount that had been registered exceeded the required minimum of four pounds gold.[1] The military registers themselves, however, were in existence long before the years 945–59. For instance, when the Khurramite (Babekite) officer Theóphovos-Nasr took refuge in the East Roman Empire, with his troops, in 834,[2] and when he and his men were taken into the Imperial service by the Emperor Theóphilos, the Emperor 'had them registered in the military ledgers' (κώδιξι στρατιωτικοῖς αὐτοὺς ἀναγράφεται)[3]—the formula that reappears, verbatim, more than a century later, in Constantine Porphyrogenitus's Novel No. 7.

In these ledgers, a piece of real estate was registered, under the name of its owner at the time, if this property carried with it the obligation to produce and equip a serving soldier, and this record must have been kept ever since the date at which the four corps were cantoned in Asia Minor. The corps commanders, and also the Central Government's στρατιωτικὸν λογοθέσιον[4] at Constantinople, had to have up-to-date lists of persons under the obligation to serve personally, or by proxy, in the thematic army-corps in consequence of their being the owners, at the time, of a family property (οἶκος) which carried this servitude with it.[5]

---

[1] Constantine Porphyrogenitus, Novel No. 7, section 1.
[2] See II, 1 (iii) (a), pp. 83–4.
[3] *Theoph. Cont.*, p. 112.   [4] *De Caer.*, II, p. 698.
[5] At the time of the compilation of *De Caer.*, which was probably being revised and supplemented down to the date of Constantine Porphyrogenitus's death (959), persons in certain categories of public employment, listed in *De Caer.*, Book II, chap. 50, pp. 697–8, were personally exempted from this servitude, and consequently their οἶκοι were exempted during

The personal obligation was associated with the ownership of a family property, because, in the thematic army-corps, in contrast to the regiments of the Imperial Household (the tághmata), the soldiers' pay was not a living wage. If the families under obligation to produce thematic soldiers had not been landowners, they could not have met this obligation, and then the thematic corps, which constituted the major part of the East Roman Army, would have dissolved.

The thematic troops did receive some pay in cash (rhógha), but Constantine Porphyrogenitus records[1] that, formerly, this payment had been made only once in every four years. The army-corps had been divided into four groups, and these groups had been paid in rotation, one group only being paid in any single year.[2] Constantine refers to this[3] as being 'the old practice' (τὸ παλαιὸν τύπος), with the implication that it was obsolete in Constantine's own day. Constantine does not tell us what the practice in his own day was, but his Novel No. 7 makes it clear that the economic mainstay of the men who were under an obligation to serve in the thematic corps either in person or by proxy was, not their pay, but the income from their land—a minimum amount of which was now being made legally, and no longer merely customarily, inalienable by Constantine in this piece of legislation. Evidently it was recognized that, if the men were permitted to sell this minimum residual amount of their land, they would cease to be capable of carrying out their military obligations.

It is true that, on active service, the thematic troops received rations from the Imperial Treasury.[4] It is also on record that the soldiers of various categories, including the thematic soldiers, who served in the expeditions of the years 911[5] and 949 against the Cretan Muslims received

their lifetimes. But, at their deaths, the servitude attaching to their οἶκοι automatically revived. The horse, equipment, and arms of the soldier supplied by a family property belonged to the estate, not to the individual (*Ecloga*, chap. 16, § 2, cited by Antoniadis-Bibicou in op. cit., pp. 105–6, with p. 106, n. 1.).

[1] *De Caer.*, I, pp. 493–4 (in the memorandum on Τὰ Βασιλικὰ Ταξείδια). According to Vogt, *Basile 1er*, p. 363, Ibn Khurdādbih states that privates were paid once in every three years, but sometimes only once in every four, five, or six years, while another Arab authority states that a private's pay rose by one dinar per annum from one dinar to twelve dinars.

[2] The large sums of money that the military authorities had in hand for making these annual distributions of pay were a tempting prize for the Empire's enemies. Theophanes, pp. 484–5, records sub A.M. 6301 (A.D. 808/9) that, when pay was being distributed to the troops in théma Strymón, the Bulgars made a surprise attack, captured 1,100 pounds gold, and inflicted many casualties. Officers representing 'the other thémata' (? i.e. those others that were also due to be paid in that particular year) were present, so the distribution was not confined to the troops belonging to théma Strymón. On another occasion, thirteen kentenária of gold, destined for paying the troops of théma Armeniakoí, suffered the same fate (Kedhrênós, vol. ii, pp. 36 and 40).   [3] In *De Caer.*, loc. cit.

[4] St. Luke the Stylite, on active service, did not draw, ὡς ἔθος τοῖς στρατευομένοις . . . ὀψώνιον ἢ βασιλικὸν σιτηρέσιον (Biography of St. Luke, cited by Lemerle, 'Esquisse', vol. ccxx, p. 64).

[5] For this date 911, see Vasiliev, *Byzance et les Arabes*, ii, I, p. 199.

special pay in cash, besides rations, for the duration of these expeditions.[1] The author of Περὶ Παραδρομῆς Πολέμου emphasizes the importance of issuing the troops' pay and rations punctually and in full, and he recommends that these emoluments should be supplemented by bounties in excess of those that are customary and of those that are prescribed. This treatment will not only enable the men to acquire first-rate horses and equipment; it will raise their morale.[2] All the same, as far as the thematic soldiers were concerned, their rations (ἀννῶναι, σιτηρέσια, ὀψώνια), their pay (ῥόγα, μισθός), and the occasional Imperial bounties (δωρεαί, εὐεργεσίαι, σολέμνια)[3] were no more than windfalls that supplemented their staple income from their real estate. The possession of this property in the form of land was their essential means of support.[4]

The oldest of the military estates in Asia Minor must have been coeval with the arrival in Asia Minor of the four army-corps that were quartered there in consequence of the Arabs' conquest of Syria and of the Roman part of Armenia. The Anatolic and Armeniac corps must have beaten a hasty and disorderly retreat. The titanic impetus of the Arabs' onslaught had driven these corps to find shelter behind the natural ramparts of the Távros and Andítavros Ranges. The transfer of the Thracenses and the Obsequium to western and north-western Asia Minor, to support the two battered eastern corps that were still in the front line, must have been almost as hasty and as disorderly an operation. The East Roman Imperial administration and financial organization must have been temporarily paralysed. The Empire had not had time to begin to recover from the terrible Romano-Persian war of 604–28 when it was overtaken by the Arabs' impetuous attack. At the time of the four army-corps' arrival in Asia Minor, the Imperial Government cannot have had the means of providing them even with rations, not to speak of pay. For the troops, the only alternative to starvation or disbandment must have been to occupy as much vacant and unclaimed land within reach of their new cantonments as each man found himself able to cultivate and defend.[5]

The amount of land at the soldiers' disposal, just for the taking, must have been virtually unlimited; for, at the moment of the four corps'

---

[1] *De Caer.*, Book II, pp. 654, 655, 667–9.   [2] Π.Π.Π., p. 239.

[3] See Lemerle, 'Esquisse', vol. ccxx, p. 60; H. Glykatzi-Ahrweiler in loc. cit., on p. 7, n. 2.

[4] In contrast to the situation of the taghmatic soldiers, who were able to live on their pay (Glykatzi-Ahrweiler, loc. cit., p. 8, and p. 12, n. 3; Antoniadis-Bibicou, op. cit., pp. 100–1).

[5] The institution of στρατιωτικὰ κτήματα and the institution of thémata had no connection with each other according to some scholars, e.g. Lemerle ('Esquisse', vol. ccxix, pp. 70–1 and 257) and Karayannopulos (*Die Entstehung der byzantinischen Themenverfassung* (Munich, 1959, Beck), pp. 15–17, 71–5, 82–8). The question is one of nomenclature. The army-corps that were concentrated in Asia Minor in the seventh century were not yet called thémata, and it was some time before their commanders became the governors of the districts in which they were stationed. The lands which the soldiers had occupied may not have been called στρατιωτικὰ κτήματα before the tenth century. But it does not follow that the troops who settled in Asia Minor in the seventh century did not take possession of lands there at that date.

arrival, the depopulation of Asia Minor was at its nadir-point. Though there had been no permanent Persian occupation of Asia Minor, a Persian expeditionary force had reached Chalcedon at least twice in the course of the war—first in 609[1] and again in 626. The Persians may also have reached Chalcedon on another expedition *circa* 616.[2] As for eastern and central Asia Minor, it had repeatedly been a theatre of hostilities. A large part of the population must have perished or fled. The arrival of the four army-corps at some date after the fall of Antioch in 636 was the first step towards the re-peopling of Asia Minor. If the troops helped themselves to vacant and unclaimed land there, the Government is likely to have acquiesced in the accomplished fact. From the Government's point of view, the seizure by the troops of property that was not theirs by right was a lesser evil than the alternative, which was to see the Army disintegrate while the land remained derelict. The troops' seizure of the land will have been condoned and ratified by the Government retrospectively when the Government opened its ledgers for registering both the families under obligation to produce a thematic serving soldier and the estates from which these families were making their living. The Government must have opened these ledgers as soon as it had time to turn round. It was of vital importance for the Government to ensure that the army-corps now quartered in Asia Minor should be kept up to strength and that the families which were under obligation to produce serving soldiers should have the means of maintaining and equipping these.[3]

In Ostrogorsky's opinion, the establishment of the military estates 'was the *causa efficiens* of the spread of the system of peasant proprietorship'[4] in the East Roman Empire. The ratio of peasant proprietors in the rural population of Asia Minor and Thrace will have been increased when the original soldier-immigrants into Asia Minor were reinforced by later batches of settlers; for all these later settlers will have been given allotments of land. Some of these allotments will have carried with them the obligation to produce a serving soldier. Whatever the origins of the rural military families (οἶκοι στρατιωτικοί) may have been, they were peasant families, like the civilian families (οἶκοι πολιτικοί),[5] and these two sets of

---

[1] Stratós, op. cit., p. 65.   [2] Ibid., p. 115.

[3] In my dating of the formation of the oldest of the στρατιωτικὰ κτήματα, I am in agreement with Ostrogorsky, 'Die wirtschaftlichen und sozialen Grundlagen des byzantinischen Reiches', p. 131. Like Ostrogorsky, I date this event in the last years of Heraclius's reign. I do not think, however, that it is likely that these oldest military estates in Asia Minor were created and distributed by Heraclius himself, as Ostrogorsky, ibid., holds that they were. No doubt the lands obtained by later batches of settlers in Asia Minor—Armenian and Syrian Christian and Eastern Muslim refugees and Slav deportees—were allotted to them by the Imperial Government. But, by the time when these later settlements were made, conditions in the East Roman Empire were already less chaotic than they had been at the end of Heraclius's reign.

[4] Ostrogorsky in loc. cit., p. 133.

[5] The distinction between these two kinds of families is drawn in *De Caer.*, Book II, p. 695.

peasant families lived side by side in the same villages and were fellow members in the same communities—the communities, that is to say, whose members were responsible collectively for the payment of the total amount of tax at which each community as a whole was assessed. The military families, like the civilian families, had to pay the land-tax (τοῦ δημοσίου τέλους),[1] and door- and windows-tax (ἀερικόν),[2] and perhaps the hearth-tax (καπνικόν, meaning literally, 'chimney-smoke' tax) as well; but Leo VI ruled[3] that the military families were to be exempt from all other public services (δουλειῶν) and corvées (ἀγγαρειῶν), such as constructing fortifications, ship-building, bridge-building, road-making, and other public works. (If local funds were forthcoming, such public works were to be carried out by paid labour.)

Every military estate had to present a living member of the family that owned the estate for registration in the military ledgers as a thematic soldier who would serve either in person or by proxy. For instance, St. Efthýmios the Younger, who was born in A.M. 6332 (A.D. 823/4), was presented for registration by his widowed mother because the family's estate was a military one and the widow had no other son to perform the military service for which she had to provide. Accordingly, Efthýmios's name[4] was in the ledger from that time onwards, though, in the event, Efthýmios never actually served, since he absconded at the age of eighteen, in order to become a monk on the Mysian Mount Olympus.[5] From time to time there were musters (ἀδνούμια)[6] of all persons in an army-corps district who were under the obligation to serve, and the men were inspected in order to discover whether they were or were not properly equipped. The returns of these musters and inspections were, no doubt, used for keeping the entries in the military ledgers up to date. If a corps was going to be mobilized for active service, the inspection was strict, and the penalty for not being properly equipped might be severe.[7]

Usually, however, only an élite, among the men who were under obligation to serve, was called up for actual service,[8] and the Emperor Leo

---

[1] Leo VI, *Taktiká*, Dhiat. 4, § 1, col. 700, and Dhiat. 20, § 71, col. 1032.

[2] Dhiat. 20, § 71, col. 1032. For the meaning of ἀερικόν, see Ostrogorsky, 'Die ländliche Steuergemeinde', p. 53.

[3] *Taktiká*, Dhiat. 4, § 1, col. 700, and Dhiat. 20, § 71, col. 1032.

[4] i.e. his original secular name Nikḗtas.

[5] L. Petit, 'Vie et Office de Saint Euthyme le Jeune', in *Revue de l'Orient Chrétien*, 8ᵐᵉ année (1903), Avant-propos et Vie, pp. 155–205; Office, pp. 503–36. The present references are to pp. 172 and 173.   [6] Leo VI, *Taktiká*, Dhiat. 9, § 4, col. 768.

[7] See 'Anonymus Vári', p. 50, which is illustrated by Nikḗtas of Amnía's story in his biography of his grandfather St. Philáretos, on pp. 125–7 of Fourmy and Leroy's edition. Only the sick were excused from being called up. Malingerers were punishable. On return home from a campaign, there was to be a second muster before any general dismissal of the mobilized troops ('Anon. Vári', loc. cit.).

[8] Leo VI, *Taktiká*, Dhiat. 18, §§ 149–53, cols. 988/9, limits the strength, for active service, of 'the so-called στρατιωτικὸν θέμα' to 4,000 picked cavalrymen. The rest of the troops

VI, in his *Taktiká*,[1] instructs corps-commanders that to pick out good soldiers and good officers is one of a commander's most important duties. The commander is instructed to pick out well-to-do men (εὐπόρους), 'in order that, on mobilization, that is to say, at the assemblage of the corps (ἐν τῷ ἐξπεδίτῳ ἤγουν ἐν τῇ συναγωγῇ τοῦ φοσσάτου), they may be able to give all their time and attention to their military service'. If they are to be able to do this, 'they must have, in their own households (ἐν τοῖς ἰδίοις οἴκοις) other men both for cultivating the land and for providing the soldier with his equipment and his arms'.[2]

Well-to-do persons who were under an obligation to produce a serving soldier were a godsend to a corps-commander if he was suffering from a shortage of arms for his troops. In this situation, 'order the men who are well-to-do, but who are not presenting themselves for service, to produce one horse and one soldier each as their proxies if they do not wish to serve in person. By this means, poor men who are warlike will get their arms, while rich men who are unwarlike will bear their fair share of the burden with the serving soldiers.'[3]

Private soldiers, as well as officers, in the tághmata, and the more well-to-do soldiers (τοὺς δυνατωτέρους) in the thematic regiments (βάνδα), were to bring batmen (either slaves or freemen) with them on campaign, and, on occasions when pay was being distributed or when a muster was being held, the soldiers' batmen, as well as the soldiers' arms, were to be strictly inspected and listed.[4] However, the mobilization of a thematic *corps d'élite* consisting of well-to-do soldiers exclusively was an ideal that was never achieved in practice. There would also be poorer soldiers, and these were to share one slave or servant, and one pack-animal, among three or four men.[5] If there were not enough batmen, the worst soldiers were to do batmen's work.[6]

In reality, the differences in degree of affluence or indigence were as great in the military families as they were in the civilian families, and this is not surprising. In the original land-grabbing by the soldiers of the corps concentrated in Asia Minor, and even in the subsequent allotments of land by the Imperial Government to later batches of settlers, the values of the holdings, in terms of units of productivity (*iugationes*), are not

furnished by the corps should be assigned to other arms and other duties. Even in a serious emergency, the strength of the élite cavalry of each corps should be kept within the limit of 4,000 men, because of the now prevalent lack of training, lack of keenness, and paucity of numbers of the common run of thematic soldiers.

[1] Dhiat. 4, § 1, col. 700.   [2] Ibid.
[3] Leo VI, *Taktiká*, Dhiat. 20, § 205, col. 1069.
[4] Op. cit., Dhiat. 6, § 15, col. 725, copying 'Mavríkios', *Stratēghikón*, Part 1, chap. 2, p. 24 Scheffer, p. 54 Mihăescu.
[5] Dhiat. 6, § 16, col. 725. This passage is copied, almost verbatim, from 'Mavríkios', *Stratēghikón*, Part 1, chap. 2, pp. 24–5 Scheffer, p. 54 Mihăescu.
[6] Leo VI, *Taktiká*, Dhiat. 4, § 38, cols. 705–7.

likely to have been more than approximately equal; and, with the passage of time, the inequality between them must have grown greater. Some fathers of military families will have had large families and will have bequeathed a fraction of their estates to each of their sons. They were free to do this,[1] so long as it was understood that each fraction carried with it its quota of the tax-obligation and the military obligation of the previously undivided estate. On the other hand, there will have been military families that had suffered heavy casualties, and whose estates had consequently been preserved undivided.

The story, cited above, in Nikĕtas of Amnía's biography of his grandfather St. Philáretos,[2] tells of the plight of an indigent thematic soldier. This poor man possessed nothing but a single horse and his arms, and, on the eve of an inspection that was to be the prelude to a mobilization, the poor man's horse dropped down dead. He then borrowed Philáretos's horse 'in order . . . to get through the muster' (ἵνα . . . διαβῇ τὸ ἀδνοῦμιν), but he tells Philáretos that, after passing muster, he will have to abscond —whereupon Philáretos makes a gift to him of the horse that his indigent neighbour had borrowed for this harassing occasion. Evidently, absconding was the last resort for a representative of a military family who was too poor to equip himself properly. In the returns that were made of the findings of a muster, there was a column for men who had absconded, besides columns for the sick, for the malingerers, and for the men who had duly responded to the mobilization order.[3] The penalty for truancy after the end of the close season was condemnation to permanent garrison duty (εἰς διηνεκῆ ταξατίωνα).[4] An officer who gives a soldier leave of absence in wartime is to pay a fine graduated according to the officer's rank.[5]

The indigence of the military families can be gauged by the difficulties that the military authorities encountered in trying to prevent the men from neglecting their military duties in order to earn their living by devoting all their time and resources to cultivating their lands. It has been noted already that Leo VI recommended a corps-commander to pick soldiers who were sufficiently well-off to be able to afford to have their agricultural work done for them, and to have their equipment and arms provided for them, by other hands. In the East Roman code of

---

[1] See Constantine Porphyrogenitus's Novel No. 7 of some date between 945 and 959, in *Jus Graeco-Romanum* (hereafter *J. G.-R.*), Part III, p. 262.

[2] Fourmy and Leroy's edition, pp. 125-7.

[3] 'Anonymus Vári', p. 50.

[4] Leo VI, *Taktiká*, Dhiat. 8, § 4, col. 764. In the passage of 'Mavríkios's' *Stratēghikón* that Leo VI is copying here, the penalty is expulsion from the Army. The offender is to be handed over as a civilian (ὡς παγανός) to the civil authorities (Part 1, chap. 6, p. 35 Scheffer, p. 62 Mihăescu).

[5] Leo VI, ibid., § 26, col. 768. In the passage from which this is copied, 'Mavríkios' sets the fine at 30 nomísmata (Part 1, chap 7, p. 37 Scheffer, p. 64 Mihăescu).

military punishments (Περὶ στρατιωτικῶν ἐπιτιμίων),[1] it is laid down categorically[2] that soldiers must not give any of their time to agriculture or to trade, and that they must not undertake any public responsibilities, because these activities divert their attention from soldiering and from soldierly pursuits. Evidently this injunction was difficult to enforce. Leo VI[3] advises a corps-commander to keep his men busy with military training-exercises, and the 'Anonymus Vári', who is thought to have been an officer who had served under the Emperor Nikêphóros II Phokás (963–9),[4] explains the reason why.[5]

> To exercise and muster the army . . . is beneficial and is very much to the point. . . . To stay at home, (militarily) inactive, without either taking part in training-exercises or going on campaign annually in the campaigning season, is fatal for soldiers. It reduces them to the level of traders and of the common herd of yokels. They will sell their military equipment and their best horses and will buy oxen and the rest of the paraphernalia for agriculture, and then they will soon acquire such a habit of (military) inactivity that they will find this unstrenuous sheltered life more to their taste than battles and toils in the service of Christendom. Then, if there is an enemy invasion and the Army has to be mobilized for active service—an emergency that is bound to overtake the (East) Romans constantly—it will be impossible to find anyone imbued with proper soldierly energy . . .

Constant soldierly activity and training are the making of good soldiers.

This point is illustrated by the soldierly spirit of the akrítai, who are the enemy's immediate neighbours. The ceaseless unremitting warfare that is the akrítai's lot makes them spirited and valiant. Our soldiers must be trained and be sent on active service, and their families must be protected from abuses of all kinds; but this is not enough; they ought to be paid their due meed of honour as champions of Christendom.

The author immediately goes on to denounce the arch-abuse that saps a soldier's morale.

> It is of the first importance that the soldiers should not be humiliated and insulted by some (petty) taxation-officer. . . . Penalties and contemptuous treatment and humiliations make soldiers slack and unadventurous and poor-spirited.

---

[1] Text published by W. Ashburner, under the title 'The Byzantine Mutiny Act', in *J.H.S.*, vol. xlvi, Part I (1926), pp. 81–109.

[2] In Article 56.   [3] *Taktiká*, Dhiat. 11, § 5, col. 793.

[4] 'Anonymus Vári', Preface, p. 5.

[5] 'Anonymus Vári', *De Re Militari*, chap. 28, pp. 48–9. Cf. Περὶ Παραδρομῆς Πολέμου, p. 187: commanders of thémata on the frontier must not allow their men δι' αἰσχρὸν κέρδος οἴκοι καθίζεσθαι.

The same point is made at greater length and in still more vigorous language by the contemporary author of Περὶ Παραδρομῆς Πολέμου.[1]

The best and the most necessary of all provisions for the soldiers' welfare—the treatment that stimulates their keenness, heightens their valour, and gives them the heart to do unprecedented deeds of daring—is to ensure that their families, the families of the men in their service, and every member of their households, shall enjoy complete freedom. This right of theirs was protected and safeguarded from time immemorial, and you will find it laid down in the legislation of the Emperors of olden times, and written into their taktiká.[2] The soldiers must not only be free; they must receive their due meed of honour, and must not be treated contemptuously or be humiliated. I am ashamed to have to report that men of this stamp are subjected to beatings—men who are ready to give their lives for the service of the Emperors and for the freedom and defence of Christendom. And they suffer these indignities at the hands of petty tax-collectors—creatures who contribute nothing to the public welfare, and who do nothing but oppress and evict the poor—raking in a pile of money for themselves by their iniquitous bleeding of the poor. The soldiers ought not to be humiliated by the thematic judges either, nor to be dragged about like slaves, nor to be flogged nor to be loaded with chains and to be put in the stocks (shameful treatment) . . . The law itself lays it down that every officer shall exercise authority over his own people and shall be their judge. And to what other officer do the people of a théma belong except to the commander (τοῦ στρατηγοῦ), whom the Emperor has appointed to this post? Consequently, according to the law, the commander of a théma has always been invested with the authority over his own théma. It is the commander's prerogative to be the judge in cases concerning military affairs and to deal with anything that arises in the théma. It is the thematic judge's function to be the commander's colleague and to give the commander his cooperation.

The two military handbooks from which these passages have been quoted were probably written soon after the beginning of the last quarter of the tenth century. The passages indicate that, by this date, the taxation-officers had gained the support of the thematic judges in their proceedings for assessing and collecting the taxes payable by the military families, and that, between them, these civil servants had defeated the corps-commanders' attempts to protect the soldiers of their corps—in spite of the fact that a corps-commander was also the governor of his corps-district. The blame for this lies with the Emperor Leo VI; for his limitation of the taxes and corvées due from the military families had not amounted to much. Leo VI had not relieved them of the land-tax,[3]

---

[1] pp. 239–41.

[2] This passage of the *Π.Π.Π.*, and the passage of the 'Anonymus Vári's' *De Re Militari* that has been quoted above, refer direct to Leo VI's *Taktiká*, Dhiat. 4, § 1, col. 700, where Leo rules that the (thematic) soldiers are to have their families freed from all public services (δουλειῶν) with the single exception of the land-tax (τοῦ δημοσίου τέλους).

[3] Leo VI, *Taktiká*, Dhiat. 4, § 1, col. 700.

which was the major tax, and, as an after-thought, he had left them subject to the door- and windows-tax as well.[1] It is true that Leo had relieved the military families of surcharges and corvées, but this amount of relief cannot have offset adequately the obligation, imposed on the owners of military estates, to equip and arm themselves and to absent themselves from their properties for a large part of the year in order to take part in training exercises and to serve on campaigns. A civilian family, subject to tax-surcharges and corvées, but not to military service, must have been decidedly better off than a military family that owned the same amount of property.

It is no wonder that the serving members of military families spent as much of their time as their officers allowed on the non-military work of making a living from their land, or that the majority of them were hard put to it to provide themselves with equipment and arms up to the standard that their officers required. It is significant that Leo VI instructs his corps-commanders to make a survey during the winter vacation from hostilities (ἐν τῷ καιρῷ τοῦ παραχειμαδίου) of the horses and arms needed by their corps,[2] and that the corps-commanders sometimes found themselves in difficulties over the arming of their troops.[3] The expedient[4] of obliging a rich owner of a military estate to equip, arm, and mount a substitute for himself might improve the quality of the serving soldier produced by that particular estate, but this would not solve the problem of obtaining adequately equipped serving soldiers from poorer military estates. A corps-commander was responsible for making sure that a soldier who was under obligation to equip himself had sufficient resources, reckoned in terms of real estate of a minimum value.[5] (This minimum would be different for different branches of the service.)

If a military estate had become too poor to produce a serving soldier, the first recourse for relieving it was to grant it exemption (ἀδόρεια) from fiscal charges.[6] The next recourse was to compel a number of impoverished persons who were under obligation to serve in person or by proxy to club together to equip one among them for serving.[7] The invention of this expedient is attributed to Nikêphóros I (802–11), who had been a treasury official before he had become Emperor.[8] Constantine Porphyrogenitus was aware that this was an innovation, and that the original rule had been that soldiers should equip themselves out of their own resources,

---

[1] *Taktiká*, Dhiat. 20, § 71, col. 1032.　　　　[2] Op. cit., Dhiat. 11, § 50, col. 805.
[3] Op. cit., Dhiat. 20, § 205, col. 1069.　　　　[4] See ibid.
[5] Op. cit., Epíloghos, col. 1083.
[6] Glykatzi-Ahrweiler in loc. cit., p. 14.
[7] χορηγεῖν διὰ κοινωνίας καὶ συνδόσεως (Glykatzi-Ahrweiler in loc. cit., pp. 5–6). The contributors were called συνδόται (ibid., p. 14).
[8] This is number two in Theophanes's list (on pp. 486–7) of ten oppressive measures taken by Nikêphóros I. Δευτέραν . . . κάκωσιν, προσέταξε στρατεύειν πτωχοὺς καὶ ἐξοπλίζεσθαι παρὰ τῶν ὁμοχώρων. Cf. Kedhrênós, vol. ii, p. 37.

and should not be equipped by a consortium of contributors.[1] However, Constantine notes[2] that, in his day,

when they are poor, contributors (συνδόται) are assigned to them in order that, with the contributors' help, the recipient of the contributions may have the means to perform his own service. If, however, they are so utterly penurious that, even with the aid of the contributors that have been assigned to them, they are unable to perform their own service, they are given their discharge (ἀδορεύονται) and are transferred to the irregulars (ἀπελάτας, literally 'cattle-lifters'), who provide dzékones (τζέκωνες) for (garrisoning) forts. The lands belonging to soldiers who have suffered this mishap are left unexpropriated. Their boundaries are marked out and they are made over to the Treasury. The intention is that, if one of these discharged soldiers manages to retrieve his fortunes, he should recover his own land and should be re-instated in his own military estate (στρατείαν).[3]

It will be seen that, by Constantine Porphyrogenitus's time, vigorous and effective intervention by the Imperial Government on behalf of the thematic military families offered the only hope—but this only a forlorn hope—of keeping the thematic military formations in being.

(e) *The Encroachments of the Δυνατοί on the Land-holdings of the Πένητες and the Emperors' Agrarian Legislation*

It has been noted already[4] that the starting-date of the series of enactments for the protection of freehold peasant communities against the encroachments of large-scale landowners was approximately contemporaneous with the opening, in 926, of the East Roman counter-offensive on the Empire's eastern fronts, and it has been suggested[5] that the reason why the δυνατοί were so eager to invest in rural real estate, as soon as this became a safe field for investment, was because their openings for investment in urban trade and industry were narrowly restricted. The Emperor Rhomanós I was a man of humble origin, and his personal experience made him sympathetic towards the poor. He was, however, also a borderer, if his surname Lekapênós is evidence that his family had come from the village of Lakápê, which lay to the east-south-east of the frontier

---

[1] *De Caer.*, II, p. 695.   [2] Ibid., pp. 695–6.

[3] The word στρατεία has two meanings: (i) military service (Lemerle, 'Esquisse', vol. ccxx, p. 49 and p. 60, n. 4); (ii) a piece of land saddled with the obligation to produce a serving soldier (Lemerle in loc. cit., p. 49; Glykatzi-Ahrweiler in loc. cit., p. 13). A strateía in meaning (ii) was the real estate, belonging to an οἶκος στρατιωτικός, that was saddled with the servitude of providing a soldier. Antoniadis-Bibicou suggests (op. cit., p. 101) that strateíai in this sense were coeval with the institution of thémata in the sense of army-corps districts. I have suggested, above, that the strateíai were coeval with the cantonment of the army-corps themselves in Asia Minor.

[4] In II, 1 (i), on p. 34.

[5] In II, 1 (ii), on p. 54.

fortress Sozópetra, on one of the headwaters of the Kharínas tributary of the River Euphrates. If Lakápé was in truth Rhomanós I's place of origin, he or his ancestors[1] had come from a village that had passed into East Roman hands out of Muslim hands within Rhomanós's own lifetime, when the new East Roman théma Lykandós had been carved out of territory previously under Muslim rule by the Armenian free-lance borderer Mleh (*Graecè* Melías). This would explain Rhomanós's concern to take advantage of the 'Abbasid Caliphate's decadence in order to expand the East Roman Empire's domain still farther eastwards, as soon as the danger from Tsar Symeon of Bulgaria had been surmounted. Rhomanós I's success (won for him by the ability of his general John Kourkoúas) was commemorated in the name Rhomanópolis, which was given to a fortress guarding a kleisoúra on the Empire's new frontier beyond the Euphrates.[2] In adopting this policy of eastward expansion, Rhomanós, whatever his motive may have been, was unintentionally playing into the hands of the δυνατοί in the economic and social struggle on the East Roman Empire's domestic front.

Nature, too, played into the hands of the δυνατοί by afflicting the Empire with the terrible winter of 927/8.[3] The weather caused a famine, and the mortality was high. All versions of the Byzantine chronicle are in

---

[1] Rhomanós himself had come from théma Armeniakoí, according to *Georg. Mon. Cont.*, p. 911, and *Theoph. Cont.*, p. 419.

[2] For the location of this Rhomanópolis, see Vasiliev, *Byzance et les Arabes*, vol. iii (1935), pp. 190–2.

[3] In Rhomanós I's Novel No. 5 of September 934, section 2, the date of the beginning of the famine is placed in the first indiction in the current series (*J.G.-R.*, III, pp. 247–8). It is placed, that is to say, in the year 1 September 927–31 August 928. In this section of the act, it is provided that grandees (περιφανεῖς) in the categories enumerated in section 1 are to be evicted, in favour of the original owners, from lands that they have acquired 'in or after the first indiction in the current series, i.e. from the date of the beginning of the famine onwards' (ἀπὸ τῆς παρελθούσης πρώτης ἰνδικτιῶνος, ἤτοι τοῦ λιμοῦ καταλαβόντος ἢ παρελθόντος). On the other hand, all versions of the Byzantine chronicle state that the bout of bitter weather that caused the famine started on Christmas Day, Indiction 6 (i.e. on Christmas Day, 932). If this date for the onset of the famine were correct, the date of Rhomanós I's Novel No. 2 would be, not April 922, which is the date attached to the text of Novel No. 2, but April 933 at the earliest, and the co-Emperor Christopher's name would have to be expunged from the title, since Christopher had died in August 931. Alternatively, we should have to conclude that Novel No. 2 is spurious and that Rhomanós I's first genuine act of agrarian legislation was his Novel No. 5 of September 934. This choice of alternatives would confront us, because we are informed by a trustworthy authority, Theódhoros Dhekapolítês, that the series of acts of agrarian legislation did not start before the time of the famine (see pp. 148–9). However, Dhekapolítês also informs us (see ibid). that there was an interval of eighteen years between the date of the earliest piece of Imperial agrarian legislation and the promulgation of Constantine Porphyrogenitus's Novel No. 6 of March 947, and this piece of evidence tells decisively in favour of Novel No. 5's date for the famine, namely 927/8, as against the chronicles' date for it, namely 932/3. Dhekapolítês's two statements, read together, also tell us that Novel No. 5 of September 934 was not the earliest of the agrarian laws; that there is therefore a presumption that Novel No. 2 is genuine; but that, if it is genuine, its date is likely to have been, not 922, but 929.

accord[1] in praising Rhomanós for the measures that he took, in this emergency, for the relief of the victims of the famine in Constantinople. He provided physical shelter for them by boarding up the arcades, and he raised funds for distribution to them to which he made the city churches contribute. The urban poor had no reserves on which they could draw; but the famine was not confined to the cities, and the rural poor had land to sell. The δυνατοί took advantage of the peasant freeholders' straits. The subsequent legislation makes it clear that, in the transfer of the ownership of land in the East Roman countryside, the winter of 927/8 marked a turning-point. When the δυνατοί 'saw that the poor were hard pressed by the famine, they bought up the properties of the poor at bargain prices (εὐώνως) in exchange for specie or corn or other commodities. They took ruthless advantage of the straits to which the poor had been reduced.'[2]

The way had been opened for the δυνατοί by ill-advised legislation in the reign of Leo VI (886–912). Previously, it had been the Government's policy to protect the property of the freeholding peasant communities, and the law had made two main provisions for this purpose. The law had limited a peasant freeholder's freedom to sell his land by giving the right of first refusal (προτίμησις) to the other members of his community, either individually or collectively. The intention had been to preserve peasant estates—which were a sure source of tax-money, and of soldiers too in the case of military estates—from being acquired by new owners of other classes, from whom taxes and soldiers would be harder to extract, either because the new owners would be privileged *de jure* (as monasteries, for instance, were), or because they would be influential enough to defy the taxation-officers *de facto* (as influential laymen could). The second safeguard[3] had been a veto on business transactions by public officers during their term of office. They were prohibited, while in office, from buying any real or movable property and from starting any building-work without the Emperor's express permission, and also from receiving gifts, if such gifts were not confirmed by the donor in writing after the officer's term of office had expired or even after the lapse of a further five years.

Leo VI, in his Novel No. 84, cancelled this restriction totally for metropolitan public officers, on the ground that, in the metropolis, an aggrieved party could easily appeal to the Emperor himself. For provincial officers

---

[1] See *Georg. Mon. Cont.*, pp. 908–9; Leo Grammaticus, pp. 318–20; *Theoph. Cont.*, pp. 417–18; pseudo-Symeon, pp. 743–4.

[2] Novel No. 5, dated September 934, of the Emperors Rhomanós, Constantine (son of Leo VI), and Stephen and Constantine (sons of Rhomanós), section 1, in *J.G.-R.*, Part III, p. 247. The first of the two co-Emperors Constantine who are named in the title must be the Porphyrogenitus, for Rhomanós's son Constantine would not have been given precedence over his older brother Stephen.

[3] Justinian, *Cod.* I, 53, 1 (*Vassiliká*, VI, 3, 51), cited by P. Noailles and A. Dain, *Les Nouvelles de Léon VI le Sage* (Paris, 1944, Soc. d'Ed. les 'Belles Lettres)', p. 282, n. 4.

Leo ruled that a commander (stratêghós) of an army-corps district should continue to be bound by the previous restrictions, but that the commander's subordinates should henceforth have a free hand—subject to the commander's being empowered to review their transactions and to cashier a subordinate or to maintain him in office, at his discretion.[1] In his Novel No. 114,[2] Leo VI struck at the peasant freeholding communities' right to have the first refusal. He gave the peasant owner of real property who had paid his tax on this property up to date an untrammelled and incontestable freedom to alienate this property, and he limited to the first six months of the first year (after the transaction) the right of the seller's neighbours to buy the property back from the purchaser at the price which the purchaser had paid. Leo defended this serious restriction of the historic right of first refusal on the specious ground that it might be abused. A would-be seller's neighbours might misuse their veto to delay the sale till they could force the seller to sell to them at a bargain price. This was true; but we may guess that, in professing to be seeking to secure a fair price for the would-be seller, Leo was in truth concerned to further the interest, not of the seller, but of the δυνατός who would be competing with the seller's community for the acquisition of the seller's land.

The texts have survived of fifteen documents dealing with the crisis[3] that had been created by the cumulative effects of Leo VI's legislation, of the East Roman Army's successful counter-offensive on the eastern front, and of the famine of 927/8. Thirteen of these documents are in the form of novels promulgated by Emperors. (One of these novels is a decision, drafted for the Emperor Rhomanós II by a máyistros, on a case that had been referred by a thematic judge.) The other two documents are siyíllia (certificates) issued by officials. The earliest of these fifteen documents is dated 922, the latest 996. We also know the gist of a novel of 1003/4.

The authenticity of the ostensibly earliest document in the series is suspect, if the date attributed to it in the text[4] of it, as this text has come down to us, is correct. This novel's alleged date, April 922, is earlier than the precipitation of the agrarian crisis by the famine of 927/8. Moreover, the máyistros Theódhoros Dhekapolítês, who drafted the decision for the Emperor Rhomanós II (959–63), interprets Constantine Porphyrogenitus's Novel No. 6 of March 947 as having restrospective effect 'back

---

[1] In his Novel No. 23, Leo VI had extended to a provincial governor's female descendants the veto, already in force with regard to his male descendants, on betrothing them (presumably by pressure) to inhabitants of his province. This Novel No. 23 was a derisory offset to Novel No. 84.

[2] In op. cit., Paraleipomena, p. 376.

[3] 'Les ordonnances ne s'occupent pas de l'évolution économique, mais de ses conséquences sociales' (Bach, 'Les Lois agraires', p. 70).

[4] Published in *J.G.-R.*, Part III, pp. 234–41.

to the year of the famine (i.e. 927/8), which is the date at which the series of acts of (agrarian) legislation started'.[1]

In the same document, however, Dhekapolîtês also states[2] that there had been an interval of eighteen years between Constantine's Novel No. 6 of March 947 and the first act of Imperial (agrarian) legislation. This reckoning would make the date of Rhomanós I's first agrarian novel 928/9, and, in the title of Basil II's Novel No. 29 of 1 January 996, the first (agrarian) legislation of the Emperor Rhomanós I is, in fact, said to have been promulgated in the second indiction (i.e. in 928/9). If these two statements are correct, Novel No. 5, dated September 934, of the Emperors Rhomanós, Constantine (Leo VI's son), and Stephen and Constantine (Rhomanós's sons) cannot have been the first. The date of the first must have been 929, and this date for Novel No. 2 of the Emperors Rhomanós, Constantine (Leo VI's son) and Christopher (Rhomanós's son) is both possible and probable. It is possible because Christopher was Emperor probably from May 921[3] till August 931 (the year and month of his death). The dating 929 is probable because the year 929 is close enough to the famine year 927/8 to warrant Dhekapolîtês's previous statement that the series of acts of agrarian legislation had started at the date of the famine. The year 929 is a probable date for the earliest of the acts for a further reason. It seems unlikely that Rhomanós would have waited for more than half-a-dozen years—from the spring of 928 to the autumn of 934— before taking action for dealing with a crisis that had evidently come to a head at the time of the famine itself. It therefore seems warrantable to

---

[1] *J.G.-R.*, Part III, p. 282. [2] Ibid., p. 284.

[3] All versions of the Byzantine chronicle date Christopher's death in the August of Indiction 4 (i.e. August 931, since Indiction 4 ran from 1 September 930 to 31 August 931). The dates on which Christopher was proclaimed Emperor and was subsequently crowned are not so well established. *Georg. Mon. Cont.*, p. 890, Leo Grammaticus, p. 304, and pseudo-Symeon, p. 731, date this pair of events in the May of Indiction 5 (i.e. May 917); *Theoph. Cont.* appears to date it in the May of Indiction 8 (i.e. May 920), since it, as well as the other chronicles, gives this indiction as the year of the crowning of Christopher's mother Theodora as avghoústa. Christopher's elevation is mentioned immediately after his mother's in all versions of the chronicle, and *Theoph. Cont.* does not give a separate date for Christopher's elevation. Of course, both Indiction 5 (916/17) and Indiction 8 (919/20) are impossible dates for the elevation of either the wife or a son of Rhomanós to Imperial rank, since Rhomanós himself did not attain this rank till 17 December 920. All versions of the chronicle state that Christopher was crowned on a Whit Sunday that fell in May, but different versions give different days of the month: 17 May (*Theoph. Cont.*; but *Georg. Mon. Cont.* and Leo Grammaticus give this as the date on which Christopher was proclaimed, before being crowned); 20 May (Leo Grammaticus); 24 May (*Georg. Mon. Cont.*). Whit Sunday fell on 20 May in 921 (see Runciman, *The Emperor Romanus Lecapenus*, p. 65, n. 2), and this seems to be the most probable year. All versions of the chronicle state that Theodora died on 20 February of Indiction 10 (i.e. on 20 February 922), and that the Emperor Christopher's wife Sophía was created avghoústa in Theodora's place before the end of the same month. Therefore Christopher must have been Emperor already by 20 February 922, and he cannot have been proclaimed or crowned before his father's coronation on 17 December 920. This seems to leave 20 May 921 as the only possible date for Christopher's coronation.

conclude that the Novel numbered 2 and dated 922[1] is authentic, but that the true date is, not 922, but 929.[2]

The preamble to this novel of the Emperors Rhomanós, Constantine, and Christopher declares that the novel's purpose is to get rid of the inconsistency between two existing laws, one of which[3] rules that no one is to be prevented by his relatives or his co-owners (of still undistributed common land)[4] from selling land to anyone to whom he chooses to sell it, and another which expressly forbids him to sell to anyone except the inhabitants of his own rural district ($\mu\eta\tau\rho\sigma\kappa\omega\mu\acute{\iota}\alpha\varsigma$).

Section I of the new novel provides that, if anyone wishes to alienate any real property belonging to him (e.g. a house or arable land or a vineyard) by selling it or making it over to another party for development ($\dot{\epsilon}\mu\phi\acute{\nu}\tau\epsilon\nu\sigma\iota\nu$) or by leasing it, he must first advertise his intention to certain parties who are to have the first refusal in the following order:[5] first, relatives who are $\dot{\alpha}\nu\alpha\mu\grave{\iota}\xi$ $\sigma\nu\gamma\kappa\epsilon\acute{\iota}\mu\epsilon\nu\sigma\iota$ (i.e. whose land is mixed up topographically with the would-be alienator's land; or who are involved in the same collective tax-liabilities as the would-be alienator?); second, co-owners ($\kappa\sigma\iota\nu\omega\nu\sigma\acute{\iota}$) who are similarly implicated; third, persons who are merely mixed up, without being in any other relation with the would-be alienator; fourth, his adjacent $\dot{\sigma}\mu\sigma\tau\epsilon\lambda\epsilon\hat{\iota}\varsigma$ (defined as being persons registered as being under the same subordinate ($\dot{\nu}\pi\sigma\tau\epsilon\tau\alpha\gamma\mu\acute{\epsilon}\nu\sigma\nu$) taxation-officer; fifth and last, persons who are merely associated with the would-be alienator in respect of some portion of his property. In order to benefit by their right of having the first refusal, these parties must pay within thirty days (or, in certain hard cases, within four months) the just price, or what the would-be purchaser offers in good faith. The right of having the first refusal is to be enjoyed, *a fortiori*, mutually as between fellow members of a community ($\dot{\sigma}\mu\acute{\alpha}\varsigma$). The right to have the first refusal is not to apply in the cases of certain non-commercial transfers of property (e.g. dowries, bequests, exchanges), but such transactions must be proved

---

[1] Text in *J.G.-R.*, Part III, pp. 234–41.

[2] Novel No. 2 purports to have been promulgated by the three Emperors Rhomanós I, Constantine (Porphyrogenitus, Leo VI's son), and Christopher (one of Rhomanós I's sons). These three Emperors were all on the Imperial throne in 929, but so also were two other sons of Rhomanós's, Stephen and Constantine, for these two had been crowned on Christmas Day 924 (*Georg. Mon. Cont.*, p. 902; Leo Grammaticus, p. 314; *Theoph. Cont.*, p. 409; pseudo-Symeon, p. 739), and their names, too, appear in Novel No. 5 of 934. In 922, on the other hand, Rhomanós, Constantine (Porphyrogenitus), and Christopher were all already on the throne, and did not yet have any other colleagues. Thus the superscription of Novel No. 2 and its dating in 922 bear each other out. But, if we accept the dating of it in 922, we have to reject the testimony of Dhekapolítês and of Basil II.

[3] i.e. Leo VI's Novel No. 114.

[4] This seems to be the most probable meaning of the word $\kappa\sigma\iota\nu\omega\nu\sigma\acute{\iota}$ in the preamble and in section I. Sharers in the collective responsibility for the payment of tax are mentioned separately; they are the $\dot{\sigma}\mu\sigma\tau\epsilon\lambda\epsilon\hat{\iota}\varsigma$.

[5] See Ostrogorsky's interpretation in 'Die ländliche Steuergemeinde', pp. 34–5.

not to have been cloaks for underhand commercial transactions. The penalties for fraud of this kind are in the first place the regular penalty for perjury and in the second place the confiscation, by the Treasury, of the seller's land and of the underhand buyer's purchase-money. Both assets are then to be sold by the Treasury to the underhand seller's neighbours.

The δυνατοί are forbidden to acquire any property, on any pretext, from poorer people, unless they are their relatives. They must not acquire anything from the owners by purchase or lease or exchange in any peasant freeholding communities (χωρίοις), or in any of the outlying farmsteads (ἀγριδίοις) attaching to these, in which the δυνατός does not already hold property of his own. There is to be no intimidation or bribery by the δυνατοί or by accomplices of theirs. The penalty for this offence is forfeiture of the property thus acquired plus a fine of the amount at which the property is valued by the Treasury.

The right to the first refusal is to hold good, not only against the δυνατοί, but also against other parties—for example, the Treasury if it is selling 'klasmatic' land[1] or any other piece of real estate (κτῆσις).

The term of the statute of limitations applying to the provisions of this novel up to this point is to be ten years, but, in the case of the past or the future alienation of στρατιωτικὰ κτήματα, the term is to be thirty years, and the property is to be handed back without any refunding of the purchase price—unless the alienation of this military property still leaves the owner (τῷ στρατιώτῃ) enough to cover the maintenance of the serving soldier (τῷ στρατευομένῳ). The alienation is to be void in so far as it leaves the military estate short of this amount.

This first piece of agrarian legislation, which may have been promulgated in the year immediately following the famine of 927/8, was supplemented in September 934 by Novel No. 5 of the Emperors Rhomanós, Constantine (Leo VI's son), and Stephen and Constantine (Rhomanós's sons).[2] The purpose of Novel No. 5 is stated, in the preamble, to be, not merely to redress recent particular abuses, but to produce a permanent general cure for the agrarian malady. It is to plug the holes that have been left open in previous enactments.

As from the date of enactment of the present law, an owner is to have free and unmolested enjoyment of his hereditary estate (τὴν λαχοῦσαν κατοίκησιν). If there has been alienation, partial or total, the inhabitants of the same or of the neighbouring lands and villages are to have the right to buy the property up. The following categories of persons are prohibited from insinuating themselves, on any pretext, into a (peasant freeholding community's) village or land: máyistroi or patríkioi; (civilian)

---

[1] For the meaning of this technical term, see II, 1 (iv), pp. 182–3.
[2] Text in *J.G.-R.*, Part III, pp. 242–52.

public officers, commanders of army-corps districts, and other civilian and military officers; senators; present or past holders of office in the thémata (army-corps districts); metropolitans, archbishops, bishops, abbots, and other ecclesiastical potentates; and the administrators of ecclesiastical or Imperial property, whether in their private or in their official capacity.[1] The penalty for future infractions of this provision is that such acquisitions shall be void, and that the property, together with any improvements to it, shall be returned, without any refund of the purchase money, to the original owner or, failing him, to his relatives or to the inhabitants of his village and land.

Persons in the enumerated categories who have gained possession, during or after the famine, of lands or villages (belonging to peasant freeholding communities), or have acquired estates (κτήσεις) there, are to be evicted—but this only after a refund of the purchase-price—in favour of the original owners or their relatives, or, failing these, in favour of the other persons collectively responsible for payment of tax or in favour of the community (τῆς ὁμάδος). The refund is to include the value of the improvements to the property, if the persons who are recovering the property have the means and the will. In any case, the evicted acquirers of the property are to be entitled to carry off the wood-work, if this has been added by them at their own expense.

Persons who have made fortunes are not to use these to damage their neighbours, but they may keep their original property. Persons who have acquired their neighbours' property before the date of the famine may keep it, but they are not to acquire (any more of) their neighbours' property, and, if they have been oppressive to their neighbours, they are to be evicted from their acquisitions and are to forfeit their own property as well.

If the persons who are entitled to re-acquire alienated property are poor, they are to be given three years' grace for making the refund of the purchase-price, and the eviction of the purchasers is then also to be subject to a three years' delay. But there is to be restitution without refund if the purchase-price is found to have been less than half the fair price. If the purchase-price has been unfairly low, but not to that degree, the value of the income already received by the purchaser from his purchase is to be deducted from the amount that is to be refunded. These provisions are not to be voided on the pretext that one of the parties has become, or intends to become, a monk and has dedicated his property to a monastery.

Future offenders are to be evicted without any refund of the purchase-price or any compensation for developments and improvements. If they belong to the enumerated categories, they are to pay the Treasury the

---

[1] This list in Novel No. 5, section 1, on p. 246, is repeated in section 8 on pp. 251-2.

value of the forfeited acquisition and the Treasury is to apply this fund to providing for the poor. Indigent offenders are to be let off the payment of this additional penalty.

We have left nothing undone, Rhomanós declares in conclusion, to liberate districts and villages and cities from the enemy. We have striven with all our might to liberate our subjects from the enemy's attacks. Now that we have achieved these magnificent successes in putting an end to the aggression of the foreign enemy, what about the domestic enemy in our own household? How can we refrain from dealing severely with him?

Constantine Porphyrogenitus resented his demotion by Rhomanós Lekapênós for the benefit, not only of Rhomanós himself, but of the intruder's[1] sons. When Rhomanós had been deposed by his own sons the co-Emperors Stephen and Constantine, Constantine Porphyrogenitus— prompted by his wife, Rhomanós's daughter Elénê—deposed the two Lekapenids in their turn and, by this stroke, made himself once again sole Emperor after having been effaced for nearly twenty-six years.[2] However, on the all-important issue of agrarian policy, Constantine Porphyrogenitus agreed whole-heartedly with his unwelcome senior ex-colleague, and, in this field, the fall of the Lekapenids in 944/5 did not bring with it any change. Constantine's Novels No. 6 of March 947 and No. 7 of some date between then and 959 are in line with Rhomanós's Novels No. 2 (?) of 929 (?) and No. 5 of 934.

Novel No. 6[3] was evoked by information about abuses in théma Thrakêsioi. This information moved Constantine to enact a new law applicable to all the thémata in the Empire.

The judges have been coerced into finding in favour of the δυνατώτεροι against the πένητες, so drastic action is required. Offenders against previous legislation in Constantine's reign (i.e. against the novels of 929 (?) and 934) are to have no claim for recovery of outlays (on property unlawfully acquired). All illegal transactions from the date of the famine down to the date of promulgation of the present law are to be void. There is to be no recovery of purchase-price. Exchanges are to be cancelled, except in cases in which the poorer party wishes the exchange to stand because—having previously been a co-owner (of undistributed common land)—he prefers to have the free hand (τὸ ἐνόχλητον) that he has gained by the demarcation of a holding of his own as his private property, and also because, in the exchange, he has got the best of the bargain. If the buyer is rich and the value of the seller's property is less than 50 nomís-mata, there is to be no refund. If the seller is not so poor as that, he is to

---

[1] 'Intruder', not 'usurper', is the correct word; for, in the Roman Empire, there could be no usurpation of the Imperial office, because this office was a revolutionary one that was not based on any constitutional rights. There was, in fact, no such thing as a legitimate title to hold the Imperial office.

[2] See p. 11, with n. 2.   [3] Text in *J.G.-R.*, Part III, pp. 252-6.

have three years' grace for repayment. If the indigent seller is not an individual but is a community (ὁμάς), the judge is to fix the number of years' grace for repayment on an estimate of the value of future harvests (which is to be set against the gross sum due). If there is evidence that there has been any resort to force or fraud, there is to be no refund, even if the purchaser is not a member of the influential classes.

However, consideration is to be shown to poor monasteries and to metropolitan officials, from the rank of spathários downwards, who have made their purchases without resort to force or fraud and without the backing of influential patrons. Such purchasers are to be re-imbursed, not only for the purchase-price, but for productive expenditure—for instance, on the planting of vineyards and on the installation of water-mills. They are also to be entitled to dismantle the wood-work of their own houses (on condition that they leave the previous state of the house unimpaired), if they do not receive compensation for this wood-work.

If the re-occupiers of the alienated property are poor, they may redeem it from the future product of the land over the number of years that it will take for the cumulative value of this product to add up to the amount due to be refunded. During this period, the creditor is to have the right to supervise the harvesting, and, if the re-occupiers are well-to-do, the whole of the harvest is to go to the creditor, but, if the re-occupiers are poor, the creditor is to get only the surplus beyond what the re-occupier needs for his own subsistence.

Alienations of property are to hold good if the parties to the transaction are approximately equal in rank (ἐν ἀξιώμασι). It is significant that relative rank, not relative wealth, is to be taken as the measure of relative standing. Alienations are also to hold good if they have been made for raising tax-money or dowry-money—but, in this case, the alienated property must be transferred only to the alienator's fellow villagers or, at a pinch, to inhabitants of villages in the same rural district (μητρο-κωμίαν) or in the same county (κωμηγούραν).

When an influential personage (δυνατοῦ προσώπου) is selling property or is alienating it in some other way, the members of the peasant free-holding community (in which the seller is involved) are to have the right of first refusal if they are co-owners with each other (ἀνακεκοινωμένοι) (of undistributed common land), or if the community cannot manage without the pasture-land, water-supply, and mountain-land of the in-tending alienator. The intended transfer of property can, however, be carried through at the price of a renunciation of the share in the common property.

Idhióstaton[1] property is not to be divided.

---

[1] For the meaning of this technical term, see II, 1 (iv), p. 182, with n. 1.

Poor freeholders who exercise retrospectively their right to have the first refusal are to have four months' grace, and they may choose either to refund the price that has actually been paid or to have the value of the property estimated and to pay the amount of the valuation.

Constantine is humane and even-handed. He can see both sides of a case, and he takes pains to avoid inflicting more than the inevitable minimum amount of hardship in evicting purchasers whose means are modest and whose conduct has been correct. The spirit of his Novel No. 6 of 947 contrasts favourably with the animus shown by his grandson Basil II in his Novel No. 29 of 996—but then, by 996, the social crisis had become still more acute.

Constantine's undated Novel No. 7 was drafted for him by a civil servant, Theódhoros Dhekapolítês, and is likely to have been promulgated towards the end of Constantine's reign, since the same civil servant was also the author of the decision, on cases in which a ruling had been asked for by a thematic judge, which was promulgated as Novel No. 15 of Constantine's son and successor Rhomanós II (959–63). Both these drafts of Dhekapolítês's are concerned with the plight of the thematic soldiers. In the preamble to the first of the two, it is put on record that the soldiers' position has deteriorated.[1]

It has already been noted[2] that Constantine, in his Novel No. 7,[3] gives the force of law, for the first time, to an unwritten custom which inhibited the owners of military estates (the στρατιῶται) from selling the pieces of property that provided for the maintenance of serving soldiers (the στρατεῖαι). It has also been noted that, in this novel, Constantine lays down, in terms of pounds gold, the amounts of the inalienable minima, namely four pounds gold for cavalrymen and for seamen in the three naval thémata, but two pounds gold only for seamen in the Imperial Fleet, since, in their case, the income from their land was supplemented by regular pay.

Novel No. 7 goes on to lay down that officers are to be disqualified *ex officio* from inheriting from soldiers.

There is to be no embargo on the alienation of a soldier's movable property unless his real estate has been very seriously diminished. In that case, as much of the impoverished soldier's movable property is to be placed under embargo as will suffice, on an estimate made by a reputable valuer, to bring the aggregate value of the soldier's inalienable property up to the minimum figure.

---

[1] Soldiers are still enumerated among the oppressors of the πένητες in the account, in *Theoph. Cont.*, p. 443, of Constantine Porphyrogenitus's efforts to help the πένητες. On the other hand, in Rhomanós II's Novel No. 15, poor soldiers and poor civilians are bracketed with each other.

[2] In II, 1 (iii) (d), on p. 134.

[3] Text in *J.G.-R.*, Part III, pp. 261–6.

The registration of real estate in the military ledgers (ἐν τοῖς στρατιω-τικοῖς κώδιξιν) is *ipso facto* to have the effect of making such property inalienable, even if the value of the amount registered is in excess of the required minimum.

No one is to be entitled to buy any military real estate—above all, no grandee such as an officer, a metropolitan, a bishop, a monastery, or any other ecclesiastical establishment, or any lay potentate (δυναστής) down to the rank of a skholários.[1] Offenders against this ruling are to be evicted without any refund of the purchase-price, but they may remove their wood-work (on condition that they leave the previous state of the house unimpaired).

Military real estate that is in excess of the inalienable minimum and that has not been registered may be alienated, but, if the value of the registered part of the alienator's property is below the required minimum, the acquirer of the unregistered part must bring the value of the inalienable part of the alienator's property up to the minimum by supplementing it with the necessary amount of real estate. If none of the real estate of the owner of a military property has been registered, the best portions of it, up to the value of four pounds gold, are to be deemed to be under embargo (σιωπηρῶς ὑποκείσθωσαν). An owner of military property who is responsible for only a share in the provision for the upkeep of a soldier is to have a proportionate amount of his property made inalienable.

Purchasers of military property are to have the benefit of the statute of limitations if it is recognized that they have possessed the property for forty years.[2]

The word 'soldiers' is to be held to cover not only those who are on the active service list, but also those who have received their discharge (ἀδορείας) in due form because they have been found to be too indigent to be able to serve.[3]

The Treasury is not to buy up military estates. This is a customary abuse that shall not be made legal.

There is also an age-old customary understanding that purchasers of military property shall be evicted without refund of the purchase-price. Soldiers' claims to the recovery of alienated military property are to be

---

[1] i.e. a soldier in the senior regiment of the tághmata (the fully professional units whose men were able to live on their pay).

[2] We do not know the date, after March 947 and before 9 November 959, at which Constantine's Novel No. 7 was promulgated, but, even if the year was 959, the forty years' term of the statute of limitations would have invalidated alienations of military property that had been made as far back as 919. This would also be the year back to which the alienations would have been invalidated by the novel numbered 2, if the date of this novel was 929, since the term of the statute of limitations is set at ten years in this novel. On the other hand, Novel No. 5 of 934 leaves valid all transactions that were earlier than the beginning of the famine—that is to say, earlier than the winter of 927/8.

[3] See *De Caer.*, II, p. 696, quoted in II, 1 (iii) (d), on p. 145.

heritable by their relatives to the sixth degree of kinship, next by their kinsmen at law (ἀγχισταί), next by their fellow contributors to the maintenance of a serving soldier and by their comrades in arms, next by their fellow tax-payers who share the same collective responsibility (τοὺς συντελεστάς)—in the first place, indigent soldiers and in the second place civilians. (This is to ensure that there shall be no default on the payment of the tax that has been assessed.)

Abuses of which army-corps-district commanders (στρατηγοί) have been guilty are then listed, and penalties are imposed. Commanders have taken bribes for letting soldiers off from serving. They have violated a soldier's rights by treating him as a serf (ἐν παροίκου λόγῳ) and by holding the property that is ear-marked for maintaining him. The penalty for this abuse is to be a fine of 36 gold nomísmata, to be divided equally between the mistreated soldier himself and the Treasury. The fine for having bought military property is to be 24 gold nomísmata payable to the Treasury. The penalty for employing able-bodied (ἱκανούς) soldiers for private service is to be a fine of six gold nomísmata per head per annum, payable to the Treasury by the officer who has given the soldier leave of absence (ὁ ἐξκουσεύσας) for this improper purpose.

In the decision that was promulgated as Rhomanós II's Novel No. 15, Dhekapolítês starts by recalling a number of points in Constantine Porphyrogenitus's agrarian legislation, together with some rulings of Constantine's on questions that this legislation had raised. For instance, military officers were not to be exempted from the obligation to refund the purchase-price of land that they had sold and were now recovering. Poor men who were recovering land that they had sold were to re-enter into possession at once and were to have five years', not three years', grace for making the refund—always supposing that they were members of a peasant freeholding community.

In rendering his present decision on points on which a ruling has been asked for by a thematic judge, Dhekapolítês rules that Constantine Porphyrogenitus's Novel No. 6 of March 947 is an epoch-making act, and that cases that have arisen during the eighteen-years period between the promulgation of this act and the earliest Imperial agrarian legislation, which dated from the time of the famine of 927/8, are to be dealt with in one way, whereas cases that have arisen subsequently are to be dealt with in another way. Dhekapolítês remarks that, before Constantine's legislation, neither poor soldiers nor poor civilians had been given the right to recover property previously sold by them without refunding the purchase-price (ἀναργύρως).[1]

---

[1] This is not accurate if the novel numbered 2 and ascribed to Rhomanós I, Constantine Porphyrogenitus, and Christopher is authentic; for this novel provides that military estates alienated either in the past or in the future are to revert to the original owners without any

In cases that have arisen within the years 929–47, former owners of alienated property who have recovered this property as a result of legislation promulgated during this period are under an obligation to refund the purchase-price within the permitted period of grace—a period which has been extended by Constantine from three years to five years. If they ask for a further extension, Dhekapolîtês recommends that they should be required to give assurances in writing that they will repay within a further period, the length of which is to be decided *ad hoc*. If they then fail, wholly or partially, to carry out these assurances, two alternative ways are proposed by Dhekapolîtês for enabling the creditor to get his rights with the minimum amount of hardship for the debtor. Dhekapolîtês's recommendations for dealing with this situation are all subject to the understanding that the utilization of the alienated land shall revert to the peasant freeholding community, and that the poor shall never lose their ownership of this land.

Dhekapolîtês prescribes a different treatment for cases that have arisen since the beginning of Constantine Porphyrogenitus's effective sole sovereignty (ἀπὸ ... τοῦ χρόνου τῆς αὐτοκρατορείας of Constantine, that is to say, since 27 January 945, when Constantine had become sole emperor once again). In cases subsequent to that date, Dhekapolîtês's draft instructs the judge who has asked for the ruling to have no hesitation in reinstating in their own property, without any refund of purchase-price (ἀναργύρως), all soldiers and civilians whose property has been purchased in violation of the law. As from that date, purchasers have no excuse.

Dhekapolîtês notes that the judge's memorandum (ἀναφορά), asking for a ruling, brings out the severity of the pressure of the famine of 927/8[1] and the complete failure of the harvest. These circumstances should be taken into consideration by the judge, and, in the light of them, he should stretch the law a little, in favour of leniency to the debtors, in dealing with cases that have arisen during the eighteen years' period preceding Constantine Porphyrogenitus's Novel No. 6 of 947.

We also have a surviving extract from Rhomanós II's Novel No. 16[2] of March 962 which was addressed to the public authorities in théma

refund of the purchase-price (ἀναργύρως). Moreover, Novel No. 5 of 934 makes the same provision in the cases of past buyers at less than half the fair price and of future offenders against the prescriptions of this novel. Constantine's Novel No. 6 of 947 voids, without right of recovery of the purchase-price, all illegal transactions, down to the date of promulgation of Novel No. 6, that have been concluded since the date of the famine of 927/8.

[1] Dhekapolîtês's words are τὴν ἄρτι ἐπικειμένην τοῦ λοιμοῦ [sc. λιμοῦ] ἀνάγκην. The famine to which he is referring here can only be the famine of 927/8. The word ἄρτι ('now') cannot mean 'at the date at which Dhekapolîtês was drafting Rhomanós II's decision'. It must mean 'at the time, following the onset of the famine of 927/8, at which the poor peasant freeholders sold their land under duress', in contrast to the pre-famine period, in which the peasants had not yet come under this pressure.

[2] *J.G.-R.*, Part III, pp. 285–7.

Thrakĕsioi—the army-corps district which had been the scene of the local abuses that had moved Constantine Porphyrogenitus to promulgate his Novel No. 6 of 947 with application to all the army-corps districts in the Empire.[1]

In this extract it is decreed that any portions of military properties that have been alienated are to revert to the original owners without any refund of the purchase-price. If the acquisition has been made in good faith, there is to be no fine, but there is to be restitution unless the property has been in the acquirer's hands for the term of years that brings the statute of limitations into operation. If, however, the property has been acquired by robbery (ἁρπαγή), there is to be a fine proportionate to the size of the area that has been seized. There is to be no fine if the purchaser from a soldier is a soldier himself; but, in a transaction between soldiers, if the seller possesses the minimum required for a soldier's maintenance (τὸ ἱκανὸν ἔχει τῆς στρατείας), and if the buyer is indigent, the seller is to recover the land and the buyer is to recover the purchase-price. There is to be no recovery of the purchase-price if the buyer is the more affluent of the two parties. If both parties are poor, there is to be a refund, with a period of three years' grace for making it.

There is to be restitution without a refund, but also without a fine, if someone has bought military land from an (Imperial) Inspector (ἐπόπτου) or from an Imperial soldier with a certificate (διὰ λιβέλλων),[2] supposing that the statute of limitations does not come into operation.

If land that is partly or wholly military has been acquired in good faith, and if the statute of limitations does not come into operation, there is to be restitution without a refund, but there is to be a fine, and this fine is to be transferred from the acquirer to the alienator—unless the alienator, too, has been found to have acted in good faith. In that case there is to be no fine for either party.

When soldiers have divested themselves completely of their hereditary military property and have resigned the whole of it, together with the obligations attaching to it, to relatives or contributors, and have then asked persons to accept them as serfs, the persons who have harboured

---

[1] Théma Thrakĕsioi, i.e. western Asia Minor, was a naturally fertile and formerly flourishing district which had been ruined, first by the Caliph Muʻāwiyah's naval offensive in the years 649–68, and then by the constant depredations of the Spanish Muslims who had established themselves in Crete in 827 or 828. In 947, théma Thrakĕsioi had still been exposed to these attacks, and Constantine Porphyrogenitus's expedition against Crete in 949 had been a failure. On the other hand, the expedition of 960–1, under the command of the future Emperor Nikêphóros II Phokás, had resulted in the conquest of Candia in March 961 and in the liquidation of the Muslim regime in Crete. We may guess that there had been an immediate rush to buy land in théma Thrakĕsioi, now that this good land had at last suddenly become a safe investment.

[2] The text now reads ἐπόπτου ἢ βασιλικοῦ στρατιώτου, but we may guess that the original text read ἐπόπτου βασιλικοῦ ἢ στρατιώτου.

them are not to be punished. Again, when soldiers have been reduced to such extreme poverty that they can no longer bear the burden of military service, and when they have consequently been accepted as serfs, neither the persons who have accepted them nor the soldiers themselves are to be punished. The punishment is to fall on the people who have driven the soldiers out and who have been guilty of ruining the soldiers and forcing them to abscond. On the other hand, anyone who has harboured a prosperous and solvent (σωζόμενον) soldier and has retained him, though aware of the soldier's true condition, is to be punished; 'for, if solvent soldiers are hindered from their due performance of active service, it is manifest that our forces will suffer no small detriment'.

In Rhomanós I's, Constantine Porphyrogenitus's, and Rhomanós II's agrarian legislation there are two features that appear consistently in each of these six novels. The paramount purpose of them all is, first, to enable the peasant freeholders to recover land of theirs that has been alienated—particularly land belonging to military estates up to the minimum value that is estimated to be required for the maintenance of a serving soldier—and then to prevent such land from being alienated in the future. Subject to this paramount aim, the secondary purpose of this legislation is to avoid inflicting more hardship than can be helped on those persons who have acquired by fair means the land that is now to be given back to its original owners—especially in cases in which the acquirers themselves are non-affluent individuals or corporate bodies. The agrarian legislation of Rhomanós II's successor Nikêphóros II Phokás (963–9) is markedly different in its objectives, and, still more markedly, in its tone and spirit.

Nikêphóros, too, was concerned to shield the πένητες from the encroachments of the δυνατοί. Nikêphóros could not have been indifferent to the thematic peasant soldiers' fate; for in his reign these troops were still the mainstay of the East Roman Army, and Nikêphóros was a professional soldier who was devoted to the Army and who was ambitious to use the Army, with all his and all its might, as an instrument for reconquering for the Empire more and more of the territories that had been wrested from it by the Arabs in the seventh century. At the same time, Nikêphóros, unlike his predecessors, had another concern that was not easy to reconcile with his concern for the peasant soldiers. He was concerned to conciliate his fellow δυνατοί, or at least to conciliate the military section of the 'Establishment' which had placed him on the Imperial Throne. (Between the civilian section of the 'Establishment' and Nikêphóros there was mutual hostility from the beginning, and, when he lost the support of the military section too, his doom was sealed.) Nikêphóros also had two incidental concerns. He had his knife into the Armenian soldiers in the Army and into the ecclesiastical owners of large-scale estates. This distraction between different objectives is the common feature of Nikêphóros II's five agrarian novels, namely his undated No. 18,[1] his Novel No. 19 of 964,[2] his No. 20 of 967,[3] and his undated No. 21[4] and No. 22.[5]

Nikêphóros does show concern for his peasant soldiers. He confirms the provision that was the essential safeguard for the preservation of the property of both the soldiers and the civilian peasants. He decrees that the δυνατοί are not to be allowed to buy property except from each other; and this all-important ruling is made in Nikêphóros's Novel No. 20 of 967, which, on the face of it, is for the benefit of the δυνατοί.[6] In No. 20 Nikêphóros also decrees that, in cases in which a transfer of property has been made by robbery (ἐξ ἁρπαγῆς), all the previous legislation is to hold good, and that, if a personage in the ruling class (ἀρχοντικὸν πρόσωπον) who has bought property from one of his own kind uses his new acquisition to the detriment of his poorer neighbours, he is not only to forfeit this new acquisition but is to be evicted from his ancestral property.

In No. 22 Nikêphóros decrees, in regard to sales that have already been made, that, if a soldier has sold part of his inalienable property up to the value of four pounds gold, he is to recover this without having to make a refund. In No. 18 he decrees that, if the owner of a military estate leaves no heir who is willing to take over his heritage, someone else is to be installed in the property and is to undertake the obligation, carried by this property, for the performance of military service. Nikêphóros also makes one quaint provision for keeping the requisite minimum part of a military property intact. A soldier who has been convicted of having committed murder is to be put to death and his victim's family are to be compensated by being given some of the murderer's movable property, but they are not to be given any of that part of the murderer's real estate that is ear-marked for the maintenance of a serving soldier. This is to be preserved intact, and, if the executed murderer has left no movable property, his heirs are to provide compensation for the victim's heirs, but not out of the ear-marked land (No. 18).

Section 2 of Nikêphóros II's Novel No. 22 must have had the effect of making almost all military property inalienable for the future. The minimum value of the inalienable portion of a military estate is, in future, to be twelve pounds gold instead of only four pounds gold. Any of this trebled minimum portion that is sold is to be recoverable without a refund. Any portion of a military estate, beyond this minimum, that is

---

[1] *J.G.-R.*, Part III, pp. 289–91. [2] Op. cit., pp. 292–6.
[3] Op. cit., pp. 296–9. [4] Op. cit., p. 299.
[5] Op. cit., pp. 299–300.
[6] Bach has not taken sufficient account of this ruling of Nikêphóros's in his judgement that 'son régime est une réaction contre la protection des paysans' ('Les Lois agraires', p. 84).

sold is also to be recoverable, but in this case the purchase-price must be refunded. In thus trebling the inalienable minimum, Nikêphóros was not acting for the protection of the small military freeholder. An estate worth twelve pounds gold was a large one, and few of the military estates will have been of so high a value. Nikêphóros's objective in raising the inalienable minimum was a technical military one. A start had been made in building up a corps of heavily armoured cavalry;[1] the Emperor was eager to promote this development; and the cost of the heavily armoured trooper's equipment—a cost that the trooper himself was to bear—was, of course, inordinately high.[2]

In some of his provisions in favour of the δυνατοί, Nikêphóros is only confirming his predecessors' legislation. For instance, soldiers who are recovering alienated lands must not only refund the purchase-price but must also pay the value of improvements that have been made by the purchasers in so far as these have been utilitarian (χρειώδεις)—e.g. such improvements as the planting of vineyards and the installation of mills, as contrasted with unproductive luxurious embellishments. In the case of embellishments, the purchasers who have installed these may remove the wood-work only, and the original owners are apparently to be allowed to recover their property without being required to pay the cost of these unproductive luxuries (No. 18). Again, as has been mentioned already, if a soldier has sold land when the minimum value of the inalienable portion of a military estate was still only four pounds gold and had not yet been raised to the new figure of twelve pounds gold, to which Nikêphóros is now raising it, the soldier is to recover, without a refund, any alienated portion of his estate by which the estate has been reduced below the four pounds minimum value, but is to refund the purchase-price as the condition for qualifying for the right to recover any land that he has sold without having reduced the estate thereby below the four pounds minimum value (No. 22).

On the other hand, in his Novel No. 18, Nikêphóros modifies, in favour of the δυνατοί, one previous piece of legislation. Where there had been an exchange of property between a soldier and a δυνατός, the δυνατός, as well as the soldier, is now to have the right to file a plea for the exchange to be cancelled, and, in Novel No. 20 of 967, Nikêphóros makes two changes in the law that are to the advantage of the δυνατοί.

---

[1] τὰ τῶν κλιβανοφόρων καὶ ἐπιλωρικοφόρων κίνησιν ἔλαβε (Nikêphóros II, Novel No. 22, section 2). See the piece περὶ τῶν καταφράκτων in Nikêphóros's own work Στρατηγικὴ Ἔκθεσις καὶ Σύνταξις, edited by J. Kulakovskij in *Mémoires de l'Académie Impériale de St.-Pétersbourg*, viii͏ᵉ série, Classe Historico-Philologique, vol. viii, (1908), No. 9, pp. 10–12.

[2] Bach holds that Nikêphóros's objective was, not military, but social. In raising the minimum capital value of a στρατιωτικὸν κτῆμα to 12 pounds gold, he was giving legal sanction to previous illegal accumulations of real estate. 'La concentration des domaines trouva donc dans la personne de Nicéphore un défenseur actif' ('Les Lois agraires', p. 84).

In this Novel No. 20, Nikêphóros is openly critical of the previous legislation that he is repealing. He notes that his predecessors' legislation was prompted by a temporary state of distress (διὰ τὴν γενομένην κατὰ τὸν τότε καιρὸν ἔνδειαν), and he concedes that they acted rightly in vetoing the purchase, by the δυνατοί, of land belonging to poor civilians and to soldiers. But Nikêphóros then censures his predecessors for having gone so far as to give the poor the right of first refusal of the purchase of the property of the rich in cases in which the rich seller is a co-owner of still undistributed common land (ἐξ ἀνακοινώσεως), and also in cases in which he is merely responsible, jointly with the members of a peasant freeholding community, for the payment of tax (ἐξ ὁμοτελείας).

Accordingly, in Novel No. 20, section 1, Nikêphóros confirms the previous agrarian legislation with two exceptions. He abrogates the right of the poor, whether soldiers or civilians, to have the first refusal of the property of a rich landowner. Henceforth, neither the rich man's involvement in the collective responsibility for the payment of tax nor his co-ownership of common land is to entitle his non-affluent associates to have the first refusal of his land. The second piece of previous legislation that Nikêphóros abrogates in his Novel No. 20 is the provision, in Constantine Porphyrogenitus's Novel No. 7, that the statute of limitations for the cancelling of acquisitions of land by the rich from the poor shall come into operation only if the date of the transaction is at least forty years earlier than the date of promulgation of this novel of Constantine's. It has been noted already that, even if Novel No. 7 was promulgated as late as 959, which was the last year of Constantine's reign, the effect would have been to invalidate all transactions that had not been completed before the year 919, and 919 was eight or nine years before the famine of 927/8, which had given the rich their opportunity to buy up the lands of the poor and had therefore given the Government its legitimate grounds for cancelling these sales that had been made under duress. In his Novel No. 20, section 2, Nikêphóros abrogates Constantine's forty years' term and validates purchases made before the famine, subject to the proviso that this concession to affluent purchasers is to apply only if the purchase has been made by fair means (not ἐξ ἁρπαγῆς). In thus making the statute of limitations come into operation as from immediately before the date of the famine of 927/8, Nikêphóros was reverting to the term set for the statute of limitations in Rhomanós I's Novel No. 5 of 934.

The tone, as well as the substance, of Nikêphóros II's Novel No. 20 is significant. The tone is defensive towards the poor and propitiatory towards the rich. The preamble opens by invoking the sanction of the Christian religion for the duty of rulers to act impartially; and in two other passages the Emperor claims that he is in fact being impartial towards all parties. He also claims that, in this novel, he is not completely upsetting the previous legislation but is preserving those features of it in which it is impartial and in which it meets a permanent need (as distinct from a temporary emergency). This reiterated claim to be acting impartially rings hollow; for to give equal weight to the interests of the rich and of the poor is a euphemism for keeping the balance tilted in the rich class's favour.

Nikêphóros appeases the rich in this novel by indicting his predecessors for having blocked all avenues to enrichment, and for having impoverished those people who were rich already, by giving the poor the right of first refusal which Nikêphóros himself is now abrogating. This policy of his predecessors spelled, according to Nikêphóros, the ruin of 'the totality of (East) Roman power' (τὸ πᾶν τῆς Ῥωμαϊκῆς δυνάμεως). Nikêphóros's youthful colleague Constantine Porphyrogenitus's grandson Basil II, on whom Nikêphóros had imposed himself and who had had no say in Nikêphóros's legislation, was to live to learn, by dire experience, that the threat of ruin for the East Roman Empire stemmed from the intruder's policy, not from the policy of Basil's own grandfather. Though Nikêphóros, to his credit, did not remove the ban on the rich acquiring the property of the poor, he did remove the ban on the rich acquiring from the rich, and this enabled the rich, through intermarriage with each other, to increase their estates to the size of veritable kingdoms and to challenge the Imperial Government itself on almost equal terms. After Basil II had been relieved of the domination of two successive intruders, Nikêphóros II Phokás (963–9) and John Dzimiskĕs (969–76), Basil himself came within an ace of being overthrown by two provincial potentates, Nikêphóros II's nephew Várdhas Phokás and John Dzimiskĕs's brother-in-law Várdhas Sklêrós.

Another of Nikêphóros II's concessions to the δυνατοί reveals how wealthy these had grown since real estate in Asia Minor had become a safe and profitable investment thanks to the liberation of the country from Muslim raids—a liberation which the rich landowners owed to the military service of the thematic peasant soldiers. In his undated Novel No. 21, which may have been promulgated in the same year as his No. 20 of 967, Nikêphóros admits that the agrarian legislation had been transgressed by the encroachment of large-scale estates on lands belonging to peasant freeholding communities (χωρίοις) and their outlying farmsteads (ἀγριδίοις). The rich purchasers already possessed ancestral real estate in the territory of these communities; they had enlarged these holdings of theirs by buying small plots from their fellow villagers (τῶν συγχωριτῶν αὐτῶν); and, on these illegally acquired plots, they had built huge mansions of immense value, at great expense.[1] Nikêphóros now rules that

---

[1] A glorified description of one of these new rural palaces, built in territory that was no longer exposed to raids, is given in Book Seven of the Byzantine Greek epic *Dhiyenês Akrítas*.

the transgressors may keep these mansions and may retain possession of their sites at the cheap cost of either paying double the purchase-price or giving, in exchange, land of twice as good a quality and of twice as large an area.

Nikêphóros promulgated one even more controversial piece of legislation than his Novel No. 20 of 967 in favour of the δυνατοί, and this was his Novel No. 19 of 964, vetoing the further endowment of monasteries, hostels (ξενῶνας), and homes for old people (γηροκομεῖα).[1]

Previous legislators had recognized that ecclesiastical corporations were as rapacious as large-scale lay landowners,[2] and they had accordingly enumerated them among the categories of δυνατοί whose encroachments on the property of peasant freeholders the legislators were striving to arrest and to reverse.[3] Nikêphóros II's motive for banning any further gifts of land to monasteries, metropolitan sees, bishoprics, and charitable foundations was not social; it was financial. Nikêphóros's policy of unlimited wars of conquest was far more costly than the policy, followed by the East Roman Government before Rhomanós I had taken the offensive in 926, of parrying attacks on East Roman territory at considerable cost in hardship to the peasantry but at a minimal cost in blood to the Army and in money to the Treasury. Nikêphóros II was hard pressed for funds; the East Roman Government's staple source of public revenue was the taxation of arable and pasture land; it was therefore important for Nikêphóros that rural land should be productive; the standard of productivity on lands owned and operated by ecclesiastical corporations and by charitable foundations was low;[4] and, since ecclesiastical property, once acquired, was inalienable,[5] Nikêphóros II sought, in his Novel No. 19, to prevent any further increase in ecclesiastical property, to arrange for a more efficient utilization of existing ecclesiastical property, and, in the last resort, to transfer inefficiently managed ecclesiastical property to competent hands (οἱ ἀρκοῦντες).

In his Novel No. 19, Nikêphóros II does not veto the establishment (συνιστᾶν; an ambiguous word) of monasteries and charitable foundations, but he does veto any further gifts to existing institutions and, *a fortiori*,

---

The legendary hero of this poem is a composite figure that stands for the host of East Roman borderers, soldiers, and generals who had won peace for the Empire on its eastern front. Dhiyenĕs's generation is equated in the epic with the period of peace that lasted from the capture of Tarsós in 965 to the first Saljūq Turkish raid on Vaspurakan in (?) 1029 (see p. 410).

[1] See Savramis, op. cit., chap. 3, section 1, 'Die soziale Tätigkeit des Mönchtums', on pp. 24–34.

[2] See Savramis, op. cit., chap. 4, section 2, 'Die Klöster als Grossgrundbesitzer', on pp. 45–52.

[3] See pp. 151–2. See also P. Charanis: 'The Monastic Properties and the State in the Byzantine Empire', in *Dumbarton Oaks Papers*, Number Four (1948), pp. 51–118, especially pp. 53–64.

[4] Savramis, op. cit., p. 51.   [5] Savramis, op. cit., p. 48.

the foundation of new institutions. Would-be donors are urged to satisfy their pious or charitable impulses by reconditioning dilapidated institutions, and they are advised, in lieu of gifts of land or buildings, to rehabilitate the dilapidated institutions by stocking these with slaves, cattle, sheep, and other livestock. In order to raise the funds for this, the benefactors of ecclesiastical and charitable institutions are given permission to sell real estate of their own to any purchaser, so long as he is a layman.

Nikêphóros expressly exempts from his veto the building of hermitages (κελλία and λαύρας) in the wilderness. Nikêphóros himself was devout and ascetic. In his Novel No. 19, as in No. 20, he opens his preamble by invoking the sanction of the Christian religion. He indicts the monasteries for their un-Christian affluence by assembling apposite texts from the New Testament. In braving the displeasure of the Church, he is still more anxiously on the defensive than he is in Novel 20, in which he exposes himself to the risk of alienating the πένητες without satisfying the lay δυνατοί. In the East Roman Empire in the tenth century the Church was a greater power than any class of the lay population, and the Church's potency was still increasing. Nikêphóros's Novel No. 19 ends on a note of defiance: 'I know that I shall be accused of shocking bad taste' (φορτικὰ λέγειν δόξω). Never mind. People who look below the surface will recognize that this legislation of mine is in the public interest.'[1]

The major part of Nikêphóros II's undated Novel No. 18 is directed against misdemeanours of Armenian soldiers in the East Roman Army. 'Instability and vagrancy are Armenian national vices which need to be corrected by legislation' of the kind that the Emperor is enacting in this novel. Evidently Nikêphóros has found his experience with his Armenian soldiers exasperating. Accordingly he decrees that, when Armenian soldiers have played truant for three years, and when they find, on eventually returning, that their land has been placed in the keeping of other soldiers and officers as a reward for good conduct, or has been given to others as remuneration for public service, the returning Armenian truant is to have no right of recovery. The truant's heirs may, however, recover his land within the next thirty years if this land proves to have been given away, not as remuneration for public service, but simply from

---

[1] Nikêphóros II's particularly controversial Novels No. 19 of 964 and No. 20 of 967 were both drafted for him by the Imperial Proto a Secretis (πρωτασηκρῆτις) Symeon, a civil servant who may have been as able as Theódhoros Dhekapolítês, but may not have been his equal in point of moral integrity. Bishop Liutprand of Cremona had an encounter with Symeon during the bishop's mission to Constantinople in 968. When, on 29 June 968, Liutprand left the table at an Imperial banquet because he had taken offence at finding that the Bulgarian ambassador had been given precedence over him, it was Symeon, together with the Emperor Nikêphóros's brother Leo, the kouropalátês and loghothétês tou dhrómou, who followed Liutprand out of the room and sent him to eat his dinner in the servants' hall (Liutprand, *Legatio*, chap. 19).

motives of partiality (διὰ μόνην προσπάθειαν)—for example to some monastery[1] or to one of the Imperial estates (κουρατωρείαις) or to one of the (lay) δυνατοί. In this case, no attention is to be paid to inspectors' certificates or to golden bulls, if these are produced as evidence for the deed of gift.

Armenians who have deserted to Syria[2] are to pay the penalty of not recovering their own lands, even if they return within one year. They may, however, be allotted other lands for their maintenance (a concession which suggests that, though Nikêphóros found his Armenians annoying, he was also conscious of their military worth).

Nikêphóros II's Novel No. 19 of 964 was repealed *in toto* by Basil II in his Novel No. 26 of 4 April 988.[3] The repeal was to take effect from the date of promulgation, and the previous legislation about ecclesiastical property that had been enacted in the reigns of Basil II's ancestors was to revive. It is surprising that the Church had not obtained the revocation of Nikêphóros II's Novel No. 19 earlier than this, but on 4 April 988 the Church had Basil II at its mercy. At that moment, Tsar Samuel of West Bulgaria was master of the interior of the Balkan Peninsula and the troops of an Asiatic pretender to the Imperial throne, Várdhas Phokás, were in occupation of Khrysópolis and Ávydhos. Basil was anxiously awaiting the arrival of the 6,000 Russian mercenaries who were being dispatched to him by his future brother-in-law Vladímir, Prince of Kiev. In these circumstances, Basil had to make peace with the Church at any price.

By the beginning of the year 996, Basil II felt himself to be strong enough to show his hand. His novel No. 29 of 1 January 996[4] was the most vehement assault on the δυνατοί that any East Roman Emperor had yet made, and in this novel Basil legislates against powerful ecclesiastics as well as against powerful laymen. He confirms the list, in Rhomanós I's Novel No. 5 of 934, of dignitaries, lay and ecclesiastical, who are to be debarred from encroaching, on any pretext, on the lands of peasant free-holding communities. Basil now adds an additional category, the πρωτο-κένταρχοι (senior centurions)—'for I have ascertained that these, too, are δυνατοί in practice'. He takes precautions, noted already in another context,[5] for preventing the ecclesiastical authorities from gaining a foothold in lands belonging to peasant freeholding communities, at the price of limiting the right of an individual peasant freeholder to dispose freely of his own real estate.

---

[1] τῇ βασιλικῇ τῆς Λακάπης μονῇ, ὡς ἔγραψας. Nikêphóros's Novel No. 18 is a decision on a set of cases that have been referred to the Emperor.

[2] i.e. presumably to the dominions of the Ihkshīd in southern Syria. The principality of Aleppo in northern Syria had come, by this time, to be too much at the mercy of the East Roman Empire to have been any longer a safe asylum for deserters from the East Roman Army. [3] Text in *J.G.-R.*, Part III, pp. 303–4.

[4] Text ibid., pp. 306–18. [5] See II, 1 (iii) (c), pp. 126–7.

Basil has not only received many complaints from the poor. He has seen with his own eyes the evidence of the wrongs that they are constantly suffering. He has been a first-hand witness on his journeys through the provinces and on his way to theatres of war beyond the Empire's frontiers. But he is bitterly aware that it is impossible for him to keep an eye on everything himself; that he cannot avoid delegating powers to the commanders of army-corps districts; that the tours of the Imperial Inspectors (ἐπόπται βασιλικοί) are infrequent; and that the Inspectors themselves are dishonest.

My Majesty has found this out by practical experience of the hard facts. The Inspectors and the other officials who are supposed to look after the public interest and who are sent on missions actually devise countless tricks for cheating the Government. There are very few of them who carry out my instructions conscientiously.

Basil notes that, all over both the eastern and the western regions of the Empire, he has discovered, in his sojourns in the provinces in the course of his campaigns, numerous cases in which δυνατοί have gained possession of Imperial water-meadows by means of fraudulent descriptions of the boundaries of lands granted to these δυνατοί in Imperial deeds of gift (χρυσοβούλλια). These descriptions had been written into the deeds, and, on the basis of them, the boundaries had then been delimited on the spot to the detriment of the Imperial domain. The officials who had drafted the deeds appear to have acted in collusion with the beneficiaries. Accordingly, in his Novel No. 29, Basil cancels all descriptions of boundaries in deeds of gift. Descriptions of boundaries are to be ignored and disregarded unless they are found recorded in the ledgers of the general secretariat (ἐν τοῖς τοῦ γενικοῦ σεκρέτου κωδίκοις) or in other documents that give confirmation of title.

Constantine Porphyrogenitus may have found better men than his grandson Basil II's officials to serve as the commissioners whom Constantine, after he had become sole Emperor again in 945, sent out into each of the army-corps districts to investigate and redress the victimization of the peasantry by the army-corps-district commanders and the thematic protonotárioi and the thematic soldiers, both infantrymen and cavalrymen.[1] But Constantine's eulogist has to admit that the relief that the peasantry obtained from the commissioners, at Constantine's instance, was short-lived, and that, though Constantine had his subjects' welfare at heart, he was undiscriminating in his indulgence to all classes, in spite of his having discovered that many of his subjects—and these could have been members of the ruling class only—had been guilty of heinous irregularities to the detriment of the public interest and of the Emperor

---

[1] *Theoph. Cont.*, Book VI, chap. 10, pp. 443–4. See the present work, I, 2, p. 19.

himself and (the eulogist might have, but has not, added) also to the detriment of the oppressed majority of the rural population. The second of the two authors of Book VI of *Theophanes Continuatus* commends Constantine for having confined his intervention to the rewarding of virtue, and for having forborne to deal sternly with misdemeanours. Basil II would certainly not have endorsed this encomium of his grandfather's lax administration. At the end of his Novel No. 29, Basil II congratulates himself on having followed in the footsteps of his great-grandfather, the Emperor Rhomanós I Lekapênós, in championing the rights of the weak against the strong in the struggle for the possession of rural real estate.

Basil II's own retort to the detection of abuses was to make deterrent examples of conspicuous offenders. In his Novel No. 29 he puts on record three of his punitory acts. He has ruined the descendants of Rhomanós Mouselé,[1] the máyistros whom his grandfather had sent as his commissioner to théma Opsíkion. Evidently Basil had a poorer opinion of his own contemporaries in this family than his grandfather had had of their ancestor. Basil also records, with gusto, his vindictive humbling of the upstart *kulak* Philokálês.[2]

In 985 Basil had deposed and banished to the Crimea his namesake and great-uncle Basil the parakoimómenos (chamberlain), an illegitimate son of the Emperor Basil II's great-grandfather Rhomanós I. This Basil had been appointed to the key position of parakoimómenos by his brother-in-law Constantine Porphyrogenitus after Constantine had become sole Emperor again in 945.[3] Basil the parakoimómenos had retained or regained his office, with the versatility of the Vicar of Bray, through all but one of the vicissitudes of the next forty years,[4] but he had succumbed to his great-nephew at last. In his Novel No. 29, Basil II recalls that, when he had disgraced the parakoimómenos, he had given instructions that all the khrysovoúllia (deeds of gift) that had been issued by the parakoimómenos Basil in the Emperor Basil's name were to be submitted to the Emperor for review. In his Novel No. 29 the Emperor cancels all khrysovoúllia that had been issued in his name by the parakoimómenos which had not been endorsed with the word 'confirmed' ($\epsilon\tau\eta\rho\dot{\eta}\theta\eta$) in the Emperor Basil's own handwriting.

In Novel No. 29 of 1 January 996, Basil does not mention one signal example that he had made in the preceding year. On his return from his campaign in Syria in 995 the Emperor had been entertained in southeastern Asia Minor with almost Imperial lavishness by a local grandee,

---

[1] This piece of information is added in the *Codices Palatini*. It may have been a marginal note added to the novel by Basil himself.

[2] See II, 1 (iii) (c), p. 123.   [3] See I, 2, pp. 20–2.

[4] Basil was out of office during the brief interval between Constantine VII's death and Nikêphóros II Phokás's accession to the Imperial throne.

Efstáthios Maleïnós, and he had noticed on his way the extensiveness of Maleïnós's properties in thémata Kappadhokía and Kharsianón. The value of these properties must have appreciated enormously in the course of the thirty years that had elapsed since 965, the year in which Tarsós, the Muslim raiders' Cilician base of operations, had been captured at last by the Emperor Nikêphóros II Phokás. This was the region that had previously been the theatre of war in which the strategy of 'dogging and pouncing'[1] had been practised by Nikêphóros's father Várdhas Phokás, when Várdhas had been stratêghós of théma Kappadhokía and théma Anatolikoí, and by a Maleïnós of Várdhas Phokás's generation, Constantine, when this Constantine Maleïnós had been stratêghós of Kappadhokía. It has been noted already that the victims of this strategy had been the local communities of peasant freeholders. The beneficiaries of the success of Nikêphóros Phokás's resumption of an offensive strategy had been the Phokádhes and the Maleïnoí. The two families were connected by intermarriage. The Emperor Nikêphóros was the nephew of the monk, Michael Maleïnós, who had inspired this Emperor to promote the foundation of the Great Lávra on Mount Athos. All this was damning for Efstáthios Maleïnós in Basil II's eyes. The Emperor expropriated Efstáthios's estates and imprisoned their former owner for life.

In the enacting clauses of his Novel No. 29, Basil II ignores the abrogation by Nikêphóros II of the term of forty years that had been fixed by Constantine Porphyrogenitus for the coming into operation of the statute of limitations. Basil II assumes that the forty years' term is still in force, and he now decrees that there is to be no time-limit for the recovery of property that has been acquired by the rich from the poor. Any time-limit, however long the term, plays into the hands of the δυνατοί. However, in a later clause of this novel, Basil II confirms the provisions of Nikêphóros II's Novel No. 20 of 967 and of Rhomanós I's Novel No. 5 of 934. Acquisitions by δυνατοί from peasant freeholding communities that date from before Rhomanós I's earliest legislation[2] are to hold good, provided that the acquirers can produce title in writing, supported by the confirmatory evidence of witnesses. Acquisitions that have been made later than this date are not to have the benefit of any statute of limitations. There is to be recovery without refund and without payment for improvements. The present legislation is to have retrospective effect and is not merely to apply to future transactions. As for encroachments by the δυνατοί on public property, there is to be no statute of limitations for these under any conditions. The Treasury is now empowered to reclaim

---

[1] See II, 1 (iii) (b).

[2] Basil's designation of Rhomanós I's earliest legislation, not the famine of 927/8, to mark the date at which the statute of limitations is to come into operation suggests, so far as it goes, that Rhomanós I's first agrarian novel may have been earlier than the famine. However, Rhomanós I's Novel No. 2 had retrospective effects.

any property of which it has been illegally deprived since the reign of the Emperor Augustus.

Basil II's Novel No. 29 of 996 was radical, but in 1003/4 he followed it up by a decree that was more radical still. He now decreed that the δυνατοί alone were to bear the collective responsibility for the payment of the total amount of tax that had been assessed on a taxation-district.[1] The poor tax-payers in the district were to be relieved of this liability for the future. Radical though this decree was, it was both just and expedient. It placed the burden of collective responsibility on shoulders that were broad enough to bear it, and it provided long overdue relief for the now desperately hard-pressed peasant freeholders.

Perhaps, however, it would be more accurate to say that this decree would have provided relief for the peasant freeholders if it had been effectively put into force. We may guess that on this point, which touched the interests of the δυνατοί to the quick, there was a conspiracy between taxation-officers, judges, and large-scale landowners to defeat the Emperor's purpose, and that this was a coalition that was more than a match for Basil II's will-power and ruthlessness. In any case, this decree survived Basil II himself by only three years, even as a dead letter in the statute-book. Basil II's own *fainéant* co-Emperor, his brother Constantine VIII, whom Basil's death in 1025 left in sole possession of the Imperial throne, decided to abrogate the decree, and this decision was carried out by Constantine VIII's son-in-law and successor, Rhomanós III Árgyros.[2] This surrender marked the end of the Imperial Government's series of attempts to arrest and reverse the encroachments of the δυνατοί on the lands of the peasant freeholders.

Basil II's treatment of Efstáthios Maleïnós reads like an incident in the career of King Henry VII of England at the other end of Europe five centuries later. Henry VII attained his and Basil's common objective of breaking the power of the δυνατοί. Why did Basil II fail?

One reason, of which Basil himself was bitterly aware, was the disloyalty and dishonesty of the officials to whom he, like his predecessors, had to delegate the execution of his decrees. This is revealed in six surviving documents from the archives of the Great Lávra on Mount Athos. Three of these are from the archives of the monastery of St. Andrew at Peristeraí, 20 kilometres to the east of Thessaloníkê;[3] the other three are from the archives of the Great Lávra itself.

In August 941 the Imperial asêkrêtis, epóptês, and anaghraphéfs at

---

[1] Kedhrênós, vol. ii, p. 456. Cf. Zonarás, vol. iii, p. 561.

[2] Kedhrênós, vol. ii, p. 486.

[3] These documents relating to Peristeraí have survived among the archives of the Great Lávra on Mount Athos, to which Peristeraí was annexed by Nikêphóros II in 963/4 (see G. Ostrogorsky, 'The Peasant's Pre-emption Right: An Abortive Reform of the Macedonian Emperors', in *J.R.S.*, vol. xxxvii (1947), pp. 117–26, on p. 118).

Thessaloníkê, Thomas Kaspákês, made two sales of klásmata[1] on the Kassándra (Kassándreia, Pallênê) prong of the Chalcidic Peninsula. Thomas apparently ignored the right of first refusal (προτίμησις) which had been assured to the members of a peasant freeholding community by Rhomanós I in his Novels Nos. 2 and 5. Thomas threw open the right of purchase to all inhabitants of théma Thessaloníkê, and he claimed that he was doing this on instructions from Rhomanós I and his three co-Emperors (instructions which, if authentic, were contrary to Rhomanós I's own provisions in his Novels Nos. 2 and 5). Thomas then sold some of the land cheap to the Peristeraí monastery and some of it to a private individual who is under suspicion of having been this monastery's agent, in view of the fact that the deed of sale to him found its way into the monastery's archives. In 942 and 943, the same Thomas Kaspákês and the stratêghós of théma Thessaloníkê settled a boundary dispute—apparently over the demarcation of klásmata that had been sold by Thomas on the same occasion—between the monks of Mount Athos and the town of Ierissós, on the neck of the Athonian prong of the Chalcidic Peninsula.

In November 952[2] the Imperial asêkrêtis and judge at Thessaloníkê, Samonás, sold a piece of public land to the Abbot of Peristeraí. Manifestly this sale was contrary to the intentions of the existing agrarian legislation; the right of first refusal ought to have come into play. Samonás disallowed the exercise of this right, not by invoking, as Thomas had done, special instructions of the Emperors, overruling the provisions of their own legislation, but by ingenious interpretations of the terms of this legislation itself.

These are striking examples of the collusion between official and private members of the ruling class, and no doubt this was one of the causes of the Imperial Government's failure to arrest the encroachment of large-scale estates on peasant freeholds. There was, however, another cause that made the failure inevitable. The peasants themselves were beginning to abandon their freeholds. At the date, round about the turn of the seventh and eighth centuries, at which the Nómos Yeoryikós was compiled, a peasant freehold was a desirable possession. This is patent in the provisions of this code. On the other hand, by March 962, which was the date of Rhomanós II's Novel No. 16, the Imperial Government was being

---

[1] For the meaning of this technical term, see II, 1 (iv), pp. 182–3.

[2] For this dating, see Ostrogorsky, in loc. cit., p. 119. The date has been identified by Dölger from the fact that Samonás, the judge who was dealing with the case, was evidently acquainted with Novel No. 2 of Rhomanós I and with Novel No. 6 of Constantine Porphyrogenitus. The document is dated November in the eleventh indiction. The earliest eleventh indiction after 947 was 952/3, and, before the next eleventh indiction after that, the monastery of St. Andrew at Peristeraí, to which Samonás had made the sale, had ceased to exist as a separate corporate body, since it had been annexed to the Great Lávra in 963/4.

confronted with cases in which soldiers had abandoned their military estates and had persuaded large-scale landowners to accept them as their serfs. Rhomanós II had condoned the conduct of both the absconding soldier and the large-scale landowner who had harboured him in two sets of circumstances: if the soldier had resigned his military estate, together with the obligations attaching to it, to relatives or to contributors, and if the soldier was too poor to be able to bear the burden of military service. The harbourer of a soldier was to be brought to book only if the soldier whom he had accepted as a serf was solvent (σωζόμενος). It is remarkable that, by the year 962, even solvent soldiers were deliberately abandoning their freeholds because they found it preferable to become a large-scale landowner's serfs. The explanation is to be found in the ill-treatment of soldiers by taxation-officers and by thematic judges which is denounced indignantly by the author of Περὶ Παραδρομῆς Πολέμου.[1] Solvent soldiers, as well as their impoverished comrades, would be exposed to this ill-treatment, and, if it was carried to outrageous lengths, they might come to feel that it was preferable to be the serfs of masters who would stand between their serfs and the officials;[2] who would be influential enough to be able to shield their protégés; and who would be concerned to shield them, since, if the serf were ill treated, his master's interests would suffer.[3]

The presence, in the Empire, of powerful large-scale landowners, lay and ecclesiastical, who needed more and more hands for making their expanding estates productive, gave the peasant freeholders an effective means of retorting, in the last resort, to their official oppressors. If this alternative to the burden of freeholding had not existed, the peasant freeholders would have had no means of self-help. The presence of the large-scale estates gave freeholders the possibility of absconding with the likelihood that they would be harboured. A threat, on their part, to abscond might therefore win better treatment for them from the military and fiscal officials, and, if it did not, the threat could be carried out. The seriousness of the threat, and the frequency with which it was in fact translated into action, are attested by a number of provisions in the taxation-laws. In certain hard cases, tax is remitted, or the demand for it is suspended, for fear that the person from whom the tax is due may abscond in desperation, and there are also provisions for dealing with the accomplished fact.[4]

It has been noted already[5] that, according to Nikḗtas of Amnía's story, the poor soldier to whom the eighth-century saint Philáretos had lent his

---

[1] See the passage quoted on II, 1 (iii) (d), on p. 143.

[2] The land-tax was paid by the landowner, not by his serfs (Dölger, 'Beiträge', p. 57).

[3] This point is made by Ostrogorsky in 'Agrarian Conditions', p. 219, and in 'Die Wirtschaftlichen und sozialen Grundlagen', p. 135. Cf. Jenkins in *C. Med. H.*, vol. iv, Part II, pp. 98–9.

[4] See II, 1 (iv), p. 181.   [5] In II, 1 (iii) (d), on p. 141.

horse for passing muster was planning to abscond and refrained only when the saint gave him the horse to keep. It has also been noted[1] that the ninth-century saint Efthýmios the Younger (*né* Nikětas) absconded at the age of eighteen after his name had been entered in the military ledger of his théma, after he had married and had had a child, and after he had found a husband for his sister. When he had thus fulfilled his duties as the male head of the family (his father was dead), he went off one day on the pretence of going to look for a horse that was out at grass,[2] and his family did not see him again till forty-two years later.[3] They had lost all trace of him, and they might never have seen him again if he had not happened to get news of them which moved him to send them a message.[4] We may assume that the clerks who kept the military and tax ledgers in the Ánkyra district, in which Nikětas's native village, Opsó, lay,[5] had been no more successful in tracking him down than his family had been. Niketas had absconded from Opsó to the monasteries on the Mysian Mount Olympus;[6] had become a monk;[7] had moved on from Mount Olympus to Mount Athos;[8] had performed there prodigious feats of austerity;[9] and had won such fame by these feats, under his monastic name Efthýmios, that, when he had to visit Thessaloníkê to attend a funeral there, he was given a popular ovation and then won still greater popularity and fame by perching, out of physical reach, on the top of a pillar just outside the city.[10] For the rest of his life,[11] Efthýmios was hounded from pillar to post by importunate admirers; but the Government's ledger-clerks never caught up with him—or at least, if they did identify him, they forbore to bring to book a truant soldier and tax-payer who by that time had become venerable and emaciated, though, as Efthýmios, he had also become richer than his alias the thematic soldier Nikětas would ever have been.

This was the exceptional career of an exceptional personality. The normal fate of truants was to become serfs, not stylites and abbots. Yet even this less glamorous alternative to continuing to be a peasant free-holder became attractive enough in the course of the tenth century to move the Imperial Government to follow up Rhomanós II's Novel No. 16

---

[1] In cap. cit., p. 139.   [2] Petit in loc. cit., pp. 172–3.   [3] Loc. cit., p. 202.
[4] Loc. cit., pp. 180–1.   [5] Loc. cit., p. 170.   [6] Op. cit., p. 174.
[7] p. 175.   [8] pp. 180 and 181–2.
[9] pp. 182–6.   [10] pp. 187–8.
[11] Before he died, Efthýmios had taken time, off his pillar, to found, on the site of a ruined shrine of St. Andrew, the monastery of Peristeraí, whose abbot was enabled in 952, by the wiles of Judge Samonás, to buy some public land cheap, thanks to the judge's astute interpretation of the law (see p. 172). Endowments had flowed to Peristeraí from the start (Petit in loc. cit., p. 197). After his family had rejoined him, Efthýmios took his male relatives into his own monastery Peristeraí and founded a new convent for the women (Petit, p. 202). Before he re-ascended his pillar, Efthýmios had made his grandson Methódhios abbot and his granddaughter Efphêmía abbess (p. 202).

of 962 by taking more stringent measures for reversing the exodus of peasants from the freeholding communities to the large-scale estates. Our evidence for this is provided by two siyíllia (certificates), one issued in September 974 by Symeon, ek prosópou of thémata Thessaloníkê and Strymón, and the other in September 975 by Theódhoros Kládhon, who held the same office.[1] The action recorded in these two documents was taken by the two local officials in pursuance of Imperial instructions (from the Emperor John Dzimiskěs) which presumably applied to all parts of the Empire.[2] These officials had been instructed to track down soldiers and peasants who, in their district, had absconded to large-scale estates, either lay or ecclesiastical. In their siyíllia they certify that they have now recovered all those truants who, by rights, are dhêmosiárioi, and have left to the monasteries to which the two siyíllia are addressed— namely, the Great Lávra on Mount Athos in the certificate of 974, and the monasteries of Kolovós, Polýgyros, and Leondía, in the certificate of 975—only those families that are, by rights, these monasteries' serfs.

Ostrogorsky argues convincingly that the 'dhêmosiárioi'[3] of these two certificates are identical with the peasant freeholders of the Imperial agrarian legislation, and he draws the conclusion that the status of the peasant freeholders had grievously deteriorated in the course of the two centuries and three-quarters that had elapsed between the promulgation of the Nómos Yeoryikós and the years 974–5. The documents show that in 974–5 the Government did not recognize the right of the nominally free peasant freeholders to change their domicile. If they had absconded to a large-scale estate, the Government now sought to track them down, and, if it succeeded in identifying and catching them, it re-instated them by force on their 'freeholds'. Ostrogorsky's comment[4] is pertinent.

In protecting the small freeholders, civilian and military, against the designs of the large-scale landowners, the East Roman Government was not contending for the rights or for the independence of the small fry. The truth is that it was defending its own rights—its rights to the peasants' payments and services, which the feudal lords were trying to capture from the Government. The tenth-century domestic contest (in the Empire) was not a contest between big and small landowners; it was a contest between the Imperial Government and the feudal potentates. The small landowners were merely the object of this contest; their payments and services were the prize that was at stake. This

---

[1] See Ostrogorsky, *Quelques Problèmes d'histoire de la paysannerie byzantine* (Brussels, 1956, Byzantion), pp. 12–19.

[2] 'Sans doute, ce fut une mesure générale' (Ostrogorsky, op. cit., p. 15).

[3] The word 'Dhêmósion' had two different technical meanings: (i) the commonweal, i.e. the state; (ii) the staple state tax, i.e. the land-tax. The word 'dhêmosiárioi' might therefore mean either state serfs (δημοσιακοὶ πάροικοι) or persons liable to pay the land-tax. The former of these two alternative possible meanings is the more probable of the two, since the land-tax was due in theory from all landowners, whatever the size of their estates.

[4] In op. cit., p. 16.

fundamental fact is brought to light more clearly in these siyíllia than in the insincere rhetoric of the Imperial novels.

Thus the once free, and freeholding, peasants had now become the object of a contest between two great powers. However, this object, being human, was not passive. The contest between the Government and the δυνατοί gave the πένητες the opportunity of choosing between their two potential masters. When an increasing number of them came to the conclusion that it was a worse fate to be the Government's serf than to be a private magnate's serf, the magnates' victory over the Government was assured. The most stringent and most detailed governmental legislation could not prevent the peasants from voting with their feet by absconding to the estates of magnates, lay or ecclesiastical, who were able and eager to harbour them.

(iv) *Taxation*

Taxation played a dominant part in the economic and social life of the East Roman Empire, and its dominance became greater when the Imperial Government's expenses increased. This happened when, in its relations with its neighbours, the Empire passed over from a defensive to an offensive military policy. The change was inaugurated on the Empire's eastern front in 926, and on all fronts the new policy was pursued *à outrance* during the years 960–1018 by Nikêphóros II, John Dzimiskés, and Basil II. The Government's expenses then increased still further. East Roman taxation was imposed effectively on tax-payers who were peasant freeholders, but not so effectively on large-scale landowners, lay and ecclesiastical; and the ratio of the Empire's productive land that was held by the large-scale landowners rose *pari passu* with the keying-up of the Government's offensive military operations. These facts go far to account for the vicissitudes in the East Roman Empire's strength, measured in terms of the contemporary strength of its Muslim and its Western Christian competitors.

During the two centuries and a quarter 700–925, the East Roman Empire was relatively strong both in appearance and in reality. From 926 to 1071, its relative strength was impressively greater in appearance, but during this period of outward success the foundations of the Empire's former genuine strength were being sapped by the progressive ruin of the peasant freeholders, who had been the Empire's surest source of both tax-money and native soldiers. In the long run a state cannot be stronger than its population; and, if the state ruins the population by short-sighted fiscal and military policies, the state will bring the same fate on itself. The nemesis of the East Roman Government's policies became manifest in 1071, the year which saw both the fall of Bári and the débâcle at

Melazkerd. What is surprising is not the breakdown but the length of time to which the subsequent decline was drawn out. The East Roman Empire's overthrow in 1204 by the Venetians and the French crusaders was retrieved, and, after the reoccupation of Constantinople in 1261, the Empire's death agonies were protracted for another 192 years before it was extinguished by the 'Osmanli Turks in 1453.

Our information about the East Roman Government's fiscal policy and history is derived from three sources. The prime source is Imperial legislation (for instance, the Nómos Yeoryikós and the tenth-century agrarian laws that have been discussed in preceding sections of the present chapter). The second source is a highly technical and authoritative, but apparently unofficial, handbook for taxation-officers which was compiled after the death, in 912, of Leo VI, but perhaps not later than the mid-point of the tenth century.[1] The third source is the incidental notices in the works of chroniclers and historians.

The two stapletaxes were the land-tax and the hearth-tax (καπνικόν, meaning, literally, a tax on chimney-smoke). The hearth-tax may have been payable by every head of a household, whether or not he was an owner of real estate.[2] The components of the land-tax are uncertain. It must have included not only a tax on arable and on vineyards, but also the pasture-tax (ἐννόμιον), the tax on mountain land (ὀρική), and the bee-tax (μελισσονόμιον).[3] Ostrogorsky holds[4] that the συνωνή—the Greek official translation of the Latin term *annona*, which had originally been a payment in kind but had been commuted subsequently to a money-payment—had become the land-tax by the date at which the handbook for taxation-officers was compiled. Dölger, on the other hand, holds[5] that the συνωνή was a variable surcharge on the land-tax, and that it was also payable by the pároikoi, though by them at a fixed rate. If the land-tax and the συνωνή were not identical, they were both included in the

---

[1] This handbook, which has been preserved in *Codex Marcianus Graecus 173*, was first published by W. Ashburner in *J.H.S.*, vol. xxxv (1915), pp. 76–84. There is a second, and better, edition of the text in F. Dölger, 'Beiträge zur Geschichte der byzantinischen Finanzverwaltung, besonders des 10. und 11. Jahrhunderts', in *Byzantinisches Archiv*, Heft 9 (Berlin and Leipzig, 1927, Teubner), pp. 113–23, with a commentary on pp. 123–56. Dölger's work has been reprinted (Hildesheim, 1960) with corrections and additions. For the dating see Dölger, op. cit., pp. 7–8; Ostrogorsky, 'Die ländliche Steuergemeinde', pp. 3–6, and 'La Commune rurale', p. 148; Lemerle, 'Esquisse', vol. ccxix, pp. 258–9. It can hardly have been an official document, since, in one passage (on p. 118 of Dölger's text), the author, after giving two alternative interpretations of his own of the apparently obsolete technical term σταθέντα λογίσιμα, remarks: βασιλικὴ δέ τις σύνταξις ἐξουσιαστικῶς (arbitrarily) ἐκέλευσε μηδαμῶς ταῦτα δέχεσθαι.

[2] Ostrogorsky, 'Die ländliche Steuergemeinde', p. 51, holds that the landless tax-payer paid nothing but the καπνικόν, but that the landowner, too, paid this as well as his other taxes. Dölger, loc. cit., pp. 52–3, doubts whether the kapnikón was payable by the free peasant freeholder.

[3] Ostrogorsky, 'Die ländliche Steuergemeinde', p. 57; Dölger, loc. cit., pp. 53–7.

[4] 'Die ländliche Steuergemeinde', p. 50.   [5] In loc. cit., pp. 57–8.

δημόσιον τέλος or δημόσιοι φόροι which, together with the ἀερικόν (door and windows tax), were the only taxes that the owners of στρατιωτικὰ κτήματα were to be required to pay, according to Leo VI's instructions.¹ The δημόσιον must also have included the hearth-tax, if this was in truth payable by every head of a family.²

Civilian peasant freeholders had to pay supplements (προσθῆκαι, παρακολουθήματα) to the δημόσιον and separate taxes to the central military accounts office (λογοθέσιον τοῦ στρατιωτικοῦ) and to the thematic administrators, and they had also to perform corvées (ἀγγαρεῖαι, δουλεῖαι).³ This bundle of extra burdens was called collectively ἐπήρεια ('imposition'), in contrast to the δημόσιον, which was the totality of the regular tax payable to the central government.⁴

There were four supplements,⁵ and they amounted, together, to a surcharge of 23 per cent on the δημόσιον. Two of these, the δικέρατον and the ἑξάφολλον, had been imposed originally by Leo III⁶ for rebuilding the walls of Constantinople but had been maintained thereafter to be used for general purposes (κοινωφελεῖς αἰτίας).⁷ The other two, the συνήθεια ('customary payment') and the ἐλατικόν (journey-money), had originally been tips pocketed by the senior taxation-officers and the itinerant tax-collectors respectively, and these unofficial supplements were still being pocketed by these officials at the time when the handbook was compiled.⁸ By the time of Aléxios I (1081–1118) they had been appropriated by the state.⁹ But we may be sure that the officials still demanded tips for themselves, and that, if the taxpayer refused to make these unauthorized additional payments to them, he would be made to suffer for his temerity. The rates at which the supplements were levied were quotas of the regular taxes, and Ostrogorsky reckons¹⁰ that they were graded on scales that let the rich taxpayer off more lightly than the poor one.

In addition to the Imperial taxes there were thematic taxes. This can be inferred from several passages in Leo VI's *Taktiká*. Though the thematic soldiers had to provide their personal arms and other equipment

¹ In his *Taktiká*, Dhiat. 4, § 1, col. 700, and Dhiat. 20, § 71, col. 1032, cited in II, 1 (iii) (d), p. 139.
² Ostrogorsky points out in 'Die ländliche Steuergemeinde', pp. 54–5, that the relative importance of the different taxes varied from age to age. There is no evidence for the door and windows tax in the time of Constantine Porphyrogenitus and his successors (p. 56) but, in a khrysóvoullon dated 1186, the hearth-tax, door and windows tax, and poll-tax are enumerated side by side with each other (pp. 52–3).
³ Ostrogorsky, 'Die ländliche Steuergemeinde', pp. 60–4; Dölger in loc. cit., pp. 59–61.
⁴ Dölger, ibid., p. 61.
⁵ Ostrogorsky, loc. cit., pp. 61–4; Dölger, loc. cit., pp. 54–60.
⁶ The δικέρατον may have been imposed by Nikêphóros I (see Dölger, *Regesten*, I. Teil, p. 37), though it is attributed to Leo III by Theophanes, p. 412, sub A.M. 6232.
⁷ Handbook, § 26.   ⁸ Ostrogorsky, loc. cit., pp. 65 and 85–6.
⁹ Ostrogorsky, ibid., p. 65.   ¹⁰ Ibid., pp. 64–5.

at their own expense, there must have been thematic funds for providing the spare weapons and tools, the catapults, and the waggons on which these weapons, tools, and machines were conveyed when the army-corps went on campaign.[1] Moreover, it was one of the duties of the corps-commander to make, during the winter break between campaigning seasons, an inventory of the horses and arms that his corps would need for the next campaign, and apparently he was responsible for making good any deficiencies.[2] Also, if there was any fortification-work or ship-building or bridge-building or road-construction or any other public work to be done, and 'if the local δημόσιον could not cover this, then the work was to be let out on contract' (εἰ . . . , καὶ οὐκ ἐπαρκεῖ τὸ κατὰ τόπον δημόσιον, διὰ μισθοῦ ταῦτα ἐργάζεσθαι).[3] All these public obligations must have cost money, and, if they were charges on the army-corps-district administrations, these administrations must have met them by levying provincial taxes of their own.

The last of the passages here quoted from Leo VI's *Taktiká* seems to imply that corvée work was remunerated, yet some, at least, of it was unremunerated, for road-service (ἀγγαρεία) and boat-building service (κατεργοκτισία) could be commuted to money payments.[4] Board and lodging for officials (ἄπληκτα) and for troops (μητάτα)[5] presumably had to be provided gratis; and, if supplies and pack-animals were requisitioned, the rates of compensation were fixed (no doubt, below the market price) by the public authorities.

These taxes, surcharges, and corvées amounted in the aggregate to a heavy burden, and this burden was aggravated by the collective responsibility (ἀλληλέγγυον)[6] that was a fundamental principle of the East Roman taxation system. The rural communities (ὁμάδες) were taxation-collectivities. The members of a community were liable, collectively and individually, for the payment of the total amount of the tax-items with which a community was assessed. The technical term for this collective total was ῥίζα χωρίου ('root of the village-community').[7] The technical term for the area of the district on which this collective total was assessed was ὑποταγὴ χωρίου.[8] When the collective total had been assessed, it was

---

[1] See Leo, *Taktiká*, Dhiat. 5, § 6, col. 720, and Dhiat. 6, § 27, col. 729.

[2] Dhiat. 11, § 50, col. 805, and Epíloghos, col. 1083, cited already in II, 1 (iii) (d), p. 144.

[3] Dhiat. 20, § 71, col. 1032.

[4] Ostrogorsky, loc. cit., p. 61.

[5] Ostrogorsky, loc. cit., p. 60; Dölger, loc. cit., pp. 60–1.

[6] This was the current technical term; the earlier term had been ἐπιβολή (attribution), but this word was now used in a different sense, namely to denote the allocation of the community's collective tax among the members of the community (Dölger, pp. 132–4).

[7] The handbook, p. 114 in Dölger's text, defines the ῥίζα χωρίου as being ἡ ὅλη ποσότης τῶν ἐν τῇ συγγραφῇ ἑκάστου χωρίου κειμένων ψηφίων ('tax-items'). The total that was allocated was the δημόσιον, not the δημόσιον plus the προσθῆκαι (Dölger, loc. cit., p. 154).

[8] Handbook, Dölger's text, pp. 114–15; cf. Ostrogorsky, loc. cit., p. 22.

then allocated among the members of the community.[1] This allocation of the community's collective tax-assessment among the individual members of the community determined the amount of the community's land that the individual taxpayer held.[2] The individual peasant freeholder's title-deeds to his holding were his portion of the community's collective tax-assessment and the receipts (if he could obtain any from the tax-collector certifying that his tax-payments were not in arrears). The tax-payer was, in fact, the owner of the land on which tax had been paid by him.[3]

Thus the validity of the individual holder's title depended on his punctuality in paying the share of the community's collective tax that had been allotted to him; yet his performance of his fiscal duty was not just a private concern of his own as between him and the taxation-officers. It also concerned his ὁμοτελεῖς, his fellow members of the community who were jointly responsible with him for the payment of his tax. If he defaulted or absconded, the tax-burden that he had let drop would fall on their shoulders. This gave his ὁμοτελεῖς a moral right, which was recognized *de facto*, if not *de jure*, by the public authorities, to take over the working of his land, and to make this land continue to be productive and so continue to yield its quota of the collective tax, if the owner failed to continue to carry out a private enterprise that was at the same time both a communal and a public duty. Situations in which the ὁμοτελεῖς have taken over the working of a truant's land, and the legal problems to which these situations give rise, are dealt with in the Nómos Yeoryikós.[4] This also explains what looks, at first sight, like high-handedness, or indeed sheer robbery, in the conduct of St. Philáretos's neighbours, according to the story. In consequence partly of a devastating enemy raid, and partly of his own feckless generosity, Philáretos became poor. Out of all his once numerous slaves and livestock,[5] 'he was left with only one pair of oxen, one horse, one donkey, one cow with her calf, one male slave, and one female slave'.[6] Thereupon, all his forty-eight estates (προάστια) were seized by neighbouring δυνασταί (large-scale landowners of the δυνατοί class) and γεωργοί (peasant freeholders).[7]

When they saw that he was impoverished and was no longer capable of maintaining these estates and cultivating his own land, they divided his land

---

[1] The technical term for this allocation of the total was ἡ τῆς ῥίζης ἱκάνωσις ('making the collective total effective') (Handbook, Dölger's text, pp. 114–15). The word ἐπιβολή was now used as a synonym for this.

[2] Dölger in loc. cit., pp. 132–4.

[3] Ostrogorsky, 'Agrarian Conditions', p. 213, and 'Die ländliche Steuergemeinde', pp. 24–5, endorsed by Lemerle, 'Esquisse', vol. ccxix, p. 61: 'Est propriétaire celui qui paye l'impôt.'   [4] See II, 1 (iii) (c).

[5] Enumerated in Fourmy and Leroy in loc. cit., pp. 113 and 115.

[6] Ibid., p. 115.   [7] Ibid.

up among themselves. Some of them seized their portions by force, others wheedled theirs out of him. They left to him only the village (χωρίον) in which he resided and his ancestral mansion.[1]

Philáretos felt that he had been relieved of a burden,[2] but his neighbours realized that he had shifted this burden on to their shoulders. Philáretos had allowed his real estate to cease to be productive, but this was not going to move the taxation-officers to lower, to a corresponding degree, the figures of the collective tax-assessments of the taxation-districts among which Philáretos's estates were distributed. According to the story, every one of these estates had a spring producing more than enough water to irrigate it.[3] If so, Philáretos's share of the collective assessments must have been large, and his default on his share therefore threatened to increase the tax-burden of his ὁμοτελεῖς very gravely. Their remedy was to take over Philáretos's neglected estates and to make them once again produce enough to yield the tax that had been assessed on them in the process of allocation. Their resort to self-help was justified, since, for them, it was the only alternative to an increase in their own tax-allocations that would have been ruinous for them.

When some single member of a taxation-collectivity defaulted, even if this member's allocation was as large a part of the total assessment on the taxation-district as Philáretos's allocation must have been, it was practicable for the defaulter's ὁμοτελεῖς to take over his land and to work it in addition to their own. They would resort to this method of self-help, and the tax-collector would be able still to extract from the collectivity the total amount of its collective assessment. But suppose that a village was wholly or partially wiped out (ἐξαλιφείσης) by an enemy raid (one of the causes of Philáretos's ruin) or by some other act of God (θεομηνίας, 'manifestation of God's wrath'), i.e. a flood, drought, pest, or some other form of natural calamity; in that event it would be beyond the power of the surviving members of the taxation-collectivity fully to restore the productivity of so extensive a part of the taxation-district. If the taxation-officers were to attempt, nevertheless, to exact the whole of the tax previously due, the surviving owners of the ruined land (if any of these were left alive) would be driven to abscond, and, if the taxation-officers then attempted to exact the tax previously due from the ruined part of the district from the tax-payers in the un-ruined part, these, too, would abscond. The taxation-officers would then have on their hands a district with no inhabitants, no production, and no tax-yield at all.

In this situation, the Government had come to the conclusion—no doubt, as a result of a number of frustrating and disconcerting experiences —that half a loaf was better than no bread. In order to dissuade the

---

[1] Ibid., p. 117.   [2] Ibid.   [3] Ibid., pp. 113–15.

surviving tax-payers in the district from absconding, the ruined part of
the district was now detached from the district and was converted into
a separate taxation-unit (ἰδιόστατον).[1] By this act of separation, the tax-
payers in the remnant of the district were released from their former
collective responsibility in respect of the detached area,[2] and, in granting
this release, the taxation-officers avoided giving the un-ruined members
of the community an incentive to abscond. Their collective and individual
tax-obligations were now limited to the amount of the assessment on the
un-ruined and undetached part of the district. In order to assure them of
this, the ἰδιόστατον that had been detached from the area of the taxation-
district was given a separate description of its boundaries (περιορισμός),
which was recorded in a separate document.[3]

The assessment of the ἰδιόστατον was now dealt with separately. If the
survivors of the former holders of land in the ἰδιόστατον were still in
residence, they might be persuaded to refrain from absconding by being
granted a partial remission. Some of the entries (στιχοί)[4] might be removed
(ἀποκεκινημένοι), and holdings that had thus been partially relieved of
tax were known as μερικῶς συμπαθηθέντα. The tax-payer then continued
to pay the unremitted part of his tax, and the remitted part was not
transferred to his neighbours.[5] If the land-holders had already absconded,
their deserted lands received total remission (i.e. were ὁλοσυμπάθητα).[6]
There might also be a temporary suspension (κουφισμός) of tax-
demand on deserted land, in the hope of inducing the truants to return
to resume cultivation and to reassume their tax-obligations.[7] If and
when the owners did return, there was a restoration (ὄρθωσις) of the tax,
but this was only gradual.[8]

The absentees were given thirty years' grace for returning; but, if and
when this period ran out without their having reappeared, an inspector—
a different one from the one who had originally created the ἰδιόστατον
and had granted the partial or total temporary or permanent remissions
of the tax payable on it—now withdrew the remissions and converted the
ἰδιόστατον into a κλάσμα, i.e. a fragment permanently broken off from
the χωρίον in which the ἰδιόστατον had originally been included. This
klásma then escheated to the Government, and the Government was
free to sell it or to give it away gratis for re-peopling and recultivation.[9]

---

[1] This was one way, but not the only way, in which an ἰδιόστατον could come into existence. The term was applicable to any taxation-district (e.g. a large-scale estate) that was
not a χωρίον, i.e. was not a taxation-collectivity of free peasant freeholders.

[2] Handbook, § 5, cited by Ostrogorsky, 'Die ländliche Steuergemeinde', p. 22.

[3] Handbook, § 5.

[4] Alias διάρια (Dölger, loc. cit., pp. 126–7).

[5] Handbook, Dölger's text, p. 119.

[6] Ibid., with Dölger's commentary, p. 148.

[7] Text, p. 119.   [8] Text, pp. 119–20.

[9] Text, pp. 118–19. See also text, pp. 120–2, with Dölger's commentary, p. 152.

A comprehensive record of the fiscal history of all parts of a taxation-district was kept in the district's assessment-register ($\tau\hat{\omega}$ λόγῳ τῆς ῥίζης).[1]

In intention, these provisions for tax-relief on lands that had suffered disasters were humane and provident. However, the provision for settling or giving away klásmata at the end of the thirty years' period of grace had one grave drawback. It opened the way for large-scale land-owners, ecclesiastical or lay, to get possession of land that had originally been held by peasant freeholders. The disposal of klásmata was in the hands of local officials, and, in the preceding sub-section of the present chapter, cases have been noted in which these local officials evidently acted in collusion with local δυνατοί and overrode the right of first refusal that was supposed to be assured to the local peasant freeholders by acts of agrarian legislation that were in force at the time.[2]

Nor was the disposal of klásmata the only opportunity that the officials had for abusing their power. From first to last, the tax-payer was at the taxation-officers' mercy. He was lucky if he received separate demand-notes for the δημόσιον and for each of the four supplementary payments. He was sometimes presented with only a single inclusive figure, known as the ἀρίθμιον,[3] and then he was in danger of being overcharged.[4] More-over, when a taxation-officer had kept a record of the inclusive figures only, and not of the separate items, and when he handed his notes over to his successor, the inclusive figure (ἀρίθμιον) might be mistaken by the successor for the net figure for the δημόσιον,[5] and this official error would impose on the tax-payer a further overcharge of 23 per cent, plus a sur-charge of another 23 per cent on the overcharge.

Emperors who, like Basil I and Rhomanós I, had not been born in the purple chamber but had made their way to the summit from humble origins, were familiar, from the experience of their own families, with the abuses by which the poor were victimized. According to Constantine Porphyrogenitus,[6] Basil insisted that, as a protection for the tax-payer, tax-demands should be presented in plain writing, with the figures un-abbreviated. According to Genesius,[7] Basil I made a practice, during Lent, after the Senate had adjourned for the day, of putting in some working-time at the tax-office in order to settle outstanding disputes between the revenue authorities and the tax-payers.

We need not doubt the genuineness of these proletarian Emperors' fellow-feeling for the suffering mass of people of their own kind who had

---

[1] Text, p. 114.   [2] See II, 1 (iii) (e), pp. 150 seqq.

[3] See Dölger, commentary on the Handbook, p. 154.

[4] Handbook, text, p. 122. Cf. p. 123 for the likelihood of overcharges on pákta (state lands included in peasant freehold taxation-districts).

[5] Handbook, text, p. 122.

[6] In his biography of Basil I (*Theoph. Cont.*, Book V, chap. 31, p. 261).

[7] Book IV, p. 126.

not succeeded, as they had, in changing their condition. Basil I had not forborne 'to wade thro' slaughter to a throne', but he had not 'shut the gates of mercy on mankind' when his murderous ascent to the summit had apparently opened up for him an opportunity for doing something to relieve the hardships of his subjects who had remained at the level from which he had raised himself by his own criminal exertions. Basil I's and Rhomanós I's experience in their attempts to redress the wrongs of the weak must have opened their eyes to the truth that reaching the summit was not the same thing as acquiring the autocratic power which was an East Roman Emperor's nominal prerogative. On the Imperial throne to which they had climbed, as in the humble surroundings in which each of them had been born, they were still—as they lived to discover—under the thumb of a corrupt and oppressive civil service. In the East Roman Empire, neither the people nor the Emperor had the last word. The true masters of the Empire were the officials acting in collusion with the δυνατοί.

2. The Palace

AN East Roman Emperor could spend as much time in the Imperial Palace as he chose, or as little as he dared. In terms of his own personal security, it was probably less dangerous for him to allow the provinces to be overrun by foreign invaders while he stayed in the Palace, keeping a look-out for intrigues there against his throne or his life, than it was for him to be absent on protracted campaigns for the defence or the extension of the East Roman Empire's frontiers. Constantine Porphyrogenitus had warlike successors—the two intruders Nikêphóros II Phokás and John Dzimiskês and his own grandson Basil II 'the Bulgar-killer'—who did, at their peril, spend a large part of their time in the field.[1] By contrast, Constantine himself was more stay-at-home in the Palace that was his birthplace than most East Roman Emperors were—more, for instance, than Michael III was.

Constantine's cloistered life was partly forced on him by circumstances and was partly an indulgence of his native temperament. During his first sole reign (913–20) he was not yet grown up. During the twenty-six years 919–44, he was deliberately kept in the background by the intruder Rhomanós I Lekapênós. Though Rhomanós had made his way to the Imperial throne through a career in the Imperial Navy, he was by temperament a politician and a diplomat rather than a fighting-man. He preferred to delegate military commands to others, and, having no military ambitions himself, he would have taken care not to let Constantine outshine him in this field, supposing that Constantine had had the

---

[1] Nikêphóros II Phokás might have been more alert to the intrigues against him in the Palace that cost him his life if he had not disliked staying in the Palace and had not preferred active service in the field (see p. 67). The eleventh-century author (a Nikoulidzás Dhelphinás?) of a set of precepts addressed to an Emperor (Aléxios I?) urges the Emperor to resist the temptation to vegetate in the Palace; he ought to be constantly touring the thémata to redress grievances and to forestall insurrections. The author scouts the suggestion that such absences from the Palace may jeopardize the Emperor's hold on the Imperial throne (see *Cecaumeni Strategicon et Incerti Scriptoris de Officiis Regiis Libellus*, ed. by B. Wassiliewsky and V. Jernstedt (St. Petersburg, 1896, Imperial Academy of Sciences) pp. 103–4. On the other hand, one of the maxims of the author of *Cecaumeni Strategicon* is ὁ γὰρ ἐν Κωνσταντίνου πόλει καθεζόμενος βασιλεὺς πάντοτε νικᾷ (p. 74). This generalization, however, is too sweeping. It is true that the effective occupation of the Imperial Palace at Constantinople was a condition *sine qua non* for securing recognition as a legitimate wearer of the Imperial crown, but it was not also a guarantee that an Emperor installed in Constantinople would not be dispossessed by an insurgent who had made a *pronunciamiento* in one of the thémata or in the Fleet. For instance, Leontius was successfully ousted by Tiberius III in 698, Theodosius III by Leo III in 717, Michael I by Leo V in 813. Nor was the occupation of the Palace a guarantee against assassination, as was proved by Leo V's fate in 820 and by Nikêphóros II's in 969.

ability and the inclination. Constantine did not have either, so there was no conflict between him and Rhomanós on this score. By the time when Constantine became sole ruler again, he was a confirmed scholar, and, as an antiquarian, he was interested, as has been noted already, in the court ceremonial, notwithstanding the heavy toll of his working time that his ceremonial duties took.

An Emperor who chose to stay in the Palace did not have to move far afield. The link between the Palace and the people of Constantinople was the Hippodrome. This immediately adjoined the Palace, to the north-west of it. There was direct private access from the Palace to the Imperial Box, which was a miniature palace in itself; and, though, in the Box, the Emperor could make himself visible to his subjects if he chose, he was still aloof from them there. The only functions that obliged the Emperor to leave the Palace's precincts were processions, and these were kept within the *enceinte* of the City. The Church of the Ayía Sophía, which was the Emperor's most frequent goal outside the Palace, was only just across the way from the main gate of the Palace, which was on the Palace's north-eastern side. The Emperor also had regular visits to pay, on fixed dates, to the Church of the Holy Apostles and to a few of the other most eminent and holy churches and monasteries in the City. The Emperor's longest regular procession was to the Church of the Theotókos and the Vlakhérnai Palace beyond the northern end of the Theodosian triple land-wall. The Emperor would make this journey either by land or by water, according to his fancy or to the state of the weather.[1] Occasional auspicious events, such as the arrival of a precious relic—e.g. the Mandḗlion, which arrived at Constantinople from Édhessa on 8 August 944[2]—took the Emperor to the Golden Gate at the City's south-west corner, where he would receive the honoured object in state, to escort it in a triumphal march from end to end of the City. Occasionally the Court would venture outside the city-walls for a formally informal picnic in a meadow outside the Palace of Iería on the Asiatic shore of the Bosphorus.[3] So far as we know, the farthest afield from his birthplace, the purple chamber of the Imperial Palace, that Constantine Porphyrogenitus ever went was on his trip, on which he died, to the Mysian Olympus; and this mountain is visible from Constantinople in clear weather.

The Imperial Palace was a world in itself, and a jealously closed and watchfully guarded world. Though its circuit was extensive, it had only

---

[1] See Constantine Porphyrogenitus, *De Caer.*, Book I, chap. 27, pp. 147–56; chap. 34, pp. 178–9.

[2] See *Georg. Mon. Cont.*, Reign of Rhomanós I, chap. 48, pp. 918–19; Leo Grammaticus, pp. 325–6; *Theoph. Cont.*, Reign of Rhomanós I, chap. 48, p. 432; pseudo-Symeon, Reign of Rhomanós I, cap. 50, pp. 748–9; Kedhrênós, vol. ii, p. 319.

[3] See *De Caer.*, Book I, chap. 78, pp. 373–5.

four or five gates. The main gate was the Iron Gate[1] of the Khalkê´ on the
Palace's north-eastern side, facing the Ayía Sophía, and whoever entered here had to run the gauntlet of the Guards' regiments' quarters
before reaching the newer south-western quarters of the Palace—largely
built by Constantine Porphyrogenitus's grandfather Basil I—in which, in
Constantine's day, the Imperial family and its eunuch household lived.[2]
The majority of the courtiers came into the Palace just for the day and
slept at night in the City in private houses of their own. The rest of
the population of Constantinople lived and died without ever entering
the Palace at all. Foreign ambassadors and other state guests, whom the
Imperial Government wanted to impress, were the only non-members of
the Court who set eyes on the throne-room's rather childish clockwork:
the golden lions that roared, the golden birds that sang in the branches of
a golden tree, and the throne that, like a lift, hoisted the Emperor, in the
twinkling of an eye, from floor to ceiling.[3] The Constantinopolitan public
never had even a glimpse of any of the buildings, secular or sacred, within
the Palace's enclosure. Constantine Porphyrogenitus, in his biography of
his grandfather the Emperor Basil I,[4] excuses himself for giving a detailed
verbal description of the 'Néa' Church and Basil's other works inside the
Palace's precincts,[5] on the ground that

to see these beautiful works for oneself would be the most accurate way of
learning about them. However, they are not open to inspection by everybody,
so they have to be brought to the ears of serious inquirers in an account set
out in writing. The object is to win for the author of these works the admiration that is his due, and to save those who are excluded from the right of entry
into the Palace from being totally ignorant of its wonders.[6]

The Palace was a fortress, and it could also be a trap. The first public
event in the first bout of Constantine Porphyrogenitus's reign as sole
Emperor was the unsuccessful *putsch* made by Constantine Dhoux,[7] the
dhoméstikos of the Skholaí, i.e. commandant of the senior Guards
regiment of the four, and, as such, the highest-ranking military officer in

---

[1] *Theoph. Cont.*, Book VI, first bout of Constantine VII's sole reign, chap. 2, p. 383.

[2] The eunuch household was known collectively as τὸ κουβούκλειον (from the Latin 'cubi-
culum').

[3] See Bishop Liutprand's account of all this in *Antapodosis*, Book VI, chap. 5. There
was a similar set of mechanical toys at Baghdad, in the Palace of the Tree, in 917. See
Al-Khatīb's and Sibt b. Al-Jawzī's accounts, translated in Vasiliev, *Byzance et les Arabes*,
ii, II, pp. 77 and 171. See also Canard in op. cit., ii, I, p. 241. At Constantinople these
costly Imperial baubles had been melted down by Michael III (*Theoph. Cont.*, p. 257).
They had been replaced by the time of Liutprand's first visit (949).

[4] *Theoph. Cont.*, Book V.

[5] Op. cit., chaps. 83–90, pp. 325–36.   [6] Op. cit., chap. 87, p. 329.

[7] *Georg. Mon. Cont.*, pp. 874–6; Leo Grammaticus, pp. 288–9; *Theoph. Cont.*, Book VI, first
bout of Constantine VII's sole reign, chaps. 2–3, pp. 381–4; pseudo-Symeon, pp. 718–20;
Kedhrênós, vol. ii, pp. 278–81; Zonarás, vol. iii, Books xiii–xviii, pp. 458–60.

the metropolitan area.[1] Dhoux, who had accomplices inside both the City and the Palace, succeeded in entering the City, occupied the gate of the Hippodrome, was beaten off from there, and then succeeded in penetrating the Iron Gate of the Khalkĕ, i.e. the principal gate of the Palace, and met his death in hand-to-hand fighting inside. Dhoux's fate may have served as an object-lesson to Rhomanós Lekapênós, who succeeded in installing himself in the Palace rather less than six years later, though, at the time, he was not dhoméstikos of the Skholaí, but merely admiral of the Imperial Fleet, which, in itself, was a less promising jumping-off ground for an attempt to seize the Imperial crown. Lekapênós succeeded, where Dhoux had failed, because he did not attempt to take the Palace by storm, but kept his armed force as a threat in the background while he insinuated himself into the Palace by diplomacy.

A little less than forty-six years before Constantine Dhoux's failure to storm the Palace, Basil I had found the seizure of the Palace a more difficult enterprise than his antecedent murder of Michael III; and the murder would have been to no purpose if Basil had not then succeeded in making himself master of the Palace immediately.

Since the scene of the murder had been on the Pera side of the Golden Horn, Basil and his accomplices had to cross the water in a rough sea and to make their way first into the City and then, through the City, into the Palace. After they had landed, apparently they had no difficulty in obtaining admission into the City by the nearest gate. Basil was co-Emperor; the news of the murder of Michael could not yet have reached the guards of the City's gates and walls; so Basil and his party could count on being able to pass this first possible obstacle without being challenged. Evidently the crux, for Basil, was to gain admission to the Palace. Presumably he had enemies there, and the sequel indicates that one of these was the papías (head-porter), who held the keys. If Basil were to present himself at the main gate (the Iron Gate of the Khalkê') and were to be interrogated there by the papías or some other unfriendly officer, and if he were to be kept waiting outside the gate till the news of the murder of Michael III reached the Palace, Basil might find that someone else had been proclaimed Emperor and had been placed in possession of the Palace, and then Basil's own position would become critical.

Consequently, Basil had made arrangements in advance for being admitted into the Palace by an accomplice of his, Ardhávazdhos, through a gate at which no one else in the Palace would be expecting him to present himself.[2] Ardhávazdhos held an important post; he was the

---

[1] See J. B. Bury, *The Imperial Administrative System in the Ninth Century* (London, 1911, for the British Academy by the Oxford University Press), pp. 47–51.

[2] We may guess that this did not count as one of the regular gates. The Palace had only three gates according to the Muslim prisoner of war Hārūn b. Yaḥyā, whose account is

commander of the Etaireía regiment of household troops; and he was also a Persian, with whom another Persian, Evlóyios, who was also one of Basil's accomplices, could communicate in Persian without the purport of the conversation being understood by any of the Palace's Greek-speaking personnel. Accordingly, Basil and his party went first to fetch Evlóyios from his house in Constantinople, and then the whole party approached the Palace via the grounds of an adjacent Imperial property called 'Marina's' (τὰ Μαρίνης). This property appears to have had no entrance opening on to the public street. It was accessible through (but apparently only through) a gate in the Palace's wall, and this gate, opening into a cul-de-sac, was the gate at which it had been arranged that Ardhávazdhos should be waiting. Basil and his party now had to break into 'Marina's', and this was not difficult; for, unlike the Palace's wall, the enclosure round 'Marina's' was flimsy, and Basil here brought into play his herculean physical strength. Supported by two of his companions, Basil kicked down and broke up a stone slab forming part of the enclosure round 'Marina's', and the party thus reached the gate of the Palace where Ardhávazdhos was waiting for them.

Evlóyios then shouted through this gate to Ardhávazdhos, in Persian, that Michael had been slaughtered and that Basil was demanding to be let in. Ardhávazdhos then went and seized the keys of the Palace from the papías and admitted Basil and his party. Basil's first act was to take possession of the keys. His next act, which he carried out before dawn, was to depose the papías who had been in office and to appoint a new one.[1]

This incident illustrates the importance of the office of papías (one of the many important posts in the Palace that were reserved for eunuchs). The success or failure of an attempted *putsch* might turn on whether the papías was or was not loyal to the Emperor of the moment. In the conspiracy that came to a head in the murder of the Emperor Leo V and the enthronement, in his stead, of his intended victim Michael II, the papías of the day had played a leading part.[2]

reproduced by Ibn Rustah (see the passage translated in Vasiliev's *Byzance et les Arabes*, ii, II, pp. 384–5). The date of Hārūn's sojourn in Constantinople is disputed. The conjectures vary from 880–90 to 912–13 (Vasiliev, op. cit., vol. cit., pp. 381–2).

[1] *Georg. Mon. Cont.*, Reign of Michael III, chap. 35, p. 838; Leo Grammaticus, p. 252; pseudo-Symeon, Reign of Michael III, chap. 48, pp. 685–6.

[2] See *Georg. Mon. Interpolatus*, p. 619; Leo Grammaticus, p. 210; *Theoph. Cont.*, pp. 37–40. See also J. B. Bury, *The Imperial Administrative System in the Ninth Century*, pp. 126–7. The head-porter was the papías of the Great Palace. The Maghnávra and the Dháphnê each had a papías of its own (op. cit., p. 128). This seems to imply that—unlike 'Marina's', apparently—each of them had a gate or gates of its own, opening on to the public street. It is, in fact, recorded that Theóktistos had an iron door made in the wall of the Dháphnê, with a special papías to guard it (see p. 190). We may perhaps also infer that the Maghnávra, at any rate, could, if desired, be sealed off from the Great Palace. If the Maghnávra had

There were situations in which it was as difficult to get out of the Palace as it always was to get into it. For instance, the loghothétês Theóktistos, who was in power at the beginning of Michael III's reign, lived in a private house that lay outside the Palace, though adjoining it. For his personal security, he had an iron door made in the wall of the Dháphnê, the older part of the Palace, and he posted a papías of his own there to guard it.[1] This was a prudent precaution, but it did not save Theóktistos eventually from being murdered in the Palace, when he was on official business there, by the Emperor's uncle Várdhas.

How did the inmates of the Palace spend their time? The extant information gives the impression that, from the Emperor downwards, the whole Court lived laborious days performing ceremonies, all of which were useless and silly, while the few that were supposed to be convivial— e.g. the Ghotthikón[2] and the Vroumália[3]—were positively ludicrous. This portentous East Roman ceremonial had behind it the momentum of a long history, the greater part of which had evolved on non-Greek ground. The ceremonial went back through a number of intermediate links—the most important of which was the Sasanian Persian court at Ctesiphon—to the Achaemenian Persian court at Susa, and the Achaemenian ceremonial, in its turn, was derived from Assyrian and Babylonian and Akkadian and Sumerian precedents. If it had been possible for Aristophanes to obtain a preview of Constantine Porphyrogenitus's enormous manual of the ceremonies of the East Roman Court, he would probably have supposed, at first glance, that this was a solemn full-dress treatise on 'a day in a Persian emperor's life'—the subject that Aristophanes himself had lampooned in the ambassador's report in *The Acharnians*. When he was told that the Emperor here depicted and his fellow performers were all Greeks, Aristophanes's laughter would have turned wry. He would not have suspected that any Greeks at any date would be captivated by such nonsense.

Yet, if Aristophanes had then thought for a moment, he would have remembered that at least one eminent Greek—and a Spartiate Heraklid at that—had already succumbed to this folly. The Regent Pausanias had no sooner defeated the Persians on the battlefield than he began to ape their manners in an improvised court of his own. In the Hellenic city of Byzantium, within a few hundred yards of the site of the future East Roman Palace, Pausanias had once strutted in procession (*proélefsis*) like

---

not been both separable from the Great Palace and accessible, direct, from the public street, it is difficult to see how it could have been converted, as it was in 863, from being a palace, closed to the public, into being the seat of a university.

[1] *Georg. Mon. Cont.*, Reign of Michael III, chap. 6, p. 816.
[2] See *De Caer.*, Book I, chap. 83, pp. 381–6.
[3] See op. cit., Book II, chaps. 16–18, pp. 600 and 603–4, and chap. 53, pp. 783–91.

a veritable Persian emperor, robed in a *skaramángion*, attended (*opsikevó-menos*) by his household (*kouvoúkleion*), and escorted (*dhiriyevómenos*) by his courtiers, after these had performed the obligatory act of prostrating themselves in adoration at his feet (*proskýnêsis*).[1] This last act was one that the Hellenes of the fifth century B.C. had already known, and had detested, under its future East Roman name. I have used the other East Roman technical terms by anticipation. The vocabulary might change, but the performance remained much the same in essentials. The startling case of Pausanias shows how infectious the taste for these pompous traditional ceremonies was, and this makes the East Roman Court's addiction to them less surprising.

The change in the meaning of the Latin word *acta* tells a tale. Originally, *acta* had meant the minutes of the proceedings of a business meeting. In the documents collected in Constantine Porphyrogenitus's *De Caerimoniis*, ἄκτα means the stereotyped formulae for acclamations, and ἀκτολογίαι means recitals of this 'book of the words'. The minutes have turned into a libretto because the business has turned into a farce.

No doubt most of the East Roman Emperor's courtiers did live laborious days, but the ceremonial part of their duties will not have been a whole-time job for any of them except the Master of the Ceremonies (ὁ ἐπὶ τῆς καταστάσεως) and the eunuch household. The rest had serious public business to do as well, and the members of the household, too, will have taken advantage of their closeness to the Emperor's ear to meddle in public business unofficially and illegitimately but by no means ineffectively. Our impression of the Court's daily round comes from Constantine Porphyrogenitus's *De Caerimoniis*. Constantine took a great interest in the ceremonial side of East Roman Court-life, and, being a scholar and a writer, he expressed this interest of his in an enduring literary form. Constantine's concern with ceremonial was not just a personal idiosyncracy. It was characteristic of Byzantine official society, and the amount of time and energy spent on ceremonial at Court was certainly excessive. Constantine could, however, if he had chosen, have written an equally large book *De Administrando Imperio*,[2] and this would have been a far more instructive work.

Bury has done all that can be done posthumously to supply what Constantine left undone. Bury's *The Imperial Administrative System in the Ninth Century* is a masterly work. He has constructed a systematic account of the East Roman Imperial administration, as it stood at the close of the ninth century, from a klêtorolóyion (table of order of precedence) that

---

[1] See further IV, 2 (iv), pp. 648–51.

[2] The book of his that goes by this name is, of course, not a treatise on the administration of the East Roman Empire. It is a treatise on the conduct of the Empire's foreign relations.

was compiled by the Imperial protospathários and atriklînês Philótheos,[1] and he has supplemented Philótheos's information by gleaning from Constantine Porphyrogenitus's works and from the other documents, besides Philótheos's klêtorolóyion, that have been appended to these. The klêtorolóyion, like Constantine's own contribution to the *De Caerimoniis* and his Τὰ Βασιλικὰ Ταξείδια, is concerned primarily with ceremonial, and the light that it throws on administration is incidental. More direct light is thrown on this by some of the documents in the miscellaneous collection[2] appended to *De Caerimoniis*, Book II, particularly the field-states of the expeditions sent against the Muslim masters of Crete by Leo VI in 911[3] and by Constantine Porphyrogenitus himself in 949,[4] and the table of the salaries paid to the governors (στρατηγοί) of the 'Eastern' army-corps districts (θέματα).[5]

Bury's findings show that the elaborateness of the hierarchy of honorary ranks at the East Roman Court at the turn of the ninth and tenth centuries does not reflect the contemporary structure of the Imperial administration. By comparison with the Diocletianic–Constantinian system of honours and offices, the hierarchy of honours has been inflated. On the other hand the hierarchy of offices has been simplified. Since the breakdown of the Diocletianic–Constantinian system in the east in the seventh century, the principle of subordination, which had been characteristic of that system, had given way here to the contrary principle of co-ordination.[6] In terms of numbers, Bury notes that sixty officers were now directly responsible to the Emperor, as against twenty-two under the previous system.[7] In the organization of the Central Government the three huge and potent ministries of the Magister Officiorum, the Comes Sacrarum Largitionum, and the Comes Rei Privatae had been broken up.[8]

The same tendency is strikingly apparent in the fields of provincial administration and military organization. The separation of military command from civil authority, which had been another characteristic of the previous regime, has been reversed.[9] Now again, as in the Age of the Principate, the army-corps commanders are also the governors of the districts in which their respective corps are cantoned, and each of them is directly responsible to the Emperor.[10] Under the previous system the gover-

---

[1] Bury's text, pp. 131–79; Bonn text, pp. 702–91 of *De Caer.* On internal evidence, Bury dates Philótheos's work in September 899 (op. cit., p. 11).

[2] *De Caer.*, Book II, chaps. 40–56 inclusive.

[3] See II, 1 (iii) (d), p. 136, with n. 5.

[4] Chaps. 44 and 45.   [5] In Book II, chap. 50.

[6] Bury, *The Imperial Administrative System in the Ninth Century*, p. 20.

[7] Op. cit., p. 19. These sixty officers are specified by Philótheos in *De Caer.*, Book II, chap. 52, pp. 136–8 Bury, pp. 712–15 Bonn.   [8] Bury, op. cit., p. 20.

[9] The movement to reunite civil governorships with military commands had been started by Justinian I, but this only in a few cases.

[10] Bury, *The Imperial Administrative System in the Ninth Century*, p. 19.

nor of a province had been responsible to the vicarius of a dioecesis, who, in turn, had been responsible to a praetorian prefect, so that, between the governor of the province and the Emperor, there had been two inter-mediaries, the higher of whom had ruled a territory that was virtually an empire in itself. Military command, as well, had, under the previous system, been concentrated in fewer hands.

It is significant that, under this previous system, military command had eventually fallen, in the west, into a single pair of hands. The western magister peditum in praesenti had overshadowed his junior colleague the magister equitum in praesenti, as well as the subordinate regional magistri utriusque militiae, and he had thus made himself virtually a military dictator dominating the Imperial Government in this half of the Roman Empire,[1] whereas, in the eastern half, the infantry and the cavalry commands in praesenti had been kept on a par with each other, and the power of these two co-ordinate central commands had been further limited by the establishment of three,[2] and eventually four,[3] regional commands which, though subordinate to the two central military authorities, were nevertheless powerful enough to serve as a counter-poise to them. This difference in army organization policy was one of the reasons why, in the west, the Roman Empire had foundered in the fifth century, while, in the east, it did not go to pieces till the seventh century.[4] The progressive decentralization of the military commands in the east by the Emperors Theodosius I and Justinian I had been carried much further, by Constantine Porphyrogenitus's time, in the rehabilitated East Roman Empire.[5]

The financial field was the only one in which, in the East Roman Empire, there had been a concentration of power[6] in hands that were not those of the Emperor himself, and this was the one field in which centralization was administratively expedient without being politically dangerous.

By Constantine Porphyrogenitus's time, an Emperor reigning in the Palace at Constantinople had the power, if he also had the ability and the will, to be a ruler in fact as well as in name; and the exercise of this power was secured for him by the daily routine of life in the Imperial Palace.

Constantine, in his account of the daily ceremony of the opening of the Palace after dawn, informs us[7] incidentally that the Emperor,

---

[1] See R. Grosse, *Römische Militärgeschichte von Gallienus bis zum Beginn der byzantinischen Themenverfassung* (Berlin, 1920, Weidmann), pp. 182 and 188–9.

[2] Op. cit., pp. 185–6.

[3] Op. cit., p. 190. [4] Ibid.

[5] See Part II, chap. 4, of the present work.

[6] See pp. 194–5. [7] *De Caer.*, Book II, chap. 1, p. 520.

immediately after being dressed and saying his morning prayers, gave an audience to the postmaster-general (loghothétês tou dhrómou) : and this must have been a business meeting of first-rate importance, considering that 'the postmaster' was virtually director of political intelligence and also minister for foreign affairs. This piece of early-morning Imperial administrative routine testifies to the importance of foreign relations for the East Roman Empire. In the 'Abbasid Caliphate likewise, intelligence was part of the postmaster-general's duties.[1] By Constantine Porphyrogenitus's time, however, the collection of provincial intelligence for the government at Baghdad must have been more or less frustrated by the progressive secession of the provinces *de facto*, even though not *de jure*.

The Caliphate, like the Empire, had a money economy, but the Baghdad Government's financial control over the provinces was probably less effective than the Constantinopolitan Government's. Unfortunately, our information about the East Roman Empire's financial organization is scanty.[2] But we do know that, by Philótheos's time, the supervision over all the Central Government's financial departments had been united, for the first time since the establishment of the Principate by Augustus, in the hands of the sakellários.[3] We also know that, in each of the army-corps districts, the district protonotários, who was the chief local finance officer, was accountable to the Central Government as well as to the local governor, and was in direct correspondence with the Emperor himself.[4] In an 'Eastern' district the local governor's salary was paid by the Central Government out of the taxes that the Central Government had collected. It was only in the 'Western' districts that the governors paid themselves their own salaries out of the local revenues;[5] and, compared with the 'Eastern' districts, the 'Western' were unimportant. The 'Eastern' districts formed a block of territory stretching from the Távros Range to the Rhodópê; the 'Western' districts were little more than a scatter of isolated beachheads.[6] In the 'Eastern' districts there was also central control over the administration of military finance. The khartoulários of a district was responsible to the

---

[1] See A. von Kremer, *Culturgeschichte des Orients unter den Chalifen* (Vienna, 1875–7, Braumüller, 2 vols.), vol. i, pp. 192–8, and G. Le Strange, *The Lands of the Eastern Caliphate* (Cambridge, 1905, University Press), *passim.*

[2] Bury, op. cit., p. 78.

[3] Op. cit., p. 82, citing Philótheos, p. 139 Bury, p. 717 Bonn. In each financial department, the sakellários had a notários who supervised the department's work and gave the sakellários written reports on it.

[4] Leo VI, *Taktiká*, Dhiat. 4, § 33, col. 705, and *Theoph. Cont.*, Book VI, chap. 17, p. 448. See also Rambaud, op. cit., p. 200, and the present work, Part II, chap. 4, p. 248.

[5] *De Caer.*, Book II, chap. 50, pp. 696–7.

[6] The three naval thémata and théma Khersón were 'Western' in status, though they were Eastern geographically. See Part II, chap. 4, p. 252, with n. 1.

Central Government's loghothétês ton Stratiotikón, as well as to the local governor.[1]

In Constantine Porphyrogenitus's day the 'Eastern' districts of the East Roman Empire were probably administered more effectively than any other area anywhere to the west of China. It might, however, be an open question whether, either for China or for the East Roman Empire, effective administration was a blessing or a curse. Effective administration can be a blessing if it does not impose on a country's economic life a burden that exceeds the economic and social benefits that it can bring with it. Effective administration is expensive, and, when imposed on a predominantly agrarian economy, it may cost more than it is worth, and may then eventually break down under its own weight. This fatality is illustrated signally by the collapse of the Roman Empire in its western provinces in the fifth century and in Asia Minor in the eleventh century, and by the similar collapse, in China, of one dynasty after another.

In any case, the administration of the East Roman Empire in the tenth century was, whether for good or for evil, more effective than that of any other state, anywhere to the west of China, in that age; and, in the light of this finding, we have to revise the first impression, given by Constantine Porphyrogenitus's *De Caerimoniis*, that the Imperial civil service spent most of its time and energy on useless and frivolous ceremonial. When we probe beneath the veneer of protocol, we find practical serious public business being transacted. The deceptiveness of the appearance that masks the reality comes out still more piquantly in Constantine's two drafts for an apparently uncompleted work on an East Roman Emperor's equipment and procedure when on campaign ($T\grave{\alpha}$ $B\alpha\sigma\iota\lambda\iota\kappa\grave{\alpha}$ $T\alpha\xi\epsilon\acute{\iota}\delta\iota\alpha$).[2]

Constantine's general (and future successor) Nikêphóros Phokás must have been grateful to his sovereign for staying at home; for the Emperor's presence in the field will have been worth at least one additional army-corps to the enemy if the protocol, prescribed in this treatise, was faithfully observed in practice.[3] It is hard to imagine Nikêphóros II himself, or his no less soldierly successors John Dzimiskês and Basil II, Constantine Porphyrogenitus's grandson, submitting to be hampered in this way when they were engaged on the serious business of making war. Yet, if these soldier-emperors did succeed in shaking this Constantinian protocol off, that victory over the Imperial eunuch-household ($\tau\grave{o}$ $\kappa o\upsilon\beta o\acute{\upsilon}\kappa\lambda\epsilon\iota o\nu$)

---

[1] Leo *Taktiká*, Dhiat. 4, § 33, col. 705. See also Rambaud, op. cit., p. 204; Bury, op. cit., p. 44.

[2] Printed in the Bonn edition of *De Caer.*, on pp. 444–508, as an Appendix to Book I. The title might be translated *The Imperial Palace en Voyage*.

[3] The burden imposed on the thémata by the Emperor's passage through them if he went on campaign was one of the points in favour of the Emperor's staying behind in the Palace that were made by members of the Imperial Court in the eleventh century (see the *Scriptor Incertus*, edited by Wassiliewsky and Jernstedt, pp. 103–4).

will have been a more signal triumph than any victory over Arabs, Bulgars, or even ferocious Russians. The Imperial protocol was the eunuch-household's *raison d'être*. If the protocol were to be allowed to lapse, the household's power and pay and perquisites would be in jeopardy. The household will therefore have fought obstinately to maintain the Imperial protocol always and everywhere; and, if an Emperor were so ill-advised as to take the field in person, the household would cling to him like limpets and would bring all the Palace's paraphernalia with them on mule-back. The equipment with which the White Knight is credited in *Alice in Wonderland* is light and simple in comparison with Constantine Porphyrogenitus's specifications for equipping a campaigning East Roman Emperor.

The list of provisions[1] includes Imperial-quality wine, máyistros-and-patríkios-quality wine, olive oil, lentils, rice, pistachio nuts, almonds, beans, lard, fat, cheese, pickled fish, goats, sheep and cows in milk, provincial wine, *verdzítikon, névron, aríthmia*, 'Cyprians'. There must be containers for housing good local wine, oil, and onions where these turn up. There must be arrangements for dealing with presents brought to the Emperor in the form of victuals. For use on excursions into enemy territory, the Emperor's manciple must not forget to bring four [portable] ovens, nets for holding the fowls, and wooden troughs for the fowls to drink out of. On these excursions the Emperor must have with him a minimum of eighty mule-loads, 'to make sure that, whatever happens, nothing shall be lacking of what is required for the Imperial service'. N.B., these requirements on enemy territory are only a bare minimum. When the Emperor crosses the frontier, he leaves the bulk of his baggage behind in Rhomanía in the care of the local Imperial authorities.[2]

The household must also bring two tents and a pair of Imperial marquees; and, so long as the Emperor is still inside the frontiers of Rhomanía, half his equipment is to be sent ahead of him on each day's march so that he shall find everything conveniently ready for him when he arrives at the next halting-place for the night. There must be folding camp-stools, each long enough to seat three persons, and folding tables to match, with plenty of plate and table-linen. There must be phoundáta prayer-rugs (ἐπεύχια φουντάτα) to recline on; item, thick felt double-dyed rugs and *ptená* for the same purpose; item, other carpets of blue-dyed linen, with the nap combed up, each weighing thirty pounds, for the Emperor's invited guests; item, goat's-hair capes for the same purpose, in quantities sufficient for the number of guests expected. N.B., on excursions into enemy territory the folding camp-stools, the surplus marquees, and one tent will be left behind as a concession to the exigencies of warfare. Not so, apparently, the Emperor's portable Magyar

---

[1] Τὰ Βασιλικὰ Ταξείδια, pp. 463–4.   [2] Op. cit., pp. 453, 486, 489.

(Τουρκικόν) bath or Pecheneg (Σκυθικόν) *dzerghá*, with its *adh̆emion*-leather cistern, twelve bronze cauldrons, of three measures' capacity each, twelve *pyromákhia* (heating machines) on the scale of the bath, bricks for the oven, folding beds, and a [portable] Imperial chapel with its complement of holy vessels.[1] Also, without fail, the Emperor's manciple must bring along with him fishermen, exempted from taxes and corvées (ἐξκουσσάτους),[2] from the Témvrês river district in théma Opsíkion, nets and all, to catch fresh fish for the Emperor in the depopulated country beyond the frontier.[3] He must also bring one hundred measures of old Níkaia wine (bottled) and thirty measures of Níkaia olive oil. The rest of the Emperor's drink and victuals while in enemy territory must also come from Rhomanía, but local produce will do.[4]

The Imperial wardrobe (complete), and other equipment, is to be packed in portmanteaux made of purple-dyed leather with polished iron bands and handles made of strips of parchment (likewise polished), to make them handy for being laded on pack-animals. Item, eight silver refrigerators, with covers, for holding vine-tendril-water (οἰνάνθην) and rose-water and plain water (νερόν), two silver *vedhoúria* for water, and a number of leather jacks (ἀσκοδάβλαι), large and small. Item, four more large polished bronze refrigerators, in the cooking-pot style, for water, two polished bronze *vedhoúria* (and do not forget the holy vessels).

Books: the liturgy of the Church; treatises on strategy; treatises on mechanics, containing chapters on siege-engines; treatises on armaments-manufacture, and others appropriate to the business in hand, which is wars and assaults on camps; historical works—in particular, Polyaenus and Syrianus; [Artemidorus's] work on the interpretation of dreams; a treatise on omens; a treatise on meteorology; in addition, a thunder-chart and an earthquake-chart and other books of the kind that seamen carry with them. For information: a work of this kind—a labour of love—has been compiled from numerous sources by me Constantine, Emperor of the Romans in Christ the eternal emperor.

Item, *phoundáta* prayer-rugs to recline on, for the Emperor's guests (as noted already). Item, a well-stocked medicine-chest, including antidotes to poisons. Item, silver salvers and sprinklers for the Emperor, and others with bronze outsides and white-metal insides, the whole polished, for dignitaries and for distinguished deserters from the enemy. Item, two thick felt double-dyed rugs and *ptená* for the Emperor to recline on. Item, two processional saddles, and gold-embroidered *holókana koukoumílion* saddles with open-work housings and with other housings on top of these to conceal chafings from wear and tear. Item, two more of the same, with silver edges, for distinguished deserters. Imperial *kafkía*, of the sort called *khalínzia*, for the Emperor's invited guests. Item, two Imperial swords, one

---

[1] Op. cit., pp. 465–6.
[2] See Savramis, op. cit., p. 47.
[3] Τὰ Βασιλικὰ Ταξείδια, pp. 488–9.
[4] p. 491.

processional, and the other just a travelling-sword. Item, an array of incenses, ointments, and perfumes. Finally, *sendás*, linen piece-goods with a fluffy nap, *sávana*, *sindónia*, and some cheap *vranaíai* and *mandília*.[1]

This preposterous inventory of an East Roman Emperor's indispensable baggage on campaign reads as if it must have been calculated to break the back of even the best equipped and best organized baggage-train; but apparently the East Roman military baggage-train could bear the load. It was, indeed, admirably well found, as this same treatise of Constantine's informs us.[2] There were enough mules, and enough army-service-corps muleteers (ὀπτιμάτοι), to cope with the Emperor's impedimenta (πεντζιμέντα)[3] and with the army's too. Nor were the Emperor's impedimenta all just for his own personal use. He also carried with him a supply of unmade-up stuffs (ἀραφίων) and ready-made garments (τῶν ἐρραμμένων) for giving away to foreigners and to East Roman officers and soldiers who had distinguished themselves.[4] At each night's halting-place, robes are to be distributed to the officers—on a more munificent scale to those of the great Roman corps than to those of the Armenian corps.[5] The soldiers are also to be tipped at regular intervals in cash, and the officers too.[6] The scale of the tips is to be raised when the army crosses the frontier into enemy territory.[7] Here the tips are to be given partly in the form of livestock for rations.[8] For keeping the army in good heart on active service, tipping evidently played as important a part as it played in the Palace for mollifying the Imperial household and the civil service; and, as Liutprand discovered, this was the Emperor's personal chore, and no light one.[9] In performing this chore, the Emperor was making some slight return for the burden that his presence was imposing on the Imperial Army. Tipping is work, though it is not a particularly martial occupation.

However, as we work our way through Constantine's pair of drafts for an Emperor's guidance when on campaign, we get revealing glimpses of serious military business. These passages in the two drafts do, in fact, provide valuable evidence for the organization and operations of the East Roman Army in the tenth century, and accordingly they are taken into account in the chapter dealing with the East Roman Army in the present book.[10] In these passages we find ourselves no longer in Wonderland but in the real world of alert, efficient, and stern East Roman military practice. These passages from Constantine Porphyrogenitus's pen

---

[1] Op. cit., pp. 466–9. See also pp. 471–2 and 474 for the equipment of the Emperor's travelling bed-chamber: the lighting arrangements; a little silver travelling clock, a bronze one for the servants, gold plate for impressing foreign guests, etc., etc.

[2] See pp. 459–63, 476–81.   [3] p. 474.   [4] pp. 469–71 and 473.
[5] pp. 485–6.   [6] pp. 471–2 and 487–8.
[7] p. 472.   [8] pp. 490–1.   [9] See p. 18.
[10] Part II, chap. 6.

might have come equally from one of the professional treatises on the East Roman art of war; the *Stratêghikón* ascribed to the Emperor Maurice; the *Taktiká* compiled by the Emperor Leo VI; the treatise by the 'Anonymus Vári'; the monograph Περὶ Παραδρομῆς Πολέμου by an anonymous officer who had seen service under the second Nikêphóros Phokás, and the Στρατηγικὴ Ἔκθεσις καὶ Σύνταξις which is ascribed to Nikêphóros Phokás himself, the brilliant soldier who had been one of Constantine Porphyrogenitus's generals before he elbowed his way on to the Imperial throne, as the Emperor Nikêphóros II, side by side with Constantine's two young grandsons.

Thus the student of East Roman public affairs has the same experience in the sphere of war as in the sphere of administration. Under a veneer of childish ceremonial he finds grown-up-minded people doing serious work.

This is the true picture, but it has to be disengaged from the records of the minutiae of ceremonial by which it is smothered. For instance, in Τὰ Βασιλικὰ Ταξείδια, the pertinent account of the security regulations in camp at night is immediately followed[1] by a full-length reproduction of the acclamations that the Emperor and the troops have to chant to each other when they meet, and three older documents that are appended to the second of the two drafts waft us back into Wonderland again. These are contemporary descriptions of three Emperors' triumphal re-entries into Constantinople: Justinian I's on 2 August of the Year of the World 6033;[2] Basil I's after two rather dubious military successes at Tephrikê and at Yermaníkeia;[3] and Theóphilos's after his victory over the Cilician Muslims. The ceremonial on these occasions included an amusing piece of play-acting. The senators met the returning Emperor and presented him with three crowns, two of them of laurel and the third of gold. The Emperor responded by paying for the gold crown, cash down, to save the welcoming-party from being out of pocket.[4] Constantine takes care to mention[5] that, when his grandfather Basil was given his gold crown, he paid out something more than the crown's value in return.

While the contents of this treatise of Constantine Porphyrogenitus's are largely either comic or pedestrian, the treatise has incorporated one moving document. When an Emperor was leaving the Palace at Constantinople for the south-eastern front, the first stage in his progress was the passage of the Bosphorus in an Imperial galley.

When the Emperor is at a sufficient distance from the Palace harbour to be able to get a view of the City, he rises from his seat, stands, facing the east, with his hands raised to Heaven, makes the sign of the Cross over the City three times, and then offers a prayer to God in the following form of words:

[1] On pp. 482–4. [2] pp. 497–8. [3] pp. 498–503.
[4] p. 497. [5] On p. 501.

'Lord Jesus Christ my God, into Thy hands I commend this City of Thine. Preserve her, I pray Thee, from the onset of all adversities and tribulations, from civil war and from foreign invasion. Keep her inviolate from capture and from sack, because it is in Thee that we have placed our hopes, and Thou art lord of mercy and father of pity and god of all consolation, and Thine it is to have mercy and to save and to rescue from trials and dangers now and always and for ever and ever. Amen'.[1]

Here, for a moment, both ceremonies and technicalities are left behind, and we are caught up into the heights. Byzantine religion had its formal side, like so much else in Byzantine life; but it was nevertheless sincere and it could rise to sublimity, as it does rise in this prayer in which the human *Aftokrátor* forgets, for a moment, his own pseudo-divinity in the awesome presence of a Pandokrátor whom he recognizes to be truly divine.

[1] p. 475.

3. The City of Constantinople

IN medieval and modern Greek parlance, Constantinople is 'the City' (ἡ Πόλις) par excellence. A native of Constantinople styles himself Πολίτης; and the fourteen-and-a-half syllables-long accentual metre, which has supplanted the quantitative metres of the Greek poetry of the Hellenic Age, is called 'metropolitan verse' (στιχοί πολιτικοί). Nevertheless, Constantinople was not, and never had been, a πόλις in the Hellenic sense of the word.

The Hellenic poleis—Athens, Sparta, and the rest, including the pre-Constantinian Byzantium—had been self-governing communities. This had, indeed, been their distinctive feature; and they had continued to enjoy municipal self-government after they had lost their sovereign independence through being incorporated in the Roman Empire. Constantinople, too, had some municipal institutions bearing names that, at Athens and in other Hellenic city-states, had once stood for political realities. Constantinople had its 'demes', and these had officers called 'demarchs' and others called 'democrats'. In the sixth century the Constantinopolitan 'demes' had been political forces with which the Imperial Government had had to reckon; but, like the Imperial office itself, the demes were a para-constitutional institution, and their political action, when they had taken it, had been revolutionary. The Constantinopolitan 'demes' were not what their name implied. They were not organic parts of a self-governing municipality. Their origin and *raison d'être* were not political; they were recreational and parasitical. The 'demes' were factions backing their respective charioteers and teams of chariot-horses in races that were organized and were paid for by the Imperial Government. The genuine municipal administration of Constantinople was conducted, not by elected representatives of the inhabitants, but by officials appointed by the Emperor. Constantinople was not a younger sister of Athens or Sparta or even Byzantium, whose site was included within Constantinople's walls. Constantinople was a city of the same type and same origin as Alexandria and Antioch. Constantinople, too, had been founded by the fiat of an autocrat to serve as the capital of a bureaucratically-governed empire.

In the ninth-century the City of Constantinople was administered by two high officials and their staffs: the Prefect (Ἔπαρχος) of the City and the Quaestor (Κυαίστωρ, alternatively spelled Κοιαίστωρ).[1] There was

[1] The positions of these two officials in the scale of rank, and the titles of the members of their staffs, as in the year 899, are given in the klêtorolóyion of Philótheos (*De Caer.*, pp. 713,

some overlapping between the Prefect's and the Quaestor's functions. The Quaestor's work was primarily judicial, but he also had some duties relating to the municipal administration of Constantinople. Conversely, the Prefect's work was primarily administrative, but he too had some judicial functions. The chief administrative overlap was that both officials were concerned with the surveillance of provincial East Roman subjects and of foreigners in Constantinople (the Prefect delegated his share of this duty to his lêghatários).[1] Again, though both officials were concerned with the municipal administration of the capital, even the Prefect may not have been confined to this field. In his judicial capacity he served as a judge of appeal, and it is not certain that this appellate jurisdiction was limited to metropolitan suits.[2] As for the Quaestor, 'he was the chief legal authority in the state and the legal adviser of the Government',[3] and his municipal administrative duties in the capital were an excrescence on his main activity.

These two posts, whose holders, between them, conducted the municipal administration of Constantinople, had had different histories. The Prefect's title ἔπαρχος τῆς πόλεως was the official equivalent, in Greek, of the Latin title *praefectus urbi*, and both the office and the title had been instituted by the Emperor Augustus for the government of the City of Rome—a new post that had been one of Augustus's most radical administrative innovations. On the other hand, the ninth-century Quaestor seems to have derived his functions from a conflation of two posts: the Diocletianic–Constantinian Quaestorship of the Palace and the post of Quaesitor (ἐρευνητής) which had been created by Justinian I.[4]

The *praefectus urbi* at Rome and his younger counterpart at 'the New Rome', Constantinople, were bound to be important officials in virtue of their work. If the municipal administration of the Empire's two capital cities were to fail to function efficiently and smoothly, the stability and security of the Imperial Government itself might be imperilled. Under the Diocletianic–Constantinian regime, the two metropolitan prefects were the peers of the four praetorian prefects, who, between them, administered the whole of the Empire beyond the radius of the jurisdiction of the prefects of the two capitals. By the year 899, the date of the compilation of Philótheos's klêtorolóyion, the Prefect of Constantinople had dropped to the fifteenth place in the East Roman official hierarchy, and thereafter his relative standing continued to decline. Yet the *Vasiliká* contain a provision

---

717, 717–18 Bonn text; Bury's text in *The Imperial Administrative System*, pp. 139 and 140). For the Prefect's department, see Bury, ibid., pp. 69–73; Nicole, *Livre du Préfet*, pp. 87–90; Stöckle, *Spätrömische und byzantinische Zünfte*, pp. 90–4; for the Quaestor's department, see Bury, ibid., pp. 73–7.

[1] *Livre du Préfet*, chap. 20, § 1, p. 56.
[2] Bury, op. cit., p. 69.
[3] Bury, op. cit., p. 73.
[4] Bury, op. cit., p. 74.

that all corporate bodies in Constantinople, the citizens, and the whole population are to be subject to the authority of the Prefect of the City.[1] In Leo VI's reign (886–912) his post was still highly important and responsible, and the discretion allowed to him in the discharge of his administrative duties was wide. This is evident from the notices of his duties and prerogatives in *The Prefect's Book*—a handbook dealing with the Prefect's relations with the Constantinopolitan guilds. Since this handbook happens to be the principal relevant document that has survived, our picture of the Prefect's functions has to be pieced together largely from this source; but his supervision of the metropolitan guilds was only one of his functions, and it was not the most important of them. The Prefect's essential task was to ensure that there should be no disturbance of the peace in the Imperial capital. This was police-work, but it could not be carried out successfully by mere vigilance and repression. Popular discontent had to be forestalled by ensuring that the population of Constantinople should be supplied with sufficient food, and this at prices which it could afford to pay.[2] The solution of this economic problem was, for the Prefect, the key to the successful performance of his role as chief of police.

The Prefect discharged his police-duties, as far as was practicable, by devolving them on the heads and the members of the metropolitan guilds. These were not only required to take responsibility for obeying the regulations imposed on them; they were also called upon, in certain cases of ascertained or suspected misconduct among persons outside their own ranks, to do the Prefect's work for him by investigating and reporting.[3] The guildsmen were coerced into performing these police-duties for the Prefect by the imposition of savage penalties for non-compliance.[4] However, the Prefect and his staff had to do the major part of their police-work themselves.

In the first place, they had to exercise surveillance over the activities of guildsmen and any other persons engaged in business in Constantinople, in order to see to it that the regulations were being obeyed. To facilitate this, the Prefect designated the places where the various kinds of business might be done, and he centralized the transaction of business in a single place in all cases in which the nature of the business made this practicable. For instance, a goldsmith may not do his work at home; he may do it only in the workshops on the Mésê (the main street of Constantinople).[5] A silversmith must not go off to make a valuation without the Prefect's knowledge. Penalty for non-compliance: flogging and cropping, plus

---

[1] πάντα τὰ ἐν Κωνσταντινουπόλει σωματεῖα καὶ οἱ πολῖται καὶ ἀπὸ τοῦ δήμου παντὸς τῷ ἐπάρχῳ τῆς πόλεως ὑποκείσθωσαν (*Vasiliká*, VI, 4, 13).

[2] See II, 1 (ii) pp. 53 and 55–6.   [3] See ibid., pp. 62–3.   [4] See ibid.

[5] *Livre du Préfet*, chap. 2, §11, p. 24.

expulsion from the guild.[1] A dealer in raw silk (metaxoprátês) may sell his goods in the forum only, not at home, to ensure that this commodity shall not be conveyed clandestinely to people who are prohibited from buying it.[2] A silk-weaver (sêrikários, sêrikoprátes) who is caught selling to foreigners (ἐθνικοῖς) without the Prefect's knowledge is to have the goods confiscated.[3] Candle-manufacturers must do their business in their own workshops, and there must be no secret dealings in wax, worked or unworked.[4] The butchers may not buy livestock anywhere except in the Stratḗghion, and there only with the Prefect's knowledge. The slaughtering and chopping-up are to be done in the Prefect's presence.[5] Lambs are to be sold only in the Távros market. The dates, as well as the places, at which lambs and other livestock are to be bought are designated by the Prefect.[6] The appraisers and valuers of livestock (βόθροι) may buy what has been brought into market and has been left unsold, but they and other dealers may make such purchases only in the Forum Amestrianoú, 'and not in the City's corners and alleys', to make sure that animals that have been stolen or lost shall not be sold clandestinely without this being detected.[7] Fish may be sold only in the 'great halls' (μέγισται καμάραι), each under its own foreman (προστατεύων), who is to supervise the purchases from the fishermen and the sales, and is to receive a commission for doing this.[8] The foremen are to report the amount of the night's catch to the Prefect daily at dawn (penalty for non-compliance: flogging and cropping plus expulsion from the guild),[9] and the foremen of the tavern-keepers are to report to him when wine comes into the city.[10]

Another means by which the Prefect exercised surveillance was by requiring that certain objects—for instance, weights and measures and luxury goods intended for export[11]—shall be presented for sealing or stamping by his voullotaí (sealers), to certify that the weights and measures are correct and that the luxury goods are not of kinds that are on the embargo list. The penalty for being caught using unsealed weights and measures is flogging and cropping.[12] It is the same for refusing to give access to the Prefect's sealer or to his inspector of textile-fabrics[13] (μιτωτής).[14] Garments found rolled up in packing-stores (ἐν κυλισταρείοις) without the Prefect's seal on them are to be confiscated, and there is to be the same penalty for the packers who have received them.[15] (Anyone who has introduced into an Imperial packing-store garments that have been manufactured outside the Imperial factories is to be flogged and cropped.)[16]

---

[1] *Livre du Préfet*, chap. 2, §11, p. 24. [2] 6, 13, p. 33. [3] 8, 5, p. 37.
[4] 11, 1, p. 43. [5] 15, 1 and 2, p. 50. [6] 15, 5, p. 51.
[7] 21, 3, p. 58. [8] 17, 1, p. 52. [9] 17, 4, p. 53.
[10] 19, 1, p. 55. [11] 4, 4, p. 27. Cf. 8, 5, p. 37.
[12] 6, 4, p. 32. [13] 8, 3, p. 37.
[14] For this interpretation of this word, see Nicole, *Le Livre du Préfet*, p. 89.
[15] 8. 9, pp. 37-8. [16] 8, 11, p. 38.

Flogging and cropping is the penalty for using unsealed weighing-machines and for fraudulent weighing.[1]

The most direct way in which the Prefect intervened in commercial business in Constantinople was by taking measures to secure for the population of the capital the amplest possible food-supply at the cheapest possible prices.[2] He promoted the import of food-supplies and restricted the export of them from the City. He also penalized hoarding—in general,[3] but particularly the hoarding of food-supplies. The Prefect's lêghatários is to denounce to the Prefect the hoarders of imports, and the penalty for the offence is flogging and cropping, plus the confiscation of the hoard.[4] The grocers (saldhamárioi) are to denounce to the Prefect non-members of the guild who hoard.[5] The penalty for buying pigs and storing the meat is flogging and cropping plus rustication.[6] When droves of pigs are brought into Constantinople from outside, the foremen (πρωτοστάται) of the pig-dealers are to give the Prefect an assurance that they will not sell to middlemen, but will sell only to the general public (κοινῶς) in the Távros Market. The penalty for non-observance is flogging and cropping, and there is the same penalty for hiding pigs in a magnate's mansion and selling them clandestinely,[7] and for any hoarding of meat.[8] On the other hand, peasants who brought livestock to the Constantinopolitan market were protected against being squeezed out by the wholesale dealers.[9] They were also protected against the risk of being left with unsold stock on their hands.[10] As for exports of food-stuffs from Constantinople, the fishmongers are forbidden to pickle fish (a form of hoarding) and are also forbidden to sell fish to non-Constantinopolitan buyers for conveyance outside the City, unless there is a surplus that will go bad if it is not thus disposed of.[11]

One of the Prefect's objectives in exercising a strict surveillance over the trade in food-stuffs was to fix the prices. For instance, the sales of livestock in the Stratĕghion had to be at prices fixed by him.[12] By supervising personally the slaughtering and the chopping-up, he was able to ensure that the butchers' profit should be limited to keeping heads, hooves, and offal as their perquisites. The rest of the meat had to be sold by them at the purchase price.[13] The object of the reports, which the Prefect required, of the nightly catch of fish and of the occasional imports of wine was to enable him to fix the price of these commodities.[14] The

---

[1] 16, 6, p. 52. Cf. 11, 9, p. 49; 12, 9, p. 47; 13, 2, p. 48.   [2] Stöckle, op. cit., p. 15.
[3] For instance, linen-dealers (othonioprátai) must not hoard coin (9, 5, p. 40); druggists (myrepsoí) must not hoard their raw materials (10, 2, p. 42); candle-manufacturers must not hoard oil (11, 3, p. 44).
[4] 20, 3, p. 57.   [5] 13, 4, p. 48.   [6] 15, 6, p. 51.
[7] 16, 4, p. 52. (See the present work, II, 1 (ii), p. 55.)   [8] 16, 5, p. 52.
[9] 15, 4, pp. 50–1. (See the present work, II, 1 (ii), p. 44.)   [10] 21, 1, p. 51.
[11] 17, 2, p. 53.   [12] 15, 1, p. 50.   [13] 15, 2, p. 50.
[14] 17, 4, p. 53, and 19, 1, p. 55.

bakers' profits were limited to one kerátion for themselves plus two miliarêsia for the maintenance of their employees and their animals.[1] As an offset, the bakers and their animals were exempted from all corvées.[2] Changes in the price of wheat must be reported to the Prefect, to enable the sýmbonos[3] to make corresponding adjustments in the measures used in the sale of bread.[4] Stöckle notes[5] that none of the guilds concerned with the victualling trades demanded an entrance-fee from candidates for membership.

It looks as if, among the Prefect's manifold concerns, food-supply and food-prices had first priority at the turn of the ninth and tenth centuries,[6] and this is indeed what was to be expected, considering Constantinople's history. After the Roman Empire's economic collapse in the third century, it had been a rash act, on Constantine the Great's part, to saddle the Empire, which Diocletian had just nursed into convalescence, with a duplicate capital city. This was all the more rash because, if the New Rome was to be a counterpart of the Old Rome, it, too, had to be endowed with 'bread and shows' for its populace as a charge upon the whole Empire's productive capacity—a capacity that was already being over-taxed by a steep increase in the size and cost of the Army. The provisioning of the new duplicate capital also doubled the strain on the Mediterranean merchant-marine, which now had to carry cereals from the southern shores of the Mediterranean to feed, gratis, the inhabitants of a pair of parasitic capitals.

It is true that Constantine had shown genius in his choice of the site for his new capital for the Roman Empire—though Constantine was not the first statesman to notice the felicity of Byzantium's location. This had been recognized already, before the close of the sixth century B.C., by a sharp-sighted Persian statesman, according to a fifth-century-B.C. Greek historian.[7] Constantinople was, indeed, far better placed than Rome for serving as the capital of a circum-Mediterranean empire in the Roman Age of the Mediterranean basin's history.

Rome had been well placed for winning the hegemony over Peninsular Italy by military operations on land. But Rome's site had become

---

[1] 18, 1, pp. 53–4. [2] 18, 2, p. 54.

[3] Presumably this sýmbonos was attached to the bakers' guild, since the sýmbonos who was the Prefect's second-in-command according to Philótheos and Constantine Porphyrogenitus is called the Prefect's lêghatários in the *Livre du Préfet* (see the present work, II, 1 (ii), p. 60, with footnote 4).

[4] 18, 4, p. 54. Instead of the price being raised, the weight or quantity sold at the same price was diminished.

[5] Stöckle, op. cit., p. 61.

[6] See Jenkins in *C. Med. H.*, vol. iv, 2nd ed., Part II, p. 86.

[7] See Herodotus, Book IV, chap. 144, for the remark, attributed to Megabazos, that the founders of Khalkêdhón had been blind in overlooking the site on which Byzantium had been founded seventeen years later. See further Polybius, Book IV, chap. 38.

inadequate for serving Rome's needs when Rome had taken to the sea in the First Romano–Carthaginian War, when she had gone on to win the naval command of the Mediterranean, and when she had finally brought under her rule, direct or indirect, the whole perimeter of the Mediterranean, with as much of its hinterland as could be conquered and held by Roman infantry based on the shores of the Mediterranean itself and of its backwaters. Rome had dominated Peninsular Italy thanks to her command of the lowest-down bridge over the Tiber, which was the Peninsula's principal river, but this lowest-down bridge was too far up the river to be accessible for sea-going vessels, whether merchant-ships or warships, in the post-Alexandrine Age, when the size of ships had increased, while the lowest reach of the Tiber had been silting up. Cargoes destined for Rome had now to be trans-shipped into lighters that could be towed up the river, and this had to be done in the open sea till eventually—at a cost that could be met only by drawing on the public revenue of the whole Mediterranean World—an artificial port for sea-going vessels, where trans-shipment could be carried out in all weathers, had been excavated and had been linked up with the river.

This local inconvenience of Rome's site for access by water was a serious handicap for Rome so long as communication was quicker and cheaper by water than by land, as it continued to be till the invention of railways; but Rome's geographical position in the Mediterranean basin was a still more serious drawback for a city that had become the political capital of the Mediterranean World. Rome's access to the sea, such as it was, opened on to the western basin of the Mediterranean, and, in the Roman Age of Mediterranean history, the western half of the Mediterranean World, including Peninsular Italy itself, was under-developed and under-populated by comparison with the contemporary development of the Levant. In that age the Levant was the Mediterranean World's economic and demographic centre of gravity. Egypt, Syria, and western Asia Minor were the Mediterranean World's industrial and commercial power-houses. The economic capital of the Roman Empire was not Rome-on-Tiber; it was Alexandria-on-Nile.

Constantinople was nearer than Rome to these three key Levantine regions and was also more accessible than Rome was from each of them. Julius Caesar and Augustus were believed by their contemporaries to have played with the idea of transferring the capital of their empire from Rome to Alexandria Troas or to Troy itself. These two sites commanded the approaches from the Aegean to the Dardanelles, as well as the ferries, across the Dardanelles, between Asia and Europe. Since Augustus's day, the main crossing between the two continents had shifted northward, by Constantine the Great's time, from the Dardanelles to the Bosphorus, and accordingly, if the Mediterranean World was to be given a new capital on one of the two straits linking the Aegean with the Black Sea, Byzantium was now the inevitable site. Byzantium was singled out not only by its geographical location but by the local topography. Troy, like Rome, was not on the coast; Alexandria Troas had no natural harbour; Byzantium had a uniquely serviceable natural harbour in the Golden Horn, a deep-water inlet into which a ship coming from the Black Sea was wafted by the current of the Bosphorus[1] unless its steersman deliberately set its course for the Sea of Marmara. The Golden Horn was the topographical treasure which the founders of Khalkêdhón had been thought by Megabazos to have overlooked.

Byzantium could be reached by sea-going ships from anywhere in the Mediterranean basin and its backwaters, and, conversely, a government seated in Byzantium could send soldiers or administrators by sea to any point on the Mediterranean coasts of the Roman Empire. Byzantium also commanded the ferries across the Bosphorus on the shortest route between the lower course of the River Danube and the middle course of the River Euphrates; and, in Constantine's day, these were the two sections of the Roman Empire's frontier that were under the heaviest pressure from external enemies.

Thus by Constantine the Great's day the site of Byzantium had become still more important strategically than it had been in Megabazos's day, rather more than eight centuries earlier. On the other hand, the economic importance of the waterway on which Byzantium stood had diminished by the time when Constantine decided to plant his New Rome there.

In the pre-Alexandrine Age of Hellenic history, the water-route between the Aegean and the Black Sea had been one of the two main thoroughfares of the Hellenic World. It had, indeed, surpassed in economic importance the route from the head of the Gulf of Corinth across the Straits of Ótranto to south-eastern Italy and Sicily. The narrow seas between the Black Sea and the Aegean had been the route by which, from the seventh century B.C. onwards, the industrial and commercial Greek city-states in the Aegean basin had imported cereals from the Black Earth zone of the Ukraine in exchange for exports of Greek manufactures. The rapid increase, in and after the seventh century B.C., of the population and wealth of Corinth and the other circum-Isthmian city-states of Continental European Greece, and the corresponding contemporary development of Miletos and other city-states on the west coast of Asia Minor and on the adjoining islands, would have been impossible if their food-supply had continued to be limited to the meagre produce of their own territories. In that case they could not have made their economic revolution from the agrarian economy of the ordinary Greek city-state

---

[1] See Polybius, Book IV, chaps. 43 and 44, and Th. Fischer, *Mittelmeerbilder* (Leipzig and Berlin, 1913, Teubner), Part I, chap. 1, 'Konstantinopel', pp. 3–4.

to an industrial and commercial economy with distant markets and sources of supply. The development of these Greek city-states was made possible by their access to sea-borne imports of grain from the Black Earth zone of the Ukraine.

The Black Earth zone extends north-eastwards across Eurasia from the north-eastern face of the Carpathians round the southern end of the Urals to the foothills of the Altai Mountains. This Black Earth is one of the planet's chief potential granaries. In natural fertility this Eurasian soil is on a par with the irrigated alluvium of Egypt and 'Iraq and with the North American Black Earth of Iowa. However, the translation of this potential economic productivity into an effective economic fact depends on political factors. The Black Earth zone, the Steppe zone that intervenes between it and the north coast of the Black Sea, and the ports along this coast, especially those on or near the mouths of the rivers flowing into the Black Sea from the north, must be under a political regime that encourages both the production of an exportable surplus of cereals on the Black Earth and the water-borne conveyance of this surplus to foreign markets.

These political conditions existed during the century ending in the outbreak of the First World War in 1914. During that century the Black Sea port of Odessa, founded by the Russians in 1792,[1] became one of the principal grain-exporting ports of the World. The Russians were a sedentary agricultural people. The western bay of the Steppe, together with the north coast of the Black Sea which this extremity of the Steppe adjoins, had been annexed by the Russian Empire from the Ottoman Turkish Empire and from its dependency the Tatar Khanate of Krim, after the Russo-Turkish war of 1768–74. Before that, the western end of the Eurasian Steppe, like the rest of the Steppe, had been occupied by a series of nomadic pastoral peoples, the latest of whom had been the Tatars,[2] and the economic fortunes of the Black Earth zone to the north of the Steppe had depended on the nomads' policy. Most of the successive nomad occupants of the Black Sea Steppe, including the Crimean Tatars, had treated the Black Earth zone to the north of them as a

---

[1] This new port on a new site was christened Odessa after the Greek colonial city-state Odhêssós on the west shore of the Black Sea in present-day Bulgaria. The commercial equivalent of nineteenth-century Odessa in the Hellenic Age had been the Greek colonial city-state Olbia ('the Affluent', alias Borysthenes), at the mouth of the River Hypanis (the Bug that flows into the Black Sea), on the site on which the Russians founded the port of Nikolayev in 1789.

[2] The Tatars of the Crimea, Astrakhan, and Qazan derived their name from the Tatars who were neighbours and subjects of the Mongols, and these three Tatar khanates were successor-states of the Golden Horde, the westernmost of the appanages of the descendants of Chingis Khan. The western Tatars were, however, Turkish-speaking descendants of the Cumans (called Polovtsi by the Russians and Qipchaq by the Muslims), whom the Mongols had conquered.

raiding-ground, and this economically improvident policy had put the Black Earth zone out of action as a source of export of cereals. The nomad raids had impoverished the Black Earth zone and had discouraged agricultural production there; and, even if the Black Earth had had a surplus of cereals to export, the natural route for export, down the rivers to the Black Sea, was closed by the predatoriness of the nomads who bestrode it.

The Skyths were the sole nomad horde, among all the successive nomad masters of the Black Sea Steppe, that had had the power to impose its suzerainty over the south-western end of the Black Earth zone and had also had the economic wisdom to exploit this suzerainty by encouraging agriculture on the Black Earth and taking tribute from it in the form of cereals for export in exchange for foreign manufactures;[1] and the Skyths were not the earliest of all the nomad occupants of the Black Sea Steppe.[2] The Skyths, migrating westward from the interior of the Steppe, had crossed the River Don in the seventh century B.C. Simultaneously, the commercial Greek city-states in the Aegean basin—principally Miletos and Megara—had planted colonies round all the shores of the Black Sea except its eastern shore, and the Greek colonial city-states along the north shore of the Black Sea had gone into partnership with the Skyths in handling the export of grain from the Skyths' tributary territories on the Black Earth to the Aegean basin and the import of manufactures to Skythia from the commercial Greek city-states who bought the Skyths' grain-tribute from the Black Earth.

The importance of this trade is brought out in the story of a decision that is attributed to the Persian Emperor Xerxes by Herodotus.[3]

When Xerxes was at Ávydhos [in 480 B.C., preparing to cross the Dardanelles], he saw some grain-ships making their passage down the Dardanelles, bound for Aíyina and the Pelopónnêsos. When the Emperor's counsellors learnt that these were enemy vessels, their impulse was to capture them, and they kept looking for the Emperor to give the order. Xerxes asked them what the ships' destination was. The answer was: 'These ships are en route to Your Majesty's enemies, and they are bringing them grain.' Xerxes's rejoinder was: 'Well, aren't we bound for the same destination, and aren't we, too, carrying with us supplies of grain? So what is the objection to these shippers conveying grain, when we are going to be the consumers?'

This trade had been profitable both to the Skyths and to the nucleus

---

[1] M. Rostovtzeff, *Iranians and Greeks in South Russia* (Oxford, 1922, Clarendon Press), pp. 211–13.

[2] The Cimmerians had preceded the Skyths here, and had left their name—The Cimmerian Bosphorus—on the Straits of Kerch. The Cimmerians themselves may have had nomad predecessors whom they had evicted, as they were evicted by the Skyths.

[3] Herodotus, Book VII, chap. 147.

of the Hellenic World to the east of the Straits of Ótranto,[1] but it had lasted no longer than the Skyths' ascendancy on the Black Sea Steppe, and it had declined when, *circa* 225 B.C., the Skyths' eastern nomad neighbours, the Sarmatai, had pushed the Skyths off the Black Sea Steppe and had cooped up the remnant of them in the Crimea.[2] It is not a coincidence that Continental European Greece became impoverished at this time. (The Greek city-states along the west coast of Asia Minor continued to prosper, thanks to the restoration of their economic links with their hinterland by Alexander the Great.) Nevertheless, the trade between the Ukraine and the Aegean basin continued to be important enough to cause a fratricidal Greek war when, *circa* 220 B.C.,[3] Byzantium started to levy a toll on shipping passing through the Bosphorus in order to raise funds for paying her tribute to the neighbouring barbarians.[4] At this date the Greek city-states in the Aegean basin were still exporting their oil and wine to the region to the north of the Black Sea, and they were receiving in exchange cattle (a product of the Steppe) and slaves, honey, and wax (products of the northern forests); but grain was now being shipped sometimes from south to north, and no longer only in the opposite direction.[5]

After two centuries of depression, the export of cereals from the ports along the north coast of the Black Sea revived, on a smaller scale, for about two and a half centuries following the establishment, in 31 B.C., of the Augustan Peace. The grain conveyed from these ports to the Roman Empire during the Age of the Principate may not have come from as far afield as the broad acres of the Ukraine. The Sarmatai, who had now replaced the Skyths on the Black Sea Steppe, lacked their Skyth predecessors' economic sense. But there was a nearer source of cereals in the Kuban basin, and this lay in the dominions of the Roman Empire's protectorate the Kingdom of the (Cimmerian) Bosphorus, which bestrode the Straits of Kerch. The grain-exports from this kingdom sufficed for supplying both Greece and the units of the Roman Army in Pontic and Inland Cappodocia, which held the northern section of the Roman Empire's eastern frontier.[6] However, this revived export of grain from the north shore of the Black Sea suffered a mortal blow during the half century of anarchy in the Roman Empire between A.D. 235 and A.D. 284. Both the Kingdom of the Cimmerian Bosphorus and the Greek colonial cities to the north-east of the Danube delta were wrecked during this terrible half-century by the Goths.[7]

[1] The colonial Greek city-states to the west of the Straits of Ótranto produced enough cereals to meet their own needs.
[2] See Rostovzeff, op. cit., p. 147.
[3] See Polybius, Book IV, chaps. 47–52.
[4] Polybius, Book IV, chaps. 45–7.
[5] Polybius, Book IV, chap. 38.
[6] Rostovzeff, op. cit., pp. 153–4.
[7] Rostovzeff, op. cit., p. 155.

Thus the import of cereals into the Roman Empire from the north shore of the Black Sea through the Thracian Bosphorus past Byzantium had come to an end nearly a hundred years before Constantine the Great selected Byzantium as the site for his new Levantine capital of the Roman Empire. So long as this trade had survived, Byzantium had had the first refusal of the grain that had been the cargo carried by the ships on their southward voyage. 'First come, first served.' If cargoes of grain had still been entering the Bosphorus from the Black Sea in Constantine the Great's time, the creator of the New Rome would have found a food-supply for his new city ready to hand without needing to poach on the sources of supply previously drawn upon by the Old Rome. However, this deterioration of Byzantium's once unusually favourable economic circumstances did not deter Constantine the Great from enlarging this small colonial Greek city-state into a duplicate capital for the Mediterranean World.

Even after the temporary collapse from which it was recovering in Constantine the Great's day, the Roman Empire still had vast sources of food-production. Constantine the Great provided the bread-dole for Constantinople by diverting to the new capital the cereals exported from Egypt, leaving to the Old Rome the export from North-West Africa and Sicily. After Justinian I had reconquered the Roman Empire's Vandal successor-state, these sources, too, of cereals were at the Constantino-politan Roman Government's disposal, if required, for the provisioning of Constantinople.

After Justinian I's death in 565, his successors held, for a few years, about two-thirds of the area over which the Roman Empire had extended in 395, the date of the death of the Emperor Theodosius I. But the strain that had been put on the economy of the Empire's previously prosperous Levantine dominions by Justinian I's wars brought its nemesis in 602, when the Constantinopolitan Roman Empire collapsed. The Persian occupation of Egypt in 616 suddenly cut off Constantinople's source of food-supply, and the bread-dole was discontinued, provisionally in 618 and definitively in 626.[1]

In this crisis, the populace of Constantinople would have welcomed even a trickle of grain from the northern hinterland of the Black Sea, but the export of grain from that quarter was not resumed, on any appreciable scale,[2] for another twelve hundred years. In the tenth century, when Constantine Porphyrogenitus was compiling his *De Administrando*

[1] See II, 1 (ii), pp. 44–5, with p. 45, n. 2.

[2] According to Teall, in loc. cit., p. 119, there were exports of grain to Constantinople from Russia in the twelfth century, but these must have ceased when the Mongols conquered and absorbed all but a refugee remnant of the Cumans in the thirteenth century. The Golden Horde's staple export was not Russian grain to Rhomanía; it was Russian slaves to Egypt.

Imperio, Khersón (i.e. the Megarian colony Khersónêsos), which by that date had been for many centuries the only surviving Greek city-state on the north shore of the Black Sea, was importing its food-supplies, not from the Ukraine nor even from the Kuban basin, but from northern Asia Minor.[1] The Khersonites were paying for this food by serving as middlemen for handling goods exported by the Pechenegs, who, in the tenth century, were the pastoral nomad occupants of the Black Sea Steppe, but the Pechenegs, unlike their long since vanished Skyth predecessors, did not export grain from the Ukraine; their exports were hides—presumably those of animals bred by the Pechenegs themselves on the Steppe—and wax,[2] which they must have obtained, by raiding or trading, from the northern forests, but which was an unprofitable substitute for the grain that the Skyths had once drawn from the Black Earth.

The threat of famine which had overtaken Constantinople suddenly in 616, and had been chronic ever since, had been aggravated by the very success of Constantine the Great's new capital city. The influx of population had been immediate and prodigious, and this for several reasons.

In the first place, Constantinople, as a capital, had become the compulsory residence of a host of civil servants and a number of units of household troops. These metropolitan government employees probably received their pay regularly; negligence of this set of the Imperial Government's financial obligations would have promptly put the Government itself in jeopardy. This governmental pay-roll, supplemented by unofficial perquisites, 'squeeze', and bribes, enabled the Government's employees in Constantinople to become employers of labour on their own account on a large scale, partly in the direct form of buying slaves and hiring servants, and partly in the indirect form of making it possible, through their purchasing power, for practitioners of many kinds of trade, not only in necessities but in luxuries, to do profitable business in the Empire's new metropolis. For an inhabitant of the Levantine half of the Roman Empire, which was the populous half, to move into Constantinople (so easily accessible by sea) was an attractive option. Even if he failed to prosper there, the bread-dole gave him an assurance that he would not starve there. He would also be sure of finding security within the new capital's walls, and this was an important additional attraction in an age in which the provinces were suffering more and more severely from Persian invasions and from barbarian raids.

In combination, these diverse attractions of the new capital exerted a powerful pull. By the opening of the fifth century the population of Constantinople had reached a peak.[3] The plague of 541–2 had started a

---

[1] *De Adm. Imp.*, chap. 53, p. 270 (Bonn edition).
[2] Ibid.
[3] Teall in loc. cit., p. 91.

recession;[1] the plague of 619[2] must have alleviated further the problem of feeding the population. (It may also have been partly a consequence of under-nourishment due to the sudden stoppage, in 618, of the practice of feeding the Constantinopolitans gratis.) After 746–7, the years of the third bout of plague within two centuries, the population of Constantinople had dwindled to a figure which the Emperor Constantine V deliberately increased by bringing in settlers from other parts of his dominions.[3]

In what sense had the population of Constantinople become too small by the time when the plague of 746–7 had taken its toll? In 330, the year in which Constantinople had been dedicated, the new city had been laid out for housing the central administration of the more populous and prosperous half of a circum-Mediterranean Roman Empire. For a short span of years, in and immediately after the reign of Justinian I, it had been the capital of about two-thirds of the area, and perhaps three-quarters of the population, that the Empire had comprised in the year 330 and in the year 395. But by 747 the territory administered from Constantinople had shrunk to the limits of Asia Minor to the north-west of the Távros range, together with a scattering of European beachheads and islands. It is hard to believe that the population of the capital had become too small to service the central administration of a territory of this drastically reduced size.

Moreover, from the point of view of the Prefect of the City, the population of the capital could never be small enough now that the bread-dole had been discontinued. The Prefect's primary task was to see to it that the Imperial Government should not be overthrown by a metropolitan bread-riot. The reduction of the population of Constantinople by the three successive bouts of plague, and no doubt also, after the discontinuance of the bread-dole, by a voluntary exodus, must have been partly offset by a continuing influx of refugees into the only major city left to the Empire whose inner line of fortifications might reasonably be expected to prove impregnable. However considerable the net decrease in the population may have been, it can hardly have been great enough to balance the loss of the former grain-supply from Egypt; and no adequate substitute for this was to be found in Constantinople's immediate vicinity.

In the Thracian hinterland of Constantinople the quality of the soil is poor. By contrast, the Bithynian riviera along the north shore of the Gulf of Ismit (Nikomédheia) is fertile enough and extensive enough to have been capable of producing all the loaves that had been needed for feeding the Greek colonial city-state Khalkêdhón. (*Pace* Megabazi, the founders of Khalkêdhón had not been blind; they had been searching for good agricultural land, and they had found it; they had not been interested in

---

[1] Teall, ibid., p. 92.　　[2] Ibid., pp. 100–1.　　[3] See II, 1 (iii), p. 94.

a good commercial harbour with unfertile shores.[1]) Now, however, that Khalkêdhón had become just one of Constantinople's Asiatic suburbs, what, among so many mouths to feed, were the loaves of the Bithynian riviera or even the fishes[2] of the Bosphorus and the Marmara? The official for whom the population of Constantinople had become too small by the year 747 was not the Prefect of the City and was not the sakellários or the loghothétês tou yenikoú (whichever of these two officials we may consider to have been the equivalent of a head of the East Roman Imperial civil service);[3] it was the military officer who was responsible for keeping the fortifications of Constantinople repaired and manned.[4]

Artificial fortifications, in contrast to natural defences such as precipices or, better still, marshes, are of no avail unless they are effectively manned, and therefore the rulers of a city whose defences are man-made are caught in a dilemma when (and this was Constantinople's case after the year 616) the city does not have a source of food-supply that is sufficient for its population and that cannot be cut off. In that situation the official responsible for feeding the urban population will seek to reduce to a minimum the numbers of both the civilian population and the garrison, whereas the official responsible for defending the same population will seek to keep its numbers large enough to repair and to man the fortifications. When the walls of Constantinople were damaged by earthquake and flood,[5] the Emperor Leo III found that the inhabitants of the City had not sufficient funds and hands to repair their own city-walls for themselves, so he levied, throughout the Empire, a surcharge (the dhikératon), amounting to one-twelfth of the basic tax, for financing this indispensable piece of metropolitan public work.[6]

Moreover, the installations required for the defence of a city are not limited to ramparts; they include aqueducts and also cisterns, inside the perimeter of the ramparts, as an alternative source of water-supply in case the aqueducts are cut. In the Constantinian–Theodosian Age,

[1] See Fischer, op. cit., Part I, chap. 2, 'Landschaftsbilder von der bithynischen Riviera', pp. 24–32.

[2] See Fischer, op. cit., Part I, chap. 1, pp. 9–10.

[3] See Bury, *The Imperial Administrative System*, pp. 84–90; Philótheos, pp. 714 and 717 in the Bonn text, pp. 137 and 139–40 in Bury's text.

[4] The question whether the Kómês or dhoméstikos ton teikhéon was in charge of the walls of Constantinople, or of the Anastasian long wall, or of both, is discussed by Bury in op. cit., pp. 67–8. See also Philótheos, pp. 714 and 719 Bonn, pp. 137 and 141 Bury.

[5] See Theophanes, p. 412; Nic. Patr., p. 59. M. V. Anastos, in *C. Med. H.*, vol. iv, 2nd ed., Part I, p. 65, dates this disaster 740/1; Teall dates it, in loc. cit., 732. Theophanes's dating is A.M. 6232, in the twenty-fourth year of Leo III's reign (which was 740/1, i.e. Anastos's dating).

[6] Theophanes, ibid.; Handbook for taxation-officers, § 26. See also Ostrogorsky, 'Die ländliche Steuergemeinde', pp. 61 and 104; Dölger, 'Beiträge', p. 59; and the present work II, 1 (iv), p. 178.

Constantinople had been equipped with aqueducts and cisterns on a scale to match the Theodosian triple wall, and these equally indispensable installations likewise were laid out on a scale that implied the assumption that the amount of man-power needed for keeping them in repair would always be forthcoming. However, owing to a dearth of hands and funds, the aqueduct of Valens, which had been destroyed by the Avars in 626, remained out of action till 766; and, when Constantine V was stimulated by a drought to repair this aqueduct in that year, he had to mobilize artisans from Asia, Póndos, the Islands, Ellás, and Thrace in order to get the work done.[1] By the date of the plague of 746–7, a number of the cisterns in Constantinople had also ceased to be water-tight and had been allowed to fall into disuse, and in this emergency they were used as dumping-places for corpses.[2] A cistern in the Great Palace, another in the Maghnávra, and another in the Iería Palace on the Asiatic shore of the Bosphorus, all of which are said to have been put out of action deliberately by Heraclius, were not reconditioned till the reign of Basil I (867–86).[3]

Thus by Leo III's time the East Roman Government was a prisoner of the magnitude that the population of Constantinople had attained at its fifth-century peak; for the growth of the City's population had been matched by an extension of the length of its artificial fortifications and by an increase in the installations for its water-supply. The site of Constantinople was as excellent for defence as it was for food-supply from overseas. Byzantium, of which Constantinople was an enlargement, had been built on the tip of a triangular peninsula between the Sea of Marmara and the Golden Horn, and this peninsula was an excrescence on a larger peninsula (not triangular but snub-nosed), which was bounded by the Marmara, the Bosphorus, and the Black Sea. The coasts of both the smaller and the larger peninsula could be defended so long as the Empire had a strong enough navy to be able to dominate the maritime approaches, but the necks of the two peninsulas could be defended only by building artificial fortifications. The lie of the land made it possible to enclose areas of different sizes by land-walls of different lengths.

When Constantine the Great was laying down the line for his land-wall between the Marmara and the Golden Horn, the onlookers were amazed at the extent of the area that he was enclosing; this dwarfed the area that had been contained within the walls of tiny Byzantium. However, by the Emperor Theodosius II's time (he reigned from 408 to 450) the growth of the City's population had burst the founder's far-flung bounds, and accordingly Theodosius II—perhaps taking warning from the fall of the Old Rome in 410—had replaced Constantine I's wall with a triple wall

---

[1] Theophanes, p. 440; Nic. Patr., pp. 75–6, cited by Teall in loc. cit., pp. 102–3.
[2] Theophanes, p. 423; Nic. Patr., p. 63, cited by Teall in loc. cit., p. 103.
[3] *Theoph. Cont.*, pp. 337–8, cited by Teall, ibid.

which was appreciably longer, since it ran from the Marmara to the Golden Horn considerably nearer to the base of the triangle, i.e. nearer to an imaginary line drawn from the head of the Golden Horn to a point on the Marmara's northern shore.

The area enclosed within the Theodosian triple wall of Constantinople is approximately equal to the area of Old Rome within the Aurelianic Wall,[1] and the Theodosian triple wall continued to be the rampart of Constantinople on the landward side until the capture of the City by Mehmet the Conqueror in 1453. Till then, Constantinople had never been taken by assault from the landward side, and only once from the seaward side, namely in 1204, when the Venetians and their accomplices the French crusaders escaladed the sea-walls that had been built—like the triple land-wall, in Theodosius II's reign—by the Prefect of the City, Cyrus, in 439. However, the Emperor Anastasius I (491–518) sought to make assurance doubly sure by building, in either 507 or 497, a long wall across the neck of the larger of the two peninsulas from the Marmara to the Black Sea. This long wall ran from Selymvría on the Marmara to a point on the shore of the Black Sea between Podhima and Lake Dherkos. The *tracé* of Anastasius I's long wall was almost identical with the Chataljá (Čatalcá) line along which the Turkish army arrested the Bulgarian army's advance in 1912.

The Anastasian long wall itself arrested the advance of the Avars in 582/3,[2] but there does not seem to be a record of any later occasion on which an invader from the European hinterland of Constantinople was brought to a halt at any point short of the formidable outer face of the Theodosian triple wall of Constantinople itself; and, on the Bithynian peninsula, there was no obstacle, artificial or natural, to arrest an invader's advance anywhere short of the eastern shore of the Bosphorus. Constantine I and Theodosius II and Anastasius I, each in turn, had set in store grave embarrassments for their successors by laying out the landward defences of Constantinople on a scale that they had planned on the assumption that these defences would have at their disposal, for manning them and keeping them in repair, the whole of the revenue and the military man-power of the eastern half of the Roman Empire, including the entire area that this eastern half had comprised in each of those three reigns. By the year 747 the population of Constantinople had probably dwindled to a figure at which it could have been housed in a smaller area than had been enclosed within Constantine I's land-wall, not to speak of Theodosius II's. Yet, when once Theodosius II's magnificent fortifications had been erected, to abandon and dismantle them would have been unthinkable; and anyway at this date the Empire did not command either the resources or the skill for building a rampart, to

---

[1] Teall, in loc. cit., p. 134.   [2] See II, 1 (iii) (a), p. 73, and Annex III, p. 634.

the rear of Theodosius II's, of anything like the same strength, however greatly the length that had to be defended might have been reduced by drawing the new line closer to the tip of the peninsula.

Accordingly, the Theodosian triple wall continued to be Constantinople's landward rampart for another seven centuries, and, throughout this period, its retention was justified by results. Anastasius's hope of holding an enemy at arm's length was abandoned. From the seventh century onwards, his successors were content to arrest the advance of a European assailant at the line of the Theodosian triple wall, and the advance of an Asiatic assailant at the Asiatic shore of the Bosphorus. In the dire year 626 the East Roman Navy was able to prevent the Avars and the Persians from joining hands across the Straits, and it was also thanks to East Roman naval power that successive Arab and Russian assaults on Constantinople all ended disastrously for the assailants.

The efficacy of Constantinople's maritime defences and lines of communication—so long as the East Roman Empire retained its command of the narrow seas, or possessed allies who could command these seas on the Empire's behalf—is illustrated by the length of the time for which a government, seated in Constantinople, succeeded in holding out on each of two occasions on which a hostile power in north-western Asia Minor had expanded its dominions across the Dardanelles into Europe and, by thus encircling Constantinople, had cut all the City's overland lines of communication with the rest of the world. The Latin regime in Constantinople held out for twenty-six years (1235–61) after the refugee East Roman Government that had installed itself at Níkaia had extended its domain into Constantinople's Thracian hinterland. As for the East Roman Government that recovered Constantinople in 1261, it held out for no less than a century (1352–1453) after the 'Osmanlis, expanding their dominions from a nucleus in the vicinity of Níkaia, had won the beachhead on the Gallipoli Peninsula from which they made their swift conquest of south-eastern Europe. The 'Osmanlis reached the Danube and the Távros before they entered Constantinople. On both occasions, the narrow seas, commanded by sea-power supporting the beleaguered government at Constantinople, continued to serve as an effective life-line even after they had ceased to be an effective insulating moat.

To retain command of the narrow seas, besides continuing to hold the Theodosian land-wall, was as much as could be undertaken for the defence of Constantinople when the population of the City was reduced to its lowest figure by the plague of 746–7. In the ninth century the population increased again till, by Leo VI's reign (886–912), the City had come, once more, to be over-populated[1]—that is to say, from the standpoint of the Prefect of the City, not of the military and civil

---

[1] Teall in loc. cit., pp. 105–7.

engineers. The *Livre du Préfet* rules[1] that the candle-manufacturers' work-shops must not be closer to each other than 30 fathoms (ὀργυιαί), except for those adjacent to the Ayía Sophía. This regulation indicates that, by that time, building-room in the area enclosed within the Theodosian land-wall was becoming so scarce and so dear that there was now a temptation to crowd even buildings containing inflammable materials dangerously close to each other. The same tendency to overcrowding is indicated in Leo VI's Novel No. 113,[2] in which it is laid down that the minimum distance of 10 feet between the walls of buildings, which was already prescribed by law, shall also apply to projecting balconies. In his Novel No. 71,[3] Leo VI gives the force of law to a decision, made by Basil I, that new buildings on land previously occupied by vineyards or by arable shall be at least one bow-shot, and, where possible, two bow-shots, distant from each other. These measures are evidence that the unbuilt-up areas within the Theodosian land-wall, which had become extensive in the seventh century, had been filling up during the century and a half that had elapsed since the plague of 746–7.

This increase in the population of Constantinople eased, no doubt, the problems of defence and public works, but this at the expense of ag-gravating the problem of food-supply. Moreover, from the provincial tax-payer's point of view, Constantinople was parasitic.[4] Her main export was a host of unwelcome taxation-officers and other officials. Her main industry was the production of luxury goods for the Imperial Palace and for the metropolitan churches. These luxuries were purchased with the revenues that the Imperial Government drew from the 'Eastern' army-corps districts, and Constantinople was a heavy incubus on these; for her population in the ninth century, unlike contemporary Rome's, was perhaps not much smaller than it had been when she had been the capital of half—and, for a short time, of two-thirds—of the Mediter-ranean basin, while the area of the territory that had to support her had now dwindled to the limits of Cis-Tauran Asia Minor, and Thrace.[5] No others, among the few big cities that were in existence in the tenth century, rested on so small an economic basis. Baghdad had the irrigated alluvial soil of 'Irāq to draw upon; Fustāt, the predecessor of Cairo, could draw on the equally rich and well-cultivated soil of Egypt. The successive capitals of China were supplied from the basins of the Yellow River and the Yangtse. Western Christendom, at this date, did not con-tain any large city; and as late as 1204, the year in which Constantinople was conquered by Western 'crusaders', the sight of Constantinople was

[1] 11, 4, p. 44. [2] Noailles and Dain, pp. 372–5. [3] Ibid., pp. 256–7.
[4] Jenkins in *C. Med. H.*, vol. iv, 2nd ed., Part II, p. 93.
[5] Jenkins, in *C. Med. H.*, vol. iv, 2nd ed., Part II, p. 74, estimates that the population of Constantinople was something between 500,000 and 800,000 during the five centuries ending in 1204.

awe-inspiring for Franks.[1] Constantinople was a capital that was too big for the East Roman Empire within its tenth-century frontiers, even though the Empire's territory was now once again beginning to expand.

As a capital, Constantinople was a mixed blessing. On the other hand, as a fortress it was incomparable—on condition that the power which held this fortress should also hold the naval command of the narrow seas that insinuate themselves between Asia Minor and the Balkan Peninsula.

For a naval power, Constantinople was also a secure and well-planned base for distant naval operations. Even after the loss of all but one of the East Roman Empire's last footholds in Sicily at the beginning of the tenth century, the Imperial Navy still managed to carry out naval operations in the western basin of the Mediterranean; and, after the Empire's final loss, in 680, of its frontier along the south bank of the lower Danube, the Imperial Navy, operating from Constantinople, continued to be able to sail up the Danube in the rear of the Slavs and Bulgars who had established themselves to the south of the river. Thanks to its ability to command this waterway at will, the Imperial Navy was able, *circa* 837, to rescue the Adrianopolitan deportees whom the Bulgars had marooned in what is now Wallachia; it was able in 895 to ferry the Magyars across the lower Danube to attack the Empire's Bulgar assailants in the rear; it would have ferried the Pechenegs across for the same purpose in 917 if the admiral, Rhomanós Lekapênós, had carried out his orders. On the other hand, Constantinople was far less well placed for overland military or commercial operations.

So long as the Roman Empire had had hard-pressed frontiers to defend along the lower Danube and the Middle Euphrates, Constantinople—standing, as it stood, on the shore of the narrow seas on the route along which the distance between the Euphrates and the Danube is shortest—was the best military base for operations on whichever of these two frontiers might be in greater danger at any given moment. Constantinople was not, however, a convenient coastal base for reaching the interior of either Asia Minor or the Balkan Peninsula. Its site was at one of the extreme corners of each of these two regions, and each of these two corners came to a point in a peninsula—the Bithynian Peninsula on the Asiatic side and the Thracian on the European side. These two peninsular approaches to Constantinople would have been useful for the city's defence if they could have been sealed off effectively at their necks, by the Anastasian long wall in Europe and by a corresponding wall in Asia carried from the head of the Gulf of Ismit to the southern shore of the Black Sea; but, as has been noted already, the East Roman Empire's resources were no longer ample enough, after the collapse in 602, to

---

[1] See Geoffroi de Villehardouin, *Conquête de Constantinople*, chap. 26, § 128 (3rd ed. of N. de Wailly's text and translation (Paris, 1882, Didot), p. 72).

defend Constantinople at this distance away and on this scale. The City's assailants always managed to reach the outer face of its land-wall and to occupy its Asiatic suburbs, whereas troops or traders setting out from Constantinople overland for Asia Minor or for south-eastern Europe were compelled, by the lie of the land, to follow long and roundabout routes to their destinations. Emperors and armies en route from Constantinople for the south-eastern frontier shortened their overland journey by by-passing the Bithynian peninsula and landing at Pylai, on the south shore of the Gulf of Ismit; but the distance thus saved was inconsiderable. Smyrna, Éphesos, and Milêtós offered better-placed coastal bases than Constantinople for reaching the interior of Asia Minor, and Thessaloníkê offered a far better-placed coastal base for reaching the interior of south-eastern Europe.

Thus Constantinople's excellence for serving as a fortress and as a naval base was partially offset by this city's drawbacks for serving as a base for overland operations, military or commercial. Conversely, however, the toll that Constantinople took from the East Roman Empire after 602 as a capital that was on too grand a scale for the Empire's drastically reduced circumstances was partially offset by this city's cultural and philanthropic services.

Before the ruin of the Graeco-Roman civilization, Constantinople had providently been made into a museum for preserving the ruined civilization's relics. The greatest of the works of Hellenic art that had escaped destruction by Christians and barbarians had found sanctuary within this Christian city's walls, and here they survived till they were destroyed by the 'crusaders' who seized and sacked Constantinople in 1204. Till then, these beautiful and famous relics of Hellenic antiquity co-existed in Constantinople side by side with the works of the Byzantine Christian school of art and architecture whose origins were approximately coeval with the foundation of the City itself. These two styles of art were not only different; they were antithetical to each other;[1] and for the inhabitants of Constantinople this was confusing morally as well as aesthetically. Officially, the Christian Church condemned Hellenism and all its works. In the mouth of a 'Roman' ('Ρωμαῖος), i.e. of a medieval Greek, 'Hellene' now signified 'Heathen'.[2] Yet, while Hellenism was deprecated, it was also treasured.[3] A Byzantine writer who had any pretensions to style would eschew the 'Rhomaic' Greek that was his mother-tongue and that served his needs in everyday life. When he took up his pen, he imitated, as faithfully as he knew how, the Atticizing Greek of the Age of Augustus, which was itself an imitation of the genuine Attic of the

---

[1] See IV, 2 (v), pp. 543–6.
[2] Hellenism was one of the charges brought against Phótios (see Annex 1, p. 609).
[3] See Jenkins in *C. Med. H.*, vol. iv, 2nd ed., Part II, pp. 81–3.

fifth and fourth centuries B.C. Even in the field of the visual arts the naturalistic style of the post-Alexandrine Age of Hellenic art held its own, for decorative secular purposes, against the hieratic Syrian style that had driven the Hellenic style off the field for solemn ecclesiastical purposes.

Besides being a museum, Constantinople was an educational centre. Bréhier's study of the lives of ninth-century Byzantine saints has brought out the fact[1] that, in that period of East Roman history, country-bred boys were uneducated. For instance, Ioanníkios the Great, a son of free peasant parents, who was born in 754 in the village of Marykatos near Lake Apollonía, and who had had a military career in the Excubitors before he became a monk, remained illiterate till the age of forty-seven.[2] St. George of Amastrís and the Cretan St. Nikólaos the Studite (born in 793) did each obtain an education in his native town; yet few provincials attained high office, either civil or ecclesiastical; most bishops came from Constantinople and other large cities; and between the standards of education in the provinces and those in Constantinople there was a great gulf.[3] Even in the seventh and eighth centuries, when education in the East Roman Empire was at its lowest ebb, Constantinople still managed to produce enough literate laymen to staff the civil service. In 863 the Caesar Várdhas re-established the University of Constantinople that had been founded in 425 by the Emperor Theodosius II.[4] The revived university outlasted Várdhas's downfall and death, and Constantine Porphyrogenitus is praised by his critics, as well as by his friends, for having carried on the work that Várdhas had begun. In the Rhomaic-speaking world, Constantinople was henceforth a centre for the study of Hellenic literature and philosophy. Yet a more serious study of Hellenic philosophy, and of Hellenic science as well, was being carried on, by now, in the Islamic World; and Western Christendom was eventually to get more of its knowledge of Aristotle via Muslim and Arabic-speaking Toledo and Palermo than via Christian and Greek-speaking Constantinople.

The East Roman Empire was probably in advance of most contemporary states in its possession of social services. These were not confined to Constantinople; every monastery, anywhere in the Empire, served as a charitable institution to some extent,[5] even though Nikêphóros II Phokás may have been right in holding that, in his time, at any

---

[1] See Bréhier, 'Les Populations rurales', p. 189.
[2] Ibid., pp. 182–3 and 188–9.   [3] Ibid., p. 189.
[4] For the foundation of the Maghnávra university, and for the career of its first chancellor Leo the Mathematician, see *Georg. Mon. Interpolatus*, Reign of Theóphilos, chap. 23, p. 806; *Theoph. Cont.*, Book IV, Reign of Michael III, chaps. 26–9, pp. 185–92; pseudo-Symeon, Reign of Theóphilos, chap. 20, p. 640.
[5] See Savramis, op. cit., chap. 3, section 1, 'Die soziale Tätigkeit des Mönchtums', pp. 24–34.

rate, the monasteries were making an inadequate return to society for their endowments. However, philanthropy, like education, was concentrated in Constantinople. An orphanage had been founded there, at some date before 472, by a private benefactor named Zotikós, and in 571/2 Justin II and his consort Sophía refounded Zotikós's orphanage and founded a new one of their own.[1] The orphanotróphos—an office which existed already in the reign of Leo I (457–74)—was put in charge of both these foundations, and he was an important personage in Constantinople, though he did not administer all the philanthropic foundations in the capital, and is not known to have been in charge of any in the provinces.[2]

Besides the orphanages, there were homes for infants ($\beta\rho\epsilon\phi o\tau\rho o\phi\epsilon\hat{\iota}a$), homes for old people ($\gamma\eta\rho o\kappa o\mu\epsilon\hat{\iota}a$), homes for the poor ($\pi\tau\omega\chi o\tau\rho o\phi\epsilon\hat{\iota}a$), hospitals ($\nu o\sigma o\kappa o\mu\epsilon\hat{\iota}a$), and hostels ($\xi\epsilon\nu\hat{\omega}\nu\epsilon s$, $\xi\epsilon\nu o\delta o\chi\epsilon\hat{\iota}a$).[3] Rhomanós Lekapênós founded and equipped a hostel in ta Mavrianoú, in order to provide board and lodging for indigent provincials who had to come to Constantinople, and perhaps might have to make a long stay there, for lawsuits.[4] In an earlier chapter[5] it has already been noted that Zotikós's hospital (his foundation seems to have been converted into a hospital from an orphanage by Justin II and Sophía)[6] was enlarged by Constantine Porphyrogenitus, and that the stables of the Porphyrogenitus's frivolous brother-in-law the Ecumenical Patriarch Theophýlaktos were converted by Constantine, after Theophýlaktos's death, into a home for old people.[7] Constantine Porphyrogenitus also endowed and chartered a hostel and a home for old people that had been founded by his wife Elénê in the Old Petríon.[8]

This is a highly creditable aspect of East Roman social life, and, though it was not an exclusively metropolitan phenomenon, it is also true that philanthropic foundations, as well as educational activities, were concentrated in Constantinople, within the shelter provided there by the Theodosian land-wall and the Imperial Navy.

---

[1] Theophanes, p. 244, sub A.M. 6064.

[2] For the orphanotróphos, see Bury, *The Imperial Administrative System*, pp. 103–5.

[3] Ostrogorsky, 'Die ländliche Steuergemeinde', p. 73; Jenkins, loc. cit., p. 91.

[4] *Theoph. Cont.*, Book VI, p. 430. This humane provision for social justice is credited by Constantine Porphyrogenitus, not to his unwelcome co-Emperor Rhomanós I, but to his own grandfather Basil I. See *Theoph. Cont.*, Book V, chap. 31 (cited again in the present work, Part V, chap. 2, p. 592).

[5] I, 2, p. 20.

[6] Bury in op. cit., p. 103.

[7] *Theoph. Cont.*, Book VI, p. 449.

[8] *Theoph. Cont.*, Book VI, pp. 458–9.

4. The Army-Corps Districts (Θέματα)

CONSTANTINE PORPHYROGENITUS gives, in his *De Caerimoniis,*[1] a list of twenty-seven army-corps districts (θέματα) and four fortified defiles (κλεισοῦραι)[2] into which the East Roman Empire had been divided, for both civil and military purposes, in Leo VI's day. If the reader happens to be a student of Hellenic and Roman history, but not of Byzantine history, he will find some of the names of these thirty-one late-ninth-century districts familiar, while others may be enigmatic for him at first sight.

The familiar names—taking them in the order of Constantine Porphyrogenitus's list—will be Kappadhokía, Pamphlaghonía [*sic*], Thrákê, Makedhonía, Mesopotamía, Sevásteia, Seléfkeia, Sámos, Aiyaíon Pélaghos, Pelopónnêsos, Nikópolis, Ellás, Sikelía, Strymón, Kephalênía [*sic*], Thessaloníkê, Dhyrrhákhion, Dhalmatía. These are names of countries, cities, islands, a sea, and a river that appear on the map of the pre-seventh-century Graeco-Roman World. The classical scholar will also detect the name of the once obscure town Kibyra, on the south coast of Asia Minor, in the official title of ὁ στρατηγός τῶν Κιβυρραιωτῶν, and the name of the Tauric city-state Khersónêsos in Khersón.

On the other hand, the classical scholar may be puzzled by the plural names Anatolikoí, Armeniakoí, Thrakἔsioi, Voukellárioi, by the collective name Opsíkion, and by the singular names Kharsianón, Khaldhía, Kolóneia, Lykandós (Likandós), Leondokómês (Leondókomis), and Laghouvardhía. In Kolóneia he will recognize, of course, the Latin word 'colonia', but this Roman colony planted in Pontic Cappadocia will not be the first in the long list of Roman colonies that will occur to him. In

---

[1] Book II, chap. 50, pp. 696–7. The document is one of those in the dossier, at the end of *De Caer.*, Book II, which Constantine had not yet incorporated in the text of this work when, in 959, he was overtaken by death.

[2] Formally, this is a list of the officers who, in each of these thirty-one districts, combined the two functions of military commandant and civil administrator, together with a note of the salaries of those of them whose salaries were paid by the Central Government of the Empire and were not taken direct from the revenue raised in the officer's own district. Constantine notes that the four kleisourárkhai of Leo VI's day had all been raised to the rank of stratêghoí, and that their districts had been simultaneously converted from kleisoúrai into thémata, by the time when Constantine edited this document. This list omits the commander of one district, the Optimátoi, which was already a théma in Leo VI's day, and in which, as in the other thémata, the commander of the military unit stationed there was also the governor of the district. The reason for the omission of théma Optimátoi is that this corps was a non-combatant army service corps, and its commander's title was, not stratêghós, but dhoméstikos or kómês. In Philótheos's klêtorolóyion, the dhoméstikos ton Optimáton ranks twelve places below the lowest of the rest of the army-corps commanders (p. 714 Bonn, p. 137 Bury).

the outlandish-sounding name 'Laghouvardhía' he may detect the Lango-bards who founded the Duchy of Beneventum not long after their irruption into Italy in A.D. 568. For an interpretation of the name Khaldhía, he will have to go back to Urartian, Assyrian, and Achaemenian Persian records of the eighth, seventh, and sixth centuries B.C. Who would have expected that an ethnikon that had gone under ground since then would come to the surface again 1,400 years later? For an interpretation of the name Kharsianón, the student will have to go back still farther—to Hittite records of the fourteenth and thirteenth centuries B.C.

These pre-Hellenic names of East Roman army-corps districts, like the Hellenic names, are historical curiosities; the plural names Anatolikoí, Armeniakoí, Thrakḗsioi and the collective name Opsíkion are those of the original[1] East Roman army-corps districts; all the other districts[1] are later additions, created either by sub-dividing the original districts, by maintaining the Empire's European insular possessions and consolidating its European beachheads,[2] or by extending the Empire's domain at the expense of the Muslims, the Armenians, and the previously independent city-state Khersón on the east and at the expense of the Slavs[3] and the southern Lombards on the west.[4] The names of the four original army-corps districts are the key to the origin of the institution itself.

These four names give us a clue for reconstructing the lost history of the administrative revolution that, in and after the seventh century, had substituted the East Roman system of thémata and kleisoúrai for the utterly different Diocletianic–Constantinian system that had preceded it.

Under the Diocletianic–Constantinian regime, under which the Roman Empire had lived from 284 to 602, the military commands and the civil governorships had not been united in the same pairs of hands, as they were in the East Roman Empire in Leo VI's and Constantine VII Porphyrogenitus's time, and as they had been in the Roman Empire in the Age of the Principate (31 B.C.–A.D. 284). In the Diocletianic–Constantinian Age, military commands and civil governorships had been kept separate from each other by being placed in different pairs of hands.

In the eastern half of the Roman Empire, the Emperor Theodosius I (379–95) had divided the military high command between two co-equal magistri militum praesentales (i.e. corps-commanders whose commands were attached to the Emperor's person) and three subordinate regional

---

[1] Including Voukellárioi and also Optimátoi. The Optimátoi do not appear in *De Caer.*, Book II, chap. 50, but they do appear in Philótheos's klêtorolóyion, pp. 714 and 719 Bonn, pp. 137 and 141 Bury. For the Optimátoi, see also Bury, *The Imperial Administrative System*, pp. 66–7.

[2] See II, 1 (iii) (a), pp. 90–8.   [3] See ibid., pp. 98–105.

[4] Antoniadis-Bibicou, op. cit., p. 69, n. 1, notes that the names of the thémata are of three different types: (i) geographical corps-names (e.g. Armeniakoí); (ii) non-geographical corps-names (e.g. Opsíkion); (iii) non-corps geographical names (e.g. Ellás).

corps-commanders whose areas were respectively the dioecesis Oriens (Syria, in the widest sense of the word, and Mesopotamia), the dioecesis Thracia (the eastern half of the Balkan Peninsula), and the Praetorian Prefecture of Eastern Illyricum (the rest of the Balkan Peninsula).[1] Theodosius I's organization had been elaborated by Justinian I (527–65).[2] Justinian had increased the number of magistri militum praesentales from two to three and had doubled Theodosius I's number of regional commanders. Justinian had detached from the command per Orientem the Roman portion of Armenia, which had previously lain within the magister militum per Orientem's sphere, and had created a new command per Armeniam,[3] with an area which combined Roman Armenia with some adjacent Roman territory to the west and north of the Euphrates. Justinian had created two other new commands, per Africam[4] and per Italiam, for the defence of the former Roman territories in the West that he had recovered by liquidating the Empire's Vandal and Ostrogothic successor-states.

Justinian had also created[5] a new regional command,[6] with its headquarters at Odhêssós on the west shore of the Black Sea and with an area that was peculiar in two respects. Its commander, who was styled the quaestor Iustinianus exercitûs, held the command over troops stationed in two groups of provinces that were remote from each other geographically—Moesia Secunda and Scythia to the north-west of the Straits and the Cyclades, Caria, and Cyprus to the south-east of them—and this military officer was made the governor of the five provinces in which his troops were quartered. This was a reminiscence of the pre-284 regime and an anticipation of the regime in force in (and before) the reigns of Leo VI and Constantine VII Porphyrogenitus.

In Constantine Porphyrogenitus's list, Theodosius I's and Justinian I's magister militum per Orientem is recognizable in the stratêghós[7] ton

---

[1] A. Pertusi, *Costantino Porfirogenito De Thematibus: Testo Critico, Commento* (Città del Vaticano, 1952, Biblioteca Apostolica Vaticana), Studi e Testi, No. 160, on p. 105. See also Grosse, op. cit., pp. 185–6, and the present work, p. 193.

[2] Pertusi, op. cit., pp. 105–6.

[3] *Cod. Just.*, I, 29, 5; John Malalas, pp. 429–30; Procopius, *De Aedificiis*, III, 1, 16. Cf. A. H. M. Jones, *The Later Roman Empire, 284–602*, vol. i, pp. 280–1, and Grosse, op. cit., p. 190. The following magistri militum (stratêghoí) per Armeniam are mentioned by Procopius in *Bella*: Sittas, simultaneously per Armeniam and in praesenti (I, 15, 3); Valerianus (II, 14, 8; 24, 6; VII, 27, 3; VIII, 8, 22); Bessa (VIII, 9, 4).

[4] *Cod. Just.*, I, 27.

[5] In his Novel No. 41 of 18 May 536, published in Latin only.

[6] See E. Stein, *Studien zur Geschichte des byzantinischen Reiches* (Stuttgart, 1919, Metzler), pp. 165–8.

[7] The Latin title magister militum was rendered as stratêghós or stratêlátês in Greek already in the fifth and sixth centuries. See H. Zilliacus, *Zum Kampf der Weltsprachen im Oströmischen Reich* (Helsingfors, 1935, Mercator), p. 157; J. Karayannopulos, *Die Entstehung der byzantinischen Themenverfassung* (Munich, 1959, Beck), p. 49; and Diehl, *Études byzantines* (Paris, 1905, Picard): 'L'Origine du régime des thèmes dans l'Empire byzantin', pp. 276–92, on

Anatolikón (i.e. the corps-commander of the Orientales); their magister militum per Thraciam in the stratêghós ton Thrakêsíon (i.e. the corps-commander of the Thracenses); and their magistri militum praesentales in the stratêghós or kómês tou Opsikíou. Justinian I's magister militum per Armeniam is recognizable in the stratêghós ton Armeniakón or Armeniákon.

The units commanded by magistri militum had been called in Latin 'exercitûs'[1] and in Greek 'stratoí'.[2] The term 'exercitus' still appears in Justinian II's Latin letter of 17 February 687 to Pope Conon.[3] The corresponding Greek term appears in the Patriarch Nikêphóros's chronicle, sometimes as 'stratós'[4] and sometimes as 'stráteuma'.[5]

Justinian II's letter of 687 was written to inform the Pope that the Emperor had just obtained the ratification of the acts of the Sixth General Council of the Church, which had been held in 680, by an assembly of notables that had been convened at Constantinople *ad hoc*. The Emperor enumerates the groups that were represented on this occasion, and his list names all but one of those army-corps that, in Justinian I's reign, had been commanded by magistri militum. Only the army-corps of the Eastern Illyricum has dropped out. The passage in Justinian II's letter runs:

insuper etiam quosdam de Christo dilectis exercitibus, tam a Deo conservando imperiali obsequio quamque ab Orientali, Thraciano, similiter et ab Armeniano, etiam ab exercitu Italiae, deinde ex Cabarisianis [*sic*] et Septensianis, seu de Sardinia et de Africano exercitu.

The Obsequium is the aggregate of the troops commanded by Justinian I's three magistri militum praesentales; the exercitus Orientalis is the command of Justinian I's magister militum per Orientem; the exercitus Thracianus is the command of his magister militum per Thraciam; the exercitus Armenianus is the command of his magister militum per Armeniam; the Calarisiani[6] and the Septensiani are identified respectively,

p. 289. When the Latin terminology ceased to be used in the East Roman Army, stratêghós continued to be the title of the commander of an East Roman army-corps. The only exceptions were the dhoméstikos or kómês ton Optimáton (see p. 224, n. 2) and the commander of the Opsíkion (Obsequium), who is styled stratêghós in Constantine Porphyrogenitus's list in *De Caer.*, II, p. 696, but kómês in Philótheos's klêtorolóyion (p. 713 Bonn, p. 136 Bury).

[1] Diehl, op. cit., p. 287, citing *Lib. Pont.* 389 (exercitus Siciliae), Pope Gregory I, *Epist.*, Book V, Ep. 39 (Italiae), and the Emperor Justinian II's letter of 687 to Pope Conon.

[2] Diehl, op. cit., citing Nic. Patr., pp. 37 and 52 (Anatol.), p. 61 (Armeniak.), p. 47 (Opsik.), p. 64 (Kivyr.).

[3] In the Codex Bellovacensis, in which the text of this letter has been preserved, the document is said to come from the Papal archives in the Lateran.

[4] As 'stratós' on pp. 47, 52, 61, 64.　　　　　　　[5] As 'stráteuma' on pp. 37.

[6] The 'Cabarisiani' of the text cannot be correct as it stands, and 'Calarisiani' is the emendation that we are bound to make, since this body of troops is identified expressly by Justinian II with the garrison of Sardinia. This was Gelzer's original emendation in his edition

by Justinian II himself, with the garrison of the island of Sardinia and
with the exercitus Africanus, and these are two surviving fragments of
the command of Justinian I's magister militum per Africam. By 687 the
Arabs had already pressed so hard on Roman Africa that the headquarters of what was left of the main body of the African army-corps had
been moved westwards to Septem (Ceuta) on the African side of the
Straits of Gibraltar, and a fragment of the same corps had taken refuge at
Caralis (Cagliari) in Sardinia[1]—an island which must have been included in the area of Justinian I's magister militum per Africam, since
Sardinia had been part of the Vandal Kingdom, centred on Africa, which
Justinian I had liquidated.

Of the corps enumerated in Justinian II's letter of 687, the exercitus
Africanus ceased (except in Sardinia) to exist—as the exercitus of the
Eastern Illyricum had ceased before 687—when, in 711, the Arabs
crossed the Straits of Gibraltar.[2] The exercitus Italiae ceased to exist
when, in 751, the Lombards took Ravenna. But, in the first four entries in
Constantine Porphyrogenitus's list of the salaries of corps-commanders
(stratêghoí) in Leo VI's reign, the exercitus Orientalis appears as the
Anatolikoí, the exercitus Armenianus as the Armeniakoí, the exercitus
Thracianus as the Thrakêsioi,[3] the Obsequium as the Opsíkion.

When we note the location of these four thémata in Leo VI's and
Constantine VII Porphyrogenitus's time, our identification of their
names with those of army-corps in Theodosius I's and Justinian I's
military organization tells us what happened to the principal units of
the Roman army in the east when the Roman Empire was hit by the

---

(Leipzig, 1890, Teubner) of Georgius Cyprius's *Descriptio Orbis Romani*, p. 43, and it is
rightly endorsed by Antoniadis-Bibicou in op. cit., pp. 63 and 65. Diehl, op. cit., p. 285
and p. 289, n. 2, emends 'Cabarisiani' to 'Carabisiani', and H. Gelzer has accepted Diehl's
emendation in *Die Genesis der byzantinischen Themenverfassung* (Abhandlungen der Kön.
Sächs. Gesellschaft der Wissenschaften, 1899; reprint: Amsterdam, 1966, Hakkert), pp. 11,
20, and 29. If this emendation were not ruled out, as it is, by Justinian II's elucidation 'seu
de Sardinia, etc.', it would be convincing. A stratêghós ton Karávon figures in the *S.D.
Miracula*, Book II, cols. 1369–73, on an occasion which, at the latest, cannot have been later
that about 645, and a stratêgos Caravisianorum is mentioned in the *Liber Pontificalis*, 223,
18–20, (Mommsen), sub anno 711. It is strange that the Karavisianoí are not mentioned
by Justinian II as having been represented at his assembly of notables in 687, considering the
importance of the part that they had played, during the thirty years 649–78, in saving
the East Roman Empire from being extinguished, and also considering that it would have
been easy to convene at Constantinople some representatives of such a relatively mobile
force. However, the problem of their absence cannot be solved by making an untenable
emendation of Justinian II's text.

¹ See Gelzer's edition of Georgius Cyprius, pp. xliii–xliv.
² Gelzer notes in his edition of Georgius Cyprius, pp. xliii–xliv, that Julian of Ceuta, who
let the Arabs through, was the last East Roman exarch of Africa.
³ Antoniadis-Bibicou, op. cit., pp. 69 and 76, points out that Justinian II's Thraciani
are the Thracenses (*Graecè* Thrakêsioi), not the troops of the subsequently created théma
Thrákê—*pace* Diehl, op. cit., p. 283, n. 6.

tremendous impact of the Muslim Arabs' eruption almost immediately after the Prophet Muhammad's death in 632.[1] The remnant of the corps commanded by the magister militum per Orientem (i.e. the corps hitherto stationed in Palestine, Syria, Mesopotamia, and Cilicia) saved itself from annihilation by retreating to the north-western side of the Távros and halting there, in échelon, along the road leading diagonally across Asia Minor towards Constantinople from the relatively easily defensible Cilician Gates. The corps commanded by the magister militum per Armeniam (i.e. the corps hitherto stationed in what had been the Roman fraction of Armenia and in the adjoining part of north-eastern Asia Minor)[2] had beaten a shorter retreat westwards, abandoning Theodosiopolis, which its Arab conquerors labelled Arz-ar-Rum (i.e. the Armenian country that had previously been under Roman sovereignty).[3] The corps commanded by the magister militum per Thraciam (i.e. the corps hitherto stationed in the eastern quarter of the Balkan Peninsula, from the Aegean and the Straits to the south bank of the lower Danube), had been transferred to western Asia Minor to support the Anatolikoí and to cover them against attack by enemy forces landed on the west coast of the peninsula.

Both the Anatolikoí and the Armeniakoí had a further support in the Opsíkion. In Justinian I's time the Obsequium—i.e. the troops of the three magistri militum praesentales—had already been cantoned in north-western Asia Minor.[4] Units belonging to the Obsequium were apt to be moved from one side of the Straits to the other, as Justinian moved some of the Skholárioi from Asia Minor to Thrace in 562.[5] In reply to the Arabs' onslaught, any units of the Obsequium that had been stationed in Thrace at the time are likely to have been moved back into Asia Minor,[6] and this may also have been the occasion on which the Opsíkion was reinforced by the enigmatic optimátoi and by the Voukellárioi,[7] who had originally been, not Imperial troops, but the private retainers of senior Imperial military commanders. Our evidence that these units had once been brigaded with the Opsíkion in north-western Asia Minor is their

---

[1] See A. Pertusi, 'La Formation des thèmes byzantins', in *Berichte zum XI. internazionalen Byzantinisten-Kongress München 1958* (Munich, 1958, Beck), pp. 1–40, on pp. 31–2.

[2] See p. 226.

[3] An alternative form and interpretation of the name is Arzan-ar-Rum, meaning a settlement of refugees from Arzanênê in the upper Tigris basin, who had fled from the Saljūqs in 1045 (Pauly–Wissowa, Zweite Reihe (R–Z), 10. Halbband (1934), col. 1928).

[4] Diehl, op. cit., p. 279, citing Justinian's Novel No. 8, 3; Theophanes, p. 236 (Skholárioi in Nikomědheia, Kíos, Proúsa, Kýzikos, Kotyáeion, Dhoryláïon; Procopius, *Secret History*, p. 137, dhoméstikoi and protectores in Galatia.

[5] Theophanes, loc. cit.

[6] There was still a magister militum praesentalis in 626 (George Pisides, *Bellum Avaricum*, line 314, cited by Pertusi, 'La Formation', p. 26).

[7] A nickname meaning 'hard-tack eaters'. The etymology is given correctly in *De Them.* p. 28.

subsequent appearance there as separate thémata adjoining the Opsíkion. The Voukellárioi are mentioned separately for the first time in 766/7[1] and the Optimátoi in 773.[2]

The civil wars, the Avar and Slav migrations, and the Persian invasion that had followed the overthrow and murder of the Emperor Maurice in 602 had, we know, resulted in the virtual dissolution of the East Roman Army; and the civil administration too must have been put out of action in those East Roman territories—Roman Persarmenia, Roman Armenia, the dioecesis Oriens, and Egypt—that were occupied by the Persians for a number of years on end. We may guess, however, that after 628, the year in which peace between the East Roman Empire and the Persian Empire had been made on the basis of the *status quo ante bellum*, the pre-war organization of the civil administration and of the cadres of the Army had been re-established by Heraclius during the Empire's short breathing-space between the Persians' withdrawal and the Arabs' attack.[3] The geographical location in Asia Minor of the four army-corps that had survived from Justinian I's time indicates that it was the Arab, not the previous Persian, assault that drove these corps into the areas in which we find them stationed before the close of the seventh century. We need not question Constantine Porphyrogenitus's statements that the fragmentation of the East Roman Army's units ($\tau\acute{a}\gamma\mu\alpha\tau a$) primarily ($\mu\acute{a}\lambda\iota\sigma\tau a$), and of the Empire's territory secondarily, dated from the time of the Emperor Heraclius's successors,[4] and that the event that had forced these Emperors to carry out this reorganization was the constriction ($\sigma\tau\epsilon\nu\omega\theta\epsilon\acute{\iota}\sigma\eta\varsigma$) and truncation ($\dot{a}\kappa\rho\omega\tau\eta\rho\iota\alpha\sigma\theta\epsilon\acute{\iota}\sigma\eta\varsigma$) of the Empire, in Heraclius's own reign, as a result of the Arabs' offensive.[5]

By the time, in Leo VI's reign (886–912), when the table of salaries of corps-commanders ($\sigma\tau\rho\alpha\tau\eta\gamma o\acute{\iota}$) and Philótheos's klêtorolóyion were compiled, the corps, which had once been known in Latin as 'exercitûs' and in Greek as 'stratoí', had long since undergone two changes: a change of nomenclature and a much more important extension of functions. They had now come to bear a different Greek name, 'thémata', and they had also become the instruments for the civil administration of the areas in which they were respectively stationed.

Each corps-commander had now become at the same time the governor of the district in which the corps resided and from which its troops were recruited, and these new districts, in which the civil authority was combined with the military command in the same pair of hands, had superseded—at any rate for practical purposes—the praetorian

---

[1] Theophanes, p. 440.   [2] Theophanes, p. 447.

[3] This is Pertusi's view ('La Formation', p. 34).

[4] οἱ ἀπ' ἐκείνου (sc. Ἡρακλείου) κρατήσαντες, . . . εἰς μικρά τινα μέρη κατέτεμον τὴν ἑαυτῶν ἀρχὴν καὶ τὰ τῶν στρατιωτῶν τάγματα μάλιστα (*De Them.*, pp. 12–13).

[5] Constantine, op. cit., ibid. and p. 16.

prefectures, dioeceses, and provinces which, under the Diocletianic–Constantinian dispensation, had been administered by civil governors who did not have any troops under their command. The change in official terminology had thus been accompanied by two changes of substance: the administrative map of what was left of the East Roman Empire had been transformed, and at the same time the local civil administration had been combined with the local military command. It will be convenient to investigate the origin of the new term 'théma' before examining the new geographical areas of administration which had now come to be called by the same new name—'themata'—as the old army-corps whose commanders had become the new administrative areas' governors.

Constantine Porphyrogenitus correctly observes that the word 'théma' is Greek, not Latin.[1] He might have added that, unlike the other Greek word 'stratós', which it had superseded, the word 'théma' is not the Greek equivalent for any Latin term in the technical vocabulary of the Roman Army, and this is remarkable, considering that, as Zilliacus points out, the Roman Army had always been used as an instrument for both linguistic and psychological Romanization,[2] and that the military and legal fields had been those in which Roman-Latin influence in the East Roman Empire had been the most persistent.[3]

In introducing the term 'théma', Constantine Porphyrogenitus observes that it 'denotes the act of placing (ἀπὸ τῆς θέσεως ὀνομαζό-μενον)'. There was originally a distinction of meaning between these two Greek forms of the verbal noun. The form in '-ις' (e.g. πρᾶξις) signified an action or process; the form in '-μα' (e.g. πρᾶγμα) signified a product of action, which might be something static and concrete. Since the verb τιθέναι means 'to place', the noun 'thésis' should mean 'placing' and the noun 'théma' a 'placement' or a 'receptacle'. It means 'receptacle' in the modern Cretan Greek compound word βοϊδόθεμα (cow-byre),[4] and on this analogy it might mean a military unit's winter-quarters[5] or even the barracks in which the troops are housed.[6] However, its actual meaning is a military corps (exercitus, στρατός) and eventually an administrative district governed by the commander of a corps that was stationed there. 'Placement'—the alternative meaning to 'receptacle' for the word 'théma'—might be either a placement in a topographical

[1] Op. cit., p. 13.   [2] Zilliacus, op. cit., pp. 128–9.

[3] Op. cit., p. 170.

[4] See J. Karayannopulos, *Die Entstehung der byzantinischen Themenordnung* (Munich, 1959, Beck), p. 90.

[5] See W.-H. Haussig, 'Anfänge der Themenordnung', in Fr. Altheim and R. Stiehl, *Finanzgeschichte der Spätantike* (Frankfurt a.M., 1957, Klostermann), pp. 82–114, on pp. 86, 89, 109.

[6] This is St. P. Kyriakídês's interpretation in Ἐπετ. Ἑτ. Βυζ., Σπ. 23 (1953), pp. 392–4, cited by F. Dölger, 'Zur Ableitung des byzantinischen Verwaltungsterminus θέμα', in *Historia*, 4. Band (1953), pp. 189–98, on pp. 189 and 193.

location, i.e. a cantonment, or a placement in a ledger, i.e. an entry or booking.

Ostrogorsky[1] construes 'théma' as 'placement' in the topographical meaning, and he was followed at first by Pertusi.[2] But the actual meaning is not this either. Théma is used to mean, not cantonment, but, first, the corps that is cantoned and eventually also the district of which the corps-commander has come to be the governor. Dölger[3] opts for the meaning 'entry in a ledger'. He notes that, in the vocabulary of the East Roman bureaucracy, a θέσις is a synonym for a κῶδιξ, and that this means a dossier containing a numbered series of documents all dealing with the same piece of official business. Θέματα are 'Festsetzungen' ('entries', 'bookings')—in the case in point, they are bookings in the λογοθέσιον τῶν στρατιωτικῶν. The θέματα that were entered in the dossiers of this registry were the military units of the East Roman Army. In the eyes of East Roman officials resident in Constantinople, the realities were the entries in their ledgers, not the corps of soldiers for whom these entries stood, and not the districts that the commanders of these corps eventually came to administer. In the sight of the Central Government, the troops were ledger-entries (θέματα) or numbers (numeri, ἀριθμοί). Dölger's explanation of the term 'théma' is convincing. It has been adopted by Karayanno-pulos,[4] by Ahrweiler,[5] and, on second thoughts, by Pertusi too.[6]

In the ledgers of the East Roman Central Government's bureaux in Constantinople the term 'théma' must have come to be used to mean 'army-corps' after the government departments at Constantinople which were responsible for the East Roman Army's organization and pay had taken to doing their business, and keeping their records, in Greek instead of Latin, and this must have happened very soon after the virtual destruction of the Latin-speaking part of the population of the Balkan Peninsula through the Slav invasions, under Avar leadership, which overwhelmed the Eastern Illyricum and Thrace in the years 581/2–586/7.[7]

In the Army itself, the use of Latin military terminology evidently survived longer than in the government departments at Constantinople that dealt with military affairs. The author of 'Mavríkios's' *Stratêghikón*,

---

[1] In 'Die wirtschaftlichen und sozialen Entwicklungsgrundlagen', p. 130.

[2] In his edition of *De Them.*, p. 111.

[3] In 'Zur Ableitung', pp. 194–6.

[4] In op. cit., pp. 89–97, 'Die Ableitung des Wortes Thema', on pp. 95–6.

[5] In 'L'Asie Mineure et les invasions arabes', p. 20, n. 4.

[6] A. Pertusi, 'La Formation des thèmes byzantins', in *Berichte zum XI. Internazionalen Byzantinisten-Kongress München 1958*, vol. i (Munich, 1958, Beck), pp. 1–40, on pp. 16, 23, 24. Pertusi here cites on p. 16 Leo VI's *Taktiká*, Dhiat. 18, § 149, col. 988: τῶν τετρακισχιλίων ὁ ἀριθμός ἐπιλέκτων.

[7] See II, 1 (iii) (a), pp. 71–6, and Annex III, pp. 633–6. See also Zilliacus, op. cit., pp. 21 and 129.

which was written *circa* 600,[1] notes, in his introduction,[2] that, for the sake of clarity, he has made frequent use of 'Latin and other (non-Greek) terms that are established, by age-old practice, in military usage'.[3] All the same, the book itself was written and published in Greek, and the author felt himself called upon, at the outset,[4] to apologize for his Latinisms on the ground that he was producing a handbook for practical use, not a literary work. This shows that in the Army *circa* 600 the Latin terminology was still the normal current one, though the Latin terms now had recognized Greek equivalents.[5] But it also shows that the mother-tongue of the members of the officers' corps was already Greek, and that they had had a Greek literary education of a standard that made Latinisms and other barbarisms eyesores for them.[6]

However, at the time when 'Mavríkios's' *Stratêghikón* was published, the term 'théma' had not yet found its way into the East Roman Army's Greek terminology. In the one place in which the word occurs in Scheffer's text of 'Mavríkios',[7] this is manifestly a slip made by a copyist writing at a date at which the word had become familiar. In the corresponding passage in Leo VI's *Taktiká*[8]—a passage in which, as in so many others, Leo is copying 'Mavríkios' verbatim—the word used is not 'théma'; it is 'tághma'; and this must have been the word here in the original text of the corresponding passage of 'Mavríkios'.[9] If the original had read 'théma', Leo VI certainly would not have substituted 'tághma' for it, considering that, by Leo VI's time, 'théma' had become, long since, the official term for both an army-corps and an army-corps district. More-over, the unit with which 'Mavríkios' is concerned in this passage is a 'vándon', for which he uses the word 'tághma' as a synonym,[10] and the 'vándon' was the smallest unit in the East Roman Army in both 'Mavríkios's' and Leo VI's time,[11] whereas the term 'théma', when it came into use, was always used to denote the largest unit, namely the 'stratós' (exercitus) that was commanded by a stratêghós (magister militum).[12]

---

[1] For the date, see Zilliacus, op. cit., p. 120.   [2] On p. 3 of Scheffer, p. 44 Mihăescu.
[3] ʽΡωμαϊκοῖς πολλάκις καὶ ἄλλαις ἐν τῇ στρατιωτικῇ συνηθείᾳ τετριμμένοις κεχρήμεθα λέξεσι.
[4] p. 3. Scheffer, p. 44 Mihăescu.   [5] Zilliacus, p. 133.   [6] Zilliacus, ibid.
[7] Part 1, chap. 2, p. 25 Scheffer.   [8] Dhiat. 6, § 18, col. 725.
[9] Τάγμα, not θέμα, is, in fact, the reading in Mihăescu's text, p. 54. Mihăescu does not mention Scheffer's reading in his apparatus. Presumably the word here is τάγμα, not θέμα, in all the five manuscripts on which Mihăescu's text is based.
[10] 'Mavríkios's' 'tághma' meaning 'vándon' is to be distinguished from 'tághma' meaning one of the regiments of the household troops. Theophanes, p. 437, mentions the tághmata in this second sense, sub A.M. 6257 (November 764). He contrasts them, on p. 442, with τοῖς ἔξω θέμασι, i.e. the army-corps districts, sub A.M. 6259. Cf. p. 449, sub A.M. 6268, where he contrasts τῶν θεμάτων with τῶν ἔσω ταγμάτων.
[11] 'Mavríkios', Part 1, chap. 3, p. 27 Scheffer, p. 56 Mihăescu; chap. 4, p. 30 Scheffer, p. 58 Mihăescu; Leo VI, Dhiat. 4, §§ 2–3, col. 700, and § 6, col. 701.
[12] This conclusive proof that the word 'théma' did not occur in the original text of 'Mavríkios' is given by Dölger, 'Zur Ableitung', p. 191, n. 1.

At about what date did the term 'théma', which had originated as a technical term in the registries of government departments, become current in the ordinary vocabulary of the Greek language? This had certainly happened by Constantine Porphyrogenitus's time; for Constantine evidently assumed that his readers would know, without any explanation being required, that 'théma' meant 'army-corps' and 'army-corps district' in the salary list that had been compiled in Leo VI's reign, and that it had the same pair of meanings in Constantine's own treatise *De Thematibus*. We can indeed be sure that the term 'théma' was already well established in ordinary usage in the life-time of the chronicler Theophanes, who was born in the reign of Constantine V (741–75) and who died in 817. Theophanes uses this term 'théma' in recording events in and after, though not before, Heraclius's reign (610–41). However, in using the term already apropos of Heraclius's reign, it seems probable that Theophanes is committing an anachronism.

Heraclius's own panegyrist, George of Pisidia, never uses the word; he always uses some Greek equivalent of the Latin 'exercitus'.[1] Moreover, Heraclius himself does not use 'théma' in his kélefsis of April 628 to the Senate.[2] When Theophanes, in a passage for which George of Pisidia is his source,[3] describes[4] Heraclius's start on his counter-offensive campaign against the Persians, and when he makes Heraclius arrive ἐπὶ τὰς τῶν θεμάτων χώρας on landing at Pýlai on the south shore of the Gulf of Ismit[5] after travelling to there by sea from Constantinople, manifestly Theophanes is thinking in terms of τὰ βασιλικὰ ταξείδια of the post-Heraclian age, as described, for instance, by Constantine Porphyrogenitus.[6] The τῶν θεμάτων χῶραι, i.e. the districts occupied by the Asiatic army corps, are here contrasted with the metropolitan area, in which the troops were not the thémata but the tághmata, and which was administered by a civil governor, the Prefect of the City of Constantinople.

In this passage, Theophanes's anachronism is obvious.[7] We may perhaps infer[8] that Theophanes is likewise using the terminology of his own day, not of Heraclius's day, when he says[9] that in 611 Heraclius found, 'in all the thémata', only two survivors of the soldiers who had marched with Phokás against Maurice in 602, and when he writes of 'the three tourmárkhai of the Persians',[10] and of the [*sic*] tourmárkhês of the

---

[1] Pertusi, 'La Formation des thèmes', p. 19.
[2] *Chron. Pasch.*, cited by Pertusi, ibid., p. 20.						[3] Pertusi, ibid.
[4] On p. 303, sub A.M. 6113, April 622.
[5] For the location of this Pylai, see *De Them.*, p. 25.
[6] See *De Caer.*, pp. 444–508, discussed in II, 6, pp. 300–2.
[7] W. Ensslin, 'Der Kaiser Herakleios und die Themenverfassung', in *Byzantinische Zeitschrift*, vol. xlvi (1953), pp. 362–8, on pp. 364–5, in agreement with Baynes. Cf. Haussig in loc. cit., pp. 85–6, with p. 86, n. 19.
[8] With Ensslin, ibid., p. 366.
[9] Theophanes, p. 300, sub A.M. 6103.						[10] pp. 318–19, sub A.M. 6118.

Armeniakoí'.[1] So far as we know, the Persians never had any military officers bearing the Greek title 'tourmárkhai'; and in the East Roman army-corps of Leo VI's day, as described by Leo in his *Taktiká*,[2] the tourmárkhai were identical with the merárkhai of 'Mavríkios',[3] and a corps consisted of more than a single toúrma. The standard number of toúrmai in a corps was three, and there had likewise been three mérê in a corps in the organization of the East Roman Army *circa* 600 as described by 'Mavrikios'.[4] It seems unlikely that there was ever a time when the corps of the magister militum per Armeniam (*alias* the στρατηγὸς τῶν Ἀρμενιακῶν) consisted of a single toúrma or méros only.

In contrast to Theophanes, his contemporary fellow chronicler the Patriarch Nikêphóros (Nicephorus) never uses the term 'théma'. Nikêphóros's Greek equivalent for the Latin 'exercitus' is στρατός or στράτευμα, as has been noted already;[5] but it does not follow from this that the term 'théma' was not current at the time when Nikêphóros and Theophanes were writing their respective chronicles. While Theophanes seems to have used the terminology of his own day anachronistically, Nikêphóros seems to have been a purist who eschewed even well-established neologisms.

Thus there is no conclusive evidence for the date at which the word 'théma' became the normal term for 'army-corps'. The older term 'stratós' did not cease to be correct, though it may gradually have become unusual. The most that we can say is that the term 'théma' seems to have become current in the course of the eighth century. Fortunately the dating of the change of nomenclature is less important than the dating of the administrative change from the Diocletianic–Constantinian dispensation, under which military commands and civil administration were kept in different pairs of hands, to the regime of Leo VI's and Constantine VII Porphyrogenitus's day, under which the commander of an army-corps was *ex officio* the governor of a district in which the corps was stationed and from among whose population it was recruited. On this point we have rather more, and more definite, information.

The earliest important recorded case of a reversion from the Diocletianic–Constantinian dispensation to the Augustan dispensation is Justinian I's creation, noted already,[6] of a post—the quaestor Iustinianus exercitûs —in which a military command and the administration of an area were united in the same pair of hands. This curious arrangement, under which a military governor, stationed at Odhêssós in Lower Moesia, administered not only Lower Moesia and Scythia but the distant provinces Cyclades, Caria, and Cyprus, was still in existence in 575 in the reign of Justin II

[1] p. 325, sub A.M. 6118.   [2] Dhiat. 4, § 6, col. 701.
[3] 'Mavríkios', Part I, chap. 3, p. 27 Scheffer, p. 56 Mihǎescu.
[4] *Stratêghikón*, Part I, chap. 4, p. 31 Scheffer, p. 58 Mihǎescu.
[5] On p. 227, with footnotes 4 and 5.
[6] On p. 226.

(565–78),[1] but evidence is lacking for confirmation of the conjecture that there was an unbroken continuity between this administrative innovation of Justinian I's and one or other of the non-territorial naval commands and the territorial naval thémata that were created at disputable dates in and after the seventh century.[2] It is, however, certain that the Emperor Justinian I also created the post of praetor of the island of Sicily, and that, here too, he invested the newly created officer with both civil and military powers.[3] It is also certain the Emperor Maurice (582–602) gave the commander-in-chief of the troops in all the Empire's surviving holdings in Italy the supreme authority over the civil administration as well, and that he signalized this newfangled combination of military and civil powers by creating for it the new title 'exarch' ('viceroy'). A parallel exarchate of Africa, invested with the same combination of powers,[4] was created at about the same time.[5] Maurice's innovation had no direct effect on the combination of powers in other parts of the East Roman Empire; for, by 751, nothing was left of either of the two western exarchates except the island of Sardinia. But these four examples show that the innovation eventually embodied in the East Roman Empire's territorial thémata had already been introduced, in four special cases, before the term 'théma' itself had been coined; and in Sicily, which remained under East Roman rule till the ninth century, the Justinianean stratêghós could become the military governor of a territorial théma without any change at all in his powers or even in his title.

Like the quaestor Iustinianus exercitûs and the praetor Iustinianus Siciliae and the magistri militum per Italiam and per Africam, the magistri militum ($\sigma\tau\rho\alpha\tau\eta\gamma o\acute{\iota}$) per Orientem, per Armeniam, per Thraciam, and in praesenti, whose corps were concentrated in Asia Minor under pressure of the Arabs' assault, eventually acquired the non-military additional function of serving as the governors of the areas in which their corps had come to be stationed. Was this a sudden and deliberate replacement of the previous Diocletianic–Constantinian civilian provincial organization, or did it come about gradually and unintentionally in response to the logic of events? In the case of three, at least, out of the four original

---

[1] As the ἀρχὴ τῶν νήσων καὶ τῶν ἐπὶ Σκυθίας τε καὶ Μυσίας στρατιωτικῶν ταγμάτων of Justin II's Novel No. 163.

[2] Diehl, *Études byzantines*, pp. 290–1; Karayannopulos, op. cit., p. 68; Haussig in loc. cit., p. 88, n. 32, see here the origin of the Karavisianoí.

[3] See p. 266 with footnote 7.

[4] Diehl, op. cit., p. 277, followed by P. Goubert: *Byzance avant l'Islam*, vol. ii, Part II: *Rome, Byzance, et Carthage* (Paris, 1965, Picard) chap. 2, section 1. Goubert's date for the elevation of the magister militum per Italiam to the status of exarch is 584 (p. 35). He holds that the conferment of the same title on the magister militum per Africam likewise signalized his investiture with civil as well as military authority (p. 183).

[5] According to Karayannopulos, op. cit., p. 69, the date of the earliest mention of the exarch of Africa is 594.

thémata in Asia Minor, we have to distinguish between the withdrawal of these corps from former East Roman territories that had been lost— in Asia to the Arabs and in Europe to the Slavs—and the subsequent acquisition, by their commanders, of civil administrative functions in addition to their military duties.

The withdrawal of the Anatolikoí to the north-west side of the Távros Range and the withdrawal of the Armeniakoí from those of their former stations that had lain beyond the east and south bank of the upper Euphrates must have been sudden, though it will certainly not have been deliberate. The Anatolikoí must have evacuated the whole of their former area in Palestine, Syria, and Mesopotamia when Heraclius abandoned Antioch to the Arabs *circa* 636; the Armeniakoí must have withdrawn to their stations to the west and north of the upper Euphrates, and to other territories, still farther west, at least as early as 653, when Theodore Reshtuni made a treaty with Muʻāwīyah on behalf of all the Armenians—i.e. those of Persian Persarmenia, those of Roman Pers-armenia, and those of Roman Armenia as well.[1] The transfer of the Thrakěsioi from Thrace to western Asia Minor is likely to have been equally sudden, though this transfer, unlike the other two, must have been deliberate. But there is no evidence that the sudden migration of these three corps to Asia Minor was the occasion on which their respective commanders became the governors of the areas in Asia Minor in which the three corps came to rest.

Such evidence as we have indicates that the investment of these corps commanders, and of the commander of the Opsíkion as well, with civil administrative authority, in addition to their original military function, was not only subsequent to their migration but was also, not a sudden event, but a gradual process. Constantine Porphyrogenitus is failing, in the case of the théma Armeniakoí, to distinguish between the migration of this corps to its new territory and the affixing on this territory of the Armeniac corps' name after the commander of the corps had come to be also the territory's governor. Constantine notes correctly that the term 'théma Armeniakoí', as the name for a territory in north-eastern Asia Minor, was unknown to all the ancient authors, down to Procopius, Agathias, Menander, and Hesychius inclusive, and he therefore conjec-tures that this territory acquired the name 'théma Armeniakoí' only in and after the time of Heraclius.[2] The Armeniac army-corps did evacuate Justinian I's Armeniae III and IV and settle in his Helenopontus and perhaps in his Cappadociae, besides continuing to occupy Justinian's Armeniae I and II, and this migration did probably take place either

[1] Laurent, op. cit., p. 33; Pertusi, 'La Formation', pp. 34–5.
[2] δοκῶ δὲ εἰπεῖν ὅτι ἐπὶ Ἡρακλείου τοῦ βασιλέως καὶ τῶν κάτω χρόνων τὴν τοιαύτην προσηγορίαν ἐκληρονόμησεν (*De Them.*, p. 18).

before the end of Heraclius's reign or very soon after. On the other hand, the Justinianean provinces that had thus become this corps' new habitat probably retained not only their previous names, but also their previous civil administrations, for an appreciable time longer.

Among modern students of the subject, Ostrogorsky is in a minority in holding that the territorial thémata were substituted for the Diocletianic–Constantinian and the Justinianean civil provinces by Heraclius,[1] that the στρατιωτικὰ κτήματα were allotted by Heraclius as part of the same sudden revolutionary act of administrative and social reform,[2] and that Heraclius carried out this revolution, not after the restoration of peace in 628, but before he embarked on his counter-offensive in 622.[3] Stein, too, attributes to Heraclius the creation of at least one territorial théma, the Obsequium,[4] and also the allotment of the στρατιωτικὰ κτήματα, though he dates this allotment 629–34, not 622.[5] Most of the other modern authorities hold that, in Asia Minor in and after the seventh century, the army-corps in their new stations and the old provinces, with their civilian administrative staffs, co-existed for some time before the army-corps commanders took over the civilian governors' former functions. This is the view taken by Karayannopulos,[6] by Gelzer,[7] by Antoniadis-Bibicou,[8] by Enslin[9] in agreement with Baynes, by Pertusi,[10] by Haussig,[11] by Dölger,[12] by Stratós.[13] There is, in fact, evidence that in Italy and Africa[14] and the Eastern Illyricum, as well as in Asia Minor, the old prefectures[15] and provinces, with their civilian officials, did not suddenly disappear.

In Italy, for example, where the magister militum per Italiam had been elevated to the status of an exarch with supreme civil as well as military powers, the Justinianean praetorian prefect of Italy continued—now in subordination to the exarch—to exist until at least as late as 602.[16] Karayannopulos finds evidence for his survival in 641 and 681.[17] Similarly, the praetorian prefect of Africa survived, as a subordinate official,

[1] Ostrogorsky, 'Die wirtschaftlichen und sozialen Entwicklungsgrundlagen', p. 130.

[2] Ostrogorsky, 'Agrarian Conditions', p. 207.

[3] Ostrogorsky, 'Sur la date de la composition du Livre des Thèmes et sur l'époque de la constitution des premiers thèmes d'Asie Mineure', in *Byzantion*, tome xxiii (1935), pp. 31–66, on pp. 46–56.   [4] *Studien*, pp. 130–1 and 134.   [5] Op. cit., pp. 134–5.

[6] Karayannopulos, op. cit., p. 9, p. 29, n. 6, pp. 35, 58, 59, 70–1, 88.

[7] *Die Genesis*, pp. 8 and 65–72.

[8] *Études d'histoire maritime de Byzance*, p. 53. Here the author says that the thémata became territorial between 622 and 665, but on p. 118 she says that the non-naval territorial thémata were created by Heraclius.

[9] W. Ennslin in loc. cit.

[10] In his introduction to his edition of *De Them.*, pp. 103–11, and in 'La Formation', pp. 14–15.

[11] In loc. cit., p. 87.   [12] 'Zur Ableitung', p. 190.   [13] Op. cit., pp. 274–6.
[14] See Gelzer, op. cit., pp. 7–8.   [15] See Diehl, op. cit., p. 288.
[16] Goubert, op. cit., vol. ii, Part II, chap. 2, pp. 56–7.
[17] Karayannopulos, op. cit., p. 56.

after the magister militum per Africam had been made an exarch with the supreme civil power that had been conferred on his counterpart in Italy.[1] The praetorian prefect of the Eastern Illyricum is mentioned ten times in the *Sancti Demetrii Miracula*, Book I,[2] which was written by John, Archbishop of Thessaloníkê, *circa* 600.[3] The date of the latest mention, in East Roman legislation, of a praetorian prefect of Oriens is 629.[4] Yet this official still figures in 680 in the Acts of the Sixth Ecumenical Council,[5] though, by then, the office must have been a sinecure for at least forty-five years.

Archbishop John's 'Macedonians', 'Thessalians', and 'Achaeans'[6] are the inhabitants of the three Roman provinces Macedonia, Thessalia, and Achaïa, and therefore these provinces must have been going concerns when John was writing.[7] The Acts of the Sixth Ecumenical Council of 680 and of the Quinisext Council of 693 show that the Old Diocletianic–Constantinian provinces survived at these dates in the territories that the East Roman Empire then still retained.[8] According to Gelzer,[9] the bishops who signed the Acts of these two councils were signing as representatives of the civil provinces, not of their own ecclesiastical sees. The province Bithynia[10] was still in existence in 694–6.[11] As late as the reign of Anastasius II (713–15), some civilian provinces appear still to have survived, side by side with some already established army-corps districts. Theophanes records[12] that Anastasius 'appointed highly efficient commanders (στρα-τηγούς) to the cavalry (καβαλλαρικά) thémata, and highly educated (commanders) to the civilian (πολιτικά) (thémata)'.

---

[1] Goubert, ibid., p. 199; Karayannopulos, op. cit., p. 56, finds evidence for the praetorian prefect of Africa's survival in 645.

[2] See Lemerle, 'Invasions et migrations', p. 271, with his list of the mentions on p. 271, n. 2. Cf. Karayannopulos, op. cit., p. 56. See *S.D. Miracula*, cols. 1204, 1217, and 1220 (the πραιτόριον of the ὕπαρχος (i.e. the prefect) at Thessaloníkê near the church of St. Demetrius), col. 1220 again, col. 1260 (four times), cols. 1265, 1268, 1272, 1276 (an official who was in charge of the Δακικὸν σκρίνιον of the ὕπαρχος of Illyricum), col. 1292–3 (the staff of the πραιτόριον of the prefect), col. 1293 (the heads of the σκρίνια of the prefecture of Illyricum). The ἐπάρχους Θεσσαλονίκης in col. 1260 seems, from the context, to be the praetorian prefect of Illyricum whose seat was now at Thessaloníkê. On the other hand, Lemerle, ibid., p. 272, holds that the three mentions of a ὕπαρχος (not ἔπαρχος) in *Miracula*, Book II, refer, not to the prefect of Eastern Illyricum, who had probably ceased to exist by the time when the various components of this book were written, but to the governor of the city of Thessaloníkê (e.g. col. 1340, the ὕπαρχος who arrests Pervoúnd, and cols. 1365–8, the ὕπαρχος on the occasion, at an earlier date, when Thessaloníkê was in danger from the repatriated descendants of the deportees).

[3] Lemerle, ibid., p. 271.   [4] Karayannopulos, op. cit., p. 55, n. 5.

[5] Διοικητὴς τῶν Ἀνατολικῶν Ἐπαρχιῶν (Karayannopulos, op. cit., p. 56).

[6] *S.D. Miracula*, cols. 1272 and 1292.

[7] Charanis, 'Hellas in the Greek sources of the sixth, seventh, and eighth centuries', p. 171.

[8] Gelzer, op. cit., p. 65.   [9] Ibid. Cf. Pertusi, 'La Formation', p. 28.

[10] Ἐπαρχία τῶν Βιθυνῶν.   [11] Pertusi in his edition of *De Them.*, p. 110.

[12] On p. 383, sub A.M. 6206.

The extant seals of the kommerkiárioi (the officials charged with the local supervision of trade) provide evidence of the transition from the old civilian provincial organization to the new organization in the form of army-corps districts. The inscriptions on the kommerkiárioi's seals name the administrative districts for which the kommerkiários was responsible, and on seventh-century seals dating from the reign of Constans II (641–68) the districts named are those of the old provinces:[1] e.g. Cappadociae I and II, Lycaonia, Pisidia, Lycia, Caria, Asia.[2] Towards the close of the seventh century the names of other old provinces—e.g. 'the Islands',[3] and Galatia[4]—still appear, but there also now appears the name 'Ellás',[5] which was never the name of a Roman province but which was the name of one of the earliest of the East Roman army-corps districts in Europe. The most informative of all these later-seventh-century seals of kommerkiárioi are those bearing the name of the Armeniakoí, i.e. one of the three army-corps that had been drawn or pushed out of their previous stations by the Arabs' onslaught on the East Roman Empire. Seals bearing this name are dated 650/1, 665/6,[6] and 668/9.[7] These seals show that, by the dates at which they were made, the Armeniakoí had become an administrative district, besides being an army-corps. The same seals also show that, in their case at least, the district for which a kommerkiários was responsible had been made to fit the new administrative map of the East Roman Empire.

This was one of the ways in which a transition was made from the old civilian provincial administration to the new military one. An old set of civilian officials was retained to perform its old functions within the new administrative boundaries. Another device for easing the change was to

---

[1] See Diehl, *Études byzantines*, p. 288; Gelzer, op. cit., p. 71; Pertusi, 'La Formation', p. 36, n. 163; Antoniadis-Bibicou, op. cit., p. 82.

[2] See the following entries in G. Schlumberger: *Sigillographie de l'Empire byzantin* (Paris, 1884, Leroux): p. 279, a seal of Peter, kommerkiários of Cappadocia, Lycaonia, and Pisidia, and a seal of Kosmás, kommerkiários of Cappadocia II, both dated the third and fourth indictions in the reign of Constans II (644/5 and 645/6, or 645/6 and 646/7; alternatively 659/60 and 660/1, or 660/1 and 661/2); p. 735, a seal of George, γενικὸν κομμερκιαρίων ἀποθήκης Ἀσίας [καὶ] Καρίας, dated the fifth and sixth indictions in the reign of Constans II (646/7 and 647/8 or 647/8 and 648/9; alternatively 661/2 and 662/3 or 662/3 and 663/4); p. 264, two specimens of a seal of George, kommerkiários of Caria, Lycia, Rhodes, and Chersonese, dated respectively the eighth and ninth indictions in the reign of Constans II (649/50 and 650/1 or 650/1 and 651/2; alternatively 664/5 and 665/6 or 665/6 and 666/7).

[3] Schlumberger, op. cit., p. 195, No. 12, under théma Aiyaíon Pélaghos. This is a seal of the Imperial Customs Service for a district which is, apparently, not this East Roman théma but the Diocletianic-Constantinian Roman province of the Islands. For this province see A. H. M. Jones, *The Later Roman Empire, 284–602*, vol. i, (Oxford, 1964, Blackwell), p. 43.

[4] Schlumberger, op. cit., p. 303, a seal κουμερκιαρίου ἀποθήκης Γαλατήας. This seal bears no date. Schlumberger dates it in either the seventh or the eighth century.

[5] Schlumberger, op. cit., p. 165.

[6] Antoniadis-Bibicou, op. cit., p. 81. Cf. Karayannopulos, op. cit., p. 51.

[7] Pertusi, 'La Formation', p. 36, n. 163. According to Pertusi in this passage, 668/9 is the earliest date of a kommerkiários's seal bearing the district name 'Armeniakón'.

create new sets of officials for these new administrative areas of which the army-corps commanders had become the governors. 'The proconsuls and prefects of the thémata' (ἀνθυπάτους τῶν θεμάτων καὶ ἐπάρχους), accompanied by '*the* Praetorian Prefect' [*sic*] and 'the Kouaístor', appear, in the next batch of dignitaries after the corps commanders (στρατηγούς), in the libretto in Constantine Porphyrogenitus's *De Caerimoniis* for the celebration of the Feast of Pentecost;[1] the same functionaries also appear in the *Taktikón Uspenski*, which was compiled about half way through the ninth century.[2] However, we do not know whether these two sets of civilian thematic officials were ever more than ciphers. They are not mentioned by Leo VI in any of the passages in his *Taktiká* in which he describes the administration of the army-corps districts. Nor do they figure in any of the Imperial novels or in any of the versions of the Byzantine chronicle.

How did the transition from the Diocletianic–Constantinian to the thematic provincial administrative system come about? Gelzer, like most other students of the subject, rejects the conjecture that the thematic system was substituted for its predecessor by an act of the Emperor Heraclius. Gelzer, too, believes that there was a chronological overlap between two systems. However, he also believes that, when the thematic system had taken shape, the administrative functions which the corps-commanders had gradually acquired were ratified 'by an epoch-making legislative act in the eighth century',[3] and he holds that the old civilian administration was abolished by the Emperor Leo III.[4] However, Gelzer admits[5] that he cannot cite any direct evidence for these guesses, and they are indeed no more convincing than the guess that the change was made by a similar sudden and comprehensive act of Heraclius's a century earlier. It seems more likely that the old system was not ever formally abolished and that the new one was not ever formally substituted for it.[6] 'A Byzance, comme en beaucoup d'autres pays, c'est le provisoire, qui avait la chance de durer.'[7] There is, of course, no doubt that, for practical purposes, the thematic system had become, by Leo VI's time, the only one that was a going concern; but it does not follow from this that the new system had ever been formally instituted and inaugurated.

It is conceivable that the Diocletianic–Constantinian system of civilian provincial administration gradually faded out in the course of the seventh century, but that appointments still continued to be made to the posts after these posts had become sinecures which no longer carried any obligation to perform an active administrative service, and which were

---

[1] *De Caer.*, Book I, chap. 9, p. 61.   [2] Pertusi, 'La Formation', pp. 12 and 28–9.
[3] Gelzer, *Die Genesis*, p. 3.   [4] Op. cit., p. 75.   [5] On pp. 4 and 77.
[6] See Lemerle, 'La Chronique improprement dite de Monemvasie', p. 30, n. 47.
[7] Goubert, *Byzance avant l'Islam*, vol. ii, Part II, p. 36.

therefore probably also no longer remunerated with more than a nominal salary. The sinecure-holders may have continued, nevertheless, to figure in successive Imperial klêtorolóyia (schedules of the official order of precedence at Imperial functions) for another quarter of a millennium, until the schedule was brought up to date, at the end of the ninth century, by the Imperial protospathários and atriklínês Philótheos. In the introductory note to his revised klêtorolóyion,[1] Philótheos refers to 'the many titles of offices that have become obsolete in the course of time' (αἱ πολλαὶ τῶν ἀξιωμάτων ἀμαυρωθεῖσαι τῷ χρόνῳ προσκλήσεις), and he notes that, in compiling his own up-to-date schedule, he has 'deliberately omitted, not indeed all his predecessors' entries, but those which time had made obsolete' (τὰς τῶν ἀρχαίων ἐκθέσεις οὐχὶ πάσας, ἀλλ' ὅσας ὁ χρόνος ἀμαυρωθῆναι ἐποίησεν, ἑκόντι παρεδράμομεν). In thus pruning the klêtorolóyion to cut out dead wood, Philótheos was acting in line with the Emperor Leo VI. In his Novel No. 46,[2] Leo VI abolished the municipal curiae and the obligations and prerogatives of the decurions; in his Novel No. 47[3] he abolished the election of praetors by the Senate and of duumviri by the municipal decurions. In both novels, Leo VI justifies his abrogation of traditional institutions on the ground that these had become obsolete. Moreover, in his preface to his *Taktiká*,[4] Leo notes: 'In many cases I have clarified Greek military terms that are out of date, and I have translated Latin terms. I have substituted other terms that have become customary in military circles. My purpose has been to enable the reader to comprehend the meaning clearly.'

In this passage, as in so many others, Leo VI is modelling himself on 'Mavríkios', but, in this particular case, with a difference. In 'Mavríkios's' day, *circa* 600, the technical terminology of the East Roman Army was still Latin, though Greek was already the vernacular language of the officers and men.[5] In the course of the next three centuries, Greek had superseded Latin to a large extent even in the East Roman military vocabulary, and, though Latin had not been entirely eliminated, the process of Graecization had gone far enough by this time to move Leo VI to use the current Greek terminology in order to achieve his model, 'Mavríkios's', objective of producing a handbook that would be of practical use.[6] Though Leo VI was in many ways a pedant, practicality was his ideal, as he declares in this passage of his *Taktiká* and in his Novels Nos. 46 and 47. It therefore seems probable that the Diocletianic–Constantinian civilian provincial organization received its quietus in Leo VI's reign (886–912), It also seems probable that Leo VI did not

---

[1] In *De Caer.*, Book II, chap. 52, pp. 702 and 704 Bonn, pp. 131 and 132 Bury.
[2] Noailles and Dain, pp. 182–4.
[3] Ibid., pp. 184–7.   [4] Preface, § 5, col. 676.   [5] See pp. 232–3.
[6] See the passage of 'Mavríkios' that has been cited on p. 233.

abolish the old order by legislation. Its abolition is not decreed in any extant novel of Leo's own, or in any of the extant novels of his predecessors or successors. Leo VI seems to have left it to Philótheos to do the job by the anodyne method of omitting the titles of the officials of the ancient civilian provincial administration from Philótheos's new edition of the Imperial klêtorolóyion.

The creation of two new sets of civilian officials—the 'proconsuls' and the 'prefects' of the thémata—perhaps indicates that the Imperial Government had felt some misgivings when it had acquiesced in the assumption of administrative as well as military powers by the commanders of the army-corps. This is also indicated by Constantine Porphyrogenitus's way of describing the effect on the Empire of the combination of local administrative and military powers in the same pairs of hands. As Constantine sees the course of past history in retrospect,[1] the Romans' achievement of uniting formerly independent peoples under a single government[2] had been undone when the thémata—in the sense of districts administered by army-corps commanders—had come into existence, in the days of Heraclius's successors, as a result of the Arabs' onslaught and of the abandonment, by the Emperors, of their original practice of taking the field in person as commanders-in-chief.

Until the reign of the Emperor Justinian, all mankind was under a single government, and this unity was maintained till the reign of the Emperor Maurice—as witness Belisarius, who was commander-in-chief ($\mu o\nu o\sigma\tau\rho\acute{a}\tau\eta\gamma os$) of the whole of the East[3] . . . Naturally, when the Emperor was with the Army, there was no question of appointing any general ($\sigma\tau\rho\alpha\tau\eta\gamma\acute{o}\nu$) . . . The whole conduct of war depended on the Emperor's will, and the whole people looked to the Emperor solely and exclusively. But when the Emperors gave up going on campaign, then they instituted local generals and thémata ($\sigma\tau\rho\alpha\tau\eta\gamma o\grave{v}s$ $\kappa\alpha\grave{\iota}$ $\theta\acute{e}\mu\alpha\tau\alpha$ $\delta\iota\omega\rho\acute{\iota}\sigma\alpha\nu\tau o$), and this is what the Roman Empire has ended in ($\epsilon\grave{\iota}s$ $\tau o\hat{v}\tau o$ $\kappa\alpha\tau\acute{e}\lambda\eta\xi\epsilon\nu$) down to the present day[4] . . . Mankind was divided up [again, this time] into thémata ($\delta\iota\eta\rho\acute{e}\theta\eta\sigma\alpha\nu$, $\kappa\alpha\grave{\iota}$ $\dot{\epsilon}\gamma\acute{e}\nu o\nu\tau o$ $\theta\acute{e}\mu\alpha\tau\alpha$), when the Roman Empire began to be mutilated and truncated and reduced to a small compass by the Arabs[5] . . . When the Arabs began to take the offensive against the Romans and to devastate their villages and cities, the Emperors of that day were compelled to cut up the [previously] unitary Empire into small fragments[6] . . . The successors of Heraclius cut up their Empire into small fragments—and cut up, in particular, the military formations ($\tau\grave{a}$ $\tau\hat{\omega}\nu$ $\sigma\tau\rho\alpha$-$\tau\iota\omega\tau\hat{\omega}\nu$ $\tau\acute{a}\gamma\mu\alpha\tau\alpha$)—because they had no place or means for exercising their own Imperial authority.[7]

Evidently Constantine is retailing here the Central Government's traditional view about the effect of the establishment of territorial

---

[1] In *De Them.*, pp. 12–13 and 16. These passages have been cited already on p. 230.
[2] pp. 12 and 16.   [3] p. 16.   [4] p. 12.
[5] p. 16.   [6] p. 16.   [7] pp. 12–13.

thémata. This view was that the acquisition of the control over local administration by corps-commanders was tantamount to a partition of the Empire. Military officers who had become local governors as well had acquired virtually sovereign powers.

We may guess that this view reflected the crisis through which the East Roman Empire had passed during the civil war of 742–3. For a few months it had looked then as if the Empire might break up into two separate states, notwithstanding the gravity of the menace from the Arabs that still impended over the Empire as a whole. In this civil war the senior théma, the Anatolikoí, together with its subordinate théma, the Thrakếsioi, was challenged by the second senior théma, the Armeniakoí, which had been reinforced with Armenian volunteers from the Arab side of the frontier and—what was much more serious—by théma Opsíkion and by the troops in Thrace. This formidable combination had been built up by Artávazdhos, who had been stratêghós of the Armeniakoí in 717, and whose support of Leo III, who had at that time been stratêghós of the Anatolikoí, had then enabled Leo to occupy Constantinople and to make himself Emperor. In return, Leo had made Artávazdhos commander (kómês) of théma Opsíkion and had secured his loyalty, so he supposed, by giving him his daughter in marriage. Artávazdhos had retained influence over his own original command, the Armeniakoí, and he had won the allegiance of the commander of the troops in Thrace, which, at this date, was probably still subject, *ex officio*, to the commander of the Opsíkion.

Thrace and Opsíkion, between them, dominated Constantinople; so, when Artávazdhos rebelled against Leo III's heir and successor, Constantine V, in 742, he was able to occupy the capital and to have himself proclaimed Emperor. Constantine defeated Artávazdhos and thus made good his own title to the Imperial Crown and re-established the unity of the Empire; but the Empire had come within an ace of splitting into two, and its narrow escape made a lasting impression that had an enduring effect on Imperial policy thenceforward. The impression has left its mark on Constantine Porphyrogenitus's treatise on the thémata. The consequent policy had been successful, by his time, in ensuring that the Central Government's control over the thémata should be effective, notwithstanding the combination of administrative with military powers in the hands of the thematic stratêghoí.

However, Constantine Porphyrogenitus's thesis that the unity of the Empire had been destroyed by the corps-commanders' acquisition of territorial administrative powers has distorted his vision of the course of Roman Imperial history. In reality, the concentration of military power —as, for instance, in the hands of Artávazdhos's family or in the hands of Belisarius, which is the case that the Porphyrogenitus cites—was so far from being evidence of the Empire's unity that it was actually a menace to its survival. This was demonstrated by Artávazdhos, and it might have been demonstrated by Belisarius if Belisarius had taken the opportunity of the 'Níka' riots in 532 to overthrow Justinian I instead of saving the situation for him, as he did. One of the several causes of the Roman Empire's collapse in the west in the fifth century had been the fatal success of one of two western magistri militum in praesenti, the magister peditum, in overshadowing his colleague the magister equitum in praesenti and his regional colleagues and thus making himself virtually a permanent military dictator.[1] In the eastern half of the Empire, this concentration of military power had been avoided, thanks to the dispositions that had been made successively by Theodosius I and Justinian I.[2] This 'cutting-up' of the East Roman Empire into a number of separate military commands had not been the end of the Empire; on the contrary, it had been the Empire's salvation.

Moreover, Theodosius I's decentralization of military power in the east had been carried out nearly a quarter of a millennium before the date of the Arab onslaught; and the effect of this onslaught and of the Slav *Völkerwanderung* had been to diminish, not to increase, the number of East Roman military commands. The liquidation of the command of the magister militum per Illyricum and the fusion of the three magistri praesentales in the single command of the Opsíkion had reduced Justinian I's seven commands to four, and, of these four, two had gained in power: the Anatolikoí by having the Thrakḗsioi subordinated to them after the transfer of the Thrakḗsioi from Thrace to western Asia Minor; the Opsíkion by being given the responsibility for the defence of Thrace.[3] The civil war of 742–3 had shown that the regional commands were not perilously too small but were still perilously too big. Constantine V and his successors learned the lesson of Artávazdhos's rebellion and acted on it. The cutting-up of the East Roman Empire into small pieces was a sequel to the civil war of 742–3,[4] not to the Arab onslaught in the 630s.

The Thrakḗsioi were now released from their subordination to the Anatolikoí,[5] and eventually the three giant thémata Anatolikoí, Armeniakoí, and Opsíkion were split up into fourteen by detaching Seléfkeia from the Anatolikoí, detaching the Optimátoi, Thrákē, Makedhonía, the Voukellárioi, and Paphlaghonía from the Opsíkion, detaching Khaldía,

---

[1] See II, 2, p. 193.

[2] See II, 2, p. 193, and the present chapter, pp. 225–6.

[3] In 680 the kómês tou Opsikíou was at the same time, *ex officio*, ypostrátêghos of Thrace (Pertusi, 'La Formation', p. 39).

[4] This comes out in Tavola II (Tavola reassuntiva della formazione dei temi) in Pertusi's edition of the *De Them.*

[5] Gelzer, *Die Genesis*, p. 92, and Anastos in *C. Med. H.*, vol. iv, 2nd ed., Part II, p. 64, hold that this had been done already by Leo III.

Kolóneia, Kharsianón, and Sevásteia from the Armeniakoí, and detaching Kappadhokía either from the Armeniakoí[1] or, more probably, from
the Anatolikoí.[2] By the time when Constantine Porphyrogenitus was
editing Leo VI's schedule of the salaries of statêghoí of thémata and
kleisourárkhai of kleisoúrai, there were thirty-one full thémata,[3] each of
whose commanders was directly responsible to the Emperor; and the
total number of public servants who were directly responsible to the
Emperor was sixty in 899 (the date of Philótheos's revision of the Imperial klêtorolóyion), as compared with only twenty-two under the
Diocletianic–Constantinian dispensation.[4] Moreover, by Philótheos's
time, all the financial departments of the Central Government had been
brought under the effective control of a single high official, the sakellários.[5]

It will be seen that, so far from there having been anything like a
break-up of the East Roman Empire, the Central Government's control
over the provinces was more effective in Leo VI's time than it had been
under the Diocletianic–Constantinian regime; and this conclusion is
confirmed by our information about the internal organization of a
théma, and about the Central Government's control over a théma's
internal affairs, at the turn of the ninth and tenth centuries.

Information on these points is given in some of those rare passages of
Leo VI's *Taktiká* that are not copied verbatim from earlier authors and
that therefore presumably describe the actual state of affairs in Leo VI's
own day. One of these original passages gives a careful and precise
definition of the office of statêghós and of this office's functions.

A statêghós is the officer who wields, over the province under his rule,
an authority that is superior to everyone else's except the Emperor's. A
statêghós is the head of the administration (κορυφαῖος ἄρχων) of the military
théma of which he is in charge. He is appointed by the Emperor. Some of the
statêghós's subordinates are sent out to him by the Emperor after the statêghós
has [been consulted and has] agreed;[6] others are recommended by the statêghós

---

[1] Gelzer, *Die Genesis*, pp. 91 and 94–6, holds that Kappadhokía was detached from the
Armeniakoí, and that the Armeniakoí were broken up, not after 743 by Constantine V, but
after 793 by Eirēnē.

[2] More probably from the Anatolikoí, as Constantine Porphyrogenitus states in *De Adm.
Imp.*, p. 224; for théma Kappadhokía marched with the Arab Empire along the section of
the Romano-Arab frontier that included the Cilician Gates. Théma Sevásteia, which had
certainly once formed part of théma Armeniakoí, marched with the Arab Empire along the
section of the frontier that included the pass over the Uzun Yayla to Sevásteia (Sivas) from
Malatīyah. This pass and the Cilician Gates were the two main gateways through the
Távros and Andítavros Ranges for the Arab invasions of Asia Minor. It seems unlikely that
the Armeniakoí had been required to hold both passes, and that the Anatolikoí had been
given no section of the frontier to defend.

[3] Including théma Optimáton, which this schedule omits.

[4] See the citation of these figures of Bury's in II, 2, on p. 192.

[5] See the citation from Bury in II, 2, on p. 194.

[6] τοὺς μὲν ψήφῳ τῇ αὐτοῦ, ἐκ βασιλέως δὲ καταπεμπόμενος.

himself at his own discretion[1] . . . One of the prerogatives and duties of a stratêghós is that all the administrative business of his province—military, private, and public—(τὰς διοικήσεις, ὅσαι τε στρατιωτικαὶ καὶ ὅσαι ἰδιωτικαὶ καὶ δημόσιοι) shall be referred to him.[2]

The formidableness of a stratêghós's powers since he had become a governor as well as a military commander had moved the Central Government to impose on him restrictions designed to ensure, as far as possible, that his powers should not be abused by him. Like a Chinese imperial official, an East Roman stratêghós was debarred from holding office in his own native province.[3] During his tenure of office, a stratêghós was not allowed to buy or build anything in his théma for his private use, and he was debarred from accepting gifts.[4] He was also debarred from executing contracts and from betrothing any members of his family, either male or female.[5] The veto on executing contracts and on betrothing female relatives was an addition of Leo VI's to the restrictions on a stratêghós's freedom of action that were already in force, and this is noteworthy, considering that, in a later novel,[6] Leo had repealed the previous veto on buying and building while in office for all other thematic officials (both military, apparently, and civilian),[7] as well as for all metropolitan officials. Leo's only proviso had been that a stratêghós should have discretion to dismiss any subordinates of his who misused the free hand that Leo VI had now granted to them. In this context it is all the more significant that Leo had not only confirmed the previous restrictions on a stratêghós's activities but had actually added to them.

The stratêghós of a théma had a staff (προέλευσιν, literally meaning 'escort'). Philótheos enumerates[8] eleven grades of thematic officers, military and civilian, who were subordinate to the doyen of the thematic stratêghoí, namely the stratêghós of the Anatolikoí. Presumably the other stratêghoí had corresponding staffs. Leo VI[9] mentions two of these grades —the kómês tês kórtês (the stratêghós's aide-de-camp—literally, the officer who was in charge of his 'tent') and the dhoméstikos of the théma —but Leo refrains from making a complete enumeration, in order to concentrate[10] on the arrangements by which the Central Government exercised its control over the thematic administrative services.

---

[1] A stratêghós was empowered to dismiss, at his own discretion, any of his subordinates whom he had found guilty of misconduct (Leo VI, Novel No. 84, *ad fin.*, in Noailles and Dain, pp. 282–5).

[2] Leo VI, *Taktiká*, Dhiat. 1, §§ 9, 10, 12, col. 680.

[3] Glykatzi-Ahrweiler, loc. cit., p. 44, citing Zepos's reprint of Zachariä's *J.G.-R.*, vol. v, p. 104.

[4] Leo VI, Novel No. 84, p. 285; Zepos's reprint of Zachariä, vol. v, p. 105.

[5] Leo VI, Novel No. 23, p. 91 (see the present work, II, 1 (iii) (e) p. 148, n. 1).

[6] No. 84. [7] Leo's formula is τῶν κατ᾽ ἐπαρχίας ἀρχόντων.

[8] p. 139 Bury, p. 716 Bonn. [9] *Taktiká*, Dhiat. 4, § 32, col. 705.

[10] Ibid., § 33, col. 705.

The protonotários of the théma and the khartoulários, and also the praítor, i.e. the thematic judge (δικαστής)[1]—the first mentioned of these three officials is in charge of the civil administration, the business of the second of them is the registration (καταγραφήν) and identification (ἀναζήτησιν) of the [soldiers of the thematic] army-corps (στρατοῦ), while the third settles law-suits—well, it is true that, on certain points, these three thematic officials have to take their orders from the stratêghós, but, all the same, they also have to deal [direct] with My Majesty. They have to render to My Majesty an account of the performance of their respective duties, in order to enable My Majesty to keep Itself informed about the state and the conduct of civil and military affairs [in the théma]. We consider that this is a necessary precaution.

Constantine Porphyrogenitus has been given high marks[2] for his diligence in studying these reports and for the good use that he made of the information that he thus acquired.

He read the reports that were sent in by the stratêghoí in all parts [of the Empire] and by the Imperial protonotárioi and by the [authorities] in the villages, provinces, and cities, and also by the princes of foreign nations. He was able thus to discern immediately what was in their minds and to see what had to be done about the east and about the west. In most cases he went after them with the speed of a bird, receiving embassies, sending instructions to officials, and correcting [ill-advised] precipitate new departures. By these means Constantine played, in his own person, the diverse roles of counsellor, moderator, governor, soldier, military commander, and sovereign (ἡγεμών).

Leo VI's and *Theophanes Continuatus*'s accounts of the control exercised by the Central Government over the thematic administrations are borne out by Philótheos in his klêtorolóyion. Here the khartoulários of a théma appears as one of the officials subordinate to the stratêghós of the théma,[3] but he also appears again among the subordinates of the loghothétês tou stratiotikoú,[4] which was one of the financial departments that were under the control of the sakellários. The protonotários of a théma does not appear among the subordinates of the stratêghós, but only among the subordinates of the khartoulários of the sakéllion,[5] another of the financial departments that were under the sakellários's control.

An enigmatic post is that of the ἐκ προσώπου τῶν θεμάτων, which appears in Philótheos's klêtorolóyion as one of the posts to which the appointments were made by the Emperor. This post appears first in the singular, as the office of τοῦ ἐκ προσώπου τῶν θεμάτων,[6] but later in the plural as the protospathárioi who are ἐκ προσώπου τῶν θεμάτων κατὰ τὸ ἴδιον ἑκάστου θέμα.[7] Ἐκ προσώπου means 'representative'.[8] But whose

---

[1] Usually called 'kritĕs'.—A. J. T.

[2] In *Theoph. Cont.*, Book VI, chap. 17, pp. 448–9, cited in II, 2, on p. 194, n. 4.

[3] p. 139 Bury, p. 717 Bonn.   [4] p. 140 Bury, p. 718 Bonn.

[5] p. 141 Bury, p. 719 Bonn.   [6] p. 137 Bury, p. 714 Bonn.   [7] p. 149 Bury, p. 732 Bonn.

[8] In Theophanes, p. 415, line 3, it seems to be a translation of *in praesenti*, but it cannot mean this when it is the title of a thematic officer.

representatives were these officers? The Emperor's? Or the stratêghós's? The second of these two alternative possible interpretations is compatible, in the light of the passage of Leo VI's *Taktiká* that has been quoted above, with the ἐκ προσώπου being an appointee of the Emperor, not of the stratêghós himself; and this interpretation is supported by another passage in the klêtorolóyion: the schedule of tips payable, on appointment, to the atriklînês, which specifies the ἐκ προσώπου στρατηγοῦ ἢ κλεισουράρχου ἢ κατεπάνω Παφλαγονίας, and which also mentions that these officials receive a periodical ῥόγα (salary).[1] However, the ἐκ προσώπου does not appear in Philótheos's list of the members of a stratêghós's staff; and Bury holds[2] that the ἐκ προσώπου were representatives, not of the commanders of army-corps districts, but of the Emperor, and that they were temporary *remplaçants* of a stratêghós, not regular subordinates sent out to him. The question at issue seems to have been answered since 1911—the date of Bury's publication of his epoch-making work on *The Imperial Administrative System*—in two documents that were afterwards brought to light, namely the siyíllia issued in 974 and 975 by officials who each held the office of ἐκ προσώπου of thémata Thessaloníkê and Strymón.[3] These officials were evidently not temporary *remplaçants* of a stratêghós. They were resident thematic officials[4] who had carried out a detailed local investigation and had then taken action on it. Moreover, in the story of the quarrel between Stavrákios the katepáno of the Mardaïte community in théma Kivyrrhaiótai and the ἐκ προσώπου Efstáthios,[5] the ἐκ προσώπου is appointed by the Emperor, as a stratêghós would have been, and, like a stratêghós, he is permanently resident in the théma and considers himself to be its stratêghós in effect ('the théma of the Kivyrrhaiótai cannot have two stratêghoí'—i.e. not Stavrákios as well as Efstáthios himself).

The Central Government's strongest hold on the thematic administrations was fiscal. The assessment and collection of the Imperial taxes were in the hands of officials who were completely independent of the stratêghoí of the thémata and of their staffs. In Philótheos's klêtorolóyion, the ἐπόπται τῶν θεμάτων appear as members of the staff of the loghothétês tou yenikoú, and the yenikón was one of the central financial departments that were controlled by the sakellários. Ἐπόπται βασιλικοί was the full title of these officers, and they were not just Imperial inspectors of finance. They were the East Roman counterparts of those officials of the First Persian Empire whose title was 'the Emperor's eye'. They were, in fact, the Emperor's agents for inspecting, and reporting on,

---

[1] p. 178 Bury, p. 788 Bonn.   [2] In *The Imperial Administrative System*, pp. 46–7.
[3] See II, 1 (iii) (e), p. 175.
[4] This is what the ἐκ προσώπου of a théma were according to Glykatzi-Ahrweiler, 'Recherches', pp. 39–40.
[5] See *De Adm. Imp.*, pp. 228–31.

the whole conduct of the thematic administrations. Basil II complained that his epóptai were corrupt and that he could not rely on them.[1] No doubt his complaint was based on experience. All the same, we may guess that some of these Imperial inspectors were both honest enough and able enough to serve as an effective curb on the misconduct of the stratêghoí and of the subordinate thematic officials.

The Central Government's policy of keeping the assessment and collection of Imperial taxation in the hands of its own taxation-officers enabled it to maintain a financial hold over the stratêghoí of thémata of the 'Eastern' class. These 'Eastern' stratêghoí were paid their salaries by the Central Government at rates that the Central Government fixed,[2] and this arrangement gave financial security to the stratêghoí in this class at the cost of placing them financially at the Central Government's mercy. Constantine Porphyrogenitus does not tell us whether the 'Eastern' stratêghoí were paid only once in every four years, as he tells us, in another passage,[3] that, in the past, the thematic troops had been paid only once in every four years. However, on the analogy of the annual self-remuneration of the stratêghoí of the 'Western' thémata, we may infer that the 'Eastern' stratêghoí, too, were paid annually by Leo VI's time. Philótheos tells us that the stratêghoí of the 'Eastern' thémata had to tip the atriklînês each time that they were paid,[4] and he implies that the normal term of their tenure of office was the period covered by a single salary-payment, but that the term might be extended.[5]

Note: the stratêghoí in the West did not receive salaries [from the Central Government] because they took their own gratuities (συνηθείας) out of their own thémata annually.[6]

In this note, Constantine does not tell us whether the funds, raised in their own thémata, out of which the 'Western' stratêghoí paid themselves were thematic tax-money or Imperial tax-money. We have noticed indications that the thémata did have funds of their own, which must have been raised by local taxes levied by the thematic administrations themselves.[7] If the 'Western' stratêghoí drew their salaries from these thematic funds, the drain upon them must have been severe. On the

---

[1] See II, 1 (iii) (e), p. 168.

[2] Leo VI's schedule of the salaries of stratêghoí and kleisourárkhai, edited by Constantine Porphyrogenitus in *De Caer.*, Book II, chap. 50, pp. 696–7.

[3] In *De Caer.*, Book I, Appendix, pp. 493–4, cited in II, 1 (iii) (d), p. 136.

[4] p. 178 Bury, p. 788 Bonn.

[5] εἰ δὲ ἐπιμένουσι στρατηγοί, οἱ μὲν Ἀνατολικοὶ ἀνὰ νομίσμ. ιβ′ [i.e. a tip of 12 nomísmata].

[6] Leo VI's schedule, p. 697. The stratêghoí of the 'Western' thémata had to tip the atriklînês each time that they visited Constantinople. The amount of the tip was the same for them as for the 'Eastern' stratêghoí, namely twelve nomísmata (p. 178 Bury, p. 788 Bonn).

[7] See II, 1 (iv), pp. 178–9.

other hand, if the 'Western' stratêghoí helped themselves to a 'gratuity', of an amount that they themselves determined, out of locally raised Imperial tax-money before the balance of this was transferred to Constantinople, the Imperial tax-officials must have been less potent in the 'Western' thémata than in the 'Eastern'; and, indeed, we may guess that the distinguishing mark of thémata of the 'Western' class was that, in these thémata, the stratêghoí were, in general, less firmly under the Central Government's thumb than their 'Eastern' colleagues were.

In the following table,[1] Philótheos's enumeration of the stratêghoí of thémata, in their order of precedence, as set out in Philótheos's list of the sixty officials who were appointed directly by the Emperor,[2] is placed side by side with Constantine Porphyrogenitus's edition of Leo VI's schedule of the 'Eastern' stratêghoí's salaries.[3]

Philótheos's Klêtorolóyion	Leo VI's Schedule of Salaries	
[I. *Thémata of the* 'Eastern' Class]	[I. *Thémata of the* 'Eastern' Class]	Salaries in pounds gold
1. Anatolikoí	1. Anatolikoí	40
2. Armeniakoí	2. Armeniakoí	40
3. Thrakésioi	3. Thrakésioi	40
4. Opsíkion	4. Opsíkion	30
5. Voukellárioi	5. Voukellárioi	30
6. Kappadhokía	6. Kappadhokía	20
7. Kharsianón	7. Kharsianón	20
8. Kolonía	8. Paphlaghonía	20
9. Paphlaghonía	9. Thrákê	20
10. Thrákê	10. Makedhonía	30
11. Makedhonía	11. Khaldhía	10[4]
12. Khaldhía	12. Kolóneia	20
	13. Mesopotamía	0[5]
[II. *Thémata of the* 'Western' Class]	14. Sevásteia[6]	5
	15. Likandós[6]	5
13. Pelopónnêsos	16. Seléfkeia[6]	5
14. Nikópolis	17. Leondókomis[6]	5

[1] See further Pertusi's edition of *De Them.*, Tavola I, for a synoptic table of eight lists of East Roman thémata, namely those given by Ibn Khurdādbih, Ibn al-Fakīh, Kudāmah, the *Hudūd al-'Ālam*, the *Taktikón Uspenski*, Philótheos's klêtorolóyion, Leo VI's schedule of salaries, and the *Taktikón Beneševič*.

[2] *De Caer.*, Book II, chap. 52, pp. 136–7 Bury, p. 713 Bonn.

[3] *De Caer.*, Book II, pp. 696–7.

[4] Ten pounds only, because he took another ten for himself out of the customs receipts [e.g. those received at Trebizond].

[5] In lieu of a salary, the stratêghós Mesopotamías took the whole of the customs receipts [e.g. at the point where the frontier was crossed by the road from Qālīqalā (Theodosiópolis) to Sevásteia].

[6] Constantine notes that, in Leo VI's reign, these four districts had been still only kleisoúrai; they had not yet been raised to their present status of ranking as thémata.

Philótheos's Klêtorolóyion	Leo VI's Schedule of Salaries	
		Salaries in pounds gold
'Western' class (cont.):	*'Eastern' class* (cont.):	
15. Kivyrrhaiótai	18. Kivyrrhaiótai[1]	10
16. Ellás	19. Sámos[1]	10
17. Sikelía	20. Aiyaíon Pélaghos[1]	10
18. Strymón		
19. Kephalenía	[II. *Themata of the*	
20. Thessaloníkê	*'Western' Class*]	
21. Dhyrrhákhion	21. Pelopónnêsos	
22. Sámos	22. Nikópolis	
23. Aiyaíon Pélaghos	23. Ellás	
24. Dhalmatía	24. Sikelía	
25. Khersón	25. Laghovardhía	
	26. Strymón	
[III. *Anomalous Districts*]	27. Kephalênía	
26. Optêmátoi	28. Thessaloníkê	
27. Ta Teíkhê	29. Dhyrrhákhion	
	30. Dhalmatía	
	31. Khersón	

PART II, CHAPTER 4, APPENDIX

A Gazetteer of the Thémata

1. ANATOLIKOÍ. This was the corps of the magister militum per Orientem. Its original stations had been in Syria, Palestine, and Mesopotamia. In 636 it had retreated north-westwards through the Cilician Gates, and had settled in new stations along the south-eastern sections of the road running north-westward from the Cilician Gates to the Asiatic shore of the Bosphorus. This corps is called the exercitus Orientalis in the Emperor Justinian II's letter of 687 to Pope Conon. The date of the first mention of a théma ton Anatolikón is 669;[2] a stratêghós ton Anatolikón is mentioned first *circa* 690.[3]

The Anatolikoí were the senior théma (τὸ α' θέμα,[4] i.e. entry No. 1 in the list, paraphrased as ὁ πρῶτος κατάλογος τῆς στρατιωτικῆς τῶν λεγομένων θεμάτων φάλαγγος),[5] and its stratêghós was unique among all the

---

[1] In Leo's schedule, these three naval thémata are included in the class in which the salaries of the stratêghoí are paid by the Central Government; they are not assigned to the 'Western' class, as they are in Philótheos's klêtorolóyion.

[2] Theophanes, p. 352.   [3] Theophanes, p. 368; Nic. Patr., p. 37.

[4] Genesius, at the beginning of Book I of his Βασιλεῖαι, refers to the future Emperor Leo V on p. 4 as Λέοντός γε τηνικαῦτα στρατηγοῦντος τῶν Ἀνατολικῶν and on p. 5 as Λέων ὁ τοῦ α' θέματος ἐξηγούμενος.

[5] Ighnátios, *Life of the Patriarch Nikêphóros* (de Boor, pp. 162–3).

stratêghoí in taking precedence over the dhoméstikos ton Skholón,[1] who was the commander of the senior regiment of the household troops and who acted as the commander-in-chief of the whole East Roman Army on occasions when a commander-in-chief was needed.

2. ARMENIAKOÍ (ARMENIÁKOI).[2] This was the corps of Justinian I's magister militum per Armeniam. By 653 at the latest, this corps had evacuated its original stations to the south and the west of the upper Euphrates, but had retained those to the north and the north-west of the river and had also settled in additional territories farther to the north-west. The date of the first mention of a stratêghós ton Armeníakón is 687,[3] but there are seals of kommerkiárioi of the Armeniakoí that bear the dates 650/1, 665/6, and 668/9.[4] This corps is called the exercitus Armenianus in Justinian II's letter of 687.

3. THRAKḖSIOI (REPRESENTING THE LATIN NAME THRACENSES). This was the corps of the magister militum per Thraciam. It was transferred from Thrace to Asia Minor at some date not earlier than the withdrawal of the Anatolic corps in 636 from Syria to the north-west side of the Távros Range.[5] The father of Pope Conon (*fungebatur* 687–8) is said to have been 'natione Graecus, oriundus patre Thracesio',[6] but this may mean no more than that this Pope's father was born in the dioecesis of Thrace, and, even if it is taken to mean that he was a soldier serving in the Thracensian army-corps, this would not tell us whether this corps was stationed in Thrace or in Asia Minor at the time. In Justinian II's letter of 687, this corps is called the exercitus Thracianus.[7] A tourmárkhês of the Thrakḗsioi is mentioned in 711,[8] and a stratêghós of the théma ton Thrakêsíon in 742.[9] By the year 771 (A.M. 6262/3) it is obvious that the stratêghós of the Thrakḗsioi, Michael Lakhanodhrákon, is not merely the commander of a corps but is also the governor of an administrative district, since it is part of his duty to persecute all monks and nuns ὑπὸ τὸ θέμα τῶν Θρακησίων ὄντας, and he receives the thanks of the Emperor Constantine V for this service.[10]

---

[1] Philótheos, Klêtorolóyion, p. 136 Bury, p. 713 Bonn.

[2] Armeniákoi is the correct accentuation according to Gelzer, *Die Genesis*, p. 23; Pertusi, 'La Formation', p. 32; de Boor in his edition of Theophanes. The normal Greek accentuation would be Armeniakoí; the Latin accentuation would be Armeníaci. Pertusi, in his edition of *De Them.*, pp. 118 and 119, puts the accent on the last syllable.

[3] Theophanes, p. 348.

[4] See p. 240.

[5] Heraclius had transferred his forces from Europe to Asia in 621, after having persuaded the Avars to make peace (Theophanes, p. 302), but it cannot be assumed that the Thracenses had not subsequently been re-transferred to their proper stations in Thrace after the conclusion, in 628, of peace with the Persian Empire.

[6] *Liber Pontificalis*, Book I, p. 368.

[7] Cf. the form exercitus Armenianus in the same letter.

[8] Theophanes, p. 378.　　　　　　　　　　[9] Theophanes, p. 414; Nic. Patr., p. 60.

[10] Theophanes, pp. 445–6.

When the Thrakĕsioi were transferred to Asia Minor, they appear to have been subordinated to the Anatolikoí, but they were released from their dependence on the Anatolikoí either by Leo III or else by Constantine V after the civil war of 742–3.[1]

4. THE OPSÍKION (REPRESENTING THE LATIN NAME OBSEQUIUM). This corps was a union of the troops that had been commanded by the three Justinianean magistri militum praesentales. These troops had been stationed in north-western Asia Minor already in Justinian I's reign.[2] The title of the commander of the united Opsíkion was kómês, but he had the status of a stratêghós of the 'Eastern' class. After the transfer of the Thrakĕsioi from Thrace to Asia Minor, the kómês tou Opsikíou was also, *ex officio*, ypostrátêghos of Thrace, and he bears this double title in the Acts of the Ecumenical Council of 680.[3] In Justinian II's letter of 687, the Obsequium appears in the original Latin form of the name. The kómês tou Opsikíou had taxátoi, belonging to his théma, in Thrace in 713,[4] and in 742 the kómês of the Opsíkion was presumably still in command of Thrace. After Artávazdhos had been appointed kómês tou Opsikíou, he had secured the allegiance of the troops of Thrace.[5] We may guess that Thrace was detached from the Opsíkion and was erected into a separate théma by Constantine V after his victory over Artávazdhos in 743.[6]

5. VOUKELLÁRIOI. These had originally been the private retainers of East Roman generals. The literal meaning of the word is 'hard-tack eaters'. At some unknown date, the voukellárioi must have been taken over by the Imperial Government into its own service, have been brigaded with the Opsíkion, and have been settled to the east of the Opsíkion in north-western Asia Minor. The date of the first mention of a stratêghós ton Voukellaríon is 766/7.[7] This date indicates that the Voukellárioi had been detached from the Opsíkion by Constantine V after 743.

6. KAPPADHOKÍA. The first mention of this district is by Ibn Khurdādbih,[8] the earliest of the Arabic writers who have given lists of East Roman thémata. Ibn Khurdādbih's list is dated *circa* 850 by Brooks.[9] Kappadhokía was originally a toúrma of the Anatolikoí.[10] It may have been detached from the Anatolikoí by Constantine V after 743, but its erection into a separate théma is ascribed to the Emperor Theóphilos (829–42) by Anastos.[11] It was a théma in 863.[12] Leo VI transferred to

---

[1] See p. 245. [2] See p. 229. [3] Pertusi, *De Them.*, p. 125.
[4] Theophanes, p. 383. This is the first passage in Theophanes's chronicle in which the Opsíkion is called a théma, but it was already an administrative district in 688/9, when Justinian II planted his Slav deportees εἰς τὰ τοῦ Ὀψικίου μέρη (Theophanes, p. 364, cited on p. 90). [5] See p. 244. [6] See p. 245.
[7] Theophanes, p. 440, sub A.M. 6258. [8] Pertusi, *De Them.*, p. 120.
[9] E. W. Brooks, 'The Arabic Lists of the Byzantine Themes', in *J.H.S.*, vol. xxi (1901), pp. 67–77, on p. 67. [10] *De Adm. Imp.*, p. 224.
[11] In *C. Med. H.*, vol. iv, 2nd. ed., Part II, pp. 102–3. [12] *Theoph. Cont.*, p. 181.

Kappadhokía four vánda from the Voukellárioi and three from the Anatolikoí.[1]

7. KHARSIANÓN. The first mention of this district is by Ibn Khurdādbih.[2] It was originally a toúrma of théma Armeniakoí.[3] It is listed as a kleisoúra in the *Taktikón Uspenski*, and it was still only a kleisoúra, not a théma, in 863.[4] Genesius calls the commander of this unit a merárkhês in his account of the campaign in that year.[5] According to Leo VI,[6] a merárkhês, in the current meaning of the term, is the equivalent of the now obsolete term ypostrátêghos, meaning the deputy commander of a corps.[7] Kharsianón appears as a théma in Philótheos's klêtorolóyion (899), in Leo VI's schedule of salaries, and in the *Taktikón Beneševič*. Kharsianón had originally been a toúrma of théma Armeniakoí.[8] Anastos guesses[9] that it was detached from théma Armeniakoí by Théophilos. It was probably promoted to the status of a théma by Leo VI, who transferred to Kharsianón three vánda from the Voukellárioi, two from the Armeniakoí, and one complete toúrma and one vándon, which included the city of Kaisáreia, from Kappadhokía.[10]

8. PAPHLAGHONÍA (PAMPHLAGHONÍA). This district is listed by Ibn Khurdādbih and it appears as a théma in the *Taktikón Uspenski*, in the record of the campaign of 863,[11] and in each of the three later Greek lists. The commander of théma Paphlaghonía is styled 'katepáno' in *De Caer.*, Book II, p. 788, and in *De Adm. Imp.*, p. 178. Bury infers[12] that théma Paphlaghonía had previously been a 'katepanate' of théma Voukellárioi, and both he and Anastos[13] attribute its elevation to the status of a théma to the Emperor Théophilos.

9. THRÁKÊ. The officer who was in command of Thrace and who declared for Artávazdhos in 742 is described as στρατηγοῦντα τῆς Θράκης by Theophanes,[14] and as κατὰ τὴν Θράκην τότε στρατηγοῦντα by the Patriarch Nicephorus.[15] In 742, as in 680, Thrace was probably still just a sub-command of théma Opsíkion. It is named, however, as a separate district in all four Arabic lists, and it is called a théma in the *Taktikón Uspenski* and in the three later Greek lists. We may guess that Thrákê was detached from the Opsíkion and was erected into a separate théma by Constantine V after his victory over Artávazdhos in 743. A

---

[1] *De Adm. Imp.*, p. 225.
[3] *De Adm. Imp.*, p. 225.
[5] Genesius, Book IV, pp. 94–6.
[7] In 'Mavríkios', 'merárkhês' is the equivalent of Leo VI's 'tourmárkhês', i.e. the commander of the largest of the subdivisions of a corps, and the term 'ypostrátêghos' is not yet obsolete (see 'Mavríkios', *Stratêghikón*, Part I, chap. 3, p. 27 Scheffer, p. 56 Mihăescu).
[8] *De. Adm. Imp.*, p. 225.
[9] In *C. Med. H.*, vol. iv, 2nd ed., Part I, pp. 102–3.
[10] *De Adm. Imp.*, pp. 225–6.
[12] In *A History of the Eastern Roman Empire*, p. 222.
[13] In loc. cit.
[14] p. 415.

[2] Pertusi, *De Them.*, p. 123.
[4] *Theoph. Cont.*, pp. 861 and 863.
[6] *Taktiká*, Dhiat. 4, § 9, col. 701.
[11] *Theoph. Cont.*, p. 181.
[15] p. 60.

monostráteghos of Thrákê and Makedhonía was appointed in A.M. 6293 (A.D. 801/2),[1] and this indicates that both these thémata were already in existence in that year. Constantine Porphyrogenitus says[2] that théma Thrákê was created, and was placed under the command of a strateghós, when the Bulgars, who had previously been called the Onoghoundoúroi, crossed to the south bank of the Danube. The date of their crossing was *circa* 680.[3] It looks as if Constantine has confused the creation of théma Thrákê with the appointment of the kómês tou Opsikíou to serve simultaneously as ypostráteghos of Thrace—a combination of commands that was already an accomplished fact by the date of publication of the Acts of the Ecumenical Council of 680.[4]

10. MAKEDHONÍA. A théma Makedhonía seems to have been in existence by 801/2 (A.M. 6293), since a 'monostráteghos' of Thrákê and Makedhonía was appointed in that year. We may guess that Makedhonía had originally been included in théma Thrákê, but had been detached from it at some date between 743 and 802.[5] There was a separate strateghós Makedhonías in 813.[6] The capital of théma Makedhonía was Adrianople, and the capital of théma Thrákê was Arkadhiópolis. The Arabic authorities interpose Makedhonía between Thrákê and the Sea of Marmara,[7] and on the north they make Makedhonía march with Bulgaria exclusively.[8] If these indications are correct, the eastern end of the boundary between Makedhonía and Thrákê must have abutted on the Anastasian Long Wall, at some point to the north of this wall's southern end on the Marmara coast, and the boundary must have run from there first westwards and then northwards till it struck the southern frontier of Bulgaria. The western boundary of théma Makedhonía is indicated by an inscription, dated 926, at Kavalla (Khristópolis), recording the rebuilding of the walls of Kavalla by the stratêlátês of théma Strymón.[9] We may infer that the boundary between thémata Makedhonía and Strymón coincided with the former boundary between the dioecesis of Thrace and the praetorian prefecture of Eastern Illyricum, which followed the course of the River Nestos.[10] If so, the area of the East Roman théma Makedhonía did not even overlap with the area of the former Roman province Macedonia, whose eastern boundary was identical with the eastern frontier of the previous Kingdom of Macedon.

11. KHALDHÍA. Khaldhía was a théma in 863,[11] and it is given the status of a théma in all four Greek lists. It is mentioned as a separate district in all

---

[1] Theophanes, p. 475.

[2] In *De Them.*, Book II, pp. 45–6.

[3] For the chronology, see Obolensky in *C. Med. H.*, vol. iv, 2nd ed., Part I, p. 484, with note 3.

[4] See p. 254.

[5] See Diehl, *Études byzantines*, p. 283, n. 4.

[6] Theophanes, p. 501.

[7] Pertusi, *De Them.*, p. 157.

[8] Ibid., p. 158.

[9] Pertusi, *De Them.*, p. 163, citing Lemerle and Kyriakídhês.

[10] Pertusi, ibid., p. 164.

[11] *Theoph. Cont.*, p. 181.

four Arabic lists. The date at which it was detached from théma Armenia-koí is unknown. This may have been done after 743 by Constantine V or after 793 by Eirênê,[1] or else by Theóphilos.[2]

12. KOLÓNEIA (KOLONÍA). This district seems to have continued to be part of théma Armeniakoí during the reign of Theóphilos. An officer called Kállistos Melissênós was sent by Theóphilos to serve there as dhoux,[3] and the same Kállistos is styled 'tourmárkhês',[4] which is the title of an officer commanding one of the three major subdivisions of a théma, not the title of a commandant of a separate unit. A théma Kolóneia is not mentioned in any of the Arabic lists or in the *Taktikón Uspenski*, but there was a stratêghós of Kolóneia in 863,[5] and this théma appears in all three later Greek lists.

13. MESOPOTAMÍA. This district is not mentioned in any of the Arabic lists or in the *Taktikón Uspenski* or by Philótheos, but it appears in Leo VI's schedule of salaries and in the *Taktikón Benešević*. It was an addition to the East Roman Empire's territory. It was carved out of Armenian territory that had previously been under Arab suzerainty. It had been founded as a kleisoúra and had subsequently been raised to the status of a théma by Leo VI according to Constantine Porphyrogenitus.[6] At the same time, Leo VI transferred to his new théma Mesopotamía the toúrma Keltzênĕ from théma Khaldhía and the toúrma Kámakha from théma Kolóneia.[7] Rhomanós Lekapênós (920–44) enlarged théma Mesopotamía further by adding to it Rhomanópolis and Khanzit, which had formerly been a kleisoúra of Malatīyah.[8]

14. SEVÁSTEIA. This district is not mentioned in any of the Arabic lists or in the *Taktikón Uspenski* or by Philótheos, but Constantine notes, in his edition of Leo VI's schedule of salaries, that it had been a kleisoúra in Leo VI's reign but has become a théma since then. It appears as a théma in the *Taktikón Benešević*. It must have been detached from the Armeniakoí at some date between 899 and 912.

15. LYKANDÓS (LIKANDÓS). Like Sevásteia, Lykandós is not mentioned in any of the Arabic lists or in the *Taktikón Uspenski* or by Philótheos, but Constantine Porphyrogenitus has left a detailed record[9] of the stages by

---

[1] See p. 246, n. 1.

[2] This is Anastos's dating in *C. Med. H.*, vol. iv, 2nd ed., Part I, pp. 102–3.

[3] Bury, *The Eastern Roman Empire*, p. 222, n. 3, citing the Acts of the Amorian martyrs, 27, 29.

[4] *Georg. Mon. Interpolatus*, Reign of Theóphilos, chap. 22, p. 805; Leo Grammaticus, p. 224.

[5] *Theoph. Cont.*, p. 181.   [6] *De Them.*, pp. 30–1; *De Adm. Imp.*, p. 226.

[7] *De Adm. Imp.*, pp. 226–7.

[8] *De Adm. Imp.*, pp. 226 and 227. The Arab amirate of Malatīyah had capitulated to the East Romans in 934 and had been converted into a kouratoría (i.e. an Imperial estate) (Vasiliev, *Byzance et les Arabes*, ii, I, pp. 269–70).   [9] In *De Adm. Imp.*, pp. 227–8.

which the Armenian akrítas Melías (Mleh) carved out this district, first from a base at Lykandós and then from one at Tsamandós, in the reign of Leo VI. Tsamandós was on the head-waters of the Zamanti su, to the east of Kaisáreia, and apparently just within the south-eastern border of théma Kharsianón. Melías expanded his domain south-eastwards at the expense of the Arab amirate of Malatīyah, in which at one time he had been a refugee. Leo VI gave Melías's domain the status of a kleisoúra at some date between 899 and 912. Lykandós was raised to the status of a théma in the joint reign of Constantine Porphyrogenitus and his mother Zoê (913/14–919).[1] Melías figures as one of the characters in the Byzantine epic *Dhiyenês Akrítas*.[2]

16. SELÉFKEIA. This district is mentioned in all the Arabic lists, but not in the *Taktikón Uspenski* or by Philótheos. It was, however, a kleisoúra by the year 863,[3] and it figured as a kleisoúra in Leo VI's schedule of salaries. It was raised to the status of a théma by Rhomanós Lekapênós,[4] and it appears as a théma in the *Taktikón Beneševič*. Anastos holds[5] that it had been made into a kleisoúra by Theóphilos. It is uncertain whether, originally, Seléfkeia had been part of théma Anatolikoí or part of théma Kivyrrhaiótai.

17. LEONDÓKOMIS (LEONDOKÓMÊS). This district appears first in Leo VI's schedule of salaries, as a kleisoúra which had become a théma by the time when the schedule was edited by Constantine Porphyrogenitus. It appears as a théma in the *Taktikón Beneševič*. It is unknown otherwise, and the only indications of its location and of its origin are its name and its position in the schedule between Seléfkeia and Kivyrrhaiótai. The position in the schedule suggests that Leondókomis was a district adjoining the East Roman Empire's south-eastern frontier which had been temporarily detached, as Seléfkeia had been permanently. The name suggests that it had been called after a kómês Leo. This could have been Leo Phokás the son of the first Nikêphóros Phokás. The Phokádhes were Cappadocians; the first Nikêphóros Phokás had made his name on the eastern frontier, and he had been stratêghós of théma Kharsianón before his appointment in 885 to the command of five western thémata. This first Nikêphóros Phokás's son Leo may have served, like his father, on the eastern frontier before the unlucky last chapter of his career in 917–19 as dhoméstikos ton Skholón.

18. KIVYRRHAIÓTAI (KIVYRHAIÓTAI). The name of this naval théma was derived from the little Pamphylian coastal town Kívyrrha,[6] not from

---

[1] *De Adm. Imp.*, p. 228.

[2] See J. Mavrogordato's edition, *Digenes Akrites* (Oxford, 1956, Clarendon Press), Introduction, pp. liii and lxxvii.

[3] *Theoph. Cont.*, p. 181.   [4] *De Them.*, p. 36.   [5] In loc. cit.

[6] *De Them.*, p. 38 bis. Constantine, naming the coastal towns of théma Kivyrrhaiótai from west to east, locates Kívyrrha east of Cape Anemoúrion and Antioch-on-Krághos,

the larger and more famous city of the same name in the upper basin of the River Indós. This other Kívyrrha[1] was land-locked, and it lay on the Thrakesian side of the boundary between théma Kivyrrhaiótai and théma Thrakêsioi.[2] It is not known why théma Kivyrrhaiótai was named after the obscure Pamphylian Kívyrrha. The administrative headquarters of the théma were not there; apparently they were at Attáleia.[3] Constantine says that the name was given as an insult, but this explanation is not convincing.

The date of the earliest mention of the district is 698, apropos of Apsimar's being made Emperor under the name Tiberius III. At the time, Apsimar was the dhroungários of the Kivyrrhaiótai at the Kouri-kiótai (εἰς Κουρικιώτας), according to Theophanes,[4] while, according to the Patriarch Nicephorus,[5] he was the dhroungários in command (ἄρχοντα) of the corps (στρατοῦ) of the Kourikiótai, belonging to the district (χώρας) under (ὑπὸ) the Kivyrrhaiótai. In these two variants of the description of Apsimar's command, the relation of the Kourikiótai to the Kivyrrhaiótai is obscure. Both variants seem to imply that the Kourikiótai were a subdivision of the Kivyrrhaiótai; yet, if they were, it is difficult to explain how the officer commanding a subdivision can have been the dhroungários of the whole district; and Leo VI informs us[6] that the commanders of the three thematic fleets had originally been dhroun-ghárioi before they had been promoted to the rank of stratêghoí. Possibly Apsimar held the post of dhroungários of the Kivyrrhaiótai concurrently with the local command of one of the subdivisions of this district; but it seems more likely that Kórykos was the place where the dhroungários of the Kivyrrhaiótai had his naval headquarters, and that this is why Apsimar was there. If the Kórykos here in question is the townlet adjoining Attáleia,[7] an admiral stationed there would be within easy reach of Crete, where the *pronunciamiento* was made by the crews of the fleet that

---

and west of Selinoús, but the true geographical sequence, from west to east, is Kívyrrha, Selinoús, Krághos, Anemoúrion. According to Strabo, *Geographica*, Book XIV, chap. 4 § 2 (C. 667), who also proceeds from west to east, ἡ τῶν Κιβυρατῶν παραλία τῶν μικρῶν lies close to Sídhê, between Sídhê and the River Mélas.

[1] Steph. Byz., s.v.

[2] This boundary is sketched by Constantine Porphyrogenitus in *De Them.*, p. 38.

[3] See Ibn Hawkal, quoted in II, 1 (ii), on pp. 48–9, and *De Adm. Imp.*, p. 229. It looks as if the stratêghós of théma Kivyrrhaiótai had his headquarters at Attáleia as well as the kat-epáno of the Mardaïte community in this théma.

[4] Theophanes, p. 370.　　　　　　　　　　　　　　　　　　[5] Nic. Patr., p. 40.

[6] Leo VI, *Taktiká*, Dhiat. 19, § 24, col. 997.

[7] This Kórykos is described by Strabo, *Geographica*, Book XIV, chap. 4, § 1 (C. 667), as πολίχνιον ὅμορον to Attáleia. See also chap. 3, § 8 (C. 666). There was another Kórykos in Western Cilicia (ibid., chap. 5, § 5 (C. 670)), but Constantine informs us (*De Them.*, p. 35) that this eastern Kórykos was in théma Seléfkeia. There was a third Kórykos in the territory of Erythraí, but Erythraí lay beyond the north-western boundary of théma Kivyrrhaiótai (originally in Thrakêsioi, eventually in Sámos). The Kórykos that adjoined Attáleia seems

was on its way back from Carthage. Both variants of the narrative imply that Apsimar himself had not taken part in the expedition, and that this was why the crews preferred him.

In any case, Nicephorus's formula indicates that in 698 the Kivyr-rhaiótai were already an administrative unit (χώρα),[1] besides being a naval unit, while the title dhrounghários indicates that at this date the Kivyrrhaiótai were not a separate unit, but were under a higher com-mand—and in fact there was, at this date, a commander-in-chief of the whole East Roman Navy[2] who ranked as a stratêghós[3]—namely the stratêghós John, who had sailed 'with the whole fleet' to Carthage. One of the stratêghós's subordinates, the dhrounghários of the Kivyrrhaiótai, may have been left behind at Kórykos to parry any diversionary Arab naval attack from Syria that might be launched while the rest of the fleet was far away in West Mediterranean waters.

The στρατηγὸς τῶν ῾Ρωμαϊκῶν πλοϊμάτων of the year 697/8 evidently held the same post as the στρατηγὸς τῶν καράβων who, at some date in the 630s or 640s, had come to the rescue of Thessaloníkê when the city was in danger of being seized by the repatriated descendants of the deportees who had been marooned in Sirmia.[4] He reappears in 711 as the strategus Caravisianorum who received Pope Constantine I.[5] The headquarters and command-post (μητρόπολιν . . . καὶ ἀρχήν) of this former unitary θέμα τῶν πλωϊζομένων had been on the island of Sámos, but, unlike the subordinate district of the Kivyrrhaiótai, the θέμα τῶν πλωϊζομένων had not possessed any territory on the mainland.[6]

By the year 732 there was a stratêghós ton Kivyrrhaiotón;[7] so, between 711 and 732, the Kivyrrhaiótai had become a separate naval command, and the unitary Imperial Navy had been broken up.[8] The Kivyrrhaiótai appear as a théma, commanded by a stratêghós, in all four Greek lists. On the other hand, by the date of compilation of the *Taktikón Uspenski* (*circa* mid ninth century) the commander of the Imperial Fleet (τοῦ πλοΐμου) had sunk to being a dhrounghários instead of a stratêghós, and,

to have lain on the west coast of the Gulf of Attáleia, between Phaselis and Olympus (see Strabo, Book XIV, chap. 5, § 7 (C. 671)). See also Magie, *Roman Rule in Asia Minor* (Prince-ton, 1950, University Press, 2 vols.), vol. i, p. 288, and vol. ii, pp. 1133 and 1168, with the map at the end of vol. ii.

[1] At the time, *circa* 934-44, at which *De Them.* was being written, the territory of théma Kivyrrhaiótai extended from the western boundary of the Seléfkeia district as far north-westward as Miletós inclusive (*De Them.*, p. 36).

[2] ἅπαντα τὰ ῾Ρωμαϊκὰ πλόϊμα (Nicephorus, p. 39) ; πάντων τῶν ῾Ρωμαϊκῶν πλοϊμάτων (Theophanes, p. 370).

[3] Nicephorus, ibid.　　　　　　　　　　[4] *S.D. Miracula*, Book II, chap. 5, col. 1369.
[5] *Liber Pontificalis*, p. 390.　　　　　　　[6] *De Them.*, p. 41.
[7] Theophanes, p. 410.

[8] See L. Bréhier: 'La Marine de Byzance du viiie au ixe siècle', in *Byzantion*, vol. xix (1949), pp. 1-16, on p. 4.

in Philótheos's edition of the klêtorolóyion,[1] this officer's position in the order of precedence is seven places below the lowest of the stratêghoí, namely, the stratêghós of Khersón.

19. SÁMOS. Théma Sámos must have been detached from the Aiyaíon Pélaghos district at some date in the second half of the ninth century. Théma Sámos does not appear in the *Taktikón Uspenski*, but it does appear in all the three later Greek lists. It was formed by detaching mainland territory, extending from as far south as Tralleis and Maghnêsía-on-Maeander to as far north as Adhramýttion inclusive, from théma Thrakêsioi. The new théma was divided into two toúrmai, one centred on Éphesos and the other on Adhramýttion. The stratêghós of théma Sámos has his seat of government ($\pi\rho\alpha\iota\tau\dot{\omega}\rho\iota\sigma\nu$) at Smyrna.[2]

20. AIYAÍON PÉLAGHOS. This district was probably detached from the former unitary naval command ($\tau\hat{\omega}\nu$ $\kappa\alpha\rho\dot{\alpha}\beta\omega\nu$, $\tau\hat{\omega}\nu$ $\pi\lambda\sigma\dot{\iota}\mu\omega\nu$) at the same date as the Kivyrrhaiótai, for the chronicler Theophanes's father, who died in 780,[3] had been in command of the Aiyaiopelaghêtai.[4] Unlike the Kivyrrhaiótai, however, Aiyaíon Pélaghos was not raised in status from a dhroungários's to a stratêghós's command at the time when it was made into a separate unit. As has been noted, the commander of the Kivyrrhaiótai was already a stratêghós in 732, and he appears as such in the *Taktikón Uspenski*, but, in this list, the commander of the Aiyaíon Pélaghos is still only a dhroungários. In the three later Greek lists, however, he appears as a stratêghós, like the commanders of thémata Kivyrrhaiótai and Sámos. Constantine Porphyrogenitus informs us[5] that, notwithstanding its name, théma Aiyaíon Pélaghos extended through the Dardanelles into the Sea of Marmara. It included the island of Prokónnêsos and, on the Asiatic mainland, Párion, Kýzikos, and Dhaskýlion.

21. PELOPÓNNÊSOS. The east side of the Pelopónnêsos, from Corinth to Cape Maléa inclusive,[6] and a few smaller enclaves of territory on other coasts of the Pelopónnêsos, had held out against the Slav *Völkerwanderung*, and these Peloponnesian districts, which are probably embraced under the collective name $\tau\dot{\alpha}$ $\kappa\alpha\tau\omega\tau\iota\kappa\dot{\alpha}$ $\mu\acute{\epsilon}\rho\eta$, had presumably been attached to théma Ellás, i.e. east-central Greece, Éῠvoia, and eastern Thessaly, which was the largest piece of territory in the southern part of the Balkan Peninsula over which the East Roman Government had succeeded in retaining its hold without interruption.[7] The *Chronicle of Monemvasía* indicates that the East Roman Imperial Government re-established its authority effectively over the Pelopónnêsos as a whole in either 804/5 or 805/6,[8] and the Emperor Michael I is recorded to have appointed a

---

[1] p. 137 Bury, p. 713 Bonn.
[2] *De Them.*, p. 41.
[3] Pertusi, *De Them.*, p. 149.
[4] *Vita Theophanis*, p. 28.
[5] In *De Them.*, pp. 43–4.
[6] *Chronicle of Monemvasía*, Ivĕron MS., lines 55–7.
[7] See II, 1 (iii) (a), p. 94.
[8] See II, 1 (iii) (a), pp. 75 and 96.

stratêghós of the Pelopónnêsos *circa* 811.[1] Pelopónnêsos appears as a théma in all four Greek lists.

However, some puzzling problems arise out of the following passage in the *Chronicle of Monemvasía* :[2]

The eastern part of the Pelopónnêsos, and this part only, remained un-contaminated by (καθαρεύοντος τοῦ) the Slav nation because of its rockiness and of the difficulty of access to it. In this part, a stratêghós of the Pelopón-nêsos used to be sent down (κατεπέμπετο) [from Constantinople] by the Em-peror of the [East] Romans. One of the sestratêghoí who came from Little Armenia and was a member of the clan named Sklêroí made war on the Slav nation [in the Pelopónnêsos], conquered it, and completely annihilated it, and thus opened the way for the repatriation of the original inhabitants.

According to this passage, stratêghoí of the Pelopónnêsos were being appointed before the terminal date of the independence of the Pelopon-nesian Sklavinías, which the Chronicle dates in A.M. 6313 (i.e. 804/5) or in the fourth year of the reign of Nikêphóros I (i.e. 805/6). These stratêghoí of the Pelopónnêsos were in effective control of the never conquered eastern part only, till one of them conquered the Peloponnesian Sklavinías in Nikêphóros I's reign; but the first stratêghós of the Pelopónnêsos of whom we have a record, apart from this passage of the *Chronicle of Monemvasía*, was appointed by Michael I, apparently near the beginning of his reign, in or soon after 811.[3] It is conceivable that the author of the Chronicle is using the word stratêghós in the non-technical general mean-ing of 'commander' or 'governor', but, in East Roman usage, στρατηγός had a precise technical meaning. It was the official Greek rendering of the Latin 'magister militum', and it meant 'commander of an army-corps', a post that eventually came to carry with it, *ex officio*, the governorship of the district in which the stratêghós's corps was cantoned.

Thus the Chronicle implies that théma Pelopónnêsos was already in existence not only before 811, but before the subjugation of the Pelo-ponnesian Sklavinías in 804/5 or in 805/6. Constantine Porphyrogenitus assumes[4] that it was already in existence by the date, in Nikêphóros I's reign, of the Peloponnesian Slavs' insurrection and their siege of Pátras that had followed their subjugation. The stratêghós who was in office at the time had his seat at Corinth, 'at the extremity of the théma'. Alter-natively, the stratêghoí who were sent down to the eastern part of the Pelopónnêsos before the conquest and reannexation of the Peloponnesian Sklavinías, and also the stratêghós who was in office at the time of the insurrection, may have been stratêghoí, not of théma Pelopónnêsos, but of théma Ellás, who exercised authority in the eastern part of the

---

[1] Scriptor Incertus de Leone Armenio in the Bonn edition of Leo Grammaticus, p. 336.
[2] Ivĕron MS., lines 55–6, cited already in II, 1 (iii) (a), on pp. 95–6.
[3] Scriptor Incertus de Leone in the Bonn edition of Leo Grammaticus, p. 336.
[4] In *De Adm. Imp.*, chap. 49, p. 217.

Pelpoónnêsos because this was attached to théma Ellás as its κατωτικὰ μέρη. After the subjugation of the Peloponnesian Sklavinías and at the time of the consequent insurrection, the Pelopónnêsos as a whole may still have been part of théma Ellás, governed by a stratêghós Elládhos stationed at Corinth. A separate théma Pelopónnêsos may not have been created before the appointment of a stratêghós Peloponnḗsou by Michael I in or soon after 811.

Before the creation of théma Pelopónnêsos, Corinth seems likely to have been included in théma Ellás and indeed to have been its capital; for Corinth had been the capital of the Roman province Achaïa throughout the period of about six centuries that elapsed between the date of the creation of this province by Augustus and the date of its obliteration by the Avars' raids and the Slavs' *Völkerwanderung*. Théma Ellás had been constituted out of the fragments, still remaining under East Roman rule, of the three Roman provinces—Achaïa, Thessalia, and Epirus Vetus— which, together, had constituted Ellás (Greece) in the popular meaning of this name. If it is true that Corinth remained continuously under East Roman rule, it must have been included in the original area of théma Ellás, and we may guess that τὰ κατωτικὰ μέρη signified the Peloponnesian districts of théma Ellás 'below' Corinth, i.e. on the far side of Corinth from Constantinople.

According to the Chronicle, the stratêghós of (eastern) Pelopónnêsos who conquered the Peloponnesian Sklavinías in Nikêphóros I's reign, either in 804/5 or in 805/6, was a Sklêrós. According to the Scriptor Incertus de Leone, the stratêghós of théma Pelopónnêsos who was appointed by Michael I in or soon after 811 was named Leo 'tou Sklêroú'. Were there two stratêghoí surnamed 'Sklêrós'—one who subjugated the Peloponnesian Sklavinías for Nikêphóros I, and another who was appointed stratêghós of théma Pelopónnêsos by Michael I? Or are these merely two different notices of one and the same person? If Leo Sklêrós was the first stratêghós of a separate théma Pelopónnêsos, it is conceivable that the author of the *Chronicle of Monemvasía* may have erroneously attributed to him the antecedent subjugation of the Peloponnesian Sklavinías—the achievement that had made the creation of a separate théma Pelopónnêsos feasible. In that case, the name of the actual conqueror of the Peloponnesian Sklavinías is unknown.

The answer to this question partly turns on the interpretation of the relevant sentence in the work of the Scriptor Incertus de Leone. As the sentence stands in the text of the Scriptor as we have it, Michael I expelled Leo 'tou Sklêroú' from the Imperial Palace and made him stratêghós of the Pelopónnêsos—presumably as a face-saving way of exiling him. But this sentence begins by stating that Michael I recalled all the people to whom Nikêphóros I had been hostile; and in the immediately following sentence the Scriptor records that Michael I and his wife Prokopía recalled Leo the Armenian (the future Emperor Leo V) and made him stratêghós of théma Anatolikoí. Leo the Armenian's appointment was obviously a reward and not a punishment, so the Scriptor may have intended to say, in his clumsy language, that Leo 'tou Sklêroú', likewise, was one of the people whom Michael I and Prokopía recalled, not (like Theodhótê's brothers) one of the people whom they expelled. If Leo 'tou Sklêroú' had been in disgrace in Nikêphóros I's reign, it seems unlikely that he had been made a stratêghós by Nikêphóros I—unless, of course, he had been guilty, when in office, of some failure that had led to his being cashiered. If he was in truth the conqueror of the Peloponnesian Sklavinías, he had covered himself with glory in 804/5 or 805/6; but, if he was still in office in 807 or whatever the date of the Peloponnesian Slav insurrection may have been, he may then have fallen into disgrace for having failed to prevent the insurrection from breaking out and for having then also failed to take energetic action. The people of Pátras saved themselves by routing their Slav besiegers three days before the stratêghós arrived at Pátras from Corinth; and the Emperor Nikêphóros I gave the credit for the Patrans' surprising victory —and also gave the spoils—to the city's patron saint, St. Andrew. Perhaps the stratêghós was being reprimanded implicitly.

We are left with three unanswered questions: Were there two Sklêroí or only one? And was there, before the subjugation of the Peloponnesian Sklavinías, already a separate théma Pelopónnêsos under a stratêghós, appointed direct by the Emperor, whose effective authority was limited in practice to the eastern part of the Pelopónnêsos? Or was the eastern part of the Pelopónnêsos till then an appendage—τὰ κατωτικὰ μέρη—of théma Ellás? Thirdly, was Corinth, the ancient capital of provincia Achaïa, also the capital of théma Ellás till the creation of a théma Pelopónnêsos in which the former independent Peloponnesian Sklavinías had been reunited with the continuously East Roman eastern side, from Corinth to Cape Maléa inclusive?

22. NIKÓPOLIS. This théma is not mentioned in *Taktikón Uspenski* nor apropos of Prokópios's expedition to south-eastern Italy in 880, though Prokópios is said to have taken with him 'all the western thémata',[1] and thémata Sikelía, Kephalênía, Dhyrrhákhion,[2] Thrákê, and Makedhonía[3] are all named in this connection. Nikópolis does, however, appear as a théma in all the three later Greek lists.

---

[1] *Georg. Mon. Cont.*, p. 845; Leo Grammaticus, p. 258.

[2] *Georg. Mon. Cont.*, loc. cit.

[3] *Theoph. Cont.*, p. 305. The contingents from Thrákê and Makedhonía are said in *Theoph. Cont.* to have been commanded by Leo Apostýppês, who, according to *Georg. Mon. Cont.*, was one of the two commanders of the contingent from Pelopónnêsos.

23. ELLÁS. Among the thémata bearing geographical names—as contrasted with those bearing the names of army-corps—Ellás appears in all four Greek lists, and it is also the earliest théma with a geographical name to appear in any of our surviving records. An appointment to the post of stratêghós Elládhos was made in 695.[1] There must therefore have been a théma Ellás in or before that year; and thus Ellás is the earliest case in which we can be sure that a théma has acquired its eventual meaning and function of being an administrative district as well as a military corps. A théma bearing a geographical name could not be—as, for example, théma Opsíkion could be—solely a military corps whose commander was not also the governor of a district.

Unlike some other thémata with geographical names—for instance, Kappadhokía (Cappadocia)—Ellás had not been the name of any province of the Roman Empire either in the Age of the Principate or under the subsequent Diocletianic–Constantinian regime. In popular non-technical usage, the name Ellás had designated Continental European Greece and the adjacent islands to the south of the southern border of the Roman province of Macedonia, and Ellás in this non-technical sense had been divided into three Roman provinces: Achaïa, Thessalia, and Epirus (Vetus). As the official name of an East Roman administrative district, Ellás was an innovation.

The eventual area of théma Ellás included east-central Continental Greece, the island of Évvoia, and eastern Thessaly. Before the creation of théma Pelopónnêsos, théma Ellás perhaps also included, under the name τὰ κατωτικὰ μέρη, those coastal enclaves of Peloponnesian territory that had not been submerged by the Slav *Völkerwanderung*.

Ellás cannot have been a théma yet in 687, since it is not named in the enumeration of exercitûs in Justinian II's letter of that year to Pope Conon. Yet, before Ellás was given the status of an army-corps district, there may already have been a piece of East Roman territory bearing the name Ellás and also have been a local military force called the Elladhikoí. In Justinian II's letter of 687, the former corps of the magister militum per Illyricum, as well as théma Ellás, is missing. The army-corps of the Eastern Illyricum, which, in Justinian II's language, would have been styled the 'exercitus Illyricianus', must have disintegrated either during the Avaro-Slav invasion of the Balkan Peninsula in 581/2–586/7 or, at the latest, after the overthrow of the Emperor Maurice in 602, and, thereafter, any still surviving East Roman territories in the Balkan Peninsula to the west of the dioecesis of Thrace (i.e. to the west of the area defended by the magister militum per Thraciam) must have been left temporarily to defend themselves out of their own resources as best they could. From 581/2 onwards, the East Roman Empire's military

---

[1] Theophanes, p. 368; Nic. Patr., pp. 37–8.

priority in Europe was the defence of the European hinterland of Constantinople up to the south bank of the lower Danube, in so far as this historic frontier of the Empire could still be held. Ellás, i.e. the only remnant, besides Thessaloníkê, of the territory previously defended by the magister militum per Illyricum and administered by the praetorian prefect of the Eastern Illyricum, must have been defended and administered by the local population, with the help of the Imperial Navy,[1] until, in or before 695, it was made a théma. In 695, the appointment to the command and the governorship of théma Ellás was still such an undesirable fate that the appointee, Leóndios, revolted and deposed Justinian II, the Emperor who had appointed him.[2]

A seal has survived, inscribed τῶν βασιλικῶν κομμερκίων Ἑλλάδος and bearing the effigies of Justinian II and his son Tiberius IV, who reigned as co-Emperor from 705 to 711.[3] There is another seal, inscribed Κωνσταντίνου ἀπεπάρχων καὶ γενικοῦ κομμερκιαρίου ἀποθήκης Ἑλλάδος, which Schlumberger[4] dates in the reign of Constans II (641–68). It is a striking piece of evidence of the disintegration of the East Roman Empire to the west of Thrace that a former praetorian prefect of the Eastern Illyricum should have accepted the humble post of commercial counsellor for this prefecture's surviving south-eastern fragment. This seal indicates, if Schlumberger's dating is correct, that there was at least one minor Imperial official in Ellás before the district was given the status of a théma.

The Elladhikoí combined with the forces of the Kykládhes Islands to mount an unsuccessful naval attack on Constantinople in 727,[5] and in 799 the Elladhikoí instigated an abortive *putsch* against the Empress Eirénê.[6]

24. SIKELÍA. After Justinian I's reconquest of the Roman provinces that had been occupied by the Ostrogoths, Sicily appears to have been separated from Italy and to have been placed under a stratêghós who was given military as well as civil powers.[7] This was an anticipation of the thematic régime, and the transition to this must have been easy. There was a stratêghós of Sicily in 717/18,[8] and, after the irruption of the Lombards

---

[1] The στρατηγὸς τῶν καράβων sailed from Ellás via Skíathos to Thessaloníkê in some year in the 630s or 640s (*S.D. Miracula*, Book II, chap. 5, col. 1369).

[2] Theophanes and Nic. Patr., in locc. citt.   [3] Schlumberger, *Sigillographie*, p. 165.
[4] Ibid.   [5] Theophanes, p. 405; Nic. Patr., p. 57.

[6] Theophanes, pp. 473–4. For the part played in this affair by the chieftain of the Sklavinía Velzêtía, see II, 1 (iii) (a), pp. 98–9, with n. 1 on p. 99.

[7] See A. H. M. Jones, *The Later Roman Empire, 284–602*, vol. i (Oxford, 1964, Blackwell), p. 283, and Bury, *The Later Roman Empire*, vol. ii, p. 37, with n. 1, citing Justinian I's Novel No. 79. In this context the Greek word stratêghós represented the Latin word 'praetor', according to Bury. At this date it was normally used to represent 'magister militum', but Sicily was by far too small a region to have had a magister militum of its own.

[8] Theophanes, p. 398.

into Italy and the consequent disruption of the surviving East Roman possessions there, the 'toe' of Italy had been attached and subordinated to théma Sikelía as the 'ducatus Calabriae'.[1]

The Muslims of North-West Africa won their first foothold in Sicily in 827, and their conquest of the island was virtually completed in 902.[2] Since the death of Justinian I in 565, the East Roman Government had prudently left the remnants of its Continental European possessions to the west of Mount Rhodhópê to fend for themselves, but the East Romans made a stubborn, though eventually unsuccessful, effort to hold Sicily in the ninth century, as, in the seventh century, they had striven to hold North-West Africa.

From 902 onwards, the East Roman Empire barely retained a foothold on Sicilian soil, yet théma Sikelía still appears in Leo VI's schedule of salaries and in the *Taktikón Benešević*, as well as in the two earlier Greek lists.

25. LAGHOUVARDHÍA (LONGIVARDHÍA). This théma extended over the lowlands along the Adriatic coast of south-eastern Italy from Ótranto as far north-westward as the Gargano Peninsula inclusive, with an intermittent and precarious suzerainty over the three South Lombard principalities of Benevento, Capua, and Salerno and over the three non-Lombard city-states Amalfi, Naples, and Gaeta.

This was the only major territorial acquisition in Continental Europe to the west of Mount Rhodhópê that was made by the East Roman Empire during the four centuries and a half that elapsed between Justinian I's reign (527–65) and Basil II's (976–1025).

Basil I was goaded into taking the offensive against the Muslims in south-eastern Italy by his predecessors' and his own failure to bring the Muslims' conquest of Sicily to a halt. In 839/40, sixty-two years before the virtual completion of the Muslim conquest of Sicily in 902, the Muslims had already been able to use Sicily as a base for the conquest of Táranto, and in 841 the Venetians had tried and failed to dislodge them from there. In 842 the Muslims had taken Bari, and from this base they besieged Ragusa, on the eastern shore of the Adriatic in théma Dhalmatía, in 866–8. In 868 Basil I sent a naval expedition, in response to an appeal from the Ragusans, which raised the siege.[3] In 869 he made an alliance with the Carolingian Emperor Lewis II. Lewis took Bari from the Arabs in 871, and, after Lewis's death in 875, the East Romans occupied Bari on 25 December 876, on an invitation from the city's

---

[1] *De Adm. Imp.*, p. 225. The original Calabria had been the 'heel' of Italy, not the 'toe'. The 'toe' had been attached to the 'heel' while both 'heel' and 'toe' had still been in East Roman hands. After the Lombards had conquered the 'heel', the name 'Calabria' was retained by the 'toe'.

[2] See Vasiliev, *Byzance et les Arabes*, ii, I, pp. 145–50.

[3] *De Them.*, Book II, pp. 61–2; *De Adm. Imp.*, chap. 29, p. 130.

Lombard inhabitants. The troops of five western thémata were mobilized for a campaign in south-eastern Italy in 880.[1] Táranto was captured by the East Romans *circa* 881. In 883 contingents from thémata Makedhonía, Thrákê, Kappadhokía, and Kharsianón were mobilized for a further campaign.[2] This expedition failed to dislodge the Muslims from Amándeia and Santa Severina in 'Calabria', but in 885–6 the conquest of south-eastern Italy was completed by Nikêphóros Phokás the Elder;[3] and, though the imposition of East Roman suzerainty on the three principalities and on the three city-states was ephemeral, the East Roman Empire maintained its hold over the Apulian lowlands and over the 'toe' of Italy ('Calabria')[4] till the conquest of théma Laghouvardhía by the Normans in the eleventh century.

Théma Laghouvardhía does not appear either in the *Taktikón Uspenski* or in the klêtorolóyion (except in the Jerusalem manuscript of this),[5] but it does appear in the two later Greek lists.

There were stratêghoí at Bari in 876–86 and at Táranto in 887–8.[6] The date of the earliest record of a stratêghós Laghouvardhías is 891. In that year this post was held by Symvatíkios simultaneously with the governorships of thémata Kephalênía, Makedhonía, and Thrákê.[7] An East Roman katepáno of Italy is heard of first in 975.[8]

26. STRYMÓN. The kleisoúra Strymón may have been created by Justinian II on his expedition from Constantinople to Thessaloníkê in 688/9.[9] Constantine Porphyrogenitus says[10] that Justinian II planted 'Skyths' (i.e. Slavs) there to fill the place of the original Macedonian inhabitants. In stating that the Strymón district τῇ Μακεδονίᾳ συντέτακται,[11] Constantine must be referring to the ancient Macedonia, not to the East Roman théma that had been given the same name. Constantine certainly means the ancient Macedonia when he goes on to say that théma Thessaloníkê καὶ αὐτὸ μέρος Μακεδονίας τυγχάνει.[12] The Strymón district cannot have been detached from théma Makedhonía; for, in Leo VI's schedule of salaries, Makedhonía ranks as an 'Eastern' théma whose stratêghós's salary is paid by the Central Government, whereas Strymón ranks as a 'Western' théma. Strymón appears as a théma not only in the schedule of salaries but also in the klêtorolóyion and in the *Taktikón Beneševič*, in spite

---

[1] *Georg. Mon. Cont.*, p. 845, and *Theoph. Cont.*, p. 305, cited already on p. 264.

[2] *Theoph. Cont.*, p. 312.   [3] *Theoph. Cont.*, pp. 312–13.

[4] According to *De Them.*, p. 60, and *De Adm. Imp.*, p. 50, Calabria, which had been a ducatus of the lost théma Sikelía, was not incorporated in the new théma Laghouvardhía, but was made a stratêghís, i.e. a separate théma. However, it does not appear as such in any of the lists.   [5] See Pertusi, *De Them.*, p. 180.   [6] Pertusi, *De Them.*, p. 181.

[7] Pertusi, ibid., p. 180.   [8] Pertusi, ibid., p. 181.

[9] See Theophanes, p. 364; *De Them.*, Book II, p. 50; and the present work, II, 1 (iii)(a), pp. 79–80 and 91.

[10] In *De Them.*, loc. cit.   [11] Ibid.   [12] Ibid.

of Constantine's assertion[1] that there is no question of its ever having ranked as a théma. The *Taktikón Uspenski* is the only one of the Greek lists in which théma Strymón is missing.

27. KEPHALLÊNÍA. Constantine says in one place that Kephalênía has never ranked as a théma,[2] and in another place[3] that it was raised to the rank of a théma by Leo VI. In this latter passage, Constantine also says that Kephalênía had previously been a toúrma of Laghouvardhía. This can hardly be correct; for Kephalênía appears as a théma in all four Greek lists, and the date of the earliest of the four, the *Taktikón Uspenski*, is earlier than the date of the creation of théma Laghouvardhía.

28. THESSALONÍKÊ. This district appears as a théma in the 'Life of St. Gregory Dhekapolítês' *circa* 826 and in the 'Life of St. Ilarión', 876–86. It also appears as a théma in all four Greek lists.

29. DHYRRHÁKHION. This district appears as a théma in all four Greek lists.

30. DHALMATÍA. This district appears as an arkhondía in the *Taktikón Uspenski* and as a théma in the three later Greek lists.

According to Constantine Porphyrogenitus,[4] the Emperor Heraclius had recovered for the East Roman Empire Dhalmatía and its hinterland, which had been conquered and depopulated by the Avars. To expel the Avars, Heraclius had called in the Croats and Serbs. In return for having been authorized by Heraclius to occupy this ex-Roman territory, the Croats and Serbs had acknowledged the East Roman Government's suzerainty and had accepted conversion to Christianity. However, the Emperor Michael II (820–9) had allowed not only the Croats and Serbs and other peoples in the interior, but also the Roman cities on the coast and on the offshore islands, to become independent.[5] According to Constantine again, the situation had been saved by Basil I. Basil had responded to a request from the still pagan Slavs in the hinterland of Dhalmatía, including the piratical Arentanoí, for missionaries to be sent to convert them.[6] He had responded to an appeal from the Ragusans to him to rescue them from their Muslim besiegers.[7] Basil had then induced the peoples of the interior, as well as the coastal cities of Dhalmatía itself, to co-operate with the East Roman forces in a counter-offensive against the Muslims in Apulia. The contingents from the interior had been ferried across the Adriatic in Ragusan ships.[8] We may guess that the arrival of a Muslim expeditionary force on the east shore of the Adriatic

---

[1] In *De Them.*, in loc. cit.   [2] *De Them.*, Book II, p. 54.
[3] *De Adm. Imp.*, chap. 50, p. 224.   [4] *De Adm. Imp.*, pp. 128, 148–9, 150, 152–4.
[5] Op. cit., p. 128.   [6] Op. cit., p. 129.
[7] Op. cit., p. 130, and *De Them.*, Book II, pp. 61–2, cited on p. 267. See also E. Eickhoff, *Seekrieg und Seepolitik zwischen Islam und Abendland: Das Mittelmeer unter byzantinischer und arabischer Hegemonie (650–1040)* (Berlin, 1966, de Gruyter), pp. 215–16.
[8] *De Adm. Imp.*, pp. 130–1.

had been the alarming event that had moved the peoples of the interior, as well as the coastal cities, to seek the East Roman Imperial Government's friendship and support. Evidently Basil I was statesmanlike in his use of the opening that the Muslim offensive had given to him. At the request of the cities of Dhalmatía, he consented to their paying to the peoples of the interior (e.g. the Croats, the Zakhloúmoi, and the prince of Tervounía) the taxes that the cities had paid previously to the strateghós of théma Dhalmatía. Basil stipulated only that they should make a token payment to the strateghós as well, as an acknowledgment of the Imperial Government's continuing sovereignty.[1] This was politic; for, at the price of forgoing effective sovereignty over the coastal cities, which anyway it would not have been worth the Emperor's while to attempt to re-establish, Basil I secured the lasting goodwill and co-operation of the peoples of the interior.

31. KHERSÓN (TA KLÍMATA). Khersón (i.e. Khersónêsos) had been an independent city-state, in friendly relations with the East Roman Empire, till 833. In that year the Emperor Theóphilos converted Khersón into a théma under a strateghós.[2] The official title of this théma was *Tὰ Κλίματα*.[3] The native árkhondes still survived under the East Roman strateghós,[4] and they appear to have resented their enforced subordination; for in 891 the Khersonítai revolted and killed the strateghós.[5] The East Roman Imperial Government was evidently aware that the Khersonítai were disaffected. Constantine Porphyrogenitus's concluding instructions for his son in *De Administrando Imperio*[6] are on how to bring the Khersonítai to heel by the application of economic sanctions if they revolt or if they are refractory to the Imperial Government's commands.

The following districts are not included in Leo VI's schedule of salaries:

32. OPTIMÁTOI. This district appears in the other three Greek lists and in all four Arabic lists. Its location was on the Bithynian Peninsula, at the north-west corner of Asia Minor, and, like the Voukellárioi and théma Paphlaghonía, the Optimátoi must have been brigaded originally with the Opsíkion.

The Optimátoi resembled other thémata in being both a corps and an administrative district of which the commander of the corps was the governor *ex officio*. Moreover, the members of the Optimátoi corps, like those of other corps, were endowed with stratiotikà ktḗmata.[7] (An

---

[1] *De Adm. Imp.*, pp. 146–7. In this passage, Constantine gives the figures of the annual payments made to the peoples in the interior by six of the Dalmatian cities out of the nine.

[2] *De Adm. Imp.*, pp. 178–9; *Theoph. Cont.*, pp. 123–4. The considerations that moved Theóphilos to take this step are discussed in III, 5 (iii).

[3] *Taktikón Uspenski*, p. 115.

[4] *Theoph. Cont.*, pp. 123–4.

[5] *Georg. Mon. Cont.*, p. 855; *Theoph. Cont.*, p. 360.

[6] pp. 269–70.

[7] Constantine Porphyrogenitus, *Tὰ Βασιλικὰ Ταξείδια*, p. 476.

Optimátos forfeited his estate if he lost an animal that had been committed to his care.)[1] The Optimátoi were singular in being non-combatants. They were an army service corps. When the Emperor went on campaign, the dhoméstikos of the Optimátoi had to provide the number of men required for looking after the Emperor's baggage animals.[2] When the household troops went on campaign, one Optimátos was assigned as a batman to each combatant soldier.[3] Since the Optimátoi were non-combatants,[4] they were not divided into toúrmai and dhroúngoi,[5] as were the soldiers of the combatant thémata.

'I do not know', Constantine writes,[6] 'how the so-called théma Optí-matos came to be called a théma. It has nothing in common with thémata.' Its commander's title was not 'stratêghós' but 'dhoméstikos', and, according to Constantine,[7] this title was a mark of the corps' inferiority. A dhoméstikos, Constantine here says, ranked below a stratêghós and was under a stratêghós's command. However, this statement of Constantine's is open to challenge. It is true that, in Philótheos's order of precedence, the dhoméstikos ton Optêmáton comes twelve places below the stratêghós Khersónos, who was the junior thematic stratêghós.[8] Yet 'dhoméstikos' was also the title of the commanders of three of the four regiments of household troops, and the commander of the senior regiment, the dhoméstikos ton Skholón, served as the commander-in-chief of the whole East Roman Army when a commander-in-chief was required. Like the commanders of all four household regiments, the dhoméstikos ton Optimáton had under him a topotêrêtĕs (lieutenant). Like these and like the stratêghós of the Anatolikoí, he had a khartou-lários. Like the stratêghós of the Anatolikoí, he had a protomandátor. These facts show that the dhoméstikos ton Optimáton was—or, at least, had been originally—a grander dignitary than Constantine admits that he was.

The corps's name is on a par with their commander's title. The word 'Optimátoi' may mean either 'a *corps d'élite*' (Latin *optimi*) or a corps of nobles (Latin *Optimates*). According to a Greek historian, Olympiodorus,[9] the second of these two alternative possible interpretations of the word 'Optimátoi' is the right one. The original Optimátoi had been the nobles in the war-band with which the Teutonic barbarian Radagaisus had invaded Italy in 405. They had been taken into the Roman service by Stilicho after Radagaisus's capitulation in Etruria. This account of the corps's origin seems far-fetched. How and when did these troops make the

---

[1] See ibid.   [2] See ibid.
[3] *De Them.*, Book I, p. 26.
[4] Constantine's statement that the Optimátoi were non-combatants is confirmed by Ibn al-Fakîh, Ibn Khurdādbih, and Kudāmah (Pertusi, *De Them.*, p. 131).
[5] *De Them.*, Book I, p. 26.   [6] Ibid.   [7] Op. cit., pp. 26–7.
[8] Philótheos, p. 137 Bury, p. 714 Bonn.   [9] *F.H.G.*, iv, 50, fr. 9.

long journey from Etruria to Bithynia? And why were they transferred from the Western to the Eastern Roman Government's service? It seems more probable that the Optimátoi were so named because, like the Voukellárioi, they were a *corps d'élite*, and that, like the Voukellárioi again, they had been brigaded with the Opsíkion for this reason. The geographical location of the Optimátoi, nearest to Constantinople of all the Asiatic corps, also suggests that they had originally been a privileged corps, not a dishonoured one. At the date of composition of 'Mavríkios's' *Stratêghikón*, the Optimátoi were not only still combatant troops but were first-class troops. In two passages they are explicitly contrasted with inferior troops and are associated with the Phoidherátoi, whose high quality is not in doubt.[1]

If so, the Optimátoi must have been deliberately degraded[2] as a punishment for some signal offence. Perhaps we may guess that they had played a prominent part in the seizure of Constantinople, and of the Imperial Crown, in 742 by Artávazdhos, who was kómês of the Opsíkion at the time. If the Optimátoi did side on this occasion with the rebel commander of the corps with which they were then still brigaded, their geographical location in Bithynia is likely to have made the seizure of Constantinople devolve on them together with 'Mónotios's' son Nikêphóros, who was Artávazdhos's agent in Thrace. It has been suggested already[3] that, after Artávazdhos's defeat in 743, the victorious Emperor Constantine V probably broke up théma Opsíkion by detaching from it Thrákê and the Voukellárioi. Probably the Optimátoi were detached from the Opsíkion on the same occasion. A stratêghós of the Voukellárioi makes his first appearance in 766/7;[4] a stratêghós of Thrákê makes his in 801/2.[5] The Optimátoi are mentioned first in 773.[6] It seems likely that these three districts were detached from the Opsíkion and were created into separate thémata at one and the same date.

There had been no need for Constantine V to disarm the Voukellárioi. This corps's district was not in the immediate neighbourhood of Constantinople, and the Voukellárioi were good soldiers. The troops that were the most dangerous politically were those stationed in Thrace and in Bithynia, next door to Constantinople. The troops in Thrace could not be disarmed; they were an indispensable buffer between Constantinople and Bulgaria. On the other hand, the Optimátoi could be disarmed without weakening the Empire's defences against any of its foreign neighbours. Constantine V did call up the Optimátoi—apparently as combatants—when, in 773, he concentrated the 80,000 troops with which he won his

---

[1] 'Mavríkios', *Stratêghikón*, Part 2, chap. 5, p. 60 Scheffer, p. 84 Mihăescu. The tághmata of the Optimátoi, ἐν ἐπιλογῇ ὄντα, need to be formed only five deep. See also Part 2, chap. 10, p. 66 Scheffer, p. 88 Mihăescu.

[2] This is also Pertusi's guess in *De Them.*, p. 132. [3] On pp. 245 and 254.

[4] See p. 254. [5] See p. 256. [6] Theophanes, p. 447.

victory at Lithosória. This concentration was, however, an exceptional measure. We may guess that the Optimátoi had been degraded to non-combatant service after 743, and that the campaign of 773 was the only occasion on which arms were ever put into their hands again.

33. THE WALL (THE WALLS) (TĀFLĀ, TALĀKĀ).[1] All four Arabic sources, but none of the Greek sources, mention this district, and they also say that it includes Constantinople. No convincing Greek original has been suggested for the Arabic name Tāflā or Talākā, but Kudāmah says that this district extends from Constantinople to a wall that is two days' march distant from the capital; Mas'udi, whose list differs considerably from those of the other four Arabic authorities,[2] agrees with them in mentioning this district; and, in describing the district's western boundary, Mas'udi,[3] as well as Ibn al-Fakīh, transliterates the Greek name Μακρὸν Τεῖχος and gives the correct translation of it. This long wall can only be the Anastasian Wall. Bury points out[4] that Justinian I mentions ὁ βικάριος τοῦ Μακροῦ Τείχους in his Novel No. 16 of 535; that, in his Novel No. 25, published two months later in the same year, he mentions that there had been two βικάριοι τοῦ Μακροῦ Τείχους, one military and the other civil, and he decrees that the two posts shall now be combined in the hands of a single πραίτωρ Ἰουστινιανὸς ἐπὶ Θρᾴκης.[5] In the list of provinces, given in the *Sancti Demetrii Miracula*, Book II,[6] which were devastated, and whose populations were deported to Sirmia, in 582/3 or 586/7[7] the writer mentions separately 'Thrace' and 'the Long Wall adjacent to Byzantium'.[8]

We may infer that the Arabic authorities are correct—though their information may have been out of date—in stating that there had once been an administrative district and military command called 'the Long Wall'. We may guess that this district and command had been created by Anastasius I when he had built the Long Wall, and that they had been incorporated in théma Thrákê when Thrace had been detached from the Opsíkion and had been created into a separate army-corps district. At the time at which Constantine Porphyrogenitus was compiling his *De Thematibus*, the district in which Constantinople was included was no longer 'the Long Wall'; it was théma Thrákê.[9] In 718/19 there was still an ἄρχων τοῦ Τειχίου[10] or Τειχῶν,[11] and in 899, the year in which Philótheos brought out his new edition of the klêtorolóyion, there was still a kómês

---

[1] See Gelzer, *Die Genesis*, pp. 82 and 86–8.   [2] See Brooks, 'Arabic Lists', p. 69.
[3] Gelzer, op. cit., p. 86.   [4] In *The Imperial Administrative System*, p. 68.
[5] Compare Justinian's creation of the post of praetor of Sicily, with the same combination of powers and the same title.
[6] Book II, chap. 5, col. 1361.
[7] See II, 1 (iii) (a), p. 73 and Annex III, pp. 633–6.
[8] ἔτι μὴν καὶ Θρᾴκης, καὶ τοῦ πρὸς Βυζαντίου Μακροῦ Τείχους.   [9] *De Them.*, p. 44.
[10] Theophanes, p. 401.   [11] Nic. Patr., p. 56.

ton teikhéon, who ranked immediately below the dhoméstikos ton Optêmáton.[1] The office may have been a sinecure since the creation of théma Thrákê, but Philótheos claims that he has omitted obsolete posts, and the kómês (alias dhoméstikos)[2] ton teikhéon still had on his staff, among other subordinates, a topotêrêtḗs and a khartoulários, like the commanders of each of the regiments of household troops, and a proto-mandátor, like all of them except the dhoméstikos ton Skholón and like the stratêghós ton Anatolikón. The kómês ton teikhéon also had six portárioi,[3] and this seems to indicate that he still had the gates in the Long Wall under his charge, though the references to him[4] make it clear that he himself was stationed, not on the Anastasian Wall, but in the Palace at Constantinople.

34. THÉMA KHARPEZÍKION. This théma was as ephemeral as théma Leondókomis. Théma Kharpezíkion is mentioned only in Constantine Porphyrogenitus's account of the expedition sent against Crete in 949, but here it is named in four places,[5] and it appears to have had the regular organization of a cavalry théma. There is a present-day village named Kharpezuk sixteen kilometres west-north-west of 'Arabkir.[6] Honigmann guesses[7] that théma Kharpezíkion had been carved out of the territory of the former amirate of Malaṭīyah, but he is inclined to locate it to the east of the River Euphrates.

---

[1] Klêtorolóyion, p. 137 Bury, p. 714 Bonn. On p. 141 Bury, p. 719 Bonn he is styled dhoméstikos.

[2] He is styled 'kómês' in the *Taktikón Uspenski*, p. 119, and in *De Caer.*, Book I, p. 6. He is called ὁ τειχεώτης in *De Caer.*, Book I, p. 295; in Τὰ Βασιλικὰ Ταξείδια, p. 460; and in *Theoph. Cont.*, pp. 175 and 398.

[3] Klêtorolóyion, p. 141 Bury, p. 719 Bonn.　　　　　　　　　　　[4] See footnote 2.

[5] *De Caer.*, Book II, pp. 662, 665, 667, 669.

[6] E. Honigmann in Vasiliev, *Byzance et les Arabes*, vol. iii, p. 76.

[7] In loc. cit.

5. The Autonomous City-States (Khersón, the nine Dalmatian Cities, Venice, Amalfi, Naples, Gaeta)

THE East Roman Imperial Government was efficient enough—especially in the raising of taxes—to be an incubus on its subjects, and it weighed most heavily on them in those of its possessions and dependencies that were the most thoroughly under its control. This control was at its maximum in the thémata of the 'Eastern' class, and, among these, the remote and mountainous Khaldhía and Mesopotamía were perhaps the least strictly regimented. The stratêghoí of these two thémata, like the stratêghoí of thémata of the 'Western' class, did not have the whole of their salaries handed out to them by the Imperial Treasury but drew the salaries for themselves out of local sources of revenue—the stratêghós of Mesopotamía the whole of his salary and the stratêghós of Khaldhía the half of his. In Khaldhía, as in the ex-sovereign city-state Khersón, local notables had retained some power, and an Imperial official who had business to do in Khaldhía needed to secure the Khaldhian notables' support.[1] Among the three naval thémata, the Kivyrrhaiótai seem to have had the freest hand. The European thémata of the 'Western' class were probably freer still.[2] But the freest of all the East Roman Government's subjects were the citizens of the autonomous city-states on the Empire's fringes: Khersón on the north shore of the Black Sea,[3] the nine Dalmatian cities and Venice in the Adriatic, and Amalfi, Naples, and Gaeta on the Tyrrhene coast of Peninsular Italy.

These fourteen city-states had diverse origins. Khersón and Naples were pre-Roman Greek colonies. Khersón was a colony of Herakleia Pontica, which was itself a colony of Megara. Naples was a colony of the neighbouring colonial Greek city-state Cumae, which was said to have been the earliest of all the Greek colonies in Peninsular Italy. Of the nine Dalmatian city-states, Iadera (Constantine Porphyrogenitus's Dhiádhera, present-day Zadar, Zara),[4] Tragurium (Constantine's Tetranghoúrin, present-day Trogir, Tráu)[5], and Kattaros (Constantine's Dhekátera, present-day Kotor)[6] also date from before the *Völkerwanderung* Age, and so, on the Tyrrhene coast of Italy, does Gaeta. The rest, however,

---

[1] *De Adm. Imp.*, p. 209. [2] See II, 1 (ii), p. 48–9.
[3] At the south-west corner of the Crimea, near the entrance to the magnificent harbour on which the Russians founded Sevastopol in 1783. This was the nearest of the first-rate harbours on the north shore of the Black Sea to the north coast of Asia Minor.
[4] *De Adm. Imp.*, pp. 128, 139–40, and 147.
[5] Ibid., pp. 128, 138, 147. [6] Ibid., pp. 128, 139, 147; *De Them.*, p. 61.

were new cities founded in natural fastnesses or artificial fortresses,
by refugees who had been evicted from their former homes by barbarian
invaders. In Dalmatia, Árvê, Vékla, and Ópsara[1] were off-shore
islands in the Gulf of Quarnero, and Loumbrikáton[2] was another
island towards the south-eastern end of the Dalmatian archipelago.
Aspálathon (the present-day Split, Spalato)[3] was the palace that had been
built by the Emperor Diocletian to be his retreat after his abdication.
The palace had been occupied by refugees from Salonae and other places
in the interior who had been attracted by the palace's intact and massive
walls.[4] Ragusa (Constantine's Raoúsin, the present-day Dubrovnik)
had been founded, by refugees from the Dalmatian Epidaurus and from
Salonae, on a rock, projecting into the Adriatic, which had originally
been insulated from the mainland by a narrow channel.[5] Amalfi had
been founded on the barely accessible south coast of the Sorrento Peninsula. Venice had been founded, on islands in a lagoon, by refugees from
the former continental province Venetia. These refugee city-states were
counterparts of Monemvasía, Akhaḯa, and Arkadhía in the Pelopónnêsos[6] and the 'isles of refuge' off the coasts of the Pelopónnêsos and Attica
and in the Gulf of Itéa.[7] The Peloponnesian refugee communities too
might have become autonomous, and perhaps eventually independent, if
the East Roman Imperial Government had not re-established its direct
authority over the Pelopónnêsos as a whole in 804/5 or in 805/6.

The fates of the autonomous city-states were as diverse as their origins.
Venice became a commercial and naval Great Power. By 1204 she had
grown powerful enough to be able, in alliance with a band of French
'crusaders', to take Constantinople by storm and to partition with her
French confederates the Empire of which she had once been an outlying
possession. Ragusa became Venice's miniature replica and bitter enemy.
Venice retained her independence till 1797 and Ragusa hers till 1805.
Naples lost to the Normans the self-government that she had enjoyed
ever since her foundation; but eventually she was compensated for
having ceased to be a city-state by becoming, after 1282, the capital city
of the Kingdom of Sicily ultra Farum in South-Eastern Italy, and at last,
in 1738, the capital of the whole Kingdom of the Two Sicilies. Khersón,
Gaeta, Amalfi, and the Dalmatian cities, except for Ragusa, had no
great future, though, in the tenth century, Amalfi was still competing
with Venice for capturing the maritime trade of the Levant. Amalfi
traded as far afield as the Black Sea,[8] and in 972 she was singled out by
Ibn Hawkal as being the richest, most distinguished, and most active

---

[1] *De Adm. Imp.*, pp. 128, 140, and 147.   [2] Ibid., p. 140.
[3] Ibid., pp. 128, 137–8, 147.   [4] Ibid., p. 138.
[5] Ibid., pp. 128, 136–7, 147.   [6] See Annex III, p. 638, n. 5, and p. 650.
[7] See Sinclair Hood in *The Annual of the British School at Athens*, No. 65 (1970), pp. 37–45.
[8] Eickhoff, op. cit., p. 109.

city in Langobardia.[1] Khersón, whose trade was at the East Roman Empire's mercy, lost her independence to the East Roman Empire but retained a substantial measure of autonomy.[2]

Naples was the first of the East Roman Empire's client city-states to pursue her own interests at her suzerain's expense.[3] During the Empress Eirēnê's reign (797–802), Naples deliberately loosened her political ties with the East Roman Government and confirmed her ecclesiastical ties with Western Christendom. At Naples, the Greek language had survived, for more than eleven centuries, this colonial Greek city's subjection to Roman rule, but, at the turn of the eighth and ninth centuries of the Christian Era, Naples was now at last Latinized.[4] Naples's progress towards independence was assisted by the North-West African Muslims' progressive conquest of Sicily from the East Romans from 827 onwards. Already in 812, Naples had refused to supply a contingent to an East Roman fleet that had been sent to protect Sicily against a Western Muslim naval assault.[5] In 836 Naples called in the North-West African Muslim invaders of Sicily who had established themselves at Palermo to rescue her from her neighbour the Lombard Duke Sicard of Benevento,[6] and she thus opened the way for the Muslims to win a foothold in south-eastern Italy. Moreover, in return for the Sicilian Muslims' aid, Naples helped them, in 842/3, to extend their hold on Sicily by conquering Messina.[7]

The Frankish and East Roman counter-offensive in and after 869 against the Muslim invaders of southern Italy was offset, and was partly counteracted, by the aid that the invaders received from the local East Roman city-states and South Lombard principalities. One band of Muslims was harboured first by Naples, in its own territory, and then, from 881 onwards, by the principality of Salerno at Agropoli. Another band had been installed by Gaeta, first at Fondi, in the Papal territory, and then, in Gaeta's own territory, at Traetto ('the crossing'), a strategic position commanding the right bank of the River Garigliano, near its mouth. A third band had established itself at Sepino, in the territory of the remnant of the principality of Benevento, under the aegis of the central Italian Lombard duchy of Spoleto.[8] The re-imposition of East Roman suzerainty over Naples, Gaeta, and Amalfi in 885–6 was ephemeral. In 956, Naples was reduced to submission again by an East Roman

---

[1] Eickhoff, op. cit., p. 111.   [2] See Part II, chap. 4, Appendix, p. 270.

[3] See A. R. Lewis: *Naval Power and Trade in the Mediterranean, A.D. 500–1100* (Princeton, 1951, University Press), p. 117; Eickhoff, op. cit., p. 108.

[4] Bury, *A History of the Eastern Roman Empire*, pp. 309–10.

[5] Eickhoff, op. cit., p. 57.

[6] Bury, op. cit., pp. 311–12; Vasiliev, *Byzance et les Arabes*, vol. i, p. 181.

[7] Bury, op. cit., pp. 305–6; Vasiliev, *Byzance et les Arabes*, vol. i, pp. 204–5.

[8] Eickhoff, op. cit., pp. 218 and 225–6; Canard in Vasiliev, *Byzance et les Arabes*, ii, I, pp. 152–3.

expeditionary force,[1] but Naples's short-lived independence was finally extinguished, not by the East Romans, but by the Normans.

The origins of Venice[2] were humbler than those of Naples, though Venice became not only an independent city-state but an imperial power that was able to bully and exploit its former suzerain. An inscription of the year 639 proves that, at that date, the refugee Venetian community in the lagoon was still being governed by a dux or a magister militum who was responsible to the East Roman exarch at Ravenna.[3] The Venetian tribuni were subordinate to East Roman officials, and the demarcation of the Venetian territory on the mainland in the reign of the Lombard King Liutprand (712–39) was carried out by East Roman officials, the exarch and the local magister.[4] When the East Roman Empire's Italian subjects rebelled, the rebellion was suppressed successfully at Venice, as elsewhere. The extinction of the East Roman Exarchate of Ravenna in 751 was followed at Venice by a bout of anarchy,[5] as the self-assertion of Naples was, half a century later.

After the incorporation, in 774, of the Lombard Kingdom (including the former East Roman Exarchate) in the dominions of the Frankish crown, the pressure of Venice's hinterland on Venice increased. In 787, Charlemagne placed an embargo on Venice's trade with his dominions—presumably with the intention of forcing Venice, under this economic duress, to transfer her allegiance from the East Roman Empire to himself.[6] In 804 there was a pro-Frank revolution at Venice,[7] and in 805 the dukes of Venice and Dalmatia did homage to Charlemagne.[8] In 807 an East Roman naval expedition compelled Venice to resume her allegiance to Constantinople,[9] and the East Roman admiral Nikḗtas came to terms with Pepin, Charlemagne's son and representative in the Lombard Kingdom;[10] but a second East Roman naval expedition to the head of the Adriatic in 808–9 had no success with either Pepin or the Venetians.[11] In 810 Pepin occupied the Venetian islands at the invitation of one local faction, but he was expelled by a popular insurrection.[12] Venice's liberation of herself by her own exertions made her virtually independent, and her position was now strengthened by the synoecism of the hitherto scattered refugee Venetian settlements[13] on the unoccupied but

---

[1] Canard in Vasiliev, *Byzance et les Arabes*, ii, I, pp. 371–2.

[2] See *De Adm. Imp.*, p. 124.

[3] R. Cessi, 'Venice on the Eve of the Fourth Crusade', in *C. Med. H.*, vol. iv, 2nd ed., Part I, pp. 250–74, on pp. 250–1.

[4] Cessi, ibid., pp. 253–4.   [5] Cessi, ibid., pp. 254–5.

[6] Bury, op. cit., p. 323.   [7] Op. cit., loc. cit.

[8] Cessi in loc. cit., p. 257.

[9] Cessi, ibid., p. 258; Bury, op. cit., p. 324.

[10] Cessi, ibid., p. 258.   [11] Cessi, ibid., p. 259.

[12] Cessi, ibid. See also *De Adm. Imp.*, pp. 123–5.

[13] A list of the early insular Venetian settlements is given in *De Adm. Imp.*, p. 122.

fertile island of Rialto[1] (the site of the city of Venice from then till today).

However, since 800 Charlemagne's paramount aim, in his dealings with the East Roman Empire, had been to obtain the East Roman Government's recognition of the legitimacy of his assumption of the title 'Emperor of the Romans'. A settlement was achieved by an East Roman diplomat, Arsáphios. He went first to Venice, where, on the East Roman Government's behalf, he recognized the new regime as a *fait accompli*. Arsáphios then went on to Pavia, the capital of the Lombard Kingdom, and, finding there that Pepin was no longer alive, he went on again, farther still, to Aachen, and there negotiated with Charlemagne in 811–12 a comprehensive settlement that was ratified in 814.[2] In exchange for the East Roman Imperial Government's recognition of his title, Charlemagne now evacuated the Venetian holdings on the mainland, together with the East Roman possessions in Istria, Liburnia, and Dalmatia that were under Frankish occupation. The Frankish dominions were now thrown open again to Venetian trade, but Venice undertook to pay to the Frankish government at Pavia an annual tribute of thirty-six pounds silver on account of her mainland territories, and this tribute was still being paid in Constantine Porphyrogenitus's day.[3] Venice's *quid pro quo* was a licence to offer for sale, at the annual fair held at the capital of the Lombard Kingdom, Pavia, the silks and purples that she imported from Constantinople. Amalfi and Gaeta, too, were admitted to this fair, but not Naples.[4]

Venice's reaction to the Muslim invasion of Sicily in and after 827 was different from that of Naples. In 827 the Venetians sent ships to help the East Romans to resist the Muslim attack, and the first Venetian squadron appears to have been followed by a second,[5] but Venice's intervention in Sicily was evidently half-hearted. She did not feel that her own direct interests were at stake there. When, however, Muslims from Sicily seized first Brindisi and then Táranto in the 'heel' of Italy *circa* 838–40, the Venetians responded to an appeal from the Emperor Theóphilos by sending a naval expedition to Táranto. This further Muslim encroachment was indeed menacing Venice's own vital interests by threatening to bring the exit from the Adriatic under Muslim control. However, in 841 the Venetians suffered a crushing defeat off Táranto, and in 841–2 the Muslims followed up this victory by naval raids to the head of the

---

[1] Cessi, pp. 259–60; Eickhoff, op. cit., p. 54. In *De Adm. Imp.*, p. 122, Rhívandon (i.e. Rialto) is said, correctly, to be the present seat of the Doge; but both Rialto and Torcello are enumerated, incorrectly, among Venice's possessions on the mainland.

[2] Bury, op. cit., pp. 324–5; Cessi in loc. cit., pp. 260–1.

[3] *De Adm. Imp.*, pp. 124–5.

[4] Eickhoff, op. cit., p. 110. Cf. Liutprand, *Legatio*, chap. 55, quoted in II, 1 (ii), pp. 65–7.

[5] Bury, op. cit., pp. 301–2; Eickhoff, op. cit., pp. 75 and 104.

Adriatic.[1] Venice did not lend a hand for the relief of Ragusa in 868,[2] and it was the Ragusan, not the Venetian, navy that helped the East Roman fleet in 869 to make its counter-attack on the Muslim holdings in Apulia. Moreover, Ragusa provided seven ships for guarding the coast of théma Dhyrrhákhion, as well as théma Dhalmatía, in 949.[3]

Though it suited the Venetians, longer than it suited the Neapolitans, to be loyal to their suzerain, the Venetians, too, did not hesitate to give priority to their own interests. For instance, they carried on a profitable trade in European naval stores with the Muslim naval powers,[4] and thus made a major contribution to a Muslim naval ascendancy that lasted for more than two centuries, reckoning from the simultaneous Muslim invasions of Sicily and Crete in 827. The Muslim countries produced esparto grass for making ropes, but they were not well off for timber, tar, and pitch, and their navies might have been paralysed if their European victims had placed an effective embargo on these materials. Venice continued to supply them in defiance of Constantinopolitan prohibitions and Western Christian indignation.

The commercial advance of Venice was not impeded by her domestic strife and turbulence, which she did not overcome before the eleventh century. Part of the nemesis of the over-taxing of the East Roman Empire's resources by the ambitious military policy of the Emperors Nikêphóros II Phokás and John Dzimiskěs and Basil II was the pair of concessions that Basil II was constrained to make to Venice in exchange for services from her which his policy required. When, in 992, he gave to Venice exceptionally favourable tariff terms for her trade in the East Roman Empire,[5] this was a bad day for native East Roman commerce and industry. In 1000, Venice took prompt advantage of a free hand that Basil II had given her in Dalmatia. In that year the Venetian Doge Peter II Orseolo launched a naval expedition that gave Venice the mastery over the Dalmatian coast, and the Doge of Venice assumed the second title of Dux Dalmatiae from then onwards. By the year 1000, coming events were already casting their shadows before them. To outward appearance the East Roman Empire was then rising towards a higher peak of power than it had attained at any earlier date since the overthrow of the Emperor Maurice in 602. But the

---

[1] Bury, op. cit., pp. 312–13; Vasiliev, *Byzance et les Arabes*, vol. i, pp. 182–3; Eickhoff, op. cit., p. 184.

[2] Eickhoff, op. cit., p. 219.   [3] *De Caer.*, Book II, chap. 45, p. 664, line 9.

[4] Lewis, op. cit., p. 116. See also the present book, II, 7, p. 328.

[5] See Lewis, op. cit., p. 214, and Eickhoff, op. cit., pp. 371–2. For Venetians, the import-toll at Ávydhos was reduced, in 992, from a maximum of 30 nomísmata to 2 nomísmata, but this privilege was to be forfeited if the Venetians misused it for smuggling Amalfitan, Lombard, or Apulian goods into the Empire. (N.B. Apulia was a théma of the Empire at this date, so the Venetians were now being favoured above the Empire's own direct subjects.) In return, Venetian ships were to be provided for transporting East Roman troops to southern Italy.

contemporary commercial and naval progress of Venice at the Empire's expense throws light on the weakness of the economic basis of the Empire's military exertions in that only superficially glorious age.

The Italian city-states that were nominally under East Roman sovereignty—particularly Venice, Amalfi, Naples, and Gaeta—were the beneficiaries from the economic war between the East Roman Empire and the Umayyad Caliphate that was started by the East Roman Imperial Government during and after the second Arab siege of Constantinople in 717–18. This economic war accentuated the tendency, which was innate in the êthos of the East Roman Imperial regime, to impose a strict governmental regulation on the private economic activities of East Roman subjects. These restrictions handicapped traders whose homes were in the territory under direct East Roman administration. The autonomy of the nominally subject city-states enabled them to elude or defy Constantinople's control, and this freedom of action made their economic fortunes. From the eighth century onwards, they captured progressively the Empire's internal carrying trade, as well as its trade with the Muslims and the Western Christians.[1]

---

[1] See Lewis, op. cit., pp. 121, 122, 177.

6. *The Army*

AFTER the overthrow of the Emperor Maurice in 602, the East Roman Army had virtually disintegrated. It had been re-created by the Emperor Heraclius, and, after the restoration of peace between the East Roman and Persian Empires in 628 on the basis of the *status quo ante* the war of 604–28, Heraclius appears to have reconstituted the Diocletianic–Constantinian Army, and to have re-installed its pre-war units in their pre-war stations,[1] during the brief breathing-space before these dispositions were wrecked once again by the Arabs' onslaught. The reconstituted Roman Army survived this second shock within the drastically reduced territory that it managed still to hold. By 926, the Army was strong enough to take the offensive again, first on its eastern front against the waning power of the 'Abbasid Caliphate and its successor-states, and eventually on its western front too, against Bulgaria.

For a century ending at the death of the Emperor Basil II in 1025, this was the best army in the World. Yet in 1071, when the Empire's territory had been extended farther eastwards in Armenia than ever before since the Emperor Trajan's equally ill-starred expansion of his dominions in this quarter, the Army suffered as shattering a débâcle as it had suffered after 602 and, before that, in and after 251. In 1071 the Emperor Rhomanós IV Dhioyénês was defeated and taken prisoner by the Saljūqs, and in the same year, at the opposite end of the Empire's dominions, Bari, the capital of théma Laghouvardhía, was captured by the Normans.

Between the reign of the Emperor Philip (244–9) and the reign of Rhomanós IV (1068–71), the Army's successive collapses and recoveries went, indeed, to extremes, and this rhythm continued to repeat itself. The Comnenian recovery was followed by the débâcle of 1204, in which Constantinople itself was taken, for the first time, by a foreign assailant, and the débâcle of 1204 was retrieved by the refugee East Roman Imperial Government at Níkaia. Each of the successive recoveries was remarkable, yet not one of them fully restored the *status quo ante* the previous collapse. The general effect, in military terms, was thus a death-agony that was protracted over a term of more than twelve centuries by the dying patient's heroic series of rallies.

In technical terms, the whole of this phase of the Army's history was characterized by the persistent predominance of the cavalry arm, in contrast to the period that had ended in the third century of the Christian

---

[1] Except perhaps, for the former command of the magister militum per Illyricum (i.e. the praetorian prefecture of the Eastern Illyricum).

Era. From the beginning till the débâcle in A.D. 251, the infantry had been the Roman Army's puissant arm, and its complement of cavalry had always been inadequate. From the latter part of the third century of the Christian Era onwards, the relative importance and status of the infantry and the cavalry were reversed.

The penetration of the interior of the Empire by invaders, many of whom were mounted, constrained the Empire to build up a strong arm, of considerable mobility, for defence. The Roman infantry's age-old prestige was finally shattered by the Gothic cavalry at Adrianople in 378, and from then onwards, at the latest, the ascendancy of the cavalry arm in the Roman Army was taken as a matter of course. Yet, during the three centuries and a quarter that followed the Arabs' onslaught on the Empire in the 630s, there were still certain key roles which could not be played by cavalry and for which the infantry arm therefore continued to be indispensable. During this period it was of vital military importance for the East Roman Empire to hold Constantinople and the fortresses on the East Roman side of the Romano-Arab frontier, and fortifications cannot be manned by troops on horseback. Moreover, the East Roman infantry had also an indispensable role in the tactics of 'dogging and pouncing', which had been found by experience to be the Army's best resort for coping with the Arabs' perennial raids.[1] The 'dogging' was, of course, the cavalry's task; but the purpose of 'dogging' was to be able eventually to 'pounce' at the most favourable moment and in the most promising place. The desired and awaited occasion was the last stage of the enemy's withdrawal, when, wearied by a war of rapid movement and encumbered and preoccupied with his loot, the enemy was seeking to make his way back home, through one or other of the defiles that traverse the Távros and Andítavros Ranges. This was the East Roman Army's opportunity to make the enemy raiders pay for their temerity; but the raiders might slip through their opponents' fingers if they had to deal only with the East Roman cavalry following at their heels. If the enemy was finally to be trapped and mauled, the East Roman cavalry must detain him long enough to enable the East Roman infantry to get ahead of him and to occupy the heights commanding the defile through which the enemy had to pass—heights that, like fortress-walls, would be out of court for operations on horseback.

Thus in the East Roman Army the infantry still had at least two vital functions to perform.[2] Yet the superior prestige of the cavalry is reflected

---

[1] See II, 1 (iii) (b), pp. 109–12.

[2] It is noteworthy that the Emperor Nikêphóros II Phokás—whose *forte* was offensive warfare and whose favourite arm was the most heavily-armoured type of cavalry (κατά-φρακτοι), which he himself had fostered (see his Novel No. 21 of 967, in *J.G.-R.*, vol. iii, p. 300)—devotes the first two out of the six chapters of his Στρατηγικὴ Ἔκθεσις καὶ Σύνταξις to the infantry before going on to deal with the cataphracts in the third and fourth chapters.

in the East Roman Army's technical terminology. While the terms 'stratós' and 'théma' were applicable to all arms, the term 'toúrma', which denoted the largest of the subdivisions of a 'théma', was a word of Latin origin that had originally meant specifically a squadron of cavalry. In spite of its original meaning, this term had come to be applied to the organization of all arms, including the fleets of the naval thémata. The subdivisions of these, too, were called 'toúrmai', just as if they had been thémata of the 'cavalry' class.[1]

Since the reorganization of the East Roman Army after the Arabs' assault, it had come to consist of two sections. The bulk of it was constituted by the thémata. These were distributed all over the Empire's non-metropolitan territory, and the thematic soldiers depended for their subsistence and their equipment on income from real property, though they also received intermittently some precarious and inadequate pay in money from the Central Government.[2] By contrast, the tághmata, i.e. the household troops,[3] were concentrated, with the exception of one detachment, in or near Constantinople, and their pay was ample enough and regular enough for them to be able to live on it. Presumably they, too, were at liberty to own land, but this was not an indispensable condition, as it was with the thematic troops, for enabling them to serve.

The seamen of the Imperial Fleet were in an intermediate position.[4] Like the taghmatic land-troops, they received regular pay, but not a living wage. They were partly dependent, as the thematic troops were mainly, on income from real estate. In Constantine Porphyrogenitus's Novel No. 7, which must have been promulgated at some date between 947 and 959, the minimum amount of inalienable real estate is fixed at two pounds gold for seamen of the Imperial Fleet,[5] in contrast to the four pounds gold that is the minimum required for seamen in the three naval thémata and for soldiers in the cavalry thémata. We do not know where the estates of the seamen of the Imperial Fleet were situated. Unlike the naval thémata, the Imperial Fleet did not have a district of its own of which its commander was the governor.[6]

---

[1] See for instance, *De Them.*, p. 41.

[2] See II, 1 (iii) (d), pp. 135–7.

[3] In 'Mavríkios's' *Stratéghikón*, the term tághmata has a quite different technical meaning. It means the smallest unit in an army-corps, the unit which is called a vándon in Leo VI's *Taktiká*.

[4] See H. Ahrweiler, *Byzance et la mer* (Paris, 1966, Presses universitaires de France), p. 66.

[5] See II, 1 (iii) (d), p. 134, and II, 1 (iii) (e), p. 155.

[6] When, at some date in the second half of the ninth century (after the compilation of the *Taktikón Uspenski* and before Philótheos's revision of the klêtorolóyion), Sámos was erected into a naval théma of the same type as théma Kivyrrhaiótai and théma Aiyaíon Pélaghos, coastal territory on the mainland, formerly belonging to théma Thrakĕsioi, was transferred to the new théma Sámos—presumably in order to endow the seamen of théma Sámos with στρατιωτικὰ κτήματα situated in the transferred territory.

The tághmata[1] proper consisted, in the ninth and tenth centuries, of four cavalry regiments, the Skholaí, the Exkoúvitoi, the Arithmós, and the Ikanátoi. The Skholaí were the first of the four in order of precedence, and, when a commander-in-chief was required, the commander (dhoméstikos) of the Skholaí usually received the appointment.[2] The Ikanátoi were perhaps the youngest regiment of the four. They may have been created by Nikêphóros I (802–11). They appear already in the *Taktikón Uspenski*.

The term tághmata was sometimes used in a wider sense to include not only the four taghmatic regiments but also the Noúmeroi and the seamen of the Imperial Fleet. For instance, in a procession on the day after the Vroumália which was formed in double columns that chanted antiphonally, the officers (ἄρχοντες) of the Skholaí, the Arithmós, and the Noúmeroi marched in one column, and the officers of the Ikanátoi and the Imperial Fleet in the parallel column, and these are designated collectively as 'the officers of the tághmata'.[3] The Noúmeroi were an infantry regiment.[4] According to Bury,[5] they were the permanent garrison of Constantinople. There was also an Imperial bodyguard, the Vasilikề Etaireía. This was divided into a 'Great' and a 'Middle' wing. It was recruited partly from foreigners,[6] and two bodies of purely foreign guardsmen, the Khazars and the Phargánoi,[7] were associated with them.[8] The Maghlavítai, who are mentioned in the same passage, might be Western Muslims.[9]

Service as a guardsman was so desirable (presumably because it was lucrative) that places had to be purchased. The minimum entrance-fees were sixteen pounds gold for the Great Etaireía, ten for the Middle Etaireía, and seven for the Phargánoi or for the Khazars.[10]

---

[1] For these, see, above all, Bury, *The Imperial Administrative System*, pp. 47–66. See also Glykatzi-Ahrweiler, 'Recherches', pp. 23–31.

[2] Usually in the tenth century, at any rate. Bury points out in op. cit., p. 5, n. 2, that the army which won the historic victory over the Amīr of Malatīyah in 863 was commanded by the stratêghós of the Thrakἔsioi, Petronás.

[3] *De Caer.*, Book II, p. 604.

[4] According to Kudāmah, following al-Garmi, whose description relates to the period *circa* 838–45 (Bury, op. cit., p. 48, with n. 1). The Noúmeroi also appear in the *Taktikón Uspenski*. Bury produces evidence (in op. cit., pp. 65–6) which suggests that the Noúmeroi may have been in existence already before the ninth century.

[5] In op. cit., p. 48.

[6] *De Caer.*, Book I, Appendix: Τὰ Βασιλικὰ Ταξείδια, p. 478. Some of the non-foreign guardsmen in the Great Etaireía were recruited from théma Makedhonía (*De Caer.*, Book II, p. 586).

[7] From Farghānah, in the upper valley of the Central Asian River Jaxartes.

[8] For these, Bury cites (op. cit., pp. 107–8) *De Caer.*, I, p. 576; II, p. 660; Philótheos's klêtorolóyion, p. 772; *Vita Euthymii*, i, 12; and *Theoph. Cont.*, p. 358 ('the Khazars from the Emperor Leo's Etaireía').

[9] i.e. men from the Maghrib, which is the Arabic word for 'the West'.

[10] *De Caer.*, II, pp. 692–3.

Bury[1] is inclined to identify the Etaireía with the Phoidherátoi, who are listed by Kudāmah as the fourth of the (household) cavalry regiments stationed in Constantinople.[2] Stein contests this.[3]

The several sets of bodyguards were stationed in the Imperial Palace in Constantinople. There were detachments of all the tághmata in themáta Thrákê and Makedhonía,[4] and detachments of the Exkoúvitoi and the Ikanátoi, at any rate, in Bithynia as well.[5] As for the Phoidherátoi, Kudāmah's source may be correct in locating them at Constantinople, but at least one detachment of the Phoidherátoi was stationed in the neighbourhood of Lykaonía.[6] This was the first district traversed by the road running from the Cilician Gates to the Asiatic shore of the Bosphorus. The Foederati had been good troops at the date of composition of 'Mavríkios's' *Stratêghikón*,[7] shortly before the disintegration of the Army in 602. Evidently they had been posted deliberately just behind the section of the Romano-Arab frontier on which the pressure from the Arabs was the most severe, in order to lighten the load on the Anatolikoí, who were holding this section of the new frontier after having been pushed back to the north-west side of the Távros.

The numerical strength of the household troops must have been small, and the strength of the Etaireía and the associated components of the Imperial bodyguard must have been still smaller. Troops who were paid regularly and whose pay was a living wage must have been expensive, and, in so far as they were stationed in the capital, they must have aggravated the Prefect's always acute problem of food-supply. This was, no doubt, one of the reasons why detachments of the household regiments were posted, outside Constantinople, in its European and Asiatic environs.[8] Kudāmah's source reckoned the strength of the four household regiments at 4,000 men each, but Bury is surely right[9] in rejecting this figure. Bury applies Nikêphóros II Phokás's figure of fifty troopers for a cavalry vándon[10] as holding good for the tághmata as well as for the

---

[1] In op. cit., p. 107. [2] See Bury, op. cit., pp. 48, 63–4, and 107.

[3] In *Studien*, pp. 135–6.

[4] Glykatzi-Ahrweiler, 'Recherches', p. 31, suggests that the enigmatic Arabic name Tāflā (طافلا) or Tāflatā (طافلتا) for the Anastasian Long Wall district may be a corruption of tághma (طاغما) and tághmata (طاغمتا).

[5] Bury, op. cit., p. 52, citing *De Caer.*, II, chap. 45 (on the expedition to Crete in 949), p. 666.

[6] In both the *Taktikón Uspenski* and Philótheos's klêtorolóyion, the tourmárkhês ton Phiveráton [*sic*] is placed just above the tourmárkhês Lykaonías (see Stein, *Studien*, pp. 136–7). Philótheos says 'Lykaonías kai Pamphylías'. Stein, op. cit., pp. 137–8, emends 'Pamphylías' to 'Pisidhías'—a convincing emendation, since Pamphylía lay in théma Kivyrrhaiótai, and the Phoidherátoi are called Lycaonians and Pisidians by Kedhrênós (vol. ii, p. 546). See also Glykatzi-Ahrweiler in loc. cit., pp. 29–30.

[7] See 'Mavríkios', Part 2, chap. 5, p. 60 Scheffer, p. 84 Mihăescu, and chap. 10, p. 66 Scheffer, p. 88 Mihăescu. [8] See Teall in loc. cit., p. 111.

[9] In op. cit., p. 54. Cf. Teall in loc. cit., pp. 100–11.

[10] *Stratêghikḕ Ékthesis kai Sýntaxis*, p. 12.

thémata, and, on this basis, he assesses the total strength of the thirty vánda of the Skholaí at not more than 1,500. The Skholaí were the senior household regiment and therefore possibly also the strongest in numbers. Bury points out[1] that, in 949, the strength of the whole tághma of the Exkoúvitoi, including the officers, was only 700, and the strength of the whole tághma of the Ikanátoi only 456.[2]

In the thematic part (the major part) of the army in Leo VI's reign (886–912) the organization described in 'Mavríkios's' *Stratêghikón* survived with some changes of nomenclature,[3] and this is corroborative evidence that the thémata were the old Diocletianic–Constantinian commands of magistri militum under a new name. Before 602 a stratêghós's (i.e. a magister militum's) command ($\pi\alpha\rho\acute{\alpha}\tau\alpha\xi\iota\varsigma$, i.e. stratós, standing for the Latin term 'exercitus') had been divided into three brigades ($\mu\acute{\epsilon}\rho\eta$, alias $\delta\rho o\hat{\upsilon}\gamma\gamma o\iota$) of equal strength;[4] these were subdivided into moírai, and the moírai into tághmata (alias arithmoí, alias vánda), each of which was commanded by a kómês (alias trivoúnos).[5] 'Mavríkios's' 'mérê' survived in the Army of Leo VI's day under the Latin name 'toúrmai'; 'Mavríkios's' 'moírai' survived with no change of name; 'Mavríkios's' smallest units survived under the name 'vánda' ('Mavríkios's' synonyms for 'vánda', namely 'tághmata' and 'arithmoí', had in the meanwhile been given other technical meanings).

With these changes of name, the pre-602 cadres had survived, but the numerical strengths had shrunk. In the pre-602 army, the minimum strength for the smallest unit (Leo VI's vándon) was 200[6] and the maximum strength 400, 300 to 400 being the normal figure.[7] The strength of a moíra was 2,000 to 3,000. The strength of a méros (Leo VI's 'toúrma') was 6,000 to 7,000.[8] The normal strength of an army-corps was therefore about 20,000. Leo VI, copying 'Mavríkios', says that the maximum strength of a vándon should be 400, its minimum strength 200, and its average strength 300.[9] In another passage in which he is again copying 'Mavríkios', Leo sets the maximum strength for a vándon (he here reproduces 'Mavríkios's' term tághma) at 256.[10] But in a different context,[11] in one of those rare passages in which he is thinking and prescribing in terms of the actual army of his own day, Leo VI sets the maximum strength in cavalry for a théma at 4,000. Evidently the normal strength of an East Roman corps was, *circa* A.D. 900, only about one-fifth of what

---

[1] In op. cit., pp. 52 and 54.   [2] See *De Caer.*, Book II, chap. 45, p. 666.
[3] See IV, 3 (vii), p. 570–2.
[4] 'Mavríkios', Part I, chap. 3, p. 27 Scheffer, p. 56 Mihăescu, and chap. 4, p. 31 Scheffer, p. 58 Mihăescu.
[5] Op. cit., ibid.   [6] 'Mavríkios', p. 32 Scheffer, p. 60 Mihăescu.
[7] Op. cit., pp. 30 and 31 Scheffer, p. 58 Mihăescu.   [8] Op. cit., ibid.
[9] Leo VI, *Taktiká*, Dhiat. 4, § 43, col. 708.   [10] Dhiat. 4, § 65, col. 713.
[11] Dhiat. 18, §§ 149–53, cols. 988–9, cited already in II, 1 (iii) (d), p. 139, with n. 8.

it had been *circa* A.D. 600. The author of Περὶ Παραδρομῆς Πολέμου rates the full (cavalry) strength of a corps as low as 3,000,[1] and this shrinkage would correspond approximately to the reduction of the strength of the smallest unit, the vándon, from 'Mavríkios's' average figure of 300 men to Nikêphóros II Phokás's figure of fifty.

However, in the East Roman Army, there cannot have been in reality an 'average' or 'normal' strength for a corps. *Circa* 900, as *circa* 600, the districts from which the corps were recruited differed greatly in area and in productivity, and therefore in populousness. Among the thémata of the 'Eastern' class, small mountainous districts, such as Seléfkeia and Mesopotamía, cannot have been capable of maintaining as many cavalrymen as large thémata containing extensive tracts of good agricultural land, such as the Thrakêsioi and the Opsíkion and the Armeniakoí were, even after the Opsíkion and the Armeniakoí had been cut down to their eventual sizes. The Anatolikoí, whose lot had fallen in the relatively arid interior of the Asia Minor plateau, were compensated for this by the extensiveness of their domain even within its reduced dimensions. When a unit which had started as a kleisoúra—Seléfkeia and Mesopotamía are instances—was raised to the status of a théma, we may guess that one of the required qualifications will have been the ability to muster a minimum number of cavalrymen of some sort. We may also guess that, in the two cases in point, the requisite minimum must have been far less than Leo VI's ideal figure of 4,000.

On the other hand, we could have guessed, even if we had not been informed, that the most productive and populous thémata's contingents of picked cavalrymen must have been more than 4,000 strong. Fortunately, Kudāmah, in reproducing Ibn Khurdhādbih's list of thémata of the 'Eastern' class, has given figures for the strengths of each théma which range from a minimum of 4,000 (Kappadhokía, Kharsianón, Armeniakoí, Khaldhía, and the non-combatant Optimátoi) through 5,000, 6,000, and 8,000 to 15,000 (the Anatolikoí).[2] Kudāmah gives an aggregate strength of 70,000 for the eleven Asiatic thémata, including the Optimátoi, but he does not tell us what categories of troops he is including in his count. Leo VI reckons that, if the Emperor were to mobilize the élite cavalry of all the 'Eastern' thémata up to a strength of not more than 4,000 from each théma, this would produce more than 30,000 good troops.[3] Leo VI calls a force, composed exclusively of cavalry, that is only from 5,000 to 10,000 or 12,000 strong a small army,[4] but here he is copying 'Mavríkios'. The 'Anonymus Vári' holds that the Emperor should

[1] Π.Π.Π., pp. 227 and 229.

[2] These figures are reproduced by Gelzer, *Die Genesis*, p. 97. Cf. Bury, op. cit., p. 42.

[3] Leo VI, *Taktiká*, Dhiat. 18, § 153, col. 989.

[4] Leo VI, *Taktiká*, Dhiat. 12, § 32, col. 816 ('Mavríkios', *Stratêghikón*, Part 2, chap. 4, p. 56 Scheffer, p. 82 Mihăescu).

not go on campaign with so small a force as 8,200 cavalry,[1] but the author of Περὶ Παραδρομῆς Πολέμου considers that, for a general, 5,000–6,000 is enough.[2] In discussing the organization of the infantry, Leo VI gives different instructions if the force is under or is over 24,000.[3] Since these instructions are addressed to a stratêghós in the singular, this strength of 24,000 men plus or minus ought to represent the infantry strength of a single théma, but the figure seems much too high for this.

If we exclude the Optimátoi and also exclude Sevásteia, Lykandós, Seléfkeia, and Leondókomis, which were still only kleisoúrai, not thémata, in Leo's day,[4] there would be nine Asiatic thémata, and these would in fact produce, at the rate of 4,000 picked cavalrymen each, a total of 36,000. This is approximately half the aggregate figure, for the same set of thémata, that Kudāmah arrives at by adding up his diverse figures for individual thémata. Kudāmah may have been assuming that the second-class troops were equal in numbers to the first-class troops or, if his figures are intended to represent first-class troops only, they may be far too high. Kudāmah reckons the total strength of the East Roman Army to be 120,000.[5] Constantine V did manage to concentrate 80,000 troops (including the Optimátoi) in Thrace in 773, but evidently this was a quite exceptional *tour de force*.[6] In any case, in principle, Kudāmah's attribution of different strengths to different thémata must be right. This is, indeed, implied in Leo's figures for the corps-commanders' salaries. These range from forty to twenty pounds gold, and the salary-scale for the corps-commanders presumably corresponds more or less to the scale of strengths of the corps themselves.

Leo VI[7] follows 'Mavríkios'[8] in ruling that the second-class troops should be kept separate from the picked troops and should be given other duties. Leo's expedient for producing a bigger East Roman force to match a bigger enemy force is to mobilize, not the total strength of any single théma, but the élite cavalry of more thémata than one—indeed, of all the 'Eastern' thémata, if necessary. No doubt the second-class cavalry were called up in emergencies, and a quota of first-class infantry, both heavy and light, must always have been mobilized, simultaneously with the first-class cavalry, to perform those indispensable services, noted already, that could not be performed by cavalry. All troops of all categories that were mobilized seem to have been organized in the same

---

[1] 'Anonymus Vári', chap. 8, p. 17.
[2] Π.Π.Π., p. 230. Cf. p. 238.
[3] Dhiat. 4, §§ 70–1, col. 713.
[4] De Caer. II, p. 697.
[5] In De Goeje's *Bibliotheca Geographorum Arabum*, vol. vi (1889), p. 109, cited by Teall in loc. cit., p. 109.
[6] Theophanes, p. 447, cited already in II, 4, Appendix, p. 272.
[7] *Taktiká*, Dhiat. 18, §§ 149 and 153, cols. 988 and 989.
[8] *Stratêghikón*, Part I, chap. 4, p. 31 Scheffer, pp. 58–60 Mihăescu.

cadres as the picked troops. At any rate, these are the only cadres that are mentioned in our sources.

When we pass on from the consideration of cadres and strengths to consider questions of discipline and tactics, we find that, in the East Roman Army, the severe traditional Roman spirit still governed the provisions for security, both in camp and on the march, but that the tactics were new. While the sanction for the security-provisions was still severity, the inspiration of the tactics was intellectual. The tactics were determined partly by the lie of the land[1] in the principal war-zone, which from *circa* 636 to 926 was eastern Asia Minor; partly by the spirit and the tactics of the Arabs, who were the Empire's principal adversaries during this period; and partly by the temperament and attitude of the East Romans themselves.

For East Roman minds, war was an intellectual activity, and the essence of the art of war was to attain objectives by a maximum use of intellectual acumen and a minimum use of brute force.[2] This was already the fundamental principle of East Roman military policy before 602, and it survived the seventh-century military collapse and the subsequent recovery. The author of 'Mavríkios's' *Stratêghikón* was alive to the merits of using one's wits, for all they are worth, in the conduct of hostilities. Pitched battles (οἱ δημοπόλεμοι) are hazardous when the enemy is valiant, is a match for the East Roman Army in tactics, and is daring. An enemy of this calibre should be countered by strategy, intellect, improvised surprises (αἰφνιδιάσματα), tricks, ruses. Make good use of patrols (σκοῦλκα), spies, and scouts.[3] Tricks, ambushes, raids, and the cutting off of supplies are better means than pitched battles for waging war.[4] Leo VI has taken over from 'Mavríkios' this enthusiasm for the use of wits. Defeat the enemy by intellect. Be trickier.[5] In action, the general is not to exert himself physically; he is to keep his mind alert.[6]

However, the most effective military use of East Roman wits was their application, not to the details of military operations, but to a study of the

---

[1] 'Mavríkios's' *Stratêghikón*, Part 8, chap. 2, pp. 183 and 197 Scheffer, pp. 206 and 218 Mihăescu.

[2] Leo VI, *Taktiká*, Dhiat. 12, § 140, cols. 841–4, copying 'Mavríkios', Part 7, chap. 1, p. 138 Scheffer, pp. 166–8 Mihăescu. See II, 1 (iii) (b), p. 109, with n. 3, for the reiterated warnings against fighting pitched battles.

[3] 'Mavríkios', Part 7, chap. 4, p. 139 Scheffer, p. 168 Mihăescu: Περὶ τὸ πολυπραγμονεῖν τὰ κατὰ τοὺς ἐχθρούς.

[4] 'Mavríkios', op. cit., Part 8, chap. 2, p. 183 Scheffer, p. 204 Mihăescu. Part 10, chap. 2, p. 241 Scheffer, p. 252 Mihăescu.

[5] Leo VI, *Taktiká*, Dhiat. 12, §§ 3–4, cols. 805–8, and Dhiat. 20, §§ 8–22, cols. 1017–22, following 'Mavríkios', Part 7, chap. 4, p. 139 Scheffer, p. 168 Mihăescu. 'Mavríkios' devotes to ambushes the fourth of the twelve parts of his book.

[6] Leo VI, *Taktiká*, Dhiat. 14, §§ 2–3, cols. 848–9, (cf. §§ 27–8, col. 857; Dhiat. 17, § 79, col. 933; Dhiat. 20, § 2, cols. 1013–16), following 'Mavríkios', Part 7, chap. 1 bis, pp. 149–50 Scheffer, pp. 174–6 Mihăescu.

enemy. This was a study, not just of the enemy's equipment and tactics, but of his psychology, and the purpose was practical, not academic. The various enemies of the East Roman Empire were to be studied in order to adapt (ἁρμόζεσθαι) the East Roman Army's tactics to each enemy's idiosyncrasies. The most able and instructive passage of 'Mavríkios's' *Stratéghikón* is Part 11[1] 'On the habits and tactics of each of the foreign peoples' (with whom the East Romans may find themselves at war). Leo VI, in his *Taktiká*, has a corresponding passage, Dhiátaxis 18,[2] and here, as usual, he copies 'Mavríkios', in some places verbatim. Yet even Leo VI substitutes contemporary foreign peoples for those of 'Mavríkios's' day, and, on these, some of his observations and his instructions are based on genuine contemporary experience.

'Mavríkios' studies four foreign peoples: the Persians, the Eurasian nomads (Σκύθαι), the fair-haired peoples (Franks, Lombards, and the like), and the Slavs and Antai. Leo VI substitutes the Arabs for the Persians, but he follows 'Mavríkios' in dealing with the other three peoples in 'Mavríkios's' inventory.

The Persians were the only foreign people whom the East Romans had felt to be their equals, and they were at war with the Persians intermittently for nearly four centuries ending in 628. In the 630s the Arabs supplanted the Persians and conquered from the East Roman Empire—permanently, for the most part—the territories, south-east of the Távros and Andítavros Ranges, that the Persians had occupied temporarily in the climacteric Romano-Persian War of 604–28. By the close of the seventh century, the Arabs had gone on to conquer the East Roman dominions in North Africa to the west of Egypt. In 827 they had embarked on the conquest of Sicily, and in 826 or 827 refugee Muslims from Spain (conquered from the Visigoths) had seized Crete. In Leo VI's reign (886–912) the Arabs virtually completed their conquest of Sicily, and in 911 the East Romans made their sixth unsuccessful attempt to evict the Muslims from Crete.[3]

Thus the Arabs had proved themselves to be an even more potent and formidable adversary for the East Roman Empire than their Persian predecessors had been. Leo VI declares that it was the Arab peril that had moved him to write his *Taktiká*.[4] Moreover, though the man-power of the seventh-century Arab armies had been recruited from pastoral nomad barbarians of the same social type as those on the Eurasian Steppe, the leadership had been in the hands of citizens of the commercial city-state Mecca. Muʿāwiyah had been as sophisticated a politician as any contemporary Persian—or as any contemporary East Roman, for that

---

[1] pp. 252–90 Scheffer, pp. 261–91 Mihăescu.
[2] Cols. 945–89. [3] See II, 7, p. 343.
[4] Leo VI, *Taktiká*, ὑπόθεσις ἐπιλόγῳ, § 71, col. 1093.

matter. The education of the Arab conquerors who had settled in the conquered population's fields and cities had been completed by the conquerors' sedentary subjects, and, by the ninth and tenth centuries, the Arabs had come to be regarded by the East Romans as being, like their Persian predecessors, antagonists who were the East Romans' cultural equals. The Arabs in their turn now aroused ambivalent feelings of hostility[1] and respect in East Roman hearts. It has already been noted[2] that Eastern Muslim renegades were the most highly prized of all additions to East Roman man-power, military or civilian.

The details of the East Roman Government's warfare with the Eastern Muslims and the Slavs are dealt with in other contexts.[3] The present chapter is concerned with the survival of original Roman traditions and the development of new East Roman military tactics and techniques in the East Roman conduct of war, whoever might be the East Roman Army's adversary at the moment. The period here in question is the century beginning in 886, the first year of Leo VI's reign. At an early date in this century, Leo VI himself (886–912) compiled his *Taktiká* and instructed the máyistros Leo Katákylas to write his memorandum on the procedure when the Emperor goes on campaign.[4] At some date before 959, Constantine Porphyrogenitus wrote his own shorter memorandum on the same subject.[5] The Emperor Nikêphóros II Phokás wrote his *Stratêghikě̀ Ékthesis kai Sýndaxis* at some date before 969. The author of *Perì Paradhromês Polémou*, who wrote this work under instructions from Nikêphóros II and who praises both Nikêphóros II himself and his father Várdhas Phokás,[6] may have finished writing it before the Emperor John I Dzimiskês's death in 976, but he is unlikely to have been able to publish it before that date. The 'Anonymus Vári' is a work of about the same date.

The last three of these six works were written by professional soldiers for practical use by their brother officers, and it seems safe to assume that they represent the actual facts and practices of the writers' own day. It also seems safe to make the same assumption about 'Mavríkios's' *Stratêghikón*, a work, dating from *circa* 600, which was also written by a professional soldier. This work, too, gives the impression of being a genuine account of the actual facts and practices of the writer's day. On the other hand, Leo VI's *Taktiká*, which is the longest and the most systematic account of the East Roman art of war in the century beginning in 886, is mainly composed of paraphrases or verbatim reproductions of earlier works. There are few passages that bear the stamp of being Leo's own

---

[1] See Leo VI, *Taktiká*, Dhiat. 18, § 142, col. 981.   [2] See II, 1 (iii) (a), pp. 82–5.
[3] Warfare with the Eastern Muslims in II, 1 (iii) (b) *passim* and in III, 3, *passim*; with the Slavs, both before and after the Slav *Völkerwanderung* south of the Danube, in II, 1 (iii) (a), pp. 89–107, and in Annex III *passim*.
[4] *De Caer.*, I, Appendix, pp. 455–95.
[5] Ibid., pp. 444–54.   [6] *Π.Π.Π.*, p. 185.

original work,[1] and that can therefore be taken to reflect the situation as it actually was at the turn of the ninth and tenth centuries.

Leo's paraphrases or excerpts of pre-Diocletianic works can, of course, be ignored as irrelevant indulgences in archaism. But Leo's principal source is 'Mavríkios's' *Stratêghikón*, and, when Leo is reproducing 'Mavríkios', we cannot tell whether, *circa* 900, an item taken from this late-sixth-century work was out of date, like all the items taken by Leo from his older sources, e.g. Plutarch, Arrian, Aelian, Polyaenus, or whether some of the items taken from 'Mavríkios' by Leo were still valid after the lapse of three centuries. Leo's reproduction of an item taken from 'Mavríkios' is not, of course, in itself a guarantee that this item was not a dead letter in Leo's own day. On the other hand, the post-seventh-century East Roman Army had an affinity with the Diocletianic–Constantinian Roman Army that it did not have with the Roman Army of the times of the Principate and the Republic or with the Macedonian Army of Kings Philip II and Alexander III and their successors. An item taken from 'Mavríkios' by Leo may therefore be authentic for *circa* 900 as well as for *circa* 600.

However, the East Roman Army certainly cannot have been immune from change throughout the intervening three centuries. The seventh century had been revolutionary. In that century the East Roman Empire had gone into the melting-pot, and, though it had not dissolved, it had re-emerged with a diminished territory, new frontiers, and new adversaries.

---

[1] R. Vári, in his magnificent edition of Leo VI's *Taktiká*, has not only given us a text, based on a thorough mastery of the manuscripts, of the *Taktiká* itself; he has traced Leo's sources and has printed the texts of these above Leo's text, and has thus shown up the extent of Leo's plagiarisms. Long passages of Leo's work have been copied by him verbatim from earlier authors. Unfortunately Vári did not live to finish his edition of Leo's *Taktiká*. It breaks off at the end of § 38 of Dhiátaxis 14, and for the rest of Leo's work, i.e. Dhiátaxis 14, §§ 39–106, and the whole of Dhiatáxeis 15–20, we still have nothing better than Migne's text in *P.G.*, vol. cvii, cols. 860–1094. However, Vári's text, as far as it goes, extends to 189 out of Migne's 423 columns, and therefore the quota of apparently original passages (i.e. not plagiarisms) that Vári's edition enables us to identify is a fair sample for the whole work. I reckon that, in this portion of Leo's work, the following passages are original: Preface §§ 1–4 and 9; Dhiat. 1, §§ 8–15; Dhiat. 2, §§ 44–9 (doubtful) and Dhiat. 3 (doubtful); Dhiat. 4, §§ 1–2, 6–9, 32–3, 40; Dhiat. 5 (the whole); Dhiat. 6, § 24; Dhiat. 7, §§ 8–9 and 78–9; Dhiat. 10, §§ 19–20; Dhiat. 11, §§ 6–11, 24–6, 50–1; Dhiat. 12, §§ 1 and 71; Dhiat. 14, § 34. Of these apparently original passages, Dhiat. 1, §§ 9–10, and Dhiat. 4, §§ 32–3, give valuable information about the administration of a territorial théma and the relations of the thematic administrative officials with the Central Government. Dhiat. 11, § 11, on the importance of agriculture, and § 25, on a diversionary raid, are also interesting. In the rest of Leo VI's *Taktiká*, the original passages (i.e. not plagiarisms) appear to be Dhiat. 15, §§ 36–9; Dhiat. 17, §§ 81–3; Dhiat. 18, §§ 24, 74–80, 99, 101, 110–42, 149–53; Dhiat. 19 Περὶ Ναυμαχίας; Dhiat. 20, §§ 71, 116, 137, 205; Epíloghos, §§ 39 and 71. The more interesting of these passages are Dhiat. 17, §§ 81–3, on a diversionary raid; the passages cited from Dhiat. 18 which appear to give authentic contemporary information about certain foreign peoples; Dhiat. 19 (the whole); Dhiat. 20, § 71, on the taxes payable by thematic soldiers; Dhiat. 20, §§ 116 and 137, with Epíloghos, § 39, on a self-made man, not an aristocrat, making the best commander.

It has been noted already in this chapter that, between *circa* 600 and *circa* 900, there had been a drastic reduction in the East Roman Army's numerical strength. There may have been other proportionately great changes which we cannot bring to light. We shall have less hesitation in regarding an item taken by Leo from 'Mavríkios' as being still valid if we find the same item re-appearing in one or more of the three works that were written by professional soldiers in the third quarter of the tenth century. Yet this corroborative evidence is not conclusive. Archaism was inveterate in the Byzantine literary tradition; and even a professional soldier, sitting down to write a treatise for practical use, may have succumbed to this characteristic Byzantine form of intellectual infirmity when, in place of his sword, he was wielding a pen. A present-day writer who is attempting to make a survey of East Roman military practice in the century beginning with Leo's reign must start by warning his readers that neither the writer nor they can be sure that their feet are on firm ground.[1]

Leo VI copies out long passages of earlier books on the art of war verbatim, and this regardless of whether his plagiarisms are relevant to the conditions of warfare and the conduct of war in his own time. This is not surprising; for Leo VI was not a soldier, and, as a result of his having been given a thorough education in the classical Greek language and literature, he succumbed to archaism in writing on subjects of which he had no personal experience, though in some of his legislation, in which he abolished out-of-date Roman institutions in stilted neo-Attic prose, he proves himself to have been a realist as a civil administrator.

Leo VI's proneness to archaism in his *Taktiká* is illustrated by the following particularly flagrant example. It has been mentioned that Leo follows the precedent set by 'Mavríkios' in describing the equipment, tactics, and psychology of the principal foreign peoples by whom the East Roman Empire was confronted in his day, and that, in selecting the peoples whom he is to survey, he does bring his survey up to date in some cases. For instance, instead of reproducing 'Mavríkios's' account of the Persians,[2] Leo substitutes an account of the Persians' supplanters the Arabs,[3] and here Leo seems to be giving his readers authentic contemporary information. When he comes to the Magyars, he observes[4] that the East Romans had learnt about the Magyars' tactics when in 895 they had had the Magyars as their allies against the Bulgars, after the Bulgars had invaded Thrace. Certainly the East Romans must have known a great deal about the Magyars by the time when East Roman

---

[1] See further Annex II.
[2] 'Mavríkios', *Stratêghikón*, Part 11, chap. 1, pp. 254–60 Scheffer, pp. 262–9 Mihăescu.
[3] Leo VI, *Taktiká*, Dhiat. 18, §§ 23–4, col. 952, and §§ 110–42, cols. 972–81.
[4] Ibid., § 42, col. 956.

diplomatists had hired the Magyars' services, and when the Imperial Fleet had ferried the Magyars across the Danube. Leo's opening remark leads his readers to expect that, in his account of the Magyars, as in his account of the Arabs, he will be giving authentic contemporary information. So far from that, Leo's account of the Magyars[1] is a close copy—in many passages verbatim—of 'Mavríkios's' account of the Avars.[2]

Where 'Mavríkios' has written 'Avars', Leo has substituted 'Turks'; Leo calls the Magyars 'Turks' throughout, and this practice of his has been followed by his son Constantine Porphyrogenitus.

The use of the name 'Turks' to mean 'Magyars' has been a puzzle for modern scholars, but it is explained by Leo's archaistic preference for copying out 'Mavríkios's' work instead of using the contemporary information about the Magyars which, on Leo's own testimony, was at his disposal if he had chosen to draw on it. The title of 'Mavríkios's' chapter is 'How to adapt to the Skýthai, that is to say to the Avars and the Turks and the rest of the Hunnic peoples who lead the same kind of life' (i.e. the Eurasian pastoral nomads in general). 'Mavríkios' starts by pointing out the contrast between the Avars and the Turks in temperament and conduct. The Turks are innocent of subtlety ($\pi o \iota \kappa \iota \lambda \iota a$) and cleverness ($\delta \epsilon \iota \nu \delta \tau \eta s$), and this is all that 'Mavríkios' has to say about them. The rest of the chapter is concerned with the Avars alone. The Avars are thoroughly bad. They are highly experienced in dealing with their enemies. They are ingenious, they do not show their hand. Their behaviour is underhand and treacherous. They are avaricious. They do not keep their word.[3] They prefer trickery, surprise, and starving-out to pitched battles (the self-same practice that is recommended for East Roman commanders by the Byzantine writers on the art of war, from 'Mavríkios' onwards). When 'Mavríkios' passes on from psychology to equipment and tactics, he leaves the Turks out altogether and deals with the Avars exclusively. 'Mavríkios's' account of the Avars' psychology, equipment, and tactics is the part of his chapter on the nomads that Leo VI has copied with the change of names from 'Avars' to 'Turks'.

The reason for this change of names is clear. It was notorious that, between 791 and 805, i.e. perhaps a century before the date at which Leo was writing, the Avars had been exterminated by converging attacks concerted between the Franks and the Danubian Bulgars. Leo was also aware that, between the year 895 and the date at which he was writing, the Magyars had migrated from the western end of the Steppe along the north coast of the Black Sea to the enclave of Steppe in what is now Hungary, in which the Avars had been living before they were wiped

---

[1] Ibid., §§ 45–74, cols. 957–64.
[2] 'Mavríkios', Part 11, chap. 2, pp. 260–8 Scheffer, pp. 268–75 Mihăescu.
[3] 'Mavríkios', *Stratéghikón*, p. 261 Scheffer, p. 268 Mihăescu.

out. Leo notes[1] that the Magyars are now neither neighbours nor enemies of the East Roman Empire. Nevertheless, Leo has used 'Mavríkios's' account of the Avars to serve as his own account of the Magyars by making his surreptitious change of names. Leo has chosen the name 'Turks' for his Magyars because the Turks are the other nomad people, besides the Avars, with whom 'Mavríkios' is concerned in the plagiarized chapter. It is true that, in this chapter, there is not much about the Turks, who were remote. The chapter is mainly about the Avars, who were the East Roman Empire's aggressive neighbours in 'Mavríkios's' day. Still, the Turks do put in an appearance in this chapter of 'Mavríkios's' work; and Leo could call the Magyars of his day 'Turks' without committing an anachronism because the Turks, unlike the Avars, were then still on the map. Indeed, in the ninth century, the 'Abbasid dynasty's Turkish palace guards had won notoriety by making themselves virtually masters of the Caliphal Government. Leo VI does not confess his sleight of hand to his readers, but he does attempt to justify it to himself by remarking that 'the Skythic peoples have a practically identical way of life ($\dot{a}\nu a\sigma\tau\rho o\phi\hat{\eta}s$) and system of tactics.'[2]

This is not true. For instance, the Skyths—that is to say, the nomad people who actually bore this name—were light-armed horse-archers, whereas the Skyths' eastern neighbours and eventual supplanters, the Sarmatians, were cataphracts whose weapon was not the bow but the lance, and who charged home instead of skirmishing with their enemy at a bow-shot's distance. There is no evidence that the ninth-century Magyars' equipment and tactics were truly the same as the sixth-century Avars'. All that we know is that Leo VI has applied 'Mavríkios's' account of 'Mavríkios's' own sixth-century Avar contemporaries to Leo's ninth-century Magyar contemporaries.

Leo VI's neglect to use his contemporary information about the Magyars is disconcerting; but it is still more disconcerting to find the same archaïzing attitude of mind inhibiting a late-tenth-century East Roman diplomatist and military commander, Nikêphóros Ouranós,[3] from using information that was not only contemporary but that had been gained by him from his own military experience. In the year 995, Nikêphóros Ouranós had won a victory over the troops of Tsar Samuel of West Bulgaria by taking them by surprise on the River Elládha (Sperkheiós) in Central Greece.[4] Besides being a man of action, Nikêphóros Ouranós was an author. He wrote a *Taktiká* which has survived, and the subject of chapters 76 and 122 of this work of his is the crossing of rivers.

---

[1] Leo, Dhiat. 18, § 74, col. 964.　　　　　　　[2] Leo, Dhiat. 18, § 43, cols. 956–7.
[3] For Nikêphóros Ouranós's career, see A. Dain's edition of Nikêphóros Ouranós's *Taktiká* (Paris, 1937, Soc. d'Ed. les 'Belles Lettres'), pp. 134–6.
[4] Dain in op. cit., p. 136.

Yet, in this context, he makes no mention of his own victory on the River Elládha,[1] though an account of this operation would have been instructive for readers who were professional soldiers. Nikêphóros Ouranós's silence about his own military achievement was not imposed on him by modesty; it just did not occur to him to mention it. His *Taktiká* is a purely antiquarian work. It is an anthology of extracts from previous writers on the subject, ranging in date from as recent a work as the Emperor Nikêphóros II Phokás's Στρατηγικὴ Ἔκθεσις καὶ Σύνταξις to the fourth-century-B.C. writer Aeneas Tacticus.[2]

The so-called *Inedita Leonis Tactica*[3] is another anthology of the same kind, consisting of excerpts from the same repertory as Nikêphóros Ouranós's.

A preoccupation with an academic study of the past, to the neglect of contemporary experience, thus got the better of at least one successful soldier, Nikêphóros Ouranós, besides the non-martial Emperor Leo VI. Even the professional soldiers who were writing in the third quarter of the tenth century lapse occasionally into Leo-like plagiarisms from 'Mavríkios', as will appear from some of the footnotes to later pages of the present chapter. One of these soldiers, namely the author of Περὶ Παραδρομῆς Πολέμου,[4] does show an awareness of the danger of being hide-bound by tradition.

The exposition that I have been giving is based on the teachings of experience, but what *you* must do is to make your dispositions in accordance with the requirements of the situation with which you are confronted by the emergency of the actual moment. Tradition does not give the answer (οὐ γὰρ ἡ παράδοσις δίδωσιν). The degree of the strength of God's help [i.e. of the commander's capacity for intuitive improvisation] is the determining factor in deciding the outcome of war.

This is, of course, the truth; but it is a truth that was uncongenial to the Byzantine mind. The compulsiveness of the Byzantines' archaistic bent makes it frequently difficult for students of the works of Byzantine Greek literature to diagnose whether a writer is recording contemporary facts or is retailing some conventional tradition. The following account of East Roman military practice must be read in the light of this necessary reservation.

The first concern of the East Roman art of war was to gather 'intelligence' (in the military usage of the word). Gather as much of it as

---

[1] See Dain in op. cit., p. 144.
[2] See the list of Nikêphóros Ouranós's sources, ibid., pp. 19 seqq.
[3] *Anon. Svlloge Tacticorum quae olim 'Inedita Leonis Tactica' Dicebantur*, edited by A. Dain (Paris, 1938, Soc. d'Ed. les 'Belles Lettres'). See Dain's description of this work on his p. 8.
[4] Π.Π.Π., p. 229. Cf. p. 235.

possible before going into action,[1] and go on gathering it all the time;[2] but beware of credulity. Check deserters' statements by prisoners' statements.[3] Give credence to the reports of old hands (ἔμπειροι) only (e.g. on the difficult business of estimating the enemy's numbers).[4] Send out spies.[5] Ibn Hawkal complains that *soi-disant* East Roman traders from Attáleia, whose real objective was not commercial profit but military intelligence, were given the entrée into the heart of Dār-al-Islām.[6] On the other hand, the East Roman military authorities welcomed visits from enemy traders when an enemy offensive was imminent, because they reckoned that they would be able to elicit from their guests more information than they themselves would disclose.[7] East Roman agents behind the enemy's front would win good marks from their principals if, besides obtaining information, they contrived to sow dissension in the enemy's ranks.[8] The description, by 'Mavríkios',[9] of a drill for detecting the presence of enemy spies in an East Roman camp has been reproduced not only by Leo VI[10] but also by Nikêphóros II[11] and by the 'Anonymus Vári'.[12]

Survey a future battlefield beforehand to detect traps, natural or artificial.[13] Post watches (βίγλας),[14] but, better still, the general should be his own scout.[15] When infantry are advancing, the kambidhoúktor and the mandator should go ahead of them.[16] Watches should carry rations for fifteen days and should be sent out in relays. Troops on patrol must be kept in hand by efficient roll-calls (ἀδνουμιαζομένους) and be strictly inspected. They must have a perfect knowledge of the roads. Special road-patrols (καμινοβίγλια) and spies are needed. Armenians are no good for this, even if they are well paid and provisioned and are relieved at short intervals.[17] Send out scouts (τραπεζίτας, in Armenian ταρσιναρίους)

---

[1] Constantine Porphyrogenitus seeks to give this practice prestige by ascribing it to Constantine I (*Τὰ Βασιλικὰ Ταξείδια*, pp. 445–8).

[2] Leo VI, *Taktiká*, Dhiat. 13, § 3, col. 844.

[3] Ibid., Dhiat. 20, § 38, col. 1024. Cf. 'Mavríkios', Part 9, chap. 5: Do not trust the reports of scouting-parties (σκούλκαι) on enemy numbers. You will get better information from deserters or prisoners (pp. 229 and 230 Scheffer, p. 242 Mihăescu). Beware of prisoners and deserters who are fraudulent. Check their statements against each other (Part 9, chap. 3, p. 213 Scheffer, p. 230 Mihăescu).

[4] Leo VI, *Taktiká*, Dhiat. 16, § 92, col. 937.

[5] Nikêphóros II Phokás (N. Ph.), Στρατηγικὴ Ἔκθεσις καὶ Σύνταξις, p. 17; 'Anonymus Vári', pp. 29 and 43–4.   [6] See II, 1 (ii) p. 57.   [7] Π.Π.Π., p. 196.

[8] Leo, Dhiat. 12, §§ 132–3, col. 841 (from M. ('Mavríkios'), Part 7, chap. 1, p. 136 Scheffer, p. 166 Mihăescu). Leo, Dhiat. 15, § 36, col. 896, and § 56, col. 901; Leo, Dhiat. 20, § 21, col. 1020.

[9] M., Part 9, chap. 5, pp. 234–5 Scheffer, p. 246 Mihăescu.

[10] Leo, Dhiat. 17, §§ 109–10, cols. 941–2.   [11] p. 20.   [12] p. 9.

[13] Leo, Dhiat. 20, § 68, col. 1032.

[14] Leo, Dhiat. 17, §§ 95–108, cols. 932, 937, and 941; *Τὰ Βασιλικὰ Ταξείδια* (*T.V.T.*), p. 447.

[15] Leo, Dhiat. 20, § 68, col. 1032.   [16] Leo, Dhiat. 14, § 67, col. 869.

[17] Π.Π.Π., chaps. 1–2, pp. 186–9. Cf. Leo, Dhiat. 12, § 55, col. 831; Dhiat. 17, § 71, col. 932, and § 104, cols. 940–1.

continually,[1] especially when the Eastern Muslims' summer-raid season is approaching.[2] When a corps-commander receives intelligence of an enemy raid, he should send a force ahead to occupy the heights quickly.[3] Feints, decoys, and ambushes are strongly recommended by all our authorities.[4]

The enemy's numbers could be estimated from the quantity of the hoof-marks that he left in his trail, from the size of his abandoned camps, and from the amount of dung, animal and human, that he had dropped. These indications are noted by 'Mavríkios',[5] and are copied from him by Leo VI[6] and by the author of Περὶ Παραδρομῆς Πολέμου.[7] The interrogation of prisoners and deserters is also considered to be indispensable,[8] in spite of the risk of fraud that has been mentioned already.

An ingenious apparatus for giving the Imperial Government at Constantinople prompt information about enemy action at, or on the Roman side of, the Cilician Gates had been invented by Leo the Philosopher,[9] and had been installed by the Emperor Theóphilos (829–42). A chain of nine beacons[10]—the first at Loúlon (Lu'lu'a), the fort commanding the north-western exit from the Cilician Gates, and the ninth in the Ἡλιακὸς τοῦ Φάρου inside the Imperial Palace at Constantinople—had been set up across Asia Minor, and at either end a dial, like a clock-dial, had been placed, with the numbers of the twelve hours inscribed on it. Each of the twelve hours stood for one of twelve alternative possible events, and the particular event that had actually occurred could thus be signalled by lighting the chain of beacons at the appropriate hour of the night.[11] Michael III is alleged to have put this apparatus out of action, and to have done this for a frivolous reason,[12] but the story may have been fabricated as an item in the systematic denigration of Michael III by

---

[1] Π.Π.Π., p. 188; 'Anonymus Vári' ('A.V.'), pp. 28–9 (τραπεζῖται is an eastern-frontier name for χωσάριοι).

[2] Π.Π.Π., p. 196. [3] Π.Π.Π., pp. 194–5.

[4] Leo, Dhiat. 14, §§ 39–60, cols. 860–8; Π.Π.Π., pp. 235–6; 'A.V.', pp. 45–7.

[5] M., Part 9, chap. 5, p. 233 Scheffer, p. 244 Mihǎescu.

[6] Leo, Dhiat. 17, §§ 94 and 105, cols. 937 and 941.

[7] Π.Π.Π., pp. 195 and 220–1.

[8] Leo, Dhiat. 17, §§ 39 and 94, cols. 921 and 937; Dhiat. 20, § 38, col. 1024; N. Ph., pp. 6 and 17; Π.Π.Π., pp. 189 and 224; 'A.V.', p. 29 (prisoners may be induced to become spies) and pp. 28 and 43–4.

[9] Afterwards the first head of the university that the Caesar Várdhas established in 863 in the Maghnávra Palace at Constantinople.

[10] The sites of these nine beacons were (i) Loúlon, (ii) Mount Arghaíos, (iii) Mount Sámos (or Isámos), (iv) the Kástron Aíyilon, (v) Mount Mámas (T.V.T. substitutes the Mysian Mount Olympus for this), (vi) Mount Kýrizos, (vii) Mount Mókilos (T.V.T. Moúkilos), above the Pýlai on the south shore of the Gulf of Ismit, (viii) Mount Saint Afxéndios, (ix) the Ἡλιακὸς τοῦ Φάρου in the Palace at Constantinople.

[11] See pseudo-Symeon, pp. 681–2; Theoph. Cont., pp. 197–8; T.V.T., pp. 492–3.

[12] In locc. citt. and in Kedhrênós, vol. ii, p. 175; Glykás, p. 543. Cf. pseudo-Symeon, p. 660.

writers in the service of Basil I and of later emperors of Basil I's dynasty. The story is ignored by Symeon Magister et Logothetes, as reproduced by Leo Grammaticus and in *Georgius Monachus Continuatus*.

When the Imperial Government received intelligence, by whatever means, that an enemy invasion was on foot on a scale that called for the mobilization and concentration of some or all of the Asiatic thémata, logistics were the key to success for the East Roman Army. The Amīr of Malatīyah's invading army was annihilated in 863,[1] the Paulician leader Khrysókheir's in 872,[2] and a Tarsan raiding-party of 4,000 men in 878,[3] as the result of a skilful convergence of East Roman corps at the right point at the right moment. In 863 the East Roman commander-in-chief Petronás (an uncle of the Emperor Michael III and brother of the Caesar Várdhas) assembled the Armeniakoí, Voukellárioi, and the Kolóneia and Paphlaghonía corps on the enemy's northern flank, the Anatolikoí, the Opsíkion, the Kappadhokía corps and the troops of the Seléfkeia and Kharsianón kleisoúrai on his southern flank, and Petronás's own corps, the Thrakěsioi, together with the Thrákê and Makedhonía corps and the four Imperial tághmata, on the enemy's western front. In 872 Khrysókheir was encircled at Vathyrýax (which was apparently to the north-west of Sevásteia)[4] by the Armeniakoí and the troops of Kharsianón, who occupied the heights commanding Khrysókheir's camp. In 878, five East Roman forces, under the command of Andréas 'the Skyth', converged on the Tarsans at Podhandós (Bozanti). Two of these five were the troops of Kharsianón and Seléfkeia.

These concentrations and converging movements would have been impracticable if East Roman Asia Minor had not been equipped with *étapes* (ἄπληκτα) linked with each other by a network of roads. Constantine Porphyrogenitus has given[5] a list of the *étapes* along each of the Emperor's two routes leading from Constantinople respectively to the south-western and the north-eastern sections of the Empire's eastern frontier, with notes of the units that joined the Emperor at each *étape*. In another passage,[6] he has also informed us that each théma was responsible for supplying the Army during its passage through that

---

[1] *Georg. Mon. Cont.*, p. 825; Leo Grammaticus, pp. 238–9; Genesius, Book IV, pp. 94–7; *Theoph. Cont.*, pp. 179–83; pseudo-Symeon, p. 666; Kedhrênós vol. ii, p. 164. The site of the battlefield on which the Amīr was brought to bay has not been located. See J. B. Bury's discussion of it in *J.H.S.*, vol. xxix (1909), pp. 124–8, and H. Grégoire's in *Byzantion*, vol. viii (1933), pp. 534–9 (supported by Vasiliev, *Byzance et les Arabes*, vol. i, p. 253).

[2] *Theoph. Cont.*, Book V (Constantine Porphyrogenitus's biography of Basil I), pp. 272–6; Genesius, Book IV, pp. 121–6. For the date, see Canard in Vasiliev, *Byzance et les Arabes*, ii, I, p. 49.

[3] Genesius, pp. 114–15; *Theoph. Cont.*, pp. 284–5. For the date, see Canard in loc. cit., pp. 82–4. See also II, 1 (iii) (b), p. 111.

[4] See the map in Gelzer, *Die Genesis*.

[5] In *T.V.T.*, pp. 444–5.

[6] Ibid., pp. 476–7.

théma's territory, but that there was a subsequent settlement of accounts between the thematic and the Imperial finance officers. Unfortunately, the text of the passage enumerating the *étapes* has fallen into such confusion that the facts cannot be elicited from it with any certainty.

On the route leading from the Pýlai on the south shore of the Gulf of Ismit to the Pýlai Kilikías (the Cilician Gates), the first *étape* was Malayína, on the west bank of the River Sangários, to the east-south-east of Níkaia; the second was Dhoryláïon; the third was Kavórkin, which appears to have lain a short distance to the north-west of Amórion (the principal fortress on this route, which would thus have shielded troops concentrating at Kavórkin). According to Constantine, the Anatolikoí and the Seléfkeia corps join the Emperor at Kavórkin, and this is what we should have expected. These two corps would have exposed themselves perilously to enemy attack if their rendez-vous with the main body of the Imperial Army had been at any point to the south-east of Amórion. However, according to Constantine's text as we have it, the Anatolikoí also join the Emperor at Malayína (which must be wrong), and so do the Thrakḗsioi, whereas the dhoméstikos ton Skholón joins him at Kavórkin. Geographical considerations suggest that the Skholaí's true rendez-vous must have been at Malayína, and the Thrakḗsioi's at Dhoryláïon. Constantine goes on to state (in the text as we have it) that, when the Emperor is heading for Tarsós, the rest of the thémata concentrate at Kolóneia, and this, too, cannot be right, since Kolóneia is far away in north-eastern Asia Minor.

Constantine's fourth *étape* is Kolóneia, his fifth Kaisáreia, and his sixth Dazimón. These must be the *étapes* on the Emperor's route to 'the regions of the East' (i.e. to Tephrikḗ and Malatīyah), but the order, as we have it, must be wrong. Dazimón lies on the road to Kolóneia from the Asiatic shore of the Bosphorus via the north shore of the Gulf of Ismit. Kaisáreia lies to the south-west of Kolóneia, about two-thirds of the distance along the road from Kolóneia to the Cilician Gates. The text says that, for attacking Tephrikḗ, 'the Armeniac thémata' (i.e. the rump of the original théma Armeniakoí, together with Khaldhía, Kolóneia, Sevásteia, and Kharsianón) should concentrate at Vathrýax, and this is what we should have expected. But, in the preceding sentence, the text also says that, when the Emperor is heading for the East, the Kappadhokía and Kharsianón and Voukellárioi corps should join the Emperor at Kolóneia, and the Armeniakoí and the Paphlaghonía and Sevásteia corps should join him at Kaisáreia; and this, again, must be wrong.

Kaisáreia lay within théma Kharsianón, so the Kharsianón corps's meeting-place with the Emperor must surely have been at Kaisáreia, in the corps's own territory, and the Kappadhokía corps's meeting-place must have been at Kaisáreia too, since théma Kappadhokía lay to the south-west of théma Kharsianón. The Voukellárioi's meeting-place can have been at Kolóneia, as the text states, but then Kolóneia must have been the meeting-place for the Paphlaghonía corps and for the Armeniakoí too (and also for the Kolóneia corps itself and for the Khaldhía corps, neither of which is named). If the corps had headed for Kolóneia and for Kaisáreia according to the instructions as we have them, they would have crossed each other's paths and have obstructed each other's march.

Evidently any attempts to reconstruct so desperately muddled a passage can be no more than tentative. However, the passage does inform us that the *étapes*, the roads linking them with each other, and the rendez-vous given to the Asiatic corps were realities, and the East Roman successes in 863, 872, and 878 tell us, further, that the East Roman Army's logistical arrangements worked well on at least three occasions.

The East Roman Army's logistical problems were not easy to solve. The public authorities did their best. For the Emperor and for the tághmata they provided pack-mules for transport from the Imperial ranches (μητάτα) in (the old Roman provinces of) Asia and Phrygia.[1] They also provided an army service-corps, the Optimátoi,[2] for loading and unloading the animals, conducting them on the march, and taking them out to graze when the Army was in camp. For Optimátoi who were put in charge of the Imperial pack-mules, the Imperial kómês tou stávlou provided one sýndrophos (mate) for every ten of these optimátoi from the Imperial stables at Malayína.[3] The optimátoi led their mules; the sýndrophos walked behind to adjust any packs that threatened to slip off. (The costly and sacred Imperial baggage must be safeguarded against risks.) As for the thematic soldiers, they had to provide their own pack-animals and batmen, and, if they could not produce enough batmen to go round, even by sharing one man between several soldiers, the worst soldiers had to do batmen's work.[4]

The quantity of the Emperor's baggage was preposterously huge,[5] and when the tághmata, as well as the Emperor, went on campaign, the number of non-combatants employed on looking after the Army's baggage

---

[1] *T.V.T.*, pp. 448, 476, 488–9. These ranches were administered by the loghothétês ton ayelón, who ranked fortieth among the sixty officials who were directly appointed by the Emperor and were directly responsible to him (see Philótheos's klêtorolóyion, p. 137 Bury, p. 713 Bonn). This official's staff consisted of one protonotários each for Asia and Phrygia, together with a number of managers, kómêtes, and inspectors (see ibid., p. 141 Bury, p. 718 Bonn). In the Age of the Principate, the principal Imperial stud-farms had been in Cappadocia, but since the seventh century Cappadocia had come to be so close to the Romano-Arab frontier that livestock kept there would have been an easy prey for Arab raiders.

[2] See II, 4, Appendix, pp. 270–3.

[3] *T.V.T.*, pp. 474 and 476–8.   [4] See II, 1 (iii) (d), p. 140.

[5] See II, 2, pp. 195–8. The mules provided for the Emperor's baggage at Malayína by the loghothétês ton ayelón had to be supplemented by contributions of extra mules from the senior thematic and taghmatic military officers and the senior civil servants (*T.V.T.*, pp. 460–1).

and after the pack-mules that carried it must have fallen not far short of the number of combatant troops. Yet, if the non-combatants had been left behind and if the soldiers had had to lead their own mules, to groom their own horses, and to take the animals out to grass, these fatigue-duties would have been almost a full-time occupation—and the combatants had not the time to spare, for the East Roman method of waging war by the tactics of 'dogging and pouncing'[1] was an exacting full-time occupation in itself.

For an East Roman Army on campaign, its baggage and its animals— cavalry-horses as well as pack-mules—were a serious, though indispensable, encumbrance. On the march they lengthened the column of route and slowed down its pace. In camp, they occupied precious space. When out grazing, they and their attendants had to be guarded by combatant troops,[2] since they were a tempting target for enemy attack. If the army did find sufficient pasture, it could count itself lucky; for, in depriving the enemy of pasture by the tactics of 'scorched earth', the East Romans were depriving themselves as well. To carry fodder gave a better assurance of supply,[3] but this remedy was self-defeating, since the fodder had to be transported on the backs of additional animals which then consumed their share of it.[4] Worst of all, the soldiers' anxiety for the safety of their animals and of their baggage was likely to distract them from their proper business,[5] which was, not to guard property, but to wage war.

Of course, these handicaps impeded the enemy too; and, for him, they were aggravated, so long as the war-zone lay in East Roman territory, by his burdening himself with loot—and it was the opportunity for looting that made the risks of raiding worth incurring. Looting enriched the adherents of the right religion and mulcted the adherents of the wrong religion, and both these results were satisfactory from the raider's standpoint. At the same time, his risks increased in proportion to the amount of the loot that he accumulated. He became particularly vulnerable when he was attempting to withdraw through the passes with his baggage-train swollen by prisoners and captured livestock. When, on the Romano-Arab front, the tide of war turned after the close of the first quarter of the tenth century, the roles of Arabs and East Romans were reversed. It was now the East Romans' turn to taste the raider's exhilarating but hazardous experience.

---

[1] See II, 1 (iii) (b).

[2] Leo, Dhiat. 16, §§ 65–6, col. 929; 'A.V.', pp. 21 and 41–2. Collecting fodder was particularly hazardous when the combatant troops were in action (Leo, Dhiat. 14, § 16, cols. 852–3).

[3] Fodder and rations should be carried in enemy country (Leo, Dhiat. 13, § 16, col. 848; Dhiat. 16, § 36, col. 921).

[4] It is not possible to carry more than twenty-four days' supply of κριθή for the animals ('A.V.', p. 37).

[5] Leo Dhiat. 10, § 2, col. 788, copying M., Part 1, chap. 5, p. 121 Scheffer, p. 150 Mihăescu.

Much consideration was given to the problem of reducing the nuisance of the baggage (τοῦλδον) to a minimum. 'Mavríkios' had devoted to this subject the fifth of the twelve parts of his work. Leo VI follows suit.[1] Nikêphóros II is greatly concerned to reduce the amount of baggage and the number of non-combatants,[2] and so is the author of *Perì Para-dhromês Polémou*,[3] but Nikêphóros also insists on carrying with the army an ample stock of spare arrows, in containers holding fifty arrows each, loaded on mules. He also insists on carrying portable mangonels and other kinds of field artillery, portable siphons for squirting napalm, and a supply of this stuff (τοῦ σκευαστοῦ καὶ κολλυτικοῦ πυρός: 'artificial[4] fire that is adhesive'),[5] and these items must have required, not mules, but waggons, to transport them.

Spare weapons and spare tools were, in fact, essential components of an East Roman army's equipment.[6] Leo VI's and the 'Anonymus Vári's' lists include the same items as Nikêphóros's list. Leo adds caltrops, wooden ladders, inflatable skins, tents,[7] and smiths with their tools. The 'Anonymus Vári' requires every infantryman to have eight caltrops[8] roped together, and every squad of ten infantrymen to have a small iron stake to which a string of caltrops can be fastened. These mule-loads and waggon-loads of war-material had perforce to accompany an East Roman Army wherever it went.

A characteristic feature of the East Roman art of war which was also a Roman tradition was the strictness of the provisions for security both on the march and in camp.

On leaving camp, perfect order should be maintained,[9] and, even if the day's march is to be over level ground, an advance-guard, flank-guards, and a rear-guard are to be organized.[10] Leo VI devotes the ninth of his twenty parts to the same subject.[11] Great importance is attached to advance-parties and guides. If you have no local guides (ἐντόπιοι), and if there is no immediate fear of an enemy attack, dhoukátores (guides)

---

[1] Leo, Dhiat. 10, Περὶ Τούλδου, cols. 788–92. Cf. Dhiat. 4, § 55, col. 709; Dhiat. 9, § 37, col. 776.

[2] N. Ph., p. 5. For the heavy infantry, there is to be only one mule per two men and only one servant per four men to look after their animals and baggage (p. 5). Cf. 'A.V.', p. 26.

[3] p. 226.

[4] An alternative possible meaning of σκευαστοῦ is 'composite'. Σκευασία means 'mixture' or 'composition' in Modern Greek. See J. R. Partington: *A History of Greek Fire and Gunpowder* (Cambridge, 1960, Heffer), pp. 17–18.

[5] N. Ph., pp. 4–5.

[6] Leo, Dhiat. 4, § 56, col. 709, Dhiat. 6, § 21, col. 725, and § 27, col. 729; T.V.T., p. 494; 'A.V.', pp. 9 and 52.

[7] 'A.V.' insists that junior officers should not be allowed to bring tents, especially not when the war-zone is Bulgaria (pp. 27–8), where no local food-supply is to be found (p. 37). Rations are more useful than tents (p. 28).

[8] Cf. M., Part 12, p. 357 Scheffer, p. 362 Mihăescu.   [9] 'A.V.', pp. 18–19.

[10] Ibid., pp. 19–22. Cf. T.V.T., pp. 452–4.   [11] Leo, Dhiat. 9, cols. 768–88.

and minsorátores (surveyors) are to be sent one day's march ahead to choose the site for the next camp and to mark it out.[1] In enemy country, the minsorátores must be given an escort.[2] The dhoukátores must not only know the roads; they must also be capable of piloting the army through kleisoúrai. They must know the right distances between camps and the right locations for camps—locations with plenty of water and plenty of room. They must also have precise knowledge of enemy terrain.[3] Advance-parties (ἀντικένσωρες, from the Latin antecessores) should also go one day's march ahead. Their duty is to discover where water and pasture are to be had.[4] For the main body of the army there are alternative dispositions on the march, according to whether the enemy is far away or near.[5] Cover your infantry with detachments of cavalry.[6] The commander, with his staff (προέλευσις) and his escort, must always be in the van.[7]

Additional security measures are taken when the route for the day's march runs over broken ground or through defiles or when it crosses rivers.[8] Do not traverse defiles or broken ground at night, even for the sake of reaching a safer site for your next camp.[9] On approaching rough country, road-builders are to be sent ahead, and these are to be released from patrol service and from other fatigue duties.[10] On approaching rivers that have to be crossed, the tourmárkhai and dhroungárioi, as well as the andikénsores, are to go ahead, test the ford, and report back[11]—but this only if the enemy is not near. If he is near, the officers are to stay with their units, and the units are to refrain from trying to get ahead of each other.[12]

If the terrain ahead is particularly dangerous and difficult, you yourself, commander-in-chief, should go off, reach the critical spot, and remain there till the whole of your force has got through safely.

We know of an example that has been given by our father the Emperor Basil [I] of glorious memory. On his expedition against Yermaníkeia, the city in Syria, he went ahead of everyone into the Paradheisós River and remained standing in mid stream, by the side of the ford, with lamps. Thanks to his being there and obviously not being in danger, he was able to pilot his troops across the river easily and with no losses. He kept on giving a hand to soldiers who were in difficulties. He saved them by his personal exertions.[13]

---

[1] Leo, Dhiat. 9, § 7, col. 769. Cf. §§ 39–40, col. 777, and Dhiat. 12, § 56, col. 821. Cf. also *T.V.T.*, p. 452.

[2] 'A.V.', p. 2. [3] 'A.V.', pp. 28–9. [4] Leo, Dhiat. 9, § 12, col. 769.

[5] Leo, Dhiat. 9, §§ 29–36, col. 776; Dhiat. 12, §§ 58–62, cols. 821–4. Cf. *T.V.T.*, pp. 452 and 489–90.

[6] N. Ph., pp. 2 and 5. [7] Leo, Dhiat. 9, § 10, col. 769.

[8] 'A.V.', pp. 24–5. [9] 'A.V.', p. 15. [10] Leo, Dhiat. 9, § 9, col. 769.

[11] Leo, Dhiat. 9, § 12, col. 769. Cf. 'A.V.', p. 30.

[12] Leo, Dhiat. 9, § 15, col. 772. Cf. *T.V.T.*, pp. 484–5, and 'A.V.', pp. 24–5.

[13] Leo, Dhiat. 9, §§ 13–14, cols. 771–2, one of the rare original passages in Leo VI's *Taktiká*.

Have materials with you for bridging rivers that are not fordable.[1] When you are traversing a kleisoúra,[2] or when an enemy invader is going to traverse one,[3] send troops ahead to occupy commanding points. These should be light troops armed with missile weapons (archers and javelin-men).[4] It is imprudent to commit your army to difficult country, even if the dhoukátores and spies and khosárioi who have gone ahead have reported back that this country has not been occupied by the enemy. If you find that you must traverse it nevertheless, send an infantry force ahead, two or three days in advance. If the terrain permits the cavalry to participate, this will raise the infantry's morale.[5]

The most difficult and dangerous of all contingencies for an East Roman Army is to find that a kleisoúra on the Army's line of retreat from enemy territory has been occupied by the enemy. Keep away from any occupied kleisoúra. It is the terrain, not the enemy himself, that creates the danger. Terrain can enable a weaker force to defeat a stronger one. If you can, compel the enemy to evacuate the kleisoúra by sending infantry through other kleisoúrai, that he has not occupied, to take him in the rear. If the enemy cannot be forced or tempted to evacuate, and if his position is impregnable, take one of the side-roads; take difficult roads that are known only to your own dhoukátores.[6]

At the end of your day's march, whether the march has been difficult or easy, do not break formation till the camp has been fortified.[7]

There are four extant sets of instructions about camps that were written within the century beginning in the year 886. The subject is dealt with by Leo VI in his *Taktiká*,[8] by Constantine Porphyrogenitus in his version of Leo Katákylas's monograph,[9] by Nikêphóros II Phokás,[10] and by the 'Anonymus Vári'.[11] These four sets of instructions are consistent with each other, and their affinity with Polybius's description of a second-century-B.C. Roman camp[12] is unmistakable.

Notwithstanding the length of the time-span between the dates of these treatises and Polybius's, the medieval treatises give the impression that the affinity is due to a genuine historical continuity of professional military practice; for, though the general picture is the same, there are differences of concrete detail which correspond to the changes that have taken place, in the meantime, in the art of war, in the categories of troops, and in the relative importance of the different categories. All the same, the compulsiveness of the Byzantine penchant for archaism constrains

---

[1] *T.V.T.*, pp. 447–8.

[2] Leo, Dhiat. 9, § 27, col. 773 (copied from Onesander), and §§ 36–9, cols. 776–7.

[3] Leo, Dhiat. 9, § 28, col. 773. [4] 'A.V.', p. 15. Cf. pp. 30, 31, and 32.

[5] 'A.V.', p. 30. [6] 'A.V.', pp. 31–3. See the whole of his chap. 20, pp. 31–6.

[7] Leo, Dhiat. 9, § 77, col. 788. [8] Leo, Dhiat. 13, Περὶ Ἀπλήκτων, cols. 792–805.

[9] *T.V.T.*, pp. 481–2. [10] N. Ph., pp. 18–20.

[11] 'A.V.', chaps. 1–7, pp. 1–17. [12] Polybius, Book VI, chaps. 27–42.

us to allow for the possibility that the medieval treatises' affinity with Polybius's may be due, not—or, at least, not solely—to an historical continuity of practice, but, in part, at any rate, to literary plagiarism.

Descriptions of Roman camps, or instructions about them, had been composed by a series of authors who bridge the time-span between Polybius's generation and the generation of Nikêphóros II Phokás and his officers. The latest set of instructions in the series before the great break in continuity in the seventh century of the Christian Era is presented by 'Mavríkios'.[1] Leo VI copies 'Mavríkios' in his instructions about camps, as he does in the rest of his compilation; and even Nikê-phóros II and his two fellow professional soldiers may have succumbed to some extent to the Byzantine temptation to plagiarize, in spite of their declared, and no doubt sincere, intention to give their readers the results of their own first-hand experience.

With this reservation in mind, we may now survey the four sets of medieval East Roman instructions about camps and take note of the points on which these conform to 'Mavríkios's' instructions. This conformity may be due to the persistence of the same professional practice or it may be due to an archaistic-minded plagiarism which would be no valid evidence for the true state of affairs in the plagiarists' lifetimes. On the whole, we may perhaps guess that, in the instructions about camps, plagiarism is at its minimum and a genuine continuity of practice is at its maximum.

The two synonymous East Roman names for a camp are to be found already in the title[2] of 'Mavríkios's' chapter on the subject. One is 'phossáton',[3] meaning an area surrounded by a trench, for which the Latin word is 'fossa'. The synonym for 'phossáton' is 'áplikton' (áplêkton), a syncopation of the Latin word 'applicatum', perhaps meaning something that has been 'pitched', i.e. a tent or a number of tents. In this chapter the word 'áplêkton' has already appeared in the meaning of a permanent camp serving as an *étape*. It was also used to mean the temporary camp of any army on the move.

Any description of an East Roman camp and any instruction about it falls, by the nature of the subject, into four distinct parts: the site of the camp, the method of fortifying it, the lay-out of the area enclosed within the camp's enceinte, and the provisions for security.

The siting of the camp was as important as its fortification and as its internal lay-out, and for this the commander was dependent on the experience, judgement, and skill of his minsorátores. The site must be clean

---

[1] M., Part 12, chap. 22, pp. 344–58 Scheffer, pp. 354–63 Mihăescu, with the explanation of a missing diagram on pp. 363–4 Scheffer, p. 366 Mihăescu.

[2] Reproduced in Leo VI's corresponding chapter-heading.

[3] In East Roman Greek, the meaning of this word 'phossáton' came to be extended to denote not only a camp but the army that a camp harboured.

and healthy. Avoid woods, mud, and marshes.[1] The site should have a sufficient water-supply of its own close at hand.[2] If there is a small fordable river, include it within the enceinte, but site the place for watering your horses farther downstream.[3] Site your camp on terrain that will provide natural defences for it, on one side or on two sides, in the shape of an unfordable river or a lake or a precipice or a cañon ($\phi\acute{a}\rho\alpha\gamma\xi$).[3] Do not site your camp near a mountain, a swamp, a thicket, or a hill that would give access to enemy infantry.[3] A site that is cramped and is also commanded at close quarters by a mountain is dangerous.[4] Rather than remain on a site like that, divide your army; this is the lesser evil.[5] Keep on moving camp.[6] The accumulation of ordure in a camp quickly makes it uninhabitable.[7]

The best shape for a camp is a square,[8] and this was, of course, the traditional Roman shape. The circular shape is dangerous;[9] but, when the army is investing an enemy city, the square shape is impracticable; the besieging army and its camp will have to be drawn out thin in order to encircle the besieged city.[10] In this situation, the camp should be protected by a trench both on its inner face, confronting the city, and on its outer face, in case an enemy force from outside should attempt to come to the besieged city's rescue.[10] Moreover, the square shape may prove to be incompatible with the lie of the land;[11] and the nature of the terrain may determine not only the shape of the camp but the method of fortifying its perimeter.

The proper way to fortify your square camp is to dig a trench,[12] five or six feet wide and seven or eight feet deep, and to heap the earth from the trench inside, to make an embankment.[13] In enemy country, this is imperative, even if you are intending to make only a single night's stay.[14]

---

[1] Leo, Dhiat. 11, § 3, col. 793 (cf. M., loc. cit., p. 353).

[2] N. Ph., p. 18.

[3] 'A.V.', p. 3, following M., loc. cit., p. 354.

[4] Leo, Dhiat. 11, § 1, col. 792, and § 37, col. 801; 'A.V.', pp. 14–15.

[5] 'A.V.', p. 16.

[6] Leo, Dhiat. 11, §§ 4 and 31, cols. 793 and 801, following M., loc. cit., p. 353.

[7] Leo, Dhiat., 11, § 4, col. 793. M.'s instruction, in loc. cit., p. 353, that men must go out of bounds to obey the calls of nature is a counsel of perfection, considering the rigour of the security regulations.

[8] 'A.V.', p. 1.

[9] 'A.V.', p. 2.

[10] 'A.V.', p. 40.

[11] 'A.V.', p. 14.

[12] Leo calls this a $\tau\acute{a}\phi\rho\sigma$ in Dhiat. 11, §§ 2 and 8 (col. 793) and in § 15 (col. 796), and in § 8 he gives, as a synonym, the Latin word $\phi\acute{o}\sigma\sigma\alpha$. 'A.V.', however, on p. 4, in a passage parallel to Leo's Dhiat. 11, § 15, and derived, like it, from M., substitutes for $\tau\acute{a}\phi\rho\sigma$ the word $\chi\acute{a}\rho\alpha\xi$, which properly means, not a trench, but a stockade, and is used in this meaning by Leo in Dhiat. 11, § 9 ($\chi\acute{a}\rho\alpha\kappa\alpha$ $\pi\acute{\eta}\xi\epsilon\iota s$).

[13] Leo, Dhiat. 11, §§ 2 and 15, cols. 793 and 796, and 'A.V.', p. 4, copying M., Part 12, chap. 22, p. 349 Scheffer, p. 354 Mihǎescu.

[14] Leo, Dhiat. 11, § 2, col. 793, and Dhiat. 18, § 25, col. 952. Cf. N. Ph., p. 19.

However, you must carry caltrops with you (loaded on pack animals, in case you have had to leave your waggons behind).[1] *Chevaux de frise* made with caltrops will serve instead of earthworks if the terrain is rocky or if you arrive too late in the evening to do the digging.[2] In any case, if an enemy attack is not in prospect, earthworks can be dispensed with. The troops should not be put to the fatigue of constructing works of this kind unnecessarily.[3] The Emperor Nikêphóros II's grandfather of the same name had invented, for campaigning in Bulgaria, a portable substitute for earthworks in the shape of wooden caltrops with swords projecting from them.[4]

Even if the camp is being fortified with earthworks, it is a good plan to surround these with a waggon-laager, if you have your waggons with you, or alternatively with a stockade (χάρακα).[5] *Chevaux de frise* made with caltrops are as good an outer line of defence as a waggon-laager.[6] Outside the outer defences, dig, at intervals, leg-breaking pits, with a wooden stake planted in each of them. Your own troops should be saved from falling into these traps for catching the enemy by setting markers.[7] Also, surround the stockade with a string of bells strung on ropes.[8] Patrols coming into camp to report must duck under the bells without making them ring—which might create an uncalled-for panic.[9]

The camp should have four 'public' gates the traditional Roman number), and a larger number of small postern gates.[10] The approaches should be slanting, not straight.[11] Each main gate should have its own officer in charge, and his quarters should be close to it.[12] So, too, should be the quarters of the monavlátoi, the archers, and the slingers.[13]

The area enclosed within the camp was laid out on a grid plan, just as it had been in Polybius's day.[14] The light infantry's tents were to be

[1] Leo, Dhiat. 11, §§ 47 and 48, col. 804.

[2] Leo, Dhiat. 11, § 28, col. 800, copying M., Part 12, chap. 22, p. 352 Scheffer, p. 358 Mihăescu.

[3] N. Ph., pp. 19–20.

[4] Leo, Dhiat. 11, § 26, col. 800.   [5] Leo, Dhiat. 11, § 9, col. 793.

[6] Leo, Dhiat. 11, § 48, col. 804, copying M., Part 12, chap. 22, p. 349 Scheffer, p. 354 Mihăescu.

[7] Leo, Dhiat. 11, § 15, col. 796; 'A.V.', p. 9, following M., Part 12, chap. 22, p. 349 Scheffer, p. 354 Mihăescu.

[8] 'A.V.', p. 10.   [9] 'A.V.', p. 12.

[10] Leo, Dhiat. 11, § 15, col. 796, copying M., Part 12, chap. 22 ,pp. 349–50 Scheffer, pp. 354–6 Mihăescu, verbatim.

[11] 'A.V.', p. 4.   [12] Leo, Dhiat. 11, § 16, col. 796.

[13] N. Ph., p. 19. Monávlia were weapons with shafts of the maximum thickness that a human hand can grasp. They were effective against cataphracts (N. Ph., pp. 3–4).

[14] For the details, see M., loc. cit., pp. 350–1 Scheffer, pp. 354–6 Mihăescu; Leo, Dhiat. 11, §§ 16–18, cols. 796–7; N. Ph., p. 19; 'A.V.', pp. 3–8 and 11. The medieval authors follow 'Mavríkios' closely on this topic, but 'A.V.' gives details that appear to be authentically contemporary.

pitched just inside the waggon-laager.[1] Between this outer ring of light infantry and the rest of the troops, there was to be an empty zone 300 or 400 feet wide[2] (i.e. wide enough to put the main body of the troops in camp beyond the range of enemy arrows,[3] if the enemy were to mount a night-attack on the camp). The camp was to have a central plateía (i.e. open space, piazza), of cruciform shape, forty to fifty feet broad.[4] The commander-in-chief's quarters should be in the middle of the camp, i.e. in the plateía.[5]

In camp at night-time, security regulations were severe. After the celebration of the evening mass, there is to be silence in camp, no dancing or other sport, and no din, and no soldier is to call a comrade out loud by his name. Silence facilitates the detection of enemy spies.[6] The same object is to be attained by forbidding men to stray from their units and by enforcing this rule by means of strict daily roll-calls.[7] In camp, every officer is to have a mandátor of his own in attendance on his immediate superior, so that orders can be passed down quickly.[8] When the Emperor is in camp, the dhroungários tês víghlês[9] will be there too, and the orderlies-in-attendance (αἱ παραμοναί) of the corps-commanders and other officers are to be present in the tent of the dhroungários tês víghlês day and night.[10] 'Going the rounds' (τὰ κέρκιτα) was taken very seriously.[11] When the Emperor was in camp, the dhroungários tês víghlês conducted the outside watch (τὴν φῖναν[12] τὴν ἔξω, τὰ ἐξώβιγλα) and the commandant of the Etaireía the inside watch (φῖναν ἔσω, τὰ ἐσώβιγλα),[13] which went the rounds in the vacant zone inside the enceinte.[14]

---

[1] This instruction appears to assume either that the waggon-laager was the camp's main fortification, or that it was drawn up just inside, not outside, the earthworks, which would, indeed, have been a safer location for the waggons if there had been time and materials for building a stockade to serve as the outer line of defence.

[2] 'A.V.' divides this empty zone into three zones, each of the first two 132 feet broad and the third 36 feet broad.

[3] 'A.V.', p. 11. N. Ph., p. 19, directs that the infantry's animals are to be tethered a bow-shot's distance away from the stockade (τῆς σούδας, 'the stake').

[4] Leo, Dhiat. 11, § 17, col. 797, copying M., loc. cit., p. 350 Scheffer, p. 356 Mihăescu. Cf. 'A.V.', p. 5, and N. Ph., p. 19. Presumably the reason why it was cruciform was that here the camp's two main streets crossed each other at right angles.

[5] Apparently at the mid point of the plateía according to A.V., p. 5, but expressly *not* at its mid point according to M., loc. cit., p. 350 Scheffer, p. 356 Mihăescu.

[6] Leo, Dhiat. 11, § 22, col. 797, copying M., loc. cit., pp. 351–2 Scheffer, pp. 356–8 Mihăescu.   [7] 'A.V.', p. 9.

[8] Leo, Dhiat. 11, § 20, col. 797, copying M., loc. cit., p. 351 Scheffer, p. 356 Mihăescu.

[9] The thirty-sixth, in order of precedence, of the officials directly responsible to the Emperor (Philótheos's klêtorolóyion, p. 137 Bury, p. 713 Bonn).

[10] 'A.V.', p. 7.

[11] T.V.T. (Constantine's version of Leo Katákylas's monograph), p. 481; 'A.V.', pp. 11–12.

[12] Φῖναν looks like the Latin word 'finem', meaning the end or term of a period of duty. Leo, Dhiat. 14, § 34, cols. 857–60, directs that the watch should be divided into groups to relieve each other, and that soldiers on watch-duty should be kept on their feet and should not be allowed to sit or to lie down.   [13] T.V.T., p. 481; 'A.V.', pp. 11–12.

[14] 'A.V.', p. 10. For the exóvighla, see also N. Ph., p. 20.

The Emperor Nikêphóros II decrees, with characteristic rigour, that non-attendance at the celebration of the evening mass is to be punished by degradation to a lower rank,[1] and that, after dark, no one at all is to be allowed out of camp.[2] Leo VI[3] copies 'Mavríkios'[4] (verbatim) in decreeing that, after the evening mass, after the signal for silence, and after the setting of the watches, no one is to leave camp without the general's permission. Leo Katákylas is more explicit.[5] The dhroungários tês víghlês receives from the Emperor a watchword (σίγνον) that is changed every evening,

and, from the moment at which the dhroungários sets out on his rounds, no one is free to leave camp—not an Imperial chamberlain, not a member of the Etaireía, no one, great or small, exalted or humble, without having received the watchword from the Emperor and having then reported to the dhroungários. If anyone takes it upon himself to leave camp without the watchword, they shackle him and bring him to the dhroungários, and the Emperor is informed, for taking whatever action he may wish. If the man does obtain the watchword from the Emperor, he must re-enter at the same point at which the dhroungários has let him out. He may not re-enter at any other point. If he does, he is shackled by the pedhitoúroi and is handed over to the Emperor at dawn. These regulations are observed until the end of the campaign.

In the medieval East Roman Army there were originally only three categories of troops: ordinary cavalry, light infantry, and heavy infantry. Of these, the heavy infantry were manifestly the least useful for the 'dogging and pouncing' form of warfare. The Emperor Nikêphóros II Phokás re-introduced cataphracts, i.e. cavalry whose horses, as well as the troopers themselves, were armed cap-à-pie.[6] For East Roman purposes, cataphracts were probably no more useful than heavy infantry, and they were certainly far more expensive.

Leo VI remarks[7] that Aelian's distinction between cataphracts and ordinary cavalry is now obsolete. However, he contradicts himself by

---

[1] N. Ph., p. 21.   [2] N. Ph., p. 20.   [3] Leo, Dhiat. 11, § 19, col. 797.
[4] M., loc. cit., p. 351 Scheffer, p. 356 Mihăescu.
[5] *T.V.T.*, pp. 481–2.
[6] This equipment had been invented in Iran. It had been worn already in 331 B.C., at the Battle of Gaugamela, by the Indian and Bactrian cavalry in the army of Darius III; it had been developed in the armies of the Arsacids and their successors the Sasanids (Heraclius's opponent the Sasanian Emperor Khusraw Parviz is portrayed in full cataphract equipment in the equestrian figure, representing him, at Naqsh-i-Rustam); and it had been adopted in the Roman Army in the fourth century of the Christian Era; we have descriptions of it dating from the reigns of Constantine I (Nazarius, 'Panegyricus Constantino Augusto Dictus', chap. 22, in G. Baehrens's *XII Panegyrici Latini* (Leipzig, 1911, Teubner), p. 173), Constantius II (Ammianus Marcellinus, Book XVI, chap. 10), and Justinian I (Procopius, *A History of the Wars of Justinian*, Book I, chap. 1).
[7] Leo, Dhiat. 6, § 29, cols. 729–32.

prescribing that the 4,000 picked cavalrymen in each théma are to be cataphracts.[1] In any case, cataphracts, in the full meaning of the term, were deliberately re-introduced into the East Roman Army by Nikê-phóros II Phokás.[2] He devotes one chapter to prescribing, in detail, the armour for both the men and the horses. The horses are to be so thoroughly armoured that only their eyes and nostrils and the lower parts of their legs will remain visible. Their armoured skirts are to be split in front, to enable them to move freely. The troopers are to wear závai (byrnies, mail coats, *jebe* in Ottoman Turkish) of double or treble thickness, and these are to cover their heads as well as their bodies, so that their eyes, like their horses' eyes, will be the only visible parts of their faces.[3] In action, Nikêphóros II's cataphracts are to be drawn up in a triangular formation,[4] and the triangle is to be flanked by two lines of ordinary cavalry, with the apex of the cataphract triangle projecting.[5] The cataphracts are to attack at a slow steady pace ($\mu\epsilon\tau\grave{a}$ $\pi o\lambda\lambda\hat{\eta}s$ $\gamma a\lambda\eta$-$\nu\acute{o}\tau\eta\tau os$),[6] and they are not to join the ordinary cavalry in the pursuit if the enemy is defeated.[7] The weight of a cataphract's armament for horse and man was, in fact, incompatible with speed.

It looks as if Nikêphóros II's cataphracts were not worth their cost. They could be used only for charging home in a pitched battle, and even Nikêphóros II decrees that, if the enemy's numerical strength is equal to the East Roman force's, and *a fortiori* if it is superior, the East Roman commander must avoid pitched battles and hand-to-hand fighting ($\chi\rho\hat{\eta}$ $\dot{\epsilon}\kappa\phi\epsilon\acute{v}\gamma\epsilon\iota\nu$ $\tau\grave{o}\nu$ $\delta\eta\mu\acute{o}\sigma\iota o\nu$ $\pi\acute{o}\lambda\epsilon\mu o\nu$ $\kappa a\grave{\iota}$ $\tau\grave{a}s$ $\sigma\nu\mu\pi\lambda o\kappa\acute{a}s$) and must resort to tricks ($\dot{\epsilon}\pi\iota\tau\eta\delta\epsilon\acute{v}\mu a\tau a$) and ambushes ($\dot{\epsilon}\nu\acute{\epsilon}\delta\rho a\iota$).[8]

A 'triangle' of cataphracts was an attempt to produce the mounted equivalent of a phalanx of heavy infantry. But an infantry phalanx was effective only in a pitched battle on an unbroken stretch of open level ground. Thus heavy infantry that fought in phalanx formation was not an appropriate arm for employment in the 'dogging and pouncing' tactics of the medieval East Roman art of war, and cataphracts were inappropriate *a fortiori*. 'Mavríkios' testifies indirectly that, by the close of the sixth century of the Christian Era, the East Roman heavy infantry had relapsed into the phalanx formation and tactics which the Roman infantry had discarded in the fourth century B.C. in favour of the more flexible manipular formation and tactics; for 'Mavríkios' observes shrewdly that, for cavalry, infantry phalanx tactics are not practicable, 'because horses cannot push, with their faces, the ranks in front of them

---

[1] Leo, Dhiat. 18, § 150, col. 988.
[2] See the reference to his Novel No. 22 in II, 1 (iii) (e), p. 162, with n. 1.
[3] N. Ph., p. 11.   [4] N. Ph., pp. 8 and 14.
[5] N. Ph., pp. 14, 15, 16.   [6] N. Ph., p. 8.
[7] N. Ph., pp. 8 and 16.
[8] N. Ph., pp. 17–18.

in unison (συμφώνως), as men on foot can'.[1] In a cavalry formation in depth, the troopers cannot use their weapons effectively, not even bows;[1] so a depth of four files is enough, though the optimum depth will vary according to the quality of the troops.[2] Nikêphóros II Phokás himself rules that cavalry shall always form only five files deep—in three ranks of lancers and two of archers[3]—and that there shall be sixty archers in a force of 300 prokoursátores.[4] Nikêphóros's attempt to re-introduce cataphracts seems to have failed, for cataphracts do not figure in the extant pictures of medieval East Roman cavalry or in the Byzantine chroniclers' and historians' accounts of their performance on particular occasions or in the descriptions of what is expected of them in the directions for 'dogging and pouncing' in, for example, *Perì Paradhromês Polémou* and in the 'Anonymus Vári's' treatise.

Leo VI's description of the armour of an ordinary East Roman cavalryman and his horse[5] does make him at least a semi-cataphract, for the horse is given a nose-guard, a frontlet, a breastplate, and a gorget. This description, however, must be discounted, for it is copied from 'Mavríkios',[6] and, in the plagiarized passage, 'Mavríkios' says, four times over, that this equipment is 'modelled on the Avars' style'.[7] This is entirely credible, since, next to the Persians, the Avars were the East Romans' most formidable antagonists *circa* 600, which is the approximate date of 'Mavríkios's' work. By Leo VI's time, the Avars had been extinct for the best part of a century, so Leo's reproduction of 'Mavríkios's' description of the Avars' style of equipment can be dismissed as an anachronism. The pictures of East Roman cavalrymen in the Psalter of Theodore of Kaisáreia,[8] which was illuminated in 1066, are likely to be truer to life, not only for that date, but for the tenth century too. The cavalrymen here depicted are not heavily armoured, and their horses wear no armour at all. This was a light enough type of cavalry to be able to travel the long distances at the high speed that the tactics of 'dogging and pouncing' required.

The Eastern Muslims did continue to use cataphracts. (Presumably they, like the East Romans, had adopted this type of cavalry from their Persian predecessors.) Nikêphóros II Phokás gives directions[9] for the tactics to be adopted if enemy cataphracts are encountered, and there is a firsthand account[10] of a splendidly equipped Muslim cataphract challenging

---

[1] M., Part 2, chap. 5, pp. 58–9 Scheffer, pp. 82–4 Mihăescu, copied by Leo, Dhiat. 12, §40, col. 817.

[2] M., ibid., pp. 59–60 Scheffer, pp. 84 Mihăescu.   [3] N. Ph., p. 14.

[4] N. Ph., p. 13.   [5] Leo, Dhiat. 5, §3, col. 717.

[6] M., Part 1, chap. 2, pp. 20–3 Scheffer, pp. 50–2 Mihăescu.

[7] κατὰ τὸ σχῆμα τῶν Ἀβάρων—a piece of tell-tale information that Leo imitates in plagiarizing 'Mavríkios' here.

[8] Now in the British Museum.   [9] N. Ph., p. 17.

[10] Quoted by Ibn al-Tiqtaqā in *Kitāb al-Fakhrī* (Cairo edition, p. 72).

a wretchedly equipped Mongol horseman in 1258, in the overture to the battle that resulted in the fall of Baghdad and in the liquidation of the last remnant of the 'Abbasid Caliphate. However, the Eastern Muslim cavalry who raided East Roman Asia Minor for more than three centuries, from *circa* 640/1 to 965, were certainly not cataphracts. Their horses were not armoured; for, in two passages,[1] Leo VI directs the East Romans to shoot at their Eastern Muslim antagonists' horses. Moreover, the Muslim raiding-parties of cavalry unaccompanied by infantry[2] travelled at high speed. They never encamped for a whole night long— they halted only just long enough to rest and feed their horses. The Muslims' horses were swifter than the East Roman troops' horses.[3] The equipment of this Muslim raiding-cavalry must have been the lightest possible.

It is evident that the two serviceable categories of East Roman troops were the ordinary cavalry and the light infantry. The ordinary cavalry 'dogged' the enemy raiders; the light infantry 'pounced' on them from the heights commanding the defiles through which the enemy had to try to regain their own country. Only infantry, and light infantry, could operate on the broken mountainous terrain from which the 'pounce' was made. Here the light infantry came into their own, while the cavalry, even ordinary cavalry, were out of their element. The problem for the East Roman high command was to get their light infantry into position at the strategic point before the retreating enemy raiding-force arrived there. Nikêphóros II Phokás directs[4] that infantrymen who cannot keep up with the cavalry are to have one mule each for them to ride and for carrying what they need. Leo VI directs that the heavy infantry should not be required to make long marches, and should not be kept standing. When they halt, let them sit.[5] The light infantry would be likely to reach the strategic point first.

This strategic point is one of the exits from Rhomanía through a defile.[6] Occupy the heights commanding the defile—on both sides, if possible, and on one side at least.[7] The infantry component of the army should be concentrated at the difficult stretches of the roads (εἰς τὰς δυσχωρίας τῶν ὁδῶν).[8] The cavalry should join up with the infantry for the kill,[9] but the light infantry is to give the enemy the *coup de grâce*.[10]

The light infantry are to be archers.[11] Nikêphóros II Phokás wants his archers to be 4,800 strong in a mixed force that would also include

---

[1] Leo, Dhiat. 18, §§ 24 and 136, cols. 952 and 980.
[2] Μονόκουρσα, πεζῶν ἄνευ (N. Ph., p. 194).   [3] N. Ph., pp. 8 and 17.
[4] N. Ph., p. 5.   [5] Leo, Dhiat. 14, §§ 80 and 91, cols. 873 and 877.
[6] Leo, Dhiat. 17, § 77, cols. 932–3, quoted already in II, 1 (iii) (b), p. 110.
[7] Π.Π.Π., pp. 189–90.   [8] Op. cit., pp. 204, 213–14, and 256–8.
[9] Op. cit., p. 251.   [10] Op. cit., pp. 255–6.
[11] Leo, Dhiat. 6, § 26, col. 728.

11,200 heavy infantry.[1] Each archer is to have two quivers (one to take forty arrows, the other to take sixty), two bows, four bowstrings, a mini-shield (χεροσκούταρον), a belt-sword, an axe, and a sling.[2] Leo VI's archers are not to have shields or spears.[3] (Their hands must be kept free for shooting.)

Archery is all-important. The javelin-men can be Rhos or other foreigners,[4] but, for East Roman national troops, bows and arrows head the list of the spare weapons with which they must provide themselves.[5] Bows with bow-cases and arrows with quivers are the first items on Leo VI's list of weapons for cavalry.[6] The bows must not be too stiff for the individual soldier to bend.[7] The middle ranks of the cavalry should be armed with bows, and, like the infantry archers, these horse-archers should not be allowed to have lances or shields.[8]

What is more, every young East Roman is to learn to shoot.[9] Even men who are exempt from military service are to have bows in their homes.[10] 'Archery is a great weapon and an effective one, especially for use against Saracens and Turks' (i.e. Magyars).[11] Leo VI[12] instructs every corps-commander to order all the forts and villages and market-towns (κωμοπόλεσι) and, in a word, everyone under the corps-commander's jurisdiction to see to it that in every house there shall be one bow and forty arrows. Moreover, these civilians are to practise shooting, both in broken country and in open country, in kleisoúrai and in the bush.[12]

It hardly needs saying that, in insisting on archery for all, Leo VI is taking his cue from 'Mavríkios'. This sixth-century authority prescribes that all young Romans (not foreigners), up to the age of forty, are to be compelled, whatever their degree of expertise in archery, to carry bows and quivers and to possess spears (κοντάρια) as well,[13] in order that if, as may happen, one of these two weapons miscarries, they shall still have the other ready for use.[14] 'Mavríkios' says this once; Leo VI, in copying him, says the same thing three times, and this suggests that archery for all was still a genuinely live issue in Leo VI's day.

Order of battle receives great attention from all our authorities.[15] They go into minute detail, but their instructions can be summed up in

---

[1] N. Ph., pp. 1 and 2.   [2] N. Ph., p. 2.   [3] Leo, Dhiat. 18, § 30, col. 953.
[4] N.Ph., p. 2.   [5] Leo, Dhiat. 6, § 21, col. 725.   [6] Leo, Dhiat. 5, § 2, col. 717.
[7] Leo, Dhiat. 6, § 2, col. 721, copying M., Part 1, chap. 2, p. 20 Scheffer, p. 50 Mihăescu.
[8] Leo, Dhiat. 12, § 49, col. 820.   [9] Leo, Dhiat. 6, § 5, col. 724.
[10] Leo, Dhiat. 11, § 50, col. 805.   [11] Leo, Dhiat. 18, §§ 22–3, col. 952.
[12] Leo, Dhiat. 20, § 81, col. 1036.
[13] Copied in Leo, Dhiat. 6, § 6, col. 724.
[14] M., Part 1, chap. 2, p. 21 Scheffer, p. 52 Mihăescu.
[15] See M., Parts 2, 3, 6, 12; Leo, Dhiat. 12, §§ 7–49, cols. 808–20; §§ 58–60, cols. 823–4;
§§ 75–94, cols. 829–33; Dhiat. 14, §§ 6 and 67–79, cols. 849 and 869–73 (infantry); N. Ph.,
pp. 6–7, 8, 9, 12–18; Π.Π.Π., p. 230.

a single maxim: 'Do not put all your eggs into one basket. To marshal all your troops in one single line of battle is to invite disaster. Marshal them in at least two lines, or, better still, in three, and throw out a vanguard, flank-guards, and, above all, a rearguard (σάκα).'

This had, of course, been the cardinal principle of the Roman art of war ever since the date, some time before the close of the fourth century B.C., at which the Roman Army had abandoned the phalanx for the manipular formation and tactics. This principle may have survived the transformation of the Roman Army in and after the third century of the Christian Era—a transformation in which the cavalry, hitherto subsidiary, had become the key arm, while the infantry had come to play the secondary role that had formerly been the cavalry's. However, the holding in reserve of part of a force engaged in action has been, at all times and places, a matter of course in any system of tactics in which intellect, as well as mere brute force, has been applied to warfare. Reserves played an important part in the tactics of some of the East Romans' antagonists—not only those antagonists whom the East Romans regarded as their equals, such as the Eastern Muslims and their predecessors the Persians, but also others, such as the Eurasian pastoral nomads, who were barbarians in East Roman eyes.

The East Roman treatises on the art of war call for operations that are elaborate and that are likely to miscarry if they are not performed with precision. This is true of the prescriptions, not only for order of battle, but for column of route, for pitching, guarding, and breaking camp, and for the tricks (feints, ambushes, and traps) that were of the essence of the tactics of 'dogging and pouncing'. If these manœuvres were to be successful in action, they needed to be practised in advance, and all the treatises assume that, when the troops are not on campaign, their time should be spent on exercises. The first chapter of the first part of 'Mavríkios's' *Stratêghikón* is devoted to this,[1] and the whole of Part 6[2] is concerned with exercises in four varieties of tactics, the Eurasian Nomad (Σκυθική), the Alan, the African, and the Italian. The 'Anonymus Vári' recommends[3] that, in the close season, both marching and camping should be practised three or four times on home territory. Leo VI devotes one of the twenty parts of his *Taktiká*[4] to close-season exercises. He recommends, as an example for soldiers, the assiduity and asceticism with which athletes perform their training.[5] He returns to the subject at the beginning of a part, modelled on the corresponding part of 'Mavríkios's' work, on the practice of various foreign and East Roman

[1] M., pp. 18–19 Scheffer, pp. 48–50 Mihăescu.
[2] M., pp. 126–33 Scheffer, pp. 156–61 Mihăescu.   [3] 'A.V.', p. 51.
[4] Leo, Dhiat. 7, cols. 733–61, and Dhiat. 8, § 1, col. 764.
[5] Leo, Dhiat. 14, § 61, cols. 868–9, copying M., Part 4, chap. 5, p. 119 Scheffer, p. 148 Mihăescu.

orders of battle.[1] The author of *Perì Paradhromês Polémou*[2] and the 'Anony-mus Vári'[3] take up the same theme.

The East Roman Army with which 'Mavríkios' was concerned was a professional army which lived on regular pay and which was therefore under an obligation to carry on with its professional duties in season and out of season. In the medieval East Roman Army the tághmata had the same duty and the same opportunity for performing it. But the major part of the medieval East Roman Army consisted of the thematic troops, and, in the off-season, a thematic soldier's first concern was, not to train for the next campaign, but to attend to the cultivation of his estate in order to raise the money for paying his taxes.[4] We may guess that, in seeking to impose peace-time training on soldiers who were only semi-professional, the thematic military authorities were fighting a losing battle. The thematic soldier is likely to have given the taxation-officers' demands the priority.

The greater part of the four medieval treatises on the East Roman art of war is taken up by the consideration of operations on the East Roman side of the frontier. This is true not only of Leo VI's *Taktiká*, but also of the three treatises that were written in or after the reign of Nikêphóros II Phokás (963–9)—that is to say, in a period in which the East Roman Army was taking the offensive.

In the preceding period, most of the rare East Roman operations in enemy territory had been diversionary. Leo refers twice[5] to a brilliantly successful diversionary raid into Cilicia that was made by Nikêphóros Phokás the elder, and this operation is described in detail in *Perì Para-dhromês Polémou*.[6] The operation achieved its objective, which was to force the Cilician Muslims to raise their siege of the East Roman fortress Místheia. Incidentally, Nikêphóros collected a quantity of loot and prisoners, and managed to bring these, as well as his troops, back into Rhomanía unscathed. Though his force was large—he had with him the tághmata as well as all the Asiatic thémata except the Anatolikoí and the Opsíkion—he moved at high speed, and he eluded the Muslim besiegers of Místheia (who had hoped to catch him on his way home as a con-solation for their having had to raise the siege) by returning through a different defile from the one through which he had sallied out. The same diversionary tactics had been practised against the Tarsans at an earlier date by the stratêghoí of the Anatolikoí and of Kappadhokía, and by the stratêghós of Lykandós against both the Tarsans and the Hamdanid Amīr of Aleppo, Sayf-ad-Dawlah.[6]

---

[1] Leo, Dhiat. 18, § 2, col. 945. [2] pp. 238–9. [3] 'A.V.', p. 48.
[4] See II, 1 (iii) (d), pp. 141–2.
[5] Leo, Dhiat. 11, § 25, col. 800, and Dhiat. 17, § 83, col. 933.
[6] *Π.Π.Π.*, pp. 241–3.

The Cilician Muslims were amphibious, but they were few in numbers (except in the season in which they were reinforced by volunteers from the interior of Dār-al-Islām). Therefore send spies to find out, in advance, whether they are going to invade by land or by sea (they are not numerous enough to be able to invade in both ways simultaneously). When they invade by sea, make a diversionary raid against them on land. When they invade by land, tell the stratêghós of the Kivyrrhaiótai to attack them by sea. If you can make a simultaneous attack on them by both sea and land, as Basil I did, that will be best of all.[1]

Though Nikêphóros Phokás the elder, in his diversionary raid, reached the gates of Adhanah and devastated the inhabitants' vineyards, orchards, and fields, he did not attempt to take Adhanah or any other fortified enemy stronghold. Nor did Andréas and his four colleagues when they followed up their victory at Podhandós in 878[2] by raiding Tarsan territory up to the gates of Tarsós itself.[3] Basil I dismissed Andréas for having neglected to follow up their victory by taking Tarsós. Andréas's successor Kestás Styppiótês made the attempt and suffered a disaster.[4]

The medieval East Roman Army was not good at besieging and capturing enemy fortresses. Since 'Mavríkios' has a rather perfunctory passage on this topic,[5] Leo VI and the 'Anonymus Vári' feel constrained to take it up,[6] but it is manifestly distasteful to them.

The 'Anonymus Vári' insists on the difficulty of supply for the besieging army. You must start by devastating the enemy's vineyards, gardens, and parks. You must reduce the besieged city by starvation, but you must keep your own army supplied, and, since you will have devastated the enemy's country, you will have to import your own supplies from Rhomanía[7]— even for besieging a city in the productive Saracen country, and *a fortiori* for a siege in Bulgaria. Where your supply-route runs through kleisoúrai, it will have to be guarded; your convoys, too, will have to be escorted.

The 'Anonymus Vári' declares outright that an attempt to take a fortress by assault will fail if the besieged have not been first softened up by being starved. Leo clutches at any possible alternative to an assault. Offer tempting conditions for capitulation. Proclaim, in the local language, an amnesty for non-combatants. Welcome traitors. And, when you have gained possession of an enemy city, treat it mildly. This was Nikêphóros Phokás the elder's policy towards the (southern) Lombards. First he

---

[1] Leo, *Dhiat.* 18, §§ 138–40, cols. 980–1. See also *Dhiat.* 20, § 124, col. 1049.
[2] See II, 1 (iii) (b), p. 111, and the present chapter, p. 300.
[3] Canard in Vasiliev, *Byzance et les Arabes*, ii, I, p. 85.
[4] *Theoph. Cont.*, Book V (Constantine Porphyrogenitus's biography of Basil I), pp. 286–8. Cf. *Georg. Mon. Cont.*, p. 847; Leo Grammaticus, p. 261.
[5] M., Part 10, chap. 1, pp. 237–41 Scheffer, pp. 248–51 Mihăescu.
[6] Leo, *Dhiat.* 15, §§ 1–39, cols. 885–97; 'A.V.', chap. 21, pp. 37–41.
[7] For the consequent domestic food-shortage in the East Roman Empire, see II, 1 (i), pp. 27–8.

subjugated them by effective military operations, but then he treated them generously. He granted them exemption from tribute and from any other imposition that might have been felt humiliating.[1]

After the turn of the tide on the East Roman Empire's eastern front, the East Roman Army did capture and retain some enemy cities that had been a menace to the Empire's security. Malatīyah capitulated in 934, Qālīqalā (Theodosiópolis) was taken in 949, Adhatá in 957,[2] Samosata in 958,[3] Candia in 961 (at last), Tarsós in 965 (surprisingly late), Antioch in 969. With Antioch, the East Romans acquired a coastal strip of Syria, to the west of the River Orontes, that extended almost as far south as the northern end of Mount Lebanon.[4] Aleppo (captured temporarily by Nikêphóros II Phokás in 962)[5] saved its autonomy by submitting in 969/70 to pay an annual tribute to Constantinople.[6] Urfa (Édhessa) was a precarious outlying enclave of East Roman territory from 1031 to 1098.[7] But, in the rest of Syria and Mesopotamia, the tenth-century and eleventh-century East Roman raids, like the former Arab raids in Asia Minor, came and went without resulting in any permanent conquests. In 942–4 John Kourkoúas momentarily occupied Amida (Diyarbakr), Mayyāfāriqīn (Martyropolis), Dara, and Nisībīn. On this occasion, Urfa (Édhessa) bought immunity for itself, and for Sarūj, Harrān, and Samosata as well, by surrendering the Mandēlion.[8] These successes were striking, but they were ephemeral. The East Romans never succeeded in reconquering permanently Amida, the mighty fortress in the upper basin of the River Tigris,[9] or Nisībīn, which had been the frontier fortress of the Roman Empire before 363, or Tarābulus (Tripolis) in Syria; Tarābulus was not ever occupied, even momentarily; and neither Nikêphóros II Phokás nor John Dzimiskēs ever succeeded in reaching Jerusalem. Moreover, offensive warfare was a luxury that the East Roman Empire could not afford. Both successful sieges and long-distance raids overtaxed the Empire's resources. They were one of the causes

---

[1] Leo, Dhiat. 15, § 38, col. 896. Cf. Kedhrênós, vol. ii, p. 354.

[2] Canard in Vasiliev, *Byzance et les Arabes*, ii, I, p. 361. Constantine Porphyrogenitus plumes himself on the taking, in his own reign, of Adhatá, which had successfully withstood Constantine's grandfather Basil I (Constantine Porphyrogenitus's biography of Basil I in *Theoph. Cont.*, Book V, pp. 281–2). Adhatá was taken by Constantine's dhoméstikos ton Skholón Várdhas Phokás according to Yahyā b. Sa'īd (Vasiliev, op. cit., ii, II, pp. 97–8).

[3] Vasiliev, op. cit., vol. cit., pp. 362–3.

[4] See Honigmann in Vasiliev, op. cit., iii, pp. 95–7.

[5] Honigmann, ibid., p. 97, n. 1.　　　　　　　　　　　　[6] Honigmann, ibid., p. 94.

[7] Honigmann, ibid., pp. 134–46.

[8] For the surrender of the Mandēlion and its solemn reception at Constantinople by the co-Emperors, the Patriarch, and the Senate, see *Georg. Mon. Cont.*, pp. 918–19; Leo Grammaticus, pp. 325–6; *Theoph. Cont.*, p. 432; pseudo-Symeon, pp. 748–9.

[9] In 950/1 the East Romans made an unsuccessful attempt to take Amida by tunnelling under the walls (Ibn al-Azraq al-Fāriqī in Vasiliev, op. cit., ii, II, pp. 115–16; Dhahabī, ibid., pp. 242–3).

of the Empire's eleventh-century collapse at an illusory peak of its fortunes.

This apparent peak was illusory because the price of the East Roman Empire's expansion during the years 926–1045 was not limited to the imposition of an intolerable strain on a taxable peasant free-holding population that had already been over-taxed and that was now being supplanted by big landowners who could defy the Imperial taxation-officers. An even more serious part of the price was the deliberate disbanding of the thematic part of the East Roman Army. This force of peasant-soldiers had given the East Roman Empire a new lease of life by saving Asia Minor from being conquered by the Arabs and being incorporated, as the trans-Tauran Roman provinces and the Persian Empire had been, in the dominions of the Caliphate. The thémata had saved the Empire at a minimal financial cost; for the thematic military estates had not only provided the serving soldiers with their arms, equipment, and horses but had also yielded the staple Imperial taxes for the Treasury. But the system that had worked so well during the period, *circa* 641–926, during which the Empire had been on the defensive was abandoned after the recovery that had been due to this system's success. The thematic army was thrown over just because it had accomplished its task.[1]

This semi-professional army had been admirably well suited for parrying Arab raids on its home territory by engaging in brief 'dogging and pouncing' campaigns. But it did not answer to the requirements of ambitious conquerors, such as Nikêphóros II Phokás, John Dzimiskês, and Basil II. The thematic army was not an adequate instrument for besieging fortresses or for fighting pitched battles, and it could not afford to neglect the agricultural source of its income by soldiering for twelve months in the year. For their new purposes, Nikêphóros II and his two martial successors required fully professional troops who could live on their pay and could therefore give their whole time to their work. They therefore expanded the tághmata and enlisted foreign mercenaries—for example, the 6,000 Russians who enabled Basil II to suppress the fronde of 976–89 in Asia Minor[2]—and the three martial Emperors' unwarlike successors carried still farther the disastrous transformation of the East Roman Army that the martial Emperors had inaugurated.

Nikêphóros II is said to have augmented his resources by keying-up the taxes and corvées exacted from each category of his subjects to the previous level of the next highest category.[3] But the most facile expedient for raising the additional revenue needed for paying professional troops was to commute for additional tax-payments the obligation to produce

---

[1] Ahrweiler, *Byzance et la mer*, pp. 137–8.   [2] See p. 167.
[3] Zonaras, vol. iii, p. 505.

a serving soldier that had previously been carried by the owner of a military estate. This reduced the former thematic soldier, or former provider of a serving thematic soldier, to being a tax-payer and nothing else.[1] The process, once started, was carried farther and farther.[2] For instance, in 1050—when the Saljūqs were already making conquests in the East Roman Empire's new dominions in Armenia—the Emperor Constantine IX (1042-55) disbanded the corps of the two thémata Ivéría (Taik') and Mesopotamía and commuted the obligations of the ex-soldiers from military service to an additional tax-payment.[3] While the thémata thus declined both in prestige and in numerical strength, the tághmata—now financed by the thematic ex-soldiers' additional tax-payments[4]—gained proportionately. The *Taktikón Oikonomídhês*, which was compiled *circa* 975-9, reveals that by this date taghmatic units, commanded by dhoúkes who were directly dependent on Constantinople and were independent of the stratêghoí of the thémata in which they were stationed, were now cantoned all over the Empire.[5] The stationing of a detachment of the Phoidherátoi in théma Anatolikoí had formerly been an exceptional arrangement; this had now become the general rule. The thémata continued to exist as administrative districts, but now they were no longer army-corps as well. In consequence, the thematic stratêghoí lost power and importance, and the leading role in an administrative théma came to be assumed by the thematic judge (kritěs), who had been originally the senior civilian member of the stratêghós's staff.

This change, which was an accompaniment of annexation, was naturally resented in Armenia, where annexation was inevitably unpopular in itself. The Armenian Christians were non-Greek and non-Orthodox, and, though the previous native regime had been arbitrary and turbulent, the Armenian princes and barons had had the merit of being of the same nationality and religion as their subjects. The replacement of these national authorities by East Roman military commanders, civil administrators, and taxation-officers was bound to be grievously irksome, and it is not surprising that, in thémata Ivéría and Mesopotamía, part of the population, at any rate, welcomed the Muslim Turkish invaders as liberators from its unwanted East Roman rulers.[6]

[1] See Glykatzi-Ahrweiler, 'Recherches', pp. 17, 19, 20, 23, 90; Ahrweiler, *Byzance et la mer*, pp. 144-5 and 148; Antoniadis-Bibicou, *Études d'histoire maritime de Byzance*, p. 121.

[2] See Antoniadis-Bibicou, op. cit., p. 121.

[3] Michael Attaleiátês, p. 44; Kedhrênós, vol. ii, p. 608; Michael Glykás, p. 598; Zonarás, vol. iii, p. 647; Kekavménos, *Stratêghikón*, p. 18. See also Glykatzi-Ahrweiler, 'Recherches', p. 23; Ahrweiler, *Byzance et la mer*, p. 146; Antoniadis-Bibicou, *Études d'histoire maritime de Byzance*, p. 122; Vasiliev, *Byzance et les Arabes*, vol. iii, p. 178.

[4] Glykatzi-Ahrweiler, op. cit., pp. 23 and 90; Ahrweiler, op. cit., p. 149.

[5] Glykatzi-Ahrweiler, p. 90; Ahrweiler, pp. 117-18.

[6] Kekavménos, p. 18.

It is more significant that the Greek-speaking Orthodox Christian population of Asia Minor had also become alienated from the Imperial Government at Constantinople. The rebellions in Asia Minor in 963, in 970, in 976–9, and in 987–9, and Basil II's inability to get the better of the rebels without the aid of Iberian mercenaries in 979 and of Russian mercenaries in 988–9, are indications that here the population must certainly have acquiesced in Nikêphóros Phokás's and Várdhas Sklêrós's and Várdhas Phokás's successive *pronunciamientos*. Indeed, it looks as if the rebels had the people's active support. The fronde in 976–9 foreshadowed the Saljūq Turkish conquest of the interior of East Roman Asia Minor in and after 1071. Already in the second generation after the Saljūq conquest, the Greek-speaking Orthodox Christian inhabitants of the islands in Lake Beyshehir in south central Asia Minor resisted by force of arms an attempt to 'liberate' them that was made by the Emperor John Komnênós (1118–43). 'They were so friendly with their Turkish neighbours that they regarded the East Romans as being their enemies.'[1] This testimony from the pen of an East Roman historian speaks for itself.

[1] Nikĕtas Khoniátês, p. 50 (Bonn). Cf. John Kínnamos, p. 22 (Bonn).

7. The Navy

THE Roman Empire has made its mark on the mind of posterity as a land power which gave mobility to its invincible infantry by constructing and maintaining a magnificent network of roads. Yet, in truth, sea-power, not land-power, was the instrument with which the Romans extended their empire from Italy to the whole perimeter of the Mediterranean Sea. They succeeded in expanding their empire into the hinterlands of the Mediterranean as far as, but no farther than, they could convey their infantry overland into the interior from bases round the shores of the Mediterranean and its backwaters.

The Romans wrested the naval command of the western basin of the Mediterranean from the Carthaginians in the First Romano-Carthaginian War (264–241 B.C.). They extended their command to Levantine waters as well when, in the Romano-Seleucid War of 192–190 B.C., the Romans, with their allies Rhodes and Pergamon, broke the Seleucid Empire's naval power, in spite of the combination in Seleucid hands of the naval resources of Phoenicia with those of northern Syria and southern Asia Minor since Antiochus III's conquest of Coele Syria from the Ptolemaic Empire in 198 B.C. From 190 B.C. till A.D. 648/9, when the East Roman Navy's command of the Mediterranean was challenged by Muʿāwiyah, the Romans held this command with only two breaks in its continuity.

The first break was during the century 167–67 B.C., when, as a result of having reduced Rhodes, in succession to the Seleucid Empire, to impotence at sea, the Romans left a naval power-vacuum for Cilician and Cretan pirates to fill. The second break was during the century A.D. 439–533, during which the Vandal conquerors of the Roman dominions in North-West Africa revived the thalassocracy in the western basin of the Mediterranean that the Carthaginians had exercised for two and a half centuries ending in the First Romano-Carthaginian War. Like the Carthaginians, the Vandals did not attempt to extend their thalassocracy to the Levant, but in 468 they defeated the East Roman Government's first attempt to liquidate them. The second attempt, however, was successful. In 533 the swift and cheaply bought overthrow of the Empire's Vandal successor-state not only reunited the best part of North-West Africa with the Empire for more than a century and a half (533–698); it also re-established the Empire's naval command over the whole basin of the Mediterranean, up to the Straits of Gibraltar. Justinian I's conquests in Spain and the greater part of his conquests in Italy were ephemeral, and the price of his war of annihilation against the Ostrogoths (535–53) was the Avaro-Slav invasion of the Balkan Peninsula in and after 581/2 and the collapse of the Empire in 602. The recovery of the naval command over the whole of the Mediterranean basin was the Empire's one substantial gain from Justinian I's wars.[1]

This Roman control of the sea was not challenged by the Persians in the Romano-Persian War of 604–28. The Persians reached the north coast of Syria in 611,[2] completed their occupation of Syria and Palestine in 613–14,[3] invaded Egypt in 616,[4] and held the whole seaboard of this occupied East Roman territory till 629,[5] yet they never seized their opportunity to launch a fleet on Mediterranean waters.[6] Mu'āwīyah seized his opportunity in 648/9, within twelve years of the Arabs' conquest of Syria in 636 and within seven years of their first conquest of Alexandria in 641. From 648/9 onwards, the East Roman Navy was never again the unchallenged mistress of the Mediterranean basin,[7] though it regained the upper hand temporarily from 747 to 827. When, in the course of the eleventh century, the Muslims lost the thalassocracy in their turn, it was captured from them, not by the East Romans, but by the maritime Italian city-states.

Mu'āwīyah's challenge was met by the Emperor Constans II.[8] Indeed, Constans had replied by naval action to the Arabs' overland conquest before the Arabs took to the sea as well. In 645 an East Roman naval expeditionary force had momentarily reoccupied Alexandria. This had been a major naval operation, and it may have been carried out by Constans II's new navy, a unitary force[9] whose commander-in-chief bore the title stratêghós ton Karávon (of the ships) or ton Karavisianón (of the seamen). However, the first appearance of this officer and his fleet in our surviving records is on the occasion of his being ordered to sail from Ellás to Thessaloníkê[10] to make sure that Thessaloníkê should not be occupied by the repatriated descendants of the East Roman deportees whom the Avars had planted in Sirmia.[11] The repatriation is said to have taken place more than sixty years after the deportation,[12] and the deportation appears to have been carried out at some date between the

---

[1] This point is made by E. Eickhoff, *Seekrieg und Seepolitik zwischen Islam und Abendland: Das Mittelmeer unter byzantinischer und arabischer Hegemonie (650–1040)* (Berlin, 1966, de Gruyter), pp. 9 and 47–8.

[2] Stratós, op. cit., p. 104.   [3] Ibid., pp. 107–8.   [4] Ibid., pp. 113–14.
[5] Ibid., p. 246.   [6] Eickhoff, op. cit., p. 12.   [7] Eickhoff, op. cit., p. 11.
[8] J. B. Bury, 'The Naval Policy of the Roman Empire in Relation to the Western Provinces, from the seventh to the ninth century', in *Centenario della Nascita de Michele Amari* (Palermo, 1910, Virzi), pp. 21–34, on p. 24 (4); Antoniadis-Bibicou, *Études*, pp. 79–81.

[9] Antoniadis-Bibicou, op. cit., pp. 80 and 84.
[10] *S.D. Miracula*, Book II, chap. 5, col. 1369.
[11] Ibid., col. 1361.
[12] Ibid., col. 1364.

years 582/3 and 586/7.[1] If this dating is correct, Constans II's navy must have been already in being in the 640s.[2]

The administrative history of the Karavisianoí has been touched upon already in another context.[3] Like the original four army-corps of land-troops that were concentrated in Asia Minor in consequence of the Arabs' assault on the East Roman Empire in and after 633, Constans II's unitary navy was a large unit. Like these other large units, it was eventually split up; but, unlike these, the Karavisianoí never became a territory as well as an armed force.[4] Constantine Porphyrogenitus informs us[5] that, before the creation of théma Sámos, the headquarters (μητρόπολιν ... καὶ ἀρχήν) of the θέμα τῶν πλωϊζομένων had been on Sámos, but he does not say that the civil administration of the island had been in the hands of the naval commander-in-chief. The three thémata that were detached from the Karavisianoí (alias Ploïzómenoi)—Kivyrrhaiótai, Aiyaíon Pélaghos, and Sámos—did all become thémata in the eventual territorial meaning of the word.[6] Their stratêghoí, like those of the 'cavalry thémata', came to combine the governorship of a district with the command of an armed force. The peculiar feature of the history of the splitting-up of the Karavisianoí is that the mother-unit not only remained non-territorial but was also reduced to a lower rank when the units that were detached from it were raised to a higher one.

The stratêghoí of the three naval thémata had originally been only dhroungárioi[7]—i.e. vice-admirals of the commander-in-chief of the originally unitary Imperial Fleet. For instance, in 698 Apsímaros, who became the Emperor Tiberius III in that year, had been dhroungários of the Kivyrrhaiótai.[8] On the other hand, the commander of the curtailed Imperial Fleet, τὸ βασιλικὸν πλώϊμον, was reduced in rank from stratêghós to dhroungários. In Philótheos's list of the sixty officials who took their orders direct from the Emperor the δρουγγάριος τῶν πλοΐμων is the thirty-eighth in order of precedence, whereas the stratêghoí of the Kivyrraiótai, Sámos, and Aiyaíon Pélaghos rank respectively twenty-first, twenty-eighth, and twenty-ninth.[9]

Besides the three naval thémata, some of the other thémata had naval forces of their own, e.g. Ellás, Pelopónnêsos, Paphlaghonía, Sicily, and Kalavría;[10] and these squadrons, like the naval thémata, appear to have

[1] See the present work, II, 1 (iii) (a), p. 73, and Annex III, pp. 633–6.
[2] Antoniadis-Bibicou, op. cit., p. 78, dates its creation between 648 and 654.
[3] In II, 4, Appendix, on p. 260.
[4] Antoniadis-Bibicou, op. cit., p. 78; Ahrweiler, *Byzance et la mer*, p. 25.
[5] In *De Them.*, p. 41. [6] Antoniadis-Bibicou, op. cit., p. 86.
[7] See Leo VI, *Taktiká*, Dhiat. 19, § 24, col. 997.
[8] See II, 4, Appendix, pp. 259–60.
[9] Philótheos's klêtorolóyion, pp. 136–7 Bury, pp. 713–14 Bonn.
[10] Bury, *The Imperial Administrative System*, p. 109, n. 2; Ahrweiler, *Byzance et la mer*, pp. 32–3; Eickhoff, op. cit., pp. 84–5.

been independent of the dhroungários of the Imperial Fleet.[1] In the field-states of the expeditions sent against Crete in 911[2] and in 949,[3] the ships provided by théma Ellás on the first occasion and by théma Pelopónnêsos on the second occasion are listed separately from those of both the Imperial Fleet and the three naval thémata. In 827 the commander of the naval squadron of théma Sikelía, the tourmárkês Efthýmios, was able to desert, with his squadron, to the Aghlabid ruler of North-West Africa,[4] and thus to open the way for the North-West African Muslims' conquest of Sicily. In théma Kalavría *circa* 965[5] the local authorities' attempt to build a provincial squadron was sabotaged by the people of Rossano.[6]

There were also permanent coastguard-squadrons stationed at Ávydhos and in théma Dhalmatía.[7] The commander at Ávydhos was styled kómês Avydhikós, alias κόμης τῶν Στενῶν, and eventually officers styled 'Avydhikoí' were also posted at Attáleia, at Corinth, on the island of Évvoia, at Thessaloníkê, and at Amisós.[8] Their title indicates that they exercised, at their respective posts, the same functions as the kómês at Ávydhos (? protection against enemy attack by sea, and the levying of customs dues on merchant shipping). There was also a κόμης τῶν Στενῶν Ποντικῆς Θαλάσσης, who is mentioned, together with the κόμης Ἀβύδου, in an inscription of the Emperor Anastasius I dating from *circa* A.D. 492–4.[9] Eickhoff identifies him with the parathalassítês who is listed in Philótheos's klêtorolóyion as a member of the staff of the Éparkhos of Constantinople[10] and who has to produce 1,200 soldiers for Leo VI's naval expedition of 911 against Crete[11] and one mule for the Emperor's baggage-train when the Emperor goes on campaign.[12] According to Eickhoff,[13] the parathalassítês was posted at Iérion, on the Asiatic shore of the Bosphorus.

The title and the official standing of the dhroungários of the Imperial Fleet were not on a par with his actual importance. This is indicated more clearly in Philótheos's schedule of his staff.[14] The holder of this ostensibly inferior post had at least three advantages over the stratêghoí

---

[1] The Paphlagonía squadron may have been under his command (Ahrweiler, *Byzance et la Mer*, pp. 110–11).

[2] *De Caer.*, Book II, chap. 44, pp. 651–64.   [3] Ibid., chap. 45, pp. 664–78.

[4] *Theoph. Cont.*, pp. 81–3.   [5] For the date, see Eickhoff, op. cit., p. 358.

[6] *Life of St. Neilos* in Migne, *Patrologia Graeca*, vol. cxx, cols. 105–8. They not only refused to supply ships; they came down to the shore, burned the Government's ships that were beached there, and killed their captains (πρωτοκάραβοι). St. Neilos interceded for them with the Government's representative. See J. Gay, *L'Italie méridionale et l'Empire byzantin (861–1071)* (Paris, 1904, Fontemoing), pp. 280–1.

[7] Eickhoff, op. cit.. p. 85.   [8] Op. cit., loc. cit.

[9] Antoniadis-Bibicou, *Études*, pp. 159–60.

[10] p. 139 Bury, p. 717 Bonn. See also Bury, *The Imperial Administrative System*, p. 73.

[11] *De Caer.*, II, p. 660.   [12] *De Caer.*, I, Appendix, p. 461.

[13] Ibid.   [14] Klêtorolóyion, p. 140 Bury, p. 718 Bonn.

of the three naval thémata. In the first place, the sea-fronts of Constantinople were included in the area under his command. The capital looked mainly to him for its naval defence,[1] and it was therefore in no position to defend itself against him if he turned against the government of the day. The command of the Imperial Fleet was the stepping-stone from which Rhomanós Lekapênós mounted the Imperial throne by stages in 919–20. In the second place, the waters of the Black Sea and the Danube were the Imperial Fleet's preserve, and this fleet was therefore responsible for the naval operations, discussed below, that played an important part in any hostilities between the East Roman Empire and Bulgaria. In the third place, the Imperial Fleet seems to have retained, at least till 726,[2] a monopoly of the possession of napalm (τὸ σκευαστὸν καὶ κολλυτικὸν πῦρ, 'the artificial[3] adhesive fire' known as 'liquid fire' (ὑγρὸν πῦρ or 'sea fire' (θαλάσσιον πῦρ) or 'Greek fire' ('feu grégeois') in non-technical language). Moreover, in 822, the thematic fleets, which had sided with the rebel Thomas[4] and had sailed to Constantinople to participate in his attempt to take the City, were armed only with stone-slinging mangonels[5] and were eventually destroyed, like their predecessors in 726, by the Imperial Fleet armed with napalm.[6]

---

[1] Mainly, but not entirely. On the occasion of the expedition against Crete in 949, the naval force left behind to guard Constantinople consisted of one pámphylos and 24 ousíai from the Imperial Fleet, 6 pámphyloi and 4 ousiaká khelándia from théma Aiyaíon Pélaghos, and 6 khelándia pámphyla and 6 ousiaká khelándia from théma Sámos (see the analysis of Constantine Porphyrogenitus's figures in Antoniadis-Bibicou, op. cit., p. 94).

[2] In 726 the naval squadrons of Ellás and the Kykládhes attacked Constantinople and were destroyed by the Imperial Fleet with τῷ σκευαστῷ πυρί ('Greek fire') (Theophanes, p. 405). By 733, however, the fleet of théma Sikelía was armed with 'Greek fire' according to the Arabic authorities (Eickhoff, op. cit., p. 37, n. 11). 'Greek fire' ('le feu grégeois') was the Western crusaders' name for this stuff. This name was not used by the Greeks themselves (Partington, *A History of Greek Fire and Gunpowder*, p. 11).

[3] Or 'composite' (see p. 304, n. 4).

[4] *Theoph. Cont.*, p. 55; Genesius, p. 37.

[5] *Theoph. Cont.*, p. 62.

[6] Ὁ βασιλικὸς . . . πυρφόρος στόλος (*Theoph. Cont.*, p. 64). Cf. Genesius, Book II, p. 41; *Georg. Mon. Cont.*, p. 786; Leo Grammaticus, p. 212; pseudo-Symeon, p. 621. Apparently the Imperial Fleet, if it had once had a monopoly of 'Greek fire', no longer had this by 733 (see above, n. 2). Perhaps the regional fleets had been armed with 'Greek fire' after they had been made into independent commands. However, even when the Imperial Fleet had been deprived of the monopoly of 'Greek fire', and when this weapon had been acquired by the Muslims, the Imperial Fleet still had prior access to one of the constituents of the mixture, namely petrol, which the East Romans obtained from the hinterland of the north-east shore of the Black Sea (see p. 329). The Imperial Fleet must also have had prior access to the factory where the compound was made, for the manufacture of this secret weapon must have been carried on, under strict security conditions, at a single place only, and this place must have been within the walls of Constantinople. Rations of Greek fire may have been issued to all the East Roman fleets, but they may purposely have been kept on short rations, to make sure that they should have no reserve of 'Greek fire' if they revolted. This may explain the fact, which comes out clearly in the chroniclers' narratives, that the rebel thematic fleets were not armed with 'Greek fire' when they attacked Constantinople in 822, and that they were therefore afraid of engaging the loyal Imperial Fleet, which did have this annihilating weapon.

Navies cannot be built, equipped, and maintained without supplies of naval stores,[1] and, in the age of wooden warships, propelled by sails or by oars, the essential materials were timber, pitch, tar, and vegetable fibres for making sails and ropes. In this point the East Roman Navy had the advantage over the navies of the Arab Caliphate and its successor-states, though not over the navies of the Italian city-states, when, in the latter half of the eleventh century, these won the command of the Mediterranean. Dār-al-Islām produced cotton for sail-making and esparto grass for rope-making, but it was ill-supplied with timber. The forests on Mount Lebanon and on Mount Amanos had been drawn upon, since at least the third millennium B.C., to meet the respective demands of Egypt and 'Irāq; and in any case these forests were not at the disposal of the Arab conquerors of Syria until after the withdrawal of the Mardaïtes to the Roman side of the Romano-Arab frontier under the terms of the treaty of 688/9 or 689/90.[2] Egypt, whose Copt craftsmen and seamen were the mainstay of the Arab navy in the Umayyad Age, had always been destitute of good home-grown ship-building timber. Dār-al-Islām was ill provided with native timber as far westwards as Ifrīqīyah (Tunisia) inclusive.[3] In North-West Africa the most easterly forests that could at all compare with those of Asia Minor and Europe were in Kabylia. The Atlas Range, of course, could produce timber in greater quantities and varieties than Kabylia, and the Aghlabids did procure timber from both these sources.[4] But even Kabylia, and, *a fortiori*, the Atlas Range, was remote and was also beyond the limits of the Aghlabids' effective political control.[5] The East Roman fleets based on Asia Minor and the Muslim fleets based on Syria and Cilicia used mainly cypress-wood for their ships' timbers.[6] Dār-al-Islām as a whole had a smaller range of home-grown timber to draw upon than Christendom had,[7] and therefore the export trade in European timber was profitable for the Italian city-states that were under East Roman suzerainty.[8] In 971 the Emperor John Dzimiskēs put pressure on Venice to stop exporting timber to the Eastern Muslims.[9]

When, in 648/9, Mu'āwīyah launched his fleet, he made Cyprus his first objective. The forests on Mount Troodhos may have been the prize that he had in view, and, forty years later, the wish to have unimpeded

---

[1] See the illuminating map in Antoniadis-Bibicou, *Études*, p. 22.

[2] See II, 1 (iii) (a), p. 87.   [3] Eickhoff, op. cit., p. 133.

[4] Op. cit., pp. 119 and 124.

[5] The Spanish Umayyad Caliph 'Abdarrahmān III (912–61) was better off when, in the mid tenth century, he built a fleet to challenge the Aghlabids' Fatimid successors. There were then still forests in Spain, and the Atlas timber was nearer to Almeria than to Tunis (see Eickhoff, op. cit., pp. 293–4).

[6] Op. cit., p. 145.   [7] Op. cit., p. 156.   [8] See II, 5, p. 280.

[9] F. Dölger, *Regesten der Kaiserurkunden des Oströmischen Reiches von 565–1453*, I. Teil (Munich and Berlin, 1924, Oldenbourg), p. 94, No. 738.

access to this source of supply may have been one of the Caliph 'Abd-al-Malik's motives for agreeing to the neutralization of Cyprus in his treaty with the Emperor Justinian II. The East Roman Empire was far better provided with timber.[1]

The mountains overhanging both the north and the south coasts of Asia Minor are still well wooded today. But, for the East Roman Navy, the key material was petrol (áptha), which was the least easily procurable ingredient in East Roman napalm.[2] Till far into the nineteenth century, the best-known oil-wells in the world were those round Baku, in what is now Soviet Azerbaijan.[3] These lay within the frontiers of the Caliphate, but the use of petrol for manufacturing an atrocious weapon was the East Roman Government's jealously guarded secret; and, even when the North-West-African Muslims had discovered it, they would have found it difficult to import petrol from the west shore of the Caspian in any appreciable quantities.

In the closing chapter of his *De Administrando Imperio*,[4] Constantine gives a gazetteer of the oil-wells that were accessible for the East Roman Imperial Government. There were many of them outside the city of Tamátarkha, on the eastern shore of the Straits of Kerch, a region that was still in the Khazars' hands in Constantine's day. Constantine also notes eleven wells at the north-western end of the Caucasus Range in Zikhía and in its hinterland, nine of them near a place called Pághai (a word that means 'wells' in Doric Greek). Supplies from these sources would depend on the Khazars' and the Zikhians' good will, and the East Romans could usually count on having this. Finally, Constantine mentions two wells in districts that must have been under East Roman

---

[1] In 949, théma Aiyaíon Pélaghos kept at home one ship of the class called 'ousíai', and théma Kivyrrhaiótai two ships of the same class, for felling ship-building timber for use in the financial year (indiction) immediately following the financial year in which the expedition was being made (*De Caer.*, Book II, p. 665).

[2] See Partington, op. cit., pp. 28–32, 'What was Greek Fire?' 'It is very probable that the basis of the earliest Greek fire was liquid rectified petroleum or volatile petrol' (p. 31). 'The recipe from Anna Comnena [*Alexias*, Book XIII, chap. 3, on pp. 182–3 of vol. ii of Reifferscheid's edition] shows that the solids were pine resin and sulphur, but the essential ingredient, petrol, she deliberately omits' (pp. 29–30; cf. p. 32). Saltpetre was *not* one of the ingredients (pp. 14 and 32), *pace* Eickhoff, op. cit., pp. 143–4, and Haussig, *A History of Byzantine Civilization*, p. 208. Nor was quicklime (Partington, op. cit., p. 30). See also the bibliographical note in Moravcsik's and Jenkins's *Commentary on De Adm. Imp.*, p. 66.

The siphon through which the 'Greek fire' was discharged seems to have been a 'double action force pump' (Partington, op. cit., pp. 15–16). If the basic ingredient was petrol, this could not have been discharged effectively without being thickened. 'The particular mixture (or mixtures) used, and the mechanical means of projecting it, together constituted the invention of Greek fire' (Partington, p. 32).

[3] Perhaps this is why East Roman napalm is called 'Median fire' by Leo Diaconus, Book IX, chap. 10, p. 156, and by Cinnamus, Book VI, chap. 10, p. 165 Bonn. Codinus, p. 14 Bonn, mentions two baths, outside Constantinople, that were heated μετὰ τοῦ Μηδικοῦ πυρός (Partington, op. cit., p. 30).

[4] *De Adm. Imp.*, chap. 53, p. 269 Bonn.

rule at the time, since he calls them 'thémata'. One is Dherxênĕ, on the northern arm of the upper Euphrates, between Erzinjan and Erzerum ;[1] the other is Tziliápert (location unidentified).

'Greek fire' was invented by Kallínikos, a refugee Syrian engineer (ἀρχιτέκτων) from Heliópolis,[2] and was communicated by him to the East Roman Government just in time to enable the Emperor Constantine IV to build a fleet of ships, fitted with apparatus for discharging napalm,[3] in anticipation of the arrival of the Arab fleet in the Sea of Marmara for the first Arab siege of Constantinople (674–8). With this new and terrible weapon, Kallínikos 'burnt the Arab ships, crews and all'.[4] This was one of the causes of the Arab siege's failure.

Secret weapons cannot be kept secret for ever. Leo VI was bolting the stable door long after the steed had fled when, in his Novel No. 63,[5] he prescribed severe penalties for East Roman nationals who exported military equipment to an enemy country. Theophanes laments[6] that, when the Bulgars took Mesêmvría and Dheveltós in 812, they found there thirty-six bronze squirting-tubes (σίφωνας) and large stocks of the 'liquid fire' that was discharged from them. By the year 835, North-West-African Muslim warships, equipped for discharging napalm, were operating in the Tyrrhene Sea.[7] The Spanish Umayyads had 'Greek fire' by 844.[8] The secret may have been given away to the Aghlabid Government by Efthýmios, the turn-coat dhroungários of the local fleet of théma Sikelía. Unlike the ninth-century Bulgars, the ninth-century Muslims may have been capable of analysing East Roman 'composite' or 'liquid' fire and manufacturing it for themselves. The reason why the use of it was not perpetuated in the naval armaments of the North-West-African Muslims and in those of their Western Christian antagonists may have been their inability to obtain supplies of one of the ingredients, namely petrol. The Aghlabids and their successors the Fatimids were unaware of the vast subterranean reserves of mineral oil, lying waiting to be tapped, on the eastern fringe of their North-West-African dominions.

---

[1] The East Roman Empire re-annexed Erzerum in 949 (see Part III, chap. 4, pp. 408–9).

[2] Theophanes, p. 354, sub A.M. 6165; Constantine Porphyrogenitus, *De Adm. Imp.*, chap. 48, pp. 216–17. Theophanes calls the stuff πῦρ θαλάσσιον; Constantine calls it τὸ διὰ τῶν σιφώνων ἐκφερόμενον πῦρ ὑγρόν. Both writers use the word κατασκευάσαι to describe the preparation or manufacture of the mixture by Kallínikos.

[3] διήρεις εὐμεγέθεις κακκαβοπυρφόρους καὶ δρόμωνας σιφωνοφόρους (Theophanes, p. 353, sub A.M. 6164). Partington, pp. 12 and 14, points out that Theophanes records the building of the warships equipped with siphons in his entry for the year *preceding* the year in which he records Kallínikos's arrival and his manufacture of the stuff that was squirted from the siphons. It looks as if Theophanes has drawn on two different sources without having co-ordinated them.

[4] τὰ τῶν Ἀράβων σκάφη ἐνέπρησε καὶ σύμψυχα κατέκαυσεν (Theoph., p. 354, sub A.M. 6165).

[5] Noailles and Dain, pp. 230–3.   [6] Theophanes, p. 409, sub A.M. 6305.

[7] French translation of Dozy's text of Ibn-al-'Idārī, p. 98, in Vasiliev, *Byzance et les Arabes*, vol. i, p. 375. See also the same volume, p. 132, with n. 3, and Lewis, *Naval Power and Trade*, pp. 134 and 156; Eickhoff, op. cit., pp. 154 and 173.   [8] Eickhoff, op. cit., p. 197.

Leo VI, in his prescriptions for naval warfare,[1] seems to be uncertain whether his ships are to be used mainly for manœuvring or for shooting or for hand-to-hand fighting in the style of a battle on land. He expounds a manœuvre by which two dhrómones, working together, can capsize an enemy ship.[2] His standard warship is a dhrómon with two banks of oars (ἐλασίας) and with fifty benches, each seating two rowers.[3] There is to be a bronze-sheathed siphon (for discharging napalm) in the prow,[4] and one of the two bow rowers is to serve as siphonátor, while the other is to be in charge of the anchors.[5] The enemy ships are to be set on fire by the napalm squirted from the siphons.[6] They are to shoot 'mini-arrows',[7] containers (χύτρας) filled with reptiles,[8] containers filled with asbestos,[9] caltrops,[10] and containers filled with 'composite fire' (πυρὸς ἐσκευασμένου),[11] and they are to use hand-guns (χειροσίφωνα), 'which have been invented recently by Our Majesty'.[12] The ships are also to be provided with larger caltrops made of iron and with wooden balls studded with nails concealed under a wrapping of tow. The tow is to be set alight and the burning ball is then to be tossed on board an enemy vessel. The enemy crew will try to tread out the fire and will get foot-wounds from the hidden nails.[13]

However, the hundred rowers on a standard dhrómon are also to be soldiers.[14] The look-out at the prow (πρωρεύς) is to sit there clad in armour,[15] and the crew manning the fore part of the ship are to wear armour likewise.[16] Moreover, there are to be some dhrómones with crews 200 men strong, 150 marines on the upper deck and 50 rowers on the lower deck.[17] The least good combatants are to be stationed on the lower deck.[18] The men on the upper deck are to have the same armour as the most heavily armoured land-troops (i.e. they are to be cataphracts).[19]

The term 'dhrómon' is used occasionally in fifth-century Byzantine records and frequently in those dating from the sixth century.[20] The term

---

[1] Leo, Dhiat. 19, Περὶ Ναυμαχίας, cols. 989–1013. See also Eickhoff, op. cit., pp. 135–51, with the bibliography on p. 145, n. 40.

[2] Leo, Dhiat. 19, § 61, col. 1009.   [3] Leo, Dhiat. 19, § 8, cols. 992–3.

[4] By 949, an East Roman dhrómon carried three siphons (De Caer., Book II, p. 672). The siphons carried by the East Roman warships in the Romano-Pisan naval battle between Patára and Rhodes in 1103 could swivel (Anna Comnena, Alexias, Book XI, chap. 10, lines 19–21 on p. 134 of vol. ii of Reifferscheid's edition).

[5] § 8, col. 993.   [6] § 45, col. 1005.

[7] 'Flies' (μυιάς), § 52, col. 1008.   [8] § 53, col. 1008.   [9] § 54, col. 1008.

[10] § 55, col. 1008.   [11] § 56, col. 1008.

[12] § 57, col. 1008. Hand-guns, with a supply of napalm for squirting from them, were also to be carried in waggons by the land-army (see II, 6, p. 304). In 927/8 the East Roman Army was using, for besieging Dvin, siphons of a calibre that could plaster twelve men with napalm at one discharge (Ibn al-Athîr, VIII, 129–30, translated in Vasiliev, Byzance et les Arabes, ii, II, p. 350).

[13] § 59, cols. 108–9.

[14] § 8, col. 993.   [15] Ibid.   [16] § 13, cols. 993–6.

[17] § 9, col. 893.   [18] § 18, cols. 996–7.   [19] § 65, col. 1012.

[20] Ahrweiler, Byzance et la mer, pp. 411–12.

'khelándion' does not appear in Byzantine records before the ninth century, and it is not used by Leo VI in his *Taktiká*, but it is the only term used in Arabic records for describing East Roman warships.[1] Besides the two kinds of dhrómones, Leo VI mentions two other types of warship: the ghalaía ('cat-fish'), i.e. galley, which was small and swift,[2] and the pámphylon or pámphylos, which, according to Leo, was used as the admiral's flagship.[3]

Leo's specifications can be, and should be, checked by the actual facts and figures given in the field-states of two of the East Roman expeditions against the Cretan Muslims—the first in 911, in Leo's own reign, and the second in 949, in Constantine Porphyrogenitus's reign—that have been preserved by Constantine.[4]

In the field-state for 911 the ship's complement for a dhrómon in both the Imperial Fleet and the three thematic fleets is given as 200 rowers and 70 combatants ($\pi o \lambda \epsilon \mu \iota \sigma \tau \hat{\omega} \nu$). Moreover, the pámphylon is not just the admiral's ship. There are as many as 75 pámphyla in the armada, as compared with 102 dhrómones; each of the fleets except théma Kivyrrhaiótai has a contingent of pámphyla; and in each fleet there are pámphyla of two classes, with ships' complements of 160 and 130 men respectively. In the whole armada there are 33 first-rate pámphyla and 42 second-raters.

In the field-state for 949, three new terms appear: ousíai ('entities'), khelándia ousiaká, and khelándia pámphyla. Here the pámphyla are classified as khelándia, for the 7 pámphyla and 33 khelándia ousiaká which the Imperial Fleet is contributing to the expedition against Crete are reckoned as being 'forty khelándia in all'. The strengths of the ships' complements of both the khelándia pámphyla and the khelándia ousiaká differ for each of the three naval thémata (the strengths for the ships of the Imperial Fleet are not given). For khelándia pámphyla the strengths are 120 men in théma Aiyaíon Pélaghos and 150 in thémata Sámos and Kivyrrhaiótai. The strengths for khelándia ousiaká are 108 men in thémata Aiyaíon Pélaghos and Sámos and 110 in théma Kivyrrhaiótai.[5] The strengths for the dhrómones of thémata Sámos and Kivyrrhaiótai (théma Aiyaíon Pélaghos has no dhrómones) are 220. Only théma Kivyrrhaiótai has galleys.

The term ousíai (meaning literally 'entities'), which makes its first appearance in the field-state for 949, is used in this document in both

---

[1] Ahrweiler, op. cit., p. 412, n. 3.

[2] § 10, col. 993; § 68, col. 1012; §74, col. 1013.   [3] § 39, col. 1004.

[4] In *De Caer.*, Book II, chaps. 44 and 45 respectively. The contents of these two field-states are presented in a convenient tabular form by Antoniadis-Bibicou, op. cit., on pp. 92–3 and 94, but it should be noted that Constantine's figures for the number of ships in 949 have gone awry. The totals that he gives do not tally with his items.

[5] Constantine does not specify the class of the three Samian khelándia that were sent to Africa and the four Peloponnesian khelándia that were sent to Crete in 949.

a generic and a specific sense. In the statement that the Imperial Fleet consisted of 150 ousíai,[1] of which eight were pámphyloi and 100 were khelándia ousiaká,[2] the word is evidently being used generically to mean vessels of all kinds. On the other hand, in the statements that one pámphylos and 24 ousíai were left to guard Constantinople, and that the 20 dhrómones that took part in the expedition to Crete each had two ousíai attached to it, making 40 ousíai in all, the same word is no less evidently being used to denote a particular kind of ship.[3] The kind denoted is not revealed in the name; but the duties on which ships of this kind were employed suggest that they were not primarily designed for combat. In 949, three ousíai (in the specific sense) were sent to fell timber, 34 were kept as coastguard vessels for Constantinople, Kalavría, Dhyrrhákhion, and Dhalmatía; three were sent to do observation work off the coast of Spain; 40 were assigned as tenders to the 20 dhrómones of the Imperial Fleet that went to Crete. Probably the ousíai were smaller vessels than either the dhrómones or the khelándia pámphyla; for the khelándia ousiaká had complements of 108 men each in thémata Aiyaíon Pélaghos and Sámos, and 110 in théma Kivyrrhaiótai, whereas the complements of the pámphyla (alias khelándia pámphyla) varied from 120 (théma Aiyaíon Pélaghos) to 150 (thémata Sámos and Kivyrrhaiótai), and the complement of a dhrómon was 220 (thémata Sámos and Kivyrrhaiótai). The khelándia ousiaká seem, to judge by their name, to have been khelándia of the ousíai size, as constrasted with khelándia of the pámphyloi size.

The field-state for 949 also makes it clear that dhrómones were bigger ships than khelándia of either the pámphylon or the ousiakón class. However, Constantine Porphyrogenitus mentions three cases of transfers of personnel between the Imperial Fleet and the Emperor's private flotilla of yachts,[4] and, in the case that he records first, the crews of the Emperor's two private dhromónia, together with the two protokáravoi

---

[1] But the items for the Imperial Fleet add up to only 138 ships.

[2] But only 33 ousiaká khelándia are mentioned among the items. The other items, besides the eight pámphyloi, are 20 dhrómones and 77 ousíai.

[3] R. H. Dolley, in 'The Warships of the Later Roman Empire' (*J.R.S.*, vol. xxxviii (1948), pp. 46–53, on p. 48), interprets the word ousía as meaning, not a ship, but a ship's complement of the minimum size, i.e. 108 men. He then construes Constantine's "δρόμονες κ′ ἀνὰ οὐσιῶν β′ „ as meaning 'twenty dhrómones of two ships' complements each', i.e. with complements of 216 men each (see the ticket on Dolley's model, shown in Plate V). The context shows, however, that this cannot be Constantine's meaning, for he goes on to give the sum of these twenty pairs of ousíai as being forty ousíai, and these ousíai must be, not 'ships' complements', but ships, which is the meaning of ousíai in the rest of the document, whether the word is used for ships in general or for ships of one particular kind. Moreover, if these forty of the ousíai in the Imperial Fleet are not to be reckoned as being separate ships, the items add up, not to 138 ships, but to 98, which is not 12 short, but as much as 52 short, of Constantine's total for the Imperial Fleet in 949.

[4] *De Adm. Imp.*, chap. 51, pp. 237–8 Bonn.

of the first of them, were seconded to vessels of the Imperial Fleet that were khelándia (εἰς χελάνδια πλώϊμα).[1] Anyway, an East Roman dhrómon, which was a bireme, cannot have been bigger or heavier than a Greek trireme of the fifth and fourth centuries B.C., for, in A.D. 868, Admiral Ooryphas repeated the classical Greek practice of hauling his fleet from sea to sea over the Isthmus of Corinth.[2]

East Roman tactics at sea were as cautious as they were on land. At sea, too, do not risk engaging in a pitched battle (δημόσιον πόλεμον) with the whole of your fleet, or even with part of it if you can avoid this;[3] and, when you do give battle, engage off the enemy coast, not off our own. If the crews know that the coast that is within their reach is friendly, they will be tempted to seek shelter ashore.[4] 'Do not behave atrociously or disgracefully or inhumanly to your prisoners.'[5] This instruction does credit to Leo VI, but the atrocity would have been committed already if the prisoner had been sprayed with East Roman napalm before being captured.

The Arabs' challenge to the East Roman Navy was audacious, and the achievements of Arab fleets in Mediterranean waters were remarkable, considering the superiority of East Roman warships in build and armament[6] and the superiority of East Roman mariners in seamanship.[7] Of course, the Arabs were not without previous experience in navigation. For centuries, and indeed for millennia, before the seventh century of the Christian Era, when, for the first time, the Arabs acquired possession of sea-fronts on the Mediterranean, their ancestors along the Arabian shore of the Persian Gulf and along the coasts of the Yaman had navigated the Indian Ocean, and in the 'Abbasid Age the Arabs extended the range of their voyages in the South Seas far down the east coast of Africa as well as eastwards, into the Pacific, as far as the south-east coast of China.[8] But, when the Arabs eventually launched out on to the Mediterranean as well, they did not employ here the naval architecture that they had developed in Arabian waters. They adopted the naval architecture of their East Roman opponents.

The Arab koumbária in the Mediterranean were inferior copies of the East Roman biremes, and they could not compete with these in speed.[9] The crews of the Umayyads' Egyptian fleet were recruited mainly from Copt converts to Islam, though Arabs (including representatives of the

[1] The word πλώϊμα here must mean, not 'seaworthy', but 'belonging to the πλώϊμον βασιλικόν'.
[2] *Theoph. Cont.*, pp. 300–1.　　　　[3] Leo, Dhiat. 19, §§ 32 and 33, col. 1001.
[4] § 35, col. 1001.　　　　　　　　　　　　　　　[5] § 34, col. 1001.
[6] Eickhoff, op. cit., pp. 58–9. Until at least as late as the turn of the tenth and eleventh centuries, the superiority of East Roman warships was recognized and admired in Western Christendom (op. cit., pp. 59 and 150).
[7] Op. cit., pp. 337 and 394.　　　　　　　　　[8] See II, 1 (ii), p. 56.
[9] Eickhoff, op. cit., pp. 4, 15, 151–3.

Medinese Ansar and the Meccan Quraysh) also served.[1] All the ship-wrights and all the manufacturers of ship's tackle must have been Copts, and, after the definitive Arab conquest of East Roman North-West-Africa (Ifriqīyah) in 698, the Umayyad Caliph 'Abd-al-Malik instructed his brother the governor of Egypt to send to Tunis 1,000 Copt shipwrights to construct there a local fleet, arsenal, and naval bases.[2] The fate of Ifriqīyah had just been decided by sea-power, not by land-power; 'Abd-al-Malik recognized that a province that had been won by sea-power would have to be held by it; and, to make sure of this, he mobilized Egyptian subjects of his who had inherited the East Roman naval tradition.

As late as the turn of the ninth and tenth centuries, some of the most brilliant of the Muslim naval officers of that time were ex-East Roman renegades. For instance, Leo of (the Syrian) Tripoli, who took Thes-saloníkê in 904, was a native of Attáleia.[3] Dhamianós of Tarsós, the henchman and successor of the Tarsan sea-dog Yazaman,[4] was also of East Roman origin to judge by his name, but this did not deter him in 911/12 from taking savage reprisals on the Greek-speaking Christian population of Cyprus for the East Roman admiral Imérios's breach of Cyprus's neutrality in 910.[5]

The East Roman Navy experienced many changes of fortune between the mid point of the seventh century, when its command of the Mediter-ranean was challenged by Mu'āwiyah, and the last decade of the tenth century, when the Emperor Basil II found himself constrained to pur-chase, at a high price, the services of the Venetian merchant marine for transporting East Roman troops, and of the Venetian Navy for playing, in the Adriatic, the role that, by then, the East Roman Navy was no longer capable of playing there for itself. Through all the vicissitudes of these three and a half centuries, the East Roman Navy was continuously successful in achieving at least two of its objectives. It saved Constan-tinople from falling, and it prevented the East Roman Empire's enemies on opposite fronts from joining hands to take concerted action.

It has been noted already[6] that Constantinople can be defended only so long as the power that possesses it holds the naval command over the waters embracing the peninsula on which the city stands. The indis-pensability of naval defence for Constantinople was demonstrated by the City's fall in 1204. The efficacy of the East Roman Empire's naval defence of its capital was revealed on seven earlier occasions. The East Roman Navy saved Constantinople from the Persians and Avars in 626, from

---

[1] Op. cit., p. 15.
[2] Op. cit., p. 120. These Copts' families were sent with them, so they were intended to be permanent settlers.
[3] Op. cit., p. 83.
[4] Op. cit., p. 257.
[5] Op. cit., p. 263.
[6] In II, 3, *passim.*

the Arabs in 674–8 and 717–18, from the insurgent anti-iconoclasts in 726, from the insurgent Thomas in 821–2, and from the Russians in 860 and probably in 907 as well.

In 626 the Navy saved Constantinople by preventing the Persians and the Avars from joining forces across the Bosphorus, and it intervened effectively on similar critical occasions at later dates. In the siege of Pátras in or about the year 807, North-West-African Muslims did give aid to the insurgent Peloponnesian Slavs.[1] We may guess that the East Roman Navy's intervention was more efficacious than St. Andrew's in the parrying of this formidable joint attack; for the African Muslims could reach the Pelopónnêsos by sea only. The rescue of Ragusa by Ooryphas's naval expedition in 868 prevented the North-West-African Muslims from joining hands, across Sicily and Apulia, with the still pagan and piratical Arentanoí,[2] and the subsequent East Roman naval counter-offensive, supported by the Ragusans and by some of the peoples in the hinterland of Dalmatia, enabled the East Roman Empire eventually to debar the North-West-African Muslims from gaining their coveted foothold on the eastern shore of the Adriatic. The East Roman Navy's power in the Adriatic made it possible for the East Roman Empire to create the new théma Laghouvardhía and to retrieve Kalavría; and this greatly enlarged and strengthened East Roman dominion in south-eastern Italy proved to be an effective barrier to any further north-eastward advance of the African Muslims, in spite of the East Roman Navy's failure to prevent them from capturing the last East Roman footholds in Sicily.[3] The Navy did enable the East Roman Empire to hold Kalavría, the Vasilikáta, and Apulia; and the mountains of northern Kalavría and western Lucania proved to be insurmountable barriers to a further northward advance of the Western Muslims.[4]

The East Roman Empire's success in replacing its lost dominion in Sicily by a new dominion in south-eastern Italy saved the Empire from the most dangerous threat of a concerted converging assault to which it had been exposed since the East Roman Navy had prevented the Persians and Avars from joining hands in 626.

In or shortly before 924, at the climax of the Romano-Bulgarian war of 913–27, Khan Symeon of Bulgaria sent an embassy to the Fatimid Government in North-West Africa, proposing that they and he should join forces against the East Roman Empire and should partition it. The Fatimid Government took up Symeon's suggestion, and dispatched a ship, with envoys of their own, as well as the Bulgar envoys, on board, to ratify the agreement with Symeon in Bulgaria. The East Roman Navy

---

[1] *De Adm. Imp.*, chap. 49, p. 217. See II, 1 (iii) (a), p. 99.
[2] See II, Appendix, p. 267.
[3] See Eickhoff, op. cit., pp. 251–2.   [4] Op. cit., pp. 396–7.

intercepted and captured this ship off Kalavría, and this gave the Emperor Rhomanós Lekapênós an opening which he exploited skilfully. He imprisoned the Bulgar envoys, but sent the Fatimid envoys home with presents. This nicely calculated magnanimity moved the Fatimid Caliph Al-Mahdi not only to drop the project of a Fatimid–Bulgar joint offensive, but to halve the East Roman Empire's annual tribute to him of 22,000 nomísmata, which had fallen into arrears owing to the strain of the war with Bulgaria on the Empire's finances.[1] Al-Mahdi's favourable response to Rhomanós I's gesture can be explained partly in the light of the Fatimid dynasty's general policy. Its main objective was neither Italy nor the Balkan Peninsula but Egypt,[2] with the ultimate ambition of overthrowing the 'Abbasid Caliphate, and, against the 'Abbasids, the East Roman Empire, not Bulgaria, was the Fatimids' natural ally.[3]

Symeon also made contact with the Eastern Muslims.[4] The date is uncertain, but we may guess that this was in 924, after his negotiations with the Fatimids had fallen through. A combined squadron of Cilician, Syrian, and Egyptian ships, under Tarsan command, first made an unsuccessful attempt to get in touch with Symeon on the Thracian coast on the Marmara side of the Dardanelles, and then did succeed in meeting some Bulgar troops at the head of one of the gulfs between the prongs of the Khalkidhikḗ peninsula. The Muslim squadron took a party of Bulgars on board and conveyed them to Tarsós, but there is no evidence that this rencontre, either, achieved any practical results.

Manifestly Symeon had realized, from his experience in the two Romano-Bulgarian wars of 894–6 and 913–27, that victories on land in Europe would not enable him to take Constantinople or, short of that, to defeat the East Roman Empire decisively, unless he could obtain from an ally the naval force that he himself lacked, and the only possible effective naval allies for Bulgaria were the Muslims, either Western or Eastern.

In seeking to encircle the East Roman Empire by combining Bulgar operations on land and Muslim operations at sea, Symeon was attempting to turn the tables on the Empire; for Bulgaria had been contained and enveloped by the East Roman Navy in every Romano-Bulgarian war since the Bulgars' lodgement in 680 on the south bank of the lower Danube. So long as the East Roman Navy commanded the Straits, Constantinople remained impregnable to Bulgar assaults; for the Bulgars did not possess the siege-apparatus for breaching the city's triple land-wall, and the population could be supplied from the Empire's dominions in Asia Minor, which were out of the Bulgarian land-army's reach. The

---

[1] For this episode see Kedhrênós, vol. ii, pp. 356–7.
[2] Eickhoff, op. cit., p. 397.　　　　　　　　　　[3] Op. cit., pp. 302 and 304.
[4] See Mas'ūdī, *Murūj-adh-Dhahāb*, II, pp. 16–18, French translation in Vasiliev, *Byzance et les Arabes*, ii, II, p. 32, and Canard in op. cit., ii, I, pp. 253–4.

East Roman coastal fortresses Ankhíalos and Mesêmvría, which had been on the frontier since Justinian II's cession of the Zagora (Zagorje) to Khan Tervel in 705,[1] could also be supplied by sea so long as they remained under East Roman rule.[2] On the other hand, in a Romano-Bulgarian war, the East Roman Navy was able to compensate for the weakness of the East Roman Army in this theatre.

Invaders of Bulgaria could not live off what was then an unproductive country,[3] and the passes through the Balkan (Aímos) Range were dangerous[4] for the transit of troops, and still more so for the forwarding of supplies; but an invading East Roman Army could be kept supplied by the Navy from the sea, if the army hugged Bulgaria's Black Sea coast. Better still, the Navy could convey an invading East Roman force up the Danube and could land it on the river's south bank to take Bulgaria in the rear. Alternatively, the Navy could ferry across the Danube a nomad horde from the western bay of the Eurasian Steppe if the Imperial Government had succeeded in hiring the nomads to do the East Roman Army's work for it in Bulgaria.

The Roman Empire had maintained naval flotillas on the Rhine and the Danube ever since the Empire's frontiers had been advanced to these two river lines. The Roman Rhine flotilla must have been put out of action abruptly and once for all when the Germans crossed the Rhine—this time, never to withdraw—in the winter of 406/7. The Danube flotilla may have had a longer life, and in any case the lower Danube was navigable for sea-going warships. 'Mavríkios', writing *circa* 600, gives directions for crossing rivers[5] and for constructing floating bridges,[6] and he devotes a whole chapter[7] to instructions for carrying out naval operations in rivers and for crossing rivers in the face of enemy opposition. In a river campaign, marshal your ships on as broad a front as the river can hold.[8] If you want to occupy the opposite bank of a river when the enemy is holding it, start building a bridge of boats from your own bank, and, when your bridgehead has come within a bowshot of the enemy's bank, post your mangonel-carrying dhrómones in front of your bridgehead and drive the enemy off by laying down a barrage. Then carry your bridge

---

[1] The authenticity of this cession of the Zagorje at this date is doubted by V. Beševliev: *Die Protobulgarischen Inschriften*, pp. 59–60. It is mentioned by Georgius Monachus only in a passage that may be an interpolation. There is no mention of it in Theophanes, Nicephorus Patriarcha, or the *Suda*.

[2] For the date of the abandonment of these fortresses, see III, 2, p. 418, n. 3.

[3] 'Anonymus Vári', p. 37.

[4] Op. cit., p. 26.

[5] M., Part 8, chap. 1, p. 177 Scheffer, p. 200 Mihăescu.

[6] M., Part 11, chap. 5, p. 277 Scheffer, pp. 280–2 Mihăescu (apropos of campaigns against the Slavs and Àntai in what is now Wallachia).

[7] M., Part 12, chap. 21, pp. 345–9 Scheffer, pp. 352–4 Mihăescu.

[8] M., loc. cit., p. 348 Scheffer, p. 354 Mihăescu.

forward to the shore, fortify and garrison a camp on the enemy side, and, after that, build towers to cover your bridge.[1]

Of course the enemy who was being threatened with invasion would take defensive counter-measures. In 895, when the East Roman Navy was preparing to ferry the Magyars from the north to the south bank of the lower Danube for them to take the Bulgars in the rear, Khan Symeon fortified the south bank with a strong cordon of ropes and chains. An East Roman petty officer won the Magyars' admiration by leaping on shore from his khelándion and cutting a passage through the obstructions with his sword.[2]

In the Romano-Bulgarian war of 755–75, the Emperor Constantine V invaded Bulgaria from the lower Danube at least three times: with 500 ships in his first offensive;[3] with 800 khelándia, each carrying twelve horses, in the campaign following the accession of Khan Teletz;[4] and with a fleet of 2,000 khelándia in 773. This time, again, Constantine V sailed with the fleet to the Danube, but he sent the cavalry thémata overland to the passes through the Balkan Range to catch the Bulgars in a vice.[5] In the campaign of 766, an East Roman army advancing overland made a junction with a fleet of 2,600 ships which put in at Mesêmvría and Ankhíalos, but this fleet was wrecked by a storm.[6] According to Theophanes, the same thing happened again nine years later.[7]

In the reign of Theóphilos (829–42), perhaps *circa* 836–8,[8] an East Roman fleet sailed to the Danube and succeeded in rescuing the descendants of the Adrianopolitan deportees who had been marooned in Bulgarian territory somewhere to the north of the Danube. This operation had been preconcerted, by emissaries from the deportees, with the Imperial Government.[9]

In 895 the East Roman Navy retorted to Khan Symeon's assault overland by ferrying the Magyars across the lower Danube;[10] and the East Roman Government tried to repeat this well-tried manœuvre in 917 in its second war with Symeon (913–27). Since 896 the Pechenegs had replaced the Magyars at the western end of the Eurasian Steppe. In 917 an East Roman official, John Voghás, undertook to hire this horde, in

[1] M., loc. cit., pp. 348–9 Scheffer, p. 354 Mihăescu.
[2] *De Adm. Imp.*, chap. 51, pp. 238–9.　　　　　　　　　[3] Nic. Patr., p. 66.
[4] Nic. Patr., p. 69; Theophanes, pp. 432–3, sub A.M. 6254.
[5] Theophanes pp. 446–7, sub A.M. 6265.
[6] Nic. Patr., p. 73; Theophanes, p. 437, sub A.M. 6257.
[7] Theophanes, pp. 447–8, sub A.M. 6266.
[8] This is Bury's date. See *A History of the Eastern Roman Empire, 802–867*, p. 371, with n. 3. But Bury's dating rests on the assumption, challenged since then by Adontz, that Basil I was one of the deportees. See N. Adontz, 'L'Âge et l'origine de l'empereur Basile I', in *Byzantion*, vol. viii (1933), pp. 475–500.
[9] *Georg. Mon. Interpolatus*, pp. 817–19; Leo Grammaticus, pp. 231–3.
[10] Symeon in *Georg. Mon. Cont.*, pp. 853–4, and in Leo Grammaticus, pp. 267–8; *Theoph. Cont.*, pp. 358–9; Kedhrênós, vol. ii, p. 255.

turn, to play the same role; his mission was successful;[1] the Pechenegs arrived at the north bank of the Danube; and the Imperial Fleet, commanded by its dhroungários Rhomanós Lekapênós, also duly arrived there with orders to ferry the Pechenegs across. The East Romans were now in dire need of the Pechenegs' intervention; for the dhoméstikos ton Skholón, Leo Phokás, who had marched north with a large army in the expectation that the Pechenegs would be assaulting the Bulgars from the opposite quarter, had just suffered a crushing defeat at the Bulgars' hands on the River Akhéloos, near Ankhíalos. At this critical moment, however, Rhomanós Lekapênós failed to carry out his orders, and he sailed back to Constantinople without even attending to the second part of his instructions, which had been to rescue Leo Phokás, who, after his defeat, had taken refuge in Ankhíalos.

John Voghás accused Rhomanós Lekapênós of having deliberately sabotaged the Government's strategic plan. Lekapênós was sentenced to have his eyes put out, and he only just succeeded in getting the sentence rescinded.[2] We may guess that John Voghás's indictment was justified. Though the Pechenegs had arrived too late to forestall Leo Phokás's defeat at the Akhéloos, they could still have averted his second defeat at Katasýrtai. It looks as if Rhomanós had deliberately delayed the ferrying of the Pechenegs till he had provoked them into returning home in disgust, and as if his objective had been to leave Leo Phokás in the lurch. If the dhoméstikos ton Skholón were discredited, the way would be open for the dhrounghários ton ploïmon to exploit the political opportunity presented by a crisis in the Empire's fortunes at a time when the throne was occupied by a child. In fact, we may guess that, in behaving as he did in 917, Rhomanós already had his eye on the goal that he was to attain in 920.[3] We may also guess that, if Rhomanós had done his duty in 917, the manœuvre would have been as effective as it had proved to be on at least four earlier occasions.

The East Roman Navy did play a decisive role in the Danube, once again, in the Emperor John Dzimiskês's campaign in 971 against the Rhos conqueror of Bulgaria, Svyátoslav. In 967[4] the Rhos had forced their way across the Danube in spite of the Bulgars' attempt to bar their passage,[5] but in 971 the Rhos were prevented from withdrawing across

---

[1] *Georg. Mon. Cont.*, p. 879; Leo Grammaticus, p. 293; *Theoph. Cont.*, Book VI, p. 387; pseudo-Symeon, p. 722.

[2] *Georg. Mon. Cont.*, p. 882; Leo Grammaticus, pp. 295–6; *Theoph. Cont.*, p. 390; pseudo-Symeon, p. 724.

[3] Of course there is an alternative possible explanation of Lekapênós's misconduct on this occasion which does not require us to credit him with looking and planning so far ahead. He may simply have been bribed by Khan Symeon to disobey the instructions that he had received from his own Government.

[4] For the date, see Obolensky in *C. Med. H.*, vol. iv, 2nd ed., Part I, p. 513, n. 3.

[5] Leo Diaconus, Book V, chap. 2, pp. 77–8.

the river by the presence of the East Roman fleet. John Dzimiskês had dispatched the fleet, armed with napalm, from Constantinople to the Danube before he himself had started on his march northward overland.[1] He cornered Svyátoslav in Dhorýstolon (Dhrístra) between his own army and the fleet,[2] and forced him to capitulate. Svyátoslav had to pay this humiliating price for a guarantee that the East Roman fleet would not attack him with napalm on his way out.[3]

The medieval East Roman Navy's operations in the Danube were its most signal successes. Its failures to save first North-West Africa and then Sicily and Crete from being conquered by the Muslims were its most conspicuous reverses.

North-West Africa is virtually an island; for, on the landward side, it is insulated by deserts almost as effectively as it is, along its coastline, by the sea; and, though the Arabs—inured, as they were, to operating in steppes and deserts—succeeded in invading North-West Africa overland, their definitive conquest of this virtual island in 698 was achieved by a fleet which the East Roman fleet dared not face.[4] This poor performance of the East Roman Navy is not surprising, considering that in 698 the Umayyad Caliphate was still at the height of its strength at sea as well as on land. But in 747 Constantine V gave a parting kick to the then tottering Umayyad power by winning an annihilating naval victory off Cyprus. The Umayyads were supplanted by the 'Abbasids in 750, and neither the 'Abbasids nor their Western Christian contemporaries the Carolingians attempted to enter into the Umayyads' naval heritage. Both powers backed away from the shores of the Mediterranean. Their interests and ambitions were not maritime; they were continental.[5] Sicily and Crete were conquered from the East Romans, not by either of these two great powers, but by Muslims from North-West Africa and from Spain. The cause of the abrupt reversal of naval fortunes in the Mediterranean in and after 827 was not the Western Muslims' naval strength; it was the self-destruction of the East Roman Navy in a fratricidal conflict between opposing components of it in the East Roman civil war of 821–3.

The naval thémata had taken the insurgent Thomas's side,[6] and, at the turn of the years 821 and 822, Thomas brought their fleets into the Sea of Marmara to play their part in his siege of Constantinople. Thomas rightly judged that Constantinople could be taken only by combined operations on sea and land, but he seems to have failed to reckon with the overwhelming superiority that the Imperial Fleet, which had remained loyal to the Emperor Michael II, enjoyed over all the other East

[1] Op. cit., VIII, 1, p. 129.
[2] Op. cit., VIII, 10, p. 140, and IX, 2, p. 144, and 7, p. 151.
[3] Op. cit., IX, 10, pp. 156–7.
[4] Theophanes, p. 370, sub A.M. 6190; Nic. Patr., p. 39.
[5] See Lewis, op. cit., pp. 98 and 103.   [6] *Theoph. Cont.*, p. 55.

Roman fleets thanks to its command of a supply of napalm, to which the rebel fleets no longer had access. Evidently this disparity was manifest to the seamen themselves on both sides. The record indicates that the thematic fleets shrank from drawing the Imperial Fleet's fire, and that the Imperial Fleet, on its side, was reluctant to use this annihilating weapon against its sister fleets, even though these were temporarily in revolt.

In the course of the siege there seem to have been three confrontations between the opposing naval forces, and on the first two occasions the insurgents refused battle.[1] Indeed, on the second occasion, some of the insurgent seamen deserted, while others took refuge on shore in the camp of Thomas's land-forces. Each time, the Imperial Fleet appears to have held its fire. When, however, the fleet of théma Ellás arrived in the Marmara to replenish Thomas's naval forces, the Imperial Fleet intercepted it and destroyed it by using napalm this time.[2] Since the Asiatic thematic fleets had gone to pieces already, without going into action, at their second confrontation with the Imperial Fleet, the destruction of the fleet of théma Ellás sealed Thomas's fate; but this decision of the civil war was reached at the cost of crippling the East Roman Navy. The undisputed command of the Mediterranean, which the East Roman Navy had regained in 747, was thrown away by it in 822. The nemesis of this suicidal act was the beginning of the gradual Muslim conquest of Sicily in 827 and the facile Muslim conquest of Crete in 827 or 828.[3]

The Muslim conquest of Sicily was stubbornly contested. It took three-quarters of a century (827–902), during which there were many East Roman counter-attacks and Muslim setbacks, and the East Romans were not evicted from Rametta, their last foothold on this island, till 964.[4] On the other hand, Crete was conquered with astonishing speed and ease, and it was held by its Spanish Muslim conquerors with equally remarkable tenacity, though it lay so much nearer than Sicily to the East Roman Navy's bases and was so much sharper a thorn in the Empire's flesh throughout the 134 years (827–961) during which Crete remained in Spanish Muslim hands.

In 814/15 a band of 15,000 unsuccessful insurgents against the Umayyad Amīr of Spain established itself, with its women and children, in Egypt, near Alexandria, and in 816 these refugees seized Alexandria itself. In 825 an 'Abbasid expeditionary force reconquered Egypt from a pretender and brought the intruding Spaniards to terms. It was agreed that they should evacuate Alexandria and should make a new home for

---

[1] See *Theoph. Cont.*, pp. 60 and 62. [2] See the references on p. 327, n. 6.
[3] See Vasiliev, *Byzance et les Arabes*, i, pp. 55–7. The strength of the invading fleet was only 40 ships (ibid., p. 55).
[4] See Eickhoff, op. cit., pp. 2–3 and 145–9. In 964, an East Roman expeditionary force suffered two crushing defeats—the first on land outside Rametta and the second at sea during its retreat.

themselves by conquering some piece of East Roman territory.[1] The Spaniards chose Crete; they reconnoitred it in 826 or 827, and conquered it in 827 or 828, apparently without resistance.[2] Three unsuccessful attempts to reconquer Crete were made before the death of the Emperor Michael II in 829.[3] Further unsuccessful attempts were made in 843, in 866 (the expedition in 866 was broken off after the murder of the Caesar Várdhas), in 911–12, and in 949. Crete was conquered at last, at the eighth attempt, by Nikêphóros Phokás (the future Emperor) in 960–1.[4]

Throughout the duration of the Spanish Muslims' hold on Crete, all coasts and islands in the Aegean basin that remained under East Roman rule were constantly exposed to naval raids at short range from the strongly fortified Cretan Muslim naval base at Candia. From 827 till 961, the East Roman Navy was on the defensive in the Aegean as well as in Sicilian waters. Though Constantine Porphyrogenitus's figures for the disposition of the East Roman Navy in 949 have fallen into some confusion, they make it clear that a very considerable quota of the Navy's strength had to be left behind in that year for home defence. Not only Constantinople but théma Kivyrrhaiótai, including the islands of Rhodes and Kárpathos, had to be strongly guarded.[5]

The East Roman Navy's fratricidal conflict in 821–2 may go far towards accounting for the Muslims' initial successes in Sicily and Crete, but it does not account for the length of the subsequent spell of East Roman naval adversity.[6] The most disgraceful incident was Rhomanós Lekapênós's apparently deliberate non-fulfilment of his duty in 917. The failures to save Syracuse from falling in 878[7] and Thessaloníkê from falling in 904[8] were hardly less shameful, though these seem to have been cases of

---

[1] See Vasiliev, op. cit., vol. i, pp. 49–54 and 287.

[2] See Genesius, pp. 46–8; *Theoph. Cont.*, p. 77; Constantine Porphyrogenitus, *De Adm. Imp.*, chap. 22, pp. 104–5.

[3] Vasiliev, op. cit., vol. i, pp. 59–61; Eickhoff, op. cit., pp. 67 and 133.

[4] See *Theoph. Cont.*, pp. 473–8 and 480–1; pseudo-Symeon, pp. 758–60. The Cretan Muslims begged for help from their Spanish and North-West-African co-religionists. These sent galleys to reconnoitre, but, when the galleys reported that the Cretans' prospects were hopeless, the Western Muslims decided not to intervene. The captive Amīr of Candia and his family were treated handsomely by Rhomanós II. The Amīr was given large presents of gold and silver, and was endowed with land. He would have been made a member of the Senate if he had been willing to be baptized. See also III, 3, p. 384.

[5] See the tabular presentation, in Antoniadis-Bibicou, op. cit., p. 94, of the field-state given by Constantine Porphyrogenitus in *De Caer.*, Book II, chap. 45.

[6] This has been pointed out to me by Professor Robert Browning.

[7] Eickhoff, op. cit., p. 222. See *Theoph. Cont.*, pp. 309–12. According to *Georg. Mon. Cont.*, p. 843, and Leo Grammaticus, pp. 256–7, Basil had detained the crews of the Imperial Fleet to do navvies' work at Constantinople for the building of the 'Néa' church. Cf. pseudo-Symeon, p. 691. According to *Georg. Mon. Cont.*, pp. 860–1, Leo Grammaticus, p. 274, and *Theoph. Cont.*, pp. 364–5, a similar misuse of the seamen's labour by Leo VI was responsible for the loss of Tavroménion in 902. See also pseudo-Symeon, p. 704.

[8] Eickhoff, op. cit., pp. 258–9. See John Kameniátês's account of this in the Bonn edition of *Theoph. Cont.*, pp. 485–600.

negligence or incompetence or cowardice or all three,[1] and not of deliberate sabotage. Basil I's disastrous dilatoriness in sending naval aid to Syracuse in 878 contrasts strangely with his promptness in relieving Ragusa in 868.

The failure to save Thessaloníkê in 904 was the more inexcusable considering that, as recently as 900, the Eastern Muslims had crippled their own naval power, as the East Romans had done in 822. In 900 the 'Abbasid Caliph Mu'tadid had made a punitive expedition to Cilicia in pursuit of a rebel and had burnt the Tarsan fleet, together with its equipment.[2] This had been a terrible blow for the most dynamic of the East Roman Empire's Eastern Muslim naval adversaries.[3]

There are, however, also some credit entries in the East Roman Navy's account for this period. Our Arabic sources have recorded an East Roman naval raid on Damietta in 853, followed up by two further raids on the Nile Delta in 853/4 and 859.[4] (The Byzantine writers in the service of Basil I's dynasty have ignored this spirited East Roman naval counter-offensive, to avoid giving due credit for it to Basil I's benefactor and victim Michael III.) It is also noteworthy that, even after the virtually complete loss of Sicily, the East Roman Navy was still capable of operating in the Tyrrhene Sea. In 915 it co-operated with the Empire's satellites in south-eastern Italy and with other Italian states in the destruction of the Muslim stronghold that had been planted in 882 at the mouth of the River Garigliano.[5] In 942[6] it delivered, in co-operation with Hugh of Provence, an attack on the Spanish Muslim stronghold Fraxinetum (La Garde Freinet).[7]

The tardy reconquest of Crete in 960–1 inaugurated a revival of East Roman naval power. Cyprus was conquered and re-annexed in 965. (According to Constantine Porphyrogenitus, Basil I had held Cyprus for

---

[1] See, for instance, *Georg. Mon. Cont.*, pp. 862–3; Leo Grammaticus, pp. 707–8; *Theoph. Cont.*, pp. 366–8: apropos of the fall of Thessaloníkê.

[2] See the translations, in Vasiliev, *Byzance et les Arabes*, ii, II, of the relevant passages of Tabari, on pp. 14–17, and Mas'ūdī, on p. 42.

[3] In Basil I's reign (for the date, see Canard in Vasiliev, *Byzance et les Arabes*, ii, I, p. 56, n. 1) a Tarsan fleet had attacked Khalkís in Évvoia (*Theoph. Cont.*, pp. 298–9). By 924, the Tarsans had already replaced the ships that had been burnt by their own 'Abbasid suzerain in 900; for in 924 a Tarsan squadron made contact with a Bulgarian land-army in Khalkidhikê (see the present chapter, p. 337).

[4] See Vasiliev, op. cit., vol. i, pp. 212–18 and 315–17; Grégoire, 'Études sur le neuvième siècle', pp. 515–17; Eickhoff, op. cit., pp. 202–3, with the bibliography on p. 202, n. 2.

[5] See Canard in Vasiliev, op. cit., ii, I, pp. 236–8, and in *C. Med. H.*, vol. iv, 2nd ed., Part I, p. 729.

[6] The true date is 944 or 945, according to Eickhoff, op. cit., p. 318, n. 55.

[7] Vasiliev, ii, I, p. 310, with n. 2, and 377, with n. 3. This operation was abortive. The Muslims at Fraxinetum were not smoked out till 973 (Eickhoff, op. cit., p. 371) or 972 (Lewis, op. cit., p. 184). According to A. Schaube, *Handelsgeschichte der romanischen Völker des Mittelmeergebiets bis zum Ende der Kreuzzüge* (Munich and Berlin, 1906, Oldenbourg), p. 98, there had been a previous unsuccessful joint attack on Fraxinetum in 931.

seven years,[1] but it had then been retaken by the Muslims.[2]) However, this revival of East Roman naval power was brief, and it was abortive to the west of the Straits of Ótranto. The Navy's last conspicuous achievement was its participation in the cornering of Svyátoslav at Dhrístra in 971.

The Asiatic naval thémata sided with Várdhas Sklêrós in the fronde of 976–9, as they had sided with Thomas in the insurrection of 821–3, and it seems likely that, once again, their dissidence had an adverse effect on their fortunes. As for the Imperial Fleet, Basil II would have had a use for it if, in the Romano-Bulgarian war of 976–1018, the geographical core of the Bulgarian state had still been the region between the south bank of the lower Danube and the eastern end of the Balkan Range, as it had been from 680 to 967. The Imperial Fleet could then have played, again, the effective part that it had played so often in the past in subjecting the Bulgars to attacks from two sides simultaneously. However, the nucleus of the Bulgarian resistance movement in and after 976 was far away inland south-westward, in the Sklavinías which Bulgaria had annexed in the course of the ninth century.

For overcoming this resistance, what Basil required was not warships and not semi-professional thematic troops, either naval or military. He needed expensive full-time professional soldiers, practised in the difficult and hazardous art of offensive warfare in a heavily forested mountainous country. In waging a war of annihilation against the Bulgarian resistance movement, Basil II emulated, with the same disastrous after-effects, Justinian I's error of waging a war to the death with the Ostrogoths in Italy. Once again, the Empire's already heavily taxed resources were being overstrained for the sake of achieving a conquest that was both unnecessary and eventually untenable. Basil II's war with Tsar Samuel left Basil with no margin to spare for any other purposes. He let the East Roman Navy decay. Venice was the beneficiary.

---

[1] *De Them.*, p. 40. This East Roman occupation of Cyprus is dated 874–80 by Canard in *C. Med. H.*, vol. iv, 2nd ed., Part I, p. 714.

[2] According to Mas'ūdī, translated in Vasiliev, *Byzance et les Arabes*, ii, II, p. 43, an Eastern Muslim punitive expedition was sent to Cyprus in 911/12 to chastise the Cypriots for the breach of Cyprus's neutrality in 910 by the East Roman admiral Imérios (see p. 335). We do not know whether Cyprus then fell completely under Muslim sovereignty, or whether it reverted to the neutral status accorded to it in the Romano-Arab treaty of 688/9 or 689/90.

PART III

THE EAST ROMAN IMPERIAL GOVERNMENT'S FOREIGN RELATIONS

1. *The Historical Background to the Situation in Constantine Porphyrogenitus's Day*

THEORETICALLY it should have been impossible for the East Roman Empire to have any foreign relations; for, like the contemporary Chinese Empire, the East Roman Empire was co-extensive with the whole civilized world in the eyes of its inhabitants, from the Emperor downwards.[1] A hundred years later than Constantine Porphyrogenitus's time, the East Roman Emperor was still being described, by a Byzantine pen, as 'lord of the whole Earth' ($κύριον$ $πάσης$ $τῆς$ $γῆς$),[2] and the capital of the Empire, Constantinople, is frequently referred to, by Constantine himself, as 'the Empress City' ($ἡ$ $βασιλεύουσα$). Beyond the penumbra of civilization, on the outermost fringes of the world-state's territory, there were, of course, remote and backward barbarians, wallowing in outer darkness, to whom the world-ruler had not condescended to extend the blessing of civilized administration. He had left to their native chiefs the thankless task of keeping these barbarians in order in compliance with Imperial instructions. But the communication of these instructions could not be dignified with the title of 'foreign relations'.

This was the theory, in both the East Roman Empire and the Chinese Empire, from first to last. At Constantinople the theory was still being maintained during the century ending in A.D. 1453—a century during which 'the Empress City' was encircled, and was under virtually constant siege, by the expanding Ottoman power, while the Imperial Government had become the suppliant of the schismatic barbarian Franks. The maintenance of the corresponding theory in China did not fly quite so fantastically in the face of the facts. The huge domain in which the Chinese civilization was prevalent, and the hardly smaller area of the territory that was under the Chinese world-state's rule, did not dwindle in the course of time; they continued to expand; they are still expanding today; and, though China, like the East Roman Empire,

---

[1] See Rambaud, op. cit., pp. 299–300.   [2] Kedhrênós, vol. ii, p. 192.

suffered attack, invasion, and conquest at the hands of barbarians who, in theory, ought not to have had the power or the audacity to commit this sacrilege, China succeeded, each time, in either expelling or assimilating her barbarian conquerors.

During the East Roman Emperor Constantine Porphyrogenitus's reign (*imperabat* 913–59), the Chinese world-state happened to be passing through one of those 'intermediate periods' of temporary breakdown and break-up which also occurred at intervals in the history of the East Roman Empire, and had occurred in the history of the Pharaonic Egyptian world-state too. After the fall of the T'ang dynasty in A.D. 909, China had split politically into five fragments, and she was not reunited till A.D. 960, the year that saw the establishment of the Sung dynasty. Yet this politically divided China did not lose her cultural unity and did not cease to radiate her culture beyond the frontiers of the T'ang dynasty's local successor-states; and each of these splinters of the Chinese world-state was singly almost on a par with Constantine Porphyrogenitus's world-state in point of civilization, wealth, population, and even area.

Thus the Chinese Empire was better justified than the East Roman Empire in claiming to have no foreign relations; yet even China had one set of neighbours who were not only out of her control but who could not be ignored by her because they were a menace to her security. These were the Eurasian nomad peoples, who were also neighbours of the East Roman Empire.

Actually, neither the Chinese nor the East Roman Imperial Government was ever completely the dupe of their identical unrealistic theory. Constantine Porphyrogenitus, for instance, was aware that his 'world-state' comprised, in his day, a much smaller part of the World than it had comprised in the time of some of his less recent predecessors. He quotes[1] a passage of Theophanes's chronicle describing the Empire's loss of Britain, Gaul, Spain, and North-West Africa in the fifth century. (As seen from the standpoint of Constantinople, the loss, in the fifth century, of the backward western provinces had been no loss to speak of, whereas the loss, in the seventh century, of Syria and Egypt had been crucial.) Constantine notes[2] that in Heraclius's reign the Empire had lost territory on the west as well as on the east, and that in consequence it had undergone a transformation. Latin had been replaced by Greek as the language of the Imperial administration. In truth, Constantine Porphyrogenitus was aware that the Roman Empire had been transformed in a fundamental way. He recognized that it had ceased to be a world-state and had become one local state among a number of others.

Constantine Porphyrogenitus not only admitted this tacitly; he took account of the Empire's new situation in a practical way by taking

[1] *De Adm. Imp.*, chap. 25, pp. 110–13.   [2] In *De Them.*, pp. 12–13.

a lively personal interest in the Empire's foreign policy and compiling a manual on this for the instruction of his son and colleague Rhomanós II: the treatise that has been given the misleading title *De Administrando Imperio* by its modern Western editors. The instructional and the descriptive parts of this book of Constantine's, taken together, reveal the extent of the geographical field of the East Roman Empire's more intimate and important relations with foreign countries. An inner field within this field is indicated by the set of formulae in the *De Caerimoniis*[1] for greetings from the ambassadors of select foreign states, and for polite responses to these by the Emperor's spokesman. The total field is covered in the much more extensive set of forms of address to be used by the East Roman Government in its correspondence with foreign rulers.[2] This total field not only includes all the successor-states of the Roman Empire that had sprung up in its lost territories; it also extends, beyond the Empire's widest former limits, to embrace most of the countries, outside these limits, with which the Empire had been in diplomatic relations at the height of its power. The East Roman Empire's foreign relations in Constantine Porphyrogenitus's time, as displayed in this comprehensive schedule, range from India and the Yaman to Andalusia and Saxony.

It is natural that the East Roman Empire's foreign relations should have been numerous; for, when we look at a map of the Old World as it was in the tenth century of the Christian Era, we see that the area then covered by the East Roman Empire, and the slightly larger area covered by the Byzantine civilization, were relatively small by comparison, not only with the contemporary areas of the Chinese Empire and civilization, but also with the area of contemporary Western Christendom.

During Constantine's reign, Western Christendom, like China, was in adversity. Charlemagne's Empire, like the T'ang Empire, had broken down and broken up. Its economic foundations had been too frail to bear the weight of its ambitious political structure. Western Christendom was suffering more severely than Byzantine Christendom from the raids of the Scandinavian seafarers and the Magyar horsemen.

The Magyars did make abortive attacks on Constantinople in A.D. 934, 943, 959, and 961, and the Rhos (i.e. the Scandinavian overlords of the Slav people in the Dniepr basin) did the same in A.D. 860, 907 (?), and 941. The devastation that was perpetrated by the Rhos on the Asiatic side of the Straits was cruel. It was, however, only local, and, on the whole, the Byzantine World got off a good deal more lightly than Western Christendom from this pair of ninth-century and tenth-century barbarian scourges. It was easier for the Scandinavian raiders to penetrate continental Western Europe and the British Isles by following the coasts and rowing

---

[1] *De Caer.*, Book II, chap. 47.   [2] In op. cit., Book II, chap. 48.

up the tidal rivers than it was for them to by-pass the Dniepr cataracts and then run the gauntlet of the Pecheneg nomads on the Steppe, on their arduous way to the Black Sea and the Bosphorus.

The East Roman Empire was also screened to some extent against Magyar raids coming from the Hungarian Alföld—a western enclave of Steppe-land that the Magyars had occupied *circa* A.D. 896. The Alföld was insulated from the East Roman Empire's dominions in south-eastern Europe by the domains of three ex-nomad peoples, the Bulgars, Serbs, and Croats, who had imposed themselves on the Slav settlers in the former Roman territories in the interior and who had by now become Slavonic-speaking and sedentary. In order to get at Constantinople or any other East Roman territory, the Magyars had to purchase or conquer a passage through the territories of these buffer-states.

Thus, in retrospect, it looks as if, during the century and a half follow-ing Charlemagne's death in 814, Western Christendom was in greater straits than the East Roman Empire. It might even be held that the collapse of government and civilization in the West at this time was more grievous than the previous collapse in the fifth century had been. Yet Liutprand, who was born *circa* 920, who spent most of his life in his native Lombardy, and who must have been a witness of some of the Magyar raids into Italy, was struck by the plight of the East Roman Empire. He notes[1] that the Empire was hard pressed on all sides, and the implication is that it seemed, to his contemporary eyes, to be more hard pressed than his own Western Christendom.

The East Roman Empire was, indeed, being assailed, like Western Christendom, on three fronts: by the northern barbarians, by the Muslims on land, and by the Muslims at sea. The Empire's Muslim neighbour, the 'Abbasid Caliphate of Baghdad, commanded a far larger territory and far greater resources than Western Christendom's neigh-bour the Umayyad Caliphate of Córdoba; and the Western Muslims' piratical stronghold in Crete was a sword pointed at the East Roman Empire's heart. In the course of the ninth century the 'Abbasid Caliphate began to lose its grip, but the consequent gradual relaxation of the pressure on the East Roman Empire from the south-east was more than offset by the rapid rise of Bulgaria on the north-west. No doubt Liutprand would have had Bulgaria, as well as Crete, in mind when he was assessing the East Roman Empire's position. Though Bulgaria was a buffer between the East Roman Empire and the nomad peoples on the Steppe, she was at the same time, like Muslim Crete, a menace to the East Roman Empire at close quarters. Tenth-century Western Christendom did not have any problem that was so acute and so intractable as the East Roman Empire's Bulgarian problem.

[1] *Antapodosis*, Book I, chap. 11.

These hard facts of East Roman life call in question the East Roman Empire's apparent advantage over Western Christendom at this time in the field of foreign relations. In any case, the advantage was only temporary. The Western Christian kingdoms of West Francia and Wessex eventually succeeded in bringing the Scandinavian invaders to a halt; in A.D. 955 the Saxon rulers of East Francia broke the power of the Magyars; and, after that, both the Magyars and the Scandinavian settlers in France and England and Ireland were converted to Roman Christianity and, therewith, to the Western Christian civilization. Thus Western Christendom survived; and it had three long-term advantages over Eastern Orthodox Christendom which, in combination, told more and more heavily in its favour as time went on. Western Christendom was larger; it was more compact and homogeneous; and its internal cleavages did not cut so deep.

In Constantine Porphyrogenitus's time, Western Christendom was at least three times as big as Eastern Orthodox Christendom, even when we have taken account of the states and peoples—e.g. Iberia, Alania, and Bulgaria—that were Eastern Orthodox Christian in religion and Byzantine in culture though politically independent of the East Roman Empire, and even if we do not deduct from the account those East Roman possessions and dependencies in south-eastern Italy, Dalmatia, and the Venetian lagoon that were Western Christian in religion, not Orthodox.

The ratio between the respective areas of these two Christendoms did not change when, at the turn of the tenth and eleventh centuries, Hungary and the Scandinavian countries to the west of the Baltic were converted to Roman Christianity, while Russia was converted simultaneously to Eastern Orthodox Christianity. Eastern Orthodox Christian Russia, with her open frontiers on the east and the south, was going to dwarf Western Christian Scandinavia eventually; but the conversion of Russia did not bring to the East Roman Empire the accession of strength that the conversion of Hungary and Scandinavia brought to Western Christendom. The enlarged Eastern Orthodox Christendom that embraced Russia was not geographically compact. Orthodox Christian Russia was still insulated from the older Orthodox Christian countries by pagan Eurasian nomads on the western bay of the Eurasian Steppe. This bay extended to the eastern foot of the Carpathian Range and thus intervened between the forests and fields of Russia and the northern shores of the Black Sea and the Sea of Azov. Moreover, conversion to Eastern Orthodox Christianity did not bring with it as high a degree of ecclesiastical and cultural assimilation as conversion to Roman Christianity brought.

When a pagan barbarian people was converted to Western Christianity, at any date from the eighth century onwards, the converts became, as a matter of course, ecclesiastical subjects of the Roman Patriarchate;[1] they adhered to the Roman rite and received Roman canon law; and they adopted Latin, not only as the language of their Christian liturgy, but as the language of a higher secular culture as well. The Roman Church was strongly opposed to the celebration of the liturgy in any language other than Latin in any territory under its ecclesiastical jurisdiction. The only exception that it allowed, and this reluctantly, was the use of a Slavonic version of the liturgy, conveyed in the Glagolitic alphabet,[2] in certain Roman Catholic dioceses in Dalmatia, Croatia, and Istria;[3] and its persistence, in this quarter, in waiving its general rule was forced upon the Roman Church by its local competition with Eastern Orthodox Christianity, whose policy was more liberal than the Roman Church's in regard to both liturgical languages and ecclesiastical government.

The Eastern Orthodox Christian churches were linked with each other, as the Roman See's ecclesiastical subjects were, by a common rite and by a common canon law, but they were linked by these alone. They were not all under the ecclesiastical jurisdiction of the Patriarch of

[1] The East German barbarians who overran the western provinces of the Roman Empire in the fifth century had been converted in the previous century to the Arian version of Christianity, which had been favoured by the Emperor Constantius II (*imperabat* A.D. 337–61). The Burgundians were not converted to the Roman Christianity of their Roman subjects till the second quarter of the sixth century, the Visigoths not till A.D. 589, the Lombards only in the course of the first half of the seventh century. (The Vandal and Ostrogoth Arian Christian conquerors of Roman territory had been exterminated by Justinian.) The only German barbarians settled on ex-Roman territory who were converted to Roman Christianity from paganism direct were those West Germans—Franks and English—who had been still pagans when they had arrived. The English pagan barbarian invaders of Britain had insulated both the surviving Christians in western Britain and the newly converted Irish from the Roman See; these Far Western Christians' rite, in consequence, had not kept in step with the changes in the Roman rite, and their allegiance to the Roman See had become dubious. In the seventh century, Rome had to contend with Iona for the allegiance of the English Kingdom of Northumbria. In A.D. 664, at the Synod of Whitby, Rome won this battle; Iona itself submitted to Rome in A.D. 716, and the Picts, Irish, Welsh, and Bretons also accepted the Roman method of fixing the date of Easter and the Roman form of tonsure in the course of the eighth century. At the conversion of the still pagan German peoples beyond the Rhine (Alemanni, Bavarians, Thuringians, Frisians, Saxons) there was no question of their adopting any form of Christianity other than the Roman.

[2] This, and not the later-made alphabet that is now known as the Cyrillic, was the original alphabet that had been created for the Moravian Slavs by the two Thessalonian missionary brothers Constantine-Cyril and Methódhios. See p. 105.

[3] The survival of a Slavonic version of the liturgy in this corner of the Papacy's ecclesiastical domain was the relic of an ambition—cherished by Pope Nicholas I (858–67) and his two immediate successors, Hadrian II (867–72) and John VIII (872–82)—to foster in Central Europe, in between Eastern Orthodox Christendom and the Papacy's own aggressive East Frankish ecclesiastical subjects, a Slavophone missionary church that would be, not merely under the Roman See's jurisdiction, but actually under its direct control. For this ninth-century Papal policy and its eventual failure, see A. P. Vlasto, *The Entry of the Slavs into Christendom* (Cambridge, 1970, University Press), pp. 52–85. For the subsequent history of the Slavonic liturgy, conveyed in the Glagolitic alphabet, in Dalmatia and Croatia, see op. cit., pp. 194–207. See also F. Dvornik, *Byzantine Missions among the Slavs* (New Brunswick, 1970, Rutgers University Press), *passim*.

Constantinople; though he had assumed the title 'Ecumenical',[1] he never claimed, and was never acknowledged, to be more than *primus inter pares* among the heads of the churches that observed the Eastern Orthodox rite, and, while he himself did not acknowledge the Roman See's supremacy, he did recognize its primacy in status over his own. The Eastern Orthodox churches were reciprocally autonomous, and they did not all employ the same language for their common liturgy. The Attic Greek *koinē* had not sought the monopoly that Latin had acquired in the domain of the Roman Patriarchate.

The jurisdictional and linguistic unity of the Roman Church and the jurisdictional and linguistic diversity of the Eastern Orthodox churches were alike the outcome of local circumstances. In the former Roman provinces lying to the west of the Straits of Ótranto and the Syrtes, the City of Rome had had no rival. By contrast, in Eastern Orthodox Christendom, jurisdictional plurality had been inevitable. It would have been inconceivable that either Alexandria or Antioch should have accepted the supremacy of the other, or that either of these once imperial cities should have subordinated itself to its much younger sister Constantinople. Thus there had had to be at least three autonomous Eastern Orthodox churches, and consequently there had been no logical reason why Jerusalem, Cyprus, and any number of other churches of the Eastern Orthodox communion should not be autonomous likewise.

The non-establishment of the Attic Greek *koinē* as the universal liturgical language is, at first sight, more surprising, considering that, at the time when Christianity had come to birth, the *koinē* had been the universal language of higher culture in the Latin-speaking provinces of the Roman Empire as well as in the Greek-speaking provinces and in the regions farther to the east in which the indigenous cultures had been overlaid by a veneer of Hellenism. From the second century B.C. to the third century of the Christian Era, every Latin-speaker who had received a higher education would have some acquaintance with the Greek as well as the Latin language and literature. After that, the Greek *koinē* had receded. The temporary political and economic breakdown of the Graeco-Roman society in the third century of the Christian Era had resulted, in the western provinces of the Roman Empire, in a permanent lowering of the level of culture. One symptom of this was the loss of command of Greek in the Latin-speaking World. At the turn of the fourth and fifth centuries, even so great a Latin intellectual genius as Augustine was not at home in Greek; and, though, in sixth-century

---

[1] This title may have been assumed as early as the Patriarchate of Akákios (472–89), though it did not become a matter of acute controversy between the sees of Constantinople and Rome till the Patriarchate of John IV the Faster (582–95) (see F. Dvornik in *C. Med. H.*, vol. iv, 2nd ed., Part I, p. 439).

Italy, Boethius was sufficiently well versed in Greek to be able to translate works of Aristotle into Latin, the reason why Boethius embarked on his big translation programme was because he realized that Greek philosophy in the original Greek had now become a closed book for Western minds. Meanwhile, Greek had also been receding from the eastern section of its former domain.

In the fifth century the peoples of Egypt, Syria, Mesopotamia, and Armenia had begun to revolt against the age-long imposition on them of the Greek language. Their revolt had declared itself in the Nestorian and Monophysite secessions from the Eastern Orthodox Church and in the substitution of their own languages for Greek in the liturgies of their dissident churches. These new non-Greek-speaking churches had then come into competition with the Eastern Orthodox churches for the conversion of still unconverted peoples in the Caucasus who were accessible from both quarters; and this competition had had the same liberalizing effect on the linguistic policy of the Eastern Orthodox churches in and after the fifth century as the Roman Church's competition with Eastern Orthodoxy had on the Roman Church's local linguistic policy in Dalmatia, Croatia, and Istria in and after the ninth century. If the Eastern Orthodox missionaries in Lazica, Iberia, Abkhazia, Tzania, Zikhia, and Alania had insisted on their converts celebrating the liturgy in Greek and not in their mother-tongues, they might have lost these countries to the Nestorians or to the Monophysites. Accordingly, the Orthodox missionaries allowed them to celebrate the liturgy in their own languages, conveyed in alphabets of their own, devised for the purpose.

This concession in the debatable north-eastern borderland of the Eastern Orthodox World set a precedent in other regions. In the ninth century this precedent was followed by Constantine-Cyril as a matter of course. On his first missionary enterprise, which was for the conversion of the Khazars, his first step was to set himself to learn the Khazars' Turkish language. When he set out to convert the Slavs, he prepared himself for the mission that was to be his life-work by reducing the Slavonic dialect of the hinterland of his native Greek city Thessaloníkê to literary form; and this indicates his intention to make this dialect fit to serve as a liturgical language and not simply as a medium of oral communication with prospective converts.

This linguistic and jurisdictional pluralism of Eastern Orthodox Christianity was liberal, even though the liberalism had been dictated by circumstances. Yet, just because of its liberalism, Eastern Orthodoxy was not so potent a unifying force as Roman Catholicism was, with its single centre of ecclesiastical authority in the Roman See and its single liturgical and cultural language in the shape of Latin. In the tenth century, Roman Christendom was not only more compact geographically than

Eastern Orthodox Christendom; it was also more homogeneous. The Italian-speaking bishop Liutprand of Cremona and the Plattdeutsch-speaking emperors Otto I and II of Saxony were more at home with each other than the East Roman Emperor Constantine Porphyrogenitus and his contemporary the Tsar Peter of Bulgaria could be. The Italian and the German, like the Greek and the Bulgar, were sundered by speaking different vernaculars, but at the same time they were united by having, in Latin, a common liturgical and cultural language, whereas the Greek and the Bulgar had different liturgical languages as well as different vernaculars. In consequence, the bond created by their common Eastern Orthodoxy was relatively weak.

Moreover, the political cleavage between the East Roman Empire and the Bulgarian Empire went deeper than any contemporary political cleavage in Western Christendom, and the reason for this is to be found in the impressiveness and the genuine solidity of the East Roman Empire's structure. In the West since the collapse of the Roman Empire there in the fifth century, there had been no effective resuscitation of the Roman Empire. Charlemagne's ambitious attempt had been a failure; and, during the quarter of a millennium that elapsed between the date of Charlemagne's death and the rise of the North Italian city-states, there was no state in Western Christendom that was effective enough to capture its subjects' imagination and to become the paramount object of their loyalty. In this age, the paramount loyalty of a Western Christian was given, not to the local state in which he happened to find himself, but to the Roman Church, and this master institution was common to the whole of Western Christendom. In the West in this phase of its history, the local states were too feeble and too uninspiring to be capable of challenging the common feeling of Western Christian unity. By contrast, the East Roman Empire had been such an effective resuscitation of the Roman Empire that it constituted something like a closed world of its own which did not readily coalesce with neighbouring countries when these were converted to the Eastern Orthodox Christianity that was the East Roman Empire's religion. Pagan states converted to Eastern Ortho-doxy tended to become closed worlds on their own account, in imitation of the East Roman Empire, which was the archetypal Eastern Orthodox Christian state.

After the long-drawn-out recession of East Roman power in Italy between A.D. 568 and 751, and after the subsequent collapse of the Carolingian power in the West, the Papacy had found itself unprotected and consequently uncompromised by any form of secular imperial tutelage. The Papacy now had to fend for itself, and, while, on the political plane, this compelled it to live dangerously, it profited on the ecclesiastical plane, because the act of becoming an ecclesiastical subject of the Roman See now no longer carried with it the implication of becoming the political subject of an imperial power to which the Papacy itself professed allegiance. Meanwhile, the Ecumenical Patriarchate of Constantinople had become more and more closely tied to the East Roman Imperial Government.

The histories of the Papacy and the Constantinopolitan Patriarchate had, indeed, followed different lines from the outset. The Papacy had found its opportunity for greatness in the prestige of the Rome of St. Peter and St. Paul, and these two most eminent of the Apostles had been drawn to Rome and had suffered martyrdom there because, in their day, Rome had been the capital of the Mediterranean World. Rome had won this ecumenical position for herself a hundred and fifty years before the inauguration of the Imperial regime by Augustus; no emperor had had any hand in building up the Papacy's power either; this had been achieved by the Roman Church itself, with the aid of the prestige with which Rome had been invested by Peter and Paul and the Fabii and the Scipios. By contrast, the New Rome, Constantinople, had been created by the fiat of a Roman Emperor. If Constantine I had not founded Constantinople, the bishop of Byzantium would have remained obscure; and the bishop of Constantinople would never have risen to become a patriarch if it had not been Imperial policy to give this status to the bishop of the new Imperial capital, and if the Imperial Government had not had the power to carve out a domain for this parvenu patriarchate in between the already existing patriarchates of Rome and Antioch.

This ecclesiastical creation of the Constantinopolitan Imperial Government's was in danger, from the beginning, of becoming the Imperial Government's creature. The Patriarch of Constantinople took to styling himself 'Ecumenical' because the Emperor whose capital was this Patriarch's see claimed to be a world-ruler. The identification of the Constantinopolitan Patriarchate with the Constantinopolitan Empire was not conspicuous so long as the other four patriarchal sees—Rome, Antioch, Jerusalem, and Alexandria—together with the autocephalous church of Cyprus, were all still included within the Constantinopolitan Empire's frontiers; but, after the three eastern patriarchates had been lost to the Arabs in the reign of Heraclius, and after the Papacy had transferred its allegiance from the East Roman Empire to the Austrasian Frankish power in the eighth century, only the patriarchal See of Constantinople was left within the shrunken East Roman Empire's frontiers.

Meanwhile, it had become the policy of the Constantinopolitan Government to make the frontiers of the Ecumenical Patriarchate coincide with those of the East Roman Empire itself. The fragment of the Patriarchate of Antioch in Western Cilicia which the East Roman

Empire still retained was transferred to the Patriarchate of Constantinople in order to remove the awkwardness of leaving a piece of East Roman territory under the ecclesiastical jurisdiction of a patriarch who had now become the subject of a foreign government that was non-Christian and unfriendly. In 732 or at some date after 751,[1] Leo III or Constantine V had transferred to the Patriarchate of Constantinople from the Patriarchate of Rome those portions of the Roman Patriarchate in the Balkan Peninsula, in the 'toe' of Italy, and in Sicily that were then under East Roman rule, together with the Sklavinías in the interior of what had once been the praetorian prefecture of the Eastern Illyricum. In Constantine Porphyrogenitus's day the Ecumenical Patriarchate's domain coincided with the East Roman Empire's domain except for its excluding Venice, Istria, théma Laghouvardhía to the north of Kalavría, and possibly also Dalmatia, while including the independent Caucasian countries Lazica, Iberia, Abkhazia, Tzania, Zikhia, and Alania. One effect of this had been to make the Patriarch of Constantinople look like an East Roman civil servant who was answerable to the Imperial Government for the conduct of the Empire's ecclesiastical affairs. The Ecumenical Patriarch's chief business administrator (sýnkellos) was, in truth, virtually an Imperial civil servant, since he was appointed, not by the Patriarch himself, but by the Emperor.[2]

It might have been possible to prove that, *de jure*, the Ecumenical Patriarch, though politically he was an East Roman subject, was independent of the Imperial Government in his own ecclesiastical sphere; and, in truth, there had been three recent occasions on which a patriarch had had the courage to debar a Caesar or an Emperor from holy communion as a penalty for a breach of morals. In 858 the Patriarch Ighnátios had laid this ban on the Caesar Várdhas for his having had sexual relations with his daughter-in-law;[3] in 867 the Patriarch Phótios had laid the same ban on the Emperor Basil I for his having murdered Michael III;[4] in 906 the Patriarch Nikólaos had laid it on the Emperor Leo VI for his having contracted a fourth marriage.[5] All three protests had been spirited assertions of the Church's independence in its own sphere; but

---

[1] For this later dating, see Ostrogorsky, 'The Byzantine Background of the Moravian Mission', in *Dumbarton Oaks Papers*, Number Nineteen, p. 12. Ostrogorsky notes, on p. 13, n. 30, that Dalmatia was probably transferred on the same occasion.

[2] For the procedure of appointment, see *De Caer.*, Book II, chap. 5, pp. 530–2.

[3] *Georg. Mon. Cont.*, Reign of Michael III, chap. 20, p. 826; Leo Grammaticus, p. 240; *Theoph. Cont.*, Book IV, Reign of Michael III, chaps. 30–1, pp. 193–5; pseudo-Symeon, Reign of Michael III, chap. 28, pp. 667–8.

[4] *Georg. Mon. Cont.*, Reign of Basil I, chap. 5, p. 841; Leo Grammaticus, pp. 254–5; pseudo-Symeon, Reign of Basil I, chap. 6, pp. 688–9; Zonarás, vol. iii, Books XIII–XVIII, p. 418.

[5] *Georg. Mon. Cont.*, Reign of Leo VI, chap. 34, p. 865; Leo Grammaticus, p. 279; *Theoph. Cont.*, Book VI, Reign of Leo VI, chap. 23, p. 370; pseudo-Symeon, Reign of Leo VI, chap. 18, p. 709.

on all three occasions the Patriarch had paid for his stand by being deposed by the Caesar or Emperor whom he had censored; and the fact that the Emperor's action had been uncanonical had only thrown into higher relief the reality of his arbitrary power. The *de facto* relation of political subjection to the East Roman Imperial Government into which the Ecumenical Patriarchate had fallen is part of the explanation of the unhappy sequel to the conversion of Bulgaria to Eastern Orthodox Christianity.

2. Relations with Bulgaria

THE Bulgars had risen in the World—in the Byzantine World, that is to say—in the course of the quarter of a millennium ending in the reign of the East Roman Emperor Constantine Porphyrogenitus (*imperabat* 913–59).

The original Bulgars had been Turkish-speaking nomads. Their name makes its first appearance in our records after the disintegration of the ephemeral empire of the Western-Hun war-lord Attila. The region in which we then find them is the western bay of the Eurasian Steppe.[1] In A.D. 680 the Bulgars, without abandoning their pasture-lands, had crossed the lower Danube and had imposed their rule on the Slav tribes that had settled in the former Roman territory between the river and the Aímos (Balkan) Range. At the same time they had secured a foothold to the south of the Aímos by planting one of the Slav tribes whom they had subjected at the southern exit from the pass of Veregava.[2] By Constantine Porphyrogenitus's time the Bulgarian state had expanded beyond this modest nucleus both westwards and southwards. Along the south bank of the Danube it now extended westwards as far as Belgrade (the former Roman fortress Singidunum) inclusive. In its southward expansion it had spread not only farther beyond the Aímos (Balkan) Range[3] but also beyond the former Roman Imperial highway that had once linked Constantinople with Singidunum via Adrianople and Philippopolis and Sardica. It had even spread beyond the former Roman Via Egnatia that had once

---

[1] See further III, 5 (i), p. 425.

[2] Theophanes, p. 359. See also the present work, Annex III, p. 625.

[3] According to the anonymous author of *Theoph. Cont.*, Book IV, Biography of Michael III, chap. 15, pp. 164–5, and Kedhrênós, vol. ii, p. 153, Michael's mother, the Empress Theodora, had ceded to Bulgaria a strip of territory to the south of the eastern end of the Aímos Range, from Sidhêrá to Dheveltós (the district called Zagorá (Zagorje) in the local Slavonic dialect, which seems to have included the sites of the two derelict East Roman coastal fortresses, Mesêmvría and Ankhíalos), as a reward to the Khan Borís for his conversion to Christianity. Theodora had, however, been deposed and relegated to a convent long before the conversion of Borís, which did not take place till A.D. 864. The tonsuring of Theodora and the conversion of Borís are recorded in the right order by *Georg. Mon. Cont.*, Reign of Michael III, chap. 14, p. 823, and chap. 16, p. 824; by Leo Grammaticus, pp. 237 and 238; and by pseudo-Symeon, Reign of Michael III, chap. 13, p. 658, and chap. 25, p. 665. Pseudo-Symeon, Reign of Michael III, chap. 25, p. 666, states that the Zagorá (Zagorje) was ceded to Borís by Michael III after the conversion of Borís and his subsequent suppression of the consequent revolt in Bulgaria. Runciman, *A History of the First Bulgarian Empire*, pp. 90–1, holds that the cession was made by Theodora, but that the date was after Borís's accession in 852, not after his conversion in 864. Runciman suggests, in op. cit., p. 104, that the territorial concession which the East Roman Empire made to Bulgaria in 864 was the recognition of the already accomplished fact of Bulgaria's expansion south-westward. For the alleged cession of the Zagorje by Justinian II in 705, see p. 338, n. 1.

linked Constantinople with Dhyrrhákhion via Thessaloníkê. Dhyrrhákhion and Thessaloníkê, and Nikópolis and Thessaloníkê too, were now insulated from each other no longer just by a welter of Sklavinías but by the Bulgar state that had now incorporated all the Balkan Slavs as far south as southern Macedonia (in the original meaning of the name) and north-eastern Epirus.[1]

By comparison with the rudimentary political structure of the Slav tribes before these had lost their independence, the Bulgarian state in Constantine Porphyrogenitus's time was highly organized.[2] By comparison with the contemporary East Roman Empire, on the other hand, it was still backward, and this not only politically but also economically and culturally. As late as the year A.D. 1018, in which the incorporation of West Bulgaria in the East Roman Empire was completed by Constantine's grandson Basil II, West Bulgaria had not yet achieved a money economy.[3] All the same, the economic and political structure of tenth-century Bulgaria was probably not more backward than the structure of the majority of the states of contemporary Western Christendom, and, since her conversion to Eastern Orthodox Christianity in 864, and especially since her reception of the Slavophone Methodhian missionary clergy who had been expelled from Moravia in 885, Byzantine culture had been seeping into Bulgaria in Orthodoxy's wake. Indeed, before the conversion of Bulgaria, the still pagan khans Krum and his son Omurtag (*regnabant circa* 803–31) had been employing the services of East Roman prisoners of war and renegades to introduce the rudiments of Greek culture into their kingdom. Their palaces at Pliska were built for them by Greek architects, and the work was commemorated in inscriptions in contemporary vernacular Greek.[4] Meanwhile, the Bulgar state-builders and the far more numerous Slavs on whom these had imposed their rule had been coalescing into a single nation that remained Bulgar in name but had become Slav in language.

Tenth-century Bulgaria was thus strong by comparison with the rabble of un-united and unorganized independent Slav communities that it had replaced, and this change had been a serious change for the worse from the standpoint of the East Roman Empire. The occupation of the interior of the Balkan Peninsula by the Slavs in and after the later decades of the sixth century had been a calamity for the Empire; but, so long as the Slavs had remained in their pristine state of virtual anarchy, the Empire's

---

[1] See II, 1 (iii) (a), pp. 102–7.

[2] For the origins of the first Bulgarian dynasty, see J. B. Bury, *A History of the Later Roman Empire* (London, 1889, Macmillan, 2 vols.), vol. ii, p. 333, with n. 2. See also Bury's *editio minor* of Gibbon, vol. iv, Appendix 15, on p. 537; Runciman, op. cit., pp. 272–81; and the present work, III, 5 (iii). [3] See Kedhrênós, vol. ii, p. 530.

[4] See Runciman, op. cit., pp. 75–9; Beševliev, *Die Protobulgarischen Inschriften*, especially his *Einleitung*, pp. 84–5.

situation in the peninsula had not been irretrievable. In addition to its beach-heads it had retained some of its fortresses in the interior—for instance, Adrianople, Philippopolis, and even Sardica—and the possibility had remained open that the Imperial Government might re-establish its authority over the northern ex-Imperial territories occupied by the Slavs, as it had, in fact, successfully re-established its authority over the Pelopónnêsos.[1] The progressive expansion of Bulgaria over the Slav settlements had ruled this possibility out, and the substitution of the unitary Bulgarian state for the former innumerable Sklavinías had transformed what had been an inconvenience for the East Roman Empire into a menace to it. Adrianople, Thessaloníkê, Nikópolis, and Dhyrrhákhion were now insulated from each other by a single organized state, and the frontier between this state and the Empire now ran within a few miles of these four important East Roman cities. In the Balkan Peninsula, Bulgaria held the interior lines. The Sklavinías had been thorns in the Empire's flesh; the expanded Bulgaria was, like Muslim Crete, a sword pointed at the Empire's heart. In the balance of power between the Empire and Bulgaria, the Empire's superior political and economic and cultural strength was offset by Bulgaria's commanding 'geopolitical' position in relation to the Empire's scattered European dominions.

Since A.D. 927 the East Roman Government's consciousness of Bulgaria's power had been reflected in some startling new departures in East Roman protocol. In that year, which was the fifteenth year of a continuous state of war between Bulgaria and the East Roman Empire, the East Roman Emperor Rhomanós I Lekapênós had bought peace from Bulgaria[2] on the basis of the territorial *status quo ante bellum* by making some extraordinary concessions on hallowed East Roman maxims of state.

Rhomanós had given formal recognition to two provocative Bulgarian unilateral acts. In 925, Symeon—having failed, after thirteen years of war, to conquer Constantinople and to mount the East Roman Imperial throne there—had proclaimed himself 'Emperor of the Romans and Bulgars'.[3] In 926 he had proclaimed the archbishop of his capital city Preslav[4] the patriarch of his empire.[5] In the peace settlement of 927, Rhomanós had condoned these two high-handed acts of Symeon's.

In the first place, Rhomanós had gazetted Symeon's son and now

---

[1] See II, 1 (iii) (a), pp. 92 and 98–101.

[2] *Georg. Mon. Cont.*, pp. 905–6; Leo Grammaticus, pp. 316–17; *Theoph. Cont.*, pp. 413–15; pseudo-Symeon, pp. 740–1; Kedhrênós, vol. ii, p. 309.

[3] A.D. 925 is Obolensky's date in *C. Med. H.*, vol. iv, 2nd ed., Part I, p. 508, n. 3. There is a lead seal inscribed Συμεὼν ἐν Χρισ(τῷ) βασιλ(εὺς) 'Ρομέον (No. 89a in Beševliev, op. cit., pp. 330–1).

[4] Symeon had moved the capital of Bulgaria to Preslav from Pliska.

[5] See Runciman, op. cit., pp. 173–4; Obolensky in *C. Med. H.*, vol. iv, 2nd ed., Part I, p. 508. Symeon's proclamation of the archbishop of Preslav as patriarch is dated 917 or 919 by Vlasto in op. cit., p. 173.

reigning successor Peter as an emperor.[1] This act did have one precedent.[2] The East Roman Government had gazetted Charlemagne as an emperor in 811, as part of the price of a settlement with him. However, the two concessions were not quite comparable; for Charlemagne, after all, had been *de facto* the ruler of the whole of Western Christendom except Britain and Asturias. Moreover, the East Roman Government had discontinued the use of the title in addressing Charlemagne's divided and enfeebled successors in 871,[3] and they never conceded the title to Otto I or to any subsequent Western 'Roman Emperor of the German Nation'. When, in 968, Liutprand came to Constantinople on a second diplomatic mission—this time on behalf of Otto I, who was a much more powerful ruler than Liutprand's previous principal, Berengar of Ivrea— the reigning Emperor Nikêphóros II's brother, the kouropalátês and grand loghothétês Leo, vastly annoyed Liutprand by making a point of referring to Otto I, not as 'emperor' (βασιλεύς), but as 'kinglet' (ῥῆξ),[4] and, later, the Emperor Nikêphóros himself spoke to Liutprand with displeasure of Otto's 'intolerable, unmentionable' presumption in assuming the Imperial title. Indeed, after the East Roman Government had ceased to give the title to the declining Carolingians, it did not ever give it to any foreign ruler except the sovereign of Bulgaria.

Rhomanós's second concession in the Romano-Bulgarian peace settlement of 927 had been to recognize the archbishop of the Bulgarian See of Dhrístra (Durostorum, Dhorýstolon)—not the archbishop of the Bulgarian capital city Preslav—as a patriarch independent of the Ecumenical Patriarch of Constantinople and supreme over the Orthodox Church within the Bulgarian Emperor Peter's dominions.[5] It is true that,

[1] See Runciman, op. cit., Appendix XI. If Rhomanós had not conceded to Peter in A.D. 927 the title of 'Emperor' that Symeon had already assumed, it seems improbable that Rhomanós would have given his granddaughter in marriage to a non-Imperial barbarian ruler. However, Rambaud, in op. cit., p. 342, points out that the original formula of address, in which the sovereign of Bulgaria was styled 'árkhon', not 'vasiléfs', was still in use after Constantine Porphyrogenitus had associated his son Rhomanós II with himself, i.e. in or after 945. This formula and the revised formula are set out on p. 370 of the present work.

Peter himself styled himself first βασιλεὺς Βουλγάρων and later simply βασιλεὺς εὐσεβής on his own lead seals (Nos. 91 and 92 in Beševliev, *Die Protobulgarischen Inschriften*, pp. 332–4 of text; cf. his *Einleitung*, p. 80).

[2] It had not one, but two precedents, the second of which was the more pertinent of the two, if it is true that, in 913, the Patriarch of Constantinople and regent of the East Roman Empire, Nikólaos Mystikós, had recognized Symeon as being βασιλεὺς καὶ αὐτοκράτωρ τῶν Βουλγάρων. However, the evidence for this is not conclusive. See Obolensky in *C. Med. H.*, vol. iv, 2nd ed., Part I, p. 506, with n. 1; Vlasto in op. cit., p. 173, with n. 75 on p. 373. See further the present chapter, p. 366, n. 2.

[3] See Moravcsik and Jenkins's *Commentary* on Constantine Porphyrogenitus's *De Adm. Imp.*, p. 83.

[4] Liutprand, *Legatio*, chap. 2. In East Roman official Greek, the word ῥῆξ had a depreciatory connotation. To translate it as 'king', without putting 'king' into the diminutive, would be to miss the word's contemptuous nuance.

[5] Before long, the Emperor Peter retransferred the Bulgarian Patriarch from the see of

in Eastern Orthodox Christendom, in contrast to Roman Christendom, there had always been a number of mutually independent churches united in rite and doctrine but not in ecclesiastical government. However, the East Roman Government's recognition of the see of Dhrístra's independence of the see of Constantinople was not covered by this precedent; for, though, down to 732 or 751, the territory that had now become western Bulgaria had been under the ecclesiastical jurisdiction, not of the Constantinopolitan Patriarchate, but of the Roman See, north-eastern Bulgaria, which was the original nucleus of the Bulgarian state and was the region in which Dhrístra lay, had been part of the Patriarchate of Constantinople's domain before this territory had been occupied by pagan Slavs and then by the pagan Bulgars who had followed at the Slavs' heels. Thus the Patriarchate of Constantinople was now formally conceding the ecclesiastical independence of territory that had once been its own.

Rhomanós had made a third concession in 927. He had given his grand-daughter María in marriage to the Emperor Peter.[1] By this date Peter and his predecessors on the Bulgarian throne had been Christians for sixty-three years; and, now that the reigning sovereign of Bulgaria had been gazetted as an Emperor by the East Roman Government, he had per-haps become technically eligible, according to East Roman protocol, for obtaining an Imperial bride. All the same, this concession of Rhomanós's was subsequently censured by Constantine Porphyrogenitus in a passage that has been quoted already.[2]

In this context, Constantine cites one precedent for this third con-cession of Rhomanós's in order to disallow it. According to Constantine, the Emperor Leo III had 'made a marriage-alliance with the Khaqan of the Khazars, and had taken his daughter to wife'. The Khazar princess in question, who was baptized under the name Eirếnê, must have been a pagan till then;[3] so, on this point, the precedent was still more shocking than María's marriage to a Christian Bulgarian Emperor. But, then, what could you expect of an Emperor who had already 'put himself outside the fear of God and His commandments'[4] by attacking the veneration of the holy eikóns? After that, Leo III would have been capable of any enormity.

Dhrístra to the see of Preslav, but the East Roman Government seems never to have recognized any archbishop of Preslav as being a patriarch (see Runciman, op. cit., pp. 181–2).

[1] According to Vlasto, op. cit., p. 173, the date of this marriage, and also the date of the East Roman recognition of the Bulgarian Patriarchate, may have been as late as 932.

[2] On pp. 16–17. Constantine, as has been noted there, does mention, as a mitigating circumstance, that the Bulgars were Christians of the Eastern Orthodox rite.

[3] This marriage could not have been contracted after the Khazar royal family's conversion from paganism to Judaism. A Jewish princess would not have apostatized to Christianity—not even for the sake of becoming an East Roman empress.

[4] *De Adm. Imp.*, chap. 13, p. 87.

Constantine Porphyrogenitus is here in error on several points of fact. To begin with, the iconoclast Emperor who had married the Khazar princess had been, not Leo III, but that great man's worthy son and successor Constantine V. This does not affect Constantine Porphyrogenitus's polemical argument, since Constantine V had gone to greater lengths in his iconoclasm than Leo III. There were, however, two other precedents that were older than the one that had been set by Constantine V. Justinian II had married a Khazar Khaqan's sister, and Heraclius had promised to give his own daughter in marriage to the Khaqan of the Khazar's Turkish overlords, or perhaps even to the Turkish Khaqan's second in command.[1] Justinian II's act could be ignored with greater justification than Constantine V's. Justinian II had not been an iconoclast, but he had been a homicidal maniac. Heraclius was more difficult to dispose of. He had not only been an Orthodox Christian; he had also been a hero who had saved the Empire from destruction. It would have been hard for any of his successors to maintain that a precedent set by Heraclius counted for nothing,[2] considering that, if it had not been for Heraclius's heroism, the line of Roman Emperors would probably have ended in Heraclius's execrable predecessor Phokás.

An unimplicated observer will probably judge that, in making peace between the East Roman Empire and Bulgaria on the terms set out above, Rhomanós I had done a good service to both countries and to the whole Byzantine World. That his peace-settlement turned out eventually to have been no more than a truce was not Rhomanós's fault. An eventual catastrophic dénouement of the issue between the East Roman Empire and the Bulgarian Empire was almost foredoomed by the relation—discussed in the first chapter of this part of the present book—that had previously been established between the East Roman Imperial Government and the Ecumenical Patriarchate of Constantinople.

If the East Roman Empire and Bulgaria had been two Western Christian countries, the conversion of Bulgaria to Christianity would have broken down the barriers between them and have opened the way for their fusion with each other. This had been the effect of the conversion of Saxony on the Saxons' relation with the Franks, notwithstanding the fact that Christianity had been forced upon the Saxons at the sword's point by Charlemagne. The Saxon resistance had been so obstinate that the Franco-Saxon war had dragged on for thirty years. Yet, within little more than 150 years of the final subjugation of the Saxons by the Franks, a Saxon Western Roman Emperor was seated on Charlemagne's throne.

[1] Nic. Patr., pp. 15–16, read together with Theophanes, pp. 315–16. See the present work, p. 441.

[2] Ostrogorsky, 'The Byzantine Empire in the World of the Seventh Century', p. 18, notes that East Roman Emperors did not disdain to contract matrimonial alliances with Khazar Khaqans.

The East Roman Emperor Leo VI felt that the conversion of Bulgaria to Christianity in 864, or at any rate her eventual definitive choice of the Eastern Orthodox, in preference to the Western, form of Christianity in 870, had carried with it a moral obligation for both Bulgaria and the East Roman Empire to live in a fraternal relation with each other which had been out of the question so long as Bulgaria had still been pagan. In a striking passage of his *Taktiká*,[1] Leo announces that he is going to refrain from describing the tactics that the Bulgars and the (East) Romans use against each other, 'because we are brothers in virtue of our common faith and therefore . . . we have no intention of arming against the Bulgars'. These words were written by Leo VI notwithstanding the unhappy fact that the conversion of Bulgaria had not averted the Romano-Bulgarian war of 894–6—a war that had been waged in Leo VI's own reign, and this already before the date at which Leo was writing this passage in his *Taktiká*.[2] It was a tragedy for Eastern Orthodox Christendom that, here, the peaceful conversion of Bulgaria to Christianity[3] resulted, not in an improvement, but in a worsening, of Bulgaria's relations with the East Roman Empire, as a consequence of the Ecumenical Patriarch's political subjection to the East Roman Imperial Government.

By this time, as has been noted, the Ecumenical Patriarch had been virtually reduced to the status of an official of the East Roman state, and, as a logical accompaniment of this development, his territorial domain had been made conterminous with the Empire's. Consequently, an acceptance of the ecclesiastical jurisdiction of the East Roman Emperor's subject and official the Ecumenical Patriarch might be interpreted as implying a submission to the political sovereignty of the East Roman Emperor himself. This point had not been a stumbling-block for the princes and peoples of Lazica and Iberia and Abkhazia and Tzania and Zikhia and Alania. The ruler of Iberia had explicitly recognized the East Roman Emperor's sovereignty by accepting the title of an East Roman kouropalátês *ex officio*. Alania was guaranteed by the natural rampart of the Caucasus Range against any practical interference, on the

---

[1] Leo VI, *Taktiká*, Dhiat. 18, § 44, col. 957.

[2] The chronological sequence is made clear by Leo's previous reference, in § 42, col. 956, to the ferrying of the Magyars across the Danube in 895.

[3] Borís had yielded, without fighting, to an East Roman military demonstration, and he had taken at his baptism the name Michael, which was the name of the reigning East Roman Emperor Michael III (Kedhrênós, vol. ii, pp. 151–3). A sister of Borís's, who had been taken prisoner by the East Romans and had been converted to Christianity, had been released in an exchange of prisoners (Kedhrênós, vol. ii, p. 151 ; cf. pseudo-Symeon, p. 664). *Theoph. Cont.*, pp. 162–3, gives credit to her for the conversion of Borís. Symeon, in Leo Grammaticus, p. 238, and in *Georg. Mon. Cont.*, p. 824, gives the credit to the East Roman Army's annihilation of the Amīr of Malatīyah's raiding force in 863. When the Bulgars heard the news of this, 'they were thunderstruck and caved in'. Symeon also mentions, in locc. citt., that Bulgaria was prostrated by a famine.

East Roman Government's part, with its *de facto* independence. The point had, however, been a stumbling-block to the Bulgar Khan Borís after his conversion to Eastern Orthodox Christianity in 864. One of the conditions stipulated in the Romano-Bulgarian treaty of that year had been that Bulgaria should come under the ecclesiastical jurisdiction of the Ecumenical Patriarchate.[1] The recognition of the East Roman Government's political sovereignty, which might be held to be implicit in this ecclesiastical stipulation,[2] was unacceptable to Borís, and, to avoid this awkward political implication, Borís broke the treaty in 866 by transferring Bulgaria's ecclesiastical allegiance from the Ecumenical Patriarch to the Pope, who was not the political subject of any secular prince during the interval between the collapse of the Carolingian Western Roman Empire and its revival by the Saxon dynasty and its successors.

This move of Borís's was astute, but it did not succeed. Its failure may have been partly the Papacy's fault. The Papacy seems not to have been well-enough informed or alert enough to exploit the opportunity with which Borís had presented it. The Pope and his representatives in Bulgaria may, on occasions, have been obtuse and tactless. But probably the fundamental obstacle that stood in the way of Bulgaria's joining the Roman Church definitively was that already, before her conversion, she had committed herself to the reception of the Byzantine culture.[3] Culturally, tenth-century Constantinople was impressive and tenth-century Rome was not.[4] In any case, Borís, whatever may have been his reasons, did voluntarily re-transfer his allegiance from the Papacy to the Ecumenical Patriarchate in 870 and accepted a Greek archbishop and Greek bishops at the hands of the Patriarch Ighnátios;[5] and, though the East Roman Emperor Basil I awarded Bulgaria to the See of Rome in A.D. 879,[6] Borís clinched Bulgaria's adherence to the Ecumenical Patriarchate when he accepted the services of the Slavophone Methodhian

[1] Runciman, op. cit., p. 106.
[2] Symeon in Leo Grammaticus, p. 238, and in *Georg. Mon. Cont.*, p. 824, says outright that, in 864, the Bulgars Χριστιανοὶ γενέσθαι καὶ ὑποτάττεσθαι τῷ βασιλεῖ καὶ Ῥωμαίοις ᾐτήσαντο. He is assuming that conversion was tantamount to submission.
[3] See pp. 359–60.
[4] See Dvornik, *Les Slaves, Byzance, et Rome*, pp. 255 and 264; Runciman, op. cit., p. 122.
[5] In Philótheos's klêtorolóyion, the Archbishop of Bulgaria occupies a high place in the order of precedence. He ranks below the sýnkellos of the Patriarch of Constantinople but above all the stratêghoí of the thémata and commanders of the tághmata (p. 146 Bury, p. 727 Bonn).
[6] This move of Basil I's was, on the face of it, a volte face. At the Ecumenical Council that had met in Constantinople in A.D. 869–70 on Basil I's initiative, the Emperor had seen to it that the Papal legates should be outvoted by the representatives of all four eastern patriarchates when the Council was asked by the Bulgarian Government for a judgement on the question whether Bulgaria's ecclesiastical allegiance ought to be given to the See of Rome or to the See of Constantinople. In 879, Basil persuaded the Papal legates, and no doubt ordered the Ecumenical Patriarch, to accept him as arbitrator. Presumably, when he gave his judgement in Rome's favour, he was aware that Bulgaria was not going to act on it.

clergy who had been expelled from Moravia in 885.[1] Borís, like the Eastern Orthodox Christian princes in the Caucasus, was evidently content to let sleeping dogs lie; but his son and second successor Symeon (*regnabat/imperabat* 893–927) raised the political issue, with tragic results for all parties eventually.

In 913—immediately after the Emperor Alexander's death and the beginning of Constantine Porphyrogenitus's first reign as sole Emperor—Symeon went to war with the East Roman Empire for the second time, reached the land-walls of Constantinople, and did not withdraw till he had obtained from the Ecumenical Patriarch Nikólaos, the president of the board of regency that was acting for the child-Emperor, a promise of an Imperial marriage—perhaps a promise that one of Symeon's daughters should eventually become Constantine Porphyrogenitus's wife. It looks as if Symeon was planning to do what was actually done, six and seven years later, by Rhomanós Lekapênós. (Symeon's abortive move may, indeed, have put the idea into Rhomanós's head.) If Symeon had been able to obtain confirmation of his acceptance at Constantinople as Constantine's future father-in-law, this would have given him a leverage for installing himself as president of the board of regents in the Patriarch's place, and from this it would have been a short step to transforming himself from a regent into a co-Emperor who would have been virtually sole Emperor as the colleague of a minor. This plan of Symeon's—if he did so plan[2]—miscarried. After Symeon's withdrawal from East Roman territory, Constantine's mother Zoe succeeded in wresting the Imperial Government out of the Patriarch Nikólaos's hands, and she repudiated

---

[1] See p. 359.

[2] For this interpretation of Symeon's stipulations in 913–14, see Runciman, op. cit., p. 157, with Appendix X. The evidence for this plan of Symeon's is slight. In a letter of Nikólaos's (No. 16, col. 112), addressed to Symeon in the winter of 920/1, after Rhomanós Lekapênós had been crowned vasiléfs, Nikólaos reminds Symeon that Symeon had once asked for an Imperial marriage-alliance and that his request had been refused. Nikólaos does not say who was to have married whom, and he does not give the date. His meeting with Symeon when Symeon was investing Constantinople in 913 is, no doubt, the most likely occasion. According to *Georg. Mon. Cont.*, p. 878, Leo Grammaticus, p. 292, and *Theoph. Cont.*, p. 385, Nikólaos crowned Symeon at this meeting, but with the Patriarch's own cowl (ἐπιριπτήριον), not with a crown or a diadem. None of these versions of the Byzantine Chronicle states whether this coronation was genuine or sham, or whether the Patriarch crowned the Khan as 'Caesar' or as 'Emperor of the Romans' or as 'Emperor of the Bulgars' or just as 'Emperor'. The one thing certain is that Nikólaos made some promise or performed some act that induced Symeon to raise his siege of Constantinople without attempting to storm the triple land-wall (which, anyway, would have been beyond Symeon's power). Nikólaos may have achieved this result by speaking or acting in bad faith, and he and the chroniclers may not have divulged just how far he had gone in order to weather the emergency with which he had had to cope in 913. See *C. Med. H.*, vol. iv, 2nd ed., Part I, p. 135 (Grégoire) and pp. 505–6 (Obolensky). For Nikólaos Mystikós's correspondence on Bulgarian affairs, see Obolensky in loc. cit., p. 506, n. 2, and Vlasto, op. cit., chap. 4, n. 75 on p. 373. There are 29 extant letters on Bulgarian affairs, 26 of which are addressed to Symeon. They are printed in Migne, *P.G.*, vol. cxi, cols. 40–196. Vlasto, in loc. cit., draws particular attention to letter No. 18 of 921 and letter No. 28 of 925.

Nikólaos's promise (whatever this may have been) to Symeon, at the price of prolonging the Romano-Bulgarian war for fourteen more years.

On a long view, it would have been best for the East Roman Empire, as well as for Bulgaria and for Eastern Orthodox Christendom as a whole, if Symeon had succeeded in forestalling Rhomanós Lekapênós in insinuating himself on to the Imperial throne at Constantinople. As an East Roman Emperor, Symeon would have been acceptable to East Roman public opinion, for, though he was an alien by birth, he was a Byzantine by education and by predilection. Symeon had been brought up in Constantinople. He seems to have lived in the Imperial Palace and to have attended the Caesar Várdhas's university in the Maghnávra, as well as the Patriarch Phótios's school of Slavonic studies. His addiction to Byzantine culture had earned him the nickname 'semi-Greek' ($\dot{\eta}\mu\dot{\iota}\alpha\rho\gamma\circ\varsigma$) ;[1] and, when he had come to the throne in Bulgaria, he had not only promoted the translation of Christian Greek literary works into the literary form of the Macedonian Slavonic dialect that had been created by the Thessalonian missionaries Constantine-Cyril and Methódhios; he had made some of these translations himself.[2] Symeon the Bulgar was more highly cultivated than his successful competitor Rhomanós Lekapênós, the self-made East Roman from the Armeniac army-corps district. He would have been at least as well equipped for playing an East Roman Emperor's role as the provincial Rhomanós or the 'displaced persons' Basil I and Leo III. If Symeon had succeeded in uniting the East Roman Empire with Bulgaria in a personal union, the opposition would have been likely to come, not from his East Roman subjects, but from his Bulgar fellow-countrymen. As the legitimate representative of the Bulgarian dynasty, Symeon would probably have got the better of his Bulgar opponents—to judge by the success of his father Borís and his son Peter in dealing with attempted revolutions. In that event, his reign might have seen the beginnings of a fusion between the East Roman Empire and Bulgaria with a minimum of resistance and of bloodshed.

When the possibility of a union of the two crowns on Symeon's head had been ruled out by Rhomanós Lekapênós's acquisition of the East Roman crown, the next best settlement was the compromise, outlined above, that was negotiated in 927 between Rhomanós and Symeon's son and successor Peter. Unhappily the coexistence of two empires, each with a tame patriarchate of its own, could not be a permanent solution for the problem of Romano-Bulgarian relations. The East Roman Empire had inherited, and the Bulgarian Empire had acquired from it, the ideology of the Roman Empire of Augustus and Diocletian and

---

[1] 'Hunc etenim Simeonem emiargon, id est semigrecum, esse aiebant' (Liutprand, *Antapodosis*, Book III, chap. 19).

[2] See p. 522, n. 3.

Constantine I. Any empire that claimed to be the Roman Empire's heir was thereby committing itself to claiming to be a world-state; and, while there had been just room enough for the East Roman Empire to coexist for a few decades with Charlemagne's Western Roman Empire at the other end of Europe, there was not room for the permanent coexistence of two world-states interlocked with each other within the bounds of the Balkan Peninsula.

So long as the East Roman Empress of Bulgaria, María, lived, the compromise that her grandfather had negotiated with her husband worked. Its working was facilitated by an annual subsidy that the East Roman Government now paid to the Bulgarian Government under the 'face-saving' label of a personal allowance to María from her family. The Emperor Rhomanós I was sincerely anxious to preserve the peace with Bulgaria that he had re-established with such difficulty. The still more unwarlike Constantine Porphyrogenitus might disapprove on paper of his wife's niece María Lekapênê's unsuitable marriage,[1] but in practice he was glad to profit by it when, in 945, the deposition of his Lekapenid colleagues had left him solely responsible for conducting the Empire's foreign policy. Constantine did nothing to disturb the peace of which this marriage, and the financial arrangements that went with it, were the guarantee, and, if he had outlived María, he would have felt anxious.

The peace was, in fact, preserved until María's death in 965. Thereupon the Emperor Peter was so ill-advised as to demand from the East Roman Government a continuance of his deceased wife's annual allowance on the ground that it was 'a customary tribute'. Peter now had to deal with the Emperor Nikêphóros II Phokás; and Nikêphóros II was not Constantine Porphyrogenitus, as the East Roman officials pointed out to Otto I's ambassador Liutprand in A.D. 968.[2] The consequence was half a century of devastating and exhausting warfare. The year 972 saw the extinction of the Bulgarian Empire and the abolition of the Bulgarian Patriarchate. The co-extensive domains of the East Roman Empire and the Ecumenical Patriarchate now stretched northwards up to the line of the lower Danube for the first time for 370 years. The year 1018 saw the final overthrow and annexation of the West Bulgarian power that had arisen in 976 in the extinguished Bulgarian Empire's derelict western territories.

In this fifth trial of strength between the East Roman Empire and Bulgaria,[3] the East Roman Empire was bound to emerge as the victor in

---

[1] See pp. 16–17.   [2] See pp. 18 and 67.

[3] The first bout had been between the Emperor Constantine V and a series of Bulgar khans; the second had been between Khan Krum and the Emperor Nikêphóros I; the third had been between Khan Symeon and the Emperor Leo VI; the fourth had been between the Khan-Emperor Symeon and the Emperor Rhomanós I Lekapênós.

the limited and elusive military sense. Since 924, when Symeon had been foiled by the fortifications of Constantinople for the third time,[1] the East Roman Government had been taking advantage of the truce on its Balkan front to establish its ascendency over the declining power of the Eastern Muslims and to destroy the Western Muslims' stronghold in Crete. By 965, when the Emperor Peter delivered his rash challenge, Nikêphóros II had his hands free to concentrate against Bulgaria a military strength for which she was no match. On a wider view, however, the outcome of this fifty-two-years-long war (966–1018) was a defeat for both the two principal states of the Byzantine World, and therefore a defeat for the Byzantine Society itself. In the end, Bulgaria was incorporated in the East Roman Empire by the 'methods of barbarism' by which Saxony had been incorporated in the Carolingian Empire; and the social consequences were more serious because, in Basil II 'the Bulgar-killer's' and Tsar Samuel's war, the two contending states were better organized for bleeding each other and themselves white than the Franks and Saxons had been two hundred years earlier. This eventual solution of the problem of Romano-Bulgarian relations was by far the worst of the three alternatives. It was worse than the possible peaceful union under the Emperor Symeon which had remained unachieved, and it was worse than the coexistence, negotiated between the Emperor Rhomanós I and the Emperor Peter, which had broken down.

Meanwhile, the protocol reflecting the compromise of A.D. 927 was observed punctiliously at the East Roman Court, and the observance of it survived the rupture of 965, as Liutprand found, to his annoyance, in 968.

One consequence, in the sphere of protocol, of the East Roman recognition of the sovereign of Bulgaria as the only emperor in the World besides the East Roman Emperor himself was that Bulgarian ambassadors now took precedence over all others except the legates of the Roman See.[2]

---

[1] The two previous occasions had been in 913 and in 922.

[2] Though the Pope and his legates are given precedence over all other potentates and all other envoys in the protocol of the East Roman Imperial Government, His Holiness can hardly have been content with the terms in which he is described. In answer to the legates' greetings, the Imperial loghothétês asks: 'How is the most holy Bishop of Rome, the spiritual father of our holy Emperor?' (*De Caer.*, Book II, chap. 47, p. 680); and the form of East Roman address to the Pope is: 'To the most holy Pope of Rome, our spiritual father'. Moreover, the golden bull attached to a letter to the Pope is worth only one solidus (p. 686) or, at most, two solidi (p. 688). Two solidi is the lowest stated value of the bull attached to a letter addressed to any potentate (e.g. the Kouropalátês of Iberia, the Exousiokrátor of Alania, the ruler of Sardinia). The Patriarchs of Alexandria, Antioch, and Jerusalem get bulls worth three solidi each. The Caliph (ὁ πρωτοσύμβουλος, i.e. 'the President of the Council') and the Amīr of Egypt get bulls worth four solidi each (pp. 686 and 689). 'The bull attached to the letter sent [to the Amīr of Egypt] by the Porphyrogénnetoi Constantine and Rhomanós weighed eighteen exáyia' (p. 189). These figures reveal the Pope's real rating at the East Roman Court.

The precedence of the Roman See's representation over all other foreign envoys is expressly established by Philótheos,[1] and it is also indicated by the Roman See's being given first place both in Constantine Porphyrogenitus's schedule of formulas for greetings to the Empire by envoys from divers nations (together with the respective responses of the loghothétês tou dhrómou)[2] and in his converse schedule of forms of address by the Imperial Government to foreign rulers.[3]

In the first of these two schedules, Bulgaria comes next after the Roman See. In the second schedule, Bulgaria does not have even the second place. She comes below all the Eastern Orthodox patriarchates; below the Muslim potentates, greater and lesser; below the princelings of Armenia, Caucasia, and Western Christendom, for instance 'the Kinglet of Saxony' (ῥῆγα Σαξωνίας); and even below the Doge of Venice and the rulers of the six autonomous principalities attached to the East Roman army-corps district of Laghouvardhía.[4] It is significant, however, that, in this second context, Constantine gives, in addition to the original formula, a revised one that corresponds to the concessions made to Bulgaria in the compromise of 927.[5] The original formula is:

To the God-appointed ruler (ἄρχοντα) of Bulgaria: 'In the name of the Father, the Son, and the Holy Spirit, our one and only true God: we, Constantine and Rhomanós [II],[6] Emperors of the Romans, true believers in the selfsame God, to our well-beloved spiritual son the God-appointed ruler (ἄρχοντα) of the most Christian nation of the Bulgars.'[7]

This is almost the same formula as is used in the Imperial loghothétês's response to the Bulgarian envoys' greetings: 'How is our holy Emperor's spiritual grandson [subsequently changed to 'son'] the God-appointed ruler of Bulgaria?'[8]

But, in the schedule of forms of address, Constantine has added, after giving the original formula: 'The present-day version is: "Constantine and Rhomanós [II], pious autocrat Emperors in Christ our God, to our well-beloved spiritual son the lord so-and-so *Emperor* of Bulgaria."'[9]

The increase in the degree of the respect that the East Roman Government felt it politic to pay to the Bulgarian Government can be traced in

---

[1] In *De Caer.*, Book II, chap. 52, p. 739 Bonn, p. 155 Bury.

[2] *De Caer.*, Book II, chap. 47, pp. 680–6.

[3] Op. cit., Book II, chap. 48, pp. 686–92.

[4] The Prince of Benevento, the most important of the three South Lombard principalities, is omitted from the list ibid., p. 690.

[5] See J. B. Bury, 'The Ceremonial Book of Constantine Porphyrogenitus', in *The English Historical Review*, no. lxxxvi (April 1907), pp. 209–27, on p. 226, n. 49.

[6] The association of these two names with the original formula suggests that the formula was not revised till 945, at the earliest. This point, and the difficulties in the way of accepting the later date, have been noticed on p. 361, n. 1.

[7] *De Caer.*, Book II, chap. 48, p. 690.

[8] Op. cit., Book II, chap. 47, pp. 681–2.   [9] Op. cit., Book II, chap. 48, p. 690.

the records of the seating of the guests of honour at Imperial banquets on state occasions.

In 968 the Bulgarian ambassador's precedence over all other foreign envoys (always excepting Papal legates, no doubt, if these were present) was being stiffly upheld by the East Roman Imperial officials, as Otto I's envoy Liutprand discovered. After having been seated fifteen places away from the Emperor at one banquet,[1] Liutprand left the room when, at another banquet, he found himself placed below a Bulgarian ambassador 'with his head cropped like an Hungarian and a brass chain doing duty for a belt'.[2]

Liutprand was unaware of the status accorded to Bulgaria by East Roman protocol, and he also did not take the point that his Bulgarian colleague's appearance in Bulgar national dress was a deliberate act of national self-assertion, and that the East Roman officials' acquiescence in this gave the measure of the extent to which they felt it necessary to humour the Empire's formidable Bulgarian neighbours.[3] This was a conspicuous and disagreeable exception to the otherwise rigidly enforced rule that anyone, East Roman or foreign, who was to appear in the Emperor's presence must wear the change of clothes ($\dot{a}\lambda\lambda\dot{a}\xi\iota\mu\rho\nu$), or the successive changes ($\dot{a}\lambda\lambda\alpha\xi\iota\mu\alpha\tau\alpha$ [sic]), prescribed for that person, according to his rank.[4] Even Muslim envoys or visitors, who in other respects were treated almost as deferentially as Bulgar envoys and visitors, had to appear in white, without belts, and properly shod.[5] By contrast, the Bulgars had the privilege of retaining their national costume.[6] When Liutprand took offence, he was betraying his ignorance of these niceties of East Roman protocol. As he left the room, the Emperor's brother, the kouropalátês and grand loghothétês Leo, with the protonotários Symeon, ran after Liutprand, shouting at him that the Bulgarian ambassador enjoyed precedence over all other foreign envoys by treaty right, and that the present Bulgarian ambassador, in spite of his cropped head, unwashed body, and brass chain, was nevertheless a patríkios and must therefore take precedence over a bishop—especially a bishop who was also a Frank. They would not let Liutprand come back. They sent him off to take his dinner in the servants' hall.[7]

Before the agreement of 927, Bulgarian envoys had not enjoyed this unique precedence. In the standard order of seating of foreign envoys at an Imperial banquet at the close of the ninth century, as set out by Philótheos,[8] the foreign clergy take first place among them, the Roman clergy have precedence, with the clergy of the three eastern patriarchates

---

[1] *Legatio*, chap. 11.   [2] *Op. cit.*, chap. 19.   [3] *De Caer.*, Book II, chap. 52, p. 768.
[4] See the inventory of alláxima [sic] in *De Caer.*, Book II, chap. 41.
[5] Philótheos in *De Caer.*, Book II, chap. 52, pp. 743 and 768 Bonn, pp. 157 and 169 Bury.
[6] Ibid., p. 768 Bonn, p. 169 Bury.   [7] *Legatio*, chap. 19.
[8] In *De Caer.*, Book II, chap. 52, pp. 739–40 Bonn, 155–6 Bury.

coming next and the clergy of the Ecumenical Patriarchate coming below the foreign clergy, out of courtesy. All the clergy take precedence over guests of the rank of máyistroi, but the Archbishop of Bulgaria comes below the sýnkelloi of all the patriarchates, and only just above the eunuch patríkioi and the governor of the Anatolic army-corps district.[1] Among the lay envoys the Muslims take first place (the Eastern Muslims ranking higher than their Western co-religionists). 'The Hun, i.e. Bulgar, envoys' take second place. Only the Franks are placed below them. All the lay envoys have to wait for their dinner till the second service, but they rank with patríkioi and with governors of East Roman army-corps districts.

This was the Bulgarian envoys' place at the close of the ninth century in the standard order of precedence for the seating at Imperial banquets. At particular banquets the Bulgars came off well. The test of an ambassador's status was whether he was seated among the guests of honour at the great golden table, and, if he was, what place he was given there. At the Imperial banquet on the Feast of Pentecost,

> If ambassadors of great powers happen to be at Court, and if the Emperor invites them to dinner, the little golden table is placed above, where the [golden] *pendapýryion*[2] stands, and the Emperor sits at that, while the ambassadors sit at the great golden table.[3]

At the banquet on Christmas Day, however, at the close of the ninth century, when Philótheos was compiling his table of precedence, two Bulgarian envoys were included among the twelve eminent guests, representing the twelve Apostles, who were seated at the Emperor's own table.[4] At the banquet on Easter Day the two Bulgarian envoys were not included among the fourteen guests seated at the Emperor's own table, but they were among the thirty seated at the great golden table on this occasion.[5] The Easter Day protocol was repeated at the banquets on the third and the sixth day of the week after Easter.[6] At the reception before the banquet on the sixth day, the Bulgarian ambassadors presented

---

[1] Philótheos, *De Caer.*, Book II, chap. 52, p. 727 Bonn, p. 146 Bury.

[2] A glorified 'dumb-waiter'.

[3] *De Caer.*, Book I, chap. 9, p. 70. This passage gives the protocol at the banquet on the Feast of Pentecost at the time when Constantine Porphyrogenitus was writing, which may have been in the sixth decade of the tenth century. But we may guess that the Emperor normally dined at a separate table of his own on most occasions at all dates. According to Philótheos in *De Caer.*, Book II, chap. 52, pp. 726–7 Bonn, pp. 145–6 Bury, the only dignitaries who dined with the Emperors at their majesties' separate (ἀποκοπτῇ) table were the Patriarch of Constantinople, a caesar, a novelísimos, a kouropalátês, a vasileopátor, and a belted patríkia. Normally, therefore, ambassadors will not have been admitted to this ultra-select company. However, Liutprand seems to have dined at Constantine Porphyrogenitus's own table in 949 and at Nikêphóros II's in 968.

[4] Philótheos in *De Caer.*, Book II, chap. 52, p. 742 Bonn, p. 157 Bury.

[5] Op. cit., cap. cit., pp. 766–7 Bonn, p. 168 Bury.

[6] Op. cit., cap. cit., pp. 769 and 771 Bonn, 169 and 170 Bury.

their gifts, and, after this day's proceedings, they were not seen again. They were not invited to the banquet on the Sunday after Easter, and, on the Tuesday following, they were packed off home,[1] and the Court was relieved of their presence.

The truth is that the Bulgar envoys' company was not relished by their East Roman hosts any more than it was by their Frankish colleague Liutprand. They were honoured solely for East Roman reasons of state; and it is evident that, though they were not given such high precedence before A.D. 927 as after the agreement arrived at in that year, they were already being treated with considerable respect in the ninth century. We may guess that this exceptionally indulgent treatment of Bulgar envoys at the East Roman Court was a consequence of the events of 811–13, when Khan Krum and his men had destroyed an East Roman army, killed the hapless Emperor Nikêphóros I himself, captured Mesêmvría, Dheveltós, and Adrianople, and deported Adrianople's inhabitants. After this East Roman disaster, it must have become clear to the East Romans that the Bulgars were neighbours who could not be treated cavalierly.

A ninth-century incident which illustrates both the indulgence of the East Romans to Bulgar envoys and their dislike of them is recorded by Constantine in his biography of his grandfather the Emperor Basil I. This incident was trivial in itself, but it was historic in its political consequences. It gave the strong-limbed young groom from Adrianople his opening for hewing his blood-bespattered path to the Imperial throne.

One day the patríkios and dhoméstikos ton Skholón Andíghonos set up a banquet on a sumptuous scale in the Imperial apartments containing the [banqueting-]hall adjoining the Imperial Palace, and invited his own father Várdhas to be the guest of honour at the dinner. The Caesar went to the feast, bringing with him the more important members of the Senate and his own personal friends and companions. He brought along, too, the ambassadors from Bulgaria, who were customarily resident in the Imperial City at that season of the year. One of the guests was Basil's master Theóphilos in virtue of his, too, being a kinsman of the Caesar's. Another guest was the patríkios Constantine, the father of the patríkios Thomas, who in our reign is loghothétês tou dhrómou and is distinguished for his prowess in philosophy and for his financial integrity.

The Bulgars have the national failing of being conceited and boastful. On this occasion they happened to have with them a countryman of theirs who had a reputation for physical hardiness and who was a first-class wrestler. Up till then, he had hardly ever been thrown by anyone who had tried a fall with him. The Bulgarian ambassadors displayed an insufferable pride in this champion of theirs. They went beyond the limit in their insolence.

[1] Op. cit., cap. cit., pp. 773–4 Bonn, 171 Bury.

As the drink went its rounds and the atmosphere at the table became lively, Theóphilos said to the Caesar: 'Your highness, I have a man who will do the trick if you will give the word for him to take on this fabulous Bulgar. If the fellow goes home to Bulgaria unbeaten, it will be a terrible disgrace for the Romans, and the Bulgars' insolence will increase beyond all bearing.' The Caesar gave the order, and the aforementioned patríkios Constantine, who was extremely well disposed towards Basil because he was himself of the same Armenian origin, now did Basil a good turn. Constantine noticed that the place where the match was to take place was swimming in water, and he was afraid that Basil might perhaps slip, so he asked the Caesar to have it seen to that the surface should be sprinkled with sawdust. When this had been done, Basil closed with the Bulgar, quickly squeezed him in a paralysing grip, lifted him off the ground, and hurled him on to the table as easily as if he had been as light as a sheaf of desiccated hay or a flock of dry wool.

This feat won for Basil the warm admiration of the whole company. As for the Bulgars, they were dumbfounded at the superlativeness of Basil's dexterity and strength. It struck them dumb. From that day onwards, Basil's reputation began to spread all over the City at an increasing tempo. His name was on everyone's lips. He had already become a marked man.[1]

Basil was profiting by the Bulgars' unpopularity. In the World as seen with East Roman eyes, Bulgaria, pagan or Orthodox, was always a blot on the landscape. It was, though, much too big a blot to be ignored. Already, in the chronicles of Theophanes and the Patriarch Nikêphóros, Bulgaria receives as much notice as the mighty Arab Empire,[2] yet Nikêphóros had laid down his pen before reaching the year 811, while Theophanes, who does carry his record down to the East Roman Empire's disastrous collision with Khan Krum, lived to witness only this first demonstration of Bulgaria's waxing strength. Khan Symeon (893–927) revealed Bulgaria's full potentialities. Constantine Porphyrogenitus, who had grown to manhood during the Romano-Bulgarian war of 913–27, was well aware that the presence of Bulgaria, within point-blank range of Constantinople and of the Empire's continental European thémata, was the Empire's most importunate problem. Constantine's

---

[1] Constantine Porphyrogenitus, Biography of Basil I, chap. 12, in *Theoph. Cont.*, Book V, pp. 229–30; cf. Kedhrénós, vol. ii, pp. 193–4. This incident had already been recorded by Genesius, Book IV, pp. 110–11, with one difference. Genesius makes Basil throw, on this occasion, not a Bulgar but the winner in a match between wrestlers in the service of Michael and Várdhas. Genesius gives the name of the particular hold to which Basil resorted (τῇ κατὰ πόδρεζαν προσπλοκῇ, ὡς ὁ ἐπιχώριος λόγος). Genesius makes Basil throw the Bulgar champion after he had become sole Emperor, and accordingly makes him enter the ring incognito this time (Book IV, p. 127). Constantine's version of the story is the more convincing of the two. Even if the true date of this physical feat of Basil's is 856, not 867 or after, the incident, if historical, bears out Adontz's contention that the date of Basil's birth was 836, not 813 or earlier. (See N. Adontz, 'L'Âge et l'origine de l'empereur Basile I', in *Byzantion*, vol. viii (1933), pp. 475–500.)

[2] Ostrogorsky, 'The Byzantine Empire in the World of the Seventh Century', p. 15.

grandson, Basil II, resolved to rid the Empire of a problem that, by his time, had been besetting the Empire for three hundred years. His drastic solution was as fatal for the Empire as it was for Bulgaria.

From first to last, the East Romans looked down upon the Bulgars as barbarians, in contrast to their respect for the Eastern Muslims, whom they recognized as being their cultural equals, in spite of their being the militant champions of a religion that was Christianity's opponent and rival. Yet, after the conversion of the Bulgars to Christianity in 864 and their decision in 870 to embrace Christianity in its Eastern Orthodox and not in its Western form, the East Romans felt that their Bulgar barbarian fellow Orthodox Christians were linked with them by a closer moral bond than the Western barbarian Christian deviationists.

The Emperor Leo VI wrote Part Eighteen of his *Taktiká* after the Romano-Bulgarian war of 894-6,[1] which Leo had brought on himself by his own impolitic behaviour. In this context, Leo concedes that, though the ex-nomad Bulgars are in other respects birds of the same feather as the abominable nomad Magyars, they are distinguishable from the Magyars 'in so far as, thanks to their adoption of the Christian faith, they have also modified their standards of conduct (ἤθεσι) by adopting East Roman standards in place of their own to some slight extent. In shedding their paganism they have shed, with it, some of the savagery of their nomad tradition.'[2]

In an earlier passage, cited already, of the same part of his *Taktiká*, Leo VI goes farther. He deliberately refrains from describing the tactics that the Bulgars and the East Romans employ against each other; and the reason that he gives for this omission is that the two peoples 'are brothers in virtue of the identity of their religious faith' (διὰ τῆς μίας πίστεως), and therefore 'we have no intention of arming for war against the Bulgars'.[3] This omission is the more remarkable in view of the fact that, in the same part of his *Taktiká*, Leo does describe the military practice of the Western Christian barbarians (the Franks and the Southern Lombards) and also discusses the East Roman practice that is appropriate for dealing with both the strong and the weak points in the Frankish way of waging war.[4] Leo opens his sub-section on the Franks and Lombards by protesting[5] that the East Romans have no intention of attacking them. 'There is no question of this, considering that they are at peace with us and are our allies[6] and co-religionists (ὁμοθρήσκων) and

---

[1] In his *Taktiká*, Dhiat. 18, § 42, col. 956, Leo mentions the Magyars' military co-operation with the East Romans in 895.

[2] Leo VI, *Taktiká*, Dhiat. 18, § 61, col. 960.

[3] Leo VI, *Taktiká*, Dhiat. 18, § 44, col. 957. See the present chapter of the present work, p. 364.

[4] Leo, Dhiat. 18, §§ 78-98, cols. 964-8.   [5] Leo, Dhiat. 18, § 78, col. 964.

[6] i.e. the Franks.

subjects.'[1] However, in this case Leo does not impose on himself the silence that he maintains about the conduct of hostilities between the East Romans and the Bulgars. He does go into details about the conduct of possible hostilities between the East Romans and the Franks.

We need not question the sincerity of Leo VI's profession of benevolent intentions towards all of the East Roman Empire's Christian neighbours. An observer writing at the turn of the ninth and tenth centuries could not have foreseen the Romano-Bulgarian wars of 913–27, 966–72, and 976–1018; still less could he have foreboded the irruption of the Normans into the Mediterranean or the taking and sacking of Constantinople in 1204 by Latin 'crusaders' among whom the East Roman Empire's Venetian ex-subjects would be the moving spirits.

[1] i.e. the Southern Lombards.

3. Relations with the Eastern Muslims

IN area, the Bulgarian Empire, at its widest extent, was no larger than a single one of the major provinces of the 'Abbasid Caliphate of Baghdad, which, in Constantine Porphyrogenitus's time, was the East Roman Empire's immediate neighbour in the opposite quarter to the Empire's Bulgarian front. Nominally, the 'Abbasid Caliphate still extended, at this date, from the lower Indus and the upper Jaxartes on the east to the western borders of Egypt. It was thus, on paper, by far the largest empire in the contemporary world, and it was also the most populous; for, though it included the deserts of Arabia and Central Iran, it also included the irrigated alluvial lands of 'Irāq and Egypt; and, at this date, 'Irāq, as well as Egypt, was still one of the most productive agricultural regions in the whole of the Old World.

Throughout this vast extent of territory, parts of it highly fertile, the 'Abbasid Caliph's name was still being mentioned in the place of honour in the *khutbah* (the Friday bidding-prayer), and the local rulers were governing in the Caliph's name in virtue (so they professed) of certificates of legitimacy that they had obtained from him. The upkeep of these formalities was evidence of the 'Abbasid Caliphate's enduring prestige. By this time, however, the real state of affairs in the territories that had once been ruled effectively from Baghdad bore little resemblance to the theory which was being maintained by both the Caliph and his supplanters for their respective purposes. Since before the close of the eighth century, one province after another, beginning with those in North-West Africa and in Eastern Iran and Central Asia, had been passing out of the 'Abbasid Government's effective control *de facto*, until its writ had virtually ceased to run anywhere beyond the boundaries of the metropolitan province, 'Irāq, itself; and, even here since 945, the Caliph's government had been under the control of the Buwayhid dynasty from Daylām, the westernmost of the Iranian provinces along the south coast of the Caspian Sea. The Buwayhids were exercising their mastery over the Caliph by professing to be executing his commands as his legally appointed humble servants.

The political disruption of the Islamic World was aggravated by the recrudescence of a religious schism that had originated in a political conflict. 'Alī, the fourth of the Prophet Muhammad's khalīfahs (i.e. the inheritors of his political, as distinct from his religious, powers) had been the last of those whose legitimacy was recognized by all Muslims retrospectively. ('Alī was not recognized universally in his own lifetime.)

'Alī's partisans claimed, on his behalf, that he and his descendants were the Prophet Muhammad's sole legitimate heirs in virtue of 'Alī's having been the Prophet Muhammad's cousin and 'Alī's wife Fātimah's having been the Prophet's daughter. To begin with, this party had been worsted and had been driven underground. As a minority, it was branded as 'the Shi'ah' (i.e. 'the sect') by the majority, who claimed to be 'Sunnis' (i.e. 'walkers in the beaten track'). 'Alī's Umayyad opponent and successor Mu'āwīyah and his descendants had, of course, been Sunnis, but so were the 'Abbasids, who, in 750, had supplanted the Umayyads by force in all the Umayyads' dominions except Andalusia. Politically, 'Abbasids and Umayyads were at daggers drawn; in 929, 'Abdarrahman III, the Umayyad amīr at Cordoba, formally reassumed the title of 'Caliph' that his ancestors had borne at Damascus before 750; but, on the issue between Sunnah and Shi'ah, there was no difference of opinion between Umayyads and 'Abbasids.

However, the 'Abbasids' progressive loss of grip had given the Shi'ah its chance to raise its head. A number of the usurpers who had seized power in outlying parts of the 'Abbasid dominions had been Shi'is: e.g. the Idrisids, who, in 788, had established themselves in Morocco; the 'Fātimids' who, in 909, had established themselves in the rest of North-West Africa, and were now poised to swoop down from there upon Egypt; the 'Fātimids'' fellow Isma'ili (Seven-Imam) Shi'is the Carmathians, who had been terrorizing Syria and 'Irāq from their fastnesses in Arabia since the close of the ninth century; and finally the Buwayhids. These latter were adherents of some different sect of the Shi'ah,[1] and there was no co-operation between the several Shi'i powers; but their emergence had been more damaging to the 'Abbasid Caliphate than the emergence of local Sunni usurpers had been; for all the Shi'i powers except the Buwayhids denied the 'Abbasids' legitimacy, and the Buwayhids recognized this only with their tongues in their cheeks, as a device for ruling 'Irāq in the 'Abbasids' name.

Before the close of the ninth century, the 'Abbasid government at Baghdad had ceased to be able either to assert its authority effectively over the local rulers of the provinces or to aid the rulers of frontier provinces effectively in the warfare between these and their non-Muslim neighbours. Yet these local rulers, though now left to fend for themselves, had been displaying a remarkable vigour and vitality. The two strongest of the Muslim principalities that were the East Roman Empire's immediate neighbours were Tarsūs (Tarsós), on the East Cilician plain, and Malatīyah, on the principal western affluent of the Upper Euphrates. Each of these two minor Muslim powers was well placed strategically for invading the East Roman Empire's Asiatic territories. Tarsós lay close to

[1] See p. 477, n. 5.

the south-eastern end of the Cilician Gates; Malatīyah lay on the high road from the Tigris valley to Kaisáreia, the most important city in Eastern Asia Minor.

After the break-up of the 'Abbasid Caliphate *de facto*, its successor-states at Tarsós and Malatīyah were bound to succumb to the East Roman Empire sooner or later. They were too small, and their situation was too dangerously exposed, to allow them to hold their own permanently. Their inevitable fall was, however, postponed by two successive pieces of good fortune.

The first of these was the East Roman Government's decision, after its final abandonment of iconoclasm in 843, to complete the re-establishment of religious uniformity in the Empire by suppressing the Paulician religion, which had a considerable following in the Empire's eastern marches, just to the north of the Muslim principality of Malatīyah. The Imperial Government's intolerance, and the brutality with which it pursued its policy of repression, threw the Paulicians into the Malatīyah Muslims' arms, and these took advantage of this favourable situation that had been created for them by the East Roman Government's religious fanaticism. Malatīyah gave asylum to the Paulician resistance movement, and, from bases in this Muslim territory, the Paulicians were able to establish fortified posts in their own country on the East Roman side of the frontier.[1] With the Malatīyah Muslims thus supporting the Paulicians, the war dragged on; and, though the Emperor Basil I made a determined effort to win it after he had got rid of Michael III in 867,[2] he was foiled. When, in 871/2, he reached the walls of the Paulicians' principal fortress Tephrikĕ (Divrig), he found it too strong for him to venture to attempt an assault,[3] and, when he invaded the territory of Malatīyah, he fought shy, here too, of attempting to storm the fortifications of the city.[4] The war was brought to an end by the death of the Paulicians' leader Khrysókheir on the field of battle in 872.[5] After that, Tephrikĕ was evacuated by the Paulicians, and the whole of their country, up to the northern frontier of the principality of Malatīyah, had been reoccupied by the East Roman forces by *circa* 875.[6]

---

[1] See *Theoph. Cont.*, Book IV, Reign of Michael III, chaps. 16–17, pp. 165–8; Kedhrênós, vol. ii, pp. 153–5.

[2] For this phase of the Romano-Paulician war, see *Georg. Mon. Cont.*, Reign of Basil I, chap. 6, p. 841; Leo Grammaticus, p. 258; pseudo-Symeon, Reign of Basil I, chaps. 13 and 15, p. 692; Genesius, *Basileíai* (Bonn, 1834, Weber), Book IV, pp. 115 and 120–6; Constantine Porphyrogenitus in *Theoph. Cont.*, Book V, chaps. 36–43, pp. 266–76. The poorness of Basil's military performance is glozed over by Constantine's employee Genesius and by Constantine himself.   [3] *Theoph. Cont.*, chap. 37, p. 267.   [4] Op. cit., chap. 40, p. 270.

[5] Op. cit., chap. 43, pp. 274–6. Genesius, Book IV, pp. 122–6, gives a vivid account of the campaign in which Khrysókheir met his death. This account goes into details and must have been derived from a first-hand report.

[6] Qudāmah, writing *circa* 930, reproaches the Muslims of Malatīyah for having failed to save the Paulicians from being driven out by the East Romans. The consequent territorial

The Muslim border principalities owed their second respite to the aggressive policy of Bulgaria towards the East Roman Empire during Symeon's reign. The East Roman Empire had to concentrate its military efforts on its Bulgarian front from 894, the year in which Symeon started the first of his two wars against the Empire, till 924, the last year of active operations in his second war. In this latter year, Symeon reached the land-wall of Constantinople for the third time and had a conference with the Emperor Rhomanós I on the south-west shore of the Golden Horn just outside Vlakhérnai.[1] The talks were inconclusive, but, after this third experience of Constantinople's impregnability, Symeon turned his arms against the East Roman Empire's allies on his opposite flank, the Serbs and the Croats, and, though in 925 he overcame the Serbs, he was heavily defeated by the Croats in 926, and he died in 927. Thus, in effect, the East Roman Empire was relieved from pressure on its Bulgarian front after 924, though a peace settlement was not concluded till 927, after Symeon's death.[2] After 924, therefore, the East Roman Government had its hands free, at last, to take the offensive against its Muslim adversaries on the south-east, Malatīyah and Tarsós.

Of the two, Tarsós proved to be the hardest nut to crack. The annual springtime raids from Tarsós through the Cilician Gates into East Roman territory had become an Islamic institution after the Muslims had given up hope of making permanent conquests beyond the Távros, and, till after the close of Constantine Porphyrogenitus's reign, the only substantial East Roman success in this quarter was the conquest, in 956, of Adhatá, a frontier fort which Constantine's grandfather Basil I had tried and failed to take.[3]

On the Malatīyah front the East Roman offensive produced its results more quickly.[4] On this front the Armenian general John Kourkoúas was in command continuously, as dhoméstikos ton Skholón, for twenty-two years and seven months,[5] ending in 944. In 926/7–929/30 he compelled the Muslim principalities Malatīyah, Amida, Mayyāfāriqīn, and three others in the heart of Armenia as well, temporarily to submit to the East

---

vacuum had been filled by the Armenian Mleh (Melias), to the Muslims' detriment (Canard in Vasiliev, *Byzance et les Arabes*, ii, I, pp. 42 and 216–17).

[1] *Georg. Mon. Cont.*, Reign of Rhomanós I, chaps. 17–22, pp. 898–902; Leo Grammaticus, pp. 310–14; *Theoph. Cont.*, Reign of Rhomanós I, chaps. 15–16, pp. 405–9; pseudo-Symeon, Reign of Constantine VII, chaps. 29–30, pp. 735–9.

[2] See pp. 360–3.

[3] Constantine Porphyrogenitus in *Theoph. Cont.*, Book V, chap. 48, pp. 280–2. Constantine claims this military achievement for himself, but the actual conqueror of Adhatá was his general Várdhas Phokás, the father of another general of Constantine's, the future Emperor Nikêphóros II Phokás, who was to conquer Tarsós in 965. See also Rambaud, op. cit., p. 140, and the present work, II, 6, p. 319, n. 2.

[4] See pp. 121–2.

[5] *Theoph. Cont.*, Book VI, Reign of Rhomanós I, chap. 40, p. 426.

Roman Empire's suzerainty.[1] Under the terms of their capitulation, the Muslims of Malatīyah sent a contingent to serve in the East Roman army, and they marched in triumphal processions in Constantinople parading the Muslim prisoners that they had taken.[2] In 931, however, Malatīyah repudiated its allegiance to the Empire; and in 934, after the city had been taken by John Kourkoúas, the principality was annexed to the Empire and was administered thereafter direct, as a 'kouratoría'.[3] John Kourkoúas's crowning achievement was to bring the principality of Édhessa to terms in 944. Édhessa bought peace by submitting to the Empire's suzerainty and handing over its palladium the Mandělion.[4] The brilliance of John's achievements resulted in his being retired from his command. The story[5] is that the Emperor Rhomanós I had wanted to reward John by arranging a marriage between his own grandson Rhomanós[6] and John's daughter Efphrosýnê, and that this had made the junior Emperors so jealous that they had insisted upon John's being disgraced. Whatever the cause of his dismissal may have been, the consequence was to halt the expansion of the East Roman Empire into Mesopotamia.

The Empire's expansion was carried farther during the years 961–1045,[7] yet the temporary diminution of the area of Dār-al-Islām as a result of the Empire's expansion during the 120 years 926–1045 was slight when measured in terms of the Islamic World's vast extent, and, for the Empire, the financial, economic, and social price of these relatively modest territorial acquisitions proved to have been exorbitantly high. There was never any prospect, or any expectation on either side, that the Empire would ever succeed in regaining, in Asia and Africa, the frontiers that it had held before 604 and then again during the years 629–33.

However, the gains in this quarter that had been made by 944 have to be measured, not only in terms of the additional territory that had been won, but also in terms of the improvement of the situation in territories that had previously been in the marches but now found

---

[1] Rambaud, op. cit., p. 422, following *De Adm. Imp.*, chap. 44, pp. 193–4. The three Muslim principalities in Armenia were: (i) Melazgerd (Manzikiert); (ii) Khliat, Arjish, and Perkri; (iii) Dzermadzoú (for the two possible locations of Dzermadzoú, see Runciman in Jenkins's *Commentary*, p. 68).

[2] *Georg. Mon. Cont.*, Reign of Rhomanós I, chap. 35, p. 907; Leo Grammaticus, pp. 317–18; *Theoph. Cont.*, Book VI, Reign of Rhomanós I, chap. 24, pp. 415–16; pseudo-Symeon, Reign of Constantine VII, chap. 35, pp. 741–2; Kedhrênós, vol. ii, pp. 703–11.

[3] Leo Grammaticus and pseudo-Symeon, ibid.   [4] See II, 6, p. 319, with n. 8.

[5] See *Georg. Mon. Cont.*, Reign of Rhomanós I, chap. 52, pp. 916–17; Leo Grammaticus, pp. 324–5; *Theoph. Cont.*, Reign of Rhomanós I, chaps. 40–1, pp. 426–8; Kedhrênós, vol. ii, pp. 317–18.

[6] i.e. the Rhomanós whose father was Rhomanós I's son Constantine, not Rhomanós II, the son of Rhomanós I's daughter Elénê Lekapênê by the Emperor Constantine Porphyrogenitus.   [7] See p. 319.

themselves in the interior. The territories of Sevásteia, Lykandós, Seléfkeia, and Leondókomis, that had been kleisoúrai in Leo VI's reign, had been transformed into army-corps districts by the time when Constantine Porphyrogenitus was incorporating Leo's salary-list in the *De Caerimoniis*.[1]

The Arabs, like their Persian predecessors, were regarded by the East Romans as being the most formidable of their foreign adversaries. Leo VI, in his *Taktiká*, takes the Arabs very seriously; and, though he was writing before the East Roman Army had started to take the offensive on the Empire's eastern front—the date of this was 926—he was writing after the crushing defeat of the Amīr of Malatīyah in 863, and it was manifest in his reign (886–912) that the power of the Eastern Muslims was already far gone in its decline. Yet, in a passage that has been cited earlier,[2] Leo declares that he has been moved to write his *Taktiká* by his concern over the Arab peril.

In Leo's judgement[3] the Arabs excel all other foreign nations in the intelligence and the organization that they apply to the conduct of military operations (χρῶνται δὲ εὐβουλίᾳ καί καταστάσει πρὸς τὰς πολεμικάς μεθόδους τῶν ἄλλων ἁπάντων ἐθνῶν δοκιμώτερον). Leo has learnt this, he tells his readers, from three sources: from interrogation of his own lieutenant-generals (ὑποστρατηγῶν), who have frequently been in action against the Arabs; from written reports made to his Imperial predecessors; and from his father the Emperor Basil I, who was often at war with the Arabs.

The Arabs have adopted East Roman weapons and equipment,[4] and to a large extent they copy East Roman tactics. 'The Arabs make a point of learning, from the reverses that the East Romans have inflicted on them, how to retaliate in kind.'[5] 'They show great endurance when they are being hit by missiles. They keep their formation, and then, when the enemy attack slackens, they go into action and fight with vigour.'[6] They also keep their formation both when pursuing and when pursued.[7]

Shoot at the Arabs' horses.[8] Use poisoned arrows.[9] This is good policy, because the Arabs' horses have a high money value,[10] and the Arabs' motive for raiding is economic. They raid to win loot, because they do not make a living by agriculture.[11] They are moved by the profit motive

---

[1] See *De Caer.*, Book II, chap. 50, p. 697.

[2] In II, 6, p. 291, with n. 4.   [3] Leo, Dhiat. 18, § 123, col. 976.

[4] Dhiat. 18, § 115, col. 973.   [5] Dhiat. 18, § 119, col. 973.

[6] Dhiat. 18, § 121, col. 973. They behave in the same way in sea-fights (Dhiat. 18, § 122, col. 976; Dhiat. 19, § 15, col. 996).

[7] Dhiat. 18, § 116, col. 973, and § 135, cols. 977–80.

[8] § 23, col. 952, and §§ 135–6, col. 980.

[9] § 136, col. 980.   [10] § 23, col. 952.   [11] § 137, col. 980.

(φιλοκερδίᾳ). The plain truth is that they are out for plunder, and they go on campaign of their own volition (ἐλευθερίᾳ). They are not conscripts and are not holders of lands that carry the obligation of military service (οὐ γὰρ δουλείᾳ καὶ στρατείᾳ ἐκστρατεύουσι).[1] So, for the Arabs, the fear of losing valuable horses is an effective deterrent.

In going to war, the Arabs do not think solely in terms of profit and loss. They are also actuated by a superstitious impulse to fight for their faith, but this religious motive cuts both ways. It gives them confidence when they have hopes of victory, but it also makes them lose their morale completely when they despair of victory. They take a reverse as a sign that God is against them, and they accept defeat as being God's will. This makes them unable to take punishment with fortitude.[2]

Thus the East Romans' respect for the Eastern Muslims was tempered by a touch of contempt; but the feeling of respect was paramount, and it is revealed in the position assigned to the Eastern Muslims in the section of Philótheos's klêtorolóyion which lays down the order of precedence for foreign ambassadors.[3] Christian ecclesiastical dignitaries rank highest— representatives of the Roman See higher than the sýnkelloi of Antioch and Jerusalem, and all foreign ecclesiastics take precedence over East Roman ecclesiastics of equal rank. Next come 'Muslim friends' (οἱ ἐξ Ἀγάρων φίλοι). These are assimilated to the class (ὑποπίπτουσι τάξει) of patríkioi and stratêghoí, but, within this bracket, Eastern Muslims are given precedence over Western Muslims. 'Bulgar friends' come below 'Muslim friends' in the list, but they receive almost identical honours. Frankish envoys come below both Muslims and Bulgars. Friends from all other nations take the lowest place.

The esteem in which Eastern Muslims were held by their East Roman antagonists showed itself still more strikingly when the Eastern Muslims whom the East Roman Government had on its hands were, not ambassadors, but prisoners of war. A noteworthy feature of the relations between the East Roman Empire and the Eastern Muslims is the generosity with which the East Roman Government treated its Eastern Muslim prisoners. Evidently it regarded them as valuable human material, and its aim and hope was to win them for the Empire by persuading them to apostatize. The rewards for apostasy were tempting.[4]

When Constantine Porphyrogenitus's general Leo Phokás had captured a Muslim prince, Constantine celebrated a triumph over this royal prisoner of war according to protocol. He placed this foot on the prisoner's neck in the style of an Iranian pādishāh. This, however, was the worst that the distinguished prisoner had to suffer. After the due observance of the protocol, Constantine made much of him; he loaded

[1] § 24, col. 952. [2] § 24, col. 952, and § 117, col. 973.
[3] pp. 155–6 Bury, pp. 739–40 Bonn. [4] See II, 1 (iii) (a), pp. 82–3.

him with honours and gifts.[1] Sulla would not have made himself ridiculous by putting his foot on his prisoner's neck, but, after parading him in the triumphal procession, he would have sent him remorselessly to be strangled in the Tullianum.

A still more remarkable instance of East Roman generosity to a captured Muslim prince was the treatment of the Amīr of Candia when, at the eighth attempt,[2] Crete was reconquered by the East Roman Empire in 960–1. The Cretan Muslims were Western Muslims and they were also pirates. On at least one past occasion in the reign of Basil I, Cretan Muslim prisoners—at any rate those who had refused to apostatize—had been horribly tortured to death.[3] By the year 961 the Cretan Muslims had been tormenting the East Romans for 134 years, and it would not have been surprising if the victims had reacted vindictively when, at last, they had these inveterate enemies of theirs at their mercy. The captured Amīr and his family were duly paraded in the triumphal procession of the victorious East Roman general Nikêphóros Phokás, but, after that, 'the Amīr received lavish gifts [in kind] and in gold and silver from the Emperor and was given an estate in the country as a residence for himself and his children. He was not promoted to senatorial rank because the family declined to receive baptism.'[4]

The rank and file of Eastern Muslim prisoners of war who did apostatize were settled on the land on generous terms.[5]

If a triumph was celebrated at the time of a race-meeting, the proceedings took place in the Hippodrome. They began with a procession and culminated with the singing of a victory hymn by all the East Roman participants. 'As soon as the singing begins, all the prisoners fall flat, face downwards, on the ground, and the troops hold the prisoners' arms—their spears, with the pennants—reversed until the singing is over. When it is over, the prisoners stand up, and their arms are held the right way up again. If the Emperor [then] orders that the prisoners are to join the spectators of the races, the prisoners mount to the tiers of the Hippodrome below [those reserved for] the deme of the Greens. This is where the prisoners usually stand for watching the races. If the Emperor orders that they are to join the previous batch of prisoners held in the Praetorium, then they stand either below the deme of the Blues or somewhere else.'[6]

On Easter Sunday, eighteen of the Muslim prisoners in the Great Praetorium were given a ticket of leave to attend the Emperor's Easter

[1] Kedhrênós, vol. ii, pp. 330–1.   [2] See p. 343.
[3] Constantine Porphyrogenitus, Biography of Basil I in *Theoph. Cont.*, Book V, chap. 61, pp. 300–1.
[4] Pseudo-Symeon, Reign of Rhomanós II, chap. 4, p. 760. See also II, 7, p. 343, n. 4.
[5] For the details, see pp. 82–3.
[6] *De Caer.*, Book II, chap. 20, p. 615.

banquet in the Golden Tríklinos. They were supplied with the proper dress clothes (white, without belts) and shoes.[1] On Christmas Day, twenty-four of them were given leave from the Great Praetorium to attend the Emperor's Christmas banquet in the Tríklinos of the Nineteen Couches, and were seated, facing the Emperors, at the sixth and seventh tables. On this occasion, too, the Muslim prisoners wore the same costume: a white dress, no belt, but shoes.[2] The Christmas festivities continued for twelve days, from Christmas Day to Epiphany.[3] The Muslim prisoners' participation in the Christmas celebrations is attested by Hārūn b. Yahyā, as reproduced by Ibn Rustah.[4] Before the prisoners were served— and the service was of gold and silver plate—the Emperor's herald declared: 'I swear, by the Emperor's head, that these dishes contain no pork.'[5] On the twelfth day of the feasting, the Muslim prisoner-guests were tipped two dinars and three dirhems each.[6] They also took part in the Emperor's procession to the Ayía Sophía, were conducted into the church, wished the Emperor (three times) 'Many years', and were then given robes of honour by the Emperor's command. There were mosques in Constantinople for the prisoners' use.[7] 'The East Romans (Rūm) treat their Muslim prisoners generously and give them rations.'[8]

According to Tabari,[9] when Khan Symeon's army appeared before the land-walls of Constantinople in the Romano-Bulgarian war of 894–6, relations between the Muslim prisoners in Constantinople and the East Roman Government were so good that the Emperor Leo VI invited his prisoners to take a hand in the City's defence. The prisoners agreed, the Emperor gave them arms, and they acquitted themselves well. The Emperor then became nervous and not only disarmed the prisoners but dispersed them in the provinces as a precautionary measure.

This story does not appear in the Greek sources, and the Arabic sources reveal that there was another side of the picture. Muqaddasi, writing in the latter part of the tenth century, observes:[10]

The only Muslim [prisoners] that are lodged in the Dār al-Balāt [? the Great Praetorium][11] are V.I.P.s. These are maintained, looked after, and

---

[1] Philótheos in *De Caer.*, Book II, chap. 52, pp. 767–8 Bonn, pp. 168–9 Bury.
[2] *De Caer.*, Book II, chap. 52, p. 743 Bonn, p. 157 Bury.   [3] Ibid., p. 757 Bonn, p. 164, Bury.
[4] Translated in Vasiliev, *Byzance et les Arabes*, ii, II, pp. 387–91. It is in dispute whether the date of Hārūn's sojourn in Constantinople was *circa* 880–90 or *circa* 912–13 (Canard in Vasiliev, *Byzance et les Arabes*, ii, II, pp. 381–2).
[5] Cf. Muqaddasi, translated ibid., p. 423.
[6] The prisoners, both male and female, were tipped three nomísmata each on Good Friday by Rhomanós I according to *Theoph. Cont.*, p. 430.
[7] Ishāq b. Al-Husayn (tenth century), in Vasiliev, op. cit., vol. cit., p. 426.
[8] Ishāq b. Al-Husayn, ibid.
[9] Sub A.D. 896/7, translated in Vasiliev, op. cit., vol. ii, II, pp. 11–12. See also the present work, II, 1 (iii) (a), p. 79.
[10] This passage is translated in Vasiliev, op. cit., vol. cit., p. 423.
[11] The location of the Dār al-Balāt is discussed in Vasiliev, op. cit., vol. ii, II, p. 289, n. 1.

entertained there. The common run of the Muslim prisoners are enslaved and employed in manufacturing industries. Canny prisoners do not divulge what their trade is, when they are asked. [However], sometimes the Muslim prisoners do business among themselves and make some money by this. The East Romans do not force any of them to eat pork, and they do not slit their noses or their tongues.

According to Hārūn b. Yaḥyā,[1] there were four prisons inside the Palace, in the vestibule leading in from the gate which Hārūn calls the gate of al-Mankabah.[2] One of these four prisons was for the Tarsans, one for other Muslims, and the third for East Roman subjects, while the fourth was at the disposal of the commandant of the guards (? the Etaireiárkhês). According to Ibn Hawkal, who was writing in the middle decades of the tenth century, there were, in addition to the Dār al-Balāt, four prisons for Muslim prisoners: one in théma Thrakěsioi, one in théma Opsíkion, one in théma Voukellárioi, and one in Al-Nūmerah, i.e. τὰ Νούμερα. This appears to have been a regiment of the tághmata that was stationed in the Palace, and, according to *Theophanes Continuatus*,[3] its quarters contained one of the three prisons inside the Palace, which were the prisons of the Noúmera, the Khalkě, and the Praetorium. According to Ibn Hawkal,

The prisons in thémata Thrakěsioi and Opsíkion are the mildest. The prisoners in these are not in chains. The prisons in the Voukellárioi and in the Noúmera are harsher. The prisoners lodged in the Dār al-Balāt start in the Noúmera prison and are transferred to the Dār al-Balāt from there. The Noúmera prison is harsh, depressing, and dark.[4]

The Eastern Muslim and East Roman Governments both showed a humane concern for the prisoners of their own nationality who were held by the enemy.

Tanūhī (949–94) reports, at fourth hand,[5] that 'Alī b. 'Isā, who was the 'Abbasid Caliph Muqtadir's wazīr in 913–16 and again in 926–8, had heard from the governor of the frontier province a rumour that Muslim

---

[1] See Vasiliev, op. cit., ii, II, pp. 384–5 with p. 384, n. 5, and p. 385, nn. 1 and 2.

[2] Hārūn's 'al-Mankabah' has been emended to 'al-Mankana', i.e. 'the Arsenal', but there does not seem to be any other reference to an 'Arsenal Gate' of the Palace. If the emendation is correct, no light is thrown on it by the mention of the κουράτωρ τῶν Μαγγάνων in Philó-theos's klêtorolóyion (p. 714 Bonn, p. 137 Bury), or by Constantine Porphyrogenitus's notice of ὁ τὰ Μάγγανα καλούμενος οἶκος βασιλικός, which Basil I κατεσκεύασεν (*Theoph. Cont.*, Book V, chap. 91, p. 337 Bonn). The vestibule within the particular gate of the Palace, whichever gate it was, where Hārūn locates the four prisons was manned, according to Hārūn, by members of the Emperor's Khazar guard. Hārūn's mention of the Khazar guard is corroborated by other evidence for their existence (see the references in Bury, *The Imperial Administrative System*, pp. 107–8), but there does not seem to be any further information about the place, within the Palace, where the Khazars were usually stationed.

[3] p. 175. See also Bury, *The Imperial Administrative System*, p. 65.

[4] Translation in Vasiliev, op. cit., ii, II, p. 412.

[5] See Vasiliev, op. cit., ii, II, pp. 286–90.

prisoners in Rūm, who had formerly been well treated, were now being treated badly. A friend of the wazīr's who was a qādī advised the wazīr to bring pressure to bear on the East Roman Government through the Eastern Orthodox Patriarchs of Antioch and Jerusalem. The Patriarchs sent an envoy with a letter of remonstrance to the Emperors, and this envoy was accompanied by a representative of the governor of the Caliphate's frontier province. The 'Abbasid official, as well as the Patriarchs' envoy, eventually obtained an audience with the Emperors, and they gave him a permit to visit the prisoners in the Dār al-Balāt. The prisoners' physical appearance, and hints that they dropped, convinced the visiting 'Abbasid official that the report of their having been ill-treated was true, and that the delay in his being given access to them had been for the purpose of improving their conditions (e.g. by issuing new clothes to them).

Of course the official had no means of ascertaining whether the improvement in their treatment was maintained after his departure. But, if there is any truth in the story, it shows that the 'Abbasid Government could bring pressure to bear on the Eastern Orthodox Patriarchs whose sees lay within the 'Abbasid dominions, and that the Patriarchs, in their turn, could influence the East Roman Government—if only because it would have been invidious for the Government to expose these ecclesiastical dignitaries, who were hostages in the Muslims' hands, to the risk of being made the victims of reprisals for the East Roman Government's misbehaviour.

Another story reported, likewise at fourth hand, by al-Tanūhī,[1] is that a Muslim prisoner, in a party that had been suffering severe hardships on its road to East Roman territory, recorded that when they arrived at one village a monk brought woollen clothes and blankets for each of them. They were allowed to stay in this village for several days, and were continuously well treated there. At the next village their hardships began again. They were told that a Baghdadi businessman had arranged for the clothes and blankets to be sent to the monk for him to use for the benefit of Muslim prisoners who passed through his village. This was expensive for the philanthropist; but, in addition, he had guaranteed to the monk to make an annual payment to a Christian church in Muslim territory for as long as the monk continued to carry out his part of the agreement.

The East Roman Emperor Leo VI (886–912), for his part, showed solicitude for East Roman subjects who were prisoners in enemy hands. He repealed three pieces of existing legislation by which prisoners had been penalized. In his Novel No. 33,[2] he ruled that, when either a husband or a wife had been taken prisoner, this was not in future to entitle the

---

[1] See Vasiliev, ibid., pp. 290–1.   [2] Noailles and Dain, pp. 130–6.

other party to the marriage to re-marry. In his Novel No. 36,[1] Leo ruled that in future a child should be entitled to inherit from his parents, even if both of them had died as prisoners of war, subject to the possibility that one or both of them might have made a valid will in which the whole of the property was not bequeathed to the child. In his Novel No. 40,[2] Leo ruled that in future a prisoner should be entitled to make a will—and this with a minimum of formalities, in view of the difficulty of the prisoner-testator's situation. Moreover, if the prisoner died intestate and without heirs, his slaves should not in future become the property of the state but should be emancipated, supposing that any debts due from the estate could be paid off out of other assets.

While both East Romans and Eastern Muslims were thus concerned to alleviate the lot of their compatriots who were prisoners in the other power's hands, both were also concerned to secure their respective compatriots' liberation. Consequently, truces for the exchange of prisoners were almost as characteristic a feature of Romano-Saracen wars as the hostilities in which the prisoners were taken. The exchanges were made individual for individual, and accordingly Leo VI recommends that, though the general practice should be to sell prisoners into slavery, some should be kept in hand till the war is quite over, in order to exchange them for East Roman prisoners in enemy hands.[3] The exchanges were made across the River Lámos (Lāmis), which was the frontier between the Caliphate and the East Roman Empire on the south coast of Asia Minor. One of Tabari's sources records[4] that, for the exchange in 845, two bridges were built across the river, one by each party, and that individuals were released to cross the bridges simultaneously, man for man.

The calendar of exchanges of prisoners, in the Appendix to the present chapter, indicates that, more often than not, the East Romans had larger numbers of prisoners in hand than the Muslims had. At first sight, this is surprising. The whole population of Amórion was carried away captive in 838, and the whole population of Thessaloníkê—a much larger city than Amórion—in 904. No such wholesale captures of Muslim populations are recorded. Moreover, so long as Crete was in Muslim hands (i.e. from 827 or 828 to 960–1), the number of East Romans taken prisoner in Cretan Muslim raids on the coasts and islands of the Aegean must have been far greater than the number of Muslims taken in East Roman counter-raids by sea. This suggests that the East Roman Army's tactics of 'dogging and pouncing' must have been effective, and that the Muslim raiders overland usually had to pay for having taken the offensive by losing more

[1] Noailles and Dain, pp. 144–6.   [2] Ibid., pp. 156–64.
[3] Leo VI, *Taktiká*, Dhiat. 16, §§ 10–11, col. 909.
[4] Vasiliev, *Byzance et les Arabes*, i, pp. 202 and 314. Cf. Ya'qūbī, ibid., pp. 276 and 277.

prisoners than their East Roman antagonists. It is not so surprising that the East Romans held an excess of prisoners in 938 and 946; for from 926 to 965 the raiding was reciprocal. It is, however, remarkable that the East Romans held an excess of prisoners in 845; for this was before the turn of the tide in Romano-Arab land-warfare in 863 and before the taking of the offensive by the East Romans in 926.

The repeated exchange of prisoners had a humanizing effect on Romano-Muslim relations. The prisoners' recovery of their freedom mitigated, for both belligerents, the sufferings inflicted by chronic hostilities, and the negotiations for the exchanges, and the conduct of these when they had been agreed, created opportunities for friendly meetings between officials over a transaction that benefited both parties and in which the two parties therefore had a common interest. When embassies for negotiating exchanges were sent by either party to the other party's capital, they were treated with honour and were given sumptuous hospitality. The cordial reception of Khoirospháktês's embassy to Baghdad in 905–6, and of the subsequent East Roman Embassy in 917,[1] was matched by the cordiality of the receptions at Constantinople, in 946, of a Tarsan embassy to negotiate an exchange of prisoners, and of a joint embassy, three months later in the same year, from Sayf-ad-Dawlah and the Amīr of Amida and the Daylamites, who, by that date, were in control of the 'Abbasid Government at Baghdad.[2]

Cultural relations were still more amicable. The Emperor Michael III gratified the Caliph Wāthiq's wish to send a Muslim scholar to visit the Cave of the Seven Sleepers at Éphesos, the scene of a Christian legend that figures prominently in the Qur'ān.[3] The Muslim visitor was provided with a guide. The Emperor Theóphilos had been importuned by the Caliph Ma'mūn to lend him the East Roman mathematician and philosopher Leo,[4] but the Emperor politely parried the Caliph's repeated requests, and Leo eventually became the first head of the college that the Caesar Várdhas founded in the Maghnávra Palace in 863.[5]

The principal cultural interest which the Muslims shared with the Byzantine Greeks was in the revival of the study of pre-Byzantine Greek science and philosophy. Pre-Byzantine Greek works in these two fields were translated into Arabic in the 'Abbasid Age either direct or via translations into Syriac. These translations from Greek into Arabic differed from the contemporary translations from Greek into 'Old

[1] See II, 1 (ii), p. 57, n. 3, and the Appendix to the present chapter, pp. 39–21.
[2] For these two embassies, see further III, 7, pp. 499–504.
[3] See Vasiliev, *Byzance et les Arabes*, vol. i, pp. 8 and 12.
[4] Vasiliev in loc. cit.; Canard in *C. Med. H.*, vol. iv, 2nd ed., Part I, p. 735.
[5] See *Theoph. Cont.*, pp. 185–91; Kedhrênós, vol. ii, pp. 165–71. Cf. *Georg. Mon. Cont.*, p. 806; Leo Grammaticus, p. 225. Dölger, *Regesten*, I. Teil, p. 51, dates Theóphilos's refusal 832/3.

Slavonic' (i.e. the Slavonic dialect current in the ninth century in the hinterland of Thessaloníkê) in two respects.

The translations into Arabic were made on the initiative of the Arabs and their Syriac-speaking Christian subjects. The translations into 'Old Slavonic' were made possible by the work of the two Thessalonian Greek scholar-missionary brothers Constantine-Cyril and Methódhios, who had reduced the local Slavonic dialect to literary form and had devised the Glagolitic alphabet for conveying it. Thanks to this Greek pioneer work, Greek texts began to be translated into 'Old Slavonic' in Bulgaria by Slavs when Methódhios's Slavophone clergy were given asylum there *circa* 886 after they had been evicted from Moravia. These translations were actively promoted by the Bulgar Khan Borís-Michael, and more actively still by Borís's Byzantine-educated son and successor Khan Symeon, who did some translating work himself.

The second difference between the Arabic and the Slavonic translations of Greek works was that the Muslims and the Slavonic-speaking Christians were interested primarily in different portions of the vast repertory of Greek literature. The Muslims were mainly concerned with pre-Christian Greek philosophy and science, the Slavonic-speaking Christians mainly with Christian Greek theology, hagiography, and historiography, including not only works dating from the Patristic Age but also contemporary Byzantine Greek literature in these genres. Thus the translations into Slavonic from Greek had more effect than the translations into Arabic in fostering cultural relations between the translators and their Byzantine Greek contemporaries.

PART III, CHAPTER 3, APPENDIX

Calendar of Exchanges of Prisoners between the Eastern Muslims and the East Roman Empire

Date	Mas'ūdī's Number	
769	?	Theophanes, p. 444.
797	?	Mas'ūdī, in Vasiliev, ii, II, p. 408.
804/5	?	Tabari in Brooks, 'Byzantines and Arabs in the Time of the Early 'Abbasids, I', p. 744.
807/8		Tabari, ibid., p. 747.
810	?	Mas'ūdī, in Vasiliev, ii, II, p. 408.
816	?	Mas'ūdī, ibid.

Date	Mas'ūdī's Number	

845 III Ya'qūbī, in Vasiliev, I, pp. 275–6; Tabari, ibid., pp. 310–15; Mas'ūdī, ibid., pp. 336–7; Ibn al-Athīr, ibid., pp. 353–4; summary in the text of Vasiliev, pp. 198–204. The East Romans held many more prisoners than the Muslims; so the Caliph Wāthiq had to buy up East Roman slaves at Baghdad and Raqqah and even to contribute East Roman slave women from his own household. According to one of Tabari's sources, the Muslims recovered 4,600 persons, of whom 600 were women and children and 500 were dhimmīs (i.e. non-Muslim subjects of the Caliphate). Ibn al-Athīr's corresponding figures are 4,460 and 800 and 100.

856 IV Ya'qūbī, ibid., pp. 276–7; Tabari, ibid., pp. 317–18; Mas'ūdī, ibid., pp. 336–7; summary ibid., pp. 222–6. According to Tabari, the East Romans had 20,000 Muslim prisoners in hand. The Muslims recovered 789 men and 125 women (Tabari); 2,200 men, or 2,000 men and 100 women (Mas'ūdī).

860 V Mas'ūdī, ibid., p. 337; summary ibid., pp. 239–40. The Muslims recovered 2,367 men and women.

861/2 ? Mas'ūdī, in Vasiliev, ii, II, p. 408.

867 ? Mas'ūdī, in Vasiliev, ii, II, p. 405.

872 ? Mas'ūdī, ibid., p. 408.

896 VI Tabari, ibid., p. 12; Sibt b. al-Jawzī, ibid., p. 167; Mas'ūdī, ibid., p. 405; summary in Vasiliev, ii, I, p. 125. The Muslims recovered 2,504 men, women, and children according to Tabari and al-Jawzī, 2,495 in all (or 3,000 men) according to Mas'ūdī.

905 and 908 VII and VIII Mas'ūdī, in Vasiliev, ii, II, pp. 43 and 405–6; Ibn al-Jawzī, ibid., p. 168; summary in Vasiliev, ii, I, pp. 181–94. The East Romans broke off the exchange in 905. Relations were re-established by the East Roman diplomatist Leo Khoirospháktês, who records in his letter No. 25 (see Vasiliev, ibid., p. 191, n. 1) that, on this occasion, he spent two years abroad. Thanks to his diplomacy, the exchange was completed in 908. The Muslims recovered 1,154 or 1,155 men and women in 905, and 2,842 in 908 (Mas'ūdī); about 3,000 (Tabari and

Date	Mas'ūdī's Number	

'Arīb). Khoirospháktês's embassy is noticed by Tabari in Vasiliev, ii, II, p. 21, and by 'Arīb, ibid., p. 58.

917   IX   The way for this exchange, too, was prepared by an East Roman diplomatic mission to Baghdad. The magnificent display with which this mission was received is described by 'Arīb, in Vasiliev, ii, II, pp. 60–1; by Miskawaih, ibid., pp. 66–9; by al-Khatīb al-Baghdādī, ibid., pp.73–9; by Ibn al-Athīr, ibid., pp. 146–7; by Sibt b. al-Jawzī, ibid., pp. 169–71. For the exchange itself, see Ibn al-Athīr and al-Jawzī in locc. citt., and Mas'ūdī, ibid., p. 406. The Muslims recovered 5,500 persons according to al-Jawzī, 3,336 men, women, and children according to Mas'ūdī. Summary in Vasiliev, ii, II, pp. 238–42.

925   X   Mas'ūdī, in Vasiliev, ii, II, p. 406 (cf. Makrīzī, ibid., p. 261); summary in Vasiliev, ii, I, p. 254. The Muslims recovered 3,983 persons (2,933 according to Makrīzī).

938   XI   Ibn al-Athīr, in Vasiliev, ii, II, p. 156; Mas'ūdī, ibid., pp. 406–7. For the preparatory exchange of notes between Rhomanós Lekapênós and the Ikhshīd, see Ibn Sa'īd, ibid., pp. 203–13; summary in Vasiliev, ii, I, p. 314. The Muslims recovered more than 6,300 men, women, and children, but the East Romans held a further 800 Muslims, representing the excess of the number of Muslim prisoners in East Roman hands over the number of East Roman prisoners whom the East Romans had recovered from the Muslims. The truce was therefore prolonged for six months, to give the Muslims time to ransom, for money payments, the remaining 800 Muslim prisoners, in batches. When the exchange of 938 had been under consideration, the Ikhshīd had made an appeal at Fustāt for subscriptions for a fund for ransoming Muslim prisoners, since the number of these was known to exceed the number of East Roman prisoners, but this appeal had met with no response (Ibn Sa'īd, in Vasiliev, ii, II, p. 203).

946   XII   Ibn al-Athīr, in Vasiliev, ii, II, p. 157; Mas'ūdī,

Date	*Mas'ūdī's* *Number*

ibid., pp. 407–8; summary in Vasiliev, ii, I, pp. 314–16. The Muslims recovered 2,482 prisoners of both sexes, but the East Romans held a further 230. Sayf-ad-Dawlah's representative ransomed these, for money payments, out of a sum of 80,000 dinars that Sayf-ad-Dawlah had given to him for this purpose. Sayf-ad-Dawlah had received 30,000 of these 80,000 dinars from the Ikhshīd's posthumous representative, Kāfūr. See also *Theoph. Cont.*, p. 443.

953 — Makrīzī, in Vasiliev, ii, II, pp. 261–2. This exchange took place at Alexandria. The Muslims recovered 60 persons.

954 — East Roman embassy to Sayf-ad-Dawlah to negotiate an exchange. Kedhrênós, vol. ii, p. 331.

966, 23 June — Yaḥyā b. Sa'īd, cited by G. Schlumberger in *Un Empereur byzantin au dixième siècle: Nicéphore Phocas*, 2nd edition (Paris, 1923, Boccard), pp. 423–5. This exchange was negotiated by Sayf-ad-Dawlah with a representative of the Emperor Nikêphóros II Phokás. The exchange was carried out at Samosata (Samsāt). The River Lámos had ceased to be the frontier between the East Roman Empire and Dār-al-Islām since the reconquest of Eastern Cilicia by the East Romans in 961–5. This time there was an excess of 3,000 Muslim prisoners in East Roman hands. Sayf-ad-Dawlah had to ransom these at the price of 270 gold pieces per head. He produced 240,000 gold pieces, and, when his cash ran out, he secured the release of the still unransomed Muslim prisoners by giving a valuable cuirasse and an important hostage.

post 969 — After the partition of Syria, in this year, between the East Roman Empire and the Fatimid Caliphate, exchanges of prisoners were made between these two powers, as they had been made previously between the East Roman Empire and the 'Abbasid Caliphate or its representatives in Cilicia (see Eickhoff, op. cit., p. 287).

4. Relations with the Armenian and Caucasian Principalities

In 732 Abkhazia, along the east coast of the Black Sea, submitted to the suzerainty of the Arab Caliphate,[1] and from then onwards, till this suzerainty became a dead letter, the East Roman Empire was confronted by the Caliphate along the entire length of its eastern frontier, from the mouth of the River Lámos on the south coast of Asia Minor north-eastwards to the mouth of the River Chorokh at the south-east corner of the Black Sea. However, the situation along the north-eastern sector of this frontier was not, at any stage, the same as it was along the south-western sector. There, from Malatīyah to Tarsós, the Empire was confronted, directly and exclusively, by the Caliphate or by its local Arab Muslim representatives. Farther to the north-east, the Empire had to deal, besides, with Christian principalities that had not been extinguished by the Arab conquest.

This political situation was exceptional, though the contemporary religious situation was not. In all the regions to the west of Iran that were conquered by the Arabs, the majority of the population was Christian at the time of the conquest. In the seventh century, Christendom extended in 'Irāq south-eastwards to the head of the Persian Gulf, and in the Caucasian Albania north-eastwards to the western shore of the Caspian Sea. Westwards, Christendom extended across northern Africa and southern Europe to the shore of the Atlantic and beyond the sea into the British Isles. This vast area was partitioned among different Christian sects. In 'Irāq a majority of the Christian population was Nestorian, though Monophysite pre-Chalcedonian Christianity had been gaining some ground here at Nestorianism's expense. Monophysitism was prevalent in the Caucasian Albania, Armenia, Mesopotamia, Syria, Egypt, and up the Nile into Nubia and the Kingdom of Axum. Orthodox, alias Catholic (i.e. Chalcedonian), Christianity was the prevalent form in the territories conquered by the Arabs in North-West Africa and the Iberian Peninsula, as it was in the East Roman Empire and in the Roman Empire's barbarian successor-states in those parts of western Europe that the Arabs failed to subjugate.

In all the Christian countries that the Arabs did subdue, the conquerors assumed political control; but, on the religious plane, the conversion of their Christian subjects to Islam was gradual. In the Qur'ān, Christians,

---

[1] See Laurent, *L'Arménie entre Byzance et l'Islam*, p. 20, n. 4, and p. 206.

like Jews, are designated as being 'People of the Book', that is to say the people professing religions whose scriptures are valid as far as they go. 'People of the Book' are to be tolerated and protected if they submit to Muslim government and pay a surtax, and the prospect of losing this surtax took the edge off the Islamic state's zeal for winning converts to its rulers' own Muslim faith. Meanwhile, on the political plane, the Arab Caliphate's non-Muslim subjects were deprived of all political authority except in one region, namely Armenia and the Caucasian principalities to the north of Armenia, as far as the Arabs succeeded in imposing their sovereignty on these. In this region, a number of local Christian rulers survived, by agreement, under the suzerainty of the Caliphate, throughout the period during which the Caliphate was here the paramount power.

Armenia and the Caucasian principalities obtained these exceptionally favourable terms from the Arabs for three reasons. One reason was the nature of the terrain. The Armenian plateau is higher, and is encased in, and is traversed by, more obstructive mountain ranges, than the plateaux of Asia Minor and Iran, by which Armenia is flanked. This terrain is difficult to conquer, and is still more difficult to hold, without the acquiescence of its inhabitants. Moreover, in the seventh century Armenia and Caucasia were adjoined by the territories of two states— the East Roman Empire and Khazaria—which reacted vigorously against Arab attempts to conquer them. Between 633 and 642, the Arabs had conquered Syria, up to the Amanos Range, Egypt, Mesopotamia, 'Irāq, and Iran with amazing speed and ease. They are said to have made an incursion into East Roman Asia Minor as early as 640/1,[1] and into Khazaria, to the north of the eastern end of the Caucasus Range, in 642.[2] But, in both these directions, the Arabs were foiled. The Khazaro-Arab war lasted for a hundred years; the Romano-Arab war lasted as long as the Arab Empire itself. The Arabs did not succeed in pushing their frontier forward from the foot of the Amanos to the foot of the Távros till the turn of the seventh and eighth centuries. In 652, their first serious invasion of Khazaria met with a defeat.[3] These checks to the impetus of the Arabs' assaults in these two quarters were, no doubt, one of the considerations that induced the Arabs to grant relatively favourable terms to the Armenians in 653,[4] and to allow the Armenian and Caucasian princes a large measure of autonomy thereafter. Another reason why the Armenians stipulated for autonomy in 653, and continued to assert their autonomy, is to be found in Armenia's previous history.

[1] See II, 1 (iii) (b), p. 107.
[2] See D. M. Dunlop, *The History of the Jewish Khazars* (Princeton, 1954, University Press), p. 50.
[3] See Dunlop, op. cit., pp. 55–6.
[4] See the present work, pp. 85, 108, 398. 678.

The history of Armenia, and of the Caucasian countries to the north of her, had been different from the histories of Mesopotamia and 'Irāq and Syria and Egypt, which the Arabs had conquered so easily. The populations of these countries to the south of Armenia had all been under foreign rule for most of the time since they had been conquered by the Assyrians between the tenth and the seventh century B.C. 'Irāq had never been under the rule of a national dynasty since 538 B.C., and Egypt never since 343/2 B.C. In these countries the memory of political independence had faded away long ago, and, with it, the ambition to recover this lost heritage. By contrast, the Assyrians had never succeeded in conquering Armenia's predecessor Urartu, and, though Urartu, like Assyria, had fallen in the seventh century B.C., and though the subsequent progressive encroachments of the Armenians had partly changed the ethnic composition of Urartu's population and had wholly replaced Urartu's Hurrian language,[1] the region itself had recovered its political independence partially or even completely from time to time.

The original Armenians seem to have been Phrygians (Muski) from north-eastern Asia Minor who had crossed the upper Euphrates and had occupied the upper basin of the Tigris[2] when the Assyrian Empire had collapsed. The Armenian language is Indo-European, and presumably it is derived from the Thraco-Phrygian branch of the Indo-European linguistic family, though it has been strongly influenced by the non-Indo-European languages of the peoples on whom the Armenians imposed themselves.[3] The first, but not final, fate of the Armenian migrants was to be engulfed in the successive empires of the Medes, the Persians, and the Seleucidae. The creation of the Kingdom of Armenia was an indirect consequence of the shattering of the Seleucid Empire's prestige through its defeat by the Romans in 190 B.C.[4]

In that year the governors of the Seleucid Empire's two Armenian satrapies declared their independence. The nucleus of the dominions of Artaxias, the ruler of the more north-easterly of these two provinces, was in the valley of the River Aras (Araxes), along the middle reaches of its course. Artaxata, the capital that Artaxias laid out and named after himself,[5]

---

[1] The Urartians' own name for themselves seems to have been Khaldi. This long-submerged ethnikon had re-emerged in the name of the East Roman army-corps district Khaldhía.

[2] This district was known as Nairi by the Assyrians, and by the Arabs as Diyār Bakr, after the name of the Arab tribe Bakr which had established itself there—before the Muslim Arab conquest, according to G. Le Strange, *The Lands of the Eastern Caliphate* (Cambridge, 1905, University Press), p. 86.

[3] In *The Cambridge Ancient History*, vol. i, 3rd ed., Part I, pp. 142–3, it is suggested that the Indo-European element in Armenian is probably not Thraco-Phrygian but Hittite-Luvian, and that, in spite of appearances, Armenian is not really a member of the *satem* group of Indo-European languages.

[4] Strabo, *Geographica*, Book XI, chap. 14, § 5 (C. 528) and § 15 (C. 531–2).

[5] Strabo XI, 14, § 6 (C. 528).

was near Dvin. From this starting-point, Artaxias and his successors enlarged Armenia—previously 'as mall country'[1]—into a big kingdom which, in Strabo's day, extended from the east and south bank of the north-western arm of the upper Euphrates eastward to the western shore of the Caspian Sea round the debouchure of the Rivers Aras and Kur, and from the southern face of the watershed between the upper basin of the Tigris and the basin of the Khabur tributary of the Euphrates northward to the south bank of the River Kur and to the farther side of the Kur's headwaters.[2] This enlarged Armenia included not only the Seleucid Empire's other Armenian satrapy, Sophênê, but also some previously non-Armenian territories—for instance, some extensive tracts of Media Atropatênê (Azerbaijan); but Strabo informs us that the Armenian language became the common language of the Artaxiad Kingdom of Armenia as a result of the political unification of this heterogeneous population under the Armenian Crown.[3]

The Kingdom of Armenia had no sooner been built up in the political vacuum created by the disintegration of the Seleucid Empire than it was threatened by the approach of the Seleucid Empire's two principal successors in south-west Asia, the Roman Empire from the west and, from the east, the Parthian (or, more accurately, Parnian) Empire, which had swallowed up the Seleucid Empire's former dominions in Iran, 'Irāq, and Mesopotamia. After Rome and Parthia had contended inconclusively for the political control of Armenia for about a century and a quarter, the two powers agreed in A.D. 63 that the Armenian Crown should be worn by a member of the Arsacid House (the royal family of the Parthian Empire) but that each successive Arsacid king of Armenia should have to receive a formal investiture from the Roman Emperor in order to validate his title to his throne. The Arsacids managed to secure for their house the crowns of the Caucasian Albania and Iberia, as well as the crown of Armenia,[4] before the senior branch of the Arsacid House was supplanted in its own dominions, as it was in the third decade of the third century of the Christian Era, by the Sasanids from Fars.

The junior branches of the Arsacid House that had been installed in Armenia and in the two adjoining Caucasian kingdoms survived the extinction of the senior branch; but in 387 the Kingdom of Armenia was partitioned between the Persian and Roman Empires, and the Arsacid kingship was abolished in Roman Armenia *circa* 390[5] and in Persarmenia in 428.[6] In the Romano-Persian peace-treaty of 591, the Persian Emperor Khusraw II, who had been reinstalled on his throne thanks to East Roman

---

[1] Strabo XI, 14, § 5 (C. 528).
[2] Strabo XI, 14, § 5 (C. 528) and XI, 14, § 15 (C. 531–2).
[3] Strabo, XI, 14, § 5 (C. 528).
[4] See C. Toumanov in *C. Med. H.*, vol. iv, 2nd ed., Part I, chap. 14, p. 594.
[5] Toumanov, ibid., p. 598. [6] Ibid., pp. 598–9.

military support, paid for this service by ceding to the East Roman Empire the western half of Persarmenia, and Roman Persarmenia, as well as Roman Armenia, reverted to the East Roman Empire in the peace-settlement of 628, which re-established the territorial *status quo ante* the Romano-Persian war of 604–28. Each of the two empires then appointed an Armenian grandee to serve as viceroy of its portion of Armenia.[1]

After a number of Armenian and Caucasian cantons had made separate capitulations to the Arabs,[2] a general capitulation, on behalf of all three fractions of Armenia, together with Albania (Aghovanía) and Iberia (Ivêría), was made in 653 with the Arab viceroy of Syria, Mu'āwīyah, by Theodore Reshtuni, an Armenian grandee who had been in the East Roman Imperial Government's service but had fallen out with the East Romans and had then taken the lead in a movement for coming to terms with the Arabs. The terms, as given by the Armenian historian Sebeos,[3] were that the Arabs should refrain from posting governors or garrisons in Armenia, that they should come to Armenia's aid in the event of an East Roman attack on her, and that the Armenians, on their side, should supply the Arab Empire with a force of 15,000 cavalry. In these terms, political autonomy for the Armenians, Albanians, and Iberians was implied. Toleration for their religion was apparently taken for granted.

In order to understand why the Armenians and their Caucasian neighbours took this historic step, their previous religious and cultural, as well as political, history has to be taken into account. The Armenians and Caucasians found themselves in the same position as the Bulgars and the Khazars. They were held in a vice between neighbours who were more powerful than they were, and they were striving to preserve their separate corporate identity. The Bulgars solved this common problem by becoming converts to Christianity in its Eastern Orthodox form, but with linguistic and cultural safeguards. They adopted 'Old Slavonic', not Greek, as their liturgical and literary language and they invented, for the conveyance of 'Old Slavonic', a new alphabet, the so-called 'Cyrillic', that was simpler than the Glagolitic alphabet that had been invented by the Thessalonian Greek missionary Constantine-Cyril. The Khazars sought for a higher religion that was neither Christianity nor Islam, and they found this in Judaism. Armenia, caught between the pre-Christian Roman Empire and the Zoroastrian Persian Empire, had followed suit to its southern neighbour Osrhoene in adopting Christianity. Armenia was converted in 314, and Iberia in 337.[4] The Albanians were converted by the Armenians.[5]

---

[1] Toumanov, *C. Med. H.*, vol. iv, 2nd. ed., Part I, chap. 14, p. 605.
[2] See Laurent, op. cit., p. 33, n. 1.
[3] See the résumé in French in Laurent, op. cit., p. 34.
[4] Toumanov, ibid., p. 595, n. 1.   [5] Laurent, op. cit., p. 26, n. 4.

Christianity served well for asserting the separateness of the Armenians and Caucasians from the Zoroastrian Iranians. In the fifth century the Sasanids tried and failed to impose Zoroastrianism on the Armenians and Caucasians who were now under Sasanid suzerainty. The Armenians and Caucasians revolted, and, though their successive revolts were crushed, the Persians abandoned their attempt to impose their own national religion on them. After the military disaster that the Persians suffered in 484 at the hands of the Ephthalite Huns, they had to concede both religious toleration and political autonomy to their Armenian and Caucasian subjects.[1]

The Roman Empire presented the Armenian and Caucasian Christians with a more difficult problem when, in the last two decades of the fourth century, the Roman Imperial Government, in its turn, made Christianity its established religion. How were the Christian Armenians and Georgians to maintain their separate identity from the henceforth Christian Romans? The Armenians solved this problem in the same way as their Syrian-speaking southern neighbours in Mesopotamia and in Syria and as the Copts. The fifth-century Christological controversies gave the Armenians, too, the opportunity of espousing a version of Christianity that was different from the official Roman version, and they, too, now translated the Christian liturgy into their own national language, in place of Greek, and conveyed it in a non-Greek alphabet. The Armenian alphabet was invented *circa* 400,[2] and this endowment of the Armenian language with a script of its own was followed by an outburst of literary activity, secular as well as religious, which produced original works in Armenian, as well as translations from the Greek.[3]

The Armenian Christian Church had originally been subordinate to the episcopal see of the Cappadocian Kaisáreia. The title 'katholikós', which continued to be borne by the head of the Armenian Church after it had established its ecclesiastical independence, had originally signified the representative of an ecclesiastical superior (i.e. the Bishop of Kaisáreia in Armenia's case).[4] But in the later decades of the fourth century, when, in the Roman Empire, Christianity was advancing from being tolerated to becoming established, the Armenian Church severed its connection with the see of Kaisáreia.[5] The Armenians ignored the ruling of the Ecumenical Council of Chalcedon (451), which assigned Armenia to the domain of the Patriarchate of Constantinople. They also ignored all

---

[1] Toumanov, ibid., pp. 600–1.

[2] Toumanov, ibid., p. 599; Laurent, op. cit., p. 133, with n. 3. The Armenian alphabet, like the Coptic and like the two ninth-century Slavonic alphabets, was inspired by the Greek alphabet. On the other hand, the Syriac alphabet was derived from the Aramaic.

[3] Toumanov, ibid., p. 599.

[4] Laurent, op. cit., p. 140, n. 9.

[5] Laurent, op. cit., pp. 132 and 307–8.

theological innovations adopted by the Chalcedonian Church from those of 451 inclusive. They remained pre-Chalcedonian.[1]

An overt breach with the established church of the Roman Empire was staved off by the promulgation of the Emperor Zeno's *Enotikón*, a semi-Monophysite formula which did cause a breach between the East Roman Church and the Western Roman Church from 484 to 519. The Chalcedonian doctrine was in abeyance in the East Roman Empire when, in 491, it was condemned at a regional council, held at Vagharshapat in Persarmenia, which was attended by representatives of the Iberian as well as the Armenian Church.[2] The *Enotikón* was accepted in 506 at a regional council held at Dvin (the capital of Persarmenia), on behalf of the Churches of Armenia, Albania, and Iberia,[3] but the Armenians did not follow the East Roman Emperor Justin I when, in 519, he mended the Eastern Orthodox Church's breach with the West by reverting from the formula of the *Enotikón* to the unmitigated Chalcedonian doctrine,[4] and, at another council held at Dvin in 555, the Armenians of Persarmenia declared positively for the Armenian form of Monophysitism. The Armenians of Roman Armenia, too, were Monophysites at heart, even at times when they were forced into conforming with Chalcedonianism by the Imperial Government's pressure. The latest and most impolitic exercise of this pressure was Heraclius's in 632/3.[5] This East Roman intolerance partly accounts for the Armenians' capitulation to Mu'āwiyah in 653; for the Arabs granted to all Monophysites who came under their rule the toleration that the East Romans had grudged to them.[6]

The Caucasian kingdoms were parties to the capitulation of 653; they, too, were powerless to resist the Arabs, and, for the time being, the East Romans were powerless to help them. However, Lazica (the former Kolkhís) and Iberia had followed the East Roman Government when it had reverted to unalloyed Chalcedonianism in 519, and in 607-9 there had been a breach between the Iberian and the Armenian Church on this account.[7]

The consideration in the Iberians' minds was their wish to preserve their separate identity. Just as the Armenians wished to preserve their identity against the Persians and the Romans, so the Iberians wished to preserve theirs against the Armenians. Armenia threatened to overshadow her Caucasian neighbours, as she was threatened, herself, with being overshadowed by the East Roman Empire and by Iran. Armenia was much larger and more populous than any of the Caucasian king-

---

[1] Laurent, op. cit., pp. 132-5.　　　　　　　　　　[2] Laurent, op. cit., p. 32, n. 4.
[3] Toumanov, ibid., p. 604.　　　　[4] Ibid.　　　　[5] Toumanov, ibid., p. 605.
[6] 'Les Arméniens redoutaient encore plus les Grecs que les Arabes' (Laurent, op. cit., p. 220).
[7] Toumanov, op. cit., p. 604; Laurent, op. cit., p. 37.

doms; she was less remote, geographically, from the centres of higher civilization, and, inevitably, civilization had reached Caucasia through an Armenian channel. For instance, the national alphabet which the Iberians created to convey their own (non-Indo-European) language had been inspired by the Armenian alphabet. The Bible had been translated into Iberian from the Armenian version.[1] The exquisite standard of masonry that the Armenians had inherited from the Urartians had been transmitted by them to the Iberians, and, with it, the distinctive Armenian style of ecclesiastical architecture.[2]

The potency of this Armenian cultural influence on Iberia moved the Iberians to assert their separate identity; and they asserted this, as the Armenians had asserted theirs, by adopting a different religion from that of their more powerful neighbours. For the Caucasian peoples, the only practical alternative to the Armenian form of Monophysite Christianity was Chalcedonian Christianity. They chose this because, for them, the consequent ecclesiastical association with the East Roman Empire seemed to be less of a menace to their national identity than an ecclesiastical association with Armenia.

The Albanians would have liked to assert themselves against Armenia in the Iberian way;[3] but their geographical location was less favourable. They made at least two attempts to change over from the Armenian form of Monophysitism to Chalcedonianism, for the first time in the reign of the Emperor Maurice (582–602) and with his support,[4] and for the second time in 702–4.[5] On this second occasion the pro-Chalcedonian movement in Albania was suppressed by the Armenian Monophysite Church with Muslim Arab military aid. The Armenian Katholikós went to Bardaʿah, the capital of Arrān, the Arab portion of Albania; he there deposed the Albanian Katholikós, and the Arabs then carried off this Albanian prelate in chains to Damascus. In the Arabs', as in the Armenians', eyes, Chalcedonianism was the religion of the East Roman Empire; the adoption of Chalcedonianism was therefore tantamount to political secession, and the Arabs were determined not to permit the establishment of an East Roman outpost on the Caliphate's north-eastern frontier over against the Khazars. In general, the Arabs favoured the spread of their Monophysite Christian Armenian subjects' ecclesiastical, cultural, and political influence over the Armenians' Albanian and Iberian fellow-subjects.[6] But they supported the Albanians against the Orthodox Christian Armenian Bagratid sovereigns of Iberia.[7]

---

[1] Laurent, op. cit., p. 31. [2] Toumanov, ibid., p. 615.
[3] Laurent, op. cit., pp. 24–7.
[4] Ibid., p. 26, n. 5.
[5] Ibid., p. 166, n. 3; Toumanov in loc. cit., p. 606.
[6] Laurent, op. cit., pp. 11–12.
[7] Laurent, op. cit., p. 113.

Thus there were two rival and mutually hostile forms of Christianity in the Armenian and Caucasian dominions of the Arab Caliphate, and, during the period of Muslim Arab rule, the religious and political map of this region came to be variegated still farther by the progressive intrusion of Muslim garrisons, settlements, and principalities.[1]

After the capitulation in 653, the Arabs seem immediately to have planted a permanent Arab garrison at Tiflis, a key position, on their northern frontier, in the trough that intervenes between the Armenian plateau and the Caucasus Range.[2] They made Dvin, the former capital of Persarmenia, into the capital of their own viceroyalty comprising Armenia and the two Caucasian countries that had now submitted to their rule,[3] and Dvin attracted a considerable Muslim population. Moreover, the upper basin of the Tigris, which had probably been the Armenians' earliest acquisition to the east of the Euphrates, was detached from Armenia and was incorporated in the Arab Caliphate's province Jazīrah (Mesopotamia)—first under governors appointed by the Caliphs and then, when the Caliphate lost its grip, under virtually independent Muslim amīrs in Arzanênĕ, to the east of the Tigris's Batman su tributary, and in Amida, to the west of it. At some unknown date, perhaps after the crushing of the Armenian insurrection of 771–2 against the 'Abbasid regime, a Qaysid Arab amirate was established in the heart of Armenia, at Melazgerd (Manzikiert) in the upper basin of the southern branch of the upper Euphrates, with footholds along the northern shore of Lake Van at Khliat and Arjish and Perkri.[4]

The religious and cultural and linguistic map of Armenia and the adjoining Caucasian countries was complex, but the political map was more complex still, and was also perpetually in flux. The common political characteristic of the whole region was its political fragmentation.[5] It was a congeries of small principalities, each of which was struggling to preserve its *de facto* independence, and, if possible, to enlarge its own domain at its neighbours' expense. This political dispensation was a patent weakness, but it was also a latent source of strength.

An effectively united Armenia could have played the part of a great power, but, each time that the opportunity offered itself, it was missed, because the nominal sovereigns of all Armenia were not truly in command of their feudatories. The Artaxiads had more than a century, dating from the prostration of the Seleucid Empire in 190 B.C., for building up

---

[1] See Laurent, op. cit., pp. 10, 154–5, 176–8, and Appendix III, pp. 317–31.

[2] Toumanov, ibid., p. 605; Laurent, op. cit., p. 13, n. 2.

[3] Toumanov, ibid. However, according to Laurent, op. cit., p. 178, Dvin was the Arab capital for Armenia only; the capital for the whole viceroyalty, including Albania and Iberia, was Barda'ah, in Arrān (the portion of Albania that was under Arab rule).

[4] See *De Adm. Imp.*, chap. 44, and Laurent, op. cit., pp. 94, 101, 322–6. See also the present work, p. 381, n. 1.   [5] Laurent, op. cit., p. ? and p. 23, n. 5.

their kingdom before the Romans and the Parthians closed in on them; yet they failed to hold their own against these new powers. When, in 885, the ʿAbbasid Caliph Muʿtamid recognized Ashot Bagratuni as King of Armenia, and when the Emperor Basil I followed suit to the Caliph by sending Ashot a crown,[1] the Bagratids had 135 years for building up their kingdom before the Emperor Basil II and his successors were able to turn their attention to the annexation of the still independent major part of Armenia after having completed their annexation of Bulgaria. Yet Armenia missed her opportunity once again, and for the same reason.[2]

It is instructive to compare the history of Armenia under the Bagratunis with the contemporary history of Bulgaria. Ashot the Great was a contemporary of Khan Borís-Michael of Bulgaria. Borís-Michael reigned from 852 to 889; Ashot became high constable of Armenia in 856, and was recognized by the ʿAbbasid Government as 'Prince of Princes' in 862[3] and as King in 885. The Armenians were as martial a people as the Bulgars, and Armenia surpassed Bulgaria in point of area, population, and maturity of culture. But the Bagratuni dynasty produced no counterparts of Khans Borís-Michael and Symeon or of Tsar Samuel. Symeon was able to make a bid for winning the East Roman Crown, and Samuel was able to make an heroic fight for independence, because each of these Bulgar rulers was the leader of an effectively united people. The Armenian princes had asked the Caliph to make Ashot their king, but they had had no more intention of subordinating themselves to the Bagratunis than they had had of submitting to their ʿAbbasid suzerain. Consequently, ninth-century and tenth-century Bulgaria was a near-great power, but contemporary Armenia was not.

At the same time the internal disunity of Armenia, which inhibited her from playing the role of a great power, also inhibited her conquerors and suzerains from extinguishing her amorphous independence. When the Arsacid Crown had been liquidated, the local principalities had survived;[4] and when, in 852–5, the Caliph Mutawakkil's Turkish general Bugha had re-subjugated the whole of the Caliphate's Armenian–Caucasian viceroyalty except Sper and Iberia,[5] and had deported the subjugated

---

[1] The East Roman Government continued to call the Bagratid King of Armenia ἄρχων ἀρχόντων, which was the equivalent of the previous title, 'Prince of Princes', that King Ashot I (V) the Great had received from the Caliph. See *De Caer.*, Book II, chap. 48, p. 687. The title conferred on Ashot the Great by the Caliph in 885 had been 'Shahanshah' ('King of Kings'). See Rambaud, op. cit., pp. 506–7; Runciman in Jenkins, *Commentary on De Adm. Imp.*, p. 158.

[2] See Laurent, op. cit., pp. 2, 80, 83, 265, and 283–93. The Bagratid Kings of Armenia never succeeded in imposing their authority on the Ardzrunis of Vaspurakan.

[3] Between November 862 and April 863 (Laurent, op. cit., p. 267, n. 7).

[4] Laurent, op. cit., pp. 66 and 68.

[5] No Iberian names are included in the Arabic authorities' lists of Armenian and Albanian notables deported to Sāmarrā by Bugha (J. Marquart, *Osteuropäische und ostasiatische Streifzüge* (Leipzig, 1903, Dieterich), p. 424).

princes to Sāmarrā,[1] this re-assertion of the Caliph's authority had been as superficial as the Armenian princes' recognition of the authority of King Ashot I(V) and his successors was in the next chapter of Armenia's history. Armenia's independence was hydra-headed, and it was therefore indestructible. Arab viceroys and native 'Princes of Princes' or 'Kings' could not govern Armenia without the local princes' acquiescence. After the murder of the Caliph Mutawakkil in 861, the 'Abbasid government found that the line of least resistance for maintaining control over Armenia was to release the princes who had been interned at Sāmarrā since 853[2] and at the same time to recognize one of them, Ashot Bagratuni, as 'Prince of Princes'.[3] The 'Prince of Princes' and his fellow princes duly neutralized each other, and the princes' power, in turn, was neutralized by the power of their own nominal subordinates. The princes could not govern their principalities without the acquiescence of the local barons. The terrain of Armenia favours fragmentary local independence *de facto*, and the terrain was exploited industriously for securing this. The country bristled with castles,[4] and every Armenian châtelain was virtually sovereign within his own miniature domain. He could defy his superiors with impunity because the task of reducing all these innumerable strongholds was beyond the strength of any suzerain power.

It is significant that the territory that, under the Arab regime, was lost to Armenia and was incorporated in the Arab province Jazīrah was approximately conterminous with the portion of the Arsacid kingdom that had been annexed by the Roman Empire in the partition of 387. In Roman Armenia the Emperor Justinian had liquidated the local principalities in 532 after having created, in 528, the new command of the *magister militum per Armeniam*. In 536 he had reorganized Roman Armenia into two regular Roman provinces, Armenia I and Armenia IV.[5] In thus destroying the historic structure of Armenian society on the Roman side of the partition-line, Justinian had deprived the Armenian people of its survival-power within these limits. However, Roman Armenia was only a small fraction of the former Artaxiad kingdom. In Persarmenia the princes and the barons maintained themselves, and this ensured here the survival of the Armenian people under the subsequent Arab regime.

During this phase of Armenian and Caucasian history, the nominally comprehensive Arab viceroyalty was in truth a mosaic of insubordinate and discordant principalities, and the political struggle for existence

---

[1] Laurent, op. cit., pp. 118–28.   [2] Laurent, op. cit., p. 183, n. 4.
[3] Op. cit., p. 217.   [4] Op. cit., pp. 52–3.
[5] Toumanov, ibid., pp. 601–2; Laurent, op. cit., p. 67, n. 1, p. 68, n. 2, and pp. 488, 528, 536; Bury, *A History of the Later Roman Empire*, vol. ii, pp. 28–9. Justinian's Armenia II and Armenia III lay to the west of the Euphrates, and had not ever been included in the former Kingdom of Armenia.

among these cut across all affinities and antipathies of religion and nationality. It was natural that the Armenians and Iberians should co-operate with the Caliph Mutawakkil's general Bugha in liquidating the Arab Muslim Amīr of Tiflis[1]—the Arab military outpost that had been planted in Iberia by Mu'āwiyah. The Amīr Ishak was obnoxious to the 'Abbasid Mutawakkil because he was of Umayyad origin or affiliation and because he had repudiated his allegiance to the 'Abbasid Caliphate for twenty years. In helping to liquidate him, the Christians were reliev-ing themselves of a Muslim thorn in their flesh.[2] It was also natural that the Armenians should co-operate with their Arab viceroys in defending the Caliphate's north-east frontier against the Khazars,[3] since the raids of these still only partially civilized ex-nomads were more devastating for the Armenians than they were for the Armenians' Arab masters. It is also not surprising that, while some Armenians emigrated to the East Roman Empire, some of those who had chosen to stay at home under Arab rule fought for the Arabs against the East Romans. For instance, in 838, there were Armenians in the army of the Caliph Mu'tasim that took and sacked Amórion.[4] The Armenians who had stayed at home—and these were, of course, the great majority—were those who felt that to be coerced into accepting Chalcedonianism was a greater evil than sub-mission to an Arab suzerainty that left them free to practise their own national Monophysite form of Christianity.

On the other hand, it is surprising to find that, in the Arab–Armenian wars of 771–2 and 852–5, there were Armenian princes who played their Arab overlords' game against their own insurgent fellow countrymen and co-religionists. In 771 the leader of the insurrection, who was a Mami-konian, was defeated by the Caliph's high constable of Armenia, who was a Bagratuni; and, though this Smbat Bagratuni eventually joined the insurrection, the Ardzrunis, who were another of the Armenian princely houses, held aloof.[5] In 852–5, again, another Smbat Bagratuni, who was the Caliph's high constable of Armenia on this occasion, co-operated with the Caliph's Turkish general Bugha, whereas the Muslim Amīrs of Arzanênĕ and Tiflis were on the rebel side, and the Amīr of Arzanênĕ had actually been accessory to the murder of Bugha's predecessor Yusuf by the Armenians of Taron.[6] When this insurrection was quelled in 855, the

---

[1] Laurent, op. cit., pp. 102–3, 174, and 320–1.

[2] Op. cit., p. 321. See also Marquart, *Osteuropäische und ostasiatische Streifzüge*, pp. 188, 410–12, 421–3, 508.   [3] Laurent, op. cit., p. 171.

[4] Laurent, op. cit., p. 212. This Armenian contingent in Mu'tasim's army was led by Bagarat Bagratuni, Prince of Taron, who had been given the title of 'Prince of Princes' in 830 by the Caliph Ma'mūn (see *Theoph. Cont.*, p. 127; Genesius, p. 67). This service to the Caliphate did not save Bagarat from being deported to Sāmarrā in 851 (see Laurent, p. 336). The Ardzruni Armenian prince of Vaspurakan also served in Mu'tasim's army in 838 (Genesius, ibid.).

[5] Laurent, op. cit., p. 95.   [6] Laurent, op. cit., pp. 118 and 121–2.

loyalist (or, from the Armenian standpoint, traitorous) high constable Smbat, with his son Ashot, was deported to Sāmarrā like the conquered insurgents who were these Bagratunis' fellow princes; but Smbat Bagratuni's services to the 'Abbasid cause in 852–5 subsequently won for his son the titles of 'Prince of Princes' in 862 and of 'King' in 885.

Ashot the Great's chief successes in asserting the authority with which the Caliph had invested him were gained at the expense of the Muslim enclaves in Armenia,[1] but this may have been not inconvenient for Ashot's 'Abbasid suzerain; for the Amīrs of Arzanênê and Tiflis were not the only, or the earliest, Armenian and Caucasian Muslim rebels against the Caliphate. For instance, in 813, the Qaysids of Melazgerd had seized Dvin, which was the seat of the Caliph's viceroy.[2]

The Qaysids extended their dominions through marriages with Armenian Christian princesses.[3] So did the Amīrs of Arzanênê.[4] At least one dynasty—a branch of the Bagratids that had moved into Iberia after the Arabs' suppression of the Armenian insurrection of 771–2—changed its creed for the sake of winning a crown. These Bagratids went over from pre-Chalcedonian Christianity to Chalcedonianism, because this was an indispensable condition for making themselves into acceptable rulers of a Chalcedonian Christian country. By the turn of the eighth and ninth centuries the Iberian Bagratids had become predominant in Iberia. In 813 the East Roman Government conferred the title Kouropalátês on a member of this house;[5] and one of them, Adarnase IV, assumed the title of King in 888,[6] three years after this title had been conferred on his relative Ashot I(V), the first of the Bagratid Kings of Armenia.[7]

In Armenian and Arab eyes, adhesion to the Chalcedonian Christian Church was tantamount to submission to the East Roman Empire, but the East Romans' Caucasian co-religionists did not allow the East Romans to harbour this illusion.

In the reigns of the Emperors Leo VI and Constantine VII Porphyrogenitus, the Iberians persistently rejected the East Roman Government's request to agree to a temporary East Roman military occupation of the Iberian city Katzéon, through which supplies were reaching the Muslim garrison of Qālīqalā (Theodosiopolis), and the Iberians also refused to take part in military operations against the Amirate of Melazgerd.[8] The

---

[1] Laurent, op. cit., pp. 280–2. [2] Op. cit., pp. 323 and 324.
[3] Op. cit., p. 324. [4] Op. cit., p. 327. [5] Toumanov, ibid., p. 610.
[6] Toumanov, ibid., p. 613, with the list of Bagratids of Iberia on p. 782. The East Roman Imperial Government recognized Adarnase's claim to the title Kouropalátês in 891 (ibid., p. 613).
[7] See Marquart, *Osteuropäische und ostasiatische Streifzüge*, Exkurs IV: 'Die Ursprung der iberischen Bagratiden', pp. 391–465, with the genealogical table on pp. 438–9 and the notes on this on pp. 438–65. See also the genealogical table in Jenkins's *Commentary on De Adm. Imp.*, facing p. 172.
[8] *De Adm. Imp.*, chap. 45, pp. 199–205.

Iberians did not want to see their relatively weak Muslim neighbours supplanted by their East Roman co-religionists in an age in which the East Roman Empire's political and military strength was on the increase.

The Abkhazians, like the Iberians, were Chalcedonians, and, unlike them, they had never adhered to any other form of Christianity; for the Abkhazians had not been converted to Christianity before the reign of Justinian I,[1] and by that time the East Roman Government had abandoned the *Enotikón*. However, the Abkhazians clashed politically with the East Roman Empire in the reign of Rhomanós I (920–44). By that time Abkhazia had not only thrown off the suzerainty that the Arabs had imposed on her in 732;[2] since the last decade of the eighth century she had expanded southwards into Iberia, and this Greater Abkhazia was called Avasyía by the East Romans.[3] The Abkhazian Crown dominated Iberia from 912 to 975.[4] During this more than usually chaotic phase of Iberian history, Rhomanós I, taking advantage of a local dynastic feud, managed to introduce a small East Roman garrison into the city of Ardhanoúdzin, and to raise the Imperial standard on the walls. Thereupon, the Iberians threatened to make common cause with the Muslims against the Empire if the East Roman garrison of Ardhanoúdzin was not withdrawn; and this threat moved Rhomanós to disown his representative's action and to instruct him to evacuate Ardhanoúdzin, though he had occupied the place on previous instructions from the Emperor. Thus a small Orthodox Christian Caucasian state, at a time when it was under the control of another Orthodox Christian Caucasian state, forced the East Roman Empire, which professed the same faith as Iberia and Abkhazia and was officially their suzerain, to beat a humiliating retreat.

This reverse was the more galling for the Imperial Government because, besides losing face, it was being compelled to relinquish a valuable prize which it had held momentarily in its grasp.

Ardhanoúdzin (Ἀρδανούτζιν) is an extremely strong fortress; it has an outer enceinte (ῥαπάτιν)[5] of the size of a provincial city (χωρόπολιν); trade-routes converge on it from Trebizond, Iberia, Avasyía, and all districts of Armenia and Syria; and this trade brings to Ardhanoúdzin an enormous customs revenue. The territory of Ardhanoúdzin, the 'arzyn', is extensive

---

[1] Laurent, op. cit., p. 19, n. 4.

[2] According to Marquart, op. cit., p. 422, the Abkhazians, as well as the Iberians, had been under the suzerainty of the Arab governor of Tiflis till Ishak was defeated and killed by Mutawakkil's general Bugha in 853.

[3] Toumanov, ibid., p. 610, with n. 2.

[4] *C. Med. H.*, vol. iv, 2nd ed., Part I, p. 782.

[5] In this passage, ῥαπάτιν looks as if it were, like 'arzyn' '(territories'), an Arabic word transliterated. The Arabic word 'rabad' means the outer zone of a city, and 'rhapátin' is, in fact, interpreted as meaning προάστειον (Honigmann, cited by Runciman in Jenkins's *Commentary*, p. 178).

and productive, and it is the key to Iberia and Avasyía and the Moskhian country.[1]

Ardhanoúdzin was a big enough prize to spur the East Roman Empire and its Orthodox Christian Caucasian satellites into contending with each other for it.

Thus the East Roman Empire's expansion into the Caliphate's Armenian–Caucasian viceroyalty was unwelcome to the Orthodox Christian, as well as to the pre-Chalcedonian Christian and the Muslim, princelings and kinglets and amīrs in this intricate mosaic of petty local states; but the political fragmentation of this region created a political vacuum there; and therefore, when the Arab Caliphate receded, the East Roman Empire inevitably advanced.

The way had been opened for this advance by the re-subjugation of the Paulicians' holdings on East Roman territory in and after 872. The first East Roman re-encroachment on the territory of the historic Kingdom of Armenia was the creation of théma Mesopotamía[2] in the reign of Leo VI, perhaps in 900.[3] Leo coaxed the local Armenian prince and his sons out of their ancestral patrimony by giving them high rank and office in the Empire.[4] The annexation of the amirate of Malatīyah in 934 opened the way for enlarging théma Mesopotamía by adding to it Khanzit, to the south of the southern arm of the upper Euphrates, and some further territory to the east of Khanzit, including the headwaters of the Tigris. The way was also now open wider for East Roman diplomacy to spin a spider's web round the Armenian principality of Taron, along the middle course of the southern branch of the upper Euphrates. Constantine Porphyrogenitus devotes a chapter to this, and he goes into detail.[5] In spite of this, his narrative does not enable us to identify conclusively all the persons and occasions to which he alludes, but it does reveal the intensity of the East Roman Government's concentration on its objective here. Taron was, indeed, like the Ardhanoúdzin district, a key area. It commanded the access, both from the west and from the south, to the comparatively open country to the north of Lake Van which had been occupied by the Muslim amirate of Melazgerd.

Constantine did not live to see the annexation of Taron to the East Roman Empire in 968,[6] but he did see, in 949, the annexation of Qālīqalā

---

[1] *De Adm. Imp.*, chap. 46, pp. 207–8. See the whole of this chapter.

[2] The East Roman théma Mesopotamía included only the extreme north-western corner of the Arab province Jazīrah, and did not overlap with the original Greek and Roman Mesopotamía, which was bounded by the southern frontier of Armenia and the northern frontier of Babylonia.

[3] See *De Adm. Imp.*, chap. 50, pp. 226–7, with Jenkins's *Commentary*, p. 189; Honigmann in Vasiliev, *Byzance et les Arabes*, vol. iii, pp. 69–70.

[4] See *De Adm. Imp.*, ibid.   [5] *De Adm. Imp.*, chap. 43, pp. 182–91.

[6] Toumanov in loc. cit., p. 616. According to Honigmann in Vasiliev, *Byzance et les Arabes*, vol. iii, pp. 148–9, the date may have been as early as 966/7.

(Theodosiopolis),[1] which the Iberians had delayed but eventually had not been able to prevent. Thus, before the close of Nikêphóros II Phokás's reign (963–9), the East Roman Empire had incorporated in itself the whole valley of the northern arm of the upper Euphrates and the lower half of the valley of the southern arm. The Empire now reached almost, but not quite, to within sight of the western shore of Lake Van. As compared with the slice of Armenia that had been annexed to the Roman Empire in 387, East Roman Armenia extended in 968 rather farther towards the east, but not nearly so far towards the south. Amida and Mayyāfāriqīn were not included in it.

This was the limit of effective East Roman sovereignty in 968, but the East Roman diplomatic protocol[2] implied that the Emperor was sovereign over whichever Armenian prince he was recognizing, at the moment, as being ἄρχοντα ἀρχόντων τῆς Μεγάλης Ἀρμενίας;[3] over all the local princes in Armenia, as far to the east as Vaspurakan and as far to the south as Mokk' (Móex); over the Kouropalátês of Iberia (whose own title for himself was 'King'); over four Iberian princes who were tributary to the Kouropalátês of Iberia, and over four more who were not; over the Exousiokrátor of Alania; over the Exousiastês of Avasyía; over the Arkhon of Albania; and over the chieftains of sundry tribes in the recesses of the Caucasus Range. The East Roman claim to sovereignty over the rulers of all these territories was asserted by addressing communications to them in the form of 'orders' (κελεύσεις), and the notional bounds of the area in which the East Roman Emperor's writ was deemed to run extended eastwards to the western shore of the Caspian Sea and northwards to within range of the Sea of Azov.

So long as the East Roman claim to sovereignty over this area was asserted only in forms of words, it did no harm either to the local peoples and their rulers or to the East Roman Empire itself. The damage began when the Emperor Basil II started to turn these innocuous East Roman pretensions into military and political realities. Between the years 1000 and 1045, all the Armenian principalities except Qars and Muslim Khliat (though not most of the Iberian principalities) were annexed to the East Roman Empire, and their rulers were compensated for their enforced abdication by being endowed with appanages to the west of the River Euphrates.[4]

In thus liquidating the local principalities whose preservation had ensured Armenia's survival under all previous regimes, the East Roman Imperial Government was working, not for itself, but for unforeseen new

---

[1] Runciman in Jenkins, *Commentary on De Adm. Imp.*, pp. 176–7.
[2] As set out in *De Caer.*, Book II, chap. 48, pp. 686–8.
[3] When Constantine was drafting this passage, the title was being given, not to the Armenian Bagratids, but to the Ardzruni kings of Vaspurakan (*De Caer.*, II, p. 687, lines 4–5).
[4] See Honigmann in Vasiliev, *Byzance et les Arabes*, vol. iii, pp. 147–79.

arrivals from the east, the Muslim nomad Saljūq Turks. When, in 1021, the Armenian king of Vaspurakan ceded his kingdom to the Empire, it may already have been suffering from Saljūq raids.[1] In the year 1045, the last Bagratid King of Armenia (nominally the King of the whole of Armenia) ceded his actual dominions to the Empire. In the year 1049 the Saljūqs began, not merely to raid Armenia, but to occupy one piece of it after another permanently.

When in 1071 the Emperor Rhomanós IV Dhioyénês was defeated and taken prisoner by the Saljūq war-lord Alp Arslan, not only Armenia but also Asia Minor west of the Euphrates was at the Saljūqs' mercy. For 227 years, from 636 to 863, the East Roman Empire had waged, and had eventually won, a stubborn war to save Asia Minor, and, with Asia Minor, the Empire itself, from being conquered by the Arabs. In the forty-six years 1000–45, the Empire condemned itself to lose Asia Minor, its heartland, by making the fatal mistake of annexing Armenia. Both under Arab rule and after the Arab regime had evaporated, Armenia —persistently disunited but obstinately indestructible—had served, un-intentionally but effectively, as a buffer that had broken the shock of the Muslims' impact on the Empire's close-drawn eastern frontier. This buffer had now been destroyed deliberately by the East Roman Imperial Government itself. In the years 1000–45, Basil II and his successors made, on a far larger geographical scale, the mistake that Justinian I had made when, in 532, he had liquidated the Armenian princes and barons in the Roman Armenia of his day. The nemesis of the repetition of this error was proportionate to its geographical magnitude.

[1] Toumanov in loc. cit., p. 619. But, according to C. Cahen, *Pre-Ottoman Turkey* (London, 1968, Sidgwick & Jackson), pp. 67–8, the date of the first Saljūq raid on Vaspurakan was 1029. Cahen's dating seems more likely than Toumanov's to be the right one, and, *a fortiori*, more likely than 1016/17, which is the date suggested, on the authority of Kedhrênós, by Sp. Vryonis Jr., *The Decline of Medieval Hellenism in Asia Minor and the Process of Islamisation from the Eleventh through the Fifteenth Century* (Berkeley, Los Angeles, and London, 1971, University of California Press), p. 81.

5. Relations with Peoples to the North

(i) The Eurasian Pastoral Nomads

WHEN the Emperor Augustus carried the Roman Empire's East-European frontier northward to the south bank of the Danube, he brought the Empire into direct contact with the Eurasian Steppe along the line of the lower Danube, from the Iron Gates down to the delta through which the Danube discharges into the Black Sea. Thereby, Augustus made the Roman Empire a next-door neighbour of the pastoral nomads who dominated the Eurasian Steppe from an early date in the second millennium B.C. till the fourteenth century of the Christian Era and who, in our day, are still not quite extinct. While the East Roman Empire was in being, the Eurasian nomads were normally both the nearest of the peoples to the north of it and the most important of these peoples from the Empire's standpoint.

The Eurasian Steppe extends, from west to east, from the eastern foot of the Carpathians to the western foot of the Khingan Range. For peoples that have equipped and trained themselves for travelling over the Steppe, the Steppe is almost as conductive as the sea. Consequently, the fortunes of the East Roman Empire might be affected by any disturbance at any point on the Steppe, even as far away as the Steppe's eastern extremity in north-eastern Asia.

Nomadism is the antithesis of the sedentary way of life, yet it is also the antithesis of random vagrancy. The Greek term 'nomad' (νομάς), meaning a non-sedentary pastoralist, is derived from a word (νομός) that means 'pasture' or 'allotment', and this noun, in its turn, is derived from a verb (νέμειν) which means 'to take, to allot, to dispose'. Thus 'nomadism' connotes a systematic purposeful way of life and method of earning a livelihood. Nomads make their living by circulating repetitively in a constant orbit.

In the course of human history there have been three varieties of nomadism so far. For the first million years after Man had become human, and for an unknown length of time, before that, in the pre-human stage of mankind's evolution, our ancestors were pre-agricultural nomads who lived by food-gathering, hunting, and fishing. The second variety of nomadism has been the pastoral nomadism of the Steppe, which was invented after the invention of agriculture and has been dependent, throughout, on a symbiosis with contemporary agricultural societies. The third variety of nomadism is post-agricultural. It is the nomadism of the workers in urban factories and offices.

Different varieties of nomadism have different time-spans for circulating round the nomads' orbit. The food-gathering and the pastoral nomads' cycle is annual; the urban nomads' is daily. The urban nomads travel between their dormitories and their workshops twice in every twenty-four hours, in contrast to the pastoral and the food-gathering nomads, who either change their location twice a year or keep on the move, in time with the seasons, all the year round. In our day both the food-gathering and the pastoral varieties of nomadism are almost extinct. The exception (and it is a big exception) is food-gathering in the form of fishing, but already a time can be foreseen at which the crude technique of hunting wild fish will have been superseded by the more rational and productive technique of breeding and shepherding domesticated fish as sheep and cattle have been bred and shepherded on land during the last eight or ten thousand years. By contrast, it looks as if urban daily nomadism is going to become the way of life of a majority of mankind.

It is hard to imagine how human beings could have tamed animals if they had not been able to tempt them into domestication by sharing with them the food that their human patrons had won for themselves. Dogs appear to have been domesticated during the hunting stage of human economy by being given a share of the hunter's game. The domestication of sheep, goats, cattle, horses, camels, and elephants must have been achieved by sharing the fruits and seeds and roots of cultivated plants with these domesticated animals' wild ancestors. If this guess hits the mark, agriculture must be older than mixed farming, and mixed farming must be older than pastoral nomadism.

The opening for pastoral nomadism is in country that is too dry for raising crops but is not too dry for pasturing sheep and cattle if the flocks and herds are kept constantly on the move, in an annual circuit, from one pasture to another in time with the seasons at which each successive pasture is ripe for grazing. The subsoil of such steppe and desert lands may prove to be rich in minerals (as, for instance, it has proved, in our day, to be in Sa'ūdī Arabia and in Libya); but pastoral nomadism is the only practicable method of utilizing the Steppe's and the Desert's surface; and, in order to make semi-arid land productive, the shepherd or herdsman has to give up the agricultural side of the mixed farming that his ancestors practised on land which was well enough watered, by rainfall or by irrigation, for bearing crops.

However, the pastoral nomad cannot live exclusively on the produce of his flocks and herds. He needs also to procure vegetable food-stuffs, and metals and metal implements as well, from sedentary societies within his range. Pastoral nomadism cannot be maintained without an exchange of products between the nomads and their sedentary neighbours; and a trade in material commodities opens the way for the transmission of ideas and ideals. In this spiritual intercourse, too, there is reciprocity, but on this plane the nomads usually receive, on the whole, more than they give to their sedentary neighbours, and this disequilibrium in the balance of non-material payments is particularly striking in the sphere of religion. Buddhism, Judaism, Christianity, Manichaeism, Islam, and other higher religions that have arisen in some of the sedentary societies within the last 2,500 years have made converts among the nomads. On the other hand, there have been few, if any, cases in which the indigenous religion of a pastoral nomad people has been adopted by a sedentary society with which the nomads have traded, or even by one which the nomads have subjugated.

If pastoral nomadism becomes extinct (as seems probable) by the year A.D. 2000, it will have been a going concern during a time-span of rather less than four millennia. In most years out of these approximately forty centuries, the nomads have moved in their normal regular annual orbits within the bounds of the Steppe and, on the Steppe, within the limits of the seasonal pasture-ranges that have been the mutually recognized and respected domains of each of the nomad peoples. In these normal circumstances the commercial and cultural relations between the nomads and their sedentary neighbours have been peaceful, and the nomads' presence has therefore been taken for granted, and has been hardly noticed, by the sedentary observers and recorders of public events. The occasions on which the nomads have made an impression on their sedentary neighbours have been the rare and exceptional disturbances of the nomads' normal regular way of life in their own element (for the Steppe can properly be regarded as a distinct element on a par with water and air and cultivable land). The nomads' occasional outbreaks out of their own element into the world of fields and cities are the events that have created the sedentary peoples' conventional picture of the nomads' behaviour. For the sedentary peoples, the nomads' outbreaks have been disasters, and consequently the sedentary peoples' picture of the nomads has been lurid.

The nomads' outbreaks have been due to a number of different causes. These causes have not been mutually exclusive; and, when more than one of them has been at work, their simultaneous operation has produced outbreaks of special violence.

One cause of conflict between the nomads and their sedentary neighbours has been the lack of a clear-cut demarcation-line between 'the Desert' and 'the Sown'. There have been border-zones in which pastoral nomadism and agriculture have been practicable alternatives. These economically indeterminate zones have been debatable territories. They have changed hands between nomads and peasants in accordance with the changes in the relative political and military strength of the two parties. These changes in the ownership of the debatable territories, and in the use to which these territories have been put, have produced collisions between societies of the two types, and, for each, these collisions have been disturbing.

When there has been a concentration of power in a sedentary society adjoining the Steppe, the sedentary society's empire-builders have not only appropriated the debatable territories but have sought to dominate or subjugate the nomads on the Steppe itself. In campaigns on the Steppe between nomads and the armed forces of sedentary powers, the nomads had the advantage of operating in their own element till the recent invention of mechanized wheeled vehicles and aeroplanes put the world's steppes and deserts (though not its jungles and forests) at the mercy of powers that have modern industrial technique at their command. In the sixth century B.C. the founder of the First Persian Empire, Cyrus II, lost his life in attempting to subjugate the Saka nomads on the middle section of the Eurasian Steppe, and subsequently Darius I, in his attempt to subjugate the Skyth nomads on the western section, escaped a disaster only by abandoning the enterprise just in time. In the second century B.C. the Chinese Emperor Wuti similarly failed, on the eastern section of the Steppe, to subjugate more than a portion of the Hiungnu (Huns), though Wuti commanded the resources of a united China.

Even in the fourteenth century of the Christian Era, when the tide was beginning to take what has proved to be a permanent turn in the sedentary societies' favour, the Transoxanian war-lord Timur Lenk merely defeated the Golden Horde on the middle and western sections of the Steppe, without succeeding in incorporating them in his empire. It is only within the last three or four hundred years that the Eurasian Steppe has been first encircled and then subjugated by the Russians and the Chinese. It is only in our own day that the subjugated Eurasian nomads are being converted into agriculturists and industrial workers as the alternative to being exterminated.

Before the fourteenth-century recession of the Mongol wave of expansion, the Eurasian nomads were more successful empire-builders than their sedentary neighbours. The nomadic pastoral way of life is, in itself, an education in the arts of war and administration. It requires discipline, organization, planning, and at least an elementary mastery of logistics, and, when a nomad horde breaks out of 'the Desert' into 'the Sown', these arts, acquired for the pasturing of cattle on the Steppe, can be applied to the government of conquered human sedentary populations. The potential capacity for large-scale organization can be turned to account first for building up a union of nomad peoples on the Steppe itself, and then for directing this concentration of nomad power against the nomads' sedentary neighbours.

In the thirteenth century of the Christian Era the political genius of Chingis Khan created an empire that eventually came to embrace not only the whole of the Eurasian Steppe but also all the rest of the Eurasian continent except for its Indian, Arabian, and European peninsulas. The earliest nomad empire about which we have direct information is the one that was established by the Skyths in the seventh century B.C. From the pastures that they had occupied at the western end of the Steppe, between the River Don and the Carpathian Range, the Skyths dominated the peasants in the debatable zone to the north of their pastures and even some of the forest peoples to the north of their peasant subjects. A similar empire, based on the pastures between the lower Don and the lower Volga, was established by the Khazars in the course of the middle decades of the seventh century of the Christian Era.[1] The Skyth Empire lasted for about four centuries, the Khazar Empire for about three and a half. The Khazar Empire, so long as it lasted, was one of the East Roman Empire's most important neighbours.

The attempts—first abortive but eventually successful—to subjugate the nomads and to abolish the nomadic way of life have been made by adjoining sedentary societies when there has been a concentration of power in these. Cases in point are the offensives undertaken by the First Persian, Chinese, and Russian empires. Conversely, the nomads have imposed their rule on their sedentary neighbours at times when these have been politically disunited and have therefore been impotent. In the thirteenth century of the Christian Era, Chingis Khan and his successors might not have been able to make such rapid and extensive conquests if, at that time, China had not happened to be split between two mutually hostile empires and if the Kievan Russian principality and the 'Abbasid Caliphate had not each already dissolved into a number of mutually hostile successor-states. The East Roman Empire exposed itself in the reign of Justinian I (527–65) to invasions by the Bulgar nomads through its preoccupation with the conquest of Italy. It exposed itself to invasions by the Avars through its preoccupation with the Romano-Persian wars of 572–91 and 604–28. Its preoccupation with the subsequent assault of the Arabs, which culminated in 674–8 in the first Arab siege of Constantinople, enabled one fraction of the Bulgars to gain a permanent foothold to the south of the lower course of the Danube.

Because of the conductivity of the Steppe, any disturbance of the normal regular rhythm of pastoral nomadic life at any point on the Steppe may produce effects at distant points, not only on the Steppe, but beyond its borders. When one nomad people has broken out of its regular annual orbit, or has been driven out of it by pressure either from adjoining nomad peoples or from neighbouring sedentary powers, the

[1] See p. 441.

original disturbance is apt to produce a chain-reaction, in which one nomad people after another is dislodged from its established pasturage-domain by the impact of neighbours who have been dislodged from theirs.

The westward movement of the Skyths, driving the Cimmerians ahead of them, in the seventh century B.C., both to the north and to the south of the Caspian, has been explained by Herodotus as having been caused by the pressure on the Skyths of another nomad people on the Skyths' eastern flank, either the Massagetai[1] or the Issedones.[2] In the third and second centuries B.C. the Skyths were driven off the Steppe, into cramping asylums in the Crimea and in the Dobruja, by a westward advance of their eastern neighbours the Sarmatai, who had previously occupied the pastures to the east of the Don. About half way through the sixth century of the Christian Era, the Avars, who appear to have been a splinter of the Juan Juan, fled westwards when the Juan Juan, who had previously been dominant on the eastern section of the Steppe, were overthrown by a successful revolt of the Turks. The Turks then occupied the Steppe's middle section as well, and the Avars, in their flight from them, overran the Bulgar nomads at the western end of the Steppe and the Slavs (a non-nomadic agricultural people) in Moldavia and Wallachia. Finally the Avars crossed the Carpathians, annihilated the Gepidae in the isolated enclave of steppe-country in what is now Hungary, and seized this patch of pasture-land, the Hungarian Alföld, for themselves.

In A.D. 889 an unsuccessful attempt by the Khazars (between the lower Volga and the lower Don), in concert with the Ghuzz[3] (to the east of the River Yaik) to crush the Pechenegs[4] (between the Yaik and the Volga) resulted in the Pechenegs' fleeing from the Ghuzz westwards across the Volga and the Don and driving the Khazars' allies the Magyars westward to beyond the Dniepr. In 896 the Pechenegs, in concert with the Danubian Bulgars, drove the Magyars out of their last foothold on the main body of the Steppe, between the Dniepr and the Carpathians, and pushed them into the Alföld, where they exterminated the Alföld's Moravian Slav occupants, as, three centuries and a half earlier, the Gepidae had been exterminated on the Alföld by the Avars.

No doubt the range of these chain-reactions was of a different extent on different occasions. It was possible for a chain-reaction to propagate itself all the way from one extremity of the Steppe to another. It has been suggested[5] that a number of the barbarian assaults on the European frontiers of the Roman Empire—either by Eurasian nomad peoples direct or by non-nomadic East-European and North-European peoples

---

[1] Herodotus, Book IV, chap. 11.   [2] Ibid., chap. 13.
[3] The Arabic for Oghuz (the native Turkish form) and Οὖζοι (the Greek form).
[4] The Western form (Πατζινακῖται in Greek).
[5] See F. J. Teggart, *Rome and China: A Study of Correlations in Historical Events* (Berkeley, 1939, University of California Press).

who had been propelled by westward nomad outbreaks—can be proved, when allowance has been made for a time-lag, to correspond in date with antecedent Chinese offensives against nomad peoples at the Steppe's eastern end. According to this theory, the pressure applied to the Eurasian nomad world by China was transmitted westward, from one nomad people to another, till it eventually impinged on the Roman Empire at the opposite end of the Continent.

Of course the disturbances on the Steppe did not always travel from east to west, and they were not always produced by the pressure of some neighbouring sedentary society. The western Huns, who established themselves on the Hungarian Alföld before it was occupied successively by the Avars and by the Magyars, were forced, by a revolt of their German subjects, to recoil back eastwards. The Calmucks, who had overrun the Kazaks on the middle section of the Steppe and had broken through the Cossack cordon along the River Yaik and through the Russian frontier along the lower Volga in 1616, likewise recoiled back eastwards in 1771 and found asylum within the western fringe of the Manchu Empire. In these two cases, a movement on the Steppe from west to east was produced by pressure from sedentary peoples outside the Steppe; but there have also been eruptions out of the Steppe that have been caused by changes in the distribution of power among the nomad peoples themselves. The overthrow of the Juan Juan's Steppe-empire and the foiling of the Khazars' attempt to crush the Pechenegs account respectively for the westward eruptions of the Avars and the Magyars. The eruption of the Mongols out of the Steppe into all the adjoining seats of sedentary civilization is accounted for, as has been noted already, by the political genius of Chingis Khan. We may guess that it was some unknown Hun (Hiungnu) political genius who, nine centuries before Chingis Khan's generation, built up the Huns' power on the Steppe to a height that enabled the Huns to erupt, in the course of the fourth century of the Christian Era, first into northern China on the east and then simultaneously into Transoxania and India on the south and into Europe on the west.

These exceptional disturbances of the normal routine of nomadic pastoral life on the Steppe have been the occasions on which the nomads have made their greatest effect on the fortunes of the rest of mankind. This effect has usually taken the form of raids that, though devastating, have been ephemeral. Less frequently it has taken the less transitory form of the establishment of empires that have been based on part or on the whole of the Steppe but that have also included some or all of the adjoining sedentary societies. The Mongol Empire is the classic example of this.

The histories of these occasional outbreaks of the nomads are of greater general importance than the log of the nomads' normal annual routine, but these dramatic disturbances of the regular course of the nomads' life present difficult problems to the historian. All aspects of these episodes are elusive. Even the names of the erupting nomad peoples are volatile. The erupting peoples also repeatedly split, and their splinters sometimes combine with splinters of other peoples to form new associations. These combinations sometimes bear a new name and sometimes retain the original name of one or other of their components. Migrating nomad peoples also sometimes abandon their original language and adopt either one of the other languages current on the Steppe or else the language of one of the sedentary peoples whom the migrant nomads have subjugated. There is not any uniformity, either, in the nomads' physical race. The Eurasian nomads have been recruited from two races, the 'Caucasian' and the 'Mongoloid'. Some of them have been more or less pure-blooded representatives of one or other race, while others have been racially mixed in any number of different proportions.

The elusiveness of the Eurasian nomad peoples' names is illustrated by the case of the Magyars.[1] These call themselves Magyars today and probably have done so ever since the period of unknown length, ending in A.D. 889,[2] during which, as allies of the Khazars, they occupied the Steppe to the west of the Don and took tribute, on the Khazars' behalf, from the Slav and Finn peoples in the Black Earth Zone to the north of the Magyars' own domain on the Steppe, and in the forest zone to the north of that. The evidence for the use of the name Magyar by this date is its survival in a number of place-names in this trans-Steppe region of northerly European Russia.[3] These place-names presumably mark the sites of former Magyar garrisons and outposts.[4] However, the foreign peoples on whom the Magyars have impinged have called them by other names than 'Magyars', which is the Magyars' own name for themselves.

The commonest of the foreign names for the Magyars is 'Hungarian', 'Ungarn', 'Hongrois' in the Teutonic and Romance languages of Western Europe, 'Ugrian' in the Slavonic languages of Eastern Europe,

---

[1] See H. Grégoire, 'Le Nom et l'origine des Hongrois', in *Zeitschrift der deutschen morgenländischen Gesellschaft*, Band 91 (N.F. Band 16) (1937), pp. 630–42. Grégoire here analyses the components of Constantine Porphyrogenitus's notices of the Magyars (Τοῦρκοι), Pechenegs, and Kávaroi in *De Administrando Imperio*.

[2] *Reginonis Abbatis Prumiensis Chronicon*, sub anno 889. The passage is quoted, in translation, by C. A. Macartney, *The Magyars in the Ninth Century* (Cambridge, 1930, University Press), p. 70.

[3] See Macartney, op. cit., p. 33, with n. 1. The place-names, compounded with the ethnikon Mažar or Možar, occur in the (former Imperial Russian) Governments of Kazan, Tambov, Simbirsk, and Saratov. A majority of them are to the west of the Volga. See also I. Boba, *Nomads, Northmen, and Slavs: Eastern Europe in the Ninth Century* (The Hague, 1967, Mouton), pp. 92–3.

[4] Boba's view, ibid., that they mark the location of the Magyars' original habitat is not convincing.

and Οὔγγροι in Greek.[1] Possibly both 'Hungarian' and 'Ugrian' stand for Onogur, the Turkish name, signifying 'the Ten Ogur tribes', which was borne, in the sixth and seventh centuries, by a Bulgar nomad people whose pastures were at that time on the Steppe to the east of the Sea of Azov. 'Ugrian' could be derived from 'Onogur' by a Slavonic nasalized contraction of the 'nog' of 'Onogur'.[2] However, it is also possible that the name 'Ugrian' may have nothing to do with the name 'Onogur', but may be derived from the name 'Iyrkai', which is recorded by Herodotus[3] as having been borne by a forest people on the route to China from Olbia (Borysthenes), the Greek colony at the mouths of the Dniepr and the southern Bug. This route skirted the northern edge of the middle section of the Eurasian Steppe. The habitat of the Iyrkai seems to have been the southern end of the Ural Range, and the Finnish-speaking peoples whose dialects have the closest affinity with the Magyar language are the Voguls and the Ostiaks, whose present habitat is along the eastern slopes of the Urals.[4] The ethnikon 'Iyrkai' might be the original form (Graecized by Herodotus) of the ethnika '-Ogur', '-Igur', and 'Uigur'.

Some medieval Muslim writers identify the Magyars with the 'Bashkirs'.[5] In the thirteenth century, a people bearing the ethnikon 'Bashkirs' occupied the country, to the east of Volga Bulgaria, between the middle course of the River Volga and the southern end of the Ural Range, and this same people, bearing the same name, is still living in the same country today.

It was somewhere in this neighbourhood that, on the eve of the Mongols' westward eruption that culminated in the Mongol invasion of Russia in 1237/8, a pagan 'Great Hungary' was located by some Danubian Hungarian Dominican friars.[6] They believed that this 'Great Hungary' was the Magyars' original home, and they had been intending to convert these supposed kinsmen of theirs to Christianity in its Western form. Their activities are reported in two extant letters written by one of

---

[1] Boba holds (op. cit., pp. 75–7) that the Ugrians and the Magyars were different peoples, speaking different languages, who did not merge with each other till the close of the ninth century.

[2] See J. Moravcsik, 'Zur Geschichte der Onoguren', in *Ungarische Jahrbücher*, vol. x (1930), pp. 53–90, on p. 81; Boba, op. cit., p. 74.

[3] Herodotus, Book IV, chap. 22.

[4] According to Vernadsky, *Ancient Russia*, p. 234, the Russian chronicles call the Voguls 'Ugrii', and the Voguls are certainly not Onogurs. M. von Miechow, *De Duobus Sarmatiis* (1517), says that a people in the Urals called Juhra (i.e. Ugrians) speak a language akin to the Hungarians' language. H. von Herberstein, *Rerum Muscovitarum Commentarii* (1549) also reports this, but notes that he has not been able to confirm it. See J. Szinnyei, *Die Herkunft der Ungarn* (Berlin and Leipzig, 1920, de Gruyter), p. 3.

[5] See the passages cited by Macartney in op. cit., on pp. 33–8.

[6] See Macartney, op. cit., Excursus II, 'Magna Hungaria', on pp. 156–73, and H. Paszkiewicz, *The Origin of Russia* (London, 1954, Allen & Unwin), Appendix 12, 'The Hungarian Missionary Julianus in Eastern Europe during the Great Tartar Invasion', pp. 442–7.

them, Friar Julian.[1] In his first letter, Friar Julian claims that he reached the pagan Hungarians' country, which was 'iuxta flumen Ethyl', and that he and they were able to communicate with each other 'quia omnino habent Ungaricum ydioma'. At the time of his visit, the 'Great Hungarians' were already being attacked by the Mongols but were still holding their own.[2] Julian was not able to visit 'Great Hungary' again, nor did any of his fellow missionaries succeed in reaching it; for, before Julian wrote his second letter, he and his fellow missionaries had heard 'by word of mouth' ('viva voce') that Great Hungary had been conquered by the Mongols after a long and stubborn resistance,[3] and the Mongols were now on the point of invading Russia.

Julian himself does not expressly identify his 'Great Hungarians' with the Bashkirs, but this identification is made by the Italian Franciscan Friar, Giovanni del Pian di Carpine, who travelled to the Court of the Mongol Khaqan in 1247-9 on behalf of Pope Innocent IV,[4] and by the Flemish Franciscan Friar William of Rubruck, who travelled to the Khaqan's court in 1253-5 on behalf of King Louis IX of France. In this passage, Friar William says that he had obtained this information from the Dominican friars (i.e. the Hungarian friars) who had visited the Bashkirs' country before the Mongols had invaded it.[5]

Thus the medieval Western authorities support the medieval Muslim authorities in identifying the Magyars with the Bashkirs. This identification must, however, be wrong. Magyar is a Finnish language, whereas the Bashkirs speak a Turkish dialect today, and they were speaking Turkish already in the eleventh century, on the evidence of an eleventh-century author of a Turkish grammar, Mahmūd al-Kashgharī.[6] What is the explanation of this identification which, in spite of its being mistaken, was made by medieval Muslim and Western Christian (including Hungarian) writers independently of each other? The answer seems to be that medieval Bashkiria included a Magyar-speaking population as well as the Turkish-speaking Bashkir population that gave the country its actual name. This is not just a guess. One of the original sources of the Muslim accounts of the regions to the north and north-west of the Caspian is a gazetteer—dating, apparently, from the ninth century—of the peoples whose countries are traversed by the route from Khwarizm

---

[1] The texts have been published by L. Bendefy in *Archivum Europae Centro-Orientalis*, vol. iii (1937), pp. 1–50.

[2] Bendefy, p. 24, cited by Paszkiewicz, *The Origin of Russia*, p. 443, n. 4.

[3] See the passage quoted by Paszkiewicz, ibid., from Bendefy, p. 36.

[4] See the passage quoted by Macartney in op. cit., p. 165, and the French translation of the same passage in *Les Précurseurs de Marco Polo*, ed. by A. T'Serstevens (Paris, 1959, Arthaud), p. 137.

[5] See the passage quoted by Macartney in op. cit., p. 162, and the French translation in *Les Précurseurs de Marco Polo*, pp. 246 and 247.

[6] See Macartney, op. cit., p. 39, with n. 1. See also his p. 167.

to Volga Bulgaria, and in this gazetteer it is stated that the traveller has his first encounter with the Majghar between the Pechenegs and the Volga Bulgars' subjects or associates the Ashkal.[1] Since, at the date of the gazetteer, the Pechenegs were still on the section of the Steppe between the Rivers Yaik and Volga, the habitat of the Magyars here in question must have been the southern end of the Ural Range, immediately to the east of the Bashkirs and just where Herodotus appears to locate the Iyrkai. These Magyars will have been Friar Julian's pagan Hungarians with whom he was able to communicate because their language was the 'Hungaricum ydioma'. The Hungarian missionaries will have called the common country of these pagan Magyars and the Bashkirs 'Magna Hungaria', instead of using the usual name 'Bashkiria', because these Magyar-speaking kinsmen of theirs, not the Turkish-speaking Bashkirs, were the people in whom the missionaries were interested.

Since the Bashkirs were, and are, Turkish-speakers, an interpretation of the ethnikon 'Bashkir' in terms of the Turkish language has been suggested.[2] The ethnikon 'Bashkir' may stand for 'Beshogur', meaning a group of five Ogur tribes, so named to distinguish this group from the group of ten, known as the 'Onogurs'. In Turkish, 'on' means 'ten' and 'besh' means 'five'. However, the first syllable of the word 'Bashkir' may stand, not for 'besh', but for 'bash', which is the Turkish word for 'head'. Moreover, the name 'Bashkir' is sometimes spelled 'Bashkird'. Thus the conjecture that 'Bashkir' stands for 'Beshogur' remains unproven, and, even if confirmed, it would not lend any support to the identification of the Magyars with the Bashkirs.

Constantine Porphyrogenitus says[3] that, in his day, there was a splinter of the 'Turks' (i.e. the Magyars) which had travelled eastwards, and had settled in the region of Persia, when, in 889, the main body of the Magyars had travelled westward under the impact of the Pechenegs. These alleged south-eastern Magyars' name—still current in Constantine's day—was Σαβαρτοιασφάλοι, and Constantine infers, though this conclusion evidently puzzles him, that the Magyar people as a whole bore the name Σαβαρτοιασφάλοι while it was living, to the west of the River Don, in Levedhía.

A people bearing the first part of this evidently composite name is known from other sources. A nomad people called the Saparda is located in Media, just to the north-east of the Assyrian frontier in that quarter, in Assyrian records of events in the seventh century B.C. The name reappears in the sixth and fifth centuries B.C. as the title of a Persian satrapy,

---

[1] See the passages quoted in Macartney, op. cit., pp. 30–1.
[2] See Moravcsik in loc. cit., p. 85, n. 1; D. M. Dunlop, *The Jewish Khazars* (Princeton, 1954, University Press), p. 40.
[3] In *De Adm. Imp.*, chap. 38, p. 169.

Sparda, in western Asia Minor.[1] We may infer that, in the meantime, the Saparda had migrated from Media to Lydia, and that they were associated with the Cimmerians, if they were not just another name for these. The Saparda reappear in medieval Armenian records as the Sevordik (with the Armenian plural in -*k*) and in medieval Arabic records as the Sāwardīyah.[2] They are recorded to have invaded the Caucasian dominions of the Arab Caliphate. They occupied the whole of the Ganjah district in the Caucasian Albania, and they destroyed the city of Shamkūr, to the west of Ganjah itself, but they failed to establish themselves in Bardha'ah, which was the Arabs' military and administrative headquarters in this area.[3] To this extent, the Armenian and Arabic records bear out Constantine Porphyrogenitus's statements. There are, however, two discrepancies. The Oriental authorities date the irruption of the Sevordik-Sāwardīyah 750–60, not 889; and in this connection they give this single name only; they do not couple it with the word 'Asphál̄oi'.

Constantine Porphyrogenitus himself mentions the Sávartoi-Sevordik-Sāwardīyah without the appendage 'Asphál̄oi' in a different work of his, *De Caerimoniis*,[4] and in a different transliteration: (ἄρχοντες τῶν) Σερβοτίων instead of Σάβαρτοι. This difference in the Greek spelling of an identical name, and the absence, in *De Caerimoniis*, of the *De Administrando Imperio*'s association of this name with the Magyars, show that the references in *De Caerimoniis* and in *De Administrando Imperio* have been drawn from different sources. Marquart suggests[5] that Constantine has drawn the information that he gives in *De Administrando Imperio* from an Arabic source, and that 'Asphál̄oi' is a transliteration of the Arabic adjective 'asfal', meaning 'lower'.[6] In Marquart's view,[7] this epithet was given to the Sāwardīyah on the south side of the Caucasus to distinguish them from the Magyars to the north of the Black Sea. An alternative possibility is that, if Constantine's 'Asphál̄oi' is in truth the Arabic word 'asfal', it had been added to distinguish those of the Sāwardīyah who had descended on the Albanian lowlands from kinsmen of theirs who had remained ensconced in the Caucasian highlands. However, if Constantine's 'Asphál̄oi' were an Arabic adjectival epithet of the name Sāwardīyah, it would surely have had to be preceded by the Arabic definite article 'al-', and this is missing in Constantine's Σαβαρτοιασφάλοι.

It therefore seems more probable that Constantine's 'Asphál̄oi' represents, not an epithet of Sávartoi, but a separate ethnikon. A people

---

[1] The present-day Sephardic Jews derive their name from the Jewish diaspora in this province of the Persian Empire.

[2] See Laurent, op. cit , pp. 23–4; Macartney, op. cit., pp. 87–90.

[3] See J. Marquart, *Osteuropäische und ostasiatische Streifzüge* (Leipzig, 1903, Dietrich), pp. 36–8, and Vernadsky, *Ancient Russia*, p. 288, citing Mas'ūdī, ii, 75.

[4] *De Caer.*, Book II, chap. 48, p. 687.

[5] In op. cit., p. 39.   [6] Ibid., p. 40.   [7] Ibid.

bearing this name is, in fact, mentioned by two Latin authorities, and it is located by these in the region where Constantine locates the Magyars during the time before the Magyars were expelled by the Pechenegs. Spelled as 'Spalei' or 'Spalaei', Constantine's Aspháloi are located by Pliny in the Don basin beyond the river.[1] Spelled as 'Spali', they appear to be located by Jordanes in the same region.[2] Constantine alone mentions the Aspháloi's appearance, in company with the Sávartoi, to the south of the Caucasus. Conversely, Constantine alone mentions the presence of Sávartoi to the north of the Caucasus. The Sevordik-Sāwardīyah who invaded the Arab Caliphate's dominions in 750–60 seem likely to have been a surviving fragment of the Saparda who had migrated from Iran to Asia Minor in the seventh century B.C. A number of fragments of peoples who have not survived anywhere else have been preserved in the Caucasus—a natural fastness that has served repeatedly as an asylum. An example is the survival, down to the present day, of a remnant of the Alans astride the Darial (i.e. 'Alans' Gate') Pass.

We may infer that a remnant of the Saparda which had survived in the south-eastern Caucasus invaded the Caliphate in company with a detachment of Spali from the Don basin; that the date was 750–60, not 889; and that the invasion was promoted and organized by the Khazars for their own purposes, and was not a consequence of the occupation of the Don basin by the Pechenegs more than a century later against the Khazars' will. The Oriental authorities' dating is more convincing than Constantine's. In 750 the 'Abbasids supplanted the Umayyads as the result of a hard-fought civil war. The consequent temporary paralysis of the Arab Caliphate offered the Khazars an opportunity for pushing forward the frontiers of their own empire at the Caliphate's expense, and, if they employed as their agents two of the peoples who were under their suzerainty, this was in consonance with what is known to have been the Khazars' regular policy.

This reconstruction of the course of events would explain the presence of Sávartoi and Aspháloi to the south of the Caucasus in Constantine's day. It would not account, however, for Constantine's identification of this pair of peoples with the Magyars; for both the Saparda and the Spalei are mentioned at dates that are earlier than the earliest date at which it is credible that the Magyars were sucked out of the Uralian forest on to the Steppe. It is also difficult to believe Constantine's statement that the main body of the Magyars, after it had migrated first to the west of the Dniepr and then to the west of the Carpathians, continued to

---

[1] Pliny, *Historia Naturalis*, Book VI, chap. 7 (7), § 22.

[2] Jordanes, *Romana et Getica*, section 28. Across a river, beyond some water-meadows (Oium). The location might be across the Don, beyond Levedhía.

keep up an active intercourse with its alleged kinsmen the Savartoi-aspháloi to the south of the Caucasus.[1]

Constantine VII Porphyrogenitus follows his father Leo VI in calling the Magyars 'Turks'. This name for the Magyars is peculiar,[2] but the steps by which Leo VI was led to adopt it become manifest when we compare his account of the Eurasian nomads in his *Taktiká*[3] with the account of them in 'Mavríkios's' *Stratêghikón*[4] on which Leo's account is based. For providing himself with a description of the Magyars, Leo has copied 'Mavríkios's' description of the Avars verbatim; but, since the Avars were notoriously extinct by Leo's day, Leo has replaced the name 'Avars' by the name 'Turks', which is the second of the two ethnika that are named in the title of the chapter of 'Mavríkios's' work that Leo is here plagiarizing.[5]

'Toúrkoi' and 'Savartoiaspháloi' are 'fancy names', and they are unlikely to have been current among the majority of Leo VI's and his son Constantine Porphyrogenitus's Greek-speaking subjects. Oúngroi—the Greek version of the name by which the Magyars are designated in the Slavonic, Teutonic, and Latin languages—has probably been the usual name for them among Greek-speakers from first to last. At some date in the reign of the Emperor Theóphilos (829–42) the Adrianopolitans who had been deported in 813 by Khan Krum of Danubian Bulgaria to the Bulgarian territory in what is now Wallachia were rescued and repatriated by the East Roman Imperial Fleet. The Bulgars appealed to the Magyars, who at that time occupied the Steppe from the Don to the Seret, to intercept the fugitives, and the Magyars tried to oblige the Bulgars, but this without success. The incident is recorded in *Georgius Monachus Interpolatus*,[6] and by Leo Grammaticus.[7] In both these versions of Symeon's *Chronographia* the Magyars are called successively Oúnghroi,

---

[1] See *De Adm. Imp.*, chap. 38, p. 171.

[2] Macartney points out, in op. cit., pp. 128–32, that the other Greek writers, besides Leo VI and Constantine Porphyrogenitus, who call the Magyars 'Turks' are employees or associates of one or other of these two Emperors, or else are later writers who are copying mechanically the word used by their predecessors. This usage is adopted by Nikólaos, Leo VI's confidential secretary (mystikós) who subsequently became Patriarch of Constantinople; possibly by Philótheos (p. 171 Bury, p. 772 Bonn) ; by Genesius; and by the author of the first four books of *Theoph. Cont.* It was, however, also adopted by an independent contemporary of Constantine's, Symeon Magister (in *Georg. Mon. Cont.* and in Leo Grammaticus) and by the pseudo-Symeon, and finally by later writers who are copying a usage that, by their time, had become so unintelligible that at least one of them, Zonarás (vol. iii, pp. 443 and 484 Bonn), feels it necessary to explain that by Τοῦρκοι he means Οὔγγροι.

Two Muslim writers, Ibn Rustah and Gardēzī, say (evidently drawing on an identical source) that the Magyars (Majghar) are a race of Turks (see the translation of these passages in Macartney, op. cit., p. 206). It is not clear whether the word 'Turks' is being used in its specific linguistic sense or as a generic term for Eurasian nomads.

[3] Leo VI, *Taktiká*, Dhiat. 18, §§ 47–74, cols. 957–64.

[4] 'Mavríkios', Part 11, chap. 2, pp. 260–8 Scheffer, pp. 268–75 Mihăescu.

[5] See II, 6, pp. 294–6.   [6] pp. 817–19.   [7] pp. 231–2.

Oúnnoi, Toúrkoi (twice running), and then Oúnnoi once again. Macartney makes the convincing inference[1] that 'Oúnghroi', the name first employed, was the normal Greek name for the Magyars in the tenth century, and that 'Oúnnoi' and 'Toúrkoi' were merely academic synonyms.

This multiplicity of alternative names for the Magyars illustrates the elusiveness of Eurasian nomad ethnika by an example relating to the period of East Roman history with which the present work is primarily concerned, but other examples abound.

When the Mongols suddenly emerged above the horizon of Western Christendom in the thirteenth century, the Western Christians called them Tartars, and they spelled this name with two r's in order to make the name pun with the word 'Tartarus', the classical Greek name for 'Hell' which had found its way into Latin literature. In the correct form 'Tatar', this ethnikon came to supersede the ethnikon 'Mongol' in Muslim as well as in Christian records as the name for the nomads who were incorporated in the western appanages of the Mongol Empire. However, the Tatars were not identical with the Mongols. The Tatars were a neighbouring but separate Mongol-speaking nomad people who had been subjugated by Chingis Khan at an early stage in his empire-building career. Chingis had incorporated the Tatars in his association of nomad peoples, as he had incorporated many other of these peoples besides, but the Mongols, not the Tatars, were the ruling people in the Mongol Empire so long as this empire lasted.

When, in the thirteenth century, the Mongols took possession of the middle and the western section of the Eurasian Steppe, they found there a nomad people whose proper name was Qipchaq. The Russians called the Qipchaq 'Polovtsi', which means Steppe-people. The Western Christians called the Qipchaq 'Cumans' when a section of them, fleeing from the Mongols, sought and found asylum in Hungary. Presumably this name 'Cuman' is derived from the River Kuma, which traverses the Steppe to the north of the Caucasus and discharges into the Caspian Sea.

The name Bulgars suddenly makes its appearance after the death of the Hun war-lord Attila in 453 and after the consequent recoil of the western Huns eastwards out of the Hungarian Alföld back on to the western end of the Eurasian Steppe.[2] Moravcsik guesses[3] that this was a new name for a new combination of nomad peoples. When the western Huns had migrated westwards beyond the Carpathians, and when the Ephthalite Huns had migrated south-eastwards beyond the Jaxartes and the Oxus, the vacuum that they had left in their wake had been filled by

---

[1] In op. cit., p. 130.
[2] The first mention of the name 'Bulgar' is apropos of the Emperor Zeno's enlistment of the Bulgars' help against the Ostrogoths in 482.
[3] In loc. cit., p. 69 (following J. Nemeth) and p. 70.

peoples bearing in common the ethnikon Ogurs or Igurs with a number
of distinctive prefixes (Kotrigurs, Utigurs, Sarigurs, Onogurs, and perhaps Beshigurs, i.e. Bashkirs, as well). When the western Huns ebbed
back on to the Steppe, they appear to have combined with the Ogurs
there. The Bulgars who gained a foothold to the south of the Lower
Danube in 680 were Onogurs,[1] and the first name on the list of their
Khans is Irnik, i. e. Ernakh, which was the name of one of Attila's sons.

Combinations and splits of Eurasian nomad peoples have, indeed, been
frequent.[2] Both the Magyars and the Danubian Bulgars may have been
splinters of the Onogur association of tribes, and the Volga Bulgars may
have been a third splinter of the same association. One splinter of the
Kotrigurs became one of the eight Magyar tribes;[3] another became one
of the eight Pecheneg tribes.[4] The Magyars may or may not have been
split into two splinters when, in 889, the Pechenegs hit them. It has been
noted that Constantine Porphyrogenitus's statements to this effect are
questionable. On the other hand, there is no reason for doubting
Constantine's statement that, at some date which he does not record,
the Magyars adopted into their confederacy three tribes of dissident
Khazars whose ethnikon was 'Kavar'.[5] Moreover, it is certain that, in
the thirteenth century, the Magyars adopted a section of the Cumans
(Qipchaq) who were fleeing from the Mongols. When, in 889, the
Pechenegs were hit by the Ghuzz, not all of the Pechenegs preserved
their identity by hitting and dislodging the Magyars. Some of them submitted to the Ghuzz and were absorbed by them.[6] In truth, absorption
may have been a more usual fate than eviction for defeated nomad
peoples. For instance, there seems to have been only a minimum of
displacement when the Mongols subjugated all their fellow tenants of the
Eurasian Steppe. In the Golden Horde, which was the appanage of the
House of Jöchi (Tushi), Chingis Khan's eldest son, the Mongol element
was no more than a veneer on the surface. The rank and file of the
Golden Horde consisted of the Turkish-speaking nomad peoples—
Qangli, Qarluq, Qipchaq—who had been in occupation of the middle
and western sections of the Steppe before the Mongols overran them. The
disturbances on the Steppe have been wave-like, and waves are not dis-
placements; they are upheavals that are transmitted from one stationary
piece of water to another.[7]

[1] According to the Deacon Agháthon apropos of events in 713 (see Moravcsik in loc. cit.,
p. 67). Theophanes, p. 356, and Constantine Porphyrogenitus, *De Them.*, p. 46, call the
Danubian Bulgars Οὐννογούνδουροι or 'Ονογούνδουροι, and Nic. Patr., p. 24, gives the same
form of the name to the people who revolted, under Koúvrat's leadership, against the Avars.
[2] Moravcsik in loc. cit., p. 53.   [3] *De Adm. Imp.*, chap. 40, p. 172.
[4] *De Adm. Imp.*, chap. 37, p. 66.   [5] See *De Adm. Imp.*, chaps. 39–40, pp. 171–2.
[6] See *De Adm. Imp.*, chap. 37, pp. 166–7.
[7] After I had thought of this simile, I found that it had already occurred to H. Freiherr von
Kutschera, *Die Chasaren* (Vienna, 1910, Holzhausen), pp. 28–9.

Some of the creators of new combinations of nomad peoples have left a record of their political achievement by bequeathing their own names to serve as ethnika for the combine that they have welded together. Saljūq, Chaghatay, 'Osman, Uzbek, and Nogay were the personal names of confederation-builders before they provided names for the confederations that these nomad statesmen had established.

The latest tenants of the middle section of the Eurasian Steppe have been the Kazaks, and their name indicates that originally they were outsiders beyond the pale of the Golden Horde.[1] They did not occupy the heart of the Steppe till the Uzbeks had moved off it into Transoxania. It might have been expected that these outsiders would turn out to be composed of tribes that had not been on the heart of the Steppe before; but a survey of the components of the Kazak hordes reveals that these hordes were amalgams of splinters of peoples—e.g. Qipchaq, Naiman, Qongurat (Qonqīrat) Jalair, Qangli—which had been tenants of the Steppe in earlier chapters of its history.[2]

The languages spoken by the Eurasian nomad peoples are as elusive as the names that these peoples bear. The Magyars speak an Eastern Finnish language today, but in the tenth century they were bilingual. Constantine Porphyrogenitus informs us[3] that they had become bilingual after they had absorbed the Kavars. He also informs us, in the same context, that the Kavars were Khazars, and we know that the Khazars were a Turkish-speaking people. In the thirteenth century the Magyars also absorbed some of the Cumans, who were Turkish-speaking too.[4] These accessions of Turkish-speakers have left some traces in the vocabulary of the Magyar language. There are also more than 200 loan words in Magyar from Old Chuvash,[5] the Turkish language which was spoken by the Volga Bulgars, who were the Magyars' neighbours when these were living to the west of the River Don as allies of the Khazars. However, the Magyars ceased to be bilingual long ago. Their Finnish language has been their exclusive national language since the earliest date at which their Western neighbours became cognizant of it.

The Magyars have preserved their original Finnish language in spite of their having planted themselves in the midst of Slavonic-speaking and

[1] If the term 'kazak' (Cossack, Casogian) is derived from the Turkish verb 'qazmaq' meaning 'to dig', these 'diggers' were originally the agricultural neighbours of the nomads. These were sometimes subject to the nomads (as, for instance, were Herodotus's Skythai arotêres and Skythai georgoi) and were sometimes independent. The Turkish term came to be used to describe peoples who were independent of the dominant nomad horde, rather than peoples whose way of life was sedentary agricultural, not nomadic pastoral.

[2] See A. E. Hudson, *Kazak Social Structure* (New Haven, 1938, Yale University Press), p. 14.

[3] In *De Adm. Imp.*, chap. 37, pp. 166–7.

[4] Kutschera, op. cit., p. 196, notes that the last speaker of the Cuman Turkish language in Hungary died in 1770.

[5] See Szinnyei, op. cit., p. 19.

Roumanian-speaking and German-speaking populations. On the other hand, the Bulgars have lost their original Turkish language; they now speak the language of the Slav peoples, to the south of the lower Danube, on whom the Bulgars imposed their rule in and after the year 680. The linguistic history of the Savéiroi-Savĕr-Severians has been the same. At the turn of the fifth and sixth centuries, they were Huns, presumably Turkish-speaking, on the Steppe to the north of the Caucasus.[1] We then find them transformed into a Slavonic-speaking people—by 680 to the south of the lower Danube,[2] and by 884 in the Dniepr basin.[3] The Serbs and Croats, too, have lost their original Iranian language, if it is true that they, like the Bulgars and the Savéiroi, were nomad conquerors of sedentary Slavs.

It will be seen that the history of the Eurasian nomads is beset with pitfalls.

(ii) *Distinctive Features of the Western Section of the Eurasian Steppe*

The Eurasian Steppe extends from the Carpathians to the Khingan Range without any break in its continuity. Every part of it is easily accessible from every other part. We can, however, distinguish three sections which are linked together by relatively narrow corridors. The middle section is linked with the eastern section by the Zungarian Gap between the Altai Mountains and the Tien Shan, and it is linked with the western section by the strip of steppe-land that intervenes between the southern end of the Ural Range and the north-eastern corner of the Caspian Sea. It has been noted already that the East Roman Empire's fortunes were affected to some extent by events on all sections of the Eurasian Steppe, but naturally they were affected most rapidly and most intimately by events on the western section, since this section adjoins the Crimea and the Balkan Peninsula, in both of which the East Roman Empire had dependencies and possessions. This western section of the Steppe has several distinctive features of its own, and these features played an important part in the East Roman Empire's history.

The principal distinctive feature of the western section of the Steppe is that it alone has frontages on the sea. The middle and the eastern sections are both landlocked, but the western section touches the north shore of the Black Sea—a backwater of the Mediterranean, which is a backwater of the Ocean—and, across its northern hinterland, the western section of the Steppe also communicates with the eastern shore of the Baltic, which is a backwater of the Ocean via the North Sea. Moreover, the western

---

[1] See Runciman, *A History of the First Bulgarian Empire*, pp. 7 and 10.
[2] Theophanes, p. 359.
[3] *The Russian Primary Chronicle*, Cross's and Sherbowitz-Wetzor's translation, p. 61.

section of the Steppe has a frontage along the northern and north-western shores of the Caspian; and, though the Caspian, in contrast to the Black Sea and the Baltic, is land-locked, it is by far the largest inland sea in the World, and it links the Steppe by water with Iran and, through Iran, with the rest of South-West Asia.

All sections of the Steppe, from the lower basin of the Danube to the upper basin of the Amur, are traversed by rivers, but the rivers to the west of the Urals are more serviceable media of communication than the rivers to the east of them. The western rivers flow southwards across the Steppe and discharge into the Black Sea and into the Caspian. The rivers that traverse the middle and the eastern section of the Steppe either lose themselves in the sands (e.g. the Tarim, the Chu, and the Zarafshan) or discharge into minor inland seas (e.g. the Ili, the Jaxartes, and the Oxus) or else into the Arctic Ocean. The Amur River, whose upper basin lies within the north-eastern corner of the Steppe, passes out of the Steppe a long way above its debouchure into the Pacific, and it reaches the Pacific in so high a latitude that the ocean is here almost as inhospitable for navigation as it is along the northern coast of Asia.

All these rivers offer potential means of communication by water—at least over some portions of their courses at some seasons of the year. However, the pastoral nomads in general have not taken kindly to the water. The Saka nomads on the middle section of the Steppe did learn to be watermen on the Jaxartes and the Oxus, and they then used their navigational skill to conquer the Panjab in the last two centuries B.C. by taking to the water again on the Indus and on its tributaries. This, however, is an exception which proves the rule that, normally, good riders and drivers and shepherds and herdsmen do not make good boatmen. On the whole, the steppe-rivers have been impediments for the pastoral nomads, not facilities. Wherever possible, the nomads have made their annual treks between the rivers, along the watersheds, and, when a nomad people has been pushed or pulled out of its established orbit, it has not found it easy to ferry its flocks and its herds and its carts and its portable felt-and-wattle *kibitkas* across the rivers that have previously been the boundaries of its domain. Often a dislodged horde has preferred to wait till the onset of winter has enabled it to cross the rivers, dry-shod, over the ice.

The potential means of communication that the steppe-rivers offer have been utilized chiefly by the pastoral nomads' non-nomadic neighbours. The most enterprising of all these non-nomadic Eurasian watermen have been the Cossacks. In the course of less than two centuries, beginning in the fifteenth century of the Christian Era, the Cossacks first insulated from each other the nomads on the western section of the Steppe by establishing chains of agricultural settlements along the courses of the

Dniepr and Don and Yaik. After that, they encircled the Steppe, round its northern fringe, by travelling on the water, up and down the rivers— discovering the shortest and easiest portages between them—till they arrived at the shore of the Sea of Okhotsk. The Cossacks have been the farthest-ranging of the Eurasian watermen-pioneers, but they have not been the earliest. Already, towards the close of the sixth century, when the author of 'Mavríkios's' *Stratēghikón* was campaigning in Wallachia, the East Roman Army's Slav opponents there were in their element on the lower Danube and on its north-bank tributaries. In the ninth century, and perhaps before that, the Scandinavians had crossed the Baltic, had ascended the southern Dvina and the Volkhov and the Lovat, and had discovered the portages to the upper waters of the southward-flowing rivers, the Volga first and the Dniepr later. This discovery has had a decisive influence on the subsequent history of the whole Continent.

Moreover, when the Wallachian Slavs and the Scandinavians and the Cossacks had made their way down the rivers to the sea, they all took to the salt water, as the Goths had taken to it in the third century. When the Wallachian Slavs made their *Völkerwanderung* into the Balkan Peninsula, they launched out into the Aegean Sea in the dug-out skiffs (monóxyla) that they had used on their rivers. The Scandinavians who, by invitation or uninvited, came to rule over some of the north-eastern Slav and south-western Finnish peoples from a headquarters at Kiev, on the River Dniepr, appear to have collected dug-out skiffs from their Slav subjects along the Dniepr's headwaters and to have converted these in two stages into rather more substantial vessels for their expeditions into the Black Sea.[1] The Rhos vessels that attacked Constantinople in 860 are not called monóxyla in any of the Greek accounts of this event.[2] These converted dug-out skiffs could navigate the Black Sea with impunity, and no doubt the Volga-Scandinavians used ships of much the same build[3] for their raids on the hinterland of the south-western shore of the Caspian. The boats in which the Cossacks navigated the Black Sea in the seventeenth century were likewise substantial.[4]

When, in 860, a Dniepr-Scandinavian flotilla sailed from Kiev down the Dniepr, by-passed the Dniepr cataracts, coasted along the western shore of the Black Sea, threaded its way through the Bosphorus, and suddenly assaulted Constantinople from the seaward side, it took the East Romans by surprise. However, in this first encounter, as well as on all later occasions, the Rhos vessels proved not to be a match for East Roman war-ships armed with siphons squirting napalm.

[1] See *De Adm. Imp.*, chap. 9, pp. 75 and 78, with Obolensky's notes on pp. 23–5, 36–7, and 57 of Jenkins's *Commentary*.

[2] See A. A. Vasiliev, *The Russian Attack on Constantinople in 860* (Cambridge, Mass., 1946, the Mediaeval Academy of America), p. 190.

[3] See Obolensky in loc. cit., p. 24.   [4] See Obolensky in loc. cit., pp. 36–7.

Via the Black Sea and the rivers that discharge into it from the north, East Roman shipping and Rhos shipping met, not only to fight, but also to trade with each other, and this intercourse led to the conversion of Russia to Christianity in its Eastern Orthodox form. The western section of the Steppe, which intervened between the East Roman Empire and Russia, was never an impassable barrier. The successive nomad occupants of this end of the Steppe—Magyars, Pechenegs, Ghuzz, and Qipchaqs— were able to harass the Russians *en voyage*, especially at the portage round the Dniepr cataracts, which was the point on the water-route between Kiev and Constantinople at which the watermen were most dangerously exposed to nomad assaults. In 838, Rhos envoys managed to reach Constantinople across the Steppe, but in 839 the Emperor Theóphilos sent them homeward via Germany because their return by the direct route was prevented by a ferocious people,[1] who must have been the Magyars.[2] In 972 the Rhos war-lord Svyátoslav was killed by the Pechenegs at this point on his return voyage from his military adventure in the Balkan Peninsula, after he had purchased, by a humiliating capitulation, his release from the trap in which the East Roman Navy and Army had caught him at Dhrístra on the lower Danube.[3] Such harassments were, however, ineffectual. On the western section of the Steppe, the nomads were unable to insulate their northern from their southern sedentary neighbours.

This fact brings out another distinctive feature of the western section of the Steppe. On each of the other two sections, the nomads were confronted by a sedentary society only to the south—on the eastern section by China and on the middle section by South-West Asia and India. On the other hand, on the western section of the Steppe the nomads had to cope with a sedentary society to the north as well as to the south. Physically the Eurasian Continent is traversed by a uniform series of climatic and vegetational zones all the way from the Carpathians to the Khingan Range. The southernmost zone is so arid that its surface can be put to no other use than nomadic animal husbandry. Next to the north lies a debatable zone that can make either good pasture-land or poor arable. To the north of this lies the Black Earth zone, which is first-rate soil for the raising of cereal crops. This belt of Black Earth runs north-eastward from the Carpathians to the Altai, but not beyond. To the north of the Black Earth and of the debatable zone, a belt of forest extends from the Atlantic to the Pacific Ocean. Between the northern fringe of the forest

---

[1] *Annales Bertiniani*, entry for 17 January 839. See Vernadsky, *Ancient Russia*, p. 307; A. A. Vasiliev, *The Russian Attack on Constantinople in 860*, pp. 7–8, 11, 68.

[2] Vlasto, op. cit., note 15 on p. 390, suggests that the 'ferocious people', which had made it impossible for the Rhos to return home by the route by which they had come, were insurgent Slavs. This seems less probable than that they were the Magyars.

[3] See II, 7, pp. 340–1.

and the southern shore of the Arctic Ocean there is a strip of tundra. However, the western section of the Steppe differs from the other two sections in being accessible from the relatively close and clement Baltic Sea, and not solely from the more distant and less hospitable Arctic Ocean. The northern hinterland of the western section of the Steppe is exposed to the radiation of civilization via both the Baltic and the Black Sea, and this superior accessibility has made it possible for civilized societies to establish themselves to the north of the western section of the Steppe as well as to the south of it.

At least as early as the fifth century B.C., and perhaps as early as the seventh, the Skyth nomads' peasant subjects on the Black Earth between the Carpathians and the Urals were producing a surplus of cereals which was being exported by the peasants' nomad landlords to the Aegean basin in exchange for oil and wine and manufactures. On the Black Earth between the Urals and the Altai, settlements and cultivation on an appreciable scale did not start before the later decades of the nineteenth century, and the debatable zone in Kazakhstan has been ploughed for the first time under the Soviet regime. Till the Cossack pioneers encircled the middle and eastern sections of the Steppe from the north in the late sixteenth and early seventeenth centuries, the nomads on these two sections had no northern neighbours to cope with except forest peoples who were weak both numerically and culturally. On the other hand, to the north of the western section of the Steppe the economic and demographic and cultural basis for a civilized sedentary society was in existence already in the last millennium B.C.

Here the nomads have had to contend with their sedentary neighbours for the mastery not only of the Black Earth and the forest beyond it but of the Steppe itself. This contest has been long-drawn-out, and the ascendancy has been won and lost alternately by the contending parties, time and again; but in the end the nomads have lost the battle, and the scales were weighted against them from the start. A ceiling is set on a nomad people's capacity for civilization by the rigidity of the requirements of the pastoral nomadic way of life, whereas the cultural development of a sedentary society is not hampered by any corresponding restriction. A few Eurasian nomad peoples —for instance, the Skyths, the Khazars, and the Uigurs—have attained a level of civilization that, for nomads, is exceptionally high, but they have purchased this cultural achievement at the price of losing the command of their native element, the Steppe, to rival nomad peoples or to intrusive sedentary neighbours. The Skyths were ousted by the more barbarous Sarmatians; the Khazars were partially ousted by the more barbarous Pechenegs before the Rhos, descending from the Steppe's north-western hinterland, gave the Khazars the *coup de grâce*. The decline and fall of the Khazars began in 889, when the Pechenegs established themselves to the west of the Don in the reign of Constantine Porphyrogenitus's father Leo VI, and it ended in the blows that the Khazars received from the Rhos war-lord Svyátoslav in 963,[1] in the reign of Constantine's son Rhomanós II, and perhaps also in 968–9.[2]

This episode was not the end of the story. The Russians' first occupation of the western section of the Steppe was brief. In destroying the remnant of the Khazar Empire the Russians opened the way for the Ghuzz and the Qipchaq, and, after they had been pushed off the Steppe by these next westward-moving waves of nomads, they were subjugated in their own country by the mightier following wave of Mongol conquest. All the same, the history of the western section of the Steppe and its northern hinterland in the ninth and tenth centuries foreshadowed the extinction of the pastoral nomadic way of life on the Eurasian Steppe as a whole. This last act of the drama has been played during the last five or six centuries. It is nearing its conclusion in our day.

(iii) *Events on the Western Steppe and in its Hinterlands, 453–989*

In 453 the Western Hun war-lord Attila died and his empire dissolved. In 989 the Rhos prince Vladímir of Kiev adopted Christianity in its Eastern Orthodox form[3] and imposed it on his subjects.[4] Between these two dates, three peoples that are still in existence today emerged and established themselves: the Bulgars, the Russians, and the Magyars (to name them in the chronological order of their appearance). Today there are still Bulgars both in the southern hinterland of the Steppe—in the Balkan Peninsula to the south of the lower Danube—and in the Steppe's northern hinterland astride the confluence of the Kama with the Volga. The northern Bulgars have kept their Turkish language but have lost their name. They are now known as the Qazan Tatars. The southern Bulgars have kept their name but have lost their former Turkish language. The Russian people's domain extends today from the eastern shore of the Baltic to the western shore of the Pacific and to the northern shores of the Black Sea and the Caspian. The Magyars still hold the enclave of steppe-country on the Alföld which they occupied in 896.

Though each of these three peoples had already made its mark by 989, they had not been either the most prominent or the most powerful of the

---

[1] For this dating, see G. Vernadsky, *Kievan Russia* (New Haven, 1948, Yale University Press), p. 44.

[2] Vernadsky, op. cit., p. 46.

[3] Vlasto, op. cit., pp. 258 and 259, suggests that the date of Vladímir's baptism was 987, while accepting 989–90 as the date at which Vladímir imposed Eastern Orthodox Christianity on his subjects.

[4] The account of Vladímir's conversion in *The Russian Primary Chronicle* is acutely analysed and reconstructed by Obolensky in *The Byzantine Commonwealth*, pp. 192–7.

peoples on the Western Steppe and in its hinterlands. They had been overshadowed by the Avars, the Khazars, and the East Romans. However, none of these three more conspicuous peoples proved to have a future—except in so far as the modern Greeks may be held to be the East Romans' present-day representatives.

The Avars' career in the west had been meteoric. They had appeared suddenly in 558; had won, from a base of operations on the Alföld, an empire that had been as ephemeral as Attila's, whose base had been the same as theirs; and they had been crushed between 791 and 805 by the Franks, assisted, in the delivery of the *coup de grâce*, by the Danubian Bulgars.[1] 'They perished like the Avars'[2] had become a Slavonic proverb by the date, *circa* 1113,[3] at which *The Russian Primary Chronicle* was edited in the form in which it has come down to us.

The Khazars had raised themselves to a higher level of civilization than the Avars, and their Empire had been longer-lived. The Khazar Empire had been established in the seventh century, after the Avar Empire had crumbled, and it was maintained successfully for at least a century and a half. But by the 830s the Khazars were on the defensive, and *circa* 965[4] the Khazar Empire was destroyed, and its two chief cities, Itil and Samandar, were sacked by the Rhos war-lord Svyátoslav. Thereafter, only a few remnants of the Khazars survived in holes and corners here and there,[5] as remnants of the Skyths had survived after they had been ousted from the Steppe by the Sarmatians.

The greatest and most unexpected casualty of the three was the East Roman Empire. In 965, and even more in 1016, the Empire seemed not only to have completed its recovery from its seventh-century collapse but to have attained a new peak of power. Actually, the Empire was on the point of collapsing again, and its eleventh-century collapse was more serious than any in its chequered previous history. The conversion of Russia in 989 ensured the survival of the East Roman Empire's Eastern

---

[1] See Vernadsky, *Ancient Russia*, pp. 296–7; L. Halphen, *Charlemagne et l'Empire carolingien* (Paris, 1949, Albin Michel) pp. 81–7; Runciman, *A History of the First Bulgarian Empire*, p. 52, n. 1. See further the present work, p. 622.

[2] *The Russian Primary Chronicle*, English translation by Cross and Sherbowitz-Wetzor, p. 56.

[3] Op. cit., Introduction, p. 21.

[4] The year 965 is *The Russian Primary Chronicle*'s date, and it is also Ibn Miskawayh's. On the other hand, Ibn Hawkal dates the sack of Itil and Samandar, and also the sack of Bulghar-on-Volga, not 965, but 968/9, in three passages. However, in the third of these passages (Kramers's edition, p. 393), Ibn Hawkal says that he had obtained the information about Samandar in 968/9, so he may have confused the date of the event with the date on which he had learnt about it. From 967 to 971, Svyátoslav was heavily committed in the Balkan Peninsula, and in 968/9 at Kiev itself as well, against the Danubian Bulgars, the Pechenegs, and the East Romans.

[5] A Khazaria, whose ruler's name was George Tsoulos, was conquered in 1016 by a Romano-Russian joint operation (Kedhrênós, vol. ii, p. 464 Bonn). It is uncertain whether this remnant of Khazaria was in the Crimea or was in the Caucasus. See Dunlop, op. cit., pp. 251–2.

Orthodox Christianity, and consequently the survival of its Byzantine civilization. But this could not secure the survival of the East Roman Empire itself.

Conversions of the pagan peoples on the Steppe and in the Steppe's hinterland to one or other of the higher religions were among the notable events of the age. The Uigurs on the eastern section of the Steppe were converted to Manichaeism in 762. The conversion of the Khazars to Judaism seems to have been a gradual process.[1] It cannot have even begun by 732, if this is the date of the marriage—and simultaneous conversion to Christianity—of a Khazar princess, 'the Flower' ('Chichek'), to the Emperor Leo III's son Constantine V. The Khazars' conversion to Judaism cannot have been completed until after the visit paid to the Khaqan's court by the East Roman Christian missionary Constantine-Cyril *circa* 860–2.[2] The mission would not have been worth sending if the Khaqan and his entourage had already been Jews, in the full sense, by then. Moreover, according to the Life of Constantine-Cyril, he had come by invitation.[3] Apparently the Khazars were, by that date, already believers in the Jewish–Christian–Muslim God, whom they identified with their own sky-god Tengri, and they had moved far enough towards adopting the Jewish form of the worship of Yahweh to find the Christian form no longer acceptable to them. After disappointing Constantine-Cyril, the Khaqan and his entourage must soon have taken the decisive step of becoming Jews in the full sense of having themselves circumcised and undertaking to observe the Mosaic Law.[4]

Meanwhile, the competition between the three Judaic monotheistic religions for the conversion of the Khazars had been vigorous as well as being long-drawn-out.[5] Constantine-Cyril's Eastern Orthodox Christian mission *circa* 860–2 had been preceded by an Albanian (Aghovanian) pre-Chalcedonian Christian mission in 681/2 to Warachan (? Balanjar) and by a visit in 782 by St. Abo of Tiflis (who, being an Iberian, was presumably Orthodox).[6] The conversions to Islam were not all voluntary. The Khazar Khaqan is reported to have been constrained by

---

[1] See Marquart, *Streifzüge*, pp. 5–27 and 276–305; Vernadsky, 'Byzantium and Southern Russia', in *Byzantium*, vol. xv (1940–1), pp. 67–86, on pp. 76–86. The eventual conversion to Judaism of at least the Khaqan and his entourage is amply attested by Muslim authorities. There is some doubt about the authenticity of the Hebrew documents (the Spanish Jew Hasday b. Shaprut's letter to a Khazar King Joseph, King Joseph's reply, the so-called 'Cambridge Document', and Jehudah ha-Levi's *Kosri*). Dunlop, op. cit., chap. 6, pp. 116–17, is inclined to believe in the authenticity of all except the 'Cambridge Document'.

[2] See Vernadsky, 'Byzantium and Southern Russia', p. 60.

[3] See Vernadsky, *Ancient Russia*, p. 346.

[4] See Marquart, *Streifzüge*, p. 23; Vernadsky, *Ancient Russia*, pp. 292 and 351. In 'Byzantium and Southern Russia', p. 75, Vernadsky dates the definitive conversion *circa* 864.

[5] See the calendar of Christian, Muslim, and Jewish missionary activities in Vernadsky, 'Byzantium and Southern Russia', pp. 81–8.

[6] See Vernadsky, ibid.

military force to embrace Islam on no less than four occasions. The first occasion was in 737/8, when the Umayyad Caliph Marwan II had invaded Khazaria both through the Darial Pass and through Darband and had marched up the right bank of the Volga, past Al-Baydā (Itil), the Khazars' capital, into the country of the Burtās. The Khaqan's professed conversion was part of the price paid by the Khazars for peace.[1] The second occasion was after the defeat of the Khazars by the 'Abbasid Caliph Ma'mūn at some date between 813 and 818/19.[2] The third occasion was in 965, when Khazaria was being attacked by the Rhos war-lord Svyátoslav. The Khwarizmians—presumably, the Khazars' Muslim mercenaries—are said to have refused to fight unless the Khazars themselves agreed to become Muslims.[3] The Khazars—that is to say one of the remnants of them that had survived Svyátoslav's assault in 965— are also said to have been conquered and converted *circa* 985 by the ruler of Khwarizm.[4] The dates of the alleged conversions to Islam in 965 and 985 were at least a century later than the definitive conversion of the Khaqan and his entourage to Judaism.

However, not even the whole of the Khazar 'Establishment' had adopted Judaism. The mercenary troops on whom they had come to depend for their defence seem to have been Muslims throughout, and, in the Khazar nation as a whole, the Muslims, and even the Christians, may always have outnumbered the Jews,[5] while the majority of the Khazars may always have continued to be pagans in practice.[6] Since the Mosaic Law is onerous, the Judaism even of the Jewish minority of the Khazars seems likely to have been superficial.[7] The Khazars were noted for their toleration in matters of religion in an age in which intolerance was the rule in the Christian and Muslim worlds.

The Danubian Bulgars were converted to Christianity in 864, and in 870 they definitively decided to adopt the Eastern Orthodox form of it in preference to the Roman form, with which they had been experimenting since 866; but, after the death of Methódhios in 885 and the subsequent expulsion of his Slavophone clergy from Moravia, Bulgaria gave asylum to some of these and adopted their Macedonian Slavonic liturgy.[8] An Eastern Orthodox Christian prelate had been installed in the country of the Rhos on Phótios's initiative by 867, according to Phótios himself;[9]

---

[1] See Dunlop, op. cit., pp. 80–4. The source is Balādhurī, *Kitāb Futuh al-Buldān*, p. 326 of vol. i (New York, 1916, Columbia University Press) of P. K. Hitti's translation.

[2] The source is Muqaddasī.

[3] The sources are Ibn Miskawayh and Ibn al-Athīr (see Vernadsky, in loc. cit., and Dunlop, op. cit., p. 244).

[4] The source is Muqaddasī (see Dunlop, op. cit., p. 246).

[5] Ishtakhrī, quoted by Dunlop, op. cit., p. 92. The date of Ishtakhrī's work is *circa* 932.

[6] Ishtakhrī, quoted by Dunlop, ibid.   [7] See Dunlop, op. cit., pp. 195, 217, 221, 223.

[8] See III, 2, pp. 365–6, for Khan Borís's manœuvres after his conversion.

[9] See his encyclical of 867 in his Letters in Migne, *Patrologia Graeca*, vol. cii, cols. 736–7.

and this achievement is more likely to have been Phótios's and Michael III's than to have been Ighnátios's and Basil I's, for whom it is claimed by Constantine Porphyrogenitus.[1] Like the conversion of the Khazars to Judaism, the conversion of the Rhos to Eastern Orthodox Christianity took more than a century. The Princess Olga of Kiev was baptized, either during her visit to Constantinople in 957 or previously at Kiev,[2] but her son Svyátoslav launched a pagan reaction that was more effective than the Danubian Bulgar Khan Vladímir's. The Volga Bulgars seem to have embraced Islam already before their ruler asked the ʿAbbasid Caliph Muqtadir to send a mission that arrived at Bulghar in 922.[3] In the last quarter of the tenth century the Magyars, Poles, and Scandinavians (including the distant Icelanders) were converted to Western Christianity simultaneously with the definitive conversion of the Russians to Eastern Orthodox Christianity.

Evidently, in the last quarter of the first millennium of the Christian Era, the inhabitants of the Steppe and of its barbarian hinterlands were feeling that, in order to hold their own among their more highly civilized neighbours, they must adopt one or other of the higher religions that these impressive neighbours of theirs professed. The nomads and the sedentary barbarians felt this whether they were still on the war-path or had suffered a recent military reverse (as the Rhos had in 860 and in 971, and the Magyars in 955) or had settled down and gone over to the defensive (as the Khazars had by the 860s and the Volga Bulgars by 922).

At the same time, the new converts were wary of compromising their political independence as an incidental unwelcome consequence of abandoning their ancestral national religions. The shrewdest choices were made by the Uigurs and the Khazars. They each adopted a religion that was not the established cult of any contemporary great power. The Volga Bulgars had no choice. When Judaism had become established in Khazaria, and when Eastern Orthodox Christianity was gaining ground in Russia, the Volga Bulgars could no longer afford to remain pagans, and they had to become Muslims in order to maintain their separate identity *vis-à-vis* two adjacent powers which were each more powerful than the Volga Bulgars. The Danubian Bulgars and the Russians took the precaution of giving themselves a distinctive liturgical language, Macedonian Slavonic, in preference to the East Roman Church's Greek. The

---

[1] In *Theoph. Cont.*, Book V, chap. 97, pp. 342–3. Constantine claims for Basil the credit for the conversion of the Bulgars too (ibid., chap. 96, p. 342). Photios's mission to the Rhos may have been followed up by Ighnátios (see p. 29, n. 2, and p. 59).

[2] For the points for and against each of these two mutually contradictory views, see Obolensky in *C. Med. H.*, vol. iv, 2nd ed., Part I, p. 511, n. 4. Vlasto, op. cit., p. 250, inclines towards the view that Olga had been baptized at Kiev already, perhaps in 954/5, before visiting Constantinople in 957.

[3] See Marquart, *Streifzüge*, pp. xv, 25, 149; Macartney, op. cit., pp. 14–15, and the translation of Ibn Fadlān's report on this mission ibid., pp. 224–8.

western barbarian converts adopted Western Christianity as soon as Western Christendom began to gain the upper hand over them. As obstinate pagans, they would have suffered the fate that overtook the Mecklenburg Slavs and the Prussians. As ecclesiastical subjects of the Pope, they obtained the recognition of their political sovereignty as independent members of the Western Christian family of nations.

The Bulgars' success in surviving is as remarkable as the suddenness of their emergence.[1] They began their career at a time when, on the Western Steppe, the nomads were in retreat and the sedentary barbarians were in the ascendant. After their recoil eastwards from the Alföld into the western bay of the Steppe, the Bulgars raided the East Roman Empire's Balkan provinces at least six times—in 493, 499, 502, 538, 551, and 558— and they supported Vitalian's pro-Chalcedonian insurrection in 514, but these forays are evidence, not of the Bulgars' strength, but of the Empire's weakness. Midway through the sixth century there was a fresh eruption out of the middle and eastern sections of the heart of the Steppe which was almost as violent as the eruption of the Bulgars' Hun ancestors two centuries earlier. In 558 the Avar horde, fleeing westwards, like a cat from a dog, with the Turk horde in hot pursuit, broke in among the Bulgars on the Western Steppe like a cat among the pigeons. The Avars wiped out some of the Bulgar peoples in their path, subjugated some of them, and carried others along with the Avars themselves into the Alföld. The easternmost of the surviving Bulgars had escaped by 568 from the Avars' yoke only by exchanging it for the pursuing Turks'.[2]

However, the Bulgars managed to outlive the Avars' rapid rise and fall. When the Avars' prestige had been shaken by the failure of the Avaro-Persian siege of Constantinople in 626, the Avars' Bulgar subjects, as well as their Slav subjects and their East Roman deportees, took the opportunity to revolt and secede. The return of the East Roman deportees' descendants from Sirmia to Rhomanía under the leadership of Koúver, the Bulgar whom the Avars had put in charge of them, has been noticed already in another context.[3] In 630, some of the Bulgars whom the Avars had carried with them on to the Alföld escaped to the Frankish dominions and were massacred on King Dagobert's orders.[4] Others—perhaps also from the Alföld at the same date, or possibly from the Onogur Koúvratos-Krovátos's dominions at the later date of the migration of parties of

[1] For their emergence, see III, 5 (i), pp. 425–6.

[2] See Menander Protector, Dindorf's edition of the excerpts, pp. 54–5 and 87. On pp. 54–5 these subjects of the Turks are called Ougours or Ouigours; on p. 87 they are called Outigours. Are Theophylactus Simocatta's Ogor (de Boor's edition, pp. 258 and 259) the same people?

[3] See II, 1 (iii) (a), pp. 73–5.

[4] See Runciman, *A History of the First Bulgarian Empire*, p. 19; Grégoire, 'L'Origine et le nom des Croates et des Serbes', p. 112, citing Fredegarius, IV, § 72, p. 157.

Bulgars from there to the middle course of the Volga and to the lower course of the Danube—found refuge in the Pentapolis district of the East Roman Exarchate of Ravenna,[1] and these may or may not be identical with the Bulgar refugees who sought asylum with the King of the Lombards, Grimwald (662–71), were passed on by him to his son Romwald, the Duke of Benevento, and were settled by Romwald in Saepinum, Bovianum, and Aesernia.[2] The most successful of all the Bulgar insurgents against the Avars was Koúvratos,[3] Kovrátos,[4] or Krovátos,[5] who, according to Nicephorus Patriarcha, was the ruler of the Ounoghoundoúroi and was an ally of the Avars' adversary the Emperor Heraclius.[6] Nicephorus records Koúvratos's revolt between his notices of the Arabs' attacks on Antioch and on Egypt, which points to a date *circa* 636–9. According to Theophanes and Nicephorus, Krovátos-Koúvratos was the ruler of 'the Ancient Great Bulgaria' (ἡ παλαιὰ Βουλγαρία ἡ μεγάλη) in the reign of the Emperor Constans II (641–68). The nucleus of his domain lay between the Sea of Azov and the River Don and the River Kuban (Κοῦπις, Κῶφιν), and this was also the habitat of the Bulgars' kinsmen (ὁμόφυλοι) the Kótraghoi. Koúvrat must have established himself here with the acquiescence of the Turks. These had once dominated the Utigur Bulgars,[7] and they had besieged Vósporos (Kerch) in 576;[8] but by 636–9 the Turks' hold on their more distant subjects may already have begun to weaken.

For a few years, the Bulgars on the Western Steppe, from the Kuban as far westwards, perhaps, as the Seret, were liberated from the Avars and (apparently) also from the Turks and were united with each other politically; but the unity and independence of 'Ancient Great Bulgaria' did not long survive Koúvrat's death.[9] The Khazars then conquered Koúvrat's dominions right up to the east bank of the Pruth, and subjugated Koúvrat's son Vatvaián, who stayed on the Steppe to the east of the River Don. According to Theophanes, Vatvaián pays tribute to the Khazars 'to this day'.[10] Other parties of Koúvrat's Bulgars preserved their independence by migrating. One party (not mentioned in Theophanes's and Nicephorus's account of the dispersion of the Bulgars) put itself beyond the Khazars' reach by migrating northwards to the confluence of the Volga and the Kama. Another party, led by Koúvrat's son,

---

[1] Theophanes p. 357. [2] Paulus Diaconus, V, 29.
[3] Nic. Patr., p. 24. [4] Nic. Patr., p. 33. [5] Theophanes, p. 357.
[6] Nic. Patr., p. 24. It has been conjectured that Koúvratos is identical with the anonymous Hun chieftain who, in 619, had visited Constantinople and had been baptized there (Nic. Patr., p. 12). Koúvrat's revolt is also recorded by John of Nikíou, p. 197 in Charles's translation.
[7] Menander Protector, p. 87, Dindorf. [8] Ibid., pp. 89 and 90.
[9] For the date of Koúvrat's death, see Appendix I to the present chapter.
[10] If 'this day' is Theophanes's own day, and not his sources', Theophanes must mean that the tribute is still being paid by Vatvaián's people's descendants.

Asparoúkh (who is certainly an historical person, not a mythical eponym like Koúvrat's alleged son Kótraghos), migrated westwards across the Dniepr and the Dniestr and ensconced itself in a district called the Óngklos, which was north of the Danube between other rivers and had a shoreline (ἀκτή) that could be reached by the East Roman Fleet.[1] To the west of the Dniestr (the last river that Asparoúkh's party had crossed) the next two rivers to the north of the Danube are the Pruth (Prut) and the Seret (Sirat), and we may guess that the Óngklos was the tapering strip of land between these two, and that the name 'Óngklos' itself is a Balkan-Latin rendering of the Latin word 'angulus'.[2]

Asparoúkh's Bulgars—hemmed in, as they now were, between the Khazars and the Avars in a fastness that was secure but was narrowly constricted—relieved themselves by raiding the adjacent East Roman provinces to the south of the Danube, and the East Roman Imperial Government had to put up with this nuisance from the north so long as it was fighting for its life against the advance of the Arabs from the south. When the disastrous failure of the Arabs' first siege of Constantinople (674–8) had freed the East Roman Government's hands, Constantine IV attacked Asparoúkh in 680[3] in the Óngklos by land and sea; but this operation back-fired. The East Roman forces failed to capture Asparoúkh's stronghold, which was defended by marshes on one side and by precipices on the other, and, instead of being wiped out, Asparoúkh's Bulgars delivered a successful counter-attack. They crossed the lower Danube and dug themselves in on East Roman territory. The East Romans, exhausted by their life-and-death struggle with the Arabs, were unable to dislodge the Bulgars. They had to make peace with them.[4] The Bulgars still hold the country that Asparoúkh won for them.

Thus the Bulgars evacuated the Steppe, but they survived to make their mark on the World's history to the south of the Steppe, in the Balkan Peninsula, and to the north of it, on the middle reaches of the Volga.

[1] These details are given by Theophanes on p. 358. See also Nic. Patr., p. 34. Theophanes's words in loc. cit. are τὸν Δάναπριν καὶ Δάναστριν περάσας καὶ τὸν Ὄγγκλον καταλαβὼν βορειοτέρους τοῦ Δανουβίου ποταμοὺς μεταξὺ τούτου κἀκείνων ᾤκησεν. On p. 358, lines 12–13, Theophanes says that the Óngklos was 'on the far side of the Danube' (ἐκεῖθεν τοῦ Δανουβίου) from the East Roman Empire. Both Theophanes, p. 359, and Nicephorus, p. 35, state that, after the failure of the East Roman attack on the Bulgars' stronghold in the Óngklos, the Bulgars crossed the Danube in their victorious counter-offensive. These geographical indications show that the Óngklos lay somewhere to the north of the Danube.

[2] Theophanes, in the words quoted (in footnote 1) from p. 358, line 1, appears to equate the Óngklos with rivers, north of the Danube, which were the Danube's tributaries. The Óngklos is located on an island in the Danube delta by Professor Dimitri Obolensky in *The Byzantine Commonwealth*, p. 63, but this location does not seem to be compatible with the indications in the texts of Theophanes and Nicephorus.

[3] Theophanes's dating is A.M. 6171, i.e. A.D. 679/80, and presumably Constantine IV attacked the Óngklos in the spring or summer of 680, but there is evidence that hostilities were still continuing in 681 (see Obolensky in *C. Med. H.*, vol. iv, 2nd ed., Part I, p. 484, n. 3).

[4] Theophanes, p. 359; Nic. Patr., p. 35.

The Khazars make their first appearance on the western section of the Steppe in the third quarter of the sixth century as the vanguard of the vast association of nomad peoples under the hegemony of the Turks.[1] There were also Khazars in the Turkish vanguard on the southern fringe of the middle section of the Steppe. They were fighting there for the Turks against the Persians between *circa* 567 and 578, and again *circa* 589,[2] and their name, which has long ago become extinct on the Volga and in the Crimea, is perhaps preserved in the names of the Hazaras of central Afghanistan and the Hazara district to the east of the Indus in the northern Panjab (round the present-day Abbottabad). The Turkish army[3] that broke through the Caspian Gates (i.e. Darband), perhaps in 625,[4] and joined forces with Heraclius under the walls of Tiflis in 627, seems to have been composed of Khazars,[5] though their commander 'Zievêl, who was second in rank to the Khaqan',[6] was probably not a Khazar but a Turk, and was the 'Yabgu' of the western division of the Turks, whose overlord was the Khaqan of the whole of the Turkish Steppe-empire.[7] The 40,000 Turks whom the Yabgu sent to accompany Heraclius in his invasion of Persia were perhaps Khazar subjects of the Turks. They withdrew in the following autumn.[8] Their heart was not in a campaign in which they were probably serving under orders from their Turkish masters; but this first sight of the lands to the south of the Caucasus may have given the Khazars the appetite for their subsequent invasions of these lands when they were campaigning on their own account as an independent power.

The Western Turks were crushed by their Uigur subjects and by the Chinese between 652 and 659,[9] and it was probably not till after this that the Khazars became independent.[10] The latest dates at which the Khazars are called Turks by Theophanes are 763/4 and 764/5.[11] The Khazars now began to expand westwards,[12] from the west bank of the lower Volga, at the Bulgars' expense. We know that Asparoúkh's Bulgars had been driven to the west of the River Dniestr before 680. By the close of the

---

[1] 'Mavríkios', p. 266 Scheffer, p. 272 Mihǎescu, notes that the Turks are an association of many peoples. This notice of 'Mavríkios's' is transferred, like so much else, to the Magyars by Leo VI (*Taktiká*, Dhiat. 18, §§ 66–7, col. 961).

[2] Dunlop, op. cit., pp. 25 and 26.

[3] Ὁ λαὸς τῶν Τούρκων (Theophanes, p. 316). Cf. Nic. Patr., p. 15.

[4] This is the date given in Armenian sources (see Dunlop, op. cit., pp. 28–30).

[5] Τοὺς Τούρκους ἐκ τῆς Ἑῴας, οὓς Χαζάρεις ὀνομάζουσι (Theophanes, p. 315).

[6] Theophanes, p. 316.

[7] See Dunlop, op. cit., pp. 30–1. Cf. H. W. Haussig, 'Theophylakts Exkurs über die skythischen Völker', in *Byzantion*, vol. liii (1953), pp. 275–462, on p. 307, n. 1, citing Sebeos.

[8] Theophanes, p. 317.   [9] Dunlop, op. cit., pp. 22 and 37.   [10] Dunlop, ibid.

[11] Theophanes, pp. 433 and 435. See Marquart, op. cit., p. 54, and Macartney, op. cit., p. 127. The Khazars were called Turks only so long as they were under the Turkish Khaqan's suzerainty.

[12] See Dunlop, op. cit., pp. 46 and 59.

seventh century the Khazars controlled Phanaghóreia and Vósporos[1] and the Steppe-country in the interior of the Crimea, but not yet either Khersón or Gothia.[2] In 710 there was a Khazar governor (tudun) in Khersón, side by side with the city-state's own protopolítês Zóilos.[3]

Meanwhile, before the Khazars had shaken off the suzerainty of the Turks, they had become involved in a hundred-years-war (642–737) with the Arabs.[4] The Arabs were by far the stronger of the two belligerents. After they had tried and failed in 652 to take Balanjar, the Khazars' capital in the hinterland of the western shore of the Caspian, the Khazars nevertheless moved their capital northwards to Itil (Khazarān-Atil) on the west bank of the lower Volga. The Khazars repeatedly foiled the Arabs' invasions, and also repeatedly retaliated by invading the Arab Empire, and, though in 737 the Khazars were momentarily beaten to their knees, the Arabs were not able to hold permanently any Khazar territory to the north of the Caucasus, any more than they were able to hold permanently any East Roman territory to the north-west of the Távros.

It has been noted already that the Khazars were not Turks in the political sense of being members of the people, bearing the ethnikon 'Türk', which built up, under its hegemony, a vast Steppe-empire midway through the sixth century. The Khazars were subordinate allies of these Turkish empire-builders till this Turkish empire was overthrown *circa* 652–9. The Khazars were, however, Turks in the linguistic sense of being speakers of a dialect of the Turkish language. Turkish was the language, not only of the people called Turks, but of many other of the Steppe-peoples. The Huns, for instance, had been Turkish-speakers, and so were the Huns' descendants the Bulgars. The Volga Bulgars (Qazan Tatars) speak Turkish still today, and the Danubian Bulgars spoke it till they took to speaking the language of their Slav subjects. The Pechenegs, Ghuzz, and Qipchaq, who followed on the Khazars' heels out of the heart of the Steppe, were Turkish-speaking too.

The Khazars were, however, exceptional among the Turkish-speaking pastoral nomads, and indeed among Eurasian nomads of all languages and races, in developing a taste for the civilization of the nomads' sedentary neighbours and also showing a capacity for adopting these neighbours' way of life to a considerable extent. In the four-thousand-years-long history of the Eurasian nomads, the Khazars had no cultural peers except the Skyths and the Uigurs.

---

[1] Theophanes, p. 373; Nic. Patr., p. 41. See also Moravcsik, 'Zur Geschichte der Ono-guren', p. 83.

[2] Nic. Patr., p. 45; A. A. Vasiliev, *The Goths in the Crimea* (Cambridge, Mass., 1936, The Mediaeval Academy of America), pp. 76, 84, 87; Dunlop, op. cit., p. 45.

[3] Vasiliev, op. cit., p. 84.

[4] For the details, see Dunlop, op. cit., pp. 41–87.

Our information about the Khazars' way of life after they had settled down in the country to the west of the lower Volga and the Caspian comes mainly from Muslim sources,[1] supplemented by incidental notices in those Hebrew documents concerning the conversion of the Khazars to Judaism that can be accepted as being authentic. The Muslim accounts give us a picture of the Khazar way of life as this had come to be in the first half of the ninth century. The later Muslim writers bring up to date, here and there, but not thoroughly or consistently, the primary or secondary sources that they are copying.

In the ninth century the Khazars were still leading their ancestral nomadic way of life for part of the year. They went out on to the Steppe in the spring, and stayed in the open till the autumn, but they were no longer exclusively pastoral. They had extensive agricultural lands, from which they raised crops, and at Samandar, on the western shore of the Caspian, they had vineyards. They did not have villages, but they did have cities in which they spent the winter and made their permanent homes. After 652, their capital was at Itil (Khazarān-Atil) on the River Volga, after which the city was named. The city of Itil bestrode the Volga. The Khaqan and his entourage lived in the west-bank quarter, the Muslims and the merchants in the east-bank quarter, which must have been insecure after the Steppe between the lower Volga and the Yaik had been lost by the Khazars to the Pechenegs, who were the Khazars' nomad next-door neighbours on the east. The Khazars had two rulers, one who reigned and a lieutenant who governed.[2] The Muslim authorities differ in the titles that they give them. The Khazars' own title for the *de jure* sovereign was probably 'Khaqan', and for the *de facto* ruler Bak (Bek, Beg).[3] The Khazars' religious tolerance was reflected in the composition of their judiciary. There were seven royal judges, and these

---

[1] See the passages of Mas'ūdī's *Murūj adh-Dhahāb*, translated in Dunlop, op. cit., pp. 204–14, and the passage of Ishtakrī's work that is translated in Dunlop, op. cit., pp. 91–100, and in Macartney, op. cit., pp. 219–21. See also the passages of Ibn Rustah's, Al-Bakrī's, and Gardēzī's works that are printed, in translation, in parallel columns in Macartney, op. cit., pp. 197–202. See further the table in Macartney, op. cit., p. 4, giving Macartney's reconstruction of the relation of these last-mentioned works to each other and to their common source or sources. The earliest of the Muslim writers' sources date from the first half of the ninth century (see Marquart, op. cit., p. xxxi; Macartney, op. cit., pp. 4–28; Dunlop, op. cit., pp. 100–15).

[2] The political expedient of having a sovereign who reigns but does not govern has been adopted in a number of different countries at different times, e.g. in modern Britain and in medieval and modern Japan. It had been the practice in the Kingdom of the Cimmerian Bosporos, astride the Straits of Kerch, which had been founded in 438/7 B.C. and had survived till *circa* A.D. 362 (i.e. till about 200 years before the Khazars made their appearance to the west of the Lower Volga). In the Bosporan Kingdom there had been a civil administrator (ὁ ἐπὶ τῆς βασιλείας) and a separate military commandant (ὁ χιλίαρχος). See Vernadsky, *Ancient Russia*, p. 94, and, for the dates of the beginning and end of the Bosporan Kingdom, op. cit., pp. 57–8 and 119 and 149.

[3] Ὁ . . . χαγάνος . . . καὶ ὁ πὲχ Χαζαρίας (*De Adm. Imp.*, chap. 42, p. 178).

were recruited from representatives of all the four national religions: Judaism, Islam, Christianity, and paganism.[1]

During the first two centuries of their history on the Western Steppe the Khazars were as martial as any other Eurasian nomad people. They hunted the Avars, evicted the Bulgars, and battled with the Arabs. But the Khazars must have been almost unique, among all Eurasian nomad peoples, in eventually entrusting the defence of their empire to mercenaries of foreign extraction whose religion was not that of the Khaqan and his entourage. According to Mas'ūdī, writing between 943 and 947,[2] the military force on which the ruler of the Khazars relied was the Arsīyah. These were about 7,000 strong. They were Muslims of Khwarizmian origin, and the condition on which they served was that they should be free to profess Islam openly and that they should not be called upon to fight the Khazars' Muslim enemies. We do not know the date at which the Khazars started employing the Arsīyah, but Mas'ūdī says that it was long ago. This may have been a cause, as well as a symptom, of the Khazar Steppe-empire's decline and fall. Now that the Khazars had become non-martial as well as semi-sedentary, they were bound to succumb, sooner or later, to more ferocious neighbours. The contenders for the Khazars' heritage were the Pechenegs, followed by the Ghuzz and the Qipchaq, from the east and the Rhos from the north.

The Khazars' first signal of distress was a request, made by them to the Emperor Theóphilos (829–42) at some date before 833, to build a fortress for them on the left bank of the Don,[3] on the river's lower course. Theóphilos sent Petronás Kamatêrós, and he built the fortress—it was given the name 'Sarkel'—in 833.[4] On his return to Constantinople, Petronás advised Theóphilos to convert the autonomous city-state Khersón into a théma. Theóphilos took this advice and appointed Petronás himself to be the first stratêghós.[5] Both the Khazars and the East Romans must have believed that the Khazar capital Itil (which was covered by the new Khazar fortress Sarkel) and the Greek city-state Khersón were threatened by some potential enemy who, if he attacked, would approach across the Steppe between the right bank of the Don and the Dniepr. This potential enemy must have been either the Magyars, who were in

---

[1] The seven judges, recruited from the four religions, are noted by Ishtakrī (writing *circa* 932). Mas'ūdī in his *Murūj adh-Dhahāb*, (written between 943 and 947), specifies that Judaism, Islam, and Christianity were represented by two judges each, and paganism by one judge (see the passages quoted by Dunlop on pp. 93 and 207).

[2] See the passage quoted from Mas'ūdī's *Murūj adh-Dhahāb* in Dunlop, op. cit., p. 206.

[3] The site of Sarkel has been discovered and been excavated (see Moravcsik in the *Commentary on De Adm. Imp.*, p. 155). The site is marked on the map in Dunlop, op. cit., p. 88.

[4] *De. Adm. Imp.*, chap. 42, pp. 177–8; *Theoph. Cont.*, pp. 122–4. It is uncertain whether this Petronás was the same person as Theóphilos's brother-in-law of the same name who won the victory over the Amīr of Malatīyah at Poson thirty years later, in 863.

[5] See chap. 4, Appendix, p. 270.

occupation of this piece of the Steppe at this date, or the Rhos, whose envoys reached Constantinople in 838 from some point of departure in the Western Steppe's northern hinterland. The Magyars are surely ruled out. They were the Khazars' subordinate allies, and there is no evidence that they and the Khazars had ever been in bad relations with each other.[1] The Rhos seem much more likely to have been the potential enemy on the horizon.[2]

In 839 an embassy from the East Roman Emperor Theóphilos arrived at the court of the Carolingian Lewis the Pious at Ingelheim, accompanied by some Rhos envoys who had come to Constantinople but who were unable to return by the route by which they had come because they had had to make their way, on their outward journey, through some particularly ferocious barbarians.[3] The Rhos envoys could not face the prospect of trying to return home by the same route; so Theóphilos requested Lewis to help them to make their way back by some other route to their King 'the Rhos Chachanus'. Since Western Christendom had been suffering grievously from Scandinavian raids, Lewis was curious about the Rhos envoys' identity, and was suspicious of their designs. On being questioned, the Rhos envoys proved to be Swedes, and explained that 'Rhos' was their ethnikon.[4]

The Greek ethnikon 'Rhos', representing the Slavonic 'Rus'', went through successive modifications of its meaning till it came eventually to stand for speakers of the Russian Slavonic language who were under the direct or indirect rule of princes of the House of Rurik and who professed Eastern Orthodox Christianity as the ecclesiastical subjects of the Metropolitan of Kiev;[5] but it is certain that the original meaning was 'Scandinavians', and that the term was used to mean those Scandinavians who had established themselves among the north-eastern Slavs

[1] Marquart holds, in op. cit., p. 30, that the potential enemy was the Magyars. Ibid., p. 28, he cites a statement by Ibn Rustah that the Khazars dug a ditch to protect themselves against 'al-Majgharīyah and other peoples'. However, a ditch is not the same thing as a fortress. The ditch is likely to have been dug across the isthmus between the Don and the Volga, and the enemy who might approach between these two rivers would be, not the Magyars, but 'other peoples', *videlicet* the Rhos. Another possible location for the Khazars' ditch is the isthmus of Perekop, which connects the Crimea with the Continent; but there were Magyars on the Crimean Steppe, to the south of Perekop, when Constantine-Cyril travelled that way *circa* 861–2.

[2] This is the opinion of Bury (*A History of the Eastern Roman Empire*, p. 418); Vasiliev (*The Goths in the Crimea*, pp. 109–11); Vernadsky (*Ancient Russia*, pp. 304–5); Dunlop, (op. cit., p. 187).

[3] See p. 431.

[4] Theóphilos's letter to Lewis the Pious has not survived, but its contents, and the action taken on it by Lewis, are recorded by Prudentius of Troyes in the *Annales Bertiniani*, sub anno 839, 18 May (*Monumenta Germaniae Historica*, vol. i, *Scriptores*, p. 434).

[5] See Obolensky in the *Commentary on De Adm. Imp.*, p. 22; H. Paszkiewicz, *The Origin of Russia* (London, 1959, Allen & Unwin), pp. 11–12 and 25. See also Vernadsky, *Ancient Russia*, pp. 276–8.

and had made contact, via these Slavs' country, with the East Roman Empire.[1] Liutprand of Cremona twice expressly identifies the 'Rhos' ('Rusios') with the Nordmanni,[2] and the Muslim writers identify them with the Majūs (literally, 'Magians', meaning 'pagans'), which was their name for the Scandinavians who raided Muslim Spain and Portugal and made their way, through the Straits of Gibraltar, into the Mediterranean.[3] This identification, which is made by the Muslim writers and by Liutprand independently, is confirmed by the evidence of names. The personal names Rurik, Signeus, Truvor, Oleg, Olga, Igor, are all renderings in Slavonic of Scandinavian names. In the list of Oleg's retainers appended to the Russian translation, in the *Russian Primary Chronicle*, of the Romano-Russian treaty of 912, all the names can be interpreted as being Scandinavian, and not one of them is Slavonic. A majority of the names appended to the treaty of 945 are Scandinavian likewise. In the gazetteer, in *De Administrando Imperio*, of the pairs of names for the cataracts of the Dniepr, one of the two sets of names can be interpreted convincingly as being Scandinavian and the other as being Slavonic.[4] The Rus' are also identified with the Varangians in the *Russian Primary Chronicle*,[5] and the Varangians are, for the Russian chronicler,[6] a generic name for the northernmost tier of the Teutonic-speaking peoples.[7]

Another indication that the original Rhos were Scandinavians is the fact that in the ninth century, which was the century in which the Rhos impinged on the Khazars and on the East Romans, the Scandinavians were raiding and conquering and colonizing in an immense arc that eventually extended south-westwards to some unidentified point ('Vinland') on the north-eastern coast of continental North America and south-eastwards to Ābaskūn, at the south-eastern corner of the Caspian

---

[1] The much-disputed etymology of the word 'Rhos' is historically unimportant. The most probable derivation seems to be from the Swedish word 'rödher', meaning rowers. The Finnish name for Sweden is 'Ruotsi'. Liutprand of Cremona interprets the word as meaning 'ruddy' or 'russet' (compare the Norman–French surname 'Roussel', anglicized as 'Russell') on the strength of a little-used Greek form 'Rhoúsioi' (see Obolensky, ibid., p. 21).

[2] *Antapodosis*, Book I, chap. 11, and Book V, chap. 15.

[3] e.g. Ya'qūbī apropos of the Scandinavians' attack on Seville in 843/4, and also Mas'ūdī (see Vasiliev, *The Russian Attack on Constantinople in 860*, pp. 3 and 4).

[4] *De Adm. Imp.*, chap. 9, pp. 75–7. See also Obolensky in the *Commentary*, pp. 38–44, with the map on p. 39.

[5] On pp. 59 and 63. In the Introduction to Cross and Sherbowitz-Wetzor's translation of the Laurentian text of the *Russian Primary Chronicle*, p. 50, it is pointed out that the term 'Varangian' was not in common use in Russia until after the conclusion of the Romano-Russian treaty of 945 and is not employed in the Chronicle's account of events later than 1037.

[6] Ibid., p. 59.

[7] The name Varángioi (Greek) and Variag (Slavonic) is derived from the ethnikon of the Warings (latinized as 'Varini' or 'Warni'). For the early history of the Warings, see H. M. Chadwick, *The Origin of the English Nation* (Cambridge, 1924, University Press), pp. 102–10 and 187–8.

Sea. The Scandinavian expeditions down the Atlantic coast of Western Christendom and Muslim Portugal and Spain into the Mediterranean were contemporaneous with the Rhos attack on Constantinople in 860 via the rivers discharging into the Black Sea. Vasiliev has assembled the evidence for Scandinavian raids into the eastern basin of the Mediterranean in the years 858–61.[1] After raiding Muslim Spain in 858,[2] the Scandinavians appear to have spent two winters—those of 858/9 and 859/60—in the Rhône Delta.[3] In 860 this expedition attacked Pisa and other Italian cities.[4] Luni was one of these. The Spanish Muslim historian Ibn al-Qutīyah ('son of the Gothic mother') says that the 'Majūs' reached Alexandria and Rūm;[5] the chronicle attributed to 'Sebastian of Salamanca' states that, *circa* 860, the Scandinavian sea-raiders reached Greece via the Mediterranean.[6] Johannes Diaconus in the *Chronicon Venetum* says that they 'approached' Constantinople *circa* 860,[7] and Vasiliev interprets this notice as being a record, not of the Rhos attack on Constantinople in 860 from the Black Sea via the Bosphorus, but of a simultaneous Scandinavian raid from the eastern Mediterranean through the Dardanelles.[8] Vasiliev[9] and Paszkiewicz[10] and Vernadsky[11] are inclined to believe that the two naval expeditions that thus converged on the Sea of Marmara were not only simultaneous but were concerted, and they even make a guess at the identity of the master mind that, in their view, worked out this strategic plan on the grand scale. They suggest that Rurik of Novgorod was the same person as Rorik of Jutland.

The Rhos assault on Constantinople took the East Romans by surprise. Phótios, in his account of the affair, calls the Rhos 'an unknown people' (ἔθνος ἄγνωστον).[12] This is a rhetorical exaggeration; for the East Roman Imperial Government had received envoys from the Rhos in 838[13] and had perhaps been fearing an attack by the Rhos on Khersón as early as 833. If St. George of Amastris and St. Stephen of Surozh (Soughdhaía) lived in the first half of the ninth century, their biographies would be evidence that not only the Crimea but the north coast of Asia Minor had been raided by the Rhos before their assault on Constantinople in 860. However, these two biographies cannot be dated, and therefore

---

[1] A. A. Vasiliev, *The Russian Attack on Constantinople in 860* (Cambridge, Mass., 1946, The Mediaeval Academy of America), pp. 17–34 and 55–63.

[2] Op. cit., p. 45. The date of the first Scandinavian raid on Seville is 843/4.

[3] Vasiliev, op. cit., pp. 46–7. On p. 20 he cites Prudentius of Troyes, *Annales Bertiniani*, for the wintering in the Rhône Delta in 859.

[4] Prudentius of Troyes in loc. cit.   [5] Vasiliev, op. cit., p. 18.

[6] Vasiliev, op. cit., pp. 20–2.

[7] Vasiliev, op. cit., p. 23. The word used is 'adire'.

[8] Vasiliev, op. cit., pp. 25 and 189.   [9] Op. cit., pp. 234–7.

[10] Op. cit., p. 424.   [11] *Ancient Russia*, p. 377.

[12] Φωτίου Ὁμιλίαι, ed. by V. Laoúrdhas (Thessaloníkê, 1959, Etaireía Makedhonikón Spoudhón), text, p. 42, Homily IV, chap. 2.

[13] See pp. 431 and 445.

they throw no light on the question of the time at which the Rhos first appeared above the East Romans' horizon.[1]

In 860 the Rhos perhaps came nearer to capturing Constantinople than so far they have ever come since then. However, the Russians learnt by painful experience that trading with Constantinople, and drawing pay as mercenary soldiers in the East Roman Empire's service, was more profitable—at any rate in this quarter—than raiding.[2] The Rhos principality of Kiev undertook, in the Romano-Russian treaties of 945 and 971, to supply the East Roman Government with troops on request.[3] Vladímir's honouring of this engagement in 988[4] saved the Imperial throne for the Emperor Basil II. Thereafter the Varangian Imperial Guard became a standing institution.[5] The trade between Russia and Constantinople has been noticed in an earlier chapter.[6] By Constantine Porphyrogenitus's day, the visits of the Russian trading-flotilla to Constantinople seem to have come to be annual, and the route—via the River Dniepr and the western shore of the Black Sea—is described in his *De Administrando Imperio*.[7]

There is no record of the route that was taken by the Rhos envoys in 838 and by the Rhos raiders in 860, but it seems probable that, of the several alternative inland waterways, the Dniepr was the latest to be used. The seven cataracts, extending over a more than sixty-seven-kilometres-long stretch of the river's course,[8] were a formidable deterrent. The reason why the Rhos eventually took to the Dniepr route and set up a political and commercial headquarters for themselves at Kiev cannot have been that, on this route, they were able to elude the nomads who occupied the Steppe to the west of the Volga and the Don. The ferocious barbarians whom the Rhos envoys to Constantinople encountered in 838 must, at that date, have been the Magyars, and the command over the lower course of the Dniepr passed from the Magyars to another nomad people, the Pechenegs, when, in 896, the Pechenegs drove the Magyars right off the Steppe into the Alföld. At the last of the seven cataracts the Rhos had to run the gauntlet. It was here that the Pechenegs used to attack them;[9] and it was at the cataracts that the Pechenegs killed Svyátoslav in 972 on his return journey from Dhrístra.

---

[1] In *The Goths in the Crimea* (1936), Vasiliev takes the view that these two biographies refer to events in the early ninth century (pp. 111–12); but in *The Russian Attack on Constantinople in 860* (1946), p. 13, he retracts this previous opinion of his and dates the events recorded in the two biographies later than 860.

[2] The Russian attacks on the East Roman Empire in 860, 941, and 969–71 (above all) resulted in Russian disasters. The campaigns of 907 and 944 were inconclusive.

[3] See Dvornik, *The Slavs*, p. 207.   [4] For the date, see Vlasto, op. cit., p. 258.

[5] See the Introduction to Cross and Sherbowitz-Wetzor's translation of the *Russian Primary Chronicle*, p. 50.

[6] In II, 1 (ii), on p. 62.   [7] *De Adm. Imp.* chap. 9, pp. 74–9.

[8] See Obolensky in the *Commentary*, pp. 38–54.   [9] *De Adm. Imp.*, chap. 9, p. 78.

Moreover, Kiev itself lay perilously close to the northern edge of the Steppe, and it was raided repeatedly by the nomads who were the successive occupants of the Steppe's western section. The first recorded Pecheneg raid on Kievan territory was in 915.[1] In 968, Svyátoslav had to break off his operations in the Balkan Peninsula and to hurry back from Pereyeslavetz to Kiev in order to save Kiev from falling into the Pechenegs' hands. The Ukraine suffered more severely from the Pechenegs' eleventh-century successors the Ghuzz and the Qipchaq, and worse still from the Qipchaq's thirteenth-century successors the Tatars of the Golden Horde. Even after Russia had been united, more effectively than ever before, by the Muscovites and had asserted its independence from Tatar suzerainty, the Ukraine did not become fully secure against raids from the Golden Horde's long-lived successor-state the Tatar Khanate of Krim until 1774, when Russia compelled the Ottoman Empire to renounce its protectorate over the Crimean Tatars and to leave Russia a free hand for dealing with them.

For Scandinavian pioneers in search of an inland water-route from the Baltic to the south, the portages to the headwaters of the Oka and the Volga were as convenient as those to the headwaters of the Dniepr; the portage across the isthmus between the Volga and the Don offered access, via the Volga route, to the Black Sea as well as to the Caspian; and, on the Volga and the Don, there were no cataracts. It is therefore not surprising that the route between Scandinavia and the south via the Volga and the Don was in use much earlier than the route via the Dniepr.[2] This is proved by the evidence of finds of coins in Scandinavia and at Kiev. Muslim coins minted in the ninth and tenth centuries abound in Gothland and Sweden, whereas East Roman coins of the same age are rare there.[3] The oldest East Roman coins found at Kiev were all minted later than 867.[4] The Muslim coins must have reached Scandinavia via the Volga, whether they came from Khwarizm across the Steppe to Bulghar or came via Darband or via the Caspian from Baghdad.

Why, then, did the Rhos eventually choose to brave both the Dniepr cataracts and the nomads? The answer surely must be that, at this high price, the Rhos were able to reach one of the wealthy civilized regions to the south in their own ships, for raiding or trading, whichever of these two alternative ways of making profits might prove to be the more

---

[1] The *Russian Primary Chronicle*, p. 71.

[2] See N. K. Chadwick, *The Beginnings of Russian History* (Cambridge, 1946, University Press), pp. 2 and 13–14; Boba, *Nomads, Northmen, and Slavs*, pp. 14, 18–23, 25, 30, 31; Cross and Sherbowitz-Wetzor's Introduction to their translation of the *Russian Primary Chronicle*, p. 44; Dvornik, *The Slavs*, p. 193, n. 1; Obolensky in *C. Med. H.*, vol. iv, 2nd ed., Part I, p. 495; Paszkiewicz, *The Origin of Russia*, p. 138.

[3] Paszkiewicz, op. cit., p. 138, n. 3. Cf. the Introduction to Cross and Sherbowitz-Wetzor's translation of the *Russian Primary Chronicle*, p. 44.

[4] Boba, op. cit., p. 38, n. 56.

convenient. On the Volga route, and on its variant the Don route via the portage from the Volga, the Rhos were originally at the mercy of middle-men—the Volga Bulgars on the Volga's middle reaches, and the Khazars on the lower courses of the Volga and the Don. The Rhos's ambition was to open up routes for raiding or trading along which they could travel in their own ships all the way.

The Rhos did reach Constantinople in their own ships in 860, and, after this achievement—which was a navigational success, though it ended in a military disaster—they soon compelled the Volga Bulgars and the Khazars to give their boats passage down the Volga into the Caspian, to raid the lands of the 'Abbasid Caliphate. The Rhos raided Muslim territory in the southern hinterland of the Caspian on at least four occasions.[1] Their first raid reached Ābaskūn, at the Caspian's south-east corner in Tabaristan, at some date between 864 and 884.[2] The second of these raids reached Enzeli in 909/10.[3] The third raid was carried out in 913/14. This time the Rhos reached Ardabil, three days' journey inland.[4] The fourth raid was in 943. This time the Rhos took Bardha'ah and held it for a year.[5]

The raid in 913/14 was made with the Khazars' leave, on condition that the Khazars should receive a half share of the loot won by the Rhos raiders in Dār-al-Islām.[6] By this time the Rhos had become so strong that the Khazars and the Volga Bulgars no longer ventured to refuse to grant the Rhos passage on the Volga through their respective territories. Yet this granting of the passage was embarrassing for them for two reasons. The Rhos raiders' intended victims were Muslims, and there was a Muslim element in the population of both Khazaria[7] and Volga Bulgaria. Moreover, the Volga Bulgars were trading partners of the Muslim Khwarizmians, and the Khazars' mercenaries were Muslims of Khwarizmian origin. The second embarrassing consideration was the uncertainty whether the Rhos would ever evacuate Volga Bulgaria and Khazaria, when once they had been allowed to enter. The Khazars'

---

[1] See V. Minorsky, *A History of Sharvān and Darband in the 10th–11th Centuries* (Cambridge, 1958) pp. 108 seqq., cited by Vlasto, op. cit., note 40 on p. 392.

[2] N. K. Chadwick, op. cit., p. 61; Dunlop, op. cit., p. 235.

[3] Chadwick, op. cit., loc. cit.; Vernadsky, *Kievan Russia*, p. 33. Mas'ūdī is the source.

[4] Chadwick, op. cit., loc. cit.; Marquart, op. cit., pp. 331–6; Dunlop, op. cit., p. 239; Vernadsky, op. cit., p. 33. Mas'ūdī is the source. The passage is translated in Dunlop, op. cit., pp. 209–12.

[5] Ibn al-Athīr, viii, pp. 134–5; Ibn Miskawayh, ii, pp. 62–7, cited by Dunlop, op. cit., p. 239; Chadwick, op. cit., loc. cit.

[6] Marquart, op. cit., p. 331; Dunlop, op. cit., p. 239.

[7] In 854/5, Muslim Khazar refugees were settled at Shamkūr in Arrān, that is to say in 'Abbasid territory (Balādhurī, *Kitāb Futūh al-Buldān*, p. 319 of vol. i (New York, 1916, Columbia University Press) of P. K. Hitti's translation). This suggests that the Khazar Khaqan's increasing *penchant* towards Judaism may have already been making the Muslim Khazars restive.

Arsīyah Muslim mercenaries and the Burtās and the Muslims in Volga Bulgaria attacked the Rhos on their way home from the raid in 913/14 and killed a number of them.[1] This deterred the Rhos for the next thirty years from coming again; but they did return in 943, and in 965 they attacked and conquered both Volga Bulgaria and Khazaria.

The Rhos succeeded in destroying the Khazar Steppe-empire, but the only Khazar territory that they acquired was Tmutorakan on the Taman peninsula, and this gain was ephemeral. The *Russian Primary Chronicle* records that Vladímir I gave Tmutorakan as an appanage to his son Mstislav.[2] However, as it turned out, the Rhos, in crushing the Khazars, were working, not for themselves, but for the Ghuzz and the Qipchaq, who followed after the Pechenegs in the queue of westward-drifting nomad peoples. It was not till half way through the sixteenth century that the Muscovites made a permanent conquest, for Russia, of the course of the River Volga from a point immediately below Nizhni-Novgorod to the river's debouchure into the Caspian Sea.

In the Khazars' hundred-years-war with the Rhos that ended in the destruction of the Khazar empire by the Rhos in 965, the most serious reverse that the Khazars suffered was the defeat—or the two successive defeats—of their allies the Magyars by the Pechenegs.[3] The Khazars lost touch with the Magyars in 896, when the Danubian Bulgars took their revenge for the Magyars' invasion of Bulgaria in 895 on the East Romans' behalf by inciting the Pechenegs to co-operate with the Bulgars in invading the Magyars' country in a converging movement. This drove the Magyars right out of the Steppe. In 896 they migrated—apparently via Kiev[4]—to the far side of the Carpathians and won a new home for themselves there on the Alföld.[5] After 896, the western end of the Steppe, from the west bank of the Don at least as far westward as the east bank of the Seret,[6] was occupied by the Pechenegs.

The Pechenegs were, it is true, no friends of the Rhos, but they were no friends of the Khazars either. The migration of the Pechenegs from the Steppe between the Yaik and the Volga to the Steppe between the Don and the Iron Gates had been an unintended consequence of an attempt

---

[1] Marquart, op. cit., p. 333.

[2] The *Chronicle* (p. 119) records Vladímir's distribution of appanages to his twelve sons under the year 988, but we cannot be sure that Mstislav obtained Tmutorakan before 1015, which was the year in which Vladímir died (see Vernadsky, *Kievan Russia*, p. 75). The Russians evacuated the Taman peninsula towards the end of the eleventh century (op. cit., p. 160).

[3] The vexed question of the date or dates of the eviction of the Magyars from the Steppe by the Pechenegs is discussed in Appendix II to the present chapter.

[4] See the *Russian Primary Chronicle*, sub annis 888–98 (p. 62).

[5] See *De Adm. Imp.*, chap. 38, p. 170, and chap. 40, p. 173. See also *Georg. Mon. Cont.*, pp. 853–5; Leo Grammaticus, pp. 267–8; *Theoph. Cont.*, pp. 357–9; pseudo-Symeon, pp. 701–2.

[6] See P. Diaconu, *Les Petchénègues au Bas-Danube* (Bucarest, 1970, L'Académie de la République Socialiste de Roumanie), p. 34.

that the Khazars had made to exterminate the Pechenegs in a converging movement which they had concerted with the Ghuzz, who had been the Pechenegs' neighbours on the opposite (i.e. on the eastern) side. Inevitably the Pechenegs were defeated, but, instead of being exterminated, they won a new home for themselves, to the west of the Don, at the expense of the Khazars' allies the Magyars, while the Ghuzz replaced the Pechenegs as the Khazars' next-door neighbours on the east,[1] and then proved, no doubt, to be as tiresome for the Khazars in that location as the Pechenegs had been.[2] Thus the ninth-century shifts in the respective locations of the Magyars, the Pechenegs, and the Ghuzz told against the Khazars in their struggle with the Rhos, in spite of the fact that these shifts were the unintended result of an initiative that had been taken by the Khazars themselves.

At some date earlier than 680, the Khazars had evicted the Bulgars from the Western Steppe between the west bank of the Don and the eastern boundary of the 'Óngklos', which probably ran along the lower course of the Pruth.[3] In the ninth century, down to the year 896, we find the Magyars in occupation of this portion of the Khazars' domain, and apparently of the 'Óngklos' as well.[4] At some date in the reign of the Emperor Theóphilos (829–42) the Magyars (Oúnghroi) tried, without success, to help the Bulgars to prevent the East Roman deportees from Adrianople from reaching the East Roman flotilla that was waiting to take them on board, after the deportees had crossed the river—whichever river it was at this date—that was the frontier, to the north of the Danube, between Bulgaria and the Magyars' country.[5] In 862 the Magyars (Ugri) invaded the Frankish dominions, according to Hincmar of Rheims.[6] *Circa* 861–2, the East Roman missionary Constantine-Cyril encountered Magyars in the Steppe-country in the northern part of the Crimea, according to the Slavonic biography of Constantine-Cyril. In 881 the Franks came into conflict with the Ungri and also with the 'Cowari', i.e. the Kavars, according to the *Annals of Admont*.[7] According to the *Annales Sangallenses Maiores*, sub anno 888 (889),[7] the Agareni (i.e. the Magyars) 'in istas regiones' (i.e. in the neighbourhood of East

[1] See *De Adm. Imp.*, chap. 37, p. 164, and chap. 38, p. 169.
[2] The Khazars had tried to keep the Pechenegs in check by carrying out an annual campaign against them in their previous location (see the parallel passages of Ibn Rustah and Gardēzī in Macartney, op. cit., p. 199).
[3] See p. 440.
[4] The 'Óngklos' may have fallen under the Khazars' control when, in 680, Asparoúkh's Bulgars crossed the Danube. The Seret (Sirat), not the Pruth, was the western boundary of the territory held by the Magyars immediately before their eviction by the Pechenegs to the far side of the Carpathians (see *De Adm. Imp.*, chap. 38, last paragraph (p. 171)).
[5] See *Georg. Mon. Interpolatus*, pp. 817–19, and Leo Grammaticus, pp. 231–2.
[6] Cited by Macartney in op. cit., p. 71.
[7] Cited by Macartney in op. cit., p. 76.

Francia) 'primitus venerunt' in the reign of Arnulf, who became King of East Francia in 888, was crowned Emperor in 896, and died in 899.

Constantine Porphyrogenitus[1] locates the Magyars' habitat (κατοίκησιν) in a district, 'close to Khazaria', called Levedhía, before the eviction of the Magyars from there by the Pechenegs. Constantine notes, in the same context, that, in Levedhía, there was a river called Khingilous (alias Khidhmás), and this river is evidently identical with Constantine's River Synghoúl[2] and with the river that is now called Činhul, which joins with the River Tokmak to form the Molóchnaya—a river that debouches into the Sea of Azov through a district that is now called 'Lepedika'.[3] The name 'Levedhía' looks as if it were derived from the Greek word λιβάδια (livádhia), meaning 'water-meadows';[4] and this interpretation of the name is confirmed by both Muslim and Western Christian authorities. Gardēzī says that the Magyars' country 'is all trees and standing water'.[5] Regino says, sub anno 889, that the Magyars were driven out by the Pechenegs 'from the vast marshes round the mouth of the Don'.[6] Regino also says, likewise sub anno 889, that, when they first arrived on the Alföld, the Magyars made their living by fishing and hunting,[7] and this is what we should expect if their previous habitat had been the swamp-country along the lowest reach of the Don. Moreover, Ibn Rustah's and Gardēzī's common source confirms Regino on this point. This source notes that the Magyars live, in the winter season, by fishing in one or other of the two rivers by which their territory is bounded.[8]

Thus we have evidence for the presence of the Magyars, at dates between 829 and 896, at both the eastern and the western end of the Steppe to the west of the River Don. We find them on the west bank of the Don itself, in its lowest reach, and in the Crimea. We also find them in occupation of the Steppe immediately to the east of a river, to the north of the Danube, that was the eastern frontier of Bulgaria in 829–42. We also learn, from Ibn Rustah's and Gardēzī's common source,[9] that in the ninth century, at some date before their eviction from the Steppe in 896, the Magyars dominated all their Slav neighbours (i.e. the Slavs in the northern hinterland of the western end of the Steppe). The Magyars'

---

[1] In *De Adm. Imp.*, chap. 38, p. 168.

[2] *De Adm. Imp.*, chap. 42, p. 179.   [3] See Macartney, op. cit., p. 91.

[4] See Macartney, op. cit., pp. 92–3.

[5] See the passage quoted, together with the parallel passage of Ibn Rustah's work, in Macartney, op. cit., p. 208.

[6] See the translation of this passage in Macartney, op. cit., p. 70.

[7] 'Et primo quidem Pannoniarum et Avarum solitudines pererrantes, venatu et piscatione victum cotidianum quaeritant' (Regino, sub anno 889, cited by Marquart, op. cit., p. 40, n. 2).

[8] See the translation of these passages in Macartney, op. cit., pp. 206–7.

[9] See the English translation in Macartney, pp. 208–9.

domination was oppressive. They commandeered food supplies from the Slavs and raided the Slavs' country for slaves,[1] whom they sold to the East Romans, in exchange for luxury goods, at a Black Sea port which Ibn Rustah calls Karākh (? Kerch).

The *Russian Primary Chronicle*, sub anno 859,[2] records that, at that date, the tribute from the peoples in the northern hinterland of the Western Steppe was divided between the Khazars—not the Magyars—and 'Varangians from beyond the (Baltic) Sea'. The Varangians levied tribute on Chuds, Slavs (? i.e. the northern Slovenes in the Novgorod area), Merians, Ves', and Krivichians; the Khazars levied tribute on the Polianians (i.e. the Slavs in the Kiev area), the Severians, and the Viatichians. Evidently the arrival of Scandinavian adventurers on the waterways to the east of the Baltic had provoked a competition between them and the Khazars for the political and commercial control over the forest-peoples between the east coast of the Baltic and the northern edge of the Steppe. When this notice in the *Russian Primary Chronicle* is read together with the information, in Ibn Rustah's and Gardēzī's common source, that the Magyars dominated their Slav neighbours, it suggests that the Khazars were using the Magyars as their agents (though, no doubt, the Magyars made this agency profitable for themselves as well).

We may also infer that the Magyars were in occupation of the Steppe to the west of the Don by permission of their Khazar suzerains. This is not expressly stated either by Constantine Porphyrogenitus or by any of the other witnesses to the Magyars' presence here before 896; but, since this Steppe-country had previously belonged to the Khazars, and since the Magyars were the Khazars' subordinate allies, we may conclude that the Magyars had not established themselves in this Khazar territory against the Khazars' will, as the Pechenegs did when they migrated to the west of the Volga and the Don, driving the Magyars westward ahead of them. Indeed, we may conclude that the Khazars had not merely permitted the Magyars to establish themselves to the west of the Don, but had actually planted them there to serve the Khazars' own purposes. The re-location of subject peoples for strategic reasons was a device that had been practised by previous nomad empire-builders. For instance, the Avars in the sixth century and the Danubian Bulgars in the seventh century had re-located their Slav subjects. In the ninth century the Khazars had a manifest motive for planting their Magyar allies on Khazar territory to the west of the Don. In this location, the Magyars could help the Khazars to check the south-eastward and southward advance of the Rhos. The planting of the Magyars to the west of the Don

---

[1] Gardēzī here says that they raided the country of the Rhos, as well, for slaves.

[2] p. 59.

will have been all of a piece with the building of the fortress Sarkel on the Don's eastern bank.

If the Khazars did take the initiative in placing the Magyars where we find the Magyars between 829 and 896, can we ascertain the date at which the Magyars were moved and the region that they had previously occupied?

If the name 'Ugrii-Oúnghroi' stands for 'Onogurs', we have the answer. We can infer the location of Onoguria from the list of the bishoprics in the Eparchy of Gothia that is contained in the Notitia Episcopatuum of the Patriarchate of Constantinople that was published by de Boor in 1891. When we read this list together with the account of Constantine-Cyril's itinerary in Khazaria that is given in the Slavonic biography of Constantine-Cyril, we find, by a process of elimination, that the location of the see of Onoguria must have been on the eastern shore of the Sea of Azov, between the lower courses of the Kuban and the Don.[1] If 'Ugrii-Oúnghroi' stands for 'Onogurs', the Magyars must have been that division of the Bulgar empire-builder Koúvrat's people that stayed in the nucleus of Koúvrat's dominions—stayed, that is, between the Kuban and the Don—and fell there under the rule of the Khazars.[2] If this stationary division of the Onogurs was paying tribute to the Khazars down to the date at which Theophanes was writing his account of the dispersion of the Bulgars apropos of Asparoúkh's winning of a foothold to the south of the lower Danube in 680,[3] we have a *terminus post quem* for the planting of the Magyars to the west of the Don. Theophanes carried his Chronicle down to the year 813, and he lived till *circa* 817. Therefore, if the Magyars were Vatvaián's Onogurs, they must have stayed in the country between the Kuban and the Don till after those dates.

If, however, 'Ugrii-Oúnghroi' stands, not for 'Onogurs', but for the Herodotean 'Iyrkai', we are left in the dark about the previous habitat of those Magyars who eventually made their way to the Alföld via the Steppe to the west of the Don. In this case, all that we can be sure of is that these Magyars were not the division of the Magyars whose country was traversed by the direct route from Khwarizm to the Bulgaria on the Volga.[4] The Khwarizmian common source of Ibn Rustah, Gardēzī, and Al-Bakrī is familiar with the Uralian Magyars, but his knowledge of the south-western division of the Magyars is slight and hazy.[5] This Khwarizmian geographer seems to think that the territories occupied by the two divisions of the Magyars were continuous with each other, whereas in truth they were separated from each other by Khazaria. All that the

---

[1] See Vernadsky, 'Byzantium and Southern Russia', p. 72.
[2] See Moravcsik, 'Zur Geschichte der Onoguren', p. 81.
[3] See Theophanes, pp. 356–7, cited on p. 439.
[4] This is demonstrated by Macartney op. cit., pp. 77–9.
[5] See the passages translated in Macartney, op. cit., pp. 206–7.

Khwarizmian knows about the south-western Magyars is that they lived between two rivers that flowed into the Black Sea, and that one of the two was bigger than the Jayhūn (i.e. than the Oxus).

Gardēzī names these two rivers Ītīl and Dūbā. Macartney[1] emends Dūbā to Kūbā and identifies his 'Kūbā' with the Kuban and the Khwarizmian geographer's Ītīl with the Don. Alternatively, it would be as plausible for us to emend Dūbā to Dūnā and to identify our Dūnā with the Don and the Khwarizmian's Ītīl with the Volga, which is known to have been called by that name. However, the two names may be merely Gardēzī's, or some intermediate source's, guess. In Ibn Rustah's version the two rivers are anonymous, and pairs of rivers flowing into the Black Sea abound. This anonymous pair need not be the Kūbān (which flows into the Straits of Kerch) and the Don (which flows into the Sea of Azov). The pair might just as well be the Don and the Seret or the Dniepr and the Seret, and the rivers might be the boundaries of the Magyars' habitat after, not before, the date at which the Magyars moved—or were moved by the Khazars—to the Steppe to the west of the Don on which we find them at various dates between 829 and 896.

How much of this section of the Steppe was held by the Magyars for how many years between 829 and 896 is a moot question that is discussed in the second of the appendices to the present chapter. In the text of the *De Administrando Imperio*[2] as this has come down to us, it is stated that the Magyars 'lived with the Khazars (συνῴκησαν μετὰ τῶν Χαζάρων) for three years, fighting as the Khazars' allies in all the Khazars' wars'. The word 'all' seems to imply that the Magyars were the Khazars' neighbours and allies for a longer period than three years, and in fact we have independent evidence that this implication is correct. The Magyars were still the Khazars' immediate neighbours in 861–2, when Constantine-Cyril encountered some of them in the Crimea; and the fact that they refrained from attacking him suggests that at that date they were still the Khazars' dutiful allies, for whom a foreign envoy to the Khazar Khaqan's court was sacrosanct. The earliest record of the Magyars' presence on the Steppe to the west of the Don refers to an event in the reign of the East Roman Emperor Theóphilos, and this is evidence that the Magyars were west of the Don already before 842, which was the date of Theóphilos's death. Therefore the Magyars must have been on the Steppe to the west of the Don for at least twenty years (842–61). Thus it is evident that the figure 'three' in the text of the *De Administrando Imperio* is wrong, but we do not know what is the right figure that should be substituted for it.

The displacement of the Magyars by the Pechenegs on the Steppe to the west of the Don was not only a calamity for the Magyars themselves;

---

[1] In op. cit., p. 43.   [2] Chap. 38, p. 168.

it was a reverse for the Khazars and it brought no advantage to the Rhos, for whom any nomad people astride the Dniepr was obnoxious, whether this people happened to be the Magyars, Pechenegs, Ghuzz, or Qipchaq. On the other hand, the seizure by the Pechenegs of the Steppe to the north of the East Roman Empire was a change in the military and political situation there which the East Roman Government knew how to turn to account. After the Magyars' evacuation of the Steppe in 896, the Pechenegs acquired not only their Magyar enemies' previous country to the east of the Seret immediately,[1] but also eventually, not later than the date at which Constantine was writing, the country of their momentary allies the Bulgars to the west of the Seret in Wallachia, at least as far westward as the region facing Dhrístra (Dhorýstolon), or, in the alternative terms used in a later passage in the same chapter, 'as far as the Sarát' (i.e. the Seret, Sirat), 'the Vourát' (i.e. the Pruth, Prut), 'and the rest of the districts' ($\kappa \alpha \grave{\iota}$ $\tau \hat{\omega} \nu$ $\lambda o \iota \pi \hat{\omega} \nu$ $\mu \epsilon \rho \hat{\omega} \nu$, i.e. Wallachia), to the west of the Seret, at least as far westward as a point facing Dhrístra.[2]

The Pechenegs had, in fact, made themselves masters of the great western bay of the Eurasian Steppe from the right bank of the River Don on the east to the left bank of the lower Danube, perhaps up to the Iron Gates, on the west; and in Constantine Porphyrogenitus's time they were still in possession of the whole of this extensive and commanding territory.

[1] The Seret had been the western boundary of the Magyars' domain before their eviction from the Steppe by the Pechenegs in 896 (see *De Adm. Imp.*, chap. 38, p. 171). According to Diaconu, op. cit., pp. 15–16, there is no archaeological evidence for the presence of Pechenegs in Moldavia at the close of the ninth century or in the early tenth century. Moldavia continued, during that time, to be inhabited by a sedentary population.

[2] See *De Adm. Imp.*, chap. 42, pp. 177 and 179. See also chap. 37, p. 166: one of the eight tribes of the Pechenegs now (i.e. in Constantine's day) has a common frontier with Bulgaria; another has a common frontier with the Magyars in the Magyars' new home in present-day Hungary, and, from the border of the Pechenegs' domain, it is a four days' journey to Hungary (Tourkía), but only half a day's journey to Bulgaria. Diaconu, in op. cit., pp. 22–3, rejects Constantine's account, in chap. 42 of *De Adm. Imp.*, of the extent of the Pechenegs' domain in Constantine's own day. Archaeological evidence shows that Wallachia was inhabited by a sedentary population (which, so Diaconu seems to assume, was Roumanian-speaking) till the end of the tenth century, and there is no archaeological evidence for the presence of Pechenegs in Wallachia before that date (op. cit., pp. 23 and 37). Diaconu also (op. cit., p. 34, n. 83) tries to explain away Constantine's statement in chap. 37. Diaconu's mastery of recently discovered archaeological evidence is impressive. At the same time, his rejection, on the strength of this evidence, of a well-informed tenth-century authority's statements is high-handed, and it is also suspect of being influenced by irrelevant present-day political considerations. Constantine had no such reasons for giving a false account of the extent of the Pechenegs' domain in his own time. We may guess that Wallachia passed out of Bulgarian hands into Pecheneg hands in 917, the year in which John Voghás brough: the Pechenegs to the Danube but failed to take them across the river to the Bulgarian bank (see p. 340). The cession of Wallachia may have been the price paid to the Pechenegs by Khan Symeon for their withdrawal. Perhaps Symeon also gave a bribe to Rhomanós Lekapênós for failing to ferry the Pechenegs over and for leaving Leo Phokás in the lurch.

After the Pechenegs had thus established themselves in this key position, the East Roman Government had been quick to realize that the enlistment of this formidable nomad people that had emerged so recently above the East Roman Empire's north-eastern horizon might be a winning card in their military and diplomatic conflicts with their other northern neighbours.[1] When, in 894, Khan Symeon of Bulgaria had made war on the Empire for the first time, the Emperor Leo VI's retort had been to enlist the Magyars to invade Bulgaria from the rear, and this move had proved effective. When, in 913, Symeon made war on the Empire for the second time, Leo VI's widow Zoe, who was now governing the Empire as guardian for her son Constantine Porphyrogenitus, retorted to Symeon, in her turn, by copying the move that her husband had made in 894. In 917, Zoe sent a diplomat to the Pechenegs to induce them to invade Bulgaria from the rear, together with a naval squadron to ferry the Pechenegs across the lower Danube.

This strategy missed fire on this occasion;[2] but that was not the Pechenegs' fault; nor was it the fault of the East Roman diplomat, John Voghás; the operation seems to have been sabotaged deliberately by the admiral, Rhomanós Lekapênós the future Emperor, for the furtherance of his own personal ambitions. The two East Roman officials quarrelled with each other, and the Pechenegs withdrew in disgust.[3] This fiasco was therefore no evidence that the East Roman Government's estimate of the Pechenegs' importance had been pitched too high; and Constantine Porphyrogenitus, in his manual of instructions for the conduct of East Roman foreign policy, gives priority above everything else to an exposition of the value, for the Empire, of cultivating the Pechenegs' friendship.

In my judgement, it is always greatly to the Imperial Government's advantage to make a point of keeping at peace with the Pecheneg nation; to make conventions and treaties of friendship with them; to send an envoy to them, from here, every year with gifts of appropriate value and of kinds that the Pechenegs appreciate; and to arrange that our envoy shall bring back hostages from there—in fact, hostages and an envoy as well, to confer, in this our God-protected City, with the competent official and to receive Imperial attentions and honours in consonance with the Emperor's majesty.[4]

Constantine's catalogue of the advantages of this policy[5] is impressive.

---

[1] See further pp. 506–9.   [2] See II, 7, p. 340.

[3] *Georg. Mon. Cont.*, Reign of Constantine VII, first bout of his sole reign, chap. 10, p. 879, and chap. 17, p. 882; Leo Grammaticus, pp. 293 and 295–6; *Theoph. Cont.*, Book VI, Reign of Constantine VII, first bout of his sole reign, chap. 7, p. 387, and chap. 10, pp. 389–90; pseudo-Symeon Magister, Reign of Constantine VII, first bout of his sole reign, chap. 7, p. 722, and chap. 10, p. 723; Kedhrênós, vol. ii, pp. 286–7. See also the present work, p. 340.

[4] Constantine Porphyrogenitus, *De Adm. Imp.*, chap. 1, p. 68.

[5] In op. cit., chaps. 2–8, pp. 69–74.

In the first place the Pechenegs have Khersón at their mercy. The Pechenegs act for both Khersón and the Imperial Government as their commission-agents (remunerated in advance) for trade with Russia, Khazaria, Zikhía, and the rest of that part of the world, and the Khersonites themselves make their living by buying hides and wax from the Pechenegs, selling this produce in the Empire, and buying cereals, for their own consumption, with the proceeds.[1]

The Pechenegs can also put pressure on the Rhos. These have to buy cattle, horses, and sheep from the Pechenegs, since none of this livestock is produced in Russia itself. Moreover, the Rhos cannot stir from home unless they are sure that the Pechenegs will not invade their country during their absence. Also, the Rhos cannot get at the East Roman Empire, either for war or for trade, unless they are at peace with the Pechenegs. They are at the Pechenegs' mercy at the Dniepr portages. They cannot carry their boats round the cataracts on their shoulders and fight the Pechenegs at the same time.

As for the Magyars, they are terrified of the Pechenegs, as a result of the successive crushing defeats that they have suffered at their hands. When they have been invited to attack the Pechenegs, they have been horrified at the mere suggestion.[2]

The Bulgars, when they feel inclined to attack the Empire, are deterred by the dread that they themselves may be attacked by the Pechenegs from the rear.

Taken together, these considerations make it clear that, though the Pechenegs are hard bargainers and tough customers, subsidies given to them pay better dividends than any other outlay of the East Roman Imperial funds that are allocated for use in foreign relations.

When an Imperial official makes the passage to Khersón on this service, he must immediately send to Pechenegia and demand hostages and an escort. When these arrive, he should leave the hostages in custody in the fortress of Khersón and should set off, himself, for Pechenegia, with the escort, to carry out his instructions. These Pechenegs are insatiable. Their appetite for commodities that are rarities in their country is keen, and they are uninhibited in their demands for generous presents. The hostages demand one lot of presents for themselves and another lot for their wives; the escort demand presents for their own pains, and more presents for their animals' pains. Then, when the official enters their country, their first act is to ask for the Emperor's gifts, and, when they [i.e. the official and his staff] have glutted the men, these start asking again for the gifts for their wives and for their parents. Nor is that the end of it. The Pechenegs who accompany the official as his escort on his return journey to Khersón demand wages from him for their own pains and for their animals' pains.[3]

---

[1] Chap. 53, p. 270.
[2] *De Adm. Imp.*, chap. 8, p. 74.
[3] Op. cit., chap. 7, pp. 72–3.

The Imperial official can also contact the Pechenegs by an alternative route. Instead of passing through Khersón, he can sail straight to the mouth of the Danube or the Dniepr or the Dniestr. In this case

the official stays on board ship and also keeps on board, and under guard, the Imperial gifts that he is bringing with him. The Pechenegs come down to him, and, when they come, he gives them some of his men as hostages and takes hostages from them reciprocally. He holds these hostages on board, and then he makes his bargain with the Pechenegs. When the Pechenegs have taken oaths to him in accordance with their *zakana*, he gives them the Imperial gifts, takes on board, from among them, as many 'friends' [i.e. envoys] as he chooses, and sails for home.

The gist of the bargain that is to be made with the Pechenegs is that they will perform service in whatever quarter the Emperor may call upon them to serve, either against the Rhos or against the Bulgars or against the Magyars. The Pechenegs are fully capable of making war on all these peoples, and, as they have often attacked them, they have now become a terror to them.[1]

Constantine illustrates this point with an anecdote.

A cleric named Gabriel was once sent to the Magyars by the Emperor's orders, and he delivered his message to the following effect: 'The Emperor instructs you to go and expel the Pechenegs from their country and to settle there yourselves (it was your own home once). I want you, his Majesty directs me to say, to be near my dominions, in order that, when I have occasion, I may send and find you quickly.' At this, all the chiefs of the Magyars shouted with one voice: 'We won't rush off to seek out the Pechenegs. We are not capable of going to war with them. Their country is vast; their numbers are huge; and they are devils (κακὰ παιδία). Don't say this to us again. We don't like it.'[2]

Constantine feels no doubt that paying subsidies to the Pechenegs is worth while. It is true that the business is expensive for the Imperial treasury and is disagreeable for the officials who have to transact it. Yet it is cheaper and safer to employ the Pechenegs against the Bulgars, Rhos, and Magyars than to take direct action. If the Emperor has the Pechenegs on leash, the mere threat of unleashing them will probably be enough to bring their obstreperous neighbours to heel.

---

[1] Op. cit., chap. 8, pp. 73–4.　　[2] Ibid.

Koúvrat and Koúver

In the course of the dissolution of the Avars' empire after the failure of the Avaro-Persian siege of Constantinople in 626, a Bulgar named Koúvrat or Krovát or Kovrát revolted against the Avars. The nucleus of the 'Great Bulgaria' that he built up lay to the south-east of the River Don, but he seems to have enlarged his dominions by incorporating in them other Bulgar peoples farther to the west. He may have carried his western frontier as far westward as the angle of territory between the Pruth and the Seret; for his son Asparoúkh was able to find asylum in this corner when, at some date after Koúvrat's death, Koúvrat's dominions to the east of the 'Óngklos' were conquered by the Khazars.[1] Another incident in the break-up of the Avars' empire was the successful revolt, in Sirmia, of a Bulgar named Koúver, whom the Avars had put in charge of the descendants of the East Roman deportees whom the Avars had parked there. Koúver succeeded in conducting the deportees' descendants back into East Roman territory.

Koúvrat and Koúver were both Bulgars, and they seem to have borne the same name, in spite of the difference of the rendering of it in Greek in the *Sancti Demetrii Miracula* (Koúver) and in the chronicles of Nicephorus (Koúvratos, Kovrátos) and Theophanes (Krovátos). The name, like the names Asparoúkh and Omurtag, appears to be Iranian,[2] and to be the ethnikon of the Croat people, whose name is perhaps a derivative of the province-name Harahvatiš (in Greek Arakhosía, corresponding to the ethnikon Arakhotoí) which occurs in Achaemenian Persian inscriptions. The name figures, as Khoroathos and as Khorouathos, in Greek inscriptions found on the sites of the Greek colonies along the north shore of the Black Sea. It can be interpreted in Iranian as meaning 'he who possesses trusty friends'.[3] The Iranians from whom the name was borrowed by the Bulgars were probably the Alan branch of the Sarmatians. In the Danubian Bulgar list of the Bulgar Khans, Kurt (i.e. Koúvrat) and his descendants are said to be scions of the House of Dulo, and two daughters of 'Dule the prince of the Alans' were reckoned by the Magyars to have been ancestresses of theirs.[4] Were Koúvrat and Koúver different persons

---

[1] See p. 440.
[2] Grégoire, 'L'Origine et le nom des Croates et des Serbes', p. 114, n. 33.
[3] Grégoire in loc. cit., p. 116. See the present work, Annex I, p. 623, n. 7.
[4] Marquart, *Streifzüge*, 'Analyse der Berichte des Gaihānī über die Nordländer', pp. 160–206, on p. 172, citing Simon de Keza, *Gesta Hungarorum*, I, 1, 3.

bearing the same name, or were they one and the same person? Lemerle[1] and Grégoire[2] hold that they were the same person; Ostrogorsky[3] and Ahrweiler[4] hold that they were different persons. The answer to this disputed question turns on points of locality and date.

Koúver's governorate was in Sirmia, to the west of the Carpathians, and he repatriated the deportees' descendants from there to the hinterland of Thessaloníkê. The original nucleus of Koúvrat's 'Great Bulgaria' lay to the south-east of the River Don, which was at the opposite end of the Avars' empire. However, this difference of locality does not rule out the possibility that Koúver and Koúvrat may have been the same person. When Koúver was thinking of carrying out the project, proposed by one party among his people, that he should set himself up as a Khaqan in East Roman territory, with his capital at Thessaloníkê,[5] the command over all Koúver's people was given by the Emperor to one of the conspirators named Mávros,[6] and, from then on, Koúver himself drops out of the story. It is Mávros, not Koúver, who is deposed and interned when the plot to seize Thessaloníkê is frustrated.[7] Koúver may have gone off meanwhile in pursuit of some more promising enterprise, and this alternative may have been to set himself up as the independent ruler of some of the Avars' Bulgar subjects on the Steppe. In that case he would naturally have started operations in a district that was remote from the Avars' own headquarters on the Alföld. The most remote piece of the Avars' empire was the Steppe to the south-east of the Don. Thus, as far as locality is concerned, there is no reason for ruling out the possibility that Koúver and Koúvrat may have been the same person.

The compatibility of the respective dates of Koúver's and Koúvrat's activities is less clear. Koúver is said to have been given command over the descendants of the deportees more than sixty years after the date of the deportation.[8] This date was almost certainly either 582/3 or 586/7, which were years in which the Avars invaded the Empire's European provinces, and this would make the date of Koúver's revolt later, at the earliest, than 643, and possibly later than 650. Ahrweiler dates it later than 675.[9] On the other hand, if we accept, from the list of Bulgar Khans,[10] the figures, given in this list, for the lengths of the reigns of Koúvrat and his son Asparoúkh, that is to say fifty-eight years for each of these two

---

[1] Lemerle, 'Invasions et migrations', p. 299.

[2] Grégoire, 'L'Origine et le nom,' pp. 102–4.

[3] In *Dumbarton Oaks Papers*, Number Thirteen (1959), pp. 1–21, on p. 17.

[4] Ahrweiler, *Byzance et la mer*, p. 27.

[5] *S.D. Miracula*, Book II, chap. 5, cols. 1365 and 1368.

[6] Ibid., col. 1368.   [7] Ibid., col. 1376.

[8] Ibid., col. 1364.

[9] Ahrweiler, op. cit., p. 27.

[10] See Runciman, *A History of the First Bulgarian Empire*, Appendix II: The Bulgarian Princes' List, pp. 272–9

reigns,[1] (with a possible intervening reign of only a few months' duration), Koúvrat must have died *circa* 642. On this showing, Koúvrat and Koúver must have been different persons. However, the dates cited above are not sure.

The figure of 'more than sixty years' may stand merely for a couple of generations, reckoned at thirty-three years' length (there had been time for a new generation to have grown up). The true time-interval between the deportation and the repatriation of the deportees' children may have been appreciably shorter. The dates given in the list of the Bulgar Khans are still more suspect. The lengths attributed to the reigns of Asparoúkh's successors are confirmed on the whole by independent evidence, and Asparoúkh himself, his father Kurt (i.e. Koúvrat), and their ancestor Irnik (i.e. Attila's son Ernakh)[2] are authentic persons; but the lengths attributed to the reigns of some of Asparoúkh's and Koúvrat's predecessors, including Ernik, are as fantastically long as the lengths of the lives of some of the mythical personages in the Book of Genesis,[3] and the identical figure of fifty-eight years, attributed to the reigns of Asparoúkh and Koúvrat, seems dubious. It is not impossible that both these khans reigned for a length of time that was identical and was also unusually long, but this is at least improbable.

Moreover, the dating 584–642 for Koúvrat's reign, which the list of Bulgar Khans imposes on us if we accept its figure of fifty-eight years for both Asparoúkh's reign and Koúvrat's reign, is hard to reconcile with what we know about Koúvrat from other sources. For instance, Nicephorus implies, by the context in which he inserts his notice of Koúvrat's revolt, that the date of Koúvrat's revolt from the Avars was *circa* 636–9.[4] This dating is vague, but it is the only one that we have, and it is not incompatible with the dating of Koúver's revolt, if the figure in the *Sancti Demetrii Miracula* does not have to be interpreted strictly as meaning between sixty and sixty-six years. The dating 636–9 for Koúvrat's revolt is, however, incompatible with the dating of Koúvrat's death *circa* 642. Koúvrat could not have accomplished the liberation and unification of the Bulgars within as short a maximum time-span as six years. His reign as an independent ruler must have been fairly long, though even his total reign may not have been as long as fifty-eight years. Besides, though Nicephorus, in his first mention of Koúvrat, says that he was an ally of Heraclius's, and thus informs us that the date of his revolt was before the end of Heraclius's reign (i.e. before 641), both Nicephorus[5] and Theophanes[6] date Koúvrat's reign as being contemporaneous, not with

---

[1] See Runciman, op. cit., pp. 14 and 16.

[2] See Runciman, op. cit., Appendix III, Ernach and Irnik, pp. 279–81.

[3] Irnik, who is historical, not mythical, is credited with a reign of 145 years (437–582). See Runciman, op. cit., pp. 11–12.

[4] See III, 5 (iii), p. 439.   [5] Nic. Patr., p. 33.   [6] Theophanes, p. 357.

Heraclius's, but with Constans II's. The implication is that the major part of Koúvrat's reign as an independent ruler fell within Constans II's reign—that is, within the years 641–68. This is acceptable if we throw over the datings given in the list of the Bulgar khans for Koúvrat's reign and for Asparoúkh's. The earliest certain date in Asparoúkh's career is that he and his followers were already in the 'Óngklos' by 680. Thus there does not seem to be any chronological obstacle to our identifying Koúvrat and Koúver with each other.

It might perhaps be objected that, though both Koúver and Koúvrat are represented as having been enemies of the Avars, Koúvrat is recorded to have been an ally of Heraclius's, whereas Koúver is debited with hostile designs against the East Roman Empire. However, Koúver's repatriation of the deportees' children must have been intended to be, and have been taken as being, a pro-Roman act, and there is no evidence that Koúver went all the way with Mávros in Mávros's treacherous design to seize Thessaloníkê. Koúver may have preferred to carve out the kingdom that he coveted at the Avars' expense, on the Steppe, as Heraclius's ally, and not at the Empire's expense, in the Balkan Peninsula, as Heraclius's enemy.

The identity of Koúver and Koúvrat remains non-proven, but, on the whole, it seems more probable that they are identical than that there were two contemporary Bulgar rebels against the Avars who both bore the same name.

PART III, CHAPTER 5, APPENDIX II

The Eviction of the Magyars from the Steppe by the Pechenegs in the Ninth Century

This ninth-century change in the situation on the Steppe to the west of the River Don is dealt with by Constantine Porphyrogenitus in the *De Administrando Imperio* in three different contexts: in the opening section of the book,[1] in which Constantine explains the potential usefulness of the Pechenegs to the Imperial Government in its relations with other peoples to the north; in a second section on the Pechenegs,[2] which is historical and descriptive, in contrast to the opening section, which is a prescription for diplomatic action; and thirdly in an historical and descriptive section on the Magyars.[3] The various pieces of information that are presented in these different contexts are not all consistent with

---

[1] Chaps. 1–8, pp. 67–74.   [2] Chap. 37, pp. 164–7
[3] Chaps. 38–40, pp. 168–75.

each other, and it would be a mistake to try to make them agree by arbitrary emendations and strained interpretations. The information assembled in the *De Administrando Imperio* has been gathered at different dates from different sources, and the product is not a book in which the materials have been digested and co-ordinated by an author; it is a collection of files which have been edited only perfunctorily.

The principal inconsistency in the treatment of the topic that is the subject of this Appendix is between the first paragraph of Chapter 37[1] and all the other references to Magyar–Pecheneg relations. This variant passage (which looks as if it came from a Pecheneg source) seems to imply that the defeat of the Magyars by the Pechenegs and their eviction by the Pechenegs from the Steppe into the Alföld were brought about in one war only. The passage evidently refers to the war of 896, for it states that, as a result of this defeat and eviction of the Magyars, the Pechenegs took from the Magyars the land that the Pechenegs hold today (τὴν σήμερον παρ' αὐτῶν διακρατουμένην γῆν). Reckoning back from 'today', however, the paragraph gives two different datings for this event. It says first that it happened 'fifty years ago', but it then says that, 'as has been stated', the Pechenegs have been in possession of the land that they have taken from the Magyars 'for fifty-five years, reckoning till today' (ὡς εἴρηται, μέχρι τὴν σήμερον ἔτη πεντήκοντα πέντε).

On an inclusive count, fifty-five years, running from the year 896, would make 'today' the year 950. This is a possible date for Constantine's 'today'. He dates his 'today' 948/9 in two places in the *De Administrando Imperio*[2] and 951/2 in one place.[3] Jenkins suggests that the *De Administrando Imperio* was presented by Constantine to his son the future Emperor Rhomanós II in the year 952.[4] 'Fifty years ago' would make 'today' the year 945, which is less probable. 'Fifty' may be a vague round number given by the Pechenegs themselves at the time when their own account of their acquisition of the Magyars' former country was obtained from them. There is no warrant either for emending the 'fifty' in 'fifty years ago' to 'fifty-five' or for maintaining, as Macartney does[5] in the teeth of Constantine's 'as has been said', that the two different figures in this paragraph refer to two different events. Constantine Porphyrogenitus was an industrious collector of information, but he was not a good co-ordinator of it.

In all the other passages in question, the Magyars are said to have been defeated and evicted by the Pechenegs more than once. In Chapter 3

---

[1] p. 164.

[2] In chap. 27, pp. 120–1 (lines 54–5), and in chap. 29, p. 137 (lines 234–5).

[3] In chap. 45, p. 195 (lines 39–40).

[4] See Jenkins's General Introduction to the Commentary on *De Adm. Imp.*, p. 5. See also the present work, p. 576, n. 5.

[5] In op. cit., pp. 83–6.

they are said to have been defeated by the Pechenegs 'often' ($\pi o\lambda\lambda\acute{a}\kappa\iota\varsigma$). In Chapter 38 (which looks as if it came from a Magyar source), two successive defeats and evictions are recorded, and the second of these defeats is described in greater detail in Chapter 40. As a result of the first defeat, the main body of the Magyars 'settled in the western region, in places called Atelkoúzou, in which places the Pecheneg people now lives'.[1] According to Chapter 40, 'the place in which the Magyars used formerly to be is called after the name of the river that runs through it, "Etél" and "Kouzoú". The Pechenegs live in it now.'[2] As a result of the second defeat, the Magyars settled in the country 'that is their habitat till today'[3] (and is still their habitat in 1972). In Chapters 38 and 40, Constantine Porphyrogenitus does not date either the first or the second Magyar defeat by quoting the number of years between these events and 'today', but the date of the second defeat and eviction of the Magyars is known. It is 896, if the date of the first of Khan Symeon of Bulgaria's wars with the East Roman Empire is 894–6. A date for the first defeat is given by Regino. He records, sub anno 889, the eviction of the Magyars by the Pechenegs 'from the vast marshes round the mouth of the Don', which we can identify, with some confidence, with Constantine's 'Levedhía'.[4]

There must have been, in truth, at least two defeats of the Magyars by the Pechenegs, and not just the single defeat that is implied in the first paragraph of Chapter 37 of the *De Administrando Imperio*. That there were two defeats can, indeed, be inferred from this variant passage itself; for here, as in Chapter 38,[5] the Pechenegs' victory over the Magyars is said to have been a consequence of a previous defeat of the Pechenegs by the Khazars. In Chapter 37, fuller information about this war is given than in Chapter 38. According to Chapter 37, the Pechenegs, when they were living between the Rivers Volga and Yaik, were attacked and defeated by the concerted action of their two next-door neighbours, the Khazars from the west side of the Volga and the Ghuzz from the east side of the Yaik. The Pechenegs subsequently retrieved this defeat, and won for themselves a new home to the west of the Don, by attacking and defeating the Magyars.

The second Magyar–Pecheneg war, as described in Chapter 40,[6] had two features in common with the first Magyar–Pecheneg war. In each war the Magyars were defeated, and in each war a victory was won by a converging movement concerted between two peoples who were respectively the western and the eastern neighbours of a people whom they

---

[1] Chap. 38, p. 169 (lines 29–31).   [2] Chap. 40, p. 173.
[3] Chap. 38, p. 170 (lines 57–60). Cf. chap. 40, p. 173 (lines 21 and 26–7).
[4] There is a translation of this entry in Regino's chronicle in Macartney, op. cit., p. 70.
[5] p. 169 (lines 19–26).   [6] pp. 172–3 (lines 7–25).

defeated by this strategy. However, the differences in the circumstances of the two wars are greater than the resemblances. In the first war the confederates were the Khazars and the Ghuzz; their victims were the Pechenegs; the war-zone was the country between the Volga and the Yaik, which was the Pechenegs' habitat at that time; and the consequence was the eviction of the Pechenegs from this country and their subsequent acquisition of a new home for themselves to the west of the Don at the expense of the Magyars. In the second war the confederates were the Bulgars and the Pechenegs; their victims were the Magyars; the war-zone was Atelkoúzou, which was the Magyars' habitat at the time; and the consequence was the eviction of the Magyars from Atelkoúzou and their subsequent acquisition of a new home for themselves to the west of the Carpathians at the expense of Bulgaria to the east of the River Tisza and of the people of Great Moravia to the west of the Tisza.[1]

These two wars cannot really have been the continuous single operation that seems to be implied in the first paragraph of Chapter 37. Neither the belligerents nor the war-zone were the same in the two cases. Moreover, if the Magyars had been continuously on the run from the Pechenegs from the date of the Pechenegs' first appearance on the west side of the Don until the Magyars' flight into the Alföld, the Magyars would not have had their hands free at any moment during the intervening time. But we know that in 895 the Magyars did have their hands free to invade Bulgaria on the East Roman Empire's behalf.

We are bound to conclude that there were actually two Magyar–Pecheneg wars, not one war only,[2] and that there was a time-interval between the two wars during which the Magyars were no longer in Levedhía and were not yet on the Alföld, but were in the region that Constantine Porphyrogenitus calls 'Atelkoúzou' in one passage and 'Etél and Kouzoú' in another.

If Regino's dating of the first Magyar defeat and eviction is correct, the Magyars were living in Atelkoúzou for the seven years 889–96, till in 896 the Pechenegs evicted them from Atelkoúzou too. We know the meaning of this geographical term Atelkoúzou, and Constantine tells us what the boundaries of Atelkoúzou were. In the Magyar language, 'köz' means 'a space between two limits'—for instance, between two rivers.

---

[1] Chap. 38, p. 170 (lines 58–60). Cf. chap. 13, p. 81 (line 5) and chap. 41, p. 176 (lines 20–5).

[2] Grégoire, 'Le Nom et l'origine des Hongrois', holds that there was one Magyar–Pecheneg war only (p. 633). He agrees (p. 634) with Macartney, *The Magyars in the Ninth Century*, p. 96, in holding that Atelkoúzou (Etél and Kouzoú) was identical with Levedhía, in spite of the fact that Constantine Porphyrogenitus makes them two different regions; but (p. 634) Grégoire disputes Macartney's identification of the river that Constantine calls Khingiloús and Synghoúl (see the present work, p. 453). Grégoire (p. 635) locates Levedhía in the Dniepr–Bug region. He notes that the Bug has an affluent called Ingul, and that the Dniepr has an affluent called Ingulitz.

'Atelkoúzou' is a rendering in Greek of the Magyar word 'Itilközö'; this word means 'between two itils'; and, since 'köz' implies a pair of limits, 'itil' in this compound must be the plural of a generic name for 'river',[1] not the proper name of a single river (e.g. the Volga). The Magyars' domain was literally an 'itilközö' when it extended from the Don to the Seret and included 'Levedhía', but apparently it was not given this name in practice till, as a result of their first defeat by the Pechenegs, the Magyars were driven westwards from the west bank of the Don to beyond the west bank of the Dniepr.

The place of the Pechenegs, in which the Magyars lived at that time [i.e. at the time before they were driven into present-day Hungary], is called after the nomenclature of the local rivers. The rivers are these: the first river is the one called Varoúkh [i.e. Borysthenes, Dniepr]; the second river is the one called Koúvou [i.e. Bug]; the third river is the one called Troúllos [i.e. Dniestr]; the fourth river is the one called Vroútos [i.e. Pruth]; the fifth river is the one called Séretos [i.e. Seret (Sirat)].[2]

The Itilközö that was the Magyars' habitat from 889 to 896 was the space between the Rivers Dniepr and Seret. It had been included in the Magyars' domain already before 889, as we know from the account of the Adrianopolitan deportees' repatriation at some date in the Emperor Theóphilos's reign. From 889 to 896 the Magyars were confined to this western end of their previous domain. In 896 they were evicted from even this remnant of it.

---

[1] 'Itil' is now the generic name for 'river' in the Kazan dialect of Turkish (K. Menges, 'Notes on Some Päčänäg Names', in *Byzantion*, vol. xvii (1944–5), pp. 256–280, on p. 259).

[2] *De Adm. Imp.*, chap. 38, last paragraph (p. 171). These identifications of the five rivers are accepted by Moravcsik in Moravcsik and Jenkins, *Commentary on De Adm. Imp.*, p. 149. Diaconu in op. cit., pp. 35–6, rejects the first three of these identifications. He holds that the first three rivers listed by Constantine are small water-courses somewhere between the Dniestr (*not* the Dniepr) and the Pruth. He suggests (p. 12, n. 10) that the area covered by Itilközö is limited to the southern half of the territory between the Dniestr and the Seret. Here, again, Diaconu's judgement is suspect of being influenced by irrelevant present-day political considerations.

6. *Relations with Peoples to the West*

THIS chapter can be short, and this for two reasons. The medieval East Roman Empire's relations with peoples to the west of the Straits of Ótranto did not become a matter of life and death for the Empire till the eleventh century. Till then, the Empire's interests in the western basin of the Mediterranean were marginal, and its possessions in this region were expendable, however painful the loss of them might be. A second reason for brevity in this chapter is that the treatment of parts of the subject of it has been anticipated at previous points in the book: for instance, in the notice of the establishment of théma Laghouvardhía,[1] in the account of the autonomous city-states that were under the Empire's suzerainty,[2] and in the survey of the successes and reverses of the East Roman Navy.[3]

The East Roman Government did not resign itself readily or quickly to the loss of the possessions in the western basin of the Mediterranean that had been bequeathed to it by the Emperor Justinian I. The Imperial Government, its local representatives, and, what is more significant, the local population as well, fought hard to prevent the Lombards from making conquests in Italy and the Muslims from conquering first North-West Africa and then Sicily. But the Empire did not commit its main military and naval resources in any of these West-Mediterranean areas, and it did not fight *à outrance* in contesting the possession of them with the invaders. This self-restraint was at times humiliating, but it was wise; for the Empire's existence was not endangered by the losses of the Exarchates of Italy and North-West Africa, nor even by the loss of Sicily, while, conversely, the Empire gained little or nothing from its almost effortless retention of the uninviting island of Sardinia.

The East Roman Empire maintained its presence in the western basin of the Mediterranean for about five centuries, running from Justinian I's reconquest of North-West Africa from the Vandals in 533 until the middle decades of the eleventh century; but in the western Mediterranean the Empire was not the dominant power after the turn of the seventh and eighth centuries. In 698 the Arabs had made themselves masters of North-West Africa definitively, after a struggle that had lasted for thirty-three years. In 711 they had invaded Spain and had overthrown the the Visigothic regime there. They had annexed the whole of the former Visigothic kingdom, including even the remnant of the Visigoths' dominions in Gaul, along the coast between the Pyrenees and the Rhône. The native resistance movement in the north-west corner of the

---

[1] See II, 4, Appendix, pp. 267–8.   [2] See II, 5.   [3] See II, 7.

Iberian Peninsula seemed, for the next three centuries, to have no future.

From the turn of the seventh and eighth centuries till after the opening of the eleventh century, the western Mediterranean basin's centre of gravity—not only military and political, but economic and cultural too—lay in North-West Africa and the Iberian Peninsula, not in Italy and Gaul. During this age, the Western Muslims were in the ascendant over the Western Christians, and therefore the East Roman Empire's relations in this region with the Caliphate and with its local successor-states, the Aghlabids and Fatimids in Ifrīqiyah and the refugee Umayyads in Andalusia, were more important for the Empire than its contemporary relations with the Lombards and the Franks.

If a fifth-century observer could have peered into the future, he would have found this turn of events surprising. In the fifth century it had looked as if the heirs of the Roman Empire in the west were going to be the successor states that were being carved out of the Empire's western provinces by German war-bands. If the imaginary fifth-century observer had been far-sighted, he might have guessed that these small and culturally backward groups of North European barbarian conquerors would eventually adopt the language and religion of their ex-Roman Latin-speaking Catholic Christian subjects, who were the conquerors' superiors in culture as well as in numbers. The extent of Justinian I's eventual reconquests in the west would have been surprising, and it would have been wholly unforeseeable that the predominance in the western basin of the Mediterranean was then going to be wrested out of East Roman hands by a parvenu Levantine power that would be neither Roman nor Christian.

This unpredictable turn of events was the consequence of Justinian I's unwisdom. His ambitions in the west had been extravagantly grandiose. The East Roman Empire did not have the strength either to achieve these Justinianean objectives completely or to harvest permanently even the partial results that Justinian did achieve. Justinian's achievement had been negative. He had successfully blighted the prospects of the Empire's German successor states in the western Mediterranean basin, but his triumphs had been Dead Sea fruit. The ultimate beneficiaries had been the Muslim Arabs.

There had been only one occasion on which one of the western territories that Justinian I had reincorporated had played a decisive part in the East Roman Empire's history. Thanks to Heraclius the Elder's command of the armed forces and the cereals of the Exarchate of Africa, his son and namesake had been able, in 610, to overthrow the Emperor Phokás at Constantinople and then eventually to save the core of the Empire from disintegrating.

The Emperor Heraclius is alleged to have attempted to transfer the Empire's seat of government from Constantinople to Carthage[1] before he made up his mind to adopt the contrary policy of launching a counter-attack against the Persians on the Empire's eastern front. Constans II did actually transfer the capital to Syracuse for four or five years before he was assassinated there in 668. It was natural that members of the Heraclian House should play with this idea. The dynasty had made its fortune in North-West Africa, though the family was perhaps of Armenian origin, and though the Elder Heraclius had won his military reputation on the eastern front. The pressure on this front, first from the Persians in the Romano-Persian war of 604–28 and then, with hardly a respite, from the Arabs, was so persistent and so severe that the Empire's prospects in the Levant were bound to seem dark. Yet, even after the loss of Syria and Mesopotamia and Roman Armenia and Egypt, the Levantine remnant of the Empire in Asia Minor was still the Empire's centre of gravity, and therefore neither Carthage nor Syracuse could compete with Constantinople for the role of serving as the seat of the Imperial Government. The dwindling shreds and patches of Justinian I's reconquests in the West were not substantial enough to provide the Empire with an alternative base.

Justinian I had wilfully ignored a plain truth that had been manifest to his predecessors at Constantinople ever since the division of the Empire in 395. The eastern part of the Roman Empire was more populous, productive, and prosperous than the western part; yet even the East Roman Empire's resources were not great enough to enable it to hold its own effectively on more than a single front at a time; and, after the division made in 395 had relieved the Levant of responsibility for the West, the Levant had still to defend itself in Mesopotamia against the Persians and on the lower Danube against the Eurasian nomads and the North-European barbarians, first the Goths and then the Slavs. The disastrous outcome of the East Roman naval expedition against the Vandals in 468 had demonstrated the prudence of the East Roman Imperial Government's usual policy of refraining from intervention in Western affairs.

Justinian I had burdened the East Roman Empire needlessly with three additional fronts: one in the Berber hinterland of North-West Africa, another in Spain, and yet another in Italy, which had been the heaviest commitment of all. The price of Justinian I's western conquests had been an acquiescence in the Persian Empire's predominance in the east and an exposure of the Balkan Peninsula to constant devastating barbarian raids. The price, for Justinian I's successors, of the Romano-Persian war of 572–91 had been the collapse of the East Roman Empire's

[1] See Nic. Patr., p. 12.

stand against the Slavs and Avars in the Balkan Peninsula and against the Lombards in Italy. The price of Constantine V's Romano-Bulgarian War (755–75) was the inability of this able and masterful Emperor to undo three previously accomplished facts in Italy: the annexation of Ravenna to the Lombard Kingdom in 751; Pope Stephen II's transfer of the Roman See's allegiance in 753, *de facto*, from the East Roman Empire to the Kingdom of the Franks; and the rejection of iconoclasm in all the surviving dominions of the East Roman Empire in Italy to the north of 'Calabria' (the 'toe'). Iconoclasm had been, and continued to be, rejected by the autonomous Italian city-states—Venice, Amalfi, Naples, Gaeta—that had not yet ceased to recognize the East Roman Imperial Government's suzerainty.

The price of Basil II's war to the death against Tsar Samuel of Western Bulgaria was the economic ruin and political alienation of the peasants in the 'Eastern' thémata, who, for three centuries, ending in Basil II's reign (976–1025), had been the Empire's mainstay—its prime and irreplaceable source of revenue and of military man-power. Basil II succeeded in suppressing the rebellions of Asiatic pretenders to the Imperial Crown; but he suppressed them only with the aid of Russian mercenaries. The Asiatic peasants were both impotent and unwilling to oppose the pretenders on the Crown's behalf, and they remained equally passive when, in the eleventh century, the Muslim Saljūq Turks invaded and permanently occupied the geographical heart of Asia Minor, which had been the economic and political heart of the East Roman Empire.

The East Roman Empire's sole act of reconquest, to the west of the Straits of Ótranto, between the reign of Justinian I (527–65) and the reign of Manuel I (1143–80), was the establishment of théma Laghouvardhía in the reign of Basil I (867–86); and, in thus reacquiring territory in Italy, the Empire was taking the offensive in appearance only; for actually this was a defensive measure, and, if Basil had refrained from taking it, he would have put the East Roman Empire in jeopardy. By the year 867, the Muslims of Ifriqīyah had won for themselves a strong enough base of operations in Sicily to enable them to thrust their way across south-eastern Italy and, on from there, across the Adriatic. The Muslims were threatening to join hands in the Balkan Peninsula with the East Roman Empire's local enemies the Arentanoí and the Bulgars. The Muslims might have attained this objective if Basil I had not forced them, in 868, to raise their siege of Ragusa, and if he had not then launched a counter-offensive against them in Italy. If the Western Muslims and the Bulgars had succeeded in joining hands, the East Roman Empire would have been encircled by a coalition of powerful adversaries; and this would have been an ordeal that the Empire might not have been able to survive. For the Empire, it was vitally important to insulate Bulgaria from Ifrīqīyah; Sicily had now ceased to be an effective insulator; the new théma Laghouvardhía was a substitute for the Empire's vanishing Sicilian dominion. The new dominion's area was confined to the minimum extent of south-east Italian territory that could serve this defensive purpose effectively.

The Emperor Aléxios I (1081–1118) followed Basil I's example. He kept his western commitments and exertions down to a minimum. He did not attempt to reconquer théma Laghouvardhía from the Normans, who had set the seal on their conquest of this transmarine East Roman territory by taking its capital, Bari, in 1071. Aléxios I limited himself to resisting the Normans' subsequent efforts to press on, in the wake of their Muslim predecessors two centuries earlier, from south-eastern Italy eastwards. Aléxios I defended, successfully, the Empire's dominions in the Balkan Peninsula. Aléxios I's grandson Manuel I hastened the Empire's fourth collapse[1] by repeating Justinian I's mistake. Manuel I overtaxed the Empire's now exiguous resources by taking the offensive against the Empire's Norman successor-state in Italy in the unprofitable war of 1147–58.

The principal western powers with which the East Roman Empire had to deal in the ninth and tenth centuries were the Muslim rulers of North-West Africa (Ifrīqīyah);[2] the Carolingians and their eventual successors the Ottonids; the Papacy; and the refugee Umayyad Amīrs (eventually Caliphs) in the Iberian Peninsula. These four powers have been named, and will be surveyed, in the descending order of their importance from the East Roman Empire's standpoint.

Muslim Ifrīqīyah and Andalusia did not reach their potential acme so long as they were outlying dominions of a Caliphate whose capital was in Asia. Ifrīqīyah, which was the most formidable of the western powers that the East Roman Empire encountered, did not develop its latent strength till it had become virtually independent under the rule of the Aghlabids (800–909), whose recognition of the suzerainty of the ʿAbbasid Caliphs of Baghdad was only nominal.

The East Roman Empire began to feel the pressure of the North-West African Muslims in 827, when the Aghlabids won their first foothold in

---

[1] The Roman Empire collapsed for the first time in the third century, and the East Roman Empire for the second time in the seventh century (as a result of Justinian I's over-ambitious policy) and for the third time in the eleventh century (the expansionists Nikêphóros II Phokás, John Dzimiskês, and Basil II were ultimately responsible for this third collapse). On each of these three earlier occasions the Empire had made a remarkable recovery; but it never got over its collapse in 1183–1204, though Michael VIII Palaiológhos did recapture Constantinople from the Latins in 1261 and was the founder of a dynasty that was the longest-sustained, as well as the last, of all the successive attempts to transform the essentially revolutionary Roman Imperial dictatorship into a legitimate hereditary monarchy.

[2] See E. F. Gautier, *Les Siècles obscures du Maghreb* (Paris, 1927, Payot)—a remarkable and illuminating book.

Sicily.[1] Within perhaps not more than eight years of the start of this offensive, the Muslims made a second leap—this time across the narrower seas that divide Sicily from Italy. *Circa* 835 they occupied Brindisi;[2] in 836 the Lipari Islands;[3] in 839/40 Táranto. By 841/2 they were installed in Bari; and from then till 871 they were the dominant power in south-eastern Italy. At each stage in this rapid and far-ranging expansion of Muslim power in the western and central Mediterranean, the advance-guard developed an independent capacity for carrying the expansion farther. Sicily superseded Ifrīqīyah as the main base of Muslim naval offensive operations;[4] and, when the Sicilian Muslims had won their foothold in Italy, the Italian advance-guard of the Sicilian advance-guard became, in its turn, an independent force.

The Christian powers did finally succeed in expelling the Muslim invaders of south-eastern Italy. At this distance from the Muslims' home base in Ifrīqīyah, the Christians had the advantage geographically as well as numerically; and, though some of them, especially the city-state of Naples, were often in collusion with the Muslims, while the Christians' co-operation with each other was only fitful and half-hearted, their combined strength proved decisively superior in the Italian theatre of operations on the rare occasions on which it was effectively brought to bear. On the other hand, the Muslims virtually completed their conquest of Sicily by 902, and, though, in the mountainous hinterland of Messina, the Greeks held out at Rametta till 964, the defeats that the East Roman forces suffered in that year, first on land at Rametta itself and then at sea, were the most serious of their reverses during Nikêphóros II Phokás's mostly triumphant reign (963–9).

After 902 the Aghlabids' pressure on the East Roman Empire's western front had slackened as the Aghlabids themselves had come under increasing pressure from the new Fatimid power. The Fatimids supplanted the Aghlabids in Ifrīqīyah in 909, but the respite that this change of regime in Ifrīqīyah gave to the East Romans was brief. The Fatimids captured, intact, all the installations and armaments of their Aghlabid predecessors in Ifrīqīyah, including the African part of the Aghlabids' fleet.[5] The Fatimids went on to conquer Sicily; in 911 they suppressed a Sicilian Muslim revolt; and in 914–17 they defeated a pro-Aghlabid Sicilian Muslim naval counter-attack on Ifrīqīyah.

The Fatimids differed from the Aghlabids in at least four respects. The Aghlabids' armed forces were recruited from the descendants of the Arabs who had settled permanently in Ifrīqīyah after the Arab conquest

---

[1] The Aghlabids had already conquered Malta in 820–7. In 861 the East Romans made an unsuccessful attempt to re-take it (Eickhoff, op. cit., p. 102).

[2] Vasiliev, *Byzance et les Arabes*, vol. i, p. 182.   [3] Eickhoff, op. cit., p. 103.

[4] Eickhoff, op. cit., p. 194.   [5] Op. cit., p. 274.

in the seventh century; the Fatimids' armed forces were recruited from a local Berber people, the Kutāma,[1] whose home country was Kabylia. The Aghlabids were Sunnī Muslims; the Fatimids were Shī'īs who claimed descent from the Prophet Muhammad's daughter Fatimah, and from her husband the Prophet's cousin 'Alī, through Ismā'īl, a descendant of Fatimah and 'Alī in the fifth generation.[2] Whether or not their pedigree was authentic, the self-styled Fatimids claimed, on the strength of it, to have the sole legitimate title to rule the entire Islamic World. Consequently—and this was the third of their differences from the Aghlabids—their ambition to expand their dominions was unlimited. The fourth difference was that the Aghlabids' aggression was directed mainly against non-Muslims—in the first place, against the East Romans —whereas the Fatimids were less concerned with the *jihād* than with attacking and overthrowing rival claimants to the Caliphate, and indeed the rulers of any other Muslim states within their reach that were in-dependent *de facto*.

The *jihād* overseas in the Mediterranean had been the outlet that the Aghlabids had found for their Arab warriors' energies.[3] On the African mainland they had been content to hold the territory within the *limes* that had been established by the East Romans after they had liquidated the Vandal Kingdom and had re-annexed its dominions. This territory was only a small part of the Maghrib (i.e. the western end of Dār-al-Islām), but the fenced-in area contained most of the fertile land in the Maghrib to the east of the lowlands along the Atlantic seaboard of Morocco, and, under the Aghlabid regime, the productivity of Ifrīqīyah had been raised again to a high level.[4] Under the subsequent Fatimid regime, the level was raised still higher, and the foreign trade, which had also been fostered by the Aghlabids, was carried by the Fatimids to its peak.[5] This economic prosperity was the basis of the naval power of Ifrīqīyah during the years 800–969. The Fatimids may have used their commercial strength to support their military offensives and their pro-paganda attacks against rival Muslim powers.[6]

Though the Fatimid regime in Ifrīqīyah was more potent and more dynamic than the Aghlabid regime had been, the pressure on the East Roman Empire from Ifrīqīyah does not seem to have been increased as

---

[1] See Gautier, op. cit., chap. 5.

[2] See Bernard Lewis, *The Origins of Ismā'ilism* (Cambridge, 1940, Heffer), chap. 2; eundem, *The Assassins* (London, 1967, Weidenfeld & Nicolson), chap. 2.

[3] See Eickhoff, op. cit., p. 117.

[4] To almost as high a level as it had attained in the Antonine Age, according to Eickhoff, op. cit., p. 119.

[5] Op. cit., pp. 280–3.

[6] See B. Lewis in *C. Med. H.*, vol. iv, 2nd ed., Part I, p. 648. If the Fatimids did wage economic warfare against the 'Abbasids, this may not have started till after 969, the year in which the Fatimids moved their headquarters from Ifrīqīyah to Egypt.

a result of the Fatimids' take-over. The Fatimids' aggressiveness—directed primarily, as it was, against other Muslim powers—provoked strong reactions from these, and the emergence in Ifrīqīyah of a Berber Shīʿī power in place of an Arab Sunnī power divided the Islamic World against itself. The seizure of Ifrīqīyah by the Fatimids, wielding Berber force of arms, was tantamount to a third barbarian conquest, and the tenth-century Kutāma Berber conquerors were at least as barbarous as the Vandals had been and were decidedly more barbarous than the Arabs whom the Kutāmah replaced. Indeed, one of the causes of the Sicilian Muslims' pro-Aghlabid revolts was the barbarous conduct of the Kutāmah garrison that held Sicily for the Fatimids.

The Aghlabids had not fallen foul of the Muslim states to the west of them, and in 827 the Spanish Muslims had cooperated with the Aghlabids in their first invasion of Sicily.[1] The Aghlabids had been willing to co-exist with the Rustamids in their hinterland, though this dynasty of Iranian origin was not Sunnī but Khārijī (ultra-'Dissident').[2] The Aghlabids also coexisted with the Idrīsids, a Shīʿī dynasty[3] which had founded a principality at Fez (Fās) in Morocco in 788, after having tried and failed in 786 to assert itself in the Hijāz against the ʿAbbasids. Nor was there any serious friction between the Aghlabids and the Cordoban Umayyads, who were the Idrīsids' fellow refugees in the far west of the Islamic World. The Cordoban Umayyads had been evicted by the ʿAbbasids from all the Umayyads' ancestral dominions except the Iberian Peninsula, whereas the Aghlabids were nominally the representatives of the ʿAbbasids in the west. However, the paths of the Aghlabids and the Cordoban Umayyads did not cross.

In contrast to the Aghlabids, the Fatimids took the offensive both southwards and westwards. They liquidated the Rustamids and the Aghlabids simultaneously,[4] and, after their hands had been freed by the failure, in 917, of the Sicilian Muslims' pro-Aghlabid counter-offensive, the Fatimids advanced westward to the Atlantic, drove their fellow Shīʿīs the Idrīsids into the Rīf,[5] and thus constrained them to appeal for protection to the Cordoban Umayyads. The consequence of this Fatimid aggression was a collision between the Fatimids and the Umayyads—on land for winning the allegiance of the Berber peoples of western North-West Africa, and on sea for the naval command of the western basin of the Mediterranean.[6] This conflict between the two

---

[1] See Eickhoff, op. cit., p. 75.   [2] See Gautier, op. cit., chaps. 2 and 4.

[3] See Gautier, op. cit., pp 274–91. The Idrīsids were evidently not Seven-Imām (alias Ismāʿīlī) Shīʿīs (the sect of the Shīʿah which the Fatimids represented).

[4] The overthrow of the Rustamids by the Fatimids was, in ethnic terms, a victory of the Kutāma Berber henchmen of the Fatimids over the Botr Zanātah Berber henchmen of the Rustamids (see Gautier, op. cit., pp. 301–2).

[5] In this fastness the Idrīsids survived till 985.   [6] See Eickhoff, op. cit., pp. 291–5.

profitable politically to rule in the name of a puppet Sunnī Caliphate principal Muslim powers in the West was advantageous for the East Roman Empire, which was under pressure from the Fatimids but had no quarrel with the Umayyads, who had ceased to be the Empire's neighbours and adversaries when they had lost their eastern dominions and had found asylum in distant Spain.[1]

The Fatimids' main objective was not the far western extremity of Dār-al-Islām; it was its eastern heart. The Fatimids aspired to supplant the 'Abbasids and the 'Abbasids' successor-states, as the 'Abbasids in 750 had supplanted the Damascene Umayyads. As early as 913–14 the Fatimids invaded Egypt by both land and sea. This invasion ended in a disaster[2] which gave the pro-Aghlabid Sicilian Muslims their opportunity in 914 for attacking the Fatimids in Ifrīqīyah. But the Fatimids never renounced their ambition to make themselves masters of the Muslim East, and in 969 they did conquer Egypt and went on from there to conquer southern Syria too.

For about two decades after this historic event, there was an apparent possibility that the Seven-Imam (Ismā'īlī) sect of the Shī'ah might at last succeed in uniting the whole of Dār-al-Islām under a Fatimid dynasty of Caliphs; for in 969 the Carmathians were still on the war-path along the Arabian fringes of Syria and 'Irāq; and the Carmathians were not only Shī'īs; they were adherents of the same Seven-Imam sect as the Fatimids themselves. However, the Carmathians did not always see eye to eye with the Fatimids;[3] nor, *a fortiori*, did the Buwayhids—an Iranian Shī'ī dynasty from Daylam, at the south-west corner of the Caspian Sea, who were in control of the 'Abbasid Caliphs at Baghdad at the same date. The Buwayhids were not Shī'īs of the same sect as the Fatimids and the Carmathians. The Buwayhids were not Seven-Imam Shī'īs,[4] and, apart from doctrinal considerations, the Buwayhids found it more

---

[1] It is true (see Eickhoff, op. cit., p. 198) that, *circa* 849, the Cordoban Umayyads had conquered the Balearic Islands, and that these had continued to be East Roman possessions ever since their recapture in the reign of Justinian I. But the loss of this outpost had not been a blow of the same magnitude as the loss of Sicily, and the memory of it (if it was remembered) did not deter the East Roman Imperial Government, a century later, from seeking a *rapprochement* with the Cordoban Umayyads when the opportunity for this was opened up by the Umayyads' conflict with the Fatimids.

[2] See Eickhoff, op. cit., p. 275.

[3] See Lewis, *The Origins of Ismā'ilism*, chap. 3.

[4] The Buwayhids' home province, Daylam, and the provinces to the east of Daylam between the Elburz Range and the Caspian Sea, had maintained their political independence and their Zoroastrian religion after the rest of the Sasanian Persian Empire had been incorporated in the Muslim Arab Empire. In 864 the Zaydī branch of the Shī'ah had won converts in the Caspian provinces of Iran, but apparently there is no evidence that the Buwayhids were Zaydīs. They appear to have welcomed non-Ismā'īlī Shī'īs of all persuasions, and, among the Shī'īs in 'Irāq, the Twelve-Imāmers (known as Imāmīs *sans phrase*) are thought to have been already in a majority by the time, in the tenth century, when the Buwayhids established their ascendancy over the 'Abbasids in 'Irāq, which was the last remnant of the

profitable politically to rule in the name of a puppet Sunnī Caliphate than to instal in the 'Abbasids' place a dynamic Shī'ī dynasty whose doctrine was not the Buwayhids' own.

The Fatimids did make one further leap eastwards. They took Multān.[1] But Egypt did not prove, for them, to be a stepping-stone to 'Irāq. The consequence, for the Fatimids, of their conquest of Egypt and their transfer of their capital from Mahdīyah to Cairo was not the acquisition of Muslim lands to the east of the Euphrates; the price of their migration to Egypt was the loss of their hold on the Maghrib—the region which had been the cradle of their power. In 969 the Fatimids became a power in the Middle East but consequently soon ceased to be a power in the western Mediterranean.

From the East Roman Empire's standpoint, the second most important region to the west of the Empire, after Ifrīqīyah, was the realm of the Franks and of the Carolingian Franks' Ottonid Saxon successors in the pretension to the controversial title of Roman Emperors in the west.

It was fortunate for the East Roman Empire, and for the Western Muslims too, that, among the German successor-states of the defunct Western Roman Empire, Frankland was the one that eventually incorporated or overshadowed all the others that Justinian I had not liquidated. The Frankish power had its base in a region that was remote from the geographical base of the East Roman Empire's power. The sagacious Emperor Anastasius I had advertised his recognition of this truth when he had decorated the ex-pagan Catholic Christian Frankish war-lord Clovis as a reward for his victory in 507 over the Arian Visigoths. It was equally fortunate for both the East Romans and the Western Muslims that, when Charlemagne's *soi-disant* Western Roman Empire was revived, within narrower territorial limits, by Otto I a century and a half after Charlemagne's death, the homeland of this German dynasty that had reasserted a claim to the Imperial title lay still farther northward in western Europe. The Franks' homeland bestrode the Roman Empire's former frontier along the lower course of the Rhine; the Con-

'Abbasids' dominions (see *The Encyclopaedia of Islam*, new edition, vol. i (1960), pp. 1350–2).

The Zaydī principality on the Caspian coast of Iran seems to have been small and short-lived. On the other hand, the Zaydī principality that was established in the Yaman in 901 survived, through many vicissitudes, until after the Second World War. In the Yaman in 1972 the supporters of the dynasty of the Zaydī Imāms were disputing the possession of the country with their republican adversaries.

In 1972, Zaydī Shī'ism was still represented by its adherents in the Yaman and Ismā'īlī (Seven-Imām) Shī'ism by the Khojas, whose head was the Agha Khan. But the Twelve-Imāmers had become the dominant branch of the Shī'ah. This branch was now represented by the Shī'īs of Iran, 'Irāq, and the Lebanon.

[1] See S. M. Ikram: *Muslim Civilization in India* (New York and London, 1964, Columbia University Press), pp. 14 and 26. The Fatimids held Multān from 977 to 1005, and Mansūrah, in Sind, from *circa* 985 to 1025.

tinental Saxons' homeland lay between the Rhineland and the south-west bank of the Elbe. The East Roman Empire's relations with the Franks and with their Saxon successors were sometimes strained, and, more frequently, the tone of the diplomatic correspondence between them was acrimonious, but the distance between their respective bases made for peace, and military clashes between them, and even political confrontations, were rare.

The most serious military encounter between East Roman and Frankish armies had occurred in 553–4, when Narses, the East Roman general who had completed Belisarius's work of reconquering Italy from the Ostrogoths, had inflicted a crushing defeat on one of the two Franko-Alemannic war-bands that had descended on Italy in the hope of harvesting the fruits of the victory over the Ostrogoths that had finally been won by the East Romans at an excessive price. Even Justinian I did not attempt to follow up his generals' reconquest of Italy, and their repulse of Italy's Frankish invaders, by launching a counter-offensive against the Franks for the reconquest from them of Gaul. Justinian I exterminated the Ostrogoths and assailed the Visigoths, but he left the Franks alone.

The German people that was the beneficiary of Justinian I's exhausting war with the Ostrogoths in Italy was not the Franks: it was the Lombards; and the East Roman Empire was not confronted again by the Franks at close quarters till after the conquest and incorporation of the North-Italian Lombard Kingdom in the Frankish dominions by Charlemagne in 773–4. Even then, the direct territorial contact between the two powers was only on a narrow front.

The Lombard Duchy of Benevento, which the East Roman Emperor Constans II had just failed to reconquer in 663, insulated from the Carolingian Empire the East Roman possessions in the 'toe' of Italy and in Sicily. In Charlemagne's time the Duchy of Benevento had not yet broken up, and its recognition of Charlemagne's suzerainty was only nominal and temporary. In the Balkan Peninsula the East Roman Empire was insulated from the Carolingian Empire by Bulgaria. The Bulgars had co-operated with the Franks in the extermination of the Avars on the Hungarian Alföld,[1] and the Bulgars had obtained the lion's share of the territorial spoils. The Bulgars would have been as unwilling to submit to the Franks as they were to submit to the East Romans; and, if Charlemagne had attempted to impose his suzerainty on Bulgaria, he would have failed; for Bulgaria was a more powerful state than Benevento, and both these states were beyond the effective range of a power based on the lower course of the Rhine.

Thus the front along which there was a direct confrontation between the East Roman Empire and Charlemagne was confined to Venice, Istria, and the nine surviving Roman cities on the coast of Dalmatia

[1] See pp. 295 and 434.

and on some of the offshore islands. These were all tiny enclaves of territory; but Venice, at any rate, was economically and politically important. The complicated and delicate relations between Venice, the East Roman Empire, and the Carolingian Empire at this juncture have been touched upon in a previous chapter.[1]

It was fortunate for the East Roman Empire that, in St. Peter's on Christmas Day, 800, Charlemagne had been crowned by Pope Leo III as Emperor of the Romans, and had been acclaimed as such by the congregation. (This probably consisted of the notables and of the militia of the Ducatus Romanus, who were deemed to represent the Roman Senate and People.) The confidential preliminaries to the Pope's public act are not on record, but we may guess that the Pope was pursuing what he conceived to be his own interests, and, whether or not Charlemagne had any previous cognizance of the Pope's intentions, it is certain that he was embarrassed by the *fait accompli*. This weakened his position *vis-à-vis* the East Roman Empire; for, now that he had been proclaimed Roman Emperor, his prestige required that his investiture should be recognized as being legitimate, and the key to recognition was in the East Roman Government's hands, since the legitimacy of the East Roman Emperor's title was incontestable, and he alone possessed the prerogative of adopting a colleague.

Any concession that might seem to derogate from the East Roman Emperor's claim to be the uniquely legitimate bearer of the Imperial title was painful for the East Romans. They took protocol very seriously and were highly sensitive about it. However, the Emperor Nikêphóros I in 811, like the Emperor Rhomanós I in 927, realized that it was good business for the Empire to buy peace and territorial integrity from a powerful neighbour in exchange for the concession of a form of words, even though, in East Roman estimation, the Imperial title might be as precious as the Imperial Government's gold reserves. The East Roman envoy Arsáphios's comprehensive settlement, in 811, of all questions at issue between the two powers, and the ratification of this settlement in 814, was one of the master-strokes of medieval East Roman diplomacy.[2] In exchange for the recognition of Charlemagne's title, Arsáphios secured the evacuation, by the Franks, of the Dalmatian cities, Istria, and the Venetians' continental footholds. Above all, he secured the abandonment of any Carolingian claims to sovereignty over Venice itself, and the preservation of Venetian economic interests in the Carolingian dominions that had now become Venice's hinterland. Thus Charlemagne paid a high price for a title that the East Roman Government had conceded to him personally but had not committed itself to conceding to his successors. None of these was as powerful as Charlemagne had

[1] See II, 5, pp. 278–9.   [2] See p. 279.

been, and, though the East Roman Government did recognize some of them, too, as Emperors on some occasions, these occasions were rare, and, when the title was then conceded, this was usually done with a bad grace.

Charlemagne's annexation of the Lombard Kingdom in 773–4 had elevated the Frankish realm to the status of a power of first-class calibre. There had been no power of this calibre in Western Christendom since the disintegration of the Western Roman Empire in the fifth century. Consequently, statesmen at both Aachen and Constantinople now played with the idea that the Roman Empire of Constantine I and Theodosius I might perhaps be resuscitated, in all the plenitude of its fourth-century might, majesty, and dominion, by means of a marriage-alliance between the two reigning dynasties. These projects fell through. The betrothal of Charlemagne's daughter Rotrud to the Emperor Constantine VI was broken off in 787 or 788 by the Emperor's mother Eirĕnê. Eirĕnê herself, after she had deposed her son and had blinded him with intent to cause his death, is said[1] to have received in 802 an offer of marriage from Charlemagne and to have wanted to accept, but she failed to overcome the opposition of her advisers before she herself was deposed, in her turn, by Nikêphóros I.

If either of the projected marriage alliances had been consummated, could this have resulted in an effective and enduring amalgamation of the Carolingian realm with the East Roman Empire? In an earlier chapter,[2] it has been suggested that if, in 913, Khan Symeon of Bulgaria had succeeded in his plan (if he did so plan) to make himself the father-in-law of the youthful East Roman Emperor Constantine VII Porphyrogenitus, this would have resulted in an amalgamation of Bulgaria with the East Roman Empire. But the two situations differed in two respects. Bulgaria and the East Roman Empire were interlocked with each other geographically, whereas, geographically, the Carolingian dominions and the East Roman Empire were virtually poles apart. In the second place, Khan Symeon's Bulgaria had adopted Christianity in its Eastern Orthodox form, and this conversion to Orthodoxy carried with it the definitive adoption of the Byzantine culture. Indeed, Symeon himself had had a thorough Byzantine education, and his cultural allegiance to the East Roman Empire's style of civilization was not shaken by his conflict with the Empire on the military and political planes. The infiltration of Byzantine Greek influence into Bulgaria was coeval with the lodgement of the Bulgars to the south of the Danube. It would have been difficult to reverse a tide that had been flowing for as long as that.

By contrast, Frankland and the East Roman Empire were far apart culturally as well as geographically. Frankland's geographical base was

---

[1] See Theophanes, p. 475.   [2] III, 2, pp. 366–7.

the Rhineland, the East Roman Empire's was Asia Minor. These two regions had been united in the Roman Empire through the territorial expansion of a power whose base had been in Italy, and the unity of the Roman Empire had been re-established, after its break-up in the third century of the Christian Era, by Romans who were still Roman, though the homeland of these later Romans was not Italy but was Illyricum. Only a power based on either Italy or Illyricum could have united and re-united Asia Minor with the Rhineland, but at the turn of the eighth and ninth centuries neither Italy nor the Danube basin was politically potent.

Moreover, Roman Italy had provided a cultural as well as a geographical link between the Rhineland and Asia Minor. Rome and the other Italian communities that Rome had subordinated to herself politically in the course of the fourth and third centuries B.C. had adopted the Hellenic culture and had then transmitted this, in a Latinized version, to the peoples to the west and to the north-east of Italy whom Rome had incorporated in her Empire. But, from the third century of the Christian Era onwards, this cultural unity, which had never been complete, had fallen asunder progressively. The Illyrian Romans who had reunited the Empire were ignorant of Greek; their attempt to extend the use of their own Latin tongue among the majority of the Empire's population, who spoke Greek as their mother-tongue or as their lingua franca, was foredoomed to fail;[1] and Greek-speaking and Latin-speaking Christendom subsequently became more and more alien to each other, till, by Charlemagne's time, they were sundered by an insurmountable cultural barrier.

The crux was cultural, not theological. It seems probable that, on the current issue of eikóns, a compromise could have been worked out if the two empires had been united politically. In 787 the veneration of eikóns had been reinstated in Eastern Orthodox Christendom at the Seventh Ecumenical Council, held at Níkaia. Conversely, in 794, the cult of eikóns was condemned at a synod of the Frankish Church, held at Frankfurt, and the same line was taken in the *Libri Carolini*. Both this work and the Acts of the Council of Frankfurt were drafted without reference to the Papacy and in disregard of current Papal policy. It is conceivable that, if Charlemagne had been installed on the Imperial throne at Constantinople, he might have found a solution for the question of eikóns that would have been acceptable to both the iconoclasts and the iconodules among his Eastern Orthodox subjects. But it is hardly conceivable that he could have made the East Romans feel that he himself was a fully naturalized member of their own society, as Khan Symeon could perhaps have made the East Romans accept him if, a century later, it had been Symeon's destiny to forestall Rhomanós Lekapênós.

[1] See IV, 2 (vii).

The Franks, and *a fortiori*, their successors the Saxons, could not have been assimilated by the East Romans. They were almost as alien to them as the Western Muslims were. Militarily and politically, however, the unwieldy Carolingian and Ottonian empires were not, even at the peaks of their power, such dangerous neighbours for the East Roman Empire as Ifrīqīyah was from 800 to 969. The Norman Kingdom, which was a successor state of both the East Roman Empire in south-eastern Italy and the African Muslim amirate in Sicily was the first—though not the last—Western Christian power that menaced the East Roman Empire as seriously as the Muslims of Ifrīqīyah had menaced it in their heyday. The East Romans proclaimed their awareness of this by confounding the Normans with the Muslims under the insulting sobriquet 'Children of Hagar'.

Next to Ifrīqīyah and to the Germanic Roman Empire, the Papacy was the third most important of the East Roman Empire's western neighbours. The East Roman Empire's relations with the Papacy during the six hundred years, ending in the eleventh century, during which Eastern Orthodox Christendom was more potent than Western Christendom, display two salient features. On the one hand, the Papacy, relatively weak though it still was, succeeded nevertheless in emancipating itself progressively from the political control of the East Roman Imperial Government. On the other hand, the Papacy was not able to intervene in the domestic affairs of the Eastern Orthodox Christian churches, except at times when the Eastern Christians were at odds among themselves.

The Papacy's eventual destiny did not begin to become apparent till nearly half way through the eleventh century. It was, indeed, a *tour de force* for the Roman See, at the south-eastern extremity of the medieval Western Christian World, to succeed in making itself this World's spiritual and cultural centre; and the magnetic attraction of the site of Rome was demonstrated when, in 1309, in response to the pull of fourteenth-century geographical realities, the Papal Court migrated from Rome to Avignon—a location that, unlike Rome, was close to the central nodes of fourteenth-century Western Christendom's network of communications. The Papacy's sojourn at Avignon from 1309 to 1376 was stigmatized as being its 'Babylonish captivity', and the Papal Court reverted to its hallowed but geographically eccentric original seat.

The prestige of the site of Rome has been the source of the Papacy's moral authority and of its ecclesiastical pre-eminence throughout the history of the Roman See. The primacy of the Patriarchate of Rome over the other four patriarchates has always been recognized by all non-Protestant Christians who adhere to the Chalcedonian creed. This creed was formulated, the order of precedence of the five Patriarchates was agreed, and their respective domains were delimited, at Chalcedon by the Fourth Ecumenical Council in the year 451. Ever since then, the Roman Patriarchate's primacy has always been acknowledged by the other four Patriarchates' Chalcedonian ecclesiastical subjects, even at times when their relations with the Roman Patriarchate have been strained, so long as the Roman Church has passed muster, as being impeccably orthodox, in the Eastern Orthodox churches' estimation.

On the other hand, an overwhelming majority of Eastern Orthodox Christians has always rejected the Roman Patriarchate's claim to be, not only *primus inter pares*, but paramount over the whole body of the Chalcedonian Church. After the balance of power between Eastern and Western Chalcedonian Christendom had turned decisively in favour of the West, the Papacy's supremacy over the Eastern Orthodox churches was acknowledged formally, from time to time, by some of the East Roman Emperors—for instance, by Michael VIII Palaiológhos in 1274, by John V Palaiológhos in 1369, by John VIII Palaiológhos in 1439, and by Constantine XI in 1452. The motive of these Emperors was not doctrinal conviction; it was *raison d'état*. They acknowledged Papal supremacy in the vain hope that this humiliating concession might win for them effective Western military help. But not one of them succeeded in carrying with him more than a handful of his Orthodox Christian subjects. Inside the then fast-shrinking frontiers of the East Roman Empire, as well as in the expanding non-East Roman tracts of the Orthodox Christian World, the people showed by their acts that, in their eyes, submission to the Papacy's ecclesiastical sovereignty was a greater evil than political subjugation by a Muslim power.

However, this situation, in which Western Christendom, and therefore the Papacy, held the remnant of the East Roman Empire at its mercy, did not begin to present itself until after the year 1071, when the East Roman Empire suffered the third of its successive collapses. From the third century to the eleventh century the prestige of Rome was based, not on present realities, but on memories of the past. In the third century, Rome ceased, *de facto*, to be the political capital of the circummediterranean empire that the Roman city-state had built up. The seat of government now shifted from Rome to Milan, Nikomḗdheia, Thessaloníkê, and Trier, and, in the fourth century, Byzantium was converted into a 'New Rome', Constantinople. The City of Rome itself survived its sack by the Visigoths in 410 and by the Vandals in 455, but it was devastated and depopulated during the Romano-Ostrogothic war of 535–62, and Rome did not again become a great city in the physical and demographic sense until the century following her conversion in 1870 into the capital of a politically reunited Italy.

Rome's material dilapidation during the intervening centuries makes her spiritual power all the more impressive. Her influence in the World at the height of the Papacy's fortunes may perhaps be reckoned to have been even greater than it had been during the *floruit* of the pre-Christian Roman Republic and Empire. Rome had forestalled the foundation of a 'New Rome' at Constantinople by providing herself with a new Romulus and Remus, namely Peter and Paul. This pair of reputed founders of the Christian community at Rome came into their own when the Roman Empire was converted to Christianity. The Patriarchate of Constantinople was unable to equip itself with a reputed founder of their stature. Of course the reason why Rome was sought out by the missionaries of a sect that aspired to convert all mankind was because, in their time, Rome was the political capital of the west end of the Oikoumenê. In the course of the preceding four hundred years, Rome had become the capital of the whole perimeter of the Mediterranean as a result of the cumulative achievements of a long line of pre-Christian Roman statesmen and soldiers.

At the time when the first Christian missionaries reached Rome, Juvenal's famous characterization of Rome[1] at the turn of the first and second centuries of the Christian Era was not a rhetorical exaggeration in terms of the first chapter of the Roman Church's history. Greek was the lingua franca of the City of Rome's immigrant underworld; and this was the public among whom the Christian church won its first metropolitan converts. During the first two centuries of its existence, the Roman Church was Greek-speaking, as is attested by the fact that Greek, not Latin, is the language of St. Paul's Epistle to the Romans, of Hermas's *Shepherd*, and of the theological works of the third-century Roman Christian scholar and ecclesiastical politician Hippolytus. By A.D. 451, Rome had become, once again, the predominantly Latin-speaking city that it had been before the second century B.C., but, in the drawing of the boundaries of the Patriarchates, which had been carried out at the Council of Chalcedon in that year, the Roman Patriarchate had been assigned some Greek-speaking ecclesiastical subjects who were not domiciled in the City of Rome itself.

The territorial domain assigned to the Roman Patriarchate in 451 embraced the Empire's three western praetorian prefectures, including the prefecture of the Eastern Illyricum. The fourth prefecture, Oriens, alone was left to be divided among the Patriarchates of Constantinople, Antioch, Jerusalem, and Alexandria. The Roman Patriarchate's portion was thus relatively vast in sheer extent, though, in population, productivity, and culture, fifth-century Oriens may have been a match for all the other three prefectures together. The Roman Patriarchate's domain was thinly populated and was economically underdeveloped, except in a few patches, and, apart from Greece and Italy, its domain was

---

[1] 'Graecam urbem'—Juvenal, *Satire* III, line 60.

inferior to Oriens in the level of its culture. This sprawling backward Roman Patriarchate included the whole of the Roman Empire's Latin-speaking population except for the small fraction of this whose home was Oriens's Thracian dioecesis; but, in the southern half of the Eastern Illyricum (i.e. in Continental Greece, the Kykládhes Islands, and Crete), the Roman Patriarchate also included a Greek-speaking population, and the Roman Patriarchate's Greek-speaking territory coincided with the historical nucleus of the Greek-speaking world.

After the Emperor Constantine I had taken the Christian Church under his wing, he made it clear that he expected a *quid pro quo* from the Christian ecclesiastical authorities. In return for his protection and patronage, the Church was to promote his policies by commending them to its adherents. This claim that Constantine had made on the Church was not embodied in any formal compact; but this did not make the claim any the less onerous, and, if and when the ecclesiastical authorities opposed the Emperor's will and obstructed the achievement of his purposes, they asserted their independence at their peril.

Constantine I's expectations from the Church were inherited from him by his successors, but of course the Imperial Government could not bring pressure to bear on patriarchs and bishops whose sees and flocks were not under the Government's effective political control, and in 451 the only part of the Roman Patriarchate's vast domain that was in the East Roman Government's hands was the Eastern Illyricum. In 451 the Western Empire was in its death-agonies, and most of its dominions, covering the major part of the Roman Patriarchate's domain, had already been partitioned among virtually independent German successor-states. Italy went the same way in 476, and, from that year till the incorporation of Italy in the East Roman Empire as a result of the Romano-Ostrogothic war of 535–62, the Pope was beyond the reach of the Roman Imperial Government's arm. The Roman Patriarchate's only hostage in the East Roman Government's hands during this interlude was the Eastern Illyricum, which was the easternmost fringe of the Roman Patriarchate's ecclesiastical domain.

After Justinian I had re-established the Imperial Government's rule in Italy, he and his successors assumed that they could treat Popes of Rome as they could and did treat Patriarchs of Constantinople. Popes too were expected, once more, to promote Imperial policies, and, if they were contumacious, they were to be made to suffer for this. The Imperial Government thrice succeeded in coercing a Pope who had incurred its displeasure, but the fourth attempt was a failure.

The Popes were in a different position from the Patriarchs of Constantinople in two respects. In the first place, they had been exempt from effective Imperial control for a century and a half before Justinian I succeeded in re-establishing this. Since the partition of the Empire in 395, the Western Imperial Government had been too feeble to be able to impose its will on the Popes, and, after 476, the Popes had been subject, *de facto*, to German war-lords in Italy who were only nominally the East Roman Imperial Government's vicegerents there. Neither Odovacer nor Theodoric had any interest in forcing a Pope to carry out the wishes of his and the Pope's nominal sovereign.

Accordingly, the Papacy had been able, with impunity, to reject the Emperor Zeno's *Enotikón* and to break off communion with the Eastern Patriarchates while the *Enotikón* was in force.[1] The Eastern Patriarchates had accepted the *Enotikón* willy-nilly; they were in the East Roman Government's power; but, apart from this, the Imperial policy embodied in the *Enotikón* coincided with the Eastern Patriarchates' own interests. Both the Eastern Patriarchs and the East Roman Government were deeply concerned to arrest, and if possible to reverse, the mass movement against Chalcedonianism in Egypt, Syria, and Mesopotamia, which were the East Roman Empire's most populous and most productive dominions. For Eastern statesmen and prelates, this had been an issue of vital importance. Yet the Pope, who had no Monophysite ecclesiastical subjects, had chosen, on this grave issue, to obstruct the Easterners' policy. The East Roman Imperial Government had been impotent to retaliate. For the Papacy, this had been a memorable exercise of independence.

The second of the Papacy's two advantages over the Eastern Patriarchates, and over the Patriarchate of Constantinople in particular, was that the East Roman Empire's reign in Italy was short-lived. When in 568, only three years after Justinian I's death, the Lombards broke into Italy, the Empire managed still to hold a beach-head round Ravenna and the 'toe' of the peninsula with Imperial garrisons, but it had to leave the Ducatus Romanus to fend for itself. The Pope would have welcomed an Imperial garrison if this had been forthcoming, and the Ducatus Romanus remained East Roman Imperial territory officially till in 800 Pope Leo III implicitly withdrew his allegiance from the Empress Eirĕnê by giving it to Charlemagne. Meanwhile, for more than two centuries ending in 800, the people of the Ducatus Romanus had saved themselves by their own exertions. They had thus borne the military and political burden of independence *de facto* long before they had asserted their independence formally, and naturally this experience had made them bolder in refusing to adopt East Roman Imperial policies that were distasteful to them.

The Empress Theodora was able to have Pope Silverius (536–7)

---

[1] See *C. Med. H.*, vol. iv, 2nd ed., Part I, pp. 21 and 434–5. The *Enotikón* was in force from 482 to 518; the Roman Patriarchate was out of communion with the Eastern Patriarchates from 484 to 519.

arrested, deported, deposed, and replaced by a Pope of her own choice, Vigilius (537–55). When Vigilius, in turn, proved unaccommodating, the Emperor Justinian was able to arrest him; to fetch him from Rome to Constantinople; to keep him there from 547 to 555; and to extort from him an endorsement of 'the Three Chapters', in which Justinian had condemned, in 544, certain theological works of an allegedly Nestorian complexion. The endorsement of 'the Three Chapters' was a matter of political importance for Justinian; for he, like his predecessors on the East Roman Imperial throne, had to take account of the anti-Chalcedonian feelings of the Imperial Government's Monophysite subjects (feelings that were shared by Justinian's wife, Theodora), and the promulgation of 'the Three Chapters' had been intended to be a conciliatory gesture towards them. Yet even this irresolute Pope, while he was a virtual prisoner in his sovereign's capital, far away from his own see, had the spirit to excommunicate the Patriarch of Constantinople and to refuse to attend a Council[1] that the Emperor had convened.[2]

Justinian I's treatment of Pope Vigilius was milder than Theodora's treatment of Silverius, and this was surpassed in brutality by Constans II's treatment of Pope Martin I (649–55). This Pope's offence against the Imperial Government was of the same kind as Vigilius's. He had refused to endorse an Imperial state paper which had been intended to relieve the tension between Chalcedonians and Monophysites. The controversial paper in Pope Martin I's case was the *Týpos* issued by Constans II in 648. Justinian I had tried to have Vigilius dragged from an altar in a church in Constantinople at which he had taken sanctuary; Constans II not only dragged Pope Martin to Constantinople; he imprisoned him there, and then sent him into exile at Khersón.[3] None of these three deported Popes lived to see Rome again.

Justinian I and Constans II had each succeeded in bringing a Pope from Rome to Constantinople. Constans II's Exarch of Ravenna had arrested and deported Pope Martin I in 653. But, when Leo III's Exarch, on this Emperor's orders, tried to mete out the same treatment to Pope Gregory II, he was foiled, and this time it was the Imperial official, not the Pope, who was roughly handled.[4] Pope Gregory II's offence had been his support of the Emperor Leo III's western subjects in their resistance to the imposition of additional taxes after the Imperial

---

[1] The Fifth Ecumenical Council, held at Constantinople in 553.

[2] For the affair of 'the Three Chapters', and for Justinian I's treatment of Pope Vigilius, see J. B. Bury, *History of the Later Roman Empire from the Death of Theodosius I to the Death of Justinian*, vol. ii, pp. 378–80 and 383–91, in the paperback edition (London, 1958, Constable).

[3] See J. B. Bury, *A History of the Later Roman Empire from Arcadius to Irene* (London, 1889, Macmillan, 2 vols.), vol. ii, pp. 292–7.

[4] See Bury, op. cit. in n. 3, vol. cit., pp. 440–5; Dvornik in *C. Med. H.*, vol. iv, 2nd ed., Part I, pp. 442–4.

Government had emerged from the ordeal of the second Arab siege of Constantinople in 717–18. Pope Gregory II's reassuring experience on this occasion gave him the confidence to reject Leo III's edict of 726, banning the veneration of eikóns. This edict, following upon the increase in taxation, led to widespread revolts, first in Ellás and the Kykládhes Islands and then in the surviving remnants of the Empire's possessions in Italy. Pope Gregory II (715–31) and his successor Gregory III (731–41) did their best to help the Imperial Government to re-establish its political authority,[1] but the revolts had made it evident that the Pope could be sure of being supported by his ecclesiastical subjects within the Imperial frontiers, as well as outside them, if he opposed iconoclasm uncompromisingly. The amenable Patriarch of Constantinople, Anastásios (730–54), who had been substituted by the Emperor Leo III for the recalcitrant Patriarch Yermanós I (715–30), was excommunicated first by Pope Gregory II and then again in 731 by a synod convened at Rome by Pope Gregory III. The Emperor retorted by sending the fleet of théma Kivyrrhaiótai to the west in 732/3. The Kivyrrhaiótai, unlike the Elladhikoí and the Islanders, were supporters of iconoclasm. However, this fleet was destroyed by a storm in the Adriatic.[2]

It was now clear that the East Roman Government had lost command of the Ducatus Romanus and that it no longer had the military power to arrest and deport a Pope. It therefore retaliated by transferring from the Patriarchate of Rome to the Patriarchate of Constantinople all those parts of the Roman Patriarchate's domain that were still effectively under East Roman control: that is to say, the 'toe' of Italy, Sicily, Ellás, the Kykládhes Islands, and Crete.[3] The Government also diverted from the Papal to the Imperial treasury the revenues of the Patrimony of St. Peter,[4] which were mostly derived from estates in Sicily.

The territories hitherto belonging to the Roman Patriarchate that were now transferred to the Constantinopolitan Patriarchate were those in which the population was Greek-speaking. The Papacy recovered its ecclesiastical jurisdiction over the 'toe' of Italy and over Sicily in the eleventh century as a result of the Norman conquest, but it never recovered its jurisdiction over the Eastern Illyricum. Logically, the Patriarchate of Constantinople ought to have retroceded the Eastern

---

[1] Juridically both these Popes were still the East Roman Government's subjects. Gregory II was a Roman in the topographical sense; Gregory III was a Syrian. No doubt, their juridical status counted for less than their fear of the Lombards in disposing them to remain loyal to the Emperor Leo III politically.

[2] Theophanes, p. 410, sub A.M. 6224.

[3] The date of this transfer is discussed by M. V. Anastos in *C. Med. H.*, vol. iv, 2nd ed., Part I, 4, pp. 70–1. Anastos holds that 732/3 is the most probable of the possible alternative datings.

[4] Theophanes in loc. cit.

Illyricum to the Patriarchate of Rome in 843, for in that year the conflict between iconoclasts and iconodules in Eastern Orthodox Christendom was at last resolved once for all by a compromise, and this conflict had been the cause of the transfer of the Eastern Illyricum in 732/3. However, the triumphant iconodules were in accord with the discomfited iconoclasts in being determined that the Eastern Illyricum should be retained within the Constantinopolitan Patriarchate's domain. After the conversion of Bulgaria in 864, the Papacy eventually failed in its competition with the Patriarchate of Constantinople for winning Bulgaria's ecclesiastical allegiance.[1] As for the sees of the Latin rite, paying allegiance to Rome, that were established in those portions of the East Roman Empire that were conquered by the Latins in and after 1204, they were as ephemeral as the Latin regime itself.

This is the second point, besides the rejection of the Papal claim to supremacy (as distinct from primacy), on which an overwhelming majority of Eastern Orthodox Christians have continued to agree among themselves (whatever may have been their domestic differences on other points). Today the Churches of Greece, Bulgaria, and, within Yugoslavia, of Macedonia, Serbia, and Montenegro are Eastern Orthodox in creed and in rite. Moreover, today Mount Athos is the principal holy place and pilgrimage resort for the whole of Eastern Orthodox Christendom.[2] Yet, till 732/3, Mount Athos had lain within the domain of the Patriarchate of Rome. Thus the territorial price of the Papacy's achievement of independence from the East Roman Empire has been high.

Independence enabled the Papacy thenceforward to oppose the East Roman Imperial Government's policy with impunity, but independence did not enable the Papacy to intervene effectively in the domestic affairs of either the Empire or the Patriarchate of Constantinople. In 843 the struggle over eikóns was at last brought to an end in Eastern Orthodox Christendom by a settlement that was achieved by the Eastern Orthodox Christians among themselves, without the Papacy's assistance. Yet for clerics who were still under the East Roman Emperor's sovereignty it continued to be as dangerous as it had once been for Popes to incur the Emperor's displeasure, and, when an East Roman cleric had fallen foul of an Emperor, he, or at any rate his supporters, might be tempted to appeal to the Pope as an ecclesiastical authority who, besides being now beyond the reach of the East Roman Emperor's arm, was recognized by all Eastern Orthodox Christians, including Emperors, to outrank the four Eastern Patriarchs.

However, East Roman Patriarchs or other prelates who ran into

---

[1] See III, 2. In any case the nucleus of the Khanate of Bulgaria did not fall within the limits of the Eastern Illyricum. Bulgaria's nucleus lay in the Thracian dioecese of the praetorian prefecture Oriens.   [2] See, for instance, Vlasto, op. cit., pp. 219, 226, 298–9.

political trouble found, time and again, that the Papacy was, for them, a broken reed. The fortunes of the Constantinopolitan Patriarchs Ighnátios and Phótios and Nikólaos I Mystikós were decided, not by Popes, but by Caesars and Emperors. Ighnátios was deposed in 858 for having dared to condemn the Caesar Várdhas's sexual conduct. Ighnátios was reinstated when his successor Phótios had refused to countenance the murder of the Emperor Michael III by Michael's colleague Basil I. Phótios was reinstated by Basil I when it suited the Emperor's convenience, and was deposed for the second time when, in 886, Basil I was succeeded by Leo VI. Another Patriarch, Nikólaos I, was deposed by Leo VI for having refused to countenance Leo's fourth marriage. Nikólaos I was reinstated and his supplanter Efthýmios I was deposed when, in 912, Leo VI's brother Alexander became senior Emperor in consequence of Leo's death.

The Papacy's interventions in these East Roman domestic affairs were ineffective. An East Roman Emperor, as well as a cleric, might find it convenient to appeal to Rome. The Emperor Leo VI obtained from Pope Sergius III a guarded sanction for his fourth marriage and for his deposition of the Patriarch Nikólaos I, but the Pope's pronouncement did not settle, for the East Romans, either the issue over fourth marriages or the question of the Patriarch Nikólaos's status. After the Emperor Alexander had reinstated Nikólaos, the still continuing controversy between the pro-Nikólaos and the pro-Efthýmios faction in the Eastern Orthodox Church was settled in 920 by the Vasileopátor Rhomanós Lekapênós. East Roman clerics who were brave enough to defy East Roman Emperors had to fight their own battles, as best they could, without effective Papal help or hindrance. Moreover, when Popes did intervene in Eastern Orthodox domestic quarrels, they seldom came off with flying colours. Among ninth-century and tenth-century Popes, Nicholas I (858–67) is an outstanding figure, but neither he nor his successors knew how to cope with the Patriarch Phótios and with the Emperor Basil I.

From the East Roman standpoint the fourth, in order of importance, of the powers to the west of the Empire was the Cordoban Umayyad Caliphate. At an earlier point in this chapter,[1] it has already been noted that this far western Muslim power and the East Roman Empire had no points of friction with each other, and that, from 909 onwards, they had a common interest in opposing the aggression of the Fatimids. Constantine Porphyrogenitus appears to have sent embassies to Córdoba in 945/6 and in 947, and an embassy from Córdoba appears to have been received at Constantinople in 948 or in 949.[2] There is no record that

---

[1] On p. 477.

[2] For the number and the dates of these embassies, see Canard in Vasiliev, *Byzance et les Arabes*, ii, I, pp. 323–30. In op. cit., ii, II, there are translations of Ibn Abī Usaybi'ah's

these exchanges of embassies resulted in the conclusion of a treaty. When, in 949, Constantine Porphyrogenitus dispatched his naval expedition against Crete, he detailed three ships to observe the Spanish coast.[1] This precautionary measure suggests that, in spite of the ostensible cordiality, on both sides, of the diplomatic relations that had been established between the two powers, the East Roman Government did not feel quite sure in 949 that the Cordoban Umayyad Government might not intervene on behalf of the Cretan Muslims. These Cretan Muslims were of Spanish descent, though their Spanish forebears had been rebels against the Umayyad regime and had been evicted by it. However, there is some evidence that, in 956, a combined East Roman and Umayyad naval force inflicted a defeat on the Fatimids' fleet in the narrow seas between Ifrīqīyah and the west end of Sicily.[2]

At an early point in the present chapter it has been noted that, in the ninth and tenth centuries, the African and Spanish hinterlands of the western basin of the Mediterranean were predominant over its Italian and transalpine hinterlands. This ratio of power in the western Mediterranean was unnatural, but it was not unprecedented. It was unnatural because the potential resources of North-West Africa and the Iberian Peninsula are not a match for those of Transappennine and Transpyrenean western Europe. In western Europe there are vast tracts of fertile land stretching away northwards from northern Italy to southern Sweden. The inhospitable zone beyond the Arctic Circle is far more distant from Marseilles and Genoa than the inhospitable Sahara is from Tunis and Fez and even from Córdoba. Spain and North-West Africa are relatively arid regions in which the patches of fertile soil are exceptional oases. These two regions can be predominant only when they are occupied by peoples, and are governed by regimes, that have the ability and the impulse to make the most of the two regions' limited agricultural, industrial, and commercial potentialities, and, even then, their predominance will be precarious if contemporary conditions beyond the opposite shores of the western Mediterranean are not unusually barbarous and chaotic.

For these reasons, the predominance of North-West Africa and Spain in the ninth and tenth centuries of the Christian Era was unnatural, but it did have a precedent in the predominance of the Carthaginian Empire

account of the East Roman embassy of 947 to Córdoba (on pp. 185–7) and of Maqqari's citations from the accounts of the same embassy by Ibn Hayyān and Ibn Khaldūn (on pp. 274–81). For the Spanish embassy to Constantinople, see *De Caer.*, II, pp. 571 and 580; Liutprand, *Antapodosis*, VI, 5; the present work, III, 7, pp. 499–500.

[1] See II, 7, p. 333.

[2] See Eickhoff, op. cit., pp. 332–3, citing the Cambridge Chronicle and Al-Numan. The Cambridge Chronicle's entry for the year 955/6 is printed in Vasiliev, *Byzance et les Arabes*, ii, II, p. 106.

during the two centuries and a half ending in 264 B.C., the opening year of the First Romano-Carthaginian War. During this quarter of a millennium the tide of Greek colonization was no longer flowing westward, and the gradual political unification of Italy under the hegemony of Rome had not yet been carried far enough to enable Rome to exert her power beyond Peninsular Italy's coastline. In the western basin of the Mediterranean, the ratio of power during the two hundred and fifty years ending in 264 B.C. was an anticipation of the ratio there during the ninth and tenth centuries of the Christian Era.[1]

The predominance of the Aghlabids and their successors the Fatimids in North-West Africa, and of the Cordoban Umayyads in the Iberian Peninsula, during those two centuries was a *tour de force*, and the reversal of fortunes in the course of the next two centuries is therefore not surprising, though its rapidity and its extremeness are dramatic.

North-West Africa was at the peak of its prosperity and power during the sixty-three years, 909–72, during which the Fatimids made their headquarters at Mahdīyah, before transferring them to Cairo. Muslim Spain was at its peak in the reign of the Cordoban Umayyad ruler 'Abd-ar-Rahmān III (912–61). In 929 he felt himself strong enough to re-assume, for his house, the title of Caliph, which his forebears had lost in 750, when, everywhere except in the far west of Dār-al-Islām, they had been ousted and superseded by the 'Abbasids. After 'Abd-ar-Rahmān III's death, the power of the Cordoban Umayyad Caliphate was sustained by the minister Mansūr, who rose to the summit between 967 and 981. Mansūr pressed the independent Christian principalities at the foot of the Asturian mountains and the Pyrenees harder than they had ever been pressed since the partial recession of the original wave of Arab conquest.[2] In 985, Mansūr sacked Barcelona;[3] and in 997 he raided Santiago de Compostela, which at that date was the third most sacred

---

[1] See E. A. Freeman, 'Sicilian Cycles', in *Historical Essays*, third series, second edition (1892) pp. 434–42. This essay was first published on 9 March 1898, in *The Saturday Review*.

[2] The Arabs had begun to lose their hold on the north-west corner of the Peninsula before their attempt to conquer Aquitaine had been defeated in 732 by Charles Martel, and in this quarter the Christians who had retrieved or recovered their independence had gradually gained ground from about half way through the eighth century till 916, the year in which 'Abd-ar-Rahmān opened his counter-offensive according to E. Lévy-Provençal, *Histoire de l'Espagne musulmane*, vol. i (Cairo, 1941, Institut Français d'Archéologie Orientale du Caire), p. 306. Meanwhile, at the north-eastern end of the Arab dominions in Spain and Septimania, the Franks, too, had been advancing at the Arabs' expense. The Franks had conquered Narbonne in 751 (ibid., p. 46); Gerona had seceded to them in 785 (ibid., p. 91); and they had conquered Barcelona in 801 (ibid., pp. 123 and 125–7). These territorial encroachments had not weakened the Spanish Muslims' power, as was shown in the ninth century by their lodgements in Provence and in the Alps, and in the tenth century by their offensive overland in the Peninsula itself.

[3] See Lévy-Provençal, op. cit., vol. i, p. 435; A. Schaube, *Handelsgeschichte der romanischen Völker des Mittelmeerebiets bis zum Ende der Kreuzzüge* (Munich and Berlin, 1906, Oldenbourg), p. 103.

pilgrimage resort for Western Christians. In Western Christian eyes, Santiago was surpassed in sanctity only by Rome and by Jerusalem.

If in 1002, the year in which Mansūr died on the war-path, it could have been foretold to him that, by 1086, Toledo, the central city of the Peninsula and the former capital of the Visigothic Kingdom, would be in Christian hands again, he would have been incredulous. Yet in Muslim Spain the same thing happened after Mansūr's death in 1002 as had happened in Muslim North-West Africa already after the transfer of the Fatimids' capital from Mahdīyah to Cairo. Each of these Western Muslim realms disintegrated into a mosaic of petty successor-states, and in each case the political vacuum was filled by barbarian invaders from all quarters.

The greatest material damage seems to have been done by two Arab pastoral nomad tribes, the Banu Hilāl and the Banu Sulaym. These two tribes were unleashed in 1051 by the Cairene Fatimid Government to chastise the Sanhāja Berbers of western Kabylia, who, in 1045, had repudiated their allegiance to their now remote Fatimid sovereigns. The original wave of Arab invaders of Ifrīqīyah and Andalusia had been under the command—and also to some extent under the control—of citizens of Medina and Mecca whose ancestors had made their living, not as shepherds, but as cultivators of the soil and as traders. These early Arab Muslim commanders and statesmen had therefore been alive to the importance of preserving the agriculture and the urban life of the countries that they conquered. The Banu Hilāl and the Banu Sulaym were undiluted and uncontrolled barbarians, and, as they moved westward across the Maghrib, they put the fields and cities of Ifrīqīyah out of action.[1] As for the political vacuum in Andalusia, the Murābit Muslim barbarians from the Senegal and the still more savage Muwaḥḥid barbarians from the Atlas contended for the possession of the highly civilized heart of Muslim Spain with the Christian barbarians from the Asturias and from Catalonia (the Spanish March of the Carolingian Empire).

The waves of barbarian invasion from the Senegal and from the Atlas washed not only northwards over Andalusia but also eastwards over Ifrīqīyah, in the opposite direction to the previous advance of the Banu Hilāl and the Banu Sulaym. In 1134–58, during the lull between the successive onsets of the Murābit and the Muwaḥḥid waves, the Norman conquerors of the East Roman théma Laghouvardhía and of Muslim Sicily occupied a number of beach-heads along the coast of Ifrīqīyah.

---

[1] See Gautier, op. cit., chap. 10. The lasting damage that the Banu Hilāl and the Banu Sulaym had done to Ifrīqīyah made a deep impression on Ibn Khaldūn three centuries later. See F. Rosenthal's translation of the *Muqaddimah* (London, 1958, Routledge & Kegan Paul, 3 vols.), vol. i, p. 305; also vol. ii, p. 289; vol. iii, pp. 415–20.

Mahdīyah, once the Fatimids' North-West African capital, was taken by the Normans in 1148.

This was indeed a reversal of the situation as it had been in the ninth and tenth centuries. During those two centuries, Western Christendom had been the main target of barbarians who raided Eastern Orthodox Christendom and Dār-al-Islām only occasionally. Charlemagne's over-taxing of the resources of his dominions had brought on his successors the same nemesis that, in the history of the East Roman Empire, had overtaken the successors of Justinian I and was to overtake the successors of Basil II. The Norsemen were already raiding the maritime fringes of the over-extended Carolingian Empire before Charlemagne's death in 814, and when, towards the close of the ninth century, the Norsemen's maritime onslaught on Western Christendom began to slacken, the Magyars started to raid Western Christendom overland from the east. Western Christendom's sufferings in the ninth and tenth centuries may have been more severe than its sufferings in the fifth century had been; for its fifth-century invaders (except the Franks and Angles) had already adopted their Christian victims' religion before they crossed the Roman Empire's frontiers, whereas the Norsemen and Magyars were pagans whose victimization of Christians was not restrained by any fellow feeling.

In the ninth and tenth centuries, Western Christendom was, to all appearances, at the nadir of its fortunes. The Carolingian Empire petered out, and there was a virtual interregnum, which lasted for more than a century, before the Ottonian Empire partially filled the vacuum. All Western Christian countries were now in travail, but Italy's plight was the worst of all. In the seventh and eighth centuries, Italy had escaped the Arab onslaught that had overtaken almost every other country round the perimeter of the Mediterranean. In the ninth century it was Italy's turn to be attacked by the Muslims of both Ifriqīyah and Spain, and in this century Italy barely escaped the fate that had overtaken Spain in the eighth century.

The ninth-century occupation of south-eastern Italy by the North-West African Muslim conquerors of Sicily, and their eventual eviction, have already been noticed. The African Muslims also attacked the Tyrrhene coast. The suburbs of Rome were raided in 846. In 849 Rome itself was only just saved from capture, thanks to naval aid from Naples, Gaeta, and Amalfi; but *circa* 885 the African Muslims succeeded in establishing a beach-head at the mouth of the Garigliano. Meanwhile, the Spanish Muslims nearly succeeded in severing Italy's communications overland with the Transalpine Western Christian countries. *Circa* 891–4 they occupied La Garde Freinet (Fraxinetum),[1] overhanging the coast of Provence, and from here they boldly pushed their way inland and beset

---

[1] Lévy-Provençal, op. cit., p. 386.

some of the passes over the Alps. The eviction of the African Muslims from their beach-head at the mouth of the Garigliano in 915[1] freed the interior of central Italy from Muslim raids; but the East Roman Navy's attempt in 942 to help Hugh of Provence to evict the Spanish Muslims from La Garde Freinet was unsuccessful.[2] It was not till 973 that La Garde Freinet fell and that the Alpine passes were cleared.

Unfortunately for Italy in particular, but also for the rest of Western Christendom as well, the moral standing of the Papacy was lower in the ninth and tenth centuries than it had ever been before. In these centuries, Popes of the stature of Leo IV (847–55) and Nicholas I (858–67) were rare. Leo IV was elected to save Rome from the Muslim conquest with which she had been threatened in 846; in 849 he rose to the occasion; and his service to the city is commemorated in the name of the Leonine Wall, with which he subsequently fortified the Trastevere. Nicholas I's intervention in Eastern Orthodox Christian affairs did not win him laurels; yet he, like Leo IV, was at least a commanding personality. There were, however, occupants of the Papal throne in these two centuries who were pawns in the hands of the turbulent and disreputable aristocracy of the Ducatus Romanus. This was the nemesis of the local support that the Papacy had received when, in the eighth century, it had been struggling to liberate itself from the East Roman Government's high-handed exercise of Imperial prerogatives. If, in the year 1002, the Spanish Christians' reconquest of Toledo was unpredictable, so, at the same date, was the reform of the Papacy and its recovery of its moral standing during the second half of the eleventh century.

The meteoric rise of the North Italian city-states to affluence and power in the course of the same century was equally surprising. In 1002, it could not have been foreseen that, within the next hundred years, the North Italians were going to wrest the commercial and naval command of the Mediterranean from Muslim and East Roman hands. Certainly this was not foreseen by Bishop Liutprand of Cremona. His history of his own times is a tale of disaster; yet Liutprand's mood is more sanguine than might seem to be warranted by his subject. Evidently this well-placed and shrewd observer of contemporary events was not reduced to despair by his experiences.

Liutprand did not live to witness one historic event that tipped the balance in Western Christendom's favour. At the turn of the tenth and eleventh centuries the Magyars, Poles, and Scandinavians were converted to Christianity as ecclesiastical subjects of the Patriarchate of Rome, and Western Christendom was thus relieved from barbarian invasions at the very time when the Islamic World and Eastern Orthodox Christendom were on the point of being exposed to the barbarians' full

---

[1] See II, 7, p. 344.   [2] See ibid.

fury. Even the Mongols, who devastated China and Transoxania and Iran and 'Irāq and Russia, did not advance farther westward than Western Christendom's Hungarian and Polish eastern marches.

The apparent suddenness of the turn for the better in Western Christendom's fortunes after the close of the tenth century suggests that, even in this grim century, seeds of new life must have been germinating in Western Christendom beneath the surface. One symptom of religious renewal that was recognized at the time was the Cluniac reform of Western Christian monasticism. On the cultural plane, it was not immediately evident that the tenth-century West Frankish way of life was going to captivate the Danish raiders to whom, in 911, the Carolingian Charles the Simple handed over the country that has been known, since then, as Normandy. On the technological plane, a ninth-century innovation that is not mentioned in contemporary historical records has been detected recently by modern scholars from evidence provided by Western works of visual art. In that century, western technicians made a revolutionary break with the traditional method of harnessing draught-horses. The new method may have been discovered on the Eurasian Steppe or in China. It made it possible to bring into play a far greater proportion of a horse's muscular strength than the traditional method had allowed. This invention was not only an epoch-making event in the history of traction. It was also a victory of open-minded experimentation over the uncritical acceptance of inherited custom.[1]

In our day, modern Western science applied to technology has given the post-Christian West a temporary ascendancy over all the rest of the World. Yet already, by the turn of the twelfth and thirteenth centuries, the reversal of fortunes in the relations between the Western Christians and the Western Muslims was complete; and this change of fortunes at the western end of the Oikoumenê did not leave the fortunes of the East Roman Empire unaffected. Two of the consequences for the East Roman Empire were the capture of Bari by the Normans in 1071 and the capture of Constantinople itself in 1204 by the East Romans' Venetian ex-subjects and the Venetians' French dupes and accomplices.

[1] See R. Lefebvre des Noëttes, *L'Attelage: le cheval de selle à travers les âges* (Paris, 1931, Picard) especially pp. 89 and 121–4; Lynn White: *Medieval Technology and Social Change* (Oxford, 1962, Clarendon Press), pp. 59–61; eundem in *The Fontana Economic History of Europe*, vol. i, section 4: 'The Expansion of Technology, 500–1500', p. 15. The inventors were the Chinese according to J. Needham, *Science and Civilization in China*, vol. i (Cambridge, 1954, University Press), pp. 240–1, with Table 8 on p. 242.

7. East Roman Arts of Diplomacy

FOR dealing with foreigners the East Roman Government had an unshakeable belief in the efficacy of making a dazzling impression. This may seem naïve to us. We may feel that, if we had been in those visitors' shoes, we would have insisted on probing down to the reality underlying the show, and the reality, not the show, would have been, we may suppose, our criterion for estimating the East Roman Empire's power. Some of the East Roman apparatus for making an impression will certainly seem to us still more naïve than the policy itself. Could even the most simple-minded barbarians have taken seriously the mechanical toys in the Imperial throne-room that were set working for the edification of foreign ambassadors to whom the Emperor was giving audience? Bishop Liutprand records, with some self-complacency, that, on the occasion of his embassy to Constantine Porphyrogenitus in 949, he was neither frightened nor thrilled when the dummy lions greeted him with their mechanized roar; but he admits that his imperturbability was due only to his foresight in having taken care to inform himself, in advance, of the surprises that awaited him.[1] Apparently this child's-play did usually make its intended effect. At any rate, after the spendthrift emperor Michael III had had the toys melted down,[2] they were replaced, though the material was gold and the treasury was almost empty. What is more, the Caliph at Baghdad found it worth his while to fit up his own throne-room with a similar set of contraptions.[3]

A less childish way of trying to impress the foreign visitors to Constantinople was to exhibit the architectural and artistic beauties of the Palace and the City. The East Roman Government was fond of entertaining important foreign potentates, or their representatives, at Constantinople as state guests, in order to impress them with the City's grandeur. We have an anonymous account[4] of the impression made by Constantinople on Rhos envoys in the reign of Basil I. The dispossessed Bagratuni Árkhon ton Arkhóndon of Armenia, Ashot II, was on a state visit to Constantinople at a critical stage in the second war between the

---

[1] Liutprand, *Antapodosis*, Book VI, chap. 5.

[2] *Theoph. Cont.*, Book IV, Reign of Michael III, chap. 21, p. 173; Book V, chap. 29, p. 257; pseudo-Symeon, Reign of Michael III, chap. 15, p. 659; Michael Glykás, p. 543.

[3] The East Roman ambassador who was received at Baghdad in 917 by the Caliph Muqtadir was taken to the Palace of the Tree. It contained a silver tree with eighteen branches, on which gold and silver birds sang mechanically. See the passage from al-Khatīb translated in Vasiliev, *Byzance et les Arabes*, ii, II, p. 75, and the passage from Sibt b. al-Jawzī, ibid., p. 171. Al-Khatīb claims that the ambassador was impressed.

[4] Printed in the Bonn edition of Constantine Porphyrogenitus's works, vol. iii, pp. 358–64.

East Roman Empire and Symeon.[1] The Kouropalátês of Iberia, Adarnase IV, followed at a later critical stage in the same Romano-Bulgarian war.[2] Possibly the coincidence of dates was not accidental. The East Roman Government may have gone out of its way on each occasion to make it clear to friendly rulers that, however furiously the Bulgars might rage outside Constantinople's walls, the Imperial City was impregnable and was continuing to lead its normal life, thanks to its access to the Anatolian army-corps districts' resources, which were beyond the reach of Symeon's arm. The Imperial Government was able to lend Ashot II enough troops to reinstate him. The Iberian potentate was given a royal reception, and the Aghorá and the Ayía Sophía were specially decorated for his benefit. His visit to the Ayía Sophía was the climax of his tour.

We also have detailed accounts, in Constantine VII's *De Caerimoniis*,[3] of three state visits that took place in his reign. On the first of these occasions (31 May 946) the state guests were officially ambassadors of the 'Abbasid Caliph but actually they were emissaries of the Amír of Tarsós, and their business was to negotiate for an exchange of prisoners and for the making of peace. On the second occasion (30 August 946)[4] the three guests were a representative of the Daylamite Buwayhid government,[5] the Amír of Amida, and an envoy from the Hamdanid Amír of Aleppo, Sayf-ad-Dawlah.[6] On the third occasion (9 September 957) the guest was Olga (Helga) the chieftainess (arkhóndissa) of Russia. Constantine notes in passing that, on 24 October (948 or 949),[7] there had been a reception in the same style for ambassadors from Andalusía, and that the proceedings were substantially the same on all these four occasions, except that the Andalusian ambassadors did not dine with the Emperors on the day of their reception. On the first two

---

[1] *Theoph. Cont.*, Book VI, Reign of Constantine VII, first bout of sole reign, chap. 7, p. 387; *Georg. Mon. Cont.*, Reign of Constantine VII, first bout of sole reign, chap. 11, pp. 879–880; Leo Grammaticus, p. 293; pseudo-Symeon Magister, Reign of Constantine VII, first bout of sole reign, chap. 8, pp. 722–3. The date of this visit was probably 914 (see *C. Med. H.*, vol. iv, 2nd ed., Part I, p. 136, with n. 2, and p. 717, following Canard), but it is dated 921 by Toumanoff in op. cit., p. 614.

[2] *Theoph. Cont.*, Book VI, Reign of Rhomanós I, chap. 9, p. 402; *Georg. Mon. Cont.*, Reign of Rhomanós I, chap. 11, pp. 894–5; Leo Grammaticus, p. 307; pseudo-Symeon Magister, Reign of Rhomanós I, chap. 24, p. 733; Kedhrênós, vol. ii, p. 300. The date was just after the coronation, as Avghoústa, of Rhomanós's daughter-in-law Sophía, his son Christopher's wife, on 20 February in the tenth indiction, i.e. 922.

[3] Book II, chap. 15.   [4] See III, 3, p. 389.

[5] By this date the Buwayhids were not only masters of most of Iran to the west of the Caspian Gates; they also had the 'Abbasids under their thumb.

[6] Branches of the Hamdanids were now ruling Aleppo and Mosul.

[7] *De Caer.*, II, p. 571 (see also p. 580). Constantine has recorded the day of the month, but not the year. See also Liutprand, *Antapodosis*, Book IV, chap. 5. Liutprand has recorded that the Spanish embassy had arrived in Constantinople shortly before his own arrival there. I. Bekker, in his edition of Liutprand's works (Hannover and Leipzig, 1919, Hahn), dates the reception of the Spanish embassy 949. M. Canard in Vasiliev, *Byzance et les Arabes*, ii. I, p. 330, dates it 948.

occasions the principal scene of the solemnities was the great tríklinos[1] of the Maghnávra; on the third occasion it was the tríklinos of Justinian II.

For these four receptions the Imperial Government mobilized all its decorational resources down to the last skaramángion, stikhárion, and chandelier.

For the decoration of those parts of the Palace which were to be used for the reception on each occasion, the Palace borrowed from the churches their metal-work ornaments and their hangings. The Néa[2] and the other churches inside the Palace's precincts[3] were laid under contribution in the first place. The hyper-holy Theotókos of the Pháros supplied wreaths, silver chandeliers with silver chains, a cross, and a dove;[4] Áyios Pétros supplied a golden plane-tree set with pearls;[5] Áyios Theódhoros a *khorosankhórion* embroidered with lions and griffins;[6] the Pantheon a triple-dyed purple hanging embroidered with a plane-tree.[7] The monastery church of S.S. Séryios and Vákkhos ('the Little Ayía Sophía', outside the Palace, but not far below the foot of the Hippodrome) shared with the Néa the honour of supplying the decoration for the great tríklinos of the Maghnávra[8]—the centre point of the first two receptions, since this hall contained the Solomonic throne, on which the Emperor was to sit when he received his guests. In the list of churches that lent their treasures, the Ayía Sophía and the Holy Apostles are conspicuous by their absence, but these two super-churches did send their choirs, suitably robed.[9]

The Palace also enlisted the help of the Prefect (Éparkhos) of Constantinople, not only for decorating the Hippodrome,[10] and the route of the procession through the City, in the customary way,[11] but for borrowing decorations for the Palace. The Prefect carried out his commission industriously; he combed the public hostels, homes for old people, and city churches, and he borrowed hangings, as well as gold and enamel and chased-silver work, from the silver-smiths.[12] The demes were enlisted too. The Blues and the Greens each lent their silver organ.[13]

Naturally, the Palace itself did its part. On either side of the steps leading up to the great tríklinos of the Maghnávra there was a row of Imperial standards.[14] The two standards immediately adjoining the steps were held by Imperial chief-oarsmen. The gold-embroidered silk Imperial standard was held at the top of the steps, where the two curtains of the tríklinos met, by the commandant of the Etaireía.[15] Inside the great tríklinos, on either side of the Solomonic throne, were ranged the Roman sceptres and diptychs and the rest of the golden sceptres, and,

---

[1] For the form tríklinos, see Reiske's note in the Bonn edition of *De Caer.*, vol. ii, p. 24.
[2] pp. 571, 572, 573.   [3] p. 580.   [4] pp. 580–1.
[5] p. 580.   [6] pp. 580–1.   [7] p. 581.
[8] pp. 570–1.   [9] pp. 577, 585, 589.   [10] p. 573.
[11] pp. 572 and 573.   [12] p. 572. (See also the present work, p. 43.)
[13] pp. 571 and 580.   [14] pp. 576–7.   [15] p. 576.

in a lower tier, the military ensigns (kambidhoktória, lávoura, síghna).[1] The Imperial golden organ was placed outside the curtains of the great tríklinos, with the Blues' silver organ on one side and the Greens' on the other.[2] The *pastopoioí* transformed the arboretum into an ambulatorium by a skilful arrangement of silk draperies.[3] The Palace also supplied the big skaramángia that were hung for the occasion,[4] and also the enamel-work from the Palace's strong-room[5] and an assortment of silver-ware.[6] Perhaps the priceless Persian carpets, too,[7] were the Palace's own.

Nature was called in to supplement art. There were crosses and wreaths of laurel and there were flowers in season.[8] The floors were strewn with laurel and ivy,[9] and, in the choicer places, with myrtle and rosemary.[10] The whole floor of the great tríklinos of the Maghnávra was strewn with roses.[11]

The personnel of the Court was dressed up to the nines, and the lower ranks were fitted out, for the occasion, in grander robes than they were normally entitled to wear. The máyistroi and the best-looking of the proconsuls wore the lóroi,[12] which were reserved for supreme occasions.[13] This liberated the máyistroi's stikhária, which otherwise they would have been wearing; so these were lent to those primikérioi who did not have stikhária of their own.[14] Ostiárioi who did not have paraghávdhia wore their own capes over their shirts.[15] Spatharokouvikoulárioi who did not have golden paraghávdhia wore their own shirts, with swords.[16] Protospathárioi who held an office (i.e. whose title was not merely honorary) wore their own shirts and the máyistroi's phoundáta festival capes.[17] Even the oarsmen from the Imperial galley who were holding the standards outside the great tríklinos wore officers' 'changes' (*alláxima*) of all four colours,[18] and the bath-attendants (*saponistaí*) of the Imperial bed-chamber wore *atravátika* capes.[19]

These coats of many colours were not scattered haphazard.

At the reception all the ranks above-mentioned, from the protospathárioi down to the lowest rank wearing a skaramángion, were stationed each in the place where a skaramángion of that particular colour and cut ought to be.

---

[1] p. 575.

[2] p. 571. On p. 580, the *two* Imperial golden organs and the two silver organs of the Blues and the Greens are said to have been placed in the portico of the khrysotríklinos, alias the orolóyion. Elsewhere, the Palace is credited with a single golden organ only. Michael III, for instance, had found only one to melt down (Constantine Porphyrogenitus in *Theoph. Cont.*, Book V, chap. 29, p. 257).

[3] p. 571.   [4] pp. 571 and 572.   [5] p. 571.

[6] p. 572.   [7] p. 574.   [8] p. 573.

[9] Ibid.   [10] pp. 573-4.   [11] p. 574.   [12] p. 574.

[13] e.g. the Imperial banquet on Easter Day (Philótheos in *De Caer.*, chap. 52, p. 766 Bonn, p. 168 Bury).

[14] p. 574.   [15] Ibid.   [16] pp. 574-5.

[17] p. 575.   [18] p. 577.   [19] p. 578.

Each of the styles of skaramángia had its own station assigned to it—the green and rose-coloured eagles here, the beeves (vóphous, i.e. 'boves') and polygyre eagles here, the basins here, the white lions here. In fact, as I have said, each man took up his position in the place assigned to the particular skaramángion that he was wearing.[1]

Constantine Porphyrogenitus did not hand over the responsibility for organizing this elaborate display to his master of the ceremonies. The Emperor himself went into all the details, and he has noted two of these that were his own idea.

When the Muslim ambassadors were presented,

they were wearing *spékia*—not their own, but others that were particularly beautiful and costly, with collars encrusted with precious stones and huge pearls. It is against the rules for a non-eunuch (*varvátos*) to wear a collar like that, either with pearls or with precious stones, but, for display, and for this one occasion only, they were directed to wear these ornaments by Constantine the Christ-loving lord.[2]

Constantine's second personal intervention was to order three extra wreaths: a green one in honour of the Holy Apostles; a blue one in honour of the hyper-holy Theotókos of the Pháros, and another green one in honour of the holy meghalomartyr Dhêmĕtrios—each wreath complete with cross and dove. This addition to the Palace's own stock of decorations turned out to have been fortunate. The Muslim ambassadors had been expecting that, when the formalities and festivities were over, they would be able to get down to business. However, many days passed without their hearing further from the Imperial Government. At last the ambassadors asked to see the Emperor and to have a talk with him. This threw the Court into a flurry; for it was unthinkable that the ambassadors should be received without the Palace being decorated, and, by now, all the decorations that had been put up for the reception had been taken down and been returned to their owners. It was not feasible to borrow them again so soon and at such short notice. In this crisis, the Emperor's three wreaths saved the situation. Spaced out, and eked out with their three doves (which must have been detachable), they provided, for the business meeting, the bare minimum of decoration that the Imperial protocol required.[3]

A striking and endearing feature of the proceedings is their amiability. The fitting-out of minor dignitaries of the Palace with grander robes than they were properly entitled to wear has been mentioned already. The Muslim ambassadors—who were, no doubt, all of them *varvátoi*— might have been embarrassed, and even offended, if it had been broken

---

[1] pp. 577–8.   [2] p. 584.   [3] pp. 581–2 and 586–7.

to them that the regalia into which they had changed from their own simpler clothes were, by rights, reserved for eunuchs, and that they had been given this dubious honour on the Emperor's personal instructions. The administrative staff of the municipality of Constantinople (ἡ πολιτική), together with the representatives of the demes with their officers, were admitted inside the Khalkê gate of the Palace.[1] The crowd (πάχωμα) was not; but a spectacle was provided for them too. The ruck of the naval ratings and the supernumerary Dalmatians and the baptized Rhos were paraded outside with their standards, shields, and native swords.[2]

Inside the Palace, the sequel to the obligatory formalities was jovial. After the reception the Muslim ambassadors dined with the Emperors. The two choirs—Holy Apostles and Ayía Sophía—sang lauds to the Emperors all the time, except when fresh courses were being brought in, which was a signal for the choirs to keep quiet and to let the organs have a hearing. After rising from table, but before leaving the banqueting hall, the ambassadors were tipped in both money and kind, and their retinue was not forgotten.[3] A specially fine performance in the Hippodrome was also staged for the ambassadors' benefit;[4] and the Feast of the Transfiguration, which fell on Saturday 8 August, was celebrated with some extra pomp.[5] On Sunday 9 August there was another state banquet, this time in the tríklinos of Justinian II. The chased silver dinner-service from the Karianós robing-room was brought out for this occasion, and the whole of the banquet was served on it. During dinner the company was entertained with a variety show. This time the Muslim guests included forty prisoners from the Praetorium,[6] besides the two Tarsan ambassadors and their retinue. This time too, there was a round of tips. The ambassadors each received 500 miliarésia, presented on golden salvers; their retinue received 3,000 between them; and the forty guest-prisoners 1,000 between them. A lump sum was also sent to the prisoners who were still confined in the Praetorium.[7]

The honours accorded to the Tarsan ambassadors did not go to the length of seating them at the Emperor's own table.[8] At the banquet on the occasion of the joint visit of the representatives of three non-Caliphial Muslim governments, their separate table had to be a round one, because none of the three was willing to yield precedence to either of his two colleagues. The parakoimómenos and one of the máyistroi paid them the

---

[1] p. 579.   [2] Ibid.   [3] p. 585.
[4] pp. 588–90.   [5] pp. 590–2.
[6] This was a gesture of good will on an occasion on which peace talks were on the agenda. It was, however, a regular practice to include 18 Muslim prisoners of war from the Praetorium among the guests at the Imperial banquet on Easter Sunday (Philótheos in *De Caer.*, Book II, chap. 52, pp. 767–8 Bonn, pp.168–9 Bury: see the present work, pp. 384–5.)
[7] p. 592.   [8] Ibid.

compliment of sitting at this round side-table with them.[1] On this occasion the banquet was held in the great tríklinos of the nineteen couches, in the style and order of the twelve days' festivities at Christmas.[2]

The reception and banquet for the chieftainess Olga (Helga) of Kiev were fun for the ladies of the East Roman Court. The visiting sovereign was not only a woman herself; her retinue, too, was female; the numerous male diplomats and commercial counsellors whom she had brought with her marched, self-effacingly, in the rear of the Russian delegation.[3] This procedure on the Russian side gave the cue for the East Roman protocol on this unusual occasion. Accordingly, after Olga had been received by the Emperor in the style of the receptions for the Muslim embassies, the Emperor withdrew, and Olga was then given a second reception—this time in the tríklinos of Justinian II—by the Empress Elénê and her daughter-in-law the wife of the co-Emperor Rhomanós II. The Empress sat on Theóphilos's great throne, and her daughter-in-law on a golden chair at the side. It was now the East Roman ladies' turn to be presented. The first batch were 'the belted patríkiai', who were peeresses in their own right; the other batches were the wives of male dignitaries, marshalled in their husbands' order of precedence: mayístrissai, patríkiai, ophphikialéai protospatharéai, the rest of the protospatharéai, the spatharokandidhátissai, and, last, the spatharéai and stratórissai and kandidhátissai all in one bunch. The climax was the presentation to the two Empresses of Olga herself with her kinswomen and the élite of her ladies-in-waiting. After that, Olga was given a third reception—this time by the Emperor, the Empress, and their porphyrogenite children *en masse*. The Emperor commanded Olga to be seated, and then gave her as much time as she wanted for talking business with him.[4]

The banquet that followed was served in two different banqueting halls simultaneously. The Imperial family and Olga, with a select company, were served in the tríklinos of Justinian II. When the East Roman noble ladies entered, they fell on their faces[5] before the Imperial family, according to rule. Olga remained standing, but it was noticed, with satisfaction, that she slightly but perceptibly inclined her head. She was put in her place by being seated, as the Muslim state guests had been, at a separate table. Her table-companions, were, according to rule, 'the belted patríkiai'. The male members of the Russian delegation, who were nearly one hundred strong,[6] were served in the khrysotríklinos.

[1] p. 594.
[2] p. 594. For the series of Christmas banquets, see Philótheos in *De Caer.*, Book II, chap. 52, pp. 741–59 Bonn, pp. 156–64 Bury.   [3] pp. 594–5.   [4] pp. 595–6.
[5] προσκυνησάντων (a solecism for the correct feminine form προσκυνησασῶν).
[6] There were eighty-two of them, not counting Olga's son Svyátoslav's men, whose number is not recorded. The male portion of the Russian delegation consisted of one cousin of

Constantine has not told us where Olga's six kinswomen and eighteen ladies-in-waiting dined, but they were evidently fed; for they figure among the recipients of the customary after-dinner tips. After dinner, dessert was served in the breakfasting-room on the little golden table. At this stage the Imperial family and Olga sat together, and Olga and her six kinswomen and eighteen ladies-in-waiting received their tips.

The Russian delegation's visit was a long one. It had opened on Wednesday 9 September, and on Sunday 18 October there was another pair of banquets, one for the men and the other for the ladies. Since the all-important question of protocol had been settled in principle during the opening day's proceedings, the Imperial family could now afford to be more sociable without fear of compromising their dignity. This time, the Emperor dined with the (masculine) Rhos; the Empress, her daughter-in-law and the porphyrogenites with Olga. This time, too, there was a round of tips. If the discrepancies between the figures given for the recipients on the two occasions are not just slips made by Constantine or by his copyists, two more diplomats than before, and one more commercial counsellor, managed to qualify for receiving tips this time, while Olga's personal interpreter was forgotten.

We have now passed in review the proceedings during six state visits to the East Roman Court, in which the combined resources of the Palace and the City were mobilized to impress and please the important foreign guests. How effective were such shows for furthering the purposes of East Roman foreign policy?

At the western end of the Old World in the tenth century of the Christian Era, international relations were governed, as they are governed still today, by appreciations of comparative power; and in this field there are two kinds of power that 'talk', namely effective armed force and plenty of money or of its equivalent in kind. Neither of these two essential forms of power can have been much in evidence in the formalities and festivities to which the East Roman Government's foreign guests were treated at Constantinople. The motley units of the Imperial Guard, in their gaudy uniforms, must have made on the experienced eyes of Tarsan Muslim frontiersmen and Rhos merchant-adventurers the impression that the British Crown's beefeaters would make, today, on United States marines or on Soviet paratroopers. The effect, in this case, will, in fact, have been a minus quantity. As for the tips, these were evidently handsome as tips go, but sums of that relatively modest order of magnitude would have left the Pechenegs cold. The Pechenegs certainly exacted vastly greater sums than those before they pledged themselves

Olga's, eight other kinsmen of hers, twenty diplomats (apokrisiárioi), forty-three commercial counsellors (praghmateftaí), the priest Gregory, the two interpreters, six servants of the diplomats, and Olga's personal interpreter.

to make war on the Rhos or on the Magyars or on the Bulgars at the East Roman Government's bidding. The East Roman Government did command both the financial means required for hiring the Pechenegs[1] and the seasoned troops required for repelling the Rhos—as Olga's son Svyátoslav was to discover fourteen years after the date of his mother's pacific expedition to Constantinople. But whence was it that the East Roman Empire drew its effective armed force and its adequate supplies of money?

To find the answer to this vital question, we have to look away from Constantinople and the Imperial Palace to the Empire's 'Eastern' army-corps districts. This compact block of rural territory was the tenth-century East Roman Empire's living body; 'the City' and the Palace were parasitic excrescences on it. The pomp of the Palace's protocol and of the Ayía Sophía's liturgy was all paid for by taxes levied by the Central Government from the Asiatic countryside, and this same tax-fund also produced the money for subsidizing the Pechenegs and for the other subsidy that, from 927 to 965, was paid to Bulgaria in the form of an allowance to the Empress María. The East Roman Empire's financial strength was based on the economic strength of Asia Minor and on the Imperial civil service's efficiency in raising revenue from the Asiatic districts. The two 'Eastern' districts on the European side of the Straits, namely Thrákê and Makedhonía, are likely to have produced no less good soldiers than the Asiatic districts, but these two districts' value as revenue-producers must have been reduced by the frequency of the devastating raids from which they suffered at the hands of Eurasian nomads as well as Bulgars.

The civil service's financial efficiency had its price. It enabled the Central Government to extract more revenue from Asia Minor than the country's economy could yield without damage.[2] Over-taxation was assuredly one of the causes of the progressive squeezing-out of the small holders, against which the Imperial Government legislated assiduously but ultimately without success.[3] Meanwhile, the substantial revenues that the Government was able to raise at this cost did give it the means of making money 'talk' to great effect in the conduct of its foreign relations.

The objectives for which the East Roman Government laid out money abroad were partly negative and partly positive. In subsidizing Bulgaria, the East Roman Government did not expect to purchase anything more than an exemption from Bulgar attacks. There was no expectation that the Bulgars would ever undertake to fight the East Roman Empire's

---

[1] See pp. 458–60.
[2] 'C'est de la vitalité de la monarchie que mouraient ses sujets' (Rambaud, op. cit., p. 222).
[3] See II, 1 (iii) (e) and II, 1 (iv).

battles for her at this or any other price, however high. On the other hand, the subsidies paid to the Pechenegs out of the East Roman peasants' pockets did save East Roman soldiers' lives—and this, perhaps more often than not, without costing even expendable Pecheneg lives, if it is true, as Constantine declares,[1] that the mere threat of being attacked by the Pechenegs was enough to deter the Bulgars and Magyars and Rhos from attacking the Pechenegs' East Roman paymaster.

To hire expendable barbarians to do the too precious East Roman soldier's work for him was the positive objective of the subsidies that the East Roman Government paid in Constantine Porphyrogenitus's day to the Pechenegs and perhaps to other barbarian peoples as well; and it is evident that, in Constantine Porphyrogenitus's judgement, this was a trump card in East Roman hands. Indeed, he is so much fascinated by the potentialities of the device that he cannot resist pointing out how it could also be used against inoffensive and even friendly nations.

'The Ghuzz can make war on the Pechenegs.'[2] This is both true and pertinent. No doubt the Ghuzz were as great a terror to the Pechenegs as the Pechenegs were to the Magyars, and this for the same reason. The Ghuzz had evicted the Pechenegs from their previous pasture-ranges, as the Pechenegs had then evicted the Magyars from theirs; and the experience of being evicted had had a shattering effect on morale. Constantine's observation is pertinent as well; for, considering what the Pechenegs were like, it was expedient for the East Roman Empire to have up its sleeve the means of turning against the Pechenegs the master-device of using barbarians to fight barbarians, supposing that the Pechenegs were, one day, to default on their bargain with the Empire. After they had pocketed a twelve months' subsidy, they could not be trusted not to join forces against the Empire with the Bulgars or the Magyars or the Rhos in a spring-time looting-raid into Imperial territory, instead of their threatening these neighbours of theirs with sanctions if they attempted to do just that.[3] So far, so good, but the reader is pulled up short by what follows.

The Ghuzz can [also] make war on the Khazars, and so can the Exousio-krátor of Alania. 'The nine regions' of Khazaria lie next door to Alania, and the Alan is able, supposing that he chooses, to raid and loot these regions and thereby inflict on the Khazars grave damage and death, considering that these regions are, for Khazaria, the sole source of abundance, and indeed of subsistence. If the Exousiokrátor of Alania does not keep the peace with the Khazars but considers the friendship of the Emperor of the Romans to be of

---

[1] See the passage quoted on p. 460 from his *De Adm. Imp.*

[2] *De Adm. Imp.*, chap. 9, p. 79.

[3] The Pechenegs did join forces with the Magyars in the Magyar raid in 934, according to the Arabic accounts of this affair (see Diaconu, op. cit., pp. 17–19).

greater value to him, then, if the Khazars do not choose to maintain friendship and peace with the Emperor, the Alan can do them great harm. He can ambush their roads and attack them when they are off their guard on their route to Sárkel and to 'the nine regions' and to Khersón. If the Exousiokrátor really exerts himself to restrain the Khazars, Khersón and 'the nine regions' will enjoy the most profound peace. The Khazars will be afraid of being attacked by the Alans and will not have their hands free to send an army to attack Khersón and the regions, because they are not strong enough to wage war with both adversaries simultaneously; so they will be compelled to keep the peace. 'Black Bulgaria'[1] is also in a position to make war on the Khazars.[2]

If this passage in Constantine Porphyrogenitus's manual for the conduct of the East Roman Imperial Government's foreign relations had ever fallen into the hands of the Khazar Khaqan and his ministers, they would have been indignant. They would have pointed out that nowadays Khazaria was one of the most pacific states in the World, and that, if she had been more warlike in her earlier days, her arms had never been directed against the East Roman Empire. The two powers had, in fact, never been at war with each other,[3] while, on the other hand, Khazaria had frequently been at war with the East Roman Empire's enemies, and this to the Empire's signal advantage. Indeed, the Empire may have owed it to the Khazars that she had survived the successive onslaughts of the Sasanid Persian Emperor Khusraw II Parviz and the Muslim Arabs. At the crisis of the last and deadliest of the Romano-Persian wars, the Emperor Heraclius had requested from the Khazars' Turkish suzerain, and had received from the Khazars themselves,[4] the military aid that Constantine Porphyrogenitus hoped that he himself might receive from the Pechenegs in case of need, and thereafter the pressure on the Empire of the Arabs' onslaught had been relieved by the vigour of the Khazars' offensive-defensive resistance to the Arabs' advance towards the Caucasus.[5] The friendship between Khazaria and the Empire had been symbolized and sealed in two marriage-alliances between their respective Imperial families. What, then, had been in Constantine's mind when he had been thinking out ways of tormenting Khazaria by inducing her neighbours to fall upon her?

Probably Constantine's apologia would have been that his application to the Khazars of the device of using barbarians to fight barbarians had

---

[1] i.e. the former Bulgaria astride the middle course of the River Volga, in the neighbourhood of the present day Qazan? For Black Bulgaria, see further op. cit., chap. 42, p. 180. The identification of Black Bulgaria with Volga Bulgaria is questioned by Moravcsik, *Commentary*, p. 63.

[2] *De Adm. Imp.*, chaps. 10–12, pp. 80–1.

[3] The conflict between Justinian II and his brother-in-law the Khazar Khaqan of the day did not amount to a war and did not involve the East Roman Empire; for at the time Justinian II was off the Imperial throne and was in exile at Khersón.

[4] See pp. 440–1.   [5] See p. 442.

been just an academic exercise, and had not been meant to be taken seriously, as he had meant his son to take his instructions for combating the Rhos and the Magyars and the Bulgars by threatening to set the Pechenegs on them. To this, the Khazars could have retorted that this exercise at their expense was both superfluous and tactless.

Constantine can, in truth, reasonably be criticized for playing with this particular device unseasonably, and the device itself was unheroic.[1] All the same, the subsidies to the Pechenegs were a more effective means of providing for the Empire's defence against aggressive-minded foreign nations than pageants in the Imperial Palace. One intrepid East Roman official risking his life in Pechenegia with a bag of gold was serving the Empire better than thousands of decorators and cooks and eunuchs and varvátoi working like beavers in the Palace to impress state guests by inflicting on them the tedious vanities of East Roman Imperial protocol.

---

[1] Yet the truculent warrior Nikêphóros II Phokás did not disdain to employ it against the Bulgars in 965. He enlisted the Rhos to take the Bulgars in the rear, with consequences that were nearly disastrous (see p. 518).

PART IV

THE BYZANTINE CIVILIZATION

1. *The Byzantine Civilization's Origin, Affinities, and Diffusion*

THE East Roman Empire was a state, and the upkeep of this state was burdensome for its heavily taxed subjects. This, however, was not all that the East Roman Empire was. It was also the seed-bed of a new civilization.[1]

The Eastern Orthodox Christian civilization—or the Byzantine civilization, to call it by a shorter title[2]—was one of five new civilizations that had sprouted, at the western end of the Old World, among the debris of the Roman Empire. The youngest of the five was the Islamic civilization; the other four were Christian. The Nestorian and Monophysite churches had seceded from the once unitary Catholic Church to the east and south of the domain that the Orthodox (i.e. Chalcedonian) Church had still retained. To the west of the Eastern Orthodox Christian World, another separate Christian civilization was arising, in Constantine Porphyrogenitus's time, in the ecclesiastical domain of the See of Rome.

The former domain of the Roman Empire, before its break-up, was the common ground from which these five new civilizations had sprung; but, to trace their common origin, we have to look back, behind the cultural history of the Roman Empire, to the beginnings of the cultural intercourse between two civilizations of an older generation, the Hellenic

---

[1] The point has been made by Rambaud in op. cit., p. xvi.

[2] The name 'Byzantine' is convenient, but it is also misleading in two ways. It implies that the Eastern Orthodox civilization was a product of Constantinople, whereas it was in truth a product of the East Roman Empire as a whole and of its lost dominions in Syria and Egypt as well. In the second place, the name properly belongs to the colonial Hellenic city-state Byzantium, whose history had come to an end when the history of Constantinople had begun. Byzantium had never fully recovered from its siege and capture by L. Septimius Severus in the war of the Antonine succession in the last decade of the second century. In the fourth century the remnant of Byzantium had been engulfed in the new capital of the Roman Empire which had been founded by Constantine I and had continued to grow under his successors (see II, 3).

and the Syrian (i.e. the civilization of the Canaanites, Hebrews, and Aramaeans, which had come to birth in Syria, simultaneously with the birth of the Hellenic civilization in the Aegean basin, at the turn of the second and the last millennium B.C.). The interaction between these two earlier civilizations had begun at least as early as the ninth or eighth century B.C., when the Hellenic Greeks had borrowed the Alphabet from its inventors the Canaanite Phoenicians. The reciprocal influence of the two civilizations on each other had become more intimate and more intense after Alexander the Great had annexed South-West Asia and Egypt to the Hellenic World, and the process of fusion had continued after the perimeter of the Mediterranean basin, from the west bank of the Euphrates to the shores of the Atlantic, had been united politically, under Roman rule, in an empire that was felt by its inhabitants to be virtually coextensive with civilization itself.

By the time when the Roman Empire broke up, as it did at the turn of the fourth and fifth centuries of the Christian Era, the Syrian and Hellenic civilizations had been interacting with each other for more than one thousand years. The effect of this long-continuing process had been to decompose each of the two interacting civilizations and to combine their liberated constituent elements into a culture-compost which—to pursue the metaphor—offered a rich soil for a new crop. The soil was the richer because elements of the Pharaonic Egyptian civilization and the Sumerian–Akkadian–Babylonian civilization had been incorporated in the Syro-Hellenic amalgam. This was the soil that had borne the crop of the five new civilizations that were in existence by the tenth century and that are still in existence today, more than a thousand years after Constantine Porphyrogenitus's time.

The replacement of the old set of civilizations in this quarter of the World by the new set had been a radical and revolutionary change, but the transition had not, of course, been either instantaneous or clear-cut. The shock that had precipitated this cultural revolution had been the decline and fall of the Roman Empire; for this had been a cultural as well as a political débâcle. The immediate effect had been to produce something like a cultural interregnum. By the tenth century, this interregnum was over. By this date, all the five new cultures had taken shape. They had not, however, all developed at the same pace. The Byzantine and Islamic cultures had begun to blossom in the ninth century; the Western Christian civilization did not break into flower before the eleventh century.

It is not surprising that the Byzantine and Islamic civilizations should have been relatively precocious, considering that each of them had inherited a substantial part of the ground on which the deposit of the Syro-Hellenic culture-compost was deep. By contrast, the Western

Christian civilization had originated in what had been a backward colonial annex of the Hellenic and Canaanite worlds. In the tenth century it was still an open question whether this unpropitious soil would be capable of producing an independent new civilization. It was possible that the western basin of the Mediterranean and its hinterland might now, for the second time, become a colonial annex of civilizations based on the Levant. This western extremity of the Old World might, in fact, have been partitioned between the Islamic and Byzantine civilizations, as it had been partitioned previously between the Canaanite and the Hellenic. Even so Francophile a Byzantine observer as the Emperor Constantine Porphyrogenitus could not have foreseen that within the next 250 years the Western Christian civilization was going, not only to catch up with the Byzantine and the Islamic, but to forge ahead of them —and this not only in the barbaric field of military and political power, but in the field of culture as well.

The Byzantine civilization's domain had never been confined within the military and political frontiers of the East Roman Empire. When, under the dynasties founded successively by the emperors Heraclius and Leo III, the East Roman Empire had arisen, phoenix-like, from the pyre on which the Diocletianic–Constantinian Roman Empire had been burnt to ashes, the Empire had already lost to its Muslim Arab assailants its Syrian and Egyptian dominions; but the nascent Byzantine civilization was at home in these lost territories, as well as in the East Roman Empire's surviving territory in Asia Minor. Indeed, the local forms that the Syro-Hellenic culture-compost had taken in Syria and Egypt played leading parts among the formative forces that gave the new Byzantine civilization its distinctive character.

In Syria and Egypt, however, in contrast to Asia Minor, the Byzantine civilization was, in Constantine Porphyrogenitus's time, a wasting asset. In the course of the fifth and sixth centuries the mass of the population in these two regions had seceded from the Chalcedonian Catholic Church and had established pre-Chalcedonian (Monophysite) national churches of their own, with liturgies in their national languages.[1] They had repudiated Catholic Christianity because, in their eyes, this bore the taint of being 'Melchite', that is to say 'Imperial'. The Copts and Syrians had come to think of that church as being the tool of a Graeco-Roman political regime that they felt to be alien. It was true that it was easier for them to repudiate Roman rule than to purge out of their civilization the Hellenic ingredient that by this time was age-old. The Syriac and Coptic literatures included a large quota of translations of works in Greek, and these pre-Christian as well as Christian. All the same, the Monophysites were consciously in revolt against Hellenic civilization as

---

[1] See pp. 120–1, 394–5, 399–400.

well as against Roman rule; and the Roman Empire had lost Syria and Egypt, ecclesiastically and culturally, to the Monophysite majority of the local population before it had lost the two territories militarily and politically to Muslim Arab conquerors.

In the tenth century a majority of the population of both Syria and Egypt was still Christian, not Muslim; but, within this abiding Christian majority, the 'Melchites' were now a small minority; and, since the Byzantine civilization's destiny was linked with 'Melchite' Eastern Orthodoxy's destiny, it could be foreseen that, in the domains of the Eastern Orthodox Patriarchates of Antioch, Jerusalem, and Alexandria, the Byzantine civilization had no future. The Byzantine civilization's land of promise was to be found, not to the south of Asia Minor, in the domain of Monophysite Christianity and Islam, but to the north, in those vast tracts of northern Asia and Europe that were still virgin soil—were still open, that is to say, to conversion from paganism to some higher religion and from barbarism to some higher form of culture. The two northerly regions, beyond the East Roman Empire's frontiers, in which Eastern Orthodox Christianity, carrying Byzantine civilization with it, had established itself by the tenth century were Caucasia and south-eastern Europe.

In Caucasia, Eastern Orthodoxy had won Iberia and Abkhazia on the East Roman side of the mountains and Alania on the far side,[1] but it had not managed to bring Monophysite Armenia back into the Chalcedonian fold, and it had not made any appreciable impression on Khazaria. It has been mentioned already[2] that the Khazar royal family had eventually embraced Judaism, which, from the Khazars' point of view, had the cultural merit of being a higher religion without having the political drawback of being the established religion of either of Khazaria's two powerful neighbours, the East Roman Empire and the Arab Caliphate. Among the people of Khazaria, Islam, too, had begun to win converts, but this only after the Arab offensive in the direction of the Caucasus had died down.

In south-eastern Europe, as in Britain, a mission-field had been created by the obliteration of Christianity in ex-Roman territory that had been Christian before it had been overwhelmed by pagan barbarians in the course of the fifth, sixth, and seventh centuries. The former Roman provinces between the middle and lower Danube and the shores of the Adriatic and the Aegean had been overrun by pagan Slavs, right down to the Pelopónnêsos inclusive, and a large part of this new pagan Slav

---

[1] Abkhazia had been converted to Eastern Orthodox Christianity in the reign of the Emperor Justinian I (Laurent, *L'Arménie entre Byzance et l'Islam*, p. 19, n. 4). The ruler of Alania had been converted at an early date in the tenth century (Laurent, op. cit., p. 17, n. 7).

[2] On pp. 435–6.

population had subsequently been overlaid by pagan Eurasian Nomad conquerors: temporarily by the Avars; permanently by the Croats, Serbs, and Bulgars.[1] The Croats and Serbs are said to have adopted Christianity in return for being authorized by the Roman Emperor Heraclius to supplant the Avars in the Western Illyricum;[2] and Heraclius is said to have been careful to arrange that these new converts in this quarter should come under the ecclesiastical jurisdiction of the Roman See, since the Western Illyricum, and the Eastern Illyricum too, were in the domain of the Roman Patriarchate.[3]

This had been politic; for the relations between the Roman See and the Patriarchate of Constantinople had always been delicate since the creation of the Constantinopolitan Patriarchate by the Constantinopolitan Roman Government, and especially since this Patriarchate's subsequent provocative assumption of the title 'Ecumenical'.[4] These relations had then been exacerbated by the opposition, in the Roman See's domain, to the Emperor Leo III's iconoclasm, and by the East Roman Government's reprisals. In 732, or possibly at some date later than the Lombard conquest of Ravenna in 751, the East Roman Government had transferred from the Roman See's ecclesiastical jurisdiction to the Ecumenical Patriarchate's as much of the Roman See's domain in the 'toe' of Italy, in Sicily, and in the Eastern Illyricum as was at that time under the East Roman Empire's rule, together with the whole of the rest of the former diocesis of the Western Illyricum and the former praetorian prefecture of the Eastern Illyricum,[5] most of which, apart from a few surviving enclaves of East Roman territory round the coasts, was occupied at the time by Sklavinías that were independent *de facto*.[6]

This trespass by the secular power in the field of ecclesiastical jurisdiction had been *ultra vires*, and the Roman See had never acquiesced in it or forgiven it. The injury had been aggravated when, in the early years of the ninth century, the whole of the Pelopónnêsos had been brought back under East Roman rule and the pagan part of its population had been converted;[7] for the ecclesiastical jurisdiction over this reclaimed territory, too, had been given to the Ecumenical Patriarchate and not

---

[1] See Annex III, pp. 621–5.   [2] Ibid., pp. 624–5.   [3] See ibid.
[4] See p. 355.   [5] See p. 356.
[6] This point is made by G. Ostrogorsky, 'The Byzantine Background of the Moravian Mission', in *Dumbarton Oaks Papers*, Number Nineteen, pp. 1–18, on p. 13.

[7] The majority of these Peloponnesian pagans had been the descendants of Slavs who had infiltrated into the Pelopónnêsos in the seventh century, but in the Mani the pagans had been native Greeks who, in this natural fastness, had held their own against the Christian Church as well as against the Slavs. These Maniot Hellenic pagans had not been converted till the reign of the Emperor Basil I (*imperabat* 867–86). Until then, the Maniots had been screened by the two autonomous Slav tribes, the Mêlingoí and the Ezerítai, who lay between the Mani and the part of the Pelopónnêsos that had remained, or had been brought back, under direct East Roman administration. See *De Adm. Imp.*, chap. 50, p. 224, and the present work, pp. 527, 579, and 620 with n. 1.

to the Roman See. Nor had the East Roman Government given back to the Roman See any of its sequestrated territories after 843, though the definitive repudiation of iconoclasm in that year throughout the dominions of the East Roman Empire had extinguished the cause of the quarrel between the East Roman Government and the Papacy that had moved Leo III or Constantine V to mulct the Roman See of its 'Calabrian', Sicilian, and Illyrian territories.

So long as, within the domain of the Ecumenical Patriarchate, the struggle for mastery between 'iconoclasts' and 'iconodules' had continued, this portion of Christendom had been a house divided against itself, and this disunity had inhibited the Eastern Orthodox Church from engaging in missionary enterprises. The final victory of the 'iconodules' had been advantageous for missionary work, since the representation of objects of veneration in visual form is an attraction for un-sophisticated natures; and the restoration of peace, unity, and eikóns in the Eastern Orthodox World had been followed quickly by the work of the Thessalonian missionaries, Constantine-Cyril and Methódhios, among the Slavs. Their master-stroke had been to prepare the way by shaping the local dialect of the Slavs in the hinterland of Thessaloníkê into a literary language, written in an alphabet of its own,[1] that was capable of serving as a vehicle for the liturgy of the Christian Church and for a corpus of translations of works of Greek literature, Christian and secular. At this date the various branches of the Slavonic family of languages had not yet diverged widely from each other; so, when one Slavonic dialect had been given a literary form, this could serve any other part of the huge Slav World as well.

Constantine-Cyril's and Methódhios's preliminary philological work had thus opened up a vast potential mission-field for them. Ostrogorsky points out[2] that the mission to Moravia in 863[3] had not been an isolated enterprise. The Rhos attack on Constantinople in 860 had been followed by the first of those missions to Russia that were eventually to bear so rich a harvest. In 860, or shortly after, Constantine-Cyril had gone to Khersón on a mission to the Khazars. In 864, Khan Borís of Bulgaria had been converted to Christianity as an ecclesiastical subject of the Ecumenical Patriarchate of Constantinople,[4] and, after a disillusioning flirtation with

[1] The Glagolitic alphabet that had been invented by Constantine-Cyril had no future. The alphabet in which the Macedonian Slavonic dialect has been conveyed far and wide is the so-called Cyrillic, which was invented in Bulgaria, by the school of translators and copyists that had been established near Preslav, at the monastery of Titča, after the death of both Constantine-Cyril and Methódhios and the liquidation of the Slavophone church that they had founded in Moravia (see II, 1 (iii) (a), pp. 104–5).

[2] In loc. cit., pp. 3–4 and 18.

[3] 863, not 862, is Ostrogorsky's date for Rostislav's appeal to the East Roman Government.

[4] Ostrogorsky, in loc. cit., pp. 4–5, points out that the East Roman Empire's fortunes in south-eastern Europe were governed by its fortunes in Asia Minor. The retention of Asia

the See of Rome, Borís had accepted—if he had not procured—the ruling made by the Constantinople Council of 869–70, in reply to an inquiry from Borís himself, that Bulgaria lay within the Ecumenical Patriarch's domain, not the Pope's. Serbia had accepted Eastern Orthodox Christianity under the Ecumenical Patriarch's jurisdiction a few years later than 864. In fact 'the second half of the ninth century had witnessed the most marked advance' in the radiation of the Byzantine culture.[1]

Meanwhile, Constantine-Cyril and Methódhios had been unable to avoid becoming involved in south-east European international politics. The pagan rulers of the south-east European barbarian principalities, from Bulgaria in the south-east to Greater Moravia in the north-west, had realized in the ninth century that they must accept Christianity in order to hold their own against the pressure of the rejuvenated Christian World; but, like the Khazars, they had been anxious to avoid compromising their political independence by embracing the religion and culture of a civilized power that was their immediate neighbour. They would have preferred to enter into a religious and cultural association with some power that was more remote and that would, in that degree, be less of a menace to them. It has been mentioned already[2] that Bulgaria had no sooner received Christianity from the Ecumenical Patriarchate than she had started to experiment with the alternative possibility of giving her ecclesiastical allegiance to Rome instead. Conversely, Great Moravia, which had found itself uncomfortably close up against the eastern border of an expanding Kingdom of East Francia, had applied, in 862 or 863, to the distant East Roman Empire for missionaries, and Constantine-Cyril and Methódhios had gone to Great Moravia in response to this request.[3]

Great Moravia had lain in the Western Illyricum, and Constantine-Cyril and Methódhios, like the Emperor Heraclius, and in sharp contrast to the Emperors Leo III and Constantine V, had been careful to respect the rights of the Roman See over their mission-field. They had taken the initiative in placing their newly founded Moravian church

Minor was the first charge on the Empire's resources, and its interests in Europe had to be subordinated to this, since this was a matter of life and death. However, Petronás's victory over the Amīr of Malatīyah in 863 had marked the turn of the tide of warfare between Rhomanía and the Arab Caliphate in Rhomanía's favour. The East Roman military demonstration against Bulgaria in 864, which had led to Borís's conversion, had been made in the year after Petronás's victory in Asia Minor.

[1] Ostrogorsky in loc. cit., p. 3. [2] On pp. 365–6 and 515–16.
[3] For the creation and destruction of the Slavophone Moravian Church, see F. Dvornik, *Les Slaves, Byzance, et Rome au ixe siècle* (Paris, 1926, Champion), pp. 147–81, 199–213, 262–97; eundem, *The Slavs: Their Early History and Civilization* (Boston, 1956, American Academy of Arts and Sciences), pp. 80–102; eundem, *Byzantine Missions among the Slavs: SS. Cyril and Methodius* (New Brunswick, 1971, Rutgers University Press); Vlasto, *The Entry of the Slavs into Christendom*, pp. 13–85.

under the Roman See's jurisdiction; but this had not saved their Slavo-phone clergy from being evicted from Great Moravia, after Methódhios's death in 885, at the instance of the bishops of the adjoining East Frankish sees. This treatment of the Great Moravian Slavophone Church was un-deserved; for there is no evidence that the East Roman missionaries had had any political ulterior motive. All the same, they had been East Roman subjects; they had been bringing with them the Byzantine civilization, which had the twofold attraction of being more mature than the Western civilization at this date and of being presented in the Moravians' Slavonic mother-tongue; and the ruler of Great Moravia had certainly been moved to call in the Thessalonian missionaries by a wish to associate himself politically with the East Roman Empire rather than with East Francia. This had been a powerful combination of factors making for the induction of Great Moravia into the Byzantine World; so the East Franks had had reason, though they may not have had justification, for intervening to nip the nascent Slavophone Moravian Church in the bud.

This competition for the winning of pagan Slav south-eastern Europe, extending from Great Moravia to Bulgaria inclusive, had put a strain on the relations between the Western and the Byzantine World. Indeed, in 867 the competition had produced a temporary breach between the Roman and the Constantinopolitan Church. This breach seems to have been mended towards the close of the ninth century. By that time the competition between the two churches for the allegiance of the south-east European countries had come to an end. The gravitational pull of geographical propinquity had prevailed over the political counter-pull of defensive-minded local statesmanship. Great Moravia had been an-nexed to Roman Christendom conclusively; Bulgaria had thrown in her lot with Eastern Orthodox Christendom decisively; and finally the Magyars, by breaking into the Alföld and scattering the Moravian settlers there to the winds, had reinstated an insulating wedge of paganism across the overland line of communications between the two rival Christendoms.

Throughout the tenth century the Magyars remained truculently pagan and aggressively predatory at the expense of both Christendoms impartially; and therefore, till the conversion of the Magyars to Roman Christianity at the end of that century, the competition between the two churches for converts in Continental Europe was in suspense. In the Emperor Nikêphóros II Phokás's reign (*imperabat* 963–9) there was renewed friction, on a minor scale, over ecclesiastical jurisdiction in south-eastern Italy;[1] during Constantine Porphyrogenitus's reign

[1] For details, see J. Gay, *L'Italie méridionale et L'Empire byzantin* (Paris, 1904, Fontemoing), pp. 347–64.

(912–59), on the other hand, tension between the two churches was low. It was also low between the two empires;[1] and this made it easier for Constantine to give rein to his avowed Francophilism.

Meanwhile, the biggest consequence of Constantine-Cyril's and Methódhios's work had not yet declared itself. Their Slavophone Moravian Church had foundered, through no fault of theirs; but their feat of shaping the Macedonian Slavonic dialect into a literary language had continued to bear fruit. The transfer to Bulgaria of the Slavophone clergy who had been evicted from Moravia had clinched Bulgaria's adherence to Eastern Orthodoxy,[2] but this enduring effect of Constantine-Cyril's and Methódhios's work in south-eastern Europe was to be surpassed by its coming effect in Russia. Russia's eventual conversion to Eastern Orthodox Christianity had been portended in Olga's state visit to Constantinople and in her baptism.[3] In Russia the immediate effect of a sovereign's conversion to Christianity was a pagan reaction, as it had been in Bulgaria. Olga's fierce son Svyátoslav repudiated his mother's act, and he lived to bring the East Roman Empire to the brink of destruction through the East Roman Government's own fault. The Emperor Nikêphóros II, who should have known better, resorted to Constantine Porphyrogenitus's device of using one barbarian to fight another; but, this time, the East Roman trick was played once too often. Nikêphóros called Svyátoslav in to fight Bulgaria, with the result that Nikêphóros's murderer and successor John Dzimiskês had to fight Svyátoslav. The decisive defeat of the Russians in this trial of strength with the East Roman Empire's massed 'Eastern' army-corps was a perhaps unavoidable prelude to the Russians' adoption of the East Roman form of Christianity.

Towards the turn of the tenth and eleventh centuries the competition for the allegiance of the still unconverted northern pagans was resumed. Roman Christendom now incorporated Hungary, Poland, and the Scandinavian countries; Islam incorporated 'Volga Bulgaria'; Eastern Orthodox Christendom incorporated Russia. Of these three achievements, the Islamic one was the earliest and the most remarkable, but the

---

[1] Rambaud, op. cit., p. 309.

[2] See III, 2, pp. 359 and 367.

[3] Kedhrênós, vol. ii, p. 329, and the *Russian Primary Chronicle* and *Regino Cont.* state that Olga was baptized at Constantinople during her visit in 957. (The *R.P.C.*'s dating, 955, is erroneous.) This must have been the crowning event of the visit, and it is surprising that it is not mentioned by Constantine Porphyrogenitus in his account of the proceedings in *De Caer.*, Book II, chap. 15 (see the present work, III, 7, pp. 504–5). But the inference that Olga had been baptized previously at Kiev is not accepted either by Dvornik (see *The Slavs: Their Early History and Civilization*, p. 200) or by Obolensky (see *C. Med. H.*, vol. iv, 2nd ed., Part I, p. 511, n. 4). On the other hand, Vlasto, op. cit., p. 250, thinks that, on the whole, it is more likely that Olga had been baptized at Kiev already in 954/5. Obolensky suggests, in *The Byzantine Commonwealth*, p. 195, that Olga may have undergone a preliminary ceremony of reception into the Christian community at Kiev, postponing her final christening until her visit to Constantinople.

Eastern Orthodox Christian achievement was the most far-reaching. It was remarkable that Islam should have succeeded in making a lodgement astride the Volga, on the far side of the Eurasian steppe from Dār-al-Islām; this is the more remarkable, considering that the direct route up the western shore of the Caspian Sea and on, up the lower Volga, was effectively blocked by Khazaria; Islam reached 'Volga Bulgaria' from a base of operations in its far north-easterly marches in Transoxania and Khwarizm. However, Eastern Orthodox Christianity's conversion of Russia was the winning stroke in the northward expansion of the three religions at this stage. Kievan Russia outflanked Hungary, Poland, and Scandinavia, lying, as it did, to the east of them, and Russia was so vastly larger than Volga Bulgaria that she could not fail, in the end, to overwhelm Volga Bulgaria's successor in this quarter, the Khanate of Qazan. After that outpost of Islam on the Volga had fallen, there was nothing to prevent Russian pioneers from expanding eastwards till they reached the western shores of the northern Pacific; and territorial gains for Russia were gains for Eastern Orthodox Christianity too.

Thus Eastern Orthodox Christendom, and, with it, the Byzantine civilization, has expanded far beyond the farthest limits that the East Roman Empire ever attained, and the civilization has also outlived the Empire by many centuries. The Eastern Orthodox Patriarchates of Constantinople, Antioch, Jerusalem, and Alexandria still survive; so today the Eastern Orthodox World stretches from Egypt on the south to the Arctic Ocean on the north, and from the western frontiers of the Ukraine to Vladivostok. It is true that within the last three hundred years the Byzantine civilization has been overlaid, throughout this vast region, by a Western cultural veneer of various shades. The shade is now everywhere red, except in Greece and Cyprus and the four ancient Eastern Patriarchates; and in those Patriarchates the Orthodox community is now only a diasporá. However, underneath this exotic Communist Western and Capitalist Western top-dressing, the Byzantine civilization is still alive, and who can tell whether, on its own ground, Byzantinism may not be going to have the last word? At any rate, both Eastern Orthodox Christianity and Byzantine civilization were still forces to be reckoned with in the World in 1972, 519 years after the Ottoman conquest of Constantinople and 768 years after the shattering of the East Roman Empire, beyond repair, by Western 'crusaders'.

This wide expansion and long survival of the Byzantine civilization is the fruit of Constantine-Cyril's and Methódhios's philological and missionary work in the ninth century; and it is significant that this East Roman pair of brothers, who have made so much history in the course of the last eleven centuries, came, not from Constantinople, but from Thessaloníkê.

It has already been noted[1] that Constantinople is awkwardly placed for communicating overland with the interior of either the Balkan Peninsula or Asia Minor, though it is superbly sited for serving as a fortress and as a naval base. On the coast of the Balkan Peninsula the natural point of departure for the interior is not Constantinople; it is Thessaloníkê,[2] which, for this purpose, is sited as admirably as another historic peripheral Greek city, Marseilles. Thessaloníkê, like Marseilles, is sited close to the seaward end of a river-valley that serves excellently as a route into the interior, while, like Marseilles again, Thessaloníkê is just far enough away from its river's mouth for its harbour to escape being silted up. The traveller from Marseilles up the Rhône valley finds, at the head of the valley, easy portages into the basins of the Seine and the Rhine; and the Vardar valley is equally accommodating. The watershed that divides it from the Morava valley is low, and the Morava is a tributary of the Danube.

Thus Thessaloníkê is well placed for communicating not only with the interior of south-eastern Europe but with south-eastern Europe's central European hinterland; it was 'the Empire's principal gateway to the Slavic World';[3] and this made a good case for the transference of the East Roman entrepôt for trade between the East Roman Empire and Bulgaria from Constantinople to Thessaloníkê—the more so because, after Bulgaria's annexation of the Sklavinías in Thessaloníkê's hinterland, Bulgaria's centre of gravity was shifting westward. The reason why this move on the East Roman Government's part provoked Khan Symeon into going to war with the East Roman Empire in 894 was not that the move was bad for Bulgaria intrinsically. It was unacceptable to Symeon because it had been engineered by two East Roman businessmen from the Helladic army-corps district in order to give them an opportunity for fleecing the Bulgar traders. When Symeon had complained of this to the Emperor Leo VI, he had obtained no redress, since the offending Helladic businessmen had gained Leo's ear through the agency of a eunuch belonging to Leo's father-in-law.[4]

In any case, the structure of the East Roman Empire gave the Thessalonians themselves an incentive for making the most of the legitimate commercial opportunities that their city's situation presented to them. Like Constantinople, Thessaloníkê was a fortress; if it had been unfortified, it could not have survived the *Völkerwanderung* that transformed the ethnic map of the Balkan Peninsula in the sixth and seventh centuries.

---

[1] See pp. 49 and 220–1.

[2] See *De Adm. Imp.*, chap. 42, p. 177, where it is noted that Belgrade, on the Danube, can be reached from Thessaloníkê easily in eight days.

[3] Ostrogorsky in loc. cit., p. 7.

[4] *Georg. Mon. Cont.*, Reign of Leo VI, chap. 11, p. 853; Leo Grammaticus, pp. 266–7; *Theoph. Cont.*, Book VI, Reign of Leo VI, chap. 9, p. 357; see also the present work, pp. 61–2.

Unlike Constantinople, however, Thessaloníkê was not a natural fortress, and it was not a capital city either. East Roman Constantinople lived parasitically on the taxes that the East Roman civil service collected in the 'Eastern' army-corps districts; Thessaloníkê had no such unearned income. The tiny 'Western' army-corps district of which it was the administrative centre hardly extended beyond the horizon of the sentries posted on its walls. Thessaloníkê was an unsubsidized beach-head; and, to make its living, it had to do business with the Slavs in its hinterland, however alien and barbarous and unfriendly these unwelcome new neighbours of Thessaloníkê's might be. Thessaloníkê, like Khersón, was thus constrained to come to terms with its barbarian neighbours if possible; and the most promising way of trying to get on with them was to learn their language and to become familiar with their way of life. The Thessalonians are recorded to have been bilingual in Cyril-Constantine's generation. They spoke the Slavonic language of their hinterland, as well as their ancestral Greek mother-tongue.[1]

We may guess that if Constantine-Cyril and Methódhios had been, not Thessalonians, but 'Polítai' (Constantinopolitans), they might not have felt a vocation to become missionaries and would anyway not have had the requisite experience and knowledge. Growing up, as they did, in Thessaloníkê, they must have been in touch there, since childhood, with people whose profession was to do business in the Sklavinías on the far side of the political frontier. We may also guess, however, that Thessaloníkê might not have become the base of operations for evangelizing the Slavs, as well as for trading with them, if the city had not given birth to these two men of vision.

[1] *Life* of Constantine-Cyril, chap. 5, cited by Ostrogorsky in loc. cit., p. 15. According to J. Marquart, *Osteuropäische und ostasiatische Streifzüge* (Leipzig, 1903, Dieterich), p. 190, Constantine-Cyril is recorded to have rejected the Latins' policy of recognizing only 'three privileged languages'. 'How have you the face to give recognition to three languages only, and to decree that all other peoples and races shall be blind and deaf? . . . We differ from you in having knowledge of many nations that are literate and that give praise to God, each in its own language. I can tell you which these nations are. They are the Armenians, Persians, Abkhazians, Iberians, Sugdans [i.e. the people of Soughdaia in the Crimea], Goths [i.e. the Crimean Goths], Avars, Tursi [i.e. the Tiwerci, meaning the Slavs living on the River Tyras, alias Dniestr], Arabs, Egyptians, Syrians, and many more besides.'
The East Romans lived nearer to the heart of the civilized world than the Western Christians, and they were therefore more sensitively aware of the presence of other civilized peoples with reputable languages and scripts of their own. The Syriac, Pahlawī, and Arabic alphabets, like the Greek and Latin, had been derived from the Phoenician alphabet. The Coptic alphabet had been derived from the Greek; the Armenian alphabet had been inspired by the Greek, and the Iberian by the Armenian.
The Eastern Orthodox Church had tolerated the use of the Iberian language and alphabet for conveying the Orthodox liturgy. If the Patriarchs of Antioch and Constantinople had tried to coerce the Iberians into using the Greek language and alphabet, they would have risked goading the Iberians into abandoning Orthodoxy for the Armenian form of Monophysitism (see p. 353). However, the Iberian liturgy in the Iberian language and alphabet had confronted the Greek missionaries with a *fait accompli*. The new departure—and it was

Constantine-Cyril's genius is revealed in his first enterprise. After he had decided to be a missionary he went first to Khersón, and started to learn there the Khazar dialect of Turkish.[1] Evidently Constantine-Cyril had realized already that the most promising first step towards the conversion of a non-Christian people would be to master their language; and he had started on the Khazars' language because he had also realized that the Khazar hinterland of distant Khersón was a more important mission-field than the hinterland of his own home town. At this date the Khazars' language was the key language for the evangelization of the north; for the Khazars were not only still masters of the whole of the Steppe between the Volga and the Seret; they were also still overlords of some of the Slav and Finnish peoples in the forests to the north of the Steppe. Though in this quarter the Khazars' sphere of influence had already been reduced in size by the descent upon the Dniepr valley of the Scandinavian Rhos from the Baltic, the Khazars' Steppe-empire had not yet been broken up by the migration of the Pechenegs from the east bank of the Volga to the west bank of the Don.

Eventually, Constantine-Cyril abandoned his project for evangelizing Khazaria and its northern dependencies and devoted himself to the evangelization of a Central-European Sklavinía. Why did he renounce a mission-field whose major importance he had recognized? Perhaps he had come to the conclusion that the Khazar royal family had already passed 'the point of no return' in its gradual commitment to Judaism, and that this was an insurmountable obstacle to Christian missionary work in Khazaria.[2] We can only guess at his reasons for turning his attention away from the Turkish language of the Khazars to the Slavonic language of his native city's hinterland; but we can see in retrospect, as Constantine-Cyril himself probably could not see at the time, that, in shaping the Macedonian Slavonic dialect into a literary language, he was creating an instrument that would win Slav converts for Eastern Orthodoxy[3] not only in south-eastern Europe but in Russia

a momentous one—that was taken by Constantine-Cyril was to invent a new alphabet for conveying the Orthodox (or, in Moravia, perhaps part Eastern Orthodox, part Western) liturgy in the language of a people that, till then, had been both illiterate and pagan. For the abortive Moravian Slavophone Church, see further Vlasto, op. cit., pp. 20–85 and Dvornik, *Byzantine Missions, passim.*

[1] See Bury, *A History of the Eastern Roman Empire*, pp. 394–6. This mission to the Khazars is dated 860 by Bury, ibid.; by Ostrogorsky in loc. cit., p. 17; by Obolensky in *C. Med. H.*, vol. iv, 2nd ed., Part I, p. 492; by Vlasto, op. cit., pp. 34–6.   [2] See p. 435.

[3] One effect of the making of Macedonian Slavonic into a literary language was to stimulate the growth of a Slavonic religious literature which included original works as well as translations from the Greek. Khan Symeon of Bulgaria (893–927) fostered literary activity in Macedonian Slavonic at Preslav (see Soulis, 'The Legacy of Cyril and Methodius to the Southern Slavs', p. 31; Vlasto, op. cit., pp. 174–6). Symeon himself made an anthology, in Slavonic, of the works of St. John Chrysostom and another of the works of other Greek Christian fathers (Soulis, ibid., p. 32; Vlasto, op. cit., p. 178). Methódhios's disciple Con-

too.[1] Eventually, Russia proved to be the key country in northern Europe, and, in Russia, the key language proved to be the Slavonic mother-tongue of the native population, not the Turkish and Scandinavian languages of the north-eastern Slavs' transitory alien masters.

stantine, who became bishop of Preslav, was an original writer (of poetry, as well as prose), besides being a translator (Soulis, ibid., p. 34; Vlasto, op. cit., pp. 177–8). Khrabr wrote an apologia for the Slavonic alphabet and literature (Soulis, ibid., p. 34; Vlasto, op. cit., p. 177). According to Vlasto in loc. cit. and Dvornik, *Byzantine Missions*, pp. 250–1, the alphabet that Khrabr was championing was the Glagolitic, and he was writing before the official adoption of the 'Cyrillic' alphabet at Preslav in 893. Two other translators and adapters were John the Exarch and Gregory the Priest (Vlasto, op. cit., pp. 176–7 and 178). An 'enormous' body of Slavonic literature was produced in Bulgaria during the reigns of Symeon and his successors down to the fall of the First Bulgarian Empire (Soulis, ibid., p. 35). On the other hand, few secular Byzantine Greek works were translated (p. 36). 'On the whole, the learnèd literature of Byzantium remained inaccessible to mediaeval Bulgaria' (p. 37). Of the Byzantine secular historical works, only chronicles, not any sophisticated histories, were translated in the age of the First Bulgarian Empire (Soulis, p. 37; Vlasto, op. cit., p. 176). There were no translations of, or commentaries on, pre-Byzantine Greek literature (Soulis, p. 37; Vlasto, op. cit., p. 179).

[1] The selective version of Byzantine culture in Slavonic dress that had been made in Bulgaria was disseminated from there not only to the Russians (Vlasto, op. cit., pp. 292–3) but also to the Serbs and to the Roumans (Soulis, ibid., p. 38). Though Roumanian is a Romance language, Macedonian Slavonic was the administrative, as well as the liturgical, language of the Roumanian principalities of Wallachia and Moldavia in the fourteenth century (ibid., p. 42), and it continued to be the sole liturgical language of the Orthodox Church there till 1679, when the Metropolitan of Moldavia, Dhosítheos, published at Jassy a translation of the liturgy into Roumanian. The Bible was translated into Roumanian in 1688 (see N. Jorga, *Geschichte der Rumänen und ihrer Kultur* (Hermannstadt [Sibiu], 1929, Krafft and Drotleff), pp. 233–4 and 239–40).

2. Conservatism and Innovation in Byzantine Life

(i) The Question at Issue

IF one were to ask any educated modern Westerner what was the first idea that associated itself in his mind with the word 'Byzantine', his answer would probably be 'conservatism', and this even if his acquaintance with Byzantine life went deep enough to make him aware that his considered answer might not wholly agree with his first spontaneous reaction. What is it that has set up this association of ideas in modern Western minds? One, at any rate, of its causes is the arresting contrast between two figures: 476 and 1453. The Westerner knows that, as far as his part of the World was concerned, the history of the Roman Empire came to an end in the year A.D. 476, when the last Roman Emperor in the West was deposed. He also knows that, at Constantinople, the series of Roman Emperors that had begun at Rome with Augustus ran on, officially without a break, to the year A.D. 1453. The length of this series of Roman Emperors in the Eastern Orthodox Christian World recalls, to the Westerner's mind, the lengths of the series of Chinese 'Sons of Heaven' and Egyptian Pharaohs. Such spans of time for the duration of a regime may look like evidence of stationariness to a Westerner whose norm is the comparative instability of Western political life.

This vision of Egyptian, Chinese, and East Roman constitutional history is, of course, partly an illusion. In all three series of reigns, the alleged continuity between each reign and the succeeding one was, to a large extent, an official fiction. Often—far too often for this to be in the public interest—the succession was decided, not by a loyal observance of agreed constitutional rules, but by intrigue, assassination, revolution, and even civil war. In the Roman Empire, at any rate, from beginning to end, there was not any constitutional provision for indicating incontestibly who the legitimate heir to a reigning Emperor was.[1]

This objection to taking continuity of succession to the Imperial throne at its face value might perhaps be overridden on the ground that, though the Imperial succession might often be decided by fraud or violence, the Imperial regime itself, including its concrete embodiments in the Court and the civil service, did truly continue without a break.[2] There is, however, a more serious objection to taking continuity in the succession to a crown as evidence of social immobility. Let us assume, for the sake of the argument, that the continuity in the succession has been con-

---

[1] See pp. 12–14.   [2] This point has been made on p. 13.

stitutionally impeccable throughout. It can still be objected that this tells us little or nothing about the character of the civilization that has produced the long-lasting Imperial regime. It can be argued convincingly that, in the structure of a civilization, politics are of secondary importance, and that the character of a civilization is reflected more accurately in its economics, its art, its philosophy, its religion, and the other non-political aspects of its life. When we examine the Byzantine civilization on these lines, we find our first impression changing. The conservative features do not fade out of the picture, but they no longer dominate it. Side by side with Byzantine conservatism, we become aware of a no less characteristically Byzantine readiness, and even appetite, for innovation.

(ii) *Public Administration*

We have already observed this proclivity, even in the sphere of public administration, when we have expanded our field of vision to take in other things besides the succession to the Imperial Crown. For instance, in comparing the post-Heraclian East Roman system of administration with the Diocletianic–Constantinian system, we have found that, in points of substance, it has less in common with this than with the pre-Diocletianic system of the Principate.[1] The resemblance between the East Roman system and the Diocletianic–Constantinian system, though conspicuous, is superficial. The Diocletianic–Constantinian hierarchy of ranks and titles has been maintained and indeed has been elaborated to the verge of caricature, but there has been a new departure, and a radical one, in the distribution of responsibility and power. The separation of military commands from the civil government of provinces, which had been one of the fundamental principles of the Diocletianic–Constantinian regime, has now been abandoned. The commander of an East Roman army-corps is, *ex officio*, also the governor of the district in which his corps is cantoned. Moreover, in both these capacities he—like the legatus of a military province under the Principate—is responsible to the Emperor direct, whereas another of the fundamental principles of the Diocletianic–Constantinian system had been the interposition of intermediate tiers of officials and officers between the Emperor and the governors of provinces and commanders of basic military units. In these points of substance the East Roman system is reminiscent of the Augustan, whereas the Diocletianic–Constantinian system differs, in identical points, from both its predecessor and its successor.

It is, of course, improbable that the resemblance of the East Roman system to the Augustan was the work of conscious and deliberate archaism. The Byzantines were addicted to archaism, but their ability to practise

---

[1] See II, 4.

it was limited by the inadequacy of their knowledge of the past. Constantine Porphyrogenitus's writings reveal to us that this Roman Emperor had little knowledge of the history of the Roman Empire before the reign of Constantine the Great;[1] and Constantine Porphyrogenitus was exceptional among East Roman Emperors, courtiers, and officials in taking a lively interest in the past and in being an industrious student of it. The obvious explanation of the East Roman system's points of likeness to the Augustan system is that a similar problem had been solved on similar lines twice, and the second time independently, in the long course of Roman Imperial history. In other words, the replacement of the broken-down Diocletianic–Constantinian system by the Augustan-like East Roman system was not an example of conservative-minded archaism; it was an independent piece of empirical improvisation for meeting a practical need.

This simpler and more credible explanation of the genesis of the East Roman army-corps districts is borne out by evidence of the same readiness to innovate that we meet with in other fields of Byzantine activity besides administration. The Byzantine civilization is the third that has been created by Greek-speaking people since the second millennium B.C., and, in a number of fundamental points, it is the antithesis of the Hellenic civilization that was its immediate predecessor. It differs from this at least as sharply as the Hellenic civilization differs from its own immediate predecessor, the Mycenaean. A brief review of the principal antitheses between the Byzantine and the Hellenic attitude to life will make it plain that the founding fathers of the Byzantine civilization broke radically with their Hellenic past.

(iii) *Religion*

The key-note of Hellenic spiritual life had been rationalism; the key-note of Byzantine spiritual life was religion. In the Hellenic society the priesthood had been de-professionalized and secularized as far as possible. Either it had been amalgamated with the civil power or it had been subordinated to it. In the Byzantine society, on the other hand, the Eastern Orthodox Christian clergy had become as powerful a professional corporation as the Pharaonic Egyptian clergy had been. In the East Roman Empire, as in Pharaonic Egypt, the clergy was the only institution in an otherwise autocratically governed state that, at its peril, could and did oppose the autocrat's wishes on occasion.[2] Most Byzantine bishops and courtiers would have felt more at home among the native population of Ptolemaic Egypt than among the Hellenic 'ascendancy' there.

---

[1] He did know about the distinction between the civil Senatorial provinces and the military Imperial provinces in the Age of the Principate (*De Them.*, p. 16).

[2] See pp. 356–7 and 490–1.

Phótios is a solitary exception that proves the rule. His Hellenic rationalism shocked and offended his contemporaries.[1] On the other hand, a third-century-B.C. Hellene would have found kindred spirits in the eighteenth century Western World, while in the ninth-century or tenth-century Byzantine World he would have been isolated intellectually and morally, as Phótios was.

This difference in êthos between Byzantines and Hellenes is striking, but it was at its maximum only among the minority at the apex of the social pyramid. As we descend towards the peasantry, we find the difference diminishing and the quantum of continuity gaining upon the quantum of change. A Byzantine Greek and an Hellenic Greek peasant would have found it less difficult to enter into each other's respective attitudes to life.[2] The Byzantine would have found in the local Hellenic hero a recognizable counterpart of his own local saint; the flight and the cries of birds would have been as ominous for him as they had been for his Hellenic predecessor; and the fairies and trolls who haunted the everlasting hills had survived the Slav *Völkerwanderung* as hardily as the Maniot worshippers of the Olympian gods.[3]

In the Byzantine Greek World, every city, and perhaps almost every village too, had its tutelary saint who played the same role as the tutelary god, goddess, or hero of an Hellenic Greek city-state.

This supernatural local patron might be a figure whose name was a household word throughout Christendom. For instance, the patron of the Peloponnesian city Pátras was the Apostle St. Andrew, and the Apostle was believed to have intervened visibly and energetically to save his protégés the Patrans at the crisis of their fortunes, when, at some date between 804/5 and 811, the recently repatriated descendants of those Patrans who had found asylum overseas nearly two centuries back were being besieged, in their re-founded city, by insurgent Peloponnesian Slavs who were up in arms in an attempt to recover their cherished independence.

According to the legend,[4] the Apostle had tripped up the horse of a returning Patran scout who had been sent to appeal for speedy help from the stratêghós at Corinth, and who had been instructed to signal to the city whether or not the stratêghós was on the march. Thanks to this apparent accident, which, for pious minds, had in truth been miraculously contrived, the scout unintentionally gave the signal which signified that the relieving force was approaching, and this false good news put

---

[1] See p. 4, n. 1, and pp. 609–10.

[2] See J. C. Lawson, *Modern Greek Folklore and Ancient Greek Religion* (Cambridge, 1910, University Press; New York, 1964, University Books); M. P. Nilsson, *Greek Popular Religion* (New York, 1940, Columbia University Press).

[3] For these, see pp. 514, n. 7, 579, and 619–20.

[4] Recounted by Constantine Porphyrogenitus in *De Adm. Imp.*, chap. 49, pp. 218–20.

such heart into the defenders of the city that they immediately made a sortie in the hope of catching their Slav assailants between the stratêghós's (actually still distant) troops and the Patrans themselves. Though the Patrans took the offensive against their Slav besiegers under a mis-apprehension, they routed the enemy; for, notwithstanding the absence of the Imperial troops, the Patrans did not fight single-handed. St. Andrew himself appeared on horseback; and, led by him, his protégés' charge was irresistible. Thus Pátras was saved, not by her own exertions and not by the stratêghós's, but by the Apostle's.

The Imperial Government testified by positive acts that it gave credence to the tale of St. Andrew's visible personal intervention. The routed Slav insurgents had found asylum (so it was reported) in St. Andrew's shrine. This report is hard to believe; for the shrine of the city's patron can hardly have been located outside the city walls. However, as a thank-offering for the Apostle's solicitude in saving not only his own city of Pátras but also its discomfited assailants, the re-subjugated Slav insurgents were condemned by the Imperial Government to render certain services in perpetuity both to the See of Pátras and to the Imperial Government itself, and the See was raised to metropolitan status at the expense of dilatory Corinth. The See of Corinth now had not only to put up with the presence of another metropolitan see, besides itself, within the same province; it also had to cede to the new metropolitan See of Pátras the bishoprics of Methónê and Korónê.[1]

An apostolic patron could, however, be outshone by one of less exalted rank who had the good fortune to preside over a greater and more important city and who was also reputed to have saved his city by his personal intervention not only once but repeatedly, and this in emergencies as perilous as the one that was believed to have moved St. Andrew to intervene on behalf of the city of Pátras in the reign of Nikêphóros I.

In the Byzantine World in Constantine Porphyrogenitus's day, St. Demetrius of Thessaloníkê, the next greatest East Roman city in Europe after Constantinople itself, loomed larger than the apostolic patron of the small and outlying city of Pátras. St. Demetrius was a local martyr and, though the death-sentence had, no doubt, been passed and executed by a representative of the Roman Imperial Government in execution of the policy of the vehemently anti-Christian Emperor Galerius, the contemporary pagan majority of the citizens of Thessaloníkê may have approved of the Government's action for all that we know. However, a prophet can perhaps be reconciled posthumously to having been stoned if the descendants of his murderers build him a splendid enough sepulchre and honour him with sufficiently fervent devotion.

---

[1] See the *Chronicle of Monemvasía*, Ivêron MS., lines 73–4.

In any case, when, in the sixth and seventh centuries, Thessaloníkê was exposed to the fury of the Avars' assaults and to the pressure of the Slavs' *Völkerwanderung*, the Thessalonians took it for granted that their fellow citizen whom their ancestors had put to death had made the welfare of his and their city his concern, and they were convinced that their faith in St. Demetrius's unfailing benevolence and efficacy had been vindicated by a series of dramatic miraculous performances of his for their benefit. These incidents, in which Thessaloníkê's patron saint is the hero, are the theme of the *Sancti Demetrii Miracula*, the only surviving source of information for the authentic as well as the legendary history of Thessaloníkê during this critical chapter of the city's and the East Roman Empire's history.

The *Miracula* recount interventions by St. Demetrius not only on behalf of the city that he was believed to have taken under his aegis but also on behalf of individuals—and the first case cited is the saint's cure of an individual who was not even a native Thessalonian but who happened to have been posted by the Imperial Government in St. Demetrius's domain. A senator named Marianós, who was resident at Thessaloníkê because he had been appointed praetorian prefect of the Eastern Illyricum, was prostrated there by a stroke and was then offered help by St. Demetrius in a dream in which the saint appeared to Marianós in the likeness of a Constantinopolitan friend of Marianós's who bore the saint's name. In the dream, 'Demetrius' told Marianós that, if he would visit 'Demetrius's' house, he would be cured. The dreamer then explained, in his dream, to his visitant that he was physically incapable of travelling to Constantinople, and he appealed to St. Demetrius for help. It was then revealed to Marianós that his visitant, in his dream, was not his friend at Constantinople but was the saint on the spot; that his house was the famous church in Thessaloníkê that was dedicated to him; and that 'the imperial city in which St. Demetrius is domiciled is the Heavenly Jerusalem, but that he is not parted from (οὐκ ἀπολιμπάνεται τῆς) Thessaloníkê, his native city in which he grew up'. So the prefect's servants carried their master to the church of St. Demetrius. There Marianós told them to drop him on the floor, and thereupon he was duly healed.[1]

An official in the prefect's office at Thessaloníkê who had likewise fallen ill told his family to carry him to the house of 'the patron (προστάτου) of our city—the chief one'. When he had made them understand his directions, he, too, was carried to the church of St. Demetrius and was healed there.[2]

The author of Book I of the *Miracula* adjures his readers to testify to the truth of a recent performance of St. Demetrius's of which they had

---

[1] *S. D. Miracula*, Book I, chap. 1, cols. 1204–20.
[2] Ibid., Book I, chap. 2, cols. 1220–1.

been his fellow witnesses. When Thessaloníkê had been attacked by the plague, those plague-stricken Thessalonians whom St. Demetrius visited at night recovered, but others did not. Also, nearly all those who recovered took refuge in the saint's church—a sure way, to modern thinking, of catching the infection. One of the suppliants in the church of St. Demetrius had a vision at night. 'He beheld the saint, draped in a khlamýs and displaying a rosy gracious countenance, distributing his favours to the people like some consul to whom the Emperor had delegated plenary powers.'[1] An Imperial official was cured by a healing spring, outside the city, that was dedicated to St. Demetrius;[2] but St. Demetrius has healed not only physical sickness but psychic sickness too.[3]

However, St. Demetrius's most sensational feats were not his miraculous cures of individuals; they were his interventions on behalf of the whole Thessalonian community. He saved his chosen people from famine; he saved them from civil war; and he saved the city of Thessaloníkê itself from being captured by trickery or by surprise or by assault.

In one of the sieges, the Thessalonians were in danger of being starved out. The barbarians who were investing the city had devastated the whole countryside outside the walls, and merchant ships had stopped calling, because of a rumour that the city had fallen. At this critical moment, Stéphanos, the master of a corn-ship freighted with a big cargo destined for Constantinople, had a vision, in full daylight, of St. Demetrius. (He recognized him by his likeness to the representation of him on the eikóns.) St. Demetrius was standing beside Stéphanos on board and was telling him to set his sails for Thessaloníkê. The saint then walked off on the water, ahead of the ship, which was duly making for Thessaloníkê now. Under instructions from the saint, Stéphanos shouted to the masters of other corn-ships to turn back and make for Thessaloníkê, with the result that many corn-ships arrived there.[4]

St. Demetrius also relieved Thessaloníkê during another famine—a recent one that had not been caused by a siege of the city. This was a general famine which was afflicting Constantinople too, and all foodstuffs, not merely corn, were in short supply. St. Demetrius caused ships, heavily laden with food of all kinds, to converge on Thessaloníkê just before the close of the sailing season for the winter. In this case the masters of the ships did not have visions of St. Demetrius, but an official on the staff of the kómês of Ávydhos, who was bound for Khíos to serve as governor of the island, heard a voice in which the speaker identified

---

[1] *S.D. Miracula*, Book I, chap. 3, cols. 1225–32.
[2] Ibid., Book III, chap. 4, col. 1393.   [3] Ibid., Book I, chap. 4.
[4] Ibid., Book I, chap. 8, cols. 1252–3. The author does not tell us which of the sieges of Thessaloníkê was the occasion of this miracle.

himself as Demetrius and gave the ship-masters their new instructions to make for Thessaloníkê. The official who was *en route* for Khíos assumed that the Demetrius who had been speaking was someone of that name on the staff of the praetorian prefect of the Eastern Illyricum whom the prefect had sent on this errand. Accordingly, the new governor of Khíos wrote to the prefect to complain, and to the kómês to censure the prefect for his conduct, and this censure was endorsed by the Emperor. This drew from the prefect letters to the governor of Khíos and to the Emperor informing them that he had not given any orders for diverting the ships and that he did not have anyone named Demetrius on his staff.[1]

St. Demetrius saved Thessaloníkê from the civil war and massacre that became rife, all over the Empire, after the overthrow and murder of the Emperor Maurice in 602. At news of the troubles in the eastern parts of the Empire, feelings ran high in all the cities of Illyricum too—with the one exception of Thessaloníkê. Here St. Demetrius kept the emotional temperature low. A kinsman of the praetorian prefect of the day, who had come to Thessaloníkê on a visit and had paid the call at the church of St. Demetrius which was a customary *devoir* for new arrivals, reported that he had had a vision of St. Demetrius restraining 'Lady Law and Order' (Κυρία Εὐταξία) from taking her departure. In consequence there was not, at Thessaloníkê, any breach of the peace, in spite of a series of provocations in the course of the next two years.[2]

In the sixth and seventh centuries, as in the fourteenth century, domestic strife was particularly dangerous for Thessaloníkê because it threatened to inhibit her people from making a united effort to repel attempts by alien hands to get possession of her.

The first attempt by the barbarians to take Thessaloníkê by assault[3]— the date was probably 586/7[4]—caught the city denuded of defenders. The praetorian prefect of the Eastern Illyricum, his staff, and the élite of the local troops were all absent at the time in Ellás on public duty;[5] others, including the senior officials in the prefect's office, were also absent on a mission to Constantinople;[6] the majority of the inhabitants, military as well as civil, were out in the countryside—it was the vintage season—and could not get back into the city[7] because the enemy took them by surprise by overrunning the forts and estates outside[8] and then investing the city walls at close quarters.[9] Only a small minority of the soldiers and civilians—and these the least fit physically—were inside the walls at the time.[10] The population had also been decimated by the

---

[1] Ibid., Book I, chap. 9, cols. 1256–60.
[2] Ibid., Book I, chap. 10, cols. 1262–9. [3] Ibid., Book I, chaps. 13–14.
[4] See Annex III, p. 635, n. 6. [5] *S.D. Miracula*, Book I, chap. 10, cols. 1292–3.
[6] Col. 1293. [7] Ibid. [8] Col. 1290.
[9] Col. 1293. [10] Ibid.

plague.[1] The Khaqan of the Avars had been informed by deserters of the city's defencelessness.[2]

On the other hand the Khaqan's own forces and armaments were formidable. He had mobilized the whole of the Slav and other barbarian man-power that was subject to him,[3] and he could put these masses to effective use, thanks to the Avars' considerable capacity for organization. The Khaqan had equipped himself with a powerful train of siege engines,[4] serviced by a staff of technicians who knew how to repair them when they were damaged;[5] and he launched a raft with the intention of attacking Thessaloníkê from the harbour as well as from the landward side.[6]

St. Demetrius, however, was more than equal to this almost desperate occasion. Nine or ten days before the date of the barbarians' assault, a vision of the city's patron appeared to Archbishop Efsévios in a dream.[7] When the assault was delivered, the saint appeared on the city walls in the guise of a warrior and speared the first of the assailants who were mounting a scaling ladder.[8] The assailants then panicked.[9] The stream of deserters from the Avar host was so great that they had to be interned in the city's public baths.[10] These deserters declared that the sight which had demoralized them had been the vision of a ruddy ($\pi\nu\rho\rho\acute{a}\kappa\eta\nu$) radiant man mounted on a white horse and clad in a white robe—' "Look, like this one", and the informant seized and exhibited the khlamýs of one of the consulars ($\acute{\nu}\pi\alpha\tau\iota\alpha\nu\hat{\omega}\nu$) who was standing there.'[11] Meanwhile, the enemy's raft broke up while it was being towed into the harbour by a machine,[12] and the shot from the enemy's mangonels failed to hit the city walls.[13] In fact, St. Demetrius had caused this first formidable assault on Thessaloníkê to collapse.

The enemy's next move[14]—this time, made by the Slavs independently —was to try to take Thessaloníkê by surprise, but St. Demetrius out-manœuvred them.[15] He resorted to the self-sacrificing expedient of causing a fire to break out in his own church.[16] He took care on this occasion that the disaster which overtook the church eventually in 1917 should not occur 1,300 years earlier. The whole population of the city came to the rescue, and the fire was extinguished. The problem was to get the people to evacuate the building after the danger was over, and action was taken by an official of the Dacian Desk ($\tau o\hat{v}$ $\Delta\alpha\kappa\iota\kappa o\hat{v}$ $\kappa\alpha\lambda o\nu$-$\mu\acute{e}\nu o\nu$ $\sigma\kappa\rho\iota\nu\acute{\iota}o\nu$)[17] of the praetorian prefecture of the Eastern Illyricum.

[1] Cols. 1293 and 1297. See p. 78.   [2] Col. 1297.   [3] Col. 1285.
[4] Cols. 1300 and 1309.   [5] Col. 1309.   [6] Col. 1304.
[7] Col. 1296.   [8] Cols. 1288–9.   [9] Col. 1289.
[10] Col. 1304.   [11] Col. 1313.   [12] Col. 1304.   [13] Cols. 1310–12.
[14] The date was perhaps after 602, and was anyway after the first siege (see Lemerle, 'Invasions et migrations', p. 295). 'A siege in 612 is recorded in an inscription in the church of St. Demetrius' (Vlasto, op. cit., p. 5).
[15] *S.D. Miracula*, Book I, chap. 12, cols. 1273–81.   [16] Col. 1276.
[17] Ibid. The literal meaning of 'skrínion' is, not 'desk', but 'rolls-case'.

This civil servant gave a false (he believed it to be false) alarm: 'Barbarians round the walls' (Βάρβαροι περὶ τὸ τεῖχος),[1] and the people rushed out of the salvaged church to man the allegedly threatened walls, just as the mendacious civil servant had intended. Thereupon his inspired lie turned out to be the truth after all. From the walls they descried a force of about 5,000 Slavs—a seasoned élite—approaching;[2] so the citizens sallied out and attacked them.[3] The people who were still in the church, clearing up the mess left by the fire and by the fire-fighting, were upset when they heard the sound of fighting. The civil servant then confessed that he had invented the barbarian attack as a trick for clearing the church—whereupon the news was brought to the church that the battle was authentic.[4]

Like this abortive surprise attack, the second siege of Thessaloníkê[5] —the date of this was during Archbishop John's tenure of the see[6]—was made by the Slavs independently. It was a combined operation of the Dhraghouvítai, Saghoudhátai, Veleyezêtai, Vaionêtai, Verzítai, and the rest of the Slav tribes. These Slavs had now taken to the sea for the first time. They had devastated the whole of Thessaly, the islands adjacent to Thessaly and Ellás, the Kykládhes Islands, the whole of Achaïa and Epirus,[7] the greater part of Illyricum, and a portion of Asia,[8] and they planned to sack Thessaloníkê as well.[9] They brought with them their families and property; for their intention was to settle permanently in the city.[10]

The East Roman defenders of Thessaloníkê had no ships for guarding the mouth of the harbour, and the Slavs lashed their dug-out canoes together, decked them with planks, armoured them with hides, and advanced in crescent formation.[11] St. Demetrius retorted by running round the city walls and walking on the sea, clad in his customary white khlamýs.[12] Thereupon, the Slav dug-outs capsized and the crews fought each other for survival. Khátzon, the Slav war-lord, saw an oracle that had been given to him fulfilled in an unexpected way. He had been told by the oracle that he would enter Thessaloníkê, and so he did, but as a prisoner; and his end was tragic. The Thessalonian magnates tried to hide him, but the women dragged him out and stoned him to death.[13]

The third siege of Thessaloníkê[14]—the date of this siege, as well as the date of the previous second siege, was during Archbishop John's tenure

---

[1] Col. 1276.   [2] Col. 1277.   [3] Ibid.   [4] Cols. 1280–1.

[5] Book II, chap. 1, cols. 1325–34. Was this, and not the previous abortive surprise attack, the siege dated 612? Or was it the siege of 614–16? See Vlasto in loc. cit.

[6] Col. 1325.   [7] i.e. the two Roman provinces bearing these names.

[8] i.e. the Roman province called 'Asia'.   [9] Col. 1325.

[10] Col. 1326.   [11] Col. 1328.   [12] Col. 1332.   [13] Cols. 1333–4.

[14] Chap. 2, cols. 1336–45. See also the present work II, 1 (iii) (a), p. 73, and Vlasto, op. cit., p. 5.

of the see[1]—was a more serious affair; for this time the leadership, organization, and equipment were taken in hand by the Avars. As usual, however, St. Demetrius rose to the occasion. The Avaro-Slav blockade was broken by the daily arrival of food-ships, and the masters declared that they had been diverted urgently to Thessaloníkê by a person unknown whom they had taken to be a kankellários. This was, of course, St. Demetrius in action once again.[2] The Khaqan consequently failed to starve Thessaloníkê into surrender, and he also failed to breach its fortifications with his elaborate siege-train.

At some date in the 630s or 640s, Thessaloníkê was in danger of being captured by the insidious infiltration of a disloyal faction of the repatriated descendants of the East Romans whom the Avars had deported to Sirmia.[3] To frustrate this plot, the Imperial Government had ordered the admiral of the Imperial Fleet, Sisínnios, to sail for Thessaloníkê from Ellás. Apparently, neither the Government nor the admiral was aware of the urgency of the admiral's mission. Actually it was touch and go whether Sisínnios would reach Thessaloníkê in time. Sisínnios lingered for three days on the deserted island of Skíathos, waiting for a favourable wind, but St. Demetrius was not caught napping. On the third night, he appeared to Sisínnios in a dream and told him to hurry.[4] Simultaneously, the wind changed, and the fleet reached Thessaloníkê next day.[5] Its arrival was just in time.

About three-quarters of the way through the seventh century—the date was probably 677[6]—the Imperial Government's probably unjustified arrest and execution of the Romanophil Graecized Slav chieftain Pervoúnd provoked Pervoúnd's tribesmen and their Slav neighbours into besieging Thessaloníkê.[7] This time St. Demetrius was on foot when he drove off the Slav assailants.[8] On this occasion the Slavs were less dangerous on land than at sea. Their maritime raids on East Roman shipping were far-ranging, and once again there was a risk that Thessaloníkê might be starved out. The local authorities delayed their request for food-shipments. They had actually been exporting food from Thessaloníkê, and they feared that this misconduct of theirs might be detected.[9] However, the Emperor sent food-ships to Thessaloníkê, unsolicited by the local authorities,[10] but presumably not without having been inspired by St. Demetrius. The local authorities had ventured eventually to ask for 5,000 (? módhioi); the Emperor had sent 60,000.[11]

---

[1] *S.D. Miracula*, Book II, chap. 2, cols. 1336 and 1337.   [2] Col. 1344.
[3] Chap. 5. See also the present work, II, 1 (iii) (a) pp. 74–5.
[4] Col. 1372.   [5] Col. 1373.
[6] This siege, which lasted for two years, culminated in a three days' assault which was launched on 25 July in the fifth indiction. See Lemerle, 'Invasions et migrations', p. 302.
[7] *S.D. Miracula*, Book II, chap. 4, cols. 1340–60. See also the present work, II, 1 (iii) (a), pp. 97–8.   [8] Col. 1352.   [9] Cols. 1357–9.   [10] Col. 1357.   [11] Col. 1360.

It is no wonder that the Thessalonians rejected a request for the saint's body from the Emperor Maurice. Archbishop Efsévios replied that a similar request from the Emperor Justinian I had been rejected. As a sop, some of the dust that had caught the odour of St. Demetrius's sanctity had been sent to Justinian, so Efsévios was sending another pinch of it to Maurice now.[1] The Thessalonians had a strong case for their obduracy. Constantinople's demand for the transfer of Thessaloníkê's saint was characteristic of Constantinople's aggressive egotism. Constantinople had a site which was a natural fortress in itself. She had Theodosius II's triple wall and Anastasius's Long Wall. It was, and was bound to be, the Imperial Government's policy to give Constantinople priority over all the rest of the Empire in the stationing of the Empire's inadequate defence-forces. Thessaloníkê possessed none of these assets. The exemption that she had shared with Constantinople from falling to the barbarians who had overrun the rest of the Empire's dominions in the Balkan Peninsula had been due wholly and solely to her patron St. Demetrius. Her native saint and guardian had been her 'hope and strength, a very present help in trouble'; and now Constantinople was coveting Thessaloníkê's palladium.

Constantinople's demand had invited a rebuff. When Sparta had coveted Tegea's palladium, which was the body of the Mycenaean hero Orestes, she had been more sly, and her cunning had been rewarded by success,[2] like the cunning of the mariners from Bari who in 1087 carried off the body of St. Nikólaos, the patron of the Lycian city of Myra.[3] Neither Sparta nor Bari, however, would have succeeded in filching St. Demetrius's body from Thessaloníkê; for, unlike the bodies of the hero Orestes and of St. Nikólaos, St. Demetrius's body was not passive, 'sicut cadaver'. During one of the sieges of Thessaloníkê by the Avars and/or the Slavs—probably the occasion was the first siege, which was laid to Thessaloníkê when Efsévios was archbishop[4]—the city's plight came to seem so desperate to the powers above that Christ dispatched two angels bearing orders for St. Demetrius to leave his kivórion and come away with them. The saint rejected the divine command. 'For me', was his reply, 'life is not worth having if my fellow-citizens perish.' This scene in the church of St. Demetrius was witnessed, in a vision, by one of the saint's fellow-citizens.[5]

The Thessalonians' belief in St. Demetrius's active concern for their city's salvation carried Thessaloníkê, intact, through the toil and trouble

[1] *S.D. Miracula*, Book I, chap. 5, cols. 1240–1.
[2] See Herodotus, Book I, chaps. 67–8.
[3] In Western Christendom, St. Nikólaos (Sankt Niklaus) has been transformed into 'Father Christmas'.
[4] *S.D. Miracula*, Book I, chap. 14, col. 1296.
[5] Chap. 15, cols. 1320–1.

of the seventh century, when the Imperial Government and Navy were tied down by their primary task of saving Asia Minor and Constantinople, which left them little strength to spare for succouring even the second most important city in the Empire's fast-shrinking European dominions. But Thessaloníkê's tutelary saint was defeated by the Government's and the Navy's culpable failure to defend Thessaloníkê against the Saracen assault in 904—a *coup* of which they had had ample warning in advance. All that St. Demetrius was able to do when his city was overtaken by this disaster was to make an excursion on horseback from his native city[1] in order to intercept, in the Vale of Témbê, some Italian pilgrims who were heading, hitherto unwarned, for the captured city. St. Demetrius gave the melancholy news of his city's fall to the pilgrims' supernatural companion.[2] Thanks to this timely warning, the pilgrims gave Thessaloníkê a miss and travelled, instead, to Constantinople.[3]

However, this lapse did not shake the Thessalonians' faith in their patron. Though in 904 he had failed to save them from the fell swoop of the Saracen corsairs, he had never failed to protect them against the perpetual menace of their permanent Slav neighbours. 'Still, to this day, he checks the impetus of the pernicious Skýthai like a massive unyielding ring-wall. He bars the barbarians' way with his invincible right hand and saves his city inviolate from being overrun by them.'[4]

The Slav settlers in the hinterland of Thessaloníkê had been converted and had gradually been tamed, but St. Demetrius failed the Thessalonians once again when, in August 1185, Thessaloníkê was taken and sacked for the second time by 'children of Hagar'—this time not by Eastern Muslims under the command of an East Roman renegade but by Christian Normans from Sicily, whose ferocity the East Romans stigmatized by applying to them the opprobrious biblical name that had been an appropriate term of abuse for the Muslim Arabs.[5]

---

[1] Τῆς πατρίδος ἐπαναστάς (*S.D. Miracula*, Book III, chap. 3, col. 1392).

[2] This mysterious fellow traveller's name was Akhílleios (col. 1389). He was old and on foot. More than 2,000 years had passed since Odysseus had watched him striding away over a meadow, thick with asphodel, in the abode of the dead. But the pilgrims' vision testifies that in A.D. 904 Achilles was still haunting the Pelasgikon Argos over which he had once reigned. Indeed, this primeval river-god, who had been immortalized in the *Iliad* as a pseudo-historical warrior prince, had secured for himself a second lease of glorious life under the mask of a genuinely historical personage, Akhílleios, the fourth-century bishop of Lárisa, which had been the capital of the Hellenic Greek canton Pelasgiotis. St. Akhílleios's relics were removed by Tsar Samuel of West Bulgaria from Lárisa to his capital, Prespa, when he captured Lárisa in the course of the Romano–Bulgarian war of 976–1018, perhaps in the year 986 (see Kedhrênós, vol. ii, p. 436).

[3] *S.D. Miracula*, Book III, chap. 3, cols. 1388–92. A first-hand account of the capture and sack of Thessaloníkê in 904 by one of the victims, John Kameniátês, is printed in the Bonn edition of *Theoph. Cont.*, pp. 485–600.

[4] *S.D. Miracula*, Book III, chap. 3, cols. 1392–3.

[5] An account of the Normans' capture and sack of Thessaloníkê in 1185 by the city's Archbishop, the famous scholar Efstáthios ('Eustathius'), is printed in the Bonn edition of Leo

The quarter of a millennium of anarchy in the Eastern Orthodox Christian World that set in after the death in 1180 of the Emperor Manuel I Komnênós was brought to an end by the imposition of a *Pax Ottomanica* on all the local contending parties. During this time of troubles St. Demetrius did not save Thessaloníkê, as he had saved her, during the troubles after the overthrow and murder of the Emperor Maurice in 602, from the civil war that had then broken out in all the other cities in the prefecture of the Eastern Illyricum. Thessaloníkê was rent by a savage class-war from 1342 to 1350.[1] The city's definitive occupation by the 'Osmanlis in 1430 may have spelled, for the Thessalonians, a mitigation of their lot, but, for their patron saint, it spelled a greater humiliation than those that he had suffered in 904 and in 1185. In 1495 St. Demetrius's church was converted into a mosque.

It was still a mosque—and also, fortunately for me, still intact,[2] and with fragments of the mosaics re-exposed to view since 1907–8[3]—when I visited it in June 1912. Yet I found that St. Demetrius was not only still present, but was also still potent, in the shrine that, ostensibly, was no longer his. From his tomb, which was in a chapel at the north-west corner of the mosque, with access only through the mosque itself, St. Demetrius was still performing the miraculous cures that had attracted the halt and maimed to this spot for centuries. With sublime benevolence, he now cured Christians and Muslims impartially, and his generosity to the Muslims retained a footing for his co-religionists in his church, even now that it had been turned into a mosque. If the Muslim authorities had deprived their Christian subjects of St. Demetrius's services by refusing them access to the wonder-working tomb, St. Demetrius might have decided that, since he had been prevented from healing Christians, he would refuse to heal Muslims alone, and this was a risk that the Muslims had not dared to take. In the chapel when I entered it, a red-haired little Turkish girl, still too young to feel shy, was playing about among a throng of Christian devotees.[4]

Grammaticus, pp. 362–512. It has been re-edited by S. Kyriakhídês (Palermo, 1961, Istituto Siciliano, Testi, V).

[1] For the 'Zealot' movement and regime at Thessaloníkê, see *C. Med. H.*, vol. iv, 2nd ed., Part I, pp. 358–9 and 361–2; O. Tafrali, *Thessalonique au quatorzième siècle* (Paris, 1913, Geuthner).

[2] This historic building was burned down accidentally in 1917, during the occupation of Thessaloníkê by the Western Allies. It had previously been reconverted into a church after the city had been acquired from Turkey by Greece as a result of the Balkan Wars of 1912–13.

[3] See R. S. Cormack, 'The Mosaic Decorations of S. Demetrios, Thessaloníki: a Re-examination in the Light of the Drawings of W. S. Scorfe (Plates 1–15)', in *The Annual of the British School at Athens*, No. 64 (1969), pp. 17–52.

[4] See also F. W. Hasluck, *Christianity and Islam under the Sultans* (Oxford, 1929, Clarendon Press, 2 vols.), vol. i, pp. 16 and 263–6, for the ritual at St. Demetrius's tomb during the period (1495–1912) during which the saint's church at Thessaloníkê was the Qāsimīyeh mosque (dedicated to the Sixth Imām—perhaps because St. Demetrius's Day, 26 October,

I am not acquainted with the terms which the present-day Thessalonians use in hailing, or speaking of, their city's patron in this sceptical-minded post-Christian age. But I should not be surprised if I found that the traditional language was still being used. Since the transfer of Thessaloníkê from Turkey to Greece in 1912–13, the Thessalonians have had reason to be grateful to St. Demetrius once more. In Greek hands the industry, trade, and population of Thessaloníkê have grown prodigiously, and this increasingly valuable prize has not been lost by Greece. The Bulgars failed to seize Thessaloníkê in 1913, and the occupations of the city by the Western Allies in the First World War and by the Germans in the Second World War were ephemeral. In the realm of religion, popular feelings and beliefs are apt to remain constant through the ages, and I fancy that the language used by the pious seventh-century authors of the *Sancti Demetrii Miracula* would be congenial to all but a sophisticated minority of the saint's twentieth-century fellow-citizens. This language would certainly have been both congenial and familiar to the Greeks of the Hellenic Age. It would fit the tutelary deity or hero of any Hellenic city-state whose patron was masculine, and, transposed into the feminine gender, it would also fit, like a glove, Hellenic Athens's tutelary goddess Athena Prómakhos, alias Athena Poliás.

The appellations and ejaculations by which St. Demetrius is honoured in his *Miracula* illustrate the perennial popular undercurrent of the history of the Greek people's religion. Demetrius is 'the Lord (δεσπότης) of Thessaloníkê'—'next to God',[1] but this reservation, introduced out of courtesy to censorious Eastern Orthodox Christian theologians, is manifestly only perfunctory. 'My Lord (next to God), your grace circumambulates (περιπολοῦσα) the whole district.'[2] 'Him that fighteth for our city, with whole-hearted zeal and fervour, for ever and ever; him who has been allotted, not only to the city but to the whole district, as an invincible wall.'[3] 'The veritable saviour of our city and of our citizens (ὁ σωζο-πολίτης ὄντως)—the victorious athlete (ἀθλοφόρος) of Christ.'[4] 'The guardian (κηδεμών) (after God) of our souls.'[5] 'The succourer of us all.'[6] 'The victorious athlete who shelters us.'[7] 'The Lord (after God) of the city.'[8] 'The victorious athlete's manifold care.'[9] 'In what manifold ways he contrives the salvation of his servitors.'[10] 'The devotee of our city and

happened also to be the Imām Qāsim's Day). The ritual was performed, with the words recited in Greek, for Christian Greek visitors to the tomb, by a Muslim Turkish dervish sacristan. Hasluck quotes, in op. cit., pp. 263–4, the eyewitness account of the ritual given by L. de Launay, *Chez les Grecs de Turquie* (Paris, 1897), pp. 183–4. When I visited the mosque and tomb myself in 1912, I was with Hasluck, and he explained to me the situation there under the Islamic regime.

[1] Col. 1213.
[2] Col. 1216.
[3] Col. 1221.
[4] Ibid.
[5] Col. 1233.
[6] Col. 1244.
[7] Ibid.
[8] Cols. 1245, 1260, 1297.
[9] Col. 1248 bis.
[10] Ibid.

of mankind (ὁ φιλόπολις[1] καὶ φιλάνθρωπος).'[2] 'The common ambassador to God of the whole district; the devotee of the city.'[3] 'The martyr-guarded metropolis of the Thessalonians.'[4] 'The championship of his native city (τῆς πατρικῆς ὥσπερ ἀντιλήψεως).'[5] 'The immunity-giving saviour of his native city (τὸν ἀλεξίκακον σωσίπατριν).'[6] 'This saint-guarded city.'[7] 'Demetrius the saviour of his native city.'[8] 'The saviour of the city.'[9] 'Our redeemer (λυτρωτοῦ ἡμῶν).'[10] 'The patron and redeemer of our city.'[11] 'The guardian of the city.'[12]

This belief in the potency and benevolence of a city's supernatural patron is not surprising in the Dark Age—nearly a quarter of a millennium long—that lasted from the overthrow and murder of the Emperor Maurice in 602 to the renaissance of classical Hellenic culture within the bosom of the East Roman 'establishment' in the reign of Michael III (842–67). Nor is it surprising that, even after that, the unsophisticated majority of a Byzantine city's inhabitants should appeal, atavistically, for supernatural aid when an enemy was at the gates. It is, however, surprising to find one of the founding fathers of the ninth-century renaissance, the scholar-patriarch Phótios himself, animating his distracted fellow Polítai by playing on their superstition and ostensibly sharing it with them. When, in 860, a Rhos flotilla suddenly appeared in Constantinopolitan waters, the Patriarch and the Emperor (who had run the gauntlet in a perilous passage of the Bosphorus on his hasty return from a campaign in Asia)

proceeded together to the church of the Mother of God in Vlakhérnai and there mollified and propitiated τὸ Θεῖον.[13] Then, chanting hymns, they brought out from the church the Theotókos's holy omophórion and dipped the tip of it in the sea. Immediately, calm changed to storm. Winds blew and waves rose. The ships of the ungodly Rhos were smashed. Few escaped.[14]

Whether or not the Rhos flotilla was destroyed by a change of weather that was as sudden as the flotilla's own onslaught had been, it was to be expected that Phótios and Michael would mobilize the spiritual force of superstition. Even if these two representatives of the new enlightenment had their tongues in their cheeks, their resort to the omophórion of the

---

[1] Repeated in cols. 1256, 1262, 1273, 1284, 1320, 1321, 1353–6.
[2] Col. 1253.   [3] Col. 1256.   [4] Col. 1264.   [5] Col. 1277.
[6] Col. 1285.   [7] Col. 1340.   [8] Cols. 1344 and 1353.   [9] Col. 1344.
[10] Col. 1345.   [11] Col. 1376.   [12] Col. 1393.
[13] This is, of course, a resuscitated classical Greek term which, in 860, would not have been familiar to the populace. Its comprehensiveness was, however, as convenient for bracketing God's Mother with God himself as it had been, in the pre-Christian Era, for bracketing the innumerable nameless daimónia with the Olympians and with a pervasive supra-personal divine power that was beyond and above all particular manifestations of divinity.
[14] *Georg. Mon. Cont.*, p. 827; Leo Grammaticus, pp. 241–2; cf. *Theoph. Cont.*, p. 196; pseudo-Symeon, pp. 674–5.

Theotókos was the last card in their hands for rousing the panic-stricken population of Constantinople to fight for its life. It is, however, strange to find Phótios endorsing, retrospectively, his simple-minded flock's belief that their city had been saved by the miraculous intervention of the Theotókos through the instrumentality of an article of attire that was reputed to be a relic from her wardrobe. In the second of his homilies on the deliverance of Constantinople in 860 from the deadly Russian peril, Phótios records that the whole City and he entreated the Mother of God to intercede for them with her Son, to protect ($\pi\rho o a \sigma \pi i \sigma a \iota$) her despairing people, and to do battle on behalf of ($\dot{v}\pi\epsilon\rho\mu\alpha\chi\hat{\eta}\sigma a\iota$) her own flock. They brought the Mother of God's 'wrap' ($\pi\epsilon\rho\iota\beta o\lambda\dot{\eta}v$), and the Godhead ($\tau\dot{o}$ $\Theta\epsilon\hat{\iota}ov$) relented.

This venerated garment ($\sigma\tau o\lambda\dot{\eta}$)[1] is truly the Mother of God's wrap. It made the round of the walls and the enemy mysteriously ($\dot{a}\rho\rho\dot{\eta}\tau\omega$ $\lambda\dot{o}\gamma\omega$) turned tail; the city donned this wrap and the enemy's camp broke up as if it were obeying orders ... The Virgin's garment had no sooner circumambulated the walls than the barbarians abandoned the siege and packed up.[2]

Was Phótios a *croyant* or was he a sceptic? Probably he was both at once—a state of mind which has been common at many different times and places, including Italy in the Age of the Renaissance, though it may be difficult for present-day Western students of the past to enter into it imaginatively.

Alas, $\tau\dot{o}$ $\Theta\epsilon\hat{\iota}ov$, in the form of the Christian pantheon, failed to save East Roman Constantinople in her last agony, as it had failed to save Thessaloníkê in 904 and in 1185. On 29 May 1453, which was the last day of the East Roman Empire's long-drawn-out existence, the report that Constantinople's 'Osmanli assailants had burst their way into the City was the signal for the Polítai to flock into the Great Church. Their mood was not yet one of despair, for they cherished a traditional belief that, if ever the 'Infidels' were to approach the Ayía Sophía, an angel would descend and would annihilate them.[3] The 'Osmanlis were approaching, but the angel did not appear. The Great Church became a mosque, and Constantinople became the capital of the Ottoman Empire.

The reigning religion had changed, but $\tau\dot{o}$ $\Theta\epsilon\hat{\iota}ov$ had not; for the god of the Muslims was identical with the god of the Christians. (This Muslim–Christian god was the god of the Jews.) Thus the same god continued to be the patron of Constantinople, and to be worshipped in the

---

[1] Phótios the neo-Attic stylist avoids using the post-Hellenic word $\dot{\omega}\mu o\phi\dot{o}\rho\iota ov$ ($\mu a\phi\dot{o}\rho\iota ov$ in colloquial language).

[2] Phótios, Fourth Homily, chap. 4 ($\Phi\omega\tau\dot{\iota}ov$ $'O\mu\iota\lambda\dot{\iota}a\iota$, ed. by V. Laoúrdhas (Thessaloníkê, 1959, Etaireía Makedhonikón Spoudhón), p. 45.

[3] See S. Runciman, *The Fall of Constantinople 1453* (Cambridge, 1965, University Press), pp. 134 and 147.

Ayía Sophía, until Mustafā Kemāl Atatürk defused conflicting emotions that had attached themselves to this famous fane by turning it from a place of worship into a museum.

We may conclude that, in the realm of religion, the majority of the Byzantine Greeks was conservative from first to last. Strait-laced Byzantine theologians might hold, as an article of faith, that Byzantine Christendom's breach of continuity with her pre-Christian past was absolute, and these might advertise the intransigence of the stand that they were taking by using the word 'Éllênes' as a synonym for 'pagans'. Sophisticated Hellenists, such as Phótios, might identify themselves consciously with the Byzantine Greek World's pre-Christian past. The majority of the Greek people never took either of these two opposite courses. This majority continued unselfconsciously to satisfy its religious needs and to express its religious feelings in the traditional ways that it had inherited from its Hellenic Greek predecessors and from the Mycenaean Greek and Minoan predecessors of these. The popular religious conservatism that is illustrated by the Byzantine Thessalonians' devotion to St. Demetrius and by the Byzantine Pátrans' devotion to St. Andrew is evidence, not that the Byzantine civilization was exceptionally conservative-minded, but that popular religion is tenacious at all times and places.

(iv) *Proskýnêsis*

The keynote of Hellenic political life had been a hatred of autocracy and a contempt for the servility that an autocrat exacts from his subjects. For the Hellene, everything in autocracy that he abominated had been symbolized in the ceremonial act of *proskýnêsis*, in which a subject acknowledged his servitude to his imperial lord and master by prostrating himself at his feet.[1] For a self-respecting Hellene who found himself in the unfortunate position of having to choose between performing this odious act of *proskýnêsis* and being put to death, it was a point of honour to refuse to purchase life at this unacceptable price.

An instance in which two Lacedaemonians had made this choice when it had been presented to them at the Persian Imperial Court has been recorded by Herodotus.[2] A century and a half later, Alexander the Great had raised a storm in his Hellenic entourage when—fancying himself as the heir of the vanquished Achaemenidae—he had tried to exact the performance of *proskýnêsis* from these Hellenes as well as from the Achaemenid emperors' former subjects. Among the Hellenes who were Alexander's adherents, this ill-considered demand of Alexander's had

---

[1] See pp. 190–1.
[2] Herodotus, Book VII, chaps. 134–7. The Emperor Xerxes secured the *beau rôle* for himself by refusing to put these two defiant Spartans to death, in spite of their provocation.

evoked ridicule, indignation, and disaffection, and they had made it clear to their otherwise admired and beloved leader that, on this point, they were not willing to oblige him. It had not been for this that they had overthrown the Achaemenian imperial regime. On this point, the feelings and opinions of Macedonian Greeks and city-state Greeks had been identical.

When we turn from Arrian's *Alexandri Anabasis* to Constantine Porphyrogenitus's *De Caerimoniis Aulae Byzantinae*, we find that, in this post-Hellenic Greek World, *proskýnêsis* has become an established institution. The Greek word itself has changed colour. Its literal meaning is 'grovelling like a dog at someone's feet', and the word must have originated as a slang term that had expressed Hellenic feelings in being deliberately offensive. By Constantine Porphyrogenitus's time, this opprobrious word has long since been taken seriously and has been adopted into the solemn vocabulary of East Roman Imperial protocol, while the symbolic ceremonial act itself has become an obligatory accompaniment of every phase of Court ritual, whenever a subject has the honour of finding himself in the Imperial presence.

This rite is not waived even in situations in which it is peculiarly unseasonable according to Hellenic and Western ideas. For example, at the state banquet in honour of the Rhos chieftainess Olga, the high-ranking East Roman ladies who had been invited for this occasion had no sooner found themselves in the Imperial presence than they performed *proskýnêsis* as a matter of course.[1] When the Emperor joins the army on campaign and reviews the troops on parade,

the officers dismount, while the Emperor is still quite a long way off, and give the salute, from the commanding officer and the protonotários of the corps down to the tourmárkhai and the dhroungharokómêtes and the merárkhês and the adjutant[2] and the corps's khartoulários and its dhoméstikos. All these officers fall flat on the earth, prostrating themselves (προσκυνοῦντες) in adoration of the Emperor. All the troopers, on the other hand, remain in the saddle.[3]

In general, the nearer to the throne, the greater the obligatory self-abasement. A mitigation was, however, conceded to the loghothétês tou dhrómou at his daily morning business-meetings with the Emperor,[4] and also to other high officials when the Emperor summoned these to appear before him.

When the loghothétês passes the curtain, he throws himself on the floor in adoration (πίπτει ἐπ᾽ ἐδάφους προσκυνῶν) and then goes up to the Emperor

---

[1] See III, 7, p. 504.
[2] Kómês tês kórtês, which means, literally, 'tent-officer' (see Bury, *The Imperial Administrative System*, p. 43).
[3] Constantine Porphyrogenitus, Τὰ Βασιλικὰ Ταξείδια, pp. 482–3.   [4] See p. 194.

straight away. For information: if the loghothétês leaves the room and then comes back, he does not perform *proskýnêsis* this time. For information: anyone holding office or possessing senatorial status who has been summoned by the Emperor to appear before him falls to the ground and performs *proskýnêsis* at his entry, and then retires; but, if the Emperor wants to see him again, this time he does not perform the act when he enters.[1]

(v) Dress, Architecture, and Visual Art

The antithesis between the Byzantine spirit and the Hellenic spirit is expressed in the difference of attitude towards the symbolic physical act of *proskýnêsis*; but the esoteric world of official protocol is not the only sphere in which the same contrast comes out in visual form. It also displays itself in public life in architecture, and in personal life in dress.

In contrast to the Minoan and Mycenaean past, as well as to the Byzantine future, the Hellenic ideal for dress and for architecture had been simplicity and plainness, whereas the Byzantine ideal was complexity and gorgeousness.

A Spartan king and a Seleucid emperor and a Roman princeps had worn the plain clothes worn by commoners; an East Roman courtier— not to speak of an East Roman vasiléfs and avghoústa—wore robes that would not have disgraced a Persian grandee at the Achaemenian or the Sasanian court. The typical Hellenic public building had been an oblong hall in which all the lines had been straight and all the angles, except those of the gable roof, had been right-angles. The result of this is not unlike what a child builds with his toy blocks, as a present-day observer finds when he sees the 'Theseum' at Athens or the Maison Carrée (note the name) at Nîmes or some other public building in the Hellenic style that remains intact. To modern Western eyes an Hellenic building gains in aesthetic value when it has been half ruined (as the Parthenon on the akropolis of Athens has been by the Venetian bomb that blew up the Turkish gun-powder store there in 1687). The modern Westerner appreciates the aesthetic effect of the resulting violent breach in the, to his mind, monotonous regularity of an Hellenic building's lines; and, in this aesthetic judgement, he would probably have had the support of a Byzantine connoisseur. We may infer this from the anti-Hellenic style of the architecture that is one of the visual expressions of the Byzantine spirit. In Byzantine architecture the dominant lines are not straight lines; they are curves; and the characteristic Byzantine form of roof is not a gable; it is a dome. These radical differences of physical shape express differences of mental attitude.

The Hellenic architect had compensated for the dullness of his structure by the exactness of his workmanship. Of course he was not incapable

[1] *De Caer.*, Book II, chap. 1, p. 520.

of building things out of the straight. We rightly marvel at the minute bulges that have been made deliberately in the columns and along the base of the Parthenon to produce the optical illusion of straightness. All the same, the Byzantine architect would have been justified in claiming that he had mastered technical problems that the Hellenic architect had never faced—the problem, for instance, of imposing the round base of a dome on a four-square-shaped space. Conversely, an Hellenic architect would have winced at the shoddiness of Byzantine workmanship —shoddiness, that is, according to the exacting Hellenic standards, though the same Byzantine work would have passed muster with an eighteenth-century Western architect who fancied that he was building in the Hellenic style.

Byzantine architecture does not differ from Hellenic architecture merely in the points of physical shape and technical virtuosity; it differs from it more profoundly in its psychological orientation.

The êthos of Hellenic architecture is what present-day psychologists call 'extrovert'. An Hellenic temple faces outwards towards a public that lives and works and debates and worships in the open air. Such decorations as the austere-minded Hellenic architect allows himself to introduce are all on the outside—columns, metopes, frieze, and the set pieces of sculpture in the gable-pediments. The cella may contain a majestic statue of the god, but—to translate an Hellenic temple into the terms of a Protestant church—the Hellenic place of public worship is neither the chancel nor the nave; it is the churchyard. This belongs to the living; it has not been given over to the dead. Encircling graves would not have hallowed an Hellenic temple; they would have polluted it.

By contrast, Byzantine architecture is 'introvert'. Here it is the interior that is the place of worship. The Byzantine architect has not thrown austerity to the winds; but he has confined it to the outside of his building. This exterior is so plain that it beckons the spectator to enter, in order to see whether, inside, the architect may not have a surprise for him—and indeed he has! On entering, the spectator finds that the girdle of columns which surrounds an Hellenic temple like a grove of trees has been transferred to the interior to simulate a dark forest, while the missing metopes and frieze have been transmuted into mosaics and into colour-patterns made of variegated marble slabs. These brilliant decorations line the Byzantine church's inner walls. They also conceal the roughness of the masonry—a trick that would have incensed an Hellenic architect, though not an eighteenth-century Western one.

The mosaics in the interior of a Byzantine church are characteristic samples of Byzantine art; and this art, whether employed as an adjunct to architecture or presented in independent works, is, like Byzantine architecture itself and like Byzantine dress, the antithesis of the Hellenic style. Hellenic art reflects Hellenic rationalism. It is naturalistic and realistic. (Its naturalism is still apparent; its realism escapes us now that the pictures have perished and the marble substance of the statues has lost its coating of paint.) Byzantine art has not followed Jewish and Islamic art in eschewing the representation of living creatures other than flowers and trees. The issue was raised by the iconoclasts, but it was decided against them eventually, after a struggle that had rent Byzantine society for more than a century. In Byzantine art from 843 onwards, as well as before 726, the human figure played, as it had played in Hellenic art, a very important role; but the aspects of human nature that interest the Byzantine and the Hellenic artist are not the same. The 'extrovert' Hellenic artist is interested primarily in a human being's physical appearance; the 'introvert' Byzantine artist is interested primarily in a human being's spiritual life. In fact, the antithesis between a Hellenic statue and a Byzantine eikón is like the antithesis between a Hellenic temple and a Byzantine church.

Moreover, in the field of representational art, as in that of architecture, the Byzantine craftsman might fairly claim that he has probed deeper than his Hellenic predecessor had ever probed into the mystery of human nature, and that, like the Byzantine architect, he has succeeded in expressing the ineffable by tackling and solving problems that the Hellene had never faced. The portrayal of the human figure in a Byzantine mosaic does not reproduce physical nature, as an Hellenic statue does, but it does bring the human figure to life in a way that is not open for the Hellenic artist working in the Hellenic medium.

If this sounds paradoxical, try the experiment of standing in front of the re-exposed mosaics in the Ayía Sophía and, as you gaze, keep on slightly changing your stance. As you move, the figures seem to move too. You could swear that their eyes are turning and shining and that their garments are rustling. The legendary miracle granted to Pygmalion seems now to be occurring authentically in this utterly un-Hellenic medium. The transfiguration of a realistically-painted naturalistic marble statue into living flesh and blood is something that our visual imagination cannot really envisage; but the Byzantine mosaicist has succeeded in creating the illusion that his jig-saw puzzle has come to life; and, like the Hellenic architect who has made the base of the Parthenon look flat, and its columns look straight, by warping both these architectural members into subtle bulges, the Byzantine mosaicist has achieved his miracle by a piece of deliberate technique. Instead of setting his tesserae dead flat, he has set them at minutely different angles, so that, as we move, we keep on catching different pieces in different lights. Our own movement is thus transferred to them, and it makes them flicker and shimmer. This Byzantine trick is a *chef d'œuvre* of artistic virtuosity.

The deliberateness of the Byzantines' break-away from the Hellenic tradition is as significant as the break-away itself is dramatic. All the antitheses between the two civilizations in all the different spheres at which we have now taken a glance are so many evidences of the Byzantines' ability to innovate, and of their conscious desire to put this gift of theirs into practical effect.[1] The Byzantines reveal in themselves an eager and sensitive receptivity to the outlooks and achievements of alien worlds. The inspiration of their curvilinear architecture comes, probably, from Italy,[2] and the inspiration of their soulful rendering of the human figure possibly from Syria; but the Byzantines have not been just plagiarists. They have borrowed in order to create something new that is distinctively their own. Byzantine mystical experience and architecture and art are not static; they are continually changing and developing.

At the same time, the Byzantine artist could be conservative if he chose. His abandonment of the Hellenic style in most branches of art had not been forced upon him by any loss of mastery over Hellenic technique. For instance, he could still paint in the naturalistic Hellenic style if he wanted to, as he has demonstrated by producing competent works of this kind. The post-Alexandrine Hellenic manner continued, in the Byzantine World, to be in vogue for the decoration of secular buildings where a light touch was desired. Byzantine paintings and mosaics in this Hellenic vein might be mistaken for authentic Hellenic works of art; they are poles apart, in feeling as well as in technique, from contemporary Byzantine mosaic-work in the Byzantines' own grand style.

(vi) *Rhomaic Greek*[3]

The Byzantine Hellenizing artists had their counterparts in the realm of language and literature. The only Greeks, before the twelfth-century satirists, who wrote[4] in the living Greek language of their day were the Bulgarian Crown's Greek employees. The standard literary form of

---

[1] In the sphere of religion, tradition prevailed at the popular level, but at the sophisticated level the Byzantine Greeks' break with their Hellenic Greek past was more acutely conscious and more intransigently deliberate here than in any other sphere of cultural life. It is true that Byzantine theology, once formulated, set hard, but Byzantine mystical experience did not.

[2] See J. M. C. Toynbee in *The Crucible of Christianity* (London, 1969, Thames & Hudson), pp. 172–202.

[3] See J. B. Bury, *A History of the Later Roman Empire* (London, 1889, Macmillan, 2 vols.), vol. ii, chap. 7: 'The Language of the Romaioi of the sixth century', pp. 167–74; Robert Browning, *Medieval and Modern Greek* (London,1969, Hutchinson), pp. 59–72; R. M. Dawkins, 'The Greek language in the Byzantine Period', in N. H. Baynes and H. St. L. B. Moss, *Byzantium* (Oxford, 1948, Clarendon Press), pp. 252–69; C. A. Trypanis, *Medieval and Modern Greek Poetry: an Anthology* (Oxford, 1951, Clarendon Press).

[4] Actually, engraved. The Bulgarian Crown's Greek texts are all official documents inscribed on stone in the eighth, ninth, and tenth centuries. See V. Beševliev, *Die Protobulgarischen Inschriften* (Berlin, 1963, Akademie-Verlag).

Greek was still the Attic *koinē* which was the language of the Septuagint, of the New Testament, and of the liturgy of the Greek-speaking Eastern Orthodox Christian churches. But, from the generation of the Caesar Várdhas and the Patriarch Phótios onwards down to the generation that was overtaken by the crushing disaster of A.D. 1204, there were always some Greek writers to be found who could reproduce the grammar, syntax, vocabulary, and style of the Augustan-Age imitation of fourth-century B.C. Attic Greek. Constantine Porphyrogenitus used this style in the prefaces and other formal passages of his literary works. Constantine himself is only passably good at this literary game; his father, Leo VI, was a more highly accomplished virtuoso; Constantine plumes himself on writing a simple language as a rule;[1] but one of his services to society—a doubtful service, though it is one which even his critics acknowledge[2]—was that he gave a further impetus to the literary renaissance that Várdhas and Phótios had initiated. Perhaps partly thanks to Constantine himself, Constantine had successors in the course of the next quarter of a millennium who did better than he had done in this line. Leo Diaconus (Dhiákonos), Michael Psellós, Anna Comnena (Anna Komnênê), and a series of later Byzantine historians, philosophers, and *littérateurs*, notably the pedantically revolutionary neo-polytheist George Yemistós Plēthon (*circa* 1360–1452), succeeded in writing a neo-Attic that Dionysius of Halicarnassus might not have condemned.

Some ultra-purists (Constantine Porphyrogenitus was not one of these)[3] carried their affectation to the length of excluding even contemporary technical terms[4] and contemporary ethnika from their vocabulary. For 'Serbs' they would write 'Trivalloí'; for 'Slavs' or 'Bulgars' or 'Pechenegs' or 'Ghuzz', 'Skýthai'; for 'Franks', 'Keltoí'; for 'Turks', 'Pérsai', or, with perverse ingenuity, 'Tefkroí'. This affectation grew upon Byzantine men of letters during the miserable quarter of a millennium of East Roman history that ran from A.D. 1204 to 1453. They could at least still put the current names of contemporary nations into Attic Greek fancy dress, though they were fast losing their grip on the Attic Greek grammar and syntax.

---

[1] Preface to *De Caer.*, Book I, p. 5.

[2] See p. 19.

[3] Constantine is, however, an occasional sinner. For instance, he describes Basil I's general Andréas, who won a brilliant victory over the Tarsan Muslims at Podhandós in 878 (see pp. 111, 300, and 318) as ὁ ἐκ Σκυθῶν (*Theoph. Cont.*, Book V, chap. 50, p. 284). Khazar? Magyar? Pecheneg? Bulgar? Slav? Constantine's affectation in this passage has left us in the dark. He has copied the formula from the work of his employee Genesius, but has made it still vaguer than the original. Genesius had written (in his Book IV, p. 115) οὗτος ἐκ Σκυθῶν ἑσπερίων ἐξώρμητο.

[4] Constantine Porphyrogenitus, in his preface to *De Caer.*, Book I, p. 5, claims, with truth, that he has reproduced well-established technical terms (ὀνόμασι τοῖς ἐφ᾽ ἑκάστῳ πράγματι πάλαι προσαρμοσθεῖσι καὶ λεγομένοις).

The temptation to archaïze had not yet presented itself for the writers of the gradually accumulating corpus of Bulgarian and Russian Byzantine literature that was now being written, not in Greek, but in the Macedonian Slavonic dialect that had been given literary form by Constantine-Cyril and Methódhios. The two Thessalonian philologist-missionaries' literary Slavonic was still too recent to have yet become as different from the living Slavonic dialects of the day as Byzantine neo-Attic Greek was from the living Rhomaic.

The breadth of the gulf that had come to divide the living language of Constantine Porphyrogenitus's day from his and his father's and his successors' *koinê'* and from their neo-Attic can be measured in terms of vocabulary. We cannot measure it in terms of grammar and syntax except by inference from the blunders that they have made in trying to write Hellenic Greek;[1] for neither Constantine nor any other Byzantine writer in Greek ever wrote the actual language that he spoke—not even when his literary guards were down[2] and not even when he was trying deliberately to write as he spoke, as the twelfth-century satirists did try.

Constantine's works, and the documents from other hands that have been attached to them—especially, in *De Caerimoniis*, τὰ Βασιλικὰ Ταξείδια, the field-states of the expeditions of 911 and 949 against Crete, and Philótheos's klêtorolóyion—contain, between them, a number of inventories of all kinds of things: official titles and offices; 'changes' (*allaxímata*) of official robes;[3] naval stores;[4] kitchen utensils, table-ware, and bedding;[5] military equipment;[6] industrial tools.[7] This collection of ninth-century and tenth-century Byzantine inventories, in which the objects enumerated are called by the contemporary names for them that were in common use, perhaps runs to a greater length than the aggregate of all inventories in the surviving works of Hellenic literature, including inscriptions. This Byzantine material makes it possible for us to compare the Byzantine Greek vocabulary with the Hellenic, and the comparison indicates that, of the two, the Byzantine is by far the richer, and is also by far the more exotic, in the sense of containing a much greater number of words of non-Greek origin.[8]

---

[1] See R. M. Dawkins in Baynes and Moss, *Byzantium*, pp. 256–62.

[2] Constantine Porphyrogenitus did, at least twice, so far forget himself as to write νερό (*De Adm. Imp.*, chap. 9, p. 777; Τὰ Βασιλικὰ Ταξείδια, p. 446).

[3] For these, see *De Caer.*, *passim*, but particularly Book I, chap. 37, pp. 187–91, and Book II, chap. 41, p. 641. See also p. 371 above.

[4] See *De Caer.*, Book II, chap. 44, pp. 657–61, and chap. 45, pp. 669–77.

[5] See particularly Τὰ Βασιλικὰ Ταξείδια and the accounts of banquets in *De Caer.*, *passim*, and in Philótheos's klêtorolóyion, pp. 740–83 Bonn, 132–79 Bury.

[6] *De Caer.*, Book II, chap. 44, p. 357, and chap. 45, pp. 669–73.

[7] *De Caer.*, Book II, chap. 44, pp. 658–9, and chap. 45, pp. 673–7.

[8] It might be objected that the surviving Byzantine Greek literature happens to contain a proportionately greater amount of inventory-material than the surviving Hellenic Greek literature and that, if we had a corresponding amount of Hellenic inventory-material, we

We cannot identify the provenance of the major part of this huge exotic Byzantine Greek vocabulary. Our ignorance of this is brought home to us by names of articles of official attire that occur, hundreds of times over, in Constantine's *De Caerimoniis*. Among the commonest are 'skaramángion', 'kameláfkion', 'dhivitěsion' (διβητήσιον), 'dzidzákion' (τζιτζάκιον). Out of these ubiquitous four, only the last-mentioned, 'dzidzákion', is plain sailing. 'Dzidzákion' is a Greek version of the Turkish word 'chichék'; the meaning of this word is 'flower'; and we happen to know where this word came from, and who brought it. It was brought to Constantinople from Khazaria by the East Roman Emperor Constantine V's Khazar bride. Her pet name, in Khazar Turkish, was 'the flower', and the East Roman Court was so taken with this foreign avghoústa's native costume that they adopted it as an additional article of East Roman masculine ceremonial dress and labelled it with the name of the lady who had first made them acquainted with it. Here we have an illuminating fragment of cultural history; and, if we were equally well informed about all the other foreign loan-words in Byzantine Greek, we should have a wealth of information about the East Roman Empire's cultural contacts with other parts of the World.

Unfortunately, our knowledge of the word 'dzidzákion's' history is exceptional. When we come to the word 'dhivitěsion', we may perhaps guess—but this is a guess which cannot be verified—that it is a transliteration of a hypothetical Latin word 'divitense' and that its literal meaning is 'a rich man's outfit'. Actually, the 'dhivitěsion' seems to have been rather less grand a robe than the 'skaramángion', but that would not rule out the Latin derivation here suggested for the word. As for 'kameláfkion', we know that this was originally some kind of a hat and that it turned into some kind of a canopy, but its derivation is an enigma; and so is the derivation of 'skaramángion', though the 'skaramángion' was the standard robe of state at the East Roman Court in the reigns of Constantine Porphyrogenitus and his father, Leo VI.

It is tantalizing that so much of the information latent in the Byzantine Greek technical vocabulary eludes us. However, the very existence of this vocabulary, and the vast size of it, inform us that, during the time (perhaps a long span of time) during which it was being adopted, the prevailing Byzantine attitude towards alien apparatus of all kinds must have been receptive, and that the pedantry of the ultra-Atticist Byzantine men of letters cannot have been characteristic of Byzantine society as a whole. The readiness of ships' chandlers, military commissaries, chefs,

should find that the Hellenic Greek vocabulary was richer than the surviving evidence for it suggests. This objection is not borne out, however, by the contents of such Hellenic inventories as we do possess. For instance, there is nothing very exotic in the inventory of the gifts given to the sanctuary at Delos by distinguished visitors (Dittenberger, *Sylloge*, 2nd ed., vol. ii, No. 588, pp. 320–46).

and valets to adopt foreign gadgets and to call these by their foreign names could, no doubt, be discounted by the pedants. What else, the pedants might protest, could be expected of such vulgar folk? But what could the pedants say when the same vulgarity was being exhibited by the Emperor's household? Did not the Imperial household call itself the 'Kouvoúkleion'? It seemed actually to take pride in this horrid Latin label.

Moreover, the stage directions for the performance of official cere-monies, which constitute the bulk of the Emperor Constantine's *De Caerimoniis*, are crammed full of the most outlandish vulgarisms. Yet the Imperial master of ceremonies (ὁ ἐπὶ τῆς καταστάσεως) must have been aware of what he was doing when he allowed the Court, from the Emperor downwards, to take to wearing the barbaric costumes that bore these even more barbaric names, and Constantine himself shows no symptoms of distress while he is copying out these long-winded directions *in extenso*. When the East Roman Court was as unashamedly addicted to innovation as this, how could the Byzantine World be convicted of being conservative? The Court had a better claim than purist writers to speak for Byzantine society.

Nor was it only in its vocabulary that Byzantine Greek had left Hellenic Greek behind. The transformation of the Greek language had gone far deeper than that. The pronunciation had been changing,[1] and so had the structure. Like other languages of the Indo-European family, Greek had been becoming less inflexional and more analytical in its structure, and at the same time its original pitch accent had been changing into the stress accent of Byzantine and of present-day Greek. This change in the nature of the accent had been awkward for Greek poets. These had been composing in quantitative verse since time immemorial, or at least since the time of the precursors of the authors of the *Iliad* and the *Odyssey*, and the earliest of these precursors may have been composing their poetry before the end of the Mycenaean Age. Moreover, much of the Hellenic Greek quantitative poetry is superb, and its prestige has been even more than proportionate to its genuine greatness.

---

[1] The transliteration of Latin words into the Greek alphabet in the libretti of official chants (see pp. 572–4) shows that, in the tenth century, the phonetic values of the letters of the alphabet, as well as the accentuation, were already what they are today. These phonetic changes had, indeed, already taken place by the beginning of the ninth century. This is revealed in the colloquial Greek inscriptions, dating from the first half of the ninth century, at Pliska, near Aboba, which was then the capital of Bulgaria, and at other places in Bulgarian territory (see p. 359). In these inscriptions the contemporary spoken Greek language had been written phonetically by people who were evidently entirely ignorant of the Attic *koinē*, and who therefore wrote the living language just as they spoke it and heard it spoken, with no archaistic distortions. A study of the language of these inscriptions 'shows that it presents (*darstellt*) the living vulgar tongue (*Volkssprache*), that was spoken at the time—the last step from the old *koinē* to Modern Greek' (Beševliev, op. cit., *Einleitung*, pp. 26–7).

We do not know who was the first Greek poet who had the courage to take practical account of the change in the nature of the Greek accent by composing in accentual verse in the living language of his own generation.[1] We may guess that he did not arise till long after this change in the temperament and structure of the Greek language had become an accomplished fact. We may also guess that his courage was the audacity of ignorance. We may guess, that is to say, that he was not well enough educated to be aware that he was committing a literary enormity. Since this new-fangled accentual verse bore the name 'Constantinopolitan' (στίχοι πολιτικοί),[2] we may also guess that this innovation was the work of the Imperial capital's urban proletariat. The earliest surviving specimen of it—ἰδὲ τὸ ἔαρ τὸ γλυκύ—looks, in fact, like a popular song, and it is on record that it was sung by the Blues and Greens, with the two 'demes' first singing alternate lines[3] and then repeating the performance in massed choir,[4] as part of the prescribed proceedings in the Hippodrome at Constantinople on the occasion of the Loupérkal festival. Bury dates the composition of this spring song at least as early as the reign of Michael III (*imperabat* 842–67).[5]

There were post-sixth-century Byzantine Greek poets who continued to write Hellenic Greek verse, as there were post-sixth-century Byzantine artists who continued to paint pictures and compose mosaics in the post-Alexandrine Hellenic style. With the exercise of a little ingenuity, it was possible to write verse that could be read either quantitatively as iambics or accentually as scazons. This was a favourite Byzantine literary exercise. Such compromises between the living present and the dead past are natural when the past continues to have prestige. Considering the immensity of the prestige of the Hellenic Greek literature and language, it is remarkable, not that the Byzantine Greeks should have practised linguistic and literary archaism, but that, side by side with this, they should have created a new accentual poetry in the living language of their day. If the literary merit of this Modern Greek poetry has received less generous recognition than it deserves, this is because it has had the misfortune to be overshadowed by its tactlessly immortal Hellenic predecessor.

[1] Accentual verse written, not in the contemporary form of living Greek, but in the *koinē*, was produced, from the fourth century onwards, by the Christian Greek hymnographers, the greatest of whom is the sixth-century Syrian Rhomanós the melodhós.

[2] See p. 201.

[3] *De Caer.*, Book I, chap. 72, p. 366.

[4] Ibid., p. 367. In the third line, as this is cited there, the word βασιλεῦσι does not scan. We may infer that τῷ βασιλεῖ, not τοῖς βασιλεῦσι, appeared at this place in the original version, and that the song was composed at a date at which there was only one Emperor on the throne. When there were more Emperors than one, metre had to be sacrificed to protocol.

[5] J. B. Bury, 'The Ceremonial Book of Constantine Porphyrogenitus', second instalment, in *The English Historical Review*, July 1907, pp. 417–39, on p. 435.

(vii) *East Roman Latin*

In the tenth century a knowledge of Latin was as rare in the Byzantine World as a knowledge of Greek was in the contemporary West. If any tenth-century Byzantine intellectual might have been expected to have acquired a mastery of Latin, it would have been Constantine Porphyrogenitus; for Constantine was both a scholar and a statesman, and, in both capacities, he would have found a knowledge of Latin useful to him. However, Constantine's Latin was poorer than Liutprand's smattering of Greek, of which Liutprand was so proud. Constantine communicated with Latin-speaking Liutprand through an interpreter,[1] and, every time that Constantine undertakes to interpret a Latin word himself, he betrays his ignorance.

He thinks, for instance, that the Latin original of the name 'Optimátoi' means, not an élite, but just the reverse[2] (his Greek translation of 'Optimátoi' is ἄτιμοι).[3] He says that the Opsíkion army-corps, whose name is a transliteration of the Latin word 'obsequium', means a military force that marches *ahead* of the Emperor,[4] whereas it really means a force that follows at his heels. Constantine derives the place-name Pombeió-polis from the Greek common noun πομπή,[5] which makes the reader wonder whether Constantine had ever heard of the world-famous Roman war-lord who had named the place after himself. He derives the word 'indictio' from the place-name Actium.[6] He says[7] that the Dalmatian city Diadora (the present-day Zara) is called 'iam era' in Latin, and he notes, that 'iam era[t]' means 'already was (ἀπάρτι ἦτον)'.

Here, at least, poor Constantine has atoned for a fantastic etymology by, for once, translating a pair of Latin words correctly.[8] The compiler of the 'lexicon' of non-Greek words used in the libretto of the 'Ghotthikón' mime[9] has done better. Out of the twenty-three words on his list, he has given correct translations of twelve words that are recognizably Latin; but the 'alternative interpretation',[10] in which each word is classified as being either Latin or Hebrew, is almost all sheer nonsense.

The Latin language is still called 'the language of the Romans' (ἡ Ῥωμαίων διάλεκτος) or 'Roman' (Ῥωμαῖστί) by Constantine Por-

---

[1] Liutprand, *Antapodosis*, Book VI, chap. 9.

[2] See J. B. Bury, *The Imperial Administrative System in the Ninth Century*, pp. 66–7.

[3] *De Them.*, p. 26. Constantine knows that, in his day, the 'Optimátoi' corps is a non-combatant unit that ranks below the combatant thémata (see II, 4, Appendix, pp. 270–3). He jumps to the conclusion that the inferiority of the present status of the Optimátoi is indicated by the meaning of their name. Constantine thus convicts himself of being ignorant of the meaning of the Latin word 'optimus'.   [4] Op. cit., p. 24.

[5] Op. cit., p. 30.   [6] Op. cit., p. 55.   [7] In *De Adm. Imp.*, chap. 29, p. 139.

[8] Constantine also reproduces correctly the traditional etymology of the Roman cognomen 'Caesar' (*De Them.*, Book I, p. 32).

[9] *De Caer.*, Book I, chap. 38, pp. 384–5.   [10] Ibid., pp. 385–6.

phyrogenitus and his sources. But the Romans of whom Constantine was the Emperor (βασιλεὺς Ῥωμαίων) did not speak Latin; they spoke Greek. All the same, they were, in their own eyes, the only true Romans extant;[1] and, in present-day Greek, 'Romans' (Ῥωμαῖοι) means Greeks and 'the Roman language' (Ῥωμαϊκά) means post-Hellenic Greek as it is spoken by Greeks, whose mother-tongue it is, when they are not self-consciously Hellenizing. In the tenth century the words were being used already in the modern sense as well as in the original meaning. In 924, when the Emperor Rhomanós I Lekapênós and the Bulgarian Khan (as he then still was) Symeon met for a peace-talk on the shore of the Golden Horn, just outside the land-walls of Constantinople, Symeon's guardsmen hailed him as Emperor 'in the language of the Romans' (τῇ τῶν Ῥωμαίων φωνῇ).[2] The non-Bulgarian language that the Bulgars were now talking can only have been Greek.

Indeed, Latin was a virtually unknown language in the tenth-century Byzantine World east of the Straits of Ótranto; and, even at the time when it had been current in Greek-speaking lands, there had always been a psychological resistance to it. A Hellenic Greek's attitude to Latin had been like a Frenchman's attitude to English. However rich and powerful the speakers of a barbarous language might become, that could not avail to turn that barbarous language into a cultivated one. In the second

---

[1] This claim seemed as preposterous to medieval Westerners as the assumption of the title 'Emperor' by Germans, from Charlemagne onwards, seemed to medieval Greeks. Both pretensions were easy targets for satire, and the East Roman Imperial Government's relations both with Charlemagne and his Imperial successors and with the Roman See were exacerbated, time and again, by irrelevant and childish disputes on points of protocol. The Westerners demurred to the Greeks styling themselves Romans. They felt this to be ridiculous and they found it annoying.

Pope Nicholas I (858–67) wrote to the Emperor Michael III: 'iam vero, si ideo linguam [Latinam] barbaricam dicitis, quoniam illam non intellegitis, vos considerate, quia ridiculum est vos appellari Romanorum imperatores et tamen linguam non nosse Romanam—quiescite igitur vos Romanos nuncupare imperatores' (Mansi xv, 187, cited by Zilliacus, *Zum Kampf der Weltsprachen im Oströmischen Reich* (Helsingfors, 1935, Mercators Tryckeri), p. 38).

The Greeks, for their part, found it equally annoying, as well as ridiculous, that a German 'kinglet' (ῥῆξ) should style himself 'Emperor'. Even in the critical years 869–71, when it was an imperative common interest of the East Roman Empire and the Carolingian Empire that they should co-operate to prevent the Western Muslims from making themselves masters of south-eastern Italy, Basil I and Lewis II wrangled over questions of style and title. Basil appears to have rebuked Lewis, in a letter that is no longer extant, for having styled himself 'vasiléfs'; for there is a surviving letter from Lewis to Basil, maintaining that he is as authentic an emperor as Basil, and pointing out that the Greek word 'vasiléfs' really means merely 'king' (see James Bryce, *The Holy Roman Empire* (7th ed., London, 1884, Macmillan), pp. 190–1, and, for the correspondence, Canard in Vasiliev, *Byzance et les Arabes*, ii, I, pp. 16–21). A century later, Otto I's ambassador Bishop Liutprand was outraged when Nikêphóros I's brother Leo styled Otto, not βασιλέα, but ῥῆγα, and when afterwards Nikêphóros himself twice called Otto's assumption of the title 'emperor' scandalous (Liutprand, *Legatio*, chaps. 2 and 25).

[2] *Georg. Mon. Cont.*, joint reign of Constantine VII and Rhomanós I, chap. 20, p. 900; Leo Grammaticus, p. 311; *Theoph. Cont.*, Book VI, Reign of Rhomanós I, chap. 15, p. 407; pseudo-Symeon Magister, chap. 29, p. 737; Kedhrênós, vol. ii, p. 305.

century of the Principate, when eminent Greeks who were Roman citizens were at last being made senators and governors of provinces, they must have acquired the minimum of Latin without which they could not have qualified for a Roman official career; but, if they were also men of letters, as Arrian and Dio Cassius were, they wrote, as a matter of course, in Greek for the Greek-reading public. In this they were following the practice of all their predecessors ever since the third century B.C., the century in which Rome had made her first impact on the Greeks' consciousness. Timaeus had paid due attention to Rome's rise; Polybius had made Rome's conquest of the western end of the civilized world the theme of his universal history. But these Greek historians had written about Rome in Greek, and for Greeks, as a matter of course.

The Romans' attitude towards the Greek language during those same centuries had been more complex. The Romans had been oppressively conscious that their native language was not a match for Greek. Since the generation of Alexander the Great, Greek had been a world language, whereas Latin, in the third century B.C., had not yet become a lingua franca even for Italy. Before Alexander's day, the Greek genius had made the Greek language the vehicle of a literature which, down to our own day, has never been surpassed. In face of these irreversible accomplished facts, the Romans had reacted to the Greek language in different ways on different planes of action.

Since they had established their military ascendancy progressively over the whole Hellenic and Hellenized World as far east as the west bank of the Euphrates, the Romans had insisted on using Latin as their official medium of communication in international relations. For instance, in 191 B.C., at Athens, Cato the Censor had deliberately addressed his Greek audience in Latin, and had had his speech translated into Greek,[1] though by that date Cato had already known Greek well enough to have spoken in Greek if he had not been concerned for the prestige of the national language of the great power whose official representative he then was. In 167 B.C. at Amphipolis, L. Aemilius Paullus, in his turn, had deliberately spoken in Latin when he was announcing the terms of the settlement that Rome was imposing on Macedon and on the rest of Greece,[2] but his words had been translated into Greek by a Roman member of his staff,[3] and Paullus, like Cato, could, no doubt, have spoken in Greek himself if he had chosen. Paullus was an overt connoisseur of Hellenic culture. After his victory at Pydna, in which he had overthrown the Kingdom of Macedon—the last surviving Greek great power —Paullus had made a tour of the famous sites and monuments of Southern

---

[1] Plutarch, *Cato Major*, chap. 12.
[2] Livy, Book XLV, chap. 29.
[3] Cn. Octavius, one of the praetors for 168 B.C.

Greece, and the only piece of the Macedonian spoils that he had taken for himself and his family had been the library of the defeated and dethroned King Perseus.[1]

Cato, in later life, had retreated from his earlier pose of Hellenophobia and had capitulated to Hellenic culture; and indeed all educated Romans had been Philhellenes on the cultural plane from the third century B.C. to the third century of the Christian Era. During those centuries, educated Romans had been bilingual. They had learnt to read, speak, and write Greek as fluently as in the eighteenth century an educated German or Englishman read and spoke and wrote French. Cicero's letters testify that Cicero was thinking in Greek as well as in Latin. As he writes or dictates, Greek phrases keep on welling up into the flow of Cicero's Latin. The earliest Roman men of letters who had published any works had written, not in even a Graecized Latin, but in Greek itself, and this for the same reason as their Greek contemporaries. These earliest Roman authors had been historians, and their objective had been to bring Rome, and Rome's achievements, within the horizon of the great Greek-reading public. In the third and second centuries B.C., this had been the only public of any consequence anywhere at the western end of the civilized world. The Romans had not waited long, after the beginning of their encounter with the Hellenic World, before they had started to create a literature in Latin on the Hellenic pattern; but this audacious Roman Hellenic literature in Latin dress had not ripened till the last century B.C., and, after that, it had had still to wait for the emergence of a Latin-reading public that could compete with the Greek-reading public in numbers and intellectual calibre.

Thus, for about five centuries ending in the third century of the Christian Era, Rome, her citizens, and her dominions had been incorporated in the Hellenic oikoumenê culturally; conversely, in the second century, the Greek-speaking majority of Rome's subjects and citizens had reconciled themselves, at last, to the long since accomplished fact that the Hellenic World, to the west of the Euphrates, had been given, in the Roman Empire, the political unity which the Greeks had never succeeded in establishing for themselves. This tardy but sincere concordat between Hellenism and Romanism is proclaimed in Greek, by a Greek representative of the Second Sophistic, in Aelius Aristeides's *In Romam*. The reconciling idea is that the Roman world-state has enabled the Hellenic civilization to fulfil its vocation of providing the World with an ecumenical culture. According to this concept, the ideal Roman citizen must be bilingual if his mother-tongue is Greek as well as if it is Latin. He must know Greek in order to participate in the World's cultural life (this goes without saying), but he must also know Latin in order to participate in

[1] Isidore of Seville: *Etymologiae*, Book VI, chap. 5, § 1.

the World's government. Greek is the key to culture; Latin is the key to power.[1]

Bilingualism was necessary because, in the world in which Greek-speakers and Latin-speakers had met each other, there had been not just some things that could be said only in Greek; there had also been some that could be said only in Latin—for instance, Roman military words of command and Roman legal formulas.[2] In all her dominions, including those in which Greek was the local population's mother-tongue or lingua franca, Rome had imposed the use of Latin, not in private life, but in public administration.[3] Yet in those provinces of the Roman Empire in which Greek was the native language or the current lingua franca, the use of Latin for Roman official purposes had been kept down to a minimum—and these had been the provinces that had contained a majority of the Empire's population and that had provided the major part of its industrial production and its commercial activity. The Emperor's secretariat had corresponded in Greek with the Empire's Greek-speaking subjects and citizens.[4] *A fortiori*, the Roman administrative staffs in the Empire's Greek-speaking provinces must have done the same. During these centuries, almost as much Greek had been spoken as Latin in the City of Rome itself. This latterday political capital of the Hellenic World had become virtually a Hellenic city of the same post-Alexandrine type as Alexandria-on-Nile and Antioch-on-Orontes. Moreover, to the west of Rome, the western bounds of the Hellenic oikoumenê had become conterminous with the western frontier of the Roman Empire. The Emperor Hadrian (A.D. 117–38) had been a native of Italica—a Roman colony in south-western Spain, not far distant from World's End at the shore of the boundless Ocean. Yet Hadrian's spiritual home had been the Hellenic World of his day.

Thus, till the third century of the Christian Era, the imposition of Roman rule on Greek-speaking populations had not brought with it, for them, more than a perfunctory and superficial imposition of the Latin language. When, in and after the later decades of the third century, an attempt had been made to extend the use of Latin among the Empire's Greek-speaking citizens, the Romans who had made this aggressive new departure in the Imperial Government's linguistic policy had not been the original Romans of Latium or even the Romans of the vaster ager Romanus of Augustus's day. They had been Illyrian Romans whose

---

[1] See G. Dagron, 'Aux origines de la civilisation byzantine: langue de culture et langue d'État', in *Revue Historique*, 93ᵉ année, tome ccxli (1969), pp. 23–56, on pp. 25–6.

[2] Dagron, in loc. cit., p. 24.

[3] Dagron, in loc. cit., pp 24–5 corrects, on this point, St. Augustine's statement in *De Civitate Dei*, Book XIX, chap. 7.

[4] Dagron, in loc. cit., p. 38. In the Imperial Chancery there was a section 'Ab Epistulis Graecis'.

school had been the Roman Army. These Illyrian Roman soldiers had been proud of the education, such as it was, that they had acquired in the ranks through the medium of Latin, which was the Roman Army's language. Their education might have seemed rudimentary, and their Latin uncouth, to the Emperor Gallienus (253–68), not to speak of the Emperor Hadrian. Yet this had been all the culture that the Illyrians had been able to acquire, and they would have been as unwilling to talk Greek as Cato the Censor had once been (even supposing that the Illyrians could have talked it, as Cato could, but they could not).[1]

Accordingly, the Latin-speaking Illyrian Emperors who had re-habilitated the Roman Empire after its collapse in the third century had made it their policy to extend the use of Latin in the Empire's Levantine provinces in which Greek had long since become the mother tongue, or at least the lingua franca, of the population. The Illyrian Emperors had sought to make Latin the language of the coinage of all denominations, as well as of the public administration, the law, and the army[2] throughout the Empire.[3] The Emperor Constantine I (306–37), whose family was of Dardanian Illyrian origin, had sought deliberately to Latinize the Levantine provinces of the Empire.[4] At the Council of Nicaea (325), the first of the ecumenical councils of the Christian Church, Constantine had behaved like Cato the Censor at Athens in 191 B.C. and like Paullus at Amphipolis in 167 B.C. He had spoken in Latin, and had had his speech translated into Greek by an interpreter.[5] The Emperor Valens (364–78), another Illyrian, had been ignorant of Greek.[6]

The Emperor Julian (361–3) was an Illyrian too. He was a relative of Constantine I. Julian, however, had been given a very thorough Hellenic education in Asia Minor by a conscientious and congenial tutor, and consequently he had reacted against both the Latin language and the Christian religion. Julian had been the one Roman Emperor of Illyrian

[1] At any rate, most of the Illyrian *novi homines* of the first generation could not speak Greek. Constantine I was in the second generation, and Julian in the third generation, of an Illyrian family that had risen to the political summit.

[2] For the application of this policy to the Army, see Zilliacus, op. cit., p. 128.

[3] Op. cit., p. 14.

[4] Zilliacus, op. cit., pp. 17, 23, 23 n. 1, 128. 'Cette tendance devient avec Constantin une politique' (Dagron in loc. cit., p. 38). After the overthrow of Licinius, eventually 'le latin est imposé a l'armée, l'Orient sera romain, le latin seule langue officielle'. All Constantine's speeches and official letters were in Latin (Dagron, p. 39, citing Eusebius, *Vita Constantini*, IV, 19 and 32; Philostorgius, II, 9).

[5] Zilliacus, op. cit., p. 23, with n. 1, citing Eusebius and Sozomen. Dagron, however, in loc. cit., p. 37, points out that Constantine I knew Greek and could speak it when he chose. Constantine at Nicaea (Níkaia) in 325, and Marcian at Chalcedon in 451, delivered his opening address to the Council (at the sixth session, in Marcian's case) in Latin, and then took part in debates in Greek (Dagron in loc. cit., pp. 36 and 48).

[6] Zilliacus, op. cit., p. 24, citing Themistius, XI, p. 144 Dindorf. Dagron, in loc. cit., p. 37, maintains that Valens was an exceptional case.

origin who was an ardent Hellenist,[1] and his religious and literary Hellenism had won for him the support of the Antiochene man of letters Libanius (Livánios) (314–post 391),[2] who had campaigned against the policy of Latinization.[3] However, the extant inscriptions indicate that there was a reversion to the Latinizing policy after the brief interlude of Julian's reign,[4] and Libanius had a contemporary and fellow-citizen, Ammianus Marcellinus (died later than 390) who is one of the greatest of all the historians who have written in Latin. This was a portent in a Greek; but Ammianus, as he himself tells us, was also a soldier,[5] and Latin was the language of the Roman Army—though Ammianus's Latin is more akin to Tacitus's than to the Illyrians'. A still greater portent was the Latin poetry of another Greek, Claudian of Alexandria (*floruit c.* 400). Ammianus's and Claudian's works register the high-water mark of the Latin language's penetration of the Hellenic World; for these two Greeks had not been writing under military orders. They had adopted Latin voluntarily as their medium of expression.

It has been pointed out by Zilliacus[6] that the foundation of Constantinople had been a challenge to Hellenism because 'it signified the transplantation of the Roman central administration and the Roman ideology on to Greek ground'. For the first quarter of a millennium of its history, Constantinople had been a bilingual city. The survival of the Greek language there had been assured by the excellence of the new capital's maritime communications with the Greek-speaking world, and, overland, by the proximity of Asia Minor, where the supplanting of the pre-Greek languages by Greek had been completed before the close of the sixth century. The Emperor Arcadius (395–408) had given Greek equal status with Latin at Constantinople in the law-courts.[7] However,

---

[1] According to Eutropius, X, 16, Julian was more at home with Greek than with Latin.

[2] See *Libanius' Autobiography (Oration 1)*, ed. and tr. by A. F. Norman (London, 1965, Oxford University Press).

[3] Zilliacus, op. cit., p. 81. Dagron, in loc. cit., pp. 27–8, maintains that Libanius and other fourth-century champions of Hellenism, e.g. Eunapius, were opposed, not to the official use of Latin in the Greek-speaking parts of the Empire, but to the spread of Latin, in place of Greek, studies there. He notes that the Christian Hellenist, Gregory of Nyssa (Ep. xiv, §§ 6 and 9 (written *circa* 380), in Jaeger's edition of Gregory of Nyssa's works, vol. viii, Part II, pp. 46–8) blames a student who has deserted Greek studies for Latin. Champions of Hellenism condemned this practice as being illiberal and mercenary. It is true that a mastery of the Latin language and of Roman law was, in the fourth century, a necessary qualification for entry into the Imperial public service (see Dagron in loc. cit., p. 40); and a Greek-speaking Roman citizen who declined to study Latin in that age would have been debarring himself from participation in the government of the Empire. Dagron, ibid., pp. 28–9, is no doubt correct in holding that Libanius and Eunapius were not politically disaffected.

[4] Zilliacus, op. cit., pp. 24, 41, 42.

[5] 'Haec ut miles quondam et Graecus'—Ammianus, Book XXXI, chap. 16, § 9.

[6] Zilliacus, op. cit., p. 15. Dagron, in loc. cit., p. 26, agrees on this point with Zilliacus, though, in general, he is critical of Zilliacus's treatment of his subject.

[7] Zilliacus, op. cit., p. 24; and Dagron in loc. cit., pp. 40–1, quoting *Cod. Just.* VII, 45, 12

the rival Latin language, though intrusive, was able to hold its own, side by side with Greek.

The Spanish Emperor Theodosius I (378–95) had carved a bilingual inscription on the base of the obelisk in the Hippodrome,[1] and a Latin couplet, arraigning his unsuccessful rival Maximus, above the Golden Gate.[2] All the surviving inscriptions of the Emperor Arcadius (395–408) are in Latin, except for a single one that is bilingual.[3] Theodosius II (408–50) had carved a bilingual inscription on the triple wall with which he had fortified Constantinople on the landward side.[4] In Theodosius II's reign, a Greek or Hellenized Egyptian named Cyrus, who held simultaneously the two offices of praefectus urbi for Constantinople and praefectus praetorio for the Eastern Illyricum, had broken with official tradition by giving his decisions, not in Latin, but in Greek,[5] and, by the end of Theodosius II's reign, Latin had ceased to be regularly in use at the Constantinopolitan Imperial Court.[6] In the university that Theodosius II had founded at Constantinople, mainly with a view to education for the civil service and for the law, he had allocated salaries for fifteen Latin-language professors as well as for sixteen Greek-language professors.[7] Yet in the middle decades of the sixth century a knowledge of Latin had still been an obligatory qualification for entry into the Imperial civil service.[8] The Emperor Justinian I (527–65) had promulgated in Latin those of his novels that dealt with the administration of

and 77. Yet 'jusqu'au viᵉ siècle, le protocole des actes juridiques, à tous les niveaux et dans toutes les provinces, est rédigé en latin' (Dagron, loc. cit., p. 39).

[1] *Corpus Inscriptionum Latinarum* (hereinafter *C.I.L.*), iii, 737; Dessau, *Inscriptiones Latinae Selectae*, 82.

[2] *C.I.L.*, iii, 736.

[3] Zilliacus, op. cit., pp. 43–4. This is remarkable in view of the fact that Arcadius had been given a non-Latin-speaking tutor, Themistios, by his father, Theodosius I (Dagron, in loc. cit., p. 37). Theodosius I had also appointed Themistios to the post of praefectus urbi for Constantinople, in spite of Themistios's ignorance of the Empire's official language (Dagron, ibid.).

[4] *C.I.L.*, iii, 734; Dessau, *Inscriptiones Latinae Selectae*, 283; *Inscriptiones Latinae Christianae Veteres*, 1832.

[5] John Lydus, *De Magistratibus*, Book II, chap. 12, and Book III, chap. 42. *Circa* 441, Cyrus was exiled from Constantinople by being made bishop of Kotyeion (Dagron in loc. cit., p. 41, citing Malálas, pp. 361–2 Bonn edition.

[6] Dagron in loc. cit., p. 37.

[7] *Codex Theodosianus*, XIV, ix, 3 (i). The chairs for grammar (the necessary basis for all future studies) were equal in number for the two languages, namely ten for each. There were only three chairs for Latin rhetoric, as against five for Greek. The two chairs for law were both Latin. The single chair for philosophy was Greek. See L. Bréhier, *Le Monde byzantin*, vol. iii; *La Civilisation byzantine* (Paris, 1950, Albin Michel), pp. 457–8. See also Zilliacus, op. cit., pp. 83–4.

[8] John Lydus, *De Mag.*, III, 27. John Lydus himself had been released from an administrative post in the department of the praetorian prefect of the Eastern Illyricum (op. cit., Book III, chap. 26), to take up an appointment for teaching Latin on the staff of the Constantinopolitan praefectus urbi (op. cit., III, 29). John Lydus's proficiency in Latin, and his zeal for Latin, had been appreciated by the Imperial Government. Evidently it was still the

Constantinople.[1] Justinian I had still been saluted by the spectators in
the circus at Constantinople with the Latin acclamation 'Iustiniane,
tu vincas'.[2] This traditional Latin acclamation might have been chanted
by a Greek-speaking populace; but, in the mid sixth century, Latin
must still have been a living popular language in Constantinople, side
by side with Greek; for the members of the Constantinopolitan fire-
brigade were then still being summoned in Latin with the shout 'omnes
collegiati adeste'.[3]

Zilliacus infers from this evidence that the members of the central
civil service and the troops quartered in Constantinople had originally
been Latin-speaking, but that the rest of the population of the city had
been Greek-speaking.[4] In 473, when the Emperor Leo I 'the Thracian'[5]
had associated his grandson with himself as his co-Emperor at a concourse
in the Hippodrome at Constantinople, the civilians had acclaimed Leo
in Greek, while the troops had acclaimed him in Latin.[6] The Latin
language had held its own at Constantinople so long as, on the City's
European landward side, there was a Latin-speaking population in the
Balkan Peninsula whose domain extended from the south bank of the
lower Danube, through Thrace, almost up to Constantinople's gates.

Government's policy to keep Latin alive in the civil service at Constantinople. It is also evident that a good Latinist there had acquired a rarity value.

Yet, during the reign of Anastasius I (491–518), perhaps little more than a quarter of a
century before John Lydus was seconded to the task of keeping Latin alive at Constantinople,
and little more than half a century before Gregory the Great was hard put to it to find a
competent bilingual interpreter in Constantinople (see p. 563, n. 4), the Mauretanian Latin
grammarian Priscian was living, teaching, and writing in Constantinople, and his grammar of
the Latin language, which became a standard work wherever Latin was still being spoken,
written, and read, was transcribed at Constantinople in 526/7 by one of his pupils. At Constantinople, Priscian must have had access to a well-stocked library or libraries of works of
Latin literature. The Emperor Valens had appointed three Latin and four Greek *antiquarii*
to staff the public library at Constantinople (Dagron in loc. cit., p. 42, quoting *Cod. Theod.*
XIV, 9, 2 of A.D. 372). Priscian follows his models, the great Greek grammarians, in the practice of illustrating usages by examples, and Priscian's examples are culled, not only from
popular Latin writers of the Golden and Silver Ages, but also from more recondite works
of these periods, and from archaic works which are unlikely to have been in general circulation in Priscian's time. Justinian I's nephew Germanus (Yermanós) was brought from his
father's and his uncle's home town Bederiana to Constantinople at the age of eight to receive
a Latin education in the capital (Agathias, *Historiae*, Book V, chap. 21), though Bederiana
itself was a Latin-speaking place. It lay within the southern fringe of the Latin-speaking
northern half of the praetorian prefecture of the Eastern Illyricum. In the course of the sixth
century, the recession of the Latin language at Constantinople was evidently rapid.

[1] Zilliacus, op. cit., p. 73.
[2] Reproduced in *Chronicon Paschale*, p. 338, in the Greek alphabet, but with the Latin, not
the Greek, accentuation of 'Ιουστινιᾶνε (*sic*).
[3] Τῇ πατρίῳ ῾Ρωμαίων φωνῇ (John Lydus, *De Mag.*, Book I, chap. 50).
[4] Zilliacus, op. cit., p. 32.   [5] Theophanes, p. 110.
[6] *De Caer.*, Book I, pp. 431–2. Though the civilians had acclaimed Leo I in Greek, they had
saluted both him and the newly promoted Leo II in Latin as 'Ávghouste'. On the other hand,
the praepositus, when he was crowning Leo II, had chanted in Greek a triple "εὐτυχῶς".

At Constantinople the official policy of Latinization might have been ineffectual if the Latin-speaking element in the City's population had not been constantly replenished from this neighbouring reservoir. The effectiveness of the Latin-speaking part of the population of the Eastern Illyricum in maintaining the currency of the Latin language in Constantinople, and indeed in the East Roman Empire at large,[1] had been increased by the Constantinopolitan Roman Imperial Government's policy, from the early years of the fifth century onwards, of recruiting its army from natives of the Empire instead of continuing to put itself in the hands of barbarian mercenaries.[2] The provinces along the south bank of the lower Danube, together with Thrace, had been one of the Government's principal native recruiting-grounds, and the popularity of military service in Thrace had spread the Latin language there, though Thrace had been organized as a Greek-speaking province originally after its annexation in A.D. 46.[3]

This progressive Latinization of Thrace had also been promoted, under the Diocletianic–Constantinian regime, by the concentration there of the troops under the command of the *magistri militum in praesenti*.[4] Conversely, Thracian soldiers had maintained the currency of the Latin language in the Levant by serving outside Thrace, not only in Constantinople, but elsewhere. 'Frequenter inde [i.e. a Thracia provincia] milites tolluntur.'[5] For instance, it is recorded sub A.M. 5997 by Theophanes that the Emperor Anastasius sent to the eastern front an army Γότθων τε καὶ Βέσσων καὶ ἑτέρων Θρᾳκίων ἐθνῶν.[6] Out of the twenty-two senior officers in the expeditionary force that Belisarius led against the Vandals in 533, little fewer than sixteen were natives of Thrace.[7] Justinian I, in his Novel No. 26, remarks that the word 'Thrace' stands for the martial virtues and for a fertile recruiting-ground for soldiers.

Before the débâcle of the western half of the Roman Empire in the course of the fifth century, the dioecesis of Thrace[8] and the northern half of the adjoining praetorian prefecture of the Eastern Illyricum[9] had been

---

[1] For evidence of Thracian soldiers serving outside Thrace itself, see Zilliacus, op. cit., pp. 129–30; Stein, *Studien*, p. 121.　　　　[2] See Stein, *Studien*, pp. 120–1.

[3] See Th. Mommsen, English translation, *The History of Rome: The Provinces from Caesar to Diocletian*, vol. i (London, 1886, Bentley), pp. 306–8; A. H. M. Jones, *The Cities of the Eastern Roman Provinces* (Oxford, 1937, Clarendon Press), pp. 10–23.

[4] Zilliacus, op. cit., p. 31.

[5] *Expositio Totius Mundi et Gentium*, in *Geographiae Veteris Scriptores Graeci Minores* (Oxford, Theatro Sheldoniano, 4 vols.), vol. iii (1712), pp. 1–20, on p. 12. The passage can now be found on p. 186 of J. Rougé's edition (Paris, 1966).

[6] Theophanes, p. 145.

[7] Procopius, *Bellum Vandalicum*, Book I, chap. 11, §§ 5–10.

[8] i.e. the Diocletianic–Constantinian provinces Europa, Rhodope, Haemimontis, Thracia, Moesia Secunda, Scythia.

[9] i.e. the Diocletianic–Constantinian provinces Dacia Ripensis, Dacia Mediterranea, Moesia Superior, Praevalis, Dardania.

merely the eastern extremity of the Empire's extensive, though for the most part thinly populated, Latin-speaking provinces. Even in that age, this Latin-speaking part of the Balkan Peninsula had given the Empire the Constantinian dynasty. Naïssus (Niš) had been the home town of Constantius I, Constantine I's father and Julian's grandfather. After the whole of the rest of the Latin-speaking portion of the Empire, including the dioecesis of the Western Illyricum, had been partitioned into successor states carved out by German invaders, the Latin-speaking provinces adjoining Constantinople had remained continuously under the rule (though not always under the complete control) of the Constantinopolitan Roman Imperial Government. Till the ephemeral reconquest of North-West Africa, Italy, and a fragment of Spain in the reign of Justinian I, this had been the only Latin-speaking piece of the Constantinopolitan Government's dominions, but the retention of it had sufficed to keep the Latin language alive in Constantinople and, to some extent, in the Levantine provinces as well, and, in Justinian I, this region had given the Empire another Emperor who loomed almost as large, in the eyes of posterity, as Constantine I. Justinian I's predecessor and uncle, Justin I (518–27), had been one of the Illyrian peasants—a long series—who had attained the Imperial throne through successful service in the Army. Justin's native village lay in the southern fringe of Dardania, in the upper basin of the River Axius (Vardar). Justin had migrated to Constantinople to try his luck there. Thus Justinian I had come out of a Latin-speaking community.

Justinian I, however, had compromised the East Roman Empire's future by over-taxing its resources—not least its precious resource of military man-power in its Latin-speaking provinces in the Balkan Peninsula. The blood-tax had depopulated these provinces, and their depopulation had exposed them, already within Justinian I's lifetime, to barbarian raids that had depopulated them still further. After Justinian I's death, two blows had sealed the fate of Latin as a living language in Constantinople and in the East Roman Empire as a whole.

The first blow had been the Slav *Völkerwanderung* and the Avar raids and deportations which had hit the Latin-speaking population in the European hinterland of Constantinople in and after the year 581/2. These Balkan Latin-speakers had not been exterminated. They survived to make a Latin contribution to the vocabulary of the southern Slavonic languages[1] and to become acknowledged partners of the Slavized Bulgars in a Bulgaro–Vlakh state when, in 1185–7, the two peoples joined forces to throw off the East Roman rule that had been re-imposed on the

---

[1] Zilliacus, op. cit., p. 31, cites the adoption, in Slavized forms, of the Latin words pullus, furca, clausura, fornix, campana, vigilia. He notes that the word 'Tsar' is derived from the Latin 'Caesar' direct.

northern part of the Balkan Peninsula by the Emperor Basil II. Down to this day the Vlakhs have held their own in the Balkan Peninsula as nomad pastoralists who spend the summer in the mountains and descend only for the winter to the plains. By taking to this elusive way of life, they have not only preserved their race and their language; they have also worked their way southwards, down the Pindus Range, carrying their Romance language with them, into regions that had been wholly Greek-speaking in the days of the Vlakhs' Latin-speaking ancestors.[1] These Latin-speakers were, however, lost to the East Roman Empire,[2] and the effect of this loss on the fortunes of the Latin language in Constantinople seems to have made itself felt quickly. The future Pope Gregory I, who knew no Greek[3] yet who nevertheless served as papal apocrisiarius at Constantinople during the years 579–85—the very years in which the Latin-speaking part of the population of the Balkan Peninsula was being overwhelmed—mentions, more than once, the handicap, for doing his diplomatic work, that he suffered from his ignorance of Greek.[4]

The second blow that had struck the Latin language dead in the remnant of the Empire that had survived the storms of the seventh century had been the transfer of the Thracensian corps of the Roman Army from the European hinterland of Constantinople to the Anatolian hinterland of Smyrna.[5] The Thracenses must have been the last remaining Latin-speaking corps.[6] The Anatolikoí and the Armeniakoí must have become Greek-speaking long before they had been forced to withdraw from Syria and Armenia into Greek-speaking Asia Minor. In their new cantonments, the Thracenses, too, found themselves in the Greek-speaking world—indeed, in the heart of it. At whatever date in the seventh century their transfer may have taken place, we may be sure that they, likewise, had rapidly become Greek-speaking in the sequel. In these new circumstances it is not surprising that Latin should have become a dead language

[1] In 980 the governorship of the Vlakh community in théma Ellás was an important post in the East Roman Imperial service (*Scriptor Incertus* in *Cecaumeni Strategicon*, ed. Wassiliewsky and Jernstedt, p. 96). These Thessalian Vlakhs played a leading part in the insurrection in théma Ellás in 1066–7 (*Cecaumeni Strategicon*, pp. 66–75). The author of this *Strategicon* gives an unfavourable account of the Vlakhs. They are a deceitful and untrustworthy people (op. cit., pp. 74–5).

[2] A rare exception was the patrician Mávros the Bessan (τὸν Βέσσον) who was sent by Justinian II in 710 on a punitive expedition against Khersón (Theophanes, p. 379).

[3] 'Nos nec Graece novimus' (Gregory, *Epistulae*, XI, 74).

[4] He complained of the difficulty of finding in Constantinople a competent bilingual interpreter. Gregory, *Epistulae*, VI, 27: 'Hodie in Constantinopolitana civitate qui de Graeco in Latinum et de Latino in Graecum bene transferunt non sunt'; see also Stratós, op. cit., p. 345.

[5] See p. 229.

[6] They were still speaking Latin—if not, by this time, Vlakh—in A.D. 587 (see the 'torna fratre' anecdote in Theophylactus Simocatta, Book II, chap. 15, and in Theophanes, *Chronographia*, p. 258, sub A.M. 6079).

in the East Roman Empire by Constantine Porphyrogenitus's day. What is remarkable is that Latin should have lodged itself as extensively as it did in the vocabulary of the Rhomaic Greek language.

This Latin element in the vocabulary of Rhomaic Greek was deposited in three distinct strata.

There are Latin words that, in defiance of the inhibitions of the perennial 'purist' school of Greek men of letters, have found a permanent place in the Greek language of everyday life, and some of these Latin intruders are 'basic'. Dionysius of Halicarnassus would have been shocked—and, even more, have been astonished—if it could have been foretold to him that οἶκος, the native Greek word for house, was going to be dislodged by the Latin word *hospitium* (σπίτι), and that another Latin word, *porta*, was going to become the Greek for 'gate' and 'pass'.

Most of these Latin 'basic' words, once naturalized, came to stay,[1] but there was a second category which, though more numerous, was ephemeral. This was the Latin element in the technical vocabularies of the East Roman Court, Civil Service, and Army. It was to be expected that, in these vocabularies, Latin terms would be prominent, since they were the vocabularies of East Roman institutions that were of 'Old Roman' origin; but it was also inevitable that these East Roman institutions should wither away as the East Roman Empire itself declined towards its fall; when the institutions withered, their professional vocabularies dropped out of Rhomaic Greek; and, long before they dropped out, they were being translated progressively into Greek from Latin. Greek replaced Latin 'when it acquired the capacity to replace it—that is to say, when the evolution of the language, and of Hellenism itself, made this change possible'.[2]

The tenure of this stratum of Latin in Rhomaic Greek had been precarious, because it had been esoteric. Its use had been confined to specialists; unlike such household words as σπίτι and πόρτα, it had never become current among the common run of Rhomaic-speakers. All the same, this second stratum was part of the living vocabulary of the East Roman official world so long as this world existed. In the mouths and ears of the courtiers and civil servants and soldiers, their Latin technical terms and the eventual Greek equivalents of these had intelligible meanings, and the objects and actions to which these meanings attached were of genuine importance for the performance of the users' official duties.

---

[1] Most, but not all. The Arab observer Hārūn b. Yaḥyā, who was in Constantinople either late in the ninth century or early in the tenth, notes (as reproduced by Ibn Rustah) that the horses of Rūm are so docile that you have only to say to them *sta* and they will halt and stay put. A present-day horse in Greece would not respond to the Latin word *sta* so intelligently. (See the passage of Ibn Rustah that is translated in Vasiliev, *Byzance et les Arabes*, ii, II, p. 392.)

[2] Dagron in loc. cit., p. 24. Cf. p. 54.

We can trace some of the stages by which the official stratum of Latin in the vocabulary of Rhomaic Greek was Graecized from about the ninth decade of the sixth century onwards.[1] The process of de-Latinization can be followed in the principal fields of official business. For instance, it can be illustrated from the history of the East Roman coinage, public administration, law, and Army.

The coinage was the field in which the Latin language fought its most stubborn rearguard action. For a coin to be acceptable, it has to have a familiar look as well as an intrinsic value. For this reason, mint-masters are conservative-minded, and the legends on coins are apt to change slowly.[2] Here Diocletian had given Latin a good start by putting a stop to the minting of coins with Greek legends at Alexandria.[3] No Greek legends reappeared till the reign of Heraclius (Hêrákleios) (610–41). Heraclius did coin bronze with a Greek legend, but his silver coinage bears on the reverse the moving Latin legend 'Deus, adiuta Romanis'—a cry that expresses the agony through which the East Romans were passing in Heraclius's time. The legends are Latin on the gold solidi of Justinian II (685–95 and 705–11).[4] On the coins of Constantine V (741–75) and Leo VI (775–80), and on the gold coins of Nikêphóros I (802–11) and Theóphilos (829–42), the legends are in Greek, but the Greek is presented in the Latin alphabet.[5] The title βασιλεύς was placed on coins for the first time by Constantine V,[6] though, in an official document, it had been assumed by Heraclius in 629.[7]

The advent of Basil I brought with it a resuscitation of legends in Latin. On a bronze coin minted during the brief joint reign of Michael III and Basil I (26 May 866 to 24 September 867), the legends are in Latin: on the obverse, 'Mihael imperat'; on the reverse 'Basilius Rex'.[8] On gold coins, the resumption of the use of Latin for the legend persisted from the sole reign of Basil I (867–86) until the sole reign of Constantine X's widow Evdhokía (1067).[9] This re-Latinization must have been introduced on Basil I's initiative for some particular purpose, and its maintenance for two centuries suggests that the purpose, whatever it may have been,

[1] Antoniadis-Bibicou, *Études*, gives a bibliography of the process of Graecization in the East Roman Empire on p. 157, n. 1.

[2] This general point is noted by Zilliacus, op. cit., p. 50. It could be illustrated by the tenacity of the archaic Attic 'owls' and of their replicas that were minted in the Yaman.

[3] Zilliacus, ibid.; Dagron in loc. cit., p. 38.

[4] Zilliacus, op. cit., p. 55.   [5] Op. cit., p. 56.   [6] Op. cit., loc. cit.

[7] In his Novel No. 25 (Zilliacus, op. cit., p. 37; Stratós, op. cit., p. 343).

[8] Zilliacus, op. cit., p. 56. Was the title 'rex' intended to imply that Basil was inferior to Michael in status? In its transliteration into the Greek alphabet, ῥήξ had a depreciatory connotation in East Roman usage, but the disparagement was so extreme that the word could hardly have been applied, with this connotation, to an East Roman Emperor, even if he was another's junior colleague. It seems more probable that, in this legend, 'rex' is simply a literal translation of βασιλεύς.

[9] Zilliacus, op. cit., p. 57.

was pertinent for the same period. We may guess that the purpose was to provide a coinage that would be congenial to subjects of the Empire who were accustomed to using Latin as their official language, even though their everyday language had developed from Latin into a Romance vernacular.

The East Roman Empire had lost its Latin-speaking subjects in the Balkan Peninsula in and after 581/2, those in North-West Africa in 698, and those in the Romagna in 751. But Basil I, after his raising of the Muslim siege of Ragusa in 868, had launched a counter-offensive against the Muslims in south-eastern Italy. He had occupied Bari on Christmas Day, 876, and, from then onwards until the Norman conquest, the Empire once again had an important Latin population under its rule in théma Laghouvardhía.[1] The Norman conquest began with the capture of Melfi in 1041, and it was consummated by the capture of Bari itself in 1071. The initial and terminal dates of the existence of théma Laghou-vardhía are so close to those of the re-Latinization of the legends on the East Roman gold coinage that it seems likely that there was a relation between the East Roman Government's Italian policy and its minting policy during these two hundred years. It is significant that the Latin legends disappeared from the coinage in the reign of Rhomanós IV Dhioyénês (1068–71) and that they were never reintroduced.[2]

In the field of public administration, the Roman Government in the Age of the Principate had been liberal in publishing official documents in Greek in the provinces in which Greek was the population's mother-tongue or was its customary lingua franca. The Monumentum Ancyranum, in which Augustus has given the World an account of his achievements, is bilingual, and so is Diocletian's schedule of maximum prices—a Roman official document that is about three centuries younger. Diocletian recognized the expediency of publishing a Greek version of a document that he wished to be widely read—especially in the Empire's economically dominant Levantine provinces. From the reign of Hadrian (117–38) onwards, some Roman Imperial rescripts had been issued in Greek alone,[3] but Diocletian, the Latinizing Illyrian, put a stop to this practice, and even the rebellious-minded Hellenist Julian seems to have refrained from reviving it. At any rate, no Greek rescripts or constitutiones of Julian's have been preserved.[4] Justinian I felt himself called upon to justify his publication of novels in Greek,[5] and he had his Greek novels

---

[1] It had continued to have unimportant Latin subjects in the Dalmatian cities and in Sardinia.

[2] Zilliacus, op. cit., p. 57.   [3] Op. cit., pp. 68–9.

[4] Op. cit., p. 71; Dagron in loc. cit., p. 39. However, Julian did give decisions in Greek on legal cases, and he was the first Emperor to do this (Zilliacus, op. cit., p. 76).

[5] Zilliacus cites Justinian I's Novels No. 7, § 1, and No. 66, §§ 1 and 2, and his *Institutes*, III, 7.

translated into Latin for the benefit of his Latin-speaking subjects;[1] but the only documents of Justinian's that were composed in Latin were those that were addressed to his Latin-speaking subjects exclusively.[2] The legends on sixth-century East Roman consular diptychs are in Latin,[3] and it has been noted already[4] that, in the mid sixth century, a knowledge of Latin was still an obligatory qualification for entry into the Civil Service. It has, however, also been noted[5] that, in the next generation after Justinian I's and John Lydus's, this requirement had become a dead letter, to judge by Gregory the Great's experience at Constantinople in 579–85.

In the field of administration, Latin survived, after it had ceased to be used for official documents, in the titles of ranks and offices. In Philótheos's klêtorolóyion (compiled in 899), fossilized Latin titles,[6] Greek titles, both classical[7] and new-fangled,[8] and hybrid Graeco-Latin compounds,[9] jostle with each other in a linguistic chaos. Some of the fossilized Latin titles have been grotesquely deformed.[10] Even, however, in this haven of formality and pedantry, Greek had captured from Latin the highest title of all. Heraclius styled himself βασιλεύς in a novel promulgated in 629,[11] and this Greek word for 'king' supplanted the Latin word 'imperator' as the official title for an East Roman Emperor.[12]

The de-Latinization of East Roman law is impressive evidence of the Greek language's strength; for Roman law was a native Roman product, and, though the Hellenization of Roman culture had infused a tincture of Hellenic philosophy into Roman law in the course of the four centuries culminating in the early decades of the third century of the Christian Era, both the native substance of Roman law and the Latin technical vocabulary in which this peculiar Roman institution was conveyed were

---

[1] Zilliacus, op. cit., p. 74.

[2] Dagron in loc. cit., p. 44. Justinian's Latin novels are mostly addressed to Tribonian, and his Greek novels to John of Cappadocia (Zilliacus, op. cit., pp. 29 and 73; cf. Dagron in loc. cit., p. 45).

[3] Zilliacus, op. cit., p. 47.   [4] On p. 559.   [5] On p. 563.

[6] e.g. κόμης, κυαίστωρ (κοιαίστωρ).   [7] e.g. στρατηγός, διοικητής.

[8] e.g. σπαθάριος, παρακοιμώμενος.

[9] e.g. τουρμάρχης, σπαθαροκανδιδάτος. Cf. such modern hybrid Western words as 'automobile'.

[10] e.g. Philótheos's προέξημος (i.e. proximus) and *Theophanes Continuatus*'s ἀτζυπάδες (? i.e. stipatores) (Book VI, p. 438, line 15, and p. 439, lines 1 and 6).   [11] See p. 565.

[12] Zilliacus, op. cit., p. 37, conjectures that Heraclius, in assuming the title βασιλεύς, was intending to signify that he had stepped into the shoes of the sovereign of Persia. Heraclius, however, had merely defeated the Persian Empire; he had not abolished it and had not annexed any of its dominions. It is true that the Achaemenian Persian Emperor had been styled βασιλεύς by his Greek contemporaries, but, in applying the title to him, they had used it without the definite article, and this grammatically curious usage was not adopted by the East Roman βασιλεῖς. It seems more likely that Heraclius was thinking of himself as being the heir, not of the Persian Shah Khuzraw Parviz, but of the Macedonian Greek kings Philip II and Alexander III and their Antigonid and Seleucid and Lagid successors.

less adaptable than most of the manifestations of the Roman genius. When Justinian codified in Latin the deposit of a millennium of Roman legislation and jurisprudence, he was no doubt intending to assert the Latinity of the East Roman Empire and to confirm the Latin language's hold on East Roman life. He sanctioned only word-for-word (κατὰ πόδας) Greek translations of the *Digest*,[1] and permitted the teaching of law in the schools at Constantinople, Rome, and Beirut only.[2] Yet, even in the field of law, the tide was running in favour of Greek. Wills written in Greek had been made legally valid as far back as 12 September 439, in a novel promulgated by Theodosius II on that date.[3] Justinian himself was acknowledging the Greek language's ascendancy when he promulgated novels in Greek; and already, in his reign, Greek had replaced Latin as the language of oral instruction and written commentary in the law-schools at Constantinople and Berytus (Beirut).[4]

This was remarkable, considering that Constantinople was still a semi-Latin-speaking city. As for Berytus, it had been the easternmost authentic (as distinguished from honorary) Roman colony, save for Heliopolis (Ba'lbek). The Roman settlers had been planted at Berytus by Augustus; and, though it was an age-old Phoenician city which, by Augustus's day, had been Hellenized, the descendants of Augustus's colonists had taken pains to maintain the Latinity of this isolated outpost of Latin-speakers in a Syriac-speaking and Greek-speaking Levant. However, even in the domain of Roman law, which had been cultivated at Berytus by a distinguished school of jurists,[5] the Roman law's native Latin language had had to yield to Greek at Berytus by Justinian's time, and probably long before that.

After Justinian I's death in 565, his monumental *corpus iuris* no longer answered to the needs of the barbarized and simplified East Roman society that emerged in the eighth century from the tribulations which had descended on the Empire before the sixth century's close. The *Ecloga*, promulgated in Greek by Leo III (717–41), reflects a linguistic as well as a social revolution.[6] In the *Ecloga* there are barely twenty Latin loan-words, whereas there are 400 of these in the Greek paraphrase of Justinian's *Institutes* that was made by the jurist Theóphilos before the deluge.[7] There are no Latinisms in the 'Rhodian' maritime law,[8] which is thought to have been edited in its present form at some date in the

---

[1] Constitutio *Tanta*, chap. 21, in *Corpus Iuris Civilis* (*C.I.C.*), I, p. 22.

[2] Constitutio *Omnem rei publicae*, chaps. 5 and 7, in *C.I.C.*, I, p. 11.

[3] Cp. Justinian I, novel 16, 8; *Cod. Just.* VI, 23, 21.

[4] Zilliacus, op. cit., pp. 84–5. P. Collinet: *Études historiques sur le droit de Justinien*, vol. ii: *Histoire de l'école de droit de Beyrouth* (Paris, 1925, Recueil Sirey), pp. 211–18, dates the change-over to Greek from Latin, as the language of instruction in the law school at Beirut, *circa* 380–420.

[5] See Collinet, op. cit., vol. ii, especially pp. 20–2.

[6] Zilliacus, op. cit., p. 75.   [7] Op. cit., p. 104.   [8] Op. cit., p. 105.

later decades of the seventh century. In the contemporary Nómos Yeoryikós ('Farmers' Law') Latinisms do occur,[1] but they are rare. Nor did East Roman law resume its ancestral Latin dress when, in the ninth century, the revival of social life in the East Roman Empire called for a reversion to a more elaborate system of law than the sorely harassed seventh and eighth centuries had required. In the legislation (*Prókheiros Nómos, Epanaghogh″, Vasiliká*) that was compiled and promulgated by Basil I (867–86) and Leo VI (886–912), Justinian's corpus was re-animated, but not in Justinian's language. In the preface to the *Prókheiros Nómos* the Basilian legislators describe the relation of their work to the Justinianean corpus. 'We have reduced its amplitude to reasonable compass, and we have translated into Greek the Latin vocabulary in which it is composed.'[2] In the novels promulgated by the Emperors of the Basilian dynasty, there are few Latin words except those that had become fully naturalized.[3] A comparison of the sixth-century with the ninth-century Greek juridical texts shows that, out of about 700 Latinisms, about 200 have survived,[4] or, on a stricter count, 180 out of 580.[5]

It is not surprising that the use of Latin persisted in the East Roman Army; it is all the more remarkable that, even in this special preserve of the Latin language, Greek did eventually push Latin to the wall, though, so long as the East Roman Army remained in being, Greek never succeeded here in evicting Latin completely.

The Roman Army had been consciously and deliberately used as an instrument of Latinization ever since the fourth century B.C.—the century in which, for the first time, Rome had acquired not only non-Latin-speaking allies but also non-Latin-speaking citizens. In the Roman Army for nearly a quarter of a millennium, ending in the grant of Roman citizenship to Rome's Italian allies in 90–89 B.C., non-Latin-speaking Roman citizens had served side by side with Latin-speaking citizens in the Roman legions, and non-Latin-speaking allies side by side with Latin-speaking allies in the alae that were brigaded with the legions. These polyglot fellow-soldiers had spent each night of the campaigning season within the vallum of the same camp; and, since Latin-speaking Roman citizens were in command, the effect must have been to disseminate the knowledge of Latin and the employment of it. After Augustus

---

[1] e.g. πραῖδα (§ 25), πραιδεύοντα (§ 48), πραιδεύει (§ 49), φουρκιζέσθω (§ 47), ὁρίῳ (i.e. horreo) (§ 68).

[2] τὸ μὲν πλάτος εἰς συμμετρίαν περιεστείλαμεν, τῶν δὲ Ῥωμαϊκῶν λέξεων τὴν συνθήκην εἰς τὴν Ἑλλάδα γλῶσσαν μετεποιήσαμεν (cited by Zilliacus, op. cit., p. 106).

[3] Zilliacus, op. cit., p. 107.

[4] Op. cit., p. 108.

[5] Op. cit., p. 109. See the comparative table, ibid., in which the figures of the original and the surviving Latinisms are distributed under six heads, representing six different branches of law. In the domain of administrative law, 85 out of 149 sixth-century Latinisms survived in the ninth and tenth centuries (ibid., pp. 109 and 110). See also the catalogue of Latinisms in the Byzantine legal vocabulary in op. cit., pp. 172–215.

had regularized Marius's revolutionary substitution of an army of proletarian volunteers for the traditional army of conscripted freeholders, the legions—now composed of full-time professional soldiers whose term of service was for the duration of their active life—had been brigaded with auxilia which were recruited from provincials and not, as the legions were, from Roman citizens, but which, like the legions of the Age of the Principate, were professional troops whose term of service was life-long.

Thus the Roman Army had continued to be a potent agency of Latinization, and this incidental function of the Army had survived into the age in which the Illyrian soldier-Emperors had set themselves to extend the process of Latinization from the Army to the Empire as a whole, including the Hellenized Levantine provinces. *A fortiori*, the Illyrian Emperors insisted on the use of Latin in the Army itself. Eusebius, in his biography of Constantine I,[1] records that Constantine 'made it his personal concern to teach all the troops the proper form of prayer. He commanded them all to pray in the Latin language as follows.'

In the East Roman Army, Latin was still the language of command, and also the language of the technical military vocabulary, at the date, *circa* A.D. 600, at which the author of 'Mavríkios's' *Stratéghikón* was writing. He notes, in his Introduction,[2]

> I have already mentioned that I have felt no concern for pedantic correctness or for ornate phraseology. This is[3] not a work of holy scripture; my main concern has been to be practical and concise. So I have made frequent use of Latin and other [non-Greek] terms that are current in military usage. I have done this in order to make my book clearly intelligible to my readers.

Here 'Mavríkios' is implicitly criticizing sixth-century Greek literary purists[4] such as Procopius and Agathias and the author of Πολιτικῆς πρακτικὸν μέρος ἤτοι περὶ στρατηγικῆς.[5] These purists had taken pains to avoid admitting into their text anything that might have offended the eye or ear of Isocrates, if he could have lived on to read their works or to hear them recited. They had therefore paraphrased in pseudo-classical Attic Greek any Latin or other contemporary technical terms that were part and parcel of the events that they were recording; and this tiresome unscientific mannerism left their readers uncertain of the exact manœuvre, word of command, unit, or rank to which they were alluding. 'Mavríkios',

---

[1] Chap. 4, § 19, cited by Zilliacus in op. cit., p. 128.

[2] Scheffer p. 3, Mihăescu p. 44.

[3] Scheffer's text has ἦν here; Mihăescu's has ὅν. Ἧν is grammatical; ὅν is not. Is Scheffer's ἦν an emendation, or is Mihăescu's ὅν a misprint?—A. J. T.

[4] See Zilliacus, op. cit., pp. 115–16 and 125.

[5] Text in H. Köchly and W. Rüstow, *Griechische Kriegsschriftsteller*, Zweiter Theil, Zweite Abtheilung (Leipzig, 1855, Engelmann), pp. 1–209.

on the other hand, reproduces, untravestied, the actual terms that were in use in the Army in his day. Zilliacus has counted fifty separate Latin words of command in 'Mavríkios's' treatise.[1]

'Mavríkios's' note in his Introduction tells us that, in his time, the Latin military terminology was still the usual current one, though no doubt there were already some officially recognized Greek equivalents.[2] However, the two facts that 'Mavríkios' writes in Greek, and that he feels it necessary to explain why he has not eliminated Latinisms from his text, reveal that Greek was already the vernacular language of military officers and of civilian students of military affairs. 'Mavríkios' himself says[3] that mandatores (i.e. adjutants) ought 'to know Latin, Persian (if occasion arises), and Greek'.[4] Zilliacus[5] raises the pertinent question whether 'Mavríkios' means to imply that a knowledge of Latin was needed by mandatores *only*.

Leo VI, writing his *Taktiká* about three hundred years later than the probable date of 'Mavríkios's' *Stratêghikón*, notes in his own introduction[6] that he has 'frequently clarified Greek terms and translated Latin terms'. This is consistent with the passage, already quoted,[7] from the Introduction to the *Prókheiros Nómos*, and the difference from the corresponding passage in 'Mavríkios's' Introduction is significant, considering that Leo VI, in his *Taktiká*, has copied a large part of 'Mavríkios's' *Stratêghikón* verbatim. Moreover, in these purloined passages, Leo VI does usually substitute Greek equivalents for 'Mavríkios's' Latin terms, and he repeats[8] that he has translated all the Latin words of command in his predecessor's treatise except for the two words *move* and *sta*. This is true. It can be verified by consulting Zilliacus's catalogue,[9] in parallel columns, of 'Mavríkios's' Latin words of command and Leo VI's Greek equivalents.

Leo VI's son and successor Constantine VII Porphyrogenitus records the prescribed exchange of greetings between the Emperor on campaign and the officers and men of an army-corps through whose district he is travelling.[10] He also records[11] the troops' prescribed acclamations to the Emperor when he is giving them a donative. These two libretti are

---

[1] See the catalogue, with Leo VI's corresponding Greek words of command in a parallel column, in Zilliacus, op. cit., pp. 134–6. See also the full catalogue of Latinisms in Byzantine military terminology, with their Greek equivalents, in op. cit., pp. 216–39.

[2] Zilliacus, op. cit., p. 133.

[3] *Sratêghikón*, Part 12, chap. 7, p. 307 Scheffer; Part 12, chap. 8, § 7, p. 318 Mihăescu.

[4] εἰδότες Ῥωμαϊστί, καὶ Περσιστὶ ἐὰν ἀπαντᾷ, καὶ Ἑλληνιστί. This is Zilliacus's punctuation, and it is surely right. Scheffer has inserted a comma between Περσιστὶ and ἐὰν ἀπαντᾷ, with no comma after ἐὰν ἀπαντᾷ, and has thus made these two last words apply, not to Persian, but to Greek. Mihăescu has put a comma both after and before ἐὰν ἀπαντᾷ, and has thus, like Zilliacus, made the phrase apply to Persian.

[5] In op. cit., p. 136.   [6] §6 (Migne, col. 676).   [7] On p. 569.

[8] Leo VI, *Taktiká*, Dhiat. 7, § 26, col. 741.   [9] On pp. 134–6.

[10] See Τὰ Βασιλικὰ Ταξείδια, pp. 482–4.   [11] See *De Caer.*, Book II, chap. 43, pp. 649–50.

entirely in Greek, and so is the libretto for the Sardinians' acclamations,[1] though, in the tenth century, or indeed at any date, Greek-speaking Sardinians must have been rarities. So much for Constantine I's endeavours to make the tenth-century troops' fourth-century predecessors say their prayers in Latin.

All the same, Latin died hard in the Army, as in the mint. Zilliacus points out[2] that Leo VI uses some Latin words—e.g. βιγλάτωρ and the important word τοῦρμα, used by Leo for designating the next largest unit to a théma—which are not to be found in 'Mavríkios'. Zilliacus also points out[3] that Leo VI prefers to use Latin terms—he uses the Graeco-Latin hybrid τουρμάρχης, and the Latin δοῦξ and κόμης[4]—whereas 'Mavríkios' normally uses the Greek equivalents μεράρχης, χιλίαρχος, ταγματάρχης. Moreover, there are many Latinisms in the 'Anonymus Vári' and in Nikêphóros II Phokás's Στρατηγικὴ Ἔκθεσις καὶ Σύνταξις,[5] though these two treatises were written about three-quarters of a century later than Leo's *Taktiká*. Since these works were composed, like 'Mavríkios's' *Stratêghikón*, by professional soldiers for practical use by their colleagues, we may assume that they, too, reproduce the military terminology that was current in their authors' day.

The third stratum of Latin in the vocabulary of Byzantine Rhomaic Greek was the quaintest of the three. This third stratum consisted of Latin words and phrases that were embedded like fossils in the stereotyped formulas that were recited in the ritual of some of the non-military official ceremonies. For the performers and for the audience alike, these bits of Latin were just gibberish; but, since they were inserted in the venerable 'book of the words', they continued to be mouthed out, religiously, year after year and century after century. The ceremonies themselves might, and did, change gradually in the course of ages. Anything that is open to the human understanding is consequently open to modification. But this Latin gibberish was unintelligible, so it was sacrosanct. It rolled down the ages unchanged, like the boulders that are carried by a glacier.

There is an outcrop of this garbled Latin in the standard form of procedure for a procession[6] to the Ayía Sophía in which the Emperors are participating.[7] When the Emperors enter the Avghoustéfs,

the praipósitos utters the Latin phrase[8] βίτ [i.e. *fit*], and the loud-speaker (φωνοβόλος) of the Imperial household (τοῦ κουβουκλείου) takes it up and

---

[1] See *De Caer.*, Book II, chap. 43, pp. 650–1.　　[2] On p. 139.　　[3] Ibid.
[4] Leo VI uses τριβοῦνος, which was a synonym for κόμης, once only, and he is the latest Greek writer to use it (Zilliacus, op. cit., p. 156).
[5] See Zilliacus, op. cit., pp. 124 and 139.
[6] προκένσος, i.e. *processus*, a synonym for προέλευσις.
[7] *De Caer.*, Book I, chap. 1, p. 21. Cf. chap. 9, p. 69; chap. 23, p. 136.
[8] τὴν Ῥωμαϊκὴν λέξιν.

chants, in a sonorous and harmonious tone, 'Welcome' (καλῶς). The whole staff of the household then responds with the words 'Welcome indeed, ye for whom we pray *Many years* (καλῶς ἤλθετε οἱ μουλτουσάνοι)' [i.e. *multos anni*, run together and changed from the acclamation *Multos annos* into an epithet of the Emperors, to whom the acclamation was addressed]. On the holy great Sunday—Easter Sunday, that is—and on that occasion only, they add another Latin phrase: '*Happiest years* (ἄνω φιλλικήσιμε)' [i.e. *anno felicissime*, for *annos felicissimos*].[1]

In the Imperial procession to the Ἁγία Sophía on special occasions, the Koiaístor's[2] kankellárioi chanted Latin galore.
On Christmas Day, for instance, they chanted:

"*Δὲ. Μαρίε. Βέργηνε. Νάτους*" [i.e. *De Maria virgine natus (est)*] "*ἐτ. Μάγια. δωριεντεκούμ. μούνερα. ἀδοράντες*" [i.e. *et Magi ab Oriente cum munera adorantes*]. Response: "*Κρίστους. Δέους. Νόστερ. κούμ. σέρβετ. ἠμπέριουμ. βέστρουμ. πὲρ. μουλτουσάννους. ἐτ. βόνος*" [i.e. *Christus Deus Noster conservet imperium vestrum per multos annos et bonos*].

At the Festival of the Lights (τὰ φῶτα), i.e. Epiphany, they chanted:

"*Ἰωάννες. ἐν Ἰορδάνε. βαπτίζατ. δόμηνουμ. σεκούνδουμ. ἴλλουμ. βόκατ. δὲ τὲ. βόλο.*" [i.e. *Ioannes in Iordane baptizat dominum. Secundum[3] illum vocat*: '*De te volo (baptizari)*']. Response as on Christmas Day.

On Easter Sunday they chanted:

"*κούμ. κρουκηφίξους. ἐστ. ἐτ. σεπούλτους. ἐτ. τέρξια. δίερρε. σουρρέξιτ.*" [i.e. *cum crucifixus est et sepultus et tertia die resurrexit*].[4] Response, as before.

On Whit Sunday they chanted:

"*κουμμανδαβὶτ. σπηρίτουμ. σάκτουμ. σούπερ. τούος. ἀπόστολος.*" [i.e. *commendabit Spiritum Sanctum super tuos Apostolos*]. Response as before.

At the Feast of the Transfiguration they chanted:

"*κοὺν τρανεφιγγουράτους, ἐστ. ἰν. μόντεμ.*" [i.e. *cum transfiguratus est in montem*]. Response as before.[5]

---

[1] The vocative was more familiar, since it was used in other acclamations. See, for instance, *De Caer.*, Book I, chap. 39, p. 69; chap. 43, p. 221.

[2] The Koiaístor (alternatively spelled 'Kuaístor') was the second most important official in the municipal government of Constantinople after the Prefect (ἔπαρχος) himself. The Koiaístor also had some Imperial responsibilities. His functions were judicial as well as administrative. See II, 3, pp. 201–2.

[3] In the Greek translation of this passage, two alternative renderings of σεκούνδουμ are offered: (i) ἀκολούθως [i.e. afterwards]; (ii) ἐκ δευτέρου [i.e. for the second time]. In the text of the document as reproduced in *De Caerimoniis*, there is a Greek translation of each phrase, and in most cases it is correct. But the division of the Latin words shows that, while the correct Greek translation had been preserved, the Latin itself was no longer understood.

[4] The Greek translator gives one correct and one incorrect rendering of this passage.

[5] The Koiaístor's kankellárioi's Latin chants are set out in *De Caer.*, Book I, chap. 74, pp. 369–70.

The Emperor was also acclaimed in Latin whenever he entertained guests in the Tríklinos of the Nineteen Couches.[1]

When the Emperor reclines at the table and the usual ceremonial has been performed, and when, at a nod from the praipósitos, the invited guests have to take their seats, the five voukálioi [i.e. *vocales*] chant: "κονσέρβετ. Δέους. ἠμπέριουμ. βέστρουμ" [i.e. *conservet Deus imperium vestrum*]. Then Number Five takes over, and he chants: "βόνα τοῦα σέμπερ" [i.e. *bona tua semper*]. Then Number Four chants: "βίκτωρ σῆς σέμπερ" [i.e. *victor sis semper*]. Next Number Three chants: "μούλτους. ἄννους. φικίδια θ' Δέους" [i.e. *multos annos vitae* (?) *det* (?) *Deus*].[2] Then Number Two chants: "βίκτωρ. φατζία. σέμπερ." [i.e. *victor(em) facia(t) semper*]. Finally, Number One chants: "Δέους. πρένστεθ" [i.e. *Deus praestet*].

At the mixing of the wine, when the Emperor drinks, the voukálioi chant: "βήβητε, Δόμηνι 'μπεράτορες, ἢν μούλτος ἄννος. Δέους Ὀμνήποτενς πρέστεθ." [i.e. *bibite, Domini Imperatores, in multos annos: Deus Omnipotens praestet*]. Then Number Two takes over, and chants [this time in Greek]: 'May ye lead a happy life, my lords'. After that, Number One chants: "Δέους πρένστεθ" [i.e. *Deus praestet*]. While the wine is being watered, Number One chants: "ἢν γαυδίω πρανδεῖτε, Δόμηνι" [i.e. *in gaudio prandete, Domini*]. And then Number Two chants [in Greek]: 'May ye be joyful while ye feast, Master.' While the dishes are being served, Number One chants [in Greek]: 'Give thanks to God while ye are taking your repast, My Lords.' At the close (?) (κατὰ μίσσον) Number One chants [in Greek]: 'Enjoy the gifts of God'. When the Emperor lays his napkin down on the table and the guests rise, all five chant: "βόνω Δόμνω σέμπερ" [i.e. *bono Domno* (sc. *Deo*) *semper* (*sit gloria*)].

At dawn, every day, the Army shouts, at the top of its voice, a string of acclamations, beginning with: 'So and so and so and so, Ávghoustoi, τούμβηκας [i.e. tu vincas]'.[3]

---

[1] *De Caer.*, Book I, chap. 75, pp. 370-1.

[2] But the Greek translator's rendering is: 'He will make thee *victorious* for ever'.

[3] Ibid., chap. 76, p. 372. The acclamation τούμβικας was used by civilians as well as by soldiers. For instance, at a reception given to the Senate and the Ecumenical Patriarch in the Hippodrome by the Emperor Heraclius, accompanied by the Imperial family, τούμβικας was chanted in honour of each of the Imperial persons in turn by the kouvikoulárioi (*De Caer.*, Book II, chap. 29, pp. 629-30).

Some of the stock stage directions for Imperial ceremonies are in Latin. λέβα ἐλωκ [i.e. *leva(te) e loco*] meant 'get up now and move on' (see *De Caer.*, pp. 239-40, 252, 265, 306, 342-3, 394, 406). καπλάτε, Δόμηνι seems, from the context (pp. 73, 110, 149, 158) to mean: 'Watch your step, My Lords' (? *captate*).

PART V

CONSTANTINE PORPHYROGENITUS'S
WORKS

1. *Constantine's Literary Activities and Intellectual Interests*

IF we are to appreciate Constantine Porphyrogenitus's literary activities, we need to look at them in the light of his life, his character, and his World. This is why the subject of the present chapter has been left to be treated last.

Constantine's literary activities must be held to include works that he promoted, as well as works that he wrote or compiled or edited himself. The amount of his own direct output was limited by the shortness of his life (he died at the age of fifty-four), by ill health, and by time-consuming official duties.[1] The work for which he was indirectly responsible was more voluminous. However, the two categories cannot be distinguished from each other sharply. In preparing the works of which he himself was the author, Constantine had, no doubt, research assistants and amanuenses, and at the same time he kept a tight hand over some, at least, of the works, produced under his auspices, that were published either anonymously or under other names than his. The anonymous writer of the first four books of *Theophanes Continuatus* states on his title-page that his work was written 'by Constantine Porphyrogenitus's command', and he declares in his preface, which is addressed to Constantine: 'You are the author of the present history of your predecessors. My hand has simply been used by you to serve you.'[2]

There is more in this than mere flattery. Constantine is sure to have dictated what his employee wrote about Constantine's own grandfather, the Emperor Basil I, whose reputation Constantine was determined to whitewash.[3] Constantine had previously commissioned, and presumably

---

[1] See the passage quoted on p. 6 from the preface to his biography of Basil I.
[2] ἱστορεῖς δὲ αὐτός, χεῖρα μόνως λαβὼν ἡμῶν διακονουμένην σοι (Preface, p. 4).
[3] See further, pp. 582–93.

had also supervised, the production of Genesius's history, on which the writer of the first four books of *Theophanes Continuatus* has drawn. At the beginning of his book, Genesius avows, first in verse and then in prose, that he has written the book under orders from the Emperor Constantine his master. Constantine certainly commissioned the fifty-three books of extracts from Hellenic literature, grouped according to topics; and we may guess that he took a hand in the planning and execution of this large-scale piece of work, whether or not he actually served as editor-in-chief. He also commissioned, or at least inspired, the tenth-century encyclopedia of Hellenic agricultural science called the *Geoponica*, to judge by the terms of the preface, which is addressed to him. If we reckon, as we ought to reckon, these indirect productions of Constantine's as being part of his literary activities, we shall find that his total output was considerable.

The principal components of this *corpus Constantineum* have been dated, by Bury,[1] from internal evidence, as follows:

De Thematibus	934[2]–end of 944
Genesius's history	944–948
Theophanes Continuatus, Books I–IV	*ca.* 949–950
Constantine's biography of Basil I (= *Theoph. Cont.*, Book V)	*ca.* 950 (anyway post 948)[3]
De Administrando Imperio	948[4]–952 (or 951)[5]

[1] J. B. Bury, 'The Treatise De Administrando Imperio' in *Die byzantinische Zeitschrift*, 15. Band, Heften 3 and 4 (1906), pp. 518–77, on p. 574; idem, 'The Ceremonial Book of Constantine Porphyrogenitus', in *The English Historical Review*, No. lxxxvi, April 1907, pp. 209–27, on pp. 211 and 217. See Bury's analysis, ibid., p. 227, of the contents of this book in the form in which it has come down to us.

[2] This book was written, or, at any rate, was published, after the conversion of the kleisoúra of Seléfkeia into an army-corps district. Constantine Porphyrogenitus himself, in *De Thematibus*, p. 36, attributes this change in the status of the Seléfkeia district to the Emperor Rhomanós I (920–44). Rambaud, op. cit., p. 165, dates the change 934; Pertusi, in his edition of *De Them.*, p. 48, dates the first draft of the book 933/4.

[3] 948 is Bury's date for Várdhas Phokás's capture of Adhatá, which Constantine mentions in his biography of Basil I, chap. 48, pp. 281–2. Canard's date, however, is 957 (see the present work, p. 319, with n. 2).

[4] Chaps. 13, p. 88, and 46, p. 208, were written after Rhomanós I's death, and he died on 15 July 948.

[5] This *terminus ad quem* is Bury's dating of chapter 37 ('On the Pecheneg People'). R. J. H. Jenkins, in the General Introduction to his and Gy. Moravcsik's *Commentary* on the *De Adm. Imp.*, p. 5, dates chapter 37, lines 13–14 of their text (p. 164, lines 20–1, of the Bonn text), 950–1. Moravcsik, in the *Commentary*, p. 144, dates these lines 949–51. Jenkins holds that Constantine started to write this work as an historical and antiquarian treatise, but that he subsequently converted it into a practical handbook for the guidance of his son Rhomanós II. 'At least it can be said that this method and purpose of a purely historical, topographical and antiquarian Περὶ Ἐθνῶν were being followed during the years 948–51, and that its conversion to a diplomatic vademecum did not occur until 951–2' (General Introduction, p. 6). Bury, in *B.Z.*, xv, p. 523, argues that chap. 30 of *De Adm. Imp.* was written 'after 950'. F. Dvornik, in Jenkins's and Moravcsik's *Commentary*, p. 99, holds that chap. 30 was

Τὰ Βασιλικὰ Ταξείδια   952–959
De Caerimoniis Aulae Byzantinae   –959[1]

Constantine's literary activities make his intellectual interests apparent. They also make his order of priorities, among these interests of his, fairly clear. In the third place they reveal his lack of interest in some subjects that were of importance in his world, and this not least for someone in his official position.

Constantine's life-long paramount interest seems to have been his earliest one. He had received the Hellenic education that had been revived in the ninth-century Byzantine renaissance,[2] and for him, as for many Western classical scholars since the fifteenth-century Western Renaissance, the Hellenic World, as this is mirrored in Hellenic literature, was more familiar, and, in a sense, more real, than the world into which he himself had been born.

This comes out in Constantine's *De Thematibus*. Having embarked on this treatise on the provincial administration of the East Roman Empire, and having found, apparently, no documents except a list of the army-corps districts, with notes on recent changes in the boundaries and the

written after 955 (see the whole of Dvornik's discussion of the dating of chapters 29–36 on pp. 97–101). If Jenkins and Dvornik are right, the compilation of *De Adm. Imp.* was in progress from perhaps as early as 948 to at least as late as 952 (see Jenkins in op. cit., p. 5), and perhaps till as late as 955. See also the present work, p. 465.

[1] The phrase ὅσα . . . παρ' ἡμῶν αὐτῶν ἐθεάθη καὶ ἐν ἡμῖν ἐνηργήθη in the preface to Book I is interpreted by Bury (*E.H.R.*, p. 211) to mean that this work of Constantine's was begun in Rhomanós I's reign, when Constantine was only a spectator, and was continued during Constantine's second bout of sole rule, when he was effectively sovereign. The bunch of unincorporated documents appended to Book II is an indication that Constantine was working on the *De Caerimoniis* down to the end of his life. Bury holds (ibid., pp. 211 and 217) that Book I, chaps. 96–7, is the only piece that was added after Constantine's death. Chapter 42, he thinks, is Constantine's own. He thinks that the two references here to Constantine's death are interpolations.

[2] The fathers of this renaissance had been Leo the Mathematician, the Caesar Várdhas, and the Patriarch Phótios. For Leo, see *Theoph. Cont.*, Book IV, Reign of Michael III, chaps. 26–9, pp. 185–92; *Georg. Mon. Interpolatus*, Reign of Theóphilos, chap. 23, p. 806; Leo Grammaticus, Reign of Theóphilos, p. 225; Kedhrênós, vol. ii, pp. 165–71. Genesius, *Basileiai* (Bonn, 1834, Weber), p. 98, names, in addition to Leo, three other salaried members of the new faculty: Leo's pupil Theodore for geometry, Theodhéyios for astronomy, Kométás for language and literature (τὰ γραμματικά). In this passage, Genesius admits that Várdhas 'prized and promoted culture (σοφία) enthusiastically' (περὶ πολλοῦ δὲ τῷ Καίσαρι Βάρδᾳ ἡ σοφία πεφιλοτίμητο), and that, after he had refounded the University, 'he took the trouble to pay frequent visits to it. He made himself personally acquainted with the individual qualifications of each of the students; gave them encouragement about their prospects; and gave the professors inducements for doing their duty by the students conscientiously. In fact, Várdhas sowed the seeds of an intellectual revival that has borne increasing fruit from his time to ours, and this is an enduring monument to Várdhas's memory.' Genesius's encomium of Várdhas's achievement in the field of culture is the more significant because its context is denigratory. Genesius must have been instructed by Constantine to denigrate Basil I's two victims, Várdhas and Michael III; but Genesius could insert his praise of Várdhas's cultural activities with impunity, because Constantine appreciated these.

status of some of them,[1] Constantine has filled in his blanks with re-
miniscences of his classical reading that have no relation to his subject;
and, in at least one case, this practice has led him wildly astray. Con-
stantine sees that the name of the Thracenses ($\Theta\rho\alpha\kappa\dot{\eta}\sigma\iota\iota$) army-corps
must have come from Thrace to the corps' present district in western
Asia Minor. He is unaware that the corps itself had been transferred to
Asia Minor from Thrace in the seventh century and had brought its
name with it from its original location; so he derives the name from an
alleged settlement of Thracians in Asia in the time of Alyattes King of
Lydia.[2] This story of Constantine's is doubly discredited by being associated with the folk-tale of the accomplished woman from Thrace,
which is at least as old as Herodotus.[3] Constantine's classical learning has
thus tricked him into ante-dating the arrival of the name 'Thrakēsioi' in
Asia Minor by at least 1,200 years. His classical learning was employed
to better purpose in producing the collection of classified extracts from
works of Hellenic literature.

If Hellenic literature was Constantine's paramount interest, his second
greatest interest was the ceremonial of the East Roman Court. This
comes out even more strikingly in *Tὰ Βασιλικὰ Ταξείδια* than in the *De
Caerimoniis* itself. The subject of this minor work is the Imperial ceremonial
that has to be observed in the field when an East Roman Emperor joins
the Army on active service. This is a strange approach to the study of
military affairs, and it is not surprising that Constantine should have
been hard put to it to find information about his subject, for this was
not a subject that was dealt with in any of the treatises on the East
Roman art of war.

I did a great deal of research [Constantine records in addressing the treatise
to his son Rhomanós II] without finding any memorandum on the subject in
the Palace, till at last I did manage to find one in the Sighrianēs monastery.
The máyistros Leo (surname, Katákylas) had embraced the monastic life
there. This máyistros had written on the subject by order of the Christ-loving
sagacious Emperor of the Romans Leo, my father and your grandfather. The
máyistros was quite unversed in Hellenic culture ($\mu o \upsilon \sigma \iota \kappa \hat{\eta} s \ ' E \lambda \lambda \eta \nu \iota \kappa \hat{\eta} s \ \dot{a}\mu\dot{\epsilon}\tau o \chi o s$
$\ldots \hat{\eta}\nu$). Consequently his treatise is full of barbarisms and solecisms and
grammatical errors. This did not prevent him from being devout or from having a thirst for the things of the spirit—virtues that were displayed in his life.
But, as I have said, he had no part or lot in Hellenic education, and consequently his treatise is quite culpably full of pitfalls. All the same, it has the

---

[1] See the present work, pp. 246 and 251–2 (Leo VI's schedule of salaries of stratêghoí), 255
(Kharsianón and Paphlaghonía), 257–8 (Mesopotamía and Lykandós), 261 (Sámos and
Aiyaíon Pélaghos), 268 (Strymón), 269–70 (Dhalmatía), 270–1 (Optimátoi), 274 (Kharpezí-
kion).

[2] *De Them.*, pp. 22–3.

[3] See Herodotus, Book V, chaps. 12–14.

merit of being veracious, thanks to the author's devoutness and uprightness. I found the treatise written in a slipshod style, besides being terribly vague and imprecise in its exposition of the facts. The original is less than one third of the length of my version, in which I have expanded it for clearness' sake. I now present you with this version of mine for permanent reference.[1]

Constantine's third greatest interest was foreign countries and peoples —and his interest in this subject was a lively one, in spite of its not being quite as keen as his interest in protocol and in the classics. The vast alien world outside the East Roman Empire's frontiers excited Constantine's curiosity, and, the more remote the country, the greater his zest. This interest of his in exotic places extends to outlying parts of the East Roman Empire itself, e.g. Khersón,[2] Venice,[3] Dalmatia,[4] the Slav settlements in the Pelopónnêsos,[5] the Maniots who had gone on worshipping the Olympian gods till they had been converted to Christianity in the reign of Constantine's grandfather Basil I.[6]

Constantine shows less curiosity about the history of the Roman Empire itself. Its history before the reign of Constantine I is almost beyond his historical horizon.[7] Constantine I and his successors mean more to him. Most of the Eastern Emperors, from Constantine I onwards, had been buried in Constantinople, and Constantine VII is familiar with their tombs.[8] He is definitely interested in the history of the dynasty founded by his grandfather Basil I. He would have liked to write the history of the Basilian dynasty from the reign of the founder down to his own time, but ill health and lack of time have constrained him to confine himself to covering his grandfather's reign.[9] The ill health and the lack of time were genuine obstacles. All the same, they did not prevent Constantine from producing his extracts from Hellenic literature and his *De Caerimoniis* and his *De Administrando Imperio*. What is revealed by his excuse for not achieving his ambitions as an historian is the order of his priorities. He was a classical scholar first, a student of protocol second, a geographer third. History came only fourth in the hierarchy of his interests.

Constantine's intense interest in East Roman protocol was not matched by any comparable interest in East Roman administration. For example, the chapter in *De Caerimoniis*[10] on the procedure for an Imperial inspection of the military granaries is entirely concerned with protocol except for one practical provision. The Emperor is to bring an architect with him

---

[1] *Tὰ Βασιλικὰ Ταξείδια*, pp. 456–7. [2] *De Adm. Imp.*, chaps. 1, 6, 7, 11, 42, 53.
[3] Op. cit., chap. 28. [4] Op. cit., chap. 30. [5] Op. cit., chaps. 49–50.
[6] Op. cit., chap. 50. See also the present work, p. 514, n. 7, p. 527, and pp. 619–20.
[7] See pp. 243–4.
[8] See his gazetteer of these in *De Caer.*, Book II, chap. 42, pp. 642–9.
[9] See the passage quoted on p. 6 from Constantine's preface to his biography of Basil I.
[10] Book II, chap. 50, pp. 699–701.

to measure up the cubic capacity of the store-houses, in case the Emperor may wish to check the accuracy of the figures for the amount of grain in store that the kómês ton orríon and his noumerários will have submitted to him.

An aspect of East Roman public administration that does interest Constantine is the problem of tipping. Chapters 49, 55, and 56 of Book II of *De Caerimoniis* are concerned with this, and there is a great deal about it in Τὰ Βασιλικὰ Ταξείδια too. Four or five laws of Constantine's, regulating tips, are extant.[1] Tips played an important part in East Roman official life. Newly appointed officials had to tip the praipósitos and others; and the Emperor had to tip all his officials, and his foreign state guests as well. Constantine Porphyrogenitus's conscientiousness in performing this tiresome part of his duties made an impression on Bishop Liutprand.[2] What is most tiresome about tipping is the difficulty of being quite sure of the right occasions and the right amounts; so Constantine was doing a useful service when he drew up schedules giving exact figures for each occasion. If his figures met with acceptance among those concerned, his schedules will have greased the wheels of East Roman administration as well as the palms of East Roman administrators. Fortunately for present-day students, Constantine has included, among his schedules of tips, a note[3] of the salaries of governors of the 'Eastern' army-corps districts and kleisoúrai.

The lowest priority among Constantine's interests was given to the East Roman art of war. Τὰ Βασιλικὰ Ταξείδια and the protocol for the inspection of military granaries prove this conclusively. The only grains of genuinely military information in the Ταξείδια are the table of the Emperor's *étapes* on his journey—a procession rather than a march—from Constantinople south-eastward,[4] the table of the chain of beacons between the south-east frontier and Constantinople,[5] and the notices of the security arrangements when en route through enemy territory or in camp at night.[6] Constantine is more concerned with establishing which members of the Court and of the civil service are exempt from being called up for military training (τηρωνάτος), and which are not exempt.[7]

---

[1] Rambaud, op. cit., p. 92.
[2] See p. 18 above.
[3] *De Caer.*, Book II, chap. 50, pp. 696-7.
[4] *De Caer.*, Book I, *T.V.T.*, pp. 444-5.
[5] *T.V.T.*, p. 492. This table is also given in *Theoph. Cont.*, Book IV, Reign of Michael III, chap. 35, pp. 197-8, and in pseudo-Symeon Magister, Reign of Michael III, chap. 46, pp. 681-2. Pseudo-Symeon mentions that this signalling-system could not only sound the alarm but could indicate which of twelve alternative possible eventualities had occurred. See also Kedhrênós, vol. ii, p. 174. See, too, the present work, p. 299.
[6] *De Caer.*, Book I, *T.V.T.*, pp. 481-2, 484, 489-90.
[7] *De Caer.*, Book II, chap. 50, pp. 697-9.

2. Constantine's Practical Purposes

CONSTANTINE PORPHYROGENITUS may have been academic-minded for an Emperor, but, thanks to his being an Emperor, he was practical-minded for a scholar. All his literary activities had some practical purpose.

For instance, his fifty-three books of extracts from extant Hellenic literature were not designed merely to reduce the huge bulk of this to manageable dimensions.[1] The choice of topics—e.g. 'embassies' and 'virtues and vices', which are the subjects of the two books that still survive—shows that the selection was intended to be of practical use for statesmen. The notion that literature can be turned to direct practical account is, no doubt, naïve, but the intention is characteristic of Constantine's view of the relation between literature and life.

In the *De Caerimoniis*, Constantine's general aim is to convert the *procès verbaux* of the procedure at some particular celebration of a recurrent ceremony into a generalized form which can be used on any occasion in future.[2] Constantine declares, in his preface to each of the two books of the *De Caerimoniis*,[3] that the publication of a correct account of East Roman Imperial protocol is going to enhance the Empire's prestige abroad and to foster the loyalty of the Empire's own subjects to the Imperial Government. This expectation was visionary, but Constantine's good faith in making the claim is demonstrated by his unmistakable enthusiasm for this tedious subject. He was not only an enthusiast for it on paper; his conscientious performance of his own onerous role in it kept him out of his study for hundreds of working hours per annum which he would have enjoyed far more if he had allowed himself to spend them on studying his beloved protocol instead of acting it.

De Administrando Imperio was started by Constantine as a work of descriptive geography. The countries to be described were the East Roman Empire's neighbours, to the exclusion of the Empire itself. (The modern title is a misnomer. The book has no title; only a dedication to Constantine's son Rhomanós II.) Chapter 42, in which the reader is carried round the northern frontiers of the Empire in an arc extending from Thessaloníkê to Abkhazia, is presented almost in the form of a gazetteer.

---

[1] The amount of extant Hellenic literature was much smaller in Constantine Porphyrogenitus's time than it had been before the loss of the library at Alexandria, but it was much greater than it has been since the sack of Constantinople by the Western 'crusaders' in 1204.

[2] See Bury, 'The Ceremonial Book of Constantine Porphyrogennetos', in *The English Historical Review*, April 1907, pp. 221–2. Instances of this are Book I, chaps. 1 and 37; Book II, chaps. 1, 2, and 13.

[3] See *De Caer.*, pp. 3–5 and 516–17.

Chapter 9, which describes the route of the Rhos from Kiev to Constantinople round the cataracts of the River Dniepr, is a mine of exotic information. The list of the twin names—one Scandinavian, one Slavonic —of each of the cataracts illustrates Constantine's curiosity[1] and gratifies ours. Constantine notes the locations of petroleum wells in the Caucasus and Armenia with as sharp an eye as Peter the Great, nearly 800 years later.[2] However, while this book was in the making, Constantine evidently decided to change its character. Instead of being completed as a description of the Empire's neighbours, it was to be turned into a manual of practical instructions for dealing with them. Jenkins suggests[3] that the date at which Constantine changed his plans for the book was 951/2, the year in which Rhomanós II, to whom the book is dedicated by his father, reached the age of fourteen.

The most purposeful of all Constantine's literary activities was his attempt to whitewash his grandfather Basil I. After having commissioned first Genesius and then the anonymous author of the first four books of *Theophanes Continuatus* to do this for him, Constantine took the anonymous author's task on himself and did Genesius's work all over again, with his own hand, in his biography of Basil I, which is included in *Theophanes Continuatus* as the fifth book of this composite work.[4]

Constantine had three purposes here. All three were designs to obscure the truth. He wanted to conceal the humbleness of his grandfather's origin, to conceal his lack of literary education, and, above all, to conceal his part—which was the protagonist's part—in the murders of the Caesar Várdhas and the Emperor Michael III.

All these three designs of Constantine's were perverse, though not all for the same reason. It was perversely unimaginative not to have realized that Basil's low birth and poor education had been handicaps that his grandson, or anyone else who was concerned for Basil's reputation, ought not to have concealed but ought to have advertised, considering that these initial disadvantages of Basil's enhanced the magnitude of his

---

[1] Constantine's curiosity has, in some cases, carried him beyond the limits of his knowledge. For instance, he states, in *De Adm. Imp.*, chap. 13, p. 86, that Constantine I had sanctioned Imperial marriages with the Franks, and with these alone among all foreign nations, because Constantine I himself stemmed from those parts. Constantine I actually stemmed from Naïssus (Niš) and was brought up in Britain. Constantine Porphyrogenitus also states, in op. cit., chap. 28, p. 123, that the continental ancestors of the Venetians were Franks. This certainly will not have been the Venetians' account of their ethnic origins; it must have been Constantine's own idea. Tenth-century East Romans found 'Franks' a convenient 'portmanteau word'. The author of Book VI of *Theoph. Cont.* states, in the Reign of Rhomanós II, chap. 39, p. 432, that the Rhos 'are a branch of the race of the Franks'. He can hardly have been aware of the linguistic affinity between the Scandinavian and the German branches of the Teutonic family of languages.

[2] *De Adm. Imp.*, chap. 53, p. 269.

[3] In his Introduction to the *Commentary* on his and Moravcsik's edition, pp. 5–6.

[4] See p. 5, n. 2.

eventual achievement. This self-made man had not only won the Imperial Crown; in a long reign he had shown himself fully equal to the exacting demands of the office; he had been the most statesmanlike East Roman Emperor since his self-made predecessor Leo III, with the possible exception of Leo III's son Constantine V. As for Constantine Porphyrogenitus's attempt to suppress Basil I's criminal record, this was doubly dishonest in a kinsman and successor of the criminal who was also an historian, and who was aware, as Constantine certainly was, of the standard of integrity that his chosen profession required of him. More than that, this third piece of dishonesty, besides being morally graver than the other two, was also still more ill-advised. Constantine could and did impose on Genesius,[1] and on the anonymous author of the first four books of *Theophanes Continuatus*, the same perversion of the truth that he perpetrated in his own biography of Basil I, but it was beyond Constantine's power to pervert the entire record.

Indeed, the truth shows through even Constantine's own employee Genesius's garbled version of the story. Constantine was right in judging that Genesius's work failed to fulfil Constantine's discreditable purpose. Constantine's own performance in his game of misrepresentation was abler, and he would have done better, from his own point of view, if, instead of contenting himself with duplicating Genesius's work, he had suppressed his employee's tell-tale narrative before publication.

Genesius gives the impression that he felt himself to have been set a task that was so impracticable as to be acutely embarrassing. The only passages in which he displays any zest are his narratives of Petronás's victorious campaign in 863[2] and the victory over Khrysókheir *circa* 872.[3] It looks as if Genesius had authentic information—perhaps from the same source—about the campaign in 861 in which the Emperor Michael III participated in person,[4] but in this case Genesius was inhibited by his employer's instructions. Basil had to be whitewashed, so Basil's unhappy predecessor Michael had to be denigrated. The reader of Genesius's account of Michael's reign (*imperabat* 842–67) would not guess, if this were his sole source of information, that this reign had in truth seen the turn of the tide in the East Roman Empire's favour in the Empire's chronic warfare with the Eastern Muslims.

Omissions and silences are Genesius's stock expedients for carrying out his instructions in defiance of the facts, but he is clumsier than his employer Constantine. Genesius's omissions are conspicuous and his silences are eloquent. For instance, there is not a word about the

[1] See K. Krumbacher, *Geschichte der byzantinischen Litteratur*, 2nd ed. (Munich, 1897, Beck), p. 265.
[2] Book IV, pp. 94–7 cited on p. 300, n. 1.
[3] Op. cit., pp. 120–6, cited on p. 300, n. 2.
[4] See Genesius's account of this campaign in Book IV, pp. 91–3.

chequered history of the relations between Basil and Phótios, and Basil's name is not mentioned till, on the eve of the assassination of Várdhas, Leo the philosopher interprets a portent as signifying that Várdhas is going to be replaced by Basil as 'Number Two' to the Emperor Michael.[1] In the account of the assassination,[2] Basil's presence is not mentioned, and Michael and God, between them, are saddled with the whole of the odium.[3]

Genesius's falsification of the story of the assassination of Michael is still more naïvely transparent. The blame for the rift between Michael and Basil is ascribed to anonymous intriguers, who are alleged to have warned each of the two Emperors that the other was plotting to kill him.

According to one account, Michael was definitely planning to kill Basil. In particular, he had given orders for Basil to be speared while they were out on a hunting party together. According to another account, this is untrue: Michael was [still] well disposed towards Basil, in spite of his faith in him having been shaken by slanderers. [Michael's alienation from Basil] moved some of Basil's well-wishers to urge Basil to murder Michael. They failed to persuade Basil. He was not entirely alienated from Michael and perhaps (ἢ καὶ) he also recoiled with horror from polluting himself with the crime of murder. Basil's supporters therefore did the deed themselves, to save Basil from a catastrophe in which they too would have been involved.[4]

In his next paragraph, Genesius is equally clumsy in his handling of the compromising fact that Basil, after he had become sole Emperor by murdering his benefactor and senior colleague Michael, built the 'Néa' church and dedicated it to the Archangel Michael. This was a snag that even Genesius's employer, the more adroit apologist Constantine Porphyrogenitus, subsequently found it difficult to circumnavigate. Genesius impaled himself on it.

Basil seized upon the personal advantage for himself which the murder of Michael had presented to him. He recognized that he now wore the Imperial Crown by God's grace, and not [by Michael's grace] as before. He expressed his gratitude to God by building a new church and dedicating it to the high commanders of the incorporeal hosts (τῶν ἀρχιστρατηγῶν τῶν αὔλων ταγμάτων) ... In this church, when it had been built ... and been consecrated, ..., Basil received the Imperial Crown from patriarchal hands, thus making a fresh start of his reign on a new basis. The Imperial Crown had now been conferred on him by the archangels' aid.[5]

In this passage, Genesius has carried out Constantine's instructions. He had been told to suppress the fact that the 'Néa' had been dedicated

---

[1] Book IV, p. 104.   [2] Book IV, pp. 105–7.

[3] Προμεμηχανούργητο ταῦτα ἔκ τε Θεοῦ καὶ βασιλικῆς ἐπινεύσεως (p. 103). πρὸς ἐνώπιον βασιλέως ἀνηλεῶς ἀποκτέννοντες κατακερματίζουσι Καίσαρα (p. 106).

[4] Genesius, Book IV, p. 113.   [5] Book IV, p. 113.

by Basil, not to the archangels collectively, but individually to the Archangel Michael together with Christ and Elijah. Genesius had also been told to ignore the insinuation that the building and dedication of this church had been an act, not of thanksgiving, but of atonement. Genesius has carried out these instructions to the letter, but nevertheless he has let the cat out of the bag.

Genesius is as infelicitous in hyperbole as he is in meiosis. For instance, Constantine the dhroungários—Basil's fellow Armenian and his bene-factor in the early stages of his career—may in truth have been an honourable man, but Genesius has made him suspect by invariably de-picting him as a paragon. It may well be true that, at the wrestling-match in which Basil made his fortune, Constantine did Basil a good turn by having the wet ground sprinkled with chaff to make sure that Basil should not slip.[1] This friendly precaution of Constantine's is men-tioned in Constantine Porphyrogenitus's account of this incident, be-sides Genesius's.[2] According to Genesius, however, Constantine the dhroungários was also the only member of the Senate who refused to condone[3] the Caesar Várdhas's high-handed act of deposing the Patriarch Ighnátios and installing the layman Phótios in his place. Constantine then secretly succoured Ighnátios when Ighnátios was being tortured.[4] Thereafter, Constantine excelled himself on the supremely critical occasion of the murder of Várdhas. He saved the Emperor Michael from sharing Várdhas's fate, and he averted a civil war.[5] This unbroken re-cord of virtue, moral courage, benevolence, and presence of mind seems too good to be true.

Evidently Constantine Porphyrogenitus recognized that Genesius had blundered, and this should have served as a warning to Constantine that, notwithstanding his own greater intellectual ability, he was unlikely to fare appreciably better if he now took upon himself the task to which Genesius had proved unequal. Genesius had done his best to carry out Constantine's instructions to misrepresent the truth, but he had been defeated by the notoriety of the facts.

Constantine must surely have been aware that there was current, in his time, a different version of the story of Basil I—a version that, though it may not have been the whole truth and nothing but the truth,[6] was at least less far from the truth than Constantine's apologia for his grand-father. Liutprand states, as being common knowledge, that the murderer

---

[1] Book IV, p. 110.   [2] See p. 374, with n. 1.   [3] Book IV, p. 100.
[4] Book IV, pp. 100–2.   [5] Book IV, pp. 106–7.
[6] For instance, it may not have been true that Constantine's father Leo VI was Evdhokía Ingerínê's son, not by Basil I, but by Michael III, whose mistress she had been before Michael had married her off to Basil. See *Georg. Mon. Cont.*, Reign of Michael III, chap. 33, p. 835; Leo Grammaticus, p. 249. Pseudo-Symeon makes the allegation, not about Leo, but about his brother Constantine (Reign of Michael III, chap. 46, p. 681).

of Michael had been Basil; that the crime had weighed on Basil's conscience; and that Basil had built the 'Néa' within the precincts of the Palace and had dedicated it to his victim's name-saint Michael the Archangel by way of atonement.[1] The story told to Liutprand may not be altogether true,[2] but we may guess, with some assurance, that it is true in respect of the point of substance, which is that the Emperor Michael's murderer had been Basil; and, in any case, Liutprand's knowledge of the story is evidence that it was in circulation, by word of mouth, in Constantinople in Constantine Porphyrogenitus's time. About two hundred years later, Liutprand's story turns up in identical form —including the statement that the 'Néa' was dedicated to the Archangel Michael—in the work of the twelfth-century Greek chronicler Michael Glykás.[3]

---

[1] Liutprand, *Antapodosis*, Book I, chaps. 8–10. This story is repeated in Book III, chaps. 32–4.

[2] The 'Néa' was certainly not dedicated to St. Michael exclusively. The dedication was a triple one, and two of the 'Néa's' patrons were certainly Christ and Elijah. Was St. Michael the third? Constantine Porphyrogenitus, in his biography of Basil I, names the patrons of the 'Néa' in three different passages, and in each place he mentions Christ first and Elijah last. On the other hand, he describes the middle patron differently in each case. In chap. 68, p. 308, he writes τῶν Ἀρχιστρατηγῶν (i.e. the Archangels collectively); in chap. 76, p. 319, he writes 'Michael the first [in rank] of the angels'; in chap. 83, p. 325, he writes 'Gabriel the first [in rank] of the angelic powers'.

What are we to make of this discrepancy? It looks as if the other patron of the 'Néa', besides Christ and Elijah, was, in truth, St. Michael, as Liutprand says. This dedication to St. Michael will then have given rise to the story, picked up by Liutprand, that the dedication to St. Michael was Basil's atonement for the murder of the Emperor Michael. The story will have come to Constantine Porphyrogenitus's ears, and he will have sought to scotch it by expunging St. Michael's name from his own narrative. In one of the three passages in which this correct attribution had been given by him, he substituted 'the Archangels' for 'Michael'; in another passage he substituted 'Gabriel'; but he overlooked the third passage in which the correct name 'Michael' had likewise been written by him in his original draft.

In chap. 83, p. 325, though not in the two earlier passages, Constantine states that the 'Néa' was built by Basil I εἰς ὄνομα τούτων (scilicet Christ, Gabriel, and Elijah) καὶ μνήμην ἀΐδιον, ἔτι δὲ τῆς Θεοτόκου καὶ Νικολάου τοῦ ἐν ἱεράρχαις πρωτεύοντος (which must mean Pope Nicholas I). The 'Néa' was dedicated on 1 May in the fourteenth year of Basil I's reign by the Patriarch Phótios (see Symeon the máyistros and loghothétês in Leo Grammaticus, p. 258, and in *Georg. Mon. Cont.*, p. 845, as well as pseudo-Symeon, p. 692). The ékphrasis declaimed by Phótios on this occasion is printed in Migne, *P.G.*, vol. cii, cols. 563–74. Both in the text and in the title of Phótios's oration, the 'Néa' is declared to have been dedicated to the Theotókos. No other names are mentioned, and this omission is significant.

[3] 'This Basil was conscience-stricken over his having murdered Michael the Drunkard; so, as a way of propitiating God, he built a number of new churches, at many places in Constantinople, in honour of the Archangel Michael. One of these is the so-called "Néa" in the precincts of the Palace' (Michael Glykás, *Vívlos Khronikê*, p. 549). It is curious that, in his previous account of the murder of Várdhas, Glykás does not say anything about Basil's part in that, though he states quite bluntly that it was Basil who murdered Michael (pp. 544–6). It will be noticed that the story has been improved on since Liutprand's day. Basil is now said to have dedicated to St. Michael, not only the 'Néa', but also a number of other new churches in Constantinople. In Constantine Porphyrogenitus's catalogue of new churches built by Basil besides the 'Néa' (op. cit., chaps. 87–8, pp. 329–31) there is no indubitable mention of any new dedication to St. Michael. In Constantine's record, in op. cit., chap. 88, of Basil's

It was, in fact, impossible for Constantine to prevent this story, which was being published abroad in Latin by Constantine's contemporary Liutprand, from being published in Greek eventually within the frontiers of the East Roman Empire. All that Constantine could achieve was to delay the publication of the story in his own dominions. So long as Constantine remained alive and on the throne, no one within the Empire would dare to publish it, or would perhaps even dare to put it on parchment for confidential circulation. This much could be achieved by the autocratic power that an East Roman Emperor wielded. But Constantine could have banned the publication of the truth without publishing a mendacious version of his own. It was true that, during his lifetime, his version would be the only one that could be purchased at a bookseller's in East Roman territory. But this temporary monopoly would do little good to Basil's memory if, all the time, something much nearer to the truth was in everybody's mind.

The true story was published, probably in Nikêphóros II Phokás's reign (*imperabat* 963–9),[1] by Symeon the máyistros and loghothétês;[2] and, when once the truth had found its way into the blood-stream of the unofficial Chronicle of East Roman history, it was going to circulate actively. It duly reappears in the version of the Chronicle that was produced by the pseudo-Symeon[3] as well as in *Georgius Monachus Continuatus*'s and Leo Grammaticus's transcripts of the genuine Symeon's text. Thus it did not take long for the story of Basil I to escape from the control of the defunct Emperor Constantine Porphyrogenitus's dead hand. Constantine's only notable posthumous convert among the chroniclers is the twelfth-century chronicler Kedhrênós, who adopts uncritically much of Constantine's account of Basil, though Kedhrênós is sharply critical of Constantine himself.[4]

For instance, Kedhrênós reproduces[5] Constantine's extravagant account of Basil's ancestry. According also to all other accounts but one,[6]

having built a church dedicated to St. Peter on the crown of the perídhromos of the Markianón in Constantinople, Constantine notes ᾧ καὶ τὸ τοῦ ἀρχιστρατήγου εὐκτήριον ἤνωται ('to which the oratory of the Archangel has been annexed'). This notice leaves it in doubt whether this oratory was, like the church of St. Peter itself, a new building or was an already existing one. The church of St. Michael the Archangel at the Sosthénion (alias Stenón, the present-day Istenye) on the European shore of the Bosphorus was restored by Basil I (see Constantine Porphyrogenitus in op. cit., chap. 94, pp. 340–1), but Constantine I, not Basil I, had been this church's founder.

[1] See Krumbacher, *Geschichte der byzantinischen Litteratur*, 2nd ed., pp. 348–9.
[2] Reproduced in *Georg. Mon. Cont.*, Reign of Michael III, chap. 34, pp. 836–7, and in Leo Grammaticus, Reign of Michael III, pp. 250–1.
[3] Reign of Michael III, chap. 48, pp. 684–5.
[4] See the passage quoted on p. 20.   [5] In vol. ii, pp. 183–4, of the Bonn edition.
[6] Symeon Magister, in his account of Basil's early life in *Georg. Mon. Cont.*, Reign of Michael III, chaps. 8–9, pp. 817–19, and in Leo Grammaticus, p. 231, neither asserts Basil's Armenian origin nor denies it.

Basil's family on his father's side was of Armenian origin; but Constantine makes this Armenian blood royal. He traces the family's lineage back to two members of the branch of the Arsacid house that had reigned in Armenia. He makes them enter the Roman Empire as refugees in Leo I's reign (*imperabat* 457–74).[1] Their descendants, so Constantine's story goes, had eventually been planted in Adrianople, and the family had retained its identity there down to Basil's father's generation.[2] According to Constantine, Basil's mother's blood was still bluer than his father's; she claimed descent from Constantine the Great on one side and from Alexander the Great on the other.[3] However, Constantine does not mention Basil's father's name,[4] and the twelfth-century chronicler Zonarás explicitly rejects Basil's claim to Arsacid descent in describing his rise in the world from obscure origins.[5] According to pseudo-Symeon,[6] an Arsacid genealogy, going back as far as Tiridates, was forged for Basil by Phótios.

As for Basil's education, Constantine admits that the only teacher that he ever had was his own father. He claims that even Chiron or Lycurgus or Solon could not have done better for him than his father did.[7] Constantine is here glozing over the fact that Basil did not, in his childhood, receive a literary education of the kind that had been enjoyed by his grandson. Constantine is franker in two later passages. After Basil had come to the throne, Constantine tells us,[8] he used, in such spare time as he could then command, to have works on history, political science, and ethics read aloud to him, and eventually he taught himself to read and write, and then started to read books with his own eyes. He made a point of having his children, girls as well as boys, given the education to which he himself 'had originally been a stranger owing to his circumstances'.[9] In the Kainoúryion, which was Basil's addition to the Imperial Palace, his and Evdhokía Ingerínê's children were portrayed in mosaic, with the girls as well as the boys carrying copies of portions of the Holy Scriptures.[10]

An identical account of Basil's role on the occasion of the murder of Michael III's uncle the Caesar Várdhas is given by Constantine and by his employee the anonymous author of the first four books of *Theophanes*

---

[1] Constantine, biography of Basil I, chap. 2, pp. 212–13. Genesius, Book IV, p. 107, had already made Basil an Arsacid descended from King Tiridates.

[2] Constantine, op. cit., chaps. 3–4, pp. 215–16.

[3] Op. cit., chap. 3, p. 216. Cf. Genesius, Book IV, chap. 107.

[4] Nor does Genesius mention it.

[5] Ioánnes Zonarás, *Epitomae Historiarum*, vol. iii, Libri XIII–XVIII (Bonn, 1897, Weber), pp. 407–12.

[6] Reign of Basil I, chap. 7, pp. 689–90.

[7] Biography of Basil I, chap. 6, p. 220. Genesius had mentioned only Chiron and had enlarged on Basil's physical training and prowess (Book IV, pp. 107 and 126–7).

[8] Op. cit., chap. 72, p. 314.

[9] οὐκ ἔσχεν ἐξ ἀρχῆς οἰκείως πρὸς γράμματα διὰ τὴν βιωτικὴν περιπέτειαν (chap. 89, p. 334).

[10] Op. cit., chap. 89, p. 333.

Continuatus.[1] According to this Constantinian story, the murder had been planned by Michael III and Várdhas's son-in-law Symvátios the loghothétês tou dhrómou. (The anonymus attributes the initiative to Symvátios alone.) When the Emperor (or Symvátios, according to the anonymus) gave the signal, the appointed assassins lost their nerve and took no action. The Emperor then appealed to Basil, who, by this time, was his parakoimómenos. Basil (we are intended to infer *ex silentio*) had not been implicated in the plot, but, in this crisis, Basil's first duty, and first concern, was to save the Emperor's life, which would have been in danger if the plot had missed fire and if Várdhas had thus been given a chance of dealing a counter-stroke. In these circumstances, Basil intervened. He breathed courage into the panic-stricken assassins' hearts and spurred them into doing their job. It is to be inferred (*ex silentio* again) that Basil himself took no direct hand in the killing of Várdhas.

According to Symeon Magister,[2] on the other hand,

Basil placed himself behind [the chairs on which Michael and Várdhas were sitting side by side], took his stand there, and made a threatening gesture at the Caesar. [At that moment] the Caesar suddenly turned his head and caught Basil in the act of threatening him, whereupon Basil gave him one with the sword (δέδωκεν αὐτῷ μετὰ τοῦ ξίφους), and Basil's men then hacked the Caesar limb from limb, while the Emperor looked on without saying a word.

According to this account, Basil was both the planner and the executant of the murder, with Michael's connivance, and the crime was aggravated by perjury. Before setting out on the expedition on which the deed was done, Michael, Basil, and Várdhas had received the sacrament together, at the Patriarch Phótios's hands, on the occasion of a solemn religious ceremony. Michael and Basil had dipped their fingers in the eucharistic wine, had crossed themselves with it, and had sworn, as they did so, to Várdhas that, if he came with them on the expedition, his life would be sacrosanct.[3] Pseudo-Symeon's[4] and Zonarás's[5] accounts are the same as Symeon Magister's.

Constantine's and his anonymous employee's accounts[6] of Basil's role on the occasion of the murder of Michael III on 24 September 867, are, if possible, still more disingenuous than their accounts of the murder of Várdhas. Constantine's story is that Michael's misconduct had become so flagrant that at last it goaded 'the most distinguished officers of state and all responsible-minded members of the Senate into taking concerted

[1] *Theoph. Cont.*, Book V, chap. 17, pp. 235–8; Book IV, Reign of Michael III, chap. 41, pp. 204–6. Constantine's story is adopted by Kedhrênós, vol. ii, pp. 174–80.

[2] In *Georg. Mon. Cont.*, Reign of Michael III, chap. 28, p. 831. The text of Leo Grammaticus's transcript, p. 245, tallies with *G.M.C.* verbatim, apart from the omission of a few words.

[3] *Georg. Mon. Cont.*, chap. 26, p. 829; Leo Grammaticus, p. 243.

[4] Pseudo-Symeon, Reign of Michael III, chap. 40, pp. 676–7, and chap. 42, p. 679.

[5] Zonarás, Bonn edition, vol. iii, Books XIII–XVIII, p. 414.

[6] *Theoph. Cont.*, Book V, chap. 27, p. 254; Book IV, Reign of Michael III, chap. 44, p. 210.

action. They arranged for Michael to be killed by his own domestic guards in the palace of the holy martyr Mámas. Michael was blind drunk at the time, so he died, unconscious, in his sleep.'

The anonymus could not bring himself to go quite to his employer's length in his whitewashing of this horrible affair. His version is that, after Michael's plot to have Basil killed while on a hunting-party had miscarried and had become public knowledge, there was a general concern to save Basil from suffering Várdhas's and Theóktistos's fate. Accordingly, 'either by a decision of the Senate or on the initiative of Basil's friends—whose lives, as well as Basil's, were now in danger—Michael was killed by his domestic guards in the palace of the holy meghalomartyr Mámas'.

The anonymus gives the hour—9.00 p.m.—at which Michael met his death, but he has not the nerve to say that Michael died in his sleep without regaining consciousness. It would indeed be difficult, even for a dead drunk man, to remain unconscious while his hands were being hacked off.

The ugly truth is told by Symeon Magister,[1] and his account is reproduced, in its gruesome details, by pseudo-Symeon[2] and Zonarás.[3]

According to this account, Basil and Evdhokía Ingerínê, Michael's mistress and Basil's wife, were dining with Michael, and Michael got very drunk. Basil took this opportunity to slip out of the dining-room on some excuse. He went to the Emperor's bedroom and used his immense physical strength to bend the key so that the door would no longer lock. After Michael had had more drinks and had caroused with Evdhokía, as was his habit,[4] Basil helped him to his bedroom and left after kissing his hand. Michael had with him a guard and a chamberlain. The chamberlain now tried to shut and lock the bedroom door; and, when he found that he could not, because it had been tampered with, he was in despair. He sat on the bed, tearing his hair. The Emperor, after all the

---

[1] In *Georg. Mon. Cont.*, Reign of Michael III, chap. 34, pp. 836–7, and in Leo Grammaticus, pp. 250–1.   [2] Pseudo-Symeon, chap. 48, pp. 684–5.

[3] *Epitomae Historiarum*, vol. iii in Bonn edition, Books XIII–XVIII, p. 417.

[4] Evdhokía Ingerínê's bad reputation is recorded by Symeon Magister in *Georg. Mon. Cont.*, Reign of Michael III, chap. 6, p. 816, and in Leo Grammaticus, p. 230, followed by pseudo-Symeon, Reign of Michael III, chap. 9, p. 655; but this is left unmentioned by Kedhrênós—e.g. in vol. ii, p. 198, of the Bonn edition. Constantine Porphyrogenitus mentions (*Theoph. Cont.*, Book V, chap. 16, p. 235) that, when Michael III gave Basil the post of parakoimómenos and the rank of patríkios, he also gave him Evdhokía Ingerínê to be his wife. Constantine notes the Ingerínê's beauty and her noble birth; but he credits her with respectability (κοσμιότητι) as well. He does not mention that she had been, and presumably continued to be, Michael's mistress; that Michael constrained Basil to divorce María, the wife to whom Basil was already married; and that Basil pensioned María off and sent her back to théma Makedhonía, which was María's and Basil's home country. These damaging facts are recorded in *Georg. Mon. Cont.*, p. 828; Leo Grammaticus, p. 242; pseudo-Symeon, p. 675. Genesius, like Constantine Porphyrogenitus, disposes of María by omitting to mention her existence.

wine that he had drunk, was sleeping like death. Basil, with three of his eight men, burst in; Michael's two men tried to keep them out, but they were overpowered. By this time, Michael was awake. One of Basil's men now struck at Michael with his sword and hacked off his hands, while another of them wounded Michael's guard and laid him prostrate on the floor. Five of Basil's men[1] were keeping guard outside, and none of Michael's people knew what was happening. Basil and his fellow-criminals now held a consultation. One member of the gang insisted that, now that they had maimed Michael, they could not afford to leave him alive. So this man obliged Basil by going back into the bedroom and finishing Michael off. He drove his sword into Michael's back and disembowelled him in the same stroke.

Basil I stands convicted of having been the murderer of both the Caesar Várdhas and the Emperor Michael III. His grandson Constantine Porphyrogenitus's failure to exonerate him is palpable and complete. Basil's unquestionable guilt is mitigated, however, by extenuating circumstances which were the same in both cases. Constantine, in denying Basil's guilt, has debarred himself from pleading these; he has left this service to be performed for Basil by the chroniclers who have pronounced Basil guilty. The excuse for Basil's crimes is that, on both occasions, either his victim's life or his own was forfeit. There is no reason for doubting that Várdhas had been planning to murder Basil, as is stated by Symeon Magister[2] and by pseudo-Symeon.[3] Várdhas had already succeeded in murdering Theóktistos.[4] All authorities agree[5] that, before Basil murdered Michael, Michael had made an unsuccessful attempt to murder Basil, and that Michael had also promoted an oarsman from the Imperial galley to be Emperor in Basil's place. Constantine was debarred from pleading that Basil had to strike first, before Michael struck him, since Constantine did not admit that Basil had been Michael's murderer. This plea on Basil's behalf is made by pseudo-Symeon[6] and by Kedhrênós.[7]

[1] Of these five, Marianós was Basil's brother (*G.M.C.*, p. 840; Leo Gramm., p. 244; pseudo-Symeon, p. 678); Asylaíon was Basil's nephew (*G.M.C.*, pp. 830, 837, 839–40); Symvátios was probably the late Caesar Várdhas's son-in-law; Várdhas, the fourth of the five, was Symvátios's brother (pseudo-Symeon, p. 678). It looks as if, in *G.M.C.*, p. 837, the words ὁ ἀδελφὸς Βασιλείου have been attached accidentally to Symvátios instead of to Marianós. Michael was killed either by Asylaíon (*G.M.C.*, p. 837) or by John the Khaldhian (Leo Gramm., p. 251). Some of these identifications differ from Bury's in *A History of the Eastern Roman Empire*, pp. 458–9.

[2] In *Georg. Mon. Cont.*, Reign of Michael III, chap. 23, pp. 827–8, and in Leo Grammaticus, p. 242. [3] Reign of Michael III, chap. 40, p. 675.

[4] *Georg. Mon. Cont.*, Reign of Michael III, chap. 12, pp. 821–2; Leo Grammaticus, p. 236; *Theoph. Cont.*, Book IV, Reign of Michael III, chap. 19, p. 170; pseudo-Symeon, Reign of Michael III, chap. 13, p. 657.

[5] See *Theoph. Cont.*, Book IV, Reign of Michael III, chap. 44, pp. 208 and 209–10; Book V, Reign of Basil I, chap. 24, pp. 249–50 and chap. 25, pp. 250–1; *Georg. Mon. Cont.*, chap. 33, p. 835; Leo Grammaticus, p. 249; pseudo-Symeon, chap. 47, pp. 682–3, and chap. 48, p. 683.

[6] Reign of Michael III, chap. 48, p. 684. [7] Vol. ii, p. 202.

We can almost hear Constantine's sigh of relief when, after skating over the bloodshed through which his hero had waded to his throne, he can begin to record acts of Basil's that are unquestionably to Basil's credit. With the unanimous support of the Senate, Basil reclaimed from Michael's favourites one half of the amounts that Michael had improperly lavished on them according to the evidence of the public accounts.[1] He made sweeping changes in the personnel of the Imperial administration; he fought corruption; he made himself the protector of the poor.[2] He appointed competent and honest judges in large numbers, and paid them good salaries.[3] He repaired the Khalkĕ and turned it into a *palais de justice*.[4] He provided subsistence for poor litigants from the countryside who had to come to Constantinople to have their cases heard.[5] He insisted that, as a protection for the tax-payer, tax-demands should be presented in plain writing, with the figures unabbreviated.[6]

Most of these measures with which Constantine credits Basil are, no doubt, authentic, and, since few tears will have been shed for Michael, it is also likely to be true that Basil was proclaimed sole Emperor with the unanimous approval of the Senate, the Guards, the rest of the Army, and the population of the capital.[7] Since, however, Constantine had glozed over the humbleness of his grandfather's origin, he was inhibited from mentioning one cause of Basil's popularity that, next to his common-sense efficiency, will have carried the most weight with the majority of his subjects. His appointment by Michael III as co-Emperor had been popular because the people 'were eager to see the Empire's helm in the hands of a man who knew, by experience, the trials of private life, and who was not unaware of the treatment that is inflicted on the humble by the powerful'.[8] Constantine left this telling point in his grandfather's favour to be made by a chronicler writing about 150 years after the publication of Constantine's own biography of Basil I. Though this is the best-constructed of Constantine's books, it is also the most wrong-headed.

It is surprising that Constantine did not write this book more adroitly.

---

[1] *Theoph. Cont.*, Book V, chap. 28, pp. 255–6.

[2] Chap. 30, p. 258. Cf. chap. 97, p. 348, for Basil's protection of the rural poor. Genesius, Book IV, p. 128, credits Basil with the foundation of hospitals, homes for the aged, and almshouses.

[3] *Theoph. Cont.*, Book V, chap. 31, pp. 259–60; Kedhrênós, vol. ii, p. 203; Glykás, pp. 547–8.

[4] *Theoph. Cont.*, Book V, chap. 31, pp. 259–60.

[5] Ibid. This humane measure is attributed to Rhomanós I by the author of the first portion of *Theoph. Cont.*, Book VI, Reign of Rhomanós I, chap. 44, p. 430. For the components of *Theoph. Cont.*, see p. 5, footnote 2.

[6] Constantine Porphyrogenitus's biography of Basil I, chap. 31, p. 261. According to Genesius, Book IV, p. 126, Basil made a practice during Lent, after the Senate had adjourned for the day, of putting in some working-time at the tax-office, where he settled outstanding disputes between the revenue authorities and the tax-payers.

[7] *Theoph. Cont.*, Book V, chap. 28, p. 255.

[8] Kedhrênós, vol. ii, p. 201.

Indeed, it is surprising that he felt that his grandfather needed a second coat of whitewash; for the whitewashing had been done, nearly seventy years before Constantine took it upon himself to re-do it, by Constantine's father and predecessor, and Basil I's son and successor, the Emperor Leo VI.[1] Leo VI's epitáphios on Basil I is composed not only in more elegant pseudo-classical Greek than Constantine Porphyrogenitus's biography, but also with vastly more skilful finesse. Constantine must have had a copy of the epitáphios in his files. Documentation was Constantine's forte. The epitáphios may, in fact, have been one of his sources. It is therefore hard to understand why Constantine did not decide to let well alone. Leo could not shirk his task of grasping the nettle. If Leo had failed to deliver an epitáphios on Basil in which he claimed Basil as his father and eulogized Basil's life and acts, he would have been undermining his own title to the succession; for silence, on his part, would have been taken to be tantamount to an admission that his real father was not Basil I but Michael III.

Leo VI's maiden speech was probably the ablest performance in his political as well as in his literary career. After his accession to the Imperial throne at Basil I's death on 29 August 886, Leo found himself in a difficult position both politically and emotionally. He could not feel any genuine love or admiration for Basil I, or any genuine regret for Basil's death. Since the death of Basil's eldest son, Constantine, in 879, Basil had treated Leo cruelly. Basil had given credence to an allegation that Leo had been plotting to take his (Basil's) life. Basil had been dissuaded, with some difficulty, from disqualifying Leo for succeeding him by putting out Leo's eyes. He had compromised by putting Leo in prison; and, though, before Basil's death, a formal reconciliation had been engineered and Leo had been set at liberty again, Basil's treatment of him must have rankled in Leo's heart.

The scandal had been so notorious that even Constantine Porphyrogenitus found that he could not ignore it. Constantine states the unhappy facts.[2] The best that he is able to do for Basil is to allege that Basil's suspicion of Leo was unfounded, but that it had been made to seem

---

[1] Leo states, in his epitáphios in honour of his father's memory, that this is his first public speech, and that he is twenty-two years old. Leo dates his birthday a few days before St. Thomas's Day, which is 6 October. *Georg. Mon. Cont.*, p. 835, and Leo Grammaticus, p. 249, date Leo's birth in the September of the fifteenth indiction, i.e. in September 866. (They date it precisely 1 September.) G. Ostrogorsky, *Geschichte des byzantinischen Staates* (Munich, 1940, Beck), p. 163, n. 1, and Grégoire, in *C. Med. H.*, vol. iv, 2nd ed., Part I, p. 125, hold that the date was 19 September 866. If this dating is correct, Leo VI must have delivered the epitáphios after 19 September 888—perhaps on 29 August 889, if the date was an anniversary of Basil I's death, or possibly on 29 August 888, if Leo was giving, not an exact, but an approximate figure for his own age at the time. Constantine Porphyrogenitus probably wrote *Theoph. Cont.*, Book V, *circa* 957–9. (See p. 319, n. 2, and p. 576, n. 3.)

[2] *Theoph. Cont.*, Book V, chaps. 100–1, pp. 348–51.

credible to Basil by the trickery of a villain to whom both the father and the son had fallen victim.

Constantine had not shared his father Leo's experience of having to cope personally with Basil I; for Constantine had not been born till nearly nineteen years had passed since Basil's death. Consequently, the emotional difficulty that Leo must have felt when *raison d'état* required him to eulogize Basil did not exist for Constantine. The porphyrogenitus could afford to make a hero of Basil, and no doubt his feeling for Basil was sincere; for Constantine's own life-line was his legitimacy. It was his birth in the purple chamber of the Palace that had enabled Constantine to survive the Lekapenids' intrusion. Constantine was a scion, in the third generation, of the dynasty that Basil had inaugurated. Leo, on the other hand, must have been well aware that the legitimacy of his own birth was questioned; and he may even have been in doubt about it himself. We do not know whether Leo's mother Evdhokía Ingerínê kept her own counsel about this, or whether, if she professed to be taking her son into her confidence and to be telling him the truth about his paternity, Leo believed what she told him—whatever this may have been.

The three-cornered relation between Evdhokía Ingerínê, Michael III, and Basil had been impossible to conceal. Naturally it had been notorious, and, no doubt, no less naturally, it had been alleged (whether in good faith or not) that Leo was really Michael's son. This allegation could not be made in public till Nikêphóros Phokás had made himself senior Emperor at a time when Leo VI's great-grandsons, Basil II and Constantine VIII, were still minors. But eventually the allegation was asserted as being a fact in the published work of Symeon the loghothétês (reproduced in *Georgius Monachus Continuatus* and Leo Grammaticus),[1] with the suggestive piece of information that Leo had been born while Michael had still been alive.

However, this allegation remains non-proven. If Leo was born in September 866 he could have been Basil's son. Michael had made Basil marry Evdhokía Ingerínê when he had appointed Basil to the post of parakoimómenos, and, though we do not know the exact date of this appointment, it cannot have been very many years or perhaps even many months before 20 April 866,[2] which was the date on which Basil murdered Várdhas; for we do know that Michael's appointment of Basil to the key post of parakoimómenos was the event that sparked off Várdhas's and Basil's mutual jealousy and fear. We also know that, from then onwards, the hostility between these two rivals was acute, and

---

[1] See p. 585, n. 6.

[2] See Bury, *A History of the Eastern Roman Empire*, p. 169, n. 2, and Ostrogorsky in loc. cit. Ostrogorsky holds that Leo VI was Basil I's son; that Basil did not marry Evdhokía Ingerínê till about 865; and that Basil's elder son Constantine was by his first wife, María.

it cannot have been long before this violent quarrel ended in the murder of one of the two antagonists by the other. Even so, the date of Basil's marriage to Evdhokía Ingerínê must have been long enough before September 866 for it to have been possible for a child, born by Evdhokía at this latter date, to have been Basil's child, not Michael's. (We may assume that Basil had not had intercourse with Evdhokía Ingerínê before Michael had given her to him; for Basil would hardly have dared, at this stage, to commit an imprudence that, if discovered, might have broken his career and perhaps have cost him his life.)

It is even possible that the date of Basil's marriage to Evdhokía Ingerínê may have been early enough for Basil's eldest son Constantine, as well as his second son Leo, to have been born by September 866. We do not know whether Constantine was, like Leo and Alexander and Stephen, Evdhokía Ingerínê's son. Pseudo-Symeon's statement[1] that he was can be ignored; for pseudo-Symeon gives September 866, the actual date of Leo's birthday, as the date of Constantine's birthday, and this shows that his substitution of Constantine's name for Leo's is simply a blunder. It is possible that Constantine may have been Basil's son by Basil's first wife María; but we cannot be sure of this, and it is not a necessary hypothesis for explaining the extreme difference in Basil's feelings for Constantine and for Leo respectively. Parents do sometimes have different feelings towards sons who are each other's full brothers and not step-brothers. A difference of character and temperament is as likely as a difference of mothers to account for Basil's partiality for Constantine and aversion from Leo.

Finally, even if we entertain the unverifiable but plausible suspicion that Evdhokía Ingerínê continued, after her marriage to Basil, to serve Michael as his mistress, there is no evidence that Michael ever had any children by her or indeed by any other women. Michael had none, so far as we know, by his wedded wife—another Evdhokía—whom his respectable mother Theodora had constrained him to marry in the vain hope of parting him from the insufficiently respectable Evdhokía Ingerínê.[2]

Thus there is no proof that Leo was not Basil's son, and hence no proof, either, that the supposed Basilian dynasty was a continuation of the Amorian dynasty under a spurious name. Yet the unproved allegation had been given colour by Basil's harsh treatment of Leo from Constantine's death in 879 to Basil's in 886, and Leo himself fostered the allegation still further; for his first act after his accession was, not to declaim an

---

[1] See p. 585, n. 6.

[2] Our authorities give diverse accounts of Evdhokía Ingerínê's moral character, but they are unanimous in their testimony to her physical beauty. If her father's name Inger (*Theoph. Cont.*, Book V, p. 235) is a Graecized form of the Swedish name Ingvar, the Ingerínê may have been one of those Nordic blondes who are notoriously attractive to *Vir Mediterraneus*.

epitáphios on Basil, but to send a stratêghós, accompanied by a delegation from the Senate, to disinter Michael III's body from its unworthy
grave at Khrysópolis and to transfer it, with Imperial honours,[1] to a
sarcophagus in the Church of the Holy Apostles in Constantinople itself—
the church that had been the Imperial mausoleum since Constantine I's
body had been placed there.[2]

Leo's promptness in paying this posthumous honour to Michael III—
an honour that was by then nearly nineteen years overdue—was as
creditable to Leo as Basil's failure to pay it had been damning for Basil.[3]
But, though Leo's action was creditable, it was also highly impolitic.
It not only advertised his rancour against Basil; it lent additional colour
to the allegation that he himself was the son, not of Basil I, but of Michael
III. This impolitic first public act of Leo VI's was, however, more than
counterbalanced by the masterliness of his subsequent composition of his
funeral oration (epitáphios) on Basil. (Leo must have composed this himself; it was far too delicate a task to be delegated to a 'ghost-writer'; and
the surviving texts of other literary works of Leo's bear out Constantine
Porphyrogenitus's statement[4] that Basil I had taken pains to see that all
his children, girls as well as boys, received the thorough literary education
that Basil himself had missed.)

Fortunately for Leo VI, his education had equipped him with a literary
style that was suited to a nicety for the oratorical *tour de force* that Leo now
had to perform. Leo's ultimate model was the 'Second Sophistic': the
set pieces composed in Neo-Attic by the rhetors of the second-century-A.D.
school. Leo's direct model was the fourth-century-A.D. appropriation of
this second-century-A.D. style by the Cappadocian Christian Father
Gregory of Nazianzós. In his epitáphios on Basil I, Leo is consciously
imitating Gregory's funeral orations on his brother Kaisários and on St.
Basil.[5]

The virtue of this style, for Leo's purpose, is that it is studiously im-
personal and abstract.[6] For the second-century-A.D. rhetors, the form of

[1] 'His' brothers followed the funeral cortège. 'His' leaves their identity uncertain. Were
these Michael's brothers? Or were they Leo's? They are more likely to have been Leo's.

[2] See *Georg. Mon. Cont.*, Reign of Leo VI, chap. 1, p. 849; Leo Grammaticus, pp. 262–3;
Theoph. Cont., Book VI, chap. 1, p. 353; pseudo-Symeon, p. 700. On this point, these four
versions of the Byzantine Chronicle are in accord.

[3] However, Basil I's animosity towards Michael III had not extended to Michael's relatives.
For instance, he had not deposed Michael's docile first-cousin Marianós, son of Petronás, from
the post of Éparkhos of Constantinople (see *Georg. Mon. Cont.*, p. 839; Leo Gramm., p. 253;
pseudo-Symeon, p. 687).

[4] See p. 588.

[5] See the Introduction, pp. 24 and 26, to A. Vogt's and L. Hausherr's edition and translation of Leo's epitáphios on Basil I in *Orientalia Christiana*, vol. xxvi, No. 77 (April 1932)
(Rome, 1932, Pont. Institutum Orientalium Studiorum). See also N. Adontz, 'La Portée
historique de l'oraison funèbre de Basile I par son fils Léon VI le Sage', in *Byzantion*, vol. viii
(1933), pp. 501–13. There are no grounds for disputing the editors' and Adontz's belief that
the epitáphios is an authentic work of Leo VI's. [6] Vogt and Hausherr, pp. 8–9.

their declamation had been an end in itself; and, though there cannot be form without a minimum of substance to serve as a clothes-peg, the rhetors had taken great pains to save the form from being marred by an obtrusion, through it, of any of the vulgarity of real life. Leo, in his epitáphios, follows the tradition faithfully—and his own purpose conveniently—by suppressing all proper names.[1] The persons with whom he is concerned are indicated only by description, periphrasis, and allusion. The epitáphios gives only a minimum of factual information;[2] and this is a convenient economy (in the medieval Greek as well as in the present-day English meaning of this word). The smaller the expenditure of ink, the smaller the coat of whitewash that will be required for obliterating a record which, if it had been full and frank, would have had to be written in black, with few openings for passages in Imperial purple.

'I cannot give an exhaustive account of my subject.'[3] 'If only I had the leisure to go into detail'[4]—'but I do not have it—I am preoccupied by affairs of state.'[5] 'And then I am so immature; I am only twenty-two.'[6] 'And a proper biography of my father would require a whole book—not just this oration of mine.'[7]

Leo limits himself to recounting only one of the many presages of his father's future greatness,[8] and he refrains from recounting any of the presages about his mother.[9] Basil's education: here God had practised economy (in the Byzantine theologians' sense). Basil's education had been elementary; it had been the education that is received by the masses; but this does not mean that Basil's education had been neglected. He had received the education that fortifies soul and body by arduous exercise.[10] Evdhokía Ingerínê's marriage: Michael III missed his chance of marrying her—fortunately for her, since she soon married a better man.[11] Happily united, Basil and Evdhokía eclipsed the reigning Emperor.[12] This was not intentional; they could not help it. 'They did acquire the glory of the Imperial Crown, but not by violence, and they did not covet sovereignty as a prize to be snatched.[13] They got into this position against their will.'[14] Actually, it was not Michael III who gave the Crown to Basil and Evdhokía; it was an act of God.[15] What happened to Michael? Well, 'he ceased to live as a result of crime that *non liquet*.'[16] The Church: Basil restored harmony in it.[17] The former Patriarch Ighnátios (now dead):

---

[1] Ibid., p. 28.　　　　[2] Ibid., pp. 8 and 9.　　　　[3] Ibid., p. 38.
[4] Ibid., p. 60.　　　　[5] Ibid., p. 40.　　　　[6] Ibid., p. 40.
[7] Ibid., p. 42.　　　　[8] Ibid., p. 50.　　　　[9] Ibid., p. 53.
[10] Ibid., p. 46.　　　　[11] Ibid., p. 54.　　　　[12] Ibid., p. 54.
[13] οὐδ' ἅρπαγμα τὴν ἀρχὴν ποιησάμενοι—a reminiscence of Philippians 2, 6: οὐχ ἁρπαγμὸν ἡγήσατο τὸ εἶναι ἴσα Θεῷ. The comparison might have seemed blasphemous if it had been explicit.
[14] Leo, *Epitáphios*, pp. 55–6.
[16] Λείπει τὸν βίον ἀνεικάστοις κρίμασιν—ibid., p. 56.　　　　[15] Ibid., p. 56.
[17] Ibid., p. 62.

his rigidity had kept the ecclesiatical feud alive.[1] Phótios (already deposed from the Patriarchate by Leo himself) : Leo refers to Phótios in more friendly terms than to Ighnátios. (After all, in 882 Phótios had saved Leo's life and his succession to the Imperial throne, at the risk of drawing Basil's vindictiveness upon himself.) The Patriarch whom Leo had appointed to supersede Phótios (his appointee had been his own younger brother Stephen) : Basil I had made a gift to the Church of a child; compare Abraham's readiness to sacrifice Isaac.[2]

In this deft piece of tendentious writing, Leo VI has created for himself the 'image' of a dutiful son eulogizing a distinguished father perhaps rather more handsomely than the beneficiary from this filial piety truly deserves. Imagine that one of those supremely accomplished rhetors of the Age of the Antonines has been commissioned to compose the speech that Antigonus Gonatas would have produced if he had felt it to be his duty to pay a tribute to Demetrius Poliorcetes. Dio Chrysostom or Aelius Aristeides could not have executed an academic commission of this kind with greater professional skill than Leo VI has displayed in the execution of his own highly practical task.

Leo's mother, as well as his father, was a moral liability for Leo; yet, if the admiration for her that he expresses in his epitáphios is not sincere, then this is his *chef d'œuvre* in his practice of the art of dissimulation. Whether out of true affection for her or out of bravado, he translated his indulgence towards her into action. He appointed Evdhokía Ingerínê's paramour Xylinêtós Nikĕtas to the eminent and dignified office of Oikonómos of the Great Church of the Ayía Sophía.[3]

With this document in his files, Constantine Porphyrogenitus would have done better if he had refrained from commissioning either Genesius or the anonymous author of *Theophanes Continuatus*, Books I–IV, and if he had also refrained from trying his own hand at writing his biography of his grandfather in *Theophanes Continuatus*, Book V. All that Constantine had needed to do was to insert his father's epitáphios of his grandfather, without comment, in the dossier of documents that he appended to *De Caerimoniis*, Book II. Leo VI had already done a better job for Basil I, and also incidentally for himself, than the subsequent endeavours of Constantine Porphyrogenitus and his employees. Yet the text of the epitáphios has not come down to us among the items in Constantine Porphyrogenitus's thesaurus. It has been preserved in a single manuscript that has survived on Mount Athos in the library of the Vatopédhi Monastery.[4]

---

[1] Leo, *Epitáphios* p. 62.
[2] Ibid., p. 64.
[3] Vogt and Hausherr in loc. cit., p. 12.
[4] See ibid., p. 7.

3. Constantine's Sources of Information and Ways of Working

In his preface to the second book of *De Caerimoniis*, Constantine states that, whereas the first book is a compilation of written documents, the second book is based on oral tradition that has never before been committed to writing.[1] The distinction here drawn between the respective natures of Constantine's sources for these two books is not borne out by the contents of Book II. Most of the chapters, like most of those in Book I, appear to be based on written documents and are introduced by the same formula: 'The protocol that has to be observed' ($\H{o}\sigma\alpha$ $\delta\epsilon\hat{\iota}$ $\pi\alpha\rho\alpha\phi\upsilon\lambda\acute{\alpha}\tau\tau\epsilon\iota\nu$). Moreover, in the sheaf of attached but unincorporated materials at the end of Book II,[2] almost everything is manifestly documentary, with a few such exceptions as Chapter 40, on 'How the Emperor, the máyistroi, the proconsuls, and the patríkioi wear their lóroi on Easter Sunday, and Chapter 42, in which Constantine describes the Imperial tombs in Constantinople from his own observation.

The work of Constantine's in which oral, as opposed to written, information is most in evidence is not the second book of *De Caerimoniis*; it is *De Administrando Imperio*. Chapters 7 and 8, for instance, of this book look as if they were based on oral reports from Imperial officials who had visited Pechenegia to pay the Pechenegs their subsidies. Chapter 9 looks as if it were based on an oral account by someone who had taken part in one or more of the Russian expeditions from Kiev to Constantinople. The account of the Dniepr cataracts reads like an eyewitness's. Constantine's source here may have been a Russian who had accepted baptism[3] and had stayed in Constantinople either in business or in the Imperial Guard. Chapter 26, 'the genealogy of the illustrious King Hugh', is obviously based on oral information from somebody in the suite of Hugh's daughter Bertha-Evdhokía, who had married Constantine's son Rhomanós II. Some of Constantine's other information about the Franks may be the fruit of conversations with Liutprand when Liutprand was serving as Berengar of Ivrea's representative at the East Roman Court in 949. Chapter 28, on the origins of Venice, could have been culled from Venetian traders or envoys in Constantinople. The colloquy between the East Roman clerical diplomat Gabriel and the

---

[1] *De Caer.*, p. 516.　　　　　　　　　　　　　　　　　[2] Chaps. 40–56.
[3] οἱ βαπτισμένοι 'Ρῶς (*De Caer.*, Book II, chap. 15, p. 579: see p. 29, n. 2, of the present work).

chieftains of the Magyars in Chapter 8 is obviously based on a report from Gabriel himself. The rest of Constantine's information about the Magyars may have been acquired orally from Arpad's grandson Termadzoús ($T\epsilon\rho\mu\alpha\tau\zeta\omicron\acute{\upsilon}s$) (Termácz) and the karkhás Vouldzoús ($Bov\lambda\tau\zeta\omicron\acute{\upsilon}s$) (Bulcsu), two Magyar dignitaries who came on a mission to Constantinople *circa* 948,[1] or from the gylás (gyula),[2] who came a few years later.[3]

In the field of Constantine's written sources of information, a conspicuous gap is his evident failure to obtain access to any documents relating to the genesis and development of the East Roman army-corps districts ($\theta\acute{\epsilon}\mu\alpha\tau\alpha$) when he was writing his book on this subject. His ignorance is flagrant,[4] and it indicates either that there were no relevant documents or that Constantine had been denied access to the archives at the time when he was at work on this book. The second of these alternatives cannot be ruled out if Bury is right in dating the composition of *De Thematibus* between 934 and the end of 944. The respectful style in which the Emperor Rhomanós I is referred to by Constantine in this work shows that it was written while Rhomanós was still on the throne, and, so long as Rhomanós was reigning, he was paramount over his colleagues. It was in Rhomanós's power to prevent Constantine from consulting the Imperial archives, but it seems most unlikely that Rhomanós added this purposeless insult to the injury that he had inflicted on Constantine already.

Rhomanós had been determined, at all costs, to keep his family on the throne, and he had associated with himself and with the Porphyrogenitus one member of his own family after another; but, even if it is true that Rhomanós had always reserved for Constantine Porphyrogenitus the next highest place in the Imperial college to Rhomanós's own, Rhomanós's exaltation of himself above the reigning representative of the Basilian dynasty was a dangerous game; for by this time the dynasty had acquired an abiding hold on the loyalty and affection of the people of Constantinople—as became apparent when Rhomanós was deposed by his own sons.[5] Rhomanós was an able politician, and he must have been sensitive to the odium that he was incurring. He must have been anxious to avoid adding to this unnecessarily; and, so far from his having any motive for keeping Constantine away from the Imperial archives, Rhomanós stood to gain by encouraging Constantine to bury his head in them. Historical research would give Constantine an occupation that would be harmless from Rhomanós's point of view; and, for

---

[1] Constantine, *De Adm. Imp.*, chap. 40, p. 175; Kedhrênós, vol. ii, p. 328. See Bury 'The Treatise De Administrando Imperio', p. 563.

[2] Constantine notes in *De Adm. Imp.*, chap. 40, p. 174, that gylás and karkhás were titles, not proper names.

[3] Kedhrênós, loc. cit.   [4] See pp. 577–8.   [5] See p. 12.

Constantine, a free hand to indulge in this academic pursuit might be a psychological compensation for his being debarred—as Constantine was being debarred by Rhomanós—from the exercise of political power. We may guess that, if documents concerning the history of the army-corps districts had existed, Rhomanós would have done what he could to help Constantine to lay hands on them.

It seems likely, however, that such documents were not to be found—and this because there had not ever been any. There will, no doubt, have been a continuous series of documents in the archives concerning the army-corps as military formations. In this capacity the army-corps had had a continuous history since the Diocletianic–Constantinian Age, and their existence would always have been recognized officially as a matter of course. On the other hand it is conceivable, as has been suggested at an earlier point,[1] that there had not ever been any official recognition of the corps-commanders' assumption, *de facto*, of the responsibility for the civil administration of the districts in which their troops were quartered. To have recognized this would have been tantamount to admitting that the Diocletianic–Constantinian system of provincial administration had broken down and had ceased to function; and to admit disagreeable facts officially went against the grain of the Byzantine êthos.

If this is the truth, the civil administration undertaken by the corps-commanders will have continued, in official eyes, to be nothing more than a temporary piece of improvisation, and care will have been taken to avoid setting an official seal on it. This new regime will not ever have been consecrated by being regularized in official documents, and, in default of documentation, the history of its development will have been irretrievably lost. Probably the tenth-century East Roman Imperial archives contained no more information than we possess today about the process by which a new permanent system of provincial administration had grown up, since the seventh century, out of an arrangement that had been merely provisional at the start.

De Thematibus, which is the least informative of Constantine's works, and his biography of Basil I, which is the least honest of them, are books in the ordinary sense. Each of them was constructed according to a plan. When the plan had been carried out, the book had been finished and had then, presumably, been published. On the other hand, *De Caerimoniis* and *De Administrando Imperio* are not books of that kind. They are more like a pair of files in some department of state. They are like files in having been always open for the addition of new material. The miscellaneousness and the disorder of their contents make it look as if Constantine had kept them on the boil for years on end.[2] He had certainly

[1] On pp. 241–3.
[2] See Bury, 'The Treatise De Administrando Imperio', pp. 523–4 and 525.

left both of them still in the making at the time when death overtook him.

Constantine's aim was to turn each of these files into a book in which the file's miscellaneous contents would have been sorted out under a number of different heads, each head covering some single topic. Constantine was conscious that he had found the Imperial documents concerning protocol in disorder (ἀταξία), and that the disorderliness of the files was threatening to lead to a disorderly execution of the jumbled-up instructions that the files contained.[1] Constantine was convinced that he had elicited order and clarity out of these chaotic materials that, hitherto, had been presented only carelessly and indiscriminately.[2] By laborious and painstaking work, he had collected the materials from many different sources and had set them out in a form that was synoptic and comprehensible.[3] The result—presented in the first book of *De Caerimoniis* —was, in the author's opinion, a technical masterpiece,[4] besides being a monument of exact scholarship and a labour of love.[5] In the first book, the chaotic materials have been rounded up and reduced to order in a coherent logical arrangement.[6] Few of Constantine's readers, however, will take Constantine's own sanguine view of what he has achieved. *De Administrando Imperio* and *De Caerimoniis*, in the state in which Constantine has bequeathed them to posterity, will strike most readers as being in lamentable confusion.

Why did Constantine fail to achieve his aim? In the first place, he failed because of the intrinsic difficulty of the task that he had set himself. To try to turn a file into a book is like trying to square a circle. The two things are incommensurate with each other. A book is—or ought to be, when finished—a unity with a structure. It should, in fact, be finite, whereas a file is, by its very nature, open-ended. A study of the two books as we now have them reveals what happened when Constantine was at work on them. Each time that he had begun to make progress in rearranging the documents in the file in some rational order, a disorderly sheaf of new documents would come tumbling in, and then the work of rearrangement would have to be begun all over again. Constantine never caught up with his accessions of fresh material. An unincorporated sheaf of these has been appended to the second book of *De Caerimoniis*.[7] Constantine may have been waiting to make a second

---

[1] See the preface to *De Caer.*, Book I. p. 4.

[2] ὅσα μὲν αὐτῶν συγγραφῆς παρά τισιν ἔτυχεν οὐκ ἐμμελῶς οὐδὲ κεκριμένως, ἀλλὰ χύδην τε καὶ σποράδην, ἐκτεθειμένα (*De Caer.*, preface to Book II, p. 516).

[3] Preface to Book I, p. 4. [4] φιλοτέχνημα (ibid.).

[5] ἡμετέραις ἐπιμελείαις φιλοπόνως συναθροισθέντα (Preface to Book II, p. 516, referring to Book I).

[6] εἱρμῷ τινι καὶ τάξει λελογισμένῃ περιελήφθη τε καὶ συντέτακται (ibid.).

[7] *De Caer.*, Book II, chaps. 40–56. See Bury, 'The Ceremonial Book of Constantine Porphyrogennetos', in *The English Historical Review*, April 1907, pp. 209–27, on pp. 214, 223, 227.

attempt to rearrange the contents of *De Administrando Imperio* till he had filled in four conspicuous blanks. In the book as we have it there are no descriptions of Bulgaria, Khazaria, Russia, or Germany.[1] Yet these four countries were all of prime importance in the East Roman Empire's network of foreign relations.

Constantine's task was Sisyphean, and he was handicapped by lack of time.[2] He had to give priority to his official duties; his ceremonial duties, alone, were time-consuming; and he died at the age of fifty-four. However, when full allowance has been made for these handicaps, some part of the blame for Constantine's failure has to be debited to Constantine's intellectual limitations. A week's work on tidying up *De Administrando Imperio* and a month's work on tidying up *De Caerimoniis* would be enough to enable any competent editor to rearrange their contents in the logical order that Constantine fancied that he had achieved. His blindness to his conspicuous failure to achieve this convicts him of having no gift for creating order, and no eye for detecting the lack of it. He was incurably muddle-headed and he was ill-advised in undertaking a literary enterprise for which clear-headedness was the first and last requirement.

In order to achieve what Constantine believed that he had achieved, his jumble of documents needed to be 'processed' in two stages. The first of these two necessary operations was to sort out and group together all documents dealing with a particular topic; the second necessary operation was to write, on this topic, an original composition of the compiler-author's own, incorporating all the contents of this particular set of documents without repetitions and without omissions. To judge by what Constantine claims to have accomplished, he knew what he had to do; but he has hardly begun to do it. In *De Administrando Imperio*, for example,[3] there are two uncoordinated accounts of the Caliph Mu'āwīyah,[4] the second of which is an extract from Theophanes's chronicle. Conversely, an identical account of the Avars' capture of Salóna is given twice over,[5] and an identical account of the foundation of Spalato three times over,[6] in the *De Administrando Imperio*, while an identical account of the Western Muslims' conquest of Laghouvardhía has been included by Constantine in three different works of his: *De Administrando Imperio*,[7] *De Thematibus*,[8] and the biography of Basil I.[9]

---

[1] This is pointed out by Bury in *Die byzantinische Zeitschrift*, 15. Band (1906), p. 575. Cf. ibid., pp. 542–3.
[2] See pp. 6 and 575.
[3] See Bury, 'The Treatise De Administrando Imperio', pp. 529, 531, 549–50.
[4] Chaps. 20 and 21.   [5] In chap. 29, pp. 126–8, and in chap. 30, pp. 141–3.
[6] In chap. 29, pp. 125–6; in chap. 29, p. 137; in chap. 30, p. 141.
[7] Chap. 29, pp. 130–1.   [8] pp. 61–2.
[9] Chap. 33, p. 290, and chap. 55, pp. 292–4.

When Constantine decided to convert *De Administrando Imperio* from a descriptive into an instructional work, he ought to have set himself to subsume the descriptive material relating to each topic under the instructional material relating to it. Alternatively he could have chosen an easier option. He could have collected all the instructional material, grouped according to topics, to constitute the first part of the book, and could have collected, under the same heads, in a second part, any descriptive material that proved recalcitrant to being subordinated to the instructional material. Constantine did choose this second option, but he made no more than a feeble attempt to rearrange his materials according to this new plan. The book does now start out with a series of eight instructional chapters on how to deal with the Pechenegs; and this is a promising start for a re-arrangement of the book. The instructions for dealing with the Pechenegs are rightly put first, considering that, in Constantine's opinion, the East Roman Government's relations with the Pechenegs were the key to its relations with all its other northern neighbours. Constantine's attempt to reorganize his materials has, however, been half-hearted.

The opening group of eight instructional chapters concerning the Pechenegs is followed by a chapter (9) that is purely descriptive. This is the chapter giving the fascinating description of the Russian route from Kiev to Constantinople. After this interruption of the instructional series, three more instructional chapters follow (chaps. 10–12). The next forty-one chapters (chaps. 13–53) are consistently descriptive, and we might have begun to think that, with Chapter 13, we had entered on the descriptive residue of the materials in the file. Yet, at the very end of Chapter 53, there are instructions for bringing the Khersonites to heel if they rebel. Thus, in the present arrangement of *De Administrando Imperio*, Constantine's change of plan has been carried out only partially. Yet the amount of further work required for carrying the change of plan through is so small that it is impossible to believe that Constantine never had time to do it. The reason why he did not do it must have been because he did not perceive that he had left his self-imposed task of rearrangement uncompleted.

The same half-heartedness is apparent in the composition of *De Caerimoniis*. The general structure of the two books of *De Caerimoniis* is the same. Each book starts with a series of documents containing directions for the performance of pieces of protocol that were still in force in Constantine's own day. Next comes a series that is obsolete but illustrative.[1] Finally, in Book II, there comes the sheaf of unincorporated documents, which has no counterpart in Book I.[2] Constantine has not,

[1] See Bury, in *The English Historical Review*, April 1907, pp. 211, 213, 214, 227; *E.H.R.*, July 1907, p. 419.   [2] See p. 602.

however, made any attempt to unify the two books, or even to co-ordinate their contents. For instance, each book includes protocol for both ecclesiastical and secular ceremonies. Moreover, the ecclesiastical material is not only incomplete; it is in utter disorder. The libretti for the acclamations that are to be chanted at the festivals have become detached from the directions for the ceremonial that is to be carried out at the same festivals, and there are two uncoordinated series of documents, each of them incomplete, dealing with the ecclesiastical ceremonies. Both these partial series follow the chronological order of the Christian liturgical year, but one of them begins the year with Christmas and the other with Easter Day.[1]

Our verdict on Constantine's work has to be that he has failed to do his job, but there is an extenuating circumstance that we can plead on his behalf. He has provided tools in abundance for any successor who may wish to try his hand at doing what Constantine has left undone, and this is a legacy of Constantine's for which we should be deeply grateful.

---

[1] See A. Vogt in his edition of *De Caer.*, vol. i, Part II, Commentary, pp. 1–3.

ANNEX I

The Record of the Years 813–959 in the Byzantine Chronicles[1]

BYZANTINE chronicles have a standard form. They present a narrative of the history of the World that runs from the Creation to a chronicler's date of writing or to some recent previous date. In principle the narrative follows the chronological order of events, but the chronicler (e.g. Symeon the máyistros and loghothétês) sometimes departs from this order deliberately for the sake of giving a continuous account of a series of events.[2] This grouping of events may be retrospective; it may be introduced apropos of what, in the chronicler's judgement, is the culminating event in a series. In extreme cases, the consolidated narrative of antecedent events virtually becomes an excursus.

This standard form, thus modified, corresponds to the Christian vision of the course, the meaning, and the purpose of the World's history; and this Christian vision has been inspired by an older Jewish vision which has been influenced by the Zoroastrian vision of history. The pre-Christian Hellenic form of historiography is markedly different. Hellenic historians do not set their narratives in a theological framework.

Byzantine Christian chronicles are a valuable source of historical information only for periods for which some better kind of source is not forthcoming. For the period down to the year 602—the date of the overthrow and murder of the Emperor Maurice—we have histories of world affairs, as seen from the standpoint of inhabitants of the Roman Empire, that are written in the secular pre-Christian Hellenic form, though their authors were Christians, at any rate nominally. For the period beginning in November 959—the date of the death of the Emperor Constantine VII

---

[1] See K. Krumbacher, *Geschichte der byzantinischen Litteratur*, 2nd ed. (Munich, 1897, Beck), Erste Abteilung, 2B, Die Chronisten, § 138: Allgemeine Charakteristik, pp. 319–23; J. B. Bury, *A History of the Eastern Roman Empire from the Fall of Irene to the Accession of Basil I* (*A.D. 802–867*) (London, 1912, Macmillan), Appendix II, 'George's Chronicle' (pp. 453–4); Appendix III, 'The Chronicle of Simeon, Magister and Logothete' (pp. 456–9); Appendix IV, 'Genesios and the Continuation of Theophanes' (pp. 460–1); R. J. H. Jenkins, 'The Chronological Accuracy of the 'Logothete'' for the Years 867–912', in *Dumbarton Oaks Papers*, Number Nineteen (Washington, D.C., 1965, The Dumbarton Oaks Center for Byzantine Studies), pp. 91–112. Professor Robert Browning has drawn my attention to an important series of articles on the subject of this Annex by A. P. Kazhdan in *Vizantijskij vremmenik*, new series (Leningrad, 1947 seqq.). Unfortunately I have not been able to benefit by Kazhdan's work, as I do not know Russian.

[2] See Jenkins in loc. cit., p. 92.

Porphyrogenitus—we have a new series of histories whose authors are writing self-consciously in the pre-Christian Hellenic form. The time-span 602 to 959 is therefore the period for which the chronicles that deal with this period, or with some part of it, have a maximum value.

Within this period, a chronicle that is not based on some extant predecessor is, of course, more valuable than one that is derivative. An example is the latter part of Symeon's chronicle from 813 onwards to 948, the year which is this chronicle's terminal date. From the Creation to A.D. 813, Symeon draws largely on Theophanes and on Georgius Monachus. But Theophanes's record ends with the accession of the Emperor Leo V in 813, and, though Georgius Monachus carries his record down to the death of the Emperor Theóphilos in 842, Symeon supplements our information about the years 813–42 from a written source, no longer extant, that was more informative than Georgius Monachus, to judge by Symeon's narrative for these years. Again, the records, for the years 948–61, of the fourth of the four successive contributors to *Theophanes Continuatus*[1] and of the pseudo-Symeon are valuable, because the genuine Symeon's record ends with the death of the ex-Emperor Rhomanós Lekapênós on 15 June or July 948.[2]

Bury recognizes[3] that, for the years 813–67, Symeon has drawn on a lost written source. Jenkins holds that he has used another lost written source for the years 867–913, and this second source, as discerned at second hand through Symeon, appears to have been precise, factual, and chronologically accurate.[4] Symeon's source for the reign of Michael III (842–67) appears to have been inferior both in its chronology and in its composition.[5] There are also some chronological mistakes in Symeon's record of the years 913–48, for which, according to Jenkins,[6] Symeon was drawing on his own recollections and on oral information from contemporaries.

Symeon, his oral informants, and his written sources were all independent of Constantine Porphyrogenitus. Symeon's written sources, including his particularly good written source for the years 867–913, must have been in existence already before Constantine got to work. We do not know whether they were ever published, and we may guess that Symeon's own chronicle was not published till after the death of Constantine's son the Emperor Rhomanós II in 963, though Symeon's record ends at

---

[1] For the components of *Theoph. Cont.*, see p. 5, n. 2.

[2] July was the month according to Symeon in *Georg. Mon. Cont.*, p. 924, and in Leo Grammaticus, pp. 330–1, and also according to pseudo-Symeon, p. 754. The first of the two anonymous authors of *Theoph. Cont.*, Book VI, makes the month June on p. 441, and, in this dating he has been followed by Runciman, *The Emperor Romanus Lecapenus*, p. 236, and by Grégoire in *C. Med. H.*, vol. iv, 2nd ed., Part I, p. 143.

[3] See op. cit., Appendix III, p. 458.

[4] Jenkins in loc. cit., pp. 95–8 and 112.

[5] Ibid., pp. 95–6.

[6] Ibid., p. 94.

15 July 948. Symeon tells the truth about Basil I and he testifies to the merits of Rhomanós I Lekapênós. His work was thus inimical to Constantine's cherished design of whitewashing Constantine's own grandfather Basil I and of asserting, against the Lekapenids, the legitimacy of the dynasty that Basil I had founded. Symeon would hardly have ventured to publish his dissenting account so long as Constantine and his son were still alive. As an historian, Symeon was Constantine's adversary, though if, as is probable though non-proven, he is identical with Symeon Metaphrastes, Symeon collaborated with Constantine in Constantine's non-controversial literary enterprise of promoting the compilation of anthologies and collections of works of literature that were not concerned with current political issues.

The original Greek text of Symeon's chronicle has not survived, but fortunately a translation of it into 'Old Slavonic' is extant and has been published,[1] and transcripts in Greek of the concluding portion of the Greek text, covering the years 813–48, have also been published. One of these published Greek transcripts is Leo Grammaticus's *Chronographia*;[2] another is Theodosius Melitenus's *Chronicon*;[3] a third is embedded in *Georgius Monachus Interpolatus* (for the years 813–42) and in *Georgius Monachus Continuatus* (for the years 843–15 July 948).[4] In writing the present work, I have used the Greek text of Symeon's chronicle as reproduced in Bekker's editions of Leo Grammaticus's *Chronographia* and of *Georgius Monachus Interpolatus et Continuatus*.

Considering the relatively high value of Symeon's chronicle, cannot we perhaps afford to ignore the record of the same years, 813–948, in chronicles that draw, at least partly, on Symeon's chronicle and that, in some passages, reproduce it almost verbatim? Cases in point are *Theophanes Continuatus*, Book VI,[5] and the pseudo-Symeon.[6] *A fortiori*, cannot we ignore later writers—for instance, Skylídzês, Zonarás, and Kedhrênós—who have copied *Theophanes Continuatus*? The versions of *Theophanes Continuatus* and of pseudo-Symeon are, in fact, merely separate recensions of the original chronicle;[7] and pseudo-Symeon's chronology is worthless.[8] Yet it would be a mistake to let this lead us into discarding

---

[1] Symeon's *Chronicle*, Old Slavonic version, ed. by V. I. Sreznevsky (St. Petersburg, 1905).

[2] Edited by I. Bekker (Bonn, 1842, Weber, pp. 207–331). This volume also contains a piece of a chronicle preserved in Cod. Par. 854 and Eustathius's account of the sack of Thessaloníkê by the Normans in 1185.

[3] Edited by G. L. F. Tafel (Munich, 1839).

[4] Edited by I. Bekker in the same volume as his edition of *Theoph. Cont.* (Bonn, 1838, Weber, pp. 761–924).

[5] Book VI, down to 15 July 948, Symeon's ending date, is printed in Bekker's edition of *Theoph. Cont.*, pp. 353–441.

[6] Printed in Bekker's edition of *Theoph. Cont.*, pp. 601–760. The date 15 July 948 is reached on p. 754.

[7] Jenkins in loc. cit., p. 91, n. 3.　　　　　　　[8] Jenkins, ibid.; Bury, op. cit., p. 459.

these derivative narratives without examining them; for then we shall be missing their occasional deviations from the common source, and some of these deviations are important.

This point can be illustrated by taking a synoptic view of Symeon's and his copyists' treatment of three characters, the Patriarchs Phótios and Trýphon and the general Várdhas Phokás[1].

Symeon records the main events in Phótios's career without comment, and in this he is followed by all his copyists but one. This one, however, the pseudo-Symeon, breaks the monotony by launching out into a vehement attack on Phótios's character. Is this an original contribution of the pseudo-Symeon's own? Or has he borrowed it from some source (e.g. some partisan of Phótios's enemy Ighnátios) that was independent of the genuine Symeon? We know neither the origin nor the motive for pseudo-Symeon's tirade, but we cannot afford to neglect it, since it gives us one of the views of Phótios's character that had passed into the Byzantine historical tradition.

One of pseudo-Symeon's charges against Phótios is that he was a rationalist. After there had been an earthquake, Phótios 'went up into the pulpit to preach and declared that earthquakes are caused, not by a multitude of sins, but by a multitudinous plethora of water'.[2] The second charge against Phótios is that he countenanced blasphemy. Even after he had become Patriarch, he attended and applauded the travesty of the liturgy that was performed by Michael III's disreputable boon companions.[3] Third charge: Phótios challenged Michael to a drinking-match and beat him by sixty cups to fifty.[4] Fourth charge: Phótios was a magician and, what was worse, a Hellenist. Godly John the hesychast had this information, in a dream, from a demon.[5] Phótios was keener on profane learning than he was on sacred learning.[6] Some pious clerics testified that, 'when we were performing the liturgy with him, we never heard him recite a prayer; he was whispering passages from the profane poets'.[7] 'Khazar-face', 'marzūq'![8]

Pseudo-Symeon records (how could he not?) Phótios's refusal to allow Basil to receive communion after the murder of Michael III, and his denunciation of Basil as a brigand and assassin.[9] Every chronicler was bound to mention the reason for Basil's deposition of Phótios.[10] But

---

[1] i.e. the father of the Emperor Nikêphóros Phokás and of Leo the Kouropalátês, not the Várdhas Phokás who was Leo the Kouropalátês's son.

[2] Pseudo-Symeon, Reign of Michael III, chap. 35, p. 673.

[3] Ibid., chap. 19, pp. 662–3.   [4] Ibid.   [5] Ibid., chap. 34, pp. 672–3.

[6] πρὸς τὰ Ἑλληνικὰ φιλοτιμότερον διέκειτο ἢ τὰ ἐκκλησιαστικά (op. cit., chap. 31, p. 670).

[7] Ibid., chap. 33, p. 672, cited already on p. 4, n. 1.

[8] Ibid., chap. 35, pp. 673–4. 'Marzūq is an Arabic word meaning 'fortunate'.

[9] Pseudo-Symeon, Reign of Basil I, chap. 6, pp. 688–9.

[10] Every chronicler, but not every writer. Genesius, who was writing under instructions from Basil's grandson Constantine, makes no mention of this or any other of the transactions

pseudo-Symeon gives Phótios no credit for his probity and courage on this occasion, whereas, in recording Phótios's subsequent reinstatement by Basil, he alleges that Phótios had earned it by committing a forgery.[1]

Whatever we may make of this onslaught on Phótios, it would have been a pity to overlook it.

Trýphon was the Patriarch who was placed on the Ecumenical throne (927–31) as a stop-gap, to keep it warm for Rhomanós I's scandalous clerical son Theophýlaktos while the boy was still below the canonical minimum age for holding the patriarchal office. Symeon simply mentions Trýphon's appointment to the Patriarchate for a limited term[2] and his subsequent deposition and retirement to make way for Theophýlaktos.[3] The author of the first portion of *Theophanes Continuatus*, Book VI,[4] reproduces, verbatim, Symeon's pair of notices. Symeon says, apropos of Trýphon's appointment, that 'he had a well-attested reputa-

between Basil and Phótios (see pp. 583–4). In introducing Phótios (Book, IV, pp. 583–4), Genesius remarks that Phótios's character was 'in some points better than the average, in other points lower'. This is the only reference to Phótios in Genesius's work.

[1] Pseudo-Symeon, pp. 689–90. Phótios had faked an ancient manuscript containing a genealogy that took Basil's Arsacid ancestry back to King Tiridates (see pp. 587–8), and he had inserted this fake into the Imperial library. The same story appears in Nikĕtas's biography of the Patriarch Ighnátios; and this suggests that pseudo-Symeon may have derived the rest of his anecdotes to Phótios's discredit from some pro-Ighnatian source or sources. If this is in truth the origin of these anecdotes, they are suspect.

Adontz, 'L'Âge et l'origine de l'empereur Basile I' (*suite*), pp. 234–5, draws attention to a previous passage in pseudo-Symeon's own chronicle (Reign of Theóphilos, chap. 24, pp. 643–5), in which a persecuted ecclesiastical dignitary, the future Patriarch Methódhios I (843–7), regains the good graces of a hostile Emperor, Theóphilos (829–42), by deciphering an enigmatic book that has come to light in the Imperial library. The points of similarity between the two stories are striking. The Emperor is told that there is only one person who will be able to decipher the book for him, and that the man is the disgraced cleric. The cleric duly performs the feat, and he subsequently becomes Patriarch. There are, however, two differences. Methódhios I subsequently became Patriarch for the first time, Phótios for the second time. Methódhios deciphered, *bona fide*, a genuine ancient book; Phótios had faked the enigmatic book himself and had arranged with an accomplice for it to be planted in the Imperial library and then to be brought to the Emperor's notice. Perhaps there was a folktale about an anonymous emperor and prelate which could be presented as being matter of fact by giving the two characters any pair of authentic historical names.

Vogt, *Basile Ier*, pp. 233–4, accepts, as being true history, the story as this is told of Phótios and Basil I. He suggests, ibid., that Phótios's faked genealogy was the source of the assertion that Basil I was an Arsacid. This assertion had been made, already, by Leo VI in his epitáphios on Basil I (Vogt and Hausherr's text, p. 44), before it was made by Genesius and by Constantine Porphyrogenitus (see p. 588, n. 1). Genesius carries Basil's pedigree back to Tiridates, as Phótios had done according to pseudo-Symeon. If the story of Phótios's forgery is to be accepted as being true, it seems more probable that Phótios made Tiridates Basil's ancestor because this tall story had already been put into circulation. If it had, Basil I would have been grateful to Phótios for providing him with what seemed like documentary evidence for the improbable story's truth.

[2] *Georg. Mon. Cont.*, Reign of Rhomanós I, chap. 37, p. 908; Leo Grammaticus, p. 318.

[3] *Georg. Mon. Cont.*, chap. 43, pp. 911–12; Leo Grammaticus, p. 321.

[4] *Theoph. Cont.*, Book VI, Reign of Rhomanós I, chap. 26, p. 417, and chap. 32, p. 421.

tion for piety and holiness', and *Theophanes Continuatus* repeats, verbatim, this testimonial too.

Pseudo-Symeon[1] and Kedhrênós[2] add an anecdote from some other source. Trýphon, they say, was tricked into setting his signature to a blank sheet of parchment which was then filled in by the authorities with a declaration which Trýphon could not repudiate, since he could not disown the signature that stood below it. The account of the trick is the same in both works, but it is told in different contexts, and this puts Trýphon's character in different lights. Pseudo-Symeon says that Trýphon was tricked into accepting the Patriarchate for a limited term after he had declined to accept it on this condition. This story is compatible with Symeon's testimonial, which is repeated verbatim by pseudo-Symeon as well as in *Theophanes Continuatus*. Kedhrênós, on the other hand, says that the trick was played on Trýphon at the end of his limited term of office, not at the beginning of it, and that Trýphon was tricked, not into signing his conditional acceptance, but into signing his resignation. According to Kedhrênós, Trýphon had promised originally to resign after a limited term, without having needed to be tricked into that. The trick was brought into play against him because, when the time came for fulfilling his promise, he attempted to revoke on it. Kedhrênós's Trýphon could not have earned the testimonial that Symeon's Trýphon has been given, whether deservedly or not.

A third instance of a deviation is Kedhrênós's verdict on Várdhas Phokás's professional ability. He convicts him of having been a bad commander and been a good officer only as a subordinate, and he makes this censure the more pointed by praising Várdhas's sons Nikêphóros and Leo in the same breath.[3] On the other hand, Kedhrênós[4] follows the chroniclers[5] in crediting Várdhas Phokás with a fine performance on the occasion of the Russian naval raid in 941; and Várdhas's universally acknowledged effectiveness in this emergency is all of a piece with his general reputation.[6] Constantine Porphyrogenitus's first act, after he had rid himself of the Lekapênoí, was to appoint Várdhas to the post of dhoméstikos ton Skholón,[7] i.e. commandant of the Imperial Guards and therewith, almost *ex officio*, commander-in-chief of the whole Army.

---

[1] Reign of Rhomanós I, chap. 37, pp. 742–3.

[2] Vol. ii, pp. 313–15.

[3] Vol. ii, p. 330.

[4] Vol. ii, pp. 316–17.

[5] e.g. Symeon in *Georg. Mon. Cont.*, Reign of Rhomanós I, chap. 50, p. 915, and in Leo Grammaticus, pp. 323–4; *Theoph. Cont.*, Book VI, Reign of Rhomanós I, chap. 39, p. 424; pseudo-Symeon, Reign of Rhomanós I, chap. 46, p. 747.

[6] See, for instance, Περὶ Παραδρομῆς Πολέμου, p. 185, cited on p. 612.

[7] Symeon in *Georg. Mon. Cont.*, second bout of Constantine VII's sole reign, chap. 1, p. 921, and in Leo Grammaticus, pp. 328–9; *Theoph. Cont.*, Book VI, second bout of Constantine VII's sole reign, chap. 1, p. 436, and chap. 14, p. 445; pseudo-Symeon, second bout of Constantine VII's sole reign, chap. 1, p. 753; Zonarás, vol. iii, Books XIII–XVII, p. 482.

Apropos of Várdhas's appointment to this eminent post, two of the chroniclers who record it pause to give Várdhas high praise. Symeon says that Várdhas 'had displayed his prowess in the field over a long period of time'.[1] The author of the first portion of Book VI of *Theophanes Continuatus*[2] repeats Symeon's encomium verbatim, adding 'on many occasions'. The author of the second portion of Book VI says that Constantine Porphyrogenitus appointed first-rate officers to serve under Várdhas and thus 'procured victory for the Roman Empire'.[3] When this latter writer has to record that Constantine eventually relieved Várdhas Phokás of his command of the Guards, he is careful to mention that the reason for this action was Várdhas's old age and infirmity and that Constantine gave the vacated command to Várdhas's favourite son Nikêphóros[4] and appointed another of his sons, Leo,[5] to the command of the 'Western' districts.[6] Nikêphóros's and Leo's appointments were confirmed by Rhomanós II.[7] The author of Περὶ Παραδρομῆς Πολέμου, who was himself a professional soldier, cites Várdhas Phokás as having been the supreme master of the tactics of 'dogging and pouncing', and he testifies that he had acquired his own training in these tactics by serving under Várdhas Phokás when Várdhas was stratêghós of Kappadhokía and of the Anatolikoí.[8] The weight of evidence is overwhelmingly in Várdhas Phokás's favour, and we do not know the source of Kedhrênós's solitary adverse judgement. Yet we ought to be aware of this dissenting opinion, even if we do not find ourselves convinced by it.

These and other cases of the kind show that it is advisable to notice not only the chroniclers' usual uniformity but also their occasional discrepancies.

---

[1] *Georg. Mon. Cont.*, p. 921; Leo Grammaticus, pp. 328–9.

[2] p. 436.   [3] pp. 445–6.

[4] *Theoph. Cont.*, p. 459; pseudo-Symeon, second bout of Constantine VII's sole reign, chap. 7, p. 755.

[5] Leo had been made governor of the Kappadhokía district at the time of his father's appointment by Constantine Porphyrogenitus to be commandant of the Guards (Zonarás, vol. iii, Books XIII–XVIII, p. 482).

[6] *Theoph. Cont.*, ibid.

[7] *Theoph. Cont.*, Book VI, Reign of Rhomanós II, chap. 4, p. 472; pseudo-Symeon, Reign of Rhomanós II, chap. 1, pp. 757–8.

[8] *Π.Π.Π.* in the Bonn edition of Leo Diaconus, p. 185.

ANNEX II

The Texts of 'Mavríkios's' Strateghikon *and of Leo VI's* Taktika

In the preface of this book, it has been noted that the editing of Greek texts of the Byzantine Age still lags far behind the editorial work that had been done on texts of the Hellenic Age. Good critical editions of even minor Hellenic Greek works are at the historian's disposal, whereas many Byzantine Greek texts of prime historical importance are still awaiting editors of the stature of de Boor and Vári and Moravcsik. Until the present book was in the last stage of being revised before being sent to the press, one of the most lamentable of these lacunae was in Rudolf Vári's *Sylloge Tacticorum Graecorum*. This lacuna was filled as recently as 1970 by the publication, in that year, of H. Mihǎescu's edition of 'Mavríkios's' *Stratéghikón*.[1]

The first volume of Vári's magnificent edition of Leo VI's *Taktiká* was intended, as the title-page for the whole *Sylloge* shows, to be the third volume of the *Sylloge*, and presumably the projected first and second volumes, if they had been published, would have contained an equally fine edition of 'Mavríkios's' *Stratéghikón*. Vári's preface to the first volume of his edition of Leo's *Taktiká* ends[2] with the prayer: 'Quae Sylloge ut ad finem perfectum persolveretur, bonum, faustum, felix, fortunatumque eveniat!' This prayer is followed, however, by the ominous dating 'Dabam Budapestini, Idibus Decembribus 1915'.

The *fasciculus prior* of Vári's volume ii of the *Taktiká* was not published till 1922, and this *fasciculus* breaks off at the end of §38 of Dhiátaxis 14. At the foot of the title-page of this *fasciculus* there is an instruction to the purchaser: 'Fasciculo posteriore cum fasciculo priore in unum tomum iuncto, hunc titulum abicies!' Unhappily, the *fasciculus posterior* never saw the light. Accordingly, for §§39–116 of Leo's Dhiátaxis 14 and for the whole of his Dhiatáxeis 15–20, together with the Epilogue, we have still to use the text printed by Migne in his *Patrologia Graeca*, vol. cvii, cols. 860–1094.[3] Migne's text is inadequate. It is a reprint of Johannes

---

[1] Μαυρικίου Στρατηγικόν, *Mauricii Strategicum*, Mauricius, *Arta Militară*, critical edition, with introduction and translation in Roumanian, by H. Mihǎescu (Bucarest, 1970, Academy of the Socialist Republic of Roumania).

[2] On p. xxxv.

[3] The whole of Leo's *Taktiká*, including the portion that Vári has edited, will be found in *Patrologia Graeca*, vol. cit., cols. 672–1094.

Lamius's edition (Florence, 1745), and this edition is an only moderately improved version of Johannes Meursius's edition (Leyden, 1612), which was the first printing of the whole of the text of Leo VI's *Taktiká*.[1]

'Mavríkios's' *Stratéghikón* fared worse than Leo's *Taktiká*. Until the publication of Mihăescu's edition in 1970, the one and only edition of the whole text of this work was Johannes Scheffer's, which was published in 1664.[2] Considering the date at which Scheffer was working, and the unsatisfactoriness of the materials that he had to use, the result that he produced does him great credit, but of course his edition falls very far short of attaining subsequent critical standards.

Scheffer's volume is dedicated to Queen Christina. 'Reddo tibi, Domina, Mauritium, quem, ante annos aliquot allatum Româ, clementissime curis commendare meis voluisti.' (Scheffer records that the Queen has paid him 'splendidissimum salarium'.)

In his notice to the reader, Scheffer gives illuminating information about the way in which his work was done.

> Mauricium . . . Lucas Holstenius [of Hamburg] ex Codicibus MSS. quattuor, duobus Barberinis, Mediceo et Farnesiano descriptum, annis superioribus ad nos, nil tale opinantes expectantesque ultro, unâ cum Leonis Codice ad MSS. collato, lacunisque Graeci textûs expletis pulchre restituto, transmisit. Codex satis eleganter pictus est, sed distinctus [? i.e. punctuated] pessime.

Here Scheffer tells us that he himself had not had the opportunity to study and collate the four manuscripts which are the ultimate sources of his text of the *Stratéghikón*. All that he had to work on was a manuscript written in his own day on the basis of these four older manuscripts. He implies, though he does not state this in so many words, that Lucas Holstenius, who brought him this contemporary manuscript, was also the person who had constructed it out of a collation of the older four. In order to produce a trustworthy text, a scholar must make a first-hand study of every manuscript that is not known to be a copy of an older one. He must then collate the manuscripts, must ascertain their relations with each other, and must form an expert judgement of their relative values.

Vári did do much or perhaps the whole of this exacting work. In 1906 he published, in parallel columns,[3] the text of Leo VI's Dhiátaxis 6 Περὶ ὁπλίσεως καβαλλαρίων καὶ πεζῶν,[4] and the Medicean and Ambrosian texts of the corresponding passage in 'Mavríkios's' *Stratéghikón*,

---

[1] Vári in his edition of Leo VI's *Taktiká*, vol. i, p. xxix.

[2] *Arriani Tactica et Mauricii Artis Militaris Libri Duodecim*, edited by Johannes Schefferus Argentoratensis (Uppsala, 1664, published by H. Curio, S.R.M. et Academiae Upsaliensis Bibliopola).

[3] R. Vári, 'Zur Überlieferung griechischer Taktiker', in *Byzantinische Zeitschrift*, 15. Band (1906), pp. 46–87, on pp. 50–60.

[4] Migne, cols. 721–33.

i.e. Part 1, chap. 2.[1] The Medicean MS. of the *Stratêghikón* had been one of the four sources of Scheffer's text, but Scheffer had not had the opportunity of using the Ambrosian MS., even indirectly. Vári also tells us, in the preface[2] to the first volume of his edition of Leo VI's *Taktiká*, that

in textu Leonis recensendo non solum Leonis *Tacticorum* codices inspicere, meliores conferre fuit mihi propositum, sed etiam fontium eius fundamentum utcunque certius mihi redintegrandi invaluit consilium. Leonem suis cum exemplis adeo artis vinclis cohaerere constat, ut unus sine altero haudquaquam praebeat columen stabile firmiterque collocatum.

The rest of the passage makes it clear that, by 1915, Vári had made a thorough study of the relations between the manuscripts of the *Taktiká* and those of the *Stratêghikón*, and that he had come to conclusions of his own that were definite (though not necessarily convincing to all other scholars).

In his text of the *Taktiká*, as far as his edition of them extends, Vári has printed, above the text of Leo's work itself, the texts of Leo's sources, and, in printing these, he has done some editorial work on them as well.[3] Thus we have a text, presented by Vári, of all the passages of the *Stratêghikón* that Leo has copied in his *Taktiká*, down to *Taktiká*, Dhiat. 14, § 38, which is the point at which Vári's edition of the *Taktiká* breaks off. Unfortunately, we do not have Vári's complete edition of the *Stratêghikón* itself that Vári had intended to produce. No doubt, if he had been able to produce it, he would have incorporated in it much more of his work on the manuscripts than he was able to use in the passages printed in his incomplete edition of Leo's *Taktiká*.

For the *Taktiká*, we have an admirable edition of the portion that Vári has covered, and, as far as this portion is concerned, we need not be troubled by Scheffer's information that there were lacunae in the manuscript of Leo's *Taktiká* that had been given to him by Holstenius, and that this manuscript had been 'pulchre restituto' by the filling in of these lacunae. Had they been filled in from the manuscript, also given to Scheffer by Holstenius, of the *Stratêghikón*? And were there the same lacunae in the manuscripts used by Meursius in his edition of Leo's *Taktiká*—an edition that is the basis of Migne's text? Scheffer's mention of lacunae shakes our faith in the text of the *Taktiká* from Dhiátaxis 14, § 39, down to the end—that is to say, the portion of the *Taktiká* for which we still have no later or better text than Migne's.

We now have Mihăescu's text of the *Stratêghikón* that has already been mentioned in this annex. The text is based on five manuscripts, and is

---

[1] On pp. 19–26 of Scheffer's edition; on pp. 50–6 of Mihăescu's edition.   [2] p. xxx.
[3] Vári's preface to his edition of Leo's *Taktiká*, vol. i, pp. xxxiii–xxxiv. This editorial work of Vári's on '*Mavríkios's*' *Stratêghikón* is duly praised by Mihăescu in his edition, p. 25.

provided with an apparatus criticus. The manuscripts used by Mihăescu are:

(i) *Mediceo-Laurentianus gr. LV, 4* ('M').[1] This is one of the four manuscripts that, according to Scheffer, were drawn upon for the production of the manuscript that was used by Scheffer himself. 'M' has also been used by Vári in his text of 'Mavríkios', Part 1, chap. 2, and no doubt also in the other passages of 'Mavríkios' that he has printed in his edition of Leo's *Taktiká*. Dain's dating of this manuscript is the middle, or, at latest, the second half, of the tenth century.[2] This is the oldest and the best of all the manuscripts that contain 'Mavríkios's' *Stratêghikón*.[3] 'The language of the Florence manuscript is, in general, more popular and less stylized—that is to say, more authentic.'[4] However, out of sixty-five of the sheets of 'M' that were occupied by 'Mavríkios's' *Stratêghikón*, fifteen are missing.

(ii) *Ambrosianus 139 (B. 119 sup.)* ('A').[5] Date: eleventh century or second half of tenth century. According to Mihăescu, 'A' is a free paraphrase of an older manuscript. It is not a copy of 'M' and is not derived from it. 'A' occupies an intermediate position between 'M' and the group of other manuscripts.

(iii) *Borbonico-Neapolitanus 284 (III–C–26)* ('N').[6] Date: eleventh century or close of tenth century.

(iv) *Parisinus Graecus 2442* ('P').[7] Date: eleventh century; some of its readings have been corrected in the margin to make them conform to the corresponding readings in 'N'.

(v) *Vaticanus Graecus 1164* ('V').[8] Date: mid eleventh century. Pieces, amounting to about six sheets, are missing.

According to Mihăescu, these five manuscripts fall into three markedly distinct categories. 'M' is the oldest and the best; 'A' is a free paraphrase of a manuscript closely related to 'M'; the other three are a group: all three are derived from the same single source.

Mihăescu's conception of the relations between his five manuscripts is given in the following stemma[9]

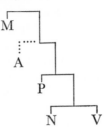

[1] See Mihăescu, pp. 15–16.
[2] A. Dain, *Les Manuscrits d'Onésandros* (Paris, 1930), p. 43.
[3] Mihăescu, p. 15. [4] Ibid., p. 16. [5] See ibid., pp. 16–18. [6] See ibid., p. 18.
[7] See ibid., p. 18. [8] See ibid., p. 19. [9] Mihăescu, op. cit., p. 19.

Here Mihăescu notes that he follows Dain,[1] and he has also used Dain's text of Leo VI's *Problemata* (Paris, 1935), which is a résumé of 'Mavríkios's' *Stratêghikón*, and Leo VI's *Taktiká*, in which long passages of 'Mavríkios' are reproduced verbatim.

I cannot appraise Mihăescu's text of 'Mavríkios'. I have no experience of my own in the editing of Greek texts. I can see that some, at any rate, of the differences between Mihăescu's Greek text and Scheffer's are due, not to Mihăescu's access to good manuscripts, but to twentieth-century, not seventeenth-century, printer's errors that could, and should, have been noticed and corrected before publication. This blemish is unfortunate, but, on a larger view, Mihăescu has done a notable service to Byzantine studies by making 'Mavríkios's' *Stratêghikón* accessible again at last—306 years after the publication of the first and sole previous edition.

Students of the East Roman art of war can feel fairly sure about certain elementary matters of fact that are of prime importance for their purposes. Leo VI's *Taktiká* were written *circa* 900; 'Mavríkios's' *Stratêghikón* was written *circa* 600.[2] Leo was not a professional soldier; 'Mavríkios' was one, and he had had practical experience of military service in campaigns in the country to the north of the lower course of the Danube (the present-day Wallachia) that was inhabited by the Slavs in his time.

Vári holds that the *Stratêghikón* was written, not at some date *circa* 600, but in the eighth century. He also holds that the author's name was Ourvíkios (Urbicius)—a different Ourvíkios, of course, from the man of the same name who was writing during the reign of the Emperor Anastasius I (491–518).[3]

On the question of the name of the author of the *Stratêghikón*, the evidence is conflicting. 'M' calls the author Ourvíkios; yet 'M' omits the Οὐρβικίου Ἐπιτήδευμα which, in other manuscripts, is included in Part XII of the *Stratêghikón*.[4] 'A' ascribes the book to Μαυρικίου . . . τοῦ ἐπὶ τοῦ βασιλέως Μαυρικίου γεγονότος. 'N', 'P', and 'V' ascribe it simply to Μαυρίκιος. The evidence is set out clearly, and is discussed judiciously, by Scheffer in his edition (see, for instance, his pp. 369 and 383–4). The question is not important. We do know, from the author's own evidence,[5]

---

[1] A. Dain, *Les Manuscrits d'Onésandros*, p. 35.

[2] Mihăescu, op. cit., p. 13, dates 'Mavríkios' within the first three decades of the seventh century. He notes, on p. 12, that internal evidence excludes a date in the second half of the seventh century. There is no mention of the Danubian Bulgars (pp. 9 and 13).

[3] Vári's views on these historical points are set out in the *Byzantinische Zeitschrift*, 15. Band (1906), pp. 61–82, and also in 19. Band (1910), p. 553, in a review, ibid., on pp. 551–4, of F. Aussaresses, *L'Armée byzantine à la fin du vi^e siècle* (Bordeaux, 1909, Feret; Paris, 1909, Fontemoing).

[4] Mihăescu, op. cit., p. 13.

[5] See 'Mavríkios', *Stratêghikón*, Part 11, chap. 5, p. 289 Scheffer; Part 11, chap. 4, p. 290 Mihăescu.

that the author was a professional soldier who had fought against the Slavs in what is now Wallachia, and we also know that no East Roman land-forces operated in this territory after the year 602. The author's claim to have had personal experience in this war-zone is borne out by the relative length and detail of his chapter on the Slavs, as compared with his chapter on the Persians. He rightly gives the Persians pride of place. So long as the Sasanian Persian Empire lasted, it was recognized by the East Romans as being their own Empire's equal in status, besides being its principal adversary. The author enlarges on the Slavs because he happens to have first-hand knowledge of them.

The prominence given to the Persians in the *Stratêghikón*, and the absence of any mention of the Arabs, shows that this treatise must have been written before the fourth decade of the seventh century. The last Romano-Persian war ended in 628. The last of the Persian troops that had been in occupation of Roman territory were evacuated in 629. By the year 641 the Persian Empire had ceased to exist. The Arabs had conquered the whole of it.

A date not later than *circa* 630 is also indicated by the prominence given to the Avars and by the coupling of the Turks' name with theirs as the other principal contemporary Eurasian nomad people. The Avars had emerged above the East Romans' horizon in 558, and they sank below it very soon after the failure, in 626, of the Avaro-Persian siege of Constantinople. Between those two dates, the Avars' impact on the East Roman Empire had been potent. The Empire's encounter with the Turks (i.e. with the sixth-century Turkish Empire on the Steppe) was brief. There were exchanges of embassies from 568 to 576, but, in the latter year, these ended in a rupture, and in the same year the Turks seized the East Roman city Vósporos, on the Crimean shore of the Straits of Kerch. In 627, outside the walls of Tiflis, the Emperor Heraclius made an alliance with Ziévêl, the Turkish Khaqan's second-in-command.[1] Soon after this, the empire of the Western Turks seems to have broken up, and the occupants of the Steppe to the west of the Lower Volga who are encountered by the East Romans and by the Arabs from the sixth decade of the seventh century onwards are no longer the Turks but the Khazars.[2]

These pieces of internal evidence are consistent with each other, and they indicate that the *Stratêghikón* was probably written not later than 602, and certainly not later than *circa* 630.

---

[1] Theophanes, p. 316, sub A.M. 6117.   [2] See III, 5 (iii), p. 441.

ANNEX III

The Slav Völkerwanderung *South of the Danube*

THE present limits of the area, to the south of the Danube, in which Slavonic languages are spoken coincide approximately with the present northern political frontiers of Turkey and Greece and northern and eastern political frontiers of Albania. To the north and east of the whole of this line, except for the northern frontier of Albania, the current Slavonic language is Bulgarian;[1] beyond the northern frontier of Albania it is Serbo-Croat.[2] However, till as recently as 1922 the Bulgarian Slav language was still being spoken as far south as the north-west shore of the Gulf of Thessaloníkê, just to the west of Thessaloníkê itself. The ninth-century form of the language of these South-Macedonian Slavs is the 'Old Slavonic' for which the Thessalonian scholar-missionary brothers, Constantine-Cyril and Methódhios, invented an alphabet. It is still the common liturgical language of the Eastern Orthodox Christian Slav peoples, and, for centuries, it was their common literary language too. The form of the Slavonic place-names that still survive, south of the Thessalonican campania, right down to the extremities of the Pelopónnêsos, tells us that an archaic form of the Slavonic language that is now called Bulgarian was spoken in all the Slav settlements in Greece that were deposited by the Slav *Völkerwanderung*.[3]

These settlements did not swamp the whole of Greece. They occupied only patches of Greece, while, in other patches, those strata of Greek population that had been in occupation since the 'Dorian' invasion—indeed, since the twentieth century B.C. in the case of Attica—continued to hold their ground.[4] Yet, geographically, the Slavs' penetration of Greece went far. There are Slavonic place-names in Kynouría,[5] near Monemvasía, where the native Greek population of the Pelopónnêsos kept the Slav invaders at bay, and even in the Máni (Taínaron)[6]—a

---

[1] i.e. not the original language of the Bulgar founders of the medieval Danubian Bulgarian state, but the language of their Slav subjects, south of the Danube, which the Bulgars themselves eventually came to speak. The Bulgars' original language was a Turkish one.

[2] M. Vasmer, *Die Slaven in Griechenland* (Berlin, 1941, de Gruyter), p. 324.

[3] Op. cit., p. 324.

[4] 'Von einer Vernichtung des Griechentums kann keine Rede sein.' The Slavonic influence on the Modern Greek language is slight (op. cit., p. 325); cf. A. Bon, *Le Péloponnèse byzantin jusqu'en 1204* (Paris, 1951, Presses Universitaires de France), p. 65.

[5] e.g. Laconia, No. 8 (p. 165), No. 12 (p. 166), and No. 43 (p. 169), in Vasmer, op. cit.

[6] Op. cit., Laconia, No. 8 (p. 165) and No. 80 (p. 174).

fastness in which not only the Greek language but the pre-Christian Greek religion survived till the reign of the Emperor Basil I (867–86).[1] As for the Latin language that had supplanted Illyrian and Thracian in the north of the Praetorian Prefecture of the Eastern Illyricum, it too survived to change into the Romance language spoken today by the Vlakhs and Roumans. Nor did the Slav settlers who spoke the Serbo-Croat variety of Slavonic swamp the whole of the dioecesis of the Western Illyricum. The Latinized population of this former Roman territory likewise continued to hold its ground and to preserve its language in some of the coastal towns and off-shore islands of Dalmatia.[2] All the same, the Slav *Völkerwanderung* produced changes in the linguistic and ethnic map of south-eastern Europe of a magnitude that had no precedent since the *Völkerwanderung* of the Illyrians, the North-West-Greek-speaking Greeks, and the Thraco-Phrygians in the post-Mycenaean Age[3] During the time-interval of perhaps eighteen centuries that intervened between these two massive changes of population, there had been barbarian invasions that had begun with the Gallic *Völkerwanderung* in the third decade of the third century B.C., and, from then onwards, these incursions of barbarians had become more frequent. Yet, though they had decimated the existing population, they had not supplanted it.[4] They had come and gone without leaving any appreciable permanent mark on the ethnic map. The Slav *Völkerwanderung* was the first invasion of south-eastern Europe for nearly 1,800 years that transformed the ethnic and linguistic map extensively and radically.

The Slavs' permanent intrusion into the two Illyrian administrative divisions of the Roman Empire was initiated, directed, and controlled, both militarily and politically, by the Avars, a well-organized and well-

---

[1] *De Adm. Imp.*, chap. 50, p. 224 (Bonn). See also the present work, p. 514, n. 7, p. 527, and p. 579).

[2] See F. Skok, 'Ortsnamenstudien zu "De Administrando Imperio" des Kaisers Konstantin Porphyrogenitus', in *Zeitschrift für Ortsnamenforschung*, Band IV (1928), pp. 213–43.

[3] It is possible that, in this previous *Völkerwanderung*, there were already some Slav participants. Some apparent indications of this, in place-names in the Balkan Peninsula dating from before the Slav *Völkerwanderung* that flooded over the Peninsula in the sixth and seventh centuries of the Christian Era, are noted in A. J. Toynbee, *Some Problems of Greek History*, (London, 1969, Oxford University Press), p. 99. Vasmer points out, in op. cit., pp. 158–9, that Srem, the Slavonic rendering of the Latin form of the city-name Sirmium, is also the name of a place in Poznań in Poland. Perhaps 'sirmium' is a Latinization of a descriptive Slavonic place-name. Bulgarian Slavonic 'srema' or 'sriema' means 'meeting', and Sirmium lay on the River Sava a short distance above its confluence with the Danube. Similarly 'sardica' may be a Latinization of a pre-Christian-Era form of the present-day Bulgarian Slavonic word 'sriedište' or 'sriedstvo', which means 'centre', and this, too, might be a descriptive Slavonic place-name, since Sardica (the present-day Sofia) is sited in a central position, namely the point at which the road from Constantinople to Sirmium crosses the road from the lower Danube valley to the Aegean up the River Isker and down the River Strúma (Strymón).

[4] Lemerle, 'Invasions', pp. 277–81.

armed Eurasian nomad people of unknown ethnic and linguistic affinities that, in the sixth decade of the sixth century of the Christian Era, had migrated westwards from Central Asia to the Steppe along the north shore of the Black Sea and, from there, to the Hungarian Alföld. The Avars' organization of the Slav *Völkerwanderung* to the south of the Danube was the chief mark that the Avars left on history. Their empire was ephemeral. They made themselves so odious to their newly-acquired subjects and neighbours at the western end of the Continent[1] that these seized every opportunity of throwing off the Avar yoke.

About the year 623, a Frankish trader named Samo led a successful resistance movement among the Avars' Moravian Slav subjects.[2] Samo's successor-state did not outlast its founder's lifetime, but the liberation of the Moravian Slavs from Avar rule was permanent. The Avars' prestige was irreparably damaged by their failure in 626 to capture Constantinople, in spite of their having had, on this occasion, the co-operation of a Persian expeditionary force just across the Bosphorus on the Asiatic shore. The East Roman Emperor Heraclius (610–41) took his revenge for this unsuccessful blow at the Empire's capital city. Like Samo, Heraclius pushed back the Avars' frontiers by engineering two successful revolts against them at opposite ends of their dominions.

At some date after the year 626,[3] Heraclius conveyed some sections of the Croat and Serb peoples to Illyricum, and helped them to install themselves there, under nominal East Roman suzerainty, in return for their ejecting the Avars and succeeding to the Avars' rule over the Slav settlers in the hinterland of the Dalmatian coast. At about the same time, Heraclius helped Koúvrat, the Khan of the Bulgar Turkish-speaking Onogurs astride the Sea of Azov and the lower Don, to make himself independent of the Avars.[4] It is questionable whether this Bulgar Koúvrat is or is not identical with the Bulgar Koúver,[5] a subordinate of the Avars who revolted at about this date against his overlords and piloted back from Sirmia to the neighbourhood of Thessaloníkê the half-caste descendants of the East Romans whom the Avars had deported to Sirmia from the south-east. In any case, this was a blow to the Avars, whether it was a single blow or a pair. Even some of the Bulgars whom the Avars had carried with them westward into Pannonia succeeded in breaking loose. The Bulgar rebel Alciocus, who sought asylum with the Franks

---

[1] See, for instance, the *Russian Primary Chronicle*, Cross and Sherbowitz-Wetzor's translation, p. 55.

[2] See Dvornik, *The Slavs: Their Early History and Civilization*, pp. 60–1.

[3] Stratós, op. cit., p. 330, notes that George Pisidês, who was writing his poem in 628, mentions the Serbs' and Croats' assault on the Avars in Book II, lines 98–100.

[4] Nic. Patr., p. 24; Theophanes, p. 357. They call the Onogurs Οὐνογουνδοῦροι.

[5] This question is discussed in III, 5, Appendix I. It has been raised in II, 1 (iii) (a), p. 74, n. 4.

in 630/1,[1] may be identical with the Alzeco who obtained asylum in the Lombard duchy of Benevento.[2]

The Avars lingered on in the Alföld till they were crushed by the Franks in two attacks—the first in 791 and the conclusive one in 795–6.[3] The Avars finally capitulated in 805. The date of the latest East Roman coins found in Avar graves is 676–7, and this is also the date of the last Avar embassy to Constantinople.[4] The Danubian Bulgars lent the Franks a hand, and were rewarded with the lion's share of the Avars' pasture-lands, up to the east bank of the River Tisza (Theiss) and perhaps beyond. 'There is to this day a proverb in Rus' which runs: "They perished like the Avars". Neither race nor heir of them remains.'[5]

In contrast to the Avars, the Slavs who migrated to the south side of the Danube and settled in south-eastern Europe have survived, though their language is no longer current over the whole of the area that they once occupied.[6] The Slavs who settled in what had been the Western Illyricum assimilated the Croats and the Serbs who had expelled the Slavs' previous Avar overlords and had stepped into the Avars' shoes. The Slavs who settled in what had been the Eastern Illyricum outlived, and perhaps absorbed, the Avars who, in this quarter, had been the organizers and leaders of their migration.[7] The Slavs went on to absorb

---

[1] Pseudo-Fredegarius, IV, § 72, p. 157, cited by H. Grégoire, 'L'Origine et le nom des Croates et des Serbes', in *Byzantion*, vol. xvii (1944–5), pp. 88–118, on p. 112. See the present work III, 5 (iii), p. 438, with n. 4.

[2] Paulus Diaconus, Book V, chap. 29, cited by Grégoire ibid., p. 112, n. 29. According to Theophanes, p. 357, one fraction of the Bulgars obtained asylum in the Exarchate of Ravenna, in the Pentapolis. See the present work, p. 439, with nn. 1 and 2.

[3] See L. Halphen, *Charlemagne et l'Empire carolingien* (Paris, 1949, Albin Michel), pp. 81–7; Vernadsky, *Ancient Russia*, pp. 296–7; Runciman, *A History of the First Bulgarian Empire*, p. 52, n. 1; and the present work, p. 434.

[4] Lemerle, 'Invasions', p. 299, n. 3.   [5] The *Russian Primary Chronicle*, p. 56.

[6] The Graecization of the southernmost of the Slav settlers in the Balkan Peninsula has been noticed in II, 1 (iii) (a), pp. 94–107.

[7] If place-names in Greece whose first two syllables are 'Avar-' denote settlements of Avars, such settlements must have been fairly numerous. However, it seems more likely that these names are derived from the (Bulgarian) Slavonic word 'avor' or 'yavor' meaning maple or sycamore tree. Examples are Ἀβαρῖκος, Ἀβαρνίτσα, Ἀβοράνη in Akarnanía-Aitolía (Vasmer, op. cit., pp. 65–6) and Navarino in Messenia.

There are, however, at least two place-names in Greece which look, on the face of them, as if they are derived from the ethnikon 'Bulgar' and which, if this is in truth their origin, are evidences—considering their locations—that the Avars brought with them into Greece some of their Bulgar subjects (see Vasmer, op. cit., pp. 320–1), as well as their Slav subjects. One of these two names is that of Lake Βούλγαρη in the north-east corner of Akarnanía (op. cit., p. 68); the other is Βουλγαρέλι in the Arta district (p. 56). These two places lie beyond the frontiers of the medieval state of Bulgaria, even at its widest extent. As for the Βουλγάρα peak in the Ághrapha district (p. 87), the Vourghar mountain and Vourgharis spring in Per-rhaivía (ibid.), Βουργάρικο in the Yánnina district (p. 25), and Μβουγαρίοβο (a Serbo-Croat form, as Vasmer notes) near Thessaloníkê (p. 208), these might all have been just inside the medieval Bulgaria's frontiers.

There are also place-names in Greece and in the Turkish part of Thrace which indicate that some of the Croats (Vasmer, op. cit., p. 319) and Serbs (pp. 319–20) were planted there,

the Turkish-speaking Bulgars who in 680 had gained a foothold to the south of the lower Danube and had then progressively subjugated as much of the Slav population there as was not subjugated by the East Roman Empire. In subjugating these Slavs, the Bulgars had saved them from being Graecized, but the Bulgars failed to save themselves from being Slavized.[1] The peoples who call themselves Bulgars, Serbs, and Croats today speak the language of the Slavs whom the original Bulgars, Serbs, and Croats had subjugated; and no doubt they have more Slav than Eurasian nomad blood in their veins. The only Slavonic-speaking people on the south side of the Danube that still retains its original name is the Slovene people at the north-western end of Yugoslavia.

Dvornik[2] has noted indications that the original Croats and Serbs may not have been Slavs but may have been Sarmatian nomads from the Eurasian Steppe. He points out that neither the name 'Serb'[3] nor the five names of Croat chiefs[4] given by Constantine Porphyrogenitus[5] are Slavonic, and he compares[6] the name 'Harvat'[7] with the name 'Harahvati' (Arachosians) of the Achaemenian inscriptions. The Harahvati may have been split into two fractions when, drifting westwards, they had run up against the obstacle presented by the Caspian Sea, and the

or planted themselves there without asking leave, instead of going on to their intended destinations in the Western Illyricum. The Croats have given their name to Χαρβάτι in Attica (p. 123), to Χαρβάτι near Mycenae, in Argholís (p. 127), and, surprisingly, to Χαρβάτα, near Khaniá, in Crete (p. 175). The Serbs have given their name to Σέρβη or Ζέρβη in Turkish Thrace, near Kirk Kilise, to Σέρβων (p. 212) on Lóngos (itself a Slavonic name meaning 'woodland'), to τὰ Σέρβια (alias Σερβία or Σερβεία), which covers the northern approach to the Pórtes Pass between the Vistríca (Aliákmon) basin and the Pêneiós (Salamvriá) basin (p. 187), to Σερβιανά in the Yánnina district (p. 50), to Σερβωτά near Tríkkala (p. 96), to Σερβιανά in Elis (p. 158), to Σέρβον in Arkadhía, near Hêraía, to Σερβοτά in Triphylía, possibly to Ζερμπίτσα (alias Ζερμπίσια) in Messenia (p. 162), and to Ζερμπίτσα (p. 168) and Σερβέϊκα (p. 173) in Laconia.

[1] F. Dvornik, *Les Slaves, Byzance, et Rome au ixe siècle* (Paris, 1926, Champion), p. 40, dates the Slavization of the Bulgars in the reign of Khan Omurtag (815–31). The process will have been made irreversible by the adoption, in the reign of Khan Borís (852–89), of the Macedonian Slavonic dialect, conveyed first in the Glagolitic alphabet invented by Constantine-Cyril, and then in the 'Cyrillic' alphabet invented at Preslav, to convey Bulgaria's liturgical and literary language (see II, 1 (iii) (a), pp. 104–5).

[2] In Gy. Moravcsik's and R. J. H. Jenkins's edition of Constantine Porphyrogenitus's *De Adm. Imp.*, vol. ii, *Commentary* (London, 1962, Athlone Press).

[3] See Moravcsik and Jenkins, op. cit., p. 132.

[4] See ibid., pp. 116–17.   [5] In *De Adm. Imp.*, chap. 30, p. 143.

[6] See Moravcsik and Jenkins, op. cit., p. 115.

[7] The personal name of Heraclius's ally the Khan of the Onogur Bulgars, Κούβρατος (Nic. Patr., p. 24) or κοβρᾶτος (op. cit., p. 33) or κροβᾶτος (Theoph. p. 357), may have been taken from the ethnikon of the Croat people. Onoguria lay on the eastern shore of the Sea of Azov. However, the name Khoroathos or Khorouathos occurs, not as an ethnikon, but as a personal name, in Greek inscriptions found at the mouth of the River Don that were engraved in the second and third centuries of the Christian Era (Dvornik, *The Slavs: Their Early History and Civilization*, p. 26; Grégoire, 'L'Origine et le nom des Croates et des Serbes', p. 116. According to Grégoire, the word means, in Iranian, 'he who possesses trusty friends').

northerly fraction may then have travelled on farther westward round the Caspian's northern shore. As for the Serbs, they are located by Pliny[1] and by Ptolemy[2] between the Volga, the Caucasus, and the Sea of Azov.[3] Rambaud notes,[4] on the evidence of Constantine Porphyrogenitus,[5] that, in the Caucasus, there were two peoples named respectively Κρεβατάδες and Σαρβάν, and that the Sarván were neighbours of the Alans. The Alans were certainly a Sarmatian people, and, if a rearguard of one Sarmatian people had stayed behind in Northern Caucasia, it is possible that rearguards of two others may have stayed there too. The name 'Serb' may perhaps also be detected in the name 'Shirvan', by which the Arab geographers called the north-eastern part of the East-Caucasian country known to Hellenic geographers as 'Albania'.

If the original Croats and Serbs were in truth Sarmatian nomads who had come from the Eurasian Steppe, they must have split, on their westward journey, (the Croats perhaps for the second time,) into two fractions: a southern one which must have travelled south of the Carpathians —and perhaps south of the lower Danube—into present-day Croatia and Serbia, and a northern one which must have travelled north of the Carpathians into 'White Croatia', i.e. southern and eastern Bohemia,[6] and into Lusatia, where there is still today an enclave of Slavonic-speaking Serbs. The northern, like the southern, Croat and Serb migrants must have subjugated a Slavonic-speaking population and have been assimilated by it.[7]

According to Constantine Porphyrogenitus,[8] the Croats expelled the Avars on their own initiative from the interior of Dalmatia and took their place there as overlords of the Slavs who had previously drifted in. According to Constantine again,[9] the Croats were acting on an invitation from the Emperor Heraclius; they acknowledged the Roman Empire's nominal suzerainty over them in their new dominions, and they submitted to being converted to Christianity by missionaries whom Heraclius procured from Rome (since both parts of Illyricum were under the ecclesiastical jurisdiction of the Roman See). According to Constantine once again,[10] Heraclius subsequently made the same terms with the Serbs.

---

[1] Pliny, *Historia Naturalis*, Book VI, chap. 2 (7), § 19.

[2] Ptolemy, *Geographia*, Book V, chap. 8, § 13.

[3] Dvornik, *The Slavs: Their Early History and Civilization*, p. 27, n. 1.

[4] In op. cit., pp. 525–6. Cf. Dvornik in Moravcsik and Jenkins, op. cit., p. 115.

[5] *De Caer.*, Book II, chap. 48, p. 688.

[6] See *De Adm. Imp.*, chap. 30, p. 143, and chap. 31, p. 148, with Dvornik's contribution to Moravcsik's and Jenkins's *Commentary*, pp. 97–8.

[7] See L. Hauptmann, 'Les Rapports des Byzantins avec les Slaves et les Avares pendant la seconde moitié du vie siècle', in *Byzantion*, vol. iv (1929), pp. 131–70, on p. 166, n. 2.

[8] *De Adm. Imp.*, chap. 30, pp. 133–4.

[9] In op. cit., chap. 31, pp. 148–9.

[10] In op. cit., chap. 33, p. 153.

After planting a detachment of them at Servía,[1] to cover the Pórtes Pass leading over the Cambunian Mountains from the Aliákmon basin into Thessaly, he sent the main body of the Serbs to evict the Avars from the Slav settlements in the Illyrian territories that have since been known as Serbia, and he arranged for the Serbs' conversion to Christianity by missionaries procured, in this case too, from Rome.

The track followed by the Slavs who settled in the Western Illyricum, to the south of the River Drava, and the extent of the territory that they occupied, are clear. Pushed south-westwards by the Avar occupants of the Alföld,[2] they moved forward till they were brought to a halt by the Adriatic Sea and the eastern Alps. They evicted or submerged all the previous Latin-speaking population except for the few enclaves that survived in Dalmatia. The Slavs who settled in the Eastern Illyricum and in the northern part of the dioecesis of Thrace between the Balkan (Aímos) Range and the south bank of the lower Danube followed several different tracks, and the ascertainment of the extent of the territory that they once occupied has been obstructed by controversies that have been inspired partly by nationalism and not solely by a disinterested quest for the truth. Fortunately, objective evidence is provided by the survival of Slavonic place-names in regions in which a Slavonic language has long since ceased to be spoken, and an exhaustive, impartial, and judicious study of the Slavonic place-names within the present frontiers of the Kingdom of Greece has been made by Vasmer.[3] Vasmer's findings are clear, and they are not contradicted by the ambiguous evidence of surviving written records.

In the Balkan Peninsula, the Slavs succeeded in penetrating the farthest, the more distant their tracks lay from the main body of the East Roman Empire in Asia Minor, with its European bridgehead in Thrace.[4]

On their easternmost southward track, the Slav settlers in the Balkan Peninsula penetrated only as far as the Zagora or Zagorje (i.e. 'the country beyond the mountains'), and they seem not to have advanced even as far as that on their own initiative. It was the Bulgars who, after establishing themselves to the south of the lower Danube in 680, posted the Severian Slavs here to cover the southern approaches to the Veregava Pass.[5] Here the East Roman Empire managed to hold against the Slavs

[1] If it is true that the Serbs were settled at Servía (alias τὰ Σέρβια), before their main body moved on westward into the country that has come to be known as Serbia, it looks as if the Serbs had approached the Balkan Peninsula from the east, and not from the north, in spite of Constantine Porphyrogenitus's attribution of a northern origin to them at the beginning of chap. 32 of *De Adm. Imp.* Constantine is supported by Stratós, op. cit., pp. 327–30.
[2] The rarity of Slavonic place-names in the Alföld indicates that the Avars drove the Slavs out of there in the second half of the sixth century (Hauptmann, 'Les Rapports', pp. 169–70).
[3] M. Vasmer, *Die Slaven in Griechenland* (Berlin, 1941, de Gruyter).
[4] This is pointed out by Vasmer, op. cit., p. 317, and by Charanis, 'Ethnic Changes', p. 40.
[5] Theophanes, p. 359 (see the present work, II, 7, p. 338, with n. 1, and III, 2, p. 358).

(though eventually not against these Slavs' Bulgar masters and managers)[1] a line running north-eastwards from the northern outskirts of Adrianople via Dheveltós to the head of the Gulf of Burgas, where the Empire had *points d'appui* in the Greek coastal cities Mesêmvría, Ankhíalos, and Sozópolis.

To the west of the western outskirts of Adrianople, the Slavs did push their way across the Balkan Range into the upper valley of the River Maríca (Évros), but, south of the Maríca valley, their way was blocked, on this sector, by the *massif* of the Rhodhópê Mountains.

To the west of Rhodhópê, there was no practicable route through the gorges of the River Mésta (Néstos)[2] before a passage was blasted through here by modern railway-engineers. But in the next two sectors, still proceeding westwards, there was always relatively good access from the south bank of the lower Danube to the north shore of the Aegean Sea. There are easy passages over the watersheds between the Isker tributary of the Danube and the River Strúma (Strymón), and between the Morava tributary of the Danube and the River Vardar (Axiós); and the Slav migrants were able to bypass the East Roman fortress Sardica, sited at the crossing of the Isker–Strúma route from north to south with the Constantinople–Sirmium route from south-east to north-west.

The Slavs who descended the Strúma valley could fan out into the patches of plain to the east of the river's lower course and, less easily, into the rugged Chalcidic Peninsula. The Slavs who moved up the Moráva valley and down into the Vardar basin, past Skopoí (Skoplje), had a choice, from Skopoí onwards, between alternative routes. Some of these westerly Slav migrants travelled on down the valley of the Vardar and reached the Thessalonican campania just to the west of the city of Thessaloníkê itself; but from here they were unable to fan out far. Thessaloníkê barred the way north-eastward; the eastern face of Mount Vérmion barred the way westward. In the eastern foothills of Vérmion, the Slavs established themselves at Náousa, as is witnessed by this town's Slavonic name,[3] but Vérrhoia's Greek name and population were saved for it by its East Roman garrison, and, south of the lower course of the River Vistríca (Aliákmon), the eastern spurs of Mount Olympus almost push the southward-bound traveller into the sea before he reaches the mouth of the gorge of Témbê. The Slavs who had descended the course

---

[1] Theophanes, p. 359, indicates that the Bulgars, like the Avars before them, moved the Slav tribes under their control, like pieces on a chessboard, to further the dominant nomad people's own military and political aims. The Bulgars' hold on the Zagorje was confirmed by the Emperor Justinian II in 705 as a reward for the Bulgar Khan Tervel's having replaced Justinian on his throne (Runciman, *A History of the First Bulgarian Empire*, p. 30; Dvornik, *The Slavs, Their Early History*, p. 66). The final cession of the Zagorje to Bulgaria by the East Roman Empire seems to have been made in the reign of Khan Borís, perhaps in consideration of Borís's conversion to Christianity in 864 (see the present work, p. 358, n. 3).

[2] Lemerle, 'Invasions', p. 276.   [3] Vasmer, op. cit., p. 209.

of the River Vardar do not seem to have succeeded in forcing their way through Témbê into Thessaly.

The Slavs who, from the neighbourhood of Skopoí, followed the apparently less promising route up-stream instead of down-stream along the Vardar proved to have made the better choice. There is an easy passage over the watershed between the headwaters of the Vardar and those of its right-bank tributary the Črna, and, from the upper basin of the Črna, the Slavs who entered it could, and did, emerge in three directions. One column followed the Roman Via Egnatia eastwards through Édhessa[1] down into the Thessalonican campania. A second column, travelling along the Via Egnatia westward instead of eastward, crossed the Pindus Range, which is the watershed between the Aegean and the Adriatic, into what is now Albania. A third column made its way from the Črna basin to the headwaters of the Vistríca to the south-east of Lake Prespa, and here this column divided. Part of it went westward across Pindus through the Tsángon Pass; another part went southward into north-western Thessaly (the Tríkkala-Kardhítsa district) over the easy passage from the Vistríca basin into the Salamvriá basin.[2]

The Slav migrants who crossed to the west side of the Pindus Range appear to have been the most numerous of all, and they certainly penetrated the farthest.

In the north-west quarter of Albania, from Elbasan on the lower Škumbi River to the west of a line running from there northwards to the left bank of the United Drin River, there are no Slavonic place-names,[3] and the absence of them there tells us that the Slavs who crossed the Pindus headed south for the basin of the Voïoússa (Aôos) River, and then ascended the Voïoússa itself and its affluents. From the headwaters of the Voïoússa, some of them crossed the Zýghos Pass into the Tríkkala-Kardhítsa district of north-western Thessaly. The main body trekked southwards into the Yánnina basin, and their trek was the longest of any. It carried them on southwards along the eastern shore of the Gulf of Préveza into Akarnanía-Aitolía and on from there, again, across the neck of the Corinthian Gulf, from Andírrhion in Aitolía to Rhíon in the Pelopónnêsos.

Thus the direction and the strength of the Slav *Völkerwanderung* into the Balkan Peninsula were determined by the contemporary geopolitical situation. The geographical factor in this twofold governing force was the structure of the landscape—a structure that always dictated the routes for human travel in this region until the techniques of modern railway

---

[1] Vódena, the Slavonic name for Édhessa, is a translation of the name which it replaced. Like 'Édhessa' in Thraco-Phrygian, 'Vódena' in Slavonic means 'Watertown'.

[2] The watershed here is so low that I failed to locate it, though I was on the look-out for it, when, on 27 July 1965, I was travelling from Kastoriá, via Ghrevená, to Kalabáka.

[3] Vasmer, op. cit., p. 324.

and motor-road engineering enabled Man, in our day, to override physical Nature's age-old dictates. The previous potency of the landscape is demonstrated by the fact that, nearly eighteen centuries earlier than the Slav *Völkerwanderung*, the *Völkerwanderung* of the Illyrian, Thraco-Phrygian, and North-West-Greek-speaking peoples had followed the same routes. The political factor that worked together with the geographical factor in channelling the Slav *Völkerwanderung* has been mentioned already. The residue of the East Roman Empire's military power, operating from Thrace, the European bridgehead of Asia Minor, pushed the Slav intruders westward and then southward. On the shores of the Adriatic and Ionian Seas, East Roman military power in the Balkan Peninsula was at its weakest; and the west side of Greece, from Épeiros down to the western Pelopónnêsos, was more remote than Sirmium from Constantinople.

These 'geopolitical' facts are reflected in the distribution and the frequency of Slavonic place-names in Greece within its present political frontiers. No doubt, the statistics of these place-names have to be discounted to some extent for several reasons. The districts to which the figures refer are unequal both in their areas and in their degrees of pastoral and of agricultural productivity per acre—a limiting factor for their capacity for providing a livelihood for a non-industrial rural population. Moreover, a greater amount of information about place-names happens, so far, to have been gathered for Épeiros than for other districts.[1] Yet Vasmer is justified in claiming, as he does,[2] that the evidence furnished by place-names is enlightening. This evidence verifies three important facts. In the first place, 'it is out of the question that there was anything like an annihilation of the Greek nationality (des Griechentums)'.[3] In the second place, 'considering how many of the geographical names prove to be Slavonic, it must be concluded that the [Slav] intruders presented themselves in very great force'.[4] In the third place, when we have allowed for the relative abundance of our information about place-names in Épeiros, 'it is still clear that eastern Greece produces less evidence of Slav influences than western Greece'.[5] In Thessaly, Slavonic place-names are rarer in the Lárisa district than in the Tríkkala-Kardhítsa district. In central Greece, they are rarer in Évvoia and Attica and Boeotia than in Phthiotís and Phokís, and much rarer than in Akarnanía-Aitolía. In the Pelopónnêsos, they are rarer in Argholís and Korinthía than in Akhaḯa, and they are particularly thick on the ground in Arkadhía and on Mount Taÿgetos.[6]

---

[1] Vasmer, op. cit., p. 317.
[2] Ibid.
[3] Vasmer, op. cit., p. 325, quoted already on p. 619, n. 4.
[4] Ibid., p. 318.
[5] Ibid., p. 317.
[6] Vasmer, ibid. In two districts, the Slav *Völkerwanderung* did not conform to the North-

Vasmer's figures fully bear out the conclusions that he draws from them. In Thrace on the Turkish side of the present-day frontier there are thirty Slavonic place-names.[1] On the Greek side of the frontier, in Western Thrace, there are only twenty of them[2] (the Rhodhópê *massif* is hard to cross). By contrast, there are 92 in the relatively small Dhráma district,[3] which is easily accessible from the lower valley of the Strúma (Strymón). In the Serrhés district, astride the lower Strúma, there are 111.[4] In the Thessaloníkê district, which bestrides the lower course of the Vardar and which includes the Chalcidic Peninsula, there are 152.[5] The middle prong of the Peninsula now bears the name Lóngos, which is the Graecized form of a Slavonic word meaning 'woodland';[6] and Πρόβλακας, the present name of the isthmus which joins the eastern prong (the Athos Peninsula) to the rump of Khalkidhikḗ, looks like a Graecization of the Bulgarian Slavonic word for 'isthmus', which is 'provlak'.[7] The Pella district, to the north-west of Thessaloníkê-Khalkidhikḗ, has 94 Slavonic place-names, though its area is much smaller.[8] The Flórina-Kastoriá district has 165.[9] (Though Flórina is on the Greek side of the Graeco-Jugoslav frontier, it lies within the basin of the Črna River.) The relatively large Kozánê (Kózhani) district, which lies to the south of the Flórina-Kastoriá district, has only 116 Slavonic place-names;[10] but, as has been noted, this region, though it lies open to the north via Kastoriá, is virtually insulated from the Thessalonican campania and from the Pierian coastal plain by the mountain-wall of Vérmion and Olympus, whose continuity is hardly interrupted by the gorge through which the Vistríca (Aliákmon) River breaks its way to the Aegean coast past the fortress of Vérrhoia.

When we come to the successive tiers of districts to the south of a line drawn from the mouth of the River Salamvriá, on the Aegean coast of Greece, to the point, opposite the island of Kórphous (Corfú), where the Graeco-Albanian frontier strikes the shore of the Ionian Sea, the contrast between the respective numbers of Slavonic place-names on the east side and on the west side of Greece becomes dramatic.

In the Maghnêsía district of Thessaly, a natural fortress, formed by Mounts Ossa and Pêlion, overhanging Thessaly's Aegean coast, there are only 15 Slavonic place-names.[11] In the Lárisa district, which adjoins Maghnêsía on the west, there are only 38.[12] But in the Tríkkala-Kardhítsa district, which adjoins the Lárisa district on the west, there are 122,[13] and the town of Kardhítsa itself bears a Slavonic name.[14] The figures then rise

West-Greek-speaking Greeks' *Völkerwanderung* in its geographical pattern. The twelfth-century-B.C. migration had left Arkadhía and Mount Taÿgetos unmolested.

[1] Vasmer, op. cit., pp. 232–4.
[2] pp. 230–2.
[3] pp. 224–9.
[4] pp. 214–23.
[5] pp. 202–14.
[6] p. 206.
[7] p. 210.
[8] pp. 197–201.
[9] pp. 189–97.
[10] pp. 178–89.
[11] pp. 108–10.
[12] pp. 99–102.
[13] pp. 86–99.
[14] p. 91.

steeply when, still proceeding westwards, we cross the Pindus Range from Thessaly into Épeiros. Here the little Arta district has 44 Slavonic names,[1] the Préveza district, between Arta and the coast, has 34,[2] while the Yánnina district of Épeiros, to the north of these two, has no less than 334.[3]

In the next tier of districts to the south, there is a corresponding rise in the number of Slavonic place-names as we pass from east to west. Évvoia is virtually part of the mainland, but, like Maghnêsía, it is a natural fortress, and in Évvoia there are only 19 Slavonic place-names.[4] In Attica there are only 18,[5] and in Boeotia there are only 22.[6] On the other hand there are 45 in Phokís[7] and 55 in Phthiotís,[8] while in the same tier, to the west of Pindus, there are 48 in Evrytanía[9] and 98 in Akarnanía-Aitolía.[10] In the Slav *Völkerwanderung*'s passage through Épeiros and Akarnanía-Aitolía, the flow of migrants was so copious that part of it spilled over into some of the off-shore islands.[11] There are eleven Slavonic place-names on Kórphous (Corfú), four on Lefkás, and three on Kephal-lênía.[12]

In the Pelopónnêsos there are no Slavonic place-names on the off-shore island Aíyina,[13] but there are 18 in Argholís,[14] 24 in Korinthía,[15] 95 (including some doubtful cases) in the Peloponnesian Akhaḯa,[16] 94 in Arkadhía,[17] 34 in Elis,[18] 42 in Triphylía,[19] 81 in Lakonía,[20] and 41 in Messenía.[21] In the vanguard of the Slav *Völkerwanderung* into the Balkan Peninsula there were two tribes, the Mêlingoí and the Ezerítai, who came to rest respectively on Mount Taÿgetos and in the marshes in the lower basin of the River Evrótas. The Ezerítai took their name from their final habitat. (᾽Εζερός seems to be a Graecized form of the Slavonic word 'ezero' meaning 'lake' and standing for the local Greek place-name 'Hélos'.[22] Alternatively, it may be a translation of the Greek word 'límnê', which is the name of a present-day village near a lakelet to the north-north-west of Gýthion.) But the course of the Ezerítai's companion-tribe's south-ward advance can be traced in place-names that they deposited on their way. There are a Μελιγγοῦς and a Μιλιγκοί in Épeiros,[23] a Μελίγγοβα in Akarnanía-Aitolía,[24] a Μέλιγος in the Tríkkala-Kardhítsa district,[25] a Μίλλιγγον in Argholís, to the south of Náfplion,[26] and a Μεληγοῦ in Kynouría.[27]

Finally there are 17 Slavonic place-names (including some doubtful cases) in Crete.[1] The Slavs had already been at home in and on the water in Wallachia before they had started on their trek beyond the south bank of the lower Danube.[2] When they reached the sea, they ventured on to the salt water in their dug-out skiffs (μονόξυλα). These were inefficient, even when specially strengthened, as was proved during the second siege of Thessaloníkê.[3] Yet, with this frail craft, they managed to raid Crete as early as the year 623.[4]

Vasmer's statistics of Slavonic place-names bear out what we learn, from the surviving written records, about the East Roman Empire's vicissitudes, after the death of the Emperor Justinian I in 565, in its south-east European dominions. These records tell us that, in this period of East Roman history, the Empire lost—in some districts only temporarily, but in most districts permanently—its possession of the whole of the interior of its former south-east European provinces, as far to the west as the western extremity of the Western Illyricum, and as far to the south as the southern extremity of the Eastern Illyricum, which terminated in the Pelopónnêsos. Along the east shores of the Adriatic and the Ionian Sea, the Empire did not retain more than a few beach-heads. On the other hand, it retained possession of the north and west shores of the Aegean, except for two breaks, one on either side of Thessaloníkê, round the mouths of the Rivers Strúma and Vardar. At these two points the Slavs arrived in force, and the territory that they occupied here fell out of the Empire's control temporarily, though the Empire was subsequently successful in re-establishing its rule over these two temporary gaps in its strip of Aegean coastal possessions. Of course the part of this coastline—and it was the major part—which the Empire did succeed in retaining without any interregnum was not exempt from enemy raids. These raids were constant, and Vasmer's gazetteer of Slavonic place-names shows that some of the raids resulted, here too, in permanent settlements of alien intruders.

The evidence of place-names tells us the extent of the area of the Slav settlements to the south of the Danube. We have still to try to ascertain the date—or, rather, the principal dates, for it seems improbable that the whole of this area was occupied in one single operation.[5] Some

---

[1] pp. 174–7. The origin of Βούργαρο, Ἄνω and Κάτω, near Khaniá, is a mystery.

[2] They had been unrivalled in their dexterity in crossing rivers ('Mavríkios', Part 11, chap. 5, p. 274 Scheffer, p. 278 Mihǎescu); they could stay under water for hours on end, breathing through hollowed reeds (ibid., pp. 274–5 and p. 278 respectively).

[3] *S.D. Miracula*, Book II, chap. 1, col. 1328.

[4] Chronicle of Thomas Presbyter of Emesa, cited by Vasmer, op. cit., p. 14.

[5] Lemerle holds that the Slav *Landnahme* took the form of 'a progressive infiltration' or of 'successive waves', rather than of 'a conquest achieved at a precise date'. 'Je ne pense pas qu'on puisse parler d'une slavisation de la plus grande partie du Péloponnèse avant la fin du viie siècle. Mais le fait lui-même n'est guère niable' (P. Lemerle, 'La Chronique improprement

of the fortified cities that fell eventually had continued to hold out long after the open countryside had been overrun far to their rear.[1] For instance, the latest date given by a contemporary authority for the Slavs' occupation of Greece is the beginning of the Emperor Heraclius's fifth year, i.e. the turn of the years 614 and 615.[2] Yet the fortress of Sardica, which lay far to the north of Greece, on the watershed between the Rivers Strúma and Isker, held out till 809, when it fell at last, not to the Slavs, but to the Danubian Bulgars.[3]

However, there are two sets of years within one, or both, of which the main events in the Slav *Völkerwanderung* and *Landnahme* seem most likely to have fallen. The later set is the years 602–26. This span of years begins with the temporary collapse of the East Roman Empire upon the overthrow and murder of the Emperor Maurice, and it ends with the Avars' failure to take Constantinople. This failure cost the Avars their domination over the Slavs whose settlement south of the Danube the Avars had instigated and directed, and, after the Slav settlers had broken loose from their Avar organizers and masters, it seems improbable that, on their own unaided initiative, they will have continued to gain much ground or to obtain many reinforcements. The later period of Slav settlement under Avar auspices (i.e. the years 602–26) includes the year 614/15, in which the Slavs took Greece from the East Romans according to Isidore of Seville.[4] The earlier set of years within which the Slav occupation of Greece, as well as of the Roman dominions to the north of Greece, may have taken place is 572–91, years during which the East Roman Empire was engaged in a war with the Persian Empire that, so long as it lasted, was the first call on the East Roman Government's attention and resources. This situation became more than ever inviting for invaders of the Empire's European dominions after the year 577, in which Romano-Persian negotiations for peace were opened but broke down. The years between 572 and 591 are those within which the Avar and Slav invasions of the Roman dominions in south-eastern Europe are dated by contemporary authorities. All but one of these invasions are dated by them after 577. But there is no conclusive evidence that the invasions in these years led to a permanent occupation; and, considering the jejuneness of our surviving records of events in the seventh century

dite de Monemvasie: le contexte historique et légendaire,' in *Revue des Études Byzantines*, vol. xxi (1963), pp. 5–49, on p. 35). 'Les Sklavènes, livrés à eux-mêmes, pouvaient poser des problèmes a l'échelle locale, mais ne posaient pas à l'Empire de vrai problème politique' (ibid., p. 34).

[1] See Stratós, op. cit. p. 320.

[2] Isidore of Seville, *Chronicon*, col. 1056 in Migne, *Patrologia Latina*, vol. lxxxiii: 'Sclavi Graeciam Romanis tulerunt.' The passage runs: 'Eraclius dehinc quintum agit annum imperii. [Eraclius dehinc sextum decimum agit imperii annum] cuius initio Sclavi Graeciam Romanis tulerunt.' The bracketed sentence seems to be an interpolation.

[3] See II, 1 (iii) (a), p. 105.　　　　　　　　　　　　　　　[4] See footnote 2.

after 602, it is not surprising that Isidore of Seville's statement that the Slavs 'took Greece from the Romans' in 614/15 is the only extant notice of a Slav settlement in Greece during the years 602–26.

A victory of the future Emperor Tiberius II over the Avars in Thrace in the fourth year of Justin II's reign is recorded by John of Biclarum,[1] but Tiberius was defeated by the Avars in 574, and the Imperial Government had to make peace with them.[2]

The Empire was invaded by 100,000 Slavs in the fourth year of Tiberius II's reign,[3] in other words the third year after the death of Justin II[4] (i.e. in 581/2). According to John of Ephesus[5] this year was signalized by the invasion of an accursed people, called Slavonians, who overran the whole of Greece and the country of the Thessalonians and all Thrace, and captured the cities and took numerous forts, and devastated and burnt, and reduced the people to slavery and made themselves masters of the whole country and settled in it by main force and dwelt in it as though it had been their own, without fear. And four years have now elapsed, and still, because the King [i.e. Emperor] is engaged in the war with the Persians, and has sent all his forces to the East, they [i.e. the Slavs] live at their ease in the land and dwell in it and spread themselves far and wide as far as God permits them, and ravage and burn and take captive. And to such an extent do they carry their ravages that they have even ridden up to the outer wall of the City and driven away all the King's [Emperor's] herds of horses, many thousands in number, and whatever else they could find.[6]

---

[1] Johannis Abbatis Biclarensis *Chronica*, in *Monumenta Germaniae Historica, Chronica Minora*, ed. by Th. Mommsen, vol. ii, p. 212. John was a Visigoth who had lived in Constantinople for 17 years and had obtained a Greek as well as a Latin education there (Isidore of Seville, *De Viris Illustribus*, chaps. 62 and 63 [44]). John's datings have gone awry (see Mommsen in vol. cit., p. 209), but he was well informed about events in the Levant until his return from Constantinople to Spain. Mommsen notes that John's latest entry giving local Constantinopolitan news is under Justin II's tenth year. Mommsen reckons John's 'Justin Year 10' to be 576, and his 'Justin Year 4' to be 570 (not the true dates 574 and 568). However, in any case, Tiberius's victory over the Avars, which John records, was before the outbreak of the Romano-Persian War in 572.

[2] Menander Protector, fr. 34, in L. Dindorf's *Historici Graeci Minores*, vol. ii (Leipzig, 1871, Teubner), p. 70; Evagrius, Book V, chap. 11; Theophanes, pp. 246–7, sub A.M. 6066. John of Ephesus, *Ecclesiastical History*, Part III, trd. by R. Payne Smith (Oxford, 1860, University Press), p. 142, records a raid by the Avars as far as 'the outer walls of Constantinople' (? the Anastasian Long Wall) at some date before Justin II's death (on 26 September 578), and on p. 207 he notes that, before Justin II's death, the Slavs and the Avars were already harrying the Empire, and that, after Tiberius II's accession, the assaults of both these peoples became more violent.

[3] Menander, fr. 47, ad fin., in vol. cit., p. 98.

[4] John of Ephesus, pp. 432–3.

[5] Ibid.

[6] The riders on this expedition are unlikely to have been the Slavs; they are more likely to have been the Slavs' Avar associates. In the passage (p. 142) cited already above, in n. 2, John of Ephesus records a raid by the Avars up to the Anastasian Long Wall ('the outer walls of Constantinople') in Justin II's reign. The cavalry raid attributed by John of Ephesus to the Slavs in the present passage (p. 432) might be either this earlier Avar raid or the Avar raid of 582/3—A. J. T.

And even to this day, being the [Seleucid Era] year 895 (A.D. 584), they still encamp and dwell there, and live in peace in the Roman territories, free from anxiety and fear, and lead captive and slay and burn. And they have grown rich in gold and silver and herds of horses and arms, and have learnt to fight better than the Romans, though at first they were but rude savages who did not venture to show themselves outside the woods and the coverts of the trees; and, as for arms, they did not even know what they were, with the exception of two or three javelins or darts.[1]

According to John of Biclarum, 'Sclavini in Thracia multas urbes Romanorum pervadunt, quas depopulatas vacuas reliquere'.[2] According to Menander,[3] Tiberius II persuaded the Avars to invade the Slav marauders' home territory (in Wallachia). The Emperor's envoy ferried 60,000 mail-clad Avar cavalry to the Roman side of the Danube, conducted them through Roman territory, and ferried them across again from there into the Slavs' country. Tiberius II ceded to the Avars the district round Sirmium, but not the city itself,[4] but the Avars took Sirmium in 582, just before Tiberius's death.[5] In the first year of Maurice's reign, 582/3, the Avars took Singidunum, ravaged the country round Ankhíalos, and threatened to destroy the Anastasian Long Wall.[6] This Avar raid is recorded by John of Biclarum. 'Avares Thracias vastant et regiam urbem a muro longo obsident.'[7] On this occasion the Avars did still more, according to Evagrius.[8]

The Avars twice made a drive right up to the so-called [Anastasian] Long Wall. They took (ἐξεπολιόρκησαν) Singidunum, Ankhíalos, the whole of Ellás, and other cities and forts. They enslaved (ἠνδραποδίσαντο) the inhabitants and destroyed and burnt everything, while the major part of the [East Roman forces] was committed in the East.

In this passage, Evagrius may be combining some of the Avars' later exploits with their operations in 582/3. However, there is archaeological evidence for the devastation of the agora of Athens *circa* 582/3,[9] and this suggests that the Avars did raid Greece in that year.

---

[1] This agrees with the description of the Slavs' military equipment in 'Mavríkios', Part 11, chap. 5, p. 275 Scheffer, p. 280 Mihăescu.—A. J. T.

[2] John of Biclarum in vol. cit., p. 214. This must be a reference to the invasion in the year 581/2, though John of Biclarum's dating for it is the tenth year of Justin II.

[3] Fr. 48 in vol. cit., pp. 98–100.

[4] Lemerle, 'Invasions', p. 289; Hauptmann, 'Les Rapports', p. 155.

[5] Menander, ibid., p. 131, cited by Theophylactus Simocatta, *Historiae*, ed. de Boor (Leipzig, 1887, Teubner), Book I, chap. 3, pp. 44–5; Theophanes, p. 252, sub A.M. 6075. Cf. John of Ephesus, Book VI, chaps. 30–3, pp. 442–5.

[6] Theophylactus, Book I, chap. 4, pp. 46–7; Theophanes, p. 253, sub A.M. 6075.

[7] John of Biclarum in vol. cit., p. 215. He dates this Avar raid in the first year of Tiberius II, i.e. 578/9. [8] Evagrius, Book VI, chap. 10.

[9] The date is indicated by coin-hoards (see Sinclair Hood in *The Annual of the British School at Athens*, No. 65 (1970), p. 42; D. M. Metcalf: 'The Slavonic Threat to Greece *circa* 580: Some Evidence from Athens', in *Hesperia*, 1962, pp. 134 seqq.).

The Empire purchased peace from the Avars at the price of a lump sum and an annual tribute,[1] but in 583/4 the Avars violated the peace settlement by secretly instigating the Slavs to invade Thrace.[2] The Slavs were defeated and expelled.[3] But in 586/7 the Avars devastated the Roman provinces of Lower Moesia and Scythia and took many cities.[4] This may also have been the campaign in which the Avars invaded Greece,[5] and in which the city of Thessaloníkê was besieged for the first time by the Avars and their Slav subjects.[6]

The Avar invasions in 582/3 and 586/7 must have been the occasions of the wholesale deportation of the Roman population of the northern part of the Balkan Peninsula to Sirmia (Pannonia Secunda in Roman official parlance) that is recorded in the *Sancti Demetrii Miracula*[7] and that is mentioned, in more general terms, by John of Ephesus, Evagrius, and John of Biclarum. By the year 582 the Avars had acquired first the countryside and then the city of Sirmium itself.[8] No doubt this ex-Roman territory had been depopulated by the series of previous barbarian raiders and temporary occupants of it, and the Khaqan of the Avars would naturally take steps to re-people this Transdanubian bridgehead of his empire with a new population that was versed in the arts of civilization.

[1] Theophylactus, Book I, chap. 6, p. 52; Theophanes, p. 253, sub A.M. 6075.

[2] Theophylactus, Book I, chap. 7, pp. 52–3; Theophanes, p. 254, sub A.M. 6076. Perhaps this is the Slav invasion that John of Biclarum is intending to record in his entry, under Tiberius II's fifth [*sic*] year: 'Sclavinorum gens Illyricum et Thraciam vastant' (vol. cit., p. 216).

[3] Theophylactus and Theophanes, locc. citt. John of Biclarum has, under the third year of Tiberius II, the entry: 'Avares a finibus Thraciae pelluntur et partes Graeciae et Pannoniae obsident.' Is he here jumbling up with the defeat of the Slavs in Thrace in 583/4 the Avars' capture of Sirmium in 582 and their campaign in 586/7?

[4] Theophylactus, Book I, chap. 8, pp. 54–5; Theophanes, p. 257, sub A.M. 6079. Theophylactus names eight, and Theophanes six, of the cities taken by the Avars in this campaign.

[5] Evagrius, Book VI, chap. 10, and John of Biclarum, p. 215, cited on p. 634, nn. 7 and 8.

[6] This siege is recorded and described in the *Sancti Demetrii Miracula* only (Book I, chaps. 13–15). The seven-days-long assault began on a Sunday 22 September in the reign of the Emperor Maurice, and the year might be either 586 or 597. Charanis, 'Ethnic Changes', p. 37, holds that 586 was the actual date. Bury, *The Later Roman Empire*, vol. ii, pp. 134–5, and Lemerle, 'Invasions' p. 290, n. 3, and p. 294, hold that the date was actually 597, not 586. Perhaps their reason for adopting the date 597 is that Efsévios was archbishop of Thessaloníkê at the time (*Miracula*, I, 14), and letters were written to Efsévios by Pope Gregory I between November 597 and the end of 603 (Lemerle, 'La Composition et la chronologie des deux premiers livres des Miracula Sancti Demetrii', p. 353). However, Efsévios may have been archbishop already in 586, and this date seems, in itself, to be considerably the more likely one of the two possibilities. We know that the Avars did invade the East Roman Empire in this year, and we also know that in 586 the major part of the East Roman Army was still tied down in Asia by the Romano-Persian War of 572–91. On the other hand, from the year 591 onwards, in which this Romano-Persian War came to an end, Maurice was able to concentrate his forces against the Avars, and, from 591 till the overthrow and murder of Maurice in 602, the Avars were being harder and harder pressed. In 597 an East Roman force was operating, beyond the Danube, in the Avars' Slav subjects' home territory in what is now Wallachia (Bury, ibid.).

[7] *S.D. Miracula*, Book II, chap. 5, col. 1361, cited already in II, 1 (iii) (a), p. 73.

[8] See p. 634, with nn. 4 and 5.

The author of Book II of the *Miracula* does not date the deportation, either absolutely or relatively to any of the other episodes described in Book II and Book I; but he does state that the exodus of the deportees' half-caste children took place rather more than sixty years after their parents had been carried away captive. If the date of the deportation was 682/3 or 686/7 or both years, this chronological note would date the exodus in some year in the 640s, and we know that, from about 623 onwards, and especially after 626, the Avars were losing control over one section after another of their unwilling subjects.

The author of Book II of the *Miracula* does not mention Greece in his list of the Roman provinces that the Slavs and Avars ravaged and depopulated, but Evagrius does write that the Avars took 'the whole of Ellás', and John of Biclarum says that they took possession of 'parts of Greece'. If in truth the Slavs and Avars had not merely raided Greece but had established themselves in Greece between 581/2 and 586/7, they must by then already have made themselves masters of the regions between Greece and the south bank of the lower Danube. Charanis has made an exhaustive study of the usages of the word 'Ellás'[1] in the works of Procopius, Agathias, Menander, Evagrius, Malalas, Hierocles, the Emperor Justinian I (in his novels), Cosmas Indicopleustes, John of Antioch, the author of the *Chronicon Paschale*, the authors of the *Sancti Demetrii Miracula*, Nicephorus Patriarcha, and Theophanes. Charanis finds that Theophanes alone is imprecise in his usage. 'To Procopius, Hellas meant the regions of Classical Greece, more especially the country south of Thermopylae, including, of course, the Peloponnesus.'[2] Charanis finds that this precise usage in Procopius's works is followed by all Procopius's successors in the series set out above, except of Theophanes alone. 'When Menander, Evagrius, and John of Ephesus speak of the devastations of Greece by the Avars and Slavs, it is of Greece proper, including the Peloponnesus, that they speak.'[3]

We need not doubt the statements that the Avars raided Greece proper. They were mobile horsemen, and, in their incursions into the Balkan Peninsula, they may have ranged far southward already within the years 572–91 and not only within the years 602–26. But, in the light of Charanis's findings about the sense in which the word 'Greece' ('Ellás') is used by the authors who record the Avars' activities, we have to ask ourselves several questions.

Just how far southward into Greece proper did the Avars penetrate in either of the periods under consideration? Their successors the Danubian

[1] P. Charanis, 'Hellas in the Greek sources of the sixth, seventh, and eighth centuries', in *Late Classical and Medieval Studies in Honor of Mathias Friend Jr.* (Princeton, 1955, University Press), pp. 161–76. Cf. eundem, 'On the Slavic Settlements in the Peloponnesus', pp. 94–5.
[2] Charanis, 'Hellas', p. 164. [3] Charanis, ibid., p. 173.

Bulgars occasionally invaded continental Greece, to the north of the Isthmus of Corinth, in the Romano-Bulgarian wars of 894–6, 813–27, and 976–1018, but the Bulgars do not seem to have set foot on the Pelopónnêsos.[1] If Evagrius's words 'the whole of Greece' are strictly accurate, they imply that the Avars, unlike the Bulgars, raided the Pelopónnêsos as well as the more northerly parts of Greece. On the other hand, John of Biclarum's words 'parts of Greece' might imply that the Avars raided the whole or part of Greece north of the Isthmus, but not the Pelopónnêsos as well. Again, we have to ask ourselves whether Evagrius's word 'took' ($\dot{\epsilon}\xi\epsilon\pi o\lambda\iota\acute{o}\rho\kappa\eta\sigma a\nu$) and John of Biclarum's word 'occupy' (occupant) mean a temporary occupation or a permanent settlement.

Finally, we have to ask ourselves whether the Avars, as distinct from the Slavs whose migrations they directed, made any permanent settlements of their own anywhere in the Balkan Peninsula, not to speak of this peninsula's southern extremity. We have ample evidence that the Slavs did make permanent lodgements in the Balkan Peninsula as far south as Greece, including parts of the Pelopónnêsos, and these settlements may have been started on the Avars' initiative, though they may have been completed on the Slavs' own initiative, after the Avars had ebbed back to the far side of the Danube. Did any Avars accompany the Slavs to the Pelopónnêsos and settle there permanently together with the Slavs? If they did, was the date some year within the period 572–91?

This last question arises because the so-called *Chronicle of Monemvasía*,[2] which is our only extant source of information about the indubitable Slav settlement and the alleged Avar settlement in the Pelopónnêsos, states that 'the Avars seized Pelopónnêsos and settled in it and lasted ($\delta\iota\acute{\eta}\rho\kappa\epsilon\sigma a\nu$) [there] for 218 years, subject neither to the Emperor of the Romans nor to anyone else, that is to say from A.M. 6096 [A.D. 587/8], which was the sixth year of the reign of Maurice. . . .'[3]

Unquestionably there was a massive Slav *Völkerwanderung* across the Danube which produced revolutionary changes in the ethnic and linguistic maps of south-eastern Europe, right down to the Pelopónnêsos inclusive, but there are differences of opinion regarding the date at which these changes began. Were they produced mainly—or short of that, primarily—by the Avaro-Slav operations during the years 581/2–586/7? Or were these merely a series of raids which were, perhaps, exceptionally

---

[1] But see p. 101, with n.

[2] Lemerle, in 'La Chronique improprement dite de Monemvasie', p. 22, points out that a more appropriate title would be 'Peloponnesian Chronicle' or 'Chronicle of the Metropolitan See of Pátras'.

[3] The *Chronicle of Monemvasía*, MS. No. 329 (5) in the Ivêron Monastery on Mount Athos (Athous MS. No. 4449), lines 50–4. The text of the Ivêron MS., which contains Part I only of the Chronicle, is printed in Lemerle, loc. cit., pp. 8–11.

prolonged and devastating, but which, like previous raids, came and went without having deposited any permanent settlements of barbarian intruders? John of Ephesus, writing in 584, says that the barbarians had been making themselves at home on Roman soil for four years,[1] but John died in 585;[2] the invaders may have withdrawn in the year after. The Slavs who invaded Thrace in 583/4 were defeated and expelled;[3] the Avar invaders of the Empire in 586/7 were made to suffer for the damage that they inflicted.[4] They, too, may have been unable to hold their ground. The permanent settlements of the invaders may not have begun until after the East Roman Empire's temporary collapse in 602.[5] This appears to be the opinion of Hauptmann,[6] Stein,[7] Stratós,[8] Bon,[9] and Lemerle,[10] so far as the Pelopónnêsos is concerned.

One consideration that might seem to tell in favour of the later of the two alternative possible datings may be discounted. From 591 to 602, the East Roman forces were carrying on a series of successful counter-offensive campaigns against the Avars and their Slav subjects. As early as 592 a Roman force crossed the lower Danube and invaded the Slavs' home territory in what is now Wallachia. From then on till 602 inclusive, Roman forces were operating in Wallachia constantly. The unknown East Roman officer who was the author of 'Mavríkios's' *Stratêghikón* gives detailed advice, suggested by his own personal experience,[11] on how to conduct offensive operations in this war-zone beyond the Empire's northern frontier.[12] Meanwhile, the Empire's former frontier on the lower Danube had been re-established; for the writer recommends that the Roman troops holding this frontier should be stationed one day's march to the south of the river.[13] The mutiny in the East Roman field-force in 602 which cost the Emperor Maurice his throne and his life was provoked by the Emperor's order that the troops should pass the winter

[1] See the passage quoted on pp. 633–4.   [2] According to Vasmer, op. cit., p. 12.
[3] Theophylactus Simocatta, Book I, chap. 7.   [4] Ibid., chap. 8.
[5] There is archaeological evidence that refugee settlements were planted on a number of off-shore islands along the coast of Greece at about the turn of the sixth and seventh centuries, e.g. on three islands in the bay of Itéa, on Ráfti Island in Porto Ráfti bay, on Péra Island in Peráni bay on the south coast of Salamis, on Pavlopétri Island off Elaphónêsos, and on Sphaktêría Island in Navarino bay in the Pelopónnêsos. But the pottery found at these sites does not give the answer to our question. Its date is the sixth or the early seventh century. On the island in the bay of Itéa, none of the pottery can be securely dated later than *circa* 600. On the other hand, the pottery on Ráfti and Péra islands does include seventh-century material (see Sinclair Hood in *The Annual of the British School at Athens*, No. 65 (1970), pp. 37 and 43–4).
[6] Hauptmann, 'Les Rapports des Byzantins avec les Slaves et les Avares', p. 158.
[7] E. Stein, *Studien zur Geschichte des byzantinischen Reiches*, p. 120.
[8] Stratós, op. cit., pp. 66 and 119, on the strength of the passage in Isidore of Seville's *Chronicon*, cited in the present Annex on p. 632. However, Stratós notes, op. cit., p. 32, that the whole line of Roman fortresses along the Danube had fallen by 587.
[9] In op. cit., p. 54.   [10] In loc. cit., p. 35. See p. 631, n. 5.
[11] 'Mavríkios', Part 11, chap. 5, p. 289 Scheffer, p. 290 Mihăescu.
[12] See op. cit., loc. cit., pp. 277–89 Scheffer, p. 280–90 Mihăescu.
[13] Ibid., p. 278 Scheffer, p. 282 Mihăescu.

to the north of the Danube in enemy territory. Is it credible that Maurice should have been conducting military operations beyond the Empire's northern frontier over a period of ten years if he had not previously evicted any of the barbarian invaders of the Empire who during the years 581/2–586/7 had planted themselves deep in the interior with the intention of establishing permanent settlements there?

This question can be answered briefly and confidently. It is entirely credible that, if such settlements had actually been made in 581/2–586/7 in the western and southern parts of the Empire's European territory, Maurice should have left them undisturbed in order to concentrate his efforts first on driving the enemy out of the Empire's Thracian dioecesis and next on deterring the enemy from embarking on further adventures by carrying the war into the aggressors' home country.[1] An East Roman Emperor's first concern was to recapture, and to make permanently secure, the European glacis of fortress Constantinople and of Constantinople's Asiatic hinterland. This war-aim necessarily had priority over all other objectives on European ground.

Whether or not we conclude from the evidence, taken as a whole, that permanent Slav settlements south of the Danube were established as early as 581/2–586/7, it will not be disputed that these sixth-century settlements, if in truth there were such, were reinforced after 602. The years 602–26 saw the Slavs take to the sea in their dug-out skiffs.[2] Now that they had thus become sea-borne, 'they ravaged the whole of Thessaly and the adjacent islands[3] and [the islands] of Ellás; also the Kykládhes Islands and the whole of Akhaḯa,[4] Épeiros, the greater part of Illyricum and part of Asia.[5] They depopulated many cities and provinces'.[6]

This reads like a resumption and extension of a previous bout of ravages, evictions, deportations, and massacres, and the date can hardly have been earlier than 602, for, at the time of the siege of Thessaloníkê —the second siege of this city[7]—in which this fresh bout of aggressive Slav activity culminated, and also at the time of the third siege,[8] which took place after at least a two years' interval, and in which the Avars

---

[1] Charanis, 'Ethnic Changes', pp. 36–7, holds that in the years 579–87 the Slavs did make permanent settlements on East Roman ground, and that there is no evidence that these settlers either withdrew voluntarily or were evicted in the years 591–601.

[2] The *S.D. Miracula*, Book II, chap. 1, col. 1325, names five Slav tribes that did this, and adds that the rest did likewise.

[3] When the East Roman admiral Sisínnios landed on the island of Skíathos *en route* from Ellás to Thessaloníkê, he found Skiáthos deserted (*S.D. Miracula*, Book II, chap. 5, col. 1369). The occasion was the arrival in Macedonia of the half-caste descendants of the East Romans who had been deported to Sirmia. The date was some year in the 630s or 640s.—A. J. T.

[4] i.e. the Roman province of Achaïa, which extended over the whole of Greece, including the Pelopónnêsos, lying to the south of Thessaly and Épeiros.—A. J. T.

[5] i.e. the Roman province of Asia in western Asia Minor.—A. J. T.

[6] *S.D. Miracula*, Book II, chap. 1, col. 1325.

[7] Described in *S.D. Miracula*, Book II, chap. 1.   [8] Described ibid., chaps. 2–3.

played the leading part, the archbishop of Thessaloníkê was John,[1] while, as recently as the end of the year 603, a letter had been addressed by Pope Gregory I to Efsévios,[2] who had been archbishop of Thessaloníkê at the time of the first siege. Moreover, the Slavs' *Völkerwanderung* and settlement south of the Danube was still in progress on the eve of the second siege; for the besiegers brought with them their families and property with the intention of establishing themselves in the city when they had taken it, as they hoped and expected to do.[3] The Slavs' offensive that reached its climax in the second and third of the three unsuccessful sieges of Thessaloníkê may well be the event which Isidore of Seville, in his *Chronicon*, dates at the turn of the years 614 and 615 and which he records in the laconic sentence 'Sclavi Graeciam Romanis tulerunt'.[4] This would be compatible with the dates at which the number of East Roman coins falls to zero in the Pelopónnêsos, outside Corinth, and dwindles sensationally at Corinth itself, even on the Akrokórinthos.

The third of the three unsuccessful sieges of Thessaloníkê[5] was made, not, like the second siege, by the Slavs acting independently, but, like the first, by the Avars together with their Slav and other subjects. The preceding two years had been spent by the Khaqan of the Avars in making elaborate preparations. He brought with him a formidable siege-train;[6] his force included Slavs and Bulgars, besides his own mail-clad Avar cavalry;[7] and this time the assault on the city was kept up for thirty-three days before it was abandoned.

None of the three sieges of Thessaloníkê is dated in the *Sancti Demetrii Miracula*, and this is our sole source of information about them, except for an inscription on the church of St. Demetrius which records a siege in the year 612.[8] If this was the second siege, not the Slavs' abortive attempt, at some date between the dates of the first two sieges, to take Thessaloníkê by surprise,[9] the third siege may perhaps be dated tentatively *circa* 614/15, which is the date indicated by the entry in Isidore's *Chronicon* for the Slavs' conquest of Greece. In any case, both the second and the third siege must have been later than 603 and earlier than 626.[10]

---

[1] *S.D. Miracula*, Book II, chap. 1, col. 1325, and Book II, chap. 2, col. 1337. In at least two manuscripts of the *S.D. Miracula* this Archbishop John is credited with the authorship of Book I (Lemerle, 'La Composition et la chronologie des deux premiers livres des Miracula S. Demetrii', p. 354).

[2] Lemerle, 'La Composition et la chronologie', p. 353.

[3] *S.D. Miracula*, Book II, chap. 1, p. 1326.   [4] See p. 632, n. 2.

[5] Described in *S.D. Miracula*, Book II, chap. 2.

[6] Ibid., col. 1340.   [7] Ibid., col. 1337.   [8] Vlasto, op. cit., p. 5.

[9] See pp. 532–3.

[10] According to Grégoire, 'L'Origine et le nom des Croates et les Serbes', p. 105, the John who was Archbishop of Thessaloníkê at the time of both the second and the third siege held office from 610 to 649. He was not the John, Archbishop of Thessaloníkê, who signed the acts of the Ecumenical Council of 681.

The strongest argument for holding that the mass-settlement of Slavs on Roman soil did not begin till after 602 is not the conduct of East Roman military operations in Europe from 591 to 602; it is the evidence of the finds—or the lack of finds—of coins, in the Aegean area in general[1] and in the Peloppónnêsos in particular—above all at Corinth, the capital city of the Roman province of Achaïa.

'For all reigns till the close of the sixth century, Byzantine [i.e. East Roman] coins, are common'[2] at Corinth, which had been the capital of the Roman province of Achaïa since its creation by Augustus. Even at Olympia, a cache of coins was deposited as late as the reign of Phokás (602–10),[3] though Olympia had lost its importance since the suppression of the pre-Christian religions of the Roman Empire and had presumably long since ceased to be fortified or defended. It is true that the latest-known pre-*Völkerwanderung* inscription in the Peloppónnêsos is one at Corinth mentioning the Emperor Justin II together with the regent Tiberius, and therefore inscribed at some date within the years 574–8,[4] but this negative evidence is outweighed by the positive evidence of the coin-finds. The cache at Olympia is particularly pertinent, since Olympia, unlike Corinth, lies in the part of the Peloppónnêsos that was overrun and occupied by Slav invaders eventually.

Thus the archaeological evidence is incompatible with the *Chronicle of Monemvasía*'s statement that the Avars had seized the Peloppónnêsos and settled in it by 587/8 and that they lasted there for 218 years. This refutation of one statement in the Chronicle raises the general question whether or not the Chronicle is a trustworthy source, but it does not, by itself, settle this question; for a document is not necessarily discredited in general by the exposure of a single error in it, even if the error relates to an important point, as it does in this case.

The *Chronicle of Monemvasía* falls into two parts, which are really two separate and independent works. Part II consists of a series of notices about the church of Lakedhaímon, and all these notices except one, which records the elevation of the See of Lakedhaímon to metropolitan status, concern the period 1261 to *circa* 1350.[5] This part has no bearing on the subject of this Annex, or indeed of this book. Part I, on the other hand, is wholly relevant. It deals with Avar and Slav activities in the

---

[1] See D. M. Metcalf, 'The Aegean Coastlands under Threat: Some Coins and Coin Hoards from the Reign of Heraclius', in *The Annual of the British School at Athens*, No. 57 (1962), pp. 14–23. 'The emphasis on coastal and island sites is pronounced . . . The large proportion of island finds from this reign is significant' (p. 14). 'The coins point to the fifth and sixth regnal years of Heraclius, that is October 614 to October 616, as being the critical period' (p. 16).

[2] A. Bon, *Le Péloponnèse byzantin jusqu'en 1204* (Paris, 1951, Presses Universitaires de France), p. 52.

[3] Bon, op. cit., p. 51.   [4] Bon, op. cit., p. 50, n. 2.

[5] Lemerle in loc. cit., pp. 24–5.

Balkan Peninsula down to, and including, the reign of Nikêphóros I (802–11), but not beyond that date.[1] Both parts of the Chronicle are included in MS. No. 220 (4) in the Koutloumousíou Monastery on Mount Athos and in the former Turin MS., of which a copy was made in 1903 before the original was destroyed in 1904 in a fire. Part I alone is included in the Ivéron MS., and Part II alone in the Rome MS., which was discovered in 1910. The best, as well as the fullest, text of Part I is the Ivéron Manuscript's.[2]

An abbreviated version of Part I of the Chronicle is given in a scholion[3] written by Aréthas of Kaisáreia in the margin of a copy of the Patriarch Nikêphóros's *Khronographikón Sýndomon*[4] which had been made for Aréthas in 931/2.[5] The scholion, as far as it reproduces Part I of the Chronicle, follows it verbatim with a few variations. Some of these (e.g. the enumeration of the districts of Greece that were overrun) are merely learnèd corrections and elaborations of the names given in the Chronicle, but there are other variations in matters of substance.

The verbatim correspondence of the two documents used to be accounted for by the hypothesis that each of the two was derived independently from a lost common source. The Chronicle certainly cannot have been derived from the scholion, since it contains material that the scholion omits; and it used to be held that the scholion, the date of which is known to have been not much later than 931/2, cannot have been derived from the Chronicle, because the Chronicle refers to the Emperor Nikêphóros I as τοῦ παλαιοῦ τοῦ ἔχοντος Σταυράκιον (as his son and successor). Manifestly this description of Nikêphóros I has been inserted in order to distinguish him from Nikêphóros II Phokás; Nikêphóros II did not come to the throne till 963; and it was therefore inferred that Part I of the Chronicle must have been written later than 963.

Lemerle, however, has suggested[6] that the description of Nikêphóros I in the Chronicle is not a part of the original text but is a gloss added after 963, and that therefore the description is evidence that the text itself was written before 963, not after it. In any case, the Chronicle, Part I, must have been written before 1082/3, the year in which the See of Lakedhaímon was raised to metropolitan status, and after the death in 806 of the Ecumenical Patriarch Tarásios, since it mentions Tarásios as being no longer alive.[7] On the assumption that the description of the Emperor Nikêphóros I is a gloss, Lemerle guesses that the date of the text (which does not mention events later than Nikêphóros I's reign) is nearer to 806 than to 1082/3; that is, in fact, earlier than 931/2; and

---

[1] See the Ivéron MS., Greek text, lines 54–76 in Lemerle, op. cit., pp. 10–11.

[2] Lemerle in loc. cit., pp. 5–8 and 22–3. See the present work, p. 337, n. 2.

[3] Translated by Lemerle in loc. cit., p. 26.

[4] Opposite the entries relating to the reign of Nikêphóros I (Lemerle in loc. cit., pp. 25–7).

[5] Lemerle in loc. cit., p. 25.   [6] Ibid., pp. 16–17.   [7] Ibid., p. 22.

that it is itself the source of Aréthas's gloss on the *Khronographikón Sýndomon*.[1]

If the Chronicle is, in truth, Aréthas's source, Aréthas must have believed that the Chronicle was authentic and trustworthy, and Aréthas was both a learnèd man and a native of Pátras, as he himself tells us in his gloss. It will be seen that, if Lemerle is right in his dating of the Chronicle, Part I, this source gains credit on two accounts: its date is much closer than had previously been supposed to the events that it records; and it has been highly regarded by a Peloponnesian scholar whose home-town, Pátras, is the focus of the chronicler's interest.

It is important to make out, if this is possible, what the Chronicle's true value is; for the Chronicle is our sole source of information about the extent, the circumstances, and the date of the Slav settlements in the Pelopónnêsos. A student's appraisal of the Chronicle's value will therefore govern his view of this critical event in the Pelopónnêsos's history. The appraisals of scholars who have studied the subject have differed radically.

The verdict of P. Charanis is that 'the Chronicle of Monemvasía is absolutely trustworthy and constitutes one of the most precious sources on the Avar and Slav penetration of Greece in the reign of Maurice'.[2] In his belief in the trustworthiness of the Chronicle, Charanis goes to considerably farther lengths than Lemerle, and Lemerle has several reservations to make regarding Charanis's judgements. Above all, Lemerle does not follow Charanis in accepting the Chronicle's statement that the occupation and settlement of the Pelopónnêsos was the work of the Avars, and that the date of this event was 587/8.[3]

At the opposite extreme to Charanis, the trustworthiness of the Chronicle has been impugned by E. P. Kyriakídhês.[4] His work is learnèd and ingenious, and he succeeds in demonstrating that, on a number of scores, the trustworthiness of the Chronicle is open to question, but unfortunately Kyriakídhês's findings are vitiated by the author's manifest partisanship in a modern nationalist controversy that is irrelevant to early medieval facts. Kyriakídhês concludes[5] that the Slavs' lodgement in the Pelopónnêsos amounted to nothing more than an infiltration of 'pastoral Slav clans' that drifted into the Pelopónnêsos peacefully *in the eighth century* [sic]. In his winding-up,[6] Kyriakídhês reveals that his work,

---

[1] Lemerle in loc. cit., pp. 26–7.

[2] 'The Chronicle of Monemvasía and the Question of Slavonic Settlements in Greece', in *Dumbarton Oaks Papers*, Number Five (1950), pp. 139–66, on p. 163; cf. eundem, 'On the Question of Slavonic Settlements in Greece during the Middle Ages', in *Byzantinoslavica* x (1949), pp. 254–8.

[3] Lemerle in loc. cit., p. 48.

[4] Οἱ Σλάβοι ἐν Πελοποννήσῳ (Thessaloníkê, 1947, No. VI in the Βυζαν· ιί Μελέται series).

[5] On his p. 94.

[6] On his p. 97.

learnèd though it is, is in truth a Greek nationalist's anti-Fallmerayer tract. The historical problem of the Slavs in Greece has suffered the same unhappy fate as the problem, in early Russian history, of the nationality of the Rhos. It has been bedevilled by modern nationalism. The distinguished American scholar Charanis (*Χαρανῆς*) is of Greek origin, to judge by his name. Yet, unlike Kyriakídhês, Charanis has made a study of the evidence which is patently objective, even if Lemerle is right in judging that, in contrast to Kyriakídhês's hyper-scepticism, Charanis is excessively credulous. Lemerle pays a handsome tribute to Kyriakídhês's learning, acuteness, and forensic ability,[1] but his verdict on this scholar's thesis is that 'il s'agit là d'un savant enchaînement d'hypothèses ingénieuses certes, mais ... dont l'ensemble ... est d'une fragilité qui non seulement n'emporte pas la conviction, mais s'écarte du vraisemblable'.[2]

Lemerle himself approaches the problem of arriving at a just valuation of the Chronicle by pointing out that its author knew, and used, the sources—Evagrius, Theophylactus Simocatta, Theophanes—that have been cited in the present annex,[3] but that these sources gave him no information about events later than the year 586/7. For his account of what happened in the Pelopónnêsos after that, the chronicler's only source was local Peloponnesian Greek tradition. He therefore has to make a new start[4] when, at line 35 of the Ivéron MS., he begins to tell the story of what happened in Greece—a part of the Balkan Peninsula that his written sources mentioned only in vague and general terms. The chronicler tacks his piece based on local tradition on to his preceding piece based on written sources by ascribing the invasion of 'the whole of Greece' (*τὴν Ἑλλάδα πᾶσαν*), which implicitly includes the Pelopónnêsos, to the Khaqan of the Avars, and he dates this alleged Avar invasion of Greece and permanent settlement there as being accomplished facts by the year 587/8, because the immediately preceding year 586/7 was the latest year in which his written sources recorded Avar activity in the Balkan Peninsula. This dating[5] is the grounds for his statement[6] that, in the Pelopónnêsos, there was an interregnum of 218 years between the date of the local barbarian *Landnahme*—allegedly by the Avars, not by the Slavs—and the date in the reign of Nikêphóros I at which the East Roman Imperial Government re-established its authority over those parts of the Pelopónnêsos that had temporarily been independent.

Why did the chronicler's written sources fail to inform him about central Greece and the Pelopónnêsos? For the reason that made the East Roman Imperial Government fail to save this outlying and expendable part of its territory from barbarian invasion and eventual

---

[1] Lemerle in loc. cit., p. 46.
[3] Ibid., pp. 11–12.
[5] Ibid., p. 35, with n. 53.

[2] Ibid., p. 48.
[4] Ibid., pp. 13, 21, 22.
[6] Ivéron MS., lines 51–5.

occupation. It has been noted in this Annex already that the East Roman statesmen's and soldiers' prime concern in the Balkan Peninsula was to retain or to recover the European hinterland of Constantinople. The East Roman historians wrote, as the statesmen and soldiers acted, from a Constantinopolitan standpoint.

They have no knowledge of what is happening in central Greece and the Pelopónnêsos. Living and writing, as they did, at Constantinople for the most part, they reflect the point of view of the capital, and the capital's interest is concentrated on the adjoining European provinces, on Thrace above all, and in a general way on the districts beyond or along the trunk road running to the Danube valley via Philippopolis, Sardica, Naïssus, Singidunum, and Sirmium. Their horizon is virtually limited to that.[1]

Lemerle points out[2] that we should have no information about the sieges of Thessaloníkê by the Avars and Slavs if the *Sancti Demetrii Miracula* had not survived. These historic sieges are not mentioned by the literary historians. How, then, could it be expected that these should have recorded what happened in the Pelopónnêsos?

The only information that we have about the Pelopónnêsos's fortunes is given to us by the *Chronicle of Monemvasía*, Part I, and by Aréthas's abridgment of it, if that is what Aréthas's scholion is. The Ivêron MS. of the Chronicle states that

in another invasion (εἰσβολῇ) they [the Avars] subjugated the whole of Thessaly and the whole of Ellás, namely Old Ĕpeiros [i.e. the Roman province Epirus Vetus], Attica, and Évvoia. They also made an invasion into the Pelopónnêsos, conquered it by act of war, drove out the noble and Hellenic peoples (τὰ εὐγενῆ καὶ Ἑλληνικὰ ἔθνη) and, when they had destroyed them, settled there themselves (καὶ διαφθείραντες κατῴκισαν αὐτοὶ ἐν αὐτῇ).[3]

In this passage, Aréthas's version differs from the Chronicle's on several points. Aréthas makes the invaders of the Pelopónnêsos Σθλαβηνοί, not Avars. In the list of invaded districts, he mentions the two Thessalies, Ainianía, and the two Lokrídhes, besides Old Ĕpeiros, Attica, Évvoia, and the Pelopónnêsos, but he does not bring in the term 'the whole of Ellás' to comprise the four last-named districts. Aréthas also, apropos of the Pelopónnêsos, writes 'the indigenous Hellenic peoples' (τὰ ἐγγενῆ Ἑλληνικὰ ἔθνη) instead of 'the noble and Hellenic peoples' (τὰ εὐγενῆ καὶ Ἑλληνικὰ ἔθνη)[4]—a version that seems more likely than the Ivêron MS.'s version to have reproduced correctly the original text of the Chronicle. Aréthas is certainly right in substituting the Σθ[?λ]αβηνοί for

---

[1] Lemerle in loc. cit., p. 33.   [2] Ibid.   [3] Ivêron MS., lines 35–8.
[4] Charanis, loc cit., p. 147; S. P. Kyriakídhês, Οἱ Σλάβοι ἐν Πελοποννήσῳ, pp. 45–6. Compare Lemerle's text of the Ivêron MS. on his pp. 8–11 with his translation of Aréthas's scholion on his p. 26.

the Avars of the Chronicle. It has been noted already that the Chronicle ascribes the invasion of the Pelopónnêsos to the Avars probably in order to link up the Peloponnesian tradition, on which it is now drawing, with the literary sources on which it has drawn up to this point for its general account of Avar activities in the Balkan Peninsula. But, after the author of the Chronicle has left these literary sources behind, he calls the barbarian settlers in the Pelopónnêsos, not Avars, but τὸ Σθ[?λ]αβινὸν ἔθνος,[1] and they were in truth Slavs, as they are called by Constantine Porphyrogenitus and as is testified by the place-names that they have put on the map.

The Chronicle (Ivĕron MS.) states, as has been mentioned in a previous chapter,[2] that the people of Pátras took refuge from the invaders at Rhíyion (Reggio di Calabria), the Argives on 'Oróvê Island', the Corinthians on Aíyina, and some of the Lákones in Sicily, where they still live at Dheménna, are called Dhemenítai instead of Lakedhaimonítai, and continue to speak the Laconian dialect. Of these exoduses, Aréthas mentions only the exodus of the people of Pátras to Reggio.[3]

The Ivĕron MS. of the Chronicle continues:[4]

Some [of the Lákones], however, found a not easily accessible (δύσβατον) site on the sea-shore, built a strongly fortified city there, named it 'Monem-vasía' because there is only a single way in by which it can be entered, and settled in this city with their own bishop. The shepherds and peasants settled in the adjacent rugged places that have recently[5] (ἐπ' ἐσχάτων) been given the name dzakoníai (τζακωνίαι).

The Ivĕron and Koutloumousíou MSS. of the Chronicle and the scholion of Aréthas then state, in almost identical words, that 'only the eastern part of the Pelopónnêsos, from Corinth to Cape Maléa,[6] remained uncontaminated by the Slav people (τοῦ Σθ[?λ]αβινοῦ ἔθνους καθαρεύον-τος) because of its ruggedness and its difficulty of access'.[7]

This statement that the east side of the Pelopónnêsos, from Corinth to Cape Maléa inclusive, remained continuously free from Slav occupation is corroborated by the distribution of Slavonic place-names in the Pelopónnêsos, and it is not contradicted by other pieces of evidence.

The Ecumenical Patriarch Nikólaos III (1084–1111), in a synodical letter addressed to the Emperor Aléxios I, declares that, 'for 218 years, no Roman was able to set foot in the Pelopónnêsos'.[8] The figure is pre-sumably derived, directly or indirectly, from the *Chronicle of Monemvasía*,

---

[1] Ivĕron MS., lines 56–7 and line 60. [2] In II, 1 (iii) (a) on pp. 75–6.
[3] Charanis in loc. cit., p. 152. [4] Lines 44–50.
[5] This is Charanis's rendering in loc. cit., p. 144, and Bon's in op. cit., p. 33, n. 3.
[6] Μέχρι Μαλαίου in the Ivĕron MS. of the Chronicle; μέχρι Μαλέας in Aréthas's scholion.
[7] Ivĕron MS., lines 55–7; translation of the scholion in Lemerle, loc. cit., p. 26.
[8] See Bon, op. cit., pp. 32–4.

and reasons for rejecting it have already been given. But this does not require us also to reject the Chronicle's statement that for a time, whatever the length of this time may have been, the barbarian settlers in the Pelopónnêsos were independent, and this is compatible with the Chronicle's further statement that the eastern side of the Pelopónnêsos remained continuously free from barbarian intrusion. The Chronicle does not say, as the Patriarch Nikólaos says, that the whole of the Pelopónnêsos was inaccessible for East Roman officials—if this is the Patriarch's meaning; if he means that the whole of the Greek population of the Pelopónnêsos had been evicted and that, for 218 years, no East Roman subject had been able to set foot in the Pelopónnêsos, the Patriarch's contention cannot be taken seriously.

It has been maintained that there is archaeological evidence for the presence of Avars at Corinth. At the foot of the Akrokórinthos, in two graves containing eight bodies in all, the objects buried with the bodies (e.g. buckles and weapons) have been held by some archaeologists to be of the same make as objects found in early-seventh-century graves in the neighbourhood of Lake Balaton in what is now Hungary. This identification of the objects from Corinth as being Avar has been accepted by Charanis.[1] However, there are archaeologists who contend that these objects are, not Avar, but Byzantine.[2]

The statistics of finds of East Roman coins at Corinth indicate that the Empire's hold on Corinth weakened in the course of the seventh century (as we should infer from the evidence of the surviving written records), but the statistics also indicate that the Empire's hold continued to remain feeble down to the reign of Basil I, though our written records testify that the Empire re-established an effective control over the whole of the Pelopónnêsos in the reign of Nikêphóros I, with the partial exception of the domains of two Slav tribes, the Mêlingoí and the Ezerítai, in southern Laconia.

From the reign of Heraclius (610–41 onwards) they [i.e. East Roman coins] become rare in the lower city but continue to be fairly numerous on the Akrokórinthos until the time of Constantine [Constans] II (642–68); from 668 until the accession of Leo VI (886), none had been found by the year 1932 on the Akrokórinthos, though a very few stray specimens [dating from this period] have been found in the lower city, especially from the reign of Nikêphóros I (802–11) onwards. They begin to become slightly more numerous again in the time of Theóphilos (829–42), and notably in the time of Basil I (867–86). When we arrive at Basil I's reign, the finds become abundant.[3]

[1] Charanis, 'On the Question of the Slavonic Settlements in Greece', p. 257.

[2] See Bon, op. cit., p. 50, with n. 1.

[3] Bon, op. cit., p. 52, with the statistical table on p. 53. According to Charanis, 'On the Question of the Slavonic Settlements in Greece', p. 257, the date of the striking diminution of

This numismatic evidence is, however, negative; there is no positive numismatic evidence indicating that Corinth was ever under Avar or Slav occupation.

The Chronicle's statement that the eastern side of the Pelopónnêsos, from Corinth to Cape Maléa inclusive, remained free from barbarian occupation is not incompatible with its previous statement that Argive refugees found asylum on Oróvê Island, and Corinthian refugees on Aíyina. The evidence of place-names indicates that the Argholís and Corinthia did not remain completely immune from Slav encroachments, but the number of the consequent Greek refugees from these two districts may have been small. If Oróvê Island is Lévinthos, it can have accommodated no more than a few refugees, and Aíyina cannot have accommodated many. There is no record that either of the two cities, Corinth and Argos, themselves, ever passed out of East Roman hands. On the other hand, it is credible that the whole population of the city of Pátras emigrated (ἡ ... τῶν Πατρῶν πόλις μετωκίσθη)[1] to Reggio di Calabria. Pátras lies on the coast of the Pelopónnêsos a very short distance to the west of the straits between Rhión and Andírrhion, at the mouth of the Gulf of Corinth. It lay right in the fairway of the Slav *Völkerwanderung*. The distribution of place-names shows that the Slavs in the seventh century of the Christian Era, like their North-West-Greek-speaking barbarian predecessors in the post-Mycenaean Age made their way into the Pelopónnêsos across these straits. It is not surprising that the people of Pátras should have emigrated *en masse*.

The Chronicle's statement that the eastern side of the Pelopónnêsos remained continuously free from Slav settlements is not impugned by the statement, in the biography of Bishop Willibald of Eichstätt, that, in the course of Willibald's travels in the years 723-8, he and his companions sailed 'ad urbem Manafasiam [i.e. Monemvasiam] in Slawinia terra, et inde navigantes in insulam nomine Coo [Kos] dimittebant Corinthios in sinistra parte'.[2] At this date, Westerners might think of the Pelopónnêsos as being one of the Sklavinías, since the west side of the Pelopónnêsos was the side on which the Slavs had settled in force. Monemvasía was within the Empire in 746-7, when the plague travelled via Monemvasía to Constantinople from Sicily and Calabria.[3]

Nor, in so far as the eastern side of the Pelopónnêsos is concerned, is the *Chronicle of Monemvasía*'s assertion that its population remained continuously Greek overridden by Constantine Porphyrogenitus's statement

the number of East Roman coins found at Corinth is, not Heraclius's reign, but the end of Justin II's, i.e. the year 578.

[1] Ivëron MS., lines 39-40.
[2] *Monumenta Germaniae Historica* (hereinafter *M.G.H.*), vol. xv, p. 93.
[3] See II, I (iii) (a), p. 94, with n. 3.

that 'the whole country was Slavized, and became barbarian,[1] when the lethal plague [of the years 746–7] preyed on the whole World'[2] in the reign of Constantine V.[3] The Slavs in this age were notoriously prolific; it is conceivable that, in the Pelopónnêsos, one effect of the plague of 746–7 may have been to incline the balance of numbers, as between Slavs and Greeks, in the Slavs' favour; and there might then have been a certain amount of peaceful penetration of the eastern Pelopónnêsos by west Peloponnesian Slavs, as is suggested by the survival of a few Slavonic place-names in this district.[4] The Greek population of the eastern Pelopónnêsos may have been depleted, not only by the plague but by subsequent emigration, if this is the district referred to as 'the lower parts' in Theophanes's notice[5] of the regions from which Constantine V drew settlers to re-people Constantinople after the plague had depopulated it. The invitation would have been particularly tempting to the refugee population of Kynouría; for the country round Monemvasía is almost as rugged and barren as the Máni.[6]

As far as Kynouría is concerned, the *Chronicle of Monemvasía*'s assertion that its population never ceased to be Greek is corroborated by present-day linguistic evidence. Kynouría is, of course, Greek-speaking today, as

---

[1] It should be noted that, in this passage, Constantine neither says nor implies that there was no part of the Pelopónnêsos that had already been Slavized and become barbarian at an earlier date than 746–7.

[2] Ἐσθλαβώθη δὲ πᾶσα ἡ χώρα, καὶ γέγονε βάρβαρος, ὅτε ὁ λοιμικὸς θάνατος πᾶσαν ἐβόσκετο τὴν οἰκουμένην (*De Them.*, II, 6, ed. Bonn, p. 53).

[3] In Constantine Porphyrogenitus's time, Peloponnesians appear to have been exposed to the taunt that they had Slav blood in their veins and that this showed in their physiognomy. Constantine vindicates his rather startling assertion that the whole country had been Slavized by quoting a jibe at the expense of a Peloponnesian contemporary of his, Nikḗtas, 'who prided himself on the nobility (I suppose I must not say non-nobility) of his ancestry'. A famous scholar, Efthýmios, had lampooned Nikḗtas by applying to him the hackneyed line of verse 'a woe-begone Slavized countenance' (γαρασδοειδὴς ὄψις ἐσθλαβωμένη). The γαρασδο- in γαρασδοειδής is most probably derived from the Bulgarian Slavonic word *gorest'*, meaning 'pain' or 'trouble'. Alternatively, it may be derived from the name Gorazd, which was borne by Methódhios's hapless successor in Moravia. Or it may be a pun on the name and the common noun.

The quotation of this line serves Constantine's turn in two ways. It makes for him his point that the Pelopónnêsos had been Slavized, and it reflects indirectly upon the social status of the Lekapenids; for Constantine hastens to inform his readers that this Peloponnesian whose pretensions had been ridiculed was the Nikḗtas who had got an Imperial son-in-law for himself by marrying his daughter Sophía to Christopher 'the son of that great gentleman the Emperor Rhomanós' (τὸν υἱὸν τοῦ καλοῦ 'Ρωμανοῦ καὶ ἀγαθοῦ βασιλέως). This ironical compliment to Rhomanós I was the nearest approach to disparaging his senior colleague that Constantine dared to make while Rhomanós was still in the saddle and Constantine was still under eclipse.

[4] See p. 630, n. 27.

[5] Theophanes, p. 429, sub A.M. 6247, cited in II, 1 (iii) (a), p. 94.

[6] I know this from first-hand experience. I passed the night of 23 April 1912 at Monemvasía after walking to there from Neápolis (Boíai) that day, and, on 24 April, I visited the site of Sparta's perioecic dependency, 'famine-stricken Epidauros' ('Επίδαυρος Λιμηρᾶ), en route for Zarax fjord and the present-day village of Yeráka.

the whole of the Pelopónnêsos now is; but the present Greek dialect of Kynouría is singular in being the only form of modern Greek that is not derived entirely from the Attic *koinê*. In this dialect, there are elements of the North-West-Greek dialect that was introduced into Laconia in the post-Mycenaean *Völkerwanderung*.

Even on the west coast of the Pelopónnêsos some new settlements founded by refugees, like Monemvasía,[2] managed to establish themselves.[3] Their names tell their story. Akhaḯa, to the west of Pátras, must have been a settlement of refugees either from the Province of Achaïa as a whole or from the district along the south shore of the Corinthian Gulf from which the province derived its name. The establishment of Akhaḯa is presumptive evidence in favour of the truth of the *Chronicle of Monemvasía*'s record of the evacuation of Pátras. Arkadhía, now called Kyparissía, close to the west coast of Messenia, must have been established by refugee Arcadians, and so must have been Mandíneia, close to the west coast of the Gulf of Kalamáta, between Kalamáta itself and Kardhamýlê. It has been noted earlier in this chapter that there is also archaeological evidence for refugee settlements, at about the turn of the sixth and seventh centuries, on Sphaktêría Island in Navarino Bay and on Pavlopétri Island, off Elaphónêsos, to the west of Cape Maléa.[4]

However, in the Pelopónnêsos as a whole, the Slav invasion resulted in a revolutionary break with the past. Such famous Peloponnesian Hellenic names as Messene, Megalópolis, and Olympia failed to survive.[5]

[1] Today, the inhabitants of Kynouría are called 'Dzákones' (*Τζάκωνες*), but the *Chronicle of Monemvasía*'s source states that the name 'dzakoníai' had been given to this district only recently (see p. 646, with n. 5). The 'Dzákones' seem to have been, not the original Greek inhabitants, but troops of some special category (see Bon, op. cit., pp. 116–17) who had been stationed in Kynouría and who gave their name to the country but who were absorbed into the existing local Greek population and thus came to speak the local dialect. The earliest mention of soldiers called dzákones is in *De Caer.*, II, p. 696, quoted on p. 145. The word is here spelled 'dzékones', and they are defined as being men, under obligation to perform military service, who are so poor that they cannot perform their service even with the help of contributions from their neighbours. They are then transferred from the regular army to the apelátai (literally, cattle-lifters), and it is from among the apelátai that dzékones are drawn for garrison duty (*ἐξ ὧν καὶ τζέκωνες ἀφορίζονται εἰς τὰ κάστρα*). See further Bon, op. cit., pp. 71–4, and *Φ. Κουκουλές, Τσακωνία καὶ Τσάκωνες*, in *Byzantinische Zeitschrift*, vol. xxvi (1926), 1. Abteilung, pp. 317–27. On p. 326, Koukoulés follows up the *Chronicle of Monemvasía*'s interpretation of the term *τζακονίαι* and Constantine Porphyrogenitus's account of the duties of *τζέκωνες* by quoting Codinus, *De Officiis*, chap. 5, p. 42 (Bonn, 1839, Weber): *ὁ στρατοπεδάρχης τῶν τζακόνων ἐπιμελεῖται τῶν εἰς τὰ κάστρα εὑρισκομένων φυλάξεων, οἵτινες τζάκονες ὀνομάζονται*. Koukoulés also cites, ibid., a *Χριστοφόρος τζάκων* on Mount Pêlion in 1270; a *Πασχάλης [Σταγηνὸς] ἐκ τῶν λεγομένων τζακώνων ἤτοι φυλάκων τῆς ἐν τοῖς Στάγοις Πέτρας* in 1346/7; and a *φύλαξιν τζακονικήν* in Thessaly in 1395.

[2] And like Ragusa and Venice in the Adriatic, and Amalfi on the south-west coast of Italy.

[3] See Bon, op. cit., p. 61.

[4] See Sinclair Hood, 'Isles of Refuge in the Early Byzantine Period', in *The Annual of the British School at Athens*, No. 65 (1970), pp. 37–45, on p. 43 and on p. 44, cited in the present work on p. 638, n. 5.

[5] Bon, op. cit., p. 59.

No pre-seventh-century monument in the Pelopónnêsos, pre-Christian or Christian, has survived intact,[1] and no new buildings were built there before the ninth century.[2] The post-*Völkerwanderung* ecclesiastical map of the Pelopónnêsos is quite different from the previous one;[3] and this suggests that, in the part of the Pelopónnêsos that was occupied by the Slavs, Christianity was temporarily extinguished, as it was in Britain in the districts occupied by the English.

[1] Op. cit., p. 50. [2] Op. cit., p. 52, with n. 3.

[3] Bon, op. cit., p. 95. The *Chronicle of Monemvasía* and Aréthas both state that, when Nikêphóros I repatriated the people of Pátras, he raised the archbishop of Pátras to metropolitan rank and placed the Sees of Lakedhaímon, Methónê, and Korónê under his jurisdiction (see Kyriakídhês, op. cit., pp. 48 and 49). This was done at the expense of the See of Corinth.

ANNEX IV

The Paulicians and the Bogomils

(i) Preliminary Considerations

RELIGION has a social as well as a personal facet; so, on its institutional side, religion is implicated in politics and economics to some extent inevitably. This is conspicuously evident in situations in which barbarians are finding that, in order to hold their own among civilizations on whose domains they have intruded, they need to adopt one or other of the higher religions that these civilizations profess. The Teutonic barbarians who invaded the Roman Empire in the fourth and fifth centuries of the Christian Era adopted Christianity either in its Arian or in its Catholic version. Their Arab counterparts adopted Islam, which was a religion created by an Arabian prophet to provide the Arabs with an equivalent of the Judaism and Christianity that, by the sixth century, were established not only along the northern borders of Arabia, all round 'the Fertile Crescent', but also in the Yaman and in some of the oases in the Hijāz. When, in and after the eighth century, both Western and Eastern Orthodox Christendom began to revive, the same need to adopt one of the higher religions began to be felt by the still pagan barbarians on the borders of Christendom and also of Dār-al-Islām. In choosing which of the alternative accessible higher religions to embrace, the barbarians were bound to be influenced by political considerations. All these barbarian peoples were bent on preserving their political independence, and they were on their guard against the danger of compromising this by adopting a higher religion that might bring them, *de facto* if not *de jure*, under the suzerainty or sovereignty of one or other of the neighbouring civilized powers.

Instances of the influence of political considerations on the choice of a higher religion have been noticed at earlier points in the present work. The rejection of the Chalcedonian formulation of Christian Orthodoxy by the majority of the Christian population of the Roman Empire to the south and east of the Távros and Andítavros Ranges was not solely the expression of theological dissent; it was also partly a manifestation of a previously latent nationalist reaction against a Greek, and subsequently Graeco-Roman, political and cultural domination to which, by A.D. 451, these peoples had been subject for nearly eight centuries.[1] The nickname

[1] See pp. 353, 394, and 399–400.

'Melchites' (i.e. Imperialists), which the Roman Empire's Transtauran subjects coined for their Chalcedonian fellow Christians, is evidence of the persistent pre-Chalcedonians' awareness of the political element in their theological stand. The Caucasian peoples opted for Chalcedonian Orthodoxy because, in their judgement, the political pressure and cultural influence of pre-Chalcedonian Armenia, not the influence of the Orthodox East Roman Empire, was the major menace to their independence.[1]

The Moravian Slavs, menaced politically by the south-eastward advance of the Western Catholic Christian Franks, applied to distant Constantinople, not to the Old Rome, for Christian missionaries, because the Franks were the Roman See's ecclesiastical subjects.[2] Conversely, the Bulgars sought a political alliance with the distant Frankish power in 862, before the East Roman Empire compelled them in 864, by a military demonstration, to adopt Christianity in its Eastern Orthodox form—a capitulation that made the Bulgars the ecclesiastical subjects of the Ecumenical Patriarch of Constantinople and therefore implicitly also the political subjects of the East Roman Emperor. After that, the Bulgars experimented with a transfer of their ecclesiastical allegiance to the Roman See, and when, in 870, this experience led them to the conclusion that they were likely to have greater freedom of manœuvre within the fold of Eastern Orthodoxy,[3] they were not satisfied till they had substituted a Slavophone for a Greek clergy and liturgy,[4] and till they had followed up this step towards ecclesiastical independence by extorting from the East Roman Imperial Government, in the peace treaty of 927, the acceptance of an autonomous Bulgarian Patriarchate and the recognition of the Khan of Bulgaria's assumption of the title of 'Emperor'.[5]

The Khazar Khaqans, caught between the Orthodox Christian East Roman Empire and the Sunni Muslim 'Abbasid Caliphate, eventually embraced Judaism in its full rigour.[6] The Khazars' choice of Judaism led the Volga Bulgars to choose Islam,[7] as the Caucasians had been led to choose Orthodox Christianity by the Armenians' choice of pre-Chalcedonian Christianity. The Khazars' previous choice of Judaism and the Volga Bulgars' previous choice of Islam left the still pagan Rhos no alternative to choosing Orthodox Christianity[8]—a choice which, for the Rhos as for the Caucasians, was not so seriously compromising as it was for the Bulgars, since, in these two cases, geographical remoteness from the heart of East Roman power made the acceptance of the Constantinopolitan Patriarch's ecclesiastical sovereignty politically innocuous.

---

[1] See p. 400.
[2] See pp. 516–17.
[3] See pp. 365–6.
[4] See pp. 104–5, 359, 365–6.
[5] See pp. 360–3.
[6] See pp. 435–6.
[7] See p. 437.
[8] See p. 518.

Similar secular factors played a part in the adoption and maintenance of higher religions, such as Paulicianism and Bogomilism, which were not the established religions of any major political power, and which were anathematized, and were sometimes actively persecuted, by both the ecclesiastical and the secular wing of the major powers' 'establishments'.

Political geography gave the dissident sects some openings. The Paulicians, who were anathema to both the Armenian pre-Chalcedonians and the East Roman Orthodox, maintained themselves in two borderlands: first in the marches between the Islamic Caliphate together with its pre-Chalcedonian Armenian client states on the east and the East Roman Empire on the west, and then in the marches between the Thracian bridgehead of the East Roman Empire and Bulgaria. The Bosnian Patarenes maintained themselves in the marches between Eastern Orthodox and Western Christendom. Political nationalism was one of the motives for the adoption of Patarenism in Bosnia[1] and also in Languedoc.[2] In these two countries, Patarenism (known as Catharism in the West) served as the expression, and as the instrument, of a distinctive separate national consciousness. In fact, it played the same political role there as had been played by pre-Chalcedonian Christianity in Armenia, by Chalcedonian Christianity in the Caucasus, by Judaism in Khazaria, and by Islam in Volga Bulgaria. In Danubian Bulgaria, after its effective annexation to the East Roman Empire in 1018, the Bogomils and the Paulicians played a leading part in the Bulgarian national resistance movement during the 168 years of East Roman rule.[3]

Paulicianism and other heresies in Armenia, Bogomilism in Bulgaria, and Bogomilism's western offshoot Patarenism-Catharism won adherents for social as well as political reasons. In Armenia, the Christian Church had been, from the beginning, a part of the aristocratic 'establishment'.[4] After the official conversion of Bulgaria to Christianity, an Eastern Orthodox Christian 'establishment' was added to the existing secular establishment, and the burden imposed on the peasantry was increased proportionately. Moreover, the Orthodox Christian Church in Bulgaria in the ninth and tenth centuries, like the Western Christian Church in the eleventh and twelfth centuries, had largely forfeited the respect of the laity because of its corruption.[5] In twelfth-century Languedoc, the masses were eager to throw off the Church's yoke, while the nobles were eager to seize the Church's property.[6] This alliance of the nobles with the masses made Catharism in Languedoc potent.[7]

---

[1] S. Runciman, *The Medieval Manichee: A Study of the Christian Dualist Heresy* (Cambridge, 1947, University Press), pp. 101, 102, 115.   [2] Op. cit., p. 147.
[3] D. Obolensky, *The Bogomils: A Study in Balkan Neo-Manichaeism* (Cambridge, 1948, University Press), pp. 109, 169, and 172–3, with p. 173, n. 2.
[4] Runciman, op. cit., pp. 30–1.   [5] Runciman, op. cit., pp. 134–6.
[6] Runciman, op. cit., p. 131.   [7] Op. cit., p. 132.

The dissenting religious communities were able to assert themselves the most vigorously in cases in which they won, as they did in Languedoc, the support, not only of a down-trodden peasantry, but also of some of the members of the 'establishment'.

The second of the Paulician heresiarchs on East Roman ground in Asia Minor, Symeon, was an East Roman official who is said to have become acquainted with Paulicianism through having been sent to suppress the Paulician community that the Armenian heresiarch Constantine of Manalali had founded at Kívossa, in East Roman territory in the neighbourhood of Kolóneia, in the seventh century. According to the story, Symeon, after he had accomplished his mission by getting Constantine killed, abandoned his official career and returned to Kívossa to become his victim Constantine's successor for three years, till he, in his turn, was martyred.[1] When, in the ninth century, the East Roman Government resumed its persecution of its Asiatic Paulician subjects, the Paulicians' two most famous and most successful military leaders in their counter-offensive were, both of them, former East Roman officials. Karvéas had been the protomandátor of the stratêghós of théma Anatolikoí. He, with 5,000 of his co-religionists, found asylum in the Muslim amirate of Malatīyah. Karvéas fled because his father had been impaled. The occasion seems to have been the intensification of the persecution of the Asiatic East Roman Paulicians by the Empress Theodora after the definitive victory of Iconodulism in the Empire in 843.[2] Karvéas was succeeded, after his death in battle, by another East Roman refugee official, the spathários John Khrysókheir.[3]

The Bogomils, whose original adherents had been recruited among the oppressed and unsophisticated peasantry of Bulgaria, won signal successes on two occasions on which the sect gained converts in the upper ranks of society. When the annexation of Bulgaria to the East Roman Empire in 1018 had removed the barrier previously presented by the frontier between the two countries, Bogomilism invaded the Empire.[4]

---

[1] The source for this story is the pseudo- or authentic Petrus Siculus: Ἱστορία χρειώδης ἔλεγχός τε καὶ ἀνατροπὴ τῆς κενῆς καὶ ματαίας αἱρέσεως τῶν Μανιχαίων τῶν καὶ Παυλικιανῶν λεγομένων, προσωποποιηθεῖσα ὡς πρὸς τὸν ἀρχιεπίσκοπον Βουλγαρίας, in Migne, *Patrologia Graeca*, vol. civ, cols. 1239/40–1303/4. The passage here in question is in cols. 1279/80–1281/2.

[2] See *Theoph. Cont.*, pp. 165–6; Runciman, *The Medieval Manichee*, p. 40; N. G. Garsoian, *The Paulician Heresy: A Study of the Origin and Development of Paulicianism in Armenia and the Eastern Provinces of the Byzantine Empire* (Paris, 1967, Mouton), pp. 125–7.

[3] See *Theoph. Cont.*, pp. 266 and 274–5, and Phótios, letters Nos. 1, 9, 19, and 26, cited in Runciman, op. cit., p. 42, with n. 1, and in Garsoian, op. cit., p. 28, n. 3. The 'John, spathários', who is the addressee of Nos. 19 and 26, seems to be identical with the John Khrysokhêrês, the addressee of No. 9, and the addressee of No. 9 is presumably identical with the Paulician leader Khrysókheir. In these letters, Phótios is trying to persuade the addressee not to apostatize from Orthodoxy.

[4] See Obolensky, op. cit., pp. 168 and 173.

Besides crossing the Straits and spreading through western Asia Minor, it lodged itself in Constantinople. According to Anna Comnena (Komnênĕ), it penetrated in Constantinople εἰς οἰκίας μεγίστας,[1] and we may guess that this partly accounts for the previously simple-minded Bogomil sect's achievement of establishing itself in the citadel of Byzantine culture. As for Paterenism-Catharism's achievement of becoming, for a time, the national religion of Bosnia, this was partly due to the adoption of Paterenism by many members of the Bosnian nobility.[2]

It has already been noted that, in Languedoc, the adhesion of the nobles to Catharism transformed Catharism from an underground popular movement into a powerful expression of nationalism.

These facts show that it would be unrealistic to ignore the secular motives for adhesion to Paulicianism, Bogomilism, Paterenism-Catharism, and other dissident sects that won adherents at the western end of the Old World in the early Middle Ages. At the same time, it would also be a distortion of the truth if we were to seek to explain the rise of these sects exclusively in secular terms[3] and were to dismiss their profession of religious beliefs and aspirations as a hypocritical mask.[4] Adhesion to these sects was usually perilous; for the times and places at which the sects were dominant were rare. Usually the sects were anathematized and persecuted by hostile religious and secular 'establishments' whose power was greater than theirs. The sects would never have come to anything—and therefore would never have alarmed the 'establishments'—if their adherents had not been inspired by convictions and enthusiasms that were not only sincere but were strong enough to move them to risk penalization and, in the last resort, to incur the death penalty rather than recant.[5] The sectarians' faith and fervour were generated by wrestling with some of Man's fundamental and perennial questions about the nature of the Universe and of what lies behind it. They believed that their own religions had found answers to these questions, and that the 'established' religions had not.

The link between the social and the religious sides of the dissident sects was their adherents' concern with the problem of evil. Man has been

---

[1] Anna Comnena, *Alexias*, Book XV, chap. 9.

[2] See Obolensky, op. cit., Appendix IV, p. 285; Runciman, op. cit., pp. 100–15.

[3] See Obolensky, op. cit., p. viii, apropos of Bogomilism. See also op. cit., p. 173, with n. 1.

[4] 'Bogomilism was not essentially a social and still less a political movement' (Obolensky, op. cit., p. 138). 'The political impulse was not everything. Behind it there was a steady spiritual teaching, a definite religion' (Runciman, op. cit., p. 171). In Bogomilism, class-war was combined with a religious renunciation of the world. See Puech in H.-C. Puech and A. Vaillant, *Cosmas le Prêtre: le traité contre les Bogomiles*, French translation, with commentary (Paris, 1945, Imprimerie Nationale et Librairie Droz), p. 274.

[5] If the nobles of Languedoc were drawn towards Catharism by covetousness, some of their sisters were drawn to it by genuine religious zeal (Runciman op. cit., pp. 131–2). Some of these ladies became martyrs (op. cit., pp. 144–5).

haunted by this problem ever since he became human in virtue of becoming conscious, but he has been tormented by the problem the most acutely during the latest five millennia, running from the dawn of civilization; for two moral enormities, social injustice and war, are coeval with civilization and have been part of its price.

Seers and thinkers have tried to cope with the problem of evil in several different ways in accordance with their respective cultural traditions. Hindus have seen the World as evil but unreal. For them, the reality is a spirit which is beyond the phenomenal world and is at the same time identical with a human being's inmost self. Buddhists have seen the World as evil but extinguishable. According to their belief, the extinction of desire enables a human being to make his exit from the World into Nirvana. For religions that see ultimate reality in the anthropomorphic form of gods or a single unique god, the problem of evil is more baffling. If God is unique, if he is the creator of the Universe, and if he is omnipotent, he himself cannot be less evil than the evil World that he himself has deliberately created. If there is a god who is good, this god cannot be the creator of the Universe in which mankind finds itself; for this Universe is shot through with evil; there is evil, as well as good, in Man himself.

A theist who faces the problem of evil frankly is driven into becoming a Dualist. The creator-god and the god who is love cannot be identical, but Dualistic theism may take one or other of two possible alternative forms. For the radical Dualistic theist, the good god and the bad god are equal in status and in power, and the war between them is consequently eternal. According to a less stark alternative version of Dualism, the good god is the ultimate spiritual reality and he is going eventually to prevail.

This diluted Dualism lacks the logicalness of absolute Dualism; for, if the ultimate god is not responsible for evil, he is not omnipotent, and if he is not omnipotent, the expectation that he will eventually prevail may be merely wishful thinking; there can be no certain assurance of his eventual victory. Alternatively, if he is omnipotent, then he is responsible for the evil that is perpetrated by the divine adversary whom he could defeat and suppress at any moment if he chose. Iranian Zervanism and Bulgarian Bogomilism are two versions of this diluted Dualism that counts on the defeat of evil in the long run.

The mythology of these two religions is identical in essence. This is no evidence that Bogomilism is affiliated to Zervanism or to Zervanism's congener, Zoroastrianism, even remotely and indirectly. The similarity is merely evidence that any form of Dualism which stops short of being radical runs into an identical difficulty and tries to solve it in an identical way. According to the Iranian myth, the good god Ahura Mazda

(Ormazd) and the bad god Angra Mainyush (Ahriman) are sons of Zervan Akarana (Endless Time); according to Bogomilism, the good god Christ and the bad god Satanael are sons of a god who, like Zervan, is prior to both of them and who is good. The good belligerent is destined to prevail over his evil adversary; time is on his side; yet, though the existence of evil is debited to the bad god's account, the god who is the ultimate spiritual reality is logically responsible for evil at one remove, since he is the father of the bad creator of the evil World besides being the father of the bad creator-god's good adversary and eventual conqueror. In fact, the diluted version of Dualism is not really more successful in solving the problem of evil than the monistic theism ('Monarchianism') for which it is offered as a substitute because it claims that it does solve this fundamental problem which monistic theism patently leaves in suspense.

The Indian and Iranian attempts to solve the problem of evil need not be examined further in this place, since there is no evidence that either Paulicianism or Bogomilism owes anything to them, even indirectly. Evil is conterminous with life, and therefore the problem of evil has wrung human hearts and has exercised human minds always and everywhere. The historical background of both Paulicianism and Bogomilism, and the *Weltanschauung* which both these sects have rejected, is the Jewish-Christian-Muslim monistic theism which credits Yahweh, originally the god of Israel and Judah, with being the creator of the Universe and being at the same time both omnipotent and good.

Yahwehism did not raise the problem of evil so long as Yahweh's worshippers saw in him merely their own tribal god; for there is nothing incongruous in a tribal god's being on no higher a moral level than his human fellow tribesmen. In the books of the Torah (the 'Old Testament') that reflect the Israelites' picture of Yahweh in the pre-Prophetic Age, this picture is as unedifying morally as the Greeks' picture of Zeus before the Greek philosophers expurgated it. The Prophets of Israel and Judah transfigured Yahweh from a badly-behaving tribal god into the righteous creator of the Universe. In thus transforming the picture of God, they raised the problem of evil; but the Prophets did not solve this problem, and it was not solved by their successors the Pharisees or by the Pharisees' successors the devisers of Christian and Islamic theology. How could the creator of this evil World be good? And, conversely, how could a good god also be the creator?

This question was insistent and topical in the second century of the Christian Era, when, at the western end of the Old World, a version of Christianity which claimed to be both the orthodox version and the 'catholic' (i.e. the universally accepted) version was in process of being established. By that time, this end of the Oikoumenê had been in trouble for at least eight centuries. The devastation and suffering that had been inflicted on south-western Asia and on Egypt by Assyrian militarism, and the contemporary local widening of the gulf, and accentuation of the tension, between the poor and the rich in Israel and Judah, had been the evils that had evoked the Prophets' searchings of heart. The temporary respite brought by the inauguration of the First Persian Empire had been cut short when the Persian Empire had been destroyed by Alexander, and when the wars between Alexander's successors for the division of the Persian Empire's territorial spoils had been followed by the Roman conquest of the perimeter of the Mediterranean basin and by the ensuing political and social revolution of 133–31 B.C. A second temporary respite had been brought to the western end of the Old World by the inauguration of the Augustan Peace; yet, though the Age of the Principate was less agonizing than the two immediately preceding centuries, no one who lived under the Roman Imperial regime could be blind to the evil in the World. The Roman Empire, like the contemporary Chinese Empire at the opposite end of the Old World, could be described, not unfairly, as an institution designed to keep the poor majority of its subjects in subjection for the benefit of a privileged minority. In the Roman Empire the injustice of the differentiation between the *humiliores* and the *honestiores* became more extreme, more conspicuous, and more invidious as time went on.

In these social circumstances there was bound to be dissent from a religion that presented the Jewish-Christian creator-god as being both omnipotent and good, without reconciling the goodness attributed to the creator with the evil in a Universe that was debited to him as being his handiwork. The version of Christianity that claimed to be Orthodox and Catholic was challenged in the second century of the Christian Era by Marcion, in the third century by Mani, in the ninth century by the Paulicians, and in the tenth century by the Bogomils. All these challenges confronted the established version of Christianity with some form of Dualism, either absolute or diluted. Marcion, Mani, and Bogomil were Dualists themselves, and the sects that they founded continued to be Dualistic throughout their history. The identity of the founder of Paulicianism is uncertain. If the founder was a Paul, we cannot ascertain which of the possible alternative Pauls he was. Our information is too scanty, and what there is of it is not unanimous. It seems to be certain that, in the East Roman Empire, Paulicianism was a Dualistic religion as early as the ninth century; and this East Roman Dualistic Paulicianism was a religion of the same species as Marcionism, Manichaeism, and Bogomilism. However, it also seems certain that Paulicianism had started as a non-Dualistic version of Christianity in its Armenian homeland, and that in Armenia the T'ondrakeçi, who, from the ninth century onwards, were the Paulicians' apparent successors there, never became

Dualists at any stage. This is the conclusion suggested by the Armenian evidence about the Paulicians and about their successors in Armenia, the T'ondrakeçi; and the earliest Armenian evidence about the Paulicians is a century older than the earliest Greek evidence about them.[1]

The belief that the World is essentially evil entails certain consequences, both practical and theoretical.

The believer's aim in life in this World must be to extricate himself from it as thoroughly and as quickly as possible. He must therefore be an ascetic, and must carry his asceticism to the furthest practicable extremes. If, like the Buddha and his Hindu opponents, he conceives of reality primarily in spiritual terms, he will concentrate his efforts on extinguishing the desires that generate self-hood and self-centredness. If, like Mani and like some, at any rate, of the Cathars, he conceives of reality primarily in material terms, he will concentrate his efforts on mortifying the flesh.[2] One of his negative duties is to eschew marriage and to abstain from procreation. For the devotee to propagate his kind would be treason; for he would then be helping to perpetuate the evil World, and not be working, as he ought to work, to liquidate it. But, whether the ascetic practises spiritual or physical ascetism or both, he has to be a devotee who dedicates his whole life and energy to his religious task.

Therefore the devotee has to have co-religionists who will minister to his needs, since he is inhibited from providing for these himself. Consequently, the members of the sect who carry out its demands in full can be no more than a minority of the sect's adherents. The majority must forgo—or be exempted from—the ascetic pursuit of perfection in order to enable a minority to follow this arduous course. Accordingly, some of those sects that have faced the problem of evil and have concluded that the counsel of perfection for Man is to extricate himself from an intrinsically evil World have been divided into two orders: an élite ('electi' in the Latin terminology of the Western Cathars) who are the only complete practitioners of the religion and therefore the only true members of the Church, and a majority whose role is the indispensable but humble one of enabling the elect to function, but who are not themselves fully within the pale of the religion in which they believe or of the sect to which they adhere. The majority of the sect's adherents disqualify themselves for the pursuit of religious perfection by marrying and giving in marriage; and it is necessary that they should thus disqualify themselves, since, if they did not, the sect would extinguish itself long before it could extinguish the World.

---

[1] See Garsoian, op. cit., p. 90.

[2] The Buddha tried this first, and then diverted his efforts from physical to spiritual asceticism when he found, by experience, that mere physical asceticism did not open for him the door for making his exit from this World into Nirvana.

This division of the community into an inner élite and an outer ministering majority is to be found in Buddhism, in Marcionism, in Manichaeism, and in Western Catharism. There is no evidence—and, indeed, no likelihood—that this striking common feature in these four religions' hierarchical organization is due to any historical connection between them. It is more likely that it is the normal social consequence of a common aversion to life in this World, and that this aversion was acquired by the adherents of each of the four religions independently, as a result of their each finding the same answer to the common human problem of evil.[1]

Though this division of the religious community into an inner and an outer circle would seem to be a logical consequence of a repudiation of the World, the division is not to be found in all sects that have translated this repudiation into the tenets of a Dualistic religion. For instance, there seems not to have been any Buddhist-like or Cathar-like élite in the Zoroastrian community, and there is no conclusive evidence for its existence in the Paulician Church either.[2] These two exceptions may have been due to special causes. The Zoroastrians are perhaps only semi-Dualists. They see the World as being a disputed territory between the battling forces of good and evil rather than as being intrinsically evil in itself. As for the Paulicians, they seem originally to have been, not Dualists, but Adoptionist Christians, and the pre-Dualistic structure of their community may have survived the conversion to Dualism of the branch of this sect that migrated from Armenia to the East Roman Empire.

Conversely, Christianity, which is not a Dualistic religion, has nevertheless gone some way towards the creation of an élite in adopting the institution of monasticism. Western Christian monks call monasticism 'religion' and themselves 'the religious', in contrast not only to the laity but also to the non-monastic clergy. The use of these words in this sense is an implicit claim that Christian monks, like Cathar 'electi', are the only complete practitioners of their religion and the only full members of their church. Moreover, Christian monks are not only celibate; some orders of them are also mendicant, like Buddhist monks and like Cathar 'electi'. However, many of the Christian orders of monks do not depend, or at any rate not wholly, on alms or on endowments, but earn their own living, at least partially, by working for it. Nor has any of the Christian churches ever ruled that an adherent who is not a monk is, on that account, not a full member.

A sect that holds the World to be so evil that it must be repudiated is likely also to think it wrong to strive for worldly power. The Bogomils

---

[1] This point is made by Puech in *Cosmas le Prêtre*, pp. 312–13. Cf. A. Borst, *Die Katharer* (Stuttgart, 1953, Hiersemann), p. 65.

[2] See Garsoian, op. cit., pp. 155, 163, 228.

appear to have lived up to their theology. They seem to have been passive, meek, and pacifist.[1] On the other hand, the Bosnian and Albigensian Cathars were militant—or, at least, they defended themselves vigorously when they were attacked. The Paulicians were notoriously martial,[2] and this trait, like the apparent absence of an élite in their organization, may have been a legacy from their pre-Dualist past.

The Marcionites, Manichees, Dualist Paulicians, and Bogomils were, all alike, reacting against the Orthodox-Catholic version of Christianity, and it is therefore not surprising that, in their theology, they have made identical departures from established Christian doctrine. There is no warrant for taking the common features of their dissenting doctrine as being evidence that the younger post-Christian Dualist sects have been derived from, or even that they have been influenced by, the older sects that have the same Christian background. Each of them may have worked out the same dissenting theology independently for itself.

One of the tenets of post-Christian Dualism is that the creator-god has created evil and therefore cannot be the good god. The creator-god is either Yahweh, the god of Israel and Judah, who, in the Old Testament, is debited with the creation of the World, or else he is Satan, the good god's adversary. If Yahweh is the creator, Yahweh must be identical with the adversary. The good god is not Yahweh. The good god is a stranger in the creator-god's World. He visits this World out of compassion, and at his peril.

Yahweh is indeed an unedifying figure as he is presented in those books of the Torah that reflect the moral standards of the Israelites of the pre-Prophetic Age. It is easy to see in this primitive Yahweh the evil creator of an evil World. The demotion of Yahweh leads to a rejection of the Old Testament, and the repudiation of Christianity's Jewish heritage[3] must have made the Dualist sects attractive to many Christians. The Old Testament was part of the national heritage of the Jewish Christian Church only; and, after the Romano-Jewish war of A.D. 66–70, this originally preponderant Jewish wing of the Christian Church dwindled into insignificance. From that time on, the majority of the Christian community consisted of Gentiles, for whom the Old Testament was an alien and incongruous component of the Christian Scriptures.

Post-Christian Dualism was also incompatible with both the Marcan Adoptionist Christianity and the Matthaean–Lucan Conceptionist Christianity that has superseded Adoptionism as the established doctrine of the Orthodox-Catholic-Protestant Church. If it is held that the World is intrinsically evil, it becomes virtually impossible to believe that the

---

[1] Vaillant in *Cosmas le Prêtre*, pp. 55–6; Puech, ibid. p. 321. See also Runciman, op. cit., p. 88; Obolensky, op. cit., pp. 143–4, 182, 190.

[2] See Runciman, loc. cit. [3] See Runciman, op. cit., p. 172.

good god has adopted a polluted human being as his son, and, *a fortiori*, that he himself has become incarnate through being conceived in a polluted human womb. If the good god had entered the bad god's evil World genuinely in either of these ways or in any other way, he would have contaminated himself, and this is unthinkable. Therefore Dualism implies Docetism. Christ's appearance in this World in human form, and his death on the Cross, are illusions; they are what Hindus would call *maya*; they are not historical realities.

In the sphere of institutions, marriage, for post-Christian Dualists, is not a sacrament; it is an offence; and it is a graver offence than irregular sexual relations, just because marriage is a regular institution which has been established deliberately for the express purpose of procreation. The ban on marriage for the Dualist élite has been noted already, and, in this connection, it has been explained that, for Dualists, to perpetuate the human race is tantamount to treason. The Dualist's duty is to promote the liquidation of an evil World. Here again the Dualist Paulicians took an exceptional stand. They did not condemn marriage and procreation.[1] In Petrus Siculus's *History* the Paulicians are not accused of any Manichaean-like asceticism.[2]

The Christian 'establishment' accused the post-Christian Dualists, including the Paulicians (pre-Dualist as well as Dualist), of practising dissimulation. They are said to have participated outwardly, but insincerely, in the rites of the Orthodox Church, and to have pretended to hold the Orthodox doctrines while privately giving them heretical interpretations of their own.[3] As far as the Paulicians are concerned, this accusation seems to be at least partially refuted by facts that are incompatible with it. The Paulicians were 'open and courageous proselytizers';[4] three of the leaders of the Paulician community at Philippopolis spoke out boldly and frankly in their disputation with the

---

[1] Obolensky, op. cit., p. 114; Garsoian, op. cit., p. 188.

[2] Obolensky, op. cit., p. 44. But Petrus Siculus does make this accusation against them in his first sermon (Migne, *P.G.*, vol. civ, col. 1308), and so does Gregory of Narek (see Puech in *Cosmas le Prêtre*, p. 263, n. 3).

[3] Apropos of the Manichee Aghápios, see Phótios, *Bibliotheca*, in Migne, *P.G.*, vol. ciii, cols. 521–5, cited by Obolensky, op. cit., pp. 25–6. Apropos of the Paulicians, see Georgius Monachus, p. 723 de Boor, cited by Runciman, op. cit., p. 51; Petrus Siculus, *History*, chap. 29 (cols. 1283/4–1285/6), cited by Garsoian, op. cit., pp. 66 and 175–7, on the colloquy between the third Paulician heresiarch, Gegnesios (Yenésios) (? in office 717–46) and the contemporary Patriarch of Constantinople; Petrus Hegumenus: Περὶ Παυλικιανῶν, passages cited (in the original Greek) by Garsoian, op. cit., pp. 51–2, nn. 94 and 95. Apropos of the Bogomils, see Cosmas the Priest, *Treatise*, pp. 55, 71, and 84, Puech and Vaillant's translation; Vaillant in op. cit., p. 30; Puech in op. cit., pp. 150–63; Obolensky, op. cit., pp. 141–2; apropos of the eleventh-century Bogomils in Asia Minor, see the letter of Efthýmios, a monk of the monastery Τῆς Περιβλέπτου in Constantinople, cited by Obolensky, op. cit., pp. 179 and 181; apropos of the Constantinopolitan Bogomils who were detected *circa* 1110, see Anna Comnena, *Alexias*, Book XV, chap. 8.

[4] Obolensky, op. cit., p. 143.

Emperor Aléxios I in 1114; some of their followers apostatized; but two out of the three leaders preferred to suffer martyrdom.[1] Already in 1084, other representatives of the Philippopolitan Paulicians, whom Aléxios had inveigled to Mosynópolis and had arrested, preferred to suffer imprisonment and the confiscation of their property rather than apostatize.[2] The accusation of practising dissimulation may, perhaps, be correct, without qualification, when it is made against the Bogomils; but, whether wholly true or partly false, this accusation is unfair. The Dualists were outlawed by the Orthodox Christian 'establishment'; the penalty for exposure followed by obduracy was extreme; and dissimulation was the sectarians' only practicable means of defence, short of the forlorn hope of taking up arms in the face of fearful odds.

The ethics of this dissimulation (in so far as it was really practised) may be controversial, but one of its effects is indisputable. It made it difficult for the 'establishment' to ascertain what the sectarians' true doctrines and practices were. The 'establishment' did have opportunities of ascertaining the facts: for instance, when the Constantinopolitan Bogomils were detected and persecuted by Aléxios I *circa* 1111,[3] and when Aléxios held his disputation with the Paulicians at Philippopolis in 1114. The most serious effort to ascertain the facts was made by the Western Christian inquisitors during the persecution of the Cathars in Languedoc in the thirteenth century.[4] Apostates are obvious sources of information. The next best source to the Western Cathars' own scriptures for the truth about the Western Cathars is the apostate Raynier (Raynerius) Sacconi, who wrote his *Summa de Catharis et Pauperibus de Lugduno* in the year 1230.[5] However, an apostate is apt to paint an unduly lurid picture of the religion that he has abandoned. He is tempted to heighten the colours partly by a sincere revulsion and partly by a wish to clear himself from the suspicion that his apostasy may not have been wholehearted. Our reservations about the indictments of Communism by ex-Communists in our day should make us cautious about taking, *au pied de la lettre*, the medieval indictments of post-Christian Dualistic sects by Dualists who had become Christians.

However, the 'establishment' usually took a course that, from their point of view, had the twofold advantage of being less laborious for them and more damaging for their sectarian victims. Since the second century

---

[1] Anna Comnena, *Alexias*, Book XIV, chaps. 8–9. See also Obolensky, op. cit., pp. 193–5; Runciman, op. cit., p. 45.

[2] Anna Comnena, *Alexias*, Book VI, chap. 2. See also Obolensky, op. cit., p. 191; Runciman, op. cit., pp. 44–5.

[3] See Obolensky, op. cit., pp. 197–206, with Appendix III on pp. 275–6.

[4] See Runciman, op. cit., pp. 116 and 147.

[5] See Runciman, op. cit., pp. 153–4 and 169–70. Text in A. Dondaine's edition of the Cathar *Liber de Duobus Principiis* (Rome, 1939, Istituto Storico Domenicano S. Sabina), pp. 64–78.

of the Christian Era a series of approved refutations of heresies—some of them confined to refuting particular heresies, and some of them encyclopedic—had been piling up in the growing corpus of Orthodox-Catholic theological literature. A heresy might be successfully suppressed or it might die a natural death from inanition, but the memory of it would still be perpetuated posthumously in the accounts of it, whether accurate or garbled, that necessarily accompanied the approved refutations of it. When a new, or at least hitherto unrecognized, heresy was detected, the simplest and most telling way of attacking it was to consult the existing corpus of Orthodox-Catholic refutational literature and to identify the contemporary heresy that was now under attack with one or more of those that were already catalogued.

This is, for instance, what the Ecumenical Patriarch Theophýlaktos—or, more probably, his 'ghost-writer'[1]—has done in a surviving letter of his to his nephew-in-law Tsar Peter of Bulgaria, in answer to a letter from the Tsar in which Peter seems to have asked the Patriarch to identify a newly discovered sect in Bulgaria (i.e. the Bogomils) and to give the Tsar guidance for dealing with it.[2] Theophýlaktos pronounces that, though the sect about which Peter is inquiring has come to light only recently ($\nu\epsilon o\phi\alpha\nu o\hat{\upsilon}s$), it is at the same time an ancient one ($\pi\alpha\lambda\alpha\iota\hat{\alpha}s$).[3] It is Manichaeism mixed with Paulianism.[4] Correspondences in trivial points of detail between Theophýlaktos's letter and Petrus Siculus's *Historia Manichaeorum* show that Petrus Siculus's compilation was one of the works on which the Patriarch's 'ghost-writer' drew.[5]

Anna Comnena defines the Constantinopolitan Bogomilism of *circa* 1111 as being Manichaeism mixed with Massalianism.[6] Efthýmios Zighavênós identifies this same Constantinopolitan Bogomilism as being 'a part of the heresy of the Massalians' with sundry variations and additions.[7]

The Orthodox Christian 'establishment' set itself to 'smear' the Paulicians by identifying them with the Manichees. The identification

---

[1] Theophýlaktos himself had a mania for horses which left him little time or attention to give to the duties of his office. He was incapacitated by a riding accident in 954, so the date of this letter of his is probably not later than that year.

[2] See Runciman, op. cit., pp. 67–8; Obolensky, op. cit., pp. 111–14.

[3] pp. 362 and 365 of the Greek text published by N. M. Petrovsky in the *Izvestiya Otdeleniya russkogo yazyka i slovesnosti Imperatorskoy Akademii Nauk*, vol. xviii, tom. 3 (1913), pp. 356–72.

[4] Loc. cit., pp. 362–3. $\Pi\alpha\upsilon\lambda\iota\alpha\nu\iota\sigma\mu\hat{\omega}$, not $\Pi\alpha\upsilon\lambda\iota\kappa\iota\alpha\nu\iota\sigma\mu\hat{\omega}$. 'Paulianism' was the heresy of the third-century Patriarch of Antioch, Paul of Samosata. Theophýlaktos directs that the (Bogomil) heretics are to be rebaptized in accordance with the nineteenth canon of the [First] Council of Nicaea. This canon is concerned with recanting adherents of Paul of Samosata. The First Council of Nicaea was held in 325, that is to say, more than three centuries before the earliest surviving record of the name 'Paulician'. See further Obolensky, op. cit., pp. 115–16; Garsoian, op. cit., pp. 215–16.

[5] Obolensky, op. cit., pp. 113–14.

[6] *Alexias*, Book XV, chap. 8.

[7] Efthýmios Zighavênós, $\Pi\alpha\nu o\pi\lambda\iota\alpha\ \Delta o\gamma\mu\alpha\tau\iota\kappa\eta$, in Migne, *P.G.*, vol. cxxx, cols. 1189/90–1243/4.

is made expressly in the titles of two of the ninth-century and tenth-century anti-Paulician polemical works in Greek, and it is tacitly assumed in two others. Petrus Hegumenus's tract[1] is called Περὶ Παυλικιανῶν τῶν καὶ Μανιχαίων. Petrus Siculus's *History*[2] is called a history of the heresy τῶν Μανιχαίων τῶν καὶ Παυλικιανῶν λεγομένων. In the titles of two of Phótius's three authentic sermons against the Paulicians[3] the name 'Manichaeans' appears alone,[4] and so it does also in the pseudo-Photian *History of the Manichaeans*.[5] The compiler of Petrus Siculus's *History* seeks to clinch his identification of the Paulicians with the Manichees by devoting eleven of his chapters[6] to Mani and Manichaeism before going on to deal with the Paulicians themselves. This identification of the Paulicians with the Manichees was the principal weapon in the Eastern Orthodox Christian polemical writers' armoury for their campaign against the Paulicians.[7]

Evidently these identifications should be regarded with extreme scepticism and should not be accepted as being veracious unless cogent independent evidence of their veracity is forthcoming.[8] All that they tell us for certain is that, in the ninth and tenth centuries, Manichaeism and Massalianism still had a particularly bad reputation in Orthodox Christian circles. We cannot infer that, at this date, there were still any Manichaeans in existence anywhere to the west of Central Asia,[9] or any Massalians anywhere at all.[10] At the same time, we cannot be sure that these two ill-famed sects were already extinct. Zighavénós gives a separate section to the Massalians,[11] in addition to his sections on the Paulicians and the Bogomils, and he would hardly have done this if he had been using the name 'Massalians' merely as a pseudonym for either of those two other sects. Again, Efthýmios the Patriarch of Bulgaria (in office *circa* 1376–1402), in his biography of St. Ilaríon, the twelfth-century Bishop of Moglena, records Ilaríon's encounters with Manichees as well as with Armenians (? i.e. Monophysites) and with Bogomils.

It is true that Efthýmios's description of St. Ilaríon's 'Manichees' is

---

[1] Text published by J. C. L. Gieseler (Göttingen, 1849, Vandenhoeck & Ruprecht), as an Appendix to Gieseler's edition (1846) of Petrus Siculus's *History*.

[2] Text in Migne, *P.G.*, vol. civ, cols. 1239/40–1303/4.

[3] Migne, *P.G.*, vol. cii, cols. 85/6–121/2, 121/2–177/8, 177/8–277/8.

[4] The other sermon in this set of three has no title.

[5] Migne, *P.G.*, vol. cii, cols. 15/16–83/4.

[6] Chaps. 11–21 in Migne, *P.G.*, vol. civ, cols. 1257/8–1271/2.

[7] Garsoian, op. cit., p. 168.

[8] This point is made forcefully by Puech in Puech and Vaillant's *Cosmas le Prêtre*, pp. 299–316.

[9] See Puech in op. cit., p. 304; H. Söderberg, *La Religion des Cathares* (Uppsala, 1949, Almqvist & Wiksell), p. 24.

[10] See Puech in op. cit., p. 372.

[11] Migne, *P.G.*, vol. cxxx, cols. 1273/87.

taken, in places verbatim, from Zighavênós's description of the Paulicians. Moreover, Zighavênós's inclusion of a section on the Massalians is not evidence that this sect was still extant in Zighavênós's own day. His *Panoplía* is an encyclopedia, and the sects that he describes and refutes in this comprehensive work may therefore include sects that were extinct long ago by his time. Yet it is not impossible that some Massalians and some Manichees may truly have survived in the Levant until the Middle Ages. Adoptionism was a version of Christianity that had been discarded in favour of Conceptionism by the Christian 'establishment' long before either Manichaeism or Massalianism had been inaugurated; yet Adoptionism did survive until the Middle Ages in at least two geographically secluded natural fastnesses at opposite extremities of Christendom. In Charlemagne's reign there was one Spanish Adoptionist, Felix of Urgel, in the Catalonian march of the Frankish Empire, and another, Elipandus, in independent Christian territory in Asturia. Felix was rebutted by Alcuin, and Elipandus by Heterius and Beatus in a letter written in 785.[1] The Paulicians likewise were Adoptionists in their Armenian homeland, and their congeners and successors the T'ondrakeçi continued to be Adoptionists and survived as such, *in situ*, into the nineteenth century. This survival of Adoptionism is a warning to us to be cautious in coming to the conclusion that any sect has become extinct.

What is more, a sect may survive without retaining its original doctrines and practices. For instance, the branch of the Paulician Church that won a foothold in the eastern marches of the East Roman Empire changed its doctrine in the ninth century from Adoptionist Christianity to some form of Dualism.[2] The branch of the rural, Slavonic, and naïve Bogomil Church that won a foothold at Constantinople in the eleventh century may have undergone some changes in this novel environment that was urban, Greek, and sophisticated. At Constantinople, the Bogomils' doctrine changed greatly, their ritual changed considerably, and even their ethics changed to some extent in Obolensky's view.[3] Though this perhaps more highly developed Bogomilism was suppressed at Constantinople, where the development had taken place, it seems to have supplanted the original version of Bogomilism in this religion's Bulgarian homeland,[4] and it was this later version of Bogomilism that spread westwards in the forms of Patarenism and Catharism.

It will be seen that both Paulicianism and Bogomilism are as elusive as Proteus.

[1] See Runciman, op. cit., pp. 116 and 165, and F. C. Conybeare's translation of *The Key of Truth* (Oxford, 1898, Clarendon Press), Introduction, pp. clxx–clxxix.

[2] See Garsoian, op. cit., pp. 174, 183, 185, and 232.

[3] See Obolensky, op. cit., p. 219.

[4] See Obolensky, ibid.

(ii) *The Paulicians*

The name 'Paulicians' is an Anglicized rendering of the Greek 'Pav-likianoí' (*Παυλικιανοί*), and this is a Graecized version of the Armenian 'Payli keank'.[1] If these two Armenian words are divided into three, as 'Payl i keank', they can be read as meaning, in Armenian, 'people who are filthy in their life',[2] but it seems likely that this is a pun, made as an afterthought, on a single word that is a proper name. If 'Paylikeank' is in truth a proper name, it means, in Armenian, 'adherents of a minor Paul'. It is, indeed, spelled 'Paulikeank' sometimes.[3] The Armenian suffix -ik is a diminutive that can be given a depreciatory or pejorative connotation.[4] The name therefore seems to signify that the bearers of it are not true followers of the greatest Paul, namely Paul the Apostle. This contemptuous name must have been coined, not by the Paulicians themselves, but by their Trinitarian Conceptionist opponents,[5] the authorities of the pre-Chalcedonian (Monophysite) established church of Armenia. The Paulicians' own name for themselves was 'True Believers'.[6]

The earliest extant explicit reference to the Paulicians in Armenian is in the *Oath of Union* taken at a council of the pre-Chalcedonian Armenian Church that was convened at Dvin in 555.[7] In this document the Paulicians are condemned in company with the Nestorians. The Pauli-cians are also condemned in the Canons and Constitution of the council held by the Aghovanians (Albanians) at Ani in either 717 or 639;[8] in Canon No. 32 of the council convened at Dvin *circa* 719 by the pre-Chalcedonian Armenian Katholikós John of Otsun (Ojun);[9] and in a sermon preached by John of Otsun against the Paulicians.[10] This Armenian evidence indicates that the Paulician sect was already in existence, and was already being nicknamed 'Paulician', before 555.

Who was the 'minor Paul' who was the sect's founder, or at any rate its eponym, according to the Paulicians' Monophysite Armenian adversaries? According to two of the Greek sources, namely Petrus Hegumenus and Petrus Siculus, in passages that derive from a single

---

[1] See Garsoian, op. cit., p. 93, in her translation of the Canons and Constitution of the Council of the Aghovanians, held at Ani *circa* 717 or perhaps *circa* 639 (op. cit., pp. 93–4).

[2] Garsoian, op. cit., p. 92, n. 36; p. 94, n. 40; p. 210.

[3] e.g. in the *Oath of Union*, which is the earliest extant document in which it occurs (Gar-soian, op. cit., p. 213, n. 145).

[4] See Runciman, op. cit., p. 47; Obolensky, op. cit., p. 55; Garsoian, op. cit., p. 213.

[5] Garsoian, ibid.   [6] Garsoian, ibid.

[7] Partial English translation in Garsoian, op. cit., pp. 88–9; complete Armenian text on pp. 236–7.

[8] See Garsoian, op. cit., pp. 92–4 and 134.

[9] John of Otsun, *Opera* (Venice, 1834), pp. 74–7, cited by Garsoian, op. cit., p. 94, n. 40, and p. 135.

[10] *Opera*, pp. 78–107.

common source,[1] the third of the Paulician heresiarchs, Gegnesios (Yenésios)-Timothy, who was in office *circa* 717–46, and who resided first in the Phanároia district of the East Roman *théma* Armeniakoí and later in the Armenian district called Manalali, on the Arab side of the Romano-Arab frontier, was the son of an Armenian named Paul who had fled to Phanároia and had established a community of his followers in a village there which he renamed 'Episparís' ('Seedbed').[2] In another context[3] the Paul who fled to Phanároia and founded the Paulician community at Episparís is said to have come from Samosata,[4] and the Paulicians are said to have been called by this Paul's name instead of continuing to be called Manichees (which is what they were alleged to have been). If these two Pauls are the same person and if Paul the father of Gegnesios is an historical, not a legendary, figure, his son's dates in office rule out the possibility that the father might be identical with the famous third-century Paul of Samosata, who was Patriarch of Antioch from 260 to 272.

However, it seems an unlikely coincidence that there should have been two Pauls of Samosata, both of whom were not only important heretical leaders but were also heretics of one and the same school. The famous third-century Paul of Samosata was an Adoptionist Christian,[5] and this was the original religion of the Paulicians and continued to be the religion of their congeners and successors in Armenia, the T'ondrakeçi, right down to the nineteenth century, to judge by their book *The Key of Truth*.[6] We cannot rule out the possibility that the third-century Paul of Samosata may be the historical eponym of the nickname that had been imposed on the Paulician sect. Indeed, the tenth-century Muslim scholar Mas'ūdi says explicitly, in two passages, that the Paulicians were the famous third-century Paul of Samosata's followers.[7] It is true that, according to Petrus Siculus in his *History*,[8] the Paulicians

---

[1] Petrus Hegumenus, 1, 60, and Petrus Siculus, chap. 21, cols. 1273/4. The passages are printed in the original Greek, in parallel columns, in Garsoian, op. cit., p. 61, n. 131.

[2] Petrus Siculus, *Historia*, chap. 28, cols. 1281/2–1283/4.

[3] Petrus Siculus, *Historia*, chap. 21, cols. 1273/4, corresponding to Petrus Hegumenus, 1, 60.

[4] This Paul's mother's name is given as Kalliníkê, and he is said to have had a brother named John.

[5] See the passages from the extant fragments of Paul of Samosata's *Discourses to Sabinus*, quoted by F. C. Conybeare in *The Encyclopaedia Britannica*, eleventh edition, s.v. 'Paul of Samosata'.

[6] See Garsoian, op. cit., p. 212.

[7] Mas'ūdi, *Le Livre de l'avertissement*, French translation by A. Carra de Vaux (Paris, 1896) p. 208, quoted by Garsoian, p. 212, and by Runciman, p. 48. Runciman also quotes Mas'ūdi's *Prairies d'or* (*Murūj-adh-Dhahab*) on p. 48, n. 1.

[8] Petrus Siculus, chap. 4, cols. 1245/6, cited by Garsoian, op. cit., p. 214, n. 147, and by Runciman, op. cit., p. 48, n. 4. See also Petrus Siculus, *Historia*, chap. 24, cols. 1277/8; Petrus Hegumenus, 3, 62; pseudo-Phótios, *History*, 4, cols. 21/2, quoted by Garsoian, p. 116, n. 10.

anathematized Paul of Samosata; but this passage, even if its date were held to be before 872 and not after 932, was in either case written about the Paulicians after they had claimed Paul the Apostle as their eponym and after the East Roman branch of the Paulicians had changed its doctrine from Adoptionist Christianity to some form of Dualism. By this time, the Paulicians will have had a double motive for anathematizing Paul of Samosata, even if, as a matter of historical fact, this was the Paul who was both the eponym of their nickname and possibly also the true source of their original Adoptionist Christian doctrine.

The political history of the Paulicians in Armenia is more obscure than their political history in the East Roman Empire and in Bulgaria. On the other hand, the doctrinal history of the Paulicians in Armenia, and of their successors in Armenia the T'ondrakeçi, is relatively clear.

It has already been noted that the Paulicians are mentioned, under this pejorative name, in four Monophysite Armenian ecclesiastical documents, the first written in 555, the second written in either 639 or 717 or perhaps conflated from two originally separate documents written respectively at these two dates, the third written (probably by John of Otsun) in 719, and the fourth certainly written by John of Otsun, the convener of the council of 719. After the time of John of Otsun, who was the Monophysite Katholikós of Armenia *circa* 719–26, the Paulicians in Armenia are not mentioned again under that name in our Armenian sources,[1] but a sect called the T'ondrakeçi is named in these sources from the tenth until the fourteenth century.[2] This sect's name is derived from the name of a district called T'ondrak, north-east of Lake Van and south of the Aladağ. The T'ondrakeçi sect is said, in our Armenian sources, to have been founded by a man named Smbat of Zarehawan, in the time of the Katholikós John and of Smbat Bagratuni. This dating might be either 833–55 or 898–914.[3]

There is a close affinity between the doctrines of the Armenian Paulicians, as these are described in the *Oath of Union* (555) and in the writings of John of Otsun, and the doctrines ascribed to the T'ondrakeçi. Nerses Šnorhali taxes the T'ondrakeçi in the twelfth century with the same heretical practices as those imputed to the Paulicians by John of Otsun. The T'ondrakeçi are expressly identified with the Paulicians by Gregory Máyistros in a letter to the Syrian Katholikós.[4] This Gregory

---

[1] Garsoian, op. cit., p. 94.   [2] Op. cit., pp. 13 and 107.

[3] See Garsoian, op. cit., pp. 140–1. The Katholikós John V reigned from 833 to 855 and Prince Smbat the Confessor from 826 to 855. The Katholikós John VI reigned from 898 to 931 and King Smbat I Bagratuni from 890 to 914. Gregory Máyistros, writing *circa* 1042–55, evidently intends the earlier of these two alternative possible dates, since he says that the T'ondrakeçi sect was founded 170 years before his own time. Stephen Asoghik of Taron, writing *circa* 991–1019, dates the sect's foundation in the reign of the Katholikós John VI.

[4] Garsoian, op. cit., pp. 139–40. For details, see op. cit., pp. 152–73.

was an Armenian nobleman who, in the reign of the East Roman Emperor Constantine IX Monomákhos (1042–55), served as dhoux of the East Roman théma Mesopotamía, which at this date extended over the former autonomous Armenian principalities Taron and Vaspurakan.[1] Gregory must have had some acquaintance with the T'ondrakeçi's doctrines, since he was a vigorous persecutor of this sect.[2]

After the fourteenth century, there is no further trace of the T'ondrakeçi for the next five centuries, but, after the Russo-Turkish war of 1828–9, a party of T'ondrakeçi emigrated from the village of Chaurm,[3] in Armenian territory on the Ottoman side of the Russo-Turkish frontier, to Ark'weli,[4] on the Russian side, bringing with them a book, *The Key of Truth*, in which their doctrines are set out and their ritual is prescribed. In 1837 this book was confiscated by the Monophysite Armenian Katholikós at Echmiadzin, and an investigation into the tenets and practices of the T'ondrakeçi refugees was carried out by the Armenian ecclesiastical authorities from 1837 to 1845. The confiscated book was placed in the library of the Armenian Holy Synod at Echmiadzin, was discovered there by F. C. Conybeare in 1891, and was published by him in 1898.[5] The manuscript—from which thirty-eight pages have been torn out—was written in the Taron district in 1782, but the terms of the surviving fragment of the colophon, together with the archaic language of the text, indicate that the work itself may have been composed as early as the ninth century, i.e. in the century in which the foundation of the T'ondrakeçi sect is dated in our medieval Armenian sources.[6]

The surviving part of *The Key of Truth*, read together with the record of the Monophysite Armenian ecclesiastical authorities' inquiry, in 1837–45, into the religion of the T'ondrakeçi refugees from Chaurm, and with the medieval Armenian accounts of the religion of the Paulicians in Armenia, and of their successors there, the T'ondrakeçi, makes it evident that the T'ondrakeçi—and therefore almost certainly also their Paulician predecessors in Armenia—were Adoptionist Christians, not Dualists. 'In almost all particulars, the doctrine of *The Key of Truth* is corroborated by the other Armenian sources which we possess.'[7]

The confession of faith in *The Key of Truth* declares that there is one true God who is the creator, and that Jesus was a creature, not a creator.[8] According to the Adoptionist Christology, Jesus became the son of God,

---

[1] Garsoian, op. cit., pp. 97–8. [2] Op. cit., pp. 98 and 144–5.

[3] See Conybeare's edition of *The Key of Truth*, Introduction, pp. cv–cvi.

[4] See Garsoian, op. cit., p. 108.

[5] *The Key of Truth: A Manual of the Paulician Church of Armenia*; the Armenian text edited and translated with illustrative documents and introduction (Oxford, 1898, Clarendon Press).

[6] See Garsoian, op. cit., p. 108; Runciman, op. cit., p. 56.

[7] Garsoian, op. cit., p. 166.

[8] *The Key of Truth*, 28–9 (93–4) and 52 (114).

not at the moment of his conception in his mother's womb, but at the moment of his baptism.[1] Though Adoptionism was rapidly driven almost completely off the field by Conceptionism, it seems probable that Adoptionism was the dominant Christology so long as the Judaeo-Christians continued to be the majority of the Christian community. In becoming Christians, the Judaeo-Christians had not ceased to be also orthodox Jews. Jesus's disciples had been orthodox Jews, and so had been Jesus himself. It is not credible that either Jesus or his Jewish adherents could have regarded him as being a 'son of God' in any sense except the figurative sense in which some of the rabbis of the Pharisaic Age felt themselves to be sons of God and called themselves God's sons as an expression of the mutual love and confidence and familiarity that was the relation between God and them. This metaphorical use of the term 'son' was not shocking to Jews because it did not offend against the Jewish belief in God's unity and uniqueness. On the other hand, Conceptionism—the belief that a man had been begotten by an act of God on a human mother, without having had a human father—was and is incompatible with Judaism. This belief was of Egyptian, not Israelitish, origin; it was the official account of the genesis of every Pharaoh since at least as early as the Fifth Dynasty; and, before this Egyptian formula was applied by the Gentile Christians to Jesus, it had been taken over from the Egyptians by the Greeks and had been applied to a number of eminent Greeks and Romans, including Plato, Alexander the Great, Scipio Africanus Major, and Jesus's own older contemporary Augustus.

The Adoptionist Christology of the third-century Patriarch of Antioch, Paul of Samosata, shows that, in Syria, Adoptionism died hard—as was to be expected in Syria, since Syria adjoins Palestine, the Jewish birthplace of Christianity, and was one of the earliest of Christianity's missionfields. Dr. Garsoian gives weight to the influence, on Christianity in Armenia, of Antioch and the Syrian church.[2] 'Syriac Christianity, with its Adoptionist character, was the first faith of Armenia.'[3] St. Gregory the Illuminator re-oriented Armenian Christianity; he attached it to Cappadocia in place of Syria, and he Hellenized it.[4] The struggle in Armenia between Syrian and Hellenic Christianity continued during the fourth and fifth centuries,[5] but eventually the Conceptionist Hellenic Christology triumphed in Armenia, as it did in almost the whole of Christendom, and in Armenia, as elsewhere, Syrian Adoptionism became heretical.[6] In Armenia, Adoptionism survived only as the heretical and persecuted religion of the Paulicians and their successors the T'ondrakeçi. Dr. Garsoian suggests that no direct connection between

---

[1] *The Key of Truth*, 12 (80), 45 (108), 11 (79).
[2] Garsoian, op. cit., p. 220.　　　　　　　　　　　　　　　[3] Op. cit., p. 223.
[4] Ibid.　　　　　　　　[5] Op. cit., p. 225.　　　　　　　　[6] Op. cit., pp. 226 and 227.

Armenian Adoptionism and Paul of Samosata's Adoptionism need be postulated. All that we need to postulate is a general connection between the original Adoptionist Christology of Christianity in Armenia and early Syrian Christianity.[1]

On the evidence of the medieval Armenian sources—for instance, King Gagik II (1042–5), as reported by Matthew of Edessa[2]—the medieval Tʻondrakeçi held the doctrine about baptism that is found in *The Key*. *The Key* insists both on the importance of baptism and also on the importance of its being delayed, following Christ's example, till the age of thirty.[3] This is, of course, the fundamental doctrine of Adoptionism. Arianism was a sophisticated revival of it, and Nestorianism was a partial reversion to it, as was recognized in 555 at the Monophysite Council of Dvin.

A corollary of the belief that Jesus was a normal human being who had been adopted as the son of God at his baptism, is the belief that other human beings too can become Christs if they are spiritually worthy. Paul of Samosata was accused of believing himself to be a potential Christ, and of being actually worshipped by his congregation.[4] The medieval Tʻondrakeçi were accused of holding this belief;[5] in *The Key of Truth* there is a liturgy for raising an adherent of the sect to the status of Christ through baptism;[6] and one of the nineteenth-century Tʻondrakeçi refugees from Chaurm deposed, in a recantation made to the authorities of the Armenian Monophysite Church, that he had heard a man named Gregory of Kalzwan, one of the adepts of the Tʻondrakeçi sect, say: 'Behold, I am the Cross; light your tapers on my two hands and give worship. I am able to give you salvation, just as much as the Cross and the Saints.'[7] The eighth-century Adoptionists in Asturia were debited with the same belief. They were said to say 'Et ille Christus et nos Christi', and this doctrine is elaborated in the *Symbolum fidei* attributed to their leader Elipandus: 'Si conformes sunt omnes sancti huic filio Dei secundum gratiam, profecto et cum adoptivo adoptivi, et cum advocato advocati, et cum Christo Christi.'[8] In the Eastern Orthodox wing of the

[1] Garsoian, op. cit., pp. 230 and 233.

[2] See Garsoian, op. cit., p. 159 and p. 212, n. 140.

[3] Garsoian, op. cit., pp. 152–4 (quoting *The Key of Truth*, 5–6 (74–5), 20–1 (87–8), 6 (75)) and pp. 159–61.

[4] According to Simeon of Beth Arsam, *Epistola de Barsauma*, in Assemani, *Bibliotheca Orientalis*, vol. i (Rome, 1719), pp. 346–58, on p. 347, quoted by Garsoian, op. cit., p. 211, n. 135, Paul of Samosata said of himself: 'Ego quoque, si voluero, Christus ero, quum ego et Christus unius eiusdemque simus naturae.'

[5] Garsoian, op. cit., pp. 161–2.

[6] *The Key of Truth*, 46 (108), 36 (100), 30 (95). See further Conybeare, Introduction, pp. xxxvii, xxxix, and cxliii–cxliv.

[7] Conybeare, *The Key of Truth*, Introduction, pp. xxvii and lii.

[8] *Epistula Heterii et Sancti Beati ad Elipandum*, cited by Conybeare in op. cit., Introduction, pp. clxxiii and clxxv.

Conceptionist Christian Church, this belief has survived the substitution of Conceptionism for Adoptionism as the doctrine of the great majority of Christians. Athanasius of Alexandria, himself, who was the arch-opponent of Adoptionism when this was revived in the sophisticated form of Arianism, has written Αὐτὸς γὰρ ἐνηνθρώπησεν ἵνα ἡμεῖς θεοποιηθῶ-μεν,[1] and deification (θέωσις) is the authorized goal of Eastern Orthodox Christian mysticism.[2]

Thus the Adoptionist Church, though it was Christian, not Dualist, was divided, like the Dualist sects, into two orders, an élite and the ordinary members.[3] It has been noted already[4] that there is a liturgy for the ordination of the electi in *The Key of Truth*. However, the two religions' respective concepts of perfection were diametrically opposed to each other. In the Dualist communities the electi were repudiating the World, which for them was intrinsically evil, by practising celibacy and asceticism, and, in virtue of their devoting themselves wholly to this course, they were the only complete practitioners of their religion. In the Adoptionist Christian Church the electi were demonstrating the possibility of redeeming and sanctifying the World, as Jesus had demonstrated this, in the act of being adopted by God as his sons. Like Jesus himself and his disciples, they were not celibates and not ascetics, and their freedom from celibacy and asceticism survived the eventual change-over of the East Roman branch of the Paulicians to a version of Dualism.[5]

The T'ondrakeçi Adoptionists in Armenia were iconoclasts. In *The Key of Truth*, the worship of images or of any other material objects, including crosses, is forbidden,[6] and iconoclasm is imputed to the Paulicians and to the T'ondrakeçi in our medieval Armenian sources.[7]

The evidence surveyed above brings out two salient features of Paulician, and subsequent T'ondrakeçi, doctrine and practice in Armenia: this sect was Adoptionist Christian, not Dualist, and in Armenia it remained true to its original tenets and practices from 555 (the date of our earliest information about these) till 1837 (the date of the beginning of the Monophysite Armenian ecclesiastical authorities' inquiry into the

---

[1] Athanasius, *Oratio de Humanâ Naturâ a Verbo Assumptâ et de Eius per Corpus ad Nos Adventu*, chap. 54, in Migne, *P.G.*, vol. xxv, col. 192. Athanasius is here following Irenaeus, *Contra Haereses*, Book III, chap. 19, § 6: εἰ μὴ συνηνώθη ὁ ἄνθρωπος τῷ Θεῷ, οὐκ ἂν ἐδυνήθη μετασχεῖν τῆς ἀφθαρσίας.

[2] See J. M. Hussey, *Church and Learning in the Byzantine Empire, 867–1185* (Oxford, 1937, University Press), chap. 2.

[3] Garsoian, op. cit., p. 155. According to Garsoian, op. cit., p. 163, n. 68, the existence of an order of the elect in the T'ondrakeçi community is indicated by the eleventh-century writer Aristakes of Lastivert in his *History*, xxiii, 123.   [4] See p. 673, with n. 6.

[5] See p. 663 of the present work. Asceticism is regarded with disapproval in *The Key of Truth* (see Garsoian, op. cit., p. 155).

[6] *The Key of Truth*, 19 (86) and 53–4 (115), quoted by Garsoian, op. cit., p. 156.

[7] References in Garsoian, op. cit., pp. 164–6 and 201–2.

religion of the refugees from Chaurm). Neither the Paulicians nor the T'ondrakeçi are accused of being Dualists by any of their earlier Conceptionist Christian Armenian opponents down to the eleventh-century historian Aristakes of Lastivert inclusive;[1] and indeed the Dualistic belief in the evilness of creation would have been incompatible with the Adoptionists' belief that human beings of flesh and blood, living normal lives in this World, could become adoptive sons of God. The accusation that they were Dualists was, however, made against the T'ondrakeçi by two Armenian writers, the monk Gregory of Narek, a contemporary of the East Roman Emperor Basil II (976–1025), and the máyistros Gregory the dhoux of théma Mesopotamía in the reign of Constantine IX Monomákhos (1042–55). Dr. Garsoian points out that both these writers were partisans of the East Roman Empire who were familiar with East Roman life and letters, and she makes the convincing suggestion that they were imputing unwarrantably to the T'ondrakeçi the Dualist doctrines that had been held, by their day, for some time past by the Paulicians in the East Roman Empire, as the two Gregories will have known.[2]

The doctrinal history of the Paulicians in the Empire is hard to elucidate, and this is unfortunate, because the East Roman Paulicians played a more important part than the Armenian Paulicians and T'ondrakeçi in the religious as well as in the political history of the western end of the Old World. The war of 843–72 between the East Roman Paulicians and the Imperial Government made a mark on the Empire's domestic history as well as on its relations with the Eastern Muslims. The East Roman Paulicians' change-over from Adoptionist Christianity to some form of Dualism seems likely to have been one of the causes of the subsequent spread of Dualism westward into Bulgaria, and beyond Bulgaria as far afield as Languedoc.

An initial difficulty that confronts us here is the uncertainty regarding the authenticity and the date and the authoritativeness of some of our Greek sources of information about the East Roman Paulicians.[3] Modern scholars have disagreed, and they have not yet arrived at a consensus. There seems at present to be a general acceptance of the authenticity and authoritativeness of the following documents: (a) the ninth-century (?) *Paulician Formula* designed to be recited by a recanting Paulician;[4] (b) the Patriarch Phótios's encyclical letter of 866;[5] (c) Phótios's four letters to John Spathários Khrysókheir (?);[6] (d) Phótios's Sermons II–IV.[7]

---

[1] Garsoian, op. cit., p. 98. [2] See Garsoian, op. cit., pp. 98–101 and 158.
[3] A detailed and penetrating study of the Greek sources has been made by Garsoian in op. cit., chap. I, pp. 27–79.
[4] Edited by G. Ficker in *Zeitschrift für Kirchengeschichte*, vol. xxvii (1906), pp. 453–5.
[5] Migne, *P.G.*, vol. cii, cols. 721/2.
[6] Migne, *P.G.*, vol. cii, Letters No. 1 (cols. 927/8), No. 9 (cols. 933/4), No. 19 (cols. 941/2), No. 26 (cols. 945/6). [7] Migne, *P.G.*, vol. cii, cols. 85/6–177/8.

The *Manichaean Formula*[1] seems to be authentic, but it is a hotch-potch of Paulician doctrine confounded with non-Paulician Manichaean doctrine, and its date is uncertain. It seems to be generally agreed that the Διήγησις περὶ τῆς Μανιχαίων ἀναβλαστήσεως,[2] which is attributed to Phótios, is spurious. Internal evidence shows that it must have been written later than 932.[3] The controversial works are (a) Petrus Hegumenus's Περὶ Παυλικιανῶν τῶν καὶ Μανιχαίων[4] and (b) Petrus Siculus's Ἱστορία χρειώδης ἔλεγχός τε καὶ ἀνατροπὴ τῆς κενῆς καὶ ματαίας αἱρέσεως τῶν Μανιχαίων τῶν καὶ Παυλικιανῶν λεγομένων,[5] accompanied by three sermons ascribed to the same author.[6] Grégoire held that Petrus Hegumenus's tract is an epitome of Petrus Siculus's *History*; other scholars—among them, Dr. Garsoian—hold that Petrus Hegumenus's tract is an authentic work of the mid ninth century,[7] and that Petrus Siculus's *History* is a compilation in which Petrus Hegumenus's tract has been laid under contribution as part of the compiler's material. A searching analysis of Petrus Siculus's work[8] leads Dr. Garsoian to the conclusion that there are a number of inconsistencies between different components of it and that at least two pieces of it are fakes. Dr. Garsoian holds that Petrus did not really visit the Paulicians' capital, Tephrikě, as he claims to have done in the year 869,[9] and the dedication of his *History* τῷ προέδρῳ τῆς Βουλγαρίας[10] is suspect, since the first Archbishop of Bulgaria was not appointed till 870. Indeed, the title of the *History* gives the lie to the alleged dedication. In the title, the *History* is said to be προσωποποιηθεῖσα ὡς πρὸς τὸν ἀρχιεπίσκοπον Βουλγαρίας, that is to say 'represented as being addressed to the Archbishop of Bulgaria'. The implication of these words in the title is that the dedication is fictional, not genuine.[11]

---

[1] Migne, *P.G.*, vol. i, cols. 1461/2–1471/2.

[2] Migne, *P.G.*, vol. cii, cols. 15/16–83/4.

[3] H. Grégoire, 'Les Sources de l'histoire des Pauliciens', in *Bulletin de l'Ac. Roy. Belge, Classe des Lettres*, 5ᵐᵉ série, vol. xxii (1936), pp. 95–114, on pp. 110–12; idem, 'Autour des Pauliciens', in *Byzantion*, vol. xi (1936), pp. 610–14, on pp. 612–13.

[4] Printed as an Appendix to J. Gieseler's edition of Petrus Siculus's *History* (Göttingen, 1849, Vandenhoeck & Ruprecht). Petrus Hegumenus's tract is identical with one of three variant versions of a chapter that has been inserted in the Chronicle of Georgius Monachus.

[5] Migne, *P.G.*, vol. civ, cols. 1239/40–1303/4.

[6] In Migne, *P.G.*, vol. cit., cols. 1305/6–1365/6.

[7] Georgius Monachus's Chronicle is thought to have been finished *circa* 866–7, and the chapter on the Paulicians, one version of which is identical with Petrus Hegumenus's tract, is included in all manuscripts of the Chronicle. The Paulicians are holding Orthodox Christian priests as prisoners (P. H., 17, 66–7), and this must have been during the war of 843–72. There are close correspondences, set out by Garsoian, op. cit., p. 53, n. 96, between P. H.'s tract and the *Paulician Formula*.

[8] Garsoian, op. cit., pp. 55–68.

[9] *History*, cols. 1241/2 and 1303/4. On this, see Garsoian, op. cit., pp. 70–3.

[10] Cols. 1241/2–1243/4.

[11] In his account of his alleged visit to Tephrikě, Petrus Siculus states (cols. 1241/2) that at Tephrikě he had heard from the Paulicians themselves that they were planning to send missionaries to Bulgaria, and (cols. 1243/4) that this is why he is addressing his work to the

However, Chapters 23–41 of Petrus Siculus's *History*, which give an account of the fortunes of the Paulicians in East Roman territory, from the heresiarchate of Constantine-Silvanus to the heresiarchate of Séryios-Tykhikós, is given credence by Dr. Garsoian, as well as by Grégoire. 'It is a systematic and orderly account of the sect's development . . . Many of the geographical locations in it can be verified, and a number of historical events mentioned are corroborated elsewhere. Finally, this section presents a homogeneous unit without repetitions or interpolations.'[1]

Dr. Garsoian suggests[2] that this section is the work of some contemporary of Séryios's who had apostatized from Paulicianism to Eastern Orthodox Christianity. She also guesses[3] that this hypothetical apostate made use, in writing this section, of Séryios's letters and also of a history of Paulicianism that had been written by the Paulicians themselves. The apostate author has given a hostile twist to this material, but its originally pro-Paulician tone can still be detected.

In any case, we have to make use of this section of Petrus Siculus's compilation; for we have no other information about the domestic history of the Paulicians in East Roman territory—in contrast to our knowledge of their political and military history, about which we are relatively well informed by East Roman chroniclers and historians.

Nothing can be made of the account of the origin of the Paulicians in Chapter 21 of Petrus Siculus's history[4]—a chapter that precedes that section of the work, namely Chapters 23–41, that is given credence by Dr. Garsoian as well as by Grégoire. The Paul who, in this passage, is credited with having been the eponym of the Paulicians' name (that is to say, of their depreciatory nickname) is said to have been a Manichee who had come as a missionary from Samosata to the Phanároia district in théma Armeniakoí and to have established there a Paulician community in a village that he renamed Episparís. The settlement at Episparís in Phanároia is likewise attributed to a Paul in Chapter 28,[5] but

Archbishop of Bulgaria. If this piece of Petrus Siculus's work is in truth a tenth-century fake, this particular item in it is at any rate *ben trovato*. In 869 Bulgaria, which had been converted to Eastern Orthodox Christianity in 864, was a bone of contention between the Constantinopolitan and the Roman Patriarchal sees, and in 867 Pope Nicholas I had noted the presence in Bulgaria of Armenian as well as Greek missionaries (*Responsa Papae Nicolai* to Khan Borís-Peter of Bulgaria in *Monumenta Germaniae Historica, Epistolae*, vol. vi, No. 106, p. 599); Migne, *Patrologia Latina*, vol. cxix, col. 1015; the reference is to Responsum No. 106). These Armenian missionaries may have been representatives of the Monophysite established church of Armenia, but alternatively they may have been Paulicians. If they were, they are likely to have come from Thrace, but they may have come from Tephrikě, and Petrus Siculus may have possessed this piece of information when he was composing his story of his fictitious mission.

[1] Garsoian, op. cit., p. 62.   [2] Op. cit., pp. 62–4.   [3] Op. cit., pp. 65–7.
[4] Petrus Siculus, cols. 1273/4, corresponding to Petrus Hegumenus, 1, 60. These two Greek texts are printed in parallel columns in Garsoian, op. cit., p. 61, n. 131.
[5] Cols. 1281/2–1283/4.

the Paul who is mentioned in this passage is said to have been an Armenian, and his migration is said to have been a flight from persecution. He is also said to have been the father of the third Paulician heresiarch, Gegnesios (Yenésios)-Timothy, who was a contemporary of the Emperor Leo III (717–41). Paul the father of Gegnesios may well be an historical figure, and, if he is, we may dismiss the Paul mentioned in Chapter 21 as a legendary doublet of the Paul of Chapter 28. The Paulicians are known to have been called by that name as early as 555; they were Adoptionist Christians; they had never been Manichees, and they never did become Manichees, though the Paulicians in the East Roman Empire did eventually become non-Manichaean Dualists. The Paul of Chapter 21 is said to have come from Samosata, not from Armenia, and this suggests that the story in Chapter 21 has been generated by a confusion of Paul the father of Gegnesios with the famous third-century Patriarch of Antioch Paul of Samosata, who was not a Manichee but was an Adoptionist Christian, as the original Paulicians in Armenia were.

The authentic history of the Paulicians in the East Roman Empire begins with the migration of an Armenian named Constantine from the district of Manalali, in Armenia,[1] to Kívossa, in the East Roman district of Kolóneia, in the reign of Heraclius's grandson, i.e. Constans II (641–68).[2] Here Constantine of Manalali ruled his Paulician community for twenty-seven years. He was killed in a persecution ordered by the Emperor Constantine IV (668–85).[3] Dr. Garsoian[4] dates the heresiarchate of Constantine 654–81. Her initial date suggests that Constantine may have fled from Armenia into the East Roman Empire because of the Armenians' capitulation to Mu'āwīyah in 653.[5] The terms included an undertaking, on the Arabs' side, to tolerate the Monophysite Armenian established church; but this stipulation may not have covered non-Monophysite Armenian Christians, so the capitulation may have given the Monophysites an opening for persecuting the Paulicians with the Arabs' acquiescence.

---

[1] Petrus Siculus, chap. 23, cols. 1275/6, calls Manalali 'a village in τῷ Σαμοσάτῳ τῆς Ἀρμενίας'. Samosata is not in Armenia; it is in the Syrian district Commagene. Manalali is a district, not a village, in Armenia, in the north-west corner of the country, on the northern branch of the upper Euphrates, to the east of the present-day town of Erzincan—that is to say, next door to the Kolóneia district of the East Roman Empire. Petrus Siculus's mistaken location of Manalali in his Chapter 28 may have been an attempt to reconcile Chapter 28 with Chapter 21. Paulicians are located in Manalali by the eleventh-century Armenian historian Aristakes of Lastivert (see Garsoian, op. cit., p. 147). Chaurm, the home of the nineteenth-century Armenian T'ondrakeçi refugees, lies close to Manalali (Conybeare, Introduction, pp. lxix–lxx).

[2] Petrus Siculus, *Historia*, chaps. 23–4, cols. 1275/6–1279/80.

[3] Op. cit., chaps. 24–5, cols. 1279/80.

[4] In op. cit., p. 121, n. 34.

[5] See pp. 85, 108, 395, and 398

According to Petrus Hegumenus,[1] the Paulicians (i.e. the Paulicians in the East Roman Empire) considered Constantine of Manalali, not Paul (the legendary Manichee from Samosata) to be their founder (τοῦτον οὖν ἔχουσιν ἀρχηγὸν τῶν διδασκάλων αὐτῶν, καὶ οὐχὶ τὸν Παῦλον). Of course, Constantine of Manalali was not in truth the founder of the sect itself. At least one hundred years before the date of his flight from Armenia to Rhomanía, the sect had already existed in Armenia and had already been known there by the nickname 'the followers of a minor Paul'. However, Constantine of Manalali did take two historic new departures. He established the first Paulician community on East Roman ground, and he responded to the challenge presented to his sect by their Armenian Conceptionist Christian adversaries' nickname for it.

The sect had been nicknamed 'followers of a minor Paul'. Constantine of Manalali claimed the greatest Paul, Paul the Apostle himself, as the sect's patron. Constantine of Manalali called himself Silvanus,[2] after the name of St. Paul's companion Silas in Macedonia,[3] and he gave the name 'Macedonia' to the church that he had founded at Kívossa. His successors in the leadership of the East Roman Paulicians followed his example by each taking the name of someone who is associated with St. Paul in the Acts of the Apostles or in St. Paul's own Epistles, and by naming each new Paulician church that they founded after one of those founded by St. Paul.

Three years after Constantine Silvanus had been killed, the leadership of the Paulicians at Kívossa-'Macedonia' was taken over by an ex-East Roman official, Symeon-Titus.[4] After three years in office, Symeon was killed, in his turn, by the Paulician apostate who had previously killed Constantine-Silvanus.[5] Evidently the East Roman Government's attitude towards the Paulician refugees in Rhomanía and towards their converts there was ambivalent. At first the Government may have welcomed them as victims of Armenians who were Monophysites and secessionists, and of Arabs who were enemies and Muslims. On second thoughts, the Imperial authorities may have reflected that the Paulicians were, nevertheless, not Orthodox Conceptionist Christians.

---

[1] Petrus Hegumenus, 2, 61.

[2] Petrus Siculus, *Historia*, in loc. cit.

[3] Acts 16: 19; 17: 4.

[4] According to Petrus Siculus, *Historia*, chaps. 24–5, cols. 1279/80, Symeon had been the official who had been sent by the Emperor Constantine IV to persecute Constantine-Silvanus. Garsoian points out, in op. cit., p. 65, that the story of Symeon is suspect. It is derived from East Roman Paulician sources dating from the time by which the East Roman Paulicians had already taken St. Paul's career as their ensample. A persecutor who is converted and eventually becomes a martyr in his turn follows in St. Paul's footsteps so precisely that the Paulician teller of the tale lays himself open to the suspicion of having taken liberties with the true history of Symeon in order to make it correspond to the history of St. Paul.

[5] Petrus Siculus, *Historia*, chaps. 26–7, cols. 1279/80–1281/2.

After this second persecution in the East Roman Empire, the Paulicians made a new start at a new point on East Roman ground. A Paulician named Paul fled from persecution (? in Armenia) to a village, renamed by him Episparís, in the Phanároia district,[1] which lay farther to the west in théma Armeniakoí than Kívossa-'Macedonia'.[2] This Paul was succeeded by his son Gegnesios (Yenésios)-Timothy, who was in office during the thirty years 717–46.[3] Gegnesios-Timothy was summoned to Constantinople by the Emperor Leo III under a safe conduct, to have a colloquy with the Ecumenical Patriarch. The heresiarch passed muster and returned safely to Episparís,[4] but he found it advisable to move out of East Roman territory into Manalali, and this was probably the site of his foundation, the church of 'Achaïa'. Gegnesios-Timothy died in 746 of the great plague.[5]

After Gegnesios's death, the Paulicians who had re-emigrated to Manalali came into conflict with the Muslims, who were the overlords of the Armenian principalities. A new leader, Joseph, succeeded in evacuating then from Manalali to Episparís, and became heresiarch under the name Epaphródhitos.[6] Here he got into trouble with the Orthodox ecclesiastical authorities, but he found asylum, within East Roman Asia Minor, far away to the south-west, at Antioch-up-against-Pisidia (a city that was commended to the Paulicians by St. Paul's missionary-work there),[7] and he founded the Paulician church of 'Philippi'.[8] Joseph-Epaphródhitos was in office *circa* 747–83.

An heresiarch who was in bad odour with the Orthodox Church could hardly have continued to live for three decades[9] in East Roman territory if the Imperial Government had not tacitly condoned his heterodoxy. Reading between the lines, we may guess that the Orthodox hierarchy, many of whom, no doubt, were crypto-iconodules under the iconoclast Emperors' regime, sought to make trouble for the Paulicians not only because these were heretics but also as an indirect way of making trouble for the Emperors. The Paulicians were heretics who were also iconoclasts. In their iconoclasm the Paulicians saw eye to eye with Leo III and Constantine V, and with Constantine V they also had in common an antipathy to Mariolatry. According to the Paulicians' belief, Jesus's mother had conceived him in the normal way as a result of sexual intercourse with a human father. However, the Paulicians' doctrine was

---

[1] Petrus Siculus, op. cit., chap. 28, cols. 1281/2–1283/4.

[2] Théma Armeniakoí included both Kívossa and Episparís until the detachment of the Kolóneia district from it, and its erection into a separate théma, at some date before 863. (See pp. 245–6 and 257.)

[3] Petrus Siculus, *Historia*, chap. 28, cols. 1283/4.

[4] Op. cit., chap. 29, cols. 1283/4.   [5] Op. cit., chap. 29, cols. 1285/6.

[6] Op. cit., chaps. 30–1, cols. 1285/6.   [7] Acts 13: 13–52.

[8] Petrus Siculus, *Historia*, chap. 31, cols. 1285/6–1287/8; chap. 38, cols. 1297/8.

[9] Op. cit., chap. 31, cols. 1285/6.

not identical with even Constantine V's, for, officially at least, Constantine V was an Orthodox Conceptionist. We may guess that Constantine V's motive for tolerating the Paulicians was more military than theological.[1] During their temporary return to Manalali the East Roman Paulicians had fallen foul of the Empire's enemies the Muslims. The Paulicians themselves were first-rate soldiers. There were Paulicians among the Armenians from Theodosiopolis and the Syrians from Malatīyah whom Constantine V planted in Thrace in 755 or 757.[2] This plantation was evidently a move in Constantine V's attempt to conquer Bulgaria in the twenty-years' war of 755–75, and this war had precedence over all other military business on Constantine V's agenda.

After Joseph-Epaphródhitos's death, there was a contest over the succession, and the Paulician community in Rhomanía split into two factions. Joseph's immediate successor Vaánês (Vahan) was Armenian, like Joseph himself and like all Joseph's predecessors in Rhomanía except Symeon,[3] but the victor, Séryios-Tykhikós, was an East Roman whose birthplace was a village near Távia in théma Armeniakoí. According to Petrus Siculus, Vaánês claimed that he, Vaánês, had remained faithful to the doctrine that had been transmitted to him by Joseph-Epaphródhitos, whereas 'You, Séryios, are a newcomer who has never seen any of our teachers or kept company with them' (Σὺ νεωστὶ κατεφάνης, καὶ οὐδένα τῶν διδασκάλων ἡμῶν ἑώρακας ἢ συμπαρέμεινας).[4] Séryios, however, was obdurate, and he 'split the sect in two'.[5] After Séryios's death, when Séryios's partisans were thirsting to massacre Vaánês's partisans, one of Séryios's disciples, Theódhotos, tried to restrain them by reminding them that, before Séryios came, 'we all held one faith'.[6]

Séryios held office from 801 to 835, and, during the last twenty-one of these thirty-five years, the Emperors were, once again, iconoclasts. Yet, after Séryios had founded one new Paulician church, 'Laodhíkeia', at Koinokhórion in the district of Neo-Kaisáreia (Niksar) in théma Armeniakoí,[7] the Emperor—either the iconodule Michael I (811–13) or his iconoclast successor Leo V (813–20)—instructed two local officials, the Bishop of Neo-Kaisáreia and a civil servant, to investigate Séryios's activities.[8] Séryios and his adherents murdered both these representatives of the East Roman Government, and they then sought and found asylum with the Amīr of Malatīyah. The Amīr settled them in his own

---

[1] See Obolensky, op. cit., p. 61.

[2] Σύρους τε καὶ Ἀρμενίους, οὓς ἤγαγεν ἀπὸ Θεοδοσιουπόλεως καὶ Μελιτηνῆς, εἰς τὴν Θρᾴκην μετῴκισεν, ἐξ ὧν ἐπλατύνθη ἡ αἵρεσις τῶν Παυλικιανῶν (Theophanes, p. 429; cf. Nic. Patr., p. 66). [3] See Garsoian, op. cit., p. 183, with n. 158.

[4] Petrus Siculus, *Historia*, chap. 40, cols. 1299/1300.

[5] Op. cit., chap. 40, cols. 1299/1300. [6] Op. cit., ibid.

[7] At this date, théma Kolóneia, in which Neo-Kaisáreia is located by Constantine Porphyrogenitus (*De Thematibus*, p. 31), had not yet been detached from théma Armeniakoí (see the present work, pp. 245–6 and 257). [8] Petrus Siculus, op. cit., chap. 41, cols. 1301/2.

territory, at Argaoún.[1] Séryios founded a second Paulician Church, 'Kolossaí', at Argaoún, and a third, 'Éphesos', at Massīsah (Mopsou-estía) in the territory of the Muslim amirate of Tarsós. From his new bases in Muslim territory, Séryios led raids into East Roman territory till 835, when he was murdered.[2] After Séryios's death in 835, his partisans almost exterminated Vaánês's partisans, in spite of Theódhotos's efforts to prevent the massacre. Moreover, Séryios's partisans now carried Séryios's innovations to greater lengths.[3]

There is a significant coincidence of dates between several events: the splitting of the Paulician community in Rhomanía in consequence of Séryios's innovations; the breach between Séryios's partisans and the East Roman Imperial Government, in spite of the fact that, in the course of Séryios's heresiarchate, the Government became once again iconoclast; the virtual extermination, after Séryios's death, of Vaánês's followers, who had remained faithful to the sect's original doctrines; and the foundation, in Armenia, of the T'ondrakeçi sect, whose doctrines appear to have been identical with the original doctrines of the Pauli-cians. If the date of the foundation of the T'ondrakeçi is the earlier of the two alternative possible dates, namely some year between the years 833 and 855, which is Gregory Máyistros's dating,[4] this event followed at the heels of the crushing of the adherents, in Rhomanía, of the original form of Paulicianism, and the carrying to further lengths there of Séryios's innovations. The original form of Paulicianism was now replaced in Rhomanía by a new form of this religion, but in Armenia the original form reasserted itself, and it maintained itself down to the nineteenth century at Chaurm, next door to the sect's Armenian homeland, Mana-lali. The ninth-century breach between the palaeo-Paulicians in Armenia and the neo-Paulicians in Rhomanía seems to have been complete. When the East Roman neo-Paulicians were fighting the East Roman Government with their backs to the wall, the support that they received from beyond the frontier came, not from their own alienated co-religionists, but from the Muslims.

What were the innovations introduced into the Paulicians' original doctrines by Séryios and his followers? There is a consensus among modern scholars that in Rhomanía, in contrast to Armenia, the Paulicians were (at least eventually) Dualists and consequently also Docetists in their Christology.[5] The mere change of location goes far towards ac-

---

[1] Op. cit., chap. 41, cols. 1301/2.

[2] Op. cit., chap. 36, cols. 1293/4; chap. 41, cols. 1301/2. See further Garsoian, op. cit., p. 68, n. 153, and p. 114, n. 5, for the locations of Séryios's three churches and for the chrono-logical order of their foundation-dates.

[3] Petrus Siculus, *Historia*, chap. 41, cols. 1301/2.   [4] See p. 670, with n. 3.

[5] The Paulician heresiarchs, down to the innovator Séryios-Tykhikós inclusive, are not accused of either Dualism or Docetism by their Orthodox Christian opponents (Garsoian,

counting for a change of doctrine. It is not surprising that there was no doctrinal change in Manalali. This district is walled-off from the rest of the World by ranges of huge mountains (I have seen Manalali from the air). Théma Armeniakoí opens out on to the coast of the Black Sea and has easy lines of communication overland with other parts of Asia Minor. Both by sea and overland, théma Armeniakoí was in touch with Constantinople. It was as natural that Paulicianism should change when it was transplanted to théma Armeniakoí as it was that Bogomilism should change when it was transplanted to Constantinople. But why did the change undergone by Paulicianism in théma Armeniakoí take the particular form of a change from Adoptionist monistic Christianity to Dualism? This particular change is perhaps sufficiently accounted for by the Paulician immigrants' and their native converts' experience in théma Armeniakoí of East Roman life. The grinding pressure of taxation, the social injustice of the widening gulf between rich and poor, and the devastation caused by the Muslim raids across the Empire's eastern border would be enough, in combination, to convince the victims of these tribulations that the World was evil and that it must therefore be the handiwork of an evil creator.

In the preliminary considerations in this chapter it has been noted that it is prudent to be sceptical about the alleged identity of a medieval heresy with some ancient heresy, when this identification is made by the medieval heresy's contemporary opponents. The ninth-century Orthodox Christian opponents of East Roman Paulicianism were determined to discredit it by identifying its Dualism with Manichaeism, but there is conclusive evidence that this identification is untenable.[1] The ninth-century Dualist Paulicians anathematized Mani.[2] The Paulicians' Orthodox opponents insinuated that this was a trick designed to put the Orthodox off the scent, but the onus of proving the truth of this insinuation lies on the shoulders of the makers of it. The twelfth-century Monophysite Armenian Katholikós Nerses IV Šnorhali (1166/7–1172/3) distinguishes between the T'ondrakeçi and the Manichees in Armenia.[3] In the 'Abbasid dominions, Manichaeism was persecuted,[4] whereas the

---

op. cit., p. 177). Séryios is alleged to have been worshipped by his adherents (Petrus Siculus, *Historia*, chap. 31, cols. 1287/8). This was traditional practice in the Adoptionist Christian church, from the third-century worship of Paul of Samosata to the nineteenth-century worship of Gregory of Kalzwan. However, Séryios is said (by Petrus Siculus, ibid.) also to have called himself Paraclete, and in this he was following a precedent set by Montanus and by Mani (see Obolensky, op. cit., p. 20).

[1] See Garsoian, op. cit., pp. 188, 193–6, 203. Cf. A. Borst, *Die Katharer* (Stuttgart, 1953, Hiersemann), p. 66, n. 31; H. Söderberg, *La Religion des Cathares* (Uppsala, 1949, Almqvist & Wiksell), p. 37.

[2] Petrus Siculus, *Historia*, chap. 4, cols. 1245/6, and chap. 24, cols. 1277/8.

[3] See Garsoian, op. cit., p. 101; Conybeare, Introduction to *The Key of Truth*, p. cxxxii, with quotations from Nerses in Appendix V.   [4] Garsoian, op. cit., p. 193.

East Roman Paulicians were welcomed as allies by the Muslim wardens of the 'Abbasid Caliphate's north-western marches.

If the Dualism that the Paulicians developed in théma Armeniakoí owed any of its inspiration to an older Dualistic sect, the most likely historical source of influence would be Marcionism.[1] Théma Armeniakoí was approximately conterminous with the former Kingdom of Pontus (Pontic Cappadocia). Pontus was Marcion's homeland; and, if his followers survived anywhere into the early Middle Ages, this is the place where we should expect to find them. The neo-Paulicians' Dualism is akin to the Marcionites'.[2] It is a spiritual contrast between two gods; it is not, like Manichaean Dualism, a contrast between light and darkness taken almost literally. Moreover, the neo-Paulicians' selective canon of Scripture seems to have been almost identical with the Marcionites'.[3] However, the hypothesis that ninth-century Paulician Dualism may have been inspired by Marcionism has been rejected by some eminent modern authorities, and it remains non-proven.[4] In théma Armeniakoí in the ninth century, the evilness of the World was manifest, and Dualism was an obvious theological inference from experience of the bitter facts of life.

(iii) *The Bogomils*

If it is true that the hardness and injustice of the conditions of daily life go far to account for the change-over to Dualism from Adoptionist Christianity in the Paulician community in théma Armeniakoí in the ninth century, the same explanation will account, *a fortiori*, for the rise and the spread, in the tenth century, of the Bogomil form of Dualism in Bulgaria.

Bulgaria was then what is called nowadays a 'developing' country; and countries that are in this stage suffer from the peculiar strain of being impelled constantly to strive to catch up with their more highly 'developed' neighbours. The region in the interior of the Balkan Peninsula over which the Danubian Bulgars had extended their rule in and after the year 680 had already been backward and afflicted before that. Except for upper Macedonia (in the classical meaning of this geographical name), the territory that was to become Bulgaria had not been incorporated in the Graeco-Roman World till the Emperor Augustus had carried the Roman Empire's frontier forward in this quarter up to the south bank of the lower Danube. This interior of the Balkan Peninsula had been poorer than the surrounding regions—Greece, Asia Minor, and Peninsular Italy—and, when the Empire had fallen into decline, this

---

[1] See Runciman, op. cit., pp. 60–1.
[2] See Obolensky, op. cit., pp. 45–8.
[3] Puech in *Cosmas le Prêtre*, p. 174, n. 3; Obolensky, op. cit., pp. 39 and 47.
[4] See Garsoian, op. cit., pp. 204–5 and 232–3.

still backward region had been drained of man-power by the demands of the Roman Army and had been devastated by repeated barbarian invasions that had culminated, but had not ceased, with the Slav *Völkerwanderung* and the subsequent lodgement of the ex-nomad Turkish-speaking Bulgars in part of the area that the Slav immigrants had re-peopled.

The establishment and maintenance of an independent Bulgarian state in the heart of the European domain of the East Roman Empire had been a *tour de force*, and Bulgaria had barely survived the East Roman Emperor Constantine V's supreme effort to reconquer it in the war of 755–75. Thus, when, in the ninth century, the East Roman Empire began to revive, Bulgaria, though still unconquered, remained relatively backward both economically and culturally. At the same time, Bulgaria could not hope to maintain its separate identity permanently unless it succeeded in diminishing the difference between itself and the East Roman Empire in their respective levels of civilization. Bulgaria could civilize itself only in so far as it could manage to adopt the Byzantine way of life. Even before the conversion of Khan Borís-Michael to Christianity in 864, his predecessors had been importing East Roman architects and artists and engravers to do the work.[1] The extravagance had been modest, but, even so, it must have imposed an excessive burden on Bulgaria's Slav peasantry. The contemporary Greek peasantry in the East Roman Empire was hard pressed, even at the peak of its prosperity, by the East Roman Imperial Government's demands, in spite of the superiority of the Empire's economy to Bulgaria's. The pressure on the Bulgarian peasantry was aggravated when in 870 Borís opted definitively for the Eastern Orthodox form of Christianity. Though one faction of the Bulgar nobility opposed the introduction of Christianity and its con-comitant the Byzantine way of life, these diehards were repeatedly defeated by the Crown and its supporters. This Byzantinizing faction in Bulgaria sought to emulate the style of the East Roman courtiers and large landowners, and the consequent increase in the expensiveness of the Bulgarian lay 'establishment' was doubled by the introduction of an Orthodox Christian hierarchy in the sumptuous East Roman style.

The Bulgarian peasantry was subjected to a further excruciating turn of the screw by the perverse policy of Khan Borís's son and second successor, Khan Symeon (893–927). Symeon's thorough-going Byzantine education at Constantinople had inspired him with both a political and a cultural ambition. His political ambition was to unite the East Roman Empire with Bulgaria under his own rule as the common Emperor of the two states, and, if he could not achieve this, he was resolved to

---

[1] The evidence is the inscriptions, in phonetically spelled Greek, that have been found in the Palace at Aboba-Pliska and elsewhere (see p. 359).

arrogate to himself the title and status of Emperor in Bulgaria, and to elevate the Eastern Orthodox Archbishop of Bulgaria to the title and status of a Patriarch who would be ecclesiastically independent of the Patriarch of Constantinople but would be subordinate politically *de facto* to the Bulgarian Imperial Crown, as the Patriarch of Constantinople was to the East Roman. At the same time, Symeon ardently pursued the expensive cultural policy of Byzantinizing the Bulgarian way of life.

Symeon's policy was a disastrous failure on its political and social side.[1] He failed to subjugate the East Roman Empire in his unprovoked aggressive war of 913–27. By 924 he had found, as he had already found in his previous, less wanton, war of 894–6, that, for Bulgarian arms, Constantinople was impregnable. When, after Symeon's death in 927, his son and successor Peter made peace with the East Roman Empire, Bulgaria's gains from a war that had been far more exhausting for her than for her opponent were only titular, not substantial. Rhomanós Lekapênós bought peace at the cheap price of recognizing the style and title of Emperor and Patriarch, which Symeon had assumed, unilaterally, for himself and for his archbishop. As corollaries, the Bulgarian Imperial ambassador was given precedence over all other lay ambassadors at Constantinople; the Emperor Peter was given an East Roman Imperial bride, Rhomanós's granddaughter María; and María's Bulgarian husband was paid an East Roman subsidy in the face-saving form of an annual allowance for his wife.[2]

These concessions in the field of protocol were, no doubt, gratifying for the Bulgarian Crown and Court, but they brought with them no relaxation of economic pressure for the Bulgarian peasantry. Nor did the peasantry—except, perhaps, in Kutmitčevica, which had been St. Clement's and St. Naum's mission-field[3]—gain any spiritual or cultural benefit from the introduction into Bulgaria of a Byzantinized Eastern Orthodox hierarchy. A great gulf remained fixed between the Bulgarian peasantry and the Bulgarian 'establishment', ecclesiastical as well as lay,[4] in spite of the fact that, from 885 or soon after, the Bulgarian Eastern Orthodox clergy and liturgy were Slavophone. Byzantinization, even in an indirect form, through the medium of the Macedonian Slavonic language, did bestow on Bulgaria the gift of a higher civilization; but, at the very time when Bulgaria had laid herself open to Byzantinization by submitting to conversion, the Byzantine civilization itself had begun to ail in its own East Roman homeland.[5]

---

[1] Obolensky's severe verdict in op. cit., pp. 90–1 and 109, is fully justified.
[2] See pp. 360–2.   [3] See pp. 104–5.
[4] See Runciman, op. cit., p. 66; Obolensky, op. cit., p. 91.
[5] See Obolensky, op. cit., p. 108.

In another context,[1] it has been noted that the turn of the tide in 863 in the perennial Romano-Muslim war on the Empire's eastern front, followed by the launching of an East Roman counter-offensive in 926, had tipped the domestic balance of social forces within the Empire in favour of the large landowners, to the detriment of the peasantry. It has also been noted[2] that, in the struggle for the land between the peasants and the large landowners in the Empire, the hard winter of 927/8 marked a turning-point, and that the tenth-century series of East Roman Imperial agrarian laws failed to arrest the agrarian revolution by which the peasantry was now being ruined. The winter of 927/8, following immediately after a fifteen-years-long war, had afflicted Bulgaria as well as Constantinople and Asia Minor.[3] The East Roman social sickness now infected Bulgaria; its carrier was the inflowing Byzantine culture. 'The Bogomil heresy was born amidst peasants whose physical misery made them conscious of the wickedness of things.'[4]

One reaction to the harshness and injustice of secular life for the masses in the Byzantine World was a great increase in the number of monks and monasteries,[5] and, in the tenth century, this movement was under way in Bulgaria as well as in Rhomanía. Monasteries became attractive as oases of peace and stability, in which the inmates could pursue the quest for holiness, thanks to their being released there from the hopeless task of fighting a losing battle against tax-officers, raiders, and landlords.[6] Members of the rich minority, who were not themselves impelled towards the monastic life by intolerable economic pressure, salved their consciences by founding and endowing new monasteries as a means of acquiring spiritual merit. In the East Roman Empire by the seventh decade of the tenth century, the Emperor Nikêphóros II Phokás was curbing this movement, at the risk, as he recognized, of incurring extreme odium.[7] The pullulation of monks and monasteries had, indeed, become a serious social evil by that date. Some monks were truly holy, and perhaps more of them were morbidly ascetic; but the increase in their numbers inevitably lowered the level of their average moral standard;[8] and corporately the monasteries, like the non-monastic ecclesiastical hierarchy, were exacting landlords and greedy land-grabbers, as the tenth-century East Roman agrarian legislation reveals. Moreover, they were, on Nikêphóros II's evidence, economically inefficient landlords by comparison with their lay counterparts. The Bogomils were attracted by the ideals of Eastern Orthodox monasticism and at the same time were repelled by the travesty and the betrayal of these ideals by

---

[1] See pp. 34–6.   [2] See pp. 145–7.
[3] Obolensky, op. cit., p. 101.   [4] See Obolensky, op. cit., pp. 103–4.
[5] See D. Savramis: *Zur Soziologie des byzantinischen Mönchtums* (Leiden/Köln, 1962, Brill).
[6] See Obolensky, op. cit., pp. 103–4.   [7] See pp. 165–6.
[8] See Obolensky, op. cit., p. 104.

the Orthodox Christian monks and monasteries in Bulgaria. Cosmas the Priest, in the second part of his treatise, in which he castigates the errors of the Orthodox, devotes one chapter[1] to the perils of the monastic life and another[2] to 'the bad monks'. Tsar Peter reaped what Khan Symeon had sown. Bogomilism was the crop.

Only the first of the three parts of Cosmas's treatise is directed against the Bogomils. The second and the third part are addressed to the Eastern Orthodox Christian 'establishment' in Bulgaria, both clerical and lay. In Part III, in which Cosmas gives his advice to the Orthodox, he catalogues their faults;[3] he points out the unperformed duties of the rich;[4] he rebukes the educated rich for deliberately keeping their culture to themselves, instead of sharing their books with the poor;[5] he laments the negligence of the priests.[6]

> Whence come these wolves, the bad dogs of the heretical doctrine? Do they not come from the negligence and ignorance of the pastors? Whence come 'the thieves and robbers'[7]—that is to say, the sins and iniquities? Is it not because people do not receive instruction from the bishops?[8] . . .
>
> It is we who are responsible for the sins of our people and for their being put to death; it is we who have to render an account of this[9]. . .
>
> Holy fathers and pastors, and every reader of this book: let none of you blame my ignorance and lack of intelligence. 'The wind bloweth where it listeth.'[10] No, you should rather praise and glorify God who performs miracles and who has put human words in my mouth, as he put them in the mouth of Balaam's ass. A dog, too, spoke to the inhabitants of Sodom to denounce their shameless ways.[11]

Cosmas has controverted the Bogomil heretics without indulging in vituperation, and he has arraigned and reproached his own co-religionists for having caused the scandal that has provoked this heretical revolt against the established Orthodox Church. Cosmas's attitude is as admirable as it is rare. Few authors of polemical works have had the clearsightedness and honesty and courage to lay the blame for heresy on the shoulders of an 'establishment' that has failed to do its duty. Few assailants of an alien religion have given their readers such objective and trustworthy information about it.

The best of all possible sources of information about the tenets and practices of a religion is, of course, this religion's own canonical literature. For the T'ondrakeçi—and therefore almost certainly for the pre-Sergian Paulicians too—we possess evidence of this first-hand kind in *The Key of Truth*. For Catharism of the Desenzano school, we possess the *Liber de*

---

[1] Chap. 23 on pp. 99–100 in Puech and Vaillant's translation.
[2] Chap. 24, pp. 100–5.   [3] Chap. 28, pp. 116–18.   [4] Chap. 29, pp. 118–20.
[5] Chap. 30, pp. 120–3.   [6] Chap. 31, pp. 123–7. Cf. Part I, chap. 8, p. 64.
[7] John 10: 1.   [8] Chap. 31, p. 124.   [9] Chap. 31, pp. 126–7.
[10] John 3: 8.   [11] Chap. 22, conclusion, p. 127.

Duobus Principiis,[1] discovered in 1939. For Bogomilism, we possess only a Latin translation of a book called *Interrogatio Iohannis*.[2] The doctrines expounded in this book are manifestly Bogomil,[3] and the book itself (presumably the Slavonic original) is said to have been brought from Bulgaria by the Cathar bishop of Concorezzo, Nazarius (1150–1235).[4] Sacconi had once met Nazarius and had been told by him that he had learned his doctrine 'ab episcopo et filio maiore ecclesiae Bulgariae' about sixty years earlier than that.[5] Our first-hand information is thus not so good in the case of the Bogomils as it is in the cases of the T'ondrakeçi and the Desenzano Cathars. At the same time, it is better than our information about the post-Sergian Dualist Paulicians, with whose doctrines we are acquainted solely through the accounts given by Orthodox Christian adversaries who falsely identify them with the probably by then extinct western Manichees. Moreover, our second-hand information about the Bogomils is contemporary and is also trustworthy, in spite of its coming from hostile sources.

For the original tenth-century Bogomilism, we have factual evidence in the treatise of Cosmas the Priest, which has already been quoted. This treatise appears to have been written in or immediately after 972,[6] and it describes the tenets and practices of the Bogomils in the writer's own day. No doubt in places Cosmas misrepresents the facts, but at any rate he does not try to identify Bogomilism with any earlier heresy.[7] For the eleventh-century Bogomils in Asia Minor, we have a first-hand account,[8] by a monk named Efthýmios, belonging to the Monastery Τῆς Περιβλέπτου

---

[1] Text edited by A. Dondaine, together with Sacconi's *Summa* (Rome, 1939, Istituto Storico Domenicano S. Sabina); French translation by R. Nelli in *Écritures cathares* (Paris, 1959, Denoël), pp. 67–201.

[2] Latin text edited by R. Reitzenstein in *Die Vorgeschichte der christlichen Taufe* (Leipzig and Berlin, 1929), pp. 297–311; French translation in Nelli, op. cit., pp. 34–66.

[3] See Puech in *Cosmas le Prêtre*, p. 130, n. 1; Nelli in op. cit., pp. 31–3; Runciman, op. cit., pp. 85–6; Obolensky, op. cit., pp. 226–8 and 242.

[4] On the Carcassonne MS. of this Latin translation, the inquisitors have noted: 'Hoc est secretum haereticorum de Concorrezio portatum de Bulgaris ⟨a⟩ Nazario suo episcopo, plenum erroribus'.

[5] Sacconi, *Summa*, Dondaine's text, p. 76.

[6] Cosmas notes (*Treatise*, Introduction, p. 54 in Puech and Vaillant's translation), that the priest Bogomil first began to preach his heresy in Bulgaria in the reign of the Emperor Peter. Since Peter reigned from 927 to 969, Cosmas must have been writing later than 969. Cosmas exhorts his readers to imitate 'the new [i.e. modern, not to be confused with John Chrysostom] priest John, whom many of you know as the former pastor and Exarch in Bulgaria' (chap. 23, p. 127). This John had dedicated a work to Symeon as 'prince', i.e. presumably before the year in which Symeon assumed the title 'Emperor' (Vaillant, in op. cit., p. 22). Symeon began to call himself 'Emperor' in 915 according to Vaillant in loc. cit., but not till 925 according to Obolensky (see the present work, p. 360). In any case, John is unlikely to have been still alive very much later than 969. Cosmas's references to the extreme tribulations through which Bulgaria is passing (these references are collected by Vaillant in op. cit., pp. 23–4) suggest that he was writing during, or very soon after, the catastrophic events of 969–72.   [7] Puech in *Cosmas le Prêtre*, p. 146.

[8] Greek text edited by G. Ficker, *Die Phundagiagiten* (Leipzig, 1908).

in Constantinople, of the trial and condemnation at Akmóneia in théma Opsíkion, Efthýmios's homeland, of a missionary of the sect of the Phoundayiayítai (τῶν Φουνδαγιαγιτῶν),[1] whom Efthýmios identifies with the Bogomils in the title of his letter. The authenticity of Efthýmios's account of the eleventh-century Bogomils is attested by Efthýmios's naïve admission that he had tried and failed to find an account of them in St. John of Damascus's *De Haeresibus*.[2] Evidently his own observation was his only source of information about them. As for the early-twelfth-century Bogomils at Constantinople who were detected *circa* 1110,[3] we have the section on them in Efthýmios Zighavênós's *Panoplía Dogmatica*.[4] Zighavênós had been commissioned to write the *Panoplía* by the Emperor Aléxios I.[5] Zighavênós had interviewed the leader of the Constantinopolitan Bogomil community, a physician named Basil, before Basil had been put to death, and he had studied the *procès verbal* of Basil's oral statement of his tenets.[6] Basil had made this statement to the Emperor Aléxios, and it had been taken down, without Basil's being aware of this, by a secretary hidden behind a curtain.[7]

Finally we have the evidence of the apostate Cathar Sacconi, writing in 1230, that in his time there were sixteen Cathar churches in all, and that two of them, the 'Ecclesia Burgaliae' (variant reading 'Bulgariae') and the 'Ecclesia Dugunthiae' (variant reading 'Dugranicae'),[8] were the original churches from which all the rest were derived.[9] There is also Western evidence that the adherents of these two mother churches of the Western Cathars—the 'Ordo de Bulgaria' and the 'Ordo de Dugrutia'—differed from each other in doctrine. The Church of Dugrutia-Dugunthia-Dugranica held that there were two gods on an equal footing with each other eternally.[10] Presumably the 'Ordo de Bulgaria' held the less radical form of Dualism that is attributed to the tenth-century

---

[1] Efthýmios of *Τῆς Περιβλέπτου* says that these heretics were called Phoundayiayítai in théma Opsíkion, but Bogomils in théma Kivyrrhaiótai and in the west. Obolensky points out that Phoundayiayítai means 'bagmen', and that it is a Greek translation of the Bulgarian Slavonic name 'Torbeshi' (op. cit., p. 178, n. 1, and pp. 166–7).

[2] See Puech in *Cosmas le Prêtre*, p. 141.

[3] See Obolensky, op. cit., p. 198, with Appendix III on pp. 275–6.

[4] Migne, *P.G.*, vol. cxxx, cols. 1289–1332, *Panoplía*, section 27, analysed by Obolensky in op. cit., pp. 206–19, and by Runciman in op. cit., pp. 74–80.

[5] Anna Comnena, *Alexias*, Book XV, chap. 9.

[6] Puech in *Cosmas le Prêtre*, p. 142.   [7] *Alexias*, Book XV, chaps. 8–9.

[8] Dondaine, op. cit., p. 63, and Obolensky, op. cit., p. 158, suggest that 'Dugranicae' may be a garbled rendering of the name of a Slav tribe, the Dragovichi. One section of the Dragovichi lived near Thessaloníkê, but there was another section near Philippopolis. The Metropolitan of Philippopolis was also Exarch *Τῆς Δραγουβιτίας*. See further Obolensky, op. cit., pp. 158–62.

[9] The Latin text of this passage is printed in Dondaine, p. 70, and Obolensky, p. 157.

[10] 'Haeretici qui habent ordinem suum de Dugrutia . . . credunt et praedicant . . . duos Dominos esse sine principio et sine fine': Bonacursus, *Contra Catharos*, cited by Obolensky in op. cit., p. 162, n. 1.

Bulgarian Bogomils by Cosmas and to the twelfth-century Constantino-politan Bogomils by Zighavênós.

In the seventh and eighth decades of the twelfth century, these two south-east European churches competed with each other for winning the adherence of the Cathar churches in the West. At a council held in 1167 by the Cathars of Languedoc at St. Félix-de-Caraman, near Albi, the radical Dualist Bishop 'Niquinta' (i.e. Nikĕtas) of Constantinople converted the Languedoc Cathars to his doctrine, after having already converted the Cathars of Lombardy. But, after the deaths of Nikĕtas and of his convert Mark the Deacon, whom Nikĕtas had installed as Cathar bishop in Lombardy and had then brought with him to the Council in Languedoc, an emissary of the less radical south-east European Dualist church re-converted the Cathars of Milan.[1] In Italy by the year 1190, there were six Cathar churches, split into three different persuasions. The Church of Milan was, by then, once again moderate Dualist; the Churches of Garda, Florence, and Spoleto were radical Dualist; the Churches of Verona and Vicenza were of the same persuasion as the Bosnian Patarenes.[2]

According to Cosmas,[3] the first preacher of the Bogomil heresy was a priest named Bogomil. Vaillant believes[4] that this is a pseudonym, like the Pauline names assumed by the Paulician heresiarchs in East Roman territory, but it may equally well have been Bogomil's baptismal name. The meaning of the name is in dispute.[5]

The tenets and the practices of Bogomil's followers are set out by Cosmas and Zighavênós. The time-interval between the dates at which these two accounts were written is about 150 years, but there is no in-compatibility between them. Zighavênós's account is the more detailed and more precise of the two, and this may indicate that, at Constantinople, the Bogomils' doctrines and rites had been elaborated; but it may also merely be due to Zighavênós's being a more expert theologian than Cosmas, and to his dealing with the Bogomils at greater length. Cosmas rightly reserves more than half of his treatise[6] for rebuking his own Orthodox Christian co-religionists.

[1] See Runciman, op. cit., pp. 72–3; Obolensky, op. cit., pp. 162 and 288–9; Borst, op. cit., pp. 96–7 and 100. [2] See Borst, op. cit., p. 101.
[3] Part I, chap. 1 (Introduction), p. 54. [4] *Cosmas le Prêtre*, p. 27.
[5] In modern Bulgarian, 'mil' means 'dear', and Obolensky, in op. cit., p. 117, n. 4, inter-prets 'Bogomil' as meaning 'dear to God', and as being a translation of the familiar Greek name Θεόφιλος. However, Vaillant, in loc. cit., n. 2, denies that 'mil' can mean 'dear' in Old Slavonic. According to him, its only Old-Slavonic meaning is 'pitiable'. He interprets 'Bogomil' as meaning 'deserving of God's pity', and this interpretation is supported by Zighavênós: Βόγον μὲν γὰρ ἡ τῶν Βουλγάρων γλῶσσα καλεῖ τὸν Θεόν, μίλον δὲ τὸ ἐλέησον. Εἴη δ' ἂν Βογόμιλος κατ' αὐτοὺς ὁ τοῦ Θεοῦ τὸν ἔλεον ἐπισπώμενος (Migne, *P.G.*, vol. cxxx, col. 1289). Cosmas's pun 'Bogu [*sic*, instead of Bogo] milu, but in truth Bogu ne milu' (see Vaillant's translation, p. 54, n. 3) leaves the issue undecided.
[6] Fifty-four out of eighty-four pages in Puech and Vaillant's translation.

The Bogomils' conviction that the World is evil is at the root of both their tenets and their practices.

Their fundamental tenet is that the creator of the World is not God;[1] the creator is the Devil,[2] and he is the prince of this World.[3] According to Zighavênós,[4] the Devil, *alias* Satan, is God the Father's first-born son and is the elder brother of the Lóghos, who[5] is Michael and Jesus and Christ.[6] Satan's name's original suffix '-el' signifies his divinity and his creative power—and, in fact, after rebelling and being cast out of Heaven, Satan created the World, including the bodies of Adam and Eve; but, to animate these, Satan had to induce the Father to infuse his spirit into them. In the Year of the World 5500, the Father sent down the Lóghos. This emissary took bodily form only 'in appearance' (ἐν φαντασίᾳ), and, in this illusory guise, he entered the World through Mary's ear,[7] was crucified, died, rose again, and bound Satan in Tartarus. He deprived him of his divinity (docking his name of its suffix '-el').[8]

It will be seen that the Bogomils' Dualism, as described by Zighavênós, is, like Zoroastrian Dualism, not absolute. The evil god and the good god are not on a par with each other. The supreme god is good, he is prior to the bad god, and he is also more potent. The good god's good emissary eventually subdues the bad god, but the Bogomils' Christology is Docetic; for the redeemer could not allow himself to be contaminated by the bad god's evil creation. Bogomilism resembles Manichaeism, and differs from Zoroastrianism and Marcionism and neo-Paulician Dualism, in equating the antithesis between good and evil with the antithesis between spirit and matter, but there is no evidence that Bogomil borrowed his doctrine from any of these earlier religions. Bogomil's doctrine could have been suggested to him by his own and his contemporaries' experience of the evilness of life in early-tenth-century Bulgaria, without his needing to seek for ideas by doing theological research.

According to Zighavênós, Satanael performed the role ascribed in the Old Testament to Yahweh. He sent the Flood; he gave the Law to Moses on Mount Sinai; he was the revealer of the greater part of the Old Testament. According to Zighavênós, the Bogomils had made a selective canon of Scripture (as the Marcionites and the Dualist neo-

---

[1] Cosmas, chap. 4, p. 59.

[2] Op. cit., chap. 4, pp. 58–9; chap. 13, pp. 74 and 77; chap. 18, p. 84.

[3] 'The Devil Prince of the World' is the heading of chap. 13, on p. 73.

[4] Cols. 1293–7.   [5] Col. 1301.

[6] According to Cosmas, chap. 13, p. 77, the Bogomils identified the Devil with the Prodigal Son, and Christ with the Prodigal's elder brother.

[7] The Bogomils took literally a statement that the Orthodox had made metaphorically, in allusion to the Annunciation (Obolensky, op. cit., p. 211, n. 3).

[8] Cols. 1301–4.

Paulicians had done), and on this point his account differs from Cosmas's,[1] who states[2] that the Bogomils rejected the whole of the Old Testament, including the Books of the Prophets, but does not state expressly that they rejected any part of the New Testament. According to Cosmas, the Bogomils debited Mary with acts of folly[3] and sin.[4] According to Zighavénos,[5] they arrogated the title 'theotókoi' to members of their own sect who 'give birth to the Lóghos' by their teaching. Cosmas and Zighavénos both state that the Bogomils hate the Cross,[6] and that they reject baptism[7] by water,[8] the cult of images,[9] the Eucharist,[10] and the Orthodox Christian hierarchy.[11] Cosmas adds that they believe that the miracles attributed to Christ were performed by the Devil.[12] Zighavénos adds that they decline to give recognition to saints, with a few exceptions.[13]

The Bogomil practice that causes Cosmas the greatest concern and alarm is the repudiation of marriage and the loathing of procreation.[14] The Bogomils say that marriage has been instituted by the creator, namely the Devil, whom they call Mammon in this context.[15] 'They have a horror of babies that are baptized. If they happen to see an infant child, they avert their eyes with horror as if they were seeing a piece of vile dung. They spit and hold their nose.'[16] They call babies 'children of Mammon'.[17]

In his Part II, in which he deals with the errors of the Orthodox, Cosmas puts his finger on the truth that this disgust with the World and repudiation of it was not confined to the Bogomils. In tenth-century Bulgaria this was in the air. There are some Christians who are contemptuous of marriage; others take the tonsure irregularly and go off to Jerusalem or Rome, and then give up and return to their wives.[18]

---

[1] On this difference, see Obolensky, p. 212.   [2] Chap. 9, p. 68, and chap. 12, p. 72.

[3] Chap. 10, p. 69.   [4] Chap. 18, p. 84.   [5] Col. 1320.

[6] Cosmas, chap. 5, p. 59, and chap. 17, p. 84; Zighavénos, cols. 1309–12.

[7] Cosmas, chap. 15, p. 81; Zighavénos, col. 1312.

[8] Zighavénos, col. 1312, describes the Bogomils' rite of initiation by baptism, not with water, but through the spirit. This rite, like their selective canon of scripture, may have been an addition to their original doctrine and practice.

[9] Cosmas, chap. 11, pp. 70–2. The heretic says: 'The venerators of images are like the pagan Greeks' (p. 71). Cf. Zighavénos, col. 1308.

[10] Cosmas, chap. 6, p. 61. 'They say: "The communion has not been instituted by a commandment of God, and the Eucharist is not really the body of Christ, as you pretend; it is just a food, like other foods. It is not Christ," they say, "who has instituted the Mass, and that is why we do not hold the Communion in honour." ' Cf. Zighavénos, col. 1313.

[11] Cosmas, chap. 8, p. 64; Zighavénos, cols. 1321 and 1329. They confess, but only to each other, not to an Orthodox Christian priest (Cosmas, chap. 20, p. 90).

[12] Cosmas, chap. 16, p. 82; chap. 18, p. 84.

[13] Zighavénos, col. 1308. Cf. Cosmas, chap. 18, p. 84.

[14] Cosmas, chap. 14, pp. 77–81.   [15] Ibid., p. 77.   [16] Chap. 15, p. 81.

[17] Cosmas, chap. 15, p. 82. Puech notes, on p. 268, that 'children of Mammon' has a double meaning. Besides meaning 'children begotten by the Devil', it means 'children born to be exploited by the rich'. Thus to bring children into the World is Devil's work. It is pandering to social injustice.   [18] Chap. 22, p. 93.

If you want to be a monk, stick to your vocation.[1] Cosmas castigates bad monks.[2] 'They only stop bickering to start drinking.'[3] He is particularly severe in condemning anchorites who live in luxury, free from discipline. He denounces their pride and their lust for power.[4] In his chapter on marriage,[5] he declares—in direct opposition to the Bogomils, who hold that marriage has been instituted by the Devil—that marriage has been ordained by God.[6] If you want to become a monk, do not do it without your wife's consent or without providing for your children—spiritually as well as materially.[7] 'If your motive for abandoning your family is a conviction that the World is a blight, and if you condemn the state of marriage because you believe that it is incompatible with being saved, then you have completely accepted the heretics' thesis.'[8]

Consistently with their repudiation of the World, the Bogomils not only condemned marriage and procreation but were ascetic in matters of food and drink. In the tenth century they abstained from meat and from wine.[9] In the twelfth century they abstained from eggs and from cheese as well.[10]

In their attitude towards society, the Bogomils are rebels.[11] They refuse to work and they refuse to obey the authorities. 'They teach their adherents not to submit to the authorities; they abuse the rich; they hate the Emperors; they mock at their superiors; they insult the nobles; they hold that God detests people who work for the Emperor, and they advise a servant not to work for his master.'[12]

At the same time, they are humble, silent, and unobtrusive,[13] and, by their humility, they attract the Orthodox insidiously.[14]

It will be seen that the early-twelfth-century Constantinopolitan Bogomils differed from the tenth-century Bulgarian Bogomils little, if at all, in either doctrine or practice. On the other hand, by the seventh decade of the twelfth century, the Dragovichian Church had come to differ radically from the Bulgarian Church in its formulation of the Bogomils' fundamental doctrine, Dualism itself. The Dragovichian Bogomils held that the good god and the bad god were on a par with each other, and this eternally.[15] We may infer that the Bulgarian Church continued to hold the doctrine ascribed to the Constantinopolitan Bogomils by Zighavênós, whose precise statements on this point are not inconsistent with Cosmas's vague allusions. It has been noted already that, according to Zighavênós, the bad god, who is the Devil, is the rebellious son of the good god, and the Devil's rebellion has been quelled

---

[1] Cosmas, chap. 22, p. 93. Cf. chap. 23, p. 100.   [2] Chap. 24, pp. 100–5.
[3] Ibid., p. 101.   [4] Ibid., pp. 103–4.   [5] Chap. 25, pp. 106–10.   [6] Ibid., p. 108.
[7] Ibid., p. 106.   [8] Ibid.   [9] Cosmas, op. cit., chap. 14, p. 77.
[10] Zighavênós, col. 1325.   [11] Cosmas, chap. 19, pp. 85–90.
[12] Ibid., p. 86.   [13] Cosmas, chap. 1, p. 55.
[14] Ibid., pp. 55–6.   [15] See p. 690, with n. 10.

by the Devil's brother, whom the good god has sent into the World as his emissary.

The Dragovichian Church's innovation in Bogomilism was not so revolutionary a new departure as the Sergians' innovation had been in Paulicianism. Séryios and his partisans had transformed Paulicianism in the eastern marches of the East Roman Empire from Adoptionist Christianity into Dualism; the Dragovichian Bogomils only keyed up a version of Dualism that was a compromise with Monarchianism into a version of Dualism that was absolute. Even so, this twelfth-century change of doctrine in one branch of Bogomilism was momentous. Can it be explained?

The explanation that has been suggested already for the origin of Bogomilism in the tenth century could also perhaps account for the accentuation of its Dualism in the twelfth century. Dualism is a reflection, in theological speculation, of the practical experience of the power of evil. In Bulgaria, between the tenth and the twelfth century, there had been further turns of the screw. To rate the power of evil higher than before would be a natural response to this aggravation of the pressure of evil on the Bulgarian peasantry's life.

Tenth-century Bogomilism had been a reaction to Khan Symeon's policy of War and Byzantinization. Tsar Peter's reign from 927 to 969 had been only a lull. The events of 969–72 had been catastrophic. The subsequent revolt of West Bulgaria, and the East Roman Emperor Basil II's consequent war of attrition, ending in the effective annexation of Bulgaria to the Empire in 1018, had been crushing; and, after that, the screw had still kept on turning.[1] A Greek hierarchy had been imposed on the Orthodox Church in Bulgaria in 1037. From 1041 onwards, the East Roman Government's officials in Bulgaria had all been Greeks. Taxation in kind, which Basil II had maintained, had been replaced by the levying of the taxes in money. The insurrection that this change had provoked in 1041 had been stamped out. The Greek prelate Theophýlaktos, who from 1078 to 1118 was Archbishop of Okhrida (a see that was originally conterminous with the former West Bulgaria),[2] writes of his see and of his Bulgarian ecclesiastical subjects with inhuman contempt.[3] At the same time, he complains of the Greek tax-officers who were his compatriots.[4] If these fleeced even a Greek clerical grandee, they must have been merciless to Bulgarian peasants, as Obolensky rightly infers. Moreover, the Byzantinization of Bulgaria was making

---

[1] See Obolensky, op. cit., pp. 170–2.

[2] See p. 107, n. 1. The Emperor Basil II had enlarged the domain of this archiepiscopal see, first to include all territories, beyond the limits of Tsar Samuel's West Bulgaria, that had once been subject politically to Tsar Peter (927–69), and then to include the sees of Vérrhoia, Sérvia, and Stághoi (Kalabáka) as well.

[3] See ibid., p. 170, n. 1.   [4] See ibid., p. 171.

headway in the country's economy as well as in its ecclesiastical government. Bulgaria was now experiencing the agrarian revolution to which, in Rhomanía, the East Roman Government had capitulated after Basil II's death in 1025, at the end of a century-long losing battle to check the great landowners' encroachments on the peasantry. In the eleventh century this aggressive class of great landowners, which was already victorious in Rhomanía, made its appearance in subject Bulgaria too. This brought with it the institution of prónoiai, and the conversion of the peasantry into the great landowners' dependants (πάροικοι).

It is not surprising that, by the seventh decade of the twelfth century, the Dragovichian Bogomil Church should have concluded that the power of evil was as strong as the power of good. Indeed, it would not have been surprising if, by this time, the Bogomils had come round, full circle, back to Monarchianism, with the Devil now invested with the omnipotence of the Jewish-Christian-Muslim God. It is remarkable that, in opposition to the Dragovichian Bogomil Church, the Bulgarian Bogomil Church remained faithful, as apparently it did, to the diluted form of Dualism that had been the Bogomils' original creed.

This explanation, in terms of experience, of the origin of Bogomilism, and of the subsequent keying-up of its Dualism in the creed of one of its churches, seems sufficient. It has, however, been suggested that the original form of Bogomilism was inspired by Paulicianism,[1] and that the radical Dualism of the Dragovichian Church was in truth Paulicianism itself.[2]

It is true that the neo-Paulician Dualism of Séryios and his followers was about a century older than Bogomilism. But the domain of this Sergian Paulician Dualism was in the eastern marches of the East Roman Empire, and here it was extirpated by the year 872, or at any rate was driven underground. It is a far cry from ninth-century théma Armeniakoí and Tephrikě to tenth-century Bulgaria, and the Paulicians whom the Emperor Constantine V had planted in Thrace in 755 or 757 can hardly have been carriers of Dualism, for they were Armenian Paulicians, and these never became Dualists; nor did the Paulicians in East Roman Asia Minor become Dualists before the ninth century. The Paulician settlement in Thrace may have passed from East Roman rule to Bulgarian rule as a result of Khan Krum's crushing defeat of the Emperor Nikêphóros I in 811.[3] If so, the interposition of a political frontier between

---

[1] For instance, Zighavênós debits Paulicianism with the Bogomils' account of the creation (cols. 1300–1) and also with the Bogomils' distinction and antithesis between the God of the Old Testament and the God of the Gospel (col. 1305). Vaillant, in *Cosmas le Prêtre*, p. 27, takes it for granted that 'l'hérésie des Bogomiles est la forme prise chez les Bulgares par l'hérésie arménienne des Pauliciens'.

[2] This is Obolensky's view, as given in op. cit., p. 124, n. 3.

[3] This is noted by Obolensky, op. cit., p. 62.

them and the Paulicians in eastern Asia Minor would have insulated the Thracian Paulicians from contact with the innovator Séryios's adherents in Asia Minor. As for the new batch of Paulicians that was planted at Philippopolis by the Emperor John Dzimiskês at some date between 972 and 976, these were, according to Anna Comnena,[1] prisoners of war from Armenia and from 'the land of the Khályves'. The traditional location of this semi-legendary nation of blacksmiths was towards the eastern end of the south coast of the Black Sea, that is to say, in country that was East Roman territory in John Dzimiskês's day; but evidently Anna thinks of them as not having been East Roman subjects, and, if they were not, they, too, will not have been Dualists.

Moreover, even if we make the unverifiable assumption that both batches of Paulician settlers in the Maríca basin did exchange their ancestral Adoptionist Christianity for the Asiatic neo-Paulicians' version of Dualism, we have no positive evidence to tell us what this version actually was. We know little more than that it was not the Manichaean version of Dualism with which the ninth-century and tenth-century East Roman Orthodox Christian polemicists malignly identified neo-Paulician Dualism in order to discredit it. We know more about the neo-Paulicians' conduct than about their tenets. We know that, in practice, the neo-Paulician Dualists, like their Adoptionist Christian palaeo-Paulician predecessors, were not celibates and were not ascetics. This practice of theirs runs counter to even a minimal form of Dualist theology.[2] It seems reasonable to infer that the Paulician version of Dualism, so far from being radical or absolute, was moderate—probably more moderate than the original form of Bogomil Dualism, and far more moderate than the Dragovichian Church's twelfth-century absolutism.

Nor have we any warrant for assuming that the Philippopolitan Paulicians shared the missionary zeal that had inspired the Paulicians in Eastern Asia Minor in the seventh, eighth, and ninth centuries. 'The Paulicians remained essentially foreigners in Bulgaria.'[3] They seem to have concentrated their energies on maintaining their own communal identity, not on making local native converts.[4] They have retained the

---

[1] *Alexias*, Book XIV, chap. 8. Cf. Kedhrênós, vol. ii, p. 382; Zonarás, vol. iii, pp. 521–2.
[2] This point is noted by Obolensky in op. cit., pp. 114, 129, n. 1, and 144.
[3] Obolensky, op. cit., p. 139, n. 2. Cf. p. 144.
[4] The name 'Populicani', 'Poplicani', 'Publicani' (i.e. Pavliciani) was affixed, by the Western Christian ecclesiastical authorities, to people convicted of heresy at Oxford in 1160, in Flanders in 1162, in Burgundy in 1167. At the Third Lateran Council, held in 1179, the Publicani were condemned under that name, and were expressly identified with the Albigenses, Cathari, and Patarini. See Runciman, op. cit., pp. 121–2; Conybeare, *The Key of Truth*, Introduction, pp. cxxxix–cxl. However, the errors with which these 'Publicani' were charged were the rejection of marriage, of Baptism, and of the Eucharist. In lieu of marriage, they were said to favour chastity or (less convincingly, but more damagingly) to favour sexual promiscuity. These charges, except for the last, agree with those made against the Bogomils by Cosmas and by Zighavênós. They do not correspond to anything that we know for

nickname Paulicians, in which the seventh-century heresiarch Constantine of Manalali taught them to take pride, down to this day.[1] By the year 1717 they had become Uniate Roman Catholic Christians, and Lady Mary Wortley Montagu, in a letter written at Philippopolis on 1 April 1717, notes that they were 'a sect of Christians that called themselves Paulines' and that 'St. Paul is their favourite saint'.

If we guess that the Bogomils discovered Dualism for themselves—including even the 'absolute' Dualism of the twelfth-century Dragovichian Church—solely in the light of their own harsh experience, we shall be on surer ground than if we guess that the Bogomils' Dualism was inspired by the Philippopolitan Paulicians.[2]

certain about the Dualist Paulicians. It is therefore possible that the Western Christian authorities merely affixed a name with which they were already familiar to heretics who, in fact, had the same tenets and practices as the Bogomils, and were, directly or indirectly, converts made by Bogomilism, not by Paulicianism. During the First Crusade, the Crusaders had found a Castra Publicanorum near Antioch in 1097, and another near Tripolis (Tarābulus) in 1099 (Runciman, op. cit., p. 46). The Crusaders' overland route ran through Philippopolis, and the Second Crusade had travelled that way in 1146–9.

[1] Obolensky, op. cit., p. 266.

[2] Borst, op. cit., p. 68, n. 12, holds that Bogomilism was not derived from Messalianism and that it was also not a direct product of Paulicianism.

BIBLIOGRAPHY (SELECTIVE)

Note: The field of this bibliography is limited to topics that are dealt with in some detail in the present book, and the book is not a comprehensive study of the East Roman Empire and the Byzantine civilization even for the period with which it is mainly concerned—that is to say, the seventh to the tenth century. For instance, architecture and visual art are treated only cursorily, and there is no systematic account of the Eastern Orthodox Church, though there are few chapters in which the Church does not figure in a prominent role. The purpose of the bibliography is merely to illustrate and supplement the book within the book's own limits; it is not an attempt to vie with the magnificent bibliographies in the second edition of Volume IV of *The Cambridge Medieval History*. These are indispensable.

CONTENTS

1. BYZANTINE CHRONICLES, BIOGRAPHIES, AND LETTERS WRITTEN BETWEEN 602 AND 913

Anonymus, i.e. *Scriptor Incertus de Leone [V] Bardae Filio*, ed. by I. Bekker, together with Leo Grammaticus's *Chronographia*: Bonn, 1842, Weber, pp. 333–62.

Basil (not identical with any otherwise known bearer of this name): 'Life of St. Euthymius (Efthýmios) the Younger', ed. by L. Petit, in *Revue de l'Orient Chrétien*, 8ᵐᵉ année (Paris, 1903, Picard), pp. 155–205.

—— Ἀκολουθία τοῦ Εὐθυμίου τοῦ Νέου, ibid., pp. 503–36.

Chronicon Paschale, ed. by L. Dindorf: Bonn, 1832, Weber, 2 vols.

Georgius Monachus: *Chronicon*, ed. by C. de Boor: Leipzig, 1904, Teubner, 2 vols. [A restoration of the genuine text of Georgius's own final edition, stripped of interpolations and continuations.]

Georgius Pisides: *Poëmata*: Giorgio di Pisidia, *Poemi*, ed. by A. Pertusi: Ettal, 1960, Ettal Buch-Kunstverlag: Studia Patristica et Byzantina, 7. Heft.

John of Nikíou: *Chronicle*: Ethiopic text edited, with French translation, by H. Zotenberg: Paris, 1883, Imprimerie Nationale; English translation by R. H. Charles: London, 1916, Oxford University Press.

Leo VI: 'Oraison funèbre de Basile I', edited, with introduction and translation, by A. Vogt and I. Hausherr, in *Orientalia Christiana*, vol. xxvi, Num. 77 (April 1932): Rome, 1932, Pont. Institutum Orientalium Studiorum.

Leo Choerosphactes [Khoirospháktês]: Letters, ed. by G. Kolias: Athens, 1939.

Nicephorus Patriarcha: Ἱστορία σύντομος ἀπὸ τῆς Μαυρικίου Βασιλείας and Χρονογραφικὸν σύντομον, ed. by C. de Boor, with Ignatius's biography of Nicephorus: Leipzig, 1880, Teubner.

Nikḗtas of Amnía: 'Life of St. Philáretos of Amnía', edited and translated, with introduction, by M.-H. Fourmy and M. Leroy, in *Byzantion*, vol. ix (1934), pp. 85–170.

Theophanes: *Chronographia*, ed. by C. de Boor: Leipzig, 1883–5, Teubner, 2 vols.

Varii auctores: *Sancti Demetrii Martyris Miracula*, Books I–III, in Migne, *Patrologia Graeca*, vol. cxvi (1891), cols. 1203–1398.

2. CONSTANTINE VII PORPHYROGENITUS'S WORKS

Biography of the Emperor Basil I = *Theophanes Continuatus*, Book V, ed. by I. Bekker: Bonn, 1838, Weber, pp. 211–353.

De Administrando Imperio, ed. by I. Bekker in C. P.'s works, vol. iii, Bonn, 1840, Weber, pp. 65–270; edited by Gy. Moravcsik and translated by R. J. H. Jenkins: Budapest, 1949, University Institute of Greek Philology; *Commentary*, ed. by Jenkins with Dvornik, Lewis, Moravcsik, Obolensky, and Runciman: London, 1962, Athlone Press; revised second edition of Moravcsik and Jenkins's text: Washington, D.C., 1967, Dumbarton Oaks Center for Byzantine Studies.

De Caerimoniis, edited, with commentary, by I. I. Reiske in C. P.'s works, vols. i and ii: Bonn, 1829–30, Weber; edited, with commentary, by A. Vogt, as far as Book I, chap. 92 (83): 4 parts in 2 vols.: Paris, 1935–40, L'Association Guillaume Budé.

De Thematibus, ed. by I. Bekker in C. P.'s works, vol. iii, Bonn, 1940, Weber, pp. 11–64; edited, with commentary, by A. Pertusi: Città del Vaticano, 1952, Biblioteca Apostolica Vaticana: Studi e Testi 160.

3. WORKS (ON PUBLIC AFFAIRS) INCORPORATED, EDITED,
OR COMMISSIONED BY
CONSTANTINE VII PORPHYROGENITUS

Anonymus: *Theophanes Continuatus*, Books I–IV, ed. by I. Bekker: Bonn, 1838, Weber, pp. 1–211.
Genesius, Joseph: Βασιλεῖαι, ed. by C. Lachmann: Bonn, 1834, Weber: reprinted in Migne, *Patrologia Graeca*, vol. cix, cols. 991–1156.
Leo Katákylas: Τὰ Βασιλικὰ Ταξείδια, ed. by C. P.: printed as Appendix to *De Caer.*, Book I, in Bonn edition, vol. i, pp. 455–508, together with a piece of C. P.'s own on the same subject, in vol. cit., pp. 444–54.
Philótheos: *Klêtorolóyion*: incorporated in *De Caer.*, Book II, Bonn edition, pp. 702–91; re-edited by J. B. Bury in *The Imperial Administrative System in the Ninth Century*: London, 1911, Oxford University Press, pp. 131–79; reprinted 1958, Burt Franklin.

4. MODERN COMMENTS, NOT MENTIONED IN SECTION 3,
ON WORKS WRITTEN, INCORPORATED, EDITED,
AND COMMISSIONED BY
CONSTANTINE VII PORPHYROGENITUS

Bury, J. B.: *A History of the Eastern Roman Empire, A.D. 802–867*, Appendix IV: 'Genesios and the Continuation of Theophanes', pp. 460–1.
—— 'The Ceremonial Book of Constantine Porphyrogenitus', in *The English Historical Review*: April 1907 (Part I); July 1907 (Part II).
—— *The Imperial Administrative System in the Ninth Century, with a Revised Text of the Kletorologion of Philotheos*: London, 1911, Oxford University Press: reprinted 1958, Burt Franklin.
—— 'The Treatise De Administrando Imperio', in *Byzantinische Zeitschrift*, vol. xv, Heften 3 and 4 (1906), pp. 518–77.
Diehl, Ch.: 'Sur la date de quelques passages du Livre des Cérémonies', in his *Études byzantines*: Paris, 1905, Picard, pp. 293–306.
Ostrogorsky, G.: 'Sur la date de la composition du Livre des Thèmes et sur l'époque de la constitution des premiers thèmes d'Asie Mineure', in *Byzantion*, vol. xxiii (1953), pp. 31–56.
Skok, P.: 'Ortsnamenstudien zu De Administrando Imperio des Kaisers Konstantin Porphyrogennetos', in *Zeitschrift für Ortsnamenforschung*, Band IV, Heft 3: Munich and Berlin, 1928, Oldenbourg, pp. 213–43.

5. CHRONICLES AND HISTORIES WRITTEN, INDEPENDENTLY
OF CONSTANTINE VII PORPHYROGENITUS,
DURING AND AFTER HIS REIGN[1]

Anna Comnena: *Alexias*, ed. by A. Reifferscheid: Leipzig, 1884, Teubner, 2 vols.
Anonymus: *Theophanes Continuatus*, Book VI, down to the notice of Rhomanós Lekapênós's death on 15 June [*sic*] 948, in I. Bekker's edition of *Theoph. Cont.*, Bonn, 1838, Weber, pp. 353–441.
Anonymus: *Theophanes Continuatus*, record of the years 948–61, ibid., pp. 441–81.

---

[1] The entries under this head are limited to works that deal, at least in part, with East Roman affairs within the period 602–976.

Glykás, Michael: *Vívlos Khronikē*, ed. by I. Bekker: Bonn, 1836, Weber.

Kedhrênós, Yeóryios: Georgius Cedrenus, Joannis Scylitzae Ope ab I. Bekkero suppletus et emendatus: *Synopsis Historiarum*, tomus alter: Bonn, 1839, Weber.

Liutprand (Liudprand) Bishop of Cremona: *Opera*, ed. by J. Becker: 3rd edition, Hannover and Leipzig, 1915, Hahn.

Nikólaos Mystikós: *Letters*, in Migne, *Patrologia Graeca*, vol. cxi, cols. 1–406.

Pseudo-Symeon Magister: *Chronographia*, ed. by I. Bekker, together with *Theophanes Continuatus*: Bonn, 1838, Weber, pp. 601–760.

Rhomanós Lekapênós: *Letters*, ed. by I. Sakkelion, in Δελτίον τῆς Ἱστορικῆς καὶ Ἐθνολογικῆς Ἑταιρείας τῆς Ἑλλάδος, vol. i (1883) pp. 658–66; vol. ii (1884), pp. 40–5.

Symeon Magister et Logothetes: *Chronographia*: the whole, translated into Old Slavonic, ed. by V. I. Sreznevsky (St. Petersburg, 1905); reproductions of the part of the Greek text that covers the years 813–948, 15 July [*sic*], in Leo Grammaticus: *Chronographia*, ed. by I. Bekker : Bonn, 1842, Weber, pp. 207–331; in *Georgius Monachus Interpolatus* (A.D. 813–42) in the Bonn edition of Theophanes Continuatus, pp. 761–810; in *Georgius Monachus Continuatus* (A.D. 843–948, 15 July [*sic*]) ibid., pp. 810–924; in Theodosius Melitenus: *Chronographia*, ed. by G. L. F. Tafel (Munich, 1859).

Zonarás: *Epitome Historiarum*: ed. by M. Pinder and B. Büttner-Wobst: Bonn 1841–97, 3 vols.; ed. by L. Dindorf: Leipzig, 1868–75, 6 vols.

6. MODERN COMMENTS ON THE *CHRONOGRAPHIA* OF SYMEON MAGISTER ET LOGOTHETES

Bury, J. B.: *A History of the Eastern Roman Empire, A.D. 802–867*, Appendix II: 'George's Chronicle', pp. 453–4.

—— op. cit., Appendix III: 'The Chronicle of Simeon, Magister and Logothete', pp. 455–9.

Jenkins, R. J. H.: 'The Chronological Accuracy of the "Logothete" for the years 867–912', in *Dumbarton Oaks Papers*, Number Nineteen: Washington, D.C., 1965, The Dumbarton Oaks Center for Byzantine Studies, pp. 91–112.

7. MODERN WORKS: GENERAL: HISTORICAL

Adontz, N.: 'L'Âge et l'origine de l'empereur Basile I', in *Byzantion*, vol. viii (1933), pp. 475–500.

—— 'L'Âge et l'origine de l'empereur Basile I', (suite), in *Byzantion*, vol. ix (1934), pp. 223–60.

—— 'La Portée historique de l'oraison funèbre de Basile I par son fils Léon VI le Sage', in *Byzantion*, vol. viii (1933), pp. 501–13.

Ámandos, K. I.: Ἱστορία τοῦ Βυζαντίνου κράτους, second edition: vol. i (395–867) 1933; vol. ii (867–1204) 1957 Ὀργανισμὸς Ἐκδόσεως Σχολικῶν Βιβλίων; third edition, vol. i: Athens, 1963.

Bréhier, L.: *Vie et mort de Byzance*: Paris, 1947, Albin Michel.

Bury, J. B.: *A History of the Later Roman Empire from Arcadius to Irene (395 A.D. to 800 A.D.)*: London, 1889, Macmillan, 2 vols.

—— *History of the Later Roman Empire from the Death of Theodosius I to the Death of Justinian*, paperback edition: London, 1958, Constable, 2 vols.

—— *A History of the Eastern Roman Empire from the Fall of Irene to the Accession of Basil I (A.D. 802–867)*: London, 1912, Macmillan.

Charanis, P.: 'Ethnic Changes in the Byzantine Empire in the Seventh Century', in *Dumbarton Oaks Papers*, Number Thirteen (1959), pp. 25–44.

——— *Studies on the Demography of the Byzantine Empire* (reprints of 22 studies published since 1946): London, 1972, Variorum Reprints.

Diehl, Ch.: *Histoire de l'Empire byzantin*: Paris, 1919, Picard.

Dölger, F.: *Regesten der Kaiserurkunden des oströmischen Reiches von 565–1453*, I Teil: *Regesten von 565–1025*: Munich and Berlin, 1924, Oldenbourg.

Gay, J.: *L'Italie méridionale et l'Empire byzantin*: Paris, 1904, Fontemoing: reprinted, Burt Franklin.

Gibbon, Edward: *The History of the Decline and Fall of the Roman Empire*, ed. by J. B. Bury: editio minor, London, 1900–2, Methuen, 7 vols.

Goubert, P.: *Byzance avant l'Islam*: Paris, 1951–65, Picard, 2 vols. in 3 Parts.

Grégoire, H.: 'Études sur le neuvième siècle', in *Byzantion*, vol. viii (1933), pp. 515–50.

Grierson, Ph., and Jenkins, R. J. H.: 'The Date of Constantine VII's Coronation', in *Byzantion*, vol. xxxii (1962), pp. 133–8.

Haussig, H. W.: *A History of Byzantine Civilization*: London, 1971, Thames & Hudson, translated by J. M. Hussey from the author's *Kulturgeschichte von Byzanz*, second revised edition: Stuttgart, 1966, Kröner.

Hussey, J. M. [ed.]: *The Cambridge Medieval History*, vol. iv; *The Byzantine Empire*, 2nd ed.; Cambridge, 1966–7, University Press, 2 Parts.

Jenkins, Romilly [R. J. H.]: *Byzantium: The Imperial Centuries: A.D. 610–1071*: London, 1966, Weidenfeld & Nicolson.

Jones, A. H. M.: *The Later Roman Empire, 284–602*: Oxford, 1964, Blackwell, 3 vols. + case of maps.

Kolias, G.: *Léon Choerosphactès, magistre, proconsul et patrice*: Athens, 1939.

Obolensky, D.: *The Byzantine Commonwealth: Eastern Europe 500–1453*: London, 1971, Weidenfeld & Nicolson.

Ostrogorsky, G.: 'The Byzantine Empire in the World of the Seventh Century', in *Dumbarton Oaks Papers*, Number Thirteen (1959), pp. 1–21.

——— *Geschichte des byzantinischen Staates*: Munich, 1940, Beck; *History of the Byzantine State*, translated by J. M. Hussey, 2nd revised edition: Oxford, 1968, Blackwell.

Rambaud, A.: *L'Empire grec au dixième siècle: Constantin Porphyrogénète*: Paris, 1870, Franck.

Runciman, S.: *The Emperor Romanus Lecapenus and his Reign*: Cambridge, 1929, University Press.

Schlumberger, G.: *Un Empereur byzantin au dixième siècle: Nicéphore Phocas*: Paris, 1890, Didot; reprint, Paris, 1923, Boccard.

Stein, E.: *Histoire du Bas-Empire*, vol. i (284–476): Bruges, 1959; vol. ii (476–565): Paris–Brussels–Amsterdam, 1949, both published by Desclée de Brouwer.

Stratós, A. N.: *Byzantium in the Seventh Century, I: 602–634; II: 634–641*: Amsterdam, 1968 and 1972, Hakkert.

Vasiliev, A. A.: *Histoire de l'Empire byzantin*, vol. i (324–1081); vol. ii (1081–1453): Paris, 1932, Picard.

Vryonis Jr., Sp.: *The Decline of Medieval Hellenism in Asia Minor and the Process of Islamisation from the Eleventh through the Fifteenth Century*: Berkeley and Los Angeles, 1971, University of California Press; chapter 1: 'Byzantine Asia Minor on the Eve of the Turkish Conquest', pp. 1–68.

8. MODERN WORKS: GENERAL: DESCRIPTIVE

Baynes, N. H.: *The Byzantine Empire*: London, 1925, Oxford University Press.

Baynes, N. H., and Moss, H. St. L. B. [edd.]: *Byzantium: An Introduction to East Roman Civilization* [symposium]: Oxford, 1948 (paperback edition, 1961), Clarendon Press.

Bréhier, L.: *La Civilisation byzantine*: Paris, 1950, Albin Michel.

Diehl, Ch.: *Byzance: grandeur et décadence*: Paris, 1919, Flammarion.

—— *Les Grands Problèmes de l'histoire byzantine*: Paris, 1947, Armand Colin.

Hussey, J. M.: *The Byzantine World*: London, 1957, Hutchinson.

Krumbacher, K.: *Geschichte der byzantinischen Literatur*, 2nd edition: Munich, 1897, Beck; reprinted 1958, Burt Franklin.

Runciman, S.: *Byzantine Civilisation*: London, 1933, Edward Arnold.

9. WORKS ON ADMINISTRATION, LAW, FINANCE, ECONOMICS

(i) SOURCES

Anonymus: Νόμος Γεωργικός, edited, with commentary, by W. Ashburner in *The Journal of Hellenic Studies*, vol. xxx (1910), pp. 85–108, and vol. xxxii (1912), pp. 68–95.

Leo VI: *Les Nouvelles*: edited and translated by P. Noailles and A. Dain; Paris, 1944, Société d'Édition les 'Belles Lettres'.

—— Τὸ 'Επαρχικὸν Βιβλίον: *Le Livre du Préfet, ou l'Édit de l'Empereur Léon le Sage sur les corporations de Constantinople*, texte grec du Genevensis 23, ed. by J. Nicole: Geneva, 1893, Georg: reprint, with translation and with facsimile of the MS.: London, 1970, Variorum Reprints.

Marcianus Codex gr. fondo antico, 173 (Venice): Treatise on Taxation: ed. by W. Ashburner in *The Journal of Hellenic Studies* vol. xxxv (1915), pp. 76–84; ed. by F. Dölger in *Byzantinisches Archiv*, Heft 9: Berlin and Leipzig, 1927, Teubner; reprinted with corrections and additions: Hildesheim, 1960.

Taktikón Benešević, in Kodex Hieros. Patr. 24, in Benešević, 'Die byzantinischen Ranglisten' (see 9 (ii)), pp. 110–11.

Taktikón Uspenskij, in Jerusalem Patriarchal Library MS. 39, ibid.

Zachariä von Lingenthal, C. E. [ed.]: *Jus Graeco-Romanum*, Pars III: *Novellae, Constitutiones*: the tenth-century novellae that deal with the agrarian question: Leipzig, 1857, Weigel pp. 220–318; reprinted in Zepos, J. and P. [edd.], *Jus Graeco-Romanum*, vol. i: Athens, 1931.

(ii) MODERN WORKS

Bach, E.: 'Les Lois agraires byzantines du Xe siècle', in *Classica et Mediaevalia*, vol. v (1942), pp. 70–91.

Benešević, V.: 'Die byzantinischen Ranglisten nach dem Kletorologion Philothei (*De Cer.*, l. II, c. 52) und nach den Jerusalemer Handschriften zusammengestellt und revidiert', in *Byzantinisch-Neugriechische Jahrbücher*, 5. Band (Jahrgang 1926/7), pp. 97–167.

Bréhier, L.: *Les Institutions de l'Empire byzantin*: Paris, 1948, Albin Michel.

—— 'Les Populations rurales au IXe siècle d'après l'hagiographie byzantine', in *Byzantion*, vol. i (1924), pp. 177–90.

Bury, J. B.: *The Imperial Administrative System in the Ninth Century, with a Revised Text of the Kletorologion of Philotheos*: London, 1911, Oxford University Press; reprinted: New York, 1963, Burt Franklin.

Charanis, P.: 'On the Social Structure of the Later Roman Empire', in *Byzantion*, vol. xvii (1944–5), pp. 38–57.

—— 'The Monastic Properties and the State in the Byzantine Empire', in *Dumbarton Oaks Papers*, Number Four (1948), pp. 51–118.

Diomedes, N. A.: 'The Development of Land-tax in Byzantium', in *Epetêrís Etaireías Vyzandinón Spoudhón*, 19 (1949), pp. 306–14.

Dölger, F.: 'Beiträge zur Geschichte der byzantinischen Finanzverwaltung, besonders des 10. und 11. Jahrhunderts', in *Byzantinisches Archiv*, Heft 9: Berlin and Leipzig, 1927, Teubner; reprinted with corrections and additions: Hildesheim, 1960.

—— 'Die Frage des Grundeigentums in Byzanz', in *Bulletin of the International Committee of Historical Sciences*, 5 (1933), pp. 5–15, reprinted in *Byzanz und die europäische Staatenwelt* (Ettal, 1953), pp. 217–31.

Glykatzi-Ahrweiler, H.: 'Recherches sur l'administration de l'Empire byzantin aux IXe–XIe siècles, in *Bulletin de Correspondance Hellénique*, vol. lxxxiv (1960), pp. 1–111.

Karayannopoulos, J.: *Das Finanzwesen des frühbyzantinischen Staates*: Munich, 1958.

—— 'Die kollektive Steuerverantwortung in der frühbyzantinischen Zeit', in *Vierteljahrschrift für Sozial- und Wirtschaftsgeschichte*, 43. Band (1956), pp. 289–322.

Khristophilópoulos: Τὸ ἐπαρχικὸν βιβλίον Λέοντος τοῦ Σοφοῦ καὶ αἱ συντεχνίαι ἐν Βυζαντίῳ: Athens, 1935 [praised by Mickwitz (q.v.), in op. cit., p. 205; inaccessible for me].

Lemerle, P.: 'Esquisse pour une histoire agraire de Byzance', in *Revue Historique*, 1958, vol. ccxix, pp. 32–74 and 254–84; vol. ccxx, pp. 43–94.

Lopez, R. S.: 'The Role of Trade in the Economic Readjustment of Byzantium in the Seventh Century', in *Dumbarton Oaks Papers*, Number Thirteen (1959), pp. 69–85.

Macri, C. M.: *L'Organisation de l'économie urbaine dans Byzance sous la dynastie de Macédoine (867–1057)*: Paris, 1925, Guillon.

Mickwitz, G.: *Die Kartellfunktionen der Zünfte*: Zweiter Teil, Kapitel VIII: 'Die byzantinische Zünfte im 10. Jhdt.', pp. 205–31: Helsingfors, 1936, Societas Scientiarum Fennica.

Ostrogorsky, G.: 'Agrarian Conditions in the Byzantine Empire in the Middle Ages', in *The Cambridge Economic History*, vol. i, 2nd ed.; Cambridge, 1966, University Press, pp. 205–34.

—— 'Die ländliche Steuergemeinde des byzantinischen Reiches im X. Jahrhundert', in *Vierteljahrschrift für Sozial- und Wirtschaftsgeschichte*, 20. Band (1928): Stuttgart, 1928, Kohlhammer, pp. 1–108.

—— 'La Commune rurale byzantine', in *Byzantion*, vol. xxxii (1962), pp. 138–66.

—— *Pour l'histoire de la féodalité byzantine*: Brussels, 1954, L'Institut de Philologie et d'Histoire Orientales et Slaves.

—— 'The Peasant's Pre-emption Right: An Abortive Reform of the Macedonian Emperors', in *The Journal of Roman Studies*, vol. xxxvii (1947), pp. 117–26.

Rouillard, G.: *La Vie rurale dans l'Empire byzantin*: Paris, 1953, Maisonneuve.

Savramis, D.: *Zur Soziologie des byzantinischen Mönchtums*: Leiden/Köln, 1962, Brill.

Setton, M. K.: 'On the Importance of Land Tenure and Agrarian Taxation in the Byzantine Empire, from the fourth century to the Fourth Crusade', in *The American Journal of Philology*, 74 (1953), pp. 225–59.

Stöckle, A.: *Spätrömische und byzantinische Zünfte* = *Klio*, Neuntes Beiheft: Leipzig, 1911, Dieterich.

Teal, J. L.: 'The Grain Supply of the Byzantine Empire, 330–1025', in *Dumbarton Oaks Papers*, Number Thirteen (1959), pp. 87–139.

Zakynthênós, D.: *Crise monétaire et crise économique à Byzance du XIIe au XVe siècle*: Athens, 1948.

Zoras, G.: *Le corporazioni bizantine: studio sull'ἐπαρχικὸν βιβλίον dell'imperatore Leone VI*: Rome, 1931, Editrice Studium.

10. THE THÉMATA: MODERN WORKS

Antoniadis-Bibicou, H.: *Études d'histoire maritime de Byzance à propos du 'Thème des Caravisiens'*: Paris, 1966, S.E. and P.E.N.

Beneševič, V.: 'Die byzantinischen Ranglisten nach dem Kletorologion Philothei (*De Cer.*, l. II, c. 52) und nach den Jerusalemer Handschriften zusammengestellt und revidiert', in *Byzantinisch-Neugriechische Jahrbücher*, 5. Band (Jahrgang 1926/7), pp. 97–167.

Brooks, E. W.: 'Arabic Lists of the Byzantine Themes', in *The Journal of Hellenic Studies*, vol. xxi (1901), pp. 67–77.

Diehl, Ch.: 'L'Origine du régime des thèmes dans l'Empire byzantin', in his *Études byzantines*: Paris, 1905, Picard, pp. 276–92.

Dölger, F.: 'Zur Ableitung des byzantinischen Verwaltungsterminus θέμα', in *Historia*, 4. Band (1955), pp. 189–98.

Ensslin, W.: 'Der Kaiser Herakleios und die Themenverfassung', in *Byzantinische Zeitschrift*, 46. Band (1953), pp. 362–8.

Gelzer, H.: *Die Genesis der byzantinischen Themenverfassung*, Amsterdam, 1966, Hakkert: originally published in *Abhandlungen der Kön. Sächs. Gesellschaft der Wissenschaften, Phil.-Hist. Klasse*: Leipzig, 1899.

Glykatzi-Ahrweiler, H.: 'Recherches sur l'administration de l'Empire byzantin aux IXᵉ–XIᵉ siècles', in *Bulletin de Correspondance Hellénique*, vol. lxxxiv (1960), pp. 1–111.

Haussig, W. H.: 'Anfänge der Themenordnung', in Altheim, Fr., and Stiehl, R.: *Finanzgeschichte der Spätantike*: Frankfurt a. M., 1957, Klostermann, pp. 82–114.

Kaegi, W. E.: 'Some Reconsiderations on the Themes (Seventh–Ninth Centuries)': in *Jahrbuch der österreichischen byzantinischen Gessellschaft*, vol. xvi (1967), pp. 39–53.

Karayannopulos, J.: *Die Entstehung der byzantinischen Themenverfassung*: Munich, 1959, Beck.

Metcalf, D. M.: 'The New Bronze Coinage of Theophilus and the Growth of the Balkan Themes', in *American Numismatic Society Museum Notes*, X (1961), p. 95.

Ostrogorsky, G.: 'Sur la date de la composition du Livre des Thèmes et sur l'époque de la constitution des premiers thèmes d'Asie Mineure', in *Byzantion*, vol. xxiii (1953), pp. 31–66.

Pertusi, A.: 'La Formation des thèmes byzantins', in *Berichte zum XI. Internationalen Byzantinisten-Kongress München 1958*, vol. i: Munich, 1958, Beck, pp. 1–40.

Stein, E.: 'Zur Enstehung der Themenverfassung', in his *Studien zur Geschichte des byzantinischen Reiches, vornehmlich unter den Kaisern Justinus II und Tiberius Constantinus*: Stuttgart, 1919, Metzler: Zweiter Teil, 6. Kapitel, pp. 117–40.

—— 'Quaestor Justinianus Exercitûs', in op. cit., Zweiter Teil, 8. Kapitel, 3. Abteilung.

11. THE EAST ROMAN ARMY AND NAVY

(i) SOURCES

Anonymus: *Incerti Scriptoris Byzantini Saeculi X. Liber de Re Militari*, edited by R. Vári: Leipzig, 1901, Teubner.

Anonymus: Περὶ Παραδρομῆς Πολέμου in *Leonis Diaconi Historiae*, edited by C. B. Haas: Bonn, 1828, Weber, pp. 179–258.

Cecaumeni Strategicon et Incerti Scriptoris de Officiis Regiis Libellus, ed. by B. Wassiliewsky and V. Jernstedt: Petropoli, 1896, Academia Caesarea Scientiarum. N.B. In these two works, only chaps. 24–78 of the *Strategicon* deal with military affairs; the rest of both these works is concerned with civilian life, both public and private.

Leo VI: *Taktiká*: Migne, *Patrologia Graeca*, vol. cvii, cols. 669–1094; edited by R. Vári down to Dhiátaxis 14, § 34 inclusive, only: Budapest, 1917–22, 2 vols.

'Mavríkios', in *Arriani Tactica et Mauricii Artis Militaris Libri Duodecim*, edited by J. Scheffer: Upsala, 1664, M. Curio, S.R.M. et Academiae Upsaliensis Bibliopola; Μαυρικίου Στρατηγικόν, Mauricii Strategicon, edidit, Dacorumanice vertit, prolegomenis instruxit H. Mihăescu: Bucarest, 1970, Academy of the Socialist Republic of Roumania.

Nikêphóros Ouranós: *Tactique*, edited by A. Dain: Paris, 1937, Société d'Édition les 'Belles Lettres'.

Nikêphóros II Phokás: Στρατηγικὴ "Εκθεσις καὶ Σύνταξις, ed. by J. Kulakovskij, in *Mémoires de l'Académie Impériale des Sciences de St.-Pétersbourg*, viiie série, Classe Historico-Philologique, vol. viii, No. 9 (1908).

Περὶ Στρατιωτικῶν 'Επιτιμίων ed. by W. Ashburner: 'The Byzantine Mutiny Act', in *The Journal of Hellenic Studies*, vol. xlvi (1926), Part I, pp. 81–109.

(ii) MODERN WORKS

Ahrweiler, H.: *Byzance et la mer: la marine de guerre, la politique, et les institutions maritimes de Byzance aux viie–xve siècles*: Paris, 1966, Presses Universitaires de France.

Antoniadis-Bibicou, H.: *Études d'histoire maritime de Byzance à propos du 'Thème des Caravisiens'*: Paris, 1966, S.E. and P.E.N.

Aussaresses, F.: *L'Armée byzantine à la fin du vie siècle*: Bordeaux, 1909, Feret; Paris, 1909, Fontemoing.

Bréhier, L.: 'La Marine de Byzance du viiie au ixe siècle', in *Byzantion*, vol. xix (1949), pp. 1–16.

Bury, J. B.: 'The Naval Policy of the Roman Empire in Relation to the Western Provinces, from the 7th to the 9th Century', in *Centenario della Nascita di Michele Amari*, vol. ii: Palermo, 1910, Virzi, pp. 21–34.

Dolley, R. H.: 'The Warships of the Later Roman Empire', in *The Journal of Roman Studies*, vol. xxxviii (1948), pp. 47–53.

Eickhoff, E.: *Seekrieg und Seepolitik zwischen Islam und Abendland: Das Mittelmeer unter byzantinischer und arabischer Hegemonie*: Berlin, 1966, de Gruyter.

Grégoire, H.: 'L'Expédition de Damiette (853)', in 'Études sur le neuvième siècle', in *Byzantion*, vol. viii (1933), pp. 515–17.

Grosse, R.: *Römische Militärgeschichte von Gallienus bis zum Beginn der byzantinischen Themenverfassung*: Berlin, 1920, Weidmann.

Koukoulés, Ph.: Τσακωνία καὶ Τσάκωνες, in *Byzantinische Zeitschrift*, vol. xxvi (1926), 1. Abteilung, pp. 317–27.

Lewis, A. R.: *Naval Power and Trade in the Mediterranaen, A.D. 500–1100*: Princeton, 1951, University Press.

Moravcsik, Gy.: 'Mauricius', in *Byzantinoturcica*, vol. i, 2nd ed.: Berlin, 1958, Akademie-Verlag, pp. 417–21.

Partington, J. R.: *A History of Greek Fire and Gunpowder*: Cambridge, 1960, Heffer.

Vári, R.: Review of F. Aussaresses: *L'Armée byzantine à la fin du VIe siècle*, in *Byzantinische Zeitschrift*, 19. Band (1910), pp. 551–4.

—— 'Zur Überlieferung mittelgriechischer Taktiker', in *Byzantinische Zeitschrift*, 15. Band (1906), pp. 46–87.

12. BULGARIA

(i) SOURCES

Beševliev, V.: *Die Protobulgarischen Inschriften*: Berlin, 1963, Akademie-Verlag.

(ii) MODERN WORKS

Dvornik, F.: *Les Slaves, Byzance et Rome au IXe siècle*: Paris, 1926, Champion.

Runciman, S.: *A History of the First Bulgarian Empire*: London, 1930, Bell.

Sergheraert, G. (Gérard, Chr.): *Syméon le Grand (893–927)*: Paris, 1960, Maisonneuve.

Soulis, G. C.: 'The Legacy of Cyril and Methodius to the Southern Slavs', in *Dumbarton Oaks Papers*, Number Nineteen, pp. 19–43.

13. THE EASTERN MUSLIMS

(i) SOURCES

Anonymus: Βασιλείου Διγενοῦς Ἀκρίτου Λόγοι 'Οκτώ, edited, with translation, introduction, and commentary, by J. Mavrogordato: Oxford, 1956, Clarendon Press.

Brooks, E. W.: 'Byzantines and Arabs in the Time of the Early 'Abbasids', in *The English Historical Review*: I in vol. xv (October 1900), pp. 728–47; II in vol. xvi (January 1901), pp. 84–92.

—— 'The Arabs in Asia Minor (641–750), from Arabic Sources', in *The Journal of Hellenic Studies*, vol. xviii (1898), pp. 182–208.

Vasiliev, A. A.: *Byzance et les Arabes*, vol. i (820–67): Brussels, 1935, L'Institut de Philologie et d'Histoire Orientales: Traduction d'Auteurs Arabes, pp. 267–394.

—— *Byzance et les Arabes*, vol. ii (867–959), Part II: Extraits des sources arabes: Brussels, 1950, L'Institut de Philologie et d'Histoire Orientales et Slaves.

(ii) MODERN WORKS

Ahrweiler, H.: 'L'Asie Mineure et les invasions arabes', in *Revue Historique*, 86ᵉ année, vol. ccxxvii (1962), pp. 1–32.

Anderson, J. G. C.: 'The Campaign of Basil I against the Paulicians', in *The Classical Review*, vol. x (1896), No. 3, pp. 136–40.

Bury, J. B.: 'Mutasim's March through Cappadocia in A.D. 838', in *The Journal of Hellenic Studies*, vol. xxix (1909), pp. 120–9.

Grégoire, H.: 'La Bataille de 863', in 'Études sur le neuvième siècle', in *Byzantion*, vol. viii (1933), pp. 534–9.

—— 'Michel III et Basile le Macédonien dans les inscriptions d'Ancyre', in *Byzantion*, vol. v (1929), pp. 327–46.

Kremer, A. von: *Culturgeschichte des Orients unter den Chalifen*: Vienna, 1875–7, Braumüller, 2 vols.

Le Strange, G.: *The Lands of the Eastern Caliphate*: Cambridge, 1905, University Press.

Marquart, J.: *Osteuropäische und ostasiatische Streifzüge*, 8: 'Die Reisebericht des Hārūn b. Jahya': Leipzig, 1903, Dieterich, pp. 206–70.

Vasiliev, A. A.: *Byzance et les Arabes*: vol. i, *La Dynastie d'Amorion (820–867)*: Brussels, 1935, L'Institut de Philologie et d'Histoire Orientales; vol. ii, *La Dynastie Macédonienne (867–959)*: Part I, Brussels, 1968, Fondation Byzantine; Part II, Brussels, 1950, L'Institut de Philologie de l'Histoire Orientales et Slaves; vol. iii, *Die Ostgrenze des byzantinischen Reiches von 363 bis 1071* (by E. Honigmann): Brussels, 1935, L'Institut de Philologie et d'Histoire Orientales.

14. ARMENIA AND CAUCASIA: MODERN WORKS

Charanis, P.: *The Armenians in the Byzantine Empire*: Lisbon, 1963, Bertrand.

Der Nersessian: *The Armenians*: London, 1969, Thames & Hudson [read by me too late to be used in writing this book].

Laurent, J.: *L'Arménie entre Byzance et l'Islam depuis la conquête arabe jusqu'en 886*: Paris, 1919, Fontemoing.

Marquart, J.: *Osteuropäische und ostasiatische Streifzüge*, Excurs IV: 'Der Ursprung der iberischen Bagratiden': Leipzig, 1903, Dieterich, pp. 391–465.

15. THE PEOPLES TO THE NORTH OF THE EAST ROMAN EMPIRE

(i) SOURCES

Anonymus [pseudo-Nestor]: *The Russian Primary Chronicle*, Laurentian Text, translated and edited by S. H. Cross and C. P. Sherbowitz-Wetzor: Cambridge, Mass., 1953, The Mediaeval Academy of America.

Phótios: *Homilies* (Nos. 3 and 4): ed. by V. Laourdhas: Thessaloníkê, 1959, Etaireía Makedhonikón Spoudhón; English translation with introduction and commentary, by C. Mango: Cambridge, Mass., 1958, Harvard University Press.

(ii) MODERN WORKS

Boba, I.: *Nomads, Northmen and Slavs: Eastern Europe in the Ninth Century*: The Hague, 1967, Mouton; Wiesbaden, 1967, Harrassowitz.

Chadwick, N. K.: *The Beginnings of Russian History*: Cambridge, 1946, University Press.

de Boor, C.: 'Der Angriff der Rhos auf Byzanz', in *Byzantinische Zeitschrift*, 4. Band (1895), pp. 445–66.

Diaconu, P.: *Les Petchénègues au Bas-Danube*: Bucarest, 1970, L'Académie de la République Socialiste de Roumanie.

Dunlop, D. M.: *The History of the Jewish Khazars*: Princeton, 1954, University Press.

Dvornik, F.: *Byzantine Missions among the Slavs: SS. Constantine-Cyril and Methodius*: New Brunswick, 1971, Rutgers University Press.

—— *Les Slaves, Byzance et Rome au IXe siècle*: Paris, 1926, Champion.

—— *The Making of Central and Eastern Europe*: London, 1949, Polish Research Centre.

—— *The Slavs: Their Early History and Civilization*: Boston, 1956, American Academy of Arts and Sciences.

Gerland, E.: 'Photios und der Angriff der Russen auf Byzanz', in *Neue Jahrbücher für das klassische Altertum*, 6. Jahrgang (1903), pp. 718–22.

Grégoire, H.: 'Le Nom et l'origine des Hongrois', in *Zeitschrift der deutschen morgenländischen Gesellschaft*, Band 91 (N.F. Band 16) (1937), pp. 630–42.

Haussig, H. W.: 'Theophylakt's Exkurs über die skythischen Völker', in *Byzantion*, vol. liii (1953) [published in 1954], pp. 275–462.

Kutschera, H. Freiherr von: *Die Chasaren: Historische Studie*, 2nd ed.: Vienna, 1910, Holzhausen.

Lemerle, P.: 'La Composition et la chronologie des deux premiers livres des Miracula S. Demetrii', in *Byzantinische Zeitschrift*, 46. Band (1953), pp. 349–61.

Macartney, C. A.: *The Magyars in the Ninth Century*: Cambridge, 1930, University Press.

Marquart, J.: *Osteuropäische und ostasiatische Streifzüge*: Leipzig, 1903, Dieterich.

Menges, K.: 'Notes on some Päčänäg Names', in *Byzantion*, vol. xvii (1944–5), pp. 256–80.

Moravcsik, J.: 'Zur Geschichte der Onoguren', in *Ungarische Jahrbücher*, 10. Band (1930), pp. 53–90.

Obolensky, D.: 'The Heritage of Cyril and Methodius in Russia', in *Dumbarton Oaks Papers*, Number Nineteen, pp. 45–65.

Ostrogorsky, G.: 'The Byzantine Background of the Moravian Mission', in *Dumbarton Oaks Papers*, Number Nineteen, pp. 1–18.

Paszkiewicz, H.: *The Origin of Russia*: London, 1954, Allen & Unwin.

Szyszman, S.: 'Le Roi Bulan et le problème de la conversion des Khazars,', in *Ephemerides Theologicae Lovanienses*, t. xxxiii, fasc. 1 (1957), pp. 68–76.

—— 'Les Khazars: problèmes et controverses', in *Revue de l'histoire des religions*, vol. clii, No. 2, Oct.–Dec. 1957, pp. 174–221.

Vasiliev, A. A.: *The Goths in the Crimea*: Cambridge, Mass., 1936, The Mediaeval Academy of America.

—— *The Russian Attack on Constantinople in 860*: Cambridge, Mass., 1946, The Mediaeval Academy of America.

Vernadsky, G.: *Ancient Russia*, in G. Vernadsky and M. Karpovich: *A History of Russia*, vol. i: New Haven, 1943, Yale University Press.

—— *Kievan Russia*, in the same series, vol. ii: New Haven, 1948, Yale University Press.

Vernadsky, G.: 'Byzantium and Southern Russia', in *Byzantion*, vol. xv (1940–1), pp. 67–86.
Vlasto, A. P.: *The Entry of the Slavs into Christendom*: Cambridge, 1970, University Press.

16. EAST ROMAN LATIN

(i) SOURCES

Johannes Lydus: *De Magistratibus*, edited by R. Wuensch: Leipzig, 1903, Teubner; English translation by T. F. Carney: Sydney, 1965.

(ii) MODERN WORKS

Dagron, G.: 'Aux origines de la civilisation byzantine: Langue de culture et langue d'État', in *Revue Historique*, 93ᵉ Année, tome CCXLI (1969), pp. 23–56.
Zilliacus, H.: *Zum Kampf der Weltsprachen im oströmischen Reich*: Helsingfors, 1935, Mercators Tryckeri.

17. THE SLAV *VÖLKERWANDERUNG* TO THE SOUTH OF THE DANUBE

(i) SOURCES

Anonymus: *The Chronicle of Monemvasía* [so-called]: text edited by P. Lemerle in *Revue des Études Byzantines*, vol. xxi (1963), pp. 8–11.
Constantine Porphyrogenitus: *De Administrando Imperio*, chaps. 29–36: *The Early History of the Slavonic Settlements in Dalmatia, Croatia, and Serbia*, edited by J. B. Bury: London, 1920, S.P.C.K.
Evagrius: *Ecclesiastical History*, edited by J. Bidez and L. Parmentier: London, 1898, Methuen.
Johannes Biclarensis: *Chronica*, in *Monumenta Germaniae Historica: Chronica Minora*, edited by Th. Mommsen, vol. ii, Berlin, 1894, Weidmann: *subsidia critica* on pp. 166–77, text on pp. 207–20.
John Bishop of Ephesus: *Ecclesiastical History*, Part III; translated from the Syriac by R. Payne Smith: Oxford, 1860, University Press.
Menander Protector: *Agathias Continuatus*, fragments, in *Historici Graeci Minores*, edited by L. Dindorf, vol. ii: Leipzig, 1871, Teubner, pp. 1–131.
Theophylactus Simocatta: *Historiae*, edited by C. de Boor: Leipzig, 1887, Teubner.
Varii auctores: *Sanctii Demetrii Martyris Miracula*, Book I–III, in Migne, *Patrologia Graeca*, vol. cxvi (1891), cols. 1203–1398.

(ii) MODERN WORKS

Bon, A.: *Le Péloponnèse byzantin jusqu'en 1204*: Paris, 1951, Presses Universitaires de France.
Charanis, P.: 'Hellas in the Greek Sources of the Sixth, Seventh, and Eighth Centuries', in *Late Classical and Mediaeval Studies in Honor of Albert Matthias Friend, Jr.*: Princeton, 1955, University Press.
—— 'On the Question of the Slavonic Settlements in Greece during the Middle Ages', in *Byzantinoslavica*, vol. x (Prague, 1949), pp. 254–8.
—— 'On the Slavic Settlements in the Peloponnesus', in *Byzantinische Zeitschrift*, 46. Band (1953), pp. 90–103.
—— 'The Chronicle of Monemvasía and the Question of Slavonic Settlements in Greece', in *Dumbarton Oaks Papers*, Number Five (1950), pp. 139–66.
—— 'The Slavic Element in Byzantine Asia Minor', in *Byzantion*, vol. xviii (1948), pp. 69–83.

Dvornik, F.: *The Slavs, their Early History and Civilization*: Boston, 1956, American Academy of Arts and Sciences.

Grégoire, H.: 'L'Origine et le nom des Croates et des Serbes', in *Byzantion*, vol. xvii (1944–5), pp. 88–118.

—— 'Un Édit de l'Empereur Justinien II daté de septembre 688', in *Byzantion*, vol. xvii (1944–5), pp. 119–124a.

Hauptmann, L.: 'Les Rapports des Byzantins avec les Slaves et les Avares pendant la seconde moitié du VIᵉ siècle', in *Byzantion*, vol. iv (1929), pp. 137–70.

Hood, Sinclair: 'Isles of Refuge in the Early Byzantine Period', in *Annual of the British School at Athens*, No. 65 (1970), pp. 37–45.

Koukoulés, Ph.: *Τσακωνία καὶ Τσάκωνες*, in *Byzantinische Zeitschrift*, vol. xxvi (1926), 1. Abteilung, pp. 317–27.

Kyriakídhês, S. P.: *Οἱ Σλάβοι ἐν Πελοποννήσῳ = Βυζαντιναὶ Μελέται* VI: Thessaloníkê, 1947.

Lemerle, P.: 'Invasions et migrations dans les Balkans depuis la fin de l'époque romaine jusqu'au VIIIᵉ siècle', in *Revue Historique*, vol. ccxi (1954), pp. 265–308.

—— 'La Chronique improprement dite de Monemvasie: le contexte historique et légendaire', in *Revue des Études Byzantines*, vol. xxi (1963), pp. 5–49.

—— 'La Composition et la chronologie des deux premiers livres des Miracula S. Demetrii', in *Byzantinische Zeitschrift*, 46. Band (1953), pp. 349–61.

Lipšic, E. E.: *Byzanz und die Slawen*: Weimar, 1951, Böhlaus Nachfolger.

Metcalf, D. M.: 'The Aegean Coastlands under Threat: some Coins and Coin Hoards from the Reign of Heraclius', in *Annual of the British School at Athens*, No. 57 (1962), pp. 14–23.

—— 'The Slavonic Threat to Greece circa 580: Some Evidence from Athens', in *Hesperia* (1962), pp. 134 seqq.

Vasmer, M.: *Die Slaven in Griechenland = Abhandlungen Preuss. Ak. Wiss.* (1941), Phil.-hist. Kl., No. 12: Berlin, 1941, de Gruyter.

18. THE PAULICIANS AND THE BOGOMILS

(i) SOURCES[1]

Anonymus: *Interrogatio Iohannis et apostoli et evangelistae in cena secreta regni celorum de ordinatione istius mundi et de principe et de Adam*, ed. by R. Reitzenstein in his *Die Vorgeschichte der christlichen Taufe*: Leipzig and Berlin, 1929, pp. 297–311: French translations of the Carcassonne MS. and the Vienna MS. in Nelli, op. cit. *infra*, pp. 34–66; introduction ibid., pp. 31–3.

—— *Liber de Duobus Principiis*, ed. by A. Dondaine, O.P.: Rome, 1939, Istituto Storico Domenicano S. Sabina: French translation in R. Nelli, *Écritures cathares*, Paris, 1959, Denoël.

—— *The Key of Truth*, edited and translated, with introduction, by F. C. Conybeare: Oxford, 1898, Clarendon Press.

Cosmas le Prêtre: *Le Traité contre les Bogomiles*, traduction et étude par H.-Ch. Puech et A. Vaillant: Paris, 1945, Imprimerie Nationale; Librairie Droz.

Nelli, R., ed. and tr.: *Écritures cathares*: Paris, 1959, Denoël.

Petrus Hegumenus: *Περὶ Παυλικιανῶν τῶν καὶ Μανιχαίων*, edited by J. C. L. Gieseler: Göttingen, 1849, Vandenhoeck & Ruprecht.

---

[1] For sources in Armenian, other than *The Key of Truth*, see the bibliography in N. G. Garsoian, *The Paulician Heresy*, pp. 244–8.

Petrus Siculus: Ἱστορία χρειώδης ἔλεγχός τε καὶ ἀνατροπὴ τῆς κενῆς καὶ ματαίας αἱρέσεως τῶν Μανιχαίων τῶν καὶ Παυλικιανῶν λεγομένων, προσωποποιηθεῖσα ὡς πρὸς τὸν ἀρχιεπίσκοπον Βουλγαρίας, edited by J. C. L. Gieseler: Göttingen, 1846, Vandenhoeck & Ruprecht; Migne, *Patrologia Graeca*, vol. civ, cols. 1239/40–1303/4.

—— *Sermons*, in Migne, vol. cit., cols. 1305/6–1349/50.

Photios(?): Διήγησις περὶ τῆς Μανιχαίων ἀναβλαστήσεως, in Migne, *Patrologia Graeca*, vol. cii, cols.15/16–83/4.

Photios: Letters 1, 9, 19, 26 in Migne, vol. cii, cols. 927, 933, 941, 945.

—— Λόγοι Β–Δ, in Migne, vol. cii, cols. 85/6–263/4.

Sacconi, O.P., Raynier: *Summa de Catharis et Pauperibus de Lugduno* (1230), in Dondaine's edition of *Liber de Duobus Principiis*, pp. 64–78.

(ii) MODERN WORKS

Borst, A.: *Die Katharer*: Stuttgart, 1953, Hiersemann.

Garsoian, N. G.: *The Paulician Heresy*: The Hague and Paris, 1967, Mouton.

Grégoire, H.: 'Les Sources de l'histoire des Pauliciens', in *Ac. Roy. Belg., Bulletin de la Classe des Lettres*, 5ᵉ série, vol. xxii (1936), pp. 95 seqq.

—— 'Sur l'histoire des Pauliciens', ibid., pp. 224–6.

Loos, M.: 'A propos des sources grecques reflétant les Pauliciens', in *Byzantinoslavica*, No. xvii (1956), pp. 19–57.

—— 'Certains aspects du Bogomilisme byzantin des 11ᵉ et 12ᵉ siècles', ibid., No. xxviii (1967), pp. 39–53.

—— 'Le mouvement paulicien à Byzance', ibid., No. xxiv (1963), pp. 258–86, and No. xxv (1964), pp. 52–68.

—— 'Origine du nom des Pauliciens', ibid., No. xviii (1957), pp. 202–17.

—— 'Où en est la question du mouvement paulicien?', in *Izvestiya na Instituta za istoriya*, Nos. xiv–xv (1964), pp. 357–71.

—— 'Zur Frage des Paulikianismus und Bogomilismus', in *Byzantinische Beiträge*, ed. by J. Irmscher: Berlin, 1964, pp. 323–33.

Obolensky, D.: *The Bogomils, a Study in Balkan Neo-Manichaeism*: Cambridge, 1948, University Press.

Runciman, S.: *The Medieval Manichee*: Cambridge, 1947, University Press.

Söderberg, H.: *La Religion des Cathares*: Uppsala, 1949, Almqvist & Wiksell.

Ter Mkrttschian, K.: *Die Paulikianer im byzantinischen Kaiserreiche und verwandte Ketzerische Erscheinungen in Armenien*: Leipzig, 1893, Hinrichs.

INDEX

INDEX TO MAPS

The first numeral in each entry (printed in bold type) gives the number of the map. The letters of the alphabet, followed by numerals in ordinary type, give the locations on the grids of Maps 2–5. Map 1 has no grid.

ERRATA AND ACCIDENTAL OMISSIONS ON THE MAPS

Errata

3 D–E2   Viatchians should be Viatichians.

5 C2   Spalata should be Spalato.

5 C2   Cattara should be Cattaro.

5 C2   Dhyrrhákion (both town and théma) should be Dhyrrákhion.

5 K2–3   Dvin (Muslin) should be Dvin (Muslim).

Omissions

2 H–J2   The district name Farghānah should have been inscribed on the north-east corner of the Arab Caliphate.

3 C1   The courses and names of the Rivers Neva and Narva, and the names of the River Lovat and of Lake Peipus, should have been shown here to illustrate the historical importance of the portages between the Baltic rivers and the Caspian and Black Sea rivers (see pp. 449–50).

           N.B. For the role of rivers and portages in the formation and expansion of Russia, see Martin Gilbert, *Russian History Atlas* (London, 1972, Weidenfeld and Nicolson), Maps 14 and 27.

ERRATA IN THE TEXT

Page 7, last line of text: Karvounópsína should be Karvounopsína.

Page 99, note 1, line 11: Southern should be southern.

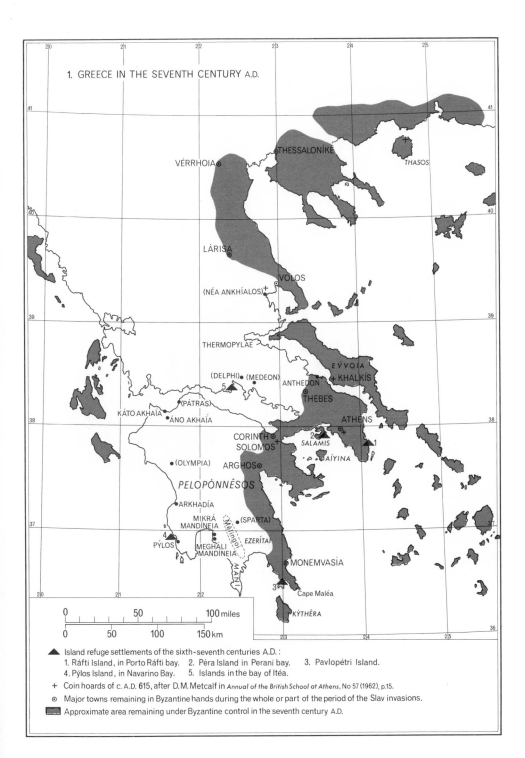

1. GREECE IN THE SEVENTH CENTURY A.D.

THESSALONÍKĒ

VÉRRHOIA⊙

THASOS

LÁRISA⊙

VÓLOS⊙
(NÉA ANKHÍALOS)+

THERMOPYLAE

(DELPHI)● (MEDEON)
5. ▲

EÝVOIA
+ KHALKÍS
ANTHEDON⊙

(PÁTRAS)

THEBES⊙

KÁTO AKHAÍA●
●ÁNO AKHAÍA

ATHENS⊙

CORINTH⊙
SOLOMOS+
2●
SALAMIS
⊕+
▲1

●(OLYMPIA)
ARGHOS⊙

AÍYINA

PELOPÓNNÊSOS

●ARKHADÍA

MIKRÁ
MANDÍNEIA●
4 ▲
PÝLOS●
(SPARTA)

Melingoi

MEGHÁLI
MANDÍNEIA●
EZERÍTAI

MANI

MONEMVASÍA⊙

3 ▲
Cape Maléa

KÝTHÊRA

0		50		100 miles

0	50	100	150 km

▲ Island refuge settlements of the sixth-seventh centuries A.D. :
1. Ráfti Island, in Porto Ráfti bay.   2. Péra Island in Perani bay.   3. Pavlopétri Island.
4. Pýlos Island, in Navarino Bay.   5. Islands in the bay of Itéa.

+ Coin hoards of c. A.D. **615**, after D.M. Metcalf in *Annual of the British School at Athens*, No 57 (1962), p.15.

⊙ Major towns remaining in Byzantine hands during the whole or part of the period of the Slav invasions.

▬ Approximate area remaining under Byzantine control in the seventh century A.D.

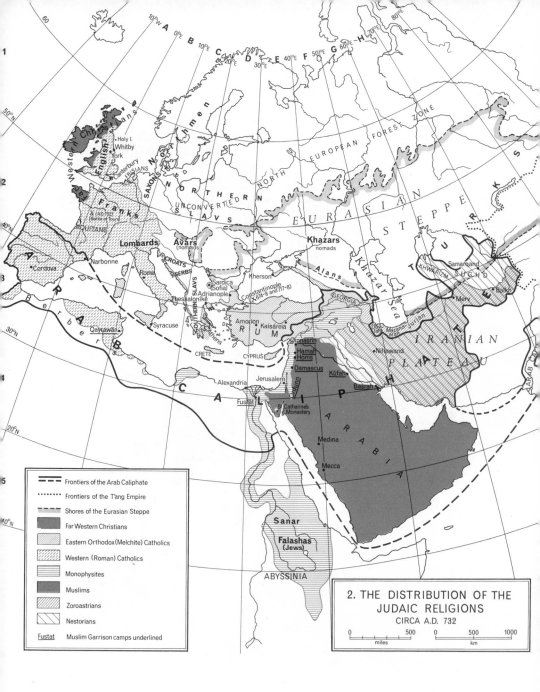

2. THE DISTRIBUTION OF THE
JUDAIC RELIGIONS
CIRCA A.D. 732

0	500	0	500	1000
	miles			km

Frontiers of the Arab Caliphate
Frontiers of the T'ang Empire
Shores of the Eurasian Steppe
Far Western Christians
Eastern Orthodox (Melchite) Catholics
Western (Roman) Catholics
Monophysites
Muslims
Zoroastrians
Nestorians

Fustat   Muslim Garrison camps underlined

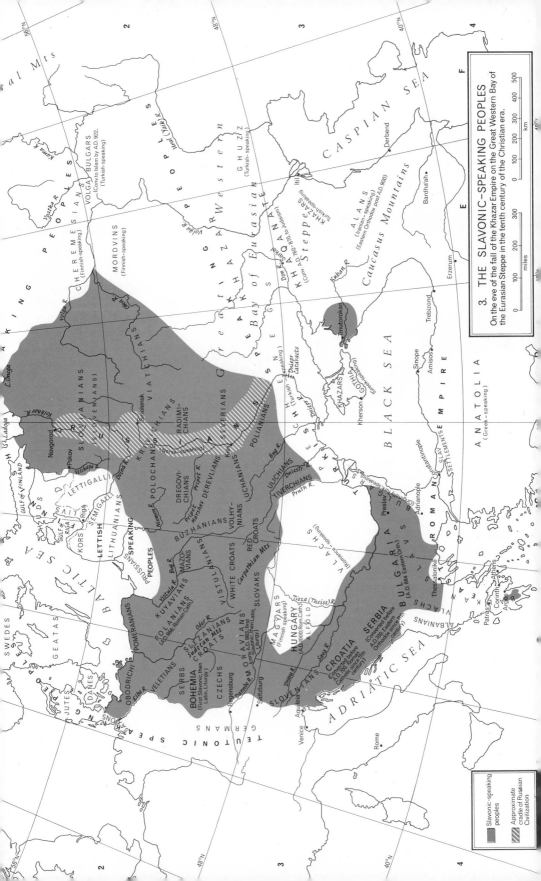

3. THE SLAVONIC-SPEAKING PEOPLES
On the eve of the fall of the Khazar Empire on the Great Western Bay of the Eurasian Steppe in the tenth century of the Christian era.

Slavonic-speaking peoples

Approximate cradle of Russian Civilization

km   0   100   200   300   400   500
miles   0   100   200   300

CASPIAN SEA

BLACK SEA

ADRIATIC SEA

BALTIC SEA

GULF OF FINLAND

L. Ladoga
L. Onega

Ural Mts

Kama R.
Vyatka R.
Ural R. (Yaik)
Volga R.

CHEREMISS
(Finnish-speaking)

VOLGA BULGARS
(Conv. to Islam by A.D. 922.)
(Turkish-speaking)

MORDVINS
(Finnish-speaking)

GHUZZ
(Turkish-speaking)

KHAZARS
(Turkish-speaking)

KHAZAR KHAGANATE
(Conv. A.D. 780-870, to Judaism)

Itil
Sarkel

ALANS
(Eastern Orthodox post A.D. 900)

Derbend

Bardha'ah

Caucasus Mountains

Kuban R.

Erzerum

Trebizond

Sinope

Amisos

ANATOLIA
(Greek–speaking)

ROMAN EMPIRE

Constantinople

Adrianople

Athens

Corinth

Patras

Argos

Thessalonike

PECHENEGS
(Turkish-speaking)

Preslav

BULGARIA
(A.D. 864 Eastern Orth.)

SLAV SETTLEMENTS

VLACHS
(Romance–speaking)

ALBANIANS

Volga R.
Oka R.
Don R.
Volga R.

Great Western Bay of Eurasia

Great Bay of Eurasia

KHAZARS

GOTHIA
(Greek–speaking)

Kherson

Dnieper Cataracts
Dnieper R.

Tmutorokan

TIVERCHIANS
ULICHIANS

Bug R.
Dniestr R.
Pruth R.
Tisza (Theiss) R.

POLIANIANS
Kiev

SEVERIANS
DEREVLIANS
VOLHY-NIANS
UCHIANS

RUSSIANS (Norse-speaking)

VIATICHIANS
RADIMI-CHIANS
KRIVICHIANS
Smolensk

SLOVENIANS
(SLOVENIANS)
Novgorod
Pskov
Velikaya R.

Volkhov R.

POLOCHANE
Drina R.
Niemen R.
Pripet R.
Pripet Marshes
DREGOVI-CHIANS
BUZHANIANS
RED CROATS
WHITE CROATS
Carpathian Mts
MAZO-VIANS
VISTULANIANS
KUYAVIANS
POLANIANS
(A.D. 966 Roman Cath.)
SILEZANIANS
Sudeten Mts
MORAVIANS
(conv. A.D. 863, first Slavonic, then Latin, Liturgy)
SLOVAKS
Oder R.
Vistula R.
Bug R.

MAGYARS
(Finnish–speaking)

HUNGARY
(A.D. 1000 Rom. Cath.)

ALFÖLD

Tisza R.

Danube R.

SLOVENIANS
CROATIA
(Conv. to Rome before Catholic A.D. 900 century.)
SERBIA
(Converted before A.D. 800 Orthodox xenith 9th century.)
Sava R.
Drava R.

Venice
Aquileia
Rome

Saltzburg
Regensburg

BOHEMIA
(First Slavonic, then Latin, Liturgy)
CZECHS

GERMANS

TEUTONIC SPEAKING PEOPLES

SERBS
VELETIANS
OBODRICHI
POMERANIANS
Elbe R.

DANES
JUTES
GEATAS
SWEDES

Riga
KORS
SEMIGALLI
LETTIGALLI
LITHUANIANS
PRUSSIANS

LETTISH SPEAKING PEOPLES

LITHUANIAN SPEAKING PEOPLES

FINNS

Eastern Orthodox (Melchite) Catholics

Western (Roman) Catholics

Monophysites

Muslims

Karluks   Muslims underlined

- - - -   Shores of the Eurasian Steppe

0   500 miles

0   500   1000 km

4. THE DISTRIBUTION OF THE JUDAIC RELIGIONS

ON THE EVE OF THE MONGOL
EXPLOSION IN THE THIRTEENTH CENTURY
OF THE CHRISTIAN ERA